D1521243

*Everyman's*

# DICTIONARY OF EUROPEAN WRITERS

---

**Addenda**

**Cecchi, Emilio:** died 1966

**Kolb, Annette:** died Munich, 1967

**Vailland, Roger:** died Meillonas, 1965

---

A volume in
EVERYMAN'S REFERENCE LIBRARY

*Everyman's Reference Library*

DICTIONARY OF QUOTATIONS AND PROVERBS
THESAURUS OF ENGLISH WORDS AND PHRASES
DICTIONARY OF SHAKESPEARE QUOTATIONS
DICTIONARY OF NON-CLASSICAL MYTHOLOGY
DICTIONARY OF DATES
DICTIONARY OF MUSIC
EVERYMAN'S ENGLISH DICTIONARY
ENGLISH PRONOUNCING DICTIONARY
DICTIONARY OF LITERARY BIOGRAPHY: ENGLISH AND
AMERICAN
EVERYMAN'S DICTIONARY OF EUROPEAN WRITERS
CONCISE ENCYCLOPAEDIA OF ARCHITECTURE
CLASSICAL DICTIONARY
CLASSICAL ATLAS
EVERYMAN'S ENCYCLOPAEDIA OF GARDENING
FRENCH-ENGLISH—ENGLISH-FRENCH DICTIONARY
DICTIONARY OF PICTORIAL ART (2 volumes)
DICTIONARY OF ECONOMICS
EVERYMAN'S ENCYCLOPAEDIA (12 volumes)

*Other volumes in preparation*

---

*Also by W. N. Hargreaves-Mawdsley*

A HISTORY OF ACADEMICAL DRESS IN EUROPE, *Clarendon Press*,
1963
A HISTORY OF LEGAL DRESS IN EUROPE, *Clarendon Press*, 1963
THE ENGLISH DELLA CRUSCANS AND THEIR AGE, 1783–1828,
*Martinus Nijhoff, The Hague*, 1967
WOODFORDE AT OXFORD, 1759–76, *Oxford Historical Society*, 1968

# *Everyman's*

# DICTIONARY OF

# EUROPEAN WRITERS

*by*

## W. N. HARGREAVES-MAWDSLEY

M.A.(Oxon.), D. Phil.(Oxon.), F.S.A.

*Lecturer in Modern History in the University of St Andrews*

LONDON: J. M. DENT & SONS LTD
NEW YORK: E. P. DUTTON & CO. INC.

SBN: 460 03019 1

# PREFACE

IN COMPOSING this *Dictionary of European Writers* I have cast my net as widely as possible, so that smaller communities and the late arrivals into European literature are adequately represented. The period covered extends from the origins of modern European literature right up to the present day, i.e. from the tenth century onwards.

I have tried to be catholic in my selection of authors, my yardstick for inclusion being that even if from the literary point of view a writer does not seem worthy of a place, yet if his work is (*a*) of historic value as illustrating the social life of his day, (*b*) if he influenced a large public and (*c*) if his work, mediocre in itself and almost dead, started a literary movement or inspired an author greater than himself, he must be included.

I soon found myself having to come to a decision about literary and non-literary writers, of philosophers and thinkers. If the criterion for inclusion in this *Dictionary* were literary quality or at least influence on the public or on greater authors, or as illustrating history, what of theologians, philosophers and other men of learning? Only some have definitely literary qualities and few of them are strictly speaking literary men. If only the minority such as Spinoza and Schopenhauer qualified on literary qualities, almost all the great names among the non-literary writers could be said to have stimulated and inspired the literary climate of Europe. On these grounds they have been included. Kant's prose is poor and rambling enough, and yet how many literary men were influenced by him! However interesting Winckelmann, the archaeologist, may be for the specialist, he would not hold a place here had it not been for his influence on new trains of thought which found their way into literature, e.g. into the work of Goethe.

Titles of English translations (except when they are so close to the original title as not to require the giving of the title) are included within the brackets following the date of the original book's first publication. After the English title follows the date of the translation. Occasionally when there is no English translation, a French, German or even Italian one is indicated as of possible use to the reader. This is of value only when the original language is very little known in the West, e.g. Polish, whose literature has often found its way westwards through French. Similarly in the last century Modern Greek literature often reached a wider public through Italian.

For the benefit of the Western reader for whom Russian, the other East European languages and Modern Greek are bound to be unfamiliar, I have given my own translations of the titles of books in those languages which have not been published in English. These appear in roman between quotation marks to distinguish them from published translations, which are in italics. In a few cases, however, I have translated other languages where the context seemed to demand it.

The bibliographical apparatus is meant as a guide for further reading. The editions usually indicated are the standard ones, the most easily obtainable, and also the most convenient to use. Editions of particular historical interest (e.g. an *editio princeps*) are also mentioned.

Accents are not employed in well-known proper names (Cadiz, not Cádiz), as otherwise they are. When the names of the great writers (e.g. Dante, Goethe, Dostoyevsky) are mentioned in other articles there is no cross-reference to them (q.v.) but cross-references are given in all other cases.

The reader will notice that I give not only dates but places of birth and death, where known.

I should like to record here my thanks to Mr R. V. Pringle, M.A., M.Litt., of the University Library, St Andrews, for his great help in proof-reading.

1968.                                                    W. N. H.-M.

# A

**Aafjes, Lambertus Jacobus Johannes** (1914–    ), Dutch poet and literary journalist, born in Amsterdam. Two of his devotional poems inspired by his fervent Roman Catholicism, *Een Voetreis naar Rom* (1946) and *In den Beginne* (1949), show a striking conception of life within a traditional framework.

**Aakjaer, Jeppe** (1866–1930), Danish poet and novelist, was born into a poor peasant family in Jutland and became a herd-boy, a harsh life which he afterwards vividly described in his novels *Bondens Søn* (1899) and *Vredens Børn*; *et Tyendes Saga* (1904). Going to Copenhagen he managed to gain some sort of education, and thereafter lived by his pen and by lecturing, until he had saved enough to buy a farm in Jutland, which became a centre of folklorist rallies. He continued his political writing, but it is as a poet that he is remembered today. The best known of his volumes of poetry is *Rugens Sange* (1906, 'Songs of the Rye'), influenced, it would seem, by Burns. He died at Jenle.

**Aarestrup, Carl Ludvig Emil** (1800–1856), Danish poet, was born in Copenhagen and died at Odense. A country physician, whose poetry was little regarded in his lifetime, it was not until his *Samlede Digte* appeared in 1877 that it was realized that here was a poet of refined taste, unashamedly erotic, who had always at his command an astringent sarcasm that restrained him from downright voluptuousness. Perhaps his elegant *Ritournelles* are his most outstanding work.

**Aasen, Ivar Andreas** (1813–1896), Norwegian philologist and poet, was the son of a peasant, and was born at Aasen, Volda. He managed to teach himself sufficiently to become a village schoolmaster, and later with a grant from the Society for the Advancement of Learning at Trondheim he was enabled to study Norwegian dialects, which resulted in his *Det norske Folkesprogs Grammatik* (1848) and *Ordbog over det norske Folkesprog* (1850). As a poet he made a great reputation with *Symra*, which was published in 1863, and is a song-cycle containing such lyrics as 'Dei gamle Fjelli' and 'Nordmannen'. He died in Kristiania (Oslo).

**Abarbanel (Abravanel), Isaac ben Jehudah** (1437–1508), Portuguese Jewish scholar, was born in Lisbon, and held high appointments at the court there. He left Portugal for Spain, becoming treasurer to King Ferdinand, but in 1492, realizing that the king was not to be diverted from expelling the Jews from his kingdom, even by a bribe

of 30,000 ducats which Abarbanel offered him, he took service under
the King of Naples. He died in Venice. One of the finest Hebrew and
Latin scholars of his time, he was responsible for the greatest Old
Testament commentary of the age (publ. Venice, 1511 onwards),
which was much studied by Christian scholars.

**Abarbanel, Leone Ebreo (Leo Judaeus)** (1460?-1535?), Italian Jewish
philosopher, eldest son of Isaac Abarbanel (q.v.). He left Spain with
his father in 1492 and lived as a physician in Genoa and then in
Naples where he died. Coming into contact with Renaissance men of
letters such as Pico della Mirandola the elder, he became a neo-
platonist, the result of this new state of mind being his *Dialoghi dell'
Amore*, in which he argues that it is spiritual love alone which guides
the world. Whether this work was written in Spanish, Hebrew or
Latin is not known, for it has come down to us only in the Italian
translation which, edited by M. Lenzi, appeared in Rome in 1535.

**Abba, Giuseppe Cesare** (1838-1910), Italian diarist, novelist and short-
story writer, born at Cairo Montenotte, is almost exclusively remembered for his vivid first-hand account of the Sicilian campaign of
1860, in which he served under Garibaldi. A great portion of his life
was spent in writing it in various forms, first as a poem, *Arrigo: da
Quarto al Volturno* (1866), then as a diary, the first and more attractive
version being entitled *Noterelle d'uno dei Mille edite dopo vent' anni*
(1880), the second, *Da Quarto al Volturno* (1891). Among his other
work, a volume of short stories, *Cosa vedute* (1887), may be mentioned.
Abba, whose style was much admired by Carducci (q.v.), died at
Brescia. See *The Diary of One of Garibaldi's Thousand* (Oxford
Library of Italian Classics).

**Abélard, Peter** (1079-1142), French prose-writer, poet, philosopher
and theologian writing in Latin. Born at Pallet near Nantes of a noble
Breton family he became a brilliant student and, taking orders, an
equally successful teacher in Paris, Peter Lombard and Arnold of
Brescia being among his most loyal pupils. Feeling himself strong
he rashly attacked his old masters, and for his bold theological
teaching was condemned at the Council of Soissons (1121). But it was
his love for the young Héloïse, his pupil, which has invested him with
such a romantic aura, providing a theme for subsequent writers,
Pope among them. His flight with Héloïse to Brittany, the birth of
his son Astrolabius, the separation of the lovers, his monastic school
at the Paraclete, his ten painful years as abbot of St Gildas were
features of his restless and unhappy life, which is described in his
moving *Historia Calamitatum*. Apart from this, and his works on
theology and philosophy, he wrote some remarkable rhythmic and
rhymed Latin poetry, of which the most noteworthy are his hymns
and elegies, especially that addressed to his son. Mercilessly attacked
by Bernard of Clairvaux (q.v.), and condemned for heresy at the
Council of Sens, he took refuge in the Priory of St Marcel, near
Châlons-sur-Saône, where he died.

**Abell, Kjeld** (1901-1961), Danish playwright born at Ribe. He worked
as an artist, often abroad, until 1936, but in that year turned to the

stage with a play satirizing the snobbery and conventions of society, *Melodien, der blev vaek* (1937), produced in London the same year. Delicate, charming and humorous, he laughs at what he despises. Remarkable above all is his technique, reminiscent of a music-hall revue. Among his other plays should be mentioned *Anna Sophie Hedvig* (1939; Eng. trans. 1944), a heavily disguised attack on totalitarian regimes. He died in Copenhagen.

**Aben-Ezra,** *see* **Ibn Ezra, A.**

**Ablesimov, Alexander Onisimovich** (1742–1783), Russian fabulist and playwright born in the Kostroma district. Apart from his fables (1769), he is the man of one work, the comic opera, *Mel'nik, koldun, obmanshchik i svat* ('The Miller, Sorcerer, Swindler and Matchmaker', written 1779; publ. 1789).

**About, Edmond François Valentin** (1828–1885), French journalist and novelist, was born at Dieuze, Lorraine. After a highly successful career at the École Normale, Paris, he went to Athens to study archaeology before returning to the French capital to make his career a literary one. His *La Grèce contemporaine* (1854) is a lively account of his impressions of Greece, but it is the other book which his Greek journey inspired, the wittily mischievous *Le Roi des montagnes* (1856; Eng. trans. *The King of the Mountains*, 1897 seqq.), which remains alive today. Among his later books should be mentioned his fantastic trilogy, *Le Cas de M. Guérin, L'Homme à l'oreille cassée* and *Le Nez d'un notaire* (1862), and *Madelon* (1863). *Le Roman d'un brave homme* (1874) is representative of his subsequent quieter, critical approach to society. He died in Paris.

**Achard, Marcel** (1899–    ), pseudonym of **Marcel Auguste Ferréol,** French playwright, born at Lyon. First interested in the puppet theatre, his earliest success, produced in 1923 at the Atelier Theatre, Paris, was a circus play with the characters as clowns, *Voulez-vous jouer avec moâ?* His fantasy and whimsicality are further revealed in *La Vie est belle* (1928), with its improbable situations and meetings, and above all in *Jean de la Lune* (1929), with its theme, to which he often later returned, of the dreamer-idealist and the faithless woman, the dreamer conquering, however, in the end. *La Belle Marinière* (1929) contains more than a touch of disillusionment, but thereafter he returned to his happier vein. Among his later plays are *Domino* (1931), *Pétrus* (1933), *Le Corsaire* (1938), *Nous irons à Valparaiso* (1948), *La Demoiselle de petite vertu* (1949) and *Auprès de ma blonde* (1952).

**Aconzio, Jacopo (Jacobus Acontius)** (1500–1567?), Italian philosopher. Born at Trent, he was forced as a Protestant to take refuge in Basel in 1557, but there he was not at rest, finding as much dogmatic intolerance among the Reformers as among the Catholics. He settled in England in 1559 and there completed his broadminded plea for toleration, *Stratagemata Satanae* (1565), one of the first of its kind, which seems to breathe the spirit of a new age.

**Adam, Paul** (1862–1920), French novelist, was born and died in Paris. Son of a wealthy family ruined by a financial crash he turned to his pen for a living. Some of his books, such as *Chair molle* (1885), are cruelly merciless attacks on contemporary society, others such as *Robes rouges* (1891), *L'Année de Clarisse* (1897) and *Lettres de malaisie* (1897) reveal their author as a profound pessimist revolted by what he sees of life about him. It is not therefore surprising to find him in his later work hiding from the crude present in a triumphant past of heroic wars or athletic prowess with mighty crowd scenes on a huge canvas. Such work is exemplified in *La Bataille d'Uhde* (1899) and the series of four novels collectively entitled *Le Temps et la vie* (1899–1903), which celebrates the French Revolution and the triumph of the Latin spirit. In his last phase he turned to travel books, *Visages du Brésil* (1915), and to colonial studies such as *La Ville inconnue* (1911), which caused him to be called the 'French Kipling'.

**Adam de la Halle** (or **Le Bossu**) (1250?–1289?), French poet and dramatist, born at Arras. Entering the service of Robert, Count of Artois, he went with him to Italy and died there, probably at Naples. Besides his miscellaneous lyrics, surprisingly fresh and in advance of their time, he wrote a farce, *Le Jeu de la Feuillée* (1276?), and a pastoral play, *Le Jeu de Robin et de Marion* (1283?).

**Adam de St Victoire** (*fl.* 1140), a Breton religious poet. Becoming an Augustinian at St Victoire, Paris, he wrote many Latin sequences for use in church at high festivals. The finest perhaps is the Easter sequence, *Zyma vetus*, perfect in form and rich in symbolism.

**Adamov**, *see* **Marković**.

**Adenet le Roi des Ménestrels** (1240?–1297?), French poet. After serving as minstrel to two kings of Brabant, he entered the service of Gui, Count of Flanders, whom in 1270 he accompanied on the eighth crusade, and visited North Africa and Sicily. He is remembered now solely for his romance *Cleomadès*, written between 1275 and 1282. An edition of it by A. van Hasselt was published in 1888.

**Ady, Endre** (1877–1919), Hungarian poet and prose-writer, born at Érmindszent. A stay while a young journalist in Paris, and his liaison there with the cosmopolitan Adèle Brüll, the 'Leda' of his poems, led to his revolt against the narrow puritanism of his family, and the selfish materialism of the Hungarian ruling class. It was the materialism which he found once again surrounding him on his return to his native land, contrasted with the freedom and idealism which he had discovered in Paris, which formed the mainspring of his poetry. The best of it is to be found in *Vér és arany* (1907, 'Blood and Gold') and *Ki látott engem?* (1914, 'Who has seen me?'). In spite of the inconsistent quality of his work Ady remains the most considerable Hungarian poet of the twentieth century. He died in Budapest.

**Aeneas Silvius**, *see* **Piccolomini**.

**Afanasyev, Alexander Nikolayevich** (1826–1871), Russian folklorist, a government official in Moscow, was responsible for gathering together one of the most important collections of Russian folk tales ever assembled, *Narodnya russkiya skazki* (1855–63; Eng. trans. *Russian Fairy Tales*, 1945).

**Afflighem, Willem van** (1210?–1297), Dutch poet, who became abbot of St-Truyen in 1277. His plain, direct poem *Sinte Lutgart*, a life of the saint of that name, is an early example of Dutch poetry. The standard edition of it is by F. van Veerdeghem (1899).

**Afinogenov, Alexander Nikolayevich** (1904–1941), Soviet playwright born at Skopino, began his career with sensational dramas on labour struggles in other countries and in earlier times, such as *Robert Tim* (1923) with its subject of the weavers' revolt in England in the early nineteenth century. After this he turned to life in his own country, melodramatically insisting on the purity of Communism and loyalty to the central government in such plays as *Volchya tropa* (1927, 'The Trail of the Wolf'). With his propagandist drama *Strakh* (1931; Eng. trans. *Fear*, in *Six Soviet Plays*, 1934) he attempted to prove that it was not a system of terror made use of by the central government which held the Soviets together. The work was discussed all over the world. In *Dalyekoye* (1935; Eng. trans. as *Remote*, 1936, and as *Distant Point*, 1941) we have reflections on the growing menace of Fascism, which in his last play *Nakanune* (1941; Eng. trans. *On the Eve*, 1946) have become reality with Germany's invasion of Russia. Afinogenov was killed in Moscow during a German air-raid.

**Afzelius, Arvid August** (1785–1871), Swedish folklorist, born at Fjällåkra in Västergötland. He was editor of a work on Swedish folk dances, *Traditioner af svenska folkdanser* (1814–15), and a huge collection of folk tales, *Svenska folkets sagohäfder* (11 vols., 1839–70), and translated the *Older Edda* into Swedish (1818). He died at Enköping.

**Aganoor-Pompili, Vittoria** (1855–1910), Italian poet, was born in Padua and died in Rome. Considered by many, Benedetto Croce (q.v.) among them, as the greatest Italian woman poet, her tender, natural lyrics are to be found in *La leggenda eterna* (1900) and *Nuove liriche* (1908).

**Agoult, Marie de Flavigny d'** (1805–1876), French author, born in Frankfurt, who used the literary pseudonym of **Daniel Stern,** is now remembered as the mistress of Franz Liszt and mother of Wagner's second wife, although she was in her own day well known for such works as *Esquisses morales* (1849). She died in Paris.

**Agricola, Rudolf (Roelof Huysmann)** (1442–1485), Dutch scholar, born near Groningen. He was a foremost humanist, who sought the new learning assiduously at Louvain and Paris, and afterwards in Italy from 1468 for eleven years. He then went to Heidelberg, and spent his time there lecturing and in writing amongst other works the famous *De Inventione Dialectica* (1480), a life of Petrarch and poetry of an occasional nature. He died at Heidelberg. His compositions were collected and published by Alard of Amsterdam in 1539.

**Agrippa, Cornelius** (1486–1535), German speculative writer, whose real name was **Nettesheim,** was born of a noble family of Cologne, and entered the imperial service. In 1506 he was sent on a diplomatic mission to France and then went to Catalonia. He is next heard of in 1509 teaching theology at Dôle in Burgundy, where for his strong criticism of the Church's credulity he earned the hatred of the clergy.

The following year he resumed a diplomatic career and was sent to
London where he was the guest of Colet, Dean of St Paul's. In 1511
he went to Italy, becoming doctor of law and of medicine at Pavia in
1515, left for Metz, and was back in Cologne in 1520 where he fearlessly denounced the Inquisition and defended a supposed witch in
public. Driven from Cologne by the clergy, he set up in medical
practice in Switzerland; but his wanderings soon continued, for in
1524 he went to Lyon as physician to the queen-dowager of France.
By now, because of his unorthodox ideas and restless life, the public
with the encouragement of the clergy fastened on him the character
of occult philosopher, and he found it advisable to make his way to
Antwerp where he was little known. There he was appointed historiographer to the Emperor Charles V, and published the two works by
which he is best known, *De Incertitudine et Vanitate Scientiarum*
(1530) and *De Occulta Philosophia* (1531–3). If the first showed him
to be a searcher after scientific truth, the second mystified the public
who considered him now as a downright magician with his black
poodle and magic mirror, and it is only in more recent times that
Agrippa has had justice done him as a thinker of integrity. For his
*De Incertitudine* he lost his appointment, and after further wanderings to Mechlin, and imprisonment at Lyon, he died in Grenoble.
His complete works were published at Lyon in 1550.

**Aho, Juhani,** pseudonym of **Johannes Brofelt** (1861–1921), Finnish
man of letters, born at Lapinlahti. Influenced by French realism, his
historical novel on seventeenth-century Finland, *Panu* (1897), yet
contains a romantic strain inspired by Selma Lägerlöf (q.v.). *Panu*
was dramatized in 1903. The author of many other novels and plays,
Aho died in Helsinki.

**Aimard, Gustave,** pseudonym of **Olivier Gloux** (1818–1887), French
novelist, born in Paris. After various adventures at sea and on land,
which included about fifteen years of nomadic life shared with
American Indians in Arkansas and Mexico, and a journey to the
Caucasus, Aimard settled in Paris to live by his pen. The French
Fenimore Cooper, on whose work he consciously modelled his own,
Aimard soon became the most popular writer of adventure stories in
France. Among his forty-three books may be mentioned *Les Trap-
peurs de l'Arkansas* (1858), *Le Guaranis* (1864), *Les Bohèmes de la
mer* (1865), *Cardenio* (1874), *Par mer et par terre* (1879) and *Le
Rastréador* (1883). During the Commune (1870–1) he organized the
Francs-tireurs de la Presse. He died in Paris.

**Aimeric de Peguilhan** (1195?–1230), Provençal troubadour, born at
Toulouse. He became the favourite of Azzo VI of Este, on whose
death he wrote two carefully written but stiff laments. His other
poetry, including his forty or so love poems, are the results of the calls
made on a professional court poet, who was expected to turn his hand
to any subject whether he felt it or not. He is said to have died a
heretic in Lombardy, having taken refuge there during the time of
the Albigensian wars.

**Akhmatova, Anna,** pseudonym of **Anna Andreyevna Gorenko** (1888–
1966), Russian poet. Born at Kiev, the daughter of an officer in the

merchant marine, her quiet, clear lyrics are to be found in such of her collections as *Chyetki* (1913, 'Prayer Beads'), *Belaya staya* (1917, 'The White Flock'), *Stikhi* (1922, 'Verses') and *Iva* (1940, 'Willow Tree'). In 1910 she married the poet N. S. Gumilyov (q.v.), but divorced him in 1918. She died in Moscow. See the English translation, *Collected Poems, 1912–1963* (1963).

**Aksakov, Sergei Timofeyevich** (1791–1859), Russian novelist and critic, was born at Ufa, and became a civil servant in Moscow where he lived for the greater part of his life and where he died. His most important work, in which he proves himself to be an absolute realist with his eyes always on the pleasantly homely and kindly aspects of life, is *Semeynaya khronika* (1856; Eng. trans. *A Russian Gentleman*, 1917). He turned his early memories to good account in *Detskie gody Bagrova vnuka* (1856; Eng. trans. *Years of Childhood*, 1916) and *Vospominaniya Bagrova vnuka* (1858; Eng. trans. *A Russian Schoolboy*, 1917), both of which contain magnificent descriptions of nature. As a literary historian he is still represented by the very much alive *Literaturnye i teatralnye* (1858).

**Alain,** *see* **Chartier, É.**

**Alain-Fournier,** pseudonym of **Henri Alban Fournier** (1886–1914), French novelist, who was born at La Chapelle d'Angillon (Cher) and was killed in action on the Meuse. His reputation rests on one book, *Le Grand Meaulnes* (1913; Eng. trans. *The Lost Domain*, 1959). In this delicate study of adolescent thought, its keynote the search for a lost land and a lost love, 'more rose and gold than reality', he succeeds almost entirely, although the ending with its account of the discovery of Yvonne and Meaulnes is somewhat disturbing and out of harmony with the remainder of the book. R. Gibson's *The Quest of Alain-Fournier* (1953) is an excellent study of the Alain-Fournier mystique.

**Alamanni, Luigi** (1495–1556), Italian poet. In his youth in Florence he joined to the full in the city's intellectual life and was a friend of Machiavelli (q.v.). On the collapse of the Florentine republic he left Italy for France, and became court poet to François I, dying at Amboise. His outstanding work is a poem in the didactic Roman manner, *Della Coltivazione* (1546).

**Alarcón, Pedro Antonio de** (1833–1891), Spanish novelist, born at Guadix. He began his career as a journalist, first becoming widely known for his *Diario de un testigo de la guerra de África* (1859), an account of the Spanish-Moroccan war in which he served. It was, however, not until 1874 that his internationally famous book appeared, *El sombrero de tres picos* (Eng. trans. *The Three-Cornered Hat*, 1918; rev. ed. 1935), which inspired Manuel de Falla's ballet. His short stories, such as those appearing in *Novelas cortas* (1881–1882) and *El capitán Veneno* (1881; Eng. trans. *Captain Venom or Poison*, 1914) contain the quintessence of Spanish humour in its authentic atmosphere. The best of his long novels is *El niño de la bola* (1880; Eng. trans. *The Infant with the Globe*, 1955), set in Andalusia. Alarcón, a well-known liberal politician, died in Madrid.

**Alarcón y Mendoza, Juan Ruiz de** (1580?–1639), Spanish dramatist. Born of good family at Tasco, Mexico, after several visits to Spain he finally settled in Madrid in 1615 where he held a lucrative government post and where he died. He wrote over twenty heroic tragedies and comedies of character in the ten years following his permanent residence in Madrid. Although he had success in his day his plays were undeservedly forgotten soon after his death, for there is little doubt that at his best he is not far short of Lope de Vega, while on occasion he can even measure up to Calderón. There is a heroic dignity about his presentation of moral problems and the nemesis that awaits the evil doer (especially the miser, the liar and the traducer) which is impressive. He was much pillaged by French playwrights, and his best work, *La verdad sospechosa*, is the absolute source of Corneille's *Le Menteur*. Alarcón's work appears in *Biblioteca de Autores Españoles*, vol. xx.

**Alas y Ureña, Leopoldo,** pseudonym **Clarín** (1852–1901), Spanish novelist and literary critic, was born in Zamora, became professor of law in Oviedo and died in that city. As Clarín he became the most influential literary critic of the day, but he is remembered now as the author of one of the finest European novels of the century, *La regenta* (2 vols., 1884–5), a tragi-comedy of life in a country town. Three of his best short stories, *Pipá, El sombrero del señor Cura* and *¡Adiós, cordera!*, have been translated into English by W. Brooks as *Retold in English* (1905). *Doña Berta* (1896; new ed. 1943) and *Su único hijo* (1913) should also be mentioned.

**Alberdingk Thijm, Josephus Albertus,** pseudonym **Pauwels Foreestier** used for some of his work (1820–1889), Dutch short-story writer and poet, born at Amsterdam, where he died. As editor of the *Volksalmanak voor Nederlandsche Katholieken* he devoted a life's work to the advocacy of Roman Catholic emancipation. Although an ardent student of the poet Vondel (q.v.), in his own poetry he followed the mercurial, inconsistent work of Bilderdijk (q.v.) with mediocre results, such as are to be seen in *De Klok van Delft* (1846). His best work can be found in his short stories, *De Organist van den Dom* (1848) and *Portretten van Joost van den Vondel* (1876), the latter containing particularly felicitous descriptions of seventeenth-century Holland.

**Albert von Stade** (1200?–1261), German poet and chronicler, writing in Latin, was first the Benedictine abbot of Stade, afterwards joining the Franciscans. Besides his *Annales*, a universal chronicle from the Creation to 1256, he wrote an epic on the siege of Troy called *Troilus*, a critical edition of which by T. Merzdorf appeared in 1875.

**Alberti, Leon Battista** (1404–1472), Italian man of letters, artist and scientist. The archetype of the Renaissance humanist, whose interests were all embracing, he was of Florentine family, and received his education at the universities of Padua and Bologna. His outstanding work is *Della famiglia* (1437–41), which, cast in dialogue, is a series of treatises on domestic life and its duties. It gives us unrivalled pictures of the family life of the greater merchant families of the period, touched with the grace of High Renaissance thought and feeling. The book did not appear in its complete form until 1845. His essays on the fine arts were all written in Latin. Alberti died in Rome.

**Alberti, Rafael** (1902–    ), Spanish poet. Born at Santa María, Cadiz, he settled in Madrid in 1917, where his volume of sea lyrics, *Marinero en tierra*, appeared in 1924. He soon fell under the influence of his friend Lorca (q.v.), but by 1929 had freed himself to publish his masterpiece, *Sobre los ángeles* (Eng. trans. *Concerning the Angels*, 1967), an introspective, melancholy work, which surrealistically attacks the spiritual and political malaise of the time. In 1934 he became so implicated in left wing politics that on the defeat of the Spanish Government by Franco (1939) he was forced to emigrate to Buenos Aires. In exile he has published two remarkable volumes of poetry, *Retornos de lo vivo lejano* (1952), elegiac and autobiographical, and *Ora marítima* (1953), a work steeped in ancient Greek legend in praise of his native Cadiz. Alberti is second only to Lorca among his contemporaries. See the English trans. *Selected Poems* by B. Belitt (1966).

**Albertus Magnus** (1206–1280), German scholar writing in Latin, the *Doctor Universalis* of the schoolmen, was born in Laningen, Swabia, of noble family having the title of Counts of Bollstadt, attended the University of Padua, joined the Dominicans, and was the master of Thomas Aquinas (q.v.) at Paris. Gaining an encyclopaedic knowledge, his aim was to place all important non-Christian philosophy and science at the service of theology. With that in mind he studied Graeco-Arabic science and thought, and became a follower of Aristotle, whose work he approached through Jewish, Arabian and Western commentators. The result of his labours was to cause that fusion of theology and Aristotelianism which is the basis of scholasticism. His most notable works are *Summa Theologiae* and *Summa de Creaturis*, in which can be seen the seeds of Thomism. For a short time Bishop of Regensburg, Albertus retired in 1262 to a monastery at Cologne where he died.

**Albov, Mikhail Nilovich** (1851–1911), Russian novelist from Petersburg. He was a follower of Dostoyevsky (q.v.), but seems to have extracted from his model only the most decadent elements. A thorough-paced nihilist, ceaselessly complaining about the drabness of daily life and indulging in the deepest introspection, his collected works (*Sobranie sochineniy*) were published in eight volumes between 1906 and 1908.

**Alcoforado, Mariana** (1640–1723), a Portuguese nun who was born and died at Beja. She was believed without any foundation to have been the author of some love-letters addressed to a French nobleman. No Portuguese original was forthcoming, but the letters appeared in French in 1669 as *Lettres Portugaises*. They are supposed to have been an invention of the publisher, but their popularity was immense, and they are best-selling paperbacks in Portugal in the twentieth century. There is an English translation by E. Prestage (1893).

**Aldana, Francisco de** ('el divino') (1537–1578), Spanish poet. Born at Alcántara, he followed a military life, accompanied King Sebastian of Portugal on his ill-starred Moroccan expedition, and was killed at Alcazar-Kebir. His poetry on a variety of subjects was collected in two volumes (1589 and 1591). His best-known poem is *Epístola a Arias Montano*.

**Aleardi, Aleardo** (1812–1878), Italian poet-patriot of Verona, who died in Florence. As a journalist he freely and openly attacked Austrian rule and was twice imprisoned. His political poems such as the didactic *Le città italiane marinare e commercianti* (1856), in which he argues that Italy must look for her regeneration to sea trade, and *I tre fiumi* (1857), in which he prophetically pronounces that liberation will come from Piedmont, are today more interesting than anything else. His love poetry, *Lettere a Maria* (1847), was immensely popular in its day.

**Alecsandri, Vasile** (1821–1890), Rumanian playwright and poet, was born at Bacău and educated at the French school at Jassy, later going to Paris to study first medicine and then law, both of which he abandoned for literature. Returning to Rumania in 1839 he began to collect Balkan peasant ballads (published 1852–3), and then turned whole-heartedly to the theatre. He had had verse plays produced at the national theatre at Jassy since 1844, for the most part light melodramas and operettas, which were collected as *Teatru romanesc* (1852). They show a pronounced French influence, particularly that of Scribe (q.v.). The plays which he wrote after this, though more finished, are less urgent, e.g. *Ovidiu* (1885, 'Ovid'). Always in close contact with France he won a prize at the Montpellier Festival in 1878 for his poem *La Gent latine*, and gained the friendship of Mistral (q.v.) who translated it into Provençal. Alecsandri, who if anything wrote with too much facility, is on the whole a superficial if polished writer, but his importance as a link between Balkan and Western European literature cannot be overestimated. He died at Mircesti, Rumania.

**Aleixandre, Vicente** (1900–      ), Spanish poet. He was born in Seville of a wealthy family. Ill health prevented his taking up a regular profession. Romantic in feeling, surrealistic in form, two characteristic volumes of his verse are *Espadas como labios* (1932) and *La destrucción o el amor* (1935). More recently he has published *El mundo a solas* (1950), *Historia del corazón* (1954), *Poesías completas* (1960) and *Presencias* (1965).

**Alemán, Mateo** (1547–1614?), Spanish novelist. born in Seville. He was of a Jewish family forcibly converted to Christianity, and was educated at Salamanca and Alcalá. In 1599 appeared the picaresque novel on which his fame depends, *Guzmán de Alfarache*, the second part coming out in 1604 (Eng. trans. *The Rogue, or the Life of Guzmán de Alfarache* by T. Mabbe, 1621, ed. J. Fitzmaurice-Kelly, 1924). The book, written in splendid prose, is the supposed autobiography of a rogue. The standpoint is pessimistic; man sins and the wages of sin are misfortunes ending in death. Alemán left Spain for Mexico in 1608 and died there having written some devotional works.

**Alembert, Jean le Rond d'** (1717–1783), French savant, born in Paris. A natural son of Mme de Tencin (q.v.) and the Chevalier Destouches, he was abandoned as an infant outside the Chapel of St Jean-le-Rond—hence his name—and was brought up by a humble couple. Thanks to the handsome annuities paid to him in secret by his real father he had an excellent education, and made such a reputation as a mathematician that in 1741 he was elected to the Académie des Sciences. In the following years he gained a European reputation with such works as *Traité de dynamique* (1743), *Recherches sur la précession des équinoxes* (1746) and *Recherches sur différents points du système du monde* (1754), in which year he became an Academician. Already (1751) he had become Diderot's foremost collaborator in the *Encyclopédie*, the famous Introduction to which, the *Discours préliminaire*, is his. A social success and one of the most influential men of letters of the day, he is a typical thinker of the rationalistic, anti-clerical age which preceded the revolution. His unrequited love for Mlle de Lespinasse is well known. He died in Paris. His *Œuvres littéraires et philosophiques* appeared in 1821.

**Alexis, Willibald,** *see* Häring, G. W. H.

**Alfieri, Vittorio** (1749–1803), Italian tragedian and poet, was born at Asti of an old noble Piedmontese family, and after a desultory education at Turin he went on a somewhat wild European tour (1767–72). So far his life had been no more than a reflection of his restless and unbalanced nature, but steeling himself to discipline he set himself to be the great tragedian of liberty. Hating the political censorship of Piedmont, he left for Pisa in Tuscan territory where he worked hard to perfect his style, and in the freer atmosphere wrote an essay against tyranny, *Della tirannide* (1777). That very year he met the Countess of Albany, the wife of Prince Charles Edward Stuart, who on her formal separation from her husband in 1784 lived with Alfieri for the rest of his life. Meanwhile his masterpiece *Saul* (Eng. trans. 1820) had been produced in 1782, before which and after which appeared such tragedies on classical themes as *Polinice* (1783), *Antigone* (1783), *Oreste* (1783), *Timoleone* (1784), *Bruto Primo* (1787) and *Bruto Secondo* (1787). Translations into English include *Agamemnon* (1854), *Philip the Second* (1815), *Merope* (1831), *Orestes* (1816) and *Rosamunda* (1856). Marred though they sometimes are by bombastic declamation, and that intentional harshness of language with which Alfieri sought to rouse his public from the cloying sweetness of Metastasio (q.v.), his tragedies of tyranny and tyrants of vast and evil dimensions and of victim-heroes have about them something ruggedly grand and never stand still. Deeply influenced by Rousseau, and a political idealist, he was profoundly shocked by the French Revolution's excesses. An inspirer of the fight for Italian freedom a generation later, he died in Florence, leaving behind him his interesting autobiography, *Vita di Vittorio Alfieri da Asti scritta da esso* (1804; Eng. trans. *Memoirs*, 1951).

**Algarotti, Francesco** (1712–1764), Italian poet and miscellaneous prose-writer. Of a Venetian mercantile family he was never at a loss

for money, and taking advantage of his opportunities travelled
throughout Europe. Cultured and socially polished to the last degree
ne found equal welcome in the *salons* of literary Paris and at the court
of Frederick the Great. As a poet he excelled as a sonneteer and writer
of blank-verse *Epistole* on various subjects, as a traveller his letters
on his journey in Russia, *Viaggi di Russia* (1738–9), are full of life,
while as a keen student of English science and thought he wrote a
popular account of Newton's *Optics*, *Newtonianismo per le dame*
(1735). He was also an art critic, and as an antiquarian of standing
was elected fellow of the Society of Antiquaries of London. He died
in Pisa.

**Aliger, Margarita Iosifovna** (1915–    ), Soviet poet, born in Odessa,
who in 1942 won the Stalin Prize for her patriotic poem *Zoya*,
describing the murder of a Russian girl by the Germans. Her *Stikhi i
poemy* ('Verses and Poems') were published in 1944.

**Almeida, José Valentim Fialho de** (1857–1911), Portuguese short-story
writer and satirist, was born and died at Vila de Frades in the Alentejo
province. A somewhat bitter satirist he lashed many abuses of his
time in *Os gatos* (1889–93) but his best work is to be found in his
attractive stories about the Alentejo in the collection, *O país das
uvas* (1893).

**Almeida Garrett, João Baptista da Silva Leitão** (1799–1854), Portuguese
poet, novelist and playwright, was born in Oporto, the stronghold of
liberalism in the country. Having taken part in a revolt against
oppressive government he was obliged to leave the country in 1820,
and in the following years lived in England and France. Imbibing the
romanticism of Byron and Hugo he published two heroic poems on
historical subjects, *Camões* (1825) and *Dona Branca* (1826), thereby
becoming the father of the Portuguese romantic movement. Returning to Portugal in 1832 he became a leading political figure as a
member of the Liberal Party, and at that party's triumph twenty
years later was given a peerage. Of his later poetry the most significant is *Folhas caidas* (1853), in which his strongly personal
touch is to be seen. As a playwright his *Frei Luís de Sousa* (1844;
Eng. trans. *Brother Luiz de Sousa*, 1909) with its simplicity of pathos
and clarity of style is his greatest work, while as a prose writer he is
best represented by his historical novel, *O Arco de Sant' Ana* (vol. i,
1845; vol. ii, 1850), and his book of travels, *Viagems na minha terra*
(1846). He died in Lisbon.

**Almqvist, Carl Jonas Love** (1793–1866), Swedish novelist, poet and
playwright, born in Stockholm. Of unsettled character, the only lasting influence on him was Swedenborg's (q.v.) mysticism, which in the
end led him to those delusions which were his ruin. He tried every
kind of career from Lutheran cleric to farmer, and made nothing of
any; but he found an opportunity to indulge his egocentricity in the
enormous literary work on which he embarked in 1832, *Törnrosens
bok*, which, in its fourteen volumes all of them published by 1851,
contains historical novels, short stories, plays and above all lyrics
(*Songes*). The most readable of his works today is his short novel,

*Det går an* (Eng. trans. *Sara Videbeck*, 1919). Published in 1839 it was written to discredit the convention of orthodox marriage. His literary career and life in Sweden came to a sudden end in 1851, when he was accused of murder and had to escape to America. Returning to Europe in 1865 he died soon afterwards at Bremen.

**Alonso, Dámaso** (1898–    ), Spanish poet and critic, was born in Madrid. As a poet he started as an imagist (*Poemas puros*, 1921), becoming later a sincere seeker after a solution to mankind's spiritual problems in such works as *Oscura noticia* and *Hijos de la ira* (both 1944). As a literary scholar he is one of the greatest of his generation, being especially appreciated for his work on Góngora (*Soledades de Góngora*, 1927) and San Juan de la Cruz (*La poesía de San Juan de la Cruz*, 1942).

**Altamira y Crevea, Rafael** (1866–1951), Spanish historian and critic, was born at Alicante, and took up a university career, first at Oviedo, where he introduced the earliest educational classes for workmen in Spain, and afterwards at Madrid. He was also a judge of the International Court of The Hague. His great work is his *Historia de España y de la civilización española* (4 vols., 1911; Eng. trans. 1949), which is also of literary value. He left Spain during the civil war and died in Mexico.

**Altolaguirre, Manuel** (1904–1959), Spanish poet. Born in Málaga, his first book of verse, *Las islas invitadas y otros poemas*, was published in 1926. He had by this time become one of Lorca's circle, and the influence of Dámaso Alonso's (q.v.) work on Góngora is reflected in further books, *Ejemplo* (1927) and *Soledades juntas* (1931). A republican during the civil war he went to Cuba, where in Havana he founded a printing works called 'La Verónica'. Later he returned to Spain and died in Burgos. Translations of some of his work appear in *Translations from Hispanic Poets* (N.Y., 1938).

**Álvarez de Cienfuegos**, *see* **Cienfuegos**.

**Álvarez Quintero, Serafín** (1871–1938) and **Joaquín** (1873–1944), Spanish playwrights whose collaboration lasted a lifetime, were born near Seville and died in Madrid, Andalusian to the core. Writing unchangingly down to their last works in the nineteenth-century *costumbrismo* tradition, their pieces range from amusing one-act plays such as *El ojito derecho* (1897) to a serious study of ingratitude like *Los galeotes* (1900), to *genre* pictures like *El patio* (1900) and to a sensitive study of a Spanish (and purer) Madame Bovary in *El amor que pasa* (1904; Eng. trans. 1932). One of the best known of their plays is the sentimentally serious study of Andalusian character, *Malvaloca* (1912; Eng. trans. 1916). *Don Juan, buena persona* (1918) is in their gayest and wittiest vein. See the Granville-Barker translations, *Four Plays* (1927) and *Four Comedies* (1932).

**Amfiteatrov, Alexander Valentinovich** (1862–1938), Russian novelist from Kaluga. His novels on intellectual circles and middle-class society, facile and superficial but very attractively written, appealed to the wide public for whom they were intended. *Vosmidesyatniki*

(2 vols., 1907–8, 'Those of the Eighties') and *Devyatidesyatniki* (2 vols., 1911–13, 'Those of the Nineties') are typical examples of his work. He left Russia in 1917, and died at Levanto, Italy.

**Amiel, Henri-Frédéric** (1821–1881), Swiss prose-writer, born in Geneva. He was early left an orphan, but was brought up by an uncle who took his duties seriously, sending his nephew first to the Académie de Genève and afterwards to Berlin University. In 1849 he joined the staff of the Académie (University) de Genève, first as professor of aesthetics, then lecturer in philosophy, and from 1854 professor of the same, a post which he held until his death. His life was uneventful and his contributions to academic philosophy no more than some articles in learned journals, so that he would have been soon forgotten had it not been for his *Journal intime* (Eng. trans. 1885), which he kept fully from 1847 until his death. In it is clearly revealed that silent tragedy of a man whose supersensitive cerebral existence has paralysed his physical one. Lack of self-confidence and a sense of the futility of all action has nullified his varied gifts and destroyed all hope of realizing his aspirations. The *Journal* is, however, by no means all gloom, some of the passages on literature and the arts being outstandingly beautiful. Amiel died in Geneva.

**Amyot, Jacques** (1513–1593), French scholar and translator, was born at Melun. He became a tutor in Greek and was so successful that he was finally (1557) invited to become royal tutor. He was patronized by both Charles IX and Henri III, becoming Grand Almoner of France (1560) and Bishop of Auxerre (1570), in which city he died. His greatest work was his faithful and sturdy translation of Plutarch's *Parallel Lives* (1599), which became a model for all future work of that kind and was a revelation to a Greekless general public. North relied heavily on it for his English Plutarch. Besides further translations of Plutarch, his most significant works were his translations of the late Greek romances of Heliodorus and Longus. Amyot translated the *Aethiopica* of the former as *L'Histoire éthiopique* in 1548 and the *Daphnis et Chloë* of the latter in 1559.

**Andersen, Hans Christian** (1805–1875), Danish short-story writer, novelist, poet and playwright, and one of the world's greatest writers of fairy-tales, was born at Odense, the son of a shoemaker. After a wretched childhood and early youth he went to Copenhagen to seek his fortune there, taking a humble job in a factory. Although he had an excellent voice, his ugly face and lanky graceless body prevented his taking up a singer's career, as likewise that of an actor. But he found friends and a patron in Jonas Collin, director of the Royal Theatre, who for six years paid for his education. In 1828 he left the school at Slagelse and turned to literature as a livelihood, publishing poetry and various prose works, among them *Fodreise fra Holmens Canal til Østpynten af Amager* (1829, 'The Walk to Amager'), which gives a foretaste of his humour and satirical skill. He brought out two volumes of his poems in 1830–1, and his German travel book, *Skyggebilleder af en Reise til Harzen* (Eng. trans. *Rambles in the Romantic Regions of the Hartz Mountains*, 1848) also appeared in 1831. In 1833 he was granted a royal travelling pension and went to Italy, and his experiences there coloured his first important work, *Improvisatoren* (Eng. trans. *The Improvisators*, 2 vols., 1845), which he wrote on his return to Denmark in 1835. But above all it was this very year that he wrote the first of those 168 fairy-tales for children, *Eventyr, fortalte for Børn*, which appeared from then on at regular intervals until 1872, and which were translated into many languages throughout the world. Among his novels produced in the succeeding years may be mentioned *Kun en Spille-mand* (1837, Eng. trans. *Only a Fiddler*, 3 vols., 1845), *De to Baronesser* (1848, Eng. trans. *The Two Baronesses*) and *Lykke-Peer* (1870, Eng. trans. *Lucky Peer*, 1871). An extensive traveller, he wrote attractive books on Sweden, Spain and Portugal, and his visit to England when he made a friend of Dickens is celebrated in *Et Besøg hos Charles Dickens i Sommeren, 1857* (1868). His correspondence with the Grand Duke of Saxe-Weimar-Eisenach is interesting, and especially his genial if egoistic autobiography *Mit Livs Eventyr* (1855, Eng. trans. *The Story of my Life*, 1871). It was out of his own life story, with its hardship, its successes and the underlying sadness at his own physical ugliness—for he is the Ugly Duckling (*Den grimme Ælling*) of his own short story—that he fashioned the famous fairy-tales. Sometimes, the master of a delicate irony, he mocks at himself, sometimes he is hopeful, a genius fighting for his rightful fame; at other times, as in *Skyggen* ('The Shadow'), he cannot restrain his bitterness as he tells of a cheat who steals a good man's love and happiness; but always he rises above his own shortcomings to give universality to his pure and charming conception of life. Andersen died in Copenhagen.

**Andersen, Tryggve** (1866–1920), Norwegian novelist and short-story writer, born at Ringsaker, is regarded as probably the greatest master of Norwegian prose. He is best known for his historical novel, *I Cancelliraadens dage* (1897), treating of the clash between officialdom and peasant culture in eastern Norway early in the nineteenth century. A neurasthenic, often in the grip of his own hallucinations, his contemporary novel, *Mod kvæld* (1900), clearly reveals the troubled state of his mind, as does his posthumous *Dagbog* (1923), with its gloomy obsession with the sea. His short stories are excellent, among the best being *Gamle folk* (1904) and *Fabler og hændelser* (1915). He died at Gran.

**Andersen Nexø, Martin,** *see* **Nexø, M. A.**

**Andres, Stefan** (1906–    ), German novelist, poet and playwright. Born near Trier, the son of a miller, he was destined for the priesthood, but left his convent school and turned to literature. He travelled much, particularly in southern Europe, was in Spain during the civil war, and lived in Italy from 1937 to 1949. Besides his love of the south his untiring theme is his inability to reconcile his longing for a life in the world and at the same time the life of contemplation in the cloister. His delight in Italy is portrayed in *Der Mann von Asteri* (1939), in Greece in *Der gefrorene Dionysos* (1943; renamed *Die Liebesschaukel* in 1951) and *Das goldene Gitter* (1943). The question of the spiritual and material world begins with his patently auto-biographical first novel, *Bruder Luzifer* (1932), the story of a novice who finds the call of the outside world too much a temptation to withstand, while in *El Greco malt den Grossinquisitor* (1936) a deeper study is made, involving as it does the conflicting claims of free inquiry and orthodoxy. Without doubt the climax of the theme and of the work of Andres is to be found in his novel set in the Spain of the civil war, *Wir sind Utopia* (1942; Eng. trans. *We are Utopia*, 1954). His trilogy, *Das Tier aus der Tiefe* (1949), *Die Arche* (1951) and *Der graue Regenbogen* (1959), collectively entitled *Die Sintflut*, is a stern account of a totalitarian regime, that of Hitler being presumed. Of his verse, *Requiem für ein Kind* (1948), is moving, while in his play *Gottes Utopia* (1950) his most urgent theme, the problem of man in a distracted world, is treated in a different medium.

**Andreyev, Leonid Nikolayevich** (1871–1919), Russian novelist, short-story writer and playwright, born at Orel. After attempting to reproduce the style of Chekhov (q.v.) and to write in the humanitarian vein of Gorky (q.v.) he turned to Dostoyevsky (q.v.) for his model, but succeeded only in extracting nihilism from his new master, as is to be seen in *Eleazar* (1904). Such works, however, appealed to the disillusioned intellectuals. Andreyev's hopes were flattened by the failure of the 1905 Revolution, and in his next novels such as *Gubernator* (1905) and *Judas Iscariot* (1907) his nihilism has vanished as he lashes society and politicians with sharp irony. He next turned to plays in the realistic manner, which added nothing to his reputation. With the coming in 1917 of the Bolsheviks, whom he hated, he left Russia and died in obscurity and poverty in Finland. See the English translation, *When the King Loses His Head* (and other stories), 1920.

**Andrić, Ivo** (1892–     ), Serbian poet and short-story writer, was born at Travnik, Bosnia, studied at four universities, one of them being Vienna, and early became a thorn in the flesh of the Austrians as an ardent patriot. After 1918, with the independence of Yugoslavia, he entered the diplomatic service, finally becoming minister in Berlin. His work may be divided into two kinds, his philosophical lyrics and prose poems, in which he seeks eagerly but painfully to solve the problem of human suffering and to understand the position of man in the universe, such as *Ex Ponto* (1918) and *Nemiri* (1921, 'Disquietudes'), and his vivid studies of all the various Balkan racial types, a meeting and mingling of East and West, such as are to be found in his collections of short stories (*Pripovetke*) appearing in 1924, 1931 and 1936, and *Travnička Chronika* (1945) which contains masterly portraits of the peasants of the region in which he was born. He received the Nobel Prize in 1961. Recent English translations include *The Bridge on the Drina* (1959), *Devil's Yard* (1964) and *The Woman from Sarajevo* (1966).

**Andrieux, François-Guillaume-Jean-Stanislaus** (1759–1833), French poet and dramatist, was born at Strasbourg and became a judge under the National Convention. His poetry, such as the tale *Le Procès du Sénat de Capoue* (1796), shows the uncompromisingly classical lingering on into the romantic era. His verse comedies, ranging in time from *Anaximandre* (1782) to *Le Manteau* (1826), are very vivacious. Andrieux, who was appointed professor of literature at the Collège de France in 1814, died in Paris.

**Angelus Silesius**, religious name of **Johann Scheffler** (1624–1677), German mystical poet, was born at Breslau into a Lutheran family. He practised as a physician, but later was converted to Roman Catholicism and was ordained. In 1657 was published *Heilige Seelenlust*, devotional mystical poems in pastoral style, many of them in use today as hymns. This and his other main work, *Cherubinischer Wandersmann* (1674; selected Eng. trans. 1932), a collection of distichs inspired by the works of Jakob Böhme (q.v.) and D. Czepko, make him one of the most considerable German poets of his age. He died at Grüssau.

**Anghel, Dimitrie** (1872–1914), Rumanian poet, born near Jassy. Deeply influenced by French symbolist literature he wrote such poetry as *Fantezii* (1909, 'Fantasies'). In collaboration with the Transylvanian poet S. O. Iosif (q.v.) he wrote *Caleidoscopul lui A. Mirea* (1908–10, 'A. Mirea's Kaleidoscope'). He died by suicide at remorse for his adultery (ending in marriage) with his friend Iosif's wife, Iosif having died the year before.

**Anghiera, Pietro Martire d'**, *see* **Martyr, Peter.**

**Angiolieri, Cecco** (1260?–1312?), Italian poet of Siena. In his sonnets he reveals his selfish, ungenerous nature. Bewailing his bad fortune in having so little money and jealously railing at Dante, there is yet a certain swagger in his verse, especially when he sings of wine and women. In his burlesques there is a wry sense of the ludicrous. *Il Canzioniere* appeared in 1946, edited by S. Blancato.

**Anker Larsen, Johannes** (1874–    ), Danish novelist. All his life connected with the Royal Theatre, Copenhagen, it was as a writer of fiction with a tendency to religious mysticism that he made his name. Among his numerous works may be listed *De Vises Sten* (1923; Eng. trans. *The Philosopher's Stone*, 1924), *Martha og Marie* (1925; Eng. trans. *Martha and Mary*, 1926), *Sognet, som vokser ind i Himmelen* (1928; Eng. trans. *A Stranger in Paradise*, 1930) and *Hansen* (1949).

**Annensky, Innokenty Fyodorovich** (1855–1909), Russian poet who was born at Omsk and died in Petersburg. His inspiration on the one hand is derived from French poetry, especially that of Mallarmé (q.v.), on the other from Tyutchev (q.v.), both symbolistic, but the first calm and of bright texture, the second inclining always to a menacing darkness. Neglected in his lifetime, it is only in later times that his work has come to be seen at its full worth, influencing among others Pasternak (q.v.). His most characteristic work is the tragedy *Thamiras Cytharede* (1916) with its classical theme used for modern ends. He may be said to have anticipated Giraudoux (q.v.) and others of the modern French school of playwrights.

**Annunzio**, *see* **D'Annunzio.**

**Anouilh, Jean Marie Lucien Pierre** (1910–    ), French dramatist, born at Bordeaux, the son of a tailor, he became a publicity agent and then the secretary of various Paris theatres. He then turned to writing for the theatre, his first successful play *L'Ermine* (Eng. trans. *The Ermine*, 1956, in *Plays of the Year*, vol. xiii) being produced in 1933; but it was not until *La Sauvage* (1934; Eng. trans. *Restless Heart*, 1958) that his full stature was revealed, and he is now regarded as the greatest dramatist of his generation. The true Anouilh flavour is produced first of all by drawing his subjects from classical mythology and then placing them either in a contemporary, near-contemporary or fanciful setting, where the tantalizing drama of happiness just within reach but never quite secured is played out. Although he can portray a relatively pleasant concept of life as in *L'Invitation au château* (1947; Eng. trans. *Ring Round the Moon*, 1950) and in *Colombe* (1951; Eng. trans. 1952), perhaps his greatest works are those which he describes as *pièces noires*, they being marked by profound pessimism. Of these the best known are *Le Voyageur sans bagages* (1937; Eng. trans. *Traveller without Luggage*, 1959), *Eurydice* (1942; Eng. trans. same title, 1951, and as *Point of Departure*, 1952), *Antigone* (1944; Eng. trans. 1951; new ed. 1957) and *Médée* (1946; Eng. trans. *Medea*, 1957, in *Plays of the Year*, vol. xiii). Among his latest plays are *Ardèle ou la Marguerite* (1949; Eng. trans. *Ardèle*, 1957), *La Répétition, ou L'Amour puni* (1950; Eng. trans. *The Rehearsal*, 1961), *La Valse des Toréadors* (1952; Eng. trans. *The Waltz of the Toreadors*, 1956), *L'Alouette* (1953; Eng. trans. *The Lark*, 1956), *Pauvre Bitos* (1956; Eng. trans. *Poor Bitos*, 1964), *L'Hurluberlu* (1957), in which he seems to have found a new and positive interpretation of society, *Becket, ou l'honneur de Dieu* (1959; Eng. trans. *Beckett, or the Honour of God*, 1960), *La Grotte* (1961; Eng. trans. *The Basement*), *L'Orchestre* (1962) and *La Foire d'empoigne* (1962). He wrote the film script of *Monsieur Vincent*, the life of St Vincent de Paul (1949). A shy and retiring man, Anouilh lives at Neuilly in complete seclusion.

**Antokolsky, Pavel Grigoryevich** (1896–       ), Russian poet. Born in Petersburg, he possessed both a lyrical and dramatic power as can be seen from his short and his narrative poems which have been twice collected, first as *Stikhotvoreniya* (1936), his subsequent work appearing in the volume *Stikhi i poemy* (1950). The two most widely known poems of Antokolsky, who early made his peace with Bolshevism, are 'François Villon' (he has always been interested in Western themes) and a monody on the death of his son killed during the German invasion of Russia in 1943.

**Anzengruber, Ludwig** (1839–1889), Austrian playwright and novelist, spent all his life in Vienna. He began his career as a bookseller's assistant and then became a clerk in the service of the police. Making a fortune with his successful play *Der Pfarrer von Kirchfeld* (1870), an attack on fanaticism in religion, he devoted himself entirely to a literary life. His later plays such as *Der Meineidbauer* (1872; Eng. trans. *The Farmer Forsworn*, 1913) and *Das vierte Gebot* (1877; Eng. trans. *The Fourth Commandment*, 1912) deal with Austrian peasant life. His best novel is *Der Sternsteinhof* (1885). From 1884 until his death he was editor of the Viennese *Figaro*. His *Gesammelte Werke* were published (10 vols.) in 1890.

Apollinaire, Guillaume, i.e. Wilhelm Apollinaris de Kostrowitski (1880–1918), French poet, was born in Rome, the illegitimate son of a Polish adventuress and an unknown father. He became naturalized as French in 1914. In 1898 he went to Paris, published his first poems in the periodicals *La Plume, La Revue blanche* and *La Grande France,* and before long was the centre of the circle of young Parisian poets who gathered at the Soirées de la Plume. Founding his own literary review, *Le Festin d'Ésope,* in 1903 he began to proclaim the new poetical ideas which were to result in literature's cubist equivalent of the cubism of painting and sculpture. With the publication of *Alcools* (1913; Eng. trans. 1964), a collection of all his poetry written since his arrival in Paris, he became the acknowledged head of the poets of his generation. In speaking for his generation, during which the sharpest transition that the modern world has known was taking place, he became the source of a new Europe-wide literary movement, its results hardly yet over. He faced as no one had done before the challenges of new inventions such as cars and aeroplanes, not refusing to deal with anything that helped to paint the portrait of his age, whose characteristics he clearly defined. An ardent patriot, he flung himself with vigour into the war of 1914, dying in Paris of wounds received in action two days before the Armistice. That same year was published his second volume of poetry, *Calligrammes,* in which visual and literary art are made to approximate to one another to their extreme limits. This is not surprising, for he saw in cubism the complete expression of the times, and had the highest regard for Picasso and his circle, hailing them in *Les Peintres cubistes* (1913; Eng. trans. 1944) and thereby founding cubism as a conscious school, with its abolition of perspective and the limits of time and place. He points also to surrealism, which term he seems to have invented. The rest of his verse appeared in *Ombre de mon amour* (1948), and among his other works may be mentioned the novels *Le Poète assassiné* (1913) and *La Femme assise* (1920), a story of the Mormons, the collection of short stories, *L'Hérésiarque et Cie* (1910; Eng. trans 1965), and the play *Les Mamelles de Tirésias* (performed 1917; publ. 1918). There are excellent verse translations into English in R. Shattuck's *Selected Writings of Guillaume Apollinaire* (1950).

Aquinas, Thomas (1225–1274), the greatest of all Christian theologians, was born of noble family at Roccasecca, near Aquino, half way between Rome and Naples. Educated by the Benedictines at Monte Cassino and at the University of Naples, he entered the Dominican Order in 1244. He continued his training under Albertus Magnus (q.v.) at Cologne until he became an acknowledged Aristotelian scholar. Called in 1252 to the University of Paris, he remained there lecturing until in 1259 he was appointed to teach in the Papal Curia. He afterwards held academic posts in Pisa and Bologna before returning to Paris in 1268. By now the uncontested leader of European theological thought, his opinions were sought in every kind of dispute within the Church. His health already weakened by continual overwork, he set out to attend the important Council of Lyon but died of fever on the way at Fossannova. As a writer he was a magnificent scholastic Latinist and his Latin verse, which is to be seen in his hymns for the Office of Corpus Christi, is of a high order. His greatest work is the *Summa Theologiae*, in which he built up a theological system of scientific magnificence, the basis of the theology of the Western Church up to the present day. His second greatest work is the *Summa contra Gentiles*, dealing with natural religion. He was canonized in 1323. The standard edition of his works is the *Opera omnia* in the 'Leonine' edition of 1882. There are English translations of the *Summa Theologiae* and the *Summa contra Gentiles* (1920) and see also *Philosophical Texts* (1951).

**Aragon, Louis** (1897–    ), French poet, novelist and essayist, was born in Paris, and studied medicine for a time before leaving it to devote himself to literature and art. Originally a cubist, he published his first work, a book of poems, *Feu de joie*, in 1920. His first novel, *Anicet, ou le Panorama* (1921), describes the breakdown of world morality, while the second, *Le Libertinage* (1924), deals sharply, even cruelly, with love and society. He was one of the founders of surrealism in 1924, and for the next six years led a purely literary life, publishing a book of poems, *Le Mouvement perpétuel* (1925), an idealist novel, *Le Paysan de Paris* (1926) and a volume of literary criticism, *Traité du style* (1928), in which his views of art and life are stated. But a growing conviction that the Western world was in decadent decline led him to Communism (1930), which he commemorated in an aggressive poem, *Front rouge* (1931; Eng. trans. *The Red Front*, 1933). It caused some stir and led to his prosecution. He had by now broken with his former friends and abandoned pure literature as bourgeois; he would now advance the possibilities of social revolution. His early books written with this in view are literary failures, and it was not until he published the first of his three masterly novels on France between the beginning of the century and the war of 1914, biased perhaps, but sombrely dignified and penetrating, that he succeeded in making literature out of his new cause. These three works are *Les Cloches de Bâle* (1934; Eng. trans. *The Bells of Basel*, 1936), *Les Beaux Quartiers* (1936; Eng. trans. *Residential Quarter*, 1938) and *Les Voyageurs de l'Impériale* (1941; Eng. trans. as *The Century was Young*, 1941, and as *Passengers of Destiny*, 1947). Aragon, who took part in the resistance, mourned fallen France in *Le Crève-Cœur* (poems) in 1941 and pilloried collaborators with the Germans in *Le Musée Grévin* (1943). Elsa Triolet (q.v.), whom he married in 1939, is the inspiration for several volumes of poems, the last being *Elsa* (1959). He has written studies of Stendhal (1954), of Soviet literature (1955) and with Maurois (q.v.), *Histoire parallèle des U.S.A. et de l'U.R.S.S.* (1962; Eng. trans. 1964). He has translated Lewis Carroll's *The Hunting of the Snark* (1928) and Petrarch's sonnets (1947). *Semaine sainte* (1958; Eng. trans. *Holy Week*, 1961), a later novel, should also be mentioned.

**Arany, János** (1817–1882), Hungarian poet and translator. Born the son of poor peasants at Nagy-Szalonta, he leapt into fame with his folk epic, the trilogy *Toldi* (1847–79), part of which was translated into English in 1914. Another epic, *Buda halála* (1864; Eng. trans. *The Death of King Buda*, 1936), confirmed his reputation as the greatest Hungarian poet after Petöfi (q.v.). A classical scholar and student of English literature, he made excellent translations of Aristophanes and Shakespeare, in the last of which he was aided by his son Lázsló. János Arany died in Budapest.

**Arason, Jón** (1484–1550), Icelandic poet, born at Grýta. He was the last Roman Catholic bishop of Iceland who fell a victim to the Reformation on the scaffold at Skálholt. His religious and secular poetry is the only poetry of value produced on the island during the period. Although Arason introduced printing into Iceland, none of his own work was published until his *Davíðsdiktr* appeared in 1612. His complete work was published only in 1918.

**Arbes, Jan Jakub** (1840–1914), Czech novelist, was born and died in Prague. He introduced into Czech literature the *romaneto* or short novel with a fast-moving plot, but his best work is his full-length novel, *Agitátor* (1893). His collected work (*Sebrané spisy*) filled forty volumes (1901–16).

**Arène, Paul** (1843–1893), French short-story writer, playwright and journalist, was born at Sisteron, and early became the friend of Alphonse Daudet (q.v.) with whom he collaborated in writing those stories which were published in book form as *Lettres de mon moulin* in 1869. His field was the life of Provence, and the kindliness and charm of his work, pervaded as it is by quiet humour and a subtle quaintness, are to be seen in such novels and collections of short stories as *Jean des Figues* (1868), *La Gueuse parfumée* (1876), *La Chèvre d'or* (1886) and *Domnine*, published a year after his death, which occurred at Antibes. Of his comedies probably the most characteristic is *Pierrot héritier* (1865).

**Aretino, Pietro** (1492–1556), Italian prose-writer, poet and playwright. Born at Arezzo, the son of a shoemaker and not the bastard of a nobleman as he later pretended, he went to Rome to support Giulio de' Medici's candidature for the papacy. He stayed on, full of wit and impudence, until the publication of sixteen obscene sonnets, *Sonetti Lussuriosi* (illustrated by Giulio Romano), forced him to leave for Venice in 1527. There he found himself, wrote his *Commedie*, the only readable Renaissance comedies, and took his revenge on the Rome that had dismissed him in *I Dialoghi* (1536), discussions on the corrupt state of Roman life, and in *I Ragionamenti* (first published 1600, but freely handed about in manuscript in Aretino's time), an attack on the morals of well-known Roman personages. He wrote romantic epics, such as *Lagrime di Angelica* (1538), and a tragedy, *Orazia* (1546). He was killed by a fall in his house in Venice.

**Argensola, Bartolomé Leonardo de** (1561–1631), Spanish poet, born at Barbastro, Aragon, became a priest, and after a stay in Naples as secretary to the Spanish viceroy, was appointed chronicler royal of Aragon at Zaragoza in 1615, and there he died. He was a thorough classicist who modelled himself on Horace, and viewed with distaste the excesses of Góngora's style. In his *Rimas* are to be found odes, epistles and satires as highly polished as anything in Spanish poetry, but too often lacking the final feeling of inspiration. He wrote also some historical works. The standard edition of his works is by Viñaza (1889).

**Argensola, Lupercio Leonardo de** (1559-1613), Spanish poet, born at Barbastro. Like his brother he took up a public career, in that capacity going to Naples where he died, and like him he took Horace for his model as a poet. Inferior to Bartolomé (q.v.), he kept strictly to classical forms except in his sonnets, which are somewhat rough.

**Aribau, Bonaventura Carles** (1798-1862), Catalan poet, who was born and died in Barcelona, became director of the Spanish treasury, and took a leading part in the Great Exhibition, London, in 1851. His *Oda a la Patria* (1833) contains his best work as a poet, and is considered as the chief starting-point of the revival of Catalan literature.

**Ariosto, Lodovico** (1474-1533), Italian poet, was born at Reggio Emilia, near Parma. He studied law and played with poetry, but on his father's death in 1500 was forced to exert himself as head of his family. In 1503 he was introduced to Cardinal Ippolito d'Este at Ferrara and became his secretary, being employed on several missions. In 1506 he began his life's work, *Orlando Furioso*, one of the greatest romantic epics of all time, a continuation of the *Orlando Innamorato* of Boiardo (q.v.), which he finished in 1516. On Cardinal d'Este's death in 1520 Ariosto took service with his brother Duke Alfonso, who in 1522 appointed him governor of the wild mountainous region of Garfagnana. After a successful rule of three years he returned to Ferrara only to retire finally to his country estate in 1527, where he prepared his final longer version of *Orlando Furioso* (1532; Eng. trans. by J. Harington, 1591; by A. Gilbert, 2 vols., 1954; and in Bohn's Illustrated Library), and collected and revised his poetry and his comedies, of which only the sonnets are valuable. Ariosto died at Mirasole, and was buried with much ceremony in a magnificent tomb in the church of San Benedetto, Ferrara. A man of commanding personal appearance and of kindness and integrity, his work in *Orlando* with its excellence of language, narrative power and characterization reveals the fine full flower of the Italian renaissance. There is a monumental three-volume edition of the various versions of *Orlando* by S. Debenedetti (1828), but there are also several handy ones including that by N. Zingarelli (1944).

**Arnault, Antoine Vincent** (1766-1834), French poet and dramatist, was born in Paris and prospered both under the old monarchy and the Empire, but under the restored monarchy he was imprisoned as a turncoat from 1815 to 1819, when a political amnesty restored him to the sun. He was secretary of the French Academy at the time of his death at Le Havre. A confirmed classicist in style, though not in feeling, for his play *Oscar* (1796) is influenced by Macpherson's *Ossian*, there is a certain intensity about the best of his seven dramas, *Blanche et Montcassin ou Les Vénitiens* (1799) His most successful work is, however, to be found in *Fables et Poésies* (4 vols., 1812-26). His autobiography, *Souvenirs d'un sexagénaire* (1833), still has some interest, and he wrote a lengthy *Vie de Napoléon* (1822).

**Arndt, Ernst Moritz** (1769-1860), German poet, was born on the island of Rügen, the son of a former serf. He was educated for the Church with the help of bursaries at the universities of Stralsund, Greifswald and Jena, at the second of which he became professor of history in 1805. A man of strong physique and convictions, his *Geschichte der Leibeigenschaft in Pommern und Rügen* (1803) led to the ending of serfdom; and in his devastating attack on Napoleon, then at the height of his power, in his *Geist der Zeit* (3 vols., 1806, 1809 and 1813, the first vol. translated into English as *Arndt's Spirit of the Times*, 1808), he gave overwhelming proof of his courage. As it was he had to lie low in Stockholm for a while. In the War of Liberation against France (1813) he was foremost in encouraging the national spirit of Germany with such patriotic songs as 'Der Rhein, Deutschlands Strom' and 'Was ist des Deutschen Vaterland?' He was engaged in liberal politics for some years, and in old age as 'Father Arndt' he became a revered legend. He died at Bonn, where he had been professor of history since the university's foundation in 1818.

**Arndt, Johann** (1555-1621), German theological and devotional writer, born at Ballenstedt, in Anhalt, he was educated at four universities, including Wittenberg. Becoming a zealous Lutheran he was appointed, after holding several less important posts, pastor of St Martin's Church, Brunswick, where he remained until his death. Several of his works are so beautifully written as to entitle them to be classed as literature, outstanding among them being *Der Paradiesgärtlein* (1612), which has been translated into English as *The Garden of Paradise* (1716).

**Arniches, Carlos** (1866-1943), Spanish playwright, who was born in Alicante and died in Madrid. Well known for his long series of short plays in which he describes popular life in Madrid, he is at his best in such character studies as *El pobre Valbuena* and *El amigo Melquiades*, these and many another work nearly as good being collected in *Teatro completo* (1948).

**Arnim, Bettina (Elisabeth) von** (1785-1859), German author, was born of a merchant family of Italian origin in Frankfurt-am-Main, the sister of Clemens Brentano (q.v.). Unbalanced and self-assertive with flashes of genius, she became a lion-hunter and pursued Goethe almost, but not quite, beyond the bounds of discretion. Marrying her brother's friend and collaborator, the upright, idealistic Prussian Junker Achim von Arnim (q.v.) in 1811, they led an unsettled and not wholly happy life. After his death in 1831 she turned more and more to literary work, bringing out her readable but for the greater part fictitious *Goethes Briefwechsel mit einem Kinde* (1835; Eng. trans. *Goethe's Correspondence with a Child*, 1837), the child being herself. She died in Berlin, leaving a mass of letters, those to her husband and to Goethe showing not only her wayward charm and her selfishness, but also her intellectual capacity.

**Arnim, Ludwig Joachim,** i.e. **Achim, von** (1781-1831), German novelist and poet. Born in Berlin, he was brought up on the family estate at Wiepersdorf, Prussia, and then studied at Halle and Göttingen, at the latter forming a lifelong friendship with Clemens

Brentano (q.v.). After journeys to France and England, neither of which pleased him, he settled in Heidelberg with Brentano and together they edited a collection of folk songs, *Des Knaben Wunderhorn* (3 vols., 1806–8), which, by tapping a source of literary riches overlooked before, had a great influence. His inhibitions and increasingly morbid isolation, expressed in a style coldly fantastic like a lunar landscape, are reflected in his novels *Armut, Reichtum, Schuld und Busse der Gräfin Dolores* (1810), with its muddled moral values, strangely at variance with the strict integrity of Arnim himself, and *Isabella von Ägypten* (1812; Eng. trans. 1927). In *Halle und Jerusalem* (1811) the doctrine of Novalis (q.v.), that God must be sought in the meanest occupations and dreariest moments of life, is applied with some effect. A Junker himself, Arnim was opposed to the exclusiveness of his class and advocated an aristocracy of spiritual merit to take the place of one of blood, but as might be expected his plea fell on deaf ears. He later tried his hand at historical novels (*Die Kronenwächter*, 2 vols., 1817). He died of heart disease on his Wiepersdorf estate.

**Arnoux, Paul Alexandre** (1884–    ), French novelist, poet and dramatist, born at Digne. Among his works, in feeling eager and optimistic and in expression purely classical, are *L'Allée des mortes* (1906), *Huon de Bordeaux* (1922), *Paris sur Seine* (1939), *L'Amour des trois oranges* (1947), which inspired the composer Prokoviev, and *Contacts allemands* (1950).

**Arriaza y Superviela, Juan Bautista** (1770–1837), Spanish poet. Born in Madrid, where he died, Arriaza served in the Spanish embassies in London and Paris. A master of metre, he used Italian-inspired poetic-rhythmic schemes to charming advantage in his description of dancing, *Terpsícore o las gracias del baile*. Ignoring the rising tide of romanticism he continued to admire Boileau (q.v.), whose *Art poétique* he translated in 1807.

**Artaud, Antonin** (1896–1948), French poet, born at Marseille. Mentally unbalanced, it was not until his visit to Mexico in 1936 that experience gave positive direction to his thoughts, and he began to hurl weird defiance at organized society, using himself and Van Gogh as the pivotal points of his arguments in *Le Retour d'Artaud le Mômo* and *Van Gogh ou le suicide de la société* which both appeared in 1948. That very year he died in Paris, his health destroyed by a long period of addiction to drugs.

**Artsybashev, Mikhail Petrovich** (1878–1927), Russian novelist, born at Ashtyrka, Kharkov. A man of uncertain character and unsettled life, he became an artist, but failing in this turned to novel writing. It was his sensational novel *Sanin* (1907; Eng. trans. 1915), with its preaching of free love and the flouting of convention, that made his reputation. This and such another as *U posledney cherty* (Eng. trans. *Breaking Point*, 1915), which was published in 1912, brought him notoriety among the older generation, but among the young he was considered a champion of revolutionary aspirations. Nevertheless he opposed the Bolshevik Revolution from the outset, and went into voluntary exile in Poland, dying in Warsaw.

**Arvers, Alexis-Félix** (1806–1850), French poet and playwright. The son of a well-to-do Paris wine merchant, his legal studies ended in nothing, and he became a dandy of the boulevards and amateur man of letters. His volume of poetry, *Mes heures perdues* (1833), was most promising, and contained the well-known sonnet, 'Mon âme a son secret'. After some attempts at writing for the theatre which gained him a certain notoriety but no real success, he turned to light comedy and vaudeville, an example of which is *Les Dames patronesses* (1837), written in collaboration with Scribe (q.v.). T. de Banville (q.v.) in 1878 brought out an edition of *Mes heures perdues*. He died in Paris.

**Asbjørnsen, Peter Christen** (1812–1885), Norwegian folklorist, who was born and died in Kristiania (Oslo), together with J. Moe (q.v.) made a great collection of Norwegian folk tales, appearing as *Norske Folkeeventyr* between 1842 and 1871 (Eng. trans. *Norwegian Fairy Tales*, 1924). The style in which they were retold had a great influence on the development of a classical Norwegian language.

**Asnyk, Adam Prot** (1838–1897), Polish lyric poet, born at Kalisz. After living in Italy and Germany for seven years he returned to Poland and settled at Cracow in 1870. His lyrics, which are deeply reflective, were published as *Poezje* in four series between 1869 and 1894. His plays on social problems are unimportant. He died at Cracow.

**Atterbom, Per Daniel Amadeus** (1790–1855), Swedish poet and philosopher, born, the son of a clergyman, at Åsbo. A thorough introvert, he fell under the influence of the vague, pantheistic, Buddhist-inspired philosophy of the later Schelling (q.v.), and began his long amorphous work *Blommorna* in 1812. Two years before in the periodical *Phosphorus*, founded by himself and some friends who called themselves the 'Aurora Society', he inaugurated the Swedish romantic age with some telling essays. Before his originality was stifled by his taking up an academic career as a professor at Uppsala he had written two formless and unactable poetic dramas, on which his fame rests, *Fågel Blå* and *Lycksalighetens Ö* (1824–7). Here in obscurely symbolistic but often beautiful poetry he writes of the earthly happiness which is won only by renunciation. Atterbom died in Stockholm.

**Aubanel, Théodore** (1829–1886), a Provençal poet, was the son of a printer of Avignon, whose trade he followed. With Mistral (q.v.) and others he founded the group responsible for the rebirth of Provençal literature in the nineteenth century. His verses, practically all contained in three collections, are for the most part love poems of great power, their sensuality ennobled by an admixture of spiritual feeling. The three volumes are *La miougrano entreduberto* (1860), *Li fiho d'Avignoun* (1885) and *Lou reire-souleu* (1899). Aubanel died at Avignon.

**Aubigné, Théodore-Agrippa d'** (1552–1630), French poet and scholar, was born into a noble, strictly Protestant, family at St Maury near Pons-en-Saintonge. At the age of nine he solemnly vowed to his father that he would devote his life to the cause of Protestantism, at thirteen took part as a soldier in the siege of Orléans, and then went to study theology under Beza (q.v.) at Geneva. At the Peace of Saint-Germain he entered the court of Charles IX (1570), but two years later, escaping the massacre of St Bartholomew by mere chance, he had to retire once more. At last he found his party triumphing with the advent of Henri de Navarre, but although he became Henri's close friend and companion, the king's outward conversion to Catholicism weakened his position, attempts were made to assassinate him, and on Henri IV's murder in 1610 he found life at court increasingly difficult. At last in 1620 he sold his property and settled in Geneva where he died, so it is said, of shock at the conversion to Catholicism of his son Constant, the father of Mme de Maintenon. Aubigné is the author of two very different collections of poetry. The first, *Le Printemps du sieur d'Aubigné* (not published until 1873), contains some beautiful secular poetry, including love poems in the manner of Ronsard (q.v.), addressed to Diane Salviati, odes, elegies and sonnets. But it is in his long religious and political poem, *Les Tragiques* (1616–19), that he rises to the stature of one of the greatest of French religious poets. Unforgettable are his soldierly attacks on every form of vanity and human wickedness, while his vision of the Last Judgment which ends the work is one of the most powerful and disturbing passages in literature. There is a good critical edition of *Les Tragiques* by Garnier and Plattard (4 vols., 1933). His *Œuvres* edited by Réaume and Caussade appeared (6 vols.) in 1877–92.

**Aubry, Octave** (1881–1946), French novelist, was born in Paris of a well-to-do family, and was educated at Paris University. His first publications were scholarly ones, and it was not until *Sœur Anne* (1912) and *L'Homme dans la Cime*, which was serialized in the *Nouvelle Revue* (1913), that he became known as a novelist. Later still he gained European fame with attractively written if somewhat sensational historical novels about the eighteenth century and the Napoleonic era, such as *Brelan de Femmes ou le Coup d'État de Brumaire* (1927). After gaining a fortune by his pen, the while working as a civil servant, he returned to serious historical writing with *La Trahison de Marie Louise* (1933), *Sainte-Hélène* (1935) and several other studies of Napoleon's later career. His travel books, nearly all dealing with Spain, include *Couleur de Sang* (1926), *Visions d'Espagne* (1927), *L'Espagne: Les Provinces du Sud de Séville à Cordoue* (1929) and *L'Espagne: Les Provinces du Nord de Tolède à Burgos* (1930).

**Audefroi le Bastart** (*fl.* early thirteenth century), French poet probably from Arras, many of whose sixteen extant poems are addressed to Jean Blondel (q.v.), sieur de Nesle (Somme), who died in 1241. The greater part are lyrics, and a few are short sentimental narratives. They are typical of the courtly poetry produced by the *trouvères* of the time.

**Audiberti, Jacques** (1899–1965), French poet, novelist and dramatist, born at Antibes. As a poet he showed the influence of Mallarmé (q.v.) as in *Race des hommes* (1937), *La Nouvelle Origine* (1942), *Toujours*

(1944) and *Rempart* (1953). As a novelist he inclined to the monstrous, to nightmarish fantasy, to baroque style and the burlesque as in *Abraxas* (1938), *Carnage* (1942), *Le Maître de Milan* (1950), *Marie Dubois* (1952) and *Les Jardins et les fleuves* (1954), although in the latter classical calm creeps in increasingly. As a dramatist he wrote plays on the whole humorous and imaginative such as *Quoat-Quoat* (1946), *Le Mal Court* (1947), both outstanding in their different ways, *Pucelle* (1950), *Les Naturels du Bordelais* (1953), *La Hobereaute* (1958) and *L'Effet Glapion* (1959). He also wrote a cinema play, *La Poupée* (1963). He died in Paris.

**Auerbach, Berthold** (1812–1882), German novelist, born of a Jewish family at Nordstetten, Württemberg, was given a rabbinical education, and attended various universities, including Heidelberg, where he turned to the study of law and philosophy. But suddenly in 1836 he was arrested for his too advanced political opinions and suffered imprisonment. So broken in spirit and mind was he after his release that a professional career (for he had abandoned the idea of becoming a rabbi long before) had to be given up. He turned to his pen for a living, first as a literary critic in the Jewish interest (*Das Judentum und die neueste Literatur*, 1836) and then as a student of Spinoza, translating his works (5 vols., 1841). While thus engaged he had discovered his latent talent as a novelist with *Das Ghetto: Spinoza* (1837; Eng. trans. 1882) and *Dichter und Kaufmann* (1839; Eng. trans. 1877); but it was with his sentimentally idealized stories of Black Forest peasant life, *Schwarzwälder Dorfgeschichten* (4 vols., 1843–54; Eng. trans. *Black Forest Village Stories*, 1869), that he made his name. His longer novels which followed, such as *Barfüssele* (1856; Eng. trans. *Little Barefoot*, 1873) and *Edelweiss* (1861), have lost all the earlier if sophisticated charm, and his last works such as *Auf der Höhe* (1865; Eng. trans. *On the Heights*, 1867) are heavy and moralizing. After a restless, wandering life Auerbach, who did more than anyone to make popular the German novel of peasant life, died at Cannes.

**Auersperg, A. A.,** *see* **Grün, A.**

**Augier, Guillaume-Victor-Émile** (1820–1889), French dramatist. Born at Valence he became librarian of the duc d'Aumale, and soon began to write for the stage in verse. Apart from his first, *La Ciguë* (1844), which is on a classical theme, all these plays devolve upon social questions and are thoroughly anti-romantic, *Gabrielle* (1849) being a prime example. In 1854 he turned to prose with a play on a family problem, *Le Gendre de M. Poirier*, in the style of Dumas *fils* (q.v.), later works in the same vein and each dealing with a different social problem being, for example, *Lions et renards* (1869), prostitution, and *Les Fourchambault* (1878), illegitimacy. The stagecraft of Augier is accomplished, and with natural dialogue and good characterization at his command he produced some very creditable work. He died at Croissy.

**Autran, Joseph** (1813–1877), French poet and dramatist, was a native of Marseille. A devotee of the classics he modelled his nature poetry on Greek and Latin verse forms, *Ludibria Ventis* (1838) and *Epîtres* *rustiques* (1861) being good examples of this unvarying, slightly precious style. His one real success was a play in the Greek manner, *La Fille d'Éschyle* (1848). He died in Marseille.

**Auvergne, Martial d'** (1430?–1508), French story writer and poet. A legal official of the Parlement of Paris, he wrote a series of short stories, *Arrêts d'amour* (1640–5), which humorously treat of love and its troubles with mock legal pomposity. His dull poetry includes *Les Vigiles de Charles VII*. He probably spent all his life in Paris, dying there.

**Aventinus, Johannes,** also known as **Johannes Thurmayr** (1477–1534), German scholar and historian, was born at Abensberg (Latin Aventinum), Bavaria. Professor of Greek and mathematics at Cracow, he died at Regensburg. He is best remembered for his attractively written history of Bavaria, *Bayerische Chronik,* finished in 1533 and published in 1566, the final edition in a Latin version, *Annales Boiorum libri VII,* appearing in 1580. It has always greatly appealed to men of letters as a source book.

**Averchenko, Arkady Timofeyevich** (1881–1925), Russian humoristic writer, born in Sevastopol. The best of his work appears in his contributions to the magazine *Satyricon* published in Petersburg from 1906 to 1917. His humour too often degenerates into buffoonery, and more than that, there is too often present a cheap vulgarity designed to appeal to the lowest type of reader. An opponent of the Revolution he did not, however, emigrate to western Europe until 1922. His work was much appreciated in Germany, translation of his bizarre sketches being published as *Grotesken* in 1914 and 1919. He died in Prague.

**Averroes,** called **Ibn-Rushd** (1126–1198), Spanish Arabic philosopher. Born in Cordoba, the son of the kadi there, he himself became kadi of that city and of Seville, but died at Marrakesh in Morocco. His chief life's work in literature was as a commentator on Aristotle, and the importance of his scholarship in this field to Western Latin thought cannot be overestimated. But his doctrine of the Universal Reason as opposed to individual reasons, one for each man, ended in his denial of the immortality of the individual, and Averroism was condemned by Pope Leo X. Most of his writings are known only through Latin translations, the great edition being the Venetian one of 1552.

**Avicebron,** i.e. **Ibn-Gabirol, Solomon ben Judah** (1020?–1070), Jewish poet and philosopher, was born in Malaga, spent the greater part of his life in Zaragoza, but died in Valencia. He composed a Hebrew grammar in about 1040, but his greatest prose work, preserved fully only in a Latin translation as *Fons Vitae,* was originally written in Arabic. Here neo-platonist philosophy is set forth in the form of dialogues, and had profound influence on Western thought in many quarters, as different as the Franciscans and Schopenhauer. His leading poetical work, *The Royal Crown,* is in Hebrew.

**Ayala,** *see* **López de Ayala.**

**Aymé, Marcel** (1902–1967), French novelist and playwright, born of a humble family at Joigny. Absolutely self-educated, he became an insurance agent, salesman and journalist before he definitely took to literature in 1929. A sceptical realist, with a dash of pessimism, and at the same time broad humour and fantasy in his work, his main characteristics are well represented in such novels and short stories as *La Table aux crevés* (1929; Eng. trans. *The Hollow Field*, 1933), *Les Contes du chat perché* (1934; Eng. trans. *The Wonderful Farm*, 1952), *La Belle Image* (1941; Eng. trans. *The Second Face*, 1951) and *Le Passemuraille* (1943). Among his plays may be named *Clérambard* (1949; Eng. trans. 1958). Other translated works include *La Jument verte* (*The Green Mare*, 1938) and *Across Paris* (1957). The best of his later dramatic work is to be found in the collection, *Le Minotaure, précédé de la Convention Belzébin et de Consommation, théâtre* (1967). He died in Paris.

**Azaña y Díaz, Manuel** (1880–1940), Spanish man of letters and statesman. Born at Alcalá de Henares, he was educated by the Augustinians, but later went to France to study law. He returned to Spain to pursue a quiet intellectual life, becoming secretary of the famous literary society, the Madrid Ateneo, in 1913. It was not until 1926 that he became known as an accomplished literary scholar with the first of his studies of Juan Valera (q.v.), the Spanish novelist, *La vida de D. Juan Valera*. Two other works on Valera were *La novela de Pepita Jiménez* (1927) and *Valera en Italia* (1929). His delicate autobiographical account of his early years, *El jardín de los frailes* was published in 1927, and the extension of his intellectual ideas and researches is to be seen in his two collections of essays, *Plumas y palabras* (1930) and *La invención del Quijote* (1934). But before this, in 1931, he had entered politics as prime minister of the second Spanish republic, resigning in 1933. In 1936 he became last president of the republic, and on the defeat of his forces went into exile in France, dying in Montauban. It is not surprising that all his later works are political, but although their interest today is documentary rather than literary, they are all invested with an acuteness of mind and distinction of style all Azaña's own. A great orator, his collection of speeches, *Discursos*, shows him at his restrained and dignified best. He translated George Borrow's *Bible in Spain* into magnificent Spanish (1921).

**Azeglio,** *see* **D'Azeglio.**

**Azorín,** *see* **Martínez Ruiz, José.**

# B

**Babel, Isaak Emmanuilovich** (1894-1941?), Russian Soviet short-story writer born of Jewish parents in Odessa. He took part in the Civil War on the Bolshevik side and later served with Budenny's Cossacks in Poland, an experience which he vividly describes in the collection of stories, *Konarmiya* (1926; Eng. trans. *The Red Cavalry*, 1929). This was followed in 1927 by another collection, *Yevreyskye rasskazy* ('Jewish Tales'). A writer of romantic contrasts, he can combine faith and scepticism, gentleness and cruelty, extreme beauty and ugliness in a single page with dazzling effect. Having rapidly attained popularity in the twenties, his ironic detachment and individualism proved too much for Stalin's Russia, and he died, by means unknown, in a concentration camp. See the English translation, *Collected Stories* (1955).

**Babits, Mihály** (1883–1941), Hungarian novelist, born at Szekszárd, was notable for his highly individualistic novel *Timár Virgil fia* (1922; Fr. trans. *Le Fils de Virgile Timár*, 1930). He died in Budapest.

**Bacarisse, Mauricio** (1895–1931), Spanish poet and novelist, was born in Madrid, where he died. In his two mature volumes of verse, *El paraíso desdeñado* (1928) and *Mitos* (1929), he introduced many new French influences into Spanish poetry with good effect. His strange novel, *Los terribles amores de Agliberto y Celedonia*, was published in the year of his death.

**Bacchelli, Riccardo** (1891–     ), Italian novelist from Bologna. At first becoming known as an advanced literary practitioner he developed into a writer in the grand manner of Manzoni's (q.v.) *I promessi sposi*. Of his early style *Il diavolo al pontelungo* (1927; Eng. trans. *The Devil at the Long Bridge*, 1929) and *La città degli amanti* (1929; Eng. trans. *Love Town*, 1930) are representative. His great work is his admirable saga of the Italian nation, stressing its unity, *Il mulino del Po* (3 vols., 1938–40; Eng. trans. *The Mill on the Po*, 2 vols., 1952), in which the best features of the nineteenth-century Italian historical novel reappear. A very fine later work is *I tre schiavi di Giulio Cesare* (1958). For the earlier novels see *Tutte le novelle, 1911–1951* (12 vols., 1952–3).

**Bachaumont, Louis Petit de** (1690–1771), French writer of literary memoirs. Born in Paris in easy circumstances he figured in many *salons*, and was a leading contributor to *Mémoires secrets pour servir à l'histoire de la république des lettres* (ed. by no means in its entirety by P. Lacroix, 1859), which is of enormous importance as containing much information about literary censorship and biographies of authors. He died in Paris.

**Baculard d'Arnaud, François-Thomas de** (1718–1805), French playwright and novelist, born in Paris, where he died. A sensationalist writer with an eye for facile stage effect and an ability to harp on sensibilities in a superficially lachrymose period, his fame by 1750 increased to such an extent as to induce Frederick the Great to invite him to his court. Baculard accepted, but his ludicrous vanity soon brought the visit to an end. It was, however, after this that his significant work was done. *Le Comte de Comminge* (1764) still keeps its place in literary history as an early and characteristic example of the horrific melodrama, which in the 1790's and later was to become one of the most spectacular forms of popular romanticism. *Euphémie*, another piece in the same manner, was staged in 1768. Thereafter he turned more and more exclusively to the novel as an adherent of the school of 'feeling' growing up in the wake of Rousseau. Representative of this last approach and style are *Les Épreuves du sentiment* (6 vols., 1772–81) and *Les Délassements de l'homme sensible* (6 vols., 1783–93), rambling novels, written generally in an inflated way. His *Œuvres* were published in 1803.

**Baena, Juan Alfonso de** (*fl.* 1410–1445), Spanish anthologist. Little is known of his life except that he held some appointment at the court of Juan II of Castile, for whom he edited an anthology of nearly six hundred poems, written during the last hundred years in Castile and Galicia, and including some by Imperial and Páez. This collection, known as the *Cancionero de Baena* (first publ. in 1851 by E. de Ochoa, q.v.), was presented to the king in 1445 and is the first important work of its kind in Spanish literature. Besides, thanks to Baena's work many poems which would otherwise have been lost were preserved, and through it we gain an insight into the taste of the period. A facsimile edition of the 1860 Leipzig one by P. J. Pidal of the *Cancionero* appeared in New York in 1926, edited by H. R. Lang.

**Baerle, Kasper van** (1584–1648), Dutch poet writing in Latin and in the vernacular, was born in Antwerp. In 1617 he was appointed a professor at Leiden, but owing to the enmity of his colleagues, they being clergymen of the Reformed Church while he was an ordained Remonstrant, he was deprived of his post two years later. In after life he held office in the Amsterdam Athenaeum and he died in that city. A convenient volume by which to assess his abilities as a Latin poet is *Poëmata* (1628), while in the lengthy *Verscheyde nederduitsche Gedichten* (1651–3) the full compass of his Dutch poetry, together with that of others, is to be found.

**Baggesen, Jens** (1764–1826), Danish poet and prose-writer, was born at Korsør, Zealand. Going to Copenhagen he became well known for his verse, such as *Comiske Fortællinger* (1785), being especially patronized by the German colony resident in the city. He married a German in 1790 and continued to write as much in German as in

Danish for some time, the former work filling two volumes as *Gedichte* in 1802. A man unsettled in purpose and always in need of a guide, Baggesen first became an uncritical devotee of Kant (q.v.). rechristening himself Immanuel; next, in 1791 he began to travel widely, his earlier experiences of his travels being turned to good account in his most enduring book, the delightfully whimsical volume of prose, *Labyrinthen* (2 vols., 1792–3; new ed. 1909), and returning to Denmark in 1806, after a number of years in France, he flung himself into the arms of Oehlenschläger's (q.v.) vivacious bluestockinged sister. Her declared purpose was to convert the laggard into a thorough-paced romantic like her brother, and she succeeded for a time; but breaking free, Baggesen turned away from such seductions, and for the rest of his life went his own, often sad, way, following in the path of that neoclassicism with a pale admixture of romanticism to be seen in such works as *Heideblumen* (1808) and *Poetiske Epistler* (1814). Family disasters, bad health and poverty had darkened his later years when he died at Hamburg. His Danish works are comprised in *Danske Værker* (12 vols., 1827–32), his German in *Poetische Werke* (5 vols., 1836).

**Bagritsky, Eduard,** pseudonym of **Eduard Dzyubin** (1897–1934), Russian Soviet poet. Born at Odessa, he is chiefly remarkable as the author of the tragic epic, *Duma ob Opanase* (1925, 'The Lay of Opanas'), set in the Ukraine at the time of the civil war (1918–20). He died in Moscow.

**Bagrynowski, S.,** *see* **Sieroszewski, W.**

**Bahr, Hermann** (1863–1934), Austrian playwright, prose-writer and critic. Born at Linz, by 1890 he had become a leading influence in letters when his *Zur Kritik der Moderne* was published. In *Dialog vom Marsyas* (1904) he investigated the relationship between art and society, and in *Expressionismus* (1914; Eng. trans. 1925) he gave a cogent account of that *avant-garde* philosophy of the arts, expressionism. So varied was his talent that he was equally at home in original literature, as was proved by his novels *Theater* (1897) and *Himmelfahrt* (1916), and by his excellent comedy *Das Konzert* (1900; Eng. trans. 1921). He died in Munich. His critical studies of three Austrian writers, Grillparzer, Stifter and Feuchtersleben (qq.v.), were published long afterwards in 1947 as *Oesterreichischer Genius*.

**Baḥya, ibn Paqūda,** known also as **Baḥya ben Joseph** (*fl.* 1040), Spanish Hebrew poet and Arabic philosopher, is said to have been born at Zaragoza, where presumably he died. He became a judge of the rabbinical court. His famous work is *Hidāyah ilā farā'id alqulūb*, in its Hebrew text, *Hovath ha-Levavoth* (mod. ed. by A. S. Yahuda, 1912; Eng. trans. *The Duties of the Heart*, 1904). In this splendid work Baḥya, while preaching observance of the Mosaic and rabbinical law, teaches as of even more account that heart is more important than body. In this he proves himself to be a neoplatonist. Much of his liturgical poetry remains in manuscript, most noteworthy being the group in the Bodleian Library, Oxford.

**Baïf, Jean Antoine de** (1532-1589), French poet. Born in Venice, he early came to Paris and joined the circle of the Pléiade. As an unending experimenter in metrical forms he made unsuccessful attempts to introduce several complicated classical metres into French poetry, failed in his bid to acclimatize the Alexandrine, and invented an ugly fifteen-syllable line called the *baïfin*. Baïf was also a musician and obtained a royal patent to found an academy of poetry and music, which began to take in pupils in 1567. His concerts were patronized by Charles IX and Henri III. He is chiefly known for his *Œuvres en rime* (4 vols., 1572-3) and *Mimes, enseignements et proverbes*, which were published in a long series between 1576 and 1597. *Poésies choisies*, a carefully selected edition of his poetry, was published in 1874, but this could do little to rehabilitate him. As a contemporary, Cardinal Perron, said of him: 'A very good man, but a very bad poet.' He died in Paris.

**Baillet, Adrien** (1649-1706), French literary critic. Born and educated at Neuville-au-Hez, Picardy, he became a priest in 1676, and after serving in the country became librarian to the Advocate-General of the Parlement of Paris. In this position he was enabled to devote much time to research, the most important result of which was his *Jugements des savants sur les principaux ouvrages des auteurs*, a scholarly review of the work of all kinds of writers, never completed. It was much used by men of letters and plundered by critics of the day. Baillet died in Paris.

**Bajza, József Ignać** (1755-1836), Slovak novelist, born at Predmier, is the author of *René mládenca príhodi a skúsenosti* (1783-5, 'The Adventures and Experiences of Young René'), part fact, part fiction, in which are most interesting descriptions of the scenery and social life of Slovakia, with sidelights on the problems confronting the nation. It is accounted the first Slovak novel. Bajza died at Bratislava. His collected works appeared between 1861 and 1863.

**Balaguer, Victor** (1824-1901), Catalan man of letters who so forcibly furthered the revival of his national literature, was born in Barcelona. While a student at Barcelona University he made a reputation as a dramatist, and soon afterwards entering politics he became a leader of the Liberal Party in his native city in 1843. The foremost advocate of Catalan nationalism, he began in 1857 to publish poetry in Catalan, a collective edition of which was brought out as *Poesías catalanas* (2 vols., 1868). He had already (1866) retired from Spain to Provence, where he found himself at home with the Provençal poets, whose revival of their literature had much in common with the Catalan renaissance. Before this he had moved to Madrid carrying his political influence with him, and thither he returned in 1869, becoming a deputy of the Cortes and minister for the colonies in 1871. Two collections of Catalan tragedies were published in 1876 and 1878, by which time he had dropped out of politics. He died in Madrid. See his *Obras* (35 vols., 1882-98).

**Balassa(-i), Bálint** (1554-1594), Hungarian poet. Born at Zólyom of a noble family, he became the greatest lyric poet of his country without rival until modern times. Well versed in classical literature, his short war poems and love lyrics, together with some devotional poetry of less urgency, make up the sum total of his work, a critical edition of which by Dézsi was published in 1923. Balassa died at Esztergom.

**Balbuena, Bernardo de** (1568–1627), Spanish poet and novelist. Born at Valdepeñas, he went out to Mexico in his early days, and apart from a short spell in Spain at a seminary at Sigüenza, remained abroad for the rest of his life. He is the author of three works, the descriptive poem on the city of Mexico, *La grandeza mexicana* (1604; ed. J. V. Horne, 1930), *El siglo de oro* (1607; modern ed., 1821), which is a pastoral novel in Italian style with an admixture of charming eclogues and an epic poem, *El Bernardo* (1624; *Biblioteca de Autores Espanoles*, xvii), inspired by Ariosto's *Orlando* (q.v.). Balbuena, who became Bishop of Puerto Rico in 1620, died there.

**Balde, Jakob** (1604–1668), German poet and dramatist, writing only in Latin. Born at Ensisheim he became a Jesuit, and before long gained a reputation as a poet in the style of Horace and a modern master of all forms of Horatian metre. His *Lyrica* (1643–6) was a collection much appreciated not only in his own day, but in the later eighteenth century, gaining a new lease of life from the praise bestowed on it by Herder (q.v.) and others. It was translated into German twice between 1828 and 1831. His odes for festivals, modelled on the *Carmen Saeculare*, catch something of the authentic ring of the original. Balde's religious drama *Jephthias* (1654), also in Latin, is of less moment. His *Opera* were collected in 1660. He died at Neuburg-am-Donau.

**Baldi, Bernardino** (1553–1617), Italian poet. A native of Urbino, he is remembered as the author of *La Nautica* (1590; modern ed. by G. Bonifacio, 2 vols., 1919), an instructive and attractive poetical account of ships and sea trade.

**Balmes Urpía, Jaime Luciano** (1810–1848), Spanish savant. Born at Vich, Catalonia, he read law at the University of Cervera, graduating in 1833. Ordained, he yet took up journalism, becoming editor of *El Pensamiento de la Nación*, in which he tried to make peace between Legitimists and Carlists. Later he took to academic life, and in 1844 published a much read and translated defence of Roman Catholicism, *El protestantismo comparado con el catolicismo* (Eng. trans. 1849), in which he sought to counterbalance the influence of the Protestant Guizot's *Histoire de la civilisation en Europe*. In this as in his *Filosofía fundamental* (1846; Eng. trans. 1856) he proves himself to be a tolerant man and a thinker of deep penetration. His apology for the Spanish Inquisition (anon. Eng. trans. 1841) is hardly convincing. His *Obras completas* were published in a definitive edition in 1948. He died in Vich.

**Balmont, Konstantin Dmitrievich** (1867–1943), Russian poet. Born at Gumichi he became prominent as a *fin de siècle* poet, influenced by Shelley, Baudelaire, Whitman and Wilde. During his best period from about 1895 to 1910 he produced poetry which displayed possibilities open to Russian poetic diction unrealized before. His collected works were published in ten volumes between 1908 and 1913. He died in exile in Paris, having long outlived his fame.

Balzac, Honoré de (1799–1850), French novelist. Born at Tours, he was educated at the Oratorian college in Vendôme (1807–13), and was afterwards put into a lawyer's office where he learned enough about criminology to be able to deal with it convincingly in his future work. His relations with his parents were never happy, and there is little doubt that his mother's openly avowed lack of love for him had the most far-reaching effects. In 1820 he broke off all connection with them and went to live in a Paris garret, existing on the miserable allowance they made him. During the two years of garret life he began to write, but neither *Les Deux Hector* nor *Mon Cousin de la main gauche* had any success; yet his meeting with Madame de Berny took place at this time. She had been at the pre-Revolutionary court at Versailles, and from her Balzac was able to build up the world of the old nobility which he was to use as the historical starting point of his *Comédie humaine*. Their liaison, which lasted for several years, was of general benefit to Balzac. Madame de Berny is the central personage in *Le Lys dans la vallée* (1835). Meanwhile the young man had tired of Bohemia and had returned to the family in 1822; but the publishing and printing business, which he started in 1825 with considerable financial aid from his father, ended in disaster three years later. But he had not ceased to write, and when affairs looked at their blackest he had his first literary success with *La Physiologie du mariage* (1829; Eng. trans. *The Physiology of Marriage*, 1925). *La Peau de chagrin* (1831; best Eng. trans. *The Fatal Skin*, 1949) brought him more than wide and almost unanimous praise—it brought him an anonymous letter, which turned out to be from the Polish Countess Hanska. This was the beginning of that romance of eighteen years which ended in marriage after the death of her husband and a few months before Balzac's own death. In the intervening years in order to meet her he travelled to Vienna, Rome, Brussels and Petersburg, and finally in 1847 stayed with her on her Ukraine estate. It was in 1833 that the idea of the *Comédie Humaine*, 'The Drama of Human Life', came to him. A gigantic conception, it was to be a huge series of novels depicting minutely every aspect of French society from the beginning of the Revolution of 1789 to the present, and this finally reached down to 1848, the fall of Louis-Philippe. Flamboyant and vital, credulous, open and moody, mentally (it would seem) tireless, Balzac's treatment of life as exemplified in the novels is the man himself, but withal he wrote always objectively. His work is essentially romantic, but so detailed as to make it appear that he is a realist. It has such faults as diffuseness and even rhetorical emptiness at times, but everything is too intensely alive to suffer from these mistakes, and this great series is one of the triumphs of literature. His output—he wrote eighty-five novels—is enormous and was only accomplished by almost superhuman work, sometimes running to sixteen hours at a stretch. No wonder he died at fifty-one. Unrecognized by the French Academy, still heavily in debt, since his extravagant tastes precluded such mundane matters as saving, this intensely attractive, vivid man died in Paris, almost literally poisoned by the unending stream of black coffee which helped him through his hours of toil. It was not until 1842 that he had definitely, as he shows in his famous preface, decided on the architecture of his *Comédie humaine*. This, which does not by any means account for all his works, consists above all of the *Études de mœurs*. These may be divided into *Scènes de la vie privée*, *Scènes de la vie de province*, *Scènes de la vie parisienne*, *Scènes de la vie politique* and *Scènes de la vie de campagne*. Of *la vie privée* novels the outstanding are *Une Fille d'Ève* (1830–9), *La Femme de trente ans* (1831–44), *Le Père Goriot* (1834–5; Eng. trans. *Old Goriot*, 1951), *La Fausse Maîtresse* (1841), *Mémoires de deux jeunes mariées* (1841–2; Eng. trans. *The Two Young Brides*, 1902), *Honorine* (1843) and *Modeste Mignon* (1844). Of *la vie de province* novels particularly to be noticed are *Le Curé de Tours* (1832), *Eugénie Grandet* (1833), *Les Illusions perdues* (1837–43; Eng. trans. *Lost Illusions*, 1951), *Pierrette* (1841), *La Rabouilleuse* (1841–2) and *La Muse du département* (1843). Then come the *Scènes de la vie parisienne*, including *L'Histoire des treize; Ferragus* (1833), *La Duchesse de Langeais* (1833–4) and *La Fille aux yeux d'or* (1834–5), *L'Histoire de la grandeur et de la décadence de César Birotteau* (1837; Eng. trans. *César Birotteau*, 1928), *Splendeurs et misères des courtisanes* (1839–47), *Un Prince de la Bohême* (1840), *Un Homme d'affaires* (1845), *La Cousine Bette* (1846; Eng. trans. *Cousin Bette*, 1948) and *Le Cousin Pons* (1847; Eng. trans. *Cousin Pons*, 1950). The *Scènes de la vie politique* are less successful but comprise *Les Chouans* (1829) and *Une Ténébreuse Affaire* (1841). Finally in the *Scènes de la vie de campagne* are *Le Médecin de campagne* (1833), *Le Curé de village* (1838–9) and *Les Paysans* (1844). The second main division of the *Comédie humaine* is that entitled *Études philosophiques*. Here belong such works as *L'Élixir de la longue vie* (1830), *La Peau de chagrin* (1831), already mentioned, *Maître Cornélius* (1831), *L'Auberge rouge* (1931), *Les Proscrits* (1831), *L'Enfant maudit* (1831–6), *La Recherche de l'absolu* (1834), *Un Drame au bord de la mer* (1835) and *Massimilla Doni* (1839). Finally come the *Études analytiques*, represented by *La Physiologie du mariage* (1829), already mentioned, and *Les Petites Misères de la vie conjugale* (three series, 1830, 1840 and 1845). The definitive edition is the *Œuvres complètes* (ed. Bouteron and Longnon, 40 vols., 1912–40). The whole *Comédie Humaine* has been translated into English (ed. G. Saintsbury, 40 vols., 1895–8), but a newly translated series is much needed. Good modern translations are noted in the course of this article.

**Balzac, Jean-Louis Guez** de (1597–1654), French prose-writer, born at Angoulême. A member of the famous literary circle at the Hôtel de Rambouillet, his collections of letters, many of which were published between 1618 and 1637, soon came to be regarded as models of French prose. He died at Balzac, Charente. His *Œuvres complètes* were published in 1665.

**Bances Candamo, Francisco Antonio de** (1662–1704), Spanish poet and dramatist, born at Sabugo, Avilés. After his student career at Seville University he turned to a literary life, becoming a dramatic critic, a lyric poet and a writer of comedies. Although he shows that he had a style of his own in the two latter spheres, it was not strong enough for him to avoid being entirely overshadowed by his acknowledged masters, Góngora in poetry and Calderón on the stage, albeit only the Calderón of the comedies. His *Obras líricas* were collected in 1720 and his *Obras cómicas* in 1722. He died at Lezuza.

**Bandello, Matteo** (1485–1561), Italian poet and writer of short stories, was born at Castelnuovo Scrivia in Piedmont and joined the Dominican Order in a minor capacity, afterwards leaving it. Driven from Milan after the Spanish victory of Pavia in 1525, he settled in France and was consecrated Bishop of Agen in 1550. He is represented as a poet by his volume of lyrics, *Il canzoniere* (1544). His 214 short stories, *Le novelle*, composed between 1512 and 1560, appeared in four volumes between 1554 and 1573. They provided a gold-mine of plots for European dramatists, none of them turned to greater account than *Giulietta e Romeo*, from which grew Shakespeare's *Romeo and Juliet*. Massinger also stood particularly in his debt for plots. Bandello died in France at Bassens, Garonne. There is an excellent collected edition, *Tutte le opere*, by F. Flora (2 vols., 1934–5). All the *Novelle* were translated into English by J. Payne (Villon Society, 6 vols., 1890).

**Bang, Herman Joachim** (1857–1912), Danish novelist. Born at Adserballe, Zealand, he became an actor, failed and took to authorship. A lonely and unbalanced man who could never reconcile himself to the realities of life, he made a tentative approach to the very problems which beset him in *Realisme og Realister* (1879), enlarging his area of review in *Kritiske Studier* (1880). It was, however, with his novel *Fædra* (1883), dramatized as *Ellen Urne* in 1885, that he found his public. Before long he came to excel in the portrayal of the drab life of ordinary people in such works as *Stille Eksistenser* (1886) and *Under Aaget* (1890). Tragedy, which underlies these novels but which remains unseen, comes nearer to the surface in *Ida Brandt* (1896, originally entitled *Ludvigsbakke*; Eng. trans. *Ida Brandt*, 1928) and *Mikael* (1904). It is actively present in *De uden Fædreland* (1906; Eng. trans. *Denied a Country*, 1927), a work which touches on topical social and political questions. *Masker og Mennesker* appeared in 1910 (Eng. trans. *A Play and Some Poems*, 1943). Bang, who for some years had led an unsettled life, died at Ogden, Utah, U.S.A.

**Banville, Théodore de** (1823–1891), French poet, playwright and short-story writer. Born at Moulins, the son of a naval officer, he soon made his way to Paris, where he came under the influence of Gautier (q.v.); but it was his study of medieval metres, which he handled with such dexterity as to gain the title of 'roi des rimes', that gave his work its special flavour. He began to publish early, his work at this time being a fusion of romantic and classical elements. *Les Cariatides* (1842), *Les Stalactites* (1846) and the later *Odes funambulesques* (1857) reveal his poetry at its best. *Dans la fournaise* (1892) is an example of his later verse. As a playwright, with his wit and taste for parody often obtruding, he wrote *Le Beau Léandre* (1856), *Gringoire* (1866), probably his best piece, *Deidamia* (1876) and *Le Baiser* (1888). As a short-story writer he was more successful than as a playwright. Daintiness, brilliance and a nice sense of form are often displayed in such collections as *Esquisses parisiennes* (1859), *Contes féeriques* (1882), *Contes héroïques* (1884) and *Contes bourgeois* (1885). A selection from his poetry was translated into English by A. T. Strong (1913). Banville died in Paris.

**Baour Lormian, Pierre Marie** (1770–1854), French poet and playwright, was born at Toulouse. Imbued with the classical concept of revolution and empire, he opened his career with an uncompromisingly classical epic, inspired at a great distance by Tasso, *La Jérusalem délivrée* (1795), while Ossian was the framework on which he built his none the less classical *Poésies galliques* (1801). As a dramatist he came forward with dull tragedies of eighteenth-century character such as *Omasis* (1806) and *Mahomet II* (1810). A zealous opponent of romanticism in all its forms, he published as late as 1847 a severe and outdated religious epic, *Le Livre de Job*. He died in Paris.

**Barahona de Soto, Luis** (1548–1595), Spanish poet. Born at Lucena, he became a physician in Cordoba, later moving to Antequera, where he died. The most famous of his works is *La primera parte de la Angélica* (1586), an imitation of Ariosto's (q.v.) *Orlando Furioso*, and he wrote a number of lyrics, whose grace was praised by Cervantes (q.v.). There is an excellent study of his life and work by F. Rodríguez Marín (1903).

**Baraković, Juraj** (1549–1628), Dalmatian poet. Born near Zara, he became a priest. His topographical poem on the history of Zara, *Vila Slovinka* (1614), is with all its imperfections a major contribution to early Slav literature. He died in Rome.

**Baratynsky, Evgeny Abramovich** (1800–1844), Russian poet. Expelled from the Royal School, Petersburg, in which city he was born, he joined the army, and after serving for eight years in Finland retired and settled in Moscow. He soon found his way into Pushkin's circle, where he became known as a thoughtful, pessimistic poet writing in a sharp, close-knit manner. He wrote narrative poetry such as *Eda*, but it is in *Sumerki* (1842, 'Dusk'), a volume of lyrics, that he most definitely reveals himself. He died of tuberculosis in Naples. His collected works appeared in the Kazan edition of 1884.

**Barberino, Andrea da** (1370?–1430?), Italian writer and compiler of prose epics, was born at Barberino, Valdelsa. He is known as the author of the collection of Carolingian epics, *I Reali di Francia* (ed. G. Vandelli, 1892–1900). He died in Florence.

**Barbey d'Aurévilly, Jules Amédée** (1808–1889), French novelist and short-story writer. Born at Saint-Sauveur-le-Vicomte of an old Norman landed family, he became a man-about-town in Paris, aping Byron and Brummell, and gained the reputation of 'dandy' (a new word hardly acclimatized in France) and satanist, which so fascinated Baudelaire (q.v.) and others. He dabbled in literature, becoming a critic and occasional contributor to *Le Pays* and other papers, displaying also an aggressive royalism and catholicism. The economic ruin of his family in 1851, however, suddenly drove him to his own resources. He turned to his pen, having made a certain reputation in some quarters with his original and unsavoury novel

*Une Vieille Maîtresse* (1849). His renewed effort resulted in *L'Ensorcelée* (1854) with its satanism, *Le Chevalier des Touches* (1864) and *Un Prêtre marié* (1865). His collection of weird stories, *Les Diaboliques* (1874; Eng. trans. *She-Devils*), pushes the theme of satanism and the black arts to the utmost limits. His *Œuvres complètes*, including all his literary criticism, were published (17 vols.) in 1926–7. Barbey died in Paris, unesteemed then. The present century has given him more than his due.

**Barbier, Henri Auguste** (1805–1882), French poet. Born in Paris, he studied for the Bar, but soon turned to authorship, gained a following with his satire *La Curée* (1830) and general recognition with *Les Iambes* (1831) which ran through over thirty editions in fifty years. Other poetic satires were *Il Pianto* (1832), scourging degenerate Italy, while *Lazare* (1833) did the same for Britain's harsh industrial revolution. His work after 1840 changes; satire dies out and is replaced by a quiet sadness. Such is to be found in *Chants civils et religieux* (1841), *Rimes héroïques* (1843) and *Les Sylves* (1864). Barbier helped to provide Berlioz with the libretto of *Benvenuto Cellini*. He died in Nice.

**Barbieri, Giovanni Maria** (1519–1574), Italian literary scholar, who lived all his life at Modena, was the first to put Romance studies on a true scientific basis. His great work dealing with the origin of rhymed verse appeared as *Arte del rimare; Dell' origine della poesia rimata* in 1790.

**Barbusse, Henri** (1873–1935), French poet, novelist and publicist. Born at Asnières, he became a journalist, the while trying his hand at symbolist poetry such as *Pleureuses* (1895) and *Les Suppliants* (1903). It was his experience of the 1914 war, however, that canalized his powers, the result being *Le Feu, journal d'une escouade* (1916; Eng. trans. *Under Fire*, 1917), a powerful anti-war novel of gigantic proportions, full of outraged feelings and human sympathies. When peace returned he became a Communist, and his new-found belief in the coming brotherhood of man is the theme of his next work, *Clarté* (1919; Eng. trans. *Light*, 1919). The consequent difficulties in bringing about the millennium in the post-war world is the burden of *Les Enchaînements* (2 vols., 1925; Eng. trans. *Chains*, 1925). *Jésus* (1927) offended some, but was a serious if ingenuous confession of faith; but *Staline* (1934) showed that he could go to almost impossible lengths in pursuit of belief. He died in Moscow while on a visit.

**Barea, Arturo** (1897–1957), Spanish novelist and literary critic. Born in the bleakest circumstances at Badajoz, he took part in the Spanish Civil War on the Government side and came to Britain as an exile in 1939. There he turned his experiences to good account and, thanks to the outstanding qualities of his wife as a translator from Spanish into English, made a name for himself with the trilogy inspired by his experiences in Spain, which appeared as *The Forge* (1940), *The Track* (1943) and *The Clash* (1946). The original Spanish text, *La forja de un rebelde*, was not published until 1951. His studies of *Lorca* (1944)

and *Unamuno* (1952) were pioneering works in the criticism of subjects which have now become much better known. *The Broken Root*
(1951) described present-day Madrid. He died at Faringdon, Berkshire.

**Baretti, Giuseppe Marc' Antonio** (1719–1789), Anglo-Italian prose-
writer. Born at Turin, he left home in 1735 and drifted into literature
for a living. Mentally trenchant, socially awkward and morose, for
him it was a happy day when, realizing a long-cherished ambition, he
landed in England, the country whose literature he had always so
much admired (1751). In London this man, impatient of the pedantry
of the Italian academies, breathed a new air. In spite of his rough
manner he soon won the confidence and friendship of Samuel Johnson
and his circle, and made something of a reputation with his *Italian
Library* (1757), an account of Italian authors and their works. His
*Italian-English Dictionary* (1760) was popular for nearly one hundred
years. In the same year he revisited the Continent, in his *Lettere
familiari*, published the same year, giving an account of Spain and
Portugal. His *Manners and Customs of Italy*, published two years
after his return to England in 1766, is entertaining and vivid. While
in Italy he had entered the literary lists against 'Petrarchan purists',
the pretensions of the periodical *Il Caffè* to lay down laws, and the
new comedy as represented by Goldoni (q.v.), with his journal *La
Frusta letteraria* ('The Literary Scourge') which he ran in Venice
(1763–5). His acquittal for stabbing a man to death in self-defence
(1769) belongs to the annals of literary biography. In 1777 he
nullified Voltaire's strictures on Shakespeare. An interesting bridge
between Italian and English culture, and a fighter for the freedom
of development of Italian literature when it seemed that academi-
cism was all-powerful, Baretti died in London. The best edition of
his works is that by Piccioni (6 vols., 1911–36).

**Bargone, Charles,** *see* **Farrère, Claude.**

**Barlach, Ernst** (1870–1938), German dramatist, born at Wedel,
Holstein. A sculptor also, the quality of whose work is still subject to
debate, he wrote some powerful plays, revealing his pessimistic belief
in man's ultimate doom, although love can go far to make this
transitory life bearable. Among them may be named *Der blaue Boll*
(1926) and *Die gute Zeit* (1930). His work was banned under the
Hitler regime, which has perhaps led to the present tendency to
overpraise him. He died at Güstrow.

**Baroja y Nessi, Pío** (1872–1956), Spanish novelist and autobiographer,
was born near San Sebastián and took up medicine. After practising
not very successfully for a time he went to Madrid where he became
manager of a bakery, and it was not until the business collapsed in
1902 that he took to writing. His novels deal for the most part with
the dispossessed of the world, but to atone for his often nihilistic
themes, which verge at times on cynicism, there are always a redeem-
ing, even though sharp, humour, a good clear style and splendid
natural descriptions. Of his enormous output his Basque novels
*Zalacaín, el aventurero* (1909) and *Las inquietudes de Shanti Andía*
(1911; Eng. trans. *The Restlessness of Shanti Andía*, 1959) are in his

very best manner. Highly characteristic of another and more strident manner are *Aventuras, inventos y mixtificaciones de Silvestre Paradox* (1903), an account of the Bohemian life of Madrid, *La feria de los discretos* (1905; Eng. trans. *The City of the Discreet*, 1917), about Andalusia, and *Paradox, rey* (1906; Eng. trans. *Paradox King*, 1931), a satirical fantasy about an expedition of eccentric Europeans to Africa. Later straight novels are *La canóniga* (1929) and *Aviraneta* (1931), and the trilogy about the Spanish Republic, *La familia de Errotacho* (1932). Very pessimistic are his masterly sketches of London, *La ciudad de la niebla* (1909, 'The City of Mist'), while his philosophy of life is presented in *El árbol de la ciencia* (1911; Eng. trans. *The Tree of Knowledge*, 1928), and in his story of lost youth, *Las noches del Buen Retiro* (1934). His *Memorias* (6 vols., 1944–9) are of extreme interest both for himself and the Spain of his time. He died in Madrid.

**Baronio(-us), Cesare** (1538–1607), Italian Latinist and historian. Born at Sora, Naples, he went to Rome in 1557 and became a pupil of St Philip Neri, joined his Congregation, and was nominated superior of it in 1593. His great work is *Annales Ecclesiastici a Christo nato ad annum 1198* (12 vols., 1588–93; other important eds. are that by Mansi, 38 vols., 1738–59; and that by Theiner, with a continuation by O. Raynaldus to 1565, 37 vols., 1864–83). It was written at the suggestion of St Philip Neri in reply to the Protestant *Magdeburg Centuries*. As such it was bound to take on a polemical note; but the nobility of its style, the tremendous critical ability displayed in the choice made from boundless material and the splendid symmetry of the whole render it a landmark in historical writing which is also literature. Baronius was made cardinal in 1596, and would have become pope in 1605 had it not been for the Spaniards, whose claim to Sicily he had sternly opposed in various works. He died, Vatican librarian, in Rome.

**Barrès, Augustin-Maurice** (1862–1923), French novelist and publicist, was born at Charmes-sur-Moselle in Lorraine. A keen French nationalist he hated the German annexation of Alsace-Lorraine and moved to Paris, where he supported Boulanger, the militant politician, and was deputy for Nancy from 1889 to 1893. At this time an outspoken individualist, his trilogy, *Le Culte de moi*, appeared as *Sous l'œil des barbares, Un Homme libre* and *Le Jardin de Bérénice* between 1888 and 1891; but seeing in the Panama scandal and the Dreyfus affair signs of decadence in France he hastened to support the bulwarks of nationalism in *Le Roman de l'énergie nationale*, the first volume of which, *Les Déracinés* (1897), sang the praises of native soil, while the second, *L'Appel du soldat* (1900), gave an appealing account of military life. Some of his best work is less personal, such as the travel pieces *Les Amitiés françaises* (1903) and the country epic *La Colline inspirée* (1913; Eng. trans. *The Sacred Hill*, 1929). *Au service de l'Allemagne* (1905) contains powerful invective against those who seek to play down the menace of Germany. *Colette Baudoche* (1909; Eng. trans. 1918) has downright charm. During the war Barrès gained enormous popularity with his patriotic articles in the *Écho de Paris*.

In his last work, *Un Jardin sur l'Oronte* (1922), he returns to a quieter style. Having exercised a profound influence on his generation, he died in Paris.

**Barrière, Théodore** (1823–1877), French dramatist. Born in Paris, he became a geographical engraver and later was a clerk in the war ministry, finally giving himself up entirely to writing for the stage. His first success was *La Vie de Bohème* (1849) in which he collaborated with Murger (q.v.), the author of the novel from which the play is taken. The most important of his other numerous plays are *Les Faux Bonshommes* (1856) in collaboration with E. Capendu, *Les Gens nerveux* (1860) with V. Sardou (q.v.), and *L'Infortunée Caroline* (1864) with L. Thiboust. He died in Paris.

**Barrili, Antonio Giulio** (1836–1908), Italian novelist. Born at Savona, he was trained for the law, but settled in Genoa as a journalist. Soon afterwards he turned novelist, and became immensely popular as the author of facile and sentimental novels about outsize heroes and heroines. By 1866, when he broke off to serve under Garibaldi in the 1866–7 campaign, he had written two highly successful books, *Capitan Dodèro* (1865; Eng. trans. 1920) and *Santa Cecilia* (1866). His best novels are generally considered to be *Val d'Olivi* (1873), *Come un sogno* (1875) and *Cuor di ferro e cuor d'oro* (1877). He became a deputy in 1876 and professor of Italian literature at Genoa in 1889. He died at Carcare.

**Barrios, Daniel Leví de,** christianized **Miguel** (1625?–1701), Spanish poet, born at Montilla. An absolute time-server, although having declared himself a Jew, he was just as ready to call himself a Roman Catholic and serve in the Spanish army in the Low Countries. Finally, however, his apostasy proved too much for him, and having settled in Amsterdam he was reconverted to Judaism. His highly intricate and often insipid poetry is to be found in his three books published in Brussels, *Flor de Apolo* (1665), *El coro de las musas* (1672) and *Poesías famosas* (1674). He probably died in Amsterdam.

**Barros, João de** (1496–1570), Portuguese prose-writer. Born at Viseu, he was brought up at the court of King Manuel and remained a courtier all his life. Inspired by the colonial conquests of his country, he wrote a grandiloquent romance of chivalry, *La Crónica do Emperador Clarimundo* (1522), in which he touches on the subject in a fictional way. In 1533 he was made head of the Portuguese colonial administration, a turning point of his life. As the glories of the empire stretched out before his eyes he decided to be its historian, taking Livy as his model. The result was *Asia*, an account of the eastern conquests in noble rolling prose, the first part of which appeared in 1552, the second in 1553, the third in 1563 and the fourth not until 1615 (the whole ed. H. Cidade, 3 vols., 1945–6). Barros's work had great influence on Camões (q.v.) in planning his *Lusíadas*. He died at Ribeira de Litém.

**Bartas, Guillaume de Salluste du,** *see* **Du Bartas, G. de S.**

**Barthélemy, Auguste Marseille** (1796–1867), French poet. Born at Marseille, he was educated by the Jesuits at Juilly, and moving to Paris in 1822 began to attack the Bourbon regime in verse satire. His epic *Napoléon en Égypte* (1828) was immensely popular with its open support for a Napoleonic revival, and the fears of the reactionary government of Charles X were increased by his elegy on the death of Napoleon's son the Duke of Reichstadt, *Le Fils de l'homme* (1829). For this he was imprisoned and became a popular hero; but two years later made his peace with Louis Philippe's government, received a pension and became a government hack. His later work was generally ignored. He died at Marseille.

**Barthélemy, Jean-Jacques** (1716–1795), French prose-writer. Born at Cassis, he settled in Paris in 1744 as assistant keeper of the royal collections of medals, becoming keeper nine years later. In literature he is celebrated as the author of the first successful attempt to construct antiquarianism, aesthetics and topography into a cohesive narrative, for his *Voyage du jeune Anacharsis en Grèce* (4 vols., 1788) 'taught while it entertained' and had a wide European success. It subtly reflects the scholarly tastes of an age on the doorstep of change. In 1789 he was elected a member of the French Academy. On the outbreak of the Terror in 1793 his age did not save him from arrest as a royalist, but he was soon freed as a man of singular unworldliness, kindliness and enormous learning. A close friend of Madame du Deffand in days past, he died in Paris. The first collected edition of his works was that by Villenave (4 vols., 1821).

**Bartrina, Joaquín María** (1850–1880), Spanish poet. Born at Reus, near Barcelona, he had a hard youth, and very early set out on a journalistic career, the exigencies of which wore him out at an early age and before long killed him in Barcelona. His biting poem, *Algo* (1874), in which he reviews human follies, made its mark. In the year of his death appeared a collection of his work, *Obras en prosa y verso de don Joaquín María Bartrina*.

**Bartsch, Rudolf Hans** (1873–1952), Austrian novelist. Born at Graz, where he died, he became a regional novelist of his native Styria, his most widely read novel in this *genre* being *Elisabeth Kött* (1909; Eng. trans. 1910), before turning to biographical novels with *Schwammerl* (1912). This romantic piece of fiction, partly anchored in fact, has for its subject the life of Schubert, and was made into an operetta as *Das Dreimäderlhaus*, eventually finding its way on to the English stage as *Lilac Time* (1922). *Der grosse alte Kater* (1929), in which a sentimentalized Schopenhauer (q.v.) appears, is perhaps the most successful of his later works in the same vein.

**Bashkirtseff, Marie Konstantinova** (1860–1884), Russian prosist writing in French, was born at Poltava, but was brought up in Italy. In 1877 she went to Paris to become an art student under Bastien-Lepage, and was successful enough to exhibit regularly at the Salon from 1880 to 1884. Her best-known painting is *L'Atelier Julian*. It is, however, her remarkable *Journal*, so self-revealing in a manner unattempted before, even by Amiel (q.v.), which has kept her name alive. Published in 1887 after her death it was translated into English in 1890. A close friend and correspondent of Maupassant, her letters to him, signed 'Russ', were published in 1891. She died in Paris.

**Basile, Giambattista** (1575?–1632), Italian short-story writer. Born in Naples he gained wide knowledge of the world as a soldier and politician, and in the course of a varied career he gathered material for his collection of fifty Neapolitan stories, many of them founded on folk tales, published in 1637 and known as *Il Pentamerone* (Eng. trans. *The Pentameron* by R. Burton, 1893; better, *The Pentamerone* by N. B. Penzer, 2 vols., 1932). It had an immense influence on folklorists, most outstandingly on the brothers Grimm (q.v.). Basile died at Giugliano.

**Bass, Eduard,** pseudonym of **Eduard Schmidt** (1888–1946), Czech novelist and short-story writer, was born in Prague and died there. He began with short stories, the most considerable collection being *Klapzubova jedenáctka* (1922; Eng. trans. *The Chattertooth Eleven*, 1943), but later turned to the full-length novel. *Cirkus Humberto* (1941; Eng. trans. *Umberto's Circus*, 1950) contains much humour, some of it uncomfortable, and fine descriptive passages.

**Bassani, Giorgio** (1916–     ), Italian poet and short-story writer, was born at Bologna. He stands out as one of the leading neo-realists. As a poet he is represented by *Te lucis ante* (1947) and *Un' altra libertà* (1951), but of recent times he has turned more and more to prose, and it is in this medium that he has matured, as in *Gli ultimi anni di Clelia Trotti* (1955), *Cinque storie ferraresi* (1956), *Gli occhiali d'oro* (1958) and above all *Il giardino dei Finzi-Contini* (1962), Proustian in its preoccupation with past time, and set in the neighbourhood of Ferrara which has proved an inspiration to him.

**Basselin, Olivier** (early fifteenth century), French poet. Born in the Val-de-Vire, Normandy, he composed drinking songs, known as *vaux-de-vire*, from which the word 'vaudeville' is derived.

**Basterra, Ramón de** (1888–1928), Spanish poet. Born in Bilbao, he became an advocate and went into the diplomatic service, settling in Madrid where he died. He endeavoured to face up to modern challenges to traditional poetry, overhauling symbolism and recasting forms of presentation in order to revivify the appeal of art. Basque folklore and classicism are attractively blended in his work, of which may be named *La sencillez de los seres* (1923), *Los labios del monte* (1924) and the two 'Virulo' books, *Las mocedades* (1924) and *Mediodía* (1927). His selected works were brought out as *Una antología poética de Ramón de Basterra* in 1939.

**Bataille, Henry** (1872–1922), French poet and dramatist, born at Nîmes. His first book of poetry, *La Chambre blanche*, was published in 1895. His best poetic production was *Le Beau Voyage* (1904), and in the same year he began his long series of stage successes with *Maman Colibri*. His dramatic essays appeared in *Écrits sur le théâtre* (1917), and his last work was *L'Homme à la rose* (1920). He died at Rueil.

**Batyushkov, Konstantin Nikolayevich** (1787–1855), Russian poet. Born at Vologda, he joined the diplomatic service and while in

Naples (1817) published *Opyty v stikhakh i proze* ('Works in Verse and Prose'), containing poetry of great tonal and metrical beauty such as had not been seen before in Russian literature. He became insane in 1822 and died in Vologda. His collected works were published (3 vols.) in 1885-7.

**Baudelaire, Charles Pierre** (1821–1867), French poet and prose-writer. Born in Paris, the son of a civil servant old enough to remember the *ancien régime* whose exquisite manners he retained, and of a kindly but superficial mother of English ancestry, the future poet was brought up in an atmosphere of peace and security which was to haunt him throughout his life (*see* 'L'Ennemi' in *Les Fleurs du mal*). The death of his father left him for a time the centre of his mother's affection, and it was a disaster for him when she married a young, vigorous and commanding army officer, Aupick, afterwards a general and ambassador. From then on Baudelaire became difficult and rebellious, and in despair his parents sent him on a sea voyage (1841). The ship was to have taken him to India but soon, tiring of the plan, he prevailed on the captain to land him at Mauritius. Here he stayed for nearly a year in the house of Madame Autard de Bragard, responding to the sensuousness of all about him and storing up those vivid impressions which he was to reproduce, deepened and seasoned by nostalgia, in such hauntingly beautiful lyrics as 'La Vie antérieure', 'Parfum exotique' and 'L'Invitation au voyage'. Many was the time that in the midst of the northern gloom of Paris he would dream of ships and the sea and the violent colours of tropical islands, and these became for him the symbols of the ultimate unobtainable ideal. In 1842 he returned to Paris to claim his inheritance, the capital left him by his father, and took a mistress, a half-caste actress in a third-rate theatre, the notorious Jeanne Duval, who became a financial responsibility to him for the rest of his life, for a long time alienating his mother's affection and draining his steadily diminishing fortune. But between 1842 and 1844, installed in fine apartments in the Hôtel Lauzun, living recklessly beyond his means, taking to poetry, experimenting with those aids to 'les paradis artificiels', opium and hashish, and cultivating the dandy with an admixture of 'satanism' derived from Byron, Baudelaire enjoyed a fleeting glimpse of that independence which was never to be his again. It was a formative experience, and out of it grew many features of those literary characteristics that he made so particularly his. The intense interest in art, the preoccupation with the fantastic and the unreal, aided by drugs, and the anatomizing as it were of the spleen produced by the great city of mists and watery skies grow out of these Lauzun years. But the time of reckoning soon came, for, realizing that if he continued at this rate all his fortune would vanish, his stepfather insisted that he should submit to guidance in the administration of his affairs. The result of this was that for the rest of his life he was forced to keep within the bounds set him by a kindly but intensely narrow-minded provincial lawyer. Already, however, as his friends testify, he had fortunately found his poetic feet, and by 1846 he had written enough to be able to announce a publication shortly. By 1849 he was adver-

tising a volume entitled *Limbes*, but this never appeared, and his
debut as a poet in print took place with two contributions to *Le
Magasin des Familles* (1850). There was still expectation of a volume
*Limbes* when in 1852 a book with the same title by someone else led
to the adoption of the famous one, *Les Fleurs du mal*, and under this
title eighteen poems were published in *La Revue des Deux Mondes* in
1855. By this time two ingredients had powerfully increased his gifts:
sensual love for the 'Black Venus', Jeanne Duval, idealistic love for
the 'White Venus', Madame Sabatier, with in between the obsession
with the actress Marie Daubrun, the character of which still remains
uncertain; while at the same time there is a revolt against the so-
called pleasures of the world, which he had found so hollow. Hence
the title of the great collection *Les Fleurs du mal*, enticing beauty
hiding corruption, which was at length published in 1857. (Many
translations have appeared.) This shared the distinction of Flaubert's
*Madame Bovary*, which appeared the same year, of being singled
out for prosecution for immorality, but was finally allowed to be
sold minus six condemned pieces. To describe *Les Fleurs* adequately
here is impossible. Suffice it to say that it is one of the greatest volumes
of lyric verse produced by a poet in modern times. There may
have been poets with wider ranges, but within his range he is inimitable. Above all no one has conveyed better than he the sickness
of mind which lies at the heart of so much of urban civilization,
the neuroses of modern life, or has identified himself with, and
so meaningfully described, 'les soleils mouillés de ces ciels brouillés'
of the north. If there are poems which are harsh and horrible such
as 'Une Charogne', then so sometimes is life. On the other hand there
is a cry to God from the heart in 'De Profundis Clamavi', there
is the tenderness of love ('Le Balcon' and 'Harmonie du Soir'), the
romantic impulse of 'L'Invitation au Voyage', the breath of autumn
and the fear of winter in 'Chant d'Automne', hopelessness in the
'Spleen' poem beginning 'Quand le ciel bas et lourd . . .', and a
nobility in which the end of 'Le Voyage' has hardly been surpassed.
'L'Horloge' marvellously conveys the idea of modern panic at the
passing of time, while in 'Recueillement' there is a note of resignation
which seems to fill the evening sky with its cadence. Some of these
poems were not written in time for the edition of 1857, but appeared
either in that of 1861 or the posthumous one of 1868. The rest of his
poetry is to be found in *Les Épaves* (1866) and in *Le Parnasse Contemporain* (1866), in which sixteen poems are grouped together under
the title *Nouvelles Fleurs du mal*, six of them having already come out in
*Les Épaves*. Everything not gathered up in the 1868 edition appears
in *Vers retrouvés* (1929). But as a prose-writer, translator and art
critic Baudelaire had enormous gifts. *Les Paradis artificiels* (1860)
shows him as a brilliant translator from Poe and others, an adapter
and a straight prosist of infinite variety, while *Petits poèmes en prose*
(1869) is a beautiful prose counterpart of *Les Fleurs*. (These three
were translated into English by A. Symons, 1925.) *Curiosités esthétiques* and *L'Art romantique* (1869) contain his notable art criticism
of the *salons*. Aphorisms and glimpses of autobiography are to be
found in *Mon Cœur mis à nu et Fusées* (1909; new eds. 1943 and

1949; Eng. trans. *My Heart Laid Bare and other Prose Writings*, 1950), and his letters are of importance. His *Journaux intimes* were first published in 1938 (Eng. trans. *Intimate Journals*, 1949). Very early in life Baudelaire had contracted syphilis and this finally led to softening of the brain of which he died in Paris. He left no true literary successors, although initially Mallarmé (q.v.) and Rimbaud (q.v.) owed much to him. In his memory Swinburne wrote one of his best poems, 'Ave atque Vale'. The definitive edition of his work is that by J. Crépet (15 vols., 1922–48). E. Starkie's edition of *Les Fleurs* (1943) is useful.

**Baudissin, Wolf Heinrich von** (1789–1878), German translator. Born at Rantzau, Slesvig, he served in the Danish diplomatic service in Sweden, Austria and France. He had already helped Tieck (q.v.) in the later stages of the Shakespeare translations into German, when in 1827 he settled in Dresden to devote himself to a literary life. Of his many translations, those from Molière (1865–7) are his finest achievement. He died in Dresden.

**Baudry de Bourgueil** (1046–1130), French prose-writer and poet. Born at Meung-sur-Loire, he went to the University of Angers, then took the vows as monk and became Abbot of Bourgueil in 1089. He was consecrated Archbishop of Dol in 1107. His interesting *Itinerarium* describes his travels in northern France and England, incidentally revealing an arresting character. Among his other prose works are lives of saints and a history of Jerusalem. Throughout his life he wrote poetry in classical Latin style, excelling in descriptive subjects. His rhymed religious poems are in manner in advance of their time. Baudry died at Preaux.

**Baum, Vicki** (1888–1960), Austrian novelist. Born in Vienna, she came forward immediately after the 1914 war as a writer of vivid if facile fiction, presented with almost flawless technique, with *Der Eingang zur Bühne* (1920; Eng. trans. *Falling Star*, 1934). With *Hell in Frauensee* (1927; Eng. trans. *Martin's Summer*, 1931) her touch seemed surer still, and in *Stud. chem. Helene Willfüer* (1929; Eng. trans. *Helene*, 1932) she showed that she could be a thoughtful writer; but it was *Menschen im Hotel* (1929; Eng. trans. *Grand Hotel*, 1931) that brought her international fame. Here the narrative is inimitable, even though on second thoughts the work as a whole may seem slick, but it was what the world at large wanted, and sniff as the highbrows might it was honest craftsmanship. The 1920's were Vicki Baum's stage, and she wrote little later; but *Kautschuk* (1944; Eng. trans. *The Weeping Wood*, 1944) shows new attainments, the author having kept abreast of new science-fiction literature. *Schicksalsflug* (1947) is semi-autobiographical. *Ballerina* (1958) was perhaps the best of her later novels. She became an American citizen and died in Hollywood, California.

**Baumgarten, Alexander Gottlieb** (1714–1762), German prose-writer and founder of the science of aesthetics, was born in Berlin, and became a pupil of J. C. Wolff (q.v.) at Marburg. Appointed professor of philosophy at Frankfurt-an-der-Oder, he made a long and detailed study of the theory of beauty and taste, which he was the first to term 'aesthetics'; and he elaborated his ideas in several treatises, the most important and most famous being *Ästhetika* (1750). In this work, conditioned by the new ideas of classical antiquity brought forward by the discoveries at Pompeii and Herculaneum (cf. L. de Brosses's *Herculaneum* (q.v.) published the same year), Baumgarten proposes that beauty should be considered without respect to moral qualities, a view to be challenged by Moses Mendelssohn (q.v.) and others later in the century. Baumgarten died at Frankfurt-an-der-Oder.

**Bayle, Pierre** (1647–1706), French prose-writer, lexicographer and critic, born at Carlat in Languedoc (Arriège), the son of a Calvinist minister, was throughout his life engaged in religious controversy. Becoming a Roman Catholic for one year (1669–70) he turned Protestant again and remained one for the rest of his life, but a very tolerant one, too much so for his Calvinist associates. He lectured on philosophy at Sedan (1675–81), and was in the latter year appointed professor of philosophy at Rotterdam University where he remained until 1693 when he was deprived quite falsely as a danger to Protestantism in Holland. This was really because of the generous spirit of his *Avis aux réfugiés* (1690) in which he included exiles of every shade of belief. His view was in line with that of Locke and gave a foretaste of the benevolent views of the eighteenth century. He was furthermore an initiator of ideas, for his standpoint on many matters became the basis for much of the thought which is associated with eighteenth-century encyclopaedism (*see* Diderot) and enlightenment. In his *Pensées sur la Comète de 1682* (i.e. Halley's Comet), published in 1682 (rev. ed. 1704; crit. ed., A. Pratt, 1911–12) he covertly attacked the supernatural in religion. His great work, the *Dictionnaire historique et critique* (2 vols. 1695–7), an encyclopaedia of knowledge, is in effect a vast attack on established ideas; by setting out facts and presenting them to the public in a scientific, dispassionate manner he taught his readers to think for themselves, not as they had been taught to think. Voltaire (whose *Candide* Bayle inspired), La Mettrie (q.v.) and Helvétius (q.v.) are only a few of those directly influenced by him. He died in Rotterdam. His *Œuvres*, edited by Desmaizeaux, appeared in 1730 (9 vols.).

**Bazán, Emilia Pardo,** *see* **Pardo Bazán, E.**

**Bazin, René** (1853–1932), French novelist and short-story writer, was born at Angers. Very much of a Catholic and influenced by his provincial background, he embarked on his literary career with *Stéphanette* (1884) under the pseudonym of **Bernard Seigny,** which proved him a realist. *La Terre qui meurt* (1899; Eng. trans. *Autumn Glory*, 1901) was a fierce lament for the decaying provinces and the turning away from nature to the cities. This note is intensified in perhaps his finest book, *Le Blé qui lève* (1907; Eng. trans. *By Faith Alone,* 1908), in which all that is good and all the deepest elements of Catholicism are connected with nature. *Les Oberlé* (1901; Eng. trans. *The Oberlé Family*, 1933) had already shown the beginning of a new theme, the importance of the family, of patriotism and dislike of Germany. It deals with the Alsace-Lorraine question, and the saga was continued in *Les Nouveaux Oberlé* (1919). In his last works such as *Baltus Lorrain* (1926) and *Magnificat* (1931; Eng. trans. 1932) all these elements are solidified into uncompromising reaction. Bazin died in Paris.

**Béatrice de Die** (*fl.* 1160?), Provençal poet, who wrote some striking love-poetry addressed to Raimbaut d'Orange. For depth of feeling it is unusual for its age. It is discussed in S. Santy, *La Comtesse de Die* (1893).

**Beaumarchais, Pierre-Augustin Caron de** (1732–1799), French drama-tist and prose-writer. Born in Paris, the son of a watchmaker named Caron, he followed his father's trade successfully enough to invent a watch escapement, but before it could be patented the idea was stolen from him. His subsequent defence of his rights became known to Louis XV, who invited him to court, and engaged him as royal watchmaker and teacher of the harp to his daughters. A handsome man and of pleasing personality, he soon made his way at court, and sealed his worldly success by marrying the wealthy widow of an official (1756), thereupon adding 'de Beaumarchais' to simple 'Caron'. By 1761 he was the close friend of a banker Duverney, who helped him to invest his fortune with such good results that he soon became master of a vast sum, increased still more by his marriage to a second rich widow in 1768. His first literary work, the play *Eugénie* (1767), was founded on his experiences in Spain, to which he had paid an unofficial visit three years before. This and its successor, the comedy *Les Deux Amis* (1770), were lukewarmly received. *Eugénie* greatly influenced Goethe in writing his play *Clavigo*. Meanwhile his bene-factor Duverney had died, and Beaumarchais became involved in a lengthy lawsuit to defend his right to succeed to certain parts of the estate as specified in the will in the face of a host of Duverney's relatives, who, having neglected the old man when alive, now pressed forward with claims. Beaumarchais' cause was eagerly followed by the public, who saw in him, rightly or wrongly, a private man defending himself against the corruption favoured by the regime. Making the most of his opportunity Beaumarchais published *Mémoires du Sieur Beaumarchais par lui-même* (1773–4), in which he nimbly attacked the French legal system and pointed to the injustice of the imprisonment that he had just suffered, and which had been contrived by his enemies to keep him out of the case. The popular hero, however, still played the courtier, and in 1774 he was employed as a political agent in Britain, Austria and Germany, in which capacity (1775–6) he gained a considerable amount of arms and raw material for the American rebels. His experiences and his views were now canalized into the two brilliant plays for which he is famous. On the side of youth and purity of purpose against the power of privilege, whether ecclesiastical, legal or feudal, he wrote *Le Barbier de Séville* (1775) and *La Folle Journée* (1778). The first was produced with success the year it was written; the second was banned on account of its even more searching attack on hereditary privilege until 1784, when it was renamed *Le Mariage de Figaro* and enjoyed a success almost without parallel. The revivified 'gentleman's gentleman' of earlier comedy, now presented in the person of Figaro, with his different roles in the two plays, is a major creation. The plays in the form of Italian libretti soon found their opera composers, Paesiello for *Le Barbier* (1780) and Mozart for *Le Mariage* (1786), Paesiello's opera eventually being superseded by Rossini's (1816). Beaumarchais' own opera *Tarare* (1787), with music by Salieri, showed that he possessed no talent in that line and was a failure. *La Mère coupable* (1792) was a feeble appendage of the Figaro plays. It was one matter to attack abuses in a stable society; another to face a revolution. The French Revolution ruined Beaumarchais, who, in spite of all, drew his breath from the *ancien régime*. He was suspected of siding with the *émigrés* and was imprisoned (1792), and on his release lived in Holland and England. He returned to Paris in 1796, and died there stone deaf and in straitened circumstances. The best edition of his *Œuvres complètes* is that by E. Fournier (1876), of the *Théâtre complet et Lettres*, that by M. Allem (1934).

**Beauvoir, Édouard Roger de** (1806–1866), French novelist, his real name being **De Bully**. Born in Paris, he took up a literary career and wrote several novels and stories of an ephemeral character. The only one remembered now is *L'Écolier de Cluny ou le Sophisme*, for the most part because Dumas *père* (q.v.) was greatly indebted to it for his play *La Tour de Nesle* (1832). Beauvoir died in Paris.

**Beauvoir, Simone de** (1908–    ), French novelist. Born in Paris, she studied philosophy, taught for a while, and then meeting Sartre (q.v.), fell completely under his influence. In her novels such as *L'Invitée* (1943; Eng. trans. *She Came to Stay*, 1949), *Le Sang des autres* (1944; Eng trans. *The Blood of Others*, 1948) and *Tous les hommes sont mortels* (1947; Eng. trans. *All Men are Mortal*, 1955) existentialism is explored. Her break with her upper middle-class surroundings for Bohemia, combined with an aggressive feminism, are subjects which appear in her most famous work, *Le Deuxième Sexe* (1949; Eng. trans. *The Second Sex*, 1952), while *Les Mandarins* (1954; Eng. trans., 1956) is a striking and uncompromising account of intellectual Paris just after the Second World War, two of the thinly veiled characters being Sartre and Camus (q.v.). *Privilèges* (1955) looks searchingly into social problems. With *Mémoires d'une jeune fille rangée* (1958; Eng. trans. *Memoirs of a Dutiful Daughter*, 1959) she began an autobiography continued in *La Force de l'âge* (1960; Eng. trans. *The Prime of Life*, 1963), *La Force des choses* (1963; Eng. trans. *Force of Circumstance*, 1965) and *Une Mort très douce* (1964; Eng. trans. *A Very Easy Death*, 1966), a moving account of her mother's death from cancer.

**Bebel, Heinrich** (1472–1518), German satirist, born at Justingen. He became a well-known scholar influenced by the Italian renaissance. It was, however, his *Facetiae* (1507, 1512 and 1514), sketches in Latin of Swabian life, mocking the follies of the time with forcefulness and crudity, which made him exceedingly popular. In 1541 they were translated into German by Sebastian Franck (1488–1542), an Ulm printer, originally a Lutheran parson. Bebel died at Tübingen. There is a critical edition of the *Facetiae* by G. Bebermeyer (1931).

**Beccaria, Cesare** (1738–1794), Italian prose-writer. Born in Milan of noble family, he eagerly imbibed French encyclopaedist ideas and opened his mind to the Enlightenment growing up in Europe. He was soon in the thick of literary life, and was a principal figure in that most influential of mid eighteenth-century Italian periodicals, *Il Caffè*, from 1764 to 1766. But it is his excellently written, epoch-making book on criminal law, *Dei delitti e delle pene* (1764; Eng. trans. *Of Crimes and Punishments*, 1965), which has made his name memorable. In it he argues for the abolition of torture and of the death penalty (both of which were abolished in Tuscany by the Grand Duke Leopold in 1786), and demands that judicial punishment should take into account the person to be punished and not simply punish according to the crime. In 1768 Beccaria became professor of political economy at Milan, where he died. His *Dei delitti e delle pene* has been edited in modern times by Calamandrei (1950). The best edition of his *Opere* is that of 1874.

**Becher, Johannes Robert** (1891–1958), German poet and prose-writer. Born of well-to-do parents in Monaco, the First World War turned him first into a Socialist, appealing to European fraternity in the books of verse, *An Europa* (1916) and *Verbrüderung* (1916), and at the end of the war into a Communist. *Päan gegen die Zeit* (1918) is a remarkable piece of expressionism, but he later became a realist, in which manner he mourned Lenin's death in *Am Grabe Lenins* (1924) and praised the new industrial advances which he believed that Communism had brought about in *Maschinenrhythmen* (1926). Twenty years later his faith in Communism was still as strong as ever, as is to be seen in his collection of 'ballads', *Dank an Stalingrad* (1943). His *Volk im Dunkel wandelnd* (1948) is a powerful collection of verse, in which Becher, by now the grand old man of East German literature—he died East German Minister of Culture—faces up to the challenges of the post-war world. In his later volumes of verse, *Schöne deutsche Heimat* (1952) and *Deutsche Sonette* (1952), he preaches the advantages of domesticity. His novels such as *Abschied* (1940) are of secondary importance, as are his essays, mere platforms for political propaganda. Some of his earlier verse appears in Deutsch's *Contemporary German Poetry* (1923). He died in East Berlin.

**Bechstein, Ludwig** (1801–1860), German poet and novelist, born at Weimar. As an original poet he produced volumes of epic verse, inspired by Thuringia's historic past, such as *Die Haimonskinder* (1830) and *Thüringens Königshaus* (publ. posthumously in 1865); but it is as the narrator in his own clear prose of the folk tales of Thuringia, Austria and Franconia that he is particularly to be remembered. Such volumes are *Fahrten eines Musikanten* (3 vols., 1836–7) and, entirely authentic, *Deutsches Märchenbuch* (1846) and *Neues Deutsches Märchenbuch*. He died at Meiningen.

**Beck, Karl** (1817–1879), Hungarian poet and dramatist writing in German. Born at Baja, Hungary, he became prominent in the Young German movement as a noisy and violent protagonist. As a poet he wrote *Nächte. Gepanzerte Lieder* (1838) and *Janko* (1846); as a dramatist the tragedy *Saul* (1841). After the 1848 revolutions he fades from view. He died at Währing-bei-Wien, Austria.

**Becker, Nikolaus** (1809–1845), German poet. Born at Bonn, he leapt to fame with his patriotic 'Rheinlied' (composed 1840), set to music well over a hundred times and parodied by Musset (q.v.). This and other poems, many of a more or less similar nature, were published as *Gedichte* (1841). His other work does not call for notice. He died at Hunshoven.

**Beckett, Samuel** (1900– ), Franco-Irish novelist and playwright, writing in French and English. Born in Dublin, he became a disciple of James Joyce, whose influence is clearly seen in *Murphy* (1938). Later resident in Paris he developed an excellent French prose style, and with *Molloy* (1951; Eng. trans., 1955) he was hailed as a major writer by his adopted country. With *Malone meurt* (1951; Eng. trans. *Malone Dies*, 1956) and *L'Innommable* (1953; Eng. trans. *The Unnameable*, 1958) he comes to tragic conclusions about human life. In *En attendant Godot* (1952), the play so well known to British theatre audiences as *Waiting for Godot* (1954), he comes to the conclusion that all hope is vain and all effort towards redemption impossible. More recent plays for the stage have included *Fin de partie* (1957; Eng. trans. *Endgame*, 1958), *Krapp's Last Tape* (1958) and *Happy Days* (1961), while for the radio he has written *All That Fall* (1957), *Embers* (1959) and *Cascando* (1963; Eng. trans. 1963).

**Becque, Henri François** (1837–1899), French dramatist, born in Paris where he died, he first became known as the librettist of the romantic opera *Sardanapalus* (1867), and the romantic was still the keynote of that little masterpiece *L'Enfant prodigue* (1868), *Michel Pauper* (1870) and *L'Enlèvement* (1871). Thereafter there comes about a complete change in his work, and in *Les Corbeaux* (1882) and *La Parisienne* (1885) he is a pitiless realist. His *Théâtre complet* was published (3 vols.) in 1899.

**Bécquer, Gustavo Adolfo** (1836–1870), Spanish poet. Born in Seville, he was left an orphan at an early age, and after trying his hand at painting in his uncle's studio, he left for Madrid in 1854. He made his living as a freelance journalist and translator, pursuing a precarious, undisciplined life which finally ruined his health and led to his early death. Many of his articles are to be found in *El Contemporáneo* and *El Museo Universal*. None of his poetry was collected during his lifetime, but appeared with his works in 1871 (mod. ed., 1942). His lyrics, few in number, have a quality more akin to the north and absent from Spanish literature; there is about them a melancholy, a restlessness, something weird and disturbing. Love, disappointment, death, are the main milestones on life's road; the first love fails, but death as the second lover will not. Among the finest are the prose-poems, 'Los ojos verdes' and 'El rayo de luna'. Bécquer died in Madrid. There is a reasonably good English translation of the *Rimas* (lyrics) and *Leyendas* (prose-poems in the manner of stories) by H. F. W. Olmstead (1907), entitled *Tales and Poems of G. A. Bécquer*.

**Beer, Johann** (1655–1700), German novelist. Born at St Georgen,

Upper Austria, he became court musician at Weissenfels in 1677 and remained there for the rest of his days. There he wrote in his own peculiar style a number of realistic novels on the contemporary scene, generally considered the best of the century after those by Grimmelshausen (q.v.). Among them may be named *Ritter Hopfensack* (1678), *Ritter Spiridon* (1679), both skits on outmoded chivalresque ways of life, *Jucundus Jucundissimus* (1680) and *Teutsche Winternächte* (1682).

**Beffroy de Reigney, Louis Abel** (1757–1811), French dramatist. Born at Laon he became a journalist and later began to write plays with *Nicodème dans la lune* (1790). He also wrote both words and music for several operas such as *La Petite Nanette* (1795), the most successful. For years he laboured at his *Dictionnaire néologique*, but it was still unfinished at his death in Paris.

**Beheim, Michael** (1416–1474?), German poet, born at Sulzbach and author of two chronicles in verse, *Das Buch von den Wienern* (1466) and *Der Leben Friedrichs I von der Pfalz* (1469). In both he reveals himself as a man who knew life to the full. He probably died at Sulzbach.

**Behmen, Jakob,** *see* **Böhmen, J.**

**Bejła, J.,** *see* **Rzewuski, H.**

**Belinsky, Vissarion Grigoryevich** (1811–1848), Russian publicist. Born at Sveaborg, his violent revolutionary play *Dmitry Kalinin* (1832) brought him expulsion from Moscow University, after which he took to journalism. In subsequent works he introduced German philosophy (especially Hegel and Feuerbach) into Russian thought. More than anything else, however, it was his championship of freedom of thought and action which made him the rallying point of many of the best elements among his countrymen. He died in Petersburg. His collected works appeared (11 vols.) in 1900–17. An English translation, *The Selected Philosophical Works of V. G. Belinsky*, was published in 1948.

**Bellamy, Jacobus** (1757–1786), Dutch poet. Born at Flushing of humble origin, he gained a university scholarship to Utrecht in 1782, in which year he published a volume of love-poetry, many of the poems rhymeless and of a variety of metres, addressed to 'Fillis', his fiancée, and entitled *Gezangen mijner jeugd*. In his two subsequent volumes, *Vaderlandsche Gezangen van Zelandus* (1783) and *Gezangen* (1785), are to be found the additional themes of friendship and patriotism. On the point of being ordained a minister he died at Utrecht.

**Bellarmine, Robert** (1542–1621), Italian prose-writer. Born at Montepulciano, near Siena, he entered the Jesuit Order in 1560 and became professor of theology at Louvain nine years later. In 1576 he was appointed a member of the staff of the Roman College, of which he was nominated rector in 1592. A man of wide culture, reasonable and a moderating influence, he more successfully than any other theologian of the age attempted to bridge the ever widening gap between Catholics and Reformers. Without personal ambition, he was against his will made cardinal in 1599 and Archbishop of

Capua in 1602. His learning and excellent Latin are well displayed in his major work, *Disputationes de Controversiis Christianae Fidei* (3 vols., 1581), a monument to the Counter-Reformation. A defender of Galileo (q.v.) against his formidable clerical opponents, Bellarmine died in Rome. A complete edition of his works appeared in Paris in 1874.

**Bellay, Joachim du,** *see* **Du Bellay.**

**Belleau, Rémy** (1528–1577), French poet. Born at Nogent-le-Rotrou, he became a member of the Pléiade. All his work evinces a delicate sensibility and an indefinable charm, apparent already in his early work, *Petites inventions* (1556); but it is in the *Bergerie* (1565; rev. and augmented ed., 1572), with its beautifully balanced short poems, that he fully reveals himself. Even more delightful is his last volume, *Amours et nouveaux échanges des pierres précieuses* (1576; mod. ed. by A. van Bever, 1909), with its ingeniously and effectively employed conceit of imagery derived from occultism and precious stones. Belleau died in Paris.

**Belli, Gioacchino Giuseppe** (1791–1863), Italian poet, often writing in dialect. Born in Rome, where he died, in his brilliant and bitter sonnets he satirized Roman society from top to bottom. These were collected as *I sonetti romaneschi di G. G. Belli* (ed. L. Morandi, 6 vols., 1886–9).

**Bellincioni, Bernardo** (1452–1492), Italian poet. A lifelong resident in Florence, except for a short spell in Milan, he was employed in the service of Lorenzo the Magnificent. A high-spirited writer, he was always inclined to satire. His *Sonetti, canzoni e capitoli* were published posthumously in 1493.

**Bellman, Carl Michael** (1740–1795), Swedish poet. Born in Stockholm he became a bank clerk, and leaving his post led a very erratic life until made court secretary by Gustav III in 1775. His duties were negligible, but he soon came to be greatly in demand as a court entertainer. The improvisations, often derived from folk-songs, which he sang at court functions, accompanying himself on the lute, resulted in his two poetical collections *Fredmans Epistlar* (1790) and the inferior *Fredmans Sånger* (1791). Full of life and colour, with delightfully contrasting descriptions of town and country, many of the skilful verses are very much alive today. Bellman died in Stockholm of drink, and penniless.

**Belloy, Dormont de,** later calling himself **Pierre-Laurent Buirette** (1727–1775), French tragedian, was born at Saint-Flour. His attempt to bring new life to that department of his country's drama by choosing stirring subjects seemed momentarily to have succeeded with *Le Siège de Calais* (1765); but his other works such as *Gaston et Bayard* (1771), another attempt to rouse enthusiasm by its nationalistic theme, were not of the calibre to halt the decay of French tragedy. He died in Paris, and in 1779 his *Œuvres complètes* with a biography were published.

**Belmonte Bermúdez, Luis de** (1587?–1650?), Spanish dramatist. Born at Seville, he went to America before settling down for good in

Madrid where he died. Since he collaborated so much with other playwrights after the fashion of several English Elizabethans and Jacobeans, very few works can with certainty be attributed to him. An exception is *El diablo predicador*, a clever and witty improvement of an earlier play of uncertain authorship, *Fray Diablo*. A modern version of it is the French one, *Le Diable prédicateur*, edited by L. Rouanet, 1901.

**Bely, Andrey,** pseudonym of **Boris Nikolayevich Bugayev** (1880–1934), Russian novelist and poet. Born in Moscow, he joined freely in the intense literary life of the capital in the years before the revolution, counting Blok (q.v.) among his friends, and regarding V. S. Solovyev as his inspirer. First becoming known as a poet, he published four volumes of verse entitled *Simfonia* between 1902 and 1908, but he gained his pre-war reputation with the striking and sombre novel *Peterburg* (1913; Eng. trans. *St Petersburg*, 1960). The year 1917 had a fundamental effect on him, and he emerged from the experiences of semi-religious enthusiasm as a master symbolist, as is to be seen in his autobiographical novel *Kotik Letayev* (1918; part of it in Eng. trans. in G. Reavey and M. Slonim, *Soviet Literature*, 1933), and in his volume of collected verse, *Stikhotvoreniya* (1923). He died at Tiflis, his ardour for the regime having greatly moderated.

**Bembo, Pietro** (1470–1547), Italian man of letters. Born at Venice, he entered the Church and in 1500 made his debut as an author with *Gli Asolani*, a series of dialogues in platonic style on ideal love, dedicated to Lucrezia Borgia. From 1506 to 1512 he was at the court of Urbino, which he left to become secretary to Pope Leo X. In 1525 in his *Prose della volgar lingua* he came forward as the champion of the use of Italian rather than Latin for general literature, maintaining that Tuscan should be the model. In this he was opposed by Castiglione (q.v.) and others who denied this restrictive attitude to the Italian language as a whole. The *Prose* in fact started a controversy which was still active in the eighteenth century when Baretti (q.v.) and others opposed the pretensions of the Florentine Accademia della Crusca. In 1529 Bembo was appointed historiographer to the Republic of Venice and director of the library of St Mark's. In 1530 was published his book of verse (*Rime*) in Petrarchan style, a work which had much influence. Made a cardinal by Pope Paul III, he later became Bishop of Bergamo. He died in Rome. The standard edition of his *Opere* is that by Classici (12 vols., 1808–10). A convenient edition of his two major works is *Gli Asolani e Prose della volgar lingua*, by C. Dionisotti-Casalone, 1923.

**Benavente y Martínez, Jacinto** (1866–1954), Spanish dramatist, born in Madrid. He began his dramatic career with *El nido ajeno* (1894), and with *Gente conocida* (1896) launched out on his brilliant social satires, others of the same type being *La noche del sábado* (1903) and *Los intereses creados* (1907). *La malquerida* (1913), founded on the personal domestic tragedy of friends of his, shows that he was capable of an intenser feeling. His *Obras completas* (8 vols.) were published in 1945–7. There is an English translation of thirteen of the plays, *Plays of Jacinto Benavente* (4 vols., 1917–24). He died in Madrid.

**Benda, Julien** (1867–1956), French prose-writer. Born in Paris, he studied letters and science before launching into literature, and soon revealed himself as an opponent of new tendencies of thought centred in Bergson (q.v.), whose philosophy he attacked in *Le Bergsonisme* (1912) and *Sur le succès du bergsonisme* (1917). This distaste for a lack of what he regarded as clear, sound thinking resulting in intellectual malaise also appears in the novels *L'Ordination* (1912; Eng. trans. *The Yoke of Pity*, 1913) and *Belphégor* (1918; Eng. trans. 1929). *La Trahison des clercs* (1927; Eng. trans. *The Great Betrayal*) was a devastating attack on insincerity in politics, and thereafter he turned his attention to the potentialities of the democracies (*La Grande Épreuve des démocracies*, 1942). The result of the Second World War left him in the state of mind shown in *La France byzantine ou le Triomphe de la littérature pure* (1945). He had, however, lost the greater part of his audience, and such last works as *Du style d'idées* (1948), *Les Cahiers d'un clerc* (1949) and *Mémoires d'infra-tombe* (1952) drew down widespread opposition on his head. This was certainly not deserved, but was due to the radical change in contemporary values. He died at Fontenay-aux-Roses.

**Benedeiz** (*fl.* 1125?), Anglo-Norman author of a French version of the *Navigatio sancti Brandani* (960?). Benedeiz's version, with its account of the strange and marvellous encountered on the voyage to the Isle of Saints, has been a source fit for poetic imaginations to play on, a notable example being Tennyson's *The Voyage of St Brandan*. There is an edition of the Anglo-Norman version by E. G. R. Waters (1929).

**Benedictsson, Victoria Maria,** sometimes using the pseudonym **Ernst Ahlgren** (1850–1888), Swedish novelist and short-story writer. Born at Alstad, she contracted (1871) an unhappy marriage with a postmaster in a village in Skåne, which resulted in a mental breakdown from which she never totally recovered (1881). Leaving Sweden and settling in Copenhagen she decided to earn her living by her pen. She showed great promise with her collection of short stories about life in the Skåne country, *Från Skåne* (1884). Her full-length novel *Fru Marianne* (1887) is a delicate study of a girl's development in face of the world. About this time she became the mistress of Georg Brandes (q.v.), the critic, but this brought her no more happiness than her marriage, and in despair she committed suicide in Copenhagen. Her collected works were published (7 vols.) in 1918–20.

**Benediktov, Vladimir Grigoryevich** (1807–1873), Russian poet, was born in Petersburg and there died. A superficial, flashy romantic, he had an eager public following. His collected poems, *Stikhotvoreniya*, appeared in 1902 (2 vols.) and in 1939 (1 vol.).

**Ben Ezra,** *see* **Ibn Ezra.**

**Bengtsson, Frans Gunnar** (1894–1954), Swedish novelist, essayist and historian. Born at Tossjö, Skåne, he made his name with the finely critical but at the same time heroically conceived *Karl den XII: s levnad* (1935; Eng. trans. *The Life of Charles XII*, 1960). His best-known volume of essays is the vigorous collection *Sällskap för en* *eremit* (1938; Eng. trans. *A Walk to an Ant-hill and Other Essays*, 1950). His lengthy Viking saga *Röde Orm* (1941; Eng. trans. *Red Orm*, 1943) carried his name even further afield. He died in Stockholm.

**Benjamin ben Jonah, of Tudela** (*d*.1173), Spanish Hebrew prose-writer and traveller, was born at Tudela where he became a rabbi. He travelled in the east from 1160 onwards, finally returning to Spain and dying in Zaragoza. His remarkable journeys embraced Catalonia, France, Italy, Greece, Syria, Palestine and Mesopotamia. His return route was by Khuzistan, the Indian Ocean, Arabia and Egypt. His intelligent observation, which embraced a clear study of the national institutions of the countries through which he passed, resulted in a book of extraordinary interest. It was first published as *Masse'oth Rabbi Binyamin* in Constantinople in 1543. There is an English translation with text by M. N. Adler (1907).

**Benn, Gottfried** (1886–1956), German poet and miscellaneous prose-writer. Born at Mansfeld, his mother being French, he took up medicine and became a specialist, the while publishing verse in the realistic manner, his two most significant collections being *Gesammelte Gedichte* (1927) and *Ausgewahlte Gedichte* (1936). He had by this latter date voiced his approval of the aims of the Nazis, believing as did so many at the time that they were the only hope in the face of threatening chaos. The point of view that led Benn to this decision is to be seen in his two books of essays, *Nach dem Nihilismus* (1932) and *Der neue Staat und die Intellektuellen* (1933); but in spite of this Hitler's regime never wholly accepted him. Thus for a considerable time he found it best to withdraw from literary limelight, and it was not until after the Second World War that he appeared again in his former stature. *Statische Gedichte* (1948) represents the best of his later poetic style, as does *Goethe und die Naturwissenschaften* (1949) of his literary criticism and *Der Ptolemäer* (1949) of his short stories. *Doppelleben* (1950, 'Double Life') is an autobiography. His complete poetical works were published in 1956. He died in Berlin. For English translations see *Primal Vision, Selected Poetry and Prose of Gottfried Benn* (1961).

**Benoît de Sainte Maure** (*fl.* 1160?), French poet, a native of Ste Maure near Poitiers, served in some capacity at the court of Henry II of England. His one work is the long and nobly presented epic, *Le Roman de Troie*, an account of the Trojan War. In it appears the episode of Troilus and Cressida, made use of in time to come by Boccaccio, Chaucer and Shakespeare. The great interest in the Troy legend which permeated so much medieval literature was certainly derived from Benoît. The standard edition of the work is that by L. Constans (6 vols., 1904–12).

**Benoît, Pierre** (1886–1962), French poet and novelist. Born at Albi, he first commanded attention with a volume of poetry, *Diadumène* (1914), containing subtly evocative 'atmospheric' work reminiscent of Baudelaire (q.v.). After the First World War he turned to adventure stories, producing *L'Atlantide* in 1919 (Eng. trans. *The Queen of Atlantis*, 1920) and *La Chaussée des géants* in 1922. A third stage in his literary career was reached with his psychological novels, *Axelle*

(1928) and *Le Soleil de minuit* (1930). He was elected to the French Academy in 1931. His later novels, such as *La Toison d'or* (1953), were comparative failures. He died at St-Jean-de-Luz.

**Benserade, Isaac de** (1613–1691), French theatre poet, was born and died in Paris. He provided the poetry, very often set to music by Lulli, for many ballets. His *Œuvres* were published in 1697, and O. Uzanne edited them in 1895.

**Bentivoglio, Ercole** (1507–1573), Italian poet, playwright and critic, born at Modena. His first works were sonnets, and an attack on the Bembo (q.v.) school for insisting exclusively on Tuscan as the literary language, entitled *Della lingua toscana*. It is, however, for his two surviving comedies, *Il Geloso* (1544) and *I Fantasmi* (1547), that he is of note. He died in Venice. There is a good modern edition of *Le Commedie* by I. Sanesi (1935).

**Bentivoglio, Guido** (1579–1644), Italian prose-writer. Born at Ferrara he became private chamberlain to Pope Clement VIII and was later head of the Inquisition, in which office he signed Galileo's (q.v.) condemnation. Often employed by the papacy as a diplomat, he was made cardinal and was entrusted with looking after French affairs at the papal court. He found time to write a very valuable history of the Spanish wars in the Low Countries, *Della Guerra di Fiandra* (1632–9; Eng. trans. *The Compleat History of the Wars of Flanders*, by Henry, Earl of Monmouth, 1654). It is, however, as a writer of letters and dispatches, as, for example, in the *Raccolta di lettere familiari e politiche* (1631; mod. ed., 2 vols., 1852) and *Lettere diplomatiche* (4 vols., 1863–70), that he proves himself to be master of a good epistolary style. On the death of Urban VIII he went to Rome to take part in the conclave to elect a new pope, and would almost certainly have himself been elected had he not suddenly died.

**Beolco, Angelo** (1502–1542), Italian playwright, called **Il Ruzzante** after his most famous character, was born in Padua, where he died. At first he wrote in the academic manner, copying Plautus, *La Vaccaria* being the best example of this; but he found himself in realistic plays of country life, homely and even crude, but reeking of the soil, such as *La Fiorina*, with an additional touch of sympathy bordering on pathos. His works were collected as *Tutte le opere del famosissimo Ruzzante* (1584; a further edition, 1598).

**Béranger, Pierre-Jean de** (1780–1857), French poet. Born in Paris, he began life as a printer's apprentice at Péronne, returned to Paris about 1800, and two years later started out on his literary career. The pension he received from Lucien Bonaparte in 1804 did not prevent him from mocking the regime in poetry—satirical, sentimental, witty, dainty, licentious—which before long made him the most widely read French poet of his time. From 1809 to 1821 he was a clerk at the University of France (Paris), being dismissed and imprisoned for his liberal views, and he was again imprisoned in 1828, but this only led to his being regarded as a still greater idol. Five collections of his *Chansons* were published between 1815 and 1833 (*Œuvres complètes*, ed. Garnier, 4 vols., 1868–75). After 1830 he became the mouthpiece of those who had no taste for the bourgeois monarchy of Louis Philippe and looked back with nostalgia to the days of Napoleon. Among his poems, which lend themselves to music and can be moving in their simplicity, are 'Le Roi d'Yvetôt', 'Souvenirs', 'Le Vieux Drapeau' and 'Le Bon Vieillard'. He died in Paris.

**Berceo, Gonzalo de** (1195?–1270?), the first known Spanish poet, was born at, or near, Berceo, Logroño, and became a priest. His devotional poetry is generally taken from Latin sources, but he added much of his own. His best work is usually considered to be *Los milagros de la Virgen*, divided into twenty-five stories of her intervention in the affairs of the world (*Milagros de Nuestra Señora*, ed. Solalinde, 1934). His works appear in *Biblioteca de Autores Españoles*, vol. lvii.

**Berchet, Giovanni** (1783–1851), Italian poet and literary critic. Born in Milan, he became an enthusiastic follower of Madame de Staël's (q.v.) theories, and in conformity with her ideas wrote *Lettera semiseria di Grisostomo* (1816), advocating that Italian men of letters should find inspiration not in French or English but in German literature. In 1821 he became a political exile and was for some years a clerk in a Milanese bank in London. Here he published his best-known work *Fantasie* (1828), a poem of an exile yearning for home. Later he returned to Italy and became a force behind the Risorgimento. He died in Turin. His collected works appeared (3 vols.) in 1911–12.

**Berdyayev, Nikolay Alexandrovich** (1874–1948), Russian philosophical writer. Born at Kiev, he was one of the young writers, Merezhkovsky (q.v.) among them, who came forward in the wake of Tolstoy at the beginning of the century as champions of a return to religious values in place of nihilistic theories. It was not, however, until after he had left Russia in 1922 and had settled in Paris that he was able to devote himself untrammelled to objective thought, which resulted in a series of thoughtfully penetrating studies. Chief among these, and exercising an enormous influence in Europe, particularly just before and just after the Second World War, are *Filosofiya svobody* (1927; Eng. trans. *Freedom and the Spirit*, 1935), *Ya i mir obyektov* (1934; Eng. trans. *Solitude and Society*, 1938) and *Mechta i deystvitel'nost'* (1938; Eng. trans. *Dream and Reality*, 1950). He died in Paris.

**Berent, Wacław,** pseudonym of **Wacław Rawicz** (1873–1940), Polish novelist. Born in Warsaw, he abandoned science for a literary life, and had one truly deserved success with his striking fictional account of medieval Poland, *Żywe kamienie* (1918; Fr. trans. *Les Pierres vivantes*, 1932). He died in Warsaw.

**Bergengruen, Werner** (1892–1964), German, poet, novelist and short-story writer, was born in Riga. A highly religious man by nature, he was converted to Catholicism and this faith was the mainspring of his work. He opened his literary career with historical novels, such as *Das Kaiserreich in Trümmern* (1927); but his three best pieces of full-length prose fiction are *Der grosse Tyrann und das Gericht* (1935;

Eng. trans. *A Matter of Conscience*, 1952), *Am Himmel wie auf Erden* (1941) and *Der letzte Rittmeister* (1951; Eng. trans. *The Last Captain of Horse*, 1952). As a poet he is represented by such books as *Die Rose von Jericho* (1936), outstandingly by *Dies Irae* (1946) and by *Die heile Welt* (1951). His 'Novellen', following on the manner of Meyer (q.v.), include *Der Starost* (1938) and *Das Feuerzeichen* (1949). Of his collections of short stories *Der spanische Rosenstock* (1940), *Die Sultansrose* (1946), *Der Teufel im Winterpalais* (1949), *Das Tempelchen* (1950), *Die Rittermeisterin* (1954) and *Die Flamme im Säulenholz* (1955) are particularly worthy of mention. His reminiscences, *Schreibtisch-Erinnerungen*, appeared in 1961. The consistency of his faith and his political and social beliefs demand respect, for he refused to compromise even in the most dangerous circumstances. He died in Baden-Baden.

**Bergerac, Savinien Cyrano de,** *see* **Cyrano de Bergerac, S.**

**Bergman, Hjalmar Fredrik Elgerus** (1883–1931), Swedish novelist, short-story writer, playwright and wireless script-writer. Born at Örebro the son of a wealthy banker of that town, he dabbled in literature, thoroughly imbibed the atmosphere of his home which he was to make good use of later, travelled much, suffered from a disease of the eyes which threatened him with blindness, but from which he recovered to a certain extent, and in 1910 was forced by his father's failure in business to make use of his hobby to earn his living. It was some time before he found his way, but in *Markurells i Wadköping* (1919; Eng. trans. *God's Orchid*, 1924) he turned his past experiences in Örebro to masterly account. He followed this up with *Farmor och vår Herre* (1921; Eng. trans. *Thy Rod and thy Staff*, 1937) and *Chefen fru Ingeborg* (1924; Eng. trans. *The Head of the Firm*, 1936), while his last novel, *Clownen Jac* (1930), showed signs of strain caused by incessant overwork. In constant demand as a script-writer, as time went on he had less and less opportunity for more durable dramatic writing, the best of which is probably *Marionettspel* (1917). He died in Berlin.

**Bergmann, Anton,** or **Tony** (1835–1874), Flemish novelist and short-story writer. Born at Lier, he became a lawyer and died there. He is the author of a collection of tales, *Twee Rijnlandse Novellen* (1870), and of a realistic novel, full of bold characterization and of colour, if somewhat loosely constructed, *Ernest Staes, advocaat* (1874), which exercised some influence on French and German fictional writing.

**Bergsøe, Jørgen Vilhelm** (1835–1911), Danish novelist. Born in Copenhagen, where he died, he became a popular novelist with such clear, vivid and fast-moving stories as *Fra Piazza del Popolo* (1867), *Fra den gamle Fabrik* (1869) and *Bruden fra Rørvig* (1872; Eng. trans. *The Bride of Roervig*, 1877). His *Romaner og Fortællinger* appeared in 6 volumes in 1913–14.

**Bergson, Henri** (1859–1941), French philosopher and prose-writer. Born in Paris of Jewish family, he was educated at the École Normale, and from 1900 to 1921 was professor of philosophy at the Collège de

France. Without going into the question of his philosophical teaching, he stands out as a fine stylist in such works as *Le Rire* (1900; Eng. trans. *Laughter*, 1911) and *L'Énergie spirituelle* (1919), while in works purely philosophical and without apparent literary content, there is a remarkable sense of the fitness of language as in *Matière et mémoire* (1896; Eng. trans. *Matter and Memory*, 1896), *L'Évolution créatrice* (1907; Eng. trans. *Creative Evolution*, 1907) and *Les Deux Sources de la morale et de la réligion* (1932; Eng. trans. *The Two Sources of Morality and Religion*, 1935). His gift of style led to this great exponent of 'vitalism' being read by many who had received no training in metaphysics, but who responded to his abilities as a man of letters. He died in Paris.

**Berlichingen, Götz (Gottfried) von** (1480–1562), German adventurer and prose-writer. Born at Jagsthausen, Württemberg, he became a soldier and was a captain of mercenaries in the Peasants' War (1525). Later he fought for the Hungarians against the Turks. As early as 1504 he had had his right hand, cut off in battle, replaced by an iron one. Retiring finally to his castle of Hornberg, where he died, he wrote his memoirs, *Lebensbeschreibung*. This vivid account of Reformation times was first published in 1731, and Goethe was inspired by it to write the rousing drama with his name as its title. There have been many editions of the *Lebensbeschreibung*, including that by A. Leitzmann (1916).

**Bermúdez de Castro, Salvador** (1817–1883), Spanish poet. Born in Cadiz of a noble family, he became a diplomat and politician, meanwhile cultivating poetry which, though outwardly romantic, was basically sceptical and even pessimistic, as is to be seen in *Ensayos poéticos* (1840). He invented a particular stanza of eight lines called the *bermudina*. He died in Rome.

**Bernagie, Pieter** (1656–1699), Dutch playwright, born at Breda. He became a physician, but his heart was in the theatre. The period of his dramatic activity was very short, lasting only from 1684 to 1686; but in the plays which he then produced he proved that he was well able to deal not only with comedy, such as in *Het studenteleven* (1684), but with tragedy also, such as in *Arminius* (1686). The success of these works led to his being appointed a member of the council of the Amsterdam theatre, but he wrote no more and died in Amsterdam.

**Bernanos, Georges** (1888–1948), French novelist and essayist. Born in Paris, he studied law, took part in the First World War and on the return of peace entered business. Retiring from that in 1925, he came forward as a novelist eager to explore shams, especially religious ones, with *Sous le soleil de Satan* (1926). In prose he attacked middle-class complacency in *La Grande Peur des bien-pensants* (1931), while in his best known work, the novel *Journal d'un curé de campagne* (1936; Eng. trans. *The Diary of a Country Priest*, 1937), he movingly explored religious experience. After the volume of essays, *Les Grands Cimetières sous la lune* (1938; Eng. trans. *A Diary of My Times*, 1938), he left France with his family, disgusted at the Munich affair, and settled in Brazil, and did not return to France until the end of the war. Thereupon he turned prolific author once more, in the two years that remained to him publishing the novel *Monsieur Ouine* (1946), *Lettre aux anglais* (1946), an appeal to Britain to be strong in peace as in war, *La France contre les robots* (1947), stressing the dangers of technical advance in the post-war world, and *Le Chemin de la croix des âmes* (1948). He died at Neuilly.

**Bernard, Tristan** (1866–1947), French novelist and dramatist, born at Besançon. Going to Paris, he soon became an established wit and *raconteur*, and much of his dry, brittle humour finds its way into both his novels and his plays. Of the former the best are generally considered to be *Le Mari pacifique* (1901), *Le Secret d'état* (1908) and *Le Voyage imprévu* (1928); of the latter *L'Anglais tel qu'on le parle* (1899), *Le Danseur inconnu* (1910), *La Volonté de l'homme* (1917) and *Jules, Juliette et Julien* (1929). He died in Paris.

**Bernard de Clairvaux** (1090–1153), French Latin prose-writer and poet. Born at Fontaines-lès-Dijon of a noble family of Burgundy, about 1113 he entered the Cistercian monastery of Cîteaux, leaving it two years later to become abbot of a new monastery at Clairvaux, Champagne. In 1128 he was secretary to the Council of Troyes, and two years later so great had his influence become that he was able to destroy the claims of the antipope Anacletus, and in 1146 was chosen to preach the Second Crusade. We see him in a very different and unpleasant light when it is remembered that he was responsible for ruining Abélard (q.v.) and Arnold of Brescia, and that he was the author of cruel and bitter attacks on St William of York. He died at Clairvaux, and was canonized in 1174. Many of his works, devotional treatises, works of exegesis, sermons, business letters, hardly deserve the name of literature, but two are fine examples of their kind. These are *De Diligendo Deo* and *De Gradibus Humilitatis*, and both have been edited as *Select Treatises of St Bernard of Clairvaux* by Williams and Mills (1926). *De Diligendo* has been translated into English by E. G. Gardner as *The Book of Saint Bernard on the Love of God* (1916). One of the greatest of Latin hymn-writers, many modern hymns are founded on his ' Jesu dulcis memoria'.

**Bernard de Morlaix** ( *fl.* 1140), Anglo-French poet. Reputed to have been born of English parents at Morlaix, Brittany, he became a monk at Cluny. He is the author of a strange and powerful poem in long, rolling metre, a satire on the vanities of the world, ' De Contemptu Mundi'. Portions of this were freely translated in *The Rhythm of Bernard of Morlaix* (1859) by J. M. Neale and were converted by him into such beautiful hymns as ' Jerusalem the Golden' and ' Brief life is here our portion', which, however, hardly reflect the strength of the original.

**Bernard Silvester** ( *fl.* 1150), French poet and prose-writer in Latin, of whom practically nothing is known, is the author of *De Mundi Universitate*, a mixture of prose and poetry, a neo-platonic allegory of the Creation. According to its dedication Bernard owed something to Chartres, probably his education. The work has been edited by C. S. Barach and J. Wrobel (1876).

**Bernardes, Diogo** (1532?–1597?), Portuguese poet. Born at Ponte da Barca in the Minho valley, he was in 1566 living as a successful lawyer at Nóbrega. In favour with King Sebastian of Portugal, he was appointed secretary to the Portuguese Embassy at Madrid, where he made a favourable impression on Philip II of Spain, who was afterwards to do him a good service. In 1578 he went to Morocco with King Sebastian's expedition and, sharing its disasters, remained a prisoner in Africa until ransomed by the special command of Philip II. Little wonder it is that henceforth Bernardes was a strong supporter of Philip's right to the kingdom of Portugal. It is after this period of his life that he seems to have written the bulk of his poetry, all of which was to be published at the very end of it. His religious poetry, which appears in *Várias rimas ão Bom Jesus, e à Virgem gloriosa sua mãe, e a santos particulares* (1594), shows undoubted sincerity, while in his eclogues and pastoral poetry, contained in *O lima* ('Lime tree') *de Diogo Bernardes* (1596) and *Rimas várias, flores do lima* (1597), he proves himself to be one of the finest poets of his age, and the only poet of his country who can be said to have approached and at times even equalled Camões (q.v.). The place of his death is uncertain. His *Obras completas* were edited by Marquês Braga (3 vols., 1945–6).

**Bernardes, Manuel** (1644–1710), Portuguese prose-writer. Born in Lisbon, he became a priest. The excellence of his style displayed in his delightful if ingenuous devotional works marks him out as a master of prose. His chief book is *Nova floresta ou silva de vários apotegmas* (5 vols., 1706–28), and among his others are *Luz e calor* (1696) and *Os últimos fins do homen* (1728). He died in Lisbon.

**Bernardin de Saint-Pierre, Jacques-Henri** (1737–1814), French prose-writer. Born at Le Havre, he became an engineer, in his spare time cultivating his keen interest in natural history and meteorology. The most formative period in his life was his three years (1768–71) as government engineer in Mauritius, where he found himself surrounded by that natural beauty on which he was later to draw for his literary work, while a reading of Rousseau (q.v.) pointed out to him the way to a sentimental Arcadia. On his return he published his *Voyage à l'Île de France* (1773), a tribute to Mauritius, but it was not until 1784 that his *Études de la Nature* (not completed until 1789) began to appear. All his love of natural beauty, heightened by the quality of his acute observation, breaks out here, rising to a height in the charming short novel, *Paul et Virginie* (1787). This last gained a European reputation and was translated into many languages (numerous Eng. trans., including that by H. M. Williams, 1795). His unfinished *L'Arcadie* was published in 1788. In 1790 there appeared two slighter works in the same style, *Le Café de Surate* and *La Chaumière indienne*. He died at Eragny. His *Œuvres* were edited by A. Martin (12 vols., 1818–20).

**Bernart de Ventadour** (*fl.* 1150–1195), Provençal troubadour. Born at Ventadour, the son of a servant of the lord of the castle there, he addressed his songs to the châtelain's wife Agnès de Montluçon. He is afterwards heard of at the court of Eleanor of Aquitaine (1152), and until 1194 he was a courtier of Raymond V of Toulouse. On Raymond's death that year he went to the monastery of Dalon, dying there soon after. Forty of his lyrics remain, and are considered to be among the finest of the world's love-lyrics. See C. Appel's edition of his work (1915) and *Chansons d'amour*, edited with an English translation by M. Lazar (1967).

**Bernart Marti** (*fl.* 1170), Provençal troubadour, known sometimes as **Le Pintor**, whose nine poems show him to have had a strong personality. Though a sceptic, he is an unprejudiced sensualist and lover of life. His ability in the presentation of his work is in advance of his time. See *Les Poésies de Bernart Marti*, edited by E. Hoepffer (1925).

**Berni, Francesco** (1497?–1535), Italian poet. Born of good family at Lamporecchio, Tuscany, he went to Rome in 1517 to enter the service of his uncle, Cardinal Bibbiena, and later of Giberti, chancellor of Pope Clement VII. It was at this time that he revised the *Orlando Innamorato* of Boiardo (q.v.) in the light of sixteenth-century taste (publ. 1541), which as late as the nineteenth century was actually preferred to the original, and wrote the bulk of his jovial *Rime giocose*. In 1532 he became secretary to Cardinal Ippolito de' Medici, but left his service a year later and went to Florence, where he became involved in court intrigues and, refusing to take part in a plot to poison Cardinal Salviati, was himself poisoned. A critical edition of his works by E. Chiorboli was published in 1934.

**Bernstein, Henry Léon Gustave Charles** (1876–1953), French playwright. Born in Paris, he found success with his first play *Le Marché* (1900), and almost up to the time of his death continued to write, in the same realistic style, works which if not great were certainly of a high quality within their range, and which have continued to hold the stage after many pretentious literary pieces have been forgotten. From this large outpouring it is difficult to make a selection, but the following may be listed as good examples: *Joujou* (1903), *Le Bercail* (1904), *La Griffe* (1906), *Samson* (1907), *Après moi* (1911), *L'Assaut* (1912), *L'Élévation* (1917), *Judith* (1922), *La Galérie des glaces* (1924), *Le Venin* (1927), *Le Cœur* (1935), *Le Voyage* (1938) and *La Soif* (1950). Bernstein died in Paris.

**Béroalde de Verville, François Vatable,** whose surname was originally **Brouart** (1556–1631?), French writer of short stories, born in Paris. He published anonymously about 1618 a quaint book of short stories, many of them rough and satirical, supposed to have been told at a feast, entitled *Le Moyen de parvenir, œuvre contenant la raison de tout ce qui a été, est et sera* (ed. C. Royer, 2 vols., 1896). It was very much read for a generation or so and exercised an influence on some branches of fictional narrative for a considerable time after that. He died at Tours.

**Béroul** (*fl.* 1180–1200), French poet of whom nothing is known, except that he is the author of a *Tristan* romance in Norman dialect, the middle portion of which, containing a reference to the siege of Acre (1191), survives. A work of strength, ranging in matter from the almost ridiculous to the tragic, it is much superior to the first German version of the *Tristan* by Eilhart von Oberg, whose likeness to it in substance suggests a common origin. Béroul's *Tristan* was edited by E. Muret, the revised fourth edition (1947) of which is the standard.

**Bersezio, Vittorio** (1828–1900), Italian playwright and novelist, was born at Peveragno, and gained a reputation with his comedies in Piedmontese dialect, the first two being *La Beneficenssa* (1862) and *La violenza a l'a sempre tort* (1862). It was with his third, *Le miserie d'monssu Travet* (1863), that his reputation spread far and wide. This comedy, often near to tears, about the poor little underpaid, overworked, bullied government clerk, who for all his cares proudly thinks of himself as a pillar of the state, at once took its place in Italian literature (it was translated into Italian in 1871), and has never lost it. Another comedy, written this time in Italian, was *La prosperità del signor Travetti* (1896). Of his very readable novels, derived particularly from Dumas *père* and Sue (q.v.), may be mentioned *L'Aristocrazia* (1881), *Il primo amore di Rosa* (1887), *Viperina* (1889) and *La parola della morta* (1898). In writing in Italian after the success of *Monssu Travet*, there is little doubt that Bersezio lost something of his spontaneity. He died in Turin.

**Bertaut, Jean** (1552–1611), French poet. Born at Donnay, he entered the Church and was for a time closely associated with the royal court. He wrote poetry throughout his life, and it is chiefly remarkable as mirroring the change from the Ronsard school to the almost entire influence of the Malherbe (q.v.) school from about 1600. His own career is adumbrated in his work from the lighthearted verse of his early days, to the serious official odes of his 'court' period, to the devotional poems of his last years. He was consecrated Bishop of Séez in 1606 and died in that city. His *Œuvres poétiques* were collected in 1601 and 1605 (complete edition by A. Chenevière, 1891).

**Berto, Giuseppe** (1914–     ), Italian novelist, born at Mogliano (Treviso), came to fame in 1947 with his novel about war in north Italy, *Il cielo è rosso* (Eng. trans. *The Sky is Red*, 1948), written when a prisoner-of-war in the U.S.A. He followed this up with *Le Opere di Dio* (1948; Eng. trans. *The Works of God*, 1949) and *Il Brigante* (1951; Eng. trans. *The Brigand*, 1951). His most recent works are *Guerra in camicia nera* (1955) and *Il male oscura* (1964; Eng. trans. *Incubus*, 1966).

**Bertolome Zorzi** (1230?–1290), Provençal troubadour. A Venetian merchant, he was taken prisoner by the Genoese in 1263 and not released until 1270 when he returned to Venice and died there. While in Genoa he was allowed to take part in several contests of troubadours, and bravely chose subjects praising his native country, which his opponent Bonifacio Calvo (q.v.), the Genoese troubadour, was magnanimous enough to praise. The consequent renown which Bertolome won led to his gaining his freedom. Among his other poetry are to be found religious, political and love songs, all written in a most simple manner, and a lament for the death of Conradin of Hohenstaufen (1268). He and his work are discussed in G. Bertoni's *I trovatori d'Italia* (1915).

**Bertram, Ernst** (1884–1957), German poet and man of letters. Born at Wuppertal, he was appointed professor of German literature at Cologne University in 1922, in which year he published a three-volume collection of poetry, *Das Gedichtwerk*. Later poetic work includes *Griechensiland* (1934), *Die Fenster von Chartres* (1940) and *Patenkinderbuch* (1949). His great work in prose was his *Nietzsche* (1918; new ed. 1929). His collected poetry appeared as *Gedichte und Spruche* (1951). He died in Cologne.

**Bertran de Bar-sur-Aube** (*fl.* 1200–1205), French poet, of whom nothing is known for certain, wrote two epic poems, *Aymeri de Narbonne* (ed. L. Demaison, 1887) and *Girart de Vienne* (ed. G. Yeandle, 1930). One of the very best narrative poets of the earlier Middle Ages, he is the master of a strong, concise style, rare in his own time and for long afterwards.

**Bertran de Born** (1140?–1215?), Provençal troubadour of Hautefort in Dordogne, where he had estates, he took part in the feuds between Henry II of England and his sons Henry and Richard, and repeatedly stirred up trouble among the nobles of southern France. On the death of Henry II (1189) he went with Richard I to Palestine, and entering the Cistercian Order in 1195 died in the abbey of Dalon. One of the greatest of the troubadours of the century, over forty of his poems, some love-poems and other satires, are extant. See A. Thomas, *Poésies complètes de Bertran de Born* (1888).

**Bertrand, Aloysius,** in reality **Jacques-Louis-Napoléon** (1807–1841), French poet in prose and verse, born at Ceva, he spent most of his life in Dijon, but died in Paris where he had become a protégé of Sainte-Beuve (q.v.). He is the man of one work, the collection of prose-poems, *Gaspard de la Nuit, fantaisies à la manière de Rembrandt et de Callot* (1842), ushered into the world by Sainte-Beuve as his literary executor. It exercised a definite influence on Baudelaire (q.v.), and is undoubtedly an unusual and exotic fruit of the very essence of the middle years of high-flying romanticism.

**Berwiński, Ryszard Wincenty** (1819–1879), Polish poet. Born at Polwica, he began to take part in politics at an early age in the interests of his country's freedom and socialism. His ardours and endurances are reflected in his *Poezje* (1844). He died, with all hopes gone, in Istanbul.

**Beskow, Bernard von** (1796–1868), Swedish dramatist. Born in Stockholm, where he also died, he became permanent secretary of the Swedish Academy in 1834. He had already fallen under the influence of German drama, especially of Schiller's, and his first play, *Erik XIV* (1828), shows his indebtedness to *Wallenstein*. Three other historical tragedies, including *Torkel Knutsson* (1836), together with *Erik*, make up the volume, *Dramatiska Studier* (1838), which had considerable influence in its day, but apart from *Erik* these dramas were not performed until 1862. His study, *Gustaf III* (5 vols., 1860–1869), is a major historical work.

**Besser, Johann von** (1654–1729), German poet. Born at Frauenburg of humble origin, he intrigued his way first into the Prussian and then into the Saxon court. His *Schriften* (1711) contains a miscellaneous collection of his somewhat salacious poetry, all of it of third-rate quality. It is a good example of the cheap and popular writing which circulated freely in the Germany of that time. Besser died in Dresden. In 1701 he had been one of the masters of ceremonies at the celebrations in connection with the crowning of Frederick I as first king of Prussia.

**Betteloni, Vittorio** (1840–1910), Italian poet and translator who lived all his life in Verona. His small store of poetry, written in a terse and telling style in opposition to *fin-de-siècle* decadence, published post-humously as *Poesie* in 1914, appealed strongly to a small but in-fluential circle of critics. As a translator he turned Byron's *Don Juan* into Italian with ingenuity and a certain power.

**Betti, Ugo** (1892–1953), Italian dramatist, born at Camerino. In his plays, which include *La casa sull' acqua* (1929), *Il diluvio* (1931), *Un albergo sul porto* (1933), *Il vento notturno* (1945) and *Marito e moglie* (1947), he dwells on the darkest side of life, but always finds enough good human souls to grapple with the evil. He died in Rome. His *Teatro* was published in 1955. An English translation, *Three Plays by Ugo Betti*, came out in 1957.

**Bettinelli, Saverio** (1718–1808), Italian dramatist, critic and historian, was born at Mantua and died there. A Jesuit whose orders lay lightly about him, he was a typical *littérateur*, aesthete and dilettante of the time. His Voltairian tragedies, his earliest published works, are little more than literary curiosities now, but his *Lettere virgiliane* (1757) is most significant both for its advocacy of pure classicism as the canon of good taste in literature and art, and for its attack on the Middle Ages, in particular Dante. This standpoint of adoration of ancient Rome and dislike of the 'undisciplined' medieval period which inter-vened is repeated in the *Lettere inglesi* (1767). To the study of aesthet-ics he contributed *L'entusiasmo delle belle arti* (1769), which clearly mirrors the taste and values of the time. That Bettinelli's dislike of medieval literature did not preclude his appreciation of the history of Middle Age Italy is to be seen in his *Risorgimento d'Italia* (1775), a subject which, written in an age of political degeneracy, looks forward to a future when the country will rise again. See his *Opere* (24 vols., 1799–1801) and the modern edition of both the *Lettere* and the rest of his critical writings (1930).

**Beyle, Marie Henri,** *see* **Stendhal.**

**Bèze (Beza), Théodore de** (1519–1605), French poet, playwright and theologian, was born into a landed family at Vézelay, Burgundy, and was a society playboy in Paris, during which time he penned erotic Latin verses (*Poemata,* 1548); but in the very year of their publication he fell seriously ill and, on his recovery, renounced his former ways, married his mistress and, going to Geneva, became a Calvinist. Much of his life and many of his writings hardly fall within the scope of literature, but he is noteworthy as the author of the first French tragedy, *Abraham sacrifiant*, written and performed in 1550 (Eng. trans. 1577). His *La Comédie du pape malade* (1561, under the pseudonym of 'Thrasibule Phénice') is an early and interesting example of politico-religious satire in dramatic form, while the Latin treatise, *De Francicae Linguae Vera Pronuntiatione* (1584; ed. A. Tobler, 1868), is a landmark in the study of phonetics. Bèze, who succeeded Calvin (q.v.) as head of the Reformed Church in Geneva, died in that city.

**Bezzola, Andrea** (1840–1897), Swiss Romansch poet. Born at Zernez, Engadine, he read law at Zürich and interested himself in politics, finally becoming head of the Swiss national council (1885) and a judge of the Federation (1893). His dignified lyric poetry, of a deep religious flavour, is contained in three volumes, *15 Chanzuns ladinas* (1889), *16 Chanzuns ladinas* (1894) and *17 Chanzuns ladinas* (1898). He died in Zürich.

**Bianco da Siena** (*fl.* 1367), Italian religious poet. Born at Anciolina in the Val d'Arno, he was a textile-worker in Siena, before becoming a member of the lay order of *Gesuati*, founded by the rich Sienese merchant Giovanni Colombini in 1367. Bianco, leaving his trade, thereupon went wandering in central Italy, composing and singing on his way his erotic quasi-religious *Laudi spirituali* (ed. Bini, 1851). He thereafter vanishes from record.

**Bidermann, Jakob** (1578–1639), German playwright and novelist, writing in Latin. Born at Ehingen, he became a Jesuit and wrote plays which were performed by schoolboys at Augsburg and Munich. Very interesting as perhaps the finest examples of German baroque symbolistic drama, they were collected as *Ludi theatrales sacri* in 1666. His chief novel is *Utopia* (1640). He died in Rome.

**Bidloo, Govert** (1649–1713), Dutch poet and dramatist, born at Amsterdam. He became a surgeon and had interests in theatres, being lessee of one of the largest in his native city. It was he who introduced plays in French classical style to the Dutch stage, the best of his works of this kind being *Karel, erfprins van Spanje* (1679) and *De dood van Pompejus* (1684). As a poet he produced descriptive verse, such as the religious subject, *Jezus leeraar buiten Capernaum* (1711). Having acted as court physician to William III of England until the latter's death in 1702, he died professor of anatomy at Leiden.

**Bielski, Marcin** (1495?–1575), Polish playwright and chronicler; was born at Biala, and followed a career which alternated between that of a soldier and a farmer. One of the pioneers of Polish literature, he is the author of *Kronika wszystkiego świata* (1551), a universal chronicle, and a verse-play, *Komedia Justyna i Konstancjej* (1557). He probably died at Biala.

**Bierbaum, Otto Julius** (1865–1910), German poet, novelist and critic. Born at Grünberg, Silesia, he appealed to a wide audience with his book of verse, *Der Irrgarten der Liebe* (1901; rev. 1906), in which he used new styles to treat of old themes. His long novel *Prinz Kuckuck* (1906–8) showed great humour with an admixture of satire. Bierbaum founded and was editor of *Die Insel*, the literary magazine, and so may be said to have been the 'godfather' of the publishing firm of Insel-Verlag which grew out of it. He died in Dresden.

**Bilderdijk, Willem** (1756–1831), Dutch poet. Born in Amsterdam, this strange personality, undisciplined and talented, was in bad health all his life and suffered from lameness. *Elius* (1785), a religious poem, gives one a good idea of his early work. His unhappy marriage and the French invasion of Holland in 1795 drove him to Britain and Germany where he led an eccentric, wandering life until recalled by King Louis Napoleon on his succession to the crown of Holland in 1806, an event celebrated in his excellent *Napoleon Ode* (1806). For the next four years, basking in the favour of King Louis until the latter's resignation in 1810, he enjoyed the only happiness of his life; and the end of the Napoleonic regime heralded at the Battle of Leipzig filled him with dismay, as he writes in a powerful poem, *Hollands Verlossing* (1813). The accession of William I did not bring him his hoped-for academic post, and he had to be content with a pension. The most ambitious work of this unsatisfactory literary performer is the epic *De Ondergang der eerste Wareld* (1820), left unfinished. He died, a strange recluse, at Haarlem. His collected works appeared (16 vols.) in 1856–9.

**Binding, Rudolf Georg** (1867–1938), German prose-writer. Born in Basel of wealthy parents, he was able to follow his own inclinations which amounted to writing and horse-racing. His best known and most characteristic works are *Reitvorschrift für eine Geliebte* (1924) and *Aus dem Kriege* (1925; Eng. trans. *Fatalist at War*, 1929). The first is a good example of his highly poetical narrative works, the second of his autobiographical style. Binding died at Starnberg.

**Birch-Pfeiffer, Charlotte Katharina** (1800–1868), German actress who turned playwright and novelist, was born at Stuttgart. She became a theatrical manager in Berlin. Nearly all her plays are derived from foreign novels, as, for example, her adaptation of *Jane Eyre*. Her sentimental novels were well suited to her middle-brow public. Her complete works, which appeared in two series between 1863 and 1880, fill twenty-six volumes. She died in Berlin.

**Birk, Sixt** (1500–1554), German dramatist, born at Augsburg, where he also died. He became a schoolmaster and wrote several religious plays of a highly didactic Protestant character, performed by his pupils. Birk was thus the first to realize the importance of this kind of propagandist work which served to instil reformed principles into actors (at a formative age) and audience. Protestants would thus beat Roman Catholics at their own game making use of the stage for the same purpose as they had done. Nearly all the plays were written in German, but Birk, in order to give them a wider audience, translated them later into Latin. As such *Sapientia Salomonis* found its way to England and was performed at Westminster School in 1566. His best work is *Susanna* (German, 1532; Latin, 1537), followed by *Judith* (German, 1532). His collected works as *Dramata Sacra* were published in 1547.

**Bitzius, Albert,** *see* Gotthelf, Jeremias.

**Bjørnson, Bjørnstjerne Martinus** (1832–1910), Norwegian man of letters. Born at Kvikne, Østerdalen, the son of a Lutheran clergyman, he went to Kristiania University in 1850, but left without a degree in 1854 to take up journalism. His first successes were the volumes of stories, *Arne* (1858; Eng. trans. 1890) and *En glad Gut* (1860; Eng. trans. *A Happy Boy*, 1896). His connection with the theatre had already begun in 1857 when he became director at Bergen, and for it he wrote *Mellem Slagene* (1858) and the very successful *Halta Hulda* in the same year. He was in Italy from 1860 to 1862, a period to which belong two further dramas, *Kong Sverre* (1861) and *Sigurd Slembe* (1862; Eng. trans. *Sigurd the Bastard*, 1888), his best. Posts at the Kristiania theatre and as a journalist sent him seeking new literary styles, but it was a return to his peasant novels with *Fisker-jenten* (1869; Eng. trans. *The Fisher Lassie*, 1890) which brought him the most success. The play *Sigurd Jorsalfar* (1872) is in the old romantic style; but from now on politics and social questions intrude, and in *Redaktoren* (1874; Eng. trans. *The Editor*, 1914), *En Fallit* (1875; Eng. trans. *The Bankrupt*, 1914) and *Kongen* (1877; Eng. trans. *The King*, 1914) we find him tackling problems, the importance of which has since faded. This is not the case with the next group, which contains his most satisfying plays both in depth and artistic competence. Among these are *Over Ævne* (1883; Eng. trans. *Beyond our Power*, 1913), *Over Ævne II* (1895; Eng. trans. *Beyond Human Might*, 1914), *Paul Lange og Tora Parsberg* (1898; Eng. trans. 1899) and *Laboremus* (1901; Eng. trans. 1914). Meanwhile he had continued to bring out more stories, which include *Kaptejn Mansana* (1879; Eng. trans. 1882), *Det Flager i Byen og paa Havnen* (1884) and *Paa Guds Veje* (1889; Eng. trans. *In God's Way*, 1890). He now frequently journeyed abroad, writing several attractive travel books. He had become a national figure and took a great part in the events leading to Norway's separation from Sweden in 1905. His poetry also, *Digte og Sange* (1870; Eng. trans. *Poems and Songs*, 1915) and *Arnljot Gelline* (1870; Eng. trans. 1917), had come to be highly regarded. He is the author of Norway's national anthem. He was awarded the Nobel Prize in 1903 and died in Paris. *The Novels of Bjørnstjerne Bjørnson* is an almost complete translation into English of the novels (ed. E. Gosse, 13 vols., 1895–1909). Of the translations of the plays those by R. F. Sharp, *Three Comedies* (1912) and *Three Dramas* (1914), may be noted.

**Blanche, August Theodor** (1811–1868), Swedish playwright, born in Stockholm, the illegitimate son of a clergyman and a housemaid. Becoming a journalist he edited the advanced paper *Freja* (1839–42), and then turned to writing for a living. He tried his hand at many kinds of writing, but it is as the author of comedies that he is remembered. Of the best are *Hittebarnet* (1847) and *Ett resande teatersällskap* (1853). In 1852 he entered the Swedish Riksdag and became very popular for his humanitarian and reforming zeal. He died in Stockholm. His complete works, edited by A. Hedin, appeared in 1889–92.

**Blanco White** (Blanco Crespo), José María (1775–1841), Anglo-Spanish poet and prose-writer. Born at Seville of Irish ancestry, he was ordained priest in 1799. Little by little losing his faith, he took the opportunity resulting from the disruption of the country caused by the French invasion and British intervention to escape to England in 1810. Having settled in London as Blanco White (the 'Doblado' = 'doubled', 'white' in Spanish and in English, as he called himself), he founded a periodical *El Español*, in which he advocated the breakaway of the South American states from the mother country, and on the review's cessation in 1814 received a pension of £250 a year for public services from the British Government. He edited another paper, *Variedades, o mensagero de Londres* (1823–5), having in the meantime not only renounced Roman Catholicism altogether but taken Anglican orders. Made a member of Oriel College, Oxford, and given an M.A. degree by decree of Convocation, he was for a time an outstanding personality in Oxford life, and was a regular contributor to the *Quarterly Review* and the *Westminster Review*. For some years before he left Spain he had written a certain amount of Spanish poetry of high quality, such as 'Los placeres del entusiasmo', 'La voluntariedad' and 'Una tormenta nocturna en alta mar', and he is entitled to a very respectable place in early romantic Spanish literature. His translation into Spanish of Hamlet's great speech, 'To be or not to be', is considered one of the finest in any language. After 1825 he wrote little more in Spanish. His noble English sonnet, 'Night and Death', was first published in the *Bijou* for 1828. His *Letters from Spain* (1822), *Evidence against Catholicism* (1825) and *Second Travels of an Irish Gentleman in Search of a Religion* (1833), throw much light on his life and personality. From 1832 to 1835 he was in Dublin as a private tutor, leaving his post abruptly, renouncing his Anglican orders, and settling in Liverpool as a Unitarian, where he died. *The Life of the Rev. Blanco White written by himself* appeared (3 vols.) in 1845. Blanco White spans the experience of two completely different ages and countries, and provides striking material for a study of the mental difficulties of those who were too honest and too clear-headed to be able to accept belief at second-hand or for convenience' sake.

**Blasco Ibáñez, Vicente** (1867–1928), Spanish novelist. Born in Valencia he became a lawyer, afterwards entering on a political career as republican deputy for his native city in the Cortes, and earning his living as a journalist. A man of action who founded colonies in Paraguay and Argentina, and who owned a publishing house whose cheap editions did much to aid the advance of popular education, he was a salutary influence on the Spain of his day, being a thorn in the side of a ramshackle monarchy and a stifling dictatorship. His finest works are those which deal with power and realism in south-eastern and southern Spain, such as *Flor de mayo* (1895; Eng. trans. *Mayflower*, 1922), *La barraca* (1898; Eng. trans. *The Cabin*, 1919), *Cañas y barro* (1902; Eng. trans. *Reeds and Mud*, 1928) and *Mare Nostrum* (1917; Eng. trans. *Mare Nostrum (Our Sea)*, 1919). About the turn of the century he changed to a more popular manner, before long gaining an international reputation with colourful novels, including *La bodega* (1906; Eng. trans. *The Fruit of the Vine*, 1923), concerned with society, and more especially *Sangre y arena* (1909; Eng. trans. *Blood and Sand*, 1913), the celebrated story of a bullfighter's life with necessary anti-clerical undertones, and *Los cuatro jinetes del Apocalipsis* (1916; Eng. trans. *The Four Horsemen of the Apocalypse*, 1918), the subject of which is the First World War, during which he supported the Allies. These two last were made into highly successful films. Blasco Ibáñez died a millionaire in exile at Menton, French Riviera. In 1933 his body was taken to Valencia by battleship with full state honours and reinterred there.

**Blicher, Steen Steensen** (1782–1848), Danish poet and short-story writer, born at Vium, Jutland. He became a clergyman, and lived for most of his life as a badly off country parson, taking refuge from his wretched domestic life in long walks over the Jutland moors, talks with peasants and drinking. Out of this life of sombre pattern grew such poetry as that contained in *Jyllandsrejse* (1817), the whole being collected as *Samlede Digte* (3 vols., 1835–40). His short stories, informed with quiet sadness and silent humour, appeared as *Noveller* in five volumes between 1833 and 1841. There is an exhaustive edition in thirty-three volumes of all his work (1920–34), and a useful *Digte og Noveller* (2 vols., 1946). Sigrid Undset (q.v.) translated some of the short stories into English as *Twelve Stories by Blicher* (1945). Blicher died at Spentrup.

**Blixen-Finecke, Karen,** sometimes using the pseudonym **Isak Dinesen** (1885–1962), Danish short-story writer, writing also in English. Born, the daughter of the author William Dinesen, at Rungsted, she married Baron Blixen-Finecke in 1914 and went to Kenya, where she remained until 1931. Her first book of value was written in English, *Seven Gothic Tales* (1934), and it appeared in Danish as *Syv fantastiske Fortællinger* the following year, being rewritten by herself. The same was the case of her next work, *Out of Africa* (1937), which was published the same year as *Den afrikanske Farm*, and of *Winter's Tales* (1942; *Vintereventyr*, 1942). Her later works, such as *Farah* (1950), *Daguerrotypier* (1951), *Babettes Gæstebud* (1952) and *Spögelseshestene* (1955), show a development away from English interests and style, but Kenya again provided the inspiration for *Shadows in the Grass* (1961). She died near Copenhagen.

**Bloch, Jean-Richard** (1884–1947), French prose-writer, born in Paris. An Alsatian Jew, Bloch became a socialist journalist of some note, and after the First World War turned Marxist. *Et Cie . . .* (1918; Eng. trans. *And Co.*, 1930) shows that already, under the influence of the possibilities which the Russian Revolution seemed to have made way for and the humanism of Romain Rolland (q.v.), he was giving his whole attention to the rôle of the intellectual, and the internationally minded Jewish intellectual in particular, in the devastated world. The pessimism of *Carnaval est mort* (1920) gives place to new enthusiasms, the most important being unified world culture, a solid core in every country to resist the forces of disintegration. The potentials of various parts of the world are investigated in *Sur un Cargo* (1924), *La Nuit Kurde* (1925; Eng. trans. *A Night in Kurdistan*, 1930) and *Cacaouettes et Bananes* (1929). In *Destin du Théâtre* (1930) he argued for people's theatres as part of the cultural basis of every nation, while in *Naissance d'une culture* (1936) and *Naissance d'une* *cité* (1937) he amplifies his creed. He fled to Russia on the French capitulation of 1940, but returned to France five years later, and died in Paris just after having completed *Moscou-Paris* (1947), when it seemed that Communism might triumph. His influence on Louis Aragon (q.v.) was extensive.

**Blok, Alexander Alexandrovich** (1880–1921), Russian poet, born in Petersburg. At first under the influence of German romanticism, especially Novalis (q.v.), he wrote mystical poetry, but the disastrous result of the 1905 revolution put an end to his idealism, and in his later work he comes out as a disillusioned realist, although using symbolism as a vehicle for his thought. He had been living a wild, apparently purposeless existence when the revolution of 1917 came to give him renewed hope in the world, a mood celebrated in his masterpiece *Dvenadtsat'* (1918; Eng. trans. *The Twelve*, 1920) and he followed this up with *Skify* (1918, 'The Scythians'), in which he welcomed the whole of the West into a brotherhood of nations. The inevitable disillusion was, however, not long in coming, and optimism and inspiration slipped away together. Blok, whose collected works, *Sobranie sochineniy*, were published (12 vols.) in 1932–6, is considered as the chief of the Russian symbolist movement. He died in Petersburg.

**Blondel de Nesle** (*fl.* 1190), French poet not easily identifiable and said by some to be Jean, seigneur de Nesle (Somme). Over twenty lyrics attributed to 'Blondel de Nesle' exist, their subjects being serious if not pessimistic. They are of slight literary value. The romantic story of Blondel's having discovered the whereabouts of the imprisoned Richard Cœur de Lion by singing a love-song composed by them together outside Dürrenstein Castle, Austria, rests solely on *Le Récit d'un ménestrel de Reims* (1280?). The Blondel poems have been edited by L. Wiese (1904).

**Bloy, Léon** (1846–1917), French novelist and publicist. Born at Périgueux in that near poverty which dogged him for most of his life, he appeared in 1884 with his *Propos d'un entrepreneur de démolitions*, which showed him to be an uncompromising opponent of the falsity of politics and society. True Catholicism was his balm, and if his anger directed against vice was always sure to hurt as it was meant to do, the balm was always ready. Of particular quality are his following books: *Le Désespéré* (1886), *La Femme pauvre* (1897; Eng. trans. *The Woman who was Poor*, 1939), *Le Sang du pauvre* (1909), *Le Pèlerin de l'absolu* (1914; Eng. trans., shortened, *Pilgrim of the Absolute*, 1947) and *Au seuil de l'Apocalypse* (1916). His letters are of much interest. Bloy died at Bourg-la-Reine.

**Blumauer, Johannes Aloys** (1755–1798), Austrian poet and dramatist. Born at Steyr, he studied for the priesthood, abandoned his plans, joined the Freemasons for purely selfish ends, and gained a post in the national censorship office (1781) which he held for a dozen years. Falling foul of the authorities, he lost this in 1793 and ended his days in Vienna as a bookseller. A typical product of the Enlightenment, very much diluted, presenting also the less reputable side of masonry, he produced a tragedy, *Erwine Steinheim* (1780), which hangs midway between the *Sturm und Drang* and Romantic movements. The bulk of his poetry, of mediocre quality, appeared as *Gedichte* (vol. i, 1782, vol. ii, 1787). His *Freimaurerlieder* (1786, ' Freemasonic Songs') are of greater interest as giving some insight into the ideals of the masonic movement in Austria. Mozart, a keen mason by this time, read them and set them to music, and they were much prized by Schikaneder, his librettist for *The Magic Flute*. Blumauer's silly burlesque of Virgil's *Aeneid* is better forgotten. His *Gesammelte Schriften* were published (3 vols.) in 1862.

**Boborykin, Peter Dmitrievich** (1836–1921), Russian novelist, born in Tambov. His collected works, which appeared in 1897, comprise fiction conveying first-hand panoramas of middle-class life, including *Kitay-Gorod* (1882) with its brilliant descriptions of mercantile life in Moscow in the 1870's. He died in Lugano.

**Bocage, Manuel Maria Barbosa du** (1765–1805), Portuguese poet. Born at Setúbal of French descent, he very soon revealed great poetic talent coupled with an unruly and unbalanced nature. As early as 1779 he joined the army, then went over to the navy, sailed to Goa (1786), led a dissipated life there, deserted in 1789, and went to Macao, where he lived on the verge of starvation, returning at last to Portugal in 1790. The next year he published his first book, *Idyllios maritimos*, an unequal collection, but showing a strong personal touch, violent, undisciplined and somewhat decadent. Election to the important Lisbon literary society, the Nova Arcadia, seemed for a time to anchor him, and in the same year as the *Idyllios* (1791) he published the first of his three volumes of *Rimas*, in which he proved his preference for the sonnet form in which to express his taste for satire and for the gloomy side of life. He, however, soon began to insult his fellow Arcadians, was expelled, and in 1797 was arrested and imprisoned for a time by order of the Inquisition as a heretic and a danger to the state because of ideas expressed in his poetry. He was later freed, published two further volumes of *Rimas* in 1799 and 1804, some of the poems highly erotic, and died in Lisbon. A strangely featured, pale-faced man, with something macabre about him, his rebellious life appealed to the young romantic generation apart from the intrinsic value of his work. The best of it, however, certainly supports his claim to be considered the greatest Portuguese poet of the eighteenth century. The first complete edition of his poetical works was published at Rio de Janeiro in 1811; the standard edition is the *Obras poéticas* (7 vols., 1849–50). The splendid studies by Teófilo Braga (q.v.) have done an immense amount for Bocage scholarship.

**Boccaccio, Giovanni** (1313–1375), Italian poet and prose-writer, was born probably in or near Florence the illegitimate son of Boccaccio di Chellino, a wealthy merchant of Florence, holding estates in Certaldo. At first his father refused to allow him to pursue his literary tastes, but later relented and allowed him to study law at Naples, where he remained from 1328 to 1340. During the latter years of this period he entered the court of Robert of Anjou where he met and loved the beautiful Maria d' Aquino, a natural daughter of King Robert, whom he immortalized as Fiammetta; she is a constant theme in his work and is the main figure in the *Decameron*. But it was study, in companionship with various scholars at the court, of Virgil, Horace and Ovid, which turned him into a major poet, and to the period from 1335 to 1340 belong *Filostrato*, a beautiful poem in *ottava rima* about Troilus and Cressida, afterwards freely used by Chaucer, and *Teseida*, an epic based on the *Aeneid* and telling the story of Palamon and Arcite. In these two works are revealed the joys and miseries occasioned by his love for Fiammetta. Then there are the charming idyll, *Ninfale fiesolano* (Eng. trans. *The Nymph of Fiesole*, 1960), the spiritual love of the Dantesque *Amorosa Visione*, and *Fiammetta*, which has been termed 'the first psychological novel of Europe'. These happy and unhappy days at Naples were cut short by his recall to Florence in 1340. His father's business had failed. There with his family in straitened circumstances he lived quietly in study and in composition, cultivating Florentine literary society. In 1348, while the Black Death was approaching north Italy, he began his most famous work, one of the greatest of world literature, the *Decameron*. This consists of a hundred stories, told on ten successive days in the garden of a villa some way from Florence, where a number of people have taken refuge from the terrible plague. In a reckless atmosphere, which always arises in periods of danger when death is near and life is of little value, the company tell one another tales of every kind, sad, romantic, amusing even to indecency; but whatever the story they recount, it is always to underline the fact that love is the guiding force of the world whatever form it takes. It enters into us, and for the noble it will be nobly conceived, for the base it will take a base form; but it is always there and cannot be avoided. The work in fact is an attack on medieval asceticism, inspired by a state of mind brought about by that great pestilence which marks the beginning of the end of the Middle Ages. But apart from such considerations the tales of the *Decameron* are of transcendent beauty, and when Boccaccio took these stories, which were known all over the Italy of his day, and transformed them into his own miracles of Italian prose, he created a fashion which revolutionized the literatures of his own country, France and England (without the *Decameron* the *Canterbury Tales* would never have been written), and which persisted far down the ages. In 1349 his father died of the Black Death, and he began to travel. His meeting with Petrarch (q.v.) in 1351 was of immense importance, for it may be said that from then on his life centred upon this friendship. Petrarch introduced him to Dante studies and directed him to further ancient classical literature. Then in 1362 came a sudden religious awakening, said to have been effected by a dying priest; but he was saved from his consequent despondency by Petrarch, who also helped him to bear with philosophy his poor financial circumstances. He had already taken part in important diplomatic missions to the Papal States, the last of these being in 1367, and in 1373 he gave a series of public lectures on Dante at the invitation of the city of Florence, but his health began to fail and he withdrew to the small family estate at Certaldo. There the following year he heard of Petrarch's death (1374) and his own was not long delayed. In his later years he had taken more and more to writing in

Latin, the *Vita di Dante*, completed in 1362, being his most prominent work in the vernacular in the final period. Of his Latin works the most attractive are the poetry of the *Eclogae* and *Epistolae* and the biographies of Livy and Petrarch. His geographical dictionary, *De montibus, silvis, fontibus*, is of much interest. There are good modern editions of the *Rime* (1914), *Teseida* (1938), *Filostrato* (1937), *Fiammetta* (1939) and the *Opere latine minori* (1928). The definitive edition of the *Decameron* is that by Bosco (1947). Montier's seventeen-volume *Opere* (1827–34) is still invaluable.

**Boccage, Marie Anne Fiquet du** (1710–1802), French poet. Born in Rouen, she went to Paris where she soon made a name for herself with her beauty and wit, and presided successfully over her *salon*. Her main works are two bulky volumes of poetry, *Le Paradis terrestre* (1748) and *La Colombiade* (1756). She died in Paris.

**Boccalini, Traiano** (1556–1613), Italian prose satirist, was born at Loreto. He served the Papal States in a judicial and political capacity until his growing hatred of increased Spanish interference led him to settle in the Venetian Republic. His famous and ingeniously presented work is that memorable satire on the affairs of men, *I Ragguagli di Parnaso* (Part I, 1612; Part II, 1613; crit. ed. G. Rua, 1910; Eng. trans. *Advertisements from Parnassus with the Politicke Touchstone*, by Henry, Earl of Monmouth, 1669). King Apollo rules on Parnassus and convokes a council of the great of all ages to discuss important questions of every kind. The findings of the council are transmitted to earth in the shape of two hundred dispatches. Boccalini, who also wrote on politics and on Tacitus, died in Venice.

**Boddaert, Marie Agathe** (1844–1914), Dutch poet and novelist, born at Middelburg. She married in 1872 and went to live in The Hague. Later she became well known as an historical novelist, her greatest success in that department being *Sturmfels* (1889). Her *Aquarellen*, a book of poetry published two years before, appealed to a limited but influential public. In later years she wrote stories for girls, a good example of which is *Roswitha* (1909). She died in The Hague.

**Bodel, Jean** (*d.* 1209), French poet and dramatist. Born at Arras, he became a municipal clerk there and a *jongleur* in his spare time. His play *Le Jeu de Saint Nicolas* was written in 1199 (crit. ed. by F. J. Warne, 1951); his epic on Charlemagne's Saxon war, *Les Saisnes*, in 1201 (crit. ed. Menzel and Stengel, 1906) and his poems, *Les Congés*, in 1202 (crit. ed. G. Raynaud, *Romania*, ix, 1880). He also wrote short pastoral poems. In 1202 he contracted leprosy in Arras and died of it there.

**Bodenstedt, Friedrich Martin von** (1819–1892), German poet and translator, was born at Peine, Hanover. In 1841 he went to Moscow as a tutor, and visited Turkey and Greece before returning to Germany in 1847. For a time he became a journalist and edited the *Weser Zeitung*, and then in 1851 suddenly sprang to fame with his book of pseudo-oriental poems which he pretended to be the work of his Tartar master which he had copied down when in the East and had now translated. The *Lieder des Mirza Schaffy* (1851; Eng. trans. *The Songs of Mirza Schaffy*, 1880) was so immensely popular that seventy years later it had reached the 264th edition. As a translator he worked on Shakespeare (1866–72), and later on Omar Khayyám, Pushkin and Lermontov. His autobiography, *Erinnerungen* (2 vols., 1888–90), is full of interest. He was appointed director of the Meiningen theatre in 1866, and died at Wiesbaden.

**Bodin, Jean** (1530–1596), French prose-writer. Born at Angers, he was educated in Toulouse and became a lawyer in Paris. In 1571 he was given an official post at Laon, and in 1581 spent a short time in England. He was already famous for his excellent *Les Six Livres de la République* (1576), which he himself later translated into Latin. This lucid inquiry into the political and legal standing of the state has been described as the only really good work on political science before the eighteenth century. Indeed one would call him a man amazingly in advance of his time if one had not read his quaint *De la démonomanie des sorciers* (1580) which contains all the medieval credulity. He died of the plague at Laon.

**Bodmer, Johann Jakob** (1698–1783), Swiss poet and literary theorist, was born at Greifensee, near Zürich. In 1725 he became professor of Helvetian history in Zürich University, holding the post until 1775. A man of keen mental powers, he was the driving force in the partnership with J. J. Breitinger (q.v.) against the continued influence of French classicism in European, especially German, literature and against the pretensions of J. C. Gottsched (q.v.) of Leipzig to be a literary dictator. His first important literary venture, in which he was aided by Breitinger, was the journal *Die Discourse der Mahlern* (1721–3). In it among other matters he investigated the relationship between the arts, especially literature and the plastic arts, and so set in motion such investigations in that field as were later to be brought to the vivid conclusions of Caylus and Lessing (q.v.). In *Von dem Einfluss und Gebrauche der Einbildungskraft* (1727) he marshals his strength, again aided by Breitinger, along these lines; but it was not until 1740 that he was ready completely to demolish the forces of pseudo-classicism. In his *Kritische Abhandlung von dem Wunderbaren in der Poesie* (1740) he shows a comprehension of the wider aspects of literature and the arts rare in his day; while his eye for the pictorial qualities of epic and the taste which he reveals when discoursing on the correct transmutation of nature into literary description is of high quality, and deserved its influence. His *Kritische Betrachtungen über die poetischen Gemälde der Dichter* (1741) concerned itself more nearly with the function of the poet. Bodmer soon became an honoured figure for the younger generation of men of letters, and to visit him was a recognized literary pilgrimage. The young Klopstock (q.v.) and later Wieland (q.v.), and later still Goethe (q.v.), among many others, journeyed to Zürich to pay their respects. As an original writer Bodmer can hardly be said to have succeeded. His plays, collected as *Schweizerische Schauspiele* (1775) and for the most part inspired by Swiss history, do not amount to much, while his religious epics (Bodmer was a clergyman) *Noah* (1750) and *Jacob und Joseph* (1751–4) are ponderous. His translation of Milton's *Paradise Lost* (1732) is creditable. He died in Zürich.

**Bødtcher, Ludwig Adolph** (1793–1874), Danish poet. Born in Copenhagen, he spent much time in Rome in the Danish artists' colony there and became a close friend of the sculptor Thorvaldsen. His three volumes of quiet tasteful poetry, lit up by a pale, late romanticism, were published in 1856, 1875 and 1876, and the whole were collected in one volume as *Samlede Digte* in 1940. Bødtcher returned to Copenhagen in later years and died there.

**Boëx, Justin,** *see* **Rosny, J.-H.**

**Bogdanovich, Ippolit Fyedorovich** (1743–1802), Russian poet who introduced La Fontaine's (q.v.) *Psyché et Cupidon* (and so the French classical style) into Russian literature with his excellent paraphrase of it, *Dushenka* (1775). Born at Perevolochnaya, he died in Kursk.

**Böhme, Jakob** (1575–1624), German mystical writer, sometimes called **Behmen,** was born the son of a peasant at Altseidenberg, near Görlitz, Lusatia, and set up as a shoemaker at Görlitz itself in 1589 where he remained for the rest of his life. Entirely self-taught, as a result of long meditation and reading, he circulated *Aurora oder Morgenröte im Aufgang* in 1612 (not published until 1634), *Drei Prinzipien göttlichen Wesens* in 1619, *Sechs mystische Punkte* and *Sechs theosophische Punkte* in 1620, *De Signatura Rerum* in 1622 and *Mysterium Magnum* in 1623. By this time he had gained a considerable following, and in the years after his death his works were translated into many languages, including English. His mysticism and personal claims to divine inspiration, however, brought him many enemies among the clergy. Behmenists later appeared in England, but were absorbed by the Quakers. The standard German edition is that of K. W. Schiebler (7 vols., 1831–47). There have been many English translations ranging from Sparrow's (1647) to Earle's (1930).

**Bohomolec, Franciszek** (1720–1784), Polish playwright and essayist. Born at Vitebsk, he became a Jesuit and taught at various Jesuit colleges, for the pupils of which he wrote comedies, their plots and style of dialogue copied from Molière (q.v.). These were collected in five volumes, 1755–60. Later he wrote in the same manner for the National Theatre, these plays being published in 1767, and showed himself to be a keen opponent of the upper classes with their frequently idle and dissipated lives. He founded a periodical, the *Monitor*, in 1765 and edited it until his death. In manner like the English *Tatler* of Addison and Steele, the *Monitor* did a great deal to improve Polish tastes and ways of life. Bohomolec died in Warsaw.

**Boiardo, Matteo Maria** (1441–1494), Italian poet. Born at Scandiano, Reggio Emilia, he was in the service of the Estes, dukes of Ferrara, all his life. His great work is his *Orlando Innamorato* which he began in 1482 for the entertainment of his patrons. The poem, an epic on Charlemagne and his captains and their fortunes in war and love, was left unfinished, was published with additions by others (1526, 1531), and rewritten early in the sixteenth century to suit prevailing tastes by Francesco Berni (q.v.). Under this high polish it remained until Sir Anthony Panizzi brought the original into public notice again (nineteenth century). The theme of Orlando's love for Angelica, the princess of Cathay, was the inspiration which set Ariosto (q.v.) to compose *Orlando Furioso*. He also wrote charming lyric poetry, generally on love themes. He died at Reggio Emilia. There is a complete edition of his works by A. Zottoli (2 vols., 1936–7), and *Orlando Innamorato, Sonetti e Canzoni*, edited A. Scaglione, appeared (2 vols.) in 1951.

**Boie, Heinrich Christian** (1744–1806), German literary journalist. Born at Meldorf, Holstein, he was educated at Jena and Göttingen, where in 1770 with F. W. Gotter (q.v.) he founded the literary periodical *Musenalmanach*, which lasted until 1775 and proved to be a nursery of much poetic and other talent. Of still greater value was his second literary journal, *Das Deutsche Museum*, which he started in 1775. Appointed a public administrator in Holstein in 1781, he dropped out of literature. He died at Meldorf.

**Boileau-Despréaux, Nicolas** (1636–1711), French poet and critic. Born in Paris where his father was a prosperous lawyer, he began to study first for the Church, and then for the Law. In 1657, however, his father died leaving him a sufficient fortune to follow his inclinations and adopt a literary career. In 1660 he wrote *Adieux d'un poète à la ville de Paris*, the first of his satires, six more of which passed about in literary circles in manuscript before being published in 1666, two more appearing in 1668. Horace's *Satires* were his models, and into such a classical framework he fitted his devastating attacks on the weaknesses and follies of society. The last three, making up the number to twelve, were written in 1694, 1698 and 1705, and were much inferior to the earlier ones. (The best ed. of the *Satires* is by A. Adam, 1941.) The year 1674 was Boileau's period of particular triumph, for in it were published not only the first five of his *Épîtres*, no less Horatian than the *Satires*, but *L'Art poétique*, that remarkable re-creation of Roman Augustan literary taste inspired by the *Ars Poetica* of Horace. So masterly was the presentation, and so authoritative the scholarship displayed, that Boileau was able to lay down rules that governed the accepted canons of dramatic and poetic style for at least sixty years. Part of *Le Lutrin*, a serio-comic epic, was also published this year, being completed in 1683. In 1675 another *Épître* appeared, the ninth had been reached two years later, and the series was rounded off with the twelfth and last in 1698. (The standard ed. of the *Épîtres* is by A. Cahen, 1937.) Boileau now reaped the harvest from the sowings of earlier years. He was on terms of close friendship with Racine (q.v.) and La Fontaine (q.v.), while the royal favour blazed on the assiduous courtier. He was appointed historiographer to the king jointly with Racine, and by Louis' special request was elected to the Academy in 1684. After this he wrote little more; *Réflexions sur Longin* (1694) provides an opportunity, while discussing the literary criticism of the later Greek philosopher Longinus, to underline his own stern classicism already formulated. His last years were sad; he outlived nearly all his friends and he suffered from deafness and other maladies. In 1705 he sold his country house where he had been living for many years and came to live in Paris again. There he died. 'The Legislator of Parnassus', whose principles were carried out in English literature, e.g. by Pope, has suffered a great decline in reputation, being considered a narrow critic who damaged literary style. Boileau, however, was necessary, and if one takes into account the slackness of diction and superfluity of language that followed the decline of the baroque, whether it was Marinism (q.v.) in Italy, Góngorism (q.v.) in Spain, the 'Pindarique' writers in England and the bad influence of Malherbe (q.v.) in France itself, one can see that his method of scrutinizing poetry for reason and common sense, mercilessly satirizing any who transgressed his rules and became precious or sentimental, was bound to have a salutary effect. That his original principles became debased and frozen into dull and groping latinisms was no fault of his own. As a critic he was the literary architect of his age; as the author of the *Satires* and *Épîtres*, he showed that with all his outward urbanity he could see, behind the disguises of periwigs and shoes with red heels, man for what he was worth. The most satisfactory of the editions of his *Œuvres complètes* is that by C. Gidel (4 vols., 1873).

**Boisgobey, Fortuné de** (1824–1891), French novelist. Born at Granville, Normandy, his real name being **Castille**, he assumed that of Boisgobey on taking up journalism, first making his name with a series of sketches, 'Deux comédiens', which he contributed to *Le Petit Journal* in 1868. From that time onwards until his death he was a successful and popular writer of detective novels, chief among them being *L'Homme sans nom* (1872), *Le Crime de l'Opéra* (1879) and *Le Fils du plongeur* (1890). Many were translated into several European languages.

**Boisrobert, François le Metel de** (1592–1662), French poet and playwright. Born in Caen, he became Richelieu's secretary and was one of the original members of the French Academy on its foundation in 1634. Soon afterwards he was appointed one of the five playwrights specially chosen by Richelieu to write propagandist pieces according to his orders. Of his plays *La Belle Plaideuse* (1654) is still readable, but it is his two collections of *Épîtres en vers* (1646 and 1659; ed. M. Cauchie, 2 vols., 1921–7) which have lasted best. He died in Paris.

**Boito, Arrigo** (1842–1918), Italian librettist and poet, who was also a musical composer. Born in Padua he became a man of letters, and gained fame as a librettist with *La Gioconda* (1876) for Ponchielli and *Otello* (1887) and *Falstaff* (1893) for Verdi. His best book of poetry is *Re Orso* (1902). He died in Milan.

**Bojer, Johan** (1872–1959), Norwegian novelist, born at Orkesdalsøren. His first work appeared in 1896, but it was not until seven years later that his books were introduced to foreign countries, the first being *Troens magt* (1903; Eng. trans. *The Power of a Lie*, 1908). Among his numerous books, usually dealing with the problems of the time, may be mentioned: *Vort rige* (1908; Eng. trans. *Treacherous Ground*, 1912), *Liv* (1911; Eng. trans. *Life*, 1922), *Fangen som sang* (1913; Eng. trans. *The Prisoner who Sang*, 1924), *Den store hunger* (1916; Eng. trans. *The Great Hunger*, 1918), *Verdens ansigt* (1917; Eng. trans. *The Face of the World*, 1919), *Vor egen stamme* (1924; Eng. trans.

*The Emigrants*, 1926), *Det nye tempel* (1927; Eng. trans. *The New Temple*, 1928), *Dagen og natten* (1935; Eng. trans. *By Day and Night*, 1937) and *Kongens Karer* (1938; Eng. trans. *King's Men*, 1940). Bojer's prose is not particularly distinguished, but lends itself well to translation, and he has always been more appreciated abroad than in Norway. His powers of description and characterization are noteworthy. He died in Oslo.

**Bolintineanu, Dimitrie,** pseudonym of **Dimitrie Cosmad** (1819–1872), Rumanian poet, was born at Bolintinul. He showed himself to be a gifted writer of ballads with a strong historical sense in his volume *Poezii* (1847). Involved in the 1848 Revolution he had to escape to exile, but returning later became foreign minister in 1857. He again successfully exploited his gifts in *Melodii române* (1858). He died of neglect in a mental hospital in Bucharest. *Poezii* (2 vols., 1877) contains his collected works.

**Böll, Heinrich** (1917–    ), German novelist. Born in Cologne, his powerful, bitterly ironical novels set in the defeated Germany of post-1945 were *Der Zug war pünktlich* (1949) and *Und sagte kein einziges Wort* (1953). A recent novel of note was *Ansichten eines Clowns* (1963). For his short stories, see the English translation, *18 Stories* (1966).

**Bonarelli, Guidobaldo della Rovere** (1563–1608), Italian pastoral poet, born at Pesaro, he was a follower in that *genre* of Tasso and Guarini (qq.v.). His best work is the pastoral drama *Filli in Sciro* (1607). His other pastoral dramas are conveniently collected in E. Camerini's edition of his *Drammi de' boschi e delle marine* (1927). He died at Fano.

**Bonaventura,** religious name of **Giovanni di Fidanza** (1221–1274), Italian Latin prose-writer, born at Bagnorea, near Orvieto, Tuscany. He became a Franciscan, taught at Paris University, and was finally made a cardinal (1273). He died while attending the Council of Lyon, exhausted by severe asceticism. His most important works, notable for their fervour, are the *Itinerarium Mentis in Deum* and *De Reductione Artium ad Theologicum*. The best edition of the works of the 'Seraphic Doctor' is that by the Franciscans of Quaracchi (1882–1902).

**Boner, Ulrich** (*fl.* 1324–1349), Swiss fabulist of Bern, who about 1349 wrote *Der Edelstein*, a collection of fables from various sources from Aesop onwards, ably retold with additional moral digressions. First printed in 1461, *Der Edelstein* survived to be grist to the mill of eighteenth-century rationalists. There is a good edition of it by F. Pfeiffer (1844).

**Bonet, Honoré** (1345?–1406?), French poet and prose-writer, of whom nothing is definitely known apart from the fact that he was a Benedictine and at one time a papal nuncio. He is the author of the prose work on the legal aspects of war, *L'Arbre des batailles* (1388; Eng. trans. *The Tree of Battles*, 1949), and the poem on the disasters of the age, *L'Apparicion maistre Jehan de Meun* (1398; mod. ed., 1926). Both are penetrating reviews of the period.

**Bonifacio Calvo** (*fl.* 1250–1270?), Genoese troubadour who served his apprenticeship at the court of Castile and then returned home. His contest with the Venetian Bertolome Zorzi (q.v.) was famous, and his chivalrous behaviour towards his rival led to Bertolome's release in 1270 from being held prisoner in Genoa. After this nothing more is heard of Bonifacio. His favourite theme, that of noble-hearted women, amounts almost to a religious cult. He and his work are discussed in G. Bertoni's *I trovatori d'Italia* (1915).

**Bonstetten, Karl Viktor von** (1745–1832), Swiss prose-writer, writing in German and French. Born in Bern of wealthy parents, he was destined for a diplomatic career and was given a careful education at Leiden and Paris. It was while on his travels in his early years that he visited Cambridge and made such an impression on the lonely, declining and somewhat pathetic poet Gray. Thereafter he spent much of his time in Italy. A man of attractive but unoriginal mind, it is probably for this very reason that he so faithfully conveys to the modern reader the climate of thought in the circles and period in which he lived. His principal works are *Über Nationalbildung* (1802) and *L'Homme du midi, et l'homme du nord* (1824), in which he sought to take the doctrine of nationalism and environment, already developed by Mme de Staël (q.v.) and A. W. Schlegel (q.v.), a step further; while in his *Briefe an Matthisson* (1827) are to be found many an echo of the literary and artistic tastes of a bygone age. He died in Geneva.

**Borberg, Svend** (1888–1947), Danish dramatist, born in Copenhagen. His carefully written, arrestingly thoughtful, though stationary plays had enormous influence in Danish literary circles. Of these *Ingen* (1920) and *Synder og Helgen* (1939) were outstanding. He died in Copenhagen shunned for collaboration with the Germans.

**Bordeaux, Henri** (1870–1963), French novelist. Born, the son of a lawyer, at Thonon-les-Bains, he first attracted attention with *La Peur de vivre* (1902; Eng. trans. *The Fear of Living*, 1914) and consolidated his reputation with *Les Roquevillard* (1906; Eng. trans. *The Will to Live*, 1916). He continued his strongly moral studies of traditional upper bourgeois life with *La Robe de laine* (1910; Eng. trans. *The Woollen Dress*, 1912) and *La Neige sur les pas* (1912; Eng. trans. *Footprints beneath the Snow*, 1913). At the outbreak of the First World War he became an artillery officer, taking part in the defence of Verdun, his account of which, *Les Captifs délivrés*, was published in 1917. In 1919 he visited London and drew crowds to his Verdun lectures, and in the same year was elected to the French Academy. He reappeared as a novelist in his former manner with *Yamilé sous les cèdres* (1923), this being succeeded by such as *La Revenante* (1932), *Andromède et le monstre* (1938), *L'Ombre sur la maison* (1942) and *Les Yeux accusateurs* (1949). The quadrilogy *Histoire d'une vie*, founded on his own experiences of life down to the middle of the First World War, was published between 1951 and 1957, and showed astonishing powers for one of his age. Later appeared *Mémoires secrets du chevalier de Rosaz* (1958). He died in Paris.

**Borel, Pétrus,** pseudonym of **J.-P. Borel** (1809–1859), French poet. Born at Lyon, he made early for Paris where he soon found himself in Gautier's (q.v.) circle. In his opposition to all established values he is a thoroughpaced romantic, the werewolf and other themes of law-lessness and disintegration being used by him with effect in such books as *Champavert* (1833) and *Madame Putiphar* (1839). After his spell of dandyism he found himself penniless and was forced to seek civil service employment in Algeria. He prospered for a while, but fell into lazy ways, was dismissed, tried unsuccessfully to return to France and died at Mostaganem. See *Œuvres complètes* (5 vols., 1921).

**Borghi, Giuseppe** (1790–1847), Italian poet, born at Bibbiena. He became a priest, a librarian in Florence and a university lecturer at Palermo. His best work is to be found in his religious *Inni sacri* (1829). Some of his secular poetry, rightly or wrongly, was taken up as Risorgimento literature. He had some influence on Giusti (q.v.). He died in Rome. His *Poesie complete* appeared in 1867.

**Borghini, Raffaello** (1541–1588?), Italian playwright, born in Florence, where he died. He was the author of several comedies, including *La donna costante* (1578), and of a pastoral play, *Diana pietosa* (1586).

**Börne, Ludwig**, originally **Löb Baruch** (1786–1837), German prose-writer. Born at Frankfurt-am-Main, the son of a Jewish money-changer, he studied medicine at Berlin, and from 1807 law and political economy at Heidelberg and Giessen. In 1809 he returned to Frank-furt, and in 1811 was appointed police actuary there, dividing his time between his duties and journalism, in which he supported liberalism against the increasingly reactionary German governments. With the end of Napoleonic rule in Germany in 1813 he was dis-missed from his post as a Jew, an event which led him still further into opposition to reaction. His conversion to Christianity in 1818, when he assumed the name of Ludwig, has given rise to accusations against him of time-serving, but as a Christian he attacked the establishment in his new journal, *Die Wage* ('The Balance'), with as much vigour as when he had been a Jew. Despairing of any political change in Germany, he moved to Paris after the revolution of 1830, was a theatre critic, quarrelled violently with his fellow exile Heine (q.v.), whom he regarded as an aesthetic indifferentist, while he was a practical enthusiast. *Die Wage* was now revived in French as *La Balance*, and contained many invectives against politically amoral Germans. His finest work as a journalist with literary abilities of a high order is to be seen in his 'Paris Letters', *Briefe aus Paris* and *Neue Briefe aus Paris* (1832–7), the final sections appearing post-humously in 1838. Wearing himself out preaching revolution, he died of consumption in Paris. His *Gesammelte Schriften* were published (12 vols.) in 1862.

**Borsi, Giosuè** (1888–1915), Italian poet and essayist. Born at Leg-horn, he developed early into a poet and made a name for himself with the highly spiritual volumes of verse, *Primus fons* (1907) and *Scruta obsoleta* (1910). His *Testamento spirituale* (1915) is a moving account of his return to orthodox Christianity. In the year of its publication he was killed on the Gorizia front.

**Borup, Morten** (1446?–1526), Danish poet writing in Latin. Born at Adslev, near Skanderborg, he became a farmer, but abandoned the country when he was nearly thirty and gained sufficient education not only to become headmaster of Aarhus cathedral school but to write the finest Latin poem in Danish literature, *Carmen vernale*, and various others of a topographical nature. He died at Aarhus.

**Bos, Charles du** (1882–1939), French essayist and diarist. Born in Paris, his mother being English, he went to Oxford where he was influenced by the aftermath of the preciousness of Walter Pater, and the style which he adopted holds a unique place in French literature. As a critic he is at his best in *Réflexions sur Mérimée* (1920) and *Byron et le besoin de la fatalité* (1929; Eng. trans. *Byron and the Need of Fatality*, 1932). His highly individualistic *Journal* appeared (3 vols.) posthumously in 1946–9. He died in Paris.

**Bosboom-Toussaint, Anna Louisa Geertruida** (1812–1886), Dutch fictional writer. Born at Alkmaar, she became a governess before turning to literature for a living, modelling her historical novels on those of Scott. Perhaps her finest work in this manner is the one, written from a strongly Protestant point of view, on the revolt of the Netherlands from Spain and the Earl of Leicester's intervention, *De Graaf van Leicester in Nederland* (3 vols., 1845–6). Other books on the subject followed, the last of the series being *Gideon Florensz* (4 vols., 1854–5). Her later works dealt with contemporary matters, a good example of such being *Majoor Frans* (1874; Eng. trans. 1885). She died in The Hague. Her collected works appeared (25 vols.) in 1885–8.

**Boscán Almugáver, Juan** (1493?–1542), Spanish poet and translator. Born in Barcelona, he became a soldier and fought for the Knights of Rhodes and for the empire before joining the diplomatic service. In 1526 he was persuaded by the Venetian plenipotentiary to try his hand at writing Spanish poetry in Italian metre. He cannot be said to have succeeded, but his attempts roused others to emulate him, including Garcilaso de la Vega (q.v.), who soon surpassed him. His only real success was his blank-verse poem on the ancient fable, *Hero y Leandro*. His translation into Spanish of the *Cortegiano* ('Courtier') of Castiglione (q.v.) is excellent. Boscán died in Barcelona. His widow, Ana Girón de Rebolledo, a woman of great intellectual abilities, unusual for her time, edited her husband's works, together with those of his friend Garcilaso, in 1543. His *Obras* appeared in a good, serviceable edition by W. Knapp (1875). There is an edition of the translation of *Il Cortegiano, Los cuatro libros del Cortesano*, by A. M. Fabié (1873).

**Bosco, Henri** (1888–     ), French novelist. Born at Avignon, all his writing is redolent of his native Provence. A subtle mingling of the sensual and the occult gives a particular quality to his work which is exemplified in *Pierre Lampédouse* (1924), *Le Très-toulas* (1935), *Hyacinthe* (1940), *Le Jardin d'Hyacinthe* (1946) and *Monsieur Carré-Benoît à la campagne* (1947). *Un Rameau de la nuit* (1950) opens a new era of his work. Gloom, storm, danger and uncertainty enter into his novels. There is a preoccupation with islands and the confrontation of antagonistic characters. The influence of such English romanticists as C. R. Maturin is strong. Later works include *Antonin* (1952), *L'Antiquaire* (1954), *Le Renard dans l'île* (1956) and *Barboche* (1957).

**Bossuet, Jacques-Bénigne** (1627–1704), French prose-writer and orator. Born at Dijon, he entered the Church, and as a canon of Metz had already (1652) made a reputation as a vigorous defender of Catholicism against the Huguenots. In 1661 he became court preacher and, gaining the particular favour of Louis XIV both for his magnificent pulpit oratory and for his belief in Gallicanism, i.e. a national state Church in France in opposition to papal interference, he began to rise rapidly in the Church, being finally consecrated Bishop of Meaux in 1681. Moderate on the whole and hopeful to reconcile Catholicism and Protestantism, he yet finally gave way and joined with Madame de Maintenon in pressing forward with the revocation of the Edict of Nantes (1685). He is seen at his worst in his anti-Protestant controversies and in his opposition to the mysticism of Fénelon (q.v.). On the other hand in such a book as *L'Histoire des variations des églises protestantes* (1688), where he does not make outright war on what he condemns but allows the evidence, which he assembles with such mastery and such cunning, to do his work, he is very powerful. But it is for his funeral orations, which rise to the magnificence of solemn grandeur, that he is generally remembered, the most famous being those on Henriette, Duchess of Orléans (1670), Turenne (1675) and Condé (1686). Bossuet died in Paris. Of editions of his *Œuvres complètes*, that by Guillaume (10 vols., 1877–85) is the standard one, while the *Œuvres oratoires* have appeared in a definitive edition by C. Urbain and E. Levesque (7 vols., 1928–9).

**Botev, Christo** (1847–1876), Bulgarian poet. Born at Kalofer, he became (1872) head of the Bulgarian revolutionary council, sworn to gain the independence of the nation. His handful of poems, considered the finest in the Bulgarian language, were published in *Pesni i stihove* (1875). He was killed on the mountain peak of Vola while leading an expedition against the Turks.

**Botta, Carlo** (1766–1837), Italian historian, born at San Giorgio Canavese, would hardly be regarded as a literary figure were it not that in his two main works he writes in a style consciously founded on late Middle-Age Italian prose. This remarkable example of bringing the archaic to life again—it must be admitted, not always with happy results, but often with much success—confronts one in *Storia della guerra d'indipendenza degli Stati d'America* (1809; final ed. revised, 1844) and *Storia d'Italia dal 1789 al 1814* (1824). Botta, who had always felt more at home in France than in Italy, died in Paris.

**Bouchet, Jean** (1476–1557?), French poetaster, a native of Poitiers and some relation of Guillaume Bouchet de Brocourt (q.v.), was a lawyer and a friend of Rabelais (q.v.). A leading light among the literary men of the town, he wrote several bombastic books of verse, including *Les Regnars traversans les périlleuses voyes des folles fiances du monde* (1500) and *Épistres morales et familières* (1545), which, unaccountably as it seems to us now, proved immensely popular. Jean Bouchet died at Poitiers.

**Bouchet de Brocourt, Guillaume** (1514?–1594), French writer of short stories, was born at Poitiers. He spent the greater part of his life on his estate of Brocourt, near Poitiers, and died in his château there. Between 1584 and 1598 were published three books of his short stories called *Les Sérées* (i.e. 'Soirées'), supposed to have been told at their evening potations by a group of townsmen of Poitiers. They are vigorous and full of life, and compare very favourably with many of the anaemic outpourings of the Hôtel Rambouillet in the following century. See the edition by C. E. Roybet (6 vols., 1873–82).

**Bouchor, Maurice** (1855–1929), French poet and playwright, born in Paris. His volume of poetry, *Les Contes parisiens* (1880), was well regarded; but his particular contribution to literature were his religious plays composed for marionettes. They were performed at the Théâtre de Marionettes, Paris, the whole series being collected and published as *Mystères bibliques et chrétiens* (1920). He died in Paris.

**Bouilhet, Louis** (1821–1869), French poet and playwright. Born at Cany (Seine Inférieure), he became the close friend and literary adviser of Flaubert (q.v.). A literary poet, learned and with un-bounded descriptive powers, though lacking fire and urgency, he first caught public notice with his long epic of the last days of the Roman Empire of the west, *Melaenis* (1851). *Les Fossiles* (1854) is a 'geological epic', a story of the Earth from the earliest times until its end. This and many other shorter poems which succeeded it appear in *Festons et Astragales* (1859). His increasing interest in the question of transferring classical historical themes into literature had much influence on Flaubert at this time, and is in major part respon-sible for the latter's Carthaginian novel *Salammbô* (1862), in which very year was published Bouilhet's last volume of poetry, *Dernières Chansons*, with a most interesting introduction by his friend Flaubert. As a playwright Bouilhet wrote pieces of a contemporary character such as *Faustine* (1864) and *La Conjuration d'Amboise* (1866). He died in Rouen.

**Bouilly, Jean Nicolas** (1763–1842), French miscellaneous writer, was born at La Coudraye, near Tours, and during the French Revolution of 1789 was employed in organizing primary schools throughout France. He was the author of many shallow, sentimental poems and books for children, but also wrote the play *Léonore* which formed the basis for the libretto of Beethoven's opera *Fidelio*. Thus by devious means he has acquired a kind of immortality. He died in Paris.

**Boularan, Jacques,** *see* **Deval, Jacques.**

**Bourbon, Nicolas** (1503–1553?), French Latin poet. Born at Ven-deuvre (Aube), he became famous for his fine Latin poems, *Nugae* (1533; second ed. much increased in size, 1538), strong and sincere evocations of classical times long past, with a highly individualized streak of sadness running through. The place of his death is unknown.

**Bourdet, Édouard** (1887–1944), French playwright, born at Saint-Germain-en-Laye, specialized in social problems, satirizing the life which produced them without becoming didactic. His wit and stage technique brought him immense success. *La Prisonnière* (1926), *Vient de paraître* (1927), *La Fleur des pois* (1932) and *Les Temps* *difficiles* (1934) are fair examples of his range of accomplishment. He died in Paris.

**Bourget, Paul Charles Joseph** (1852–1935), French novelist. Born at Amiens, he was educated in Paris where he fell under the influence of Taine (q.v.) and wrote *Essais de psychologie contemporaine* (1883). But he later rejected his master's intellectual approach, and from the publication of his novel *Le Disciple* (1889) he became both a moralist and a highly skilled investigator of human character. By *Cosmopolis* (1893) he had begun to find corruption in the high society which was the cornerstone of his plots, and by the time we reach *L'Étape* (1903) we find him safely planted behind the Catholicism which came to his aid in preaching a happy outcome to an increasingly complex social world. This, however, prevented his literary development, and although his plots are technically satisfactory, and his psychological insight into character seldom failed him, his work never rose above its immediate time, and at his death in Paris he had almost outlived his reputation. Among his later novels are *Le Démon de midi* (1914), *Le Sens de la mort* (1915), *Le Danseur mondain* (1926) and *Nos actes nous suivent* (1927).

**Boursault, Edmé** (1638–1701), French playwright and novelist. Born at Mussy-l'Évêque (Aube), he made his way to Paris to try his fortune there. He began as a prolix and sometimes sentimental novelist, *Le Prince de Condé* (1675) being a good example of this kind of work. It is, however, as a writer of the comedy of manners that he has lasted, his *Le Mercure Galant, ou La Comédie sans titre* (1683) and *Ésope à la ville* (1690) being particularly racy and vivid. He also wrote satiric verse in which he displayed scant respect for Molière, Boileau or Racine. Boursault died in Paris.

**Boutelleau, Jacques,** *see* **Chardonne, Jacques.**

**Boutens, Peter Cornelis** (1870–1943), Dutch poet, born at Middelburg, he set out as a schoolmaster, but owing to the success of *Verzen* (1898) decided to pursue a literary life. His most considerable work, which conveys his feeling for the religious mystery of life, is *Zomerwolken* (1922). A long poem in the collection *Kerstkind*, and perhaps his masterpiece, has been translated into English as *The Christ-Child* by H. J. C. Grierson (1938). Other volumes of verse particularly worthy of mention are *Beatrijs* (1908), *Carmina* (1912) and *Sonnetten* (1920). Boutens, who was a highly accomplished translator from Greek, Latin and German, died in The Hague. His collected works were published (6 vols.) between 1943 and 1951.

**Boy,** *see* **Żeleński, T.**

**Boyer, Claude** (1618?–1698), French playwright. Born at Albi, he came to Paris and turned hack dramatist. He ludicrously challenged Racine from the time when in 1665 he refurbished an old tragedy and renamed it *Le Grand Alexandre* to try to steal the thunder from Racine's *Alexandre* (q.v.), until in 1692 he wrote a play *Jephté* for Saint-Cyr in emulation of Racine's *Athalie*. An incomplete edition of his *Œuvres* was published (5 vols.) in 1688. Boyer died in Paris.

**Boylesve, René** (1867–1926), French novelist, whose real name was **René Marie Auguste Tardiveau,** was born at La Haye-Descartes (Indre-et-Loire). He excelled as a writer on the life of prosperous families in the country. Good examples of his work are *Le Médecin des Dames de Néans* (1896), *Le Parfum des Îles Borromées* (1898), *L'Enfant à la balustrade* (1903) and *Tu n'es plus rien* (1917). He died in Paris.

**Bracciolini-Poggio, Gian Francesco,** *see* **Poggio Bracciolini, G. F.**

**Brachvogel, Albert Emil** (1824–1878), German dramatist and novelist, was born at Breslau. He gained enormous success with the melodrama *Narziss* (1857), influenced by the French stage. *Friedemann Bach* (1858) is his second-best play. His short stories are of a facile, romantic kind. His collected works appeared (10 vols.) in 1879. Brachvogel died in Berlin.

**Braga, Joaquim Teófilo** (1843–1924), Portuguese poet and prose-writer. Born at Punta Delgada, he was educated at Coimbra, and came forward as a poet with *Stella matutina* (1863), later appearing as a serious literary critic with *História da poesia popular portuguesa* (1867). His finely conceived *História da literatura portuguesa* was published in twenty volumes between 1870 and 1892, but the methods employed have not always stood the test of time. His shorter and more intense studies, such as *Filinto e os dissidentes da Arcádia* (1901), *Bocage, sua vida e época literária* (1902) and *Os Árcades* (1918), all dealing with complex literary movements and thought in the later eighteenth century, show him at his best. A typical nineteenth-century intellectual liberal, he was prominent in the political events which led to the downfall of the monarchy, and became first president of the Portuguese Republic in 1910–11, being re-elected for a short time in 1915. He died in Lisbon.

**Brancati, Vitaliano** (1907–1954), Italian novelist born at Pachino, near Syracuse, whose satirical studies, generally set in Sicily, include *Don Giovanni in Sicilia* (1941), *Gli anni perduti* (1941), *Il bell' Antonio* (1949; Eng. trans. *Antonio, the Great Lover,* 1952) and *Paolo il caldo* (1955). He died in Turin.

**Brandes, Georg Morris Cohen** (1842–1927), Danish man of letters. Born in Copenhagen into a Jewish family, he studied at Copenhagen University (1859–64) and then travelled for some years in France and Italy, acquiring that cosmopolitanism of outlook which was so important an ingredient in his critical approach to life and literature. His close reading of Sainte-Beuve (q.v.) and Taine (q.v.) was particularly fruitful and led to his three works on aesthetics and literature, *Æsthetiske Studier* (1868), *Kritiker og Portraiter* (1870) and *Den franske Æsthetik* (1870). Returning from his travels in 1872, he became a member of the academic staff of his old university, and embarked on his great task *Hovedstrømninger i det nittende Aarhundredes Literatur* (6 vols., 1872–87; Eng. trans. *Main Currents in Nineteenth-Century Literature,* 6 vols., 1901–5). Meanwhile Kierkegaard's (q.v.) thought had profoundly impressed him and led him away from his earlier militant socialism and agnosticism,

*Søren Kierkegaard* (1877) celebrating the new outlook. He next turned to literary and political biography, a period marked by *Esaias Tegnér* (1878), *Benjamin Disraeli* (1878; Eng. trans. *Lord Beaconsfield*, 1880) and *Ferdinand Lasalle* (1881; Eng. trans. 1911). The next influence was Nietzsche (q.v.), and it was Brandes who, after the German philosopher's career had been closed by madness, became his great advocate. The Nietzschean spell put an end to Brandes's revolutionary views and he now became the advocate of 'aristocratic radicalism'. All this time he was as intensely unpopular in his own country as Ibsen (q.v.), whom he had met in Germany and many of whose views coincided with his own, had been in Norway. Prejudice against him had severely interfered with his own career, and it was not until 1902 that he became a full professor. At last he had come to be the idol of the younger generation, and his influence on the rising naturalistic school in Scandinavia was enormous. Already he had brought new ideas to bear on Shakespeare in *William Shakespeare* (3 vols., 1895–6; Eng. trans., 2 vols., 1898), and he touched immense literary horizons with works on Goethe (2 vols., 1914–15; Eng. trans. 1924) and Voltaire (2 vols., 1916–17; Eng. trans., 2 vols., 1930). His *Verdenskrigen* (1917; Eng. trans. *The World at War*, 1917) shows him as an apologist for neutrality; it led to a controversy with the Ibsen scholar William Archer, who replied with *Shirking the Issue: a Letter to Dr Georg Brandes* (1917). Of his latest work, *Cajus Julius Cæsar* (2 vols., 1918) and *Michel Angelo Buonarotti* (1921) are in his best style. There are also the charming travel-book *Hellas* (1925; Eng. trans. *Hellas, Travels in Greece*, 1926) and the controversial *Sagnet om Jesus* (1925; Eng. trans. *Jesus, a Myth*, 1926). He died in Copenhagen.

**Brandt, Geeraerdt** (1626–1685), Dutch prose-writer, was born probably in Amsterdam, and became a watchmaker and later a Remonstrant clergyman in that city. Besides his poems, *Gedichten* (1649), of little account, some Senecan dramas, and biographies, including an informative and excellently written life of Vondel (q.v.), *Leven van Joost van den Vondel* (1682), he is chiefly to be remembered for his well-composed *De historie der Reformatie* (1668), of a pleasingly terse and close-knit style. He died in Amsterdam.

**Branner, Hans Christian** (1903–1966), Danish novelist and short-story writer. Born at Ordrup of a middle-class family, he early moved to Copenhagen, where he made a reputation by applying psychology to plots taken from everyday life. Outstanding is the volume of short stories, *Angst* (1947), and the novel *Rytteren* (1949; Eng. trans. *The Riding Master*, 1951), both of which contain powerful studies of mental anguish resulting from a sense of danger. His comedy *Søskende* was produced in 1951. He died in Copenhagen.

**Brant, Sebastian** (1458–1521), German satirist. Born in Strassburg, he was educated at Basel and became town clerk of Strassburg. In 1494 his *Narrenschiff* was published at Basel. This satire on the follies of the time as represented by more than one hundred fools sailing in a ship to the land of folly, powerful morally, weak poetically, soon gained European fame. A Latin translation by Locher was made of it in 1497, while Alexander Barclay's poem *The Shyp of Folys of the Worlde* (1509) is partly a translation and partly an imitation of it. Henry Watson's English translation, *The Grete Shyppe of Fooles of the Worlde* (1517), is excellent. A modern English translation by E. H. Zeydel was published in 1944. Brant died in Strassburg.

**Brantôme, Pierre de Bourdeilles de** (1540?–1614), French prose-writer. Born in the province of Périgord, he was in the retinue of Mary Queen of Scots when she left France for Holyrood in 1561. He fought for the Knights of Malta against the Ottoman empire in 1565, and was later engaged as a mercenary in many fields of battle. Retiring from a military profession, he became chamberlain at the court of France, where he had ample opportunity to cull the gossip that he was later to fashion into his entertaining and well-written *Mémoires*, which he began to write as soon as he resigned from this office in 1594. He died on his estates at Brantôme. The *Mémoires* did not appear in print until his *Œuvres complètes* were assembled in 1665–6. The standard edition is by L. Lalanne (11 vols., 1864–82).

**Brecht, Bertolt** (1898–1956), German playwright, born in Augsburg It took him a long time to find his true means of literary expression, and it was by adapting the work of another, *Die Dreigroschenoper*, taken from Gay's *Beggar's Opera*, that he found his way (1928). With the advent of Hitler in 1933 the German literary world was closed to him, but he was gradually able to conquer Britain and America, although his following remained small. *Die Rundköpfe und die Spitzköpfe* (1938; Eng. trans. *Round Heads, Peak Heads*, 1939) was his most original work up to date, and the impression which he had made was deepened by *Furcht und Elend des Dritten Reiches* (1938; Eng. trans. *The Private Life of the Master Race*, 1948). *Der gute Mann von Sezuan* (1942; Eng. trans. *The Good Woman of Setzuan*, 1943) brought him full recognition by his limited circle, who for all the claims they made for him could not deny that he fatally lacked dramatic gifts and that his plays were epics. Among his later works are *Herr Puntila und sein Knecht Matti* (1948), *Der Hofmeister* (1950), *Der kaukasische Kreidekreis* (1954) and *Leben des Galilei* (1955). He died in Berlin. A complete English translation, *Plays of Bertolt Brecht*, was begun in 1960. The standard edition is the Suhrkamp *Werkausgabe* (20 vols., 1967).

**Brederoo** or **Brederode, Gerbrand Adrianensz** (1585–1618), Dutch dramatist. Born in Amsterdam, the son of a shoemaker, he first became a painter, and it was only later that he grew into a serious writer. Though there is much vigour in his work, he never learned the art of dramatic construction, *De Spaansche Brabander* (1617), his best play founded on *Lazarillo de Tormes*, a Spanish picaresque novel, for all its wit and vividness, being without real movement. He died in Amsterdam. There is a good edition of his works by J. A. N. Knuttel (3 vols., 1918–29).

**Breitinger, Johann Jakob** (1701–1776), Swiss prose-writer and literary critic. Born in Zürich, he joined the staff of the gymnasium there, and died in that city. He came to be associated with J. J.

Bodmer (q.v.) in opposition to the theories of J. C. Gottsched (q.v.) and the outworn classical school mounted on a French platform, and in advocating the merits of English literature and naturalism. He collaborated with Bodmer in *Kritische Abhandlung von der Natur* (1740) and wrote on his own *Kritische Dichtkunst* (2 vols., 1740). He was altogether of less originality than Bodmer, but his powers of elucidation were perhaps sharper. The influence on German literature of these associates can hardly be overestimated.

**Bremer, Fredrika** (1801–1865), Swedish novelist and travel-writer. Born at Tuorlo, near Åbo, Finland, she published her first work of importance, *Familjen H.*, in 1831, and concentrated her moderate gifts on producing good fictional accounts of upper middle-class life, particularly well presented in *Presidentens döttrar* (1834) and *Grannarna* (1837). All her novels up to 1845 were translated into English by Mary Howitt (11 vols., 1844–5). After about 1848 her work took on a strident feminist note, as in *Hertha* (1856), and lost the charm of her earlier manner. Her travel books, *Hemmen i den nya verlden* (3 vols., 1853–4; Eng. trans. *Homes in the New World*, 1854) and *Livet i gamla verlden* (1862; Eng. trans. *Life in the Old World*, 1862), are, if somewhat prolix, the most pleasing of her later works. She died at Årsta.

**Brenner, Sofia Elisabet** (1659–1730), Swedish poet and the first woman of her nation to live by her pen, was born at Stockholm and there died. The wife of a well-known artist, she herself was no mean scholar, writing with ease in German and Latin. As an original poet, however, she can hardly be said to have really succeeded. Her *Poetiska dikter* were published in two volumes, the first in 1713 and the second in 1732 (a collected edition in 1873).

**Brentano, Clemens Maria** (1778–1842), German poet and prose-writer. Born at Ehrenbreitstein, the son of an Italian business man and a German mother, he grew up as clever as he was unbalanced. Naturally destined to play a part in the romantic movement, he published his first work *Godwi*, steeped in ardours, in 1800. He had already begun to feel dissatisfied with life when he met in Jena and married Sophia Mereau (1803). The three following years were the happiest and most settled of his career. Having moved to Heidelberg he met (1805) Achim von Arnim (q.v.), later to become his brother-in-law, whereupon there began that collaboration in the collecting and editing of German folk-song which resulted in *Des Knaben Wunderhorn* (1806–8), one of the most momentous achievements of German romanticism. His wife's death (1806) had already shaken him, and an impulsively contracted marriage the following year proved a disaster from the start and ended in divorce (1814). The partnership with Arnim ended in 1808, and nothing seemed to take its place. None the less the knowledge of folk-song and of folk-tales produced a rich harvest in the following years. The novel *Geschichte vom braven Kasperl und dem schönen Annerl* (1816; Eng. trans. *The Story of the Just Casper and Fair Annie*, 1927) is an excellent example of his work in prose, the fairy-story raised to literature. Returning to the Roman Church in 1817, he spent six years (1818–24) recording the revelations of the 'Nun of Dül-men', Katharina Emmerich, taking them down from her lips for weeks at a time, which resulted in a devotional volume, translated into English as *The Life of Anne K. Emmerich* (1833). In his later years his mind was filled with Rosicrucianism, alchemy and astrology, mingled with religion, and he showed signs of mental derangement several years before his death at Aschaffenburg, Bavaria. His post-humously published *Märchen* (2 vols., 1846; Eng. trans. 1885) comprised the bulk of his lyrical poetry, while the *Romanzen vom Rosenkranz* (1852) contain some of his very best imaginative work. His collected works first appeared in nine volumes (1852–9), edited by his nephew. A modern edition of his poetry is that by S. Brentano and R. A. Schröder (1943).

**Bretel, Jacques** (*fl.* 1285), French poet, probably from Lorraine, who wrote *Le Tournoi de Chauvency*, a vivid account of a tournament with all the accessories of chivalry held up to view. There is a critical edition of it by M. Delbouille (1932).

**Breton, André** (1896–1966), French poet, born at Tinchebray (Orne). After studying Freud and flirting with the Dada group, he founded surrealism in 1924. Of his works, *Les Pas perdus* (1924), *Nadja* (1928), *Les Vases communicants* (1937) and *Poèmes* (1948) all reveal a master-hand in the use of word, image and language. Later he produced *La Lampe dans l'horloge* (1948), *Au regard des divinités* (1949) and *Farouche à quatre feuilles* (in collaboration, 1955). *La Clef des champs, Le Surréalisme de 1943 à 1953* (1953) is of great interest. He died in Paris.

**Bretón de los Herreros, Manuel** (1796–1873), Spanish dramatist and lyric poet. Born at Quel, Logroño, he became sub-librarian of the national library, Madrid, in 1831, maintaining that post until appointed permanent secretary of the Spanish Royal Academy in 1842, which office he held until his death in Madrid. His *Letrillas* show him to have been a composer of graceful lyrics; but it is as a writer of comedies, poking gentle fun at the follies of society, that he is generally remembered, his masterpiece being *La escuela del matrimonio* (1851). See *Obras* (5 vols., 1883–4) and *Teatro* (ed. A. Cortés, 1928).

**Bridel, Philippe** (1757–1845), Swiss poet and prose-writer. Born at Begnins, Vaud, he became a clergyman of the Reformed Church. His lifelong aspiration was to make French Switzerland aware of a distinct national heritage, natural and cultural, and he strove with enthusiasm if not with the success he merited to give the French-speaking cantons a viable claim to a literature of their own. *Poésies helvétiennes* (1782) is his most considerable claim to be regarded as a poet. *Le Conservateur suisse* (13 vols., 1855–8) comprises his vast literary output. 'Le Doyen' Bridel, as he was generally called, died at Montreux.

**Bridget**, also called **Birgitta, Bride** (1302–1373), Swedish saint and visionary. Born at Finsta of noble family, she was married at fourteen to Ulf Gudmarsson, and on his death in 1344 she retired from the world to a life of religion. She settled in Rome in 1349, later gaining permission from the Pope to establish the Brigittine order of nuns to be associated with the Augustinians. Her *Revelationes* (written in Swedish apparently, although known only in the Latin translation), in which she castigates the worldliness of popes and kings, have a sweeping power and contain passages of undoubted inspiration, reaching poetry of a high order. Bridget died in Rome. The *Revelationes Sancte Birgittae* were first published at Lübeck (1492), although they had had a wide circulation in manuscript since the fourteenth century. *The Revelations of S. Birgitta* by W. P. Cumming (1929) is a competent edition.

**Brieux, Eugène** (1858–1932), French dramatist. Born in Paris, he made his mark with *Ménages d'artistes* at the Théâtre Libre (1890), and soon gained a wide public, at the same time arousing opposition to his realistic plays on social problems. Chief of these were *Les Trois Filles de M. Dupont* (1897; Eng. trans. *The Three Daughters of M. Dupont*, 1898), on family life, *La Robe rouge* (1900; Eng. trans. *The Arm of the Law*, 1901), an attack on the legal profession, *Les Remplaçantes* (1901), on baby-farming and *Les Avariés* (1901; Eng. trans. *Damaged Goods*, 1902), on venereal disease, which caused an impression when performed in London. An inferior French Ibsen, Brieux was highly regarded by Bernard Shaw, who wrote the preface to the English translation of *Three Plays* (1911), but he has hardly stood the test of time. His later works include *La Femme seule* (1913), *Les Americains chez nous* (1920) and *La Famille Lavolette* (1926). He died at Nice.

**Brillat-Savarin, Anthelme** (1755–1826), French writer. Born at Belley, he became a lawyer and was a deputy of the States-General in 1789. In 1793 he was elected mayor of Belley, but was then forced to escape to Switzerland and afterwards to America, and for a time earned his living playing in the orchestra of a theatre in New York. Returning to France in 1796, he became a member of the Court of Cassation. His *Physiologie du goût* (1825; Eng. trans. *A Handbook of Gastronomy*, 1884) is the most elegant and witty book ever published on the subject. Brillat died in Paris.

**Brizeux, Julien Auguste Pélage** (1803–1858), French poet. Born at Lorient, Morbihan, Brittany, he was a wanderer all his life, dividing his time between his native land and Italy. An out-and-out romantic, not free from ungoverned sentimentality at times, his elegy, *Marie* (1831), is a tender and characteristic work, while in his rustic epic, *Les Bretons* (1845), he again draws inspiration from his soil, as he also did for *Histoires poétiques* (1851). In his translation of Dante (1840) he can hardly be said to have succeeded. He died at Montpellier. His collected works, edited by A. Dorchain, were published (4 vols.) in 1910–12.

**Brockes, Barthold Heinrich** (1680–1747), German poet. Born in Hamburg where he died a senator, he was educated at Halle, gaining religious principles which colour all his literary work. Whether he writes of nature or of man it is always with the view of relating

them to God, whose wisdom and goodness has made everything for
the best, perfect and therefore without need of change. He learned
his philosophy from Pope's deistic *Essay on Man*, the craft of poetic
description from Thomson's *Seasons*. His main works are *Daphnis*
(1733), and the rest of an enormous production is comprised under the
title *Irdisches Vergnügen in Gott* (9 vols., 1721–48). His complete
*Werke* appeared (5 vols.) in 1800.

**Brod, Max** (1884–    ), Austrian novelist and miscellaneous prose-
writer. Born in Prague, he joined the circle which included Werfel
(q.v.) and Kafka (q.v.), whose biography (*Franz Kafka. Eine Bio-
graphie*) he published in 1937 (Eng. trans. 1947). A key to his literary
personality is his ever-present awareness of the cleavage between
German and Jew in himself and in others of his race and country.
This informs all his work, the most significant of which is his trilogy
*Kampf um die Wahrheit*, the first part being *Tycho Brahes Weg
zu Gott* (1916; Eng. trans. *The Redemption of Tycho Brahe*, 1928),
the second *Reubeni, Fürst der Juden* (1925; Eng. trans. *Reubeni,
Prince of the Jews*, 1928) and the third, *Galilei in Gefangen-
schaft* (1948). Other novels include *Das Zauberreich der Liebe* (1928;
Eng. trans. *The Kingdom of Love*, 1930), *Die Berauschten* (1937),
*Unambo* (1949) and *The Master*, which appeared in English in 1951,
a year before the German version *Der Meister*. Among his volumes of
essays may be noticed *Heidentum, Christentum, Judentum* (1921;
Eng. trans. *Three Loves*, 1929).

**Brodziński, Kazimierz Maciej Jozef** (1791–1835), Polish poet. Born at
Królówka, he had a restless life, finally becoming a professor of
literature at Warsaw University, but dying at Dresden. He is chiefly
known for his lyrics, sad but restrained, bridging the classical and
romantic schools in Polish letters. His best verse is to be found in
*Pieśni* (1819) and *Wiesław* (1820; Eng. trans. by J. Bowring in
*Specimens of the Polish Poets*, 1827). His collected works, *Dzieła*,
were published (10 vols.) in 1842–4.

**Brofelt, Johannes,** *see* **Aho, Juhani.**

**Brofferio, Angelo** (1802–1866), Italian playwright and dialect poet.
Born near Asti, he was seriously implicated in anti-Austrian movements as early as 1831, and politics coloured all his work. His leading
dramas are, in his earlier and less stridently political manner,
*Salvator Rosa* (1827), in which the seventeenth-century artist shows
himself to be a rebel against society; while *Vitige re de' Goti* (1848)
was so inflammatory that no one would dare to produce it in Italy,
and it was staged in Paris. He died at Locarno. His collected poetry,
both in classical Italian and Piedmontese, was published in 1902
(republished 1926).

**Brosbøll, Johan Carl Christian,** with the pseudonym of **Carit Etlar**
(1816–1900), Danish novelist and short-story writer, was born at
Fredericia. The most popular Danish author of his day, he took the
elder Dumas (q.v.) for a model and produced fast-moving and highly
successful historical novels such as *Gøngehøvdingen* (1853; Eng. trans.
*The Gynga Chief*, 1931). He died at Gentofte.

**Brosses, Charles de** (1709–1777), French antiquarian, philologist and man of letters, was born in Dijon. A leader of the new humanism which resulted from the discoveries at Herculaneum, his *Lettres sur Herculaneum* (1750) had great influence on the science of aesthetics formulated that very year by Baumgarten (q.v.) and on Winckelmann (q.v.). In his *Du culte des dieux fétiches* (1760) he gave the term *fetish* its present meaning, while in *La Formation mécanique des langues* (1765) he powerfully developed the science of philology and consequently influenced Herder (q.v.). Much information about eighteenth-century artistic taste can be gained from his letters, a selected English translation of which was published in 1897. He died in Paris, *président-à-mortier* of the Parlement of Burgundy.

**Bruller, Jean,** *see* **Vercors.**

**Brunetière, Ferdinand** (1849–1906), French literary critic. Born in Toulon, he taught at the École Normale, became editor of the *Revue des Deux Mondes* (1893), and was elected to the French Academy (1894). He was thus in a strong position to influence literature. He took up a firm stand against the naturalistic school of Zola (q.v.) in *Le Roman naturaliste* (1883) and no less against the theory of art for art's sake, arguing that writers must be responsible for inculcating morality in their works. After the *fin-de-siècle* period an increasing number of writers found themselves of this opinion, and the 1914–18 war with its consequent neo-Catholicism and idealism to some extent at least answered his hopes. His most important works are *Études critiques sur l'histoire de la littérature française, 1880–1906* (9 series, 1880–1925), *Histoire et littérature* (1884), *Histoire de la littérature française classique* (4 vols., 1895) and *Un Manuel de l'histoire de la littérature française* (1898; Eng. trans. 1898). Brunetière died in Paris.

**Bruno, Giordano** (1548–1600), Italian philosopher and prose-writer, in the vernacular and Latin. Born at Nola, he was ordained in 1572 and soon set himself to overturn scholasticism and Aristotelianism. Having to leave Italy in 1576, he led a wandering life and turned up in England in 1583, where he wrote his powerful *Acromatismus* (1586) in which the main points of his philosophy are rehearsed. Bruno was a naturalistic pantheist, and argued that innumerable worlds exist besides this one. His idea of elements (monads) was afterwards revived by Leibniz (q.v.). It was understandable that the ecclesiastical authorities should be outraged at this attempt to overthrow their moth-eaten ideas, and on his incautious return to Italy in 1591 Bruno was denounced by a former friend in 1593, and, after nearly seven years of imprisonment by the Inquisition at Rome, was burnt at the stake, having refused to give up his beliefs. His Italian works, showing great vivacity and having an excellent style, are to be found in a scholarly modern edition by Gentile and Spampanato, *Opere italiane de Giordano Bruno* (second ed., 1925–7). The best collection of his Latin works is the three-volume one of 1879–81. He is also the author of the famous comedy *Il Candelaio* (1582).

**Bruyère, Jean de la,** *see* **La Bruyère, Jean de.**

**Brynjúlfsson, Gísli** (1827–1888), Icelandic poet. Born at Ketilstaðir, the son of a clergyman, he went to Copenhagen where he became lecturer in Icelandic, retaining the post until his death. His revolutionary and nationalistic poems are grouped under the title of *Frelsiskvæði íslenzk og almenn* (1890, 'Songs of Liberty, Icelandic and General'). He died in Copenhagen.

**Buchholtz, Andreas Heinrich** (1607–1671), German religious poet and novelist. Born at Schöningen, he published devotional poems, *Geistliche teutsche Poemata* (1651), and a long, rambling, purposeful novel, *Des Christlichen Teutschen Grossfürsten Herkules und der böhmischen Königlichen Fräulein Valiska Wundergeschichte* (1659), designed to counteract the influence of mundane French novels. He died in Brunswick. The popularity of Buchholtz lasted almost to Goethe's day.

**Buchholtz, Johannes** (1882–1940), Danish novelist. Born at Odense, he became a popular writer in Britain and America, both because of his narrative gifts and his delicate humour. Of his books the best known are *Egholms Gud* (1915; Eng. trans. *Egholm and his God*, 1921), *Clara van Haags Mirakler* (1916; Eng. trans. *The Miracles of Clara van Haag*, 1922), *Susanne* (1931; Eng. trans. 1934) and *Frank Dovers Ansigt* (1933; Eng. trans. *The Saga of Frank Dover*, 1939). He died at Struer.

**Büchner, Karl Georg** (1813–1837), German dramatist, born at Goddelau. He went to Giessen University where he read medicine and helped to run a political newspaper which was suppressed by the police (1834). This led him to turn to the drama as an outlet and resulted in the composition of his strong and pessimistic play *Dantons Tod* (1835; Eng. trans. 1954). Of his two other plays, *Leonce und Lena* (1836) is a satire couched in the form of a fairy-tale, and *Woyzeck* (1837; Eng. trans 1954) is a tragedy of poverty and love. This last remained unfinished at his early death in Zürich and was not published until 1879. A weird long-short story, *Lenz* (1836), dealing with the eighteenth-century German dramatist of that name (q.v.) also remained incomplete. It is only in the present century that Büchner's work has been acclaimed. Time alone will show whether the excessive praise showered on this brilliant and precocious, though immature, writer is justified. The standard edition is F. Bergemann's *Sämtliche Werke und Briefe* (1922). See also the English translation, *Plays*, by G. Dunlop (1952).

**Budé, Guillaume** (1468–1540), French scholar, to whose efforts are due the Collège de France, the library of Fontainebleau and the nucleus of the Bibliothèque Nationale, was born in Paris, where he died. The greatest Greek scholar of his time, a measure of his powers can be gained from his *Commentarii linguae Graecae* (1529) and his excellent *De transitu Hellenismi ad Christianismum* (1535), although the Latin leaves something to be desired.

**Budi, Pjetër** (1566–1623), Albanian poet and theologian. Born at Gur'i Bardhë in central Albania, he became Vicar-General of Serbia in 1599, and a bishop in 1621. He may be called the father of Albanian poetry. In his beautiful devotional verse, which is, for example, interspersed throughout the adaptation of Bellarmine's (q.v.) *Disputationes de Controversiis Christianae Fidei* which he published in 1618, he is clearly inspired by his country's folk-song. He was drowned in the River Drin.

**Buffon, Georges-Louis Leclerc de** (1707–1788), French prose-writer and natural historian. Born of a noble family at the Château de Montbard, Burgundy (Côte d'Or), he became director of the Jardin du Roi (now Jardin des Plantes) in 1739, and spent the rest of his life writing his *Histoire naturelle* (36 vols., 1749–89), additions to it by other hands bringing the total to forty-four volumes by 1804. The uniformity of style, majestic if sometimes pompous, though never ridiculously so, throughout the length of this work is remarkable, and satisfyingly blends tradition and the new scientific knowledge brought about by the Age of Reason. Literary ability and performance meant much to Buffon, who in his *Discours sur le style* (1753; mod. ed., 1926) insisted that it was style rather than content which was the factor which decided the quality of works as literature. As a scientist he is noteworthy as the propounder of what came to be known as the law of evolution in a volume of the *Histoire naturelle* entitled *Époques de la nature* (1778). He died in Paris.

**Bugayev, B. N.**, *see* **Bely, A.**

**Bulgakov, Mikhail Afanasyevich** (1891–1940), Russian Soviet novelist and short-story writer, was born at Kiev. His novel *Belaya gvardiya* (1925, 'The White Guard'; in dramatic form *Dni Turbinykh*, 1935; Eng. trans. *Days of the Turbins*, in *Six Soviet Plays*, 1935) deals with the civil war in Russia of 1918–21, treating both sides with remarkable impartiality. His short stories, *Diavoliada* (1925, 'Devilry'), are satires on the less inspiring aspects of day–to–day Soviet rule. Not surprisingly he died in obscurity in Moscow. In recent times there has been a move to rehabilitate Bulgakov, and with the publication of *Master i Margarita* (1967; Eng. trans. *The Master and Margarita*, 1967) his full stature as a novelist has begun to be revealed.

**Bulgarin, Faddey Venediktovich** (1789–1859), Russian novelist. Born at Minsk, he became editor of a newspaper, *Severnaya Pchela* ('The Northern Bee'), which he kept zealously in the service of reaction and the police. As a novelist he introduced the style of Sir Walter Scott into Russian literature, his most successful piece of fiction being *Ivan Vyzhigin* (1829; Eng. trans. 1831). He died in Petersburg.

**Bunin, Ivan Alexeyevich** (1870–1953), Russian *émigré* prose-writer, born in Voronezh. A traditionalist, he profited greatly from a sympathetic study of Turgenev, and as a novelist achieved a masterpiece with *Gospodin iz San Francisco* (1915; Eng. trans. *The Gentleman from San Francisco*, 1922, to which are added several of Bunin's short stories, some translated by D. H. Lawrence, the whole being revised and enlarged by Leonard Woolf, 1934). As a short-story writer nothing of his is more representative than *Tyemnye allei* (1943; Eng. trans. *Dark Avenue and other Stories*, 1949). *Vospominaniya* (1950; Eng. trans. *Memories and Portraits*, 1951) is an attractively written volume of reminiscences. In 1933 he received the Nobel Prize for literature, the first Russian writer to do so. He died in Paris.

**Buonarotti, Michelangelo** (1475–1564), the magnificent artist of the Italian Renaissance, born at Caprese, and who died in Rome, was also a poet of no mean order. His sonnets in particular, written in his later years when the plastic arts seemed to have failed him as elements in which to express himself, reveal the depths of his mind and are full of the light of his arresting personality. His letters also are great and tragic documents. See *Lettere e rime*, edited by Vitaletti (1930) and J. A. Symonds's English translation of the sonnets (1878).

**Burchiello, Domenico da Giovanni** (1404–1449), Italian poet. Born in Florence, he became a barber. A sturdy republican, he aimed a series of telling satires against tyrants and would-be tyrants, especially the Medici, who managed eventually to have him banished. He died in poverty in Rome. His work appears in *Sonetti del Burchiello, del Bellincioni e di altri poeti fiorentini alla burchiellesca* (1757).

**Burckhardt, Jakob** (1818–1897), Swiss prose-writer, critic and historian. Born in Basel where he died, he became professor of history at Basel in 1858, and exercised an enormous influence on the interpretation of social and cultural history and the history of art. In this way he did more than anyone else single-handed to bridge the gap between the arts and the new scientific approach to history emanating from Germany, which threatened to drag history out of the realm of the arts into that of the sciences. His chief works are: *Die Zeit Konstantins des Grossen* (1852; Eng. trans. *The Age of Constantine the Great*, 1949), *Die Kultur der Renaissance in Italien* (1860; Eng. trans. *The Civilization of the Renaissance in Italy*, 1951), *Griechische Kulturgeschichte* (1898) and *Weltgeschichtliche Betrachtungen* (1905; Eng. trans. *Reflections on History*, 1943).

**Bürger, Gottfried August** (1747–1794), German poet. Born at Molmerswende, near Halberstadt, the son of a Lutheran minister, he spent an idle boyhood and dissipated youth, went to Halle University in 1764 to read theology, but threw it up. At Göttingen, where he went to study law in 1768, he found time in the middle of a wild life to form friendships with such sober students as Voss (q.v.) and the Stolberg brothers (q.v.), who made him acquainted with classical poetry and with English literature, especially Percy's *Reliques*. After his appointment as magistrate at Altengleichen (1772) he kept in touch with his Göttingen friends and closely studied ballad technique. The result of this was his deservedly successful ballad 'Lenore' (1775) which took Germany by storm, and his volume of collected poetry, *Gedichte* (1778), containing more ballads, bold examples of hitherto untried forms of rhyme-scheme. A two-volume edition with all the poems composed in the ten-year interval was published in 1789. Meanwhile his domestic life had collapsed with the death of his second wife (the 'Molly' of his love-poems) in 1785. His marriage to Elise Hahn, the 'Schwabische Mädchen' of his poems, in 1790 was a disaster and a divorce ensued (1792). His appointment as unpaid professor at Göttingen in 1789 had been an empty honour indeed, and he was forced to continue to eke out a meagre living with hack-work, such as the translation into German of *Baron Münchhausen* (*see* R. E. Raspe), which he had completed in 1786. He was a popular lecturer, his editorship of the *Musenalmanach* (since 1779) brought him a small income and he had the pleasure of reading a discourse on his poetry by Schiller himself (1791), but he was breaking up, and drink wore down his constitution, soon leading to his death from tuberculosis at Göttingen. His collected works were published (4 vols.) between 1796 and 1802, and it was this edition which was re-edited by W. von Wurzbach in 1904.

**Burgos, Javier de** (1842–1902), Spanish playwright. Born at Puerto de Santa María, he moved to Madrid and lived by his pen. He became well known as a librettist, and was particularly successful as the author of the libretti for *zarzuelas* (a kind of light opera), then at the height of their popularity. His most admired *zarzuelas* were *El baile de Luis Alonso* (1881) and *La boda de Luis Alonso* (1897). He died in Madrid.

**Bus, Gervais du** (*fl.* 1310–1339), French poet. A lawyer by profession, he wrote a blistering satire on hypocritical priests and civil rulers in the guise of a romance called *Le Roman de Fauvel*. Begun in 1310 it was completed four years later. It has been edited by Å. Långfors (1919).

**Busch, Wilhelm** (1832–1908), German poet and artist. Born at Wiedensahl, Hanover, he joined the staff of the *Fliegende Blätter* in 1859, the German *Punch*, to which he contributed nonsense verse and caricatures in simplified style, excellent in their way. Among his humorous illustrated poetry may be mentioned *Max und Moritz* (1858; Eng. trans. 1871) and *Schnurrdeburr oder die Bienen* (1869; Eng. trans. *Buzz-a-buzz, or The Bees*, 1872). His anti-Roman Catholic verse, such as *Der heilige Antonius von Padua* (1870) and *Pater Filucius* (1873), show that he could be master of fierce satire, roused as he had been to take part in Bismarck's policy against sacerdotalism. But this phase passed, and in the *Wilhelm-Busch-Album* which he published yearly from 1884 onwards, one finds him back in his role of the good-humoured sage, surveying the fallacies of the world, a more purposeful Edward Lear. Busch died at Mechtshausen.

**Bussy-Rabutin, Roger de** (1618–1693), French prose-writer, born at Épiry, near Autun. A cousin of Madame de Sévigné (q.v.) with whom he regularly corresponded (ed. of the *Lettres*, 5 vols., 1859), he is remembered for his witty and well-written *Histoire amoureuse des Gaules* (1666; crit. ed., 2 vols., 1868). He died at Autun.

**Butor, Michel** (1926–    ), French novelist. Born at Mons-en-Barœul (Nord), he became a schoolmaster at Sens and in Egypt before taking up the post of *lecteur* in French at Manchester University (1951–3). Here he began his first novel, *Passage de Milan* (1954), following this up with *L'Emploi du temps* (1956). *La Modification* (1957) was widely acclaimed, and he has maintained his reputation with *Degrés* (1960).

**Buttet, Marc-Claude de** (1530–1586), French poet. Born at Chambéry,

Savoy, he served for many years at the palace of Marguerite de France at Annecy. His principal work is *L'Amalthée*, a sequence of Petrarchan sonnets which first appeared in 1561, together with other poetry, in *Le Premier Livre de vers de Marc-Claude de Buttet*. Another and larger edition of *L'Amalthée* was published in 1575. An edition of his *Œuvres* by A. P. Philibert-Soupé was produced in 1877. Buttet died in Geneva.

**Butti, Enrico Annibale** (1863–1912), Italian dramatist and novelist, born in Milan where he died. His thoughtful, pessimistic novels include *L'automa* (1892), which contains some self-evaluation, and *L'immorale* (1894). As a playwright he tried to introduce an Ibsenist approach to the Italian stage. His last and most impressive work is the verse-play *Il castello di sogno* (1910), in which, facing not only the futility but the definite evils of modern life, Butti teaches that only with faith in something and love of something can we survive.

# C

**Caballero, Fernán,** pseudonym of **Cecilia Böhl von Faber** (1797–1877), Spanish novelist. Born at Morges, Lake of Geneva, of mixed German-Spanish parentage, she lived in Germany until 1813 when she was brought to Spain. Three times married and a protégée of Isabel II, she depicted the manners of Andalusia in her many novels, the best of them *La Gaviota* (1849; Eng. trans. *The Seagull*, 1867), and founded a school of novelists known from its characteristics as *costumbrismo* ('*genre* writing'). She died in Seville.

**Cadalso, José de** (1741–1782), Spanish poet and prose-writer. Born at Cadiz, he entered the professional army, but found time to write and travel and, with *Ocios de mi juventud* (1773), acclimatized the anacreontic to Spain. He saw the ignorance of his countrymen, their bigotry and parochialism, and attacked them in *Los eruditos a la violeta* (1772) and the posthumous *Cartas marruecas* (1789, 'Letters from Morocco'); but his most individual work is the strange wild collection of love-poetry, *Noches lúgubres* (1792). He was killed while besieging the British at Gibraltar.

**Caillavet, Gaston Arman de** (1869–1915), French playwright. Born in Paris, he was well known for his comedies, written in collaboration with Robert de Flers (q.v.), in which he reflected the follies of the contemporary scene, such as *L'Amour veille* (1907), *Le Bois sacré* (1910), *L'Habit vert* (1913) and *Monsieur Bretonneau* (1914). He died in Paris.

**Calderón, Serafín Estébanez** (1799–1867), Spanish man of letters. Born in Málaga, in 1822 he began to lecture on literature in the University of Granada. He settled in Madrid in 1830, but it was not until the publication of *Escenas andaluzas* (1847), a vividly written account of Andalusian scenery and folklore, that his reputation was made. As a novelist he is to be seen at his best in *Cristianos y moriscos* (1838), and in fact the interplay of Christian and Arab civilization in Spain was a subject on which Calderón spent many years of research, to that end building up a magnificent library bought by the Spanish Government at his death. He died in Madrid.

**Calderón de la Barca, Pedro** (1600–1681), Spanish dramatist. Born in Madrid, he studied for six years at the University of Salamanca, was active as a playwright between 1628 and 1643, in which latter year appeared his last, supremely important drama, *El alcalde de Zalamea*, was made a knight of the Order of Santiago by Philip IV in 1637, took part in the campaign against the Catalans in their rebellion against the central government in 1640, left the army two years later, and became a Franciscan monk in 1650. Next year he was ordained priest, became a prebendary of Toledo in 1653, and in 1663 chaplain to the king. After an interval of many years he began to write plays again, and remained with faculties undimmed until his death in Madrid. He is the author of nearly 120 plays of all kinds and lengths, philosophical plays, religious ones, tragedies of honour, 'cloak and sword' plays after the manner of Lope de Vega (q.v.) and even opera. A master of allegory, he is yet, as a pure dramatist, inferior to Lope, but he is immeasurably his superior as a poet and thinker. Spanish to the marrow, he has been misunderstood by those who do not comprehend the Spanish mind and character mirrored by him so remarkably. Soon after his death his influence began to decline, and it was not until the early nineteenth century, when A. W. Schlegel (q.v.) drew attention to him in his *Dramatic Art and Literature*, that his reinstatement gradually took place. Of his regular dramas the greatest are *La vida es sueño* (mod. ed., 1909; Eng. trans. *Life's a Dream*, 1925), *El mágico prodigioso* (mod. eds., 1877 and 1931; Eng. trans. *Justina*, 1848), *El príncipe constante* (mod. ed., 1938) and *El alcalde* already mentioned. Besides his regular plays there are seventy-two *autos sacramentales*, outdoor plays for religious festivals, especially that of Corpus Christi. The finest of these are *El divino Orfeo* and *La cena de Baltasar*. His works are comprised in volumes vii, ix, xii and xiv of the *Biblioteca de Autores Españoles*. L. Astrana Marín's *Obras completas—Dramas* (1945) contains by no means all the regular plays. Various plays have been translated into English: see D. M. MacCarthy's translation, the best (*Ten Plays*, 1853–73), E. Fitzgerald's *Six Dramas of Calderón* (1853; rev., 1903) and R. C. Trench's two translations annexed to his *Essay on the Life and Genius of Calderón* (1856; second ed., 1880). N. MacColl's *Select Plays of Calderón* (1838; rev. ed., 1888) is useful.

**Calprenède, Gautier des Costes de la** (1614–1663), French novelist. Born at the Château de Toulgou, Dordogne, he was a guards officer and at one time royal chamberlain, and gained a contemporary reputation with his huge, meandering, vaguely historical novels, in the course of which there are lengthy discourses on every kind of subject. Three alone fill thirty-four volumes: *Cassandre* (10 vols., 1642–5), *Cléopâtre* (12 vols., 1646–57) and *Faramond, ou l'Histoire de France* (12 vols., 1661; left unfinished and completed by others by 1670). 'The novelist of the Frondeurs in their leisure hours', he died at Andely.

**Calvin, Jean** (1509–1564), French religious writer in the vernacular and Latin. Born at Noyon, in Picardy, where his father was secretary of the diocese and a magistrate, he followed in his footsteps reading theology at the University of Paris and law at Orléans, learned Greek at Bourges and was in 1533 drawn into religious controversy. He was not long in joining the reformers, and was obliged to escape from Paris in 1535. At Basel he published his famous *Christianae Religionis Institutio* (1536; enlarged and definitive ed., 1559; mod. ed., 1911) with its dignified and finely written introduction, which made an end of the connection of himself and his followers with the Lutherans.

His career thereafter, with several reverses, was dedicated to building up his theocratic state in Geneva, whence Calvinism spread to various parts of Europe and was accepted as the established religion of Scotland and the United Provinces. Harsh and bigoted, there is yet no disputing his honesty within his limits, or his powers of intellect which are to be found not only in his *Institutio*, but alike in his vast commentaries on the Bible and his shortest theological tracts. His services to Protestantism in disciplining it at a time when Lutheranism was weakening cannot be controverted. He died in Geneva. The first collected edition of his works appeared in Geneva (12 vols.) in 1617, while in a modern edition they are to be found in volumes xxix–lxxxvii of the *Corpus Reformatorum* (1863–1900). His works were collected and translated into English by the Calvin Translation Society, Edinburgh (52 vols., 1844–56).

**Calzabigi, Ranieri de'** (1714–1795), Italian poet and librettist, born at Leghorn, provided the libretti for Gluck's operas *Orfeo* (1762), *Paride ed Elena* (1770) and others. He was a poet in the restrained classical style. See his *Poesie e prose diverse* (1793). He died in Naples.

**Camba, Julio** (1882–1962), Spanish prose-writer. Born at Villanueva de Arosa, Pontevedra, he travelled widely as a journalist, and brought his experience and humour to bear on the physical characteristics and way of life of many parts of the world. *Londres* (1916) is perhaps his best book, others being *Un año en el otro mundo* (1917), a brilliant piece of analysis, *Aventuras de una peseta* (1923) and his most profound work, *La casa de Lúculo* (1929). Representative of his later writing is *Haciendo de república* (1934). One criticism which can be brought against him is that he was inclined to make judgments according to exclusively Spanish standards. He died in Madrid.

**Camino, León Felipe** (1884–    ), Spanish poet. Born at Sequeros, near Salamanca, he was at first an actor, was for a time a colonial civil servant, then travelled widely in America, holding temporary academic posts there. His gifts as a poet were revealed in *Versos y oraciones del caminante* (1920), the second volume of which, published in 1930, deepened the impression he had given of being a serious and unprejudiced thinker. He hailed the republic of 1931 as the dawn of justice, and mourned its fall in *El hacha* (1939) and (in the same year) in *El español de éxodo y del llanto*. In exile in America he wrote *Antología rota* (1947), *Llamadme publicano* (1950), *La manzana* (1954) and *El ciervo* (1958).

**Cammaerts, Émile** (1878–1953), Belgian poet, playwright and prose-writer, the majority of his works being written in English. Born in Brussels, he left Belgium in 1908 and settled in Britain, being appointed professor of Belgian Studies at London University in 1931. The influence of Verhaeren (q.v.) is to be noticed in much of his poetry, the principal volumes containing it being *Chants patriotiques* (1915, 1922) and *Les Trois Rois* (1916). As a playwright he is represented by *L'Adoration des soldats* (1916; Eng. trans. 1916). His prose works deal for the most part with history and are in English. He died in London.

**Camões, Luís Vaz de** (1524?–1580), Portuguese poet. Little is known for certain about his family or even the place of his birth, although it is said that he was of noble Galician ancestry and that he was educated at Coimbra. Certain it is that he was at the royal court in Lisbon about 1544 and soon afterwards fell in love with Caterina de Atayde, daughter of an important court official. Although the girl seems to have returned his affection, her father forbade the match, and owing to his machinations Camões was banished from Lisbon on a trumped-up charge, having written some lyrics in the Italian style, love-poems of some ability, published with his later short poems which he penned from time to time in later life as *Rhythmas de Luís de Camões* (1595; Eng. trans. *Camões: The Lyricks*, 2 vols., 1884). Despairing of his love affair he joined a Portuguese expedition to Ceuta, and in a battle with Moroccans lost his right eye by a splinter. He was back in Lisbon by 1550 and seems to have led a rough and tumble life there until 1552 when he was imprisoned for wounding someone in a quarrel. Pardoned in 1553 he volunteered to go to India as a soldier, and served in Goa from 1553 to 1556, when his denunciation of rapacious Portuguese officials there led to his banishment to Macao, where he seems to have held a not very demanding but highly paid post. He decided to return to Goa in 1558, but on his way was wrecked off the coast of Cambodia, and tradition has it that he lost all his possessions except the manuscript of the first part of his great epic *Os Lusíadas*, as much of it as he had written to date. Eventually reaching Goa he was immediately imprisoned by the officials he had formerly condemned, but at last, having in the meanwhile completed his *Lusíadas*, he returned to Portugal in 1570, and settled in Lisbon where he published his country's national epic in 1572. There he lived on a modest pension granted him by young King Sebastian, but on the king's death in battle and the final ruin of Portugal in 1578 the pension seems to have ended and he died almost destitute in a Lisbon public hospital. *Os Lusíadas* (Eng. trans. *The Lusiad, or Portugal's historical Poem*, by R. Fanshawe, 1655; *The Lusiads* by W. J. Mickle, 1775; by J. J. Aubertin, 2 vols., 2nd ed., 1884; by R. Burton, 1881; and by C. W. Atkinson, 1952) is as its title 'The Lusitanians' suggests, the national epic of a seafaring and commercial nation, a song of praise, in fact, to the achievements of Portugal from the time of the discovery of the sea-route to India by Vasco da Gama to the time of Camões. In its grand conception it also embraces the vision of the Christian crusading spirit, and exalts the idea of the ability of men to fight the unknown by sailing over unknown seas and fearlessly entering new countries. In spite of all its shortcomings, such as its faulty construction and its sometimes puerile use of classical mythology, it is without doubt the greatest epic of the Renaissance. His three plays, *Auto dos Enfatriões, El Rei-Seleuco* and *Filodemo*, are of little significance beyond showing his knowledge of the classics. The standard edition of his collected works is that by H. Cidade (5 vols., 1946–7).

**Campanella, Tommaso** (1568–1639), Italian prose-writer and poet, was born at Stilo, in Calabria, and entered the Dominican Order. As an opponent of the schoolmen and of Spanish domination he soon ran into trouble, being imprisoned in Naples from 1599 to 1629, and several times tortured; but the theological and political heretic rose superior to all this, composing in prison not only such Latin works as *De Monarchia Hispanica* but his idealistic political treatise *La Città del Sole* (1623; mod. critical ed., 1920; Eng. trans. *Campanella's City of the Sun*, 1937). This beautiful work, with its plea for a wide and tolerant interpretation of religion so that it might become universal, was to be an inspiration for many political thinkers in the following years. His poems were published by a German follower, T. Adami, in 1622 (mod. eds. 1915 and 1938; Eng. trans. of the *Sonnets* only, 1878). Unattractive in style they are yet of power and undoubted inspiration. Campanella settled in France in 1629 and died in Paris.

**Campistron, Jean Galbert** (1656?–1723?), French dramatist and librettist. Born in Toulouse, he followed Racine as a writer of tragedies on classical themes such as *Arminius* (1684), *Phocion* (1688) and *Tiridate* (1691), and also provided libretti for the court composers, Lulli and others. Among his libretti are *Acis et Galatée* (1686) and *Achille et Polyxène* (1687). He died in Toulouse. His *Œuvres* (3 vols.) were published in 1750.

**Campoamor, Ramón de** (1817–1901), Spanish poet, dramatist and prose-writer. Born at Navia, Asturias, he first took up medicine and then went into the civil service. All the time he wrote extensively on every kind of subject and in every form, but he suffered from standing between the old romantic school and the new realist one, and found himself happy in neither. Little of his work is of value today except his shorter poems (some of them trans. in T. Walsh's *Hispanic Anthology*, N.Y., 1920, and *Translations from Hispanic Poets*, N.Y., 1938). He died in Madrid. His complete works were published (8 vols.), 1901–3; his complete poetical works only in 1943.

**Camus, Albert** (1913–1960), French novelist, playwright and essayist, was born at Mondovi, Algeria, taught for a time and then became a journalist. His first novel, *Noces* (1938), showed him to be a nihilist, finding life vain and human powers inadequate to deal with it. *L'Étranger* (1942; Eng. trans. *The Outsider*, 1946) deepened this impression, but with *La Peste* (1947; Eng. trans. *The Plague*, 1948) he turned round magnificently in favour of the necessity of grappling with the problems which surround us (and if we are intellectuals so much the better). Other novels are *La Femme adultère* (1954), *L'Été* (1954), *La Chute* (1956; Eng. trans. *The Fall*, 1956), and *L'Exil et le royaume* (1957). His plays, *Caligula* (1944; Eng. trans. 1947), *Le Malentendu* (1944; Eng. trans. 1947), *L'État de siège* (1948) and *Les Justes* (1950), keep pace with his novels in this development, as do his important essays, *Le Mythe de Sisyphe* (1942; Eng. trans. 1955), *Lettres à un ami allemand* (1945) and *L'Homme révolté* (1951; Eng. trans. *The Rebel*, 1953). He was killed in a car crash near Paris.

**Camus, Jean-Pierre** (1584–1652), French religious novelist. Born in Paris, he became a close friend of St François de Sales, and was eventually chosen vicar-general of Rouen. He was the first to make use of the novel for religious purposes. Such didactic, moralizing books are *Élise, ou l'Innocence coupable* (1621), *La Pieuse Julie, histoire parisienne* (1625) and *Marianne, ou l'Innocente victime* (1629). He died in Paris.

**Cañizares, José de** (1676–1750), Spanish playwright, was born in Madrid, and spent some time in the army before finding powerful patrons who procured him various posts such as a theatrical censorship. He brought to perfection the *comedia de figurón*, the comedy of manners of everyday life; and no study of social conditions of life in the capital during the first part of the eighteenth century would be complete without reference to his plays, some of which were collected as *Comedias escogidas* (2 vols., 1828, 1833). He died in Madrid.

**Cankar, Ivan** (1876–1918), Slovene prose-writer. Born at Vrhnika, he started life as an engineer, but soon turned to writing. His stories, examples of which are *Hiša Marije Pomočnice* (1904, 'The House of Mary of Charity') and *Hlapec Jernej in njegova pravica* (1907; Eng. trans. *The Bailiff Yerney and his Rights*, 2nd ed., 1946), show great sympathy for the daily lives of the poor and outcast. He died at Ljubljana.

**Canth, Minna,** *née* **Vilhelmina Johnsson** (1844–1897), Finnish novelist and playwright. Born at Tampere, she married young and was early left a widow. She then (1878) turned to literary work to support her large family, the while directing the family business. Her earlier style as a novelist is to be seen in *Hanna* (1886), her later in *Novelleja* (2 vols., 1892). Her most notable play is *Anna Liisa* (1895) with Tolstoy's influence patently present. She died at Kuopoi.

**Cantoni, Alberto** (1841–1904), Italian novelist and short-story writer. Born at Pomponesco di Mantua, he showed his power of delicate humour in such collections of short stories as *Il demonio dello stile* (1887) and *Pietro e Paola* (1897). His full-length novel *L'Illustrissimo,* published posthumously in 1906, was highly regarded by Pirandello (q.v.). He died in Mantua.

**Cantù, Cesare** (1804–1895), Italian novelist, historian and critic, was born at Brivio, Como. For his liberalism he was imprisoned in 1833, and his subsequent experience of prison life inspired his novel *Margherita Pusterla* (1838), which in its day enjoyed a reputation second only to the *I promessi sposi* of Manzoni (q.v.). He had already set about his ambitious historical work, *La storia universale,* which he started in 1836, and completed in thirty-five volumes in 1842. It is a landmark in the popularization of knowledge. Another such work was *Storia degli italiani* (1854), but a further book published this year, *L'Abate Parini e la Lombardia del secolo passato,* has withstood the test of time far better, and is a well-assembled account of that formative period of the spirit of Italian nationalism. A later work in the same vein is *Monti e l'età che fu sua* (1879). The unification beginning in 1860 had a profound effect on him; *Beccaria e il diritto penale* (1862), *Gli eretici d'Italia* (1865) and *Il conciliatore e i carbonari* (1878) show a new pride in the achievements of the new state built on the work of the heroes of the past. *Reminiscenze di Alessandro*

*Manzoni* (2 vols., 1882–3) describes with great charm his friendship with that greatest of Italian novelists. Cantù died in Milan.

**Čapek, Karel** (1890–1938), Czech playwright, novelist and travel-writer, was born in the country town of Malé Svatoňovice, in Bohemia, where his father was a physician. He was a student at the universities of Prague, Paris and Berlin, and was about to come to London University when the First World War broke out. Always of delicate health he was unable to serve in the army, and during the war period became a schoolmaster and later a journalist. In 1920 he gained European recognition with two powerful plays in which he pointed out the forces of disintegration which lay beneath the surface of the seemingly satisfactory way of life and culture in Europe, *R.U.R.* (i.e. 'Rossum's Universal Robots'; Eng. trans. 1923, and in Oxford Paperbacks) and (in collaboration with his elder brother Josef) *Ze života hmyzu* (Eng. trans. *The Insect Play*, 1923, and in Oxford Paperbacks). He then turned to the novel, and in *Továrna na Absolutno* (1922; Eng. trans. *The Absolute at Large*, 1927) and *Krakatit* (1924; Eng. trans. 1925) pointed out the problems posed by an age of intensified science and materialism. Also in 1924 he produced the first of his excellent travel books, *Anglické listy* (Eng. trans. *Letters from England*, 1925), in which he made a brilliant analysis of the country. *Povídky z druhé kapsy* (1929; Eng. trans. *Tales from Two Pockets*, 1932) was a successful excursion into the detective story. More travel books followed, *Výlet do Španěl* (1930; Eng. trans., *Letters from Spain*, 1931) and *Obrazky z Holandska* (1932; Eng. trans. *Letters from Holland*, 1933), and then he entered on some of his deepest work with the trilogy concerned with humanity from within as it stood up to the external threats and challenges which he had described earlier. This trilogy consists of *Hordubal* (1933; Eng. trans. 1934), *Povětroň* (1934; Eng. trans. *The Meteor*, 1935) and *Obyčejný život* (1934; Eng. trans. *An Ordinary Life*, 1936). Another travel book, *Cesta na sever* (1936; Eng. trans. *Travels in the North*, 1939) followed, and then finally came the two poignant plays *Bílá nemoc* (1937; Eng. trans. *Power and Glory*, 1938) and *Matka* (1938; Eng. trans. *The Mother*, 1939), in which he faces the German menace which was about to engulf his country. The shock of the extinction of Czechoslovakia by the Germans killed him. He died in Prague.

**Čapek-Chod, Karel Matěj** (1860–1927), Czech novelist. Born at Domažlice, Chod, Bohemia, he was at first a journalist in Prague before turning to authorship. His best book, not typical of his work as a whole, which is concerned with drab lower middle-class life, is *Antonín Vondrejc* (2 vols., 1917–18), a keen and realistic satire on artists, would-be artists and artistic snobbery in Prague. He died in Prague.

**Capuana, Luigi** (1839–1915), Italian novelist and short-story writer, was born at Mineo, Catania, and came to be known as the first of the Italian realists with his novel *Giacinta* (1879). Before long his cool detachment and power of analysis were brought to bear on his characters in such works dealing with aberrations in love as the novel *Profumo* (1890) and the book of short stories *Le appassionate* (1893).

Another style of investigation (for Capuana investigates his characters, never feels for them and with them) is that into the psychic in *Fausto Bragia e altre novelle* (1897), such as the story contained in it, 'La Sfinge', and such tales as 'Dottor Cimbalus' in the collection *Il Decameroncino* (1901). He also wrote children's books, the best of them *C'era una volta* (1882; Eng. trans. *Once Upon a Time. Fairy Tales*, 1892). He died in Catania.

**Capus, Alfred** (1858–1922), French playwright, born at Aix-en-Provence. At the turn of the century he came forward as a successful playwright, his greatest triumphs being *L'Adversaire* (1903, acted in Britain as *The Man of the Moment*) and *Monsieur Piégois* (1905). He died in Paris.

**Caragiale, Ion Luca** (1852–1912), Rumanian playwright, born at Haimanalele, Prahova, he made his name with satirical comedies, the best of them, *O scrisoarea pierduta* (1884, 'The Lost Letter'), mocking political and social upstarts. His collected plays appeared as *Teatru* in 1889 (sixth and last ed., 2 vols., 1937). He settled in Berlin in 1902 and died there.

**Carcano, Giulio** (1812–1882), Italian novelist, poet and short-story writer. Born in Milan, he became a thorough-paced romantic, producing facile verse such as that contained in *Armonie domestiche* (1841). As a novelist, however, he found himself, and in *Il manoscritto di un vice-curato* (1850) and *Damiano* (1852) he produced two well-constructed pieces of fiction with adequate characterization. Meanwhile he was increasingly occupied with his translation of the works of Shakespeare, completed shortly before his death, and in 1871 published short stories on country life, *Novelle campagnuole. Gabrio e Camilla*, his best novel, appeared in 1874. He died at Lesa.

**Carco, Francis,** pseudonym of **F. Carcopino-Tusoli** (1886–1958), French novelist and essayist. Born at Nouméa, New Caledonia, he soon found his way to Paris, and his Bohemian experiences there led to the writing of such slangy, rough but vivacious work as the novels *L'Homme traqué* (1922; Eng. trans. *The Noose of Sin*, 1923), *Rue Pigalle* (1927), *Prisons de femmes* (1931), *Morsure* (1949), *La Belle Amour* (1952), *Compagnons de la mauvaise chance* (1954) and, in a changed style and approach, *La Danse des morts* (1954), the series *Surprenant procès d'un bourreau* (5 vols., 1955) and *Rendezvous avec moi-même* (1957). As an essayist and critic he is represented by such works as *Le Roman de François Villon* (1926; Eng. trans. *The Romance of Villon*, 1927), *De Montmartre au Quartier Latin* (1927; Eng. trans. 1929), *Verlaine* (1939), *Bohème d'artiste* (1940), *Heures d'Égypte* (1940), *Nostalgie de Paris* (1941), *L'Ami des peintres* (1944), *Dignimont* (1946), *Ombres vivantes* (1947), *Montmartre vécu par Utrille* (1947), *Verlaine, poète maudit* (1948), *G. de Nerval* (1953), *La Belle Époque au temps de Bruant* (1954), *F. Carco vous parle . . .* (1954), *Goyescas* (1954) and *Colette 'mon ami'* (1955). He died in Paris.

**Cardarelli, Vincenzo** (1887–1959), Italian poet and essayist. Born at Tarquinia, he became a journalist, and in 1919 founded *La Ronda*, a very influential literary magazine. Both in prose, *Viaggi nel tempo*

(1920), *Sole a Picco* (1929), *Il cielo sulla città* (1938) and *Solitario in Arcadia* (1947), and in poetry, the collected edition of it appearing in 1948, he evinces a love for the classical, is greatly influenced by Leopardi (q.v.) and has an immaculate style. His later works, apart from *Viaggio di un poeta in Russia* (1954), hardly call for notice. He died in Rome.

**Carducci, Giosuè** (1835–1907), Italian poet. Born at Valdicastello, in the province of Pisa, son of a physician, he was made professor of Italian literature at Bologna in 1860. He had already made his views known in his *Rime* (1875) in which he condemns the decadent state of Italian thought and literary expression, putting its weakness down to romanticism and Christianity. New strength could only come from seeking inspiration in the ancient classics and in pre-Christian values, which would bring about a long-lost Renaissance spirit. He proceeded in *Inno a Satana* (1865) to shock public opinion by voicing these ideas still more provocatively. Here is his power and also his weakness, for Carducci has the fatal tendency to make his verse the vehicle of intellectualism. *Levia Gravia* (in series, 1861–1871) and *Giambi ed epodi* (in series, 1867–79) are both volumes ruined by this preaching. But the *Odi barbari* (in series, 1877–89) is altogether artistically satisfying, for the breath of the ancient classical world has effortlessly entered into the beautiful lyrics contained here, the Italian landscape invested with the lights and shades of the changing seasons being the binding force which creates the artistic unity. The *Rime nuove* (1887) is also a collection which shows Carducci at his best. His critical works have now passed into the realm of literary history. Retiring from his chair in 1904, he was granted a pension. Awarded the Nobel Prize in 1906, he died in Bologna. See his *Opere complete* (30 vols., 1940) and *Poesie* (twentieth ed., 1937). There are English translations of his poetry by F. Sewall (N.Y., 1892), M. Holland (1907) and G. L. Bickersteth (1913).

**Carmen Sylva,** pseudonym of **Elizabeth, Queen of Rumania** (1843–1916), poet and prose-writer, writing in Rumanian, German, French and English. She was born, the daughter of Prince Hermann of Wied, at Neuwied, and in 1869 married King (then Prince) Carol of Rumania (*d.* 1914). A fine musician and an accomplished painter, she wrote much and successfully, among her best-known books being *Les Pensées d'une reine* (1882), which gained a prize from the French Academy, *Leidens Erdengang* (1882; Eng. trans. *Suffering's Journey on Earth*, 1905), a volume of short stories, *Rumänische Dichtungen* (1883), Rumanian poetry translated by her into German, and the two books of fairy stories, *Legends from River and Mountain* (1896) and *Märchen einer Königin* (1906; Eng. trans. *A Real Queen's Fairy Book*, 1909). She died in Bucharest.

**Carneiro, Mário de Sá** (1890–1916), Portuguese poet, novelist and short-story writer, was born in Lisbon. He had no success in life, and died by suicide in Paris, having published *Dispersão* (1914), a book of verse, *A confissão de Lucio* (1914), a novel, and a volume of short stories, *Céu em fogo* (1915). His work has grown in importance in

recent times, and the publication of his collected poetry (1946) was
hailed as an event in modern Portuguese literature.

**Carner, Josep** (1884–    ), Catalan poet and short-story writer.
Born in Barcelona, he entered the diplomatic service, serving the
republic as first councillor at the Paris embassy. His earlier poems,
such as *Llibre dels poetes* (1904) and *Els fruyts saborosos* (1906), are
much influenced by French symbolism, but in later works such as
*L'oreig entre les canyes* (1920) and *Les planetes del Verdun* (1918;
rev., 1929) there is a personal note, of a quality particularly Catalan
and in a great tradition. Representative of his short stories is *La
creació d' Eva i altres contes* (1922). For his verse see the English
translation, *Poems* (1962).

**Carossa, Hans** (1878–1956), German novelist, autobiographer and
poet. Born at Tölz, he became a medical practitioner, serving in the
medical corps in both world wars. Beginning as a novelist with *Die
Schicksale Doktor Bürgers* (1913), he turned to autobiography as his
most satisfactory means of expression, which was abundantly proved
in his urbane, benevolent and cultured books, faithful accounts of his
own experience of life, such as *Eine Kindheit* (1922; Eng. trans. *A
Childhood*, 1930), *Rumänisches Tagebuch* (1924; rev. as *Tagebuch im
Kriege*, 1934; Eng. trans. from the first, *A Rumanian Diary*, 1930),
*Verwandlungen einer Jugend* (1928; Eng. trans. *Boyhood and Youth*,
1932), *Das Jahr der schönen Täuschungen* (1941; Eng. trans. *The
Year of Sweet Illusions*, 1951), *Aufzeichnungen aus Italien* (1947),
*Ungleiche Welten* (1951), *Der Tag des jungen Arztes* (1955) and *Der
alte Taschenspieler* (1956). *Der Arzt Gion* (1931; Eng. trans. *Doctor
Gion*, 1933) and *Geheimnisse des reifen Lebens* (1936) do not fit into
the category of the above, being far more objective. Carossa published his collected poetry in 1951. He died at Rittsteig near Passau.

**Carrér, Luigi** (1801–1850), Italian poet, who was born and who died
in Venice. He first taught literature at Padua, and in 1846 became a
museum curator. Influenced by Foscolo (q.v.) and Byron, he published four volumes of poetry, classical in form but romantic in
content, *Saggio di poesie* (1819), *Poesie* (1831), *Ballate* (1834) and
*Poesie edite ed inedite* (1845). His two prose works do not call for
notice.

**Carrere, Emilio** (1880–1947), Spanish poet, born in Madrid. The prime
introducer of *fin-de-siècle* French poetry into Spanish literature, his
subjects are usually taken from the seamier side of life, but the sharp
outlines of reality are smoothed away by an all-pervading shadowy
sadness. Chief of his works are *El caballero de la muerte* (1909),
*Nocturnos de otoño* (1920) and *Poemas saturnianos* (1921). He died
in Madrid.

**Carvalho e Araujo, Alexandre Herculano de,** *see* **Herculano.**

**Casanova de Seingalt, Giovanni Giacomo,** or **Jacopo** (1725–1798),
Italian prose-writer. Born in Venice, he set out on a life of adventure,
mostly in eastern Europe, not returning to Venice until 1755 when
he was imprisoned as a spy. He made his escape after a year and a
half and fled to Paris, where he gained the lucrative post of director

of state lotteries and gave himself up to every kind of amorous and political intrigue. After a while he went on his way again in many different European countries, gaining favour and posts wherever he went, only to lose them again when the truth about him came to be known. In 1785 he at last settled down as librarian to Count Waldstein at the castle of Dux in Bohemia where he died. His celebrated *Mémoires* (mod. eds., 1880 and 1926; Eng. trans. *Memoirs of Casanova*, 12 vols., 1894; and (abridged) 2 vols., 1930) provide, in the midst of his own self-glorification, certain vivid comments on the life and thought of the day. As the self-revelation of a scoundrel they are perhaps unparalleled in literature—and they certainly are literature.

**Casona, Alejandro,** pseudonym of **Alejandro Rodríguez Álvarez** (1903–1965), Spanish playwright. Born at Tineo in Asturias, he was in turn a schoolmaster, an inspector of schools and a theatre producer. He went into exile on the defeat of the republic and settled in Argentina. Outstanding among his plays, which possess much charm and humour, are *Prohibido suicidarse en primavera* (1941), *Otra vez el diablo* (1943), *La barca sin pescador* (1945), *Los árboles mueren de pie* (1949) and *La tercera palabra* (1954). In 1962 he returned to Spain and died in Madrid.

**Casper von Lohenstein,** *see* **Lohenstein.**

**Cassou, Jean** (1897–      ), French novelist, poet and critic, was born at Deusto, near Bilbao, took a leading part in the resistance during the German occupation, his *33 Sonnets composés au secret* (1944) being smuggled out of his prison and published under the pseudonym of Jean Noir, and became head of the Museum of Modern Art, Paris. As a novelist he is best represented by *Les Massacres de Paris* (1936) and *Légion* (1939); as a critic and essayist by *De l'Étoile au Jardin des Plantes* (1935), *Le Centre du monde* (1945), *La Situation de l'art moderne* (1950), *Le Bel Automne* (1950) and *Le Livre de Lazare* (1955).

**Castelo Branco, Camillo** (1825–1890), Portuguese novelist. Born in Lisbon, he was left an orphan at an early age and taken to the country, to the upper Minho valley, a remote part of Portugal which made a deep impression on him. Having tried medicine and toyed with the Church, he settled down to the life of an author, becoming highly regarded in his own country and in Brazil, but little known elsewhere. He is Portuguese of the Portuguese, and is excellent when writing mystery stories (*Livro negro do padre Dinis*, 1855) and domestic tragedies (*Amor de perdição*, 1862). Best of all are his novels of the country life of the north-east of Portugal where he lived as a child (*Novelas do Minho*, 3 vols., 1875–7). He was greatly honoured in his later years, being ennobled, but he had all his life been badly balanced, and on the verge of total blindness his mind gave way and he committed suicide at São Miguel de Side.

**Casti, Giambattista** (1724–1803), Italian poet. Born at Acquapendente, Tuscany, he took orders, became a composer of operatic libretti and wrote at intervals his urbane society verse collectively known as *Novelle galanti*, the first in 1778 and the last in 1802 (critical ed. *Novelle*, 4 vols., 1925). In 1764 he was made poet laureate at Vienna and remained in that city until 1790 when he went to live in Florence on the death of his patron, Emperor Joseph II. The overrunning of Italy by the French in 1798 with their new republican ideas was welcomed by Casti who, wisely avoiding the possible danger of a reaction in his own country, settled in Paris, and there wrote his verse satire *Gli animali parlanti* (1802; critical ed., 1893; Eng. trans. (very free) *Court and Parliament of Beasts*, 1819), in which he contrasts the old and new regimes. He died in Paris.

**Castiglione, Baldassare** (1478–1529), Italian writer. Born at Casatico near Mantua, he studied at Milan under Chalcocondylas (q.v.), and then served under the dukes of Milan and Urbino and was envoy to several foreign courts, including that of England (1506). In 1507 he began *Il libro del cortegiano* (completed and publ. 1528; Eng. trans. *The Book of the Courtyer*, by Sir Thomas Hoby, 1561; Everyman's Library, 1928), one of the supreme works of the Italian Renaissance, the beauty of thought and language of which has few rivals in the whole realm of literature. Written in the form of discussion among courtiers of Urbino, it contains much about theories of right behaviour and ends with the memorable exposition of platonic love put into the mouth of Pietro Bembo (q.v.). Castiglione also wrote poetry in Italian and Latin (*Poesie volgari e latine*, 1760). Appointed Papal Nuncio in Spain, he died at Toledo.

**Castro, Eugénio de** (1869–1944), Portuguese poet. Born in Coimbra, where he was afterwards appointed to the chair of Portuguese literature, he moved freely in French literary circles, and gave new life to his country's poetry, then at a low ebb, by introducing French symbolism into it in *Oaristos* (1890). Chief among the many volumes of his poetry which followed this epoch-making book are *A nereida de Harlem* (1896), *Orei Galaor* (1897), *Constança* (1900), *O anel de Polícrates* (1907), *Canções desta negra vida* (1922) and *Ultimos versos* (1938). His *Obras poéticas* were published (8 vols.) between 1927 and 1940. He died in Coimbra.

**Castro, José María Ferreira de** (1898–    ), Portuguese novelist who has lived most of his life in Brazil and who brilliantly described life on the upper Amazon in *A selva* (1930; Eng. trans. *Jungle*, 1934). Other novels by him are *Emigrantes* (1928), *Eternidade* (1933), *Tempestade* (1940), *Sorte* (1948), *A curva da estrada* (1950), *A missão* (1954), *A experiencia* (1954) and *O Senhor dos navegantes* (1954), all concerned with Brazilian life.

**Castro, Rosalía** (1837–1885), Spanish poet. Born at Santiago de Compostela, she suffered all her life from social difficulties (she was illegitimate), lack of money and ill health. The greatest modern Galician poet, she employed that language in all her works except one. Her sad and moving books of verse include *Cantares gallegos* (1862) and *Follas novas* (1884), in which latter there is a deepened sense of things half seen and overhead, and above all of the timelessness of nature. She died at Padrón (Coruña). Her collected works appeared in 1944.

**Castro Quesada, Américo** (1885–    ), Spanish prose-writer born in

Brazil, was a professor at the University of Madrid until the end of the civil war when he settled in the U.S.A. and one of the greatest literary critics of his generation. Under the republic he held important diplomatic posts. Among his many scholarly works are: *El pensamiento de Cervantes* (1925), *Santa Teresa y otros ensayos* (1929), *España en su historia* (1948), his most important work, reissued under the title of *La realidad historica de España* in 1954 (Eng. trans. *The Structure of Spanish History*, 1954), *Aspectos del vivir hispánico* (1949), *Ensayo de historiología* (1950) and *Origen, ser y existir de los españoles* (1959).

**Castro y Bellvis, Guillén de** (1569–1631), Spanish dramatist. Born in Valencia of well-to-do family, he held some government appointments in Italy, finally retiring to Madrid in 1619 where he died. His famous work *Las mocedades del Cid* (1618) is the direct source for *Le Cid* of P. Corneille (q.v.). Several of his other forgotten plays suggested plots to such differing playwrights as Calderón (q.v.) in Spain and Fletcher in England.

**Caterina da Siena** (1347–1380), Italian prose-writer. Born at Siena, the daughter of a dyer, she became a Dominican nun. Famed for her severe life, she was soon a force in politics as in religion, and was influential enough to persuade Pope Gregory XI to return from Avignon to Rome. In 1378 she went to Rome to heal the Great Schism, dying there as a result of overwork and the severity of her asceticism. She was canonized in 1461. Her works comprise the *Lettere* (mod. ed. 6 vols., 1939–47), the *Libro della Divina Dottrina* (mod. ed., 1928), dictated in a mystical trance and containing the fundamentals of her belief, the *Dialogo della Divina Providenza* (mod. ed., 1928; Eng. trans. 1896) and devotional poetry (see *Little Flowers of St Catherine of Sienna*, 1930). Her collected works were edited by Tomasseo (1860) and Gigli (1866).

**Catherine II,** known as **Catherine the Great** (1729–1796), Empress of Russia and author. A Princess of Anhalt-Zerbst, she was born in Stettin, and was married to the future Peter III of Russia in 1745. On the latter's assassination in 1762 she succeeded him on the throne, and as a matter of policy, to give Russia a good image in the eyes of the Europe of the Enlightenment, she surrounded herself with a cosmopolitan literary circle, and corresponded with many more whom she could not win to her court. She was herself a busy author, writing plays and essays, and even fairy stories, but it is her voluminous memoirs that alone may be said to have survived. The full and reliable edition of these (they were originally composed in French) is *Sobranie sochineniya Ekateriny II* (12 vols., 1901–8; Eng. trans. abridged, *Memoirs of Catherine the Great*, 1927). At the outbreak of the French Revolution in 1789 this superficial benevolent monarch and enlightened writer became a strong reactionary and the bust of Voltaire was hastily removed from her library. She died at Tsarkoye Selo.

**Cats, Jacob** (1577–1660), Dutch poet. Born at Brouwershaven in Zeeland, he became a lawyer, was Pensionary of Holland (1636–51) and was twice ambassador to England. His house in The Hague was a literary centre, and he was editor of and contributor to an anthology of great importance in the history of Netherlands literature, *De Zeeuwsche Nachtegaal* (1623). An influence rather than a successful performer himself, his collected works appeared (19 vols.) in 1655 (mod. ed., 1862). He died in The Hague.

**Cavafy, C.,** *see* **Kavaphes, K.**

**Cavalcanti, Guido** (1250?–1300), Italian poet. Born in Florence of noble Guelf family, he was soon involved in politics, and when in 1300 the Guelfs divided into Blacks and Whites, he found himself on the side of the latter. When therefore shortly afterwards the Black Guelfs gained power he was driven into exile, and although he was able to return to Florence a few months later, he was already a sick man as the result of privations and died in his native city shortly afterwards. He left about fifty poems (*Le rime de Guido Cavalcanti*, 1902; many of his poems were trans. into English by D. G. Rossetti in *Dante and His Circle*, 1861), generally love-poems, deeply, often sufferingly, felt and expressed with unusual clarity. He and his work were greatly admired by Dante.

**Cecchi, Emilio** (1884–     ), Italian essayist and critic. Born in Florence, he soon won a reputation as a literary journalist and, with the collection of essays *Pesci rossi* (1920), consolidated his position as a prose-writer of high quality. Other books of the same kind were *La giornata delle belle donne* (1924) and *Corse al trotto* (1936). *Scrittori inglesi e americani* (1935) and *America amara* (1939) are trenchant studies of the Anglo-Saxon world. Since the war he has pursued the style of essayist in *Di giorno in giorno* (1954) and his critical bent in *La scultura fiorentina del Quattrocento* (1956), *Ritratti e profili* (1957) and *Libri nuovi e usati* (1958).

**Cecchi, Giommaria** (1518–1587), Italian poet and playwright. Born in Florence, he became a highly esteemed merchant and city official. His poetry (*Poesie*, mod. ed., 1866) is often good if not particularly striking, but his comedies (*Commedie*, 1550; mod. ed., 1883) contain much verse, and the blank verse both in them and in the religious plays (*Drammi spirituali*, mod. ed., 1895) is among the best of the age. He died at Gangalandi.

**Cela, Camilo José** (1916–     ), Spanish novelist, born at Iria Flavia, Pontevedra. His first novel, *La familia de Pascual Duarte* (1942; Eng. trans. 1946), in spite of exhibitionism has strength and character. Other novels have been *Pabellón de reposo* (1943), *El nuevo Lazarillo* (1944), *Esas nubes que pasan* (1945) and *La colmena* (1951; Eng. trans. *The Hive*, 1953). North American influences on him abound, as is particularly to be seen in *Mrs Caldwell había con su hijo* (1953).

**Céline, Louis-Ferdinand** (1894–1961), his real name being **Louis-Ferdinand Destouches,** French novelist. Born at Courbevoie, he took part in the First World War and then qualified in medicine, after which he practised in a working-class quarter of Paris (1924). In his first book, *Voyage au bout de la nuit* (1932; Eng. trans. *Journey to the End of the Night*, 1934), he indulges in a stern criticism of humanity, writing in an anarchic style, full of slang and even obscenities.

*Mort à crédit* (1936; Eng. trans. *Death on the Instalment Plan*, 1938) is in the same style, as are *L'École des cadavres* (1938) and *Les Beaux Draps* (1941). He had already in *Bagatelles pour un massacre* (1938) given voice to his violent anti-Semitism, which led him to collaborate with the Germans, with the result that he had to escape from Paris in 1944 and lived in Denmark until 1951, during which time he was employed in writing an account of his life during those years, *D'un château l'autre* (1956). He died at Meudon.

**Cellini, Benvenuto** (1500–1571), the great Italian sculptor who has a place in literature by reason of his splendid autobiography, was born in Florence. Of a quarrelsome disposition, he was early banished from his native city and was in Rome by 1519 where he took up the goldsmith's craft. He took some part—though not the enormous part he pretends—in the siege of Rome and was high in favour with Pope Clement VII. After a fall from favour in Rome he went to France to the court of Francis I, but after a time went back to Florence and died there. For all his achievement in the plastic arts—and his 'Perseus' is an excellent piece of sculpture—he is remembered for the *Vita di Benevenuto Cellini scritta da lui medesimo*, which he began to compose in 1558 (best mod. ed., O. Bacci, 1900; Eng. trans. T. Roscoe, 1822, reprinted 1927; J. A. Symonds, 1887, new ed., 1900; R. H. H. Cust, 1910, new ed. 1935), in which he sets himself with all his striking personality against the contemporary world inimitably described. His poetry and his two treatises on art are of slight value.

**Cena, Giovanni** (1870–1917), Italian poet and novelist. Born at Canavese, he made his name with such volumes of poetry as *In umbra* (1899) and *Homo* (1907). His socialistically inspired novel, *Gli ammonitori* (1904), is of a good deal of interest. As editor of the *Nuova Antologia* (1902–17) he exercised great literary influence. His collected works fill five volumes (1928–9). He died in Rome.

**Cendrars, Blaise** (1887–1961), French poet and novelist, of Swiss origin. Born in Paris, he led a wandering, changeable, active life, and was a friend of Apollinaire (q.v.). He has succeeded in investing all his work with a sense of urgency and menace, as in *La Prose du Transibérien et de la petite Jeanne de France* (1913), *L'Or* (1925), *Histoires vraies* (1937), *La Vie dangereuse* (1938), *Poésies complètes* (1944), *L'Homme foudroyé* (1945), *Bourlinguer* (1948), *Le Lotissement du ciel* (1949), *Cent et un routes* (1951) and *Emmène-moi au bout du monde !* (1956). He died in Paris.

**Cernuda, Luis** (1904–1963), Spanish poet. Born in Seville, he settled early on in Madrid, which he left towards the end of the civil war and emigrated to the U.S.A. via France and Britain. Influenced by Guillén (q.v.), he wrote on a wider variety of subjects. He found strength in compression, and the telling phrase is abundant in his work, which consists of *La realidad y el deseo* (1940), containing all his poetry written previously, *Ocnos* (1942; rev., 1949), which are prose poems set in Seville, *Como quien espera el alba* (1947) and *Tres narraciones* (1948). He finally settled in Mexico, where he published *Variaciones sobre tema mexicano* (1952), and died there.

**Cervantes Saavedra, Miguel de** (1547–1616), Spanish novelist, dramatist and poet. He was born at Alcalá de Henares, the fourth of the seven children of a surgeon and, after being educated in Madrid (he was his schoolmaster's 'most beloved pupil'), he went to Italy and took service in the household of Cardinal Julio de Acquaviva. There are stories of his high spirits at this time leading to various affrays, and it is no surprise to find him volunteering for the army and taking part in the Battle of Lepanto (1571), at which he was wounded. He saw service also in the Tunisian wars before returning to Italy. In 1575 while returning to Spain from another military expedition he was captured by Moorish corsairs and remained in captivity for five years in Algiers. Finally ransomed in 1580 he found himself back in Spain penniless and with apparently no future. He then turned to authorship for a livelihood, and settled in Madrid, managing to make ends meet with what he earned, with the addition, from 1584, when he married, of his young wife's dowry. His writings of this period include the plays *El trato de Argel*, in which he makes use of his experiences during captivity, the patriotic tragedy *La Numancia*, and *El rufián dichoso*, none of them of much value. Ten plays in all remain, eight published in *Ocho comedias y ocho entremeses* in 1615, and two more discovered and printed in 1784. His pastoral novel, *La Galatea* (1585; Eng. trans. 1901), is neither better nor worse than others of that type and period, but it brought him some recognition. Recognition perhaps, but little enough money, and he was glad to accept a government post as one of the purveyors of provisions to the Armada now being fitted up (1587). Honest himself, some of his associates were not, and he narrowly escaped imprisonment and was censured by the Archbishop of Seville, in which city he was now living. Having been cleared, and having at last made some money, disaster befell him when his banker failed and he lost not only his savings but also revenue funds, so that when he arrived at Valladolid to present his accounts he was imprisoned. The next period of his life, which is somewhat obscure, was certainly an unsettled one with periods of imprisonment for debt. But all the time he was engaged on his great work, one of the supreme achievements of literature, the novel *El ingenioso hidalgo don Quijote de la Mancha*, the first part of which he finished in 1604 and which was published in 1605 (Eng. trans., by Shelton, 1612–20, rev., 1896; Motteux, 1702; Smollett, 1755; Duffield, 1881; Watts, 2 vols., 1888–9; and Everyman's Library). Cervantes had begun it as a satire on romances of chivalry, but as he worked at it by fits and starts it became a living picture in his mind and, freeing himself from any styles and patterns of writing which he evinced in his other works, he was free to be himself and to express himself as he pleased. The greatness of *Don Quijote* is due not to its literary distinction but to its overflowing vitality. Before us we have the Spanish people in the sixteenth century, and in Don Quixote himself and Sancho Panza we have the dual nature of the visionary idealist who is ready to lose all for an act of goodness to others, and the undisguised realist which is the make-up of every Spaniard. His splendid characterization ranging from the lord to the beggar is authentic and vital, and his humour and joy in life are everywhere to be found—not that he was not capable of serious feeling too. The publication of the first part of *Don Quijote* was received with delight by the public, and although it brought Cervantes little material gain, he did win his patrons. He would not perhaps have written the second part had it not been for the publication of a spurious one; but even so he had other work in hand, and before he completed his master-piece he had written his twelve unequal but at their best really excellent stories, *Novelas ejemplares* (1613; Eng. trans. *Exemplarie Novells*, 1638; *Exemplary Novels*, 1903). The *Novels* are faultlessly written and provided mines of riches for writers all over Europe to plunder. English Jacobean dramatists, e.g. Fletcher, made use of them for plots. The second part of *Don Quijote* was also held up for his dull and unsuccessful flight into poetry, *El viaje del Parnaso* (1614); but at last it appeared in 1615 (for Eng. trans. see above) and trium-phantly rounded off the whole. In this second part Cervantes seems to be jotting down his inmost thoughts in a notebook as they occur to him; the result is like overhearing a genius at work in his study; and, besides, there is everywhere as before the breath of human life. Less than a year later he died of dropsy in Madrid. A prose romance, *Los trabajos de Persiles y Sigismunda*, in the style of the *Aethiopica* of Heliodorus, appeared posthumously in 1617 (Eng. trans. *The Travails of Persiles and Sigismunda*, 1619). The standard edition of his com-plete works is that by R. Schevill and A. Bonilla (14 vols., 1914–25).

**Cesarotti, Melchiorre** (1730–1808), Italian man of letters. Born in Padua, he became assistant professor of Greek and Hebrew in the university there in 1768. His translation of Macpherson's *Ossian* into Italian (1763) deflected Italian literature along new paths. In *Saggio sulla filosofia delle lingue* (1785) he made a plea for the loosening of all academic bonds from literature, a prompting not wasted on Alfieri (q.v.) and others of the out-and-out romantic school. One of the Italian ambassadors sent to meet Bonaparte at Campo Formio (1797), he fell completely under his influence and became the chief of his Italian apologists. He died at Selvaggiano, near Padua. His collected works appeared (40 vols.) between 1800 and 1813. There is a two-volume edition of his selected works (1945–6).

**Céspedes y Meneses, Gonzalo de** (1585?–1638), Spanish novelist. Born in Madrid, he seems to have gone south and lived in Granada, and was later in Zaragoza and Lisbon, but died in Madrid. He is remembered as the author of the autobiographical *Poema trágico del español Gerardo* (1615–7; Eng. trans. *Gerardo, the Unfortunate Spaniard*, 1622) and the picaresque *Varia fortuna del soldado Píndaro* (1626). See *Historias peregrinas y ejemplares*, edited by E. Cotarelo (1906). His historical writing is unimportant as literature.

**Chaadayev, Pyotr Yakovlevich** (1793–1856), Russian prose-writer composing much of his work in French. Born in Moscow, he turned to French literature and thought, especially to that of the ultra-montanists such as J. de Maistre (q.v.). In his *Lettres philosophiques* (1830) he attacked Russian isolation from European culture, praised the universality of Catholicism and condemned the narrow national-ism of the Russian Orthodox Church. Restraints were put upon him and he was officially called insane, but that did nothing to quieten the controversy which he had brought into being and which is not yet over. He died in Moscow and his later writings were collected with the *Lettres* in *Œuvres choisies* (1862; Russian version, 2 vols., 1913–14).

**Chalcocondylas, Laonicus** (1432?–1490?), Greek historian. Born in Athens, he was brought up at the Byzantine imperial court at Mistra, and between about 1465 and 1487 wrote in Greek a history of the Byzantine Empire from 1298 to 1453, known from the Latin title given to it by Immanuel Bekker, its first editor (1843), as *Historiarum demonstrationes*, for it is more than a mere history: it is an analysis of Greek, Roman and Ottoman power and describes the reasons for the success of the latter with a skill that is remarkable. The prose too, and in fact the whole architecture of the work, is derived from and inspired by Herodotus and Thucydides. The best modern edition is by E. Darkó (2 vols., 1922–7). The place of his death and the exact date are unknown.

**Chamfort, Sébastien Roch Nicolas** (1741–1794), French writer, born of lowly family at Clermont, he gained entrance into Paris society by reason of his wit and personal charm. His first success was scored with the sentimental comedy *La Jeune Indienne* (1764), and he won a reputation as a literary critic with his *Éloges*, of Molière (1766) and of La Fontaine (1774). His tragedy, *Mustapha et Zéangir* (1776), was performed before the court at Fontainebleau, and he gained court appointments, which did not, however, prevent his participation in the revolution. Hunted by the Jacobins, he committed suicide in Paris. He lives by reason of his brilliant epigrams which are to be found in *Pensées, maximes et anecdotes de S. R. N. Chamfort* (1803).

**Chamisso, Adalbert von,** originally **Louis Charles Chamisso de Boncourt** (1781–1838), German poet and prose-writer. Born at Boncourt in Champagne of mixed French and Portuguese descent, his family took him to Germany soon after the beginning of the French Revolution and settled in Berlin. He served in the Prussian army from 1798 to 1806, but gave up a military career, joined literary circles, including Madame de Staël's (q.v.), became a botanist of repute and later held a post at the Royal Botanic Gardens in Berlin where he died. All his life he felt a wanderer in a strange land and this is reflected in his famous and unique work *Peter Schlemihls wundersame Geschichte* (1814; Eng. trans. *The Shadowless Man*, 1824), the tale of a man who sells his shadow, symbolical of his own position. The simplicity and apparent artlessness of the work owe something to the folk tale, and the inspiration of his poetry, above all *Frauenliebe und Leben* (1831), which was set to music by Schumann, is influenced by the Volkslied. His collected works were published (6 vols.) in 1836–9.

**Champfleury, Jules,** originally **Fleury-Husson** (1821–1889), French novelist. Born at Laon, he followed Balzac (q.v.) in his novels of provincial life: *Chien Caillou* (1847), *Les Aventures de Mariette* (1851), *Les Bourgeois de Molinchart* (1855), *Les Souffrances du Professeur Delteil* (1857) and *Les Amoureux de Sainte-Périne* (1859). *Les Confessions de Sylvius* (1849) is autobiographical. An art critic of some distinction, he died at Sèvres where he had interests in the ceramics factory. His influence on Flaubert (q.v.) was considerable.

**Chapelain, Jean** (1595–1674), French prose-writer. Born in Paris, he came to be much favoured by Richelieu, and was active in the foundation of the French Academy. He was the mouthpiece of the academy on literary taste, and about 1635 wrote *Sentiments de l'Académie sur le Cid*, in which the rule of the dramatic unities, based on the Aristotelian canon, was laid down, and *De la poésie représentative*, in which he introduced the question, discussed for a century, as to whether the best poetry were that which could be transferred into graphic art (cf. the argument in Lessing's (q.v.) *Laokoön*). These critical works have been edited in modern times by A. C. Hunter as *Opuscules critiques* (1936). His poetry, such as *La Pucelle d'Orléans* (1656), is of little value; but the attacks on him by Boileau (q.v.) were the result of jealousy rather than disapproval, for their literary tastes were the same. Chapelain died in Paris.

**Chapygin, Alexey Pavlovich** (1870–1937), Russian Soviet novelist, born in the province of Olonetz of peasant family. His most satisfying book is the well-documented and amply conceived historical novel of the seventeenth century, *Razin Stepan* (1927; Eng. trans. *Stepan Razin*, 1946). He died in Leningrad.

**Char, René** (1907–    ), French poet. Born at L'Isle-sur-Sorgue, he produced a volume of surrealist poems, *Le Marteau sans maître* (1936); but his later books have contained difficult abstract thought expressed in crisp, elliptical language as in *Seuls demeurent* (1945), *Feuillets d'Hypnos* (1948), *Le Soleil des eaux* (1949), *Les Matinaux* (1950), *Poèmes de deux années* (1955), *Recherche de la base et du sommet* (1955), *La Bibliothèque est en feu* (1957) and *La Parole en archipel* (1962). See the English translation, *Poems and Prose* (1956).

**Chardonne, Jacques,** pseudonym of **Jacques Boutelleau** (1884–    ), French novelist. Born at Barbezieux of Franco-American parentage he became a publisher. His novels, traditionally domestic in content, though their treatment is modern, psychology being made much use of, include: *L'Épithalame* (1921; Eng. trans. *Epithalamium*, 1923), *Les Varais* (1929), *Éva* (1930; Eng. trans. 1930), *Les Destinées sentimentales* (3 vols., 1934–6), *Le Bonheur de Barbezieux* (1938), *Chronique privée de l'an 40* (1941), *Chimériques* (1949), *Charles Deligny ou le fatale horoscope* (1955) and *Matinales* (1956).

**Charles d'Orléans,** *see* **Orléans.**

**Charrière, Isabelle de,** *née* **van Tuyll** (1740–1805), Swiss novelist and letter writer. Dutch by birth, she was born in Utrecht, but married a French-Swiss and settled in Switzerland. A close friend of Madame de Staël (q.v.) and of Benjamin Constant (q.v.), she wrote among many other works *Lettres de Lausanne* (1785), with their almost diagnostic approach to the contemporary scene, and the novel *Caliste* (1787). She died at Colombier.

**Chartier, Alain** (1385?–1440?), French poet and prose-writer, writing also in Latin. Born at Bayeux, he was secretary to the dauphin, afterwards Charles VII. All his work is coloured by the misfortunes of his country, then at their darkest; and as in his most considerable prose work, the *Quadrilogue invectif* (1422; critical ed., 1923), he discusses the disasters of France and tries to find a solution, so in his *Livre des quatre dames* (1415–20?; critical ed., 1929) he describes the human sorrow caused by war, for here are four ladies in mourning for their lovers killed at Agincourt. His *Tractatus de vita curiali* was translated into English by William Caxton (1484). The date and place of Chartier's death are unknown.

**Chartier, Émile,** who used the pseudonym **Alain** (1868–1951), French essayist. Born at Mortagne, he taught philosophy at the Lycée Henri IV in Paris from 1909 to 1935, in which capacity he had enormous influence over pupils who afterwards became intellectual leaders of France between the wars. Incisive and inquiring, he tore to shreds many conventional prejudices in such works as *Cent-un propos d'Alain* (5 vols., 1908–29), *Quatre-vingt chapitres sur l'esprit et les passions* (1921), *Mars, ou la guerre jugée* (1921; Eng. trans. *Mars; or The Truth about War,* 1930), revealing his strong anti-militarism, *Le Citoyen contre les pouvoirs* (1928), *Les Dieux* (1934), showing his anti-clericalism, and *L'Histoire de mes pensées* (1936). He died at Le Vésinet (Seine-et-Oise).

**Chateaubriand, François René de** (1768–1848), French novelist and general prose-writer, born of noble Breton family at St Malo, at the Château de Combourg. He entered the army, but the French Revolution cut short his plans, and in 1791 he went to the United States. He was back again before long, however, and served in the army of the French *émigrés,* being severely wounded at Namur. From 1793 to 1800 he lived in London, teaching and translating for booksellers, and in 1797 came forward as an historian with *Essai sur les révolutions.* Never particularly religious before, in 1798 he suddenly became an eager supporter of the Church of Rome, from then on pressing all his literary gifts into its service. *Atala* (1801; Eng. trans. Oxford Library of French Classics), a novel in the train of 'the noble savage' literature of the last twenty years, brought him a literary reputation, and in his rehabilitation of Catholicism in his emotional and richly romantic *Le Génie du christianisme* (1802), to which another novel, *René* (separate ed., 1805; Eng. trans. Oxford Library of French Classics), was attached he produced a work eagerly seized upon by the great majority of Frenchmen who had had enough of the deification of reason. *Le Génie* was the first widely read announcement of the trend of European intellectuals to religious feeling which marked one stage of romanticism. For a time on good terms with Bonaparte, who, while consul, sent him to Rome as secretary of legation, by 1806 Chateaubriand, disgusted with the empire, had set out on his travels to the East. His best works of these years are *Les Martyrs* (1809), a prose epic of the time of Diocletian's attempt to stamp out Christianity in the Roman Empire, and the *Itinéraire de Paris à Jérusalem* (1811). He came into his own at the restoration, was ambassador to Berlin, London and Rome, and, though he posed as a liberal during Charles X's reign, showed at the revolution of 1830 that he was as much a Bourbon royalist as ever. But it is for his moving and eloquent auto-

biography, part fiction, part reality, *Mémoires d'outre-tombe*, parts
of which had already appeared in serial form in *La Presse* at the time
of his death in Paris, that he is important as a creative literary man.
There is a critical edition of this book (1948) and an English translation (1902). A poor thinker but intuitive, a writer full of literary sins
like false sentiment and tasteless extravagance, he can yet, at his
best, carry his readers completely away.

**Chatrian, Alexandre,** *see* **Erckmann-Chatrian.**

**Chekhov, Anton Pavlovich** (1860–1904), Russian dramatist and short-
story writer, born at Taganrog, the grandson of a serf and the son of
an unsuccessful tradesman who, when the boy was small, sold up and
went to try his fortune in Moscow. Chekhov matriculated at Moscow
University as a medical student in 1879, and eked out his meagre
allowance with such money as he could make by writing, under the
pseudonym 'Antosha Chekhonte', short stories for various magazines
and papers, which reveal nothing of his future greatness. He qualified
in medicine in 1884, but soon gave up all intention of practising and
devoted himself to literature, his choice being confirmed by the
success of his first and vivacious volume of short stories, *Pyostrye
rasskazy* (1886, 'Motley Stories'). Up to this time he had been
regarded as a cheerful, even humorous writer; but his first play,
*Ivanov* (1887), showed him as a pessimist who sees life as a delusion
and not worth all the struggles of humanity to improve it. Ambition
is vanity, success is vulgar, while the sensitive are driven to the wall,
and those with a conscience which is alive to the falsity of the
worldly are failures. With a sadness bordering on fatalism, bathing his
work in moods and atmospheres, he yet always preserves a taut,
clear style, and is always alive to situation and aware of dramatic
effect. He first reveals true mastery in his two volumes of short
stories, *Khmurye lyudi* (1889, 'Gloomy People') and *Skuchnaya
istoriya* (1889, 'A Dreary Story'), and he followed up these collections
with *Uchitel' slovesnosti* (1894, 'The Teacher of Literature'),
*Muzhiki* (1897, 'Peasants'), *V ovrage* (1900, 'In the Ravine') and
*Arkhierey* (1902, 'The Bishop'). *Moya zhizn'* (1895, 'My Life')
is a more hopeful piece of writing, a narrative inspired by a temporary attachment to the teaching of Tolstoy. But pride of place
goes to his four plays: *Chayka* (1896, 'The Seagull'), a failure at
first when produced at Petersburg, but a success from the
time of its production by Stanislavsky at the Moscow Art
Theatre (1898), where were also produced *Dyadya Vanya* (1899,
'Uncle Vanya'), *Tri sestry* (1901, 'The Three Sisters') and *Vishnyovy
sad* (1904, 'The Cherry Orchard'), in the last of which we are nearer
to tragi-comedy with touches of humour intermingling with pathos.
In an age of the over-theatrical and the exaggeration of hero and
heroine Chekhov avoided principal parts and filled his stage with
characters of equal importance but forming a close-knit whole, while
his technique is built not on stage effects but the interplay and
juxtaposition of character and situation. As a short-story writer his
plots are uncompromisingly realistic, and his people are not so much
individuals as states of mind. Confrontations of ideas rather than of

actions in a world of blurred impressions take the place of the dramatic. Elected to the Imperial Academy of Science in 1900, he soon resigned as a protest against the annulment of Gorky's (q.v.) election. Soon afterwards, attacked by tuberculosis, he went to live in the Crimea, but died of the disease at Badenweiler in south Germany. For his collected works see *Polnoye sobranie sochineniy* (12 vols., 1900–4; a twenty-three vol. ed., 1923), *Sochineniya* (18 vols., 1944) and *Sobranie sochineniy* (12 vols., 1950). For English translations see *Plays by Anton Chekhov* (trans. C. Fell, 1915), *The Tales of Chekhov* (trans. C. Garnett, 13 vols., 1916–22), *Select Tales of Chekhov* (trans. C. Garnett, 1925), *Three Plays: The Cherry Orchard, The Seagull and The Wood Demon* (trans. S. S. Koteliansky, 1940), *Selected Stories* (Vanguard Library, No. 18, 1953) and the *Oxford Chekhov*, in progress, vol. ii (*Platonov, Ivanov* and *The Sea-gull*), vol. iii (*Uncle Vanya, The Three Sisters, The Cherry Orchard* and *The Wood-Demon*) and vol. viii (*Stories, 1895–7*) having already been published.

**Chénier, André-Marie** (1762–1794), French poet. Born in Constantinople, the elder son of the French consul there and of his gifted Greek wife, he was brought back to Paris while still a child and grew up in the literary and artistic atmosphere that his parents enjoyed. He himself entered the diplomatic service, and in 1787 came to London as a secretary to the French Embassy where he remained until 1790. He returned to hail the revolution with delight, but after the September massacres of 1792 gradually became alienated from it and, fearlessly denouncing the Jacobins and their reign of terror, was guillotined in Paris only two days before that terror ended with Robespierre's fall. Little of his work was published during his life, and his best poetry was written in prison, such as his *Odes, Iambes*, above all *La Jeune Captive*. It was his aim to bring the beauty of the ancient Greek lyric into French verse, and such early pieces as *Le Mendiant, La Flûte* and *L'Aveugle* have amazing grace and sonority, while *Hermès* and *La Jeune Tarentine* have an added depth of feeling. His work was little known until Henri de Latouche (q.v.) brought out an imperfect edition of it in 1819. It was at once eagerly seized on by the romantics, and Chénier has been termed the link between classicism and romanticism. The standard edition is that of 1908–1919 (3 vols.).

**Chénier, Marie-Joseph** (1764–1811), French dramatist and poet. The younger brother of André Chénier (q.v.), he was born in Constantinople, but was in Paris before the outbreak of the revolution which he greeted with enthusiasm, and began to write a number of historical tragedies, many of which were receptacles for his extreme anti-clericalism. The best known are *Jean Calas* (1791), *Henry VIII* (1791), *Caius Gracchus* (1792), *Fénelon* (1793; Eng. trans. *Fenelon, or the Nuns of Cambray*, 1795) and *Timoléon* (1794). He also wrote patriotic songs, including the famous 'Chant du départ', and stood well with the Jacobins, but was unable to save his brother from the guillotine, a fact for which he was reproached for the rest of his life, although he more than once tried to defend himself in writing. He died in Paris. His *Œuvres* were collected in eight volumes (1823–7).

**Cherbuliez, Charles Victor** (1829–1899), French novelist and critic, was born of Swiss parents in Geneva, but settled in Paris in 1864 as a contributor to the *Revue des Deux Mondes*. Nearly all his fiction, of which *Le Comte Kostia* (1863), *L'Idée de Jean Têterol* (1875), *Samuel Brohl et Cⁱᵉ* (1877), *La Ferme du Choquard* (1883), *La Vocation du comte Ghislain* (1888), *Le Secret du précepteur* (1893) and *Jacquine Vanesse* (1898) are the best, appeared in serial form in the *Revue des Deux Mondes*. Among his other works may be named: *L'Allemagne politique* (1870), *Études de littérature et d'art* (1873), *L'Espagne politique* (1874), *Hommes et choses d'Allemagne* (1877) and *Choses du temps présent* (1883), the last two under the pseudonym of Gustave Valbert. He died at Combe-la-Ville.

**Chevallier, Gabriel** (1895–   ), French novelist, born in Lyon. His novels, with a humorous streak running through them, are: *La Peur* (1930), *Clarisse Vernon* (1934), *Clochemerle* (1934; Eng. trans. 1936), his best, *Durand, voyageur de commerce* (1934), *Propre à rien* (1936; Eng. trans. *Good-for-Nothing*, 1938), *Sainte-Colline* (1937; Eng. trans. 1946), *Ma Petite Amie Pomme* (1940; Eng. trans. *Cherry*, 1950), *Les Héritiers Euffe* (1945; Eng. trans. *The Euffe Inheritance*, 1948), *Le Petit Général* (1951) and *Clochemerle-Babylone* (1951).

**Chiabrera, Gabriello** (1552–1638), Italian poet, born at Savona. Holding various sinecure court appointments he was able to devote nearly all his time to cultivating the muse. Pindar was his chief inspiration, but he wrote in many poetic forms. His lyrics of the lighter kind are full of charm (see *Poesie liriche*, 1781; mod. ed., 1926). He died at Savona. His *Opere* were published (5 vols.) in 1757.

**Chiesa, Francesco** (1871–   ), Italian poet and novelist, born at Stagno, Ticino, he was a traditionalist. As a poet he is represented by the trilogy *Calliope* (3 vols., 1903–7), *Viali d'oro* (1910), *Fuochi di Primavera* (1919) and *Consolazioni* (1921); as a novelist by *Tempo di marzo* (1925), some say his best work, *Villadorna* (1928), *Compagni di viaggio* (1931), *Voci nella notte* (1935), *Sant' Amarillide* (1938), *Racconti del passato prossimo* (1941), *Ricordi dell' età minore* (1948) and *La zia Lucrezia ed altri racconti* (1956).

**Choderlos de Laclos, Pierre Ambroise François** (1741–1803), French man of letters. Born at Amiens, he entered the army and soon rose high. He mixed much in society, and gained notoriety with a novel founded on his experiences, *Les Liaisons dangereuses* (1782; Eng. trans. *Dangerous Acquaintances*, 1924), in which he held the private lives of the French aristocracy up to scorn for the benefit of the bourgeoisie, thus driving another nail into the coffin of the old regime. In 1786, for the publication that year of *Lettre à Messieurs de l'Académie Française sur l'Éloge de M. le Maréchal de Vauban*, in which he mocked the French Army for still adhering to defence methods introduced in the mid seventeenth century by Vauban, but now hopelessly outdated, he was dismissed from the army. He therefore entered politics, attaching himself to the Duke of Orléans; but seeing the power of the Girondins on the wane in 1792 prudently rejoined the army, dying at Taranto with the rank of general. His *Œuvres* *complètes*, containing the interesting *De l'éducation des femmes*, appeared in 1943.

**Choromański, Michał** (1904–      ), Polish novelist and playwright. Born at Elizavetgrad, he is best known for *Zazdrość i medycyna* (1932; Eng. trans. *Jealousy and Medicine*, 1946), a difficult but deeply thought out work couched often in symbolic language. He also wrote the play *Czlowiek czynu* (1935, 'Man of Action').

**Choynowski, Pyotr** (1885–1935), Polish short-story writer. Born in Warsaw, but educated in Russia, he was celebrated for his excellent Polish prose, which appears to full advantage in his best work, *Młodość, miłość, awantura* (1926; Eng. trans. *Youth, Love and Adventure*, 1940). He died in Warsaw.

**Chrétien de Troyes** (*fl.* 1164–1191), French romance writer of whom little is known save that he wrote one of his works for Marie de Champagne about 1164 and another for Philippe d'Alsace, who died in 1191. All his work, which while having serious religious features is usually in the realms of the fantastic and was primarily intended to entertain courtiers, is founded on the floating legends about Arthur and his knights. Five of Chrétien's romances remain: *Erec et Énide* (*c.* 1164; mod. crit. ed., 1934), *Cligès* (*c.* 1170; mod. crit. ed., 1934), *Lancelot*, also called *La Charete* (*c.* 1173, mod. crit. ed., 1899), *Yvain*, also called *Le Lion* (*c.* 1175; mod. crit. ed., 1942) and *Perceval*, also called *Le Conte del Graal* (before 1191; mod. crit. ed., 1932). See the English translation in *Arthurian Romances* by W. W. Comfort (1913).

**Christen, Ada,** pseudonym of **Christiane von Breden** (1844–1901), Austrian poet. Born in Vienna, both her marriages broke down, and she had reached the depths of degradation when she was rescued and befriended by Ferdinand von Saar (q.v.), who published her first book of lyrics, *Lieder einer Verlorenen* (1868). The effect of the dark sorrow impressed on these poems was deepened by further volumes such as *Schatten* (1872). Her novels include *Ella* (1869) and *Jungfer Mutter* (1892), and she also tried her hand at drama with *Faustina* (1871) and *Wiener Leut'* (1893). She died in Vienna. Her collected works were published in 1911.

**Christiansen, Sigurd Wesley** (1891–1947), Norwegian novelist and playwright, born at Drammen; he worked as a post office clerk for many years before gaining his public with *To levende og en død* (1931; Eng. trans. *Two Living and One Dead*, 1932), following this up with *Agner i stormen* (1933; Eng. trans. *Chaff before the Wind*, 1934). As a playwright *Edmund Jahr* (1926) and *Alexander Pavlovitsj* (1947) show the compass of his dramatic powers. He is interested in small communities and certain powerful figures that emerge to dominate the rest. He died in Drammen.

**Christine de Pisan** (1363–1431), French poet and prose-writer. Born in Venice, her father being physician to the French court, she married a royal secretary, but was left a widow in 1389 with a young family to bring up. Knowing Latin, French and Italian and their literatures, she turned to writing for her living, and thus became the first

Frenchwoman to do so. She wrote much poetry, a good deal of it of a winningly personal kind (*Œuvres poétiques*, 3 vols., 1886–96). As a prose-writer, her life of King Charles V of France, *Livre des fais et bonnes meurs du sage roi Charles V* (1404; mod. ed. S. Solente, 2 vols., 1936–41), is of great interest and is well written. See also William Caxton's English translation of some of her work, *The Book of Fayttes of Arms and of Chyvalrye* (1489; mod. ed., 1932). Christine died in the abbey of Poissy.

**Chulkov, Mikhail Dmitrievich** (1740–1793), Russian miscellaneous writer, solely remembered for the picaresque novel *Prigozhaya povarikha* (1770; Eng. trans. *The Fair Cook, or the Adventures of a Debauched Woman*, n.d.), which was undoubtedly suggested by Daniel Defoe's *Moll Flanders*.

**Cienfuegos, Nicasio Álvarez de** (1764–1809), Spanish poet and playwright. Born in Madrid, he studied at the University of Salamanca and came under the liberal influence of his professor there, Meléndez Valdés (q.v.). His best poetry is highly individualistic and shows the way to romanticism. His plays are less successful, but form an interesting bridge between neo-classicism and the nineteenth-century Spanish theatre. Involved in the political upheavals following on the Napoleonic invasion, he died in exile at Orthez, France. His *Obras poéticas* appeared in two volumes in 1816 and his collected works are to be found in *Biblioteca de Autores Españoles*, vol. lxvii.

**Cino de' Sigisbuldi da Pistoia** (1270?–1339), Italian poet. Born at Pistoia, he studied law at the University of Bologna, and soon became involved in politics. On the Emperor Henry VII's coming to Italy Cino was his eager supporter. He was later in Rome, Siena and Perugia in various capacities, but returned to Pistoia in 1333 and died there. Some have found in his abundant love-poetry a link between Dante and Petrarch. However, much as one can praise his grace, his lyrics do not contain much sense of urgency. See *Le rime di Cino da Pistoia* (ed. G. Zaccagnini, 1925).

**Cinzio,** *see* **Giraldi, G. C.**

**Cladet, Léon** (1835–1892), French novelist, born in Montauban. He was the author of realistic fiction, including short stories describing peasant and vagrant life in the region forming part of the *départements* of Lot and Tarn et Garonne. Among them should be mentioned *Le Bouscassié* (1869), *Les Va-nus-pieds* (1873), *L'Homme de la Croix-aux-bœufs* (1878), *Ompdrailles, le tombeau des lutteurs* (1879), *Urbains et ruraux* (1884), *Héros et pantins* (1885), *Gueux de marque* (1887) and the posthumous *Juive errante* (1897).

**Claretie, Jules Arsène Arnaud** (1840–1913), French man of letters. Born in Limoges, he distinguished himself for bravery during the siege of Paris (1870). He became director of the Théâtre Français in 1885, in which capacity he did much to improve the standards of the French stage. As a novelist he is best represented by *Candidat!* (1887), and his opera, *La Navarraise* (1893), was performed at Covent Garden the following year. He died in Paris.

Clarín, *see* Alas y Ureña, L.

**Claudel, Paul** (1868–1955), French poet, dramatist and prose-writer. Born at Villeneuve-sur-Fère, he entered the diplomatic service, living in different parts of the world and meeting all manner of men. However, before his travels he had come under the influence of Mallarmé (q.v.) and Bergson (q.v.) and in Paris had mixed with the symbolists, and his work throughout his literary career was invested with their imagery which, blended with his fighting style, his inclination to humour and his strength in delineating character, form the Claudel style. But his starting point was his militant Roman Catholicism, which remained the key to all his work. It was the theatre to which he first turned his attention, and in the 'mystery' play, *La Jeune Fille Violaine* (1892; subsequently expanded to four acts and called *L'Annonce faite à Marie*), he called attention to the continuity of Catholicism and the relevance of the birth of Christianity in the modern world. *L'Otage* (1909), another religious drama, continues in the same vein and is perhaps of even greater literary value. Meanwhile as a prose-writer he had plunged deep into Bergsonian philosophy in *La Connaissance de l'Est* (1895; Eng. trans. 1914), and it took him some time to clear himself of ideas that hindered his full development. With *Corona Benignitatis Anni Dei* (1913) he triumphantly showed that he was a great poet, difficult, however, and for the select, and in 1922 with *Cinq grandes odes* he underlined his poetical powers. The influence of Rimbaud (q.v.) can be traced here. Just before this he had continued *L'Otage* to form of it a trilogy, the second part being *Le Pain dur* (1918) and the third *Le Père humilié* (1919), and had completed the second volume of *Positions et Propositions* (i, 1914; ii, 1921) in which he discussed all the fine arts by the light of his Christian philosophy; while if there was any doubt as to his ability to extend his field in the drama he had just done so in *Le Soulier de satin* (1921), although in this historical play he makes arbitrary use of fact. All this time he had pursued his diplomatic career, having reached the position of ambassador when appointed to Tokyo in 1921, which he exchanged for Washington in 1927 and Brussels in 1933. He died in Paris. *L'Annonce faite à Marie*, *L'Otage* and *Le Soulier de satin* were translated into English in 1916, 1917 and 1931 respectively.

**Claudius, Matthias** (1740–1815), German poet. Born the son of a pastor at Reinfeld, he read law at the University of Jena before dabbling in literary journalism. He wrote much in a simplicity of style which often blinds one to his distinct qualities, such as his power of evoking atmosphere and describing benign nature. A poem of this kind is the famous hymn, known in English as 'We plough the fields and scatter/The good seed on the land', in which a harmonious scene of harvest is laid out before us, and in pietistic guise all men and all things are imperceptibly carrying out the will of God. He became a bank clerk in Altona in 1788 and died at Hamburg. His collected works appeared as *Asmus* (a pseudonym) *omnia sua secum portans oder Sämtliche Werke des Wandsbecker Boten* (another pseudonym) in eight volumes, 1779–1812.

**Claussen, Sophus Niels Christen** (1865–1931), Danish poet and short-

story writer. Born at Helletoft, he spent a good deal of his life in
France, where the symbolists influenced him, but unlike them his
paganism was rabid and fleshly, and what he sought in nature was
not its spirit but its external quality. Characteristic of his books of
verse are *Naturbørn* (1887), *Frøken Regnvejr* (1894), *Danske Vers*
(1912), *Fabler* (1917) and *Heroica* (1925). As a story-teller he is at his
disagreeable best in *Kitty* (1895), *Antonius i Paris* (1896), *Løvetands-
fnug* (1918) and *Foraarstaler* (1927). He died at Gentofte.

**Cocteau, Jean** (1889–1963), French poet, novelist and playwright.
Born of a wealthy bourgeois family at Maisons-Laffitte, he was always
in his youth to be found among the *avant-garde* writers, and remained
a modernist and experimenter until the end of his days. His friendships with Apollinaire (q.v.) and Picasso liberated his powers, and
after a few years of experimentation he seemed to find his path in
*Poésies* (1920), a surrealist collection. Then in 1923 he succeeded with
the novel *Le Grand Écart* (1923; Eng. trans. 1925), following this up
with *Thomas l'imposteur* (1923; Eng. trans 1925), *Les Enfants
terribles* (1929; Eng. trans. 1930), in which he proved his powers as a
psychological writer, and *Opium: Journal d'une désintoxication*
(1930; Eng. trans. *Opium: The Diary of an Addict*, 1932). By this
time his amazing literary agility had appeared in *Orphée* (1927; Eng.
trans. 1933; also film script by Cocteau, 1949; Eng. trans. Oxford
Paperbacks), an early example of ancient mythology reclothed in
modern guise (cf. Giraudoux, q.v., and Anouilh, q.v.) and this time
treated surrealistically, and he exploited this again in *Oedipe-Roi*
(1928; Eng. trans. Oxford Paperbacks) and *Antigone* (1928). In
*Mythologie* (1934) he transferred this way of thinking to poetry.
Meanwhile he had been breaking new ground in the theatre with
*La Voix humaine* (1930; Eng. trans. *The Human Voice*, 1951),
which comes near to being a direct criticism of society, and this
impression is intensified in his next play, *La Machine in-
fernale* (1935; Eng. trans. *The Infernal Machine*, 1936; and Oxford
Paperbacks). After a return to surrealism superimposed on a fable
(*Les Chevaliers de la table ronde*, 1937) he produced a slickly written,
sophisticated, ironical play, *Les Parents terribles* (1938; Eng. trans.
*Intimate Relations*, 1951). He had not abandoned the novel, and
maintained his grasp of it in *Mon premier voyage* (1936; Eng. trans.
*Round the World Again in Eighty Days*, 1937) and *La Fin du Potomak*
(1939). After the war he returned as a playwright with the brilliant
*L'Aigle a deux têtes* (1946; Eng. trans. *The Eagle Has Two Heads*,
1948), and *Bacchus* (1952). His *Poésies* (1948) showed a surprising
development along the lines propounded in his *Poésie critique* (1945).
*La Difficulté d'Être* (1947; Eng. trans. *The Difficulty of Being*, 1967)
is an autobiographical work. He died at Milly-la-Forêt. Always
a somewhat controversial figure, partly on account of his continual
experimentation, and sometimes seeming to prefer mental dexterity
to profundity, there is no doubt that Cocteau has an assured place in
literature, even though exactly what that place is is still uncertain.

**Coelho, Francisco Adolfo** (1847–1921), Portuguese author and philologist. Born in Coimbra, he became professor at Lisbon in 1878 when

he began to gain a reputation for his studies on the Portuguese language. For the general reader his most attractive work is his collection of national folk tales, *Contos populares portuguezes* (1879; Eng. trans. *Tales of Old Lusitania*, 1885). He died in Lisbon.

**Coello, Antonio** (1611–1682), Spanish dramatist, born in Madrid. He became a friend of the great Calderón (q.v.) and collaborated with him in *Yerros de naturaleza* (not publ. till 1930), a theme, on life's being no more than a dream within a dream, to which Calderón triumphantly returned in *La vida es sueño*. Of interest to English readers are Coello's *El conde de Sex*, i.e. Essex (1638), in which he shows much partiality for Queen Elizabeth, surprisingly enough, and *Los empeños de seis horas* (1657), long attributed to Calderón, but now known to be definitely by Coello, which was adapted for the English stage as *The Adventures of Five Hours* (1663) by Sir Samuel Tuke. Coello died in Madrid.

**Colette, Sidonie-Gabrielle** (1873–1954), French novelist. Born at Saint-Sauveur-en-Puysaye in Burgundy, she made use of her experiences as a particularly receptive child in her *Claudine* series (4 vols., 1900–3: *Claudine à l'école, Claudine à Paris, Claudine en ménage* and *Claudine s'en va*), while her sympathy for and understanding of animals reaches the standard of true literature in books like *Dialogues de bêtes* (1904; Eng. trans. *Creatures Great and Small*, 1951). Her divorce from Henri Gauthier-Villars (q.v.) in 1906 forced her to earn her living, which she did as a music-hall dancer. This completely new life led her into new styles of approach to her art; above all she turned to the analysis of human (particularly feminine) passion, as in *L'Ingénue libertine* (1909; Eng. trans. *The Gentle Libertine*, 1931), *La Vagabonde* (1910; Eng. trans. 1931), *L'Envers du music-hall* (1913), *Mitsou* (1919; Eng. trans. 1930) and *Chéri* (1920; Eng. trans. 1951). She returned to childhood and nature, then to the romantic sentimentalized in *La Maison de Claudine* (1922), *Le Blé en herbe* (1923), *L'Enfant et les sortilèges* (1925), *La Fin de Chéri* (1926; Eng. trans. *The Last of Chéri*, 1951), *Sido* (1920; Eng. trans. 1953) and *Ces plaisirs. . . .* (1934). In her latest work there are examples of all her styles, such as are to be found in *Gigi* (1945), *L'Étoile Vesper* (1947), *Le Fanal bleu* (1949) and *Ces dames anciennes* (1954). Her *Œuvres complètes* were published (15 vols.) in 1948–50. She died in Paris.

**Colin Muset** (thirteenth century), French minstrel, of whom nothing is known, not even his true name. About a dozen songs are all that is left of his work, but these are fresh and attractive, and vividly bring before the reader the simple, happy-go-lucky character of the author. See J. Bédier's *Les Chansons de Colin Muset* (1912).

**Collett, Jacobine Camilla** (1813–1895), Norwegian novelist. Born at Kristiansand, the sister of Henrik Wergeland (q.v.), she was brought up in the atmosphere of literary circles, and soon found herself the central figure in the paper war between her brother and the poet Welhaven (q.v.), with whom she fell in love, but who was unable to respond. An aggressive feminist, she turned to the writing of novels with *Amtmandens Døttre* (1855; altered version, 1879). In this and in others, notably in *I de lange Nætter* (1862), she hammers impotently on the door of convention. She died in Kristiania.

**Collin, Heinrich Joseph von** (1772–1811), Austrian dramatist and poet. Born in Vienna, he entered the Austrian civil service in 1795, the while cultivating literature and associating himself with the Hofburgtheater. Owing nothing to Schiller, Collin pursued the pseudo-classical drama, and his first play, the tragedy *Regulus* (1801), uncompromisingly in this style, was an enormous success. His next play, *Coriolan* (1804), impressed Beethoven so much that he wrote an overture for it, but his best work was *Bianca della Porta* (1808), which, however, had only slight success, the Viennese audiences finding it too subtle for their taste after the straight heroics of the earlier works. He joined the Austrian army in the second war against Napoleon (1809), in which year he published his patriotic verse, *Wehrmannslieder*. His *Gedichte* (1812) contain some good ballads. He died in Vienna. His collected works appeared (6 vols.) in 1812–14.

**Collin d'Harleville,** pseudonym of **J.-F. Collin** (1755–1806), French playwright specializing in comedies, was born at Mévoisins, and took up law. The success of his comedy *L'Optimiste* (1788) made him decide to devote himself to writing for the stage, which he did with further plays of the same kind, such as *Châteaux en Espagne* (1789), *M. de Crac dans son petit castel* (1791) and *Le Vieux Célibataire* (1792). His collected works came out in 1805. He died in Paris.

**Collodi,** pseudonym of **Carlo Lorenzini** (1826–1890), Italian writer for children. Born in Florence, he began his literary career as a translator of Perrault's (q.v.) *Contes* (1875), but it was with *Minuzzolo* (1878) that he made his name as a children's author. His famous work and a classic of children's literature is *Le avventure di Pinocchio*, first appearing in the *Giornale dei Bambini* in 1880 as *Storia di un burattino* (Eng. trans. *The Story of a Puppet*, 1892). He died in Florence. His collected works, *Tutto Collodi*, appeared in 1948.

**Colonna, Francesco** (1432?–1527?), Italian Latin prose-writer. His *Hypnerotomachia Poliphili* (written 1479, publ. 1499) is an unusual work containing much architectural allegory. Part of it was translated into English anonymously in 1592 (mod. ed., 1890). Except that Colonna was a Dominican, nothing is known of him personally.

**Colonna, Vittoria** (1492–1525), Italian poet. Born at Marino, she was married in 1509 to Francesco, Marquis of Pescara, whose death inspired her to write the beautiful *Rime spirituali* (mod. ed., 1882; Eng. trans. *The 'In Memoriam' of Italy. A Century of Sonnets from the Poems of Vittoria Colonna*, 1895). She became a close friend of Michelangelo (q.v.). See her correspondence (*Carteggio*), published in full in 1889.

**Columbus, Christopher,** as **Cristóbal Colón** is usually known in English (1447?–1506), born in Genoa, the son of a wool-merchant, he wrote accounts of his four famous voyages in Spanish, which though not his native language, he handled with ability. See *Raccolta colombiana* (ed.

C. de Lollis, 1892; Eng. trans. *Select Documents Illustrating the Four Voyages of Columbus*, Hakluyt Society, 2 vols., 1930–3). Columbus died at Valladolid.

**Comenius (Komenský), Jan Amos** (1592–1670), Czech prose-writer in Czech and Latin, was born of a Moravian family at Uherský Brod, and was sent to Germany to be educated, first at the Calvinist school at Herborn and afterwards at the University of Heidelberg. He was ordained a minister in 1616, having meanwhile returned to Moravia; but in 1621 he was driven from his home by the victorious Imperialists, and spent the rest of his life wandering about Europe (he was in England in 1641), known as the greatest educationalist of his age. From a literary point of view his greatest work is undoubtedly his devotional book in Czech, *Labyrint světa a ráj srdce* (1631; Eng. trans. *The Labyrinth of the World and the Paradise of the Heart*, 1901, second ed., 1951). In the same year appeared *Janua linguarum reserata* (1631; Eng. trans. *Porta linguarum trilinguis, the Gate of Tongues Unlocked and Opened*, 1631), in which he set out his new method of learning languages. In 1650 Prince Sigismund of Hungary invited him to draw up regulations for a new school at Sárospatak, and this gave rise to his writing the first illustrated textbooks for children, *Orbis Sensualium Pictus* (1654). He finally settled in Amsterdam, but died at Naarden.

**Commines, Philippe de** (1445–1511), French prose-writer. Born in the Château de Commines, near Courtrai, in 1463 he entered the court of Charles the Bold of Burgundy, where he prospered, but left in 1472 for the court of Louis XI of France where he prospered still more. The death of Louis, however, in 1483 led to his fall; he was fined and imprisoned and not freed until 1489, when he began his famous account of the reigns of Louis XI and Charles VIII, the *Mémoires*, which, completed in 1498, were published in 1524, when the first part dealing with Louis appeared, the second dealing with Charles following in 1528 (mod. crit. ed. by J. Calmette, 3 vols., 1924–5; Eng. trans. 1897). The *Mémoires* are considered the first historical work in French which is also worthy of being considered as literature. He died at Argenton.

**Compagni, Dino** (1255?–1324), Italian prose-writer. Born in Florence, he became a prosperous merchant and held high civic appointments. He is remembered for his *Cronica* (1310–12; mod. Italian ed., 1910; Eng. trans. *The Chronicle of Dino Compagni*, 1906), a lively and finely written account of the struggle between the Black and White Guelfs (he was a White), 1281–1312. A close friend of Dante, he provides the historical background for Dante's life and the writing of the *Divina Commedia*. He died in Florence.

**Comte, Auguste** (1798–1857), French philosopher. Born at Montpellier, he taught mathematics at the École Polytechnique and later became secretary to Saint-Simon (q.v.), the influence of whom turned him into a philosopher and political theorist. The philosophy, 'Positivism', which he set out in his *Cours de philosophie positive* (6 vols., 1830–42; Eng. trans. (abridged), 2 vols., 1853), his *Système de politique* *positive* (4 vols., 1851–4; Eng. trans. 1875–7) and *Catéchisme positiviste, ou Sommaire-exposition de la religion universelle* (1852; Eng. trans. 1883), had an enormous influence on French, if not European, thought during the third quarter of the nineteenth century. Essentially a philosophy based on science and socialist theory, it held the field during the height of industrial prosperity as a possible corrective of the evils of capitalism and an attempt to enthrone science in the place of religion in an age when the vast new discoveries of science seemed to warrant unqualified optimism. In his last years maintained by a pension from J. S. Mill and other British admirers, he died in Paris.

**Condillac, Étienne Bonnot de Mably de** (1715–1780), French philosophical writer, born of noble family at Grenoble, his education was delayed owing to weak health, but close study and a quiet life, even in Paris, where at one time he occupied the same building as J.-J. Rousseau (q.v.), led to his ability eventually to found his own philosophical system, 'Sensationalism', one of the few enduring schools derived from Locke. He expresses his ideas, for example, that the deciding force which creates the personality is not innate but is the result of the experience of sensations, in *Essai sur l'origine des connoissances humaines* (1746), his most important book, *Traité des systèmes* (1749), and *Traité des sensations* (1754). His collected works were first published in 1798. He was also a friend of Diderot (q.v.) and contributed to the *Encyclopédie*. Tutor to the Duke of Parma (1758–67), he was made *abbé commendataire* of Mureaux, which meant that he appeared in clerical attire, but was to all intents and purposes a layman. He died on his estate at Flux, near Beaugency.

**Condorcet, Marie-Jean-Antoine-Nicolas Caritat de** (1743–1794), French prose-writer of the Enlightenment, was born of noble family at Ribemont, near St Quentin, and had a brilliant academic career. For a mathematical treatise he was elected to the Academy in 1765, becoming perpetual secretary of it in 1777 and inspector-general of the mint. A disciple of Voltaire, whose literary executor he became, in which capacity he was responsible for the definitive edition of his works, and a friend of Turgot and Quesnay, the physiocrats, and D'Alembert (q.v.) and Diderot (q.v.), the Encyclopaedists, he took part in the *Encyclopédie*. At the outbreak of the revolution he became a prominent figure, and in 1792 was elected president of the Legislative Assembly; but he fell with the Girondins, and after eight months in hiding, during which time he composed his most durable work, *Esquisse d'un tableau historique des progrès de l'esprit humain* (1794; pocket ed., 1819), in which he demands political and civil equality between the sexes and proclaims (the idea stemming from Shaftesbury) the unlimited perfectibility of humanity, he was discovered and arrested at Bourg-la-Reine outside Paris, dying of poison, taken at the moment of arrest, a few hours later. The standard edition of his works is that of 1847–9 (12 vols.).

**Conrad of Würzburg** (*d.* 1287), German poet. Born at Würzburg, he spent a good deal of his middle life in Strassburg, but died at Basel. Little is known of him beyond his works. Of these most noteworthy are the devotional poem on the Virgin, *Die goldene Schmiede*, and the unfinished epic on the Trojan war, *Der trojanische Krieg*. Of his shorter narrative poems the most readable is *Engelhart und Engeltrut*.

**Conscience, Hendrik** (1812–1883), Flemish novelist. Born in Antwerp, he took part in the Belgian revolution for independence from the Netherlands in 1830. Thereafter a senior civil servant, he wrote voluminously and was the chief exponent of the revival of Flemish letters. He gained a European popularity in his day as above all an historical novelist, and his 'complete works' appeared in English in 1867 (the Fr. trans., 1854–88, fills 71 vols.). His reputation has greatly faded, but *De Leeuw van Vlaenderen* (1838, 'The Lion of Flanders'), about the Battle of the Golden Spurs, is still very readable, and to a lesser extent *Jacob van Artevelde* (1849). He died in Brussels.

**Constant de Rebecque, Henri Benjamin** (1767–1830), French novelist and general prose-writer. Born in Lausanne of French Huguenot ancestry, he was educated in Britain and Germany, settling down in Paris in 1795 to live by his pen. Soon he was dabbling in politics, but for criticizing Bonaparte was exiled in 1802. He now joined forces with another exile, Madame de Staël (q.v.), and travelled with her in Germany and Italy, and it was due to her intellectual stimulus that he changed from a dilettante to a serious student of comparative religion, which was later to bear fruit in *De la religion* (5 vols., 1824–31), an important contribution to the subject. He next settled in Göttingen, having in the meantime (1808) married as his second wife a member of Novalis's (q.v.) family. Enabled to return to Paris on Napoleon's fall in 1814, he soon published the work for which he is best known, the novel *Adolphe* (1816; Eng. trans. 1951), a remarkable study of the opposing forces of sensual love and reason, a conflict which Constant, who had been born in the age of reason but had lived into the romantic era, must have known so well. After some dexterous changing of sides to suit Napoleon's return and then the Bourbons', he became a deputy in 1819 and leader of the Liberal opposition. His political opinions are to be seen in the collection of his political writings, *Œuvres politiques* (1870). His *Journaux intimes*, first printed in their entirety only in 1952, help to build up a complete picture of the man, for which *Le Cahier rouge* (1907; Eng. trans. *The Red Note-Book*, 1948) is an ancillary. He died in Paris.

**Conti, Antonio** (1677–1749), Italian dramatist, poet and essayist, born in Padua, was another of the many literary *abati* of the day. A friend of Leibniz (q.v.) and Newton, a student of Plato and Shakespeare, and a translator of Virgil and Pope, he is to be remembered for his majestic 'adaptation' of Shakespeare's *Julius Caesar* and for his own three sonorous tragedies in the manner of Shakespeare (or is it not rather P. Corneille?), *Giunio Bruto*, *Marco Bruto* and *Druso*. The four were published as *Tragedie* in 1751. There were two collections of his *Prose e poesie*, the first in 1739 and the second in 1756. He died in Padua.

**Coolus, Romain** (1868–1952), French playwright, also calling himself **René Weil**, was born at Rennes. Among his plays, notorious for their unconventionality, especially as regards love and sex, may be numbered *L'Enfant Chérie* (1906), *Cœur à cœur* (1907), *L'Éternel Masculin* (1920) and *La Guêpe* (1931). He died in Paris.

Coppée, Francis-Joachim-Édouard-François (1842–1907), French poet, dramatist and prose-writer. Born in humble circumstances in Paris, he obtained a mediocre post in the Ministry of Foreign Affairs, an office he held until 1878 when he was appointed archivist to the Comédie Française. He had already gained notice with his play *Le Passant* (1869) in which Sarah Bernhardt acted, and in the following years he gained a great reputation as a poet, ringing the changes on patriotism, sympathy with the humble, and the sentimental singing of pure love in the idiom of the Parnassians. Such books of poetry were *Les Poèmes modernes* (1869), *Les Humbles* (1872), *Le Cahier rouge* (1874), *Pour le drapeau* (1883), *Les Paroles sincères* (1890), *Les Vrais Riches* (1892) and *Prière pour la France* (1900). Further plays, all couched in romantic style, were *Severo Torelli* (1884) and *Pour la couronne* (1895). His overpowering patriotism led him into a disagreeable position over the Dreyfus affair, from which he extricated himself with difficulty. His *Souvenirs* (7 vols., 1890–1910) are interesting if prolix. He died in Paris.

Corbière, Édouard Joachim, but using Tristan as his Christian name (1845–1875), French poet, born near Ploujean (Finistère). His stern, rough poetry set in Brittany is the result of a conscious turning against romanticism, and is to be found in *Les Amours jaunes* (1873; new eds. with additions 1891 and 1912). The verse is, however, far from objective, for there is the ever-present cry of the problem of the mind and heart of the individual divided against itself. Corbière died at Morlaix.

Corneille, Pierre (1606–1684), French dramatist. Born in Rouen of an old legal family prominent in Normandy, he became an advocate in 1624, but owing to his stammering he abandoned all idea of appearing at the Bar, and instead bought judicial posts in Rouen which provided him with sinecures. Interested already in the stage, he went in 1629 to Paris with the manuscript of his comedy *Mélite*, already successfully performed in his native city. It met with such success in the capital that Corneille decided to stay there, and in quick succession he produced *La Veuve* (1631), *La Galérie du palais* (1632), *La Suivante* (1632) and *La Place royale* (1633), all comedies these, and the tragicomedy, *Clitandre* (1631). He was now patronized by Richelieu, who made him one of his 'five poets' who were to write plays, often containing propaganda in favour of his policy, on plots laid down by himself; but the association did not last long, for the cardinal dismissed the young man who refused to submit to his demands. Then came his attempt at full tragedy with *Médée* (1635), a work far in advance of anything he had written before. *L'Illusion comique* (1636), a return to comedy, showed clearly that it was tragedy that was his forte. This was abundantly proved when *Le Cid* (in fact a tragicomedy) was played in 1637. It was an immense success, and was followed by four great full tragedies, *Horace* (1640), founded on the story of the ancient Roman family of the Horatii, *Cinna* (1641), *Polyeucte* (1642) and *La Mort de Pompée* (1643), in them reaching the height of his achievement. Whereas *Le Cid* is Spanish in design and feeling, being after all adapted to a large extent from Guillén de Castro's (q.v.) *Mocedades del Cid*, the four Roman tragedies are the prime examples of French classical heroic drama. When he returned to comedy for a moment with *Le Menteur* (1643) and *La Suite du Menteur* (1644), his best comedies and the finest before Molière (q.v.), Corneille again showed his affinity with the Spanish stage, *Le Menteur* being an adaptation of Alarcón's (q.v.) *La verdad sospechosa*, *La Suite* of Lope de Vega's (q.v.) *Amar sin saber a quién*. His love for complicated Spanish plots had so far proved an excellent foil for his stark tragedies, but when from now on he began to mix his two kinds of writing he destroyed himself. Already in *Rodogune* (1645) melodrama is creeping in, and the integrity of the heroic is being tempered with intrigue. In *Théodore vierge et martyre* (1645), *Héraclius* (1647), *Nicomède* (1651) and the tragi-comedies *Don Sanche d'Aragon* (1649) and *Andromède* (1650), not only are the plots so involved that the action is held up or at least diffused and weakened, but there is a steady falling off in poetical quality. *Pertharite* (1652) was damned, and Corneille, who since his marriage in 1640 had lived for the greater part of his time in Rouen, remained there entirely until 1662, when he settled in Paris for the rest of his life. He occupied his time until 1659 in study and religious meditation—he had made a translation of Kempis (q.v.) as *L'Imitation de Jésus-Christ* in 1651— before he set about winning the ground he had forfeited in the theatre with the tragedy *Œdipe* (1659) and the tragi-comedy *La Toison d'or* (1660). He had, however, lost his public for good, and when the launching of further tragedies such as *Othon* (1664), *Attila* (1667) and *Tite et Bérénice* (1670) ended in failure, he was reduced to providing Lulli with opera libretti. For one of these, *Psyché* (1671), he joined forces with Molière and Quinault (q.v.). His last play was *Suréna* (1674). He had already lived to see Racine supersede him for pride of place as France's greatest dramatist, and domestic sorrow and a steep decline in his monetary fortune spread a gloom over his last years. Had Corneille retired from the dramatic field in 1650 his reputation would have remained far higher; even so, if he is judged by his half-dozen great works, he is worthy to be called the finest author of heroic tragedy of the French stage. His heroes express nobility of soul in magnificent rhetoric, which can rise beyond dignified declamation to the highest poetry. Will triumphs over all the powers of adversity; love must be sacrificed when it is a question of duty. His style of writing forces him to play for high stakes or fail; there is no middle way, and he can descend to empty bombast. At his best, however, he is incomparable. See *Œuvres complètes* (13 vols., 1862–8) and *Théâtre complet* (2 vols., 1934). L. Lockert's *Corneille. The Chief Plays* (1952) contains good English translations of *Le Cid*, *Horace*, *Cinna*, *Polyeucte*, *Rodogune* and *Nicomède*.

**Corneille, Thomas** (1625–1709), French dramatist. Born in Rouen, a younger brother of Pierre (q.v.), he began his career as an author with a number of plays of intrigue derived from Spanish plots such as *Les Engagements du hasard* (1647), *Le Feint Astrologue* (1648),

*Bertrand de Cigaral* (1650) and *Les Illustres Ennemies* (1654), before turning to tragedy with *Timocrate* (1656), *La Mort d'Annibal* (1669) and *Ariane* (1672), all great successes. Appointed to replace Molière on the latter's death as playwright to the royal troupe, he turned more and more towards the writing of opera libretti for Lulli and other composers; such are *La Divineresse* (1679) and *Le Berger extravagant* (1690), although *Maximian* (1691) is a return to classical tragedy. His later years were given up to heavy lexicographical work such as his *Dictionnaire des termes d'art et de science* (1694) and *Dictionnaire universel géographique et historique* (1708). He died at Les Andelys. His collected plays appear in *Œuvres des deux Corneille* (1860).

**Cornelius, Peter** (1824–1874), German dramatist and poet. Born in Mainz, the nephew of Peter von Cornelius, the artist, he became a musical protégé of Liszt at Weimar and wrote the words and music for his opera *Der Barbier von Bagdad* (1858; Eng. trans. 1925), produced and conducted by Liszt himself. It failed, however, and in disgust Cornelius went to Vienna where, and afterwards at Munich, he remained under the influence of Wagner (q.v.). His sonnet cycle, *Ein Sonettenkranz für Frau Rosa von Milde* (1859), proves that he was much more at home as a lyric poet. He died in Mainz. His collected works were published (4 vols.) in 1904.

**Corral, Pedro del** ( *fl.* 1403), Spanish novelist, of whom little or nothing is known beyond the fact that his novel *Crónica del rey don Rodrigo*, about Roderick the Goth and the invasion of Spain by the Moors, appeared between 1400 and 1404. It was first published in 1511, and is the source of all the ' Roderick ' literature which came to full flower during the early nineteenth-century romantic era.

**Cossa, Pietro** (1830–1881), Italian dramatist, born in Rome. With an excellent knowledge of stagecraft he had great success with his earlier plays from *Mario e i Cimbri* (1860) to *Puschkin* (1870) in spite of their lack of historical feeling. But with *Nerone* (1871) he became far more objective, his analysis of character improved, and he allowed his plots to conform to historical fact. Among his later plays are *Lodovico Ariosto e gli Estensi* (1875), *Giuliano l'Apostata* (1876) and *I Borgia* (1877). He died in Leghorn.

**Costa i Llobera, Miquel** (1854–1922), Catalan poet, born at Pollenza, Majorca, the best of the Majorcan writers, was a priest who became canon of Palma Cathedral. His inspiration lay in the ancient classical world of the Mediterranean, and he expressed himself in Pindaric and Horatian metrical forms, proving how well Catalan fits them. Among his books of poetry there should be named : *Poesies catalanes* (1885), *Líriques* (1899), *Tradicions i fantasies* (1903), *Horacianes* (1906) and *Visions de Palestina* (1908). He died in Palma.

**Costa y Martínez, Joaquín** (1846–1911), Spanish prose-writer. Born at Monzón, he became famous in later years as one of the leaders of the disillusioned ' Generation of '98 ', who, having seen Spain that year lose the last remnants of her American empire, realized that she must be at all costs regenerated as a European power. His *Obras*

(5 vols., 1911–15), written in a strong, vivid style, are a good example of Spanish prose of the period. In his insistence that his country must become fully part of the European community and forget her Moorish background, he had great influence on the younger generation, including Unamuno (q.v.). Costa died at Graus.

**Coster, Charles Théodore Henry de** (1827–1879), Belgian prose-writer. Born in Munich, where his father held a temporary position, the family soon afterwards returned to Belgium. As a young man he was foremost among those eager to revive Flemish literature, and with *Légendes flamandes* (1857) and *La Légende d'Ulenspiegel* (1867; Eng. trans. 1943) he may be said to have originated the national movement which had such a splendid run for two generations afterwards. Always in poor circumstances, a badly paid but regular post in the civil service came too late to help him. *Le Mariage de Toulet* was published in the year of his death in Brussels. C. Potvin (q.v.) edited and published his *Lettres à Éliza* in 1894.

**Coster, Dirk** (1887–1956), Dutch prose-writer and playwright. Born at Delft, he became a literary journalist, leading the way to a new psychological and religious approach to criticism in *De nieuwe europeesche Geest in Kunst en Letteren* (1920). Two volumes of *Verzameld Proza* followed in 1925–7. His *Marginalia* (2 vols., 1919, 1929) when translated into English (2 vols., 1929–30) exerted a wide influence. A later work is the play *Het leven en sterven van Willem van Oranje* (1948).

**Cottin, Sophie,** *née* **Ristaud** (1773–1807), French novelist. Born at Tonneins (Lot-et-Garonne), she was left a widow at twenty and turned to letters for a living. Among her books may be listed *Claire d'Albe* (1799), *Mathilde* (1805) and her best, *Élisabeth, ou les Exilés de Sibérie* (1806). She died in Paris.

**Couperus, Louis** (1863–1923), Dutch novelist. Born in The Hague, he became a journalist, first in Java and then in Amsterdam, gaining a European reputation with his novels, some in a contemporary setting and others historical. Of the first kind *Eline Vere* (1889; Eng. trans. 1892), *Nordlot* (1891; Eng. trans. *The Law Inevitable*, 1921), *De stille Kracht* (1900; Eng. trans. *The Hidden Force*, 1922) and *De Boeken der kleine Zielen* (4 vols., 1901–4; Eng. trans. *Small Souls*, 1914–20), the last a family history, are the best. Of the second kind *De Komedianten* (1917; Eng. trans. *The Comedians*, 1926) should be named. *Majesteit* (1893; Eng. trans. *Majesty*, 1894) is a fantasy without parallel in his other writings. He died at De Steeg.

**Courier de Méré, Paul-Louis** (1773–1825), French writer. Born in Paris, he entered the army, settling in Florence in 1809 after being severely wounded at the Battle of Wagram. He had not been long in Florence before a quarrel with the Laurentian librarian over the authenticity of a classical manuscript led to his writing that masterpiece of irony *Lettre à Monsieur Renouard* (1810). He returned to Paris in 1812, and in 1814 settled on his estate at Varetz in Touraine, and two years later he published an exposure of the sufferings of the peasants, his *Pétition aux deux Chambres*. From this time on he was an unsparing critic of the Bourbon regime, and gained almost the position of national hero with his brilliant condemnation of court extravagance, *Simple Discours de Paul Louis, Vigneron de la Chavonnière* (1821). For this he was imprisoned for a time and got to know Béranger (q.v.), who was in a similar plight. His pungent pamphlets have been compared with Swift's *Drapier's Letters*. He was murdered by his gamekeeper.

**Courouble, Léopold** (1861–1937), Belgian novelist. Born in Brussels, he wrote about lower middle-class life in the capital with a keen eye for human oddity, usually of the pleasantly amusing kind, in such books as *La Famille Kaekebroek* (1902), *Pauline Platbrood* (1903), *Les Noces d'or de Monsieur et de Madame van Poppel* (1905) and *Prosper Claes* (1929). He died in Brussels.

**Courteline, Georges,** pseudonym of **Georges Moineaux** (1858–1929), French novelist and writer of short stories. Born in Tours, the son of a journalist, he soon found his way into the literary life, and played with humour over the weaknesses of the civil service, army and law in, among many others, the following: *Les Gaîtés de l'escadron* (1866), *Messieurs les Ronds-de-cuir* (1893), *Un Client sérieux* (1897), *Le Miroir concave* (1901), *Les Linottes* (1912) and *La Philosophie de Georges Courteline* (1917). His *Œuvres complètes* were published (13 vols.) in 1925–7. He died in Paris.

**Cousin, Victor** (1792–1867), French prose-writer. Born in Paris, he became assistant in philosophy to Royer-Collard at the University of France, where between 1815 and 1821, when he was deprived of his post by the government for liberalism, he revolutionized French philosophy by introducing the ideas of Kant (q.v.), Fichte (q.v.), Schelling (q.v.) and Hegel (q.v.) into his lectures and thereby making an end of the moribund ideas of the eighteenth-century materialistic school. Reinstated in 1827, he became the idol of the intellectuals of 1830 and the Academy's apologist for Louis Philippe's regime. He was made a peer of France in 1832, and later held a key post in the Ministry of Public Instruction. The works by which his influence spread were *Cours d'histoire de la philosophie* (1826; new ed., 1863), *Fragments philosophiques* (1826; new ed., 1847–8) and *Du vrai, du beau et du bien* (1836; new ed., 1853). Although he welcomed the revolution of 1848, he could not keep pace with it, and the following year he dropped out of politics. He afterwards lived in seclusion in his rooms in the Sorbonne, but died at Cannes.

**Creangă, Ioan** (1837–1890), Rumanian short-story writer. Born at Humulesti in Moldavia, a peasant's son, he became a clergyman, but soon turned to teaching. Between 1875 and 1882 he published his artless but wholly charming peasant tales in the literary periodical *Convorbiri Literare*. They were collected in two volumes, the first *Povestii* (1890; Eng. trans. of some, *Old Nichifor the Impostor*, 1921; and *Recollections and Other Tales*, 1930), and the second *Amînţiri din copilărie* (1892; Eng. trans. *Recollections and Other Tales*, 1930). The most popular and most national author of Rumania, he died at Jassy.

**Crébillon, Claude Prosper Jolyot de** (1707–1777), French novelist and short-story writer, was born in Paris, the son of Prosper (q.v.), and lived all his life there. His writings, which include *L'Écumoire* (1733), *Les Égarements du cœur et de l'esprit* (1736; Eng. trans. *The Wayward Head and Heart*), *Le Sopha* (1745), his best known, *La Nuit et la moment* (1755) and *Le Hasard du coin du feu* (1763), are licentious, brilliantly witty and of impeccable style. *Le Sopha* is known as 'the most elegantly immoral of all French books'.

**Crébillon, Prosper Jolyot de** (1674–1762), French dramatist, was born at Dijon and became an advocate, settling in Paris in 1695. While practising he spent all his spare time at the theatre and gradually gained entrance into theatrical circles. At length he launched out as a dramatist on his own account with *Idoménée* (1705), the first of his nine heavy bombastic tragedies, the others, coming out at increasingly long intervals, being *Atrée et Thyeste* (1707), *Électre* (1709), *Rhadamiste et Zénobie* (1711), *Xerxès* (1714), *Sémiramis* (1717), *Pyrrhus* (1726), *Catalina* (1748), a great success, and *Le Triumvirat* (1754). After the early death of his wife in 1711 he had lived as a semi-recluse, but held various official appointments, among them that of royal censor, in which capacity he came into collision with Voltaire. A genial, homely man, he died in Paris. He was the father of C. P. J. de Crébillon (q.v.) of whose writings and escapades alike he disapproved. His works appeared (3 vols.) in 1819 and (1 vol.) in 1895.

**Creutz, Gustaf Filip** (1731–1785), Swedish man of letters. Born of noble family at Anjalagård, Finland, he had a brilliant political career as a trusted friend of King Gustav III. He moved freely in European literary circles, particularly in France. His rococo idyll, *Atis och Camilla* (1761), is the best poem of its kind in the whole range of Swedish literature. He died in Stockholm.

**Croce, Benedetto** (1866–1952), Italian prose-writer. Born at Pescasseroli, in Aquila, he was orphaned early, was sent to school in Naples and entered the University of Rome. Returning to Naples in 1886 he devoted himself to study and to literary journalism, resulting in his founding of the notable literary journal *La Critica* (1903), and the writing of his great contribution to philosophy and aesthetics, *La filosofia dello spirito* (4 vols., 1902–12; Eng. trans., 4 vols., 1903–21; vol. i rev., 1922), in which he makes a distinction between logic and intuition and beauty and aesthetics, and in which he insists on the intuitiveness of art. His reputation was Europe-wide as a philosopher. Of his literary and historical works the most noteworthy, written in a careful, sometimes dignified style, sometimes, however, failing in clarity, are *La poesia di Dante* (1920; Eng. trans. 1922), *Poesia e non poesia* (1923), *La storia d'Italia dal 1871 al 1915* (1929; Eng. trans. 1929), and *La storia d'Europa nel secolo XIX* (1932; Eng. trans. 1934). He was made a senator in 1910, was minister of public instruction (1920–1), went into opposition when Mussolini appeared on the scene and retired from politics, but came forward again after 1945. He died in Naples.

**Croisset, Francis de**, pseudonym of **Francis Wiener** (1877–1937), French playwright and travel-writer, the plays, consisting of such as

*L'Épervier* (1914), *L'Éphémère* (1919) and *Le Vol nuptial* (1932), being society comedies, and the travel-books like *La Féerie cinghalaise* (1926) being penetrating accounts of his journeys in many parts of the world. He was born in Brussels and died in Paris.

**Crommelynck, Fernand** (1888–    ), Belgian playwright, born in Brussels. He followed his father as an actor and gained a thorough knowledge of stagecraft which he put to good use in *Nous n'irons plus au bois* (1906), *Le Sculpteur des masques* (1908), *Le Cocu magnifique* (1921; Eng. trans. *The Magnificent Cuckold*, 1966), later made into an excellent film by Jean-Louis Barrault, *Tripes d'or* (1930), and *Une Femme qui a le cœur trop petit* (1934). He is caustic, brusque, but a good stylist. Since the war he has written two novels, *Là est la question* (1947) and *Monsieur Larose, est-il l'assassin?* (1950).

**Cros, Charles** (1842–1888), French poet. Born in Fabrezan, he soon went to Paris, where he led a dissolute existence, writing a volume of weird prose-poems, *Le Coffret de Santal* (1873), the result of mental derangement, but in parts beautiful. He was the inventor of colour photography and of the phonograph, but his ideas were stolen by others and he profited little or nothing. He died in Paris. See *Poèmes et Proses* (1944). His work led directly to the symbolists.

**Cruz Cano y Olmedilla, Ramón de la** (1731–1794), Spanish playwright. A lifelong inhabitant of Madrid, where he found protection in the houses of the great, he made a reputation with his short one-act plays (*sainetes*), which tell us much of the everyday life of the city. Among the best are *El fandango del candil* and *Manolo*. One of them, *La presumida burlada*, is to be found as *Pride's Fall* in *Spanish One-Act Plays* (1934).

**Cueva, Juan de la** (1550?–1610), Spanish poet and dramatist. Born in Seville, he went out to Mexico in 1574, but returned to Seville three years later and remained there for the rest of his life, living by authorship. He wrote many blood-and-thunder plays, of which fourteen are extant, the best known being *El infamador*, acted about 1580. His plays were first printed in 1583. As a poet he wrote an epic, *La conquista de la Bética* (1603), and a kind of *Ars Poetica—El ejemplar poético* (1606). His influence on Lope de Vega (q.v.) is undoubted.

**Cuoco, Vincenzo** (1770–1823), Italian prose-writer. Born in Civitacampomarano, he took a leading part in the anti-Bourbon revolution of 1799 in the Kingdom of Naples, and was for a time in exile in Milan where he wrote his valuable *Saggio storico sulla rivoluzione napoletana del 1799* (1801), another milestone on the road of the Risorgimento. His chief work is *Platone in Italia* (1804–6), in which a description of Italy (supposedly from a long-lost Greek manuscript of Plato) is made the means of appealing to his countrymen to struggle for the freedom of a land with such a glorious past. He was later allowed to return to Naples, where he died. His *Opere* appeared (5 vols.) in 1924.

**Curel, François de** (1854–1928), French dramatist and novelist. Born in Metz, he became a civil engineer, and it was not till 1885 that he stood forward as a man of letters with the novel *L'Été des fruits secs*. In 1892 he entered the lists as a playwright with *L'Envers d'une sainte*. *L'Invitée* (1893) shows a deepening concern with social problems, and this preoccupation led to *Le Repas du lion* (1897), on the capital and labour conflict. Other pre-war plays were *La Fille sauvage* (1902), *Le Coup d'aile* (1906) and *La Danse devant le miroir* (1914). After the war he turned to problems of the post-war generation in such plays as *La Viveuse et le moribond* (1926). He died in Paris.

**Cyrano de Bergerac, Savinien** (1619–1655), French prose-writer and playwright. Born in Paris, he was educated at the Collège Beauvais in the University of Paris, the master of which college was to inspire his comedy *Le Pédant joué* (1654), which suggested to Molière his *Fourberies de Scapin*. Cyrano led a wandering, almost vagabond, existence—his time spent as a royal guard lasted less than two years and came to an abrupt end—fighting a number of duels, most of them, it is said, to avenge the insults from which he suffered on account of his enormous nose. His tragedy, *La Mort d'Agrippine* (1653), was neither better nor worse than the average play of its time. It is, however, as the author of the two fantastic satirical stories, *L'Autre Monde, ou Les États et Empires de la lune* (1657; Eng. trans. *Other Worlds, the Comical History of the States and Empires of the Moon and the Sun*, Oxford Library of French Classics) and *Les États et Empires du soleil* (1662; the two included in the mod. ed. *Œuvres libertines de Cyrano de Bergerac*, 2 vols., 1921), that he has lasted. Showing the influence of Lucian and Ariosto (q.v.), they suggested more than hints to Voltaire (q.v.) for his *Micromégas*, to Swift for *Gulliver's Travels* and to Jules Verne (q.v.). He died in Paris. The romantic hero of E. Rostand's (q.v.) play has little to do with the real man.

# D

**Dabit, Eugène** (1908–1936), French novelist. Born in Paris in lowly circumstances, he worked at simple trades until taken up by Gide (q.v.), with whom he went on a visit to Russia, there dying at Sebastopol. He crowded into his short life a host of novels set in Paris, such as *L'Hôtel du Nord* (1929; Eng. trans. 1931), *Petit-Louis* (1930), *Villa Oasis* (1932) *Faubourgs de Paris* (1933), *L'Île* (1934), *La Zone verte* (1935) and *Trains de vies* (1936). His self-revelatory *Journal intime, 1928–1936*, was published in 1939.

**Dacier, Anne Lefèvre** (1654–1720), French translator, was born at Saumur, and became so excellent a classical scholar that she was employed as the part-editor with her husband André Dacier of the Delphin Classics. She produced an accomplished prose translation of the *Iliad* (1699), and made successful translations into French from the work of Aristophanes, Sappho, Plautus and Terence. She took some part in the famous and Europe-wide controversy about the relative merits of ancient and modern learning. She died in Paris.

**Da Costa, Isaak** (1798–1860), Dutch poet. Born of Jewish parents in Amsterdam, he became one of the foremost representatives of the romantic movement in the Netherlands with his *Poëzy* in 1822, in which year he became a Christian. He died in Amsterdam.

**Dagerman, Stig** (1923–1954), Swedish playwright and novelist, born at Älvkarleby, became a leading exponent of new literary treatment of the theme of man's fear of life. His best works were his plays, *Den dödsdömde* (1947; Eng. trans. *The Man Condemned to Die*, 1950) and *Judas dramer* (1949), and the novel *Bränt barn* (1948; Eng. trans. *A Burnt Child*, 1950). He died in Stockholm.

**Dahn, Julius Sophus Felix** (1834–1912), German novelist and poet. Born in Hamburg, son of the actor Friedrich Dahn, he was appointed professor of jurisprudence at Königsberg in 1872 and held the equivalent chair at Breslau from 1888 to 1910, being rector of that university from 1895. Besides his academic works he wrote poetry and several rather heavy historical novels (cf. Georg Ebers, q.v.), the best *Ein Kampf um Rom* (4 vols., 1876; Eng. trans. 1878). He died in Breslau.

**D'Alembert,** *see* **Alembert.**

**Dalin, Olof von** (1708–1763), Swedish poet. Born in Halland in the south of Sweden, he became a civil servant in 1726, giving much of his spare time to authorship. His first book of significance is the satire

*Saga om Hasten* (1738), dealing with the history of Sweden from Gustavus Vasa to Charles XII. His most ambitious work was the epic *Svenska Friheten* (1742). Tutor to the crown prince and ennobled, he was suddenly banished in 1756 on an unfounded charge of conspiracy. Reinstated in 1761, he died at Drottningholm.

**Dall'Ongaro, Francesco** (1808–1873), Italian poet and dramatist. Born at Oderzo, near Friuli, he became a priest, but renounced his Orders and founded a liberal newspaper, *Favillon*, in Trieste. In 1840 he published *Poesie*, full of *stornelli italiani* (patriotic songs in dialect), and between then and 1848 these and others were on the lips of Garibaldi and his followers. Having fought with Garibaldi in 1848 he fled to Switzerland, but was able to return in 1860 and was appointed to a professorship in the University of Naples. In 1861 he published his best drama, *Il Fornaretto*, a tragedy. His *Fantasie drammatiche e liriche* appeared in 1866. He died in Naples.

**D'Ambra, Lucio** (1880–1940), Italian novelist, short-story writer and playwright. Born in Rome, where he died, he became identified with the Fascist movement, and was a prolific author in all departments of literature except poetry. His best work belongs to his last years, the novels, *L'ombra dell' amore* (1938) and *Il carro di fuoco* (1940), the collection of short stories, *Fantasie davanti a Palazzo Dario* (1939) and the plays, *Solitudine* (1936) and *Mazarino* (1937).

**Dancourt, Florent Carton** (1661–1725), French writer of comedies, was born at Fontainebleau. He became an actor, joining the Comédie Française in 1685. Following in Molière's footsteps, though far behind him, he wrote a number of attractive, sunny comedies of manners, including *Le Chevalier à la mode* (1687), *Les Bourgeoises à la mode* (1693), *Les Bourgeoises de qualité* (1700) and *Le Diable boiteux* (1707), which by an extraordinary coincidence was acted the very same year that Lesage's (q.v.) novel of the same title was published. Both are derived from *El diablo cojuelo* by L. Vélez de Guevara (q.v.). Dancourt died at Courcelles-le-Roi (Loiret). His complete works came out (12 vols.) in 1760; his *Théâtre choisi* (5 vols.) in 1884.

**Danilevsky, Grigory Petrovich** (1829–1890), Russian novelist. Born in the province of Kharkov, he is the author of two good examples of historical fiction: *Knyazhna Tarakanova* (1883; Eng. trans. *Princess Tarakanova*, 1891) and *Sozhzhonnaya Moskva* (1886; Eng. trans. *Moscow in Flames*, 1917). He died in Petersburg.

**D'Annunzio, Gabriele** (1863–1938), Italian poet, dramatist and novelist. Born of noble family at Pescara, he was early on attracted to literature, and took for his models Carducci (q.v.) for verse and Verga (q.v.) for prose. His first works were the prose *Terra vergine* (1882), and the books of poetry *Canto nuovo* (1882) and *Intermezzo di rime* (1883). After that, for a time, he was on the staff of the *Tribuna* in Rome. There followed a volume of short stories, *San Pantaleone* (1886), in which he imitated Maupassant (q.v.), while in the novel *L'innocente* (1892) the influence of Russian literature is notable. *Odi navali* (1893) is nationalistic in tone. The works of Nietzsche (q.v.) had by this time come to make a great impression on him, and this is particularly noticeable in the novels *Il trionfo della morte* (1894; Eng. trans. *The Triumph of Death*, 1898) and *Le vergini delle rocce* (1896; Eng. trans. *The Virgins of the Rocks*, 1899), both of which led to his reputation being established outside Italy. He next essayed the drama, and in a verse play with a strong love element, *Sogno di un tramontano d'autunno* (1898), he succeeded. His liaison with the great actress Eleonora Duse had already begun, and she is pictured as the heroine of the erotic novel *Il fuoco* (1900), but pure love was the theme of *La Gioconda* (1898) in which Duse had already acted. Then came the epic *La canzone di Garibaldi* (1901), but it was in 1904 that in *La figlia di Jorio* he wrote his masterpiece. The poetry of this drama revealed new untapped beauties in Italian, besides clearing away at one stroke a good deal of the deadly verbiage which hangs over so much Italian writing. In *Canzone e orazione in morte di Carducci* (1907) he pays homage to his poetic master. From about this time he began to write more and more lyric poetry, collected and published post-humously as *Laudi* (1939), and it may well be that this constitutes his most lasting creation. With the entry of Italy into the First World War on the side of the Allies in 1915 D'Annunzio the patriot sprang to practical activity. He served bravely in the Italian Air Force, losing an eye, and created an incident of international importance when in 1919, dissatisfied with the Peace Conference for not bestowing Fiume on Italy, he occupied the town and declared that it had been annexed by his country. He afterwards occupied Zara in the same way, and had to be dislodged by troops from the central Italian government. This and his subsequent activities during Mussolini's Fascist regime, of which he heartily approved, have nothing to do with literature; but it damaged his literary abilities, or perhaps he had already said most of what he had to say. He died at Gardone on the Italian Riviera, and in the year of his death the Italian Government's official edition of his works, begun in 1927, was brought to an end in forty-nine volumes. See also *Tutto il teatro* (2 vols., 1940–1) and *Prose di romanzi* (2 vols., 1940–1).

**Dantas, Júlio** (1876–1962), Portuguese playwright, born at Lagos. His plays, such as *A ceia dos cardeais* (1902; Eng. trans. *The Cardinals' Collation*, 1927) and *Rosas de todo o ano* (1907; Eng. trans. *Roses All Year Round*, 1912), very popular in their day because well constructed, are superficial and have greatly dated. Yet at the turn of the century Dantas was the best-known Portuguese dramatist in Europe. Twice Minister for Instruction and twice Minister for Foreign Affairs under the Republic before Salazar, he died in Lisbon.

**Dante Alighieri** (1265–1321), Italian poet and prose-writer, writing also in Latin, born in Florence of an old but impoverished family, tracing its descent from a certain Cacciaguida, a knight of the second crusade. By the time he was eighteen both his parents were dead, but he had from his earliest years, in spite of lack of fortune, moved among the Florentine *élite*, his most valued friendship being that with Cavalcanti (q.v.) who encouraged his first poetic attempts. By 1287 he had completed a course at Bologna University, but soon entered the Florentine army and served in the cavalry at the Battle of

Campaldino (1289). By this time he had written several pieces of poetry addressed to his spiritualized love Beatrice Portinari, who later married Simone de' Bardi and died aged twenty-four in 1290, and who throughout his life remained his guiding star. These love-poems already show originality of a high order, far beyond the realms of the general troubadour style. After Beatrice's death the exalted inspiration was intensified, and a selection of these poems, linked together by a prose narrative, formed his first work, the *Vita nuova* (1292–4; mod. eds. by Barbi, 1932, and Sapegno, 1943; Eng. trans. Dent's Temple Classics). Up to this time a not particularly deep thinker, he turned after Beatrice's death to a close study of philosophy (Aristotle and Boëthius) and to Latin poetry and prose, especially Virgil and Cicero. If this period of intellectual pursuits was important for the future, no less so was his participation in politics, which began in 1295 on his becoming purely for the title's sake (which gave him the right to take an active part in the republic's affairs) a member of the Guild of Apothecaries. By 1300 he was a member of the Signoria, the chief magistracy. It was an unlucky moment, for it was just at this point that the division within the ruling Guelf Party at Florence came to breaking point with the struggle between the 'Whites' and the 'Blacks' for control. Dante, seeing that all further compromise was impossible, turned to the 'Whites', the constitutional group who were the foes of papal intervention in the republic's affairs. For the moment the 'Whites' prevailed, the pro-papal 'Blacks' were exiled and Dante went with an embassy to Rome to parley with Boniface VIII and dissuade him from sending Charles de Valois as a peacemaker to Tuscany. During the absence of Dante and his companions, however, Charles entered Florence, the 'Blacks' were reinstated and the 'Whites' proscribed. Dante early in 1302 was in his absence declared an enemy of the Church, was heavily fined, banished for two years and excluded for ever from holding any office. Six weeks later the sentence was increased to exile for life and death by being burnt alive if ever he should be caught by the Florentine government. Dante was never to see Florence again; henceforward he was rootless, a man unjustly condemned, longing for justice. At first Dante made common cause with his fellow exiles, living with them in various cities, including Forlì and Arezzo; but in 1304, growing tired of their plots to force their way back to Florence and of their continual politics, he left them for good and went to Verona. Here, hoping to win for himself the reputation of a scholar to compensate him for all he had lost, he set about the composition of two prose works, both left unfinished: *De Vulgari Eloquentia*, a Latin treatise on the Italian language and the art of Italian poetry (mod. crit. ed. by Marigo, second ed., 1948), and *Il convivio*, a popularization of scholastic philosophy in the form of a commentary on several of his own *canzoni* or odes (mod. crit. ed. by Busnelli and Vandelli, 2 vols., 1934–7). Both were at a stand by 1308 and he never resumed them. By this time he was in Bologna where he continued his studious life and where in 1309 or thereabouts he began the *Commedia* (calling it a 'comedy' in reference to what he called his homely style), although some scholars say he did not begin it until 1313 when all his

hopes in life were finally dashed. For before that his political ideals
had suddenly revived in the person of the newly elected Emperor
Henry VII of Luxemburg who, eager to revive imperial power in
Italy, held court in Milan in 1310. Dante had an audience with him
there early in 1311 and at once recognized in him the symbol of a
united Italy. There followed many Latin letters to Henry and a Latin
treatise *De Monarchia* (1311–13; mod. crit. ed. with the *Epistolas*
by Vinay, 1950), a work on the relations between Church and state,
in which he maintains that the emperor has received his authority
direct from God. But Henry's death in 1313 destroyed all these hopes,
and the proud exile, refusing the Florentine government's new but
humiliating terms for his return (1315), spent his last years first in
Verona at the court of Cangrande della Scala and later at Ravenna,
whose ruler Guido da Polenta was his benefactor. There, surrounded
by his family—he had married very early in life, perhaps in 1285,
Gemma Donati—he continued to write the *Commedia*, completing it
shortly before his death, which was caused by an illness contracted
on his return journey from Venice, whither he had gone as Guido's
ambassador. He was buried at Ravenna. The *Commedia*, later called
*La Divina Commedia*, is divided into three parts, *Inferno*, *Purgatorio*
and *Paradiso*, each of thirty-three cantos, there being in addition an
introductory canto. It is an allegory of life, a vision in which Dante is
led by Virgil (representing philosophy, the choice of the Roman poet
showing in what high regard he was held in the Middle Ages) through
Hell and Purgatory. After that Virgil can go no further; in the spiritual
felicity of Paradise it is Beatrice, the symbol of the divine wisdom
revealed occasionally to men in life, who becomes his guide. Although
on the one hand the work is of the essence of medievalism, on the
other it has the timeless quality of great works. Logical, sparing of
unnecessary embellishments, like his master Virgil exponent of the
compendious phrase, a gifted writer of similes often drawn from
nature, clear thinking, dramatic at times, at others epic, at others
elegiac, he took what was almost a dialect and made of it one of the
world's most beautiful languages. He created Italian literature, in
fact; for some, Italian literature is Dante. He explains to us the spirit
of his age, the age of St Thomas Aquinas (q.v.), whose work was an
inspiration to him; he is master of medieval imagery and is no less a
marvellous expositor of medieval thought and dogma. To Italy he
gave a national consciousness, which, after a period of neglect in the
ages of the baroque and the classical, made him the idol of the
Risorgimento, and since then his position has never been challenged
as one of the supreme poets of the world. Of numerous editions of the
*Commedia* are those by Casini (fifth ed., 1903), Torraca (second ed.,
1908) and Scartazzini and Vandelli (1911). The greatest of *Commedia*
commentators is probably Momigliano. The verse translation into
English by H. F. Cary, first published in 1814, is a classic in its way
and has passed through many editions. But it is probably better to
turn to the prose versions, especially Dent's Temple Classics (3 vols.,
1899–1901) with Italian and English on opposite pages. J. D. Sin-
clair's translation of the *Commedia* (3 vols., 1939–46) is powerful and
the notes reveal first-rate scholarship. M. Barbi's *Dante* (1933) and

F. Maggini's *Introduzione allo studio di Dante* (1948) are the best introductions for the specialist, but for the English reader the following should be consulted: P. J. Toynbee's *Dante Alighieri, his Life and Works* (fourth ed. rev., 1910), D. L. Sayers's Introduction to a translation of the *Inferno* (1949) and U. Cosmo's *Handbook to Dante Studies* (1950). See also the ed. and trans. *Dante's Lyric Poetry* by K. Foster and P. J. Boyde (1966).

**Da Ponte, Lorenzo,** pseudonym of **Emanuele Conegliano** (1749–1838), Italian librettist. Born at Ceneda, in Venetia, he became poet to the Imperial Theatre, Vienna, and as such produced excellent libretti for Mozart, *Nozze di Figaro* (1786), *Don Giovanni* (1787) and *Così fan tutte* (1790). He settled in London in 1794, but left England abruptly in 1805 and went to New York, where he died. He left behind him untrustworthy memoirs: *Memorie* (2 vols., 1918; Eng. trans. *Memoirs of Lorenzo Da Ponte,* 1929).

**Da Porto, Luigi** (1485–1529), Italian poet and prose-writer. Born in Vicenza of good family, he had some experience of the army which he relates in his *Lettere storiche* (mod. ed., 1857). His famous tale *Romeo e Giulietta* (1524), is a source of the plot of Shakespeare's play, while among his *Rime e prose* (1539) are some excellent sonnets. He died in Vicenza.

**Dashkova, Ekaterina Romanovna** (1743–1810), Russian literary woman, the most brilliant of her day, was born in Petersburg. Her talents both scientific and literary led to her being admitted a member of many European learned societies. Going into voluntary exile after an extensive quarrel with Catherine the Great (q.v.) she travelled about Europe, visiting Britain and founding bursaries at Oxford for Russian students, especially in mathematics. Returning to Russia in 1782 she was made director of the Petersburg Academy of Arts and Sciences, and in 1784 became first president of the Russian Academy. Deprived of all her honours and offices at the death of Catherine and the accession of Paul I (1796), she retired to her estates near Moscow, where she died. She wrote prose and plays in English, her most attractive work being her *Memoirs,* which first appeared in 1840, also in English.

**Dass, Petter** (1647–1708), Norwegian poet. The founder of modern Norwegian poetry, he was born, the son of a Scottish merchant named Dundas and a Norwegian mother, on the island of Nord-Nerø. He was ordained in 1672 and in 1689 became pastor of Alstahang in the far north, where he died. His great work is *Nordlands Trompet,* a very individualistic poem, descriptive of life in Nordland. It was not published until 1739 (crit. ed., 1927). His other works, likewise published posthumously, were of no lasting importance.

**D'Aubigné,** *see* **Aubigné.**

**Daudet, Alphonse** (1840–1897), French novelist. Born at Nîmes, in Provence, the son of a silk manufacturer, he was a schoolmaster for a short time before going to Paris in 1857. The young man had singular powers of attraction and it was not long before all doors were open to him, and he became secretary to the duc de Morny, retaining that post until Morny's death in 1865. He had already dabbled in literary work when in 1866 he published with P. Arène (q.v.), using the pseudonym Gaston Marie, *Lettres de mon moulin*, built up from reminiscences of his life in Provence, and these were continued in *Le Petit Chose* (1868). (*Lettres de mon moulin* have appeared in many translations.) Provençal life and character were also the inspiration of the delightful burlesques centring upon that inimitable personage Tartarin, *Les Aventures prodigieuses de Tartarin de Tarascon* (1872; Eng. trans. *The Prodigious Adventures of Tartarin of Tarascon*, 1887), *Tartarin sur les Alpes* (1885; Eng. trans. *Tartarin on the Alps*, 1887) and *Port Tarascon* (1890; Eng. trans. 1891). Meanwhile he had discovered his powers as a social satirist, and with *Fromont jeune et Risler aîné* (1874; Eng. trans. *Fromont the Younger and Risler the Elder*, 1880) he produced a study of the commercial classes of Paris which is held to be his masterpiece. *Jack* (1876; Eng. trans. 1890) was in the same manner, but he soon turned to other elements of the social scene, and in *Le Nabab* (1877; Eng. trans. *The Nabob*, 1878) told a good deal about the duc de Morny's private life, and with increasing asperity in *Numa Roumestan* (1881; Eng. trans. 1884) dealt with politicians and Gambetta in particular, in *Sapho* (1884; Eng. trans. 1886) pilloried the sexual life of aristocrat and bourgeois, and in *L'Immortel* (1888; Eng. trans. *One of the Forty*, 1888) laid about the French Academy. *Trente Ans de Paris* and *Souvenirs d'un homme de lettres* (both 1888; Eng. trans. *Thirty Years of Paris and of my Literary Life*, 1888; *Recollections of a Literary Man*, 1889) are autobiographical. His last works, such as *Rose et Ninette* (1892; Eng. trans. 1892) and *La Petite Paroisse* (1895), still have charm but are much weaker. Daudet died in Paris after a long and painful illness. A master not only of humour but also of pathos, with a style to match his graceful turns of thought, he brought a new kind of writing into French literature, proving that satire could be charmingly cutting and burlesque could be whimsical. His *Œuvres complètes* were published in twenty volumes, 1929–31.

**Daudet, Alphonse Marie Léon** (1867–1942), French novelist and general prose-writer, was born in Paris, the son of Alphonse Daudet (q.v.). At first reading medicine he gave it up for literature, contributed articles to *Le Figaro* and *Le Gaulois*, and published his first novel, *L'Astre noir*, in 1893. His next, *Les Morticoles* (1894), was a scathing attack on the medical profession, and there followed *Le Voyage de Shakespeare* (1895), *Les Idées en marche* (1896), *Le Pays des parlementeurs* (1901), a satire on republicanism, for he had now become (and remained) a fiery royalist, and *La Lutte* (1907). His outspoken and sometimes scandalous *Souvenirs des milieux littéraires, politiques, artistiques et médicaux* (6 vols., 1914–21) brought his name before a wide public, which had also known him since 1908, in which year he founded the paper *L'Action Française*, as the chief supporter of the return of the Bourbons to the French throne. His latest works include *Le Stupide XIXième Siècle* (1922; Eng. trans. *The Stupid Nineteenth Century*, 1928), *Les Bacchantes* (1932) and *Mes Idées esthétiques* (1939). He died in Paris.

**Dauthendey, Max** (for **Maximilian**) (1867–1918), German poet and novelist. Born in Würzburg, he worked unwillingly for seven years in his father's photography business, spending all available time in literary pursuits, and publishing his psychological novel *Josa Gerth* in 1892. He soon after turned his attention to poetry and brought out three volumes of verse, *Ultra-Violett* (1893), *Schwarze Sonne* (1897), inspired by Iceland, and *Reliquien* (1899); but it was not until *Der brennende Kalender* (1905), a collection of love-songs inspired by his wife, that he showed his mastery as a lyric poet, an impression which was deepened by his subsequent poetry, sometimes with its touch of Catholic mysticism, to be found in such volumes as *Ammenbalade* (1907), *Singsangbuch* (1907), *Lieder der langen Nächte* (1908), *Lust-samgärtlein* (1910) and *Die geflügelte Erde* (1910). It was not, however, before the publication of his novel, *Raubmenschen* (1911), that he was fully recognized and gained sufficient money to allow him to set out on world travel. His love of the East had just been shown in *Lingam* (1910), a collection of twelve Asiatic stories, followed by two collections of oriental love-tales comprised under the title of *Die acht Gesichter am Bewasee* (1911), and from now on he neglected poetry for colourful and exotic prose such as that to be found in *Die Heidin Geilane* (1912), *Gedankengut aus meinen Wanderjahren* (2 vols., 1913), *Das Märchenbuch der hl. Nächte im Javanerlande* and *Erlebnisse auf Java* (both posthumously published in 1921). He was in Java when the First World War broke out, was interned in Malang on that island and died there. His view of the war appears in *Des grossen Krieges Not* (1915). His *Gesammelte Werke* were published (6 vols.) in 1925, being followed by *Letzte Reise* in 1926.

**Davila, Enrico Caterino** (1576–1631), Italian historian. Born at Pieve del Sacco, near Padua, he became a French mercenary and fought through the civil wars until the peace in 1598, after which he entered the army of the Venetian Republic. His experiences in France led to his writing his attractive if untrustworthy *Historia delle guerre civili di Francia, 1558–1598* (1630; best ed., 1807; Eng. trans. *The History of the Civil Wars of France*, 1647 and 1758). He was murdered at San Michele, in Campagna, near Verona. His other works are unimportant, but the *Historia* lives as literature.

**D'Azeglio, Massimo Taparelli** (1798–1866), Italian novelist and autobiographer, was born in Turin of noble family, took up painting, wrote two historical novels, *Ettore Fieramosca* (1833) and *Niccolò de' Lapi* (1841), both set in sixteenth-century Italy, and then entered the political arena with pamphlets on the burning questions of the day. He was prime minister of Piedmont from 1849 to 1852, when he was succeeded by Cavour. His best work is undoubtedly his book of memoirs, showing descriptive power, *I miei ricordi* (1867; mod. ed., 1944; Eng. trans. *Things I Remember*, 1966). He had died a year before its publication at Cannero.

**De Amicis, Edmondo** (1846–1908), Italian novelist. Born at Oneglia, he took some part in the liberation of Italy, and his stories, founded on his experiences, *La vita militare* (1868), brought him swift recognition. A varied collection of short stories, *Novelle*, followed in

1872. *Cuore* (1886; Eng. trans. *Cuore: an Italian Schoolboy's Journal,* 1887) was a successful, if very sentimental, story for children translated into many European languages. He died at Bordighera.

**De Coster,** *see* **Coster.**

**Dehmel, Richard** (1863–1920), German poet and prose-writer, born at Wendisch-Hermsdorf, he became a friend of Liliencron (q.v.), with whom he tried to make an end of the outworn romanticism still clinging to much German poetry by introducing daring innovations. But these 'shock tactics', to which he sacrificed a great deal of his writing, unlike Liliencron, who was more cautious, have done much harm to Dehmel's reputation, and apart from the books of poetry, *Weib und Welt* (1896), *Zwei Menschen* (1903), not because this is of particular merit, but because it is instructive to read what he himself considered his best work, and *Schöne wilde Welt* (1913), and possibly his autobiography, *Kriegstagebuch* (1919), his work is quite dead, and even the above books have greatly faded. He was an innovator, and paid the price of the rough pioneer in literature. He died at Blankensee.

**Deken, A.,** *see* **Wolff-Bekker, E.**

**Dekker, E. D.,** *see* **Multatuli.**

**Delarue-Mardrus, Lucie** (1880–1945), French poet and novelist, was born at Honfleur, and it was Normandy which lay behind the inspiration of all her works, which include the volumes of poetry, *Par vents et marées* (1911), *Souffles de tempête* (1918) and *Les Sept Couleurs d'octobre* (1930), and the novels *L'Ex-voto* (1922) and *Guillaume le Conquérant* (1931; Eng. trans. *William the Conqueror,* 1932). She died in Touraine.

**Delavigne, Jean François Casimir** (1793–1843), French dramatist. Born at Le Havre, he made a name for himself with the satires against the government of Louis XVIII, *Les Messéniennes* (1816–22), but it was with his tragedy, showing sure signs of a break with classical tradition and looking forward to the romantic movement, *Les Vêpres siciliennes* (1819), later serving as the basis for the libretto of one of Verdi's early operas, that his reputation came. To the fore at the revolution of 1830, he won his greatest literary success with historical plays like *Les Enfants d'Édouard* (1833) and *La Fille du Cid* (1839). He died in Lyon. His collected works were published in 1855.

**Deledda, Grazia** (1873–1936), Italian novelist, born at Nuoro, in Sardinia, published her first volume, *Racconti sardi,* in 1894, and in a period of regional fiction made Sardinia her field in nearly all her subsequent volumes, such as *Il vecchio della montagna* (1900), *Elias Portolu* (1903), *Nostalgie* (1905), *L'ombra del passato* (1907), *La madre* (1920), *Il tesoro* (1928) and *Annalena Bilsini* (1928), all of which are pessimistic and, except the last which is set in north Italy, deal with primitive life threatened by unfriendly, if not hostile, nature. Awarded the Nobel Prize in 1926, to some surprisingly, she died in Rome.

**Delille, Jacques** (1738–1813), French poet and translator, was born illegitimate near Aigues-Perse, in Auvergne, and was brought up in a charity school. Later he taught at Amiens. His translation of Virgil's *Georgics* (1769) gained a great reputation and was favoured by Voltaire, and, winning the patronage of the comte d'Artois, he became *abbé commendataire* of Saint-Severin. His didactic poem *Les Jardins* (1782), replete with descriptions of formalized nature, is considered his masterpiece and is one of the best pieces of French verse of the eighteenth century. He left France at the revolution, and, after travelling in Switzerland and Germany, went to London where he occupied much of his time as a translator and later wrote his original poem, *L'Homme des champs* (1800). After his return to France in 1802 he produced a volume of his own verse, *La Pitié* (1803), translations of the *Aeneid* (1804) and *Paradise Lost* (1805), and *L'Imagination* (1806), *Les Trois Règnes de la Nature* (1809) and *La Conversation* (1812), by which last date he had become blind. He died in Paris.

**De Lolme, John Louis** (1740–1806), Swiss prosist, writing in French and English. Born in Geneva, he became an advocate there, but in 1769 came to England. Living there, a bookseller's hack bordering on poverty, he yet managed to write his enthusiastic *Constitution de l'Angleterre*, first published in Amsterdam in 1771 (Eng. trans. *The Constitution of England*, 1775). Having inherited some property in Switzerland he left England in 1775 and settled in Geneva, dying at Seewen. Among other miscellaneous works, he published in English *A History of Flagellants* (1777), an abridgment of the French work by Despence Boileau, *The British Empire in Europe* (1787) and *Strictures on the Union* (1796). His influence on political theory was marked for two generations.

**De Marchi, Emilio** (1851–1901), Italian novelist, born in Milan, where he died. A follower of Manzoni (q.v.), he yet differs from him in that basically in all his work, even in his humorous passages, there is an underlying sense of tragedy, and even the humour is used for the purpose of, as it were, covering it up. His most popular work is the strange mystery story *Il cappello del prete* (1888), but his best, and incidentally one of the finest of modern Italian novels, is *Demetrio Pianelli* (1890). Other novels are *Arabella* (1892) and *Giacomo l'idealista* (1897). Among his collections of short stories are *Storie d'ogni colore* (1885) and *Racconti* (1891).

**Dennery, Adolphe** (1811–1899), French playwright. Born in Paris of Jewish descent, he produced his first play, *Émile*, in 1831. Most of his enormous output proved ephemeral. Of his earlier plays *Marie Jeanne* (1845) was the most successful, of the later *Michel Strogoff* (1883), founded on the story by Jules Verne (q.v.). Dennery provided the libretto for Massenet's *Le Cid* (1885). He died in Paris.

**De Roberto, Federico** (1866–1927), Italian short-story writer and novelist, was born in Naples, and succeeded especially with the collections of short stories *Documenti umani* (1888), *Processi verbali* (1890) and *La sorte* (1891), and the masterly historical novel *I vicere* (1894). He died at Catania, Sicily.

Déroulède, Paul (1846-1914), French poet and playwright. Born in Paris, he took part in the Franco-Prussian War, and after its conclusion became a noisy patriot, calling to witness the old glories of France and demanding vengeance against Germany. His *Chants de soldat* (1872) proved immensely popular, as did *Pro Patria* (1879), *Marches et sonneries* (1881) and *Refrains militaires* (1889). He had meanwhile become a dedicated supporter of General Boulanger and was returned to parliament as deputy. Later his patriotic militarism became too strident for governments shaken by Fashoda and Dreyfus, and he was exiled in 1900. Of his over-written historical plays the best are probably *Messire Du Guesclin* (1896) and *La Mort de Hoche* (1897). He died in Nice.

Derzhavin, Gavril Romanovich (1743-1816), Russian poet. Born at Kazan, he became a successful civil servant and died much esteemed in Petersburg. The wealth of imagery he used in the occasional poetry which he produced throughout his life was something new in Russian letters, and the quiet lingering music of the elegy on the death of Meshchersky makes it one of the greatest poems in the language. His collected works were published (9 vols.) between 1864 and 1883.

De Sanctis, Francesco (1817-1883), Italian literary critic, born at Avellino, whose *Storia della letteratura italiana* (1872; Eng. trans. *A History of Italian Literature*, 2 vols., n.d.), though brilliant and even attractive in its way, led to a weakening of the analytical faculty among Italian literary critics and a tendency to generalize and be selective which remains today. De Sanctis died in Naples.

Desbordes-Valmore, Marceline Félicité Josèphe, *née* Desbordes (1786-1859), French poet. Born at Douai, she had a sad childhood and her early marriage to F.-P. Valmore was a failure. She was for a time an actress and a singer, and appeared as a poet in *Élégies et romances* (1819) and *Poésies* (1820). Under the pain of her unrequited passion for the poet Henri de Latouche her later volumes deepened in quality, such works as *Les Pleurs* (1833), *Pauvres fleurs* (1839) and *Bouquets et prières* (1843) having undeniable depth of feeling expressed in sincere and simple terms. For some she bridges the gap between Lamartine (q.v.) and Verlaine (q.v.). She died in Paris. Her complete works were collected (3 vols.) in 1886-7.

Descartes, René (1596-1650), French philosopher, writing also in Latin, was born of a smaller landed family at La Haye, Touraine. Of delicate health at first, he was later able to go to the Jesuits at La Flèche to be educated, and even entered the army. During his travels he found the Netherlands particularly to his liking, especially in view of the studious life he promised himself. In 1628 he left France and went to Amsterdam, and until the last year of his life was based in the Netherlands, though moving about continually to avoid the unwelcome attentions which his growing fame brought him. Although the possessor of a good style, his work is hardly literature, but in literary history he holds an important place by reason of the all-pervading influence of his thought on later seventeenth- and eighteenth-century Europe. Many writers at some stage in their career came face to face with Cartesian logic, and those who did not lived in an intellectual climate permeated by it. Without him the rationalists would have been without their most powerful inspiration and without them the course of the intellectual eighteenth century would have been vastly different. He explained his search after philosophical certainty memorably in his *Discours de la méthode* (1637), and brought his method to bear on metaphysics in *Meditationes de Prima Philosophia* (1641; also in French) and on the world of nature, the physical as opposed to the metaphysical, in *Principia Philosophiae* (1644; also in French). Unexpectedly accepted by orthodox Catholics, his conclusions were generally frowned upon by the Dutch clergy, and the increasing opposition which he experienced in his adopted country led to his accepting an invitation from Queen Christina of Sweden to settle at her court in Stockholm in 1649. It was a fatal mistake. The unreasonableness of Christina in demanding that he should attend an audience three times a week at five in the morning was too much for one accustomed to stay in bed till midday. His health was undermined, and a year later he succumbed to pleurisy. The *Œuvres de Descartes* (13 vols., 1897–1913) is the standard edition replacing that by Cousin (q.v.), the first full French one, the great one of 1713 being in Latin. For English translation see E. S. Haldane and G. R. T. Ross's *Philosophical Works of Descartes* (2 vols., 1911–12). There is an English translation of the *Discours* in Everyman's Library.

**Descaves, Lucien** (1861–1949), French novelist. A lifelong Paris resident, he is seen to best advantage in his books on army life such as *Les Misères du sabre* (1887). His autobiography, *Mémoires d'un ours* (1946), is vivacious and interesting.

**Deschamps, Antoine François Marie,** generally called **Antony** (1800–1869), French poet and translator. Born in Paris, he made a brilliant translation of Dante in 1829. Volumes of his own poetry such as *Les Italiennes* (1831), *Satires* (1834), *Dernières paroles* (1835) and *Résignation* (1839) reveal his unbalanced mind, though containing much sad beauty. In 1840 his brain gave way and he died insane at Passy.

**Deschamps, Émile** (1791–1871), French dramatist, librettist and critic, was born at Bourges and was a civil servant. A friend of Victor Hugo and one of the prime figures in the early romantic movement, he set forth the movement's aims in the preface to his *Études françaises et étrangères* (1828), considered by many as its first proclamation. Among his plays may be named *Ivanhoé* (1826) and *Don Juan* (1834). He also provided the libretto of *Roméo et Juliette* for Berlioz. *Stradella* (1837) was another successful play. He died at Versailles.

**Deschamps, Eustache** (1340?–1415), French poet. Born at Vertus, near Châlons-sur-Marne, he was first a soldier, then a man of law, gained a court appointment in 1368 and travelled in Italy, Bohemia and Hungary. He was given fine estates in Champagne, but they were ruined during the Hundred Years War with England and he seems to have died comparatively poor. Besides lyrics in all manner of forms he composed a long courtly poem, *Le Miroir de mariage*. The place of his death is uncertain.

**Desmarets de Saint-Sorlin, Jean** (1595-1676), French novelist, playwright, poet and miscellaneous prose-writer. Born in Paris, he was a member of Richelieu's intimate circle and held important posts in the civil service. He was first chancellor of the French Academy. A bigot in every department of thought and action, he led French literature down a blind alley from which it was happily rescued by the rising generation. His enormous and now quite unreadable novel *Ariane* (10 vols., 1632) was dramatized in 1639, and another heavy-footed play was *Mirame* (1640). His dull religious verse includes *Clovis ou la France chrétienne* (1657; new ed., 1673), *Marie Magdeleine* (1669) and *Esther* (1670). As a critic he is to be gauged by his *Défence de la poésie et de la langue françoise* (1675), than which there can be no narrower approach to literature. He died in Paris.

**Des Masures, Louis** (1515?-1574), French dramatist. Born at Tournai, he embraced Protestantism in middle age, and published a religious trilogy on the David theme, a subject much cultivated by reformed writers. This was published in 1563, the three parts being entitled *David combattant, David triomphant* and *David fugitif* (critical ed. *Tragédies saintes* by C. Comte, 1907). He died at Sainte-Marie-aux-Mines.

**Desmoulins, Camille** (1760-1794), French political journalist, the greatest produced by the revolution, was born at Guise, Picardy. As in *La France libre* (1789), the pamphlet, and in the weekly newspaper, *Les Révolutions de France et de Brabant* (1789-91) he stimulated revolution, so later in *Le Vieux Cordélier* (1793-4) he counselled moderation and the ending of the Terror. Whatever cause he pleaded it was in a style which opened the way for that literature of journalism which was to be so significant in the course of the next century. Desmoulins, together with his friend Danton, was guillotined in Paris.

**Des Périers, Bonaventure** (1510?-1544), French miscellaneous prose-writer, was born either at Autun or at Arnay-le-Duc, and early attached himself to the court of Marguerite de Navarre (q.v.). There he cultivated letters and free thought which led to the composition of *Cymbalum Mundi* (1537), a veiled attack on current religious beliefs, in the form of dialogues. Only the influence of Marguerite shielded him from arrest. He is said to have committed suicide, but the manner and place of his death are both uncertain. His most attractive book *Nouvelles récréations et joyeux devis*, consisting of 129 short stories, some grossly amusing, others romantic, was published posthumously in 1558 (mod. ed., 1843; new ed., 1932).

**Desportes, Philippe** (1547-1606), French poet. Born at Chartres, he went to court and became the most popular poet after the death of Ronsard (q.v.). With him, however, a decline from the standards made by the Pléiade set in, largely due to his inclination towards Italian models; but if the quality declines there is much lively charm remaining, as is to be seen in the wholly delightful *Villanelle*, 'Rosette, pour un peu d'absence,/Votre cœur vous avez changé', and the neatness of *Icare*. Between 1573 and 1583 he published various collections of secular poetry (see *Premières Œuvres*, which contain all of these, 1858), but after 1590 he turned completely to religious poetry (*Psaumes*). He made several translations of Ariosto (q.v.). He died at Chartres.

**Destouches, Philippe Néricault** (1680–1754), French dramatist. Born at Tours, he became the most evenly successful playwright of the regency and earlier years of the reign of Louis XV. His particular bent was towards the comedy of manners and he had a good eye for character, but was often not content to let his characters speak for themselves, intervening through them. Among his many comedies the following should particularly be named: *L'Ingrat* (1712), *Le Médisant* (1715), *Le Philosophe marié* (1727), *Le Glorieux* (1732), generally considered his best, and *Le Dissipateur* (1736). He died at Fortoiseau. He lived in London from 1717 to 1723 and made some creditable translations of Shakespeare, the first in French, which are to be found in his *Œuvres complètes* (6 vols., 1822).

**Deval, Jacques,** pseudonym of **Jacques Boularan** (1894–    ), French playwright and novelist, born in Paris. A mixture of mordant wit and sentimentality gives a particular quality to such comedies as *Une Faible Femme* (1920), *Une Tant Belle Fille* (1925), *Tovarich* (1929) and *Mademoiselle* (1932), all of them box-office successes. He has of recent years turned to realism, examples of his new style being *Ce Soir à Samarkand* (1950), and *Charmante soirée* (1955). As a novelist he produced *Sabre de bois* (1929) and *Romancéro* (1958).

**Diamante, Juan Bautista** (1625?–1687), Spanish playwright, born the son of a Madrid merchant of Jewish descent. He gained favour at court, writing for the royal family a number of *zarzuelas* in the Calderonian manner, and historical dramas such as *La reina María Estuarda* (1660), on the Queen of Scots. He died in Madrid.

**Díaz del Castillo, Bernal** (1492–1576?), Spanish historian. Born at Medina del Campo, he joined Cortés's expedition which conquered Mexico. He later held an appointment and land in Guatemala. From 1552 onwards he was engaged in writing his *Verdadera historia de la conquista de Nueva España* (first printed 1632; Eng. trans. *The True History of the Conquest of New Spain*, Hakluyt Society, 5 vols., 1908–16), equally fine as history and as literature. The style is engaging and lively to the highest degree. Díaz died in Mexico.

**Dicenta, Joaquín** (1863–1917), Spanish playwright, born at Calatayud, became a journalist. Turning to the stage he scored a success with costume plays through which everyday problems and controversial issues loomed thinly disguised. Typical of his work are *El suicidio de Werther* (1888), *Los irresponsables* (1892), *Juan José* (1895; Eng. trans. in C. A. Turrell's *Contemporary Spanish Dramatists*, 1919), which is his best work, *Aurora* (1902), *Sobrevivirse* (1911) and *El lobo* (1913). He died in Alicante.

**Diderot, Denis** (1713–1784), French man of letters, was born at Langres, in Champagne, the son of a master cutler. Educated by the

Jesuits he afterwards refused to take up a profession, was forced to fend for himself, and for ten years (1734–44) led a hard life in Paris as a badly paid private tutor and a hack writer. Yet during this time he gained the friendship of such writers as D'Alembert (q.v.) and Condillac (q.v.) and later of J.-J. Rousseau (q.v.), and after studying Locke and English deists like Toland and the Earl of Shaftesbury, a work by whom he translated as *Essai sur le mérite et la vertu* (1745), he struck out for himself with his *Pensées philosophiques* (1746; mod. crit. ed., 1950). For his *Lettre sur les aveugles* (1749; Eng. trans. *An Essay on Blindness*, 1750), which was in accordance with Condillac's philosophical view that every human action and the very sources of knowledge lie in the physical sensations, he was imprisoned. On his release he was invited by a publisher, Le Breton, to edit an enlarged version of Ephraim Chambers's *Cyclopaedia* (1727). Diderot accepted the offer, but as soon as he took charge of the work its character was transformed. He gained many of the leading writers of the age as contributors and also called in skilled craftsmen to write articles of a technical character. It became a treasury of knowledge, while its 'philosophical' articles formed a veritable armoury to be used to refute established ideas. Not that Diderot was in any way a revolutionary, but he was a leader of that well-informed middle class grown impatient of the restraints of Church and state, and which was willing to accept nothing at its face value. The first volume of the great *Encyclopédie* appeared in 1751, the last and thirty-fifth in 1777; but the main series was completed in 1765, the later volumes being supplements in which Diderot took no part. It was thanks to his will alone that the project was carried through to the end, for such were the difficulties that D'Alembert, the assistant editor, deserted in 1759, and with the added load on his shoulders Diderot ran the constant risk of imprisonment. Meanwhile he was a novelist with *La Religieuse* (written 1760, not publ. till 1790; Eng. trans. *The Nun*, 1797), an attack on conventual life, *Jacques le fataliste* (written 1773, publ. 1796; Eng. trans. 1797), in the manner of Sterne, and *Le Neveu de Rameau* (written 1773, publ. 1805; Eng. trans. 1897; and in J. Kemp's *Diderot, Interpreter of Nature*, 1937), an imaginary dialogue between the author and a parasite, much admired by Goethe and translated by him into German. As a dramatic critic he is represented by *Entretiens sur Le Fils naturel* (1757), *Discours sur la poésie dramatique* (1758) and *Paradoxe sur le comédien* (written 1778, publ., 1830; Eng. trans. *The Paradox of Acting*, 1883), a most interesting treatise on the art of an actor, and one which had great influence on the development of the comedy of manners in the nineteenth century. His *Salons*, a series of criticisms on exhibitions of pictures which he wrote from 1759 onwards, are among the first examples of systematic fine arts criticism. Although so keen a dramatic critic, his own performances as a playwright are failures except for *Le Père de famille* (acted 1761) and *Le Fils naturel* (written 1757, acted 1771; Eng. trans. *Dorval, or the Test of Virtue*, 1767), dramas of middle-class life showing strong English influence. See *Œuvres complètes* (20 vols., 1875–9), and a handy selective edition (ed. A. Billy), 1935. Diderot died in Paris.

**Diego Cendoya, Gerardo** (1896–      ), Spanish poet, born in Santander. His poetry can be divided into two kinds. The first, such as *Manual de espumas* (1924) and *Versos humanos* (1925), are in a stridently modern style, while the second, such as *Viacrucis* (1931) and *Ángeles de Compostela* (1940), are on religious subjects expressed in a traditional manner. Going into exile on the defeat of the republic (1939), he went to Argentina in 1940 where the following year he brought out an anthology of his verse up to date, *Alondra de verdad* (1941). Since then have appeared: *Limbo* (1951), *Paisaje con figuras* (1956), *Amor solo* (1958) and *La rama* (1961).

**Dierx, Marais Victor Léon** (1838–1912), French poet, born at Saint-Denis, Île de Réunion. His quiet and mellow style is to be seen in such volumes as *Les Lèvres closes* (1867), *Les Paroles du vaincu* (1871), *La Rencontre* (1875) and *Les Amants* (1879). He died in Paris. The last and best edition of his *Poésies complètes* is that of 1920.

**Díez Canedo, Enrique** (1879–1944), Spanish poet and prose-writer. Born at Badajoz, he joined the diplomatic service and held several appointments in South America. A man of wide European culture who greatly appreciated modern French poetry, as a poet he brought external influences to bear on the generally exclusive tendencies of Spanish letters in various books, notably *La visita del sol* (1907), in the manner of the symbolists, *La sombra del ensueño* (1910), which keeps pace with latest developments, and long afterwards, still showing an awareness of current European poetry, come *Algunos versos* (1924), *Epigramas americanos* (1928) and *El desterrado* (1940), composed after he had left Spain as a result of the defeat of the republic. His critical writings, *Sala de retratos* (1920), *Conversaciones literarias* (1921) and *Los dioses en el Prado* (1931), show great distinction of mind. He died in Mexico.

**Di Giacomo, Salvatore** (1860–1934), Italian short-story writer. Born in Naples, where he spent his whole life, he is the author of *Novelle napoletane* (1883; new ed., 1914), the incomparable collection of short stories about the poor of his native city. None of his other books are of importance.

**Diktonius, Elmer Rafael** (1896–1961), Swedish-Finnish poet and novelist, writing in Swedish. Born in Helsinki of working-class parentage, he travelled much, took up music, but found himself more suited to literary journalism. After Finland's independence he became an uncompromising left-wing force in politics, his views being reflected in such books of poetry as *Min Dikt* (1921) and *Stenkol* (1927), while in his novels *Onnela* (1925) and *Janne Kubik* (1932) he gives utterance to his love of nature and sympathy with the peasantry. *Hårdbörjan* (1946) is a representative selection of his verse. Later narratives are *Medborgare i republiken Finland* (2 vols., 1935–40) and *Höstlig bastu* (1943). He died in Helsinki.

**Dinesen, I.,** *see* **Blixen-Finecke, K.**

**Dingelstedt, Franz von** (1814–1881), German poet, novelist and playwright. Born at Halsdorf, near Marburg, he became a schoolmaster and gained a considerable following as a writer of left-wing political verse such as that to be found in *Gedichte* (1838) and *Lieder eines cosmopolitischen Nachtwächters* (2 vols., 1841, 1843). As a novelist, in his earlier years he wrote *Die neuen Argonauten* (1839; new ed., 1931) and *Unter der Erde* (2 vols., 1840). After 1843 he made his peace with the powers that were and was royal librarian at Württemberg (1843–50), and afterwards director of the court theatres successively of Munich, Weimar and Vienna. He tried his hand, none too successfully, at tragedy with *Das Haus der Barneveldt* (1850), and the following year turned to a newer and tamer kind of poetry with *Nacht und Morgen*. He was more successful with his long novels, *Die Amazone* (2 vols., 1868; Eng. trans. *The Amazons*, 1868) and *Kunstlergeschichten* (1877). He was an excellent theatrical producer, and for this he was ennobled in 1876. His collected works appeared (12 vols.) in 1877–8. He died in Vienna.

**Diniz** (1261–1325), King of Portugal from 1279 until his death, Portuguese poet. An excellent monarch, he was also a lover of learning, founding the University of Coimbra in 1290 and having many ancient classics and Arabic and Castilian works translated into Portuguese. He was himself a lyric poet of the highest quality, and nearly 150 of his poems are extant (see *Das Liederbuch des Königs Denis von Portugal*, 1894).

**Döblin, Alfred,** pseudonym Linke Poot (1878–1957), German novelist. Born in Stettin of Jewish family, he took up medicine, practised in Berlin, and was for years in North and South America and in Palestine. After two unimportant attempts at fiction, he began, influenced by the work of Kafka (q.v.), then coming into view, to explore the means of displaying the post-war neurosis of Europe. He succeeded admirably in *Berge, Meere und Giganten* (1924), over which hangs a cloud of fear at the irresistible force of the coming scientific age. The grey, impersonal, seemingly purposeless life imposed by industrialized society on individuals is powerfully recorded in *Berlin Alexanderplatz* (1929; Eng. trans. *The Story of Franz Biberkopf*, 1931), while *Pardon wird nicht gegeben* (1935; Eng. trans. *Men without Mercy*, 1937) treats of the destruction of the fundamentals of civilization by totalitarianism. He then wrote two trilogies, the first *Südamerikatrilogie* (3 vols., 1937–8) and the second *November 1918* (3 vols., 1949–50). At the end of the Second World War Döblin returned to Germany after an absence of many years. He died at Emmendingen in Baden.

**Dobrolyubov, Nikolay Alexandrovich** (1836–1861), Russian critic and philosopher, was born at Nizhny Novgorod. He became an influential literary critic in 1857 in Petersburg, crowding into four years an immense amount of work. By introducing utilitarianism and materialistic philosophy into Russia he gave a new turn to Russian letters at a critical period. He died in Petersburg. His collected works were first published (4 vols.) in 1885, and there is a six-volume edition of 1934. His most important philosophical essays were republished as *Izbrannye filosofskie sochineniya* (2 vols., 1946; Eng. trans. *Nikolay Alexandrovich Dobrolyubov, Selected Philosophical Essays*, 1948). His work was anathema to Turgenev (q.v.) and his followers.

**Dobrovský, Josef** (1753–1829), Czech philologist and literary historian writing in Latin and German, was born at Gyarmat, near Raab, Hungary, of poor family. He became a Jesuit, and on the abolition of the Order a secular priest, but was foɪ the most part engaged in teaching and in literary work. In 1792 he was enabled by his patrons to visit Scandinavia and Russia to look for Czech books carried away from Bohemia in the course of the Thirty Years War. The result was *Geschichte der böhmischen Sprache und Literatur* (1792) which showed the world how rich was the Czech literature of the past. In this way he may be said to have been responsible for creating the stimulus which resulted in the rebirth of Czech letters in the nineteenth century. He produced a masterly philological work on Czech, *Ausführliches Lehrgebäude der böhmischen Sprache*, in 1809. He died mentally deranged at Brno.

**Doderer, Heimito von** (1896–1966), Austrian novelist, short-story writer, poet and essayist. Born at Weidlingen, near Vienna, he was soon involved in the First World War and spent the years 1916–20 as a prisoner of war in Siberia. In a highly artistic and masterly manner he depicts life and society in Vienna before and after 1914. As a novelist he is represented by *Das Geheimnis des Reichs* (1930), *Ein Mord, den jeder begeht* (1938), *Ein Umweg* (1940), *Die Strudel-hofstiege* (1951), *Die Dämonen* (1956; Eng. trans. *The Demons*, 1961), *Die Posaunen von Jericho* (1958) and *Die Merowinger* (1962); as a short-story writer by *Die Bresche* (1924), *Das letzte Abenteuer* (1954) and *Die Peinigung der Lederbeutelchen* (1959); as a poet by *Gassen und Land-schaft* (1923) and *Ein Weg im Dunklen* (1957); and as an essayist by *Der Fall Gütersloh* (1930) and *Grundlagen und Funktion des Romans* (1959). He died in Vienna.

**Dolet, Étienne** (1509–1546), French scholar writing in Latin, called the 'Martyr of the Renaissance', was born at Orléans, went to the University of Paris, and in Venice (1526–32) the full force of the Renaissance struck him. In 1534 he settled in Lyon and set up a press on which he printed not only editions of the classics and his own works, but the works of contemporary French writers such as Rabelais (q.v.). For long under suspicion by the Inquisition he was accused on the basis of a supposedly mistranslated passage of Plato of denying the immortality of the soul and burned at the stake in Paris. He was a victim of the Church's panic in the face of the application of the new learning to theology. His great work is *Commentarii Linguae Latinae* (1536–8).

**Doni, Anton Francesco** (1513–1574), Italian prose-writer, born in Florence. He lived entirely by his pen, writing on anything topical that came to hand in a truly modern manner. His best-known works are his axiomatic *La zucca* (1551, 'The Pumpkin') and a phantasy of a 'brave new world' *I mondi* (1552). He died at Monselice. An edition of *Scritti vari* appeared in 1913.

**Donici, Alexandru** (1806–1866), Rumanian fabulist. Born in Bess-arabia, he early went to Russia where he learned the language and studied Pushkin. He returned home and settled as a lawyer at Jassy,

where he died. His *Fabule* (1840) owe much of their form to La
Fontaine (q.v.), but their substance is wholly Bessarabian and is of
unique quality.

**Donnay, Maurice Charles** (1859–1945), French dramatist. Born in
Paris, he began his career with *Phryné* (1891) which led him on to
further subtle explorations into the interplay of the sexes in society
such as *Amants* (1895), *Le Retour de Jérusalem* (1903), *Le Ménage de
Molière* (1912), *Les Éclaireuses* (1913) and *La Chasse à l'homme* (1917).
He died in Paris.

**Dons, Aage,** (1903–    ), Danish novelist. Born at Hornsherred, he
started on a musical career, abandoned it, described it in *Koncerten*
(1935), travelled, tried his hand again as a novelist in *Soldaterbrønden*
(1936; Eng. trans. *The Soldiers' Well*, 1940), and after the war gave
expression to the disillusionment of the time in *Frosten paa Ruderne*
(1948) and *Den svundne Tid er ej forbi* (1950). Other works include
*Farvel min Anger* (1954), *Dydens Løn* (1956) and *Braende til mit
baal* (1965).

**Dorgelès, Roland,** pseudonym of **Roland Lécavelé** (1886–    ),
French novelist. Born at Amiens, he grew up with money to spend in
pre-1914 Paris, and it was the sudden transition to the trenches and
death which turned him into an author. *Les Croix des bois* (1919;
Eng. trans. *Wooden Crosses*, 1921) expressed all the horror of war and
deep sympathy for the men who suffered. *Le Cabaret de la belle femme*
(1919; Eng. trans. *The Cabaret up the Line*, 1930) deals with war-time
recreations, but with *Saint-Magloire* (1922; Eng. trans. 1923) and
*Le Réveil des morts* (1923) war gradually recedes. With *Montmartre,
mon pays* (1928) we are in the Latin Quarter, where we are again
with an author who suffers from increasing nostalgia for the almost
vanished world of his youth in *Château des brouillards* (1932) and
*Quand j'étais montmartrois* (1936). War comes again and reminds him
of another in *Retour au front* (1940). At last he takes refuge in travel
as in *Carte d'identité* (1945) and *Bleu Horizon* (1949). He turns to
reminiscences and personal evaluations in *Portraits sans retouches*
(1952), *Tombeau des poètes* (1954) and *Tout est à vendre* (1956).

**Dostoyevsky, Fyodor Mikhailovich** (1821–1881), Russian novelist. The
son of an autocratic military surgeon, later (1839) murdered by his
serfs, he was born in Moscow. After a sad childhood he entered the
school of military engineering in Petersburg, and on graduation from
it in 1843 he entered the government's service. Already epileptic
tendencies had appeared, and it was partly for this reason that he
decided that a public life was impossible for him and turned to his
pen for a living in Petersburg. His literary career opened with two
short novels, *Bednye lyudi* (1846, 'Poor Folk'), in which he showed a
characteristic compassion for the world's outcasts, influenced by
Gogol (q.v.), and *Dvoynik* (1846, 'The Double'), a powerful study of
a split personality in the manner of Hoffman (q.v.). Both books were
very successful, but in spite of this, thanks to the unscrupulousness
of his publishers, Dostoyevsky profited little, and continued as a
literary hack. Meanwhile his political interests asserted themselves

and he joined a group of idealists known as the Petrashevsky Circle, after the name of its originator, a theoretical revolutionary. On a ridiculous trumped-up charge Dostoyevsky and his associates were arrested in 1849 and sentenced to death, being pardoned while they were actually lined up in front of the firing squad, and sent to Siberia. This profound shock followed by four terrible years (1850–4) which he spent in a penal settlement at Omsk, and four more degrading years in the army at Semipalatinsk (1854–8) completely undermined him and caused permanent psychological damage. His marriage in 1857 to the hysterical invalid Marya Dmitrievna Isayeva increased his gloom. Amnestied at last in 1859, he returned to Petersburg and resumed his literary career. Silent now, embittered and suspicious, hating the bourgeoisie, but with the strongest sympathy for the lower classes whose sufferings he knew so well, he joined his brother Mikhail in publishing the literary paper *Vremya,* in which appeared *Selo Stepanchikovo i ego obitateli* (1859, 'The Family Friend'), *Uniz-hennye i oskorblyonnye* (1861, 'The Insulted and the Injured') and *Zapiski iz myortvogo doma* (1861–2, 'Memoirs from the House of the Dead'), the last a particularly powerful and terrible account of his sufferings in Sibera. The censors stopped the publication of *Vremya* in 1863, so he started another periodical *Epokha* (1864–5), for which he wrote *Zapiski iz podpolya* ('Letters from the Underworld'), a slight foretaste of the great works to come. Desperately poor, with debts crowding in on him and suffering from his ill-starred love affair with Apollinaria Suslova, he now wrote the first of his great novels, *Prestuplenie i nakazanie* (1866, 'Crime and Punishment'). In 1867 came *Igrok* ('The Gambler'), which chronicles the painful experiences of his love for Apollinaria, and in the same year he married the selfless Grigoryevna Snitkina (his first wife had died in 1864), and with her went to Germany to escape from his creditors. He lived mostly in Baden-Baden, there writing *Idiot* (1868, 'The Idiot') and gambling, and published *Besy* ('The Possessed') in 1871, the year of his return to Russia to Petersburg. Disillusioned with what he had seen of Western Europe, he came back to his country a convinced Slavophil. His popularity, which had been for some time at its height in France, from this time onwards increased progressively in Russia, and he was at last able to live in comfort. In 1873–4 he contributed to the periodical *Grazhdanin* his self-revelatory *Dnenik pisatelya* ('An Author's Diary'), with additions in 1876–7 and 1880, which made of it a Slavophil manifesto, although in his Pushkin speech of 1880 he showed a universality of feeling, later echoed by Gorky (q.v.), which promised a unity of the cultures of East and West. His life's work was crowned by *Bratya Karamozovy* (1879–80, 'The Brothers Karamazov'), one of the world's greatest novels, a splendid plea for the rebirth of mankind inspired by faith in spiritual values. His death in Petersburg was the occasion for an astonishing outburst of love and respect all over Russia, and his funeral provided an opportunity for public mourning on an unprecedented scale. This supreme novelist had at his command unerring powers of characterization and deep psychological insight, a luminous style and a love and sympathy for man such as only the greatest writers possess. Beginning as a sceptic he gradually found himself driven on towards a longing to probe good and evil and to understand the mysteries of life through a reassessment of belief in God and a desire for immortality. His influence has been profound, and such different thinkers as Nietzsche (q.v.) and his followers and the Existentialists have acknowledged him as leading the way. The exhaustive edition of his works is *Polnoye sobranie khudozhestvennykh proizvedeniy* (19 vols., 1933–4). For a complete English translation of his novels see *The Novels of Fyodor Dostoyevsky* (trans. C. Garnett, 12 vols., 1912–20). See also *Prison Life in Siberia* (1887), *The Brothers Karamazov* (1927), *The Possessed* (1931), *The Diary of a Writer* (2 vols., 1949) and *Crime and Punishment* (1886 and 1951). Of his letters there are the following English translations: *Letters of Fyodor Mikhailovich Dostoyevsky to his Family and Friends* (1917), *New Dostoyevsky Letters* (1929) and *The Letters of Dostoyevsky to his Wife* (1930).

**Drachmann, Holger Henrik Herholdt** (1846–1908), Danish poet, playwright, novelist and short-story writer. Born in Copenhagen, he dabbled in the arts until a visit to Britain in 1871 made him determined to write. The immediate result was *Digte* (1872), revealing lyric powers which increased in subsequent volumes (*Samlede poetiske Skrifter*, 12 vols., 1906–9). However attractive his poetry may be, there is always a disagreeable egoism at hand which detracts from the full effect, and this is to be found in everything he wrote, such as the plays *Renaessance* (1894) and *Melodramaer* (1895; both trans. in *Poet Lore*, vol. xix, 1908), the novels such as *Poul og Virginie under Nordlig Bredde* (1879; Eng. trans. *Paul and Virginia of a Northern Zone*, 1895) and the short stories such as *Smaa Fortaellinger* (1884; Eng. trans. *The Cruise of the Wild Duck and Other Tales*, 1891). The claims made for Drachmann such as that he is the poetic equal of Ewald (q.v.) are difficult to substantiate. He died at Hornbaek.

**Drieu La Rochelle, Pierre** (1893–1945), French novelist and essayist, born in Paris. A man of piercing intellect, between 1919 and 1939 he tracked down and analysed world political thought, rejecting in the process all ideologies until he came to Nazism, of which he became a keen supporter inside France. A marked man after the liberation in 1944, the following year on the news of Germany's final defeat he committed suicide in Paris. The best of his works are *Blèche* (1929), *Rêveuse Bourgeoisie* (1937) and *Gilles* (1939). His collections of essays provide a faithful series of vanishing pictures of a troubled period in which hopes and fears, ardours and endurances, gave place to one another in quick succession: *État civil* (1921), *Le Jeune Européen* (1927), *Genève ou Moscou* (1927), *L'Europe contre les patries* (1931), *La Comédie de Charles* (1934) and *Journalisme fasciste* (1935).

**Droste-Hülshoff, Annette von** (1797–1848), German poet and prose-writer. Born of aristocratic family at Schloss Hülshoff, near Münster, in Westphalia, she was brought up a strict Catholic and led a retired life, although having contacts through her literary-minded brother-in-law with several writers such as Uhland (q.v.) and the Grimm brothers (q.v.). Her faith and her constant awareness of the abiding sorrow of life inform all her work, the quality of which entitles her to be regarded as the greatest of all German women writers. *Dicht-ungen* (1838) contains the two narrative poems, *Das Hospiz auf dem grossen St Bernard* and *Die Schlacht in Loener Bruch*, the latter about the Thirty Years War. Her short novel *Die Judenbuche* (1842; Eng. trans. *The Jew's Beech-Tree*, 1915) is invested with the mood of noble resignation with which she bravely faced her own disappointments (her weak health and her unhappiness in love). There are some excellent lyrics in *Gedichte* (1844), but her crowning achievement is her volume of religious verse, *Das Geistliche Jahr*, published post-humously in 1852. She died at Meersburg, on the Bodensee. Her collected works were published (5 vols.) in 1925.

**Du Bartas, Guillaume de Salluste** (1544–1590), French poet. Born at Montfort, near Auch, in Armagnac, he became a soldier and was employed on various diplomatic journeys for Henry of Navarre (afterwards Henry IV of France). A religious poet, his Protestantism is to be seen in his moralizing poems of the earlier period such as *Judith* (1573; Eng. trans. *The Historie of Judith*, by T. Hudson, 1584); but it was *La Sepmaine* (1578), the second part of which remained unfinished, a finely conceived if roughly carried out narrative of the Creation, which made him famous, being translated into several languages. His complete works were translated into English by Joshua Sylvester as *Du Bartas His Divine Weekes and Works* (1592–1599). *La Sepmaine* was read with approval by Tasso (q.v.) and Milton. Du Bartas died in Paris of wounds received at the battle of Ivry.

**Du Bellay, Joachim** (1522–1560), French poet and critic. Born at Liré, near Angers, of good family, he became a friend of Ronsard (q.v.) while at school and went with him to Paris. There Du Bellay published *La Deffence et illustration de la langue françoyse* (1549), the manifesto of the famous Pléiade poets, whose aim was here explained as being to naturalize the sonnet and ode to French and to set up the ancient Greek and Latin classics as the standard for French poetry. He immediately followed this up with *Sonnetz à la louange d'Olive* and *Vers lyriques* (both 1549), in the first of which he illustrated the Petrarchan sonnet (this is the first sonnet sequence in French) and in the second the ode. His finest work, however, was inspired by his stay in Rome (1553–7) where he acted as secretary to his uncle Cardinal Jean Du Bellay. There he was unhappy, and, again turning to the sonnet, produced two memorable sequences on loneliness and the passing of time and the transitoriness of all things, *Les Regrets* and *Les Antiquités de Rome* (both 1558; and both ed., 1945), the latter translated by Edmund Spenser as *The Ruines of Rome* in 1591. Falling out of favour with his uncle he returned to Paris in 1557 and died there in very reduced circumstances. See *Œuvres* (6 vols., 1908–31). Some of his poems have been well translated by Andrew Lang in *Ballads and Lyrics of Old France* (1872). Spenser also translated further poems of his as *Bellayes Visions* (1591).

**Du Cange, Charles du Fresne** (1610–1688), French lexicographer and antiquary, was born at Amiens (where a statue to him now stands) of an old landed family. Advocate to the Paris Parlement, he is renowned for his great *Glossarium ad Scriptores Mediae et Infimae Latinitatis* (3 vols., 1678; Benedictine ed. greatly enlarged, 10 vols., 1883–7) displaying a wealth of erudition and paving the way for new assessments of medieval Latin, which until then had been to a large extent neglected as literature and philology. Less important is his companion volume on Greek as employed in the Middle Ages, *Glossarium ad Scriptores Mediae et Infimae Graecitatis* (2 vols., 1688). He also wrote with authority on numismatics and many other classical subjects, and in 1668 brought out an edition of Joinville (q.v.). He died in Paris.

**Ducasse, Isidore-Lucien,** using **Le comte de Lautréamont** as his pseudonym (1847–1870), French prose-poet. Born in Montevideo, Uruguay, where his family were temporarily living, he settled in France in 1860. He is called the father of surrealism in virtue of his posthumously published prose epic, *Les Chants de Maldoror* (1890). He died in Paris. See his *Œuvres complètes* (1946).

**Ducis, Jean-François** (1733–1816), French dramatist, writer of fugitive verses and 'adaptor' of Shakespeare for the stage. Born at Versailles, he wrote such plays on his own account as *Œdipe chez Admète* (1778) and, in a style to suit a new public, *Abufar, ou la Famille arabe* (1795). Some of his occasional poetry such as *À mon ruisseau* and *À mes pénates* is charming, but he is now remembered as the first author to bring Shakespeare on to the French stage, although his command of English was so imperfect that he could do little more than make adaptations of the tragedies such as *Hamlet* (1769), *Roméo et Juliette* (1772), *Le Roi Lear* (1783), *Macbeth* (1784) and *Othello* (1792). He died at Versailles. His *Œuvres* were published (4 vols.) in 1826.

**Duclos, Charles Pinot** (1704–1772), French novelist and writer of memoirs, born at Dinan. His salacious *Confessions du comte de —— —* (1742) is scarcely literature, but serves to show what was often read under cover of a moral purpose in the boudoirs depicted by the artist Boucher; but in *Les Considérations sur les mœurs de ce siècle* (1751) and *Mémoire pour servir à l'histoire des mœurs du dix-huitième siècle* (1752) we have valuable and excellently written documents on the social life of his own day. He died in Paris.

**Duhamel, Georges** (1884–1966), French novelist and general prose-writer, was born in Paris, the son of a chemist who qualified in medicine late in life, and took up a medical career. It was his experiences as an army surgeon at the front in the First World War that made a compelling writer of him. The suffering which he saw led him to write that eloquent and deeply compassionate work, *La Vie des martyrs* (1916; Eng. trans. *The New Book of Martyrs,* 1919) in which he faced the crimes against humanity which war brings, and he followed this up with *Civilisation* (1917; Eng. trans. 1919), in which he found Western Europe on the edge of disruption. But it was as a novelist that he stood at his full stature. In 1920 *La Confession de minuit,* the first of the five volumes of *Vie et aventures de Salavin* appeared, the fifth coming out in 1932 (Eng. trans.

*Salavin*, 1936), in which in a masterly manner he describes the career of that product of the modern world, the victim Salavin, and after two single-volume novels, *Les Hommes abandonnés* (1921) and *Le Prince Jaffar* (1924) and two pessimistic analyses of the trend of world affairs, *Le Voyage de Moscou* (1927) and *Scènes de la vie future* (1930; Eng. trans. *America: The Menace*, 1931), he turned to his masterpiece about a family founded on his own, *La Chronique des Pasquier* (10 vols., 1933–45; Eng. trans. *The Pasquier Chronicles*, 1937 seqq.), showing in it his great breadth of humanity and hatred of shams, written in an unimpeachable style. His experiences of the German occupation which he bore with dignity and courage are reflected in *Lieu d'asile* (1944). He was for a long period editor of *Le Mercure de France*. He died at Valmondois outside Paris.

**Dumas, Alexandre Davy de la Pailleterie, Dumas the Elder** (1802–1870), French novelist and playwright. He was born at Villers-Cotterets (Aisne), the grandson of comte Alexandre Davy de la Pailleterie, a creole, whose mistress, the Haitian negress Marie-Cessette Dumas, gave birth to Alexandre Davy-Dumas. This Alexandre Davy-Dumas was in the army of the revolution when in 1792 he married Marie Labouret, the daughter of a small landowner turned innkeeper of Villers-Cotterets. Alexandre was born there ten years later when his father had already had a distinguished career in the Republican army. When he died in 1806 he had reached the rank of general, leaving his child with no prospects and little enough money. His interest in writing appeared early and, although sent to a solicitor's office to serve his articles, he soon escaped, and in 1823 went to Paris to seek his fortune. Thanks to his father's name he gained a clerkship in the household of the duc d'Orléans, and began to try his hand at melodrama; his first effort, in collaboration with a friend Adolphe de Leuven, called *La Chasse et l'amour*, was staged in 1825. It was not, however, until he turned to the historical play that he began to succeed. With *Henri III et sa cour* (1829), produced at the Comédie Française, he gained fame. Forestalling by a year Hugo's (q.v.) *Hernani*, *Henri III* marks the rout of decadent classical drama (which was still hanging in the air) and the growing triumph of romanticism, although it needed Hugo's genius to set the seal on the new movement. It brought Dumas important friendships, money and the librarianship of the Palais Royal. Then in quick succession came plays of a similar kind, including *Christine* (1830), *Antony*, *Napoléon Bonaparte* and *Richard Darlington* (all 1831), the last a tremendous success, *La Tour de Nesle* (1832), his play of the most lasting quality, and *Térésa* (1832). In that same year he fell victim to the cholera epidemic then raging in Paris, and on his recovery went to Switzerland to recover, the result being contributions to the *Revue des Deux Mondes* about his travels, collected as *Impressions de voyage* (1833), the first of his highly readable travel books. Having succeeded as a playwright he now turned to fiction, and on this his reputation rests. Adventure stories and historical novels were what appealed to him. He had already made a start with *Madame et la Vendée* (1832) and proceeded with *Pascal Bruno* (1838) and *Acté* (1839), in the last of which the historical seems to be vanishing from view. After a series of what may be called historical detective novels, *Les Crimes célèbres*, begun in 1839, he embarked on his ambitious project of writing a long romantic fictional series founded on French history from the death of Henry II in 1559 to the present—finally extended to 1848. Between 1844 and 1850 the greater part of this was carried out by Dumas and a number of 'ghosts', including Auguste Maquet, Paul Lacroix, the historian and antiquary, Paul Bocage and J.-P. Malle-fille. The first series, which may be considered as the 'Henri de Navarre' series, includes *La Reine Margot* (1845), *La Dame de Monsoreau* (1846) and *Les Quarante-cinq* (1847). The 'Musketeer' series includes *Les Trois Mousquetaires* (1844), *Vingt Ans après* (1845) and the lengthy *Vicomte de Bragelonne* (3 vols., 1848–50), which carries the history to 1672 and ends with D'Artagnan's death. A few detached novels such as *La Tulipe noire* (1850) belong historically to the later seventeenth century, but the eighteenth century does not appear to have appealed to him, for the third series does not begin until the French Revolution. Of this 'French Revolution' series the most celebrated are *Mémoires d'un médecin* (3 vols., 1846–1848), *Le Chevalier de Maison-Rouge* (1846), *Le Collier de la Reine* (2 vols., 1849–50), *Ange Pitou* (1852), a splendid reconstruction of the taking of the Bastille, and *La Comtesse de Charny* (1854). His master-piece *Le Comte de Monte Cristo* (1844) is set in the earlier nineteenth century. Later and unattached novels, although continuing to illustrate French history, include *Ingénue* (1854), *Les Compagnons de Jéhu* (1857) and *Les Louves de Machecoul* (1859). Meanwhile his finances had reached their peak, but his general extravagance endangered them, and his involvement in politics on the side of the republic in 1848 militated against him after the *coup d'état* of Louis Napoleon. Theatrical ventures failed and he withdrew to Belgium for a time to consider his position. His marriage to Ida Ferrier, the actress, had broken down years before, and he was always in the clutches of some member of the *demi-monde*, e.g. the most famous, Adah Isaacs Menken, the beautiful circus rider. But he still had the spirit for literary rehabilitation, and returning to France became a journal-ist, launching two most successful newspapers, *Le Mousquetaire* (1853) and *Le Monte Cristo* (1857). In 1860 he went to Italy and offered his services to Garibaldi, and took a leading part in directing a propaganda campaign for the cause of Italian liberty in Europe. As a reward Garibaldi appointed him Director of Fine Arts at Naples. By 1864 he was back in France plunged deep in debt, but was rescued by his son who took him to live with him at Puys, near Dieppe, and there he died. A great many of his novels have been translated into English, and none of these are more readily available than in Every-man's Library, in which the following appear: *The Three Musketeers*, *The Black Tulip*, *Twenty Years After*, *Marguerite de Valois*, *The Count of Monte Cristo*, *The Forty-Five*, *Chicot the Jester*, *Vicomte de Bragelonne* and *Le Chevalier de Maison Rouge*. One of the master story-tellers of literature, any literary shortcomings are easily atoned for by his strength derived from the breath of life.

**Dumas, Alexandre, the Younger** (1824–1895), French novelist and dramatist, was born the illegitimate son of Alexandre Dumas, the Elder (q.v.) and Marie Lebay, a dressmaker in Paris. Part of his childhood was passed in poverty until his father recognized him and treated him thereafter with kindness and generosity. But the stigma of illegitimacy, for which he had been taunted at school, remained in his mind all his life and affected his whole outlook. Fundamentally a moralist in all he wrote, he had nothing of his father's improvidence and flamboyance; for him everything had a purpose. Suddenly his father's financial fortune collapsed, and the Younger Dumas found himself with debts which could not be repaid; but he had the character to stand up to the sudden change, and looked about for a profession. Letters seemed the answer, although his only literary effort up to that time, a book of verse characteristically entitled *Péchés de jeunesse* (1847), had not been a promising start. All the same the talent was there and, relying on his power of narrative, urged on by his deeply felt moral convictions (which, however, he was nearly always artist enough not to allow to intrude to the detriment of his work), he brought out in 1848 the two novels *La Dame aux camélias* (Eng. trans. *The Lady with the Camelias*, 1856) and *Le Roman d'une femme*, following them up with a third, *Diane de Lys* (1851). They were esteemed, but they brought him little money, and it was not until *La Dame aux camélias* was dramatized and produced in 1852 that his reputation was made and his financial problem solved. This masterpiece of the 'eternal feminine' (turned into an opera as Verdi's *La Traviata* in 1853) is his greatest work. *Diane de Lys* was converted into a play in 1853, and from now on the playwright took the place of the novelist. Of a host of plays the following are outstanding: *Le Demi-monde* (1855), *Le Fils naturel* (1858), *Un Père prodigue* (1859), *L'Ami des femmes* (1864), *Les Idées de Madame Aubray* (1867; Eng. trans. 1965), *Une Visite de noces* (1871), in which the famous Aimée Deselée created the heroine's part (as in *La Princesse Georges* (1872) and *La Femme de Claude* (1873)), *Monsieur Alphonse* (1874), *L'Étrangère* (1876), with one of the most brilliant casts ever assembled together on the French stage, including Sarah Bernhardt and Fèbvre, and *Denise* (1885). All of these he provided with prefaces on their being published, in which he sought to drive home his moral purpose. But even though this might appeal to a moralizing age, his popularity was due to the emotional power with which he invested his characters, to his keen sense of the dramatic situation, to his dialogue and to his consummate knowledge of stagecraft; and then he was fortunate in having at his command the finest actors and actresses of his day. This brought him renown, probably beyond his deserts, and in his lifetime he was held in higher esteem than his father. A late novel, *L'Affaire Clémenceau* (1866), is of much interest, as are his impressive pamphlets, *Nouvelle Lettre de Junius* and *Lettres sur les choses du jour* (1871–2), in which he calls France, laid low by the Franco-Prussian War, to face the future with courage and optimism. He died at Marly.

**Dumont, Pierre Étienne Louis** (1759–1829), French prose-writer. Born in Geneva, he went to England and became a private tutor in 1785. In Paris early in the revolution he became a close friend of Mirabeau, and was the inspirer or even the composer of many of his best speeches. On Mirabeau's death in 1791 he returned to England and grew to be an intimate of Jeremy Bentham, whose work he translated into French, an undertaking which had tremendous repercussions in French history. He died in Milan. His *Souvenirs sur Mirabeau* appeared in 1832 (Eng. trans. *The Great Frenchman and the Little Genevese*, 1904).

**Dupont, Pierre** (1821–1870), French poet. Born at Lyon, where he died, he gained a reputation with his ambitious *Les Deux Anges* (1842), but it was as a writer of popular political ballads such as *Le Chant des ouvriers* that he became known to the French nation as a whole.

**Durand, Alice,** *see* **Greville, Henry.**

**Duranty, Louis Émile Edmond** (1833–1880), French novelist. Born in Paris, he became a freelance writer, and with the novel *Le Malheur d'Henriette Gérard* (1860) produced a powerful realistic work, of much interest still as an exact reproduction of the life of the time. He died in Paris.

**Duras, Marguerite** (1914–     ), French novelist. Born in Saigon, Indo-China, she returned to France in 1932 and read law, mathematics and political science at the Sorbonne. During the German occupation of France (1940–4) she took part in the Resistance movement and was deported to Germany. After the war she joined the Communist Party, from which she was expelled in 1950. Her works, which are much influenced by modern American writers such as Hemingway, include: *Un Barrage contre le Pacifique* (1950; Eng. trans. *The Sea Wall*, 1953), set in Indo-China, *Le Marin de Gibraltar* (1952; Eng. trans. *The Sailor from Gibraltar*, 1966), *Les Petits Chevaux de Tarquinea* (1953; Eng. trans. 1960), *Des Journées entières dans les arbres* (1954), *Le Square* (1955; Eng. trans. 1959), *Moderato cantabile* (1958; Eng. trans. 1960) and *L'Amante anglaise* (1967).

**Dürrenmatt, Friedrich** (1921–     ), Swiss novelist, dramatist, short-story writer and essayist. Born at Konolfingen bei Bern, the son of a Protestant pastor, he read theology and philosophy at Bern and Zürich and, giving up the idea of entering the Church, settled as a writer in Neuenburg. As a novelist he is represented by *Der Richter und sein Henker* (1952; Eng. trans. 1954), *Der Verdacht* (1953; Eng. trans. 1962), *Herkules und der Stall des Augeas* (1954) and *Grieche sucht Griechin* (1955), and as a dramatist by *Es steht geschrieben* (1947), *Der Blinde* (1948), *Romulus der Grosse* (1949; Eng. trans. 1964), *Die Ehe des Herrn Mississippi* (1952; Eng. trans. 1964), *Ein Engel kommt nach Babylon* (1954; Eng. trans. 1964), a comedy, *Der Besuch des alten Dame* (1956; Eng. trans. 1956), another comedy, *Die Oper einer Privatbank* (1960) and *Die Physiker* (1962; Eng. trans. 1962) another comedy. He is also the author of radio plays, collected as *Gesammelte Hörspiele* (1961). As a short-story writer, as in *Pilatus* (1949) and *Der Nihilist* (1950), and as an essayist, as in *Die*

*Stadt* (4 vols., 1952) and *Theaterprobleme* (1955; Eng. trans. 1964), he is less well known.

**Du Ryer, Pierre** (1600?–1658), French dramatist, born in Paris, is remembered for his tragedies on biblical themes such as *Saül* (1640), and tragi-comedies on classical themes such as *Thémistocle* (1646), *Dynamis* (1649) and *Alexandre* (1653). His translation of Herodotus (1645) opened up that rich quarry to many writers, not least of them Madeleine de Scudéry (q.v.), who drew her plot of *Le Grand Cyrus* (1649) from an incident in the *History*. Du Ryer died in Paris.

**Duun, Ole Julius** (1876–1939), Norwegian novelist. Born at Fosnes, Namdalen, of farming stock, he took up schoolmastering, at the same time writing novels of a regional character, the first being published in 1907. Unfortunately they are written in the so-called New Norwegian, and this has hindered their deserved success, for there is considerable power in the way in which he handles the case of man struggling against the gigantic forces of destruction in life which he only half understands. *Det gode Samvite* (1916; Eng. trans. *Good Conscience*, 1928) is the first of his works in which he found himself; but his great work is *Juvikfolke* (6 vols., 1918–23; Eng. trans. *The People of Juvik*, 6 vols., 1930–5). He died at Botne.

# E

**Eberhard, August Gottlob** (1769–1845), German man of letters, born at Belzig, remembered for a popular idyll *Hännchen und die Küchlein* (1822), which once enjoyed a European reputation. His most ambitious work was his lengthy poem in hexameters, *Der erste Mensch und die Erde* (1828). He died in Dresden.

**Ebers, Georg Moritz** (1837–1898), German Egyptologist and novelist, born in Berlin. He studied law at Göttingen and Egyptology in Berlin, becoming professor of that subject at Jena in 1868 and in 1870, after travels in the East, at Leipzig, which post he held until 1889. His visit to Egypt in 1872–3 resulted in his discovery at Thebes of one of the finest examples of papyri, the hieratic medical 'Papyrus Ebers', which he published in 1875. With *Eine ägyptische Königstochter* (1864; Eng. trans. *An Egyptian Princess*) he had already begun to exploit his scholarship in historical fiction, and after paralysis had in 1876 precluded an active life he became a prolific novelist, his plots of a conventional nature being set either in Egypt or in sixteenth-century Germany and the Netherlands. Of these should be mentioned *Die Schwestern* (1880; Eng. trans. *The Sisters*), *Der Kaiser* (1881; Eng. trans. *The Emperor*), *Serapis* (1885) and *Kleopatra* (1894). He died at Tutzing. His collected works filled thirty-two volumes (1893–7). Practically all have been translated into English (*The Historical Romances of Georg Ebers*, trans. D. Appleton, 1915).

**Ebert, Karl Egon** (1801–1882), Czech poet and playwright, born in Prague, was for many years a librarian at Donaueschingen. A versatile if too prolific writer, his many poems and dramas were collected to fill seven volumes (1877). He died in Prague.

**Ebner-Eschenbach, Marie von** (1830–1916), Austrian novelist, was born of noble family in Zdielawitz Castle, Moravia, and in 1848 married Freiherr von Ebner-Eschenbach, later living in Vienna where she died. Her works, which show much sympathy for the poor and a great love and understanding of children, include *Die Prinzessin von Banalien* (1872), *Zwei Komtessen* (1885; Eng. trans. *The Two Countesses*, 1893), *Krambambuli* (1886; Eng. trans. 1915), *Der Kreisphysikus* (1886; Eng. trans. *The District Doctor*, 1915), *Unsühnbar* (1890; Eng. trans. *Beyond Atonement*, 1892) and *Rittmeister Brandt* (1896; Eng. trans. *A Man of the World*, 1912). She is considered as one of the greatest of women writing in German.

**Ebreo, Leone,** *see* **Abarbanel, L. E.**

**Eça de Queirós, José Maria de** (1843–1900), Portuguese novelist and short-story writer, was born the son of a judge at Póvoa de Varzim, and was educated at Coimbra, where he soon became known for radical views. He made his name with his first important work, the powerful anti-clerical novel, *O crime do padre Amaro* (1874; Eng. trans. *The Sin of Father Amaro*, 1962), which though at times falling into exaggeration is a work of much literary value. That same year, having already served as Portuguese consul in Havana, he became consul in Newcastle and later in Bristol, remaining in Britain for fourteen years, and finally in 1888 continuing his diplomatic service in Paris where he died. Portugal's greatest novelist, in many ways he profited from living at a distance from the scenes he describes, and he brings to his writing trenchant satire and keen perception. *O primo Basilio* (1878; Eng. trans. *Cousin Bazilio, 1953*) is a devastating piece of social satire, as is *A reliquia* (1887; Eng. trans. *The Relic*, 1954). In *O mandarim* (1880) he had already shown an ability to deal with oriental themes. His posthumous collection of short stories, *Contos* (1902), give a cross-section of his diverse abilities. His *Cartas familiares e bilhetes de Paris, 1893–1896* (1945) and his *Cartas de Inglaterra* (1945) show how clearly he understood the foreign countries in which he lived. His *Correspondência* is of great interest. His statue in Lisbon is one of the sights of the city. For a selection of his short stories in English translation see *The Mandarin and Other Stories* (1965).

**Echegaray y Eizaguirre, José** (1832–1916), Spanish dramatist, was born in Madrid and became a celebrated engineer. A man of great versatility, he was at various times minister of education and minister of finance, a professor and a highly successful business man. As a playwright he breathes new life into the old Spanish drama of honour, and in spite of what some modern critics are pleased to tell us, he is the starting point of the new school and not the end of an old and decaying one. His characterization sometimes fails him and his style on occasions needs bracing up, but in such plays as *O locura o santidad* (1877; Eng. trans. *Madman or Saint*, 1907), *El gran Galeoto* (1881; Eng. trans. *The World and his Wife*, 1908), produced in London in 1882 as *Calumny*, and *Mariana* (1893; Eng. trans. n.d.) he proves himself to be worthy of very serious consideration. He died in Madrid, having been awarded the Nobel Prize in 1904. His collected works appeared (9 vols.) in 1874–98.

**Eckermann, Johann Peter** (1792–1854), German prose-writer, born of poor parents at Winsen, Hanover. After serving in the war of 1813, he was employed as a clerk in the war office at Hanover and later became a student at Göttingen. The sending of his manuscript of *Beiträge zur Poesie mit besonderer Hinweisung auf Goethe* (publ. 1824) to Goethe in 1822 led to his being invited to Weimar to be the great poet's secretary. He remained with him from 1823 until his death, having ample opportunity to take notes on his daily life and conversation which resulted in the famous *Gespräche mit Goethe in den letzten Jahren seines Lebens, 1823–32* (2 vols., 1937; Eng. trans. *Conversations with Goethe*, 1850 et seqq.) one of the finest pieces of writing of its kind in any language. He died, librarian of the Grand-Ducal Library, at Weimar.

**Eckhart, Johannes,** known as **Meister Eckhart** (1260?–1327), German theologian and mystic, was born at Hochheim, Gotha, entered the Dominican Order, was elected prior of Erfurt and provincial of Thuringia in 1298, and became a professor at Cologne in 1320. Condemned as a heretic he managed to make peace with Rome before his death. His mystical writings with their strong pantheistic character both in their form and content had great influence on the thinkers and men of letters for generations to come. They consist of treatises and sermons, and are in Latin and in German. The latter, which are more important, are collected in F. Pfeiffer's *Deutsche Mystiker* (first ed., 1857; fourth ed., 1924). They were later popularized by such writers as Suso, and in such form became the most widely known German expression of ultimate faith and vision of the Middle Ages.

**Edgren, Anne Charlotte** (1849–1892), Swedish playwright. Born in Stockholm **Anne Leffler,** she married in 1872 Gustaf Edgren, from whom she was divorced in 1889. A vigorous feminist, her most powerful and characteristic play is *Sanna kvinnor* (1883; Eng. trans. *True Women,* 1885). She remarried in 1890 and died in Naples.

**Edqvist, Dagmar** (1903–    ), Swedish novelist, born at Visby. Her books such as *Kamrathustru* (1932; Eng. trans. *The Marriage of Ebba Garland,* 1933), *Rymlingen fast* (1933; Eng. trans. *Brave Fugitive,* 1935), *Fallet Ingegerd Bremssen* (1937), *Romeo i stallet* (1948) and *Penelope väntar inte* (1951) raise problems about the position of the individual in a rapidly changing society.

**Ehrenburg, Ilya Grigoryevich** (1891–1967), Russian Soviet novelist, was born in Moscow. His divided loyalties between the old and new orders after 1917 left him in permanent uncertainty, and even though he officially became a Bolshevik he always seemed to be looking beyond party to wider horizons. As he was unable to participate whole-heartedly in a political programme, so he seemed never able in his works to plunge successfully below the surface, and although as a satirist he produced a brilliant attack on the weaknesses of modern civilization in *Neobychnye pokhozhdeniya Julio Jurenito* (1921; Eng. trans. *The Extraordinary Adventures of Julio Jurenito and his Disciples,* 1930), wrote in a romantic vein *V Protochnom pereulke* (1927, 'In Protochny Lane'), was the author of outstanding propagandist journalism in *Padenie Parizha* (1941; Eng. trans. *The Fall of Paris,* 1945), and produced a war novel of stature in *Burya* (1948; Eng. trans. *The Storm,* 1949), he could never reach the height of major literature. He died in Moscow.

**Eichendorff, Joseph von** (1788–1857), German poet and prose-writer. Born at Lubowitz, near Ratibor, Silesia, of a noble Catholic family, he came into contact with the romantics at Heidelberg in 1807, while his friendship with F. Schlegel (q.v.) at Vienna deepened this influence. He was in the Prussian civil service from 1816 to 1844. Secure in faith and domestic happiness, it was this which inspired his many beautiful lyrics, such a combination of form, feeling and content as is rarely to be found. Like Mörike (q.v.) his love of nature enters deeply into his poetry, heightening its emotional content, but unlike him Eichendorff, even when sad, never loses his trust in eternal things. His freshest lyrics appeared in *Gedichte* (1837), and later work is to be found in *Julian* (1853) and *Lucius* (1857). Of his *Novellen* the choicest is *Aus dem Leben eines Taugenichts* (1826; Eng. trans. *The Happy-go-lucky*, 1889), the best known of all his works. *Das Marmorbild* (1826; Eng. trans. *The Marble Statue*, 1927) is also excellent. He died at Neisse.

**Einarsson, Indriði** (1851–1939), Icelandic dramatist. Born at Husabakki, he was educated in Copenhagen and Edinburgh and, returning to his native country, became a leading political economist and held various government posts. As a playwright he cultivated two styles, the first, exemplified by *Sverð og bagal* (1899; Eng. trans. *Sword and Crozier* in 'Poet Lore', 1912), being romantic and traditionalist; the second, exemplified by *Skipið sekkur* (1902), realistic and modern. He died at Reykjavík.

**Eiximeniç, Francesc** (1342?–1409?), Catalan theological writer, educated at Lérida University, Oxford and Paris. He became a Franciscan, was a prominent figure at the papal and Catalan courts, and died Bishop of Elna in Roussillon. His main work is *El Crestià*, completed in 1386, which is an encyclopaedia of Christian life (much of it is lost). *Libre dels Angels* and *Scala Dei* are adventures into mysticism. All his work, which is written in excellent and clear prose, is very personal and affords intimate glimpses into contemporary life from many viewpoints.

**Elisabeth, Queen of Rumania,** *see* **Carmen Silva.**

**Éluard, Paul,** pseudonym of **Eugène Grindel** (1895–1952), French poet born at Saint-Denis. The part he took in the First World War cost him his health permanently and he led a quiet life. Surrealism appealed to him from the first and Apollinaire (q.v.) became his acknowledged master. His earlier books, including *Mourir de ne pas mourir* (1924), *La Vie immédiate* (1932), *La Rose publique* (1934) and *Les Yeux fertiles* (1936), deal with love and its problems, but the outbreak of the Spanish Civil War in the latter year drove him to try to seek a way out of the political impasse into which Europe seemed to have fallen. Like so many others of his generation he found that Communism was the answer and joined forces with Aragon (q.v.). He was a member of the Resistance. With *Donner à voir* (1939) political and social thinking has taken the place of the earlier theme, but the spare diction, the imagery and the mastery of rhythmic technique remained and were even bettered in such final works as *Au rendez-vous allemand* (1944), *Poésie interrompue* (1946) and *Une Leçon de morale* (1949). He died at Charenton-le-Pont.

**Elysio, Filinto,** *see* **Nascimento, F. M. do.**

**Eminescu, Mihail,** pseudonym of **Mihail Eminovici** (1850–1889), Rumanian poet. Born at Botoşani, he ran away from school, joined some travelling players, and attended the universities of Vienna and

Berlin, doing no good at either, but gaining a great reputation with his poems contributed to a literary magazine in 1870, *Venerea și Madonă* ('Venus and the Madonna') and *Epigonii* ('The Epigones'). In 1877 he became a journalist in Bucharest, resigning when insanity threatened in 1883. On being cured he became a librarian at Jassy, but became finally insane in 1886, dying in Bucharest in mysterious circumstances. One of the greatest Balkan poets, his *Poezii* have appeared in many editions, the one of 1950 being excellent. Translations of them have been made in many languages. An English translation, *Poems*, appeared in 1930.

**Encina, Juan del** (1469–1529?), Spanish dramatist and song-writer, was born near Salamanca where he studied before entering the Church and the service of the Albas. In 1494 he won royal favour when some of his *Representaciones* were performed before Ferdinand and Isabella. Two years later he published his *Cancionero*, a collection containing work of much variety, including an essay on the art of poetry, lyrics, and both religious and secular plays. About 1498 he left Spain for Rome, in this Renaissance atmosphere developing the new, more realistic bucolic drama (*églogas*) that entitles him to be known as the father of Spanish drama. He died in León. There is an edition of his *Teatro completo* by M. Cañete (1893). A facsimile reprint of the *Cancionero* was produced in 1928.

**Engström, Albert** (1869–1940), Swedish humorist, born at Kalmar. Trained as a journalist, he produced many volumes of stories about country folk illustrated by himself. He is generally a smiling satirist of modern society. See *Twelve Tales* (trans. H. Borland, 1949). He died in Stockholm.

**Enríquez Gómez, Antonio** (1600–1660?), Spanish poet, playwright and novelist of Jewish descent, was born in Segovia. Leaving home for France in 1636, he became a royal secretary at the court of Louis XIII, and later moved to Holland where he joined the Jewish community in Amsterdam. A lyric poet of some quality, he also wrote plays in the Calderonian mode, including *A lo que obliga el honor* (1642); but it is for his prose work, *El siglo pitagórico y vida de don Gregorio Guadaña* (1644), in which he combines keen observation of the social scene with subtle wit and a fluent style, that Enríquez will be remembered. He returned secretly to Spain and continued writing plays under the pseudonym of 'Fernando de Zarate', dying in Seville in the cells of the Inquisition.

**Enzensberger, Hans Magnus** (1929–    ), German poet and prose-writer, born at Kaufbeuren (Bayern). He studied philosophy and letters at various West German universities, taking his doctorate at the Sorbonne. He has travelled widely. In his volume of poetry, *Landessprache* (1960), he proves himself to be a didactic writer concerned with the individual faced by the forces of convention. He has also edited the anthology *Museum der modernen Poesie* (1960), has made a study of Brentano's (q.v.) poetry (1961) and has translated the poetry of Seferis (q.v.).

**Eötvös, József** (1813–1871), Hungarian novelist and miscellaneous prose-writer, was born of noble family at Buda, and made his literary name as early as 1838 with his novel *A Karthauzi* ('The

Carthusian'), which revealed French romantic influence. His second
novel, *A falu jegyzöje* (3 vols., 1845–6; Eng. trans. *The Village Notary*,
3 vols., 1850), is a powerful attack on serfdom, but is more than a
veiled political tract and contains much incident, good characterization and humour, and is written in a vigorous style. He had already
made his mark in politics as a liberal and supporter of Kossuth, and
when the revolution of 1848 broke out was nominated minister of
public instruction. The following year he was forced into exile and
settled in Munich, where he wrote *A XIX. század uralkodó eszmienek
befolyása az álladalomra* (2 vols., 1851–4, 'The Influence of the Leading Ideas of the Nineteenth Century upon the State'), an important
work. On his return to Hungary he again entered politics, becoming
minister of worship and education in 1867. He died in Budapest.

**Épinay, Louise Florence Pétronille d'Esclavelles d'** (1726–1783),
French prose-writer. Born at Valenciennes, she married her cousin,
but this broke down, and she later became the mistress of J.-J.
Rousseau, for whom she built the cottage called the Hermitage in
the valley of Montmorency. After this she formed a liaison with
F. M. Grimm. She died in Paris. Her main works are *Conversations
d'Émilie* (1774), a treatise on education deeply influenced by Rousseau,
and her highly interesting *Mémoires* (1818; Eng. trans. by J. H.
Freese, 1897; and in the Broadway Library together with her
*Correspondance*, 1930).

**Erasmus, Desiderius** (1469–1536), Dutch humanist, born in Rotterdam. His father was a priest of Gouda, his mother unknown. Educated
at Deventer and 's-Hertogenbosch, he entered the Stein monastery
in 1486, finally joining the Augustinians and becoming a priest in
1492. In 1493 the Bishop of Cambrai freed him from monastic life by
making him his secretary, later allowing him to study in Paris. Here
he remained with one break until 1499, taking pupils to eke out a
livelihood. It was one of these pupils, Lord Mountjoy, who brought
him to England, where he formed lifelong friendships with More and
Colet. Living chiefly in Oxford he was introduced to Greek by Grocyn
and Linacre, and in 1500 returned to Paris with the decision to devote
his whole time to study. He led a hard life for the next six years, then
revisited England where his growing scholarship was hailed with
enthusiasm. Next he went to Italy, and returned to England at the
invitation of Fisher, Bishop of London and Chancellor of Cambridge
University. in 1509, where he was appointed Lady Margaret professor
of divinity. While in Italy he had published his *Adagia* (1508), a
collection of classical sayings, and now while happily settled at Cambridge he wrote his great satire with its rich literary qualities, the
*Moriae encomium* (Eng. trans. *Praise of Folly*, 1959), and finished
his edition of the New Testament (1516) which entitles him to be
called the father of modern biblical criticism. In the same year he
showed in the most readable and witty of all his works, the *Colloquia*
(Eng. trans. *Colloquies*, 1965), that he was not blind to the shortcomings of many of the clergy and looked for a return to purity in its
fullest sense in the Church. From 1517 to 1521 Erasmus lived at
Louvain, greatly troubled by the Reformation. Both sides urged him

to write for them, and in the end he took refuge in Basel. However much he wanted reform he wanted it within the Church: he wanted a return to fundamentals, to the Fathers, many of whose works he edited. In fact he was a scholar, not a theologian, but he refused to go Luther's way, as he declared in *De Libero Arbitrio* (1521). He then returned to pure scholarship with *Ciceronianus* (1528), a plea for a better Latin prose style among Italian scholars. Then in 1529 the Reformation caught up with him at Basel and he was forced to go to Freiburg, where he remained till 1535, publishing there amid other works *Apophthegmata* (1531), an excellently written and personal piece of scholarship. He died on a visit to Basel. Apart from being a man of letters in his own right, Erasmus did more than any other scholar to urge on intellectual liberty and the revival of true learning. There is an edition of the *Opera Omnia* by J. Le Clerc (10 vols., 1703–6). *See* P. S. Allen's edition of the *Epistolae* (1906–58; Eng. trans. of the earlier letters by F. M. Nichols, 3 vols., 1901–17).

**Erben, Karel Jaromír** (1811–1870), Czech poet. The son of a farmer, he was born at Miletín and became a lawyer, settling in Prague, where he was appointed city archivist in 1851. A student of Czech folk-literature, he was inspired by it to produce a small volume of original poetry, *Kytice* (1853, 'The Garland'), which holds an important place in Czech letters. Among his collected works (*Dílo*, 5 vols., 1938–9) is to be found the remarkable gathering of Czech ballads and lyrics which were first published in 1862–4. Erben died in Prague.

**Ercilla y Zúñiga, Alonso de** (1533–1594?), Spanish poet, born in Madrid, where he presumably died. Of noble family, he was a member of the court of Philip II and visited England. His taking part as a combatant in the war against the Araucanian Indians of Chile inspired him to write his great epic *La Araucana* (Part I, 1569, Part II, 1578, Part III, 1589). It is especially notable for magnificent descriptions, and no less for the deep sympathy for the Indians which it evinces. The best edition of the work is that by T. Medina (Santiago, Chile, 4 vols., 1916). The first part of the First Book has been translated into English by W. Owen (Buenos Aires, 1945).

**Erckmann-Chatrian**, the compound name representing Émile Erck-mann (1822–1899) and Alexandre Chatrian (1826–1890), the two Lorrainers well known for their Alsatian novels. Erckmann, born at Phalsbourg, became a lawyer in Paris, while Chatrian, born at Soldatenthal, after employment in a glass-works, took up teaching in Phalsbourg, and here the two met. Their collaboration began in 1848, but they had little success until 1859 when *L'Illustre Docteur Mathéus* brought them a wide public. Novels about the last years of the Napoleonic Wars such as *Histoire d'un conscrit de 1813* (1864; Eng. trans. *The Conscript*, 1909) and *Waterloo* (1865; Eng. trans. 1909) proved very popular. *L'Ami Fritz* (1864; dramatized 1876) is idealistic in tone, while *Le Blocus* (1867; Eng. trans. *The Blockade of Phalsbourg*, 1870) is realistic. In *L'Histoire d'un paysan* (4 vols., 1868–70; Eng. trans. *The Story of a Peasant*, 1915) the best elements of their work, the historical vision and a love and understanding of the simple life of their native region, are displayed. After the German

annexation of Alsace-Lorraine they turned their anger on the conquerors in *L'Histoire d'un plébiscite* (1872) and *Le Brigadier Frédéric*
(1874). As dramatists *Le Juif polonais* (1869), under the title of *The
Bells*, made a great impression on the British public from 1871
onwards with Henry Irving playing a leading role. The two authors
quarrelled about money and parted in 1889, Chatrian dying the next
year at Villenomble. Erckmann lived on for over eight years and died
at Lunéville. According to E. About (q.v.) they seldom met but
collaborated by post.

**Ernst, Paul Carl Friedrich** (1866–1933), German dramatist and prose-
writer, was born at Elbingerode in the Harz. In 1905 he obtained an
appointment at the Düsseldorf Theatre, and wrote for it historical
tragedies such as *Demetrios* (1905), *Canossa* (1908), *Brunhild* (1909)
and *Ariadne* (1912). As a prose-writer he cultivated the *Novelle* in such
works as *Die selige Insel* (1909), *Troubadourgeschichten* (1929) and
*Das Glück von Lautenthal* (1932). He died at St Georgen, Styria.

**Ersch, Johann Samuel** (1766–1828), German bibliographer. Born at
Grossglogau, Silesia, he became professor at Jena in 1803 and
librarian at Halle in 1808. His *Handbuch der deutschen Literatur seit
der Mitte des 18ten Jahrhunderts* (1812–14) is the pioneer work of
modern German bibliography. He was chief editor of the *Allgemeine
Encyklopädie der Wissenschaften und Künste* until his death at Halle.

**Esenin, Sergey Alexandrovich** (1895–1925), Russian Soviet poet.
Born the son of a peasant at Konstantinovo, he received practically
no education, but imbibed the rich folklore which surrounded him.
This and his deep understanding and love of age-old village patriarchal
life provided the inspiration for his first volume of poems (1915). At
first he welcomed the revolution, but when he saw that the Bolsheviks
were simply ready to exploit the countryside for the benefit of a
highly industrialized urban civilization, his spirit was broken. He
entered the wild Bohemian world of Moscow, where although making
positive strides in his art by forming the Russian Imagist group, he
damaged his health and made a disastrous marriage with the famous
American ballet dancer Isadora Duncan (1878–1927), who divorced
him. His second marriage, to Tolstoy's grand-daughter, fared little
better. His travels in the Middle East seemed to be a way of escape
for a time, but when this failed and he found himself forced to face
the ruined Eden of Russian country life or the harsh modern life of
the cities, this was too much for him and he committed suicide in
Leningrad. One of the greatest of Russian lyric poets, whether he is
describing the mad life of the towns of post-1917, mourning the
changes in pastoral life or celebrating the exoticism which he found
in Persia (*Persidskie motivy*, 1924–5, 'Persian Themes') he always
shows power and an exquisite sensibility. His collected works appeared
(4 vols.) in 1926–7.

**Espina, Antonio** (1893–    ), Spanish novelist and short-story writer,
born in Madrid. Among his works should be mentioned: *Luna de
copas* (1929), *Luis Candelas, el bandido de Madrid* (1930; Eng. trans.
in W. B. Wells's *Great Spanish Short Stories*, 1932), *Romea, o el*

*comediante* (1935), *El libro del aire* (1957) and *El libro de las montañas* (1958).

**Espina de la Serna, Concha** (1877–1955), Spanish novelist, born in Santander, she became known as a competent novelist writing in a somewhat old-fashioned style on old-fashioned themes. Of her later and most mature works perhaps *El metal de los muertos* (1920), *Altar mayor* (1926), *La virgen prudente* (1930) and *El más fuerte* (1947) are the best. She died in Santander.

**Espinosa, Pedro** (1578–1650), Spanish anthologist, whose *Flores de poetas ilustres* (1605) is one of the most important collections of verse in the language, containing as it does an exquisitely chosen selection of the poetry of Spain's golden age, was born at Antequera and died in Orders at Sanlúcar. There is a good edition of the *Flores* by Quirós and Rodríguez (2 vols., 1896).

**Espronceda, José de** (1808–1842), Spanish poet, born near Almendralejo, Estremadura, by 1826 had been involved in conspiracies against the absolutist throne and had had to take refuge in Gibraltar. He soon found his way to England, and thereafter went to Holland to stir up the Liberal cause there. He took an active part in the French Revolution of 1830, but when amnestied in 1833 on the death of Ferdinand VII hurried back to Spain and joined Isabel II's bodyguard. Not long afterwards, however, he lost his post because of continued attacks on the regime, and lived in retirement until 1841 when he became secretary of the embassy at The Hague. Elected Liberal deputy to the Cortes for Almería, he died in Madrid the same year. Espronceda is the chief Spanish representative of Byronic romanticism, and his lyrical powers are very fine, especially when dealing with patriotism, justice and freedom. His two great works are *Canto a Teresa*, the subject of which is his pilgrimage through life from a time of love and illusion to a time of thoughts of death and disillusion, and the eerie *El estudiante de Salamanca*, full of Don Juanism, both of them written at the time of his retirement during the later 1830's. *El diablo mundo* (1840), in which he attempts the Faust theme, is far less successful. There is a complete edition of his works by J. J. Domenchina (1945), although Moreno's selective edition (1923) which includes all the best works is more useful for general reading. J. Kennedy's *Modern Poets and Poetry of Spain* (1860) contains some translations. See also *Translations from Hispanic Poets* (N.Y., 1938).

**Esquiros, Henri Alphonse** (1814–1876), French novelist and political pamphleteer, also writing historical and topographical works in English. Born in Paris, he turned to a literary life and journalism, and published two romantic pieces of fiction, *Le Magicien* (1837) and *Charlotte Corday* (1840). His *Évangile du peuple* (1840) was a socialist interpretation of the life of Jesus, and with it he came into collision with the Louis-Philippe government. At the revolution of 1848 he was elected a member of the Legislative Assembly, but was obliged to escape to England at the *coup d'état* of Louis-Napoleon of 1851. There he produced several works in English, including *Religious Life in*

*England* (1867). Later he was allowed to return to France by an amnesty of Napoleon III. He became a senator in 1875, dying at Marseille the following year.

**Estaunié, Édouard** (1862–1942), French novelist. Born in Dijon, he is remembered for his psychological analytical accounts of the day to day lives of the poor, the simple and the outcast such as *L'Empreinte* (1895), *L'Épave* (1902), *La Vie secrète* (1908), *Solitudes* (1917), *L'Ascension de M. Baslèvre* (1921), *L'Infirme aux mains de lumière* (1924), *Tels qu'ils furent* (1927) and *Madame Clapain* (1940). He died in Paris.

**Estébanez Calderón,** *see* **Calderón, S. E.**

**Estella, Diego de** (1524–1578), Spanish religious prose-writer, born at Estella, became a Franciscan and died in Salamanca. Some of his devotional works, written in magnificent prose, exercised a great influence in Spain, France and Italy. *Un tratado de la vanidad del mundo* (1574) was widely read in England. A translation of it by T. Rogers, *A Methode unto Mortification called the Contempt of the Worlde*, appeared in 1586 and was reprinted in 1605.

**Estienne, Henri** (1531–1598), French humanist, born in Paris the son of the famous printer, Robert, his scholarship was revealed in his edition of the pseudo-Anacreon *(editio princeps)* in 1554. He is above all remembered for his erudite *Thesaurus graecae linguae* (1572), still very much alive today. His *Apologie pour Hérodote* (1566) reveals him in a new light, a sceptic and an amoralist. He died in Lyon.

**Etlar, C.,** *see* **Brosbøll, J. C. C.**

**Evtushenko, E.,** *see* **Yevtushenko, Y.**

**Ewald, Carl** (1856–1908), Danish novelist, born at Gram, Slesvig, he became known as a writer of historical novels, novels dealing with contemporary problems, and short stories. Good examples of these are *Fru Johanne* (1892), *De fire Fjerdingsfyrster* (1895; Eng. trans. *The Four Seasons*, 1913), *Min lille Dreng* (1899; Eng. trans. *My Little Boy*, 1908) and *Karl Peter Ulrik* (1905). He died at Charlottenlund.

**Ewald, Herman Frederik** (1821–1908), Danish novelist. Born in Copenhagen, he wrote stilted historical novels in a kind of debased Scott manner, chief of which is *Valdemar Krones Ungdomshistorie* (1860; Eng. trans. *The Story of Waldemar Krone's Youth*, 2 vols., 1867). Other representative works are *Knud Gyldenstjerne* (1875), *Anna Hardenberg* (1880), *Griffenfeld* (1888), *Caroline Mathilde* (1890) and *Daniel Rantzow* (1899). He died at Fredensborg.

**Ewald, Johannes** (1743–1781), Danish playwright, poet and autobiographer, was born in Copenhagen, the son of a strict pietistic pastor. He ran away from school to Hamburg, returned to Copenhagen and began to study theology, took some part as a volunteer to the Austrian army in the Seven Years War, obtaining his discharge and returning home in 1760. The marriage of his fiancée to someone else in 1764 completely changed his life. From being a happy-go-lucky wanderer he became a broken-down drunkard, whose reckless life made an end of him before he was forty. But his sorrows and disappointments brought out the poet in him, and he grew to be the greatest poet of Denmark. His allegorical poem *Lykkens Tempel* (1764) was successful, and it was soon seen how he could lead the way in breathing new life into the old. His work is inspired by the northern sagas, by ballads and by Shakespeare, Milton and Klopstock (q.v.). His verse plays with their fine lyrics are splendid pieces of work. Chief of these are the biblical drama *Adam og Eva* (1769), *Balders Død* (1774–5; Eng. trans. by George Borrow, *The Death of Balder*), his masterpiece inspired by his studies of old Scandinavian literature, and *Fiskerne* (1779), a drama of ordinary life, containing the majestic lyric translated by Longfellow, 'Kong Christian stod ved höjen Mast'. *Rolf Krage* (1770) is a prose tragedy. *Adskilligt af Johannes Ewald* (1771) is a volume of poetry. At his death in Copenhagen he left unfinished his vivid autobiography, *Johannes Ewalds Levnet og Meninger*, not published until 1804 (mod. ed., 1942). His collected works appeared (6 vols.) between 1914 and 1924.

**Eyth, Max von** (1836–1906), German novelist, born at Kirchheim-unter-Teck. He became an engineer, travelling in various parts of Europe, Egypt and in many parts of the American continent, not returning to Germany until 1882. Already in 1871 he had begun to publish a fictional series, turning to good account his knowledge and experiences in his *Wanderbuch eines Ingenieurs*, the sixth and last volume of which appeared in 1884. *Der Waldteufel* (1878) and *Der Kampf um die Cheopspyramide* (2 vols., 1902) are other examples of his work, which illustrate the growth of the impact of science on the general reading public. Eyth died in Ulm.

**Ezzo of Bamberg** ( *fl.* 1060), German religious poet. He was a canon of Bamberg who about 1060 composed a rhyming poem, a narrative running from the Creation to the Resurrection, known as the *Ezzolied* or *Anegenge*. Its influence on German literature was immense.

# F

**Fabre, Ferdinand** (1830–1898), French novelist. Of peasant origin, he was born at Bedarieux, and was sent to a seminary to study for the priesthood. Abandoning this he went to Paris and worked in a lawyer's office until his health broke down and he had to return home. There in retirement he tried his hand at writing and discovered his gift. When he returned to Paris in 1861 he had written *Les Courbezon*, the first of that long line of novels inspired by the country life of his native Provence. His analysis of peasant character and of priests is particularly good, as, for example, in *Julien Savignac* (1863), *L'Abbé Tigrane* (1873), *Barnabé* (1875), *La Petite Mère* (1877; renamed *Madame Fuster*, 1887), *Mon Oncle Célestin* (1881), *Toussaint Galabru* (1887) and *L'Abbé Roitelet* (1890). He was appointed director of the Mazarin Library in 1883, dying in Paris.

**Fabre d'Églantine, Philippe François Nazaire** (1750–1794), French playwright and song-writer, was born at Carcassonne and became a priest, abandoning his Orders at the outbreak of the French Revolution. He became a member of the National Convention, was president of the Cordeliers club and was Danton's secretary. An aesthete, he was responsible for introducing symbolism into republican ceremonial and he composed the republican calendar. One of the leading playwrights of the revolution, his best works are *Philinte* (1790) and *L'Aristocrate ou le convalescent de qualité* (1791). Among his songs is the charming ' Il pleut, il pleut, bergère, rentre tes blancs moutons '. One of Robespierre's victims, he was guillotined in Paris.

**Fabricius, Johan** (1899– ), Dutch novelist, born at Bandoeng, Dutch East Indies, his first important work was *Het Meisje met de blauwe Hoed* (1927; Eng. trans. *The Girl in the Blue Hat*, 1932), and among those which followed should be mentioned *Mario Ferraro's ijdele Liefde* (1929; Eng. trans. *Vain Love*, 1931), *Leeuwen hongeren in Napels* (1934; Eng. trans. *The Lions starve in Naples*, 1934), *Nacht over Java* (1942), which appeared three years after he had settled in London, and *Mijn Huis staat achter de Kim* (1951; Eng. trans. *A Dutchman at Large, Memoirs*, 1952).

**Fabricius, Johann Albert** (1668–1736), German bibliographer and literary historian, was born in Leipzig and became professor of rhetoric and ethics in the Hamburg gymnasium. He laid the foundation of modern critical methods in literature with *Bibliotheca Latina* (1697) and *Bibliotheca Graeca* (1705–28), one of the greatest pieces of scholarship of the age. With his *Codex Apocryphus* (1703) he put manuscript scholarship on a secure scientific basis. He died in Hamburg.

**Fadeyev, Alexander Alexandrovich** (1901–56), Russian Soviet novelist, born at Kimry in the province of Tver, the son of peasants, he was another of the writers who contributed to the large literary fictional output on the civil war of 1918–21 with *Razgrom* (1927; Eng. trans. *The Nineteen*, 1929). A lengthy novel set in Siberia, *Posledniy iz Udeghé* (1928, 'The Last of the Udegs') is more ambitious than successful. The patriotic war novel, *Molodaya Gvardiya* (1945, 'The Young Guard'), deals with life in the German-occupied Ukraine. President of the Union of Soviet Writers, personal attacks were made against him at the Congress of the Union in 1955, which he took so much to heart that he committed suicide in Moscow the following year.

**Faesi, Robert** (1883–    ), Swiss poet and playwright, was born in Zürich and eventually became professor of German literature there. His fastidious art is particularly well seen in the volume of poetry, *Aus der Brandung* (1917), and in his plays *Die Fassade* (1918) and *Opferspiel* (1925). His greatest work is the trilogy on his native city, *Die Stadt der Väter* (1941), *Die Stadt der Freiheit* (1944) and *Die Stadt des Friedes* (1953).

**Faguet, Émile** (1847–1916), French critic and essayist. Born at La Roche-sur-Yon, he followed an academic career, becoming a member of the faculty of letters at the Sorbonne. Perhaps the most influential literary critic of his day, especially when he succeeded to the post of editor of the *Journal des Débats*, he is at his best in the purely scholarly field in *La Tragédie française au 16e siècle* (1883), companion studies on nineteenth-century French tragedy, on that of the seventeenth century and on that of the eighteenth century appearing the first in 1887 and the other two in 1890. Other purely literary critical books, all of great power and perspicacity, are *Voltaire* (1895), *Flaubert* (1899), *Propos littéraires* (5 series, 1902–10), *La Fontaine* (1913) and the posthumous *Histoire de la poésie française de la Renaissance au Romantisme* (1923). As an essayist he proved a brilliant controversialist with robust prejudices as, for example, in *Politiques et moralistes du 19e siècle* (1891; rev., 1900), *L'Anticlericalisme* (1906), *Le Pacifisme* (1908), *La Démission de la morale* (1910) and *Les Préjugés nécessaires* (1911). He died in Paris.

**Faidit, Gaucelm** ( *fl.* 1190–1220), French troubadour. Born at Uzerche, Limousin, he gained the patronage of Richard Cœur de Lion. He left a large number of poems, outstanding among which are a lament for Richard (1199) and *Le Triomphe de l'amour*, imitated by Petrarch.

**Fallada, Hans**, pseudonym of **Rudolf Ditzen** (1893–1947), German novelist born at Greifswald. A realist whose most deeply felt and most powerfully conceived theme is the average man confronted by sharp realities, he always manages to rise above the sense of near frustration which a survey of the world around him brings. His first success, a book which he may have occasionally equalled but never surpassed aptly dealing with this theme, is *Kleiner Mann, was nun?*

(1932; Eng. trans. *Little Man, What Now?*, 1933). Of his other novels may be mentioned *Wer einmal aus dem Blechnapf frisst* (1934; Eng. trans. *Who once Eats out of the Tin Bowl*, 1934), *Der eiserne Gustav* (1938), *Der ungeliebte Mann* (1940), *In Namen des Volkes* (1946) and *Der Trinker* (1950). He died in Berlin.

**Fangen, Ronald August** (1895–1946), Norwegian novelist, born at Kragerø, who in his many successful, though technically faulty, novels posed religious answers to world problems, and was an unmerciful opponent of materialism in all its forms. Probably his best-known work is *En lysets engel* (1945; Eng. trans. *Both are my Cousins* 1949). He died at Fornebu, near Oslo.

**Fantoni, Giovanni** (1755–1807), Italian poet, born at Fivizzano, where he died on his estate. A typical cultured dilettante of the time, he was an army officer and a member of the Arcadian Academy. He later held an appointment at the University of Pisa. Between 1784 and his death he published three collections of *Odi*, Horatian in metre, but in rhyme. Musical and smooth in execution, they are perfect examples of the later stages of what may be termed Italianesque classicism. There is an edition of his *Poesie* by Lazzeri (1913).

**Fargue, Léon-Paul** (1876–1947), French poet, born in Paris, where he died, having recaptured the atmospheric qualities of his native city better than anyone since Baudelaire (q.v.). He could not have had better masters for his type of mental approach to poetry than Laforgue (q.v.) and Verlaine (q.v.), and from the time of his first considerable volume of verse, *Tancrède* (1911), onwards he proved that an inspiration derived from an honest acceptance of modern urban life as it was need not displace the classical concept. Before he was forty he had joined an active literary and artistic group, being one of those responsible for the foundation of *La Nouvelle Revue Française* (1912). In the same year his volume *Poèmes* appeared. In his post-war poetry there is an increasing preoccupation with industrial life and there are outbreaks of humour, invariably kindly; but side by side with it is that particularly effective 'analysis of atmosphere' which gives Fargue's work its special flavour. This period opens with *Pour la musique* (1919) and continues in such volumes as *Sous la lampe* (1930), *D'après Paris* (1931) and *Le Piéton de Paris* (1939). During the Second World War his publications continued with *Haute-Solitude* (1941) and *Lanterne magique* (1944; Eng. trans. *Magic Lantern*, 1946). *Méandres* was published in the year of his death.

**Farrère, Claude**, pseudonym of **Frédéric Charles Bargone** (1876–1957), French novelist. Born in Lyon, he joined the navy, making use of his varied experiences on his travels for the plots of his strong and attractively written novels. His *penchant* was particularly towards the Far East. He is at his best in such novels as *Fumée d'opium* (1904), *Les Civilisés* (1906), *La Bataille* (1909), *Thomas l'Agnelet* (1913) and *Les Condamnés à mort* (1921). Of his later work *La Seconde Porte* (1945), *Job siècle XX* (1949) and *Les Petites Cousines* (1953) may be mentioned. His study of Pierre Loti (q.v.), whom he greatly admired, appeared as *Loti* (1930). He died in Paris.

**Favart, Charles-Simon** (1710–1792), French dramatist. Born in Paris, he became director of the Opéra-Comique. Influenced by his wife, the well-known actress Marie-Justine Duronceray, whom he married in 1745, he began to insist (the first manager in Europe to do so) that actors should dress not exclusively in contemporary costume, but in dress suited to the parts they took, which led Garrick among others to adopt the same policy. Favart excelled in the pastoral play, derived from Italian sources, usually comedy, and containing a wealth of lyrics. Most typical and attractive of his works are *Bastien et Bastienne* (1753), later set to music by Mozart, *Ninette à la cour* (1755), *Annette et Lubin* (1762) and *Les Moissonneurs* (1768). There is a definitive edition of his *Œuvres* by L. Gozlan (1853). His *Mémoires et correspondance* appeared in 1809. He died at Belleville.

**Fáy, András** (1786–1864), Hungarian fabulist. Born at Kohány, he became a man of letters in Pest, where he died. His work on social questions, economics and education was important in its day, but he is remembered now for his collection of fables and aphorisms, *Fáy András eredeti meséi es aforizmái* (1820).

**Fedin, Konstantin Alexandrovich** (1892–    ), Russian Soviet novelist, born at Saratov of mixed aristocratic and peasant family. Interned in Germany during the First World War he returned to Russia in 1918 and served in the Red Army during the civil war of 1918–21. His story, *Transvaal* (1928), describes the career of a prosperous peasant of Boer origin. It took him long to acclimatize himself to Communism, but during the thirties he managed to do so; but it was not until after the Second World War that he became established as perhaps the greatest novelist of the post-war years with *Pervye radosti* (1945; Eng. trans. *Early Joys*, 1950) and *Neobyknovennoye leto* (1948; Eng. trans. *No Ordinary Summer*, 1950), both set in a small town on the Volga, the first in 1913–14, the second in 1919 after the revolution.

**Feijó, António Joaquim de Castro** (1862–1917), Portuguese poet, born at Ponte de Lima. He joined the diplomatic service, serving for many years in Sweden where he died in Stockholm. A quiet, introspective and highly cultured poet, his best work such as *Transfigurações* (1882), *Líricas e bucólicas* (1884) and above all the sensuous *Cancioneiro chinês* (1890; Eng. trans. *Songs of Li-Tai-Pé from the Cancioneiro chinês of António Castro Feijó*, 1922), approximate to the Parnassian style. After passing through a stage of half mockery and half tenderness, as in *Bailatas* (1897), he finally settled down into the sadness bordering on pessimism to be found in the posthumous *Sol de inverno* (1922).

**Feijoó y Montenegro, Benito** (1676–1764), Spanish prose-writer, born at Casdemiro, Orense, became a Benedictine and later held various posts at Oviedo University. He set himself from the first to keep abreast of the new thought, which following hard on the new science and the new philosophy, was sweeping the Europe of his day. It is not too much to say that no single Spaniard has so tremendously influenced his countrymen as he. Above all he showed that, though a rationalist and an opponent of effete scholasticism and superstition, his faith remained unimpaired. The 'Spanish Encyclopaedist' gained a European reputation in his lifetime, his two master works being *Teatro crítico y universal* (8 vols., 1726-39) and *Cartas eruditas y curiosas* (5 vols., 1742-60). He died at Oviedo. An honoured name among the intellectuals of the generation following his death, the consequent political reaction after the death of Charles III rendered him half forgotten until recent times, when he has been rediscovered and even credited with pure scientific ideas to which he would hardly have laid claim. Many English translations were made of Feijoó in the eighteenth century, several of them from larger works. Examples are: *The Honor and Advantage of Agriculture* (1764), *An Essay of the Learning, Genius and Abilities of the Fair Sex* (1774) and *Essays or Discourses* (vol. i, 1777; vol. ii, 1780).

**Feisilber, I.,** *see* Ilf.

**Feith, Rhijnvis** (1753-1824), Dutch novelist, poet and playwright, born at Zwolle, of which he later became mayor, he was well known in his day as a poet (his best work is to be found among his five volumes of *Oden en Gedichten*, 1796-1814). His tragedies, such as *Thirsa* (1784) and *Ines de Castro* (1793), have also faded; but his three love tales, *Julia* (1783), *Fanny* (1783) and *Ferdinand en Constantia* (1785), possess a particular quality, a kind of inverted Werther theme: the sorrows of love are a foretaste of the happiness of love in the hereafter. He died at Zwolle.

**Feliú y Codina, José** (1847-1897), Spanish dramatist. Born in Barcelona, he developed late as a playwright, but made a name for himself on the Madrid stage with such neo-romantic plays, many with strong characterization and interesting regional settings, as *La Dolores* (1892), his masterpiece set in Aragon, *Miel de la Alcarria* (1893), *María del Carmen* (1896) and *Boca de fraile* (1897). He died in Madrid.

**Fénelon, François de Salignac de la Motte** (1651-1715), French prosewriter. Born of a landed family near Sarlat, near Fénelon, Périgord, he was ordained priest in 1675, and from 1679 was employed in various ways as a missioner to the Huguenots. His success (occasioned sometimes by methods not above criticism) in converting Protestants at La Rochelle brought him to the notice of Bossuet (q.v.) and the court. His *Traité de l'éducation des filles* (1687) led to friendship with Madame de Maintenon, and two years later he became tutor to Louis XIV's grandson, the Duke of Burgundy. The outcome of this appointment was the composition, to help his pupil to learn about Greek literature, of *Les Aventures de Télémaque*, not published until 1699. This book, inspired by the *Odyssey*, voiced ideas far in advance of the time which were not at all pleasing to the king, and this, coupled with a mystical work, *L'Explication des maximes des saints sur la vie intérieure* (1697), condemned by the Vatican the same year that *Télémaque* was published, led to his banishment to his diocese of Cambrai (he had become archbishop in 1695). There he died in complete retirement. A controversial figure, both over-praised and over-condemned (*see*

E. K. Sanders, *Fénelon, his Friends and Enemies*, 1901), his *Dialogues des morts* (1691) remained a very influential moral work for nearly a century. His *Œuvres complètes* were published (34 vols.) in 1820–30.

**Fernández de Moratín,** *see* **Moratín.**

**Fernández de Velasco y Pimentel, Bernardino** (1783–1851), Spanish poet, born in Madrid. As the duque de Frías he took a leading part in politics as a Liberal both during the Napoleonic wars and after the return of Ferdinand VII, who threatened his life; but he survived to become Spanish ambassador first in Britain and afterwards in France. As a poet he represents a revolt against the romantics and a return to the classical. His best works are elegiac, e.g. the noble 'Llanto del proscrito' with its theme of exile. He died in Madrid. His *Obras poéticas* appeared in 1857.

**Fernández Flórez, Wenceslao** (1886–    ), Spanish novelist and short-story writer, born at La Coruña. He became a journalist and made a reputation with his collection of short stories, *Las gafas del diablo* (1918). Of his other works the most important are *Las siete columnas* (1926; Eng. trans. *The Seven Pillars*, 1934) and *Los que no fuímos a la guerra* (1930). In his later books he developed a very fast-moving style, e.g. in *El toro, el torero y el gato* (1946) and *El bosque animado* (1947). *Mis mejores páginas*, an anthology of his best passages, came out in 1956.

**Ferrari, Paolo** (1822–1889), Italian dramatist. Born in Modena, he wrote many excellent costume comedies, the best of which, historical evocations of literary personages, are *Goldoni* (1852) and *Parini e la satira* (1857). He became professor of history at Modena and later at Milan where he died. See W. Pater's *Miscellaneous Studies* (1895).

**Ferreira, António** (1528–1569), Portuguese poet and dramatist, was born in Lisbon and educated at Coimbra where he eventually held a professorship. He later became a magistrate and held offices at court. A disciple of Sá de Miranda (q.v.) he eagerly followed the poetical styles of Italy. As a poet he was best in the epistle, but it is as a dramatist that he is remembered. Above all his *Tragédia de D. Inês de Castro*, composed about 1560 but not published until 1587 (Eng. trans. 1697), is of outstanding value. His two comedies, *Bristo* and *O Cioso*, appeared in *Comédias famosas portuguesas dos doctores Francisco de Sá de Miranda e António Ferreira* (1622). Portuguese literature owes an enormous debt to Ferreira in that, at a time when writers of his nation were becoming more and more inclined to turn to Spanish as the literary language, he stood out against it, and in breathing new life into classical Portuguese preserved it during a dangerous period. After 1580 national resentment against Spain made further Castilian infiltration into Portuguese literature impossible. Ferreira, none of whose works were published in his lifetime, died of plague in Lisbon.

**Ferreira de Castro, J. M.,** *see* **Castro, J. M. F. de.**

**Ferrier, Paul** (1843–1920), French dramatist, born at Montpellier. He was the author of many operettas, comedies and revues, all vivacious and humorous, including *Joséphine vendue par ses sœurs* (1886), *La Belle Mère* (1898) and *La Fille de Tabarin* (1901). He died at Nouan-le-Fuzelier.

**Fet, Afanasy Afanasyevich** (1820–1892), Russian poet and translator. Born of a landowning family near Mtsensk, he kept out of politics and avoided social matters in his optimistic poems, being attacked for this by the radicals who between about 1860 and 1880 swamped Russian literature. At last, however, he won through to fame, and in his final years basked in the popularity accorded to him by the symbolist school. He is essentially a lyricist, his favourite subjects being country life and love. Besides these are the fine poems written at the very end of his life in which he faces death with a calm and dignity, matched by the majesty of the verse. Of his translations he excelled in those from the classics and from German, especially Goethe. His collected poetry appeared as *Polnoye sobranie stikhotvoreniy* in several editions from 1901 onwards. He died on his estate near Mtsensk.

**Feuchtersleben, Ernst von** (1806–1840), Austrian poet and prose-writer. Born in Vienna, he soon found himself at home in art circles, gaining the friendship of the composer Schubert and of Stifter (q.v.). As a poet his *Gedichte* (1836) is a quietly well-bred collection. It was as a writer of pseudo-philosophy and psychology, especially in *Diätetik der Seele* (1838; Eng. trans. *The Hygiene of the Mind*, 1933), that he gained a reputation, and proved that he was able to do that difficult thing, write popular works without sacrificing literary style and without writing down to the reader. He died in Vienna.

**Feuchtwanger, Lion** (1884–1958), German novelist, playwright and prose-writer. Born in Munich, he first made a name with his play *Hastings* (1916; Eng. trans. *Warren Hastings*, 1928), but it was his historical novels, written in modern psychological terms, that brought him fame. First came *Die hässliche Herzogin* (1923; Eng. trans. *The Ugly Duchess*, 1927), then *Jud Süss* (1924; Eng. trans. *Power*, 1926; Eng. dramatic version, *Jew Suss*, 1929; film *Jew Suss*, 1934), generally considered his masterpiece, *Drei Jahre Geschichte einer Provinz* (1930; Eng. trans. *Success*, 1930) and *Die Geschwister Oppenheim* (1933; Eng. trans. *The Oppermanns*, 1933). Already he had begun his ambitious *Josephus-Trilogie* with the first part, *Der jüdische Krieg* (1932; Eng. trans. *Josephus*, 1932). The second part, *Die Söhne* (1935; Eng. trans. *The Jew of Rome*, 1935), was written in the exile forced on him by the rise of Hitler, and the third part first appeared in English as *Josephus and the Emperor* in 1942 (German version *Der Tag wird kommen*, 1945). Another novel, *Der falsche Nero* (1936; Eng. trans. *The Pretender*, 1937), gave place to non-fiction, the result of his increased preoccupation with the political state of Europe, such as *Moskau* (1937; Eng. trans. *Moscow*, 1937), *Exil* (1940; Eng. trans. *Paris Gazette*, 1940) and *Unholdes Frankreich* (1941; Eng. trans. *The Devil in France*, 1941). Although he had scored a success with his play *Die Petroleuminseln* (1927; Eng. trans. *The Oil Islands*, 1928), he had not developed this medium. The best of his later novels is *Goya, oder der arge Weg der Erkenntnis* (1951; Eng. trans. *This is the Hour*, 1952). He made fine translations of

Aeschylus and Aristophanes, and a masterly German rendering of Marlowe's *Edward II* in 1924. He died at Pacific Palisades, California.

**Feuillet, Octave** (1821–1890), French novelist and dramatist. Born at Saint-Lô, he went to Paris and became a literary assistant to Dumas *père* (q.v.). His play *La Crise* (1848) met with favourable notice, increased by his contributions to the *Revue des Deux Mondes*, entitled *Scènes et proverbes* and *Scènes et comédies* (1853–6). Then came the outstanding success of his idealistically inclined novel, *Le Roman d'un jeune homme pauvre* (1858), which was dramatized the same year. The idol of bourgeois purposefulness and morality, he followed this up with *Histoire de Sibylle* (1862), which led to the patronage of the Empress Eugénie with the result that that very year he was elected Scribe's (q.v.) successor in the French Academy and librarian at Fontainebleau. In *Monsieur de Camors* (1867) he solemnly attacked aristocratic decadence which enormously pleased his public, and showed his affinity with Dumas *fils* (q.v.). Among his later novels are *Julia de Trécœur* (1872) and *La Morte* (1886). He died in Paris.

**Féval, Paul Henri Corentin** (1817–1887), French novelist, born at Rennes. Having made a success with his adventure stories, *Le Club des Phoques* (1841), he was invited to write a piece of sensationalism to rival Sue's (q.v.) *Mystères de Paris*. The result was *Les Mystères de Londres* (1844), which though by no means equal to Sue's thorough-paced work, brought Féval a public and money. His further attempts at the sensational novel include *Le Fils du diable* (1847). Later books, such as *Les Couteaux d'or* (1856), *Le Bossu* (1858) and *Les Habits noirs* (1863), are mysteries verging on the detective novel. He died in Paris.

**Feydeau, Ernest Aimé** (1821–1873), French novelist, born in Paris where he died. His work depicts the decadence of the brittle and glittering society of the Second Empire. *Fanny* (1858) is his most characteristic work. Others are *Sylvie* (1861), which has more genuine power, but is less well constructed, *Monsieur de Saint-Bertrand* (1863), *Le Mari de la danseuse* (1863) and *La Comtesse de Chalis* (1867).

**Feydeau, Georges** (1862–1921), French dramatist, born in Paris, whose first play, *Tailleur pour dames* (1887), proved a great success and was followed by a number of others dealing with society life, such as *Le Mariage de Barillon* (1890), *Le Système Ribadier* (1892), *L'Hôtel du libre-échange* (1894) and *Le Dindon* (1896). Best known of all was *La Dame de chez Maxim* (1899; Eng. trans. *The Lady from Maxim's*). He later turned to one-act plays, such as *On purge bébé* (1910) and *Hortense a dit 'J'm'en fous'* (1916). The greatest of all writers of the vaudeville, he died at Rueil.

**Fichte, Johann Gottlieb** (1762–1814), German philosopher and prose-writer, born the son of a weaver at Rammenau, Upper Lusatia, entered Jena University in 1780. While acting as tutor in Switzerland (from 1788) he first became acquainted with the work of Kant (q.v.), which coloured the rest of his life. After visiting Kant at Königsberg in 1791 he wrote his *Kritik aller Offenbarung* (1792) and his remarkable assessment of the moral side of the French Revolution,

*Beiträge zur Berichtigung* (1793). Appointed professor of philosophy at Jena (1794) he developed his philosophical system and gained an enormous influence on the thought of the younger generation. Driven from his chair by jealous opponents in 1799, he obtained the chair of philosophy at Erlangen in 1805. Stirred to patriotic fervour by Napoleon's invasion of Germany, he delivered a finely composed series of addresses on national regeneration. One of those mainly responsible for the foundation of the University of Berlin, he became the first rector in 1810, and died in Berlin of fever caught from his wife who had contracted it while serving as a nurse. Apart from the fact that the literary quality of his work is high, there were few German men of letters born in the generation of the 1770's who escaped his influence. His *Sämmtliche Werke* appeared (8 vols.) in 1845–6. Of English translations the most useful is *The Popular Writings of Fichte* by W. Smith (fourth ed., 2 vols., 1889).

**Ficino, Marsilio** (1433–1499), Italian philosopher and prose-writer in Latin. Born at Figline, near Florence, he was appointed by Cosimo de' Medici in 1463 to make translations of Plato, whose work Ficino considered the basis and reaffirmation of Christianity. Strange and illogical as many of his views now appear they had a wide following, and the importance of his influence can be seen when one considers that among his pupils were Poliziano (q.v.), Lorenzo de' Medici (q.v.) and Mirandola (q.v.). Some of his philosophical work was published at Basel in 1491, and his interesting *Epistolae familiares* in 1495. He died in Florence. A defective *Opera* was published at Basel in 1561. The Paris edition of 1641 is the first more or less complete one.

**Filicaia, Vincenzo da** (1642–1707), Italian lyric poet. Born in Florence and educated at Pisa, he was employed at the court of Tuscany. His famous sonnets celebrating Italy have fire, and in time to come were to be praised by Byron and others for their patriotism and longing for Italian unity. Some of his lyrics in varied metres are very musical but have little depth. Most of his poems were collected the year of his death in Florence; but the first complete edition is that of 1793.

**Filinto Elysio,** *see* **Nascimento, F. M. do.**

**Fischart, Johann** (1546–1590), German satirist. Born at Strassburg, he studied law and the classics there, and travelled widely before returning to his native city about 1572. His best works are *Der Flöhhaz, Weibertratz* (1573), a wildly comic satire on women, *Das glückhafft Schiff von Zürich* (1576), a verse account of a river journey, and a long series of stories, the *Geschichtsklitterung* (1576, but not completed until the year of his death), founded on the first book of Rabelais's (q.v.) *Gargantua*. In 1581 he was appointed advocate to the Imperial Court of Law at Speier, and four years later became magistrate at Forbach where he died. The greatest satirist of his time, rampageous and with an unending sense of humour, he is the most characteristic figure in sixteenth-century German literature.

**Flaubert, Gustave** (1821–1880), French novelist. The son of a surgeon, he was born in Rouen and studied law in Paris (1840–3), three years which left a lasting influence on him, providing much of the material for *L'Éducation sentimentale*, a draft of which he had composed by 1845. Above all it was the time of his short meeting with Élisa Schlésinger, a publisher's wife, the Madame Arnoux of *L'Éducation*. By this time he had come to realize that a recurrent illness closely resembling epilepsy made it impossible for him to pursue a normal career, and in 1846 he settled down with his now widowed mother to a quiet provincial life at Croisset. Here he continued with his writing and by 1849 had produced a draft of *La Tentation de Saint Antoine*; but on showing it to his friends on one of his visits to Paris he met with unanimous disapproval, and in disappointment set out on a tour of the Middle East. He had already (1846) entered on a liaison with Louise Collet, the poetess, and on his return from Egypt in 1850, his mind stored with what for him was barbaric splendour, he resumed the relationship which finally ended in 1854. By that time he was near the close of his great novel *Madame Bovary*, which began to appear in serial form in *La Revue de Paris* in 1856, ending the following year. The work was published in book form immediately the serial closed (1857). Here in magnificent prose with brilliant dialogue and descriptive passages was the story of a provincial doctor's wife who in a series of love affairs tries to escape from the meshes of her boring life. An unsuccessful prosecution brought against the author for writing an immoral book only led to its increased sales. He now took his place among the leading writers of the time. He had revealed himself as a romantic realist, and was now ready to adopt the same literary approach to a very different subject and period, something which had been in his mind since his visit to the East. The plot of his new story was to be ancient Carthage's life and death struggle with her mercenaries. A visit to Tunisia in 1858, followed by a close study of the history of Carthage, resulted in the publication in 1862 of *Salammbô*, another triumph. It was not until 1869 that his next book, *L'Éducation sentimentale*, an exquisite analysis of the feelings of the men of his generation, appeared. Here are his experiences of the 1840's, including the 1848 Revolution, set in Normandy and Paris, most movingly displayed. There is a blend of the early youthful version and middle-aged experience which goes to make a book of rare charm and brilliant penetration, but it was far less successful than his two former works and it was only by degrees that it came to full favour. By this time he had gained a wide circle of literary friends, including Zola (q.v.), Daudet (q.v.), Turgenev (q.v.) and the Goncourts (q.v.). Before long another Norman, Guy de Maupassant (q.v.), was to become his disciple and his phenomenal success added still further to Flaubert's reputation. In such a circle he would spend a few convivial evenings from time to time, taking the train back to Croisset and enveloping himself in the quiet life once more. Shadows were soon creeping over his life. The Franco-Prussian War of 1870 upset him so much that he was already physically weakened when he had to face his dearly loved mother's death two years afterwards. Before long he became financially reduced and, by an imprudent arrangement of his property in favour of his niece, found himself completely in the none too kindly hands of herself and her husband. Still he struggled on, publishing his charming *La Tentation de Saint-Antoine* in 1874. After an ill-starred venture into drama, Flaubert turned to the long short story, producing in 1877 *Trois Contes* with three supremely beautiful examples of his art, *Un Cœur simple, La Légende de Saint-Julien-l'Hospitalier* and *Hérodias*. Nothing more of his was published in his lifetime, although he was at work until his sudden death from a heart attack at Croisset on his biting prose satire, *Bouvard et Pécuchet* (published in its unfinished state in 1881), on human mediocrity. It was, however, little suited to his gifts and must be accounted a failure. See his *Œuvres complètes* (ed. R. Dumesnil, first ed., 22 vols., 1910–36; second ed., 10 vols., 1945–8) and his highly interesting correspondence (*Correspondance*, 4 vols., 1887–93; Eng. trans. *Selected Letters of Gustave Flaubert*, ed. F. Steegmuller, 1954). All his works have been translated into English, and *Madame Bovary, Salammbô* and *L'Éducation sentimentale* are in translation in Everyman's Library.

**Fleming, Paul** (1609–1640), German poet, writing also in Latin. Born at Hartenstein, the son of a court chaplain, he read medicine at Leipzig University, which he entered in 1623, but gave up much time to music and literature. He had a rude awakening when the city was sacked in 1633, and was glad to gain a post on the Duke of Holstein's trade mission to Russia and Persia. Apart from the interesting experiences which the journey itself brought him, his meeting with the Niehusen sisters had an immense influence on his poetry, and it is for his love poetry, and for his vigorous verses describing his zest for life, that he is really remembered. To Opitz (q.v.), whom he met in Leipzig, Fleming owes a great deal, especially evident in his first published work *Davids Busspsalme und Manasse Gebet* (1631). His other books, all posthumous, are *Poetischer Gedichte Prodromus* (1641), *Teutsche Poemata* (1642) and *Geist- und Weltliche Poemata* (1651). Returning from Persia in 1639, Fleming made for Leiden to complete his medical studies interrupted at Leipzig six years before. His intention was to settle as a physician in Reval and be near the Niehusens, but shortly after having presented his doctoral thesis and on the journey which he at once set out on to Reval, he suddenly died at Hamburg. See J. M. Lappenberg's edition of his collected works, one-third of which are in Latin (3 vols., 1863–6).

**Flers, Robert de la Motte-Ango de** (1872–1927), French dramatist and journalist, born at Pont-l'Évêque. Of noble family, he won fame with his witty comedies, including *Les Travaux d'Hercule* (1901), *L'Habit vert* (1912) and *La Belle Aventure* (1913). He was appointed editor of *Le Figaro* in 1914. He died at Vittel.

**Fleuron, Svend** (1874–    ), Danish novelist. Born at Møen, he took up an army career, and on retirement began to write. His novels, which have been compared with those by Henry Williamson, are in that class, so rarely convincing, dealing with the lives of animals. Fleuron's main characters are always animals and he triumphantly succeeds, as in *Haren den graa* (1918; Eng. trans. *The Grey Hare*

1938), *Grim* (1919; Eng. trans. *Grim. The Story of a Pike*, 1920) and
*Flax Ædilius* (1929; Eng. trans. *Flax. Police Dog*, 1931).

**Florian, Jean-Pierre Claris de** (1755–1794), French playwright,
novelist and fabulist, was born at the family Château de Florian in
the Cévennes. Coming to Paris he soon made his reputation with his
pleasant domestic comedies, *Les Deux Billets* (1779), *Le Bon Ménage*
(1782) and *Le Bon Père* (1783). He increased his public when he
turned to novel writing in 1783. His novels are of two kinds, pastoral
idylls set in Provence, such as *Galatée* (1783) and *Estelle et Némorin*
(1788), and historical ones, such as *Numa Pompilius* (1786) and
*Gonzalve de Cordoue* (1791). He left Paris at the revolution and set
about the writing of his most famous work, his *Fables* (1792), which
prove him to be the greatest fabulist since La Fontaine (q.v.). Of his
contemporaries only Iriarte (q.v.) can be compared to him as a
fabulist. He died at Sceaux. His veiled autobiography, *Mémoires
d'un jeune espagnol*, appeared in 1807 (mod. ed., 1924). *Œuvres
complètes* were published (16 vols.) in 1820, with four supplementary
volumes in 1824.

**Fogazzaro, Antonio** (1842–1911), Italian novelist, dramatist and poet,
was born at Vicenza. He first attracted notice with his poetical
romance *Miranda* (1874); but it was his first novel *Malombra* (1881)
which showed the proper direction of his high abilities. Here is to be
seen, set out in masterly fashion, the problem of the struggle between
spirit and body. *Daniele Cortis* (1885), his second novel, was variously
received both as a moral work of great if embarrassing honesty and as
a dishonest and immoral work undermining the very Catholic Church
to which he always claimed to adhere. His desire now was to bring new
life to the Church by forcing it to look the new social and scientific
challenges of the modern world in the eye, and this he seemed to
achieve triumphantly in *Il piccolo mondo antico* (1895; Eng. trans.
*The Little World of the Past*, 1962) and *Il piccolo mondo moderno*
(1901). With *Il santo* (1905; Eng. trans. *The Saint*, 1906) he reached
the peak of his achievement, movingly bringing before an enormous
and influential public his ideas on how Christianity must face all the
dangers of materialism of the new century by courageously lopping
away much of its inherited lumber. It was a great blow to him when
it was eventually placed on the Index. His last great novel, *Leila*
(1911), pleased no one, being considered by the ecclesiastics as
further proof of his uncompromising attitude and by the coming
literary generation as a token of his vacillation. Fogazzaro is also the
author of several good plays, chief among them *Il ritratto mascherato*
(1902). An excellent poet, his *Poesie* appeared in 1908. He died at
Vicenza. *Tutte le opere* was published (14 vols.) in 1931–41.

**Földes, Jolán** (1903–    ), Hungarian novelist and short-story writer.
Born at Kenderes, she won the All Nations Prize with *A halászo
macska utcája* (1936; Eng. trans. *The Street of the Fishing Cat*, 1937).
She followed this up with *Fej vagy írás* (1937; Eng. trans. *Heads or
Tails*, 1938).

**Fonseca, Cristóbal de** (1550?–1621), Spanish devotional writer in prose, was born at Olalla, near Toledo, and became an Augustinian. His two great works are *Tratado del amor de Dios* (1592), on the love of God, and *La vida de Cristo nuestro Señor* (1596; Eng. trans. *Devout Contemplations*, 1629). Both have definite literary value. He died in Madrid.

**Fontainas, André** (1865–1948), Franco-Belgian poet. Born in Brussels, he was very early influenced by Mallarmé (q.v.), whose pupil he at one time was at school, and while a law student threw in his lot with the 'Young Belgian' literary fraternity. A symbolist, his pleasantly sad, 'atmospheric', nostalgic poetry is to be found in *Le Sang des fleurs* (1889), *Crépuscules* (1897) and *La Nef désemparée* (1908). He died in Paris.

**Fontane, Theodor** (1819–1898), German novelist. Of distant French ancestry he was born at Neu-Ruppin where his father was a dispensing chemist. He also became a chemist, and settled in Berlin in 1840 where he became a member of several literary societies. He took to writing for a living in 1849 and was in England as a foreign correspondent from 1853 to 1859, and as a result of his impressions there he wrote his entertaining *Ein Sommer in London* (1854) and *Aus England* (2 vols., 1860; the second vol. trans. into Eng. as *Across the Tweed*, 1965). He served as a war correspondent in the Franco-Prussian War, and turned his experiences to good account in *Kriegsgefangen* (1871), but it was not until he produced his fine novel of the Napoleonic period, *Vor dem Sturm* (1878), that he truly revealed his qualities. Thereafter his work changed completely, for he now took to realistic fiction in a modern setting. The first in this new manner, such as *Grete Minde* (1880) and *Graf Petöfy* (1884), hardly give one any indication of what was to come. *Irrungen, Wirrungen* (1887; Eng. trans. *Trials and Tribulations*, 1917), with its strong and uncompromising realism, exercised an immediate influence, and may be said to a great extent to have directed the path of the German novel. *Stine* (1890) showed too strong a derivation from the Zola school, but with *Effi Briest* (1895; Eng. trans. 1913) came the crowning achievement of his life, for here is a plain story transformed by the poetry which grows out of his love for the region of his birthplace. *Die Poggenpuhls* (1896) is not by any means so good, but *Der Stechlin* (1898) is a remarkable work, not even taking into account the advanced age of the author. His two volumes of autobiography, *Meine Kinderjahre* (1893; Eng. trans. of extracts, *My Childhood Days*, 1913–15) and *Von zwanzig bis dreissig* (1898), are delightful. He died in Berlin. His *Gesammelte Werke und Briefe* (22 vols.) appeared between 1905 and 1911.

**Fontenelle, Bernard le Bovier de** (1657–1757), French man of letters. Born in Rouen, a nephew of Pierre Corneille (q.v.), he early on moved to Paris and soon found his place in literary circles. He was soon writing the libretti for operas in collaboration with Pierre's younger brother Thomas Corneille (q.v.), such as *Bellérophon* (1679). He tried his hand at tragedy with *Aspar* (1680), but failed, and turned to prose, and here he found his true vein. His *Dialogues des morts* (1683) proved his gifts for popularizing philosophy, and in his *Entretiens sur la* *pluralité des mondes* (1686) he introduced theological speculations backed by astronomy derived from Giordano Bruno (q.v.) into the boudoir and 'tilted at orthodox Christianity from behind the drawing-room curtains'. This work and the urbane *Histoire des oracles* (1687), dangerous by subtle implication, pointed the way to the scepticism of the coming century with its *philosophes* and the entry of the new thought into a wider world. His *Poésies pastorales* (1688) are no better and no worse than the average works of this kind of the period. His *De l'origine des fables* (1689) has proved an interesting work to many even down to this century, and is the first scientific survey of mythology. He became secretary of the Académie des Sciences in 1699, resigning forty years later, and at the age of eighty-five in 1742 he published his excellently written *Vie de P. Corneille*. He died in Paris one month before his one hundredth birthday.

**Foreestier, P.**, *see* **Alberdinck Thijm, J. A.**

**Forsh, Olga Dmitrievna**, using till 1917 the pseudonym **A. Terek** (1873–    ), Russian Soviet novelist, born at Gunib in Daghestan of aristocratic family. Of her books *Odety kamnem* (1925, 'Clad in Stone') is usually considered her masterpiece. It deals with the rise of revolutionary movements in the late nineteenth century when official reaction and mercantile wealth seemed in the ascendant. More attractive to many tastes is her long historical novel *Radishchev* (1934–9), which has the enlightened author of the *Journey from Petersburg to Moscow* as its hero (q.v.). The influence of Merezhkovsky (q.v.) is apparent in all her work.

**Forster, Johann Georg Adam** (1754–1794), German travel and natural history writer, some of whose works appeared in English. Born at Nassenhuben, near Danzig, the son of J. R. Forster of Scots ancestry, then pastor there, he was brought by his father to England when in 1766 he took up a post at Warrington Dissenting Academy; and when in 1772 J. R. was appointed as naturalist on Captain Cook's second voyage (1772–5), the boy J. G. A. accompanied him. As a result he wrote one of the masterpieces of travel literature, *A Voyage round the World* (2 vols., 1777), showing complete command of an excellent English style, and when he came to write the German version of it, *Beschreibung einer Reise um die Welt* (2 vols., 1778–80; rev., 1784), proved his equal ability with German. He continued to live a wandering life, holding academic posts at Cassel and Vilno before becoming librarian to the Elector of Mainz in 1788. An eager supporter of the French Revolution he resigned this situation and went to Paris where he wrote his excellent *Ansichten vom Niederrhein* (3 vols., 1791–4), which contains some of the finest natural description (outside fiction) in the German language. He died in Paris.

**Fort, Paul** (1872–1960), French poet and playwright. Born in Reims, he was prominent in symbolist circles in Paris before he was twenty. A poet of the country with a great sense of the historic past, he published the first volume in the series, *Ballades françaises et Chroniques* *de France*, in 1897, which by 1951 had grown to forty volumes. Easily written, even it would seem carelessly, although this is intentional, Fort's lyrical verse has great charm of manner and a true musical quality. Printed as prose, this is a mere affectation, for the verse is generally traditional in style. His plays, some of which are historical, include *La Petite Bête* (1890), *L'Or* (1924), *Ruggieri* (1925), *Le Camp du drap d'or* (1926), *Les Compères du roi Louis* (1927) and *Guillaume le Bâtard* (1928). His *Mémoires* appeared in 1944. He died at Argenlieu, near Montlhéry (Seine-et-Oise).

**Foscolo, Ugo**, his real Christian name being **Niccolò** (1778–1827), Italian poet. Born on Zante, one of the Ionian Islands, of Greco-Italian (Venetian) parentage, he was educated at Spalato, Padua and Venice. He began as an eager supporter of all things revolutionary and of Bonaparte, whom he celebrated in *Ode a Bonaparte* (1797); but his partisanship was turned to hatred when that very year, at the Treaty of Campoformio, Venice was sold by his hero to Austria, and Foscolo left Venetian territory, living in turn in Milan, Bologna and Florence. After a period of extreme depression in the latter city, he recovered his belief in the French and enlisted in the Cisalpine Legion against Austria and Russia (1799), and fought at the siege of Genoa in the following year, and he again served in the French army in an Italian division being trained for the invasion of Britain (1804–6). At last, however, he saw through Napoleon and broke with him for good. He was the arch tyrant, and in his greatest poem, *De' Sepolcri* (1807), he lashes out at this emperor who wanted to crush liberty. This fine ode, inspired by the imperial decree dealing with places of burial, was undoubtedly suggested by a poem on a similar subject by I. Pindemonte (q.v.), whom Foscolo knew, written in 1785 and directed against the burial decree of the Grand Duke Leopold of Tuscany (afterwards the Emperor Leopold II). The theme of both is the same: do earthly tyrants presume to pursue even the dead with their authority and flout the sentiments of the bereaved? Apart from the quality of the verse the message of faith in mankind is powerful and convincing. Miscellaneous work which has not stood the test of time followed, for he was neither a dramatist nor a translator. In 1809 he accepted a post at Pavia University, but the life proved uncongenial and he resigned after a few months. He moved to Milan, but the return of the Austrians in 1814 led him to go into voluntary exile, and he settled in London. At first he managed to live quite well with literary journalism (*Quarterly Review* and *Edinburgh Review*), some volumes of literary criticism on Dante, Petrarch and *Il Decamerone*, lecturing and a legacy; but his difficult temper lost him friends and his improvidence money, and he died in poverty and neglect at Turnham Green. He was reburied in Florence in 1871. For his works see *Ugo Foscolo, poesie, lettere e prose letterarie*, edited by T. Casini (1941) and E. R. Vincent, *The Commemoration of the Dead* (1936; with the text and a commentary on *De' Sepolcri*). The exhaustive *Edizione Nazionale* was begun in 1933. Foscolo's influence on the Risorgimento, and thus on one important source of inspiration for nineteenth-century Italian poets, was profound.

**Fouqué, Friedrich Heinrich Karl de la Motte** (1777–1843), German prose-writer, was born of aristocratic Huguenot ancestry at Brandenburg, grandson of the well-known Prussian general, Baron de la Motte Fouqué of Seven Years War fame. From 1794 to 1813 he was a Prussian cavalry officer, taking every opportunity he could when on leave to write his chivalric and nordic romances, which for a time were the most generally popular works produced by the German romantics. His best book, and the only one which really survives, is the delightfully written *Undine* (1811; Eng. trans. various, the best by E. Gosse, 1896), made into an opera and set to music by E. T. W. Hoffmann (q.v.). Parts of *Sintram und seine Gefährten* (1811; Eng. trans. *Sintram and his Companions*, 1820) still have a shadowy existence, the book in its day exercising particular influence on European romanticism. After these *Der Zauberring* (3 vols., 1812; Eng. trans. *A Knightly Romance*, 1846) is perhaps the best. With changing tastes he gradually lost his public, and in fact his own talent declined, revealing more clearly than ever the fact that the greater part of his success was due rather to superficial theatrical gifts than to real literary talent. He died in reduced circumstances in Berlin, writing to the last but having outlived his success by more than twenty years.

**Fournier, H. A. F.,** *see* **Alain-Fournier.**

**Fracchia, Umberto** (1889–1930), Italian novelist and short-story writer. Born in Lucca, he became a journalist and in 1925, by becoming editor of *La Fiera Letteraria*, gained a position of unrivalled influence in the literary world. He had already written two successful novels, *Il perduto amore* (1921) and *Angela* (1923), and a volume of short stories, *Piccola gente di città* (1924). Their intense individuality of style and feeling, sometimes strange and mildly uncomfortable, was continued in the novel *La stella del nord* (1930) and the posthumous collection of short stories, *Gente e scene di Campagna* (1931). He died in Rome.

**France, Anatole,** pseudonym of **Jacques-Anatole Thibault** (1844–1924), French novelist, essayist and poet, was born in Paris, the son of a well-to-do bookseller, whose shop was a meeting-place of men of letters. Having been educated at the Collège Stanislas he settled down as a literary dilettante. The works produced by him during the following years, such as the literary study *Alfred de Vigny* (1868), and the two volumes of Parnassian verse *Les Poèmes dorés* (1873) and *Les Noces corinthiennes* (1876; Eng. trans. *The Bride of Corinth*, 1920), hardly showed his strength. With the collection of short stories, *Jocaste et le chat maigre* (1879), many of his gifts of style and manner are present in embryo, and with his first novel, *Le Crime de Sylvestre Bonnard* (1881), he sailed securely into public view. It was not, however, until his meeting with Madame Arman de Caillavet that he came to regard writing as his life's work. His powers of satire now developed, and in a keen and polished style he laid bare all hypocrisy and pretence in religion and society, always ironical and brilliantly devastating; but while exposing the ridiculous and the mean, even the perverted, he was never cruel. In fact he was deeply kind, and while suffering with humanity he never allowed himself to be carried away by his feelings from the 'good form' which his love of the eighteenth century had instilled into him. He took no sides, but simply looked keenly at both and analysed both. Among his vast output should be mentioned such novels and collections of short stories as: *Le Livre de mon ami* (1885), *Balthasar* (1889), *Thaïs* (1890) with its remarkable analysis of the confrontation of Hellenism and Christianity (a theme which never left him, being deepened by his anti-clericalism, later increased by the Dreyfus affair), *L'Étui de nacre* (1892; Eng. trans. *Mother of Pearl*, 1908), *La Rôtisserie de la Reine Pédauque* (1893; Eng. trans. *At the Sign of the Reine Pedauque*, 1912), *Les Opinions de M. Jérôme Coignard* (1893), which with other satirical studies of contemporary French affairs contained in the four volumes of *Histoire contemporaine* (1896–1901) made short work of abuses such as the Boulanger affair, the Panama scandal and anti-semitism, *Le Lys rouge* (1894; Eng. trans. *The Red Lily*, n.d.), *Le Jardin d'Épicure* (1895; Eng. trans. *The Garden of Epicurus*, n.d.), *Pierre Nozière* (1899), *Sur la pierre blanche* (1905), *L'Île des Pingouins* (1908; Eng. trans. *Penguin Island*, 1947), another satirical survey of modern French society, *Les Dieux ont soif* (1912) Eng. trans. *The Gods are Athirst*, 1942), a story of the French Revolution and *La Révolte des anges* (1914; Eng. trans. *The Revolt of the Angels*, 1914). His essays are best represented by *La Vie littéraire* (5 vols., 1888–1892; new ed., 1950). He stands out as an idealist in *Vers les temps meilleurs* (3 vols., 1906). His sharp-edged Voltairean scepticism appears in *La Vie de Jeanne d'Arc* (2 vols., 1908). He left two charming volumes of reminiscences, *Le Petit Pierre* (1918) and *La Vie en fleurs* (1922; Eng. trans. *The Bloom of Life*, 1923). Anatole France died in Tours. The definitive edition, *Œuvres complètes illustrées*, began to come out in 1925 and eventually filled twenty-five volumes. There is an edition of the complete works translated into English edited by F. Chapman and J. L. May (Bodley Head, 1908 ff.).

**Francis of Assisi** (1182–1226), saint and founder of the Franciscan Order, is here considered only as a writer. Born at Assisi, his real name being **Giovanni Bernardone,** in his youth he made himself so thoroughly acquainted with the work of the French troubadours that he gained the name of Il Francesco ('the little Frenchman'). In fact until a severe illness and conversion in his earlier twenties changed his life, he lived a gay one, spending freely as the son of a rich cloth merchant could afford to do. He died in the Convent of Porciuncle. As a poet he left only the famous *Il cantico di Fratre Sole*, inspired by the Bible (Daniel, Chap. III and probably the Benedicite). He may be said to have started the great upsurge of religious verse which issued from the Franciscan movement after his death for a century. Snatches of his prose are to be found in A. Monteverdi, *Testi volgar italiani dei primi tempi* (second ed. 1948) and C. Dionisotti and C. Grayson, *Early Italian Texts* (1949).

**François, Marie Louise von** (1817–1893), German novelist, born at Herzberg. A life of misfortunes only increased her natural kindness of heart, and her compassion for the downtrodden of the world is to be found in her fine novels, above all *Die letzte Reckenburgerin* (1871; Eng. trans. *The Last von Reckenburg*, 1887) with its splendid characterization. Of her other works *Frau Erdmuthens Zwillingssöhne* (1873) and *Stufenjahre eines Glücklichen* (1877) are noteworthy. She died at Weissenfels. Her correspondence with C. F. Meyer (q.v.) is of much interest and was edited as *Briefwechsel mit C. F. Meyer* (1905). Her *Gesammelte Werke* appeared (5 vols.) in 1918.

**Franzos, Karl Emil** (1848–1904), Austrian novelist, was born a Jew in Russian Podolia, his parents shortly afterwards moving to the Polish-Jewish village of Czortkow, Galicia (the Barnow of his books). He became an orphan very early, but managed to gain a good education at the German gymnasium at Czernowitz. He later read jurisprudence, but eventually took to journalism in Vienna. He made his first mark with a series of sketches, *Aus halb Asien* (1876), in which 'demi Asia' is South Russia and Rumania. In *Die Juden von Barnow* (1877; Eng. trans. *The Jews of Barnow*, 1882) he showed his full stature and started on his main theme, the principal feature of all his other works, the problem of the Jew in Gentile society. *Ein Kampf ums Recht* (2 vols., 1882; *For the Right*, 1887) has great power, while *Der Präsident* (1884; Eng. trans. *The Chief Justice*, 1890) had such dramatic possibilities that a stage version was made of it in 1892 (Eng. trans. *The Judge: a Play in Four Acts*, 1915). *Die Reise nach dem Schicksal* (1885), *Tragische Novellen* (1886) and *Der Wahrheitsucher* (1894) deserve mention. Franzos died in Berlin.

**Fredro, Alexander** (1793–1876), Polish playwright, born of noble family at Suchorów, he joined the Polish army and served under Napoleon. In 1815 he retired and took to farming, paying long visits to Paris, where he made a study of the French stage. A gifted writer of comedies, of which he wrote nearly forty, his best known are the farce *Damy i huzary* (1826; Eng. trans. *Ladies and Hussars*, 1925), *Sluby panieńskie* (1834; Eng. trans. *Maidens' Vows*, 1940) and *Zemsta* (1834, 'Vengeance'). Sensitive to criticism he stopped publishing and refused to allow his work to be staged after 1838, although continuing to write. He died at Lwów. A critical edition of his *Komedie*, edited by E. Kucharski, appeared (6 vols.) in 1926–7.

**Freiligrath, Hermann Ferdinand** (1810–1876), German poet. Born at Detmold, he went into business in 1831, but left it when his first volume of poems, *Gedichte* (1838), proved a success. Soon afterwards he received a royal pension on the strength of which he married. A man of integrity he sacrificed his pension for his political beliefs (1842), and having joined the Liberals and written *Ein Glaubensbekenntnis* (1844), in which he praised radicalism, he was compelled to escape to Belgium and Switzerland, finally reaching London. In 1846 he praised the coming revolution in *Ça Ira*, and two years later, when the revolution was an accomplished fact, he celebrated it in such stirring works as *Die Revolution* and *Februarklänge*. He was in Germany once more in 1848 where the impact of the new state of affairs inspired him to write the political poems in the collection *Politische und soziale Zeitgedichte* (1851). By this time the leading revolutionary poet of the age, he was a marked man when reactionary government returned to power, and although acquitted of a charge of treason, he decided to go into exile in London once more, and there worked as a bank clerk from 1851 to 1867. A fund supported by subscribers from all over Germany enabled him to return in the latter year. He died at Cannstadt. His *Gesammelte Dichtungen* appeared (6 vols.) in 1877. There are English translations by K. F. Kroeker (1872) and M. F. Liddell (1949).

**Frenssen, Gustav** (1863–1945), German novelist. Born the son of the village carpenter at Barlt, Schleswig-Holstein, his lifelong home, he entered the Protestant ministry and became pastor of Hemme in Holstein. The first of his fast-moving novels, *Die drei Getreuen* (1898; Eng. trans. *The Three Comrades*, 1907), led to his spectacularly successful *Jörn Uhl* (1902; Eng. trans. 1905), 120,000 copies of which were sold in a year. In 1903, being now financially independent, he resigned from his pastorate and bought an estate, and gave himself up to literary work. His novels after this included *Hilligenlei* (1905; Eng. trans. *Holyland*, 1906), *Peter Moors Fahrt nach Südwest* (1907; Eng. trans. *Peter Moor's Journey to South-West Africa*, 1908), *Klaus Hinrich Baas* (1909; Eng. trans. 1911), *Der Pastor von Poggsee* (1921; Eng. trans. 1931) and *Otto Babendiek* (1926; Eng. trans. *The Anvil*, 1930). As early as 1899, the date of the publication of a selection of his sermons, *Dorfpredigten* (Eng. trans. *Village Sermons*, 1924), he had shown signs of marked unorthodoxy, and finally he renounced Christianity altogether. His work has a fatal inclination towards the didactic.

**Frescobaldi, Leonardo** (1350?–1420?), Italian prose-writer. Born in Florence, he became a soldier and diplomat. His visit to Palestine in 1384, financed by the King of Naples, who wished him to furnish him with a full account of the Holy Land, resulted in his famous description of his journey. It was edited by Gargiolli in 1862 in the collection *Viaggi in Terra Santa di L. Frescobaldi e d'altri del secolo XIV*. Both in style and content it is a remarkable piece of work. The place and date of his death are both unknown.

**Freuchen, Lorentz Peter Elfred** (1886–1957), Danish novelist and general prose-writer. Born at Nykøbing, he became famous as an arctic explorer. Many of his lively and imaginative novels are set in Greenland. Best known of his works are *Storfanger* (1927) and *Rømningsmand* (1928), the two being translated together into English as *Eskimo* (1931). Freuchen made the film *Eskimo* in Alaska for an American company in 1932. Other novels are *Nordkaper* (1929; Eng. trans. *The Sea Tyrant*, 1932), *Ivalu* (1933; Eng. trans. *Ivalu, the Eskimo Wife*, 1936) and *Larions Lov* (1948; Eng. trans. *The Law of Larion*, 1952). He died in Alaska.

**Freytag, Gustav** (1816–1895), German novelist and playwright, born at Kreuzburg, Silesia, he became *Privatdozent* of German philology at Breslau University (1839–47). After 1848 he became identified with liberal politics and was later a member of the Crown Prince Frederick of Prussia's circle. He was for many years a deputy of the North German Diet. He began his literary career with brilliant comedies such as *Die Valentine* (1846), and especially *Die Journalisten* (1853; Eng. trans. 1913); but it is as a novelist that he has retained his place, his masterly study of commercial life (influenced by Dickens), *Soll und Haben* (1855; Eng. trans. *Debit and Credit*, 1858), being his major work. Among his other novels are *Die verlorene Handschrift* (1864; Eng. trans. *The Lost Manuscript*, 1865) and the series *Die Ahnen* (6 vols., 1872–81; Eng. trans. of one of them *Ingo und Ingraban*, 1873). His collected works were published (22 vols.) in 1886–8. Three times married, he died at Wiesbaden.

**Frisch, Max** (1911–    ), Swiss dramatist and prose-writer. Born in Zürich the son of an architect, he travelled widely both before and after the Second World War and was fully alive to all the intellectual problems facing western civilization. Culture in a war-damaged world is the subject of his novel *Stiller* (1954; Eng. trans. *I'm not Stiller*, 1959), and the crisis is still more deeply and ironically dealt with in *Die chinesische Mauer* (new ed., 1955), a play, and *Homo faber* (1957; Eng. trans. 1959), a novel. *Andorra* (1961; Eng. trans. 1964), a controversial work about racialism and nationalism, seems to prove him to be on the road to new approaches. A variety of prose pieces (*Stücke*) appeared (2 vols.) in 1962.

**Fröding, Gustav** (1860–1911), Swedish poet. Born at Alster, he was at the University of Uppsala, but left without a degree and plunged into the world of journalism. In 1889 he suffered the first attack of that insanity which was to haunt him for the rest of his life. He was sent to a mental home at Görlitz, Silesia, and recovered, quickly maturing as a poet as his first book, *Guitarr och dragharmonika* (1891; Eng. trans. *Guitar and Concertina*, 1925), showed. He then returned to journalism and continued with it until overtaken by another attack. After 1898 he was a permanent invalid, but he was mentally in a better condition. His collected works up to that date were published in 1902 and reveal the gloom and jollity of a split personality jostling for place. Some of his objectionable near-pornography, which is rather of pathological interest than anything else, was later cried up as being a brave manifesto of freedom. This kind of work is particularly in evidence in the book entitled *Stänk och flikar* (1896). Far more important is his message of the divine purpose to be found in all things, stated with much eloquence in such volumes as *Gralstänk* (1898) and *Efterskörd* (1910). He died in a nursing home in Gröndal. His *Samlade skrifter* appeared (16 vols.) in 1917–23.

**Froissart, Jean** (1337–1410?), French chronicler and poet. Born at Valenciennes, the son of an heraldic painter, who greatly influenced him in his love of chivalry while still a child, he became secretary to Queen Philippa, consort of Edward III of England, in 1361. He later took Orders, having in the meantime visited Scotland and many Italian and French courts. The death of the queen in 1369 in no way ended the patronage, outstanding among his patrons being Espaing de Lyon, travels with whom provided much data for his *Chroniques*. His later years were spent at the brilliant court of Gaston de Foix at Orthez. He may have died at Chimay, but this is uncertain, as is also the date of his death. As a poet he is represented by his lengthy

romance, *Meliador* (ed. A. Longnon, 3 vols., 1895–9), and by a
quantity of lyrics (*Poésies*, ed. A. Scheler, 3 vols., 1869–72). It is,
however, for his *Chroniques* above all that he is remembered (ed.
K. de Lettenhove, 25 vols., 1867–77; first Eng. trans. by Lord
Berners, 1525; ed. by W. P. Ker, 6 vols., 1901–3; handily accessible
in the Globe Ed., 1913). This great work, divided into four books,
describes the history of England, Scotland, France, Spain, the papal
courts of Rome and Avignon and of the Low Countries from 1326 to
1400. Deeply influenced in the earlier part of the work by the chronicle
of Jean le Bel, Froissart after the first book branches out on his own.
His style is noble, even splendid, to match his theme, centred as it is
round the feudal lords. Very fair in his judgments, he yet does not
breathe a word of the fact that this nobility was already in decay.

**Fromentin, Eugène** (1820–1876), French prose-writer, born the son
of a physician with a taste for the fine arts at La Rochelle, he became
an art student in Paris (1839–42) and then spent four years travelling
and painting in Algeria and the Middle East. On his return he gained
a reputation both as an artist, with his pictures of exotic scenery, and
as a writer of travel books such as *Simples Pélerinages* (1856) and
*Un Été dans le Sahara* (1857). He wrote a novel, *Dominique* (1863), of
some deserved celebrity, and *Les Maîtres d'autrefois* (1876; Eng.
trans. *The Masters of Past Time*, 1883). He died at La Rochelle.

**Frugoni, Carlo Innocenzo** (1692–1768), Italian poet. Born in Genoa,
he took minor Orders, and was a leading Arcadian and poet laureate of
the court of Parma, where he died. Much in demand as a librettist, he
was a prolific writer of all kinds of occasional verse, melodious and
filled with mythological allusions. If not strength or even originality,
he possesses classical charm in abundance. His *Opere poetiche* were
collected in ten volumes in 1779, being enlarged to fifteen volumes the
following year.

**Furetière, Antoine** (1619–1688), French novelist, poet and lexicographer, was a lifelong resident of Paris. His knowledge of the higher
bourgeoisie of the capital was shown in his clever, realistic novel, *Le
Roman bourgeois* (1666; new ed. 1854), written to mock the fashionable and empty fiction of the day. As a poet he wrote *Fables morales
et nouvelles* (1671). He was elected to the French Academy in 1662,
but was expelled from it in 1685 for having edited his *Dictionnaire
universel* (finally published in Rotterdam in 1690), which his fellow
academicians regarded as the exclusive right of the institution as a
whole. They managed to prevent its publication in France, and
Furetière's revenge was his *Factums* (1685; ed. by Baudelaire's
friend Asselineau, 2 vols., 1859), in which individual academicians
are mercilessly pilloried.

**Furmanov, Dmitry Andreyevich** (1891–1926), Russian Soviet novelist,
born at Kineshma. His main works are the two novels, *Chapayev*
(1923; Eng. trans. 1935) and *Myatezh* (1925, 'The Revolt'). Both deal
with the civil war of 1918–21, the first with Chapayev's peasant army
fighting against Kolchak in the Urals, the second with the campaign
of the Bolsheviks against the Eastern and Western powers in the area
of Mongolia. Furmanov died in Moscow.

**Fustel de Coulanges, Numa Denis** (1830–1889), French prose-writer. Born in Paris, he became an academic historian, but deserves notice as a man of letters in his own right by reason of his beautifully written study, *La Cité antique* (1864). In his *Histoire des institutions politiques de l'ancienne France* (6 vols., 1872–92) scholarship has overpowered style. He died at Massy.

# G

**Gaboriau, Émile** (1835–1873), French detective novelist, was born at Saujon (Charente-Inférieure) and was destined for business, although saved from it at the eleventh hour by his success as a freelance journalist. *L'Affaire Lerouge* (1866), one of the earliest of detective novels, brought him fame and money, and in quick succession there followed *Le Dossier No. 133* (1867) and *Monsieur Lecoq* (1869), the hero being a precursor of Conan Doyle's creation of the master detective, and being perhaps derived from Vidocq, the famous detective of Napoleonic times, whose *Mémoires* appeared in 1828, *Les Esclaves de Paris* (1869) and *La Corde au cou* (1873). He died in Paris.

**Gace Brulé** (*d.* 1214?), French poet. Probably of noble family of Brittany, he attended the court of Geoffrey of Brittany. Nearly sixty lyrics of his remain on conventional themes, but expressed in an unusually serious way. See G. Huet's *Les Chansons de Gace Brulé* (1902).

**Galilei, Galileo** (1564–1642), Italian prose-writer in the vernacular and Latin, was born in Pisa of noble but impoverished family, his father a mathematician and musician. He was destined for medicine but left the University of Pisa without a degree, determined to pursue pure science. By 1592 so successful had he been as lecturer, experimenter and author that he was given the chair of mathematics at Padua, which he held till 1610, in which year his first important publication appeared, the treatise on his astronomical observations made with the telescope he had just invented, *Sidereus Nuncius* (Eng. trans. *The Sidereal Messenger*, 1880), and in which he mentioned the discovery of Jupiter's satellites, thus confirming the ideas of Copernicus. He afterwards went to Rome, where his public lectures began with praise and ended in a papal admonition in 1616, after which he retired to Florence, and there published *Il Saggiatore* (1623), a treatise on comets founded on false ideas, written against his better nature to appease the Church, which had taken fright at his toppling of the Ptolemaic system of the universe. But it was impossible for him thus to juggle with the truth, and in his famous *Dialogo sopra i due massimi sistemi del mondo* (1632; Eng. trans. *The Systeme of the World*, 1661) he exhaustively and eloquently pointed out his reasons for believing exclusively in the Copernican planetary theory. Natural philosophers, except for a few Aristotelian diehards, welcomed the book with tremendous enthusiasm, but the Church was outraged, and Galileo was ordered to Rome and forced under threat of torture to recant his confirmation of the theory. After a few months' imprisonment in Rome he was allowed his freedom, at the urgent request of the Duke of Tuscany, on the condition that he remained on Tuscan territory, and by the end of 1633 he was in Florence, where he continued to experiment in mechanics and astronomy. The *Dialoghi delle nuove scienze* was completed in 1636, being published in 1638 by the Elzevirs of Leiden (Eng. trans. *Mathematical Discoveries concerning two new Sciences*, 1730), and in it he gives a highly important summary of his work, particularly on mechanics. He became blind in 1638 just after his discovery of the librations of the moon, and even in his blindness he was busy working out the system of the pendulum for clocks. He died at Arcetri, near Florence. Not only was Galileo a great scientist but he was a great literary craftsman, and his beautiful yet forceful prose is regarded as the best in seventeenth-century Italian letters. The definitive edition of his works is that of Favaro and Del Lungo (20 vols., 1890–1909).

**Gallego, Juan Nicasio** (1777–1853), Spanish poet. Born at Zamora, he was educated at Salamanca and fell under the influence of Meléndez Valdés (q.v.) and, although going into Orders, became a liberal. His best poem is his *Al dos de mayo* (1808; Eng. trans. *The Second of May*, 1819) and he was a good sonneteer. He died in Madrid. See his *Poesías* in *Biblioteca de Autores Españoles*, vol. lxvii.

**Ganivet, Ángel** (1865–1898), Spanish essayist and novelist, born in Granada. He entered the consular service, serving in Belgium, Russia and Finland. A friend of Unamuno (q.v.), he feared like him for the future of Spain, which he felt would have to throw off her exclusiveness and join wholeheartedly in Europe, the while preserving what was best in her magnificent culture, and to this end he reviewed her maladies in *Idearium español* (1897; Eng. trans. *Spain: an Interpretation*, 1946). Here he finds a country living on its past and suffering from fatalism, the result of the Arab blood which for all the rich culture it has brought has been disastrous for a nation lying geographically in Europe. He returned to Spain's problem again in his satirical *Cartas finlandesas* (1898, 'Letters from Finland'), in which he holds up the mirror to his country's unwilling eyes, and in his extremely interesting correspondence with Unamuno, *El porvenir de España* (1903), published after his death by suicide in Riga. His two historical novels, *La conquista del reino de Maya* (1897) and *Los trabajos del infatigable creador Pío Cid* (1898), demand far more attention than they have received. His collected works fill ten volumes (1928–30).

**Gantillon, Simon** (1890–    ), French dramatist. Born in Lyon, he entered the merchant navy, finding in his experiences there matter for his exotic plays, *Cyclone* (1923), *Maya* (1924), *Départs* (1929) and *Bifur* (1931).

**García de la Huerta, Vicente** (1734–1787), Spanish dramatist. Born at Zafra, Badajoz, he was in the train of the Alba family, and later became involved in political tangles which led to exile in North Africa. His great tragedy, *Raquel* (1778; mod. ed., 1936), the finest since Calderón (q.v.), is the work by which he is remembered. He was a copious poet (*Obras poéticas*, 2 vols., 1778), but his verse is of secondary importance. He died in Madrid.

**García Gutiérrez, Antonio** (1813–1884), Spanish dramatist. Born at Chiclana, he was intended for medicine but suddenly joined the army, giving his private time to writing. He came forward as a successful playwright in the romantic manner with *El trovador* (1836) which, founded on an old Aragonese tale, provided the libretto for Verdi's *Il trovatore*. Leaving the army he devoted himself to archaeology and history and produced a masterpiece of the stage in *Venganza catalana* (1864), a tragedy suggested by an incident in Muntaner's (q.v.) *Crónica*. His plays are a mixture of prose and verse, both equally good. He died director of the archaeological museum in Madrid. See his *Teatro* (1925).

**García Lorca, Federico** (1899–1936), Spanish poet and dramatist. Born at Fuentevaqueros, Granada, where his father had a small estate, he read law at the University of Granada, but soon became well known as the founder and director of the university theatre, the Barraca, soon to be the most influential in Spain. Friend of writers, musicians and artists, he was the most vital literary influence of his time. The mainspring of his inspiration was Andalusian peasant (and gipsy) tradition, but fused with this is a sophistication always held in check by keen perception and delicacy of feeling. Few books of verse are so rich in unadulterated poetry as *Canciones* (1927), *Romancero gitano* (1928; Eng. trans. *Gypsy Ballads*, 1953) and *Poema del cante jondo* (1931). His visit to America brought him face to face with a new way of life which distressed him with its glare and restlessness, as is to be seen in the posthumous *Poeta en Nueva York* (1940; Eng. trans. *The Poet in New York*, 1940). Passion and death became more and more his preoccupation as time passed, finely expressed in the poem *Llanto por Ignacio Sánchez Mejías* (1935; Eng. trans. *Lament for the Death of a Bull Fighter*, 1937). A poem of a completely different kind is *Doña Rosita la soltera* (1935), describing the tragedy of a thwarted life. As a playwright he reached complete mastery with the trilogy consisting of *Bodas de sangre* (1933, 'Blood Wedding'), *Yerma* (1935, 'The Barren One') and *La casa de Bernada Alba* (1940, 'The House of Bernarda Alba', translated together as *Three Tragedies of Lorca* in 1947). Here the Calderonian theme of dream and reality is explored and translated into modern terms with remarkable power and beauty. At the very beginning of the civil war he was murdered in Granada by members of the Falange. His collected works edited by B. A. Losada originally came out in eight volumes (1938–42), and on this a number of later editions have been based; a very handy one is the Aguilar edition (1960). See also the English translation, *Poems* (1939).

**Garcilaso de la Vega** (1503–1536), Spanish poet. Born in Toledo, he held posts at court, was in the army, and was banished for a while by

Charles V for a small domestic misdemeanour (1532). It was while living for a time in Naples that he wrote his handful of excellent odes, eclogues, elegies and sonnets, taking Virgil, Horace and Tibullus as his models for the first three styles and the Italians for the last. He went to war again and, wounded in a skirmish near Fréjus, died in Nice. The basis of his inspiration is unhappy love, and he expressed himself with such felicity that in spite of his small output his influence on Spanish literature has been outstanding and has never declined. A friend of Boscán (q.v.), his work was published together with Boscán's by the latter's widow in 1543. The best edition of his work is that by H. Keniston (N.Y., 1925). For an English translation see *The Works of Garcilaso de la Vega* (1823).

**Garcilaso de la Vega,** called **El Inca** to distinguish him from the poet of the same name (1539–1616), Spanish prose-writer. Born at Cuzco, Peru, of mixed Spanish and Peruvian blood, he settled in Spain in 1560, and spent a great portion of his life on his *Comentarios reales* (1609; mod. crit. ed., 1943; Eng. trans. *The Royal Commentaries of Peru, in Two Parts,* 1688; of part only, *First Part of the Royal Commentaries of the Yncas,* 2 vols., 1869–71), the first half being concerned with the history of Peru before the Spanish conquest, the second with the conquest itself and its aftermath. The work is full of verve and grace, and it is particularly worthy of attention as being one of the few Spanish works on such a subject written with sympathy for the conquered people, for there is no doubt that Garcilaso felt far more an Indian than a Spaniard. He remained in Spain, however, and died in Cordoba.

**Garnier, Robert** (1545?–1590), French dramatist. Born at La Ferté-Bernard, near Le Mans, he became an advocate and finally reached the office of royal counsellor. Considered the greatest French writer of tragedy before P. Corneille (q.v.), he was highly esteemed in England and had an enormous influence on the Elizabethan dramatists, especially Thomas Kyd. Although the action is inclined to stand still, and there is too much ranting in Senecan style, his eight pieces have considerable poetic qualities and prove that he had a knowledge of stagecraft. His tragedies are *Porcie, épouse de Brutus* (1568), *Hippolyte, fils de Thésée* (1573), *Cornélie, épouse de Pompée* (1574; Eng. trans. *Pompey the Great* by Thomas Kyd, 1594), *Marc-Antoine* (1578; Eng. trans. *Antonius,* 1592) *La Troade, ou la destruction de Troie* (1579), *Antigone* (1580), *Bradamante* (1582), which tends towards comedy, and *Sédécie, ou les Juives* (1583), his masterpiece. He died at Le Mans. See his *Œuvres* (2 vols., 1923).

**Garshin, Vsevolod Mikhailovich** (1855–1888), Russian short-story writer, born in Ekaterinoslav Province. His *Chetyre dnya* (1877, 'Four Days') is a vivid and moving account of the Russo-Turkish war in which he took part. Other works such as *Krasny tsvetok* (1883, 'The Scarlet Flower') show his longing for an ideal world in which there is a common bond and brotherhood between all men. He died by his own hand in Petersburg. The fullest collection of his stories in English translation is *The Signal and other Stories* (1912).

**Gauthier-Villars, Henri,** using the pseudonym **Willy** (1859–1931), French writer. Born at Villiers-sur-Orge, he married Colette (q.v.) in 1893, and with her collaborated in the 'Claudine' series of novels. Among his critical and fictional works may be named *Art et critique* (1889), *Mémoires d'un grenadier anglais* (1897), *Chaussettes pour dames* (1905), *Mon Cousin Fred* (1916), *Ginette la rêveuse* (1919), *La Femme déshabillée* (1922), *Les Bazars de la volupté* (1926), *La Fin du vice* (1926) and *Le Troisième Sexe* (1928). He died in Paris.

**Gautier, Théophile** (1811–1872), French poet, novelist and general prose-writer. Born at Tarbes, he soon found his way to Paris and first studied painting, before long giving this up for literature. Attracting attention to himself with his eccentric manners and his unusual clothes, and his wild, undisciplined talk, he gained admittance to Hugo's (q.v.) circle as a romantic of the romantics, fighting for that king of romanticism at the 'barricades of *Hernani*' (1830) when this play of Hugo, supported by the younger generation, swept Paris and brought about his triumph. In case he had not gained notoriety enough, Gautier now shocked the bourgeois with the licentious romance in verse, *Albertus* (1830), and in that anatomy of sensualism, the novel *Mademoiselle de Maupin* (1835; Eng. trans. 1948). *Fortunio* (1837; Eng. trans. 1915) is an excursion in novel form into the grotesque, and he explored the macabre in the verse *La Comédie de la mort* (1838). He was already immersed in journalism, having become dramatic and fine arts critic of *La Presse* in 1836, a post he held until 1854. New features of his work were travel books and books on art, e.g. *Tra los montes* (1843), which first revealed his love of Spain, and *Les Grotesques* (1844) and *Caprices et zigzags* (1845) dealing with art and literature. Increasingly weighed down by domestic commitments, he had often to write against his inclination, but his best work never suffers. *Émaux et camées* (1856; crit. ed., 1947) is a splendid volume of poetry showing unclouded feeling and absolute technical grasp. In *Jettatura* (1857), a collection of stories, and that excellent piece of historical fiction *Le Roman de la momie* (1858; Eng. trans. *The Mummy's Romance*, 1908) he is at his best. *Le Capitaine Fracasse* (1863; Eng. trans. 1933) is a fast-moving novel after the manner of Dumas the Elder (q.v.), *La Belle Jenny* (1865) shows signs of weariness, but in *Ménagerie intime* (1869), semi-autobiographical, his old charm and vivacity reappear. Travel and desultory love-affairs sometimes took him from his desk, but on the whole he lived the life of an overworked journalist. The strain was already telling on him when the shock of the Franco-Prussian War came to put the finishing touches, and he died at Neuilly. A collection of his plays, of little importance, appeared in 1872 (*Théâtre*), and his *Histoire du romantisme*, containing interesting personal recollections, in 1874. Nearly all his works appear in English translations (very varied in quality) in F. C. de Sumichrast's edition (1900).

**Gay, Delphine** (1804–1855), French poet, novelist, short-story writer and playwright, was born in Aachen, in 1831 married Émile de Girardin (q.v.), the well-known journalist, and from that time on became a central figure of the high romantic *salons* of Paris. All her work is witty but superficial, and yet the best of it has life still. Among her books of verse may be named *Le Dernier Jour de Pompei* (1827) and *Napoline* (1833), of her novels and books of short stories, *Le Lorgnon* (1831) and *La Canne de Monsieur de Balzac* (1836), and of her plays, *Judith* (1843) and *Cléopâtre* (1847). She died in Paris. Her collected works were published (6 vols.) in 1860–1.

**Geibel, Emanuel von** (1815–1884), German poet, born in Lübeck. The formative moment of his life was his stay in Greece (1838–9) as tutor to the family of the Russian ambassador in Athens, which resulted in stirring poetry on ancient Greece and modern liberty which appeared in his immensely popular *Gedichte* (1840; Eng. trans. 1864). It had reached its 130th edition by the end of the century. Before 1843 he had associated with such radical poets as Freiligrath (q.v.), but his ardour quickly cooled and he became a pensioner of Frederick William IV of Prussia. In 1852 Maximilian II of Bavaria invited him to Munich where he found many congenial spirits, chief of them Paul Heyse (q.v.). One of the most read poets of his time, his command of all kinds of metre and his ability to deal with a wide variety of subjects are to be found in such works as *Neue Gedichte* (1856), the poetic dramas *Brunhild* (1857; Eng. trans. 1879) and *Sophonisbe* (1868), *Heroldsrufe* (1871), in which he glories in the new German Empire, *Spätherbstblätter* (1877) and *Echtes Gold wird klar im Feuer* (1882). He returned to Lübeck shortly before his death. He was an accomplished Spanish scholar and made some excellent translations from that language, but in his work in general he fatally lacked depth.

**Geijerstam, Gustaf af** (1858–1909), Swedish novelist. Born at Jönsarbo in Västmanland, he was best known for his somewhat sentimental domestic novels, chief of them *Erik Grane* (1885), *Pastor Hallin* (1887), *Mina pojkar* (1896; Eng. trans. *My Boys*, 1933), *Boken om lille-bror* (1900; Eng. trans. *The Book about Little Brother*, 1921) and *Kvinnomakt* (1901; Eng. trans. *Woman Power*, 1927). From 1893 onwards he was head of a publishing firm in Stockholm, where he died.

**Gellert, Christian Fürchtegott** (1715–1769), German poet and prose-writer, was born at Hainichen and was appointed to the academic staff of the University of Leipzig in 1744, immediately on completing his courses. A man of great charm, upright and benevolent, he became for his wide public a living oracle, an adviser on any and every subject. He regarded himself above all as an educator and may be considered the typical product of the philosophy of Wolff (q.v.). With leisure and comfortable means he was able to study the rapidly increasing middle classes, eager to learn, and realized how powerful a weapon for good the printed book could be. An assiduous contributor to the *Bremer Beiträge*, he wrote such didactic works as those to be found in the collections *Betrachtungen über die Religion* (1760) and *Moralische Vorlesungen* (1770). But today he is known for his verse fables, *Fabeln und Erzählungen* (1746), neat, most accomplished pieces, his best comedy *Das Los in der Lotterie* (1747), and for his novel, inspired by Samuel Richardson's moral fiction, *Leben der schwedischen Gräfin von Guildenstern* (1748; Eng. trans. *The Swedish Countess*, 1776). A curiosity is his collection of model letters for all occasions, *Briefe, nebst einer praktischen Abhandlung von dem guten Geschmack in Briefen* (1751), which was a general handbook for the German public for fifty years. Gellert died in Leipzig.

**Gelli, Giambattista** (1498–1563), Italian writer. A Florentine master-shoemaker and one of the founders of the Florentine Academy (1540), he wrote two works which are still alive, *I capricci di Giusto Bottaio* (1546; Eng. trans. *The Fearful Fansies of the Florentine Couper*, 1568) and *La Circe* (1549; Eng. trans. *Circe*, 1744), the first about a man confronted with his soul, and the second a discussion between Ulysses and the men who have been turned into animals by Circe the enchantress. Gelli died in Florence.

**Genet, Jean** (1910–        ), French novelist and playwright. Born illegitimate in Paris, abandoned by his parents and brought up in an institution, he led a vagabond life and was imprisoned several times for robbery. At last in 1947 Cocteau (q.v.) and Sartre (q.v.) befriended him and helped to make his work known. An early play, *Les Bonnes* (1945; Eng. trans. *The Maids*, 1957) had a successful run in 1954 and encouraged Genet to continue in his vigorous, anti-naturalistic style with *Le Balcon* (1956; Eng. trans. *The Balcony*, 1957) and *Les Nègres* (1958; Eng. trans. *The Blacks*, 1960), a searching analysis of the racial problem. Of his novels, the best are *Notre-Dame des fleurs* (1943; Eng. trans. *Our Lady of the Flowers*, 1949) and *Querelle de Brest* (1946; Eng. trans. 1966), which, while violently attacking conventional values, are yet strangely lyrical in expression. The autobiographical *Journal du voleur* (1949; Eng. trans. *The Thief's Journal*, 1954) is accounted by many his most profound and arresting work.

**Genevoix, Maurice** (1890–        ), French novelist. Born at Decize, he became a schoolmaster, took part in the First World War until severely wounded, and published his first book, a war novel, *Sous Verdun* in 1916 (Eng. trans. *'Neath Verdun*, 1916). Other novels, gradually changing from wartime to peace-time settings, are *Rémy des ranches* (1922), *Raboliot* (1925), his masterpiece, *La Boîte à pêche* (1926), *Rroû* (1931; Eng. trans. *Rroû, the Story of a Cat*, 1932), *La Dernière Harde* (1938; Eng. trans. *The Last Hunt*, 1940), and the two escapist works, written during the occupation, *La Framboise et Belle-Humeur* (1942) and *Éva Charlebois* (1944). After the war he continued his novel-writing with *Sanglas* (1946), *L'Écureil du Bois-Bourru* (1947), *Chevalet de campagne* (1950), *L'Aventure est en nous* (1952), *Fatou Cissé* (1954), *Mon ami l'écureil* (1957) and *Le Petit Chat* (1957).

**Genlis, Stéphanie Félicité Ducrest de St Aubin de** (1746–1830), French writer. Born at Champcéri, near Autun, she was in 1770 appointed a lady-in-waiting in the Orléans family, and soon became 'Égalité' Orléans's mistress and governess to his children, for whom she wrote educational books such as *Théatre d'éducation* (1779–80), containing short and easily acted plays for private theatricals, and the novels *Annales de la vertu* (1781) and *Adèle et Théodore* (1782). In *Zélie* (1785) she tried her hand at a Rousseauesque idyll with scant success, and in *Conseils sur l'éducation du Dauphin* (1790) proffered advice to Marie Antoinette on the education of her son, which passed not unnaturally unheeded, for Madame de Genlis was a liberal. In 1793 when the Jacobins seized power she had to escape to Switzerland, but was welcomed back by the Consulate in 1799 and received a pension. Thereafter she produced many novels, including *Mademoiselle de Clermont* (1802), short stories like *Les Veillées de la chaumière* (1823), biographies (*Madame de Maintenon*, 1806), and an informative volume of literary memoirs, *Les Dîners du baron d'Holbach* (1822). She died in Paris.

**Gentile, Giovanni** (1875–1944), Italian prose-writer, was born at Castelvetrano in Sicily. A close friend of B. Croce (q.v.) for many years until Gentile accepted Mussolini's invitation to become his minister of education, in his main work *Teoria generale dello spirito come atto puro* (1916; Eng. trans. *Theory of Mind as Pure Act*, 1922) he describes his philosophical standpoint as the mental and physical being one, with the result that there is no distinction between theory and practice. From this he went on to probe religion in *Discorsi di religione* (1920), to find the right political solution in Fascism (*Fascismo e cultura*, 1928), and to divert education to Fascist ends (*La riforma dell'educazione*, 1928). *Il pensiero italiano del rinascimento* (1940) is an example of how scholarship can be distorted to fit an ideology. He was murdered in Florence.

**George, Stefan** (1868–1933), German poet and critic. Born at Büdesheim, near Bingen, in the Rhineland, he early went to Paris where he came under the influence of the poetry of Baudelaire (q.v.) and Mallarmé (q.v.) and got to know Verlaine (q.v.). Reading the work of such perfectionists in their language brought home to him the fact that the German literary language had been abused and was in decline. His literary journal *Blätter für die Kunst*, founded in 1892, was to remedy this, and until its extinction in 1919 it exercised a healthy influence on German letters. Intellectually powerful, technically classical even to brittleness, his over-sophistication kept his work out of the reach of many; but for those who could appreciate his wide culture and his exacting cult of beauty such books of poetry as *Der siebente Ring* (1907) and *Der Stern des Bundes* (1914) were a revelation. Gradually he became a force in German literary life, and with *Das Neue Reich* (1928) he had gained the height of unrivalled prestige. He seemed to point the way to new possibilities of life and culture to be reached through Nietzsche's 'Apollonianism' leading to a humanism addressed to modern conditions and displacing outworn Christian culture. Later, disliking the changes which were leading to Nazism and indignant at the way in which his ideas were being used to support an ideology to which he was opposed, he left Germany, and going to Switzerland settled at Locarno, where he died. His collected works were published in eighteen volumes (1927–34). See the English translation, *Poems* (1943).

**Gerbert de Montreuil** (*fl.* 1228), French poet from Picardy, was the author of the smooth and charming *Roman de la Violette*, composed about 1228, which deals with ancient Britain in the time of the Roman emperor Claudius.

**Gerhardt, Paul** (1607–1676), German hymn-writer. Born at Gräfen-hainichen in Saxony, he studied theology at Wittenberg and became a Lutheran pastor. A forceful personality as well as a man of great piety, he opposed the 'Great Elector' of Brandenburg in his attempt to fuse the Lutheran and Reformed Churches and was removed from his pastorate in Berlin (1666). He died at Lübben, where he had been archdeacon since 1668. He wrote 120 hymns which prove him to be one of the world's greatest hymn-writers, certainly with Luther (q.v.) the greatest of Protestant ones. Perhaps the finest of all is 'O Haupt voll Blut und Wunden' ('O sacred Head, sore wounded') set to music as a chorale in J. S. Bach's *St Matthew Passion*. See *Pauli Gerhardi Geistliche Andachten* (10 vols., 1666–7; crit. ed., 1866).

**German, Yury Pavlovich** (1910–    ), Russian Soviet novelist whose *Nashi znakomye* (1934–6; Eng. trans. *Antonina*, 1937), a piece of eroticism, and *Alexey Zhmakin* (1937–8; Eng. trans. *Alexey the Gangster*, 1940), a police novel, have been widely read.

**Gerok, Friedrich Karl von** (1815–1890), German religious poet. Born at Vaihingen, he became a highly popular preacher in Stuttgart, where he died. Of several volumes of devotional verse, *Palmblätter* (1857; Eng. trans. *Palm Leaves*, 1869) went through 131 editions in forty-five years. Other characteristic works are *Blumen und Sterne* (1868) and *Von Bethlehem bis Golgatha* (1881).

**Gershenzon, Mikhail Osipovich** (1869–1925), Russian prose-writer. Born at Kishinev, he was one of the few intellectuals of his generation to remain faithful to religion, and with his study of Chaadayev (q.v.), published in 1908, and his contributions to literary journals he exerted an influence in another direction from the general one at a time when a corrective was needed. He survived the revolution, dying in Moscow. His final views are expressed in *Perepiska iz dvukh uglov* (1921, 'Correspondence between two Corners').

**Gerson, Jean Charlier de** (1363–1429), French devotional author, writing also in Latin, was born at Gerson, Rethel, near Reims, and as early as 1395 had been appointed chancellor of the University of Paris. He set himself to end the Great Schism in the Western Church and to reform it, and took a leading part to those ends at the Council of Constance (1414–18); but for condemning his actions, particularly as regards the murder of the Duke of Orléans, the Duke of Burgundy sought his life, and to escape the danger Gerson fled to Rattenburg in Tirol, where he wrote the most celebrated of his Latin works, *De Consolatione Theologiae*. He later returned to France and died in a monastery in Lyon. Of his works in the vernacular the best known are *La Montagne de contemplation* (mod. ed., 1927) and *La Mendicité spirituelle* (mod. ed., 1945). The standard collection of his Latin works is the 1706 edition of the *Opera Omnia*; of the French none exists.

**Gerstäcker, Friedrich** (1816–1872), German novelist. Born in Hamburg, he set out in 1837 on adventurous journeys in the United States, where he remained until 1848, his experiences providing material for such novels on the American way of life as *Die Regulatoren in Arkansas* (1845; Eng. trans. *The Feathered Arrow, or The Forest Rangers*, 1851) and *Die Flusspiraten des Mississippi* (1848; Eng. trans. *The Pirates of the Mississippi*, 1856). From 1849 to 1852 he was in America, Polynesia and Australia, and in 1860–1 in South America. A later novel is *Germelshausen* (1862; Eng. trans. *The Strange Village*, 1878). In 1862 he was in Egypt and Abyssinia, in 1867–8 again in South America and in the West Indies. He died in Brunswick.

**Gerstenberg, Heinrich Wilhelm von** (1737–1823), German dramatist and literary critic. Born at Tondern in Schleswig of an army family, he joined a Danish regiment, and gave up his spare time to literature, fired to this by a meeting with Gellert (q.v.). He is a noteworthy link in German literature, a transmitter of ideas between the first half and the second half of the eighteenth century. In his *Gedicht eines Skalden* (1766, 'Poem of a Scald', i.e. a Scandinavian bard) he introduced the Ossianic kind of poem into German literature; in *Ariadne auf Naxos* (1767), a cantata with music by Benda, he brought in this branch of Italian writing, of which Germans had been shy before, while that same year he completed his *Briefe über Merkwürdigkeiten der Literatur* (3 vols., 1766–7; mod. ed., 1888), in which beginning from the standpoint of Klopstock (q.v.), he contrasted individualism and pure lyricism with literary formalism and broken-down classicism, choosing in favour of the individual voice speaking through the lyric. Then in 1768 came his terrible tragedy of hunger, *Ugolino*, the plot suggested by an incident in Dante's *Inferno*, a powerful stimulus towards the *Sturm und Drang* ('Storm and Stress') movement just about to come into being. In a few years, therefore, Gerstenberg had touched German literature closely at many points. After that he vanished from literary ken. He was Danish Resident in Lübeck (1775–83), and died at Altona, near Hamburg.

**Gessner, Salomon** (1730–1788), Swiss prose-poet. Born in Zürich, the son of a bookseller, he followed his father's trade in Berlin for a time, and there came into contact with men of letters. But he was too much a lover of the quiet life and worshipper of nature to want to remain in the hurly-burly of such circles for long, and he returned to Zürich, where he lived as an artist and engraver. His pastoral romance *Daphnis* (1754) is a conventional piece of rococo writing, but his *Idyllen* (1756) reveals in simple, charming prose his deep love for and understanding of nature. *Der Tod Abels* (1758; Eng. trans. *The Death of Abel*, Cooke's ed., 1796) sets the biblical tragedy against a background of rustic scenery. These were the most popular books in German not only in Germany but in Europe before the appearance of Goethe's *Werther*. Gessner died in Zürich, but had ceased to write before 1777, when his collected works were published in two volumes.

**Gezelle, Guido** (1830–1899), Flemish poet. Born in Bruges, he was ordained priest in 1854, became a journalist, and published poetry of such quality as to be one of the chief pillars of the new Flemish literary movement. He specialized in nature poetry. A man of unbalanced mind, he died in Bruges. There is a selected edition of his works (4 vols., 1949), and there are English translations of some of them in *Lyra Belgica*, I (1950).

**Ghéon, Henri,** pseudonym of **Henri Vangeon** (1875–1944), French dramatist, born at Bray-sur-Seine. Associated with various literary movements and periodicals in his youth, his profession of Roman Catholic faith in 1910 led to a complete change of direction in his activity in letters. Henceforward he followed the themes and manner of the religious mystery plays of the Middle Ages as in *Le Pauvre sous l'escalier* (1921), *Jeux et miracles pour le peuple fidèle* (1922), *La Merveilleuse Histoire du jeune Bernard de Menthon* (1924), *Le Mystère du roi Saint Louis* (1935) and *Le Jeu des grandes heures de Reims* (1938). He died in Paris.

**Ghil, René** (1862–1925), French poet. Born at Tourcoing, he came under the influence of Mallarmé (q.v.), but his attempts to approximate poetry to actual music made nonsense of his verse and seemed to reduce poetry to a mere science. His antics may be compared with those of Eric Satie in music. His main works were *Dire du mieux* (9 vols., 1889–97) and *Dire des sangs* (4 vols., 1889; reprinted 1920). He died at Niort.

**Giacometti, Paolo** (1816–1882), Italian playwright. Born at Novi Ligure, he was a fertile composer of actable plays without much depth, but much appreciated by a wide public, such as *Il poeta e la ballerina* (1841), *Regina d'Inghilterra* (1853) and *Elisabetta*. His *Teatro scelto* was published (4 vols.) in 1857–63. He died at Gazzuolo.

**Giacosa, Giuseppe** (1847–1906), Italian novelist, playwright and librettist, born at Colleretto (now called Pedanea), Aosta, is best known as the author of *Novelle e paesi valdostani* (1886), *I tristi amori* (1888), a naturalistic play of great power, and, in part, of the libretti of Puccini's *La Bohème* (1896, from Murger, q.v.), *La Tosca* (1900) and *Madame Butterfly* (1904). He died at Colleretto Parella (Ivrea).

**Gide, André Paul Guillaume** (1869–1951), French novelist, playwright, poet and miscellaneous writer. Born in Paris of Protestant parents, he grew up in a restricted and even negative atmosphere. He tried his hand at poetry in such second-rate productions as *Les Cahiers d'André Walter* (1891) and *La Tentative Amoureuse* (1893), betraying severe sexual frustration and other problems in that field which were to trouble his whole life, and then was wise enough to break away from his crippling *milieu* and visit Tunisia (1893–4). On a visit to Algeria in 1895 he met Oscar Wilde, and by now the component parts which make up the characteristic Gidean manner were all assembled. It was that conflict between Protestant sexual morality and the fear of pleasure in itself on the one hand and the longing for the sensual and exotic, glimpsed at in the Arab world, complicated by a taste for homosexuality which Wilde represented, that are the ingredients of his work. As a novelist he is well represented by *Paludes* (1895; Eng. trans. *Marshlands*, 1953), *L'Immoraliste* (1902; Eng. trans. 1930),

*La Porte étroite* (1909; Eng. trans. *Strait is the Gate*, 1924; rev., 1948), *Isabelle* (1911; Eng. trans. in *Two Symphonies*, 1931), *Les Caves du Vatican* (1914; Eng. trans. *The Vatican Swindle*, 1927), *La Symphonie pastorale* (1919; Eng. trans. *The Pastoral Symphony* in *Two Symphonies*, 1931), *Les Faux-monnayeurs* (1926; Eng. trans. *The Coiners*, 1927; new ed., 1950), *L'École des femmes* (1929; Eng. trans. *The School for Wives*, 1929), *Geneviève* (1939) and *Thésée* (1946; Eng. trans. *Theseus* in *Oedipus and Theseus*, 1950). As a poet his development was arrested early, as can be seen by comparing *Les Nourritures terrestres* (1897; Eng. trans. in *Fruits of the Earth*, 1949) and *Les Nouvelles Nourritures* (1935; Eng. trans. in *Fruits of the Earth*, 1949). As a playwright he dealt with the same general problems which he had faced in his novels, often preferring in this medium a classical or biblical symbolism as in *Saül* (1903), *Oedipe* (1931; Eng. trans. *Oedipus* in *Oedipus and Theseus*, 1950), and *Perséphone* (1934). His latest plays, *Robert, ou L'Intérêt général* (1944) and *Le Retour* (1946) are very complex. Of his critical work *Dostoïevsky* (1923; Eng. trans. 1925; rev., 1949), *Journal des Faux-monnayeurs* (1926; Eng. trans. *The Logbook of the Coiners*, 1952), *Divers* (1931), *Interviews imaginaires* (1943) and *L'Enseignement de Poussin* (1945) should be named. Among his travel books are the anti-imperialistic *Voyage au Congo* (1927) and *Le Retour du Tchad* (1928), the result of his stay in the French Congo (1925-6). His change of spirit from enthusiastic support of Communism to his later hostility towards it are chronicled in *Retour de l'U.R.S.S.* (1936; Eng. trans. *Back from the U.S.S.R.*, 1937) and *Retouches à mon Retour de l'U.R.S.S.* (1937; Eng. trans. *Afterthoughts on the U.S.S.R.*, 1938). His *Journal 1889–1939* (1939), *Pages de Journal* (1944) and *Journal 1942-9* (1950) are the most candid self-revelations of a French writer since Rousseau. The three appear in English translation as *The Journals of André Gide* (vol. i, 1947; vol. ii, 1948; vol. iii, 1949; vol. iv, 1951). He died in Paris. The master of a majestic style, he reaches excellence only in his shorter works, but his influence on the literature of his time has been very great. See *Œuvres complètes* (15 vols.), 1932-9.

**Gilbert, Nicolas-Joseph Laurent** (1751-1780), French poet, born at Fontenay in the Vosges. A precursor of the romantics, he found himself entirely out of sympathy with the rationalism of his time as is to be seen in *Le Dix-huitième siècle* (1775), a satire against sceptics and materialists. His *Adieux à la vie*, written as he lay dying from the result of a riding accident in Paris, is a poem of moving beauty. A. de Vigny (q.v.) dramatized his life in *Stello* (1832). His *Œuvres complètes* were published in 1823, and there is a handy edition of *Œuvres choisies* (1882).

**Gilkin, Iwan** (1858-1924), Belgian poet and playwright. Born in Brussels, he took up law, but after a time abandoned it for literature, and together with some friends founded the journal, *La Jeune Belgique*, which soon grew to be the mouthpiece of the younger generation of Belgian writers. He had gained from Baudelaire's (q.v.) work a taste for the gloomy and wayward, but as his volumes of verse testify (*La Nuit*, 1897; *Prométhée*, 1899; and *Le Cérisier* *fleuri*, 1899) he never reached the essential message of Baudelaire and was quite unable to reproduce his style of poetry. His plays, e.g. *Savonarole* (1906) and *Le Roi Cophétua* (1919), are unactable. He died in Brussels.

**Gilm, Hermann von** (1812–1864), Austrian poet. Born in Innsbruck, he devoted much energy, both active and literary, to stirring up nationalism in the Tyrol and he was also something of an anti-clerical. It is, however, as a writer of love-lyrics that he has survived, especially in the collection *Tiroler Schützenleben* (1863). All his work is to be found in *Gedichte* (2 vols., 1864; Eng. trans. (selected only) in *Rhyme and Revolution in Germany*, 1917). He died in Linz.

**Gil y Carrasco, Enrique** (1815–1846), Spanish novelist and poet. Born at Villafranca del Bierzo, León, he entered the diplomatic service and became a close friend of Espronceda (q.v.) who encouraged his literary ambitions. A weaker poetic spirit, he was lost in the ardours of romanticism, but his novel about the Knights Templars in Spain, *El señor de Bembibre* (1844; Eng. trans. *The Mystery of Bierzo Valley*, 1938) is generally held to be the best novel of its kind in the whole range of Spanish literature. He died while a secretary of the Spanish embassy in Berlin.

**Giménez Caballero, Ernesto** (1899–    ), Spanish publicist, was born in Madrid. A man governed by the sensation of the moment, his literary career is a pure reflection of changing schools of thought and politics, to all of which he conformed. Thus he announced his opposition to the weakening regime of Alfonso XIII, condemning the Moroccan campaign and militarism, in *Notas marruecas de un soldado* (1923), showed a disagreeable national exclusiveness in *En torno al casticismo de España* (1929), the 'authenticity' of Spain being something that liberal thought had condemned for two generations, and in *Hércules jugando a los dados* (1929, 'Hercules playing at Dice') criticized the monarchy's last bid for power with the help of Primo de Rivera. He managed to ingratiate himself with the republic while turning Fascist and helping to incubate the Falangist Party. On this account see his *Roma madre: Apología del fascismo, el Duce y Roma* (1939).

**Giner de los Ríos, Francisco** (1839–1915), Spanish journalist. Born at Ronda, Málaga, he followed in the steps of Sanz del Río (q.v.) in gaining for *krausismo* (a kind of pantheism, leading to left-wing politics and anticlericalism, derived from the ideas of the German philosopher, K. C. F. Krause, 1781–1832) a wide public hearing. As an advanced intellectual with liberal political ideas it is not surprising that he was forced from his professorship in Madrid, but in his powerful articles in the daily press and periodicals and still more by founding his Institución Libre de Enseñanza (Free Institute of Education) he brought together all the forces for good in that much neglected department of Spanish life. A man of commanding character, he died in Madrid. His collected works were published (18 vols.), 1916–28.

**Giono, Jean** (1895–    ), French novelist. Born of simple family at

Manosque in Provence, he became a bank clerk, but gradually managed to emancipate himself from this daily task by the success of his novels, all set in Provence, written in an ample, melodious style: *Colline* (1929; Eng. trans. *Hill of Destiny*, 1929), *Un de Baumugnes* (1929; Eng. trans. *Lovers are never Losers*, 1932), *Regain* (1930; Eng. trans. *Harvest*, 1939), *Le Chant du monde* (1934; Eng. trans. *The Song of the World*, 1937), *Que ma joie demeure* (1935; Eng. trans. *Joy of Man's Desiring*, 1949) and *Refus d'obéissance* (1937). Prosecuted and imprisoned in 1939 for pacifism, he passed a difficult period, returning to authorship with *Un Roi sans divertissement* (1947), *Les Âmes fortes* (1949), *Les Grands Chemins* (1951), *Le Moulin de Pologne* (1952), *La Chasse au bonheur* (1953), *Le Bonheur fou* (1957) and *Angélo* (1958). A thoroughly satisfying writer, who enters with zest of spirit into the abiding things, he has kept free from temporary fashions and problems.

**Giovanni Fiorentino** ( *fl.* 1378), Italian short-story writer. Probably born in Florence, he seems to have been exiled for political reasons to Dovadola (Forlì), where in 1378 he finished a collection of stories (the usual Renaissance medley of the tragic and those verging on the indecent) called *Il Pecorone* ('The Dunce', mod. ed., 1943). It has been urged that one of the tales, that of Gianneto, suggested a major portion of the plot (Shylock) to Shakespeare for his *Merchant of Venice*; but we know nothing of how many stories filtered down to him.

**Giraldi, Giambattista Cinzio** (1504–1573), Italian poet, playwright and writer of stories, was born in Ferrara and in 1541 gained the chair of literature in Florence. He later exchanged this for that of rhetoric at Pavia. His most important work is his *Ecatommiti*, which, begun in 1528, was not published till 1565 (Eng. trans. of some tales in T. Roscoe's *Italian Novelists*, 1825). It is a collection of 130 stories of varying quality, and provided Shakespeare with his plots for *Measure for Measure* and *Othello*, and several plots of Beaumont and Fletcher. His heavy Senecan tragedies, of which the best was *Orbecche* (1541), were published together in 1583, and his epic, *Ercole*, appeared in 1557. He died in Ferrara.

**Girardin, Émile de** (1806–1881), French journalist and novelist. Born in Paris, he soon made a successful entry into newspaper life and in 1836 started *La Presse*, designed to appeal to the ordinary reader, which was the beginning of journalism for the masses in France. At first on the side of the regime of Louis Philippe, he gradually moved towards the left and finally became a Republican, voicing his opinions in another paper, *La Liberté*. In earlier years he wrote several novels such as *Émile* (1827), vivacious but little more. By the time of his death in Paris he had become a force to be reckoned with in modern journalism.

**Giraud, Albert,** pseudonym of **Albert Kayenbergh** (1860–1929), Belgian poet, born in Louvain. A member of the same circle as Gilkin (q.v.) he suffered from the same defects, with an even greater unbalance than his associate. He was obsessed by the fantastic, the far away and the decadently beautiful which is near ugliness, as may be seen in such books of verse as *Pierrot lunaire* (1884), *Pierrot narcisse* (1891), *Dernières fêtes* (1891), *La Guirlande des dieux* (1910) and *La Frise empourprée* (1912). A man of highly unpleasant nature, he died at Schaerbeek.

**Giraudoux, Jean** (1882–1944), French novelist and dramatist. Born at Bellac in the Limousin, of a well-to-do family, the good knowledge of German which he acquired on his travels carried him into the diplomatic service, but on the success of his novels he gave himself up to authorship. He began as a novelist, and in this field his best works are *Suzanne et le Pacifique* (1921; Eng. trans. *Suzanne and the Pacific*, 1923), *Juliette au pays des hommes* (1924), *Bella* (1926; Eng. trans. 1927), *Aventures de Jérôme Bardini* (1930), *Combat avec l'ange* (1934) and *Choix des élues* (1938). By this time his plays were overshadowing his novels, and before the end of his career he was accounted one of the leading playwrights of Europe. *Amphitryon 38* (1929; Eng. trans. 1938) was his first stage success. There followed many more, such as *Judith* (1932), *Intermezzo* (1933; Eng. trans. *The Enchanted*, 1950), *La Guerre de Troie n'aura pas lieu* (1935; Eng. trans. *Tiger at the Gates*, 1955), his most famous, *Électre* (1937), *Ondine* (1939; Eng. trans. 1954), *Sodome et Gomorrhe* (1943), set in the Paris of the occupation, and the posthumous *Folle de Chaillot* (Eng. trans. *The Madwoman of Chaillot*, 1947) and *Apollon de Bellac* (both 1946). Giraudoux died in Paris. His world is unreal, his plots are non-existent; he uses myths, symbols and fantasy; but in creating his own values with their essential morality he has contributed memorably to keeping basic values alive in this distracted modern age. See his *Théâtre complet* (15 vols.), 1945–8.

**Giusti, Giuseppe** (1809–1850), Italian poet. Born at Monsummano, near Florence, he early on became known as a powerful political satirist using the lyric most deftly for his purpose. His three main works are *La Ghigliottina a vapore* (1833), *Il Dies Irae* (1835), on the death of the Emperor Francis II of Austria, and *Il Gingillino* (1845), a scathing attack on proud, vain, corrupt Florentine society. He died in Florence. There are some brilliant English translations of some of his poetry in W. D. Howell's *Modern Italian Poets* (1887).

**Gjellerup, Karl Adolph** (1857–1919), Danish novelist and short-story writer. Born at Roholte, a clergyman's son, he had a highly successful career at Copenhagen University where he read theology. He gave up all idea of a clerical life and became a keen supporter of Georg Brandes (q.v.). In time he found this scientific diet too dry, and turned with relief to German idealism, Schelling (q.v.) and Schopenhauer (q.v.) leading him to oriental philosophy. He had already begun to publish novels and short stories, in which he uses ancient classical settings or eastern ones as a background for his not always clear ideas. Such are *Antigonos* (1880), *Romulus* (1883), *Tamyris* (1887), *En arkadisk Legende* (1887) and *Minna* (1889; Eng. trans. 1913). In 1892 he settled in Germany at Klotzsche, near Dresden, where he remained for the rest of his life. He wrote much after this, but little, except for *Pilgrimen Kamanita* (1906; Eng. trans. *The Pilgrim Kamanita*, 1911), is of lasting value, and it came as a surprise to all and especially to Danes when he was awarded the Nobel Prize jointly with that far greater Dane, H. Pontoppidan (q.v.) in 1917.

**Gladkov, Fyodor Vasilyevich** (1883–1958), Russian Soviet novelist, born at Chernyavka, Saratov Province, known for his realistic, propagandist fictional works, *Tsement* (1925; Eng. trans. *Cement*, 1929) and *Energiya* (1932–8). He died in Moscow.

**Glassbrenner, Adolf** (1810–1876), German satirist. Born in Berlin, he had a keen eye for the follies of politics and society and wrought havoc on the city in his two long series, *Berlin wie es ist—und trinkt* (1833–49) and *Buntes Berlin* (1837–58). He also edited the two trenchant reviews, *Don Quixote* and *Montagszeitung*. He died in Berlin.

**Glatigny, Joseph Albert Alexandre** (1839–1873), French poet and prose-writer, born at Lillebonne. He became a second-rate wandering actor before trying his literary fortune in Paris. After such tentative efforts to discover himself as a poet as *Les Vignes folles* (1857), which seems to be a derivative of Parnassianism, he broke out on his own in the collections of lyrics, *Les Flèches d'or* (1864), *Gilles et Pasquins* (1871) and *Le Fer rouge* (1872). An engaging semi-autobiographical prose work is *Le Jour de l'an d'un vagabond* (1870). Glatigny died destitute at Sèvres. His collected poetry was published in 1879.

**Gleim, Johann Wilhelm Ludwig** (1719–1803), German poet. Born at Ermsleben, near Halberstadt, he was a student at the University of Halle with Uz (q.v.) and Götz (q.v.), the three forming the so-called German Anacreontic School, since they introduced the short-lined love poetry and drinking songs associated with the name of Anacreon of Teos, into Germany. Gleim's share was afterwards collected as *Lieder nach dem Anakreon* (1766). But his fame was due to his experiences in the Silesian War, in which he served as a military secretary (1744–5). His *Lieder* (1745) dealt with military subjects in ballad form. He settled in Halberstadt in 1747 as secretary of the cathedral there, remaining in that city for the rest of his life, the house of 'Vater Gleim', as he was affectionately termed, being a favourite place of pilgrimage for young writers, to whom Gleim was unfailingly kind. The Seven Years War again stirred him to poetical activity and his most celebrated poem, *Kriegslieder von einem preussischen Grenadier*, long afterwards set to music by Schumann, appeared in 1758. *Lieder, Fabeln und Romanzen* (1758) provides a cross-section of his work. Though his poetic talent was not strong he knew how to make the most of it.

**Glück, Barbara Elisabeth,** *see* **Paoli, Betty.**

**Glückel von Hameln** (1645–1724), Jewish prose-writer born in Hamburg, who wrote the lengthy memoirs called *Zikhronot Marat Glikel Hamil* (1896; Eng. trans. 1932), a work of fascinating interest and of great literary quality. He died in Metz.

**Gobineau, Joseph-Arthur de** (1816–1882), French prose-writer, was born of noble family at Ville-d'Avray, and went into the diplomatic service, indulging in his spare time in literary work. All this is now very dated, although something of interest can still be derived from his novel *Les Pléiades* (1874; Eng. trans. *Sons of Kings,* Oxford Library of French Classics). What, however, he is well known for is his work on racialism, *Essai sur l'inégalité des races humaines* (3 vols., 1853–5), a pseudo-scientific work which extolled the so-called Aryan race to the disadvantage of others, and which in time to come was to go to the heads of the Germans from Wagner to Hitler. Gobineau, who also published works on comparative religion and oriental history, died in Turin.

**Goetel, Ferdynand** (1890–1960), Polish novelist and short-story writer, was born at Sucha. After 1923, when his collection of tales, *Pątnik Karapeta* ('The Pilgrim of Karapet'), appeared he became a foremost man of letters in Poland. He is the author of the novels *Z dnia na dzień* (1926; Eng. trans. *From Day to Day,* 1931) and *Serce lodów* (1930; Eng. trans. *The Messenger of the Snow,* 1931), in both of which he reveals his love of mankind and feeling for nature. He died in Warsaw.

**Goethe, Johann Wolfgang von** (1749–1832), German poet, dramatist and general prose-writer. Born the son of Imperial Counsellor Johann Kaspar Goethe in Frankfurt-am-Main, he was brought up in comfortable and cultured surroundings and was liberally educated by private tutors before going to Leipzig University to read law (1765–8). His sojourn in Leipzig resulted in nothing but a severe illness, but during a lengthy convalescence he laid the foundations of a store of knowledge, including science, of a humanism based on the classics, and of modern German and French literature and philosophy. On his return to full health he went to Strassburg University, and here he discovered himself. While continuing his law course he found time to study drawing, anatomy, chemistry and archaeology and made many friends, the most important of them all being Herder (q.v.), who, by introducing him to Shakespeare, folk lyrics, biblical literature and Homer, opened up new vistas to him. Meanwhile he entered the phase of pastoralism, deepened into some of the most charming lyric poetry in German literature inspired by his love for the unspoilt country girl Friederike Brion, daughter of the pastor of the Alsatian village of Sesenheim. In 1771 he became licentiate of law and visited Wetzlar, then one of the most important centres of the German law courts, but as his subsequent short legal career was to prove his heart was not in his profession, and when he should have been cultivating judges with a view to his future, he was falling in love with Charlotte (Lotte) Buff, moving in literary circles and experiencing the shock of the suicide of a friend, K. W. Jerusalem. This short stay had immense consequences, and when he returned to Frankfurt to settle down as an advocate his whole ambition lay towards literature. Gone was the pastoral idyll and the classical quest for form, the rationalism, the inquiring scientific spirit; he plunged into a world of feeling and of passion, heightened by his repugnance for an uncongenial life, and a restlessness caused by the prod of his rising genius. With *Götz von Berlichingen* (1773) he produced a tragedy that not only broke with the literary canons of the past, but gave expression to his revolt against the social conventions, amongst which and to which he had been brought up. From *Götz* is usually dated the famous *Sturm und Drang* ('Storm and Stress') movement, which is regarded as a new era in European literary and social ideas. But it was his short novel, *Die Leiden des jungen Werthers* ('The Sorrows of Werther', 1774), inspired by his experience of love and death during his stay in Wetzlar, which brought him European fame. Another tragedy, *Clavigo* (1774), partly founded on the *Mémoires* of Beaumarchais (q.v.), gives further evidence of his rebellious feelings against an environment which was suffocating him; and when he found himself being gradually ensnared into marriage with the beautiful but insipid Lili Schönemann, a rich merchant's daughter, he took refuge in a visit to Switzerland with the two counts Stolberg (q.v.) in the summer of 1775. That autumn came an invitation from the young Duke of Saxe-Weimar, Karl August, to visit Weimar. He went and stayed there for good. The change saved his genius from possible disintegration due to the disillusionment and lack of self-discipline of his life before. Soon asked to become a permanent member of the little court, presided over in reality by the remarkable dowager-duchess who was gathering together some of the outstanding minds of Germany, Goethe with the rank of privy councillor found administrative responsibilities thrust on him, bringing day-to-day problems to solve, often learning as he went. He marvellously succeeded and during the following years he explored the world of men, aided by his friend and confidante, the remarkable Charlotte von Stein, a platonic attachment which was broken by his journey to Italy in 1786. During the years 1775–86, although he began *Wilhelm Meister* in 1777 and fitfully worked at *Faust*, fragments of which were already in being before he went to Weimar, his scientific interests predominated. This was the time of his anatomical discovery, the intermaxillary bone (1784), his botanical discovery concerning plant metamorphosis, while in physics he was looking into the theory of light, in chemistry into the elements, he was a keen weather observer, a student of engineering and architecture, and as a mineralogist took a keen interest in the ducal mines of Ilmenau. He was in fact well on the way to becoming 'Europe's last universal man', when his long-cherished visit to Italy opened the southern world to him, and with the scales lifted from his eyes he saw for himself the glories of the ancient classical era in a setting of exotic nature. Having studied classical art in the work of Winckelmann (q.v.) he was well able to pick his way among what otherwise might have been bewilderment in the midst of profusion. He completely ignored the medieval; it was the Roman and Graeco-Roman which was his world. The Italian journey (1786–8) was a turning point in his life. Suddenly there came about as if by magic a union of his intellectual and creative powers. He returned to literature refreshed and strengthened in his critical faculty by years of discipline. Romantic tendencies, though investing his new classical style and feeling, were never allowed to dominate them. As a direct result of the Italian experience *Iphigenie auf Tauris* was magnificently transferred from prose to verse (1787), the monumental tragedy *Egmont*, left truncated for so long, was brought to a triumphal conclusion (1788), while *Torquato Tasso* (1790) conveys particularly the message of Italy to him. On his return to Germany he found himself isolated socially and intellectually; in two years he had grown out of touch with Weimar, that microcosm of the best and the worst of his country. Forbidding morals, freezing parochialism, a basically superficial taste for the arts—all these short-comings oppressed him. He asked to be relieved of his administrative duties, and retired from court, taking with him as his mistress the young, pretty, lowly born Christiane Vulpius (he married her in 1806). In this isolation he published the paganly sensual love poetry, *Römische Elegien* (1789) and more significantly the greater part of what he had so far written of *Faust*, as *Faust, ein Fragment* (1790). Then in 1794 came the famous friendship with Schiller (q.v.) lasting till the latter's death in 1805. To this period belong the greater part of *Wilhelm Meisters Lehrjahre* (4 vols., 1795–6; Eng. trans. *Wilhelm Meister's Apprenticeship* by Thomas Carlyle, 1824), his finest novel, the delightful epic-idyll, *Hermann und Dorothea* (1797), a poem in a contemporary setting, a host of his best ballads, literary journalism such as *Die Propyläen* (3 vols., 1798–1800), and the fine fragment in homage to Homer, *Achilleïs* (1799). *Die natürliche Tochter* (1804) is an excursion into French domestic tragedy inspired by Diderot (q.v.). In *Winckelmann und sein Jahrhundert* (1805) he ably summed up his views on classicism and the classical world which had been a main source of inspiration for close on forty years. *Epilog zu Schillers Glocke* (1805) is a moving epitaph on his friend. There was no one to replace him, but the majestic Goethe lived on for a quarter of a century, the honoured master of German letters, forced to hide his gentle benevolence behind an often chilling exterior to protect himself from his countless admirers from all over Europe. This last period opens with the publication of the complete first part of *Faust* (1808), and continues with *Die Wahlverwandtschaften* (1809, 'The Elective Affinities'), a novel generally tedious but admired for its psychological insight into character, *Zur Farbenlehre* (1810), giving his theories on light and colour, and particularly his autobiography (none too trust-worthy, but beautifully written), *Aus meinem Leben: Dichtung und Wahrheit* (4 vols., 1811–33). His *Die Italienische Reise* (1816) may be regarded as a supplement to it, for, for all its length, *Dichtung und Wahrheit* does not go beyond 1775. *Der Westöstliche Divan* (1819), inspired by a love affair even at his age, is a beautiful collection of lyrics in Eastern style. *Wilhelm Meisters Wanderjahre* (1821; Eng. trans. Thomas Carlyle, 1827) is a continuation of the earlier novel. He was at work almost to the end of his life on the second part of *Faust* (1832), and his keen interests in the arts and sciences did not diminish. He had retired from the directorship of the Weimar theatre in 1817. He is best seen in his later years in J. P. Eckermann's (q.v.) *Gespräche mit Goethe* (1836; Eng. trans. *Conversations with Goethe*, 1839, 1850 and 1925), a memorable account. Having completed further scientific and literary works he died quietly in Weimar. The universality of his genius is incomparable; Goethe is a kind of modern Leonardo da Vinci. His guiding belief, which informed all he did, was the organic wholeness of man and nature in the universe. He called his works 'fragments of a great confession', the 'confession' being the life he lived. In his life the art of living is supremely exemplified, not particularly from the moral standpoint, but because he regarded his experiences of life as stones to build the pyramid of his personality towards that pinnacle which is as near to perfectibility as mortal man can reach. Not a Christian, nor yet a materialist or mere rationalist, he is the greatest humanist of modern times. The standard edition of his works is the great Weimar edition (142 vols., 1887–1920), which includes all literary and scientific works, diaries and letters. All his major works have been translated into English in Bohn's Library (14 vols., 1848–90), and L. MacNeice's complete translation of *Faust* (1951) is well worthy of study.

**Gogol, Nikolay Vasilyevich** (1809–1852), Russian novelist, playwright and short-story writer, was born at Sorochintsy, Poltava. He had already tried his hand at authorship with the unsuccessful *Han Küchelgarten*, under the pseudonym of 'V. Alof' (1829), when he arrived at Petersburg looking for a job. He gained one as a civil service clerk, hating every moment of his work, but making mental notes of the various officials with whom he came into contact, a storehouse of characters from which he was to draw so successfully in the future. Success came to him with the delightful collection of stories about Ukrainian country life, *Vecherá na knutore bliz Dikanki* (2 vols., 1831–2, 'Evenings at a Farmhouse near Dikanka'), and this was followed by the Cossack tale, *Taras Bulba* (1834), and further collections of stories, seven in all and of high quality, contained in *Mirgorod* and *Arabeski* (both 1835). Then came his brilliant satirical comedy, *Revizor* (1836, 'The Government Inspector'), holding up to ridicule the Russian civil service, and in fact all bureaucracies, with an accompanying humour which is without parallel. His great success enabled him to visit Italy in 1836, and he lived in Rome until 1841, writing there nearly the whole of his masterpiece, *Myortvye dushi* ('Dead Souls'), which was published in 1842. Satire, humour and brilliant characterization are to be found in this depiction of provincial Russia: it is one of the few great works of fiction. Emboldened by its excellent reception he brought out the same year a miscellaneous collection of his work to date, *Sochineniya* (2 vols.), some already published, others new such as *Zhenit'ba* ('Marriage'), a highly successful farce. After this a change is discernible in his character. Always inclined to unbalance, moral scruples derived from religious mania began to impress him. He regretted that he had not employed his literary gifts to definitely moral ends, attempted to rewrite *Dead Souls* and laid bare his scruples in the distressing *Vybrannye mesta iz perepiski s druzyami* (1847, 'Selected Passages from Correspondence with Friends'). Persuaded by a priest to burn further manuscripts which he had in hand, he suddenly decided to visit Palestine in 1848, on his return settling in Moscow. There, haunted by hallucinations such as ideas of being attacked from

behind which made him walk when outside crabwise so as always to
have his back to a wall, and troubled by fear of eternal damnation,
he died. The best edition of his collected works is that (10 vols.) of
1915. For an English translation of the works see that by Constance
Garnett (6 vols., 1922–6), although D. J. Campbell's *The Government
Inspector* (1947) and G. Reavey's *Dead Souls* (1948) are in their
particular cases perhaps better. There are translations of *Taras Bulba*
and *Dead Souls* in Everyman's Library.

**Goldoni, Carlo** (1707–1793), Italian dramatist. Born in Venice, the
son of a physician who later moved to Perugia, Carlo was left to his
own devices at an early age, and made the most of his opportunity
to join a company of travelling actors. Discovered and brought home,
he was pressed to study law in Venice and did so. Between 1731 and
1748 he practised as an advocate in Venice, Pavia and Pisa, in the
latter year giving way to what was his true interest, the stage, and
accepting the post of playwright to the theatres of San Lucca and
Sant' Angelo, Venice. His knowledge of the ancient comic writer
Aristophanes, Plautus and Terence was great, and he was an enthusiastic admirer of Molière (q.v.). He looked about him and saw not
what the Gozzis (q.v.) considered the glorious traditions of the Italian
stage, but threadbare plots and obscene buffooneries fit only for
booths at fairs. Before long, with vivid, witty plays, with their living
dialogue, dealing with all aspects of Venetian life, he was revolu-
tionizing the Italian theatre. He did away with improvisation and
mask wearing, and gave tautness and direction to plots. His industry
was amazing, and of his more than 240 plays only the best can be
named here. There are *Il cavaliere e la dama* (1749), in which he
satirizes the aristocracy, *La bottega di caffè* (1750), in which coffee-
house life is laughed at, while *Pamela nubile* (1750) is more seriously
didactic, being founded on Samuel Richardson's purposeful novel;
so is *Il bugiardo* (1750). *La locandiera* (1753) contains brilliant
characterization, and he is at his most witty and inventive in *Gli
innamorati* (1759) and *La casa nova* (1760). *I rusteghi* (1760) is in
Venetian dialect, while *Le baruffe chiozzotte* (1762) glides racily
through the back streets of Venice and presents a gallery
of types. *Il ventaglio* (1762) has abundant charm and urbanity.
In this latter year events had reached a point at which he
was almost forced to leave Venice. Carlo Gozzi and the traditionalists,
with the backing of the academies, had for some time been cam-
paigning against this 'downpour of ink', as they termed the prolific
Goldoni, who now, on being offered the directorship of the Italian
Theatre in Paris, immediately accepted. He became popular at once,
and from the first was patronized by the court; but the comedies he
wrote in France such as *Le Bourru bienfaisant* (1771) have none of
the genius of the Italian ones. His one French work of importance
is his delightful *Mémoires* (1787; mod. ed., 1907; Eng. trans.
1926). By that time he had retired from his directorship and was in
receipt of a comfortable pension. This, however, ceased at the revolution, and he died in near poverty in Paris. The edition of his entire
works fills forty-four volumes in that of 1788–95, thirty-seven in that

of 1907–43, while Ortolani's (8 vols., 1935–48) is selective but of the greatest general use. The Oxford Library of Italian Classics contains English translations (in one volume) of *La locandiera* (*Mine Hostess*), *I rusteghi* (*The Boors*) and *Il ventaglio* (*The Fan*).

**Goldschmidt, Meir Aron** (1819–1887), Danish novelist of Jewish descent, was born at Vordingborg, and, breaking away from orthodox Jewry, went to Copenhagen as a journalist in 1840. He is chiefly memorable as the author of *En Jøde* (1845; Eng. trans. *The Jew of Denmark*, 1852) with its most interesting (and rare) picture of Jewish life in Scandinavia at that period, and *Hjemløs* (1857; Eng. trans. by the author himself, *Homeless, or A Poet's Inner Life*, 1861). His memoirs, *Livserindringer og Resultater* (2 vols., 1877), were much read at the time. He died at Frederiksborg.

**Goncharov, Ivan Alexandrovich** (1812–1891), Russian novelist and travel-writer, was born at Simbirsk and launched into authorship with *Obyknovennaya istoriya* (1847; Eng. trans. *A Common Story*, 1917), a work of fiction set in the contemporary world, abounding in excellent characterization and with good descriptive passages. His second and greatest novel, *Oblomov* (1855; Eng. trans. (*a*) by C. J. Hogarth, 1915, (*b*) by N. A. Duddington, 1929), powerfully contrasts the old weakening aristocratic class with the vigorous upstart capitalist one. *Fregat Pallada* (1865, 'The Frigate Pallada') is an excursion into autobiography, and contains an account of a voyage to Japan. Goncharov's third and last novel *Obryv* (1869; Eng. trans. *The Precipice*, 1915), which, although not so good as *Oblomov*, is a great work also, and contains splendidly conceived characters, satisfyingly trounces the Nihilists and the brood of intellectual malcontents of the period. He died in St Petersburg. His collected works were published (12 vols.) in 1899.

**Goncourt, Edmond Louis Antoine Huot de** (1822–1896) and **Goncourt, Jules Alfred Huot de** (1830–1870), French novelists, historians and art critics. They came of an old Lorraine family, Edmond being born at Nancy, Jules in Paris. Being of independent means they were able to follow their own inclinations in the capital and in time built up a valuable collection of French books, manuscripts and pictures, especially of the eighteenth century, and Japanese furnishings of every kind. They first made their name as historians with such works as *Histoire de la société française pendant la Révolution* (1854), *Portraits intimes du dix-huitième siècle* (1857), *Histoire de Marie Antoinette* (1858), *La Femme au dix-huitième siècle* (1862), turning to a contemporary with *Gavarni, l'homme et l'œuvre* (1868). All these, and others of the same kind, were built up slowly from documents often in their own collection to give memorable and vivid accounts written in impeccable style. Their novels were composed in the same way, in a manner which, derived from Flaubert (q.v.), they made all their own. Here they dealt entirely with contemporary affairs, specializing in neurotics of various types with powers of observation which are remarkable, naturalists in fiction, employing impressionism to prevent any tendency to reporting. Their novels, in fact, like their histories, give clear insight into character and build up the surroundings in which the particular person being dealt with lives, without exactly confronting him face to face. Generally they are written in short chapters, each one devoted to a particular aspect of the work in hand. There is no question of there being a finished plot, and indeed it is the view of the Goncourts that a novel should show that life is little more than a string of unconnected incidents. Chief of the novels written in collaboration are: *Sœur Philomène* (1861), *Renée Mauperin* (1864), *Germinie Lacerteux* (1865), *Manette Salomon* (1867) and their masterpiece, *Madame Gervaisais* (1869). Jules died in Paris, his distressing end described by his brother in the *Journal* (9 vols., 1887–95; complete Eng. trans. 1937), that valuable account of the period, morbid in its thirst for detail. Edmond worked on alone, publishing the novels *La Fille Élisa* (1877), *Les Frères Zemganno* (1879), a veiled account of him and Jules, *La Faustin* (1882) and *Chérie* (1884). Non-fictional works by him include *Watteau* (1876) and *L'Art japonais aux dix-huitième siècle* (3 vols., 1891–6). He died at Champrosay, leaving his fortune to found the Académie des Goncourt constituted in 1903.

**Góngora y Argote, Luis de** (1561–1627), Spanish poet. Born of noble family in Cordoba, he was educated at the University of Salamanca, entered the Church, and in the following years travelled much on business for the Cathedral Chapter of Cordoba. In 1611 he retired from his active life, and in seclusion composed the poetry for which he is known, *El Polifemo* and *Las soledades* (Eng. trans. *The Solitudes of Don Luis de Góngora*, 1931). This intricate, brilliant at times, but more often extravagant and overstrained poetry, attacked by Lope de Vega (q.v.) and Quevedo (q.v.), praised by Cervantes (q.v.), was ignored during the eighteenth and nineteenth centuries, but has during the last forty years become something of a cult to be compared to the cult of the 'metaphysical' poets in England. No doubt time will set the true balance, and without irresponsible claims being made for him, he will be seen in his true light as one of the most remarkable technicians in Spanish letters who exerted much influence on Spanish seventeenth-century poetry. He died in Cordoba. See *Obras poéticas* (3 vols., 1921).

**Gorbatov, Boris Leontyevich** (1908–1954), Russian Soviet novelist born at Pervomaisk, whose war book *Nepokoryonnye* (1943; Eng. trans. *Taras's Family*, 1944) was widely acclaimed. He died in Moscow.

**Gorbunov, Ivan Fyodorovich** (1831–1895), Russian short-story writer. Born at Kopnino, Moscow Province, he wrote sketches, of which he gave public readings, mocking militarists, money makers and everything that made life ugly. The fullest collection of his works was published (3 vols.) in 1904–7. He died in Petersburg.

**Gorenko, A. A.,** *see* **Akhmatova, A.**

**Gorky, Maxim,** pseudonym of **Alexey Maximovich Peshkov** (1868–1936), Russian author. Born of working-class parents at Nizhniy Novgorod (now Gorky), he was soon left an orphan and was brought up by his grandparents who apprenticed him to a shoemaker. Escaping from this bondage, he became a draughtsman's clerk and later a cook's boy on a Volga river steamer. All this time he travelled widely, and by the date his first story, *Makar Chudra*, was published in a Tiflis paper in 1892, he had mixed with all manner of men and had travelled far. It was his sympathy with the outcasts of the world, the sympathy of a fellow sufferer, that first inspired him as a writer, and it was this theme that continued to bring out all that was finest in his craft. When he tried to describe the upper classes Gorky was never successful, and when he fell into philosophical digressions, a tendency to which he was prone, he failed. It was as a writer of short stories about the sufferings of the poor and his often longer autobiographical works that he gained his fame. Thanks to the help of Vladimir Korolenko, the editor of the left-wing *Russkoe Bogatstvo*, he gained experience of journalism which disciplined him, gave him a creed, and stood him in good stead in the writing of a series of close-knit short stories published in 1897 (Eng. trans. *Tales from Gorky*, 1902). But for a time he allowed himself to be carried away by ambitions to write full-length novels on social questions. Such a book is *Foma Gordyeev* (1900; Eng. trans. 1901), which, although full of magnificent descriptions of the Volga he knew so well, and showing a remarkable gift for characterization, is badly constructed, even formless. Before long he joined the Social Democratic Party and in 1904 founded a publishing house, *Znanie* ('Knowledge'), with the purpose of bringing out well-written books on social questions. His involvement in politics lessened the quality of his work at this time, but as 'the spokesman of the workers' he was becoming a national figure and in the revolution of 1905 he was associated with Lenin. On the failure of the movement he fled to Italy, where he lived on Capri, not being allowed to return to Russia until 1913. Meanwhile he had gained world fame with passionately felt but inartistically written novels, especially *Mat'* (1907; Eng. trans. *Mother*, 1947), on which a well-known film by Eisenstein was based. As soon as he was back in Russia he resumed his revolutionary activities, and on the outbreak of the First World War took a pacifistic attitude. He had by then already published the first volume of his autobiographical trilogy, *Detstvo* (1913; Eng. trans. *Childhood*, 1915), and this was followed by the second volume, *V lyudyakh* (1915; Eng. trans. *In the World*, 1917), the last part, *Moi universitety*, not appearing until 1923. The three were translated into English as *Autobiography* in 1949. The trilogy brought him wide acclamation, and for many it is their favourite work of his. When the revolution of 1917 came, while generally glad of it, he hailed it with some reserve, being particularly on his guard against the extremists' action against the intelligentsia. His influence on Lenin was here of great importance and many works of art were saved from destruction at his instigation. He set up funds out of his own pocket to help writers, artists and scientists from threatened starvation during the famine, and by his foundation of *Mirovaya literatura* ('World Literature'), a society for the translation into Russian of foreign literary works of international reputation, he showed that he wanted the new Russia to be in touch with the outside world. But by 1921 he found himself out of sympathy with the Soviet and settled in Italy once more, this time at Sorrento, having published in 1919 his highly interesting *Vospominaniya o Tolstom* (Eng. trans. in *Reminiscences of Tolstoy, Chekhov and Andreyev*, 1934). In 1927, the year before his triumphant return to Russia, he began the monumental quadrilogy, *Zhizn' Klima Samgina* ('Life of Klim Samgin'), not completed until the year of his death. Very different from the *Autobiography*, it is a realistic work in which the origins of the clash of the old Czarist generation and the new Bolshevik generation leading to revolution are traced. The four parts have been translated into English as *Bystander* (1930), *The Magnet* (1931), *Other Fires* (1933) and *The Spectre* (1938). All this time he unceasingly produced journalistic works, plays (conspicuously *Egor Bulitchyev*, 1931), full-length novels such as *Delo Artamonovykh* (1925; Eng. trans. *The Artamonov Business*, 1948), and, most satisfying of all, numerous intensely conceived short stories, many of which have been translated into English in such collections as *A Book of Short Stories* (1939) and *Unrequited Love and Other Stories* (1949). See also *Seven Plays* (1937). He died in Leningrad in mysterious circumstances which have not yet been cleared up. The best edition of his collected works (*Sobranie sochineniy*) is that of 1949 in thirty volumes. For a generation, i.e. after the death of Tolstoy in 1910, until his own death, Gorky was the greatest figure in Russian literature.

**Görres, Jakob Joseph von** (1776–1848), German prose-writer, was born of a Roman Catholic family at Coblenz and taught physics there. Going to Heidelberg in 1806 he joined forces with Brentano (q.v.) and Arnim (q.v.) in research into German folk-poetry, the result being his *Die teutschen Volksbücher* (1807; mod. ed., 1925), in which he proclaimed the glories of old German literature and contrasted his country's past with its present condition, under the heel of Napoleon. By 1812 he had become the literary centre of the German nationalist movement which led to the War of Independence of 1813. His *Lohengrin, ein altteutsches Gedicht* (1813) was another revelation of the wealth of old German literature, and in his newspaper, the *Rheinische Mercur* (1814), he made propagandist inroads into French domination. He hoped for the liberalization of the German states after Napoleon's fall, but was disappointed, and after his book *Teutschland und die Revolution* (1821) had been condemned and himself threatened with prosecution he turned his attention to quieter channels. By 1826 when he was made professor of history at Munich he had become a convinced ultramontanist, his views being expressed in *Christliche Mystik* (4 vols., 1836–42). A man of the highest integrity and of commanding character, he died in Munich.

**Gotta, Salvator** (1887– ), Italian novelist and short-story writer. Born at Ivrea, he was a realist of the type of Zola (q.v.) and imitated him in his long series about the fortunes of a middle-class family in a small out-of-the-way town. The best of his volumes are generally considered to be *Il figlio inquieto* (1917), *L'amante provinciale* (1920), *Lilith* (1934) and *Tre donne innamorate* (1938). His short stories, of which the collection *Il diavolo in provincia* (1926) is outstanding, deal with the same subject in small compass. Later works include *Ottocento* (3 vols., 1940–2), *Il volto dell' umano amore* (1944), *I sensitivi* (1946), *Domani a te* (1950), *Tempo della regina Margherita* (1952), *Il piccolo marinaio* (1955), *Il castello di Montalto* (1958), *Cavour, uomo e genio* (1959), *I diavoli del gran paradiso* (1962), *I giganti innamorati* (1964) and *L'ultimo dei Vela* (1965).

**Gotter, Friedrich Wilhelm** (1746–1797), German playwright. Born at Gotha, he was at the University of Göttingen, where he helped to found the influential literary periodical the *Musenalmanach* (1770). He then went into the diplomatic service, but spent his spare time in literary activities. At first a writer of comedy on his own account (*Die Dorfgala*, 1772, and *Die falschen Entdeckungen*, 1774), he gradually discovered that his talent lay in adaptation of foreign works, sometimes almost rewriting them. Examples of this method are the tragedies, *Merope* (1774) from Voltaire and *Mariane* (1776) from La Harpe (q.v.), and the comedy *Das öffentliche Geheimnis* (1781) from Carlo Gozzi (q.v.). But his best play was *Die Geisterinsel* (1797), from Shakespeare's *Tempest*, which first appeared in Schiller's *Horen* (1797) and elicited the praise of Goethe. He died at Gotha.

**Gottfried von Strassburg** (*fl.* 1210), German poet. A cleric holding some civil appointment in Strassburg, he is the author of the unfinished love epic *Tristan und Isolde*, written about 1210, highly polished in style, the love verging on the mystic. Wagner (q.v.) made use of it for his opera. Modern editions of it include those by R. Bechstein (fourth ed., 1924) and A. Closs (1944). There is a shortened English translation by J. L. Weston (1899).

**Gotthelf, Jeremias,** pseudonym of **Albert Bitzius** (1797–1854), Swiss novelist and short-story writer. Born the son of a pastor at Murten in the canton of Freiburg, he read theology at Bern, became pastor of Lützelflüh in Emmenthal in 1832, and worked vigorously for the good of his parish. When he began to write tales to instruct his people he stumbled on his own genius, and soon he was writing not simply with didactic purpose but because he must. Quiet humour, masterly character drawing and charming description are the hallmarks of his tales of Swiss village life, among which should be named *Leiden und Freuden eines Schulmeisters* (2 vols., 1838), *Wie Uli der Knecht glücklich wird* (1841; Eng. trans., *Ulric the Farm-servant*, 1886, to which English translation Ruskin wrote an enthusiastic introduction), *Käthi die Grossmutter* (1847), *Uli der Pächter* (1849) and *Elsi, die seltsame Magd* (1850), which last forms one volume of *Erzählungen und Bilder aus dem Volksleben der Schweiz* (5 vols., 1850–5). He died from a chill caught through getting wet on his parish rounds at Lützelflüh.

**Gottschall, Rudolf von** (1823–1909), German poet and playwright. Born in Breslau, he joined the Young German movement but freed himself from it after 1848. His earlier poetry had been inflated and of no lasting value, yet with the two epics, *Die Göttin* (1853) and *Carlo Zeno* (1854), he gave promise of founding a new school, but this remained unfulfilled. As a dramatist his best works are *Pitt und Fox*

(1854) and *Mazeppa* (1859), but after 1864 gave himself up almost entirely to literary journalism. He died in Leipzig.

**Gottsched, Johann Christoph** (1700–1766), German critic and man of letters, born in Königsberg. Tall and handsome, he was in danger of being forced into King Frederick William I of Prussia's brigade of guards, chosen by reason of size and appearance, and so escaped to Leipzig where he was received with open arms and appointed professor of belles-lettres (1730). From this vantage point he determined to improve German literary style. An admirer of French literature, it was to the frenchified *Cato* of Addison and not to Shakespeare that he turned as a model for his literarily perfect but dramatically dead tragedy *Der sterbende Cato* (1732), which none the less had great success. It was one thing to improve German literary style; it was another to force French models on the public, and when he assumed dictatorial powers there were those who were ready to oppose him and his *Versuch einer kritischen Dichtkunst* (1732) and *Beiträge zur kritischen Historie der deutschen Sprache* (8 vols., 1732–44). First assailed by the Swiss critics Bodmer (q.v.) and Breitinger (q.v.), Lessing (q.v.) later joined these two in advocating English literature as the model for German literature, and Gottsched was left discredited. Because of his arrogant manner it is easy to dislike him, but he certainly did his country's letters a great service when in the 1730's he tried to recapture a worthy style and language which had fallen away since the Thirty Years War. *Die deutsche Schaubühne* (6 vols., 1740–5) and *Geschichte der deutschen dramatischen Dichtkunst* (1757) remain valuable if used with a certain caution. His knowledge of medieval German literature was unusual for the period. He died in Leipzig. His *Gesammelte Schriften* appear in a convenient form in the six-volume edition of 1901–6.

**Götz, Johann Nikolaus** (1721–1781), German poet. Born at Worms, he was a fellow student of Gleim (q.v.) and Uz (q.v.) at Halle, and with them introduced the anacreontic into German literature. His *Die Oden Anakreons in reimlosen Versen* (1746), though having its attractions, cannot compare with Uz's work. Götz became a clergyman and died at Winterburg. *Vermischte Gedichte* was published posthumously in 1785.

**Gozzi, Carlo** (1720–1806), Italian poet and prose-writer. Born of noble family in Venice, younger brother of Gaspare (q.v.), after some adventures in the army he returned to Venice in 1744 eager to uphold tradition in Italian thought and letters in the face of rapidly advancing French influences. Attaching himself to the diehard *Accademia dei Granelleschi*, he attacked the new realistic comedy of manners and sentimentalism of Goldoni (q.v.) in *Tartana* (1757), a satirical poem. There followed his ten *Fiabe*, written between 1761 and 1765 (mod. ed., 1885), founded on folk tales, popular puppet plays and oriental stories, by means of which Gozzi hoped to return to truly national forms of entertainment. The best of these 'Fables' are the famous *L'amore delle tre melarance* ('The Love of Three Oranges'), a popular story, and *Re Turandote*, an oriental one, the first of which has since inspired the music of Prokoviev and the second

Puccini. These are Gozzi's masterpieces, but all the *Fiabe* proved immensely popular, and had the effect of driving Goldoni from Venice. His later work is of little importance save for his *Memorie inutili* (1797; Eng. trans. *The Memoirs of Carlo Gozzi*, 2 vols., 1890), an autobiography of value and charm. He died in Venice. His *Opere* appeared (14 vols.) in 1801–3.

**Gozzi, Gaspare** (1713–1786), Italian poet, prose-writer, journalist and critic. Born in Venice of a noble but poor family, he was the elder brother of Carlo Gozzi (q.v.). Turning to writing for a living, he wrote verse satires, *Lettere famigliari* (1755) censoring the manners of the time, took Bettinelli (q.v.) to task for preferring Virgil to Dante as a model for Italian poetry in *Difesa di Dante* (1758), and published a romance, *Il mondo morale* (1760). A pioneer in journalism, he founded and wrote the greater part of *La Gazzetta Veneta* (1760–1; mod. ed., 2 vols., 1943) and *Il Osservatore* (1761–2; mod. ed., 1897), containing much literary criticism and also morally didactic in tone. As a press censor (1762) and an educational official (1764) he was directly able to put some of his ideas into practice. He died in Padua.

**Grabbe, Christian Dietrich** (1801–1836), German dramatist. Born the son of a prison governor at Detmold, he took up law, abandoned it to try to live by writing, failed, lived a wild and reckless life and died of drink at Detmold. All the same his talent was the strongest of its kind in Germany between Kleist (q.v.) and Hebbel (q.v.), as is to be seen by reading his two Hohenstaufen dramas, *Kaiser Friedrich Barbarossa* (1829) and *Kaiser Heinrich VI* (1830). His *Don Juan und Faust* (1829) is a tremendous attempt to fuse two themes, and abounds in daring flights of imagination, while *Napoleon, oder die hundert Tage* (1831) is well constructed and contains felicitous characterization. *Hannibal* shows how too exclusively Germanic he was to succeed in a work set in the ancient world of the Mediterranean, while in *Die Hermannschlacht* (1836) he fails in open competition with his master Kleist. His collected works were published (6 vols.) in 1912.

**Gracián y Morales, Baltasar** (1601–1658), Spanish prose-writer. Born at Belmonte, he became a Jesuit. His chief work, *El criticón* (Part I, 1651; Part II, 1653; Part III, 1657; mod. ed., 3 vols., 1938–40; Eng. trans. *The Critick*, 1681), written in a style at once powerful and engaging, is a commentary on human life. Among his minor works may be named a treatise on heroes, *El héroe* (1637; mod. ed., 1911) and another on how to behave to get on well in life, with a touch of irony, *El discreto* (1646). He died at Tarazona in Aragon.

**Granada, Luis de** (1504–1588), Spanish religious writer. Born of poor parents in Granada, he entered the Dominican Order and was made prior of a monastery near Cordoba. He gained a reputation as the greatest of all Spanish preachers. His enduring work is his *Guía de pecadores* (1556), which has been translated into Latin, seven modern European languages and Japanese. A delightful English translation of it was made as *The Sinners Guyde* by Francis Meres in 1598. He stressed the importance of personal religion thoroughly in character with the spirit of the Counter Reformation. He came into collision with the Inquisition on several occasions, but died in peace in Lisbon.

**Grass, Günter** (1927–     ), German novelist, poet and playwright. Born in Danzig, he came to the fore in 1959 with his satirical novel *Die Blechtrommel* (Eng. trans. *The Tin Drum*, 1962), and followed up this success with a long short-story, *Katz und Maus* (1961; Eng. trans. *Cat and Mouse*, 1963), and another full-length novel, *Hundejahre* (1963; Eng. trans. *The Dog Years*, 1965). He spent some years in Paris, but since 1960 he has lived in West Berlin. His plays include *Onkel, Onkel* (1957), and he has published two collections of poetry, *Die Vorzüge der Windhühner* (1956) and *Gleisdreieck* (1960). There is an English translation, *Selected Poems* (1966), with German originals.

**Gravina, Gian Vincenzo** (1664–1718), Italian literary critic. Born at Roggiano, Cosenza, he became a prosperous lawyer in Rome, and with Muratori (q.v.) was the greatest Italian arbiter of literary taste of his day. His *Della ragione poetica* (2 vols., 1708; crit. ed., 1921) and *Della tragedia* (1715) are still of great importance in the history of Italian literature. He was one of the founders of the Arcadian Academy and adopted Metastasio (q.v.), whom he had found in the streets of Rome reciting his poetry, as his son, leaving him his entire fortune. Gravina died in Rome. His works were collected (3 vols.) in 1756–8.

**Gréban, Arnoul** (1420–1471 ?), French dramatist, born probably at Le Mans, held the office of precentor at Notre-Dame, Paris, in 1455, together with a court appointment. His enormously long passion play, the *Mystère de la Passion* (1453 or 1454; crit. ed., 1878), is not only the greatest French devotional drama of the fifteenth century but also of Europe. He very likely died at Le Mans, where he held a canonry.

**Green, Julien** (1900–     ), French novelist. Born in Paris of American parentage, in childhood he divided his time between France and the U.S.A. and grew up perfectly bilingual. Strongly influenced by the mystical work of William Blake, and on the other hand by the strange, warped souls who float through Dickens, he dealt with maladies of the mind, the misfits in life with all their agonies, in a highly individualistic style. His output has been restricted but of excellent quality: *Suite anglaise* (1927), *Adrienne Mesurat* (1927; Eng. trans. *The Closed Garden*, 1928), *Les Clefs de la mort* (1928), *Léviathan* (1929; Eng. trans. *The Dark Journey*, 1929), *Épaves* (1932), *Le Visionnaire* (1934; Eng. trans. *The Dreamer*, 1934), *Varouna* (1940), *Moïra* (1950; Eng. trans. 1951), *Le Malfaiteur* (1956; Eng. trans. *The Transgressor*, 1958), *Chaque homme dans sa nuit* (1960; Eng. trans. *Each in his Darkness*, 1961), and *Partir avant le jour* (1967; Eng. trans. *To Leave Before Dawn*, 1967).

**Greif, Martin,** pseudonym of **Friedrich Hermann Frey** (1839–1911), German poet and dramatist. Born in Speier, he lived most of his life in Munich isolated from the literary trends of the day. He was a traditionalist, and, though having little new to say, wrote with such ease and in so attractive a style that his *Frühlingslieder* (1864) are still worth reading. He was also a very fair dramatist, as the tragedies *Bertha und Ludwig* (1861), *Konradin* (1889) and *Agnes Bernauer* (1894) show. His collected works appeared (3 vols.) in 1895–6. He died at Kufstein.

**Greville, Henry,** pseudonym of **Alice Durand** (1842–1902), French novelist. Born in Paris, she was taken by her father to Petersburg in 1857, where she married a French tutor and where she remained until her return to France in 1872. She published more than twenty novels, at their best, witty, lively and presenting out-of-the-way pictures of Russian city life; at their worst, badly constructed and so rambling as to be boring. Characteristic of her work are *Dosia* (1876) and *Fidelka* (1894). She died at Boulogne.

**Griboyedov, Alexander Sergeyevich** (1795–1829), Russian playwright. Born in Moscow he went into the diplomatic service and was murdered in a street riot in Tehran, Persia. His comedy, *Gore ot uma* (1824; Eng. trans. (a) *The Misfortune of Being Clever*, by S. W. Prig, 1914; (b) *The Mischief of Being Clever*, by B. Pares, 1925; and (c) *Wit Works Woe* in *Masterpieces of Russian Drama*, 1933), is a piercing, though outwardly good-humoured, diatribe against the follies of Moscow society.

**Grieg, Johan Nordahl Brun** (1902–1943), Norwegian poet, novelist and general prose-writer, was born in Bergen. Cosmopolitan in his tastes, he travelled far and wide, his visits to Russia in 1933 and to Spain in 1936 being of particular significance as regards his work; for the two experiences, which left him so far to the left as to be on the verge of Communism, inspired his best novel *Ung må verden ennu være* (1938), and the Spanish visit alone gave rise to a vivid piece of reporting, *Spansk sommer* (1937). But it is his war poems in the volumes *Flagget* (1945), *Friheten* (1945) and *Håbet* (1946), a selection of them appearing in English translation in *War Poems* (1944), which brought him posthumous fame, for already he had been killed flying over Berlin on a winter night raid.

**Grigorovich, Dmitry Vasilyevich** (1822–1899), Russian novelist. Born in Simbirsk, he is known for the realistic novels *Derevnya* (1846, 'The Village') and *Anton-Goremyka* (1847), but after so excellent a beginning he rapidly lost his talent, for the most part owing to his fatal mistake of trying to make his fiction the platform for political opinions. His reminiscences of his literary life (*Literaturnye vospominaniya*), first published in 1892–3 and reissued in 1929, are of considerable value. He died in Petersburg.

**Grillparzer, Franz** (1791–1872), Austrian dramatist, poet and long short-story writer. Born in Vienna, he entered the university there to read law, having to abandon it on the sudden death of his father and go teaching. In 1813 he entered the civil service, rising gradually in it until his retirement in 1856 as Director of the Imperial Archives. His life was uniformly unhappy. At the outset his mother and his brother committed suicide within two years of each other, then he hated his official career, both because he found himself in a treadmill and because in being a functionary he served Metternich's regime which denied him and other intellectuals their freedom. Even in his private life he found no compensation, for a neurosis, for ever prompting him never to commit himself to anything and so avoid what he looked upon as entanglements, made his love-affairs sordid and selfish, and the irony was that finally he became the lodger of the fiancée he had kept waiting for years and never did marry. At any rate, he had twenty years of success as a playwright, although he composed under official frowns. He achieved success with his very first play, *Die Ahnfrau* (1817), a powerful tragedy, using the supernatural in so masterly a way as completely to discredit the 'Fate Drama' of Müllner (q.v.) and Werner (q.v.). But Grillparzer disliked the romantic school, and, regretting that he had succeeded in a drama of that kind, turned to the classical style with a subject from ancient Greece, *Sappho* (1818; Eng. trans. 1858), on the price of genius: Sappho must pay for her fame by renouncing happiness on earth. His next work was a tragedy also, the trilogy, *Das goldene Vlies* (1821–2, consisting of *Der Gastfreund, Die Argonauten* and *Medea*; Eng. trans. of the trilogy, *The Golden Fleece*, 1879). It is a great drama, and the rendering of Medea is especially fine. Having gained the highest reputation, he now turned to historical drama with *König Ottokars Glück und Ende* (1825; Eng. trans. *King Ottocar, his Rise and Fall*, 1938), which has been called an Austrian counterpart of Kleist's (q.v.) Prussian *Prinz von Homburg*. In *Des Meeres und der Liebe Wellen* (1831) we are back in ancient Greece, and the story of Hero and Leander becomes a tragedy of the tyranny of love. Some of the scenes are among the most beautiful in modern literature. *Der Traum ein Leben* (1834; Eng. trans. *A Dream is Life*, 1946) was begun as early as 1817 at the same time as *Die Ahnfrau*, like it inspired by Spanish drama and like it written in the trochaic metre employed by Calderón. In fact, the title is suggested by Calderón's *La vida es sueño*. *Der Traum ein Leben* is Grillparzer's final comment on the Metternich age. Do not dare even to dream of exploits; you might be found out. Close your minds to ideals and to glory; be like all the rest of the herd; be content with peace and whatever material advantages you may have. Then came his rash attempt at comedy, and the damning of his effort, *Weh' dem der lügt* (1838). So sensitive was he that he severed all connection with the theatre. He had already published some lyric poetry, chief of it *Tristia ex Ponto* (1835), the title of Ovid's work written in exile at Tomi, and into this book the modern outcast in the midst of Vienna pours all his bitterness. In his long short-story, *Der arme Spielmann* (1847; Eng. trans. *The Poor Minstrel*, 1915), his theme is renunciation, all the more telling because so coolly written. *Esther* (1863) remains a lovely fragment. At his death in Vienna a few more plays remained unacted and unpublished, and of them, *Die Jüdin von Toledo* (1873; Eng. trans. *The Jewess of Toledo*, 1953), an adaptation from Lope de Vega, is the best. The greatness of Grillparzer lies in the fact that he was able to blend the romantic and classical, keeping an exquisite balance. See his *Werke* (6 vols., 1923–4).

**Grimm, Jakob Ludwig Karl** (1785–1863) and **Grimm, Wilhelm Karl** (1786–1859), German writers and scholars who were born at Hanau in Hesse-Cassel. Jakob read law at Marburg, paid a visit to Paris (1805), and in 1808 accepted the librarianship offered him by Jérôme Bonaparte at Cassel. Having in 1811 brought out his first book on the Meistersinger, Jakob joined forces with Wilhelm in collecting and editing the first volume of the famous *Kinder- und Hausmärchen* (1812, 'Grimm's Fairy Tales', of which there are a number of translations, including one in Everyman's Library, and by Routledge, 1959, with an interesting introduction). The second volume followed in 1814, and the third in 1822. In 1813–15 Jakob held a diplomatic secretarial post at the Congress of Vienna, but was glad to return to Cassel and to his brother, where they lived together and so continued even after Wilhelm's marriage in 1825. It was Wilhelm who was more of a literary man and who gave the 'Fairy Tales' their good plain style. In *Altdeutsche Wälder* (1813–16) the brothers again collaborated, as in *Deutsche Sagen* (2 vols., 1816–18), but Jakob alone was responsible for the valuable *Deutsche Grammatik* (1819; revised and enlarged, 1822). In 1828 they left Cassel for Göttingen, where Jakob was given the post of librarian and a lectureship and Wilhelm the sublibrarianship. Both were later given the style of professor. Here Wilhelm published his principal book written alone, *Die deutsche Heldensage* (1829), and a little before Jakob's *Deutsche Rechts-Alterthümer* had appeared (1828), inspired by Savigny, who had taught him law at Marburg. Then came Jakob's *Deutsche Mythologie* (1835; Eng. trans. 1879–88, containing additions by scholars after his death). Dismissed from their posts at Göttingen by the King of Hanover for protesting against the abrogation of the constitution in 1837, three years later they were invited to Berlin and received professorships in the university. There the brothers set to work on the great *Deutsches Wörterbuch* in 1854, and although they did not live to complete it, the original plan, carried out by others, was theirs. They both died in Berlin.

**Grimmelshausen, Johann Jakob Christoffel von** (1625–1676), German novelist, born at Gelnhausen in Hesse-Cassel, the son of an innkeeper. His parents were killed when this Protestant town was sacked by the imperialists, and the boy was carried off by Hessians, and later served in the army from 1636 to 1648, gaining experience of that brutal Thirty Years War which he was to utilize in the future. When peace returned he became bailiff to the counts of Schauenburg at Gaisbach until 1660, when he exchanged this post for a similar one at Ullenburg. Converted to Roman Catholicism about 1666, the following year he finally came to rest at Renchen on the western borders of the Black Forest as procurator of the Bishop of Strassburg. Although he had privately tried his hand at writing years before, it was not until his later years that he seriously took to it as a means of supplementing his income. His first attempt was *Der keusche Joseph* (1667), a stiff novel on the French model about court life, but it and others in the same style are stone dead. It was when, influenced by the Spanish picaresque novel, he put his own vivid experiences to good use in

*Der abenteurliche Simplicissimus Teutsch* (1669; mod. ed., 1939; Eng. trans. *The Adventurous Simplicissimus*, 1926) that he wrote a masterpiece, containing humour and dramatic and descriptive power, revealing the sufferings of the peasants and the cruelty of the soldiery during the Thirty Years War. His shorter stories, *Die Landstörzerin Courasche* (1670; mod. ed., 1925), *Der seltsame Springinsfeld* (1670; mod. ed., 1925) and *Das wunderbarliche Vogelnest* (1672), provide an excellent supplement to the great novel, which the actual *Continuatio* (1669) fails to supply. He died at Renchen.

**Grin, Alexander,** pseudonym of **Alexander Stepanovich Grinevetsky** (1880–1932), Russian novelist. Born near Vyatka, he took some part in political activities in his early years and suffered imprisonment. After the revolution of 1917 he confined himself to adventure stories and committed himself to neither literary nor political schools. *Gladiatory* (1925) and *Doroga nikuda* (1930, 'The Road to Nowhere') are fair specimens of his writing.

**Gröndal, Benedikt Sveinbjarnarson** (1826–1907), Icelandic satirist. Born at Bessastaðir, he was educated at the University of Copenhagen, was converted to Roman Catholicism and became a well-known antiquarian. He gained his place in literature by right of his clever satire on contemporary politics and the diplomatic antics of Napoleon III in particular, *Sagan af Heljarslóðarorrustu* (1861, 'The Battle of Hel's Field', i.e. the Battle of Solferino) written in prose in a mock-medieval manner. He died in Reykjavík.

**Grossman, Leonid Petrovich** (1888–1966), Russian Soviet novelist and literary historian, born in Odessa, author of a brilliant historical novel on Pushkin (q.v.), written in the form of a diary kept at the time of the duel which resulted in the poet's death by one of his opponent's seconds, D'Archiague. Its title is *Zapiski D'Arshiaka* (1930; Eng. trans. *Death of a Poet*, 1945). Further novels deal with other Russian literary figures, such as Dostoyevsky (q.v.) in *Ruletenburg* (1932), depicting the great novelist as a roulette player for high stakes. He died in Moscow.

**Grossman, Vasily Semyonovich** (1905–1964), Russian Soviet novelist, born at Berdichev. His principal works are *Stepan Kolchugin* (1937–1940; Eng. trans. *Kolchugin's Youth*, 1946), and the two war novels *Narod bessmerten* (1942; Eng. trans. *The People Immortal*, 1943) and *Gody voiny* (1945; Eng. trans. *The Years of War*, 1946). He died in Moscow.

**Grotius, Hugo,** really **Hugo de Groot** (1583–1645), Dutch man of law and letters, writing also in Latin. Born in Delft, the son of a lawyer, he read law at Leiden and Orléans, and in 1599 settled in The Hague to practise his profession. By 1613 he had risen to be Pensionary of Rotterdam, having found time to translate the Greek and Latin classics and edit them. But in 1618 his career was suddenly cut short by his taking the side of his close friend Oldenbarneveldt in his struggle against Prince Maurice of Nassau, for when the Nassau party triumphed Oldenbarneveldt was condemned to death and Grotius to perpetual imprisonment. With the help of his wife, however, Grotius managed to escape to Paris (1621), where Louis XIII granted him a pension which enabled him to finish his famous work, begun as early as 1604, *De Jure Belli ac Pacis*, which was published in 1625 (Eng. trans. 1853). It is the foundation of modern international law, and in majestic Latin deals not only with peace and war, but with the powers and duties of states, which must be bound by laws of morality and judged by them. A great intellectual force in his day, known to scholars throughout Europe, he entered the Swedish diplomatic service in 1634, becoming Swedish ambassador to France. He retired in 1645, and decided to return to his native land, but was taken ill on the way and died in Rostock.

**Grün, Anastasius,** pseudonym of **Anton Alexander von Auersperg** (1806–1876), Austrian poet. He was born of noble family at Laibach, and became conspicuous among liberals and young Germans. His *Der letzte Ritter* (1830; Eng. trans. *The Last Knight*, 1871) is romantic, but in *Spaziergänge eines Wiener Poeten* (1831) he lashed the Metternich regime, safe from molestation by reason of his aristocratic standing. The success of *Spaziergänge* was great and made him known not only in Austria but throughout Germany. Further volumes of poetry, all of it vibrant and healthy, are *Gedichte* (1837), *Nibelungen im Frack* (1843), *Der Pfaffe vom Kahlenberg* (1850), and *In der Veranda* (1875). He died in Graz. His *Sämtliche Werke* were published in six volumes in 1909.

**Grundtvig, Nicolai Frederik Severin** (1783–1872), Danish poet and prose-writer. Born at Udby in Zealand, he entered the Church and served it first at Udby and from 1822 in Copenhagen. He won his public with the prose *Nordens Mythologi* (1808) and his highly original, if not historically defensible, *Optrin af Kæmpelivets Undergang i Nord* (2 vols., 1809, 1811). As a poet he is at his best in *Roskilde-Rim* (1814), intensely nationalistic in spirit, and the collection *Sangværk til den danske Kirke og Skole* (5 vols., 1837–70) containing many good hymns and school songs. His *Haandbog i Verdenshistorien* (3 vols., 1833–43) was a piece of pioneering work of great significance in Danish education. Indeed Grundtvig devoted his life to educational reform, and as the originator of the Danish system of high schools had a great influence (and still does have) on the life of his country. He was an Anglo-Saxon scholar of no mean ability. Made a bishop in 1861, he died in Copenhagen.

**Gryphius, Andreas** (1616–1664), German poet and dramatist, born at Glogau in Silesia, where his father was a Lutheran pastor. In spite of that father's early death by poison, Gryphius gained a good education and travelled until 1650, when he returned to Glogau as town syndic and died there. As a poet his best works are *Sonn- und Feiertags-Sonette* (1637) and *Kirchhofsgedanken* (1656), which reveal him as a man who had suffered deeply and felt sincerely. But as a dramatist with undoubted gifts he was at the disadvantage of being forced to conform to hidebound Renaissance rules dragged into German literature in a debased state by Opitz (q.v.). As a result of trying to fit his tragedies into a strait jacket he failed to convey any sense of movement or even of reality, as can be seen from *Leo Armenius* (1650), *Katharina von Georgien* (1657), and even from something so compelling as *Ermordete Majestät, oder Carolus Stuardus, König von Gross-Britannien* (1657) with its contemporary setting. Only in comedy, where tradition was less insistent and left him with more freedom as in *Herr Peter Squentz* (1663), by and large an adaptation of certain scenes of *A Midsummer Night's Dream*, is Gryphius free to be himself. There is a useful selection of his dramatic works by J. Tittmann (1870).

**Guarini, Battista,** or **Giovanni Battista** (1538-1612), Italian pastoral poet and prose-writer, was born in Ferrara, was employed at the court there and succeeded Tasso (q.v.) as court poet in 1577. His chief work is the famous pastoral drama *Il Pastor Fido* (1585, twentieth and definitive ed., 1602; Eng. trans. Dymock, 1602; Fanshawe, 1647; Grove, 1782; Clapperton, 1809), which contains graceful prose and charming lyrics and possesses sufficient dramatic action to justify its being called the first step on the way to opera. To compare it to Tasso's *Aminta* is like stepping into another world. The baroque is here in full, the sensuality is unashamedly pagan. It has a rich colour all its own, and it is not surprising that it became one of the favourite pieces of Europe. After some time away from Ferrara on account of a disagreement with Duke Alfonso, he made peace with him in 1595 but retired altogether ten years later, settling in Venice, where he died. The critical edition of *Pastor Fido* is that by G. Brognoglio (1914). The best modern edition of his complete works is that of 1950.

**Guðmundsson, Kristmann Borgfjörð** (1902–      ), Icelandic novelist and short-story writer, writing also in Norwegian. Born at Lundarreykadalur, he struggled manfully to educate himself, and finding everything against him at home settled in Norway in 1924 and gained a public with his volume of short stories, written in Norwegian, *Islandsk kjærlighet* (1926). In Norwegian he also wrote a series of romantic novels, including *Brudekjolen* (1927; Eng. trans. *The Bridal Gown*, 1931) and *Livets morgen* (1929; Eng. trans. *Morning of Life*, 1929). He wrote again in Icelandic the novel *Gyðjan og uxinn* (1937; Eng. trans. *Winged Citadel*, 1940). He returned to his native country in 1939 and has since written only in Icelandic, e.g. *Kvöld i Reykjavík* (1948) and a volume of poetry, *Kristmannskver* (1955).

**Guérin, Charles** (1873-1907), French poet. Born into a comfortable family at Lunéville, he wrote such symbolistic poetry as that contained in *Le Cœur solitaire* (1898), *L'Éros funèbre* (1900), *Le Semeur de cendres* (1901) and the serious and thoughtful *L'Homme intérieur* (1905). He died at Lunéville.

**Guérin du Cayla, Georges Maurice** (1810-1839), French poet. Born of an old and distinguished family at the château of Le Cayla in Languedoc, he was educated for the Church, came under the influence of Lamennais (q.v.) and joined the community at La Chesnaye in

Brittany for a time. He married shortly before his death from tuberculosis at Le Cayla, leaving behind some scattered poetry showing great love of nature, marked pantheism and love of ancient Greece, collected as *Reliquiae* (1842). His *Journal* (1842) is a spiritual document of rare beauty. See his *Œuvres complètes* (2 vols., 1947).

**Guerra Junqueiro,** *see* **Junqueiro.**

**Guevara, Antonio de** (1490?–1545), Spanish prose-writer. Born at Asturias de Santillana, he became a Franciscan and was confessor to the Emperor Charles V. Later he was appointed an inquisitor at Valencia and died at Mondoñedo where he was bishop. His literary reputation rests on two books, both of which were widely read in western Europe, *Marco Antonio con el Relox de príncipes* (1529; Eng. trans. *The Golden Boke of Marcus Aurelius*, by Lord Berners, 1532; *The Dial of Princes*, by Sir Thomas North, 1557; revised and abridged, 1919), written in a very elaborate style and containing fictitious letters of Marcus Aurelius which have often passed for his, and *Epístolas familiares* (1539; mod. ed. abridged, 1942; Eng. trans. *The Familiar Epistles*, 1574), quaint, and full, it would seem, of intentional anachronisms and of quotations from authorities who never existed, which was very much appreciated in England and probably gave rise to that taste for the wayward, artificial style that reached its height in Lyly's *Euphues* (1578).

**Guevara, L. V. de,** *see* **Vélez de Guevara.**

**Guicciardini, Francesco** (1483–1540), Italian prose-writer. Born in Florence, he took up law, but learned the craft of diplomacy in Spain (1512–14), and held various governorships under the papacy. Considered in great part responsible for the sack of Rome by imperial troops in 1527, he was under such a cloud that in 1534 he turned to the patronage of the Medici in his native Florence, but he was not considered trustworthy, and, having been passed over for various posts which he coveted, went into the country. At Arcetri in complete retirement he set about his long-winded but realistic *Storia d'Italia,* a history of Italy from the French invasion of 1494 to the death of Pope Clement VII (1532). It was not published in his lifetime, nor was any other of his works. The first English translation of the *History* was published between 1755 and 1759, but no reliable Italian edition appeared until Rosini's (1819). It shows a mastery of cynical diplomacy rare indeed. His *Discorsi politici e ricordi* and *Ricordi politici e civili* (Eng. trans. *Counsels and Reflections,* 1890), only deepen that impression. A friend of Machiavelli (q.v.), his *Ricordi* have been called 'Italian corruption codified and elevated to a rule of life'. He died in complete neglect at Santa Margherita in Montici. The standard edition of his *Opere* is that in eight volumes (1929–33). See the English translation, *Selected Writings* (Oxford Library of Italian Classics).

**Guillaume d'Aquitaine** (1071–1126), the first Provençal troubadour, was Duke of Aquitaine and Count of Poitou. Rich and unbalanced, he led a wild and dissipated life until suddenly converted to a Christian and ascetic one by members of the mystical Order of Fontevrault. He died on a crusade. Less than a dozen of his poems remain. They deal with love in its various aspects ranging from frank sensualism to idealization. See A. Jeanroy, *Les Poésies de Guillaume IX, duc d'Aquitaine* (1927).

**Guillaume de Lorris** ( *fl.* 1235), French poet, author of the first part of *Le Roman de la Rose*, an allegorical account of a courtly winning of a lady's hand which has had incalculable influence on French and thence on European literature generally. Nothing whatever is known of his life. The work was continued and completed by Jean de Meung (q.v.).

**Guillén, Jorge** (1893–    ), Spanish poet. Born in Valladolid, he pursued an academic career, holding posts at various times at the Sorbonne, Oxford and Seville, and leaving Spain for the United States, where he has lived since 1938, when the republic's cause was hopeless. All his well-chiselled, though romantically inclined, verse is to be found in his one book, *Cántico*, first published in 1928, and subsequently added to at intervals (1936, 1945) until the edition of 1950 became the definitive one. Behind a simple exterior much complex thought lies, and the mood consequent upon the reception of the physical experience is expressed with succinctness. For translations see E. Turnbull's *Contemporary Spanish Poetry* (1945).

**Guilloux, Louis** (1899–    ), French novelist. Born of poor parents at Saint-Brieuc, he became a journalist and was the author of fiction set in working-class conditions, including *Dossier confidentiel* (1928), *Compagnons* (1930), *Angélina* (1934), *Le Sang noir* (1935; Eng. trans. *Bitter Victory*, 1938), *Le Pain des rêves* (1942), *Le Jeu de patience* (1949), *Absent de Paris* (1952) and *Parpognacco, ou la conjuration* (1954).

**Guitry, Sacha,** in reality **Alexandre Pierre Georges** (1885–1957), French actor and playwright. Born in Petersburg, he was one of the most colourful stage figures in Europe. As an author his numerous plays were clever comic pieces or historical ones designed to suit a particular actor or actress, sometimes his own father, the famous Lucien Guitry. Such were *Nono* (1905), *La Jalousie* (1915), *Béranger* (1920), *Mozart* (1926), *Jean de La Fontaine* (1928) and *Le Mot de Cambronne* (1926). None of them are of lasting value. He died in Paris.

**Guizot, François Pierre Guillaume** (1787–1874), born in Nîmes of a Huguenot family, the famous French statesman, into whose political career it is not necessary to enter, wrote during the period 1825–8, when he was deprived of his chair of modern history at the University of France, several historical works now hopelessly outdated. His views were those of an old-fashioned liberal, who found the government of Louis-Philippe exactly suited to his taste. It was after the revolution of 1848, which closed his political career, that he turned whole-heartedly to literature. *Corneille et son temps* (1852), *Mélanges biographiques et littéraires* (1868) and *Mélanges politiques et historiques* (1869) are typical of his writings. He died at Val Richer in Normandy.

**Gumilyov, Nikolay Stepanovich** (1886–1921), Russian poet, born at Kronstadt. At first a symbolist, he later became the leading figure in the Acmeist school, combining a remarkable technical mastery of verse with a sensuousness which harks back to French exotic writers like Nerval (q.v.) and Gautier (q.v.). The chief examples of his work are *Zhemchuga* (1910, 'Pearls'), *Kostyor* (1918, 'The Bonfire') and *Ognenny stolp* (1921, 'The Pillar of Fire'). He was for a time married to the poet Anna Akhmatova (q.v.), who divorced him. He was executed in Leningrad for his active opposition to the Bolsheviks. His collected works appeared (4 vols.) in Germany in 1947, and the first volume of a fuller edition (also to be in 4 vols.) was published in the U.S.A. in 1962. A selection of his poems in English translation came out in 1945.

**Gunnarsson, Gunnar** (1889–     ), Dano-Icelandic novelist and short-story writer, was born in Iceland near Fljótsdalur of a farming family, and received a scanty education. By 1910 he was struggling as a hack in Copenhagen, but two years later had embarked on his *af Borgslægtens Historie* (4 vols., 1912–14; Eng. trans. *Guest the One-eyed*, 1920), a romantic historical saga about Iceland. Others in the same vein were *Edbrødre* (1918; Eng. trans. *The Sworn Brothers*, 1920) and *Salige er de Enfoldige* (1920; Eng. trans. *Seven Days' Darkness*, 1930). Later works were the autobiographical *Kirken paa Bjerget* (5 vols., 1923–8; Eng. trans. of vols. 2 and 3, *Ships in the Sky* and *The Night and the Dream*, 1938), *Advent* (1937; Eng. trans. *The Good Shepherd*, 1940) and *Trylle og andet Smaakran* (1939; Eng. trans. *Trylle and Other Small Fry*, 1947). He returned to Iceland in 1939. Among his later works are *Salumessa* (1952) and *Brimhenda* (1954).

**Günther, Johann Christian** (1695–1723), German poet. Born at Striegau, Silesia, he went to Wittenberg as a medical student but fell into bad company, led a reckless life, was disinherited, moved to Leipzig, did not mend his ways there, and left for Jena where he died. He had become a member of a circle of poets, among them J. von Besser (q.v.), Günther's evil genius as it happened, called the Hofpoeten, who affected French ideas derived from Boileau (q.v.), and by them some of his poems were collected as *Gedichte* (1724), a further edition of which with additional poems followed in 1735 (mod. ed., 1940). Here Günther is revealed as a poet of a depth of feeling quite exceptional for his age, his love lyrics and pieces on the flight of time and death being the best before Klopstock (q.v.) if not Goethe himself.

**Gusev-Orenburgsky, Sergey Ivanovich** (1867–1963), Russian novelist. Born at Orenburg he became a priest, later renouncing his Orders. He makes use of his ecclesiastical experience in the realistic tale *Strana ottsov* (1905; Eng. trans. *The Land of the Fathers*, 1925) and his novel *Strana detey* (1928; Eng. trans. *The Land of the Children*, 1928). He died in self-imposed exile in New York.

**Gustaf-Janson, Gösta** (1902–     ), Swedish novelist, born at Saltsjö-Duvnäs, wrote several well thought-out and expressed bourgeois novels, among them *Kapitulation?—Nej!* (1932), *Gubben kommer* (1934; Eng. trans. *The Old Man's Coming,* 1936) and the remarkable success *Stora famnen* (1937). Since the war he has plunged further below the surface in *Stampen* (1951), with a consequent loss of general popularity.

**Gutzkow, Karl Ferdinand** (1811–1878), German novelist and playwright. Born in Berlin of working-class family, he had not long entered the university there and was doing excellently when the 1830 revolutions in Europe completely changed his interests and altered the course of his life. He now took to letters, and as the apostle of the new freedom which he hoped would come to Germany he turned to fiction and the theatre. His ironical romantic novel, *Maha-Gura, Geschichte eines Gottes* (1833), surprised the public and gained some attention, but the second, *Wally die Zweiflerin* (1835), scandalized this public with its scepticism and its very bold thought about social and domestic life. Here in fact is the same bid for freer commerce between the sexes which we find in F. Schlegel's (q.v.) *Lucinde* of an earlier generation. For this Gutzkow gained notoriety and suffered imprisonment. As a playwright he was feeling his way with historical plots in *Nero* (1835) and *König Saul* (1839), while he plunged into heavy, long, formless works, patently didactic, such as *Blasedow und seine Söhne* (3 vols., 1838–9), *Die Ritter vom Geiste* (9 vols., 1850–2), which could have been interesting as an account of the period of reaction that began after the revolution of 1848 had it not been so overburdened by detail and so weak in plot, and *Der Zauberer von Rom* (9 vols., 1858–61). *Hohenschwangau* (5 vols., 1867) and *Die Söhne Pestalozzi* (3 vols., 1870) are of the same uncompromising bulk. He developed into a better dramatist, a few of his large output of plays being worth reading still, especially *Zopf und Schwert* (1844; Eng. trans. *Sword and Queue,* 1915), a good historical comedy of the Prussian court of Frederick William I, influenced by Scribe (q.v.) and the French comedy of intrigue, then at its height. *Das Urbild des Tartüffe* (1847) is an engaging comedy about Molière. *Uriel Acosta* (1847; Eng. trans. 1885), in blank verse, had enormous success, really because, under the guise of an historical play about Spinoza's (q.v.) master, it was a commentary on religious controversies aroused by such anti-traditionalist theological criticism as D. F. Strauss's *Leben Jesu. Der Königsleutnant* (1849) is built round an incident in Goethe's early days, and was written for the Goethe centenary celebrations. His dramatic works fill twenty volumes (1873–5). His other works, including *Ludwig Börne* (1840), an early assessment of the man (q.v.), are no longer of any importance. He died at Sachsenhausen.

**Gyp,** pseudonym of **Sybille Gabrielle Marie Antoinette Riquetti de Mirabeau** (1849–1932), French novelist, was born at Château Koëtsal, Morbihan, Brittany, spent most of her childhood in Lorraine, and in 1869 married comte Martel de Janville. She wrote a stream of novels, including *Petit Bob* (1882), *Ohé, les Psychologues!* (1892), *Le Mariage de Chiffon* (1894), *Bijou* (1896), *Lune de miel* (1898), *Un Mariage chic* (1903), *L'Affaire Débrouillard-Delatamize* (1911), *Les Profitards*

(1918), a war satire, and two books of memoirs. Witty and unconventional and a mistress of dialogue, she threw in her lot with various political interests and was a strong anti-semite and nationalist. She died at Neuilly.

# H

**Hackländer, Friedrich Wilhelm von** (1816–1877), German man of letters. Born at Burtscheid, near Aachen, he began his literary career with such stirring collections as *Bilder aus dem Soldatenleben* (1841) and the travel book *Daguerreotypen* (1842), describing his travels in the East. He later turned his hand to comedies (*Magnetische Curen*, 1851) and novels (*Namenlose Geschichten*, 1851, and *Eugen Stillfried*, 1852). Very popular in his day, his reputation quickly faded. He died at Leoni-am-Starnbergersee.

**Hagedorn, Friedrich von** (1708–1754), German poet. Born in Hamburg of mixed German and Danish parentage, he came to London in 1729 as a secretary at the Danish Embassy, and in 1731 took up the post of secretary to an English trading company in Hamburg. He had already published *Versuch einiger Gedichte* (1729), revealing his gifts as an elegant writer of anacreontic verse. In *Versuch in poetischen Fabeln und Erzählungen* (1738) he gained a reputation as a fabulist writing in easy and urbane verse, and in *Sammlung neuer Oden und Lieder* (3 vols., 1742–52) he showed how he could broaden the field of his poetical accomplishment. He died in Hamburg. His collected works were published (5 vols.) in 1800.

**Halas, František** (1901–1950), Czech poet. Born in Brno, he became well known with his volume *Staré ženy* (1935; Eng. trans. *Old Women*, 1948) in which he deals with the problem of the seeming purposelessness of life. In *Torso naděje* (1938, 'Torso of Hope') the menace of Germany is at the door, and terrible disasters, a veritable chapter of last things, are opening out before one. He died in Prague.

**Halévy, Ludovic** (1834–1908), French playwright, librettist and novelist, was born in Paris, the son of Léon Halévy, the scholar, and nephew of Jacques Halévy, the composer. He entered the diplomatic service, but soon made a fortune as a librettist for Offenbach and other operetta composers, working often in collaboration with Henri Meilhac (q.v.), as in *La Belle Hélène* (1864), *Barbe-Bleue* (1866), *La Vie parisienne* (1866) and *La Grande Duchesse de Gérolstein* (1867). He also wrote comedies, such as *Fanny* (1868) and *Froufrou* (1869), jointly with Meilhac. His best novels are *L'Abbé Constantin* (1882; which in 1897, when an Eng. trans. came out, had reached the 176th reprinting) and *Mariette* (1893). He died in Paris. See *Le Théâtre de Meilhac et Halévy* (8 vols., 1900–2).

**Haller, Albrecht von** (1708–1777), Swiss poet. Born in Bern of an old family, he qualified in medicine at Leipzig and became a member of the academic staff of the University of Göttingen in the very year of its foundation (1737). He thereafter became a leading anatomist and botanist in Europe. But it is for his nature poems that he holds his place as a man of letters. In an age which loved *parterres* and was afraid of untamed nature, and looked upon the peasant as 'rude', Haller pointed out the magnificence of mountains in *Die Alpen* (1728), and had sympathy for the simple men who lived among such grandeurs. His *Versuch schweizerischer Gedichten* (1732), which includes *Die Alpen,* is therefore a landmark in European nature-poetry, and is an early warning of coming romanticism and a return to fundamentals. There is a modern edition of his complete poetical works (1882). His *Tagebuch* ('Diary') appeared (2 vols.) in 1787. He died in Bern.

**Hallström, Per** (1866–1960), Swedish man of letters, born in Stockholm. Although he tried his hand at many forms of writing he was at his best as a short-story writer. Romanticism is blended with realism in his *Noveller och berättelser* (12 vols., 1922–3; Eng. trans. of some in *Selected Short Stories of Per Hallström,* i, 1922; ii, 1933). He died in Stockholm.

**Halm, Friedrich,** pseudonym of **E. F. J. von Münch-Bellinghausen** (1806–1871), Austrian poet, dramatist and short-story writer, born of noble family in Cracow. His plays were very popular in his day and on the Vienna stage he was the successful rival of Grillparzer (q.v.), while his sunny, straightforward character brought him all the prizes in his civil service career that the far greater literary man failed dismally to win. Fair samples of his plays are *Griseldis* (1835; Eng. trans. 1840), *Der Sohn der Wildnis* (1843; Eng. trans. *Son of the Wilderness,* 1868) and *Der Fechter von Ravenna* (1854; Eng. trans. *The Gladiator of Ravenna,* 1861). His collected poetry, of an average quality, came out in 1850. His plays show a knowledge of stagecraft but are shallow. Nowadays he is remembered for his long short stories, nearly all of them published posthumously, the best of them, in the manner of H. von Kleist (q.v.), being *Das Haus an der Verona-brücke* (1904) and *Die Freundinnen* (1906). He died in Vienna.

**Hamann, Johann Georg** (1730–1788), German prose-writer, born in Königsberg. Travelling tirelessly about Europe, writing long turgid treatises, yet with sudden flashes of insight which set Herder (q.v.) thinking and ignited the *Sturm und Drang* movement, Hamann did indeed warrant his soubriquet of 'Wizard of the North'. He lives as an influence rather than as a writer on his own account, although three of his books should be mentioned. They are *Kreuzzüge des Philologen* (1762), which helped Herder to embark on his philological system, *Selbstgespräch eines Autors* (1773), and the highly personally religious *Golgatha und Scheblimini* (1784), whose influence can be seen on such romantics of the next generation as Novalis (q.v.) and Arnim (q.v.) Always impecunious, but always serene, he died, an excise officer, at Münster.

**Hamerling, Robert,** originally **Rupert Johann Hammerling** (1830–1889), Austrian poet and novelist. Born at Kirchberg-am-Walde, he became a schoolmaster in Trieste in 1855, but in 1866 suffered partial paralysis and spent the rest of his life in bed at Graz, where he died. His career as a poet had begun with *Venus im Exil* (1858), other books of verse being *Ein Schwanenlied der Romantik* (1862), the satires *Ahasuerus in Rom* (1866) and *Der König von Sion* (1869), the idealistic *Danton und Robespierre* (1871), *Amor und Psyche* (1882) and *Blätter im Winde* (1887). He produced one long novel, *Aspasia* (3 vols., 1876; Eng. trans. 1882).

**Hamp, Pierre,** pseudonym of **Pierre Bourillon** (1876–     ), French novelist born in Nice. The son of working people, he was self-educated, at the same time employed in a factory, where he eventually became an inspector. He describes the workman's hard lot in many novels including *Marée fraîche* (1908), *Le Travail invincible* (1916), *La Victoire mécanicienne* (1920), *Mes métiers* (1931; Eng. trans. *Kitchen Prelude*, 1932), *Gueules noires* (1938) and *Moteurs* (1942). Sometimes the feeling borders on revolutionary defiance against an unjust society, but this is usually tempered by a kind of stern romanticism. His *Hormisdas le canadien* (1952) shows a still firmer grip on his powerful style.

**Hamsun, Knut** (1859–1952), Norwegian novelist. Born, the son of peasants, at Lom, he first worked as a shoemaker and then was a clerk in the Newfoundland fisheries, before the contribution of his realistic novel, *Sult*, to a Danish magazine in 1888 and its subsequent success in book form (1890; Eng. trans. *Hunger*, 1899) brought him wide acclaim. Here is a powerful study of a man whose character is broken down by physical privations, something very different from the average work of fiction of the time, which had often come to be little more than social theory tricked out as a story. To *Sult* other novels succeeded rapidly, for instance *Mysterier* (1892; Eng. trans. *Mysteries*, 1927), *Ny Jord* (1893; Eng. trans. *Shallow Soil*, 1914), *Pan* (1894; Eng. trans. 1920), *Victoria* (1898; Eng. trans. 1929), *Svœrmere* (1904; Eng. trans. *Mothwise*, 1922), *Benoni, Rosa* (1908; Eng. trans. *Benoni and Rosa*, 1932), *Den sidste Glœde* (1912; Eng. trans. *Look Back on Happiness*, 1940), and his masterpiece *Markens Grøde* (1917; Eng. trans. *The Growth of the Soil*, 2 vols., 1920), in which for the first time the two conflicting sides of his picture of life, the choice between avoiding social commitments and throwing in one's lot with nature, or standing up against the evils of so-called civilization, are successfully reconciled. Later works include *Konerne ved Vandposten* (1920; Eng. trans. *The Women at the Pump*, 2 vols., 1928), in which he relapses into misanthropy, *Sisste Kapitel* (1924; Eng. trans. *Chapter the Last*, 1930), *Landstrykere* (1927; Eng. trans. *Vagabonds*, 1930), in which he again takes refuge in nature, *August* (1930; Eng. trans. 1932), a particular success, *Men livet lever* (1933; Eng. trans. *The Road Leads On*, 1935) and *Ringen sluttet* (1936; Eng. trans. *The Ring is Closed*, 1937). He died at Nørholm.

**Hardenberg, F. L. von,** *see* **Novalis.**

**Haren, Onno Zweir van** (1713–1779), Dutch dramatist and poet, was born at Leeuwarden, and enjoying the favour of the court became a statesman of some importance. The turning point in his life was his sudden dismissal from his offices as a result of his brother Willem van Haren's misdemeanours. It was then that as a rebel he showed his true talent, throwing off contemporary mannerisms and proving himself to be a writer ahead of his time. In the play, *Agon Sulthan van Bantam* (1769), he lashed the Netherlands East India Company for corruption, while in a tragedy, *Willem I* (1773), he gave proof of his uncompromising patriotism. His patriotic poem, *Aan het Vaderland* (1769), was later an inspiration to Bilderdijk (q.v.) who revised it (1785). His *Dichterlijke Werken* were published (2 vols.) in 1824–6. He died at Wolvega.

**Häring, G. W. H.,** *see* **Alexis, W.**

**Hartleben, Otto Erich** (1864–1905), German playwright, poet and short-story writer. Born at Clausthal, he led a shiftless existence, unable to settle to anything. Drink intervened and ruined him. As a dramatist he is to be seen at his best in *Hanna Jagert* (1893; Eng. trans. 1913) and *Rosenmontag* (1900; Eng. trans. *Love's Carnival*, 1904), as a poet in *Meine Verse* (1895; enlarged 1905), and as a short-story writer in *Vom gastfreien Pastor* (1895). He died at Salò in Italy.

**Hartmann, Carl Robert Eduard von** (1842–1906), German prose-writer. Born in Berlin, he served for a time in the army, and after completing his course of philosophy at Rostock settled in Berlin to work out a system of philosophy based on a synthesis of Hegelianism, neo-Hegelianism and Schopenhauer (q.v.) which he felt would be necessary for modern thought. The result was *Die Philosophie des Unbewussten* (1869; Eng. trans. *The Philosophy of the Unconscious*, 1884). With its pessimism as regards the future of human life, but with its optimism in consideration of how that doomed existence could be raised to the greatest heights by the evolutionary process, aided by the seemingly unending possibilities of science, it reflected the mood of a materialistic age and was eagerly read by a public of widely varying views. In this way Hartmann may be said to have entered into literature, for his own style has little quality. Books like *Die Religion des Geistes* (1882) and *Das Christentum des neuen Testaments* (1905) display the anti-Christian dogmatism of Prussianism. Hartmann died at Grosslichterfelde.

**Hartmann, Moritz** (1821–1872), Austrian poet, short-story writer and travel writer. Born of a Jewish family at Duschnik, Bohemia, he settled in Vienna, but made frequent journeys abroad writing about his experiences in and opinions about the countries visited in such attractive books as *Tagebuch aus Languedoc und Provence* (1853). As a poet he is represented by *Schatten* (1851) and *Adam und Eva* (1851); but it is above all as a short-story writer that he is worthy of remembrance, and his clear and luminous prose is at its best in his *Novellen* (3 vols., 1863). He also translated the *Contes* of

Perrault (q.v.) as *Märchen nach Perrault* (1867). He died at Ober-döbling, near Vienna. His works were collected in ten volumes (1873–4).

**Hartmann von Aue** (1170?–1215), German poet, who took the name of his Swabian master von Aue, in whose house he was minstrel. His moralizing epic *Der arme Heinrich*, about a knight who was punished for his pride by contracting leprosy, of which he was cured by repentance, was finished about 1195, and was based on a traditional story. Longfellow made use of it in his *Golden Legend*. *Erec* (1196) and *Iwein* (1203) both come from Arthurian legend via Chrétien de Troyes (q.v.). He took some part in the crusade of 1197 and this inspired a few lyrics of a religious nature but many more about love. His influence was great on both Gottfried von Strassburg (q.v.) and Wolfram von Eschenbach (q.v.). See his collected works, *Hartmann von Aue*, edited by F. Bech (third ed., 3 vols., 1891–3).

**Hartzenbusch, Juan Eugenio** (1806–1880), Spanish dramatist and man of letters, was born in Madrid, his father a German cabinet maker and his mother Spanish. He followed his father's craft until he gained an assistantship in the Biblioteca Nacional, of which he eventually became director (1862). Besides his valuable work as a textual critic of Spanish literature (especially of the plays of Tirso de Molina, q.v., Lope de Vega and Calderón), he wrote some excellent plays in the romantic style, chief of them *Los amantes de Teruel* (1837; Eng. trans. *The Lovers of Teruel*, 1938), the two plays on the occult, *La redoma encantada* (1839) and *Los polvos de la madre Celestina* (1840), and one about the Cid, *La jura de Santa Gadea* (1845). A useful edition of his selected works was published in 1873. He died in Madrid.

**Hašek, Jaroslav** (1883–1923), Czech novelist, born in Prague. A quiet nationalism invests his work, his chief creation being the typical Czech citizen Švejk in the series *Osudy dobrého vojáka Švejka* (4 vols., 1920–3; Eng. trans. *The Good Soldier Schweik*, 1930). Here the Czech man in the street walks blithely on along his humble path while the Austro-Hungarian Empire disintegrates. He died at Lipnice.

**Hasselt, André Henri Constant van** (1806–1874), Belgian poet. Of a French family, he was born at Maastricht. In 1833 he took Belgian nationality and shortly afterwards became an inspector of schools. He joined in literary circles and made the friendship of Victor Hugo (q.v.) who encouraged him to put his metrical theories—such as the use in French poetry of a much wider range of verse forms than was admitted—into practice. His most successful books were *Primevères* (1834) and *Quatre Incarnations du Christ* (1867). His influence on the technical side of French poetry was great. He died in Brussels.

**Hauch, Johannes Carsten** (1790–1872), Danish poet and novelist, was born at Frederikshald (Halden), in Norway, the son of a Danish civil servant. He was known as a zoologist in his day, but this did not prevent him from becoming professor of aesthetics at Copenhagen in 1850. Although his many dramas in the romantic manner are of little import now, his fine poetry, which reveals an unusually noble character, has retained all its freshness. The bulk of it is contained in the two volumes *Lyriske Digte* (1842) and *Lyriske Digte og Romancer* (1861). His novel *Robert Fulton* (1853; Eng. trans. 1868) shows considerable ability. He died in Rome.

**Hauff, Wilhelm** (1802–1827), German short-story writer and novelist, was born in Stuttgart, went to the University of Tübingen, and crowded into the short space of two years a remarkable number of literary achievements, chief of them *Märchen: Almanach auf das Jahr 1826* (1826; Eng. trans. *Tales*, 1905), charming stories, *Lichtenstein* (1826; Eng. trans. 1897), a somewhat heavy novel patently derived from Scott, and further collections of tales such as *Phantasien im Bremen Ratskeller* (1827; Eng. trans. *The Wine-Ghosts of Bremen*, 1889), *Die Bettlerin vom Pont des Arts* (1827; Eng. trans. *A Constant Lover*, 1893) and *Das Bild des Kaisers* (1827; Eng. trans. *The Emperor's Picture*, 1873). He was appointed editor of the well-known *Morgenblatt* shortly before his premature death in Stuttgart. Astonishingly enough, although not quite twenty-five years old, he had already written enough to fill thirty-six volumes in the collected edition of his works. A judicious selection (4 vols.) was published in 1929.

**Hauptmann, Carl** (1858–1921), German dramatist. The elder brother of G. Hauptmann (q.v.), he was born at Obersalzbrunn, Silesia, where his father owned a none too prosperous hotel. He developed late as a playwright and even then made his reputation rather by the unusual qualities of his style than for dramatic gifts. Typical of his work are *Moses* (1906) and *Napoleon Bonaparte* (1911), but his war plays, *Krieg, ein Tedeum* (1914; Eng. trans. *War*, 1916) and *Aus dem grossen Kriege* (1915; Eng. trans. 1916), are the best. Overshadowed by his famous brother, he died at Schreiberhau.

**Hauptmann, Gerhart** (1862–1946), German dramatist, novelist, short-story writer and poet, was the younger brother of Carl Hauptmann (q.v.) and was born, an innkeeper's son, at Salzbrunn, Silesia. In 1880 he went to Breslau as an art student, then left for Italy and played at being a sculptor in Rome, until a wealthy marriage in 1885 allowed him to live as he pleased. He now went to Berlin and turned writer, and as it turned out he became a pioneer of naturalistic drama. German society was sick; Hauptmann soon realized it and dramatized the ugliness of the small cruelties of modern life, the hideous results of materialism. So powerfully written were his plays, such instinct for the stage did he show, that he was forgiven his sometimes even crude realism. With his first, *Vor Sonnenaufgang* (1889), he won acclaim and maintained his reputation with those which succeeded, such as *Das Friedensfest* (1890), *Einsame Menschen* (1891), *Die Weber* (1892) and *Der Biberpelz* (1893). In this latter year he wrote one of his finest plays, *Hanneles Himmelfahrt*, and round the little girl he builds a plot in which for the first time he allows himself a modicum of romanticism. From then on his dramatic work is a mixture of the sternly naturalistic, such as *Florian Geyer* (1896) and *Fuhrmann Henschel* (1899), and the romantic, subjective,

such as *Die versunkene Glocke* (1896) and *Und Pippa tanzt* (1906).
With *Der Narr in Christo, Emanuel Quint* (1910; Eng. trans. *The
Fool in Christ, Emanuel Quint*, 1911) he entered triumphantly on
the novel, and with *Atlantis* (1912; Eng. trans. 1912) he repeated his
success. He was the Nobel Prize winner of 1912. He struck out into
the short story with *Der Ketzer von Soana* (1918; Eng. trans. *The
Heretic of Soana*, 1923), and powerful plays followed, e.g. *Indipohdi*
(1920), *Veland* (1925), *Dorothea Angermann* (1926), *Spuk* (1929) and
*Vor Sonnenuntergang* (1932). The novels also continued with *Die
Insel der Grossen Mutter* (1924; Eng. trans. *The Island of the Great
Mother*, 1925) and *Wandu* (1928), and he also attempted a verse
satire on the adventures of *Till Eulenspiegel* (1927). Tireless in
his output, an autobiographical novel, *Buch der Leidenschaft*,
was published in 1929, and two further novels, *Die Spithacke* and
*Die Hochzeit auf Buchenhorst*, in 1930 and 1931 respectively. As
the years passed Goethe became his guiding light, and Hauptmann
also sought, as he had done, artistic tranquillity in the Olympian
calm of ancient Greece. His earlier travels in Greece had made a
great impression on him, and now in his old age, after the two
dramatic experiments, *Hamlet in Wittenberg* (1935) and *Die Fin-
sternisse* (1937), he wrote the classical trilogy, *Iphigenie in Aulis*
(1944), the second and third parts, *Agamemnons Tod* and *Elektra*
coming out posthumously in 1948. A volume of poetry, *Neue Gedichte*,
appeared the year of his death, which occurred at Agnetendorf. The
greater part of his dramatic works have been translated into English
(1912–29) by L. Lewisohn.

**Haverschmidt, François** (1835–1894), Dutch poet and short-story
writer. Born at Leeuwarden, he became a clergyman, wrote such
charming and ingenuous works in a domestic setting as *Snikken en
grimlachjes* (1867) and *Familie en Kennissen* (1867), and died by
suicide at Schiedam.

**Hebbel, Christian Friedrich** (1813–1863), German dramatist, poet and
short-story writer. Born at Wesselburen, Holstein, the son of a very
poor stone-mason, his youth was one of grinding poverty, from which
he emerged mentally scarred for life, and which rendered him taciturn
and difficult in character. Thanks to the novelist Amalia Schoppe
a fund was started to enable the intelligent boy to go to school in
Hamburg, and there he worked hard and with such good result that
he was able to proceed to the University of Munich. There money
began to run short and he would have starved had it not been for the
love of a working girl, Elise Lensing, who shared her own miserable
earnings with him. He had meanwhile thrown aside all attempts to
study, but was discovering his dramatic gifts, and by 1840 had written
his first play, *Judith*. Crude as it is, Hebbel's remarkable ability is
already apparent. Pessimism like a gigantic shadow hovers over a
Hebbel play, and even the strongest characters are in the end overcome by the gloom. In fact, the remorseless current of life is too
strong for the individual to stand up against it; he will be swept
away. At first an absolute realist expressing himself in prose, he

gradually turns to blank verse, and the everyday folk of his earlier plays become distant historical characters, then mythical ones and finally gigantic northern gods filling the stormy sky, such as Aeneas saw over Troy. There is violence in his work, brute force, sometimes with a tinge of cruelty tending to sadism. Psychologically his characters are convincing at a time when little attention was paid to such a matter. His knowledge of stagecraft was amazing. *Genoveva* (1841), which strongly appealed to the composer Schumann, and *Der Diamant* (1841) followed, and the success which they brought him enabled him to visit Copenhagen, where, through Oehlenschläger (q.v.), he gained an interview with Christian VIII, who awarded him a meagre scholarship. This enabled him to visit Paris, where he wrote his first important work, *Maria Magdalena* (1843; Eng. trans. in *Three Plays*, Everyman's Library, 1914), a tragedy of humble life of rugged power. In 1844 he went with what remained of his scholarship to Italy, but the visit was a failure, for his money did not suffice and Elise Lensing's importunities allowed him no respite. Then in 1845 he made for Vienna. The rough north German found himself in a theatrical Mecca, and it became his home for the rest of his life. As before at other crises of his life a woman came to his rescue, this time a glittering one, the famous actress Christine Enghaus, whom he married in 1846. Secure socially and theatrically, his life from now on moved in calmer channels. After the not very satisfactory *Ein Trauerspiel in Sizilien* (1847), and *Der Rubin* (1849), came the magnificent blank verse tragedy *Herodes und Mariamne* (1850; Eng. trans. in *Three Plays*, Everyman's Library, 1914). With *Agnes Bernauer* (1852) he returned to prose, and after an aberration, a volume of mediocre short stories, *Erzählungen und Novellen* (1855), came forward with that masterpiece, *Gyges und sein Ring* (1856; Eng. trans. in *Three Plays*, Everyman's Library, 1914), in verse. His collected poetry was published in 1857, some of it with a sombre power such as 'Quellende, schwellende Nacht'. He then set to work on what was to be his crowning achievement, the trilogy *Die Nibelungen* (1862). His last effort was an attempt to write a tragedy on Demetrius, but like Schiller (q.v.) who did not live to complete his, Hebbel died before he could write more than half of it. He died in Vienna. The south had not changed him essentially: he was in fact still an intractable northerner and German to the core. He may be regarded as the successor of Kleist (q.v.) and the prelude to Ibsen (q.v.). The best collected edition of his dramatic works is that by Krumm (12 vols., 1900). His complete works appear in the twenty-four volume edition by Werner (1901–7).

**Hebel, Johann Peter** (1760–1826), German poet writing in dialect, the greatest of his century according to Goethe, was born, the son of a linen-weaver, in Basel. He became a clergyman and published his first considerable work, *Alemannische Gedichte*, in 1803. Full of a kindly humour also is *Schatzkästlein des Rhein* (1811). He died at Schwetzingen. His *Sämtliche Werke* appeared (4 vols.) in 1911.

**Hedberg, Carl Olof (Olle)** (1899– ), Swedish author, born at Norrköping. His best book was his first, *Rymmare och fasttagare* (1930;

Eng. trans. *Prisoner's Base*, 1932), and he wrote many more on the same theme, which is modern society and its defects. However good his characterization may be, there is a sameness of style and plot which palls. Of his other works the most notable are *Jag är en prins av blodet* (1936) and *Djuribur* (1960; Eng. trans. *Animals in Cages*, 1962).

**Hegel, Georg Wilhelm Friedrich** (1770–1831), German philosopher, born the son of a civil servant in Stuttgart. Educated at the University of Tübingen, where he numbered Hölderlin (q.v.) and Schelling (q.v.) among his friends, he was a private tutor till 1800 when, having come into a small income at his father's death, he settled down in Jena. He was appointed *professor extraordinarius* at the university there, finding time for much private study which resulted in the publication of his first major work, *Phänomenologie des Geists* (1807). This and his later and more mature publications, including *Wissenschaft der Logik* (3 vols., 1812–16, rev., 1831, Eng. trans. *Science of Logic*, 1929), *Encyklopädie* (1817), a summary of his philosophic system, and *Grundlinien der Philosophie des Rechts* (1821; Eng. trans. *The Philosophy of Right*, 1942), possess no literary graces, being often obscure and of heavy and discursive style. Consequently they took time to filter through to wider circles, but having done so had an enormous influence on the literature and thought of the nineteenth and even the twentieth centuries. The famous Hegelian dialectic (explained with rare skill by W. Wallace in his *Prolegomena to the Study of Hegel*, 1894) could be brought to bear on many political and social theories, and gave a formidable coherence to totalitarian programmes both of the right and the left. Hegel, before he died of cholera in Berlin, where he had been professor since 1818, had produced an all-embracing system of thought as attractive to Prussianism as to Marxism. The first collected edition of his works appeared in eighteen volumes between 1832 and 1845, and see the standard *Neue kritische Gesamtausgabe* (32 vols., 1952 ff.).

**Heiberg, Johan Ludvig** (1791–1860), Danish poet and playwright. Born in Copenhagen, son of P. A. Heiberg, also a playwright, he was educated there, lived in France and Germany for a short time, and then settled in the city of his birth, where from 1825 onwards, by force of personality as much as his own literary abilities, he was the acknowledged dictator of letters. As a poet his freshest work is to be found in *Poetisk Kalender* (1819) and *Nye Digte* (1841); as a playwright in his comedies *Aprilsnarrene* (1825), *De Danske i Paris* (1832), modelled on French vaudeville, and the romantic fairy play, *Alferne* (1855). He died in Copenhagen.

**Heidenstam, Carl Gustaf Verner von** (1859–1940), Swedish poet and prose-writer. Born at Olshammar, he travelled widely, and on his return, encouraged by Strindberg (q.v.), he published a volume of poetry, epoch-making in Swedish literature, *Vallfart och vandringsår* (1888). This was followed by *Endymion* (1889), a novel about Damascus under Turkish rule, and the deeply thought out *Hans Alienus* (1892). His reputation reached its height with the series of stories with Charles XII as the central figure, *Karolinerna* (2 vols., 1897–8; Eng. trans. *A King and his Campaigners*, 1902). Other works of historical fiction, such as *Heliga Birgittas pilgrimsfärd* (1901) and *Svenskarna och deras hövdingar* (1908; Eng. trans. *The Swedes and their Chieftains*, 1909), are finely written and strongly patriotic in tone. He was awarded the Nobel Prize for literature in 1916. An English translation of his selected poems appeared as *Sweden's Laureate* in 1919. He died at Övralid. His memoirs were published a year after his death.

**Heine, Heinrich** (1797–1856), German poet and prose-writer. Born in Düsseldorf of a poorish Jewish family, his rich uncle invited him into his business, but on his proving incapable that uncle paid for him to read law, and he was a student at the universities of Göttingen, Bonn and Berlin, at the last of which he completed his course in 1825. That same year he was baptized a Christian, but without conviction and only in order to acquire the full rights of a German citizen. Yet by now his thoughts were hardly on the law. He had already enjoyed some success with his volume of poetry, *Gedichte* (1822), inspired by his love for his cousin Amalie, which had been succeeded by *Tragödien nebst einem lyrischen Intermezzo* (1823), also regarded as highly promising by critics; but with the first two volumes of his *Reisebilder* (1826–7) he reached a wide and appreciative public. With *Das Buch der Lieder* (1827) he became the most popular German poet of the day. More travel followed and led to two more volumes of *Reisebilder* (1830–1), less successful than the first; but already he had turned his back on Germany. His disappointment at his failure to gain an academic post at Munich, and his sympathy with the French July revolution of 1830, led him to Paris, where he settled in 1831, there remaining for the rest of his life. He now turned to politics and was before long considered one of the leaders of that cosmopolitan society which had grown up in Paris, the place of pilgrimage of so many exiles. Besides acting as a secret agent of the French Government as regards German affairs from 1837 to 1848, for which he was in receipt of a pension, he took it upon himself to explain the intellectual and artistic aims of the French and the Germans to one another. This latter activity led to such works as the *Französische Zustände* (1833), first published in the *Allgemeine Zeitung* newspaper, *De l'Allemagne* (1835; the original French version appearing in German as *Die Romantische Schule*, 1836), and *Philosophie und Literatur in Deutschland*, this last forming a part of a miscellany, *Der Salon* (4 vols., 1835–40). He had already stirred up a nest of hornets as a result of *Die Romantische Schule*, where as the champion of the 'Young German' school of poets with their political liberal aspirations he virulently mocked the older romantic school which he accused of bowing down before thrones and German historical tradition. Now in the article, 'Ludwig Börne' (q.v.), in the last volume of *Der Salon* (1840), he turned on his late friend and compatriot, and this led to a duel and virtual isolation from the German community in Paris. Two volumes of *Neue Gedichte* (1844) and a satirical epic *Deutschland*, the same year, were followed by

*Atta Troll* (1847), his finest sustained poem, and another collection of lyrics, *Romanzero* (1851). The collection of short stories, *Lutetia* (1854), was his last work of value. In 1845 symptoms of creeping paralysis appeared and from 1848 onwards he was bedridden and in much pain. His unimpaired mental state and the devotion of the girl Elise Konnitz ('La Mouche') upheld him. At his best Heine is one of the four greatest lyric poets in Germany, the other three being Goethe, Eichendorff (q.v.) and Mörike (q.v.), but he is inclined, as the others never did, to allow a cruel aside, a rancorous twist, to obtrude, yet on the other hand his metaphor and imagery are the equal of theirs. As a prose-writer his style, disciplined by French, offers a pleasing and even a brilliant contrast to the greater part of German prose. It was his fate always to be a bridge between two conflicting ideas, a bridge between the romantic school and the 'Young German' school, between France and Germany. He is the great literary man of exile, a counterpart of Chopin, the composer in exile, also in Paris. The best edition of his works is that by O. Walzel (10 vols., 1910–15). There is a complete English translation by C. G. Leland and others (12 vols., 1891–1905).

**Heinrich von Melk** ( *fl.* 1160), Austrian poet, author of the *Priesterleben*, a stern call to good living with many undertones derived from contemporary social life. He was probably in Orders. There is an edition of his works by R. Heinzel (1867).

**Heinse, Johann Jakob Wilhelm** (1749–1803), German novelist. Born at Langewiesen, in Thuringia, he went to Jena and Erfurt universities and then started out on a wandering, undisciplined life and, attracted to the classical world as were Goethe and Wieland (q.v.), with the second of whom he had much in common, he found his natural home in Italy. Returning to Germany in 1781 he set to work on his best-known novel, fruit of his Italian experience. *Ardinghello oder die glückseligen Inseln*, published in 1787, a year after his appointment to the secretarial staff of the Archbishop of Mainz. *Ardinghello* is a discursive, sometimes brilliant novel, breathing a kind of sick eroticism, defiance of social restraint and the longing of the Teuton for southern lands. His second novel was *Hildegard von Hohental* (2 vols., 1795–6), in which Heinse dwells much on music. He died at Aschaffenburg. The old edition of his works, an attractive edition, is the ten-volume one of 1838; more serviceable is that of 1902–26 (10 vols.).

**Helvétius, Claude Adrien** (1715–1771), French philosophical writer, was born in Paris, the son of a physician to Madame de Maintenon, consort of Louis XIV. He was always in high favour at court, and in 1738 was given a lucrative farmer-general's post. Making the most of his position, he was able to retire in 1751 with a handsome fortune and set about his two main interests, philosophical study and charitable works. He gratified the first ambition in *De l'esprit* (1758; Eng. trans. 1759), written in a sharp and witty style; he pointed out, not without irony, that broad-minded egoism was what was best for society. Taken literally by a scandalized higher bourgeoisie, it was banned and burnt, and was called blasphemous and immoral by those who had not read it, and by those who had read it but did not want others to do so. As a model landlord, caring well for his peasantry, he carried out his second ambition. He left enough to fill fourteen volumes of *Œuvres* (1795), but apart from *De l'homme* (1772), which displays a thoroughgoing materialistic conception of the human being, none of it is of particular importance. A friend of Diderot, whom he had supported both with money and literary contributions when he began to publish the *Encyclopédie* in 1751, Helvétius died in Paris.

**Hemsterhuis, François** (1721–1790), Dutch prose-writer, writing in French. Born at Franeker, he became a civil servant in The Hague, but moved freely about Europe and mixed in many literary circles. His urbane treatises include *Lettre sur les désirs* (1770), *Lettre sur l'homme et ses rapports* (1772), *Sophyle, ou de la philosophie* (1778), *Aristée, ou de la divinité* (1779) and *Lettre de Dioclès à Diotime sur l'athéisme* (1787). He died in The Hague. See his *Œuvres* (3 vols., 1846–50).

**Henriot, Émile** (1889–1961), French novelist and critic. Born in Paris, he took up journalism in 1919, in which year he published a fastidiously written novel, *Le Diable à l'hôtel ou les plaisirs imaginaires*. Others are *Les Occasions perdues* (1931) and *Tout va finir* (1936). His charming essays, sketches and critiques are to be found in *Le Livre de mon père* (1938), *Naissances* (1945) and *Les Livres du second rayon* (4 vols., 1945–8). *Au bord du temps* (1958) and *On n'est pas perdu sur la terre* (1960) are autobiographical. He died in Paris.

**Henschke, A.,** *see* **Klabund.**

**Herculano de Carvalho e Araújo, Alexandre** (1810–1877), Portuguese novelist, poet and historian, born of humble family in Lisbon, was editor of *O Panorama*, a noted liberal paper, royal librarian, and active politician. His best poetical works are *A voz do propheta* (1836), *A harpa do crente* (1838) and *Poesias* (1850). As a novelist in *O monasticon: Eurico o presbitero* (1844) and *O monge de Cister* (1848) he is stridently anti-clerical; but *Lendas e narrativas* (1851) is more satisfactory as a work of art. As an historian he is at his best in his *História de Portugal* (4 vols., 1846–53), which is not only good history but excellent prose. His *História da origem e establecimento da Inquisição em Portugal* (3 vols., 1854–9) is eloquent and as impartial as his nature, fiery in the cause of freedom from fanaticism and oppression, would allow him to be. It is well documented. He died on his estate at Val de Lobos, near Santarem.

**Herder, Johann Gottfried von** (1744–1803), German critic and philologist. Born at Mohrungen, East Prussia, he read theology at Königsberg, where he met Kant (q.v.) and Hamann (q.v.). In 1764 he became a schoolmaster and assistant pastor at Riga, and in 1767, as an earnest of what was to follow, published his *Fragmente—Über die* *neuere deutsche Literatur*, in which he argued that in literature we must return to fundamentals, to the poetry and tales of the people, an argument amplified and illustrated in *Kritische Wälder* (3 vols., 1769). In 1769 he suddenly threw up his posts in Riga, sailed to France, and the following year appeared in Strassburg, where his famous meeting with Goethe took place, Herder so stimulating the younger man and affecting him with his ideas about comparative folk literatures and the evolution of literature, that Goethe, interpreting Herder's message as the necessity for turning to the essentials of feeling and expression and thereby simplifying an over-elaborate European culture, opened the doors for the *Sturm und Drang*. Appointed court preacher at Bückeburg in 1771, he showed his powers as philologist in *Abhandlung über den Ursprung der Sprache* (1772), on the origin of language, and as aesthetician in *Von deutscher Art und Kunst* (1773). In 1776, on the advice of Goethe, he was offered the post of court chaplain and superintendent in Weimar, and stayed there for the rest of his life. His views on folk literature were now given ample support by the publication of an excellent collection of folk-songs, *Volkslieder* (1778; in subsequent editions, *Stimmen der Völker in Liedern*, 'Voices of the People in Songs', more nearly giving the underlying philological-sociological purpose of the anthology). The crown of his achievement was *Ideen zur Philosophie der Geschichte der Menschheit* (4 vols., 1784–91; Eng. trans. *Ideas on the Philosophy of History of Mankind*, 1800), in which he seems to be on the edge of propounding the evolutionary theory, and philosophizes on mankind as the link between the natural terrestrial order and a series of higher existences. Herder grew more and more difficult in character as the years went by and his health grew worse. After 1790, when he quarrelled so seriously with Goethe that they were hardly on speaking terms again, he withdrew more and more into himself. He died at Weimar. Two other books of his, *Vom Geist der hebräischen Poesie* (1782 Ff.; Eng. trans. *The Spirit of Hebrew Poetry*, 1833) and his translation of *El Cid* (1803), are of much interest. The most serviceable edition of his works is that by B. Suphan (33 vols., 1877–1913).

**Hérédia, José Maria de** (1842–1905), French poet. Born at Fortuna Capeyere, near Santiago, in Cuba, of mixed Spanish and French parents, he was educated in Paris and was appointed librarian of the Arsenal Library. He soon fell in with the Parnassians, Leconte de Lisle (q.v.) becoming his closest friend. The greatest master of the sonnet in the whole range of French literature, his 118 sonnets, together with a few other pieces in other styles, were published together as *Les Trophées* (1893; Eng. trans. San Francisco, 1897). Blazing like beautifully cut gems, every word in place and every device called into service, these miniatures are rich in classical lore. Hérédia, whose daughter married Pierre Louÿs (q.v.), died at Bourdonné.

**Hériat, Philippe,** pseudonym of **R. G. Payelle** (1898–    ), French playwright and novelist. Born in Paris, he became a cinema technician before going on the stage. He published novels such as

*L'Innocent* (1931), *La Main tendue* (1933) and *Miroirs* (1936), but best of all is his trilogy about the Boussardel family, *Les Enfants gâtés* (1939), *La Famille Boussardel* (1946) and *Les Grilles d'or* (1957). Of his plays the following may be named: the controversial *L'Immaculée* (1947), dealing with the problem of parthenogenesis, *Les Noces de deuil* (1953) and *Les Joies de la famille* (1960). He is an unsparing critic of the bourgeoisie.

**Hermant, Abel** (1862–1950), French novelist. Born in Paris, he turned early to letters and gained a following with naturalistic, often didactic, novels, such as *Nathalie Madoré* (1888), *Le Sceptre* (1896) and *Le Char de l'État* (1900), before embarking on a long series of excellently written fiction set in the higher reaches of contemporary society, *Mémoires pour servir à l'histoire de la société* (18 vols., 1901–12). A later and more cosmopolitan record was comprised in *Le Cycle de Lord Chelsea* (4 vols., 1923). He was perhaps the greatest authority of his day on the use of the French language (see *Remarques de Monsieur Lancelot pour la défense de la langue française*, 6 vols., 1929–37). His autobiography, *Une Vie, trois guerres* (1943), stood him in bad stead after the war when he was accused of pro-German feelings, if not activities, during the occupation, and he was expelled from the French Academy. He died in Paris.

**Hermes, Johann Timotheus** (1738–1821), German novelist. Born at Petznick, in Pomerania, he became a clergyman and later professor of theology at Breslau, where he died. He imitated the English novel of sensibility in *Miss Fanny Wilkes* (2 vols., 1766), *Sophiens Reise von Memel nach Sachsen* (5 vols., 1769–73), his best and most successful, and *Anne Winterfeld* (1801).

**Hernández, Miguel** (1910–1942), Spanish poet. Born at Orihuela, he was employed as goat-boy and shepherd, but managed to pick up some education. His first volume of verse, *Perito en lunas* (1933), was favourably noticed, while his next, *El rayo que no cesa* (1936), was widely acclaimed. He joined the Republican Army on the outbreak of the civil war (1936) and fought until the defeat of freedom (1939) being captured and imprisoned by the Falangists and dying of ill-treatment in prison in Alicante. His most significant book of poetry is *Viento del pueblo* (1937; Eng. trans. *Wind of the Village* in *And Spain Sings*, N.Y., 1937), and he published one more, *El labrador de más aire* (1938). His collected works appeared in 1952.

**Herrera, Fernando de** (1534–1597), Spanish poet. Born in Seville, he had sufficient means to devote his life to literature, and the bulk of his work is historical, critical and on aesthetics, but apart from his edition of the works of the poet Garcilaso de la Vega (q.v.), with valuable commentary (1580), his prose is of no literary value. As a poet on the other hand he bridges the gap between Garcilaso and Góngora (q.v.), writing lyrics in an Italianate but not over-elaborate style, and stirring odes on the greatness of Spain. Of these poems he published a selection as *Algunas obras* in 1582 (mod. ed., 1908), but in the second edition of 1619 (mod. ed. in *Biblioteca de Autores Españoles*, vol. xxxii) many more were added. He died in Seville.

**Hertz, Henrik** (1798–1870), Danish poet and playwright. Born in Copenhagen, in which he was a lifelong resident, he joined the literary circle of J. L. Heiberg (q.v.). As a poet (*Lyriske og dramatiske Digte*, 2 vols., 1841, 1844; *Digte*, 4 vols., 1851–62) he particularly well succeeded in his evocations of the Middle Ages. He won a great reputation in Britain with his play, *Kong Renés Datter* (1845; Eng. trans. *King René's Daughter*, 1850).

**Hervieu, Paul Ernest** (1857–1915), French dramatist and novelist, was born at Neuilly-sur-Seine, and entered the diplomatic service. His first book was the novel *Diogène-le-Chien* (1882), and there followed sketches and stories of everyday life, such as in the collections *L'Inconnu* (1887), *Peints par eux-mêmes* (1893) and *L'Armature* (1895). He had already entered on that long association with the Comédie Française which was to last for over twenty years. Such plays, usually tragedies, as *Les Tenailles* (1895), *La Loi de l'homme* (1897), *La Course du flambeau* (1901) and *Le Dédale* (1903), his best, prove him to have been the last in the line of nineteenth-century French dramatists of society, such as Scribe (q.v.) and the younger Dumas (q.v.). Unlike them Hervieu has much pomposity but little vitality. He died in Paris. His *Théâtre complet* was published (4 vols.) between 1910 and 1922.

**Herwegh, Georg** (1817–1875), German poet. Born in Stuttgart, he soon became involved in the political movement which was to lead to the revolutions of 1848, and had to escape for a time to Switzerland. Joining forces with Freiligrath (q.v.) on his return to Germany he helped to overturn the lingering romantic movement and forced the younger poets to face up to realities. His *Gedichte eines Lebendingen* (2 vols., 1841, 1844) brought him fame and procured him an interview with the King of Prussia, in which the latter seemed ready to bargain with him. He was later exiled, but in 1848 led a band of French and German revolutionaries into Baden. This was the end of his poetical and political career. He died in Baden-Baden. His *Neue Gedichte* (1878) seem only the crumbs from under the table. See his *Werke* (3 vols., 1909).

**Herzen, Alexander Ivanovich** (1812–1870), Russian prose-writer. Born in Moscow, the illegitimate son of a wealthy lesser noble, he was educated at the university there, went into the civil service, and having been implicated in illegal political activities was sent to a remote part of Russia, but was allowed to return to Moscow in 1839. In 1847, feeling unable to continue to work effectively against the regime in Russia, he went into voluntary exile, finally settling in London in 1852. From 1855 to 1859 he edited *Polyarnaya zvezda* ('The Polar Star'), a literary journal which had a wide sale, while his radical newspaper, *Kolokol* (1857–65, 'The Bell'), was smuggled into Russia and had an influential following. As a political thinker he was in contact with all the leading revolutionaries and reformers in Europe. But he would hardly hold his place as a man of letters were it not for his *Byloe i dumy* (1861–7; Eng. trans. *My Past and Thoughts*, 6 vols., 1924–7). Herzen died in Paris.

**Hesse, Hermann** (1877–1962), German novelist, short-story writer and essayist. Born at Calw of a clerical family, he was expected to follow in his father's and grandfather's footsteps, but burst out into life along independent lines, becoming an engineering apprentice and later an assistant in a bookshop. He began to publish poetry in 1899, but it passed unnoticed, which was not the case with his romantic yet restrained novel *Peter Camenzind* (1904), the odyssey of an artist written in a prose without parallel in modern German fiction, Thomas Mann (q.v.) not excluded. So successful in fact was *Camenzind* that Hesse was able to live independently from then on, drawing on autobiography for such novels as *Gertrude* (1910; Eng. trans. *Gertrude and I*, 1915). His talent for the short story developed as was to be seen in his attractive collection, *In der alten Sonne* (1914; Eng. trans. *In the 'Old Sun'*, 1915). In 1912 he left Germany as a protest against its militarism and settled in Switzerland, remaining there for the rest of his life. *Demian* (1919; Eng. trans. 1923) was his next major novel and shows him delving deeper into character, but in *Der Steppenwolf* (1927; Eng. trans. *The Prairie-Wolf*, 1929) there was a falling off in quality due to his trying to suit his thought to the psychological idiom, popular at the time and invading literature. In *Narziss und Goldmund* (1930; Eng. trans. *Death and the Lover*, 1932) he seemed to have found his way back to the right path, the quest for harmony between opposing forces whether of character or atmosphere, while in *Morgenlandfahrt* (1932) he gave himself up to fantasies of delightful quality, deepened later in *Traumfähre* (1945), in which the dream world intrudes upon actuality. For a time he seemed to be experimenting in short stories as in the collections *Kleine Welt* (1933) and *Fabulierbuch* (1935), and then came his masterpiece, *Das Glasperlenspiel* (2 vols., 1943; Eng. trans. *Magister Ludi*, 1949), in which all his qualities are to be found: strength, tenderness, amazing awareness of every kind of beauty, the seeking after the harmony that is to unify all created things, expressed in prose capable of every kind of use to which it is put. After that he returned once more to the short story in books like *Der Pfirsichbaum* (1946). He had already expressed his fears for western civilization in *Blick ins Chaos* (1920; Eng. trans. *In Sight of Chaos*, 1923), and he now, after the Second World War, looked again at members of that civilization, what they stood for and what they might become, in *Der Europäer* (1946), a volume of thoughtful essays. Hesse and Thomas Mann stand together as without doubt the two greatest German novelists of this century. Hesse was awarded the Nobel Prize for literature in 1946. He died at Mantagnola.

**Heyermans, Herman** (1864–1924), Dutch playwright and novelist, using the pseudonyms of **I. van Jelakowitch, S. Falkland** and **K. Habbema,** was born in Rotterdam of Jewish family. A journalist and theatre director, he lived beyond his means and later in particular overwrote in order to gain the money he needed. Still, some of his work lasts, realistic and often dealing with Jewish subjects, e.g. the plays *Ahasverus* (1893; Eng. trans. *Ahasuerus*, 1934), *Op Hoop van zegen* (1901; Eng. trans. *The Good Hope*, 1928) and *De opgaande Zon*

(1908; Eng. trans. *The Rising Sun*, 1926), and the novels *Trinette* (1893) and *Diamantstad* (1898). He died at Zandvoort.

**Heyse, Paul Johann Ludwig von** (1830–1914), German short-story writer, novelist, poet and playwright. Born in Berlin of a well-known academic family, he went to Munich at the invitation of King Maximilian II of Bavaria in 1854, and apart from visits to Italy remained in Munich for the rest of his life. His literary career really began with the publication of the collection of short stories *L'Arrabiata* (1855; Eng. trans. 1867), and he then published two epics, *Die Braut von Cypern* (1856) and *Thekla* (1858), before returning to his most successful manner, the short story, with the collections, *Das Mädchen von Treppi* (1858; Eng. trans. *The Maiden of Treppi*, 1874) and *Andrea Delfin* (1859; Eng. trans. 1864), all invested with his love for Italy. He then turned to the stage and produced two plays at least which had some success, being written in well-polished style and satisfying dramatically, *Hans Lange* (1866) and *Colberg* (1868). His masterpiece, the full-length novel *Kinder der Welt* (2 vols., 1873; Eng. trans. *Children of the World*, 1882), was one of the finest of its time; and its main theme, the problem of the generation which grew up to face the bitter choice between materialism and the spiritual, science and religious orthodoxy, is handled with rare skill. A second novel, *Im Paradiese* (1876; Eng. trans. 1878), deals with the artistic world of Munich, but lacks the strong appeal of *Kinder*, while *Der Roman der Stiftsdame* (1886) is a veiled attack on all new literary movements, for Heyse mistrusted all things new), and as a work of true literature it fails. Meanwhile the flood of collections of short stories had never ceased, such as *Moralische Novellen* (series i, 1869; series ii, 1878), *Troubadour-Novellen* (1882) and *Das Buch der Freundschaft* (1883). A fine scholar in English, Spanish and Italian literature, he made many excellent translations from the literatures of these languages into German; but his finest memorial in the realm of scholarship is his *Italienische Dichter seit der Mitte des 18. Jahrhunderts* (5 vols., 1889–1905), containing felicitous translations and excellent commentaries. He was awarded the Nobel Prize for literature in 1910, the first German to be so honoured, and was ennobled the same year.

**Hilendarsky, Paissiy,** sometimes called **Otets** ('Father') **Paissiy** (1722–1793), Bulgarian prose-writer, born at Samokov. He became a monk on Mount Athos. Discovering in the library of his monastery some manuscripts dealing with early Bulgarian history, he wrote a history of his country based on this material, and then, leaving the monastery, went to Bulgaria, travelling through the land reading his work and allowing as many as cared to do so to copy from it (*c.* 1762). Long after his death these manuscript copies of the history passed from hand to hand, and it was not until 1844 that the master copy, that written by Hilendarsky himself, was published as *Istoriya Slavyanobolgarskaya* in Zagreb. It is written with spirit and good taste and judgment.

**Hippel, Theodor Gottlieb von** (1741–1796), German novelist and playwright, was born at Gerdauen, East Prussia, the son of a schoolmaster. At first he tried his hand fairly successfully with the writing of comedies, producing *Der Mann nach der Uhr* (1765) and *Die ungewöhnlichen Nebenbuhler* (1768). After this his career in the civil service took up more and more of his time, but he was able gradually to piece together his long rambling novel *Lebensläufe nach aufsteigender Linie* (4 vols., 1778–81), a mixture of the waywardly sentimental and the clear thought of the Enlightenment. Typical of his minor prose is *Über die bürgerliche Verbesserung der Weiber* (1792). In all his work there is evidence of a thorough understanding of men and society as befitted one who in 1780 became chief of police of Königsberg, in which city Hippel died.

**Hita, Arcipreste de,** *see* **Ruiz, J.**

**Hoel, Sigurd** (1890–1960), Norwegian novelist. Born at Nord-Odal, he became a schoolmaster. He entered the literary field in the mid 1920's, but it was not until *Syndere i sommersol* (1927; Eng. trans. *Sinners in Summertime*, 1930) that he gained a wide audience. His somewhat gloomy, problematical, introspective fiction was continued in such books as *En dag i oktober* (1931; Eng. trans. *One Day in October*, 1933). A later work is *Møte ved milepelen* (1947; Eng. trans. *Meeting at the Mile Stone*, 1951). His collected works appeared (8 vols.) in 1950. He died in Oslo.

**Hoffmann, August Heinrich,** known as **Hoffmann von Fallersleben** (1798–1874), German poet. Born at Fallersleben, in Lüneberg, he was appointed professor of German literature and language at Breslau in 1835, a post which he held until 1842 when he was dismissed for political poetry. His attractive, facile books of verse on love, wine, the fatherland and good fellowship entered deeply into the popular German mind, and much of the student mystique which gathered force during the nineteenth century was built up by Hoffmann. Among them may be numbered: *Bonner Burschenlieder* (1819), *Die Schöneberger Nachtigall* (1825), *Kirchhoflieder* (1827), *Jägerlieder* (1828), *Buch der Liebe* (1836), *Unpolitische Lieder* (2 vols., 1840–2), which, however, were interpreted as political and cost him his Breslau chair, *Deutsche Gassenlieder* (1843), *Fünfzig Kinderlieder* (1848), many of them excellent, and which have for a long time been treated as part of the repertoire of national nursery rhymes of origin far older than Hoffmann, and *Soldatenlieder* (1851). His famous 'Deutschland über alles' was written in 1841. He died at Corvei. Some of his poetry has been translated in J. Legge's *Rhyme and Revolution in Germany* (1918).

**Hoffmann, Ernst Theodor Wilhelm,** changing the last name to Amadeus in honour of Mozart (1776–1822), German novelist and short-story writer, was born of highly strung and ill-matched parents in Königsberg. He was educated at Königsberg University where he read law, and between 1796 and 1800 held official legal posts in Glogau, Berlin and Posen, in the last of which his propensity to satire landed him in trouble with his superiors, and he was degraded to a small post at Plozk on the Vistula. Forgiven in 1804, he was transferred to Warsaw, but he lost his office when the French occupied the city in 1806. When in 1808 he was appointed theatrical composer at the Bamberg opera house, and designer of costumes and scenery as well, he was able to show his talents in music and art. An admirable essay on Mozart's *Don Giovanni*, and early appreciations of Beethoven, prove his abilities as a music critic, while, although it was not until 1816 that his opera, *Undine* (*see* Fouqué), was staged at Berlin, he was busy at this time with several minor musical works. In 1814 he was able to return to his legal post in Berlin on the downfall of Napoleon; but his tastes had meanwhile grown extravagant and his income was insufficient for his needs. Furthermore he had been disappointed by what he now realized was his mediocrity as a musician, and then the red tape attached to his office irked him. From 1809 he had been trying his hand with short stories. He now collected them as *Fantasie-Stücke in Callots Manier* (vols. i and ii, 1814; vols. iii and iv, 1815), which gained him more attention than all his music put together. 'Jean Paul' Richter (q.v.) wrote the preface to them, and it was right that such a master of the grotesque and the whimsical should introduce such work. The reference to the French painter Jacques Callot (1594–1635) shows that Hoffmann felt that his own inspiration was in tune with this artist so preoccupied with the manners of his time, and with his idiosyncratic style. Already Hoffmann presents something quite his own, taut, vivid, with pictorial power and undertones leading towards the sinister. All these attributes of his work are brought into play in the full-length novel *Die Elixiere des Teufels* (2 vols., 1815–16), the central figure of which is a monk. This sounds like romanticism of the 1790's ('Monk' Lewis in England), until one realizes that eighteenth-century pathos and sentiment are absent. In the *Nachtstücke in Callots Manier* (2 vols., 1817) the sinister comes out of hiding with the horrible theme of the *alter ego* and the gruesome automata of Dr Coppelius (cf. *Coppélia*, the charming ballet of Delibes where this particular story has been relieved of all its darker side like a nursery edition of *Gulliver's Travels*). There followed *Seltsame Leiden eines Theater-Direktors* (1818) and *Klein Zaches, gennannt Zinnober* (1819), by which time we have reached the morbid. Gathering up all his short stories, some unpublished before, others already published, and adding to them many more, Hoffmann began to issue them as tales told to one another by members of a club, *Die Serapions-Brüder*, the first two volumes of which appeared in 1819–21 (Eng. trans. *The Serapion Brethren*, 2 vols., 1886, 1892), while four more volumes came out after his death, the last in 1825. Here as in 'Der Sandmann' and 'Das Fräulein von Scuderi' he reaches the height of his weird powers. In his last full-length work, however, *Lebensansichten des Katers Murr* (2 vols., 1820–2), which remained unfinished, a geniality appears and a maturity which has no place for the mannerisms sometimes marring his earlier work. Already he had fallen from a life of association with Chamisso (q.v.), Fouqué (q.v.) and other lights of the Berlin literary world to a round of dissipation, ending in a terrible spinal disease which literally reduced him to the size of a dwarf. Of this malady he died in Berlin. The Hoffmann manner was copied all over

Europe and became the basis for much of the neo-Gothic literature and even satanism which lasted for nearly half a century. The basic edition of his collected works is that by Ellinger (15 vols., 1912). His *Tagebücher* ('Diaries') are interesting. See the English translation (selected) *Tales of Hoffmann* (1951). Offenbach's opera is based on certain of the stories.

**Hoffmann, Heinrich** (1809–1894), German story writer for children. Born at Frankfurt-am-Main, he became a medical practitioner. He is remembered as the author of *Struwwelpeter* (1847), which he illustrated himself, and which has been translated into almost every European language. Of his other children's books the best is *König Nussknacker und der arme Reinhold* (1851). He died at Frankfurt-am-Main.

**Hofmannsthal, Hugo von** (1874–1929), Austrian poet, playwright, librettist and essayist. Born in Vienna of Jewish parentage, a fusion of German and Italian blood, he was precocious, writing good poetical dramas, such as *Der Tor und der Tod* (1893; Eng. trans. *Death and the Fool*, 1913), before he was twenty. Soon he became the leading force in the decadent culture which characterized the last years of imperial Austria. The verse play was continued in *Die Frau im Fenster* (1899), *Die Hochzeit der Sobeide* (1899; Eng. trans. *The Marriage of Sobeide*, 1913) and *Der Abenteurer und die Sängerin* (1899; Eng. trans. *The Adventurer and the Singer*, 1917); but it was with brilliant resettings of old themes such as *Das gerettete Venedig* (1905; Eng. trans. 1915), from Otway's *Venice Preserved*, and *Oedipus und die Sphinx* (1906), from Sophocles, that he became famous in Western Europe. *Christinas Heimreise* (1910; Eng. trans. *Christina's Journey Home*, 1917) revealed another kind of dramatic talent; but it is as the librettist of Richard Strauss's operas that he won permanent fame: *Elektra* (1903; Eng. trans. 1908), *Der Rosenkavalier* (1911; Eng. trans. 1912), *Ariadne auf Naxos* (1912; Eng. trans. 1913) and *Die Frau ohne Schatten* (1916). In other departments he had also been active, collecting his lyrics, *Gesammelte Gedichte*, which show the influence of Stefan George (q.v.), in 1907, and publishing a series of excellently written and interesting essays, *Die prosäischen Schriften* (3 vols., 1907–17). His later dramatic work shows a marked change in style towards symbolism, as is to be seen in *Der Schwierige* (1921), *Das Salzburger grosse Welttheater* (1922) and *Der Turm* (1927). He died at Rodaun.

**Hofmannswaldau, Christian Hofmann von** (1617–1679), German poet and prose-writer. Born in Breslau, he came under the influence of Opitz (q.v.) at school in Danzig, and during his European travels imbibed the style of work made popular by the Italians Guarini (q.v.), whose *Pastor Fido* Hofmann was to translate into German in 1678, and Marini (q.v.). A strange character, perhaps what we should now term a split personality, he could publish religious poetry such as *Hundert Grabschriften* (1643) as readily as the highly sensual work of what is generally thought of as his most characteristic volume, *Heldenbriefe* (1663; new ed. 1680), a collection of verse and prose love epistles, sometimes titillating, but often ridiculously blown up imitations of Ovid or rather Aristaenetus. He died in Breslau. The collection of his work and that of some of his contemporary poets of the 'Silesian School' made by B. Neukirch as *Herrn von Hofmannswaldau und anderer Deutschen auserlesene und bissher ungedruckte Gedichte* (7 vols., 1695–1727), a kind of Dryden's *Miscellany*, is generally regarded as the low-water mark of German poetry.

**Hojeda, Diego de** (1571–1615), Spanish epic poet. Born in Seville, he joined the Dominicans, sailed for the New World and was in Lima in 1591. His one work is *La Christiada* (1611), an epic ranging from the Last Supper to the Crucifixion, nobly conceived and finely executed (mod. ed., 1935). Hojeda died at Huanaco, Peru.

**Holbach, Paul Heinrich Dietrich d'** (1723–1789), French prose-writer. Born into a family of German origin at Heidelsheim, Baden, he settled in Paris, where he died. A member of the circle of the Encyclopédistes, he held markedly anti-religious views and stated that self-interest is the guiding principle of men's actions. *Le Système de la nature* (1770) was a work of the very widest influence. *Le Système social* (1773) is of significance as showing the climate of political thought growing up in Paris where scientific philosophy was being drawn to its ultimate conclusions.

**Holberg, Ludvig af** (1684–1754), Danish playwright, poet and prose-writer. Born at Bergen, in Norway, where his father, who was in the army, was stationed, he was left an orphan when still very young, but managed to go to Copenhagen where he attended the university, and afterwards taught. Making the most of his slender resources he was able to travel in Europe, visiting Britain in 1706 and staying in London and Oxford for eighteen months, although it was in Paris that the full impact of European culture struck him. His stay in Rome (1714–16) may be said to have completed his education. On returning to Denmark he realized how narrow was its literary life and thought, how pedantic was its academic life and how badly treated was the despised Danish language. It was his conviction that the doors should be opened and that Denmark should become a lively modern centre of European culture, and should be given the dignity of a literary tongue in its own right. In 1717 he was given a university chair at Copenhagen. A new phase of his life began with the publication in 1719 of the mock-heroic poem *Peder Paars*, a clever satire on the false and petty conventions of the time (mod. ed., 1949). Intent upon putting his theories into practice he next devoted his energy to creating a national drama. He directed the newly opened Royal Theatre in Copenhagen and for it wrote thirty-two comedies in five years; in 1727 the theatre closed through lack of support, although Holberg worked hard for its reopening and succeeded in bringing this about twenty years later. Of these comedies the most famous are *Erasmus Montanus* and *Jeppe paa Bjerget*. Molière's (q.v.) influence is there, but Holberg is great enough to make everything his own. (Of the many English translations of the best of these plays the most attractive are those by H. W. L. Hime, 1912;

O. J. Campbell and F. Schenk, 1914; and H. Alexander, 1946 and 1950.) His appointment to the chair of history, his favourite subject, in 1730 ushered in the third and last stage of Holberg's life. There followed a number of sound works on historical and geographical subjects—hardly literature, however. But in 1741 he produced a classic in the satirico-comic romance *Nicolai Klimii Iter Subterraneum* (Eng. trans. *A Journey to the World Under-Ground*, 1742). His *Moralske Tanker* (1744; mod. ed., 1943) is a model of Danish prose, and his *Epistler* (5 vols., 1748–54; mod. ed., 6 vols., 1944–51) are of much interest. His posthumous *Memoirer*, written at intervals between 1727 and 1743 (mod. ed., 1943), was translated into English as *Memoirs of Ludvig Holberg* (1827). His writings had gained him considerable wealth and he had acquired a sizeable estate. This, together with a large sum of money, he made over to the nation for educational purposes in 1747, and the same year he was made a baron. He died in Copenhagen.

**Hölderlin, Johann Christian Friedrich** (1770–1843), German poet and prose-writer. Born at Lauffen, in Württemberg, the son of a Lutheran Church bailiff, who died shortly after his birth, he was educated for the pastorate first at Maulbronn and afterwards at the University of Tübingen, where he knew Schelling (q.v.) and Hegel (q.v.), and from which he graduated Master of Theology in 1793. He now refused to enter the Church and became a private tutor to the children of Charlotte von Kalb, on the recommendation of Schiller (q.v.), who had befriended Hölderlin and who published some fragments from his future prose poem, *Hyperion*, in his literary journal, *Neue Thalia*, between 1793 and 1795. His time with the Kalb family was happy, but in 1794 he left them on amicable terms and went to Jena to see what Schiller could do for him, remaining there for nearly a year. It was because he found himself overwhelmed by Schiller's personality that he left Jena and returned to his home. At the very end of 1795 he became a private tutor once more, this time to the children of a wealthy Frankfurt banker J. F. Gontard, with whose wife Susette he fell deeply in love. Idolizing her as Diotima (after Plato), Hölderlin found his inspiration and here he wrote *Hyperion, oder der Eremit in Griechenland* (vol. i, 1797; vol. ii, 1799), published by Cotta on Schiller's advice. This long novel, or rather series of prose poems of the greatest beauty, is set in Greece at the time of the unsuccessful revolt against the Turks in 1770. Into it he puts much of his feeling of disillusionment at the disappointing course which the French Revolution, hailed with delight by him and his fellow students at Tübingen at its beginning, had taken. In the autumn of 1798 the liaison with 'Diotima' came to an abrupt end, and he suddenly left Frankfurt, dismissed, it has been generally said, from his post, though some say he went of his own free will. He went to Homberg, where friends rallied round him and where he wrote some of his finest lyric poetry. Money ran out, more tutorships followed, in Switzerland and even in Bordeaux, at the last of which a request that he should also preach in the private chapel of the Hamburg consul, who was his employer, brought on an attack of long-delayed madness. In 1806

he became permanently insane and so remained until his death at the
house of a cabinet-maker, to whom he had been entrusted by his
friends, in Tübingen. Hölderlin's earlier verse is in the rhymed, neo-
classical metres of Schiller, but his great lyrics and odes belong to the
later period. Here he exploits to the full the amazing suitability of
the German language for ancient Greek metres. He is reflective, pantheistic, pessimistic; life is short and is often spent by the few who
feel anything in longing for a Golden Age which is lost for ever.
'Hyperions Schicksalslied' (1798, 'Hyperion's Song About Destiny')
exactly describes his view of life, contrasting the blessed 'fateless
Celestials' with the mortals below who are like water 'hurtled from
boulder to boulder'. Others, among the greatest in the German language, are: 'An die Parzen' (1798, 'To the Fates'), 'Des Morgens'
(1798, 'Morning'), 'Abendphantasie' (1799, 'Evening Fantasy'),
'Mein Eigentum' (1800, 'My Lot'), 'Wie wenn am Feiertage' (1800,
'As When on Holiday'), 'An die Hoffnung' (1801, 'To Hope') and
'Hälfte des Lebens' (1805, 'Half of Life'). Two, 'Brot und Wein'
(1801, 'Bread and Wine')—dedicated to Wilhelm Heinse (q.v.),
whose *Ardinghello* (1787) influenced the plan of *Hyperion*, and whom
Hölderlin met in 1796—and *Patmos* (1802), stand apart by reason not
only of their length but their wider scope, the first with splendid
descriptions of the everyday world contrasted with the ideal one,
the second rich in symbolism. None of these poems were collected
until Uhland (q.v.), with the help of Schwab, an old friend of
Hölderlin, brought out the *Gedichte* in 1826, the first collected edition
of all his works following (2 vols.) in 1846. The six-volume critical
edition of 1919–23 was the first of true value, and indeed prior to
the 1914 war Hölderlin was little known. After 1945 Hölderlin, who
had himself condemned Germans as 'barbarians from of old', came
into wide favour. Beissner's edition (8 vols., 1946) is likely to be
definitive. Good English translations of the poems are those by J. B.
Leishman (1944) and M. Hamburger (second ed., 1952).

**Holtei, Karl von** (1798–1880), German writer of plays, operettas,
novels and poetry, was a native of Breslau. After a life of wandering
he settled in Breslau as theatre manager, and there died. His poetry,
*Schlesische Gedichte* (1830), is of small account, but his light plays
and operettas, including *Die Wiener in Berlin* (1845) and *Die Berliner
in Wien* (1846), have their attractions. Of his lengthy novels *Die
Vagabunden* (4 vols., 1842) and *Christian Lamsell* (5 vols., 1852)
contain elements of autobiography, and have passages which could
be shown to advantage if the books were severely cut.

**Holthusen, Hans Egon** (1913–      ), German poet and critic. Born at
Rendsburg, Schleswig-Holstein, son of a pastor, as a poet he followed
in the wake of T. S. Eliot, coming to full maturity in such works as
*Hier in der Zeit* (1949) and *Labyrinthische Jahre* (1952). His works on
Rilke (q.v.), especially *Der Späte Rilke* (1949; Eng. trans. *R. M.
Rilke. A Study of his later Poetry*, 1952), are of great value. Among
his latest works are *R. M. Rilke* (1958) and *Kritisches Verstehen.
Neue Aufsätze zur Literatur* (1961).

**Hölty, Ludwig Heinrich Christoph** (1748–1776), German poet. Born, the son of a pastor, at Mariensee, he grew up into a delicate and winning person, who gained many friends when he went to the University of Göttingen as a theological student, chief of them Boie (q.v.), who encouraged him to contribute his sad, gentle, technically so satisfying lyrics to the Göttingen *Musenalmanach*. His recurrent, beautifully expressed theme is the shortness of precarious life like the swallow-time and blue sky of that lovely month of May, which, sensing its shortness, we cannot enjoy without a touch of sadness even when it is here. He died of tuberculosis in Hanover, and his poetical works were gathered as *Sämtliche hinterlassene Gedichte* (2 vols., 1782), followed by *Gedichte* (1783). See the modern edition, *Werke* (2 vols., 1914, 1918).

**Holz, Arno** (1863–1929), German poet, playwright and critic, was born at Rastenburg. As a critic (*Die Kunst, ihr Wesen und ihre Gesetze*, 1891) he paved the way for the naturalists. His own earlier plays have now only historical interest, although his later ones, such as *Traumulus* (1904), *Sonnenfinsternis* (1908) and *Ignorabimus* (1913), are still very readable—and actable. It is, however, as a poet that he has lasted, especially in the volumes *Phantasus* (1898) and *Daphnis* (1914). He died in Berlin. His collected works were published (12 vols.) in 1926.

**Hooft, Pieter Corneliszoon** (1581–1647), Dutch playwright, poet and historian. Born in Amsterdam of a rich family, he was made steward of Muiden Castle in 1609. Here he gathered round him the so-called Muiden Circle, consisting of the best men of letters, artists, musicians and scholars, the very flower of that Netherlands golden age. As a playwright he is represented by his tragedy *Theseus en Ariadne* (1614), as a poet by *Granida* (1615), while his *De Nederlandsche Historien* (1642) is not only great as history, but is written in a splendid Dutch prose. He died in The Hague.

**Hora, Josef** (1891–1945), Czech poet. Born at Dobřín, he expressed his belief in Communism in two collections of lyrics, *Pracující den* (1920, 'The Working Day') and *Bouřlivé jaro* (1923, 'Tempestuous Spring'); but he was to come face to face with realities which put such theories to flight, and when the German annexation (1938) broke over him it was domestic warmth and love and not doctrines that he prized (*Domov*, 'Home'). His finest work was the epic set in old Bohemia, *Jan houslista* (1939, 'John the Fiddler'), a world of the past to which he had escaped from the hideous present. He died in Prague.

**Hostovský, Egon** (1908–      ), Czech novelist, born at Hronov. His work is steeped in the sorrows and horrors of dictatorships and consequent persecutions and war. Foremost among them are *Listy z vyhnanství* (1941; Eng. trans. *Letters from Exile*, 1942) and *Úkryt* (1943; Eng. trans. *The Hideout*, 1945).

**Houssaye, Arsène** (1815–1896), French man of letters. Born at Bruyères (Aisne), he was successful with his first novel *La Couronne de Bluets* (1836). His *L'Histoire du 41ᵐᵉ fauteuil de l'académie française* (1855) showed his ability to write effective satire, while he reached maturity as a novelist with *La Comédie à la fenêtre* (1859). He was also an esteemed art critic, the best of his publications in this line being *Léonard de Vinci* (1869). He was director of the Théâtre Français from 1849 to 1859, and died in Paris. His son Henri (1848–1911) was a well-regarded ancient historian.

**Huch, Friedrich** (1873–1913), German novelist. Born in Brunswick, he found his spiritual home in Munich, where he died. His novels, with their weird, uncomfortable atmosphere, dream and reality intermingling, peopled with half-drawn characters, consist of *Peter Michel* (1901), *Die Geschwister* (1903), *Mao* (1907), *Pitt und Fox* (1909, cf. the play *Pitt und Fox* by R. von Gottschall, q.v.), particularly interesting to British readers and making a great but not always satisfactory feature of contrasted characters, and *Enzio* (1911).

**Huch, Ricarda** (1864–1947), German poet, novelist and general prose-writer. Born in Brunswick, she made her first impact on the public with her novel, *Erinnerungen von Ludolf Ursleu dem Jüngeren* (1892; Eng. trans. *Recollections of Ludolf Ursleu the Younger*, 1913), sceptical and dry, even hard, unusual for a young woman writer in those days, and the same approach to life and belief is continued in *Fra Celeste* (1899) and *Aus der Triumphgasse* (1902). Her correct neo-classical lyrics in *Neue Gedichte* (1907) and *Liebesgedichte* (1912) seem hardly able to bear the weight of passion. She was at her best, and at that her very best, in evocations of history, in which her vision and her scholarship combine to form works of art as in *Die Geschichten von Garibaldi* (2 vols., 1906–7; Eng. trans., 2 vols., 1928–9), and *Luthers Glaube* (1916), her confession of her newly found Protestant faith. *Der Fall Deruga* (1917; Eng. trans. *The Deruga Trial*, 1929), is one of the classics of detective fiction. Later she concerned herself more and more with the essay form, being especially interested in politics (*Michael Bakunin und die Anarchie*, 1923, and *Die Revolution des 19. Jahrhundert in Deutschland*, 1944), social history (*Im alten Reich. Lebensbilder deutscher Städte*, 2 vols., 1927–8) and philosophy (*Urphänomene*, 1946), in all of which she writes with masculine crispness and directness. She died at Schönberg. She is considered the leading German woman writer of her generation.

**Huet, Conrad Busken** (1826–1886), Dutch prose-writer. Born in The Hague, he entered the Church, left it, turned journalist and proved reactionary, especially in his attitude towards the East Indies. He settled in Paris in 1876, and freed from surroundings which had troubled him personally, he was able to develop as a writer, but even then he cannot be said to have produced anything of truly lasting quality except those evocations of the history of art, *Het Land van Rubens* (1879; Eng. trans. *The Land of Rubens*, 1888) and *Het Land van Rembrandt* (3 vols., 1882–4). He died in Paris.

Hugo, Victor-Marie (1802–1885), French poet, playwright and novelist, was born in Besançon of mixed Lorrainer and Breton blood. His
father, General Léopold-Sigisbert Hugo, attached himself to Joseph
Bonaparte and took his family with him to Italy and Spain. In 1811
General Hugo was made Governor of Madrid and sent his son to the
College of Nobles, but with the downfall of Joseph Bonaparte and the
crumbling away of French power in Spain in 1812, General Hugo lost
his governorship and the boy was removed from his aristocratic
surroundings. After the empire collapsed in 1814 Victor carried with
him throughout his life a memory of the Napoleonic age which he had
barely glimpsed and which with time became a vision colouring much
of his work. Now in reduced circumstances the parents separated on
bad terms, the mother taking her children to Paris while General Hugo
went to live at Blois. In spite of Madame Hugo's strict royalism,
Victor grew into a strong opponent of the Bourbons, tempering his
nostalgia for the vanished empire with democratic leanings. His
education at the Pension Cordier was superficial but stimulated his
fondness for reading, and in 1816 he declared that his ambition was to
be Chateaubriand (q.v.) and failing that nothing, a remark which is
probably to be interpreted as admiration for that writer's romantic
conception of religion, nature and politics. He turned his back on
proposals for a military career and on the death of his cold, decided
mother in 1821 definitely embarked on an author's life, and, refusing
his father's offer of financial help, plunged into the literary world of
Paris. Life was hard, his mother's advice returned to him, and he was
not above flattering the court in the hope of advancement, as is to be
seen in such stiff, classical volumes of verse as *Odes et poésies diverses*
(1822), *Nouvelles Odes* (1824) and *Odes et Ballades* (1826), the three
volumes being collected and published together under the latter title
in 1828. At the same time he sought a wider public with the horror
stories *Han d'Islande* (1823) and *Bug-Jargal* (1826). He had married
in 1822 the beautiful but unintelligent Adèle Foucher, who later was
momentarily involved in an unedifying love affair with Sainte-Beuve
(q.v.). By 1825 he had so won the favour of the court, which was
already paying him a considerable pension, that Charles X made him
a Chevalier of the Legion of Honour. But friendship with Lamartine
(q.v.) and Nodier (q.v.) now began to change his literary opinions
and his first published play *Cromwell* (1827), with its famous Preface,
in which he repudiated Boileau (q.v.), became the rallying point for
the rising romantics. In *Les Orientales* (1828), in which he celebrated
the Greek War of Independence, not only did he show a mastery of
lyric forms unrivalled in French literature since Ronsard (q.v.) and
the Pléiade, but he revealed a new political feeling towards democracy.
The year 1830 found him ready for great changes. Early in the year
his claims for romantic drama were put to the test and were triumphantly vindicated with *Hernani*, the '*bataille d'Hernani*', literally
fought out in the Théâtre Français. He was now the acknowledged
leader of the romantic movement. In July the demagogic and near
republican Victor Hugo threw in his lot with the tolerant regime of
Louis-Philippe. He was now in his literary element. First came his
great historical novel, *Notre-Dame de Paris* (1831), which was followed

by a volume of lyrics, *Feuilles d'Automne* (1831), the plays *Marion de Lorme* (1831), *Le Roi s'amuse* (1832) and *Lucrèce Borgia* (1833), *Claude Gueux* (1834), which more eloquently than *Le Dernier Jour d'un condamné* (1829) attacked capital punishment and showed the author's humanitarianism, the play *Angelo, Tyran de Padoue* (1835), *Les Chants du crépuscule* (1835), poems, *La Esmeralda* (1835), an opera libretto, *Les Voix intérieures* (1837), another volume of verse proving still greater mastery, *Ruy Blas* (1838), a drama, and *Les Rayons et les ombres* (1840), his finest collection of poetry to date. As his poetry increased in value, so his plays declined and *Les Burgraves* (1843) failed on the stage, after which, although he continued to write drama until the end of his life (collected as *Théâtre en liberté*, 1886), his best work is to be found in poetry and the novel. The tragic death of his daughter Léopoldine (1843), and his entanglement in politics from 1845, when he was made a peer by Louis-Philippe, halted his literary activities. Now a convinced republican, he was elected to the Assembly under the Second Republic (1848) and even stood for the presidency, although without success. At the *coup d'état* of Louis Napoleon (1851) he went into exile first in Jersey, and then in 1855 settled in Guernsey, where he remained until Napoleon's fall in 1870. In the Channel Islands he returned to authorship with the satire on the new emperor, *Napoléon-le-Petit* (1852), a theme to which he was eventually to return in 1877 in *L'Histoire d'un Crime*. But pride of place for his work of these years goes to his two fine volumes of poetry *Les Châtiments* (1853), which shows him as a political idealist and fighter, and above all *Les Contemplations* (1856), in which we see the apotheosis of the poet become seer. *La Fin de Satan* and *Dieu*, written at this period but not published until 1886 and 1891 respectively, venture into the mystical. Then came the first part of the ambitious epic, *La Légende des siècles* (1859), the second part appearing in 1877 and the third in 1883. Three great novels also belong to the time of his exile, *Les Misérables* (1862, begun as early as 1848), full of broad humanity and compassion, *Les Travailleurs de la Mer* (1866), with its gigantic seascapes set in the Channel Islands, and *L'Homme qui rit* (1869). His semi-autobiographical *Victor Hugo raconté par un témoin de sa vie* (1863) and the coarse verse of *Les Chansons des rues et des bois* (1865) cannot be said to have been successful. These outwardly peaceful, but increasingly unhappy nineteen years of exile (for his wife and family had deserted him) ended in 1870 when the Third Republic was proclaimed and he returned in triumph to Paris. There, after the brief period which he spent in Brussels during the Commune, he remained for the rest of his life, being elected senator in 1878, and publishing *Actes et paroles* (1875–6), public speeches and funeral orations, and particularly *L'Art d'être Grandpère* (1877), a delightful work. His theological and quasi-philosophical books, such as *La Pitié suprême* (1879) and *L'Âme* (1880), hardly call for notice, and the volume of verse *Les Quatre Vents de l'esprit* (1881) and the drama *Torquemada* (1882) show the failing of an aged mind. His death in Paris from pneumonia was followed by an impressive funeral and burial in the Panthéon. As a dramatist Hugo has not stood the test of time, as a novelist he holds a reputation with a wide public, but it is as a poet that he has made his most abiding contribution to literature, even if one accepts that beauty often means more to him than thought. But then the poet need not be an intellectual. Energy, humanity, faith in its widest application and optimism carry him everywhere, and though not of the highest rank of men of letters he is a very good second, and can from many standpoints be appreciated by men of widely differing views and tastes. The standard edition of his works is the *Édition de l'Imprimerie Nationale* (46 vols., 1880–5). All his main works have been translated into English, the great novels appearing in countless editions.

**Humboldt, Friedrich Heinrich Alexander von** (1769–1859), German prose-writer, born of noble family in Berlin, his father being chamberlain at the Prussian court. He devoted himself to science and in 1792 became assessor of mines, giving up that post in 1799 to explore South America, making important discoveries, geographical, geological and meteorological, returning to Europe in 1804, and settling in Paris for some time. His publications were numerous and important, but until late in life he produced nothing that can be considered literature; yet in 1845 he began, after further scientific journeys, this time to the Urals, Altai and Caspian, his marvellously conceived encyclopaedic work, *Kosmos* (4 vols., 1845–58), written in lucid and majestic prose. In it he not only demonstrated the breadth of his knowledge, but showed his grasp of the whole range of the scientific achievements of his time, the while reconciling eighteenth-century idealism and nineteenth-century research. He died in Berlin. R. H. Stoddard's *The Life, Travels and Books of Alexander von Humboldt* (1860) is a useful guide to the understanding of his achievements, while his correspondence with Goethe (1876), whom he had first met in his youth at Weimar, shows how he stood in relation to the men of letters of his time.

**Humboldt, Karl Wilhelm von** (1767–1835), German philologist. Born at Potsdam, the elder brother of F. H. A. von Humboldt (q.v.), he entered the Prussian civil service, travelled much, associated with Goethe, Schiller and the Weimar circle, and in 1802 was made ambassador in Rome. Returning to Prussia in 1808, the next year he was appointed minister of public instruction, and was the virtual founder of the University of Berlin (1810). His influence on German national education was profound and lasting, and he may be said to have set the seal on the scientific approach to scholarship, which by turning culture to practical ends gave German universities their commanding position in Europe during the nineteenth century. From 1810 when he went to Vienna as plenipotentiary until 1819, when reaction set in and virtually drove him into retirement, he was one of the leading politicians of Europe. But it was when he settled down in the latter year in his castle at Tegel to a life of studious retirement that he made his name as one of the greatest philologists of modern times, especially with his work on the Basque language and on the languages of Java. Earlier, in his *Ästhetische Versuche* (1799), he had provided a model of literary criticism without parallel in his day, and he was a brilliant Greek scholar and translator. He died at Tegel. The standard edition of his works is that of 1903–36 (16 vols.).

**Hus(s), Jan** (1369?–1415), Bohemian (Czech) prose-writer, writing also in Latin. The great reformer was born of peasant family at Husinetz (Husineć)—Hus being a contraction of this—in southern Bohemia. Having graduated at the University of Prague he taught there, was ordained, and in 1402 was rector of the university, and about the same time began to win a reputation with his sermons preached in the Bethlehem Chapel (*Sermones in Bethlehem*, mod. ed., 1938–42). Invited in bad faith by the emperor to attend the Council of Constance in 1414 he went, relying on Sigismund's promise of safe conduct, but immediately on arrival was taken and imprisoned at Constance. Here, awaiting trial which the following summer was to end at the stake in Constance, he wrote the best of his vivid letters (Eng. trans. *John Hus, Letters with Introductions and Explanatory Notes*, 1904). His Czech works (*M. J. Husi Sebrané spisy české*, 3 vols., 1865–8) sometimes reproduce almost word for word passages from his acknowledged master John Wyclif.

**Hutten, Ulrich von** (1488–1523), German humanist writing in Latin. Born of noble family at Steckelberg Castle, in Hesse-Nassau, he was sent to the Benedictine monastery school at Fulda, which he left in 1505 after a good education to lead a wandering, turbulent life and throw in his lot with rebels against the papacy and in fact anything clerical. A typical German nationalist, his image as the romantic tilter against great odds is not borne out by the facts; but some of his work has enormous spirit, such as the lively letters that he contributed to the second part of the famous *Epistolae Obscurorum Virorum* (1517; Eng. trans. 1909), in which he mocks at unworthy priests and pedants, and his two short autobiographies, *Fortuna* and *Febris* (both 1519). On the other hand, his Lucianic dialogue against the papacy, *Vadiscus* (1520), has something brutal about it, and his fulsome praise of Emperor and German people in *Arminius* (1524) is unpleasant and boded ill for the course of the coming Reformation in Germany. Mistrusted by Luther (q.v.), to whom he had proffered his services, and driven from the empire by Charles V, he went to hide his head in Basel, where Erasmus (q.v.) received him coldly. At last granted shelter on Ufenau Island on Lake Zürich with the help of Zwingli, he died there of syphilis. His collected works appeared in seven volumes (1859–70).

**Huysmans, Joris-Karl** (1848–1907), French novelist and general prose-writer. Born in Paris of a Dutch father and a French mother, he became a civil servant and remained so for thirty years, writing in his leisure hours. Beginning as a follower of the Baudelaire (q.v.) of the *Petits poèmes en prose* with *Le Drageoir aux épices* (1874), he turned soon for models to the Goncourts (q.v.) and Zola (q.v.), and produced in their realist manner his first novel *Marthe* (1876), while *Les Sœurs Vatard* (1879) is dedicated to Zola. By this time the naturalist school had come into being and Huysmans's literary crusade in Zola's cause did much to bring this about. But by 1884, the date of

*À rebours* (Eng. trans. *Against the Grain*, 1920; *Against Nature*, 1965), his masterpiece, he had turned back to Baudelaire, feeling that realism was ignoring the spiritual aspect of contemporary life, and in this remarkable book he explored satanism (cf. Barbey d'Aurévilly, q.v.) as a possible means of elucidating this problem. This stage is continued in *Là-Bas* (1891). With *En Route* (1895) Huysmans reached his final stage—he had become a Catholic in 1892—of mysticism, which was further developed in *La Cathédrale* (1898) and *L'Oblat* (1903). He also wrote some books on art criticism and devotional works. His style is of extreme originality. He died in Paris.

**Ibn Ezra, Abraham ben Me'ir** (1092–1167), Spanish Hebrew poet and scholar. Born at Tudela (Navarre), he left Spain in his forties and led a wandering life mostly in Italy and the south of France, and visited London in 1158. He returned to Spain, however, at the very end of his life, dying at Calahorra (Logroño). His poetry is of two kinds, the secular, light and of little account, although he displays in it a great deal of humour, and the liturgical, deeply philosophical. One of the finest Jewish minds of the Middle Ages, lack of self-discipline never allowed him to fulfil himself. All that he wrote shows near genius, and the nervous style, even though usually revealing signs of haste, is effective. He wrote on Hebrew grammar, astrology and mathematics, but his most ambitious work is his commentary on the Old Testament. As a philosopher he was a neo-Platonist. Part of his work on the Bible was published at Naples in 1488. There is a German edition and translation of his poetry by D. Rosin (*Reime und Gedichte*, 5 vols., 1884–96), and see L. Thorndike's *The Latin Translations of the Astrological Tracts of Abraham Avenezra* (1945).

**Ibn Ezra, Moses** (1060–1139), Spanish Hebrew poet and literary critic, was born at Granada and died at a place unknown in the north of Spain. For many years he was a rich and influential official at the court of Granada. As a poet he is considered one of the finest of that fine age of Spanish Hebrew literature, and as a critic his review of Spanish Hebrew poetry written in Arabic, the *Kitāb*, is our only authentic account of the subject. A translation of some of his poetry, *Selected Poems* by S. Solis-Cohen, appeared in 1934. The *Kitāb* remains unpublished, but a Hebrew translation of it, *Shirath Yisrael* by B. Halper, was published in 1924.

**Ibsen, Henrik Johan** (1828–1906), Norwegian playwright and poet, was born at Skien, in south Norway, the son of a wealthy business man who lost his money in 1836, after which the family lived in near poverty, and the boy became an apprentice in a chemist's shop in 1843. Literature was his hobby, and in 1849, having published a volume of second-rate love-poetry and some caustic epigrams, he decided to go to Kristiania (Oslo) to try to enter the university. He did so, but soon tired of the academic work and found his way into political and theatrical circles. In 1850 he published with the monetary help of a friend his first play, the tragedy *Catilina* (Eng. trans. 1921), but could not get it performed. But he had better success with his short historical play, called *Kjæmpehøjen* (Eng. trans. *The Warrior's Barrow*, 1921), which was acted in Kristiania the same year, and led to his being appointed director of the theatre at Bergen in 1851. He was now in his element and it was here that he learned his craft. Among the dramas of the Bergen period should be named *Olaf Liljekrans* (1856; Eng. trans. 1921), and with *Fru Inger til Østeraad* (1857; Eng. trans. *Lady Inger of Ostraat*) he may be said to have entered his maturity. In 1857 he returned to Kristiania to become director of the Norske Theater. He continued his historical plays with *Hærmændene paa Helgeland* (1858; Eng. trans. *The Vikings at Helgeland*), in which year he married, but with *Kjærlighedens Komedie* (1862; Eng. trans. *Love's Comedy*), a verse-play, satirizing the conventions of love and marriage, he broke new ground, coming forward as a fearless social critic. The play scandalized the public, which boycotted the theatre, and to avert the danger of its complete collapse Ibsen returned to his former historical style, producing his powerful *Kongsemnerne* (1864; Eng. trans. *The Pretenders*), which was a success. But he was tiring of the stifling provincial atmosphere of Kristiania and eagerly accepted the travel grant now offered to him, leaving at once for Rome. With the additional poet's pension awarded him in 1866 he was free of pressing financial troubles, and was able to settle down to write as he wished. The first results of this welcome change were the verse plays *Brand* (1866) and *Peer Gynt* (1867), full of wild, powerful imagination, which made him immensely popular with his countrymen. But those who thought that his conscience was now tamed were mistaken. Living in either Italy or Germany until he returned to Norway in 1891, Ibsen now let loose on the astonished Norwegian playgoers a torrent of prose dramas with their devastating social criticism which began with *De unges Forbund* (1869; Eng. trans. *The League of Youth*) and continued with *Samfundets Støtter* (1877; Eng. trans. *The Pillars of Society*), *Et Dukkehjem* (1879; Eng. trans. *A Doll's House*), *Gengangere* (1881; Eng. trans. *Ghosts*), *En Folkefiende* (1882; Eng. trans. *An Enemy of the People*), *Vildanden* (1884; Eng. trans. *The Wild Duck*), *Rosmersholm* (1886), and *Fruen fra Havet* (1888; Eng. trans. *The Lady from the Sea*). In these plays there is an increasing use of symbolism after *En Folkefiende*. Outstandingly different from these is his great historical play with its powerful analysis of character and spiritual thought, *Kejser og Galilæer* (1873; Eng. trans. *Emperor and Galilean*), a study of the Roman emperor Julian the Apostate. At the end of his self-imposed exile Ibsen wrote that masterpiece *Hedda Gabler* (1890), a domestic drama of Kristiania life. On his return to Norway in 1891 he started on that final phase of his work, often autobiographical in inspiration, which includes *Bygmester Solness* (1892; Eng. trans. *The Master Builder*) and *John Gabriel Borkman* (1896). His genius was by now acknowledged throughout northern Europe, and two outstanding works on him, G. B. Shaw's *The Quintessence of Ibsenism* (1891) and Georg Brandes's (q.v.) *Henrik Ibsen* (1898), added to the general acceptance of the master. His work was done. For the four years previous to his death in Kristiania he was in a state of almost complete mental and physical collapse, the price he paid for years of unending nervous energy, so deeply did he associate himself with his creativeness. His influence on the European theatre was profound. He not only broke away from accepted theatrical rules, but he made people think beyond the present, turning values inside out. Nothing but love in its fullest sense was sacred and nothing evil except the denial of love. W. Archer's *The Collected Works of Henrik Ibsen* (12 vols., 1906–12) comprises English translations of practically everything he wrote. *The Oxford Ibsen* (ed. J. W. MacFarlane) is in progress.

**Iffland, August Wilhelm** (1759–1814), German dramatist. He was born into comfortable circumstances at Hanover, but left home early to join a company of strolling players. He became one of the greatest actors of the day, and it was when he was a leading tragedian at the famous Mannheim theatre that he met Schiller. From then on he acted in all his plays, and Schiller could not have found a better interpreter. A German Garrick, he had an unerring eye for stage technique, his own sentimental plays, such as *Die Jäger* (1785), being very actable, while he had a true turn for comedy, as his skit on the craze for magnetism, *Der Magnetismus* (1787), proves. His dramatic works were published in sixteen volumes between 1798 and 1802, which rose to twenty-four volumes in the definitive edition of 1843. He died in Berlin.

**Iglesias de la Casa, José** (1748–1791), Spanish satirical poet, was born and died in Salamanca, having become a priest in 1783. None of his work is first rate, but as commentaries on the social life of the Spain of his day many of his satires are incomparable. No collection was made until the latter part of the last century, and his work is most readily available in the *Biblioteca de Autores Españoles*, vol. lxi. English translations of some of his poems are to be found in T. Walsh's *Hispanic Anthology* (1920).

**Ilf**, i.e. **Ilya Arnoldovich Feisilber** (1897–1937) and **Petrov**, i.e. **Evgeny Petrovich Kataev** (1903–1942), Russian Soviet novelists born in Odessa, who collaborated in several satirical novels couched in humorous form, such as, *Dvenadtsat' stulyev* (1928; Eng. trans. *Diamonds to Sit On*, 1930), *Zolotoy Telenok* (1931; Eng. trans. *The Little Golden Calf*, 1932) and *Odnoetazhnaya Amerika* (1936; Eng. trans. *Little Golden America*, 1937). Ilf died in Moscow, and Petrov in Sebastopol.

**Ilyin, M. A.,** *see* **Osorgin, M. A.**

**Immanuel ben Solomon,** known in Italian as **Manoello Giudeo** (1270?–1331?), Italian Hebrew prose-writer and poet. A lifelong resident of Rome, where he held various posts in synagogues, he is known almost entirely for his medley of prose and verse, the *Maḥbaroth*, which is divided into twenty-eight parts, the last of them being an imitation of Dante. They tell us much of the social life of the period. The *Maḥbaroth*, first printed in 1491, has recently (1946) been edited by M. Haberman, and the twenty-eighth episode was translated as *Tophet and Eden* by H. Gollancz in 1921.

**Immermann, Karl Lebrecht** (1796–1840), German novelist, dramatist and poet, the last of, and indeed a generation behind, the true romantic school. Born in Magdeburg, he became a member of the Prussian civil service in 1817, and was appointed district judge at Düsseldorf in 1827. He had already begun to publish poetry in 1822, and had written plays, such as *König Periander* (1823) and *Trauerspiel in Tirol* (1827). At Düsseldorf he took a lively interest in the theatre, becoming for two years (1834–6) its director, but though he improved standards considerably public support was lacking. It is, however, as a prose-writer that he is now remembered, especially as the author of *Die Epigonen* (1836), a long romantic novel in a contemporary setting, and of the charming long short story of village life, the first of the kind later to be cultivated by such writers as Stifter (q.v.), Keller (q.v.) and Storm (q.v.), *Der Oberhof*, an incident in his long satirical novel *Münchhausen* (1839). *Der Oberhof* has been translated into English by P. B. Thomas in *German Classics of the Nineteenth and Twentieth Centuries* (1913–15). Immermann died very suddenly in Düsseldorf.

**Ingemann, Bernhard Severin** (1789–1862), Danish novelist and poet. Born at Torkildstrup, he became a schoolmaster in the old town of Sorø in 1822 and spent the rest of his quiet life there. His poetry, such as his *Morgen og Aftensange* (1839), full of simple, childlike devotional feeling, is little known outside his own country. But in his novels, inspired by the historic town in which he lived, he set to work to bring Denmark's Middle Ages before a much wider public. Though very far from being the Sir Walter Scott whom he emulated, he succeeded so well that during the 1840's he had a vogue in Britain and Germany as well as in his own land. Ingemann's best-known novels are *Valdemar Seier* (1826; Eng. trans. *Waldemar, surnamed Seir, or the Victorious*, 1841), *Erik Menveds Barndom* (1828; Eng. trans. *The Childhood of King Erik Menved*, 1846) and *Kong Erik og de Fredløse* (1833; Eng. trans. *King Erik and the Outlaws*, 1843).

**Ionesco, Eugène** (1912–     ), Franco-Rumanian dramatist, born in Slatina. Although his father was Rumanian he was brought up and educated in France, and after a spell in Budapest finally settled in Paris in 1938. His literary career began as a failure, and it was not until 1950 that a play of his even reached the stage. This was *La Cantatrice chauve* (Eng. trans. *The Bald Prima Donna*, 1958), and it was scarcely noticed. The same was the fate of *La Leçon* (1951; Eng. trans. *The Lesson*, 1958), another study in the terrible isolation of one human being from another, surrounded as we are by the oppressiveness, almost hostility, of the inanimate world. In *Les Chaises* (1951; Eng. trans. *The Chairs*, 1958) Ionesco mocks language and so demolishes the only link between sundered humanity, while in *Jacques* (1952; Eng. trans. 1958) he holds up to ridicule those conformities which are the props of what is generally termed society. Not content with this destructiveness, in *Victimes du devoir* (1952; Eng. trans. *Victims of Duty*, 1958) he is ready to make an end even of personal identity in a nightmare Kafka-like manner. *Amédée*

(1953; Eng. trans 1958) is a macabre confrontation of a husband and wife with the emptiness of their loveless life. In his more recent work Ionesco seems to be groping towards a moral purpose apparently lacking in the earlier works. Whether or not this is a right interpretation of plays like *Le Rhinocéros* (1959; Eng. trans. 1960), in which cowardice and 'running with the crowd' are pitilessly attacked, it seems certain that Ionesco has far to go before he becomes articulate enough to be able to stand the test of time. A recent work, *Le Roi se meurt* (1963; Eng. trans. *Exit the King*, 1964), was well received.

**Iosif, Stefan Octavian** (1875–1913), Rumanian poet, born at Braşov; the son of a schoolmaster, he took to journalism. An admirer of German poetry, he first published a book of verse, *Versuri*, in 1897, following this up with *Patriarchale* (1901) and two series of *Poezii* in 1902 and 1908, while a later work in the same sentimental and nostalgic vein, *Cântece*, appeared in 1912. A close friend of D. Anghel (q.v.), he collaborated with him in *Legendă funigeilor* (1907, 'Gossamer Legend') and *Caleidoscopul lui A. Mirea* (1908–10). He died in Bucharest broken-hearted at his wife's adultery with Anghel.

**Iriarte, Tomás de** (1750–1791), Spanish poet. Born on the island of Tenerife, at an early age he went to Madrid to be under the tutelage of his uncle, Juan de Iriarte, the scholarly librarian to Charles III, and through his influence gained a post in the secretary of state's office in Madrid, where he died. Exceedingly witty and of keen intellect, he took part in all the literary battles of the period. He is still celebrated as the greatest fabulist that Spain has produced, and the range of style of his versification is remarkable. His principal work is *Fábulas literarias* (1782), which contains such universal favourites as 'El oso', 'La mona y el cerdo', 'Los dos loros y la cotorra' and 'El burro flautista'. Iriarte's collected works appeared in 1805. There have been several translations of the *Fábulas* into English, the earliest by Belfour and Richardson, *Fables on Subjects connected with Literature* (1804). That by G. H. Devereux, *Literary Fables* (1885), is good.

**Isla, José Francisco de** (1703–1781), Spanish satirist and translator. Born at Vidones, he became a Jesuit, and for some years lectured on philosophy and theology at Santiago, Segovia and Pamplona, becoming an excellent preacher. In 1746 he produced his first great satire, *El día grande de Navarra*, in which, in a vein of subtle mockery, he attacks the worldliness and futile pursuits of churchmen and others. His famous *Fray Gerundio*, which appeared in several parts between 1758 and 1770, is a kind of picaresque novel, its satire directed against the vulgar style of preaching so prevalent at the time. The preaching friars, who were marked out for special attack, succeeded in having further publication held up for the time being by the Inquisition, but Isla had done his work already; his *Gerundio* was so widely read and proved so damaging that preaching greatly improved from then onwards. In 1767 Isla shared the lot of the Jesuits in their expulsion from Spain, went to Italy, and settled at Bologna, where he lived poor and in weak health, but as cheerful as ever and uncomplaining until his death there. His last years were spent on his excellent Spanish translation of Lesage's *Gil Blas* (published 1787–8). His collected works appear in volume fifteen of the *Biblioteca de Autores Españoles*. A good, though somewhat abridged, English translation of *Fray Gerundio* by Warner was published in 1772.

**Istrati, Panait** (1884–1935), Rumanian novelist born in Bucharest, termed by Romain Rolland (q.v.), who befriended him at one stage of his career, 'the Gorky of the Balkans'. His parentage, his father a Greek smuggler and his mother a Rumanian washerwoman, was only the bizarre beginning of a stranger career. Leaving home as a boy, he wandered about the Levant, sometimes eating hardly enough to keep body and soul together, but at the same time gaining a remarkable knowledge of life in the raw which he was to make use of in his books. He returned to Rumania in 1913, frequented Communist circles and became an enthusiastic convert, but politics did him no good in the materialistic way; his marriage and farming were alike failures. Attempted suicide was followed by the friendship of Romain Rolland, who suggested that he should write of his experiences. In 1925 he published his first novel of importance, *Kyra Kiralina*, written as were all his books in French (Eng. trans. 1930), and there followed others, such as *Les Récits d'Adrien Zograffi* (2 vols., 1925–6), *Mikhail* (*Adolescence d'Adrien Zograffi*), 1927, *Mes Départs* (1928), *Le Pêcheur d'éponges* (1930), *En Égypte* (1931) and *La Vie d'Adrien Zograffi* (1933–5). In 1927 Istrati, still an ardent Communist, went to Russia. He returned in 1929 an enemy of the whole regime, and held it up for what it appeared to be to him, an oppression of the worst kind, in *La Russie nue* (1929; Eng. trans. *Russia Unveiled*, 1931). But he was played out, lost his money, developed tuberculosis and died in destitution in Bucharest.

**Ivanov, Vsevolod Vyacheslavovich** (1895–1963), Russian novelist and short-story writer born at Lebyazhye, Semipalatinsk, who, after being a shop assistant and doing a hundred and one jobs in funfairs, at the age of twenty became a literary disciple of Gorky (q.v.). But even then his wanderings were not over, for he was involved in the revolution and in the civil war in Turkestan. In 1921, however, he settled down to literary work in Petrograd, and after severe self-training was able to turn his varied experiences to good account. Two years later his masterpiece, *Bronyepoyezd 14–69* (the Eng. trans., *Armoured Train 14–69*, appeared in 1933), was published, and in 1927 it was made into a highly successful play. His short stories of this time, written in a swift, impressionistic style, deal especially with the impact of the revolution on the peasantry of the nations on the fringe of Russia. Such are *Tsvetnyie vetra* ('Coloured Winds', 1922) and *Golubyie peski* ('Blue Sands', 1923), both showing an almost overwhelming sensitivity. Unfortunately he listened too readily to the adverse criticism of his friends, and became self-conscious, with the result that his collection of stories, *Taynoye taynykh* ('Mystery of Mysteries', 1927), reaches nothing but nihilism. Thereafter he became a hack

propagandist for the Communist Party, only shaking himself free in
his remarkable autobiographical novel *Pokhozhdeniya fakira* (1934;
Eng. trans. *I Live a Queer Life*, 1936), but it was so badly received by
the authorities that he returned to second-rate praises of the regime.
Several of his better short stories have been translated in J. Cournos's
*Short Stories out of Soviet Russia* (1929).

# J

**Jacob, Max** (1876–1944), French poet. Born at Quimper, Brittany, of Jewish family, he went to Paris early and made himself at home in artistic circles, gaining the friendship of Apollinaire (q.v.) and Picasso. He made a reputation with *Œuvres mystiques et burlesques de Frère Matorel* (1911), following this up with *La Côte* (1913). He became a convert to Roman Catholicism in 1915, and this led to greater richness and variety by providing contrasts in his still brilliant and witty books, such as *Le Cornet à dés* (1917), *La Défense de Tartuffe* (1919), *Les Pénitents en Maillot Rose* (1925), *Le Bal masqué* (1932) and *Ballades* (1938). Early in 1944 he was arrested by the German Gestapo and died not long afterwards in a concentration camp at Drancy. *Conseils à un jeune poète* appeared in 1945.

**Jacobi, Friedrich Heinrich** (1743–1819), German novelist and philosopher, born at Düsseldorf, where his father was a wealthy business man. He went into the civil service and in 1770 was appointed finance officer for Jülich and Berg. On inheriting the business jointly with his brother J. G. Jacobi, poet and literary journalist, he gave himself up entirely to philosophy, and began to elaborate a system of his own. This philosophy, to which he gave literary expression in three dull and rambling novels, *Aus Eduard Allwills Papieren* (1775), *Woldemar* (1779) and *Allwills Briefsammlung* (1781), is yet important as revealing the first attempt in Germany, and in fact in Europe, to resurrect Spinoza (q.v.) and relate him to the eighteenth-century 'sensation' school. His *Briefe über die Lehre des Spinoza* (1785) is, however, his one interesting contribution to Spinoza studies. His work had a considerable influence on Goethe, with whom he was on terms of close friendship. His brother J. G. Jacobi published some of the young Goethe's earliest lyrics in his periodical *Iris* (1774). In 1805 F. H. Jacobi was appointed professor of philosophy at Munich, retiring in 1812. He died in that city. His *Werke* were published (6 vols.) between 1812 and 1825.

**Jacobsen, Jens Peter** (1847–1885), Danish novelist, short-story writer and poet, was born at Thisted, Jutland. He went to Copenhagen, studied botany, and gained the Royal Danish Academy's gold medal in 1872, but turned aside from science and took to literature that year. Slowly, with the knowledge that he was tubercular and was a doomed man, he worked on his highly finished novel *Fru Marie Grubbe* (1876; Eng. trans. 1914), a brilliantly conceived psychological story, and this was succeeded by his second, *Niels Lyhne* (1880; Eng. trans. 1919), dealing with the problems of atheism, and a personal testament of Jacobsen's own problems of conscience. He next turned to the short story, and the collection *Mogens og andre Noveller* (1882; Eng. trans. *Mogens and other Stories*, 1921) is the highest expression of his art. After his death at Thisted appeared his volume of poetry, *Digte og Udkast* (1886; Eng. trans. *Poems*, 1920). His *Samlede Skrifter* were published (5 vols.) between 1924 and 1929.

**Jacobsen, Jørgen-Frantz** (1900–1938), Danish novelist. Born at Thorshavn, Faroe Islands, he went to Copenhagen and settled there as a journalist. He wrote two highly regarded books on the Faroe Islands, but lives as the author of a deeply individualistic piece of fiction, set in the Faroes in the eighteenth century, *Barbara* (1939; Eng. trans. 1948). He died of tuberculosis at Vejlefjord.

**Jacobus de Voragine** (1230–1298), Italian prose-writer, born at Viareggio. He became a Dominican at Genoa in 1244, grew into fame as a preacher and was in 1292 made Archbishop of Genoa. He is remembered for his collection of the lives of saints known as the *Legenda Aurea*, written between 1255 and 1265, a popular and unhistorical account, but of good literary quality and one of the best-loved books of the Middle Ages. The best critical edition of it is that by T. Graesse (1850). Caxton published English translations of it in 1483 and 1488. For the best modern English translation see *The Golden Legend* by G. Ryan and H. Ripperger (1941). Jacobus died in Genoa.

**Jacopo da Lentini** (1185?–1240?), Italian poet, born at Lentini, Sicily, he became a leading courtier of the Emperor Frederick II ('Stupor Mundi'). A small number of his love-poems survive. He is said to have invented, or at least to have been the first to use, the sonnet. His work is to be found in E. Monaci's *Crestomazia italiana dei primi secoli* (1912).

**Jacopone da Todi** (1220?–1306), Italian poet writing also in Latin, was born at Todi, Umbria, where he became a lawyer. On the death of his wife in 1268 he became a Franciscan tertiary and ten years later a lay brother. He is the more than probable author of the *Stabat Mater*. His powerful *Laude spirituali* are in Italian, and for these see G. Feri's edition in the series *Scrittori d'Italia* (1915; rev. ed., 1930). He died at Collazone.

**Jacques de Vitry** (1180–1240), French prose-writer born at Vitry-sur-Seine, who was appointed Bishop of Acre in 1217 and was later created cardinal, took part in the fifth crusade. His fascinating *Historia Orientalis et Occidentalis* is a comparative account of eastern and western civilizations, incidentally containing a first-hand account of the Holy Land (Eng. trans. *The History of Jerusalem*, by A. Stewart, 1896). He died in Rome.

**Jakemes** (thirteenth century), French poet, the author of *Le Roman du Castelain de Couci et de la Dame de Fayel*, composed about 1285, seems to have lived in Picardy. *Castelain de Couci* is a powerful story of love and vengeance in the midst of an idle pleasure-loving society. Here is to be found the legend of the eaten heart. The best edition of the work is that by M. Delbouille (1935).

**Jaloux, Edmond** (1878–1949), French novelist and literary critic. Born in Marseille, he wrote several novels, including *Le Reste est silence* (1909) and *Fumées dans la campagne* (1918), delicately conceived and composed. In 1922 he became closely associated with literary journalism, writing particularly for *Le Temps*, and there followed several beautifully constructed volumes of criticism, including *L'Esprit des livres* (1923), *Perspectives et personnages* (1931), his widely read *Introduction à l'histoire de la littérature française* (1946) and *Essences* (1949). He left France in 1940 and settled at Lutry, Switzerland, where he died.

**Jammes, Francis** (1868–1938), French poet and novelist. Born at Tournay (Haute-Pyrénées), he gave up law for literature, and for a time became a symbolist poet, until with the publication of *De l'angélus de l'aube à l'angélus du soir* (1898) he revealed himself as a deeply religious one with a great sympathy for and understanding of the peasantry and nature. As to influences on him, that of Verlaine (q.v.) is the clearest. Among his many volumes of poetry, pride of place may be given to *Le Triomphe de la vie* (1902), *Les Géorgiques chrétiennes* (vol. i, 1911; vol. ii, 1912), *Feuilles dans le vent* (1914), *Ma France poétique* (1926) and *Diane* (1928). He was also something of a novelist: *Le Roman du lièvre* (1903) and *Cloches pour deux mariages* (1924). He died at Hasparren.

**Janicius (Janicki), Klemens** (1516–1543), Polish poet writing in Latin. Born at Januszkow of humble family, he was patronized and sent to Italy where he imbibed the Renaissance to the extent of writing a collection of delightful lyrics derived from Ovid's *Tristia*, entitled *Tristium liber I, variarum elegiarum liber I, epigrammatum liber I* (1542). He died in Cracow. There is a critical edition of his *Carmina* by L. Cwikliński (1930).

**Janin, Jules Gabriel** (1804–1874), French novelist and critic. Born in Saint-Étienne, he first attracted notice with his dramatic criticism in the *Journal des Débats*, and then settled down to a freelance literary life. Few of his numerous works were of permanent value, the exceptions being the weird, half-humorous, half-serious tale *L'Âne mort et la femme guillotinée* (1829), and *Barnave* (1831), an historical novel. He died in Paris.

**Janson, Kristofer Nagel** (1841–1917), Norwegian novelist. Born at Bergen, he became a Unitarian minister and a champion of folk expressionism. His one undisputably good novel is *Den Bergtekne* (1876; Eng. trans. *The Spell-bound Fiddler*, 1880). He died in Copenhagen.

**Jarnés, Benjamín** (1888–1949), Spanish novelist and biographer. Born at Codo, Zaragoza, he abandoned all thought of the priesthood and took up a clerical post in the army. His over-literary novels include *Mosém Pedro* (1924), *El profesor inútil* (1926) and *El convidado de papel* (1928), but he struck a new mine of his talent with *Vida de San Alejo* (1928), in which there is an arresting blend of biography and autobiography (Eng. trans. *Saint Alexis* in W. B.

Wells's *Great Spanish Short Stories*). His two straight biographies, *Zumalacárregui, el caudillo romántico* (1931) and *Castelar, hombre de Sinai* (1935), both of nineteenth-century men of action, the Carlist and the republican, are his most characteristic works. He died in Madrid.

**Jarry, Alfred** (1873–1907), French poet, playwright and novelist, was born at Laval. He opened his literary career with a volume of verse, *Les Minutes du sable mémorial* (1894), and followed it up with the experimental plays *César Antéchrist* (1895), *Ubu Roi* (1896), a wild indecent farce satirizing the petty dictators of everyday life, and its sequel *Ubu enchaîné* (1900). He then turned to fiction and produced *Messaline* (1900) and a surrealist novel *Le Surmâle* (1902). Jarry died in Paris. A third novel, *Les Gestes et opinions du Dr Faustroll*, was published posthumously in 1911.

**Jasmin**, the pen name of **Jacques Boé** (1798–1864), Provençal poet. Born at Agen, where he died, he became a hairdresser, devoting his leisure to literature, and published his first poem, *Me Cal Mouri*, in Gascon dialect, in 1822. By 1835 he had written enough to be able to form a collection entitled *Las Papillotos*, reissued with additions in 1851 and 1853. Another of his works, *L'Abuglo de Castel-Cuillé* (1836, 'The Blind Girl of Castel Cuillé'), was translated by Longfellow. Jasmin may be said to have been the father of the revival of Provençal literature.

**Jaufré Rudel de Blaya** (twelfth century), French troubadour from Provence, is remembered as the author of a few of the most beautiful examples of troubadour love-poetry. From his work is derived the theme of the troubadour and the lady far away, a legend retold in Rostand's (q.v.) *La Princesse lointaine*. See A. Jeanroy's *Les Chansons de Jaufré Rudel* (rev. ed., 1924).

**Jean Clopinel de Meung**, *see* Meung.

**Jean d'Arras** (fourteenth century), French prose-writer. All that is known of him is that he was protected by Jean, duc de Berry, and for him wrote the *Livre de Mélusine* (1395?) in honour of his patron's family. The 'fairy wife' theme of this work thus for the first time finds true literary form after remaining for so long in the realms of folklore. There is an English translation of the book by A. K. Donald (1895). The standard edition of the French text is that by L. Stouff (1932).

**Jean Paul**, *see* Richter, J. P. F.

**Jedaiah ha-Penini Bedersi** (1270?–1345?), French Hebrew poet, born at Béziers. His didactic *Beḥinath 'Olam* (first publ. before 1480; Eng. trans. *An Investigation of Causes arising from the Organisation of the World*, 1806) preaches the vanity of all earthly powers and possessions.

**Jensen, Johannes Vilhelm** (1873–1950), Danish novelist and poet. Born at Farsø, Jutland, the son of a veterinary surgeon, he studied medicine before turning to letters for a living. Among his fiction is the lengthy *Kongens Fald* (3 vols., 1900–1; Eng. trans. *The Fall of the King*, 1933), and *Den lange Rejse* (6 vols., 1908–22; Eng. trans. *The Long Journey*, 3 vols., 1922). Others are *Dr Renaults Fristelser* (1935) and *Gudrun* (1936). He was awarded the Nobel Prize for literature in 1944, especially for his poetry (*Digte, 1901–43*, 1943), and died in Copenhagen.

**Jensen, Wilhelm** (1837–1911), German novelist, was born at Heiligenhafen. Among his highly popular and imaginative, though often superficial, works are *Magister Timotheus* (1866), *Eddystone* (1872), *Karin von Schweden* (1878), *Versunkene Welten* (1882), *Doppelleben* (1890) and *In majorem dei gloriam* (1905). A close friend of Raabe (q.v.), he died in Munich.

**Jiménez, Juan Ramón** (1881–1958), Spanish poet and prose-writer. Born at Moguer, Huelva, he was educated by the Jesuits and at Seville University. Of delicate health, he settled down to a quiet literary life in Madrid. Even more than the Nicaraguan poet, Rubén Darío, Jiménez is responsible for the path taken towards modern Spanish poetry. Many of Darío's innovations were brilliant but superficial, whereas Jiménez's gave it depth, although it is generally admitted that he leant too heavily on French influences, which have been a frequent pitfall for Spanish writers since the eighteenth century. His first considerable collection was *Arias tristes* (1903), and to this first period belong also such volumes as *Jardines lejanos* (1904), *Poemas májicos y dolientes* (1909) and *Elejías lamentables* (1910). With *Baladas de primavera* (1910) he entered his second period, one which to many seemed over-elaboration such as is also to be seen in *La soledad sonora* (1911); and in *Laberinto* (1913) and *Estío* (1915) he seemed to have become a symbolist; but with *Diario de un poeta recién casado* (1917) his manner again changed, and he became a remotely thinking poet using free verse and employing a very plain style, and to this third manner he afterwards adhered. Other volumes were *Sonetos espirituales* (1917), *Poesías escojidas* (1917), *Eternidades* (1918), *Piedra y cielo* (1919) and *Segunda antolojía poética* (1922). He went into exile in South America when the insurgents defeated the republicans in 1939 and there continued to publish further poetry, such as *La estación total* (1946) and *Romances de Coral Gables* (1948); but it is not to poetry at all that he owed his world-wide fame, but to that perfect piece of Spanish prose, *Platero y yo* (1917; Eng. trans. *Platero and I,* 1922 and 1958), the story of the life and death of a donkey. He was awarded the Nobel Prize for literature in 1956 and died in Puerto Rico.

**Jodelle, Étienne** (1532–1573), French dramatist and poet. Born in Paris, he became a member of the Pléiade and scored a great success with his poetic drama, *Cléopâtre captive* (1553). The play itself is not by any means of first-rate quality, but its form showed the way out of the medieval play into modern drama. It is in fact called the first French classical tragedy. A second but very inferior drama is *Didon se sacrifiant* (1555), closely following Virgil. His most considerable poem is ' Aux cendres de Claude Colet '. He died in Paris having completely outlived his powers.

**Johann von Tepl** (1350?–1415?), Bohemian prose-writer in German, was born at Šytboř, graduated at Prague University and held administrative office there and at Tepl. He is known for his solemn *Ackermann aus Böhmen* (1405?; ed. K. Spalding, 1950; Eng. trans. *Death and the Ploughman*, 1947) in prose rhythm, a discussion between a widower and Death. He probably died in Prague.

**Johansson, Lars**, called **Lucidor** (1638–1674), Swedish poet, born in Stockholm, where he died, wrote full-hearted religious poems, love lyrics and drinking songs, which have not been collected until recent times (*Samlade Dikter*, 1914).

**John of the Cross,** *see* **Juan de la Cruz.**

**Johnson, Eyvind** (1900–    ), Swedish novelist, born at Svartbjörnsbyn, Norrland, of modest family. At first he led a very active and changeable life which gave him material for his largely autobiographical *Romanen om Olof* (4 vols., 1934–7). His *Krilon* trilogy, *Grupp Krilon* (1941), *Krilons Resa* (1942) and *Krilon själv* (1943), is a denunciation of Nazi Germany. His best-known work outside his own country is *Strändernas svall* (1946; Eng. trans. *Return to Ithaca*, 1952), which translates the Ulysses theme into modern life.

**Joinville, Jean de** (1224–1317), French prose-writer. Hereditary seneschal of Champagne, he became a close friend of Saint Louis, and accompanied him on his first crusade (1248–54). While at Acre he made his beautiful French version of the *Credo*, and he was an accomplished letter-writer, as his letters to King Louis X show; but it is for his *Histoire de Saint Louis*, begun about 1280 and finished in 1309, that he is remembered. Its charming style and the wealth of glowing scenic detail which it contains render it one of the most attractive of all medieval chronicles. Perhaps the best editions are those by F. Michel (1859) and N. de Wailly (1874). There are English translations by J. Hutton (1868), E. Wedgwood (1906), F. T. Marzials (1908) and J. Evans (1938).

**Jókai, Maurus** or **Mór** (1825–1904), Hungarian novelist. Born at Rév-Komárom, he trained for a legal career, but on succeeding as an author gave up the law, although he became an active politician, being a member of the Diet (1867–96) and of the Upper Chamber (1896–1904). He brought humour and vigour to bear on his fast-moving plots, set in all kinds of climate and condition, and his celebrity soon became Europe-wide. Among his two hundred works may be named *Erdély aranykora* (2 vols., 1852; Eng. trans. *Midst the Wild Carpathians*, 1894), *Egy magyar nábob* (4 vols., 1853–4; Eng. trans. *A Hungarian Nabob*, 1898), *Az új földesúr* (3 vols., 1863; Eng. trans. *The New Landlord*, 1868), *A kőszívű ember fiai* (6 vols., 1869; Eng. trans. *The Baron's Sons*, 1900), *Fekete gyémántok* (5 vols., 1870; Eng. trans. *Black Diamonds*, 1896), *Az aranyember* (5 vols., 1873; Eng. trans. *Timar's Two Worlds*, 1888) and *Sárga rózsa* (1893; Eng. trans. *The Yellow Rose*, 1909). His reputation has rapidly declined. He died in Budapest.

**Jordan, Wilhelm** (1819–1904), German poet. Born at Insterburg, he became first a schoolmaster and afterwards a journalist. A poet of wild and undisciplined power, his epic, *Demiurgos* (1852–4), showed all his weaknesses as well as his strength, but his materialist philosophy makes unattractive poetic fare. His most notable work was *Die Nibelunge*, which appeared in two parts, the first *Sigfridssage* (1868) and *Hildebrands Heimkehr* (1874), which introduced the vogue in Germany for modernized old poetry. Another effort along the same lines was *Die Edda* (1889). Jordan died in Frankfurt-am-Main.

**Jósika, Miklós** (1794–1865), Hungarian novelist, born at Torda. Largely influenced by Sir Walter Scott, he wrote a number of historical novels in a somewhat heavy style. The best of them is *Jö a tatár* (4 vols., 1856; Eng. trans. *'Neath the Hoof of the Tartar*, 1904). He died, having outlived his popularity, in Dresden.

**Jouhandeau, Marcel**, pseudonym of **Marcel Provence** (1888–    ), French novelist, born at Guéret. He is the despiser of small-town life and the respectability and conventionalism which enmesh and destroy. He developed comparatively late, his first really successful work being *Chaminadour* (1934), his fictional name for his native town. Thereafter, casting a particularly cold and critical eye on marriage, have appeared *Chroniques maritales* (1938), *De l'abjection* (1939), *Mémorial* (1948), *Scènes de la vie conjugale* (1948) and *La Faute plutôt que le scandale* (1949). In *De la grandeur* (1952), *Réflexion sur la vieillesse et la mort* (1956) and *Carnets de l'écrivain* (1957) he presents a broader field, applying his sharp critical faculty to many aspects of life. He was a schoolmaster at Passy from 1912 to 1949.

**Jouve, Pierre-Jean** (1887–    ), French poet. Born at Arras, the disasters of the First World War had a profound effect on him, and his work is a slow pilgrimage from grief to the hope of redemption. His difficult but strangely haunting verse is well exemplified in such volumes as *Tragiques* (1923), *Le Paradis perdu* (1929), *Sueur de sang* (1933), *Kyrié* (1938), *La Vierge de Paris* (1945), inspired by the Resistance, *Diadème* (1949), which reveals his hankering after the solitude of his earlier years, *Ode* (1951), *Lyrique* (1956), *Inventions* (1958) and *Proses* (1960). His influence on younger poets has been incalculable.

**Jovellanos, Gaspar Melchor de** (1744–1811), Spanish prose-writer, poet and dramatist, born at Gijón. Made a magistrate at Seville in 1767, he began to take a leading part in the enlightened policy of King Charles III, especially after being transferred to Madrid (1778). Everything interested him, and he was always actuated by the desire for progress. In his *Elogio de las bellas artes* (1782) he tried to improve his countrymen's taste, in his play *El delincuente honrado* (1787) he put forward the plea for criminal law reform propounded twenty years before by Beccaria (q.v.), and in *Informe sobre un proyecto de ley agraria* (1794) dealt in masterly style with land reform. An accomplished classical scholar, his best poetry has a Horatian grace, as is to be seen in *Epístola de Fabio a Anfriso*; another influence on his poetry was Milton. His *Diarios* give an unsparing portrait of him unparalleled elsewhere in Spanish literature, but even then he remains an outstandingly estimable character. He was too good a European to overcome narrow Spanish prejudice, and spent his last years uncomfortably, first as a prisoner of the dictator Godoy (1801–8) and afterwards as a patriot who refused to throw in his lot with Napoleon, but who yet could not bring himself to accept the violence of the nationalists. He died at Vega de Navía. There is a fine portrait of him by his friend Goya. See his *Obras completas* in *Biblioteca de Autores Españoles*, vols. xlvi, l; *Diarios*, ed. Adellanc, 1915. See also the English translation, *The Tribunal of the Inquisition, and Bread and Bulls* (Toulon, 1813).

**Jovine, Francesco** (1902–1950), Italian novelist, was born at Campobasso. Influenced by Verga (q.v.) he took to regional studies (especially the Abruzzi), and in studying peasant life embraced a leftist anticlerical point of view which clearly obtrudes in his works. These include *Signora Ava* (1942), *L'Impero in provincia* (1945), *Tutti i mei peccati* (1948) and his masterpiece, *Le Terre del Sacramento* (1950; Eng. trans. *The Estate in Abruzzi*, 1952). He died in Venice.

**Juan de la Cruz**, real name **Juan de Yepes y Álvarez** (1542–1591), Spanish poet. Born of a simple family at Fontiveros, Ávila, he entered the Carmelite Order in 1563, and after a spell at Salamanca studying, joined Santa Teresa's (q.v.) reform movement. This was too much for the unreformed Carmelites, who from 1573 onwards for the rest of his life persecuted him. He died possibly of ill treatment, certainly of hardship, in Andalusia at Úbeda. He was canonized in 1726. His mystical poetry, accompanied by his own prose commentaries, is unparalleled in literature. In tracing the ascent of the soul from purgatory to God he shows a magnificence of conception and of language to equal it, which render the three great poems unsurpassable of their kind. He also wrote some devotional poetry, but this is of a more conventional kind. The best edition is *Obras de San Juan de la Cruz*, by P. Silverio de Santa Teresa (5 vols., 1929–31). There is an English translation, *The Complete Works of St John of the Cross*, by E. Allison Peers (3 vols., rev. ed., 1953), and see also *Poems* by Roy Campbell, 1951.

**Juan Manuel** (1282–1349), Spanish prose-writer, nephew of King Alfonso X, was born at Escalona, Toledo, and was employed on several diplomatic missions before being forced into exile until 1338. Much of his work is lost, but enough remains to prove him to have been one of the outstanding writers of his age. Above all the *Libro del Caballero y del Escudero* (ed. S. Gräfenberg, 1893) and the *Libro de los Estados*, in part a version of the Christian Buddhist tale *Barlaam and Josaphat*, entitle him to be considered as a forerunner of Boccaccio (q.v.). His command of language is the result of unusual taste and discrimination. All his surviving work is to be found in the *Biblioteca de Autores Españoles*, vol. li. There is an English translation of selected parts of his writings in T. Roscoe's *The Spanish Novelists* (vol. i, 1832). An anthology dealing with ethical problems, *Conde Lucanor*, is the only piece of Don Juan Manuel which has been well and completely translated into English (*Count Lucanor*, 1868; rev., 1924). He died in Spain, but where is not known.

**Judah ben Samuel ha-Levi** (1080?–1145?), Spanish Hebrew poet and prose-writer, writing in Hebrew and Arabic. Born at Tudela, he became a physician and lived at the Arab courts of Cordoba and Granada. He wrote poetry in Hebrew throughout his life (collected as *Diwan*, ed. H. Brody, 4 vols., 1901–30; Eng. trans. *Selected Poems*, 1924). As a prose-writer in Arabic he is represented by his *Kitāb al-Khazari*, a treatise in dialogue form on Jewish philosophy and history (Eng. trans. H. Hirschfeld, second ed., 1931; *Selections*, I. Heinemann, 1948). This was completed about 1138, shortly before he left Spain for Palestine, where he died.

**Jung-Stilling, Johann Heinrich** (1740–1817), German prose-writer using the pseudonym **Heinrich Stilling**. Born at Im-Grund in Westphalia, near Hildenbach, the son of a charcoal burner, he became the village tailor and afterwards the schoolmaster, painfully gathering together enough money to go to Strassburg University in 1770, where he studied medicine and was befriended by Goethe. On qualifying he set up practice at Elberfeld and became a renowned operator for cataract. He later held academic posts as professor of political economy at Heidelberg and Marburg. A deeply religious man, he is at his best as a writer when he charmingly describes his life in *Heinrich Stillings Jünglingsjahre, Wanderschaft, Häusliches Leben, Lehrjahre, Rückblick, Alter* (publ. in instalments between 1778 and 1816; Eng. trans. *Heinrich Stilling*, by S. Jackson, 1835–6, and abridged version by R. O. Moon, 1886) and in *Das Heimweh* (3 vols., 1794), the latter particularly popular in the United States. His quasi-mystical work such as *Theorie der Geisterkunde* (1808) brought him much patronage, including that of the Emperor Alexander I of Russia. He died in Karlsruhe.

**Jünger, Ernst** (1895–    ), German novelist, born in Heidelberg. His experiences in the First World War, in which he showed conspicuous bravery, led to the writing of *In Stahlgewittern* (1920; Eng. trans. *Storm of Steel*, 1929), and here war, without being glorified, is regarded as a necessary atonement. *Das Wäldchen 125* (1925; Eng. trans. *Copse 125*, 1930) is a harsh picture of war; but with *Auf den Marmorklippen* (1939; Eng. trans. *On the Marble Cliffs*, 1950) he reached a hatred of war which he treated as blind brute force, and thanks to his high military honours of the past even the Nazis did not touch him. *Heliopolis* (1949) and *Der Waldgang* (1951) reveal further development. *Der gordische Knoten* (1953) shows a new direction of thought, a romantic's disillusionment with a basically technical civilization.

**Junqueiro, Abílio Manuel Guerra** (1850–1923), Portuguese poet. Born at Freixo de Espada, he entered politics on the left wing and served for many years as a parliamentary deputy. His generally pompous verse, such as *Baptismo do amor* (1868), though much read in its day, is very dated now. Perhaps his best work is to be found in the satire, *A morte de Dom João* (1874), and in the collection of lyrics, *Os simples* (1892). He died in Lisbon.

# K

**Kaden Bandrowski, Juliusz** (1885–1944), Polish prose-writer. Born at Rzeszów, he exerted great influence on the inter-war literary generation in Poland, and was an unsparing critic of anything that gave signs of decadence. *General Barcz* (1923), a novel, was highly regarded in Germany also; but it is as a short-story writer that he made his greatest contribution, as in *Miasto mojej matki* (1925; Fr. trans. *Ma ville et ma mère*, 1933) and *W cieniu zapomnianej olszyny* (1926; Eng. trans. *Call to the Cuckoo*, 1948). He became secretary of the Polish Academy in 1933, and met a violent death in Warsaw.

**Kafka, Franz** (1883–1924), Austro-Czech novelist and diarist. Born in Prague, he was almost from the first the victim of weak health and a difficult family. After taking his doctorate he became a civil servant, and although the work was thoroughly uncongenial it allowed him a certain amount of free time in which to write. As the years passed and tuberculosis developed his pessimism grew to despair, but as can be seen from his remarkably self-revealing *Tagebücher* which he kept from 1910 to 1923 (*Tagebücher 1910–1923*, 1951; Eng. trans. *The Diary of Franz Kafka*, 2 vols., 1948–9) his illness only increased his keen intellect and hypersensitivity. He seemed to read the future, the coming age of dictators and secret police, of the crushing of the individual by an almighty state machine. Practically unknown in his lifetime, he himself published little, and what he did publish, such as *Die Verwandlung* (1915; Eng. trans. *The Metamorphosis*, 1937) and *Das Urteil* (1913; Eng. trans. *The Judgment*, 1945), were tentative. It was thanks to his friend Max Brod (q.v.) that his papers were preserved and his novels published. Kafka died, after a fierce struggle against disease and in the midst of a desperate love-affair, at Kierling, not far from Vienna. In the year of his death appeared *Ein Hungerkünstler*, and then his two great novels *Der Prozess* (1925; Eng. trans. *The Trial*, 1937) and *Das Schloss* (1926; Eng. trans. *The Castle*, 1930), which have had a profound influence on modern European thought and letters. In these Kafka conveys the cold, clear horror of the victim confronted with a dehumanized society. Other works are the uncompleted *Amerika* (1927) and *Beim Bau der Chinesischen Mauer* (1931; Eng. trans. *The Great Wall of China*, 1933). His *Gesammelte Werke* (1950) fill ten volumes.

**Kahn, Gustave** (1859–1936), French poet, novelist and essayist. Born in Metz, he became a leader of the symbolist movement and one of the

first, if not the first, to use *vers libre*. His first book of verse of consequence was *Chansons d'amant* (1891), and others were *Domaine de
fée* (1896), *Les Fleurs de la passion* (1900), *Odes de la raison* (1902)
and *Images bibliques* (1929), which last shows that a quarter of a
century later he was writing in much the same manner as when he
began. As a novelist he appears to the best advantage in *L'Adultère
sentimentale* (1902), *L'Aube enamourée* (1925) and *Vieil Orient, Orient
neuf* (1926). As an essayist he writes with authority and charm in
*Symbolistes et décadents* (1902). He died in Metz.

**Kaiser, Georg** (1878–1945), German dramatist and novelist, was born
in Magdeburg and there educated before becoming an electrical
engineer in Buenos Aires. Ill health cut short his career there and he
returned to Germany to pursue a literary life, but did not become
known until the phenomenal success of several expressionist plays,
*Von Morgens bis Mitternachts* (1916; Eng. trans. *From Morn to
Midnight*, 1920), *Die Koralle* (1917; Eng. trans. *The Coral*, 1929), *Gas I*
(1918; Eng. trans. 1924) and *Gas II* (1920). Of his later works for the
stage, *Oktobertag* (1928), *Mississippi* (1930), *Der Soldat Tanaka*
(1940) and *Griechische Dramen* (1949) should be mentioned. As a
novelist he is represented by *Es ist genug* (1931) and *Villa Aurea*
(1940; Eng. trans. *A Villa in Sicily*, 1949). He died at Ascona.

**Kamban, Guðmundur Jónsson** (1888–1945), Icelandic-Danish novelist, was born at Litli-Bær Álftanes in poverty, but managed to gain
some education and became a journalist in Reykjavík. Strange
ventures into the occult, such as *Úr dularheimum* (1906, 'From
Worlds of the Spirit'), brought him a following, and with the money
he earned he went to Copenhagen where he gained a degree at the
university. Later he turned to the stage, his most notable achievement in that field being *Hadda-Padda* (1914; Eng. trans. 1917), a
wildly romantic work. His most successful period of creation was,
however, his last when, writing only in Danish, he produced the long
and dignified historical novel *Skálholt* (4 vols., 1930–2; Eng. trans.
*The Virgin of Skalholt*, 2 vols., 1936). In addition may be mentioned
*Jeg ser et stort skønt Land* (1936; Eng. trans. *I see a Wondrous Land*,
1938). He was shot in Copenhagen by Danish patriots for collaborationist activities with the Germans, of which it would seem he was
innocent.

**Kant, Immanuel** (1724–1804), German philosopher and prose-writer,
born in Königsberg, the son of a saddler of Scottish descent. He gained
a great reputation as a classical scholar while at school, turning to
physics, astronomy and mathematics at Königsberg University,
which he entered in 1740. After a long struggle against poverty and
lack of influence he was at last appointed professor of logic and metaphysics in 1770. A splendid lecturer, he put his heart and soul into
his system of philosophy, which has remained indestructible to the
present day. He rehabilitated metaphysics, and by making it acceptable to men of widely varying ideas he exercised an enormous
influence on literature, especially through Schiller. His style is
for the most part poor and produces nothing of the direct effect
which his lectures must have done, but beyond the disagreeable

complexities of style rises the majesty of his whole conception of being and of thinking. His great works are *Kritik der reinen Vernunft* (1781; Eng. trans. *Critique of Pure Reason*, 1854) and *Kritik der praktischen Vernunft* (1788; Eng. trans. *Critique of Practical Reason*, 1898). He died in Königsberg.

**Karamzin, Nikolay Mikhaylovich** (1765–1826), Russian novelist, historian and journalist, was born at Mikhaylovka, province of Simbirsk, and was educated at the universities of Moscow and Petersburg. He then joined the army before setting out on several lengthy journeys through Europe, of which he gave an account in full-blown sentimental romantic style in a series of contributions to his literary magazine, *Moskovskiy Zhurnal* (1790). It was later brought out in book form as *Pis'ma russkogo puteshestvennika* (1801; Eng. trans. *Travels from Moscow through Prussia, Germany, Switzerland, France and England*, 3 vols., 1803). With his novel *Bednaya Liza* (1792, 'Poor Liza') he introduced Rousseauism (albeit diffused) to a wide Russian public. His increasing interest in historical research led to his being appointed Historiographer Royal (1803) and thereafter he gave most of his energy to *Istoriya Gosudarstva Rossiyskogo* (12 vols., 1816–29, 'General History of the Russian State'). The work reaches only to 1613, and is narrowly nationalistic and xenophobic. Karamzin, who had an enormous influence on the development of modern Russian literary prose, died in Petersburg.

**Karinthy, Frigyes** (1888–1938), Hungarian prose-writer, born in Budapest. With his gift of detached, impersonal humour he wrote a brilliant (and more cheerful) continuation of *Gulliver's Travels*, *Utazás Faremidóba* (1916, 'The Travels of Faremidob') and *Capillaria* (1921). He died at Siófok of a brain disease, of which *Utazás a koponyám körül* (1937; Eng. trans. *A Journey round my Skull*, 1939) is the remarkable record.

**Karlfeldt, Erik Axel** (1864–1931), Swedish poet. Born at Folkärna, he wrote some interesting if difficult poetry inspired by rustic life, above all *Fridolins visor* (1898) and *Fridolins lustgård* (1901). *Flora och Pomona* (1906) has as its keynote a very personal view of the countryside with an accompanying melancholy, considerably deepened in *Flora och Bellona* (1918), in which the peace of an age-old way of living is contrasted with the horrors of a distant war, because of which its integrity is for ever destroyed. He died in Stockholm, and was posthumously awarded the Nobel Prize the same year. There is an English translation of selected poems, *Arcadia Borealis. Selected Poems* (1938).

**Karr, Jean-Baptiste Alphonse** (1808–1890), French prose-writer, born in Paris. He became a schoolmaster, but having gained a public with his autobiographical novel *Sous les tilleuls* (1832) he turned to writing for a living. His sentimental novel *Geneviève* (1838) proved highly popular, and there followed a stream of fiction, witty, ironical, romantic, and withal with plenty of common sense. In 1839 he became editor of *Le Figaro* and the same year founded the sharply satirical periodical *Les Guêpes*. His best remembered work was the result of his love for his garden, *Voyage autour de mon jardin* (1845), one of the select band of gardening books of real literary value. He suddenly retired to Nice in 1855 and died at Saint-Raphael. His memoirs, *Le Livre de bord* (4 vols., 1879–80), contain most informative accounts of the Paris world of letters during the second quarter of the century.

**Kasprowicz, Jan** (1860–1926), Polish poet. Born at Szymborze into a peasant family, he gained a good education and was for a time at Leipzig University. Becoming involved in German leftist politics he was imprisoned in 1887, and on his release returned to Poland working as a journalist. His powerful volumes of poetry, *Chrystus* (1890) and *Anima lachrymans* (1894), reveal intense unhappiness and a groping after a faith he could not reach. He entered academic life in 1909 and a few years later the conflict began to abate. Retiring to the country he found himself at spiritual peace at last. His *Hymny* (1921), a republication of two earlier volumes with later work added, traces this spiritual odyssey. He died at Harenda.

**Kästner, Erich** (1899–     ), German story-writer, novelist and poet. Born in Dresden, he began his literary career with verse satires such as *Lärm im Spiegel* (1928), but his more characteristic work is in prose. He has written full-length novels such as *Fabian* (1930; Eng. trans., 1932), but it is as the author of children's books that he has made his particular reputation. Of these *Emil und die Detektive* (1928; Eng. trans. *Emil and the Detectives*, 1930), *Pünktchen und Anton* (1930; Eng. trans. *Annaluise and Anton*, 1932), *Der 35. Mai* (1931; Eng. trans. *The Thirty-fifth of May*, 1933) and *Das fliegende Klassenzimmer* (1932; Eng. trans. *The Flying Classroom*, 1934) are inimitable. A later work in the same vein is *Das doppelte Lottchen* (1949).

**Katayev, Valentin Petrovich** (1897–     ), Russian Soviet novelist and playwright, was born in Odessa. He reached literary maturity early with his powerful if loosely constructed novel *Rastratchiki* (1926; Eng. trans. *The Embezzlers*, 1929). Another novel, *Vremya vpered* (1932; Eng. trans. *Time, Forward*, 1933), is one of the most successful efforts in favour of the Stalin industrial programme. The best known and most artistically satisfying of his works is the play *Kvadratura kruga* (1928; Eng. trans. *Squaring the Circle*, 1943). His Second World War novel *Za vlast' Sovietov* (1949, 'For the Power of the Soviets') deals with the underground movement in German-occupied Odessa.

**Katerla, Józef,** *see* **Żeromski, S.**

**Katkov, Mikhail Nikiforovich** (1818–1887), Russian man of letters, a lifelong resident of Moscow. As editor of the cautious liberal paper *Russkiy Vestnik* (from 1856) he opened the literary door to Dostoyevsky (q.v.) by accepting his contributions. He later wrote powerfully, even cruelly, in the interests of the strong reaction which set in after the Polish Revolution of 1863. His collected works (25 vols.) appeared in 1897. Such vigorous Russian journalistic prose passes more often than not over the borders into literature.

**Katona, József** (1791–1830), Hungarian dramatist, was born and died at Kecskemét. All his work except his tragedy *Bánk Bán* (performed posthumously, 1833; Fr. trans. by C. de Bigault, 1910) is forgotten, but this is accounted the finest work of its kind in Hungarian literature.

**Kavaphes, Konstantinos** (1863–1933), Greek poet. Born in Alexandria, he never lived in Greece, and therefore was not involved in the nationalist movement in Greek literature which sought inspiration in the pre-classical period. The minor notes of Hellenistic and Byzantine culture were the inspiration of Kavaphes; both were elaborate and declining civilizations which in his eyes formed a clear parallel with the dying occidental civilization of his own day. Kavaphes's point of view, that we are nearing the end of the road of life which has existed for a thousand years, is forcefully and movingly set before us in such poems as *Perimenontas tous Barbarous* ('Waiting for the Barbarians'), *Polis* ('City') and *Ithaki* ('Ithaca'), all written before 1912. After that a noticeable decline in his work set in. After Solomos (q.v.) the greatest modern Greek poet, his collected poetry, *Poiemata*, appeared in 1935 (Eng. trans. 1951). He died in Alexandria.

**Kaverin, Venyamin,** pseudonym of **Venyamin Alexandrovich Zilberg** (1902–    ), Russian Soviet novelist and short-story writer. Born in Odessa, he became known as the author of a collection of weird short stories, *Mastera i podmasterya* (1923, ' Masters and Apprentices'). He followed this up with *Konets Khazy* (1926, 'The End of a Gang'), in which he deals with the seamy side of Leningrad life, always with an eye for the bizarre. *Devyat' desyatykh sud'by* (1926, ' Nine-tenths of Fate') deals with the revolution of 1917. He embarked on a journey into the psychological approach to events with his long novel *Ispolnenie zhelaniy* (1934; Eng. trans. *The Larger View*, 1938). *Dva kapitana* (1940; Eng. trans. *Two Captains*, 1942) is a children's book about an explorer.

**Keller, Gottfried** (1819–1890), Swiss poet, novelist and short-story writer, was born, a turner's son, at Zürich. Convinced that painting was his vocation, he spent two years in Munich studying it (1840–2), but, having realized that he had not enough talent, returned home and there remained with his widowed mother, drifting aimlessly along. After a time, however, he began to write poetry, a volume of which (*Gedichte*) appeared in 1846. On the strength of its quality he was given a bursary which allowed him to study at Heidelberg. Another volume of verse (*Neuere Gedichte*) was published in 1851 at Berlin, where he spent the years from 1850 to 1855. They were formative years, and in them he reached that maturity which enabled him to write a full-length autobiographical novel, *Der grüne Heinrich* (4 vols., 1854; Eng. trans. *Green Henry*, 1960). In this work, of the literary lineage of *Wilhelm Meister*, he describes a young man's struggles as an artist, his problems and his dreams up to the point at which he is ready to stand up to the fact that he has chosen the wrong path and must retrace his steps. A certain formlessness about the work, and a matter-of-fact manner as if he feared to run into sentimentality, are generally features of all his later publications; but at his best he loses this half self-consciousness and produces almost perfect short stories such as are to be found in *Die Leute von Seldwyla* (i, 1856; ii, 1874; Eng. trans. *The People of Seldwyla*, 1929), including that miniature masterpiece, *Romeo und Julia auf dem Dorfe* ('A Village Romeo and Juliet'), which inspired Frederick Delius's *The Walk to the Paradise Garden*. In 1861 he became a civil servant, a post which brought him security but somewhat detracted from his literary avocations, and from which he resigned with a pension in 1876. The charming collection *Sieben Legenden* (Eng. trans. *Seven Legends*, 1929) appeared in 1872, *Züricher Novellen* in 1878, a revised edition of *Der grüne Heinrich* in 1879, and his finest piece of narrative writing, *Das Sinngedicht*, in 1882. In 1883 he published his collected poetry, *Gesammelte Gedichte*, which proves his lyric gifts. His last work, the long novel *Martin Salander* (1886), shows his powers in decline. He died in Zürich. His collected works appeared (10 vols.) between 1889 and 1893. The standard edition is that (24 vols.) of 1926–54.

**Kellgren, Johan Henrik** (1751–1795), Swedish poet and dramatist, was born at Floby, had a distinguished undergraduate career at the University of Åbo, and later settled in Stockholm, where he founded the celebrated newspaper *Stockholms-Posten* (1778). King Gustav III soon became his patron and provided him with plots for his poetical plays. In *Stockholms-Posten* Kellgren struck out manfully for the royal party against the nobility and clergy. He died in Stockholm.

**Kempis, Thomas à** (1379–1471) German prose-writer, writing in Latin, was born Thomas Hammerken at Kempen, near Düsseldorf. Although his parents were small peasants, his mother kept the village school and Thomas had mastered the rudiments of education before being sent, thanks to Church influence, to the famous Netherlands school at Deventer in 1391. Here he showed from the first his simple yet strong devotion and his love of a retired and studious life. In 1400 he entered the Augustinian monastery of Agnetenberg, near Zwolle, professed his vows in 1407 and was ordained priest in 1413. His particular duty was that of a copyist, and he gained a reputation for the beauty of his calligraphy expended on Bibles, missals and books of hours. He wrote several books of devotion and sermons, but it is his *Imitatio Christi* which has made him famous. Begun about 1415 and finished about ten years later, it is a work of quiet simple beauty, ascetic but cheerful, and reaching the realms of poetry at times. The earliest existing manuscript is that by Thomas himself and is dated 1441. The earliest printed copy appeared in 1472 and the first English translation in 1502. Of numerous English translations John Wesley's (1735) is memorable. Over three thousand editions of the *Imitation* have been published. He died at Agnetenberg.

**Kerner, Justinus Andreas Christian** (1786–1862), German poet and prose-writer, was born at Ludwigsburg in Württemberg and followed a medical career first at Wildbad and later at Weinsberg, where he died. At first a thorough-paced romantic poet, he associated with the

'Swabian' school, being a particular friend of Uhland (q.v.), and contributed some notable poems, especially in the medieval ballad style, to the *Poetischer Almanach für 1812*. *Deutscher Dichterwald* (1813) contains his best verse. He gradually became more and more interested in the occult, publishing his famous *Die Seherin von Prevorst* (1829; Eng. trans. *The Seeress of Prevorst*, 1845, by Catherine Crowe, the 'inventor' of the English ghost story), which contains much about clairvoyance and somnambulism, and the collection of stories of the supernatural comprised in *Magikon* (5 vols., 1840–53). There are on the other hand warmth, an engaging wistfulness and quaintness in *Bilderbuch aus der Knabenzeit* (1849, 'Picture-book of Childhood'). He lived in a kind of Gothic splendour, and his house below the castle of Weibertreu, which he had had restored at his expense, became a place of literary pilgrimage, not so much because of what he wrote as because of what he represented as the link between German literary romanticism and nationalism.

**Kettenfeier, Petri,** *see* **Rosegger, P.**

**Keyserling, Hermann Alexander** (1880–1946), German prose-writer. Born at Könno, Estonia, he studied at the universities of Dorpat, Heidelberg and Vienna, and then for a while became an art critic in Paris. His purely philosophical work is not of concern here, important though its influence was at the time. It is as the author of *Das Reisetagebuch eines Philosophen* (1919; Eng. trans. *The Travel Diary of a Philosopher*, 1925) that Count Keyserling revealed himself as a most attractive stylist, propounding his synthesis of a scientific view of the world and of oriental philosophy. Deprived of his estates in 1918 he settled in Germany, founding the 'School of Wisdom' at Darmstadt in 1920. He died at Innsbruck.

**Khomyakov, Alexey Stepanovich** (1804–1860), Russian prose-writer and poet. Born in Moscow, he wrote as a believer in tradition and keenly disliked the results of the industrialization of the West, which he considered would result in its decadence. An exception to this Western decay was England, which he highly esteemed for its adherence to tradition, and he had several English friends with whom he kept up a regular correspondence. He died at Ternovskoye. From among his numerous works, many of them religious (*Polnoye sobranie sochineniy*, 8 vols., 1900–7), has been extracted *O tserkvi* (1926; Eng. trans. *The Church is One*, 1948), excellently written and of particular interest in these days of oecumenicalism.

**Kielland, Alexander Lange** (1849–1906), Norwegian novelist, was born at Stavanger of a wealthy merchant family, but branched out on his own in business, buying and managing a brick, chimney-pot and tile factory. He had meanwhile graduated at Kristiania University, where he had gained a love of literature which finally drew him away to Paris in 1878. A study there of French literature decided him, he tried his hand at writing, and on his return to Norway showed his work to Björnson (q.v.), with whose help it was published in magazines. It was acclaimed, and Kielland immediately sold his factory and devoted himself entirely to literature. His first book of stories,

*Novelletter* (1879), showed that he had unbounded grace of style with an underlying vigour springing from his keen sense of all injustice. This book was followed by *Nye Novelletter* (1880; Eng. trans. of both volumes in *Norse Tales and Sketches* by R. L. Cassie, 1896). He now laid about him purposefully, attacking (often unfairly) conditions in the civil service in *Arbeidsfolk* (1881), in schools in *Fortuna* (1884) and in the Church, *Sankt Hans Fest* (1887); but his quieter social studies *Garman og Worse* (1880; Eng. trans. *Garman and Worse* 1885), *Else* (1881; Eng. trans. 1894) and *Skipper Worse* (1882; Eng. trans. 1885) make better and more lasting literature. Like so many reformers on paper, practical experience taught him a lesson, and as governor of Romsdal he greatly modified his extreme views. He later turned to folk-story writing such as *Mennesker og Dyr* (1891; Eng. trans. in *Norse Tales and Sketches*, 1896) and to history such as *Omkring Napoleon* (1905; Eng. trans. *Napoleon's Men and Methods*, 1907). He died at Bergen. His collected works were published (12 vols.) in 1949–50.

**Kierkegaard, Søren Aabye** (1813–1855), Danish philosopher and prose-writer, was born in Copenhagen, the son of a wealthy Jewish business man of dominating personality. As a child he led a solitary, gloomy life, but managed eventually to gain parental permission to read philosophy at Copenhagen University. On graduating in theology he travelled widely before settling for the rest of his life in his native city, wrestling with the problems of belief. An anti-Hegelian, a firm believer in 'essential' Christianity but as strong an opponent of its outward forms, the work, he claimed, of mere scientific philosophers (that is, the theologians), his influence on thought and literature has been enormous, from Ibsen (q.v.) and Strindberg (q.v.) to the French existentialists and modern German religious thinkers. His most important books are: *Enten-Eller* (1843; Eng. trans. *Either-Or*, 2 vols., 1944), *Stadier paa Livets Vej* (1845; Eng. trans. *Stages on Life's Way*, 1939), *Kjælighedens Gjerninger* (1847; Eng. trans. *Works of Love*, 1946), *Sygdommen til Døden* (1848; Eng. trans. *The Sickness Unto Death*, 1941), *Til Selvprøvelse* (1851; Eng. trans. *For Self-Examination*, 1940) and *Guds Uforanderlighed* (1855; Eng. trans. *Kierkegaard's Attack upon 'Christendom'*, 1944). He died prematurely, worn out by overwork, in Copenhagen.

**Kingo, Thomas Hansen** (1634–1703), Danish poet, born at Slangerup, of part Scottish ancestry, entered the Church and later became a bishop (of Odense, 1677). A great poet in a heavily ornate style, he is still highly regarded in Denmark for his *Kirke-Psalmebog* (1699) which contains a collection of hymns in all manner of styles full of religious fervour. He had been bedridden several years before his death at Odense.

**Kinkel, Gottfried** (1815–1882), German poet. Born at Oberkassel, near Bonn, he became *Privatdocent* at the university there. As a result of his taking a prominent part as a liberal in the revolution of 1848 he was imprisoned in Spandau, from whence he escaped to London and was a private tutor there until appointed professor of archaeology at Zürich, where he died. His romantic poetry with its strong sense of history was enormously popular in its day, as, for example, *Otto der Schütz* (1846), which in fifty years passed through seventy-three editions. Other volumes of poetry were *Der Grobschmied von Antwerpen* (1872) and *Tanagra* (1883).

**Kirshon, Vladimir Mikhaylovich** (1902–1938), Russian Soviet dramatist. Born in Petersburg, he wrote many topical plays, often little more than propaganda in support of the Bolshevik regime; but *Khleb* (1930; Eng. trans. *Bread* in *Six Soviet Plays*, 1935), a study of the clash of personalities and ideals on a collective farm, is an outstanding play.

**Klabund,** pseudonym of **Alfred Henschke** (1890–1928), German poet, novelist and playwright. Born at Crossen, he had developed tuberculosis by 1914 and spent the rest of his short life struggling against the inevitable end. A worshipper of the senses, in all his work there is an all-pervading love of 'paradises' natural and artificial, often in a vague oriental setting. As a poet he is represented by such haunting volumes as *Morgenrot! Klabund! Die Tage dämmern* (1912), *Litai-pe* (1916) and *Das heisse Herz* (1923). His vividly written, sometimes breathless novels include *Bracke. Ein Eulenspiegelheld* (1918; Eng. trans. *Brackie, the Fool*, 1927), *Pjotr. Roman eines Zaren* (1923; Eng. trans. *Peter the Czar*, 1925) and *Borgia. Roman einer Familie* (1928; Eng. trans. *The Incredible Borgias*, 1929). His play *Der Kreidekreis* (1924; Eng. trans. *The Circle of Chalk*, 1929) proves that he was exploring another medium with understanding. He died at Davos, Switzerland. A selection of his poems were translated into English as *Poems of Conflict and Despair* in *German Life and Letters* (iv, 1950).

**Kleist, Ewald Christian von** (1715–1759), German poet. Born at Zeblin, Pomerania, of an old Prussian Junker family, he followed in their footsteps in the army. He took part in the War of the Austrian Succession, but at the Peace of Aix-la-Chapelle (1748) found time to pursue his taste for literature and moved in literary circles, becoming a friend of Gleim (q.v.) and corresponding with Breitinger (q.v). The latter introduced him to *The Seasons* of James Thomson, which Kleist found was just the technical guide he needed in expressing his own love of nature. The result was *Der Frühling* (1749, 'Spring'), which marks an epoch in German literature. His meeting with Lessing (q.v.) in Leipzig in 1756 was of immense importance for both, but they were not long together. Kleist's second volume, *Gedichte* (1756), had not been long published when he was recalled to the army on the outbreak of the Seven Years War. The classical influence of Lessing can be seen in his last work, *Cissides und Paches* (1759). He died in Frankfurt-an-der-Oder of wounds received at the Battle of Kunersdorf. See his *Werke*, edited by A. Sauer (3 vols., 1883).

**Kleist, Heinrich von** (1777–1811), German dramatist and short-story writer. Born in Frankfurt-an-der-Oder of an old Junker military family, the same as that of E. C. von Kleist (q.v.), he revolted against his social surroundings, and his struggle against his circumstances permanently twisted his mind. He first entered the army, but soon resigned his commission and engaged in private study until on the verge of a mental breakdown he tore himself away to travel in France and Switzerland. A broken engagement was followed by a serious attempt to find literary expression for his almost insurmountable spiritual problem, and his first play, *Die Familie Schroffenstein* (1803; Eng. trans. *The Feud of the Schroffensteins*, 1916), is romantic and disordered. *Amphitryon* (1807) is Molière's play of that title in a *Sturm und Drang* dress. *Penthesilea* (1808) is a sombre, decadent play set in Homeric times with characters 'like the shadows of giants, frightening and impalpable'. On the other hand *Der zerbrochene Krug* (1808; not publ. till 1811) is a one-act comedy, about the only German one of first-class rank. *Das Kätchen von Heilbronn, oder die Feuer- probe* (1810; Eng. trans. in *Fiction and Fantasy of German Romance*, by F. Pierce, 1927) is an excursion into the medieval, the plot ridi- culous but the poetry at times magnificent. *Die Hermannsschlacht* and his masterpiece *Der Prinz von Homburg*, although composed between 1808 and 1810, were not published till 1821. (Of the latter there are several translations, the best being that by H. Hagedorn in *German Classics of the 19th and 20th Centuries*, 1913.) In *Die Hermanns- schlacht*, the plot of which is founded on the patriotic Arminius theme, Kleist gives way to his hatred of the French occupiers of Prussia, with the result that what should have been a tragedy in the grand manner has become a nationalistic manifesto. *Der Prinz von Homburg* on the other hand is the greatest north German drama. Set in Brandenburg at the time of the Great Elector, the plot revolves upon the themes of responsibility, fate and expiation and at last Kleist has found his way towards classical Greek tragedy. As a long short-story writer Kleist is best represented by *Michael Kohlhaas* (1810; Eng. trans 1913), which together with several others appeared in the last year of his life. Here again we find the theme of expiation (albeit mistakenly undertaken), self-sacrifice in order to make the harsh world a better place. Unable to reconcile himself to life, Kleist, together with a woman whom he had met by chance a few days before and who was of similar mind, committed suicide on the shore of the Wannsee, near Berlin. His works were first collected by Ludwig Tieck (q.v.) in three volumes (1826).

**Klikspaan,** *see* **Kneppelhout, J.**

**Klinger, Friedrich Maximilian von** (1752–1831), German dramatist and novelist, was born in Frankfurt-am-Main of humble family, came to the notice of Goethe, who helped him to gain education at Giessen University, and turned to letters. Winning the Hamburg Theatre's prize for the best drama by a young writer with his tragedy *Die Zwillinge* (1776), a lurid, undisciplined but strong piece written in a strange, abrupt style, he followed this up with *Der Wirrwarr, oder Sturm und Drang* (1776, 'Storm and Stress'), which gave its name to the short-lived intense romantic movement, a revolt of the intellectuals of Germany against the petty tyrannies of the caste system, a movement which Goethe had launched with such works as *Stella, Clavigo* and *Werther,* and which was to end with

Schiller's *Die Räuber*. In a quieter style are *Stilpo und seiner Kinder* (1780) and *Konradin* (1784). In 1780 he entered the Russian army, in which he rose to the rank of general. The rest of his work is of minor importance, and of his rambling novels only *Fausts Leben, Tathen und Himmelfahrt* (1791) is worth consideration. Klinger died at Dorpat. The best selected edition of his earlier work is Berendt and Wolff's *Klingers Jugenddramen* (3 vols., 1912–13).

**Klopstock, Friedrich Gottlieb** (1724–1803), German poet. Born the son of a prosperous lawyer at Quedlinburg, he was educated first at Schulpforta, where he planned and even began his epic on Christ's life, and at the universities of Jena and Leipzig. At Jena, which he entered in 1745, he read theology, and, greatly influenced by the literary criticism of J. J. Bodmer (q.v.) who had maintained that blank verse was unsuitable for the German language, wrote the first cantos of *Der Messias* in prose. At Leipzig he came under Gottsched's (q.v.) influence, as a result of which he was induced to rewrite them in hexameters. The first three cantos were published in the *Bremer Beiträge* in 1748 and were immediately acclaimed. It was not until 1773 that the work was completed in twenty cantos, and by that time it seemed outmoded. Nevertheless it was probably the greatest monument of devotional poetry of the eighteenth century, and showed both descriptive powers and an ability to convey ideas and feelings in suitable language. Where it particularly fails is that *Der Messias* has no dramatic qualities; it is without action. Today it may be considered dead. As a lyric poet, however, Klopstock can be said to have survived. His first collection of such poetry, *An meine Freunde* (1747), is a collection of vivacious verses addressed to his Leipzig friends. This collection, enlarged and renamed *Wingolf* (1767), contains some attractive love-poetry such as *An Fanny*, and his *Oden* were published in 1771. In these last he introduced a variety of classical metres, unattempted in German literature before, and proved how well they fitted the language. In this he may be acclaimed as an innovator, heading the path that led to that triumphant use of metre by Hölderlin (q.v.). Klopstock lived in Copenhagen, a pensioner of the Danish Government from 1751 to 1770, when he moved to Hamburg where he died. During the last part of his career he was influenced by James Macpherson's *Ossian*, and wrote a 'bardic' dramatic trilogy about Germany's earliest patriot, Hermann (or Arminius), but it amounts to little. His work in this field did, however, have a long-lasting effect on the 'historical sense' in German literature, at any rate in opening up misty vistas of a nebulous past as a source of inspiration. His *Werke* were published (7 vols.) in 1798–1809.

**Kluge, Kurt** (1886–1940), German novelist, born in Leipzig. After practising as a sculptor for many years, he turned to writing and used his natural fund of humour to good advantage in *Der Glockengiesser Christoph Mahr* (1934), *Die silberne Windfahne* (1935), *Die gefälschte Göttin* (1935), *Herr Kortüm* (1938) and *Die Zaubergeige* (1940). He died at Lüttich.

**Klyuyev, Nikolay Alexeyevich** (1887–1937), Russian Soviet poet. Born the son of peasants in the Lake Onega region, he was brought up in the poverty which made him welcome the revolution of 1917, and yet also in an atmosphere of age-old quasi-Christian mysticism which made him highly suspicious of its materialistic implications. With the death of Lenin and the decline of Trotsky's influence his worst fears seemed realized. He grafted his religiosity on to his remarkable long poem *Lenin* (1924), but thereafter his was a losing battle against the ascendancy of town over the traditions of village life. After 1928 he published no more, and died nine years later in a concentration camp for his reactionary views. The whereabouts of his death are unknown.

**Kneppelhout, Johannes,** who used the pseudonym **Klikspaan** (1814–1885), Dutch prose-writer. Born in Leiden, he began to specialize in breezy accounts of student life such as *Opuscules de jeunesse* (1838), *Studententypen* (1841) and *Studentenleven* (1844). His later work shows some sign of mental derangement, yet he died sane at Oosterbeek. His *Geschriften* were published (12 vols.), 1860–75.

**Kniaźnin, Franciszek Dionizy** (1750–1807), Polish poet. Born at Witebsk, he won a secure reputation as one of Poland's finest lyric poets in the classical style with *Erotyki* (2 vols., 1779), *Carmina* (1781), *Wiersze* (1783) and the bulk of his work contained in *Poezje* (3 vols., 1787–9). He has been compared to the English poet William Collins. He died at Końskowola.

**Knigge, Adolf Franz Friedrich von** (1752–1796), German prose-writer. Born of noble family at Bredenbeck, near Hanover, he lived as a gentleman of property, but was too active in mind to vegetate at a continuous stretch in the country, and held a court appointment at Weimar, where he met Goethe, and later a high official post at Bremen, where he died. *Geschichte des armen Herrn von Mildenberg* (1789) represents him as a novelist, but a rambling and generally ineffective one, and *Die Reise nach Braunschweig* (1792) reveals him as an entertaining because inquisitive traveller. It is, however, for his attractively urbane didactic *Über den Umgang mit Menschen* (1788) that he is now remembered. In vigorous natural prose he tenders worldly wise advice on how to live the life of the 'golden mean'.

**Knorring, Sophie von** (1797–1848), Swedish novelist. Born at Erska of noble family, she produced the charming love-story *Cousinerna* in 1834, which was followed up with *Axel* (1836) and *Tante Lisbeths 19 : de Testamente* (1838). Her serious side is shown in her stinging exposure of the *nouveau riche*, who by this time were buying up Swedish country estates and flooding rural life with their vulgarity, *Torparen och hans omgifning* (1843; Eng. trans. *The Peasant and his Landlord*, 1848). She died at Skärv.

**Kochanowski, Jan** (1530–1584), Polish poet, writing in Latin and Polish, and dramatist, was born at Sycyn and was educated at Cracow and in Italy. He visited Paris before returning to Poland to hold a court appointment, rising in 1567 to become secretary to King

Sigismund. It was while abroad and at court that he wrote his so-phisticated Latin verse such as that contained in *Lyricorum libellus* (1580), probably his best Latin collection with some charming love-lyrics, and *Foricoenia sive Epigrammatum libellus* (1584) with some trenchant epigrams. In 1575 he suddenly left the court and settled down to the life of a married farmer. He now turned to plays and wrote his interesting *Odprawa posłów greckich* (1578; Eng. trans. *The Dismissal of the Greek Envoys*, 1918). He might well have produced more along the lines of this, but the death of his little daughter in 1579 turned him into an elegiac poet. His moving Polish poems reach their highest fulfilment in *Threny* (1580; Eng. trans. *Laments*, 1920) and *Pieśni* (1586; Eng. trans. *Chants*, 1932). He died at Lublin. An English translation of many of his poems was published in 1908 as *Poems by Jan Kochanowski*.

**Kock, Charles Paul de** (1793–1871), French novelist, born at Passy, the posthumous son of a banker of Dutch descent guillotined during the French Revolution. He soon abandoned all thought of a business life and took to fiction writing. In this field his keen observation, clear descriptive powers, well-constructed plots and salacity brought him a Europe-wide public. His style is slipshod. His most successful novels were his first: *L'Enfant de ma femme* (1812), *Gustave, ou le mauvais sujet* (1821), *Le Barbier de Paris* (1826), *La Femme, le mari et l'amant* (1829), *La Pucelle de Belleville* (1834), *Mon voisin Raymond* (1837), *Mœurs Parisiennes* (1837) and *Moustache* (1838). His later work is purely mechanical. He died in Paris. His *Mémoires* (1873) are of some interest.

**Kokoschka, Oskar** (1886–    ), Austrian poet and dramatist, born at Pöchlarn, Lower Austria, the son of a goldsmith. His expressionistic and psychological approach is well exemplified in his poetry, *Die träumenden Knaben* (1908), and in his plays *Der brennende Dornbusch* (1911) and *Vier Dramen*, containing *Dornbusch, Mörder, Hiob* and *Orpheus und Eurydike* (1919). Seriously wounded during the First World War, he turned more and more to art, becoming professor at the Dresden Academy (1920–4). Thereafter he travelled much, gained an extensive reputation as a portraitist and landscapist, and in 1938 settled in London, where he remained until 1953. His interesting collection of letters, *Schriften, 1907–1955*, appeared in 1956.

**Kolb, Annette** (1875–    ), German novelist, was born in Munich and produced such society fiction as *Das Exemplar* (1913). She aimed at the cosmopolitan approach with an accent on French culture, especially the work of Villiers de l'Isle-Adam (q.v.) and Giraudoux (q.v.), for after all her mother was French. She came out as an opponent of chauvinism during the First World War with *Dreizehn Briefe einer Deutsch-Französin* (1917); *Zarastro* (1921) and *Kleine Fanfare* (1930) contained interesting treatment of the contemporary scene. In 1931 she warned Europe of the coming danger of Nazism in *Alle Männer in Europa haben versagt!! Ein paar Ausrufungszeichen von Annette Kolb*, and when the disaster did come eighteen months later she made for Paris. Here she wrote her attractive story of a family, *Die Schaukel* (1934). The débâcle of 1940 forced her to

Switzerland and thence to New York. Of her later productions the best is the historical work *König Ludwig II und Richard Wagner* (1947).

**Kolbenheyer, Erwin Guido** (1878–1962), German novelist. Born in Budapest, he wrote several pieces of historical fiction, attractive as to subject but presented in a stilted style which greatly detracts from them. Best known are *Amor Dei* (1908; Eng. trans. *God-Intoxicated Man*, 1933), *Meister Joachim Pausewang* (1910; Eng. trans. *A Winter Chronicle*, 1938), dealing with Breslau in 1650, *Paracelsus* (3 vols., 1917–25) and *Heroische Leidenschaften* (1928), about Giordano Bruno (q.v.). He also wrote on philosophical matters, and composed some plays such as *Götter und Menschen* (1944). He died in Munich.

**Komenský, J. A.,** *see* **Comenius, J. A.**

**Konevskoy, Ivan Ivanovich** (1877–1901), Russian poet, born in Petersburg, contributed excellent nature poetry to various periodicals, collected after his death as *Stikhi i proza* (ed. V. Brynsov, 1904). He died in Riga.

**Konrad von Würzburg** (1220?–1287), German poet. Born in Würzburg, he settled in Basel, and under wealthy patrons produced several works of a sophisticated technique, above all the devotional *Die goldene Schmiede* and the allegorical *Klage der Kunst* (ed. together by E. Schröder, 1926). Of his short tales the best known are *Der Welt Lohn* and *Der Schwanritter* (there are two collections of them ed. E. Schröder, 1930 and 1936). Then there are the romances *Partenopier und Meliur* (ed. K. Bartsch, 1871) and *Der Trojanerkrieg* (ed. A. von Keller, 1858) with their classical undertones. Konrad died in Basel.

**Körner, Karl Theodor** (1791–1813), German poet. Born in Dresden, the son of Schiller's friend, he was brought up as an idolized prodigy in the middle of a literary and artistic circle. In 1811 he went to Vienna and wrote several plays, including *Zriny* (1812), which contain 'more of Schiller's rhetoric than his poetry'. On the outbreak of the Prussian rising of 1813 against Napoleon he took up arms writing his patriotic songs and ballads, among them ' Das Schwertlied ' (' The Song of the Sword ') composed a few hours before his death in action at Gadebusch, near Hamburg. His poetry was collected as *Leyer und Schwert* (1814; Eng. trans. *The Lyre and the Sword*, 1834).

**Korniychuk, Alexander Evdokimovich** (1910–      ), Russian Soviet dramatist, born at Chrystynivka in the Ukraine. He succeeded only in topical plays, and his two vivid ones on the German invasion of the Ukraine, *Partizany v stepyakh Ukrainy* (1942, 'Partisans in the Steppes of the Ukraine') and *Front* (1942), both of which were translated into English in *Four Soviet Plays* (1944), are remarkable contributions to Soviet literature.

**Korolenko, Vladimir Galaktionovich** (1853–1921), Russian novelist, born at Zhitomir of Russian-Polish parentage, he went in for journalism and suffered long exile in Siberia, which provided him with the raw material with which he built his first success *Son Makara* (1883;

Eng. trans. *Maker's Dream*, 1891). He was a writer of great sensibility, abundant sympathy with suffering and a deep love of nature. All these elements and his quiet humour and faith in ultimate good go to make this and other works, such as *Les shumit* (1886; Eng. trans. *The Murmuring Forest and other Stories*, 1916) and *Slepoy Muzykant* (1887; Eng. trans. *The Blind Musician*, 1890), so memorable. His very personal *Istoriya moego sovremennika* (4 vols., 1906–10, 'History of my Contemporaries') was translated by the famous Communist Rosa Luxemburg as *Die Geschichte meines Zeitgenossen* (2 vols., 1919). Korolenko, who accepted the revolution (but without enthusiasm), died at Poltava.

**Kosor, Josip** (1879–1961), Serbian playwright and poet, was born at Trebunj, Dalmatia, the son of an artisan. He entered literary life early and tried his fortune in Germany and Austria. His first successful play was *Pozar strasti* (1911; Eng. trans. *Passion's Furnace*, 1917), and other notable stage works were *Pomirenje* (1913; Eng. trans. *Reconciliation*, 1917) and *Nepobjediva ladja* (1922; Eng. trans. *The Invincible Ship*, 1917). As a poet he is represented by *Bijeli plamenovi* (1919; Eng. trans. by Kosor himself, *White Flames*, 1929).

**Kossak-Szczucka, Zofia** (1890–        ), Polish novelist and short-story writer. Born at Skowródki, she had some personal experience of the Russian Revolution and the succeeding war, which coloured her earlier work. Later she found the historical novel in the tradition of Sienkiewicz (q.v.) most suited to her particular talent. Her first really successful work was a volume of short stories, *Kłopoty Kacperka goreckiego skrzata* (1926; Eng. trans. *The Troubles of a Gnome*, 1928). Of her full-length novels outstanding are *Krzyżowcy* (1935; Eng. trans. *Angels in the Dust*, 1947), *Król trędowaty* (1937; Eng. trans. *Blessed are the Meek*, 1944) and *Przymierze* (1946; Eng. trans. *The Covenant*, 1951).

**Kostylyev, Valentin Ivanovich** (1888–1950), Russian Soviet novelist, author of the finest piece of historical fiction in modern Russian letters, the trilogy *Ivan Grozny* (3 vols., 1941–5, 'Ivan the Terrible'). Less true to fact than several other works of the same kind, it is yet more a work of art by reason of its author's being truly inspired by a fervent patriotism which carries the plot along like a whirlwind.

**Kotzebue, August Friedrich Ferdinand von** (1761–1819), German dramatist and miscellaneous writer, was born at Weimar and became a lawyer there. A man of personality and ambition, he entered the Russian legal service, in which he soon rose in rank, and by 1785 had obtained an important government post at Reval and was granted a patent of Russian nobility. He next became chief magistrate of Estonia, but retired from his post in 1795, having in the meantime made a far-reaching reputation with his fast-moving romantic plays, shallow no doubt, but with an unerring knowledge of stagecraft, the envy of Goethe and many another lesser figure who from then on could never forgive him his good fortune. His first success, launched (as were most of his other plays) in Vienna and Berlin, was *Adelheid von Wulfingen* (1788; Eng. trans. *Adelaide*, 1798), followed immediately by his greatest success of all, *Menschenhass und Reue*

(1789; Eng. trans. *The Stranger*, 1798). He turned to exotic themes, exploiting South America, and produced 'noble savage' plots in *Die Indianer in England* (1790; Eng. trans. *The Indian Exiles*, 1801), *Die Sonnenjungfrau* (1791; Eng. trans. *The Virgin of the Sun*, 1799), about Mexico, and *Die Spanier in Peru* (1796; Eng. trans. (or rather adaptation) by R. B. Sheridan, *Pizarro*, 1799). On leaving Russian government service in 1795 he was made director of the German theatre at Petersburg where he remained, with one break of a few months in 1800 when he was in detention in Siberia, until the death of the Czar Paul the following year. Thereafter he lived in Germany and became a central figure of literary activities in Berlin. Among his miscellaneous prose works may be named *Das merkwürdigste Jahr meines Lebens* (2 vols., 1801; Eng. trans. *The Most Remarkable Year in the Life of A. von Kotzebue*, 1802) and *Erinnerungen aus Paris* (1804; Eng. trans. *Travels*, 1806). His connection with Russia was to be his undoing and still more perhaps his reactionary opinions which he was never afraid of announcing, and in spite of his anti-Napoleonic pamphlets he was disliked by the rising generation of the War of Prussian Independence. He was often in Weimar, where the literary world showed its hostility, and in Mannheim, where he quarrelled with theatre managers. In 1816 he became director of the Russian foreign service in Germany, and was murdered in Mannheim by a student called Sand who hated him for his mockery of the German student movement and believed him to be a spy in Russian pay. The murder had great political consequences, leading to the suppression of liberal movements in Germany and Austria, and in fact was grist to Metternich's mill. Kotzebue's dramatic works were published (40 vols.) in 1840–1.

**Kozmian, Kajetan** (1771–1856), Polish poet, born at Gałęzów. He is known for his attractive imitation of Vergil, *Ziemiaństwo polskie* (1830; Eng. trans. *The Georgics of Poland*, n.d.). He also wrote a great variety of lyric poetry. His collected works, *Pamiętniki* (3 vols.) appeared between 1858 and 1865. He died at Piotrowice.

**Krasicki, Ignacy** (1735–1801), Polish poet and novelist, born of noble family at Dubieck, he became a member of the intimate circle of King Stanislas Poniatowski, through whose influence he was consecrated Bishop of Ermland in 1766. Imbued with all that was good in the European culture of the Age of Enlightenment, he is the best Polish writer of his time, and was highly appreciated outside his own country, especially in Germany, throughout the nineteenth century. A wit and master of a graceful style, he satirized the failings of his countrymen in such vivacious books of verse as *Myszeidos pieśni X* (1775; Fr. trans. *La souriade*, 1817), *Monachomachija* (1778; Ger. trans. *Der Mönchekrieg*, 1870), *Satyry* (1779; Ger. trans. *Satiren*, 1788) and *Bajki i przypowieści* (1779; Ger. trans. *Die älteren Fabeln*, 1914). His two novels on contemporary Polish social life are of much interest. They are *Nikołaja Doświadczyńskiego przypadki* (1776; Ger. trans. *Begebenheiten des Nicolaus Doświadczyński*, 1777) and *Pan Podstoli* (1778; Ger. trans. *Herr Unter-Truchsess*, 1779). Translated to the archbishopric of Gniezno in 1795, that fatal year during which, on the Third Partition, Poland ceased to exist as a political entity, he retired to Berlin, where he died.

**Krasiński, Zygmunt** (1812–1859), Polish poet, playwright and novelist, was born in Paris. Two years later the family, a noble one, settled in Warsaw and he eventually went to the university there, but because of his father's unpopularity in the city owing to his pro-Russian ideas, young Zygmunt was removed, and shortly afterwards the Krasińskis were on the road again, this time to Switzerland, where he found congenial friends including Adam Mickiewicz (q.v.). The rest of his life was a series of wanderings. It was in Rome that his literary talent suddenly grew, helped on by his love affair with Joanna Bobrowa, and the immediate result was the composition of his novel *Agay-Han* (1834) and his strange, unequal, though at times powerful, verse play describing the future overthrow of society, *Nieboska komedia* (1835; Eng. trans. *The Undivine Comedy*, 1924). Another play, *Irydion* (1836; Eng. trans. *Iridion*, 1927), also belongs to this period. It was, however, above all his meeting with Delfina Potocka in Naples in 1838 which really turned him into a great poet. His three fine volumes of verse, *Przedświt* (1843; Fr. trans. *L'Aube du grand jour*, 1876), *Psalmy przyszłości* (1845; second ed. enlarged, 1848; Fr. trans. in *Poètes illustrés de la Pologne au XIXe siècle*, 1880) and *Ostatni* (1847; Fr. trans. *L'Aube, le dernier*, 1863), celebrate the coming days of greatness for Poland. By 1848 the eye disease from which he had suffered since 1831 had so far worsened that he practically ceased to write, his only significant publication during his last years being *Resurrecturis* (1857). He died in Paris, where he had resided for many years. Count Krasiński is one of the greatest Polish authors both in verse and prose, his love-lyrics being the cream of his compositions. There is a French translation of his poetry, *Œuvres complètes du poète anonyme de la Pologne*, by L. Mickiewicz (2 vols., 1869).

**Krásnohorská, Eliška,** real name **Pechová** (1847–1926), Czech librettist and poet, who provided the words for many of Smetana's operas, including *Hubička* ('The Kiss') and *Tajemství* ('The Secret'). She was born and died in Prague.

**Krasnov, Peter Nikolayevich** (1869–1947), Russian novelist. He took up the army as a career, and in 1917 became an anti-Bolshevik Cossack general. He then went into exile, living in turn in Warsaw, Berlin and Paris, and published many popular books on topical subjects, such as *Ot dvuglavogo orla k krasnomu znameni 1894–1921* (4 vols., 1922; Eng. trans. *From the Two-headed Eagle to the Red Flag, 1894–1921*, 4 vols., 1923) and *S nami Bog* (1927; Eng. trans. *Napoleon and the Cossacks*, 1932). His slickly written novels include *Ponyat'-Prostit'* (1924; Eng. trans. *The Unforgiven*, 1928), *Belaya Svitka* (1928; Eng. trans. *The White Coat*, 1930) and *Largo* (1930; Eng. trans. 1933). Having helped to organize anti-Soviet Russians to fight the Red Army during the Second World War, he was captured at the end of the war by the Soviet authorities and hanged.

**Kraszewski, Józef Ignacy** (1812–1887), Polish novelist. Born in

Warsaw, he graduated at Wilno University. He became a man of letters, publicist and fiction writer, and for his pronounced liberal views was throughout his life in conflict with authority. His first successful novel was *Poeta i świat* (1839; Ger. trans. *Dichter und Welt*, 1864), and there followed a stream of over one hundred books, chief among them *Ulana* (1843; Fr. trans. *Oulana*, 1883), his best known *Jermola* (1857; Eng. trans. *Jermola the Potter*, 1891), *Caprea i Roma* (2 vols., 1866; Fr. trans. *Villa Jovis*, 1902), *Szpieg* (1864; Ger. trans. *Der Spion*, 1864), *Żyd* (1865; Eng. trans. *The Jew*, 1890), a return to the fiction of classical times *Rzym za Nerona* (1866; Fr. trans. *Chrétienne*, 1902), and more modern historical subjects *Hrabina Kosel* (2 vols., 1873; Eng. trans. *The Countess Cosel*, 1901), *Brühl* (2 vols., 1875; Eng. trans. *Count Brühl*, 1902) and *Szalona* (1880; Ger. trans. *Auf Irrwegen*). He had been forced to leave Poland in 1867 and settled in Germany, but in 1884 he was unjustly accused of spying for France, and after a spell in prison in Magdeburg he went to Switzerland, where he died in Geneva.

**Kravchinsky, S. M.,** *see* **Stepnyak, S.**

**Krestovsky, Vsevolod Vladimirovich** (1840–1895), Russian novelist, born in Kiev, became known as the 'Eugène Sue [q.v.] of Russia' with his long novel describing a Russian city underworld, *Peterburgskie trushchoby* (3 vols., 1864–7). He died in Petersburg.

**Kretzer, Max** (1854–1941), German novelist. Born at Posen, he became a leading exponent of naturalism with his first work *Die beiden Genossen* (1880). Into his novels with working-class themes he wove socialistic ideas, as in *Drei Weiber* (1885) and *Der Holzhändler* (1900). In another manner is *Die Madonna von Grünewald* (1901). Generally speaking he is a realist working under the influence of Zola (q.v.). He died in Berlin.

**Krog, Helge** (1889–   ), Norwegian playwright, born in Kristiania (Oslo), she became well known in her own country as a social satirist, and her work later reached a far wider public in translation. The best known are *Blåpapiret* (1928; Eng. trans. *The Copy*, 1934), *Konkylien* (1929; Eng. trans. *Happily Ever After*, 1934) and *Treklang* (1933; Eng. trans. *Triad*, 1934, the three translations appearing as *Three Plays*). During the German occupation of Norway she was a refugee in Sweden. Her later work has been almost entirely political propaganda.

**Krolow, Karl** (1915–   ), German poet born in Hanover. Greatly influenced by Lorca (q.v.) and Éluard (q.v.), he made his name with *Heimsuchung* (1948), steeped in his experiences of war. His collected poetry, *Unsichtbare Hände. Gedichte 1959–1962* (1962), shows him at his best, a fusion of a laconic manner with a feeling of melancholy leading to near resignation.

**Kropiński, Ludwik** (1767–1844), Polish novelist and dramatist. Born at Paszuki, in his youth he enjoyed unfailing court patronage and rose high in the army. Deeply influenced by French literature, his two outstanding works were both closely modelled on it. These are the tragedy *Ludgarda* (acted in 1816, but not printed till 1841) and the

Rousseauesque *Julia i Adolf* (1824; Fr. trans. *Juliette et Adolphe*, 1833). He died at Woronczyn.

**Krylov, Ivan Andreyevich** (1768–1844), Russian fabulist, was born a soldier's son in Moscow, and obtained a minor position in the civil service. He soon left it, became a journalist and wandered about Russia before settling in Petersburg in 1806. Having turned to translating La Fontaine (q.v.) he discovered his true bent and began to write fables of his own—lively, terse satires, contributed at first to newspapers, but collected and published as *Basni* (Eng. trans. *Krilov and his Fables*, by W. R. S. Ralston, 1868, fourth ed., 1883; *Fables* by I. H. Harrison, 1883, and B. Pares, 1926), the first volume in 1809 and the second in 1811. Krylov held the post of assistant librarian at the Imperial Public Library, Petersburg, where he died.

**Küchelbecker, Wilhelm Karlovich** (1797–1846), Russian man of letters of German origin, he was born at Gatchina, and became a member of the Pushkin (q.v.) circle. Implicated in the Decembrist Rising of 1825, he was banished to Siberia, where he spent the rest of his life. Just before his exile he had begun to gain a public with his philosophical periodical *Mnemosyne* (1824–5). Although he wrote much afterwards, practically nothing found its way into print until the twentieth century. His most important works are his poems collected as *Lirika i poemy* (2 vols., 1932), *Posledniy Kolonna* (1937, 'The Last Column'), a novel, and the play *Prokofy Lyapunov* (1938).

**Kugler, Franz Theodor** (1808–1858), German poet and prose-writer, born in Stettin. Of several volumes of verse the best is *Legenden* (1831). In the 1840's he enjoyed a vogue as an art historian (*Handbuch der Geschichte der Malerei*, 2 vols., 1837; Eng. trans. *A Handbook of the History of Art*, 1842) and as a political historian (*Geschichte Friedrichs des Grossen*, 1840; Eng. trans. *A History of Frederick the Great*, 1844). Kugler died in Berlin.

**Kuncewiczowa, Marja** (1897–    ), Polish novelist, born in Russia at Samara. A most original writer and uninhibited experimentalist, she has written such novels as *Cudzoziemka* (1935; Eng. trans. *The Stranger*, 1944) and *Zmowa nicobecnych* (1946; Eng. trans. *The Conspiracy of the Absent*, 1950). In 1946 she settled in London.

**Kuncz, Aladár** (1886–1931), Hungarian novelist, born at Arad. He is remembered as the author of *Fekete Kolostor* (1931; Eng. trans. *Black Monastery*, 1934) in which he describes the impact made on him by France and French culture and politics. He died in Budapest.

**Kunev, Trifon** (1880–1951), Bulgarian poet. Born at Aglen, he gained an early celebrity with his volume *Pesni* (1905) which contains the best collection of Bulgarian lyrics of the century. He died a victim of the Communists in a concentration camp.

**Kuprin, Alexander Ivanovich** (1870–1938), Russian novelist and short-story writer, born at Narovchat. He led a wandering life until in 1905 he settled down to a life of letters, having won success in that year with his novel *Poyedinok* (Eng. trans. *The Duel*, 1916), in which he pointed out the cruelty that lay behind glittering army uniforms.

Other works of his were *Olessia* (1898; Eng. trans. 1909), *Belyi pudel' i Slon* (1904; Eng. trans. *The White Poodle and The Elephant,* 1947), *Granatovyi braslet* (1911; Eng. trans. *The Bracelet and Other Stories,* 1919), *Yama* (1915; Eng. trans. *The Pit,* 1930), about life in a brothel in Odessa, and *Sasha* (1920; Eng. trans. 1920). He left Russia in 1917, but returned the year before his death from cancer in Moscow.

**Kurz, Hermann** (1813–1873), German prose-writer, born at Reutlingen. Educated for the Church, he was a Lutheran pastor for a time before abandoning his calling and taking to letters for a living. Of his books may be mentioned *Genzianen, ein Novellenstrauss* (1837), *Schillers Heimatjahre* (1843), *Der Sonnenwirt* (1853) and *Der Weihnachtsfund* (1856). He later became university librarian of Tübingen, where he died. His *Gesammelte Werke,* edited by H. Fischer, were published (12 vols.) in 1904.

# L

**Labé, Louise** (1520?–1566), French poet and prose-writer. Born in Lyon, the daughter of a wealthy rope-maker, she became renowned for her beauty and as a horsewoman (she took part in the Lyon tournament of 1542 disguised as a man). 'La Belle Cordière', as this daughter of a rope-maker and wife of a rope-maker was called, published one volume, *Œuvres* (1555), containing a prose dialogue, several elegies and some deeply felt Petrarchan sonnets, the latter filled with longing for unattainable love (Eng. trans. *Love Sonnets*, N.Y., 1947) and inspired by O. de Magny (q.v.). She died in Lyon.

**Labiche, Eugène Marin** (1815–1888), French playwright. Born in Paris, he became one of the most productive writers of light pieces for the stage of his day. Farce was his particular forte, and his plays on middle-class life range from the hilarious, such as *Un Chapeau de paille d'Italie* (1851; revived on the London stage in 1952 as *The Italian Straw Hat*), to the slightly more reflective, like *Le Voyage de M. Perrichon* (1860). His *Frisette* (1846) was the original of Morton's *Box and Cox*, set to music by Sullivan as *Cox and Box*, and among his other works may be mentioned *Edgar et sa bonne* (1852), *L'Affaire de la rue Lourcine* (1857) and *Les Vivacités du Capitaine Tic* (1861). He died in Paris.

**La Bruyère, Jean de** (1645–1696), French prose-writer. Born in Paris of a higher bourgeois family, he took up law, abandoned it, bought himself the sinecure post of city treasurer of Caen, and through his friendship with Bossuet (q.v.) became a retainer of the Condé family. He continued in this degrading position for the rest of his life, and put up with it for the very good reason that it provided him with excellent material for social satire. His great work, *Les Caractères de Théophraste traduits du grec, avec les caractères ou les mœurs de ce siècle* (1688), consists of a poor translation of Theophrastus of Eresus's *Characters*, followed by a brilliant medley of character studies, often bitter, always shrewd, of the public figures of La Bruyère's own time. His style is superb, his observation trenchant, but he is over-sententious, and his axioms have nothing to do with those far greater ones by La Rochefoucauld (q.v.). La Bruyère represents the growing self-assertiveness of the rising middle class which was beginning to resent the power and insolence of an exclusive court. In asking the reason why, he is on the path to eighteenth-century encyclopaedism, but there is nothing of the deep thinker about him. He died at Versailles, where his house still stands. The best edition of his collected works is that by G. Servois (6 vols., 1864–8, 1882). There is an English translation of the *Characters* (1890).

**La Calprenède, G. de C. de,** *see* **Calprenède.**

**Laclos,** *see* **Choderlos de Laclos.**

**Lacretelle, Jacques de** (1888–      ), French novelist, born at Cormatin. Introspective, with an infinite capacity for analysis and self-analysis, he projected his intense if brooding nature into such distinctive works as: *La Vie inquiète de Jean Hermelin* (1920), *Silberman* (1922), *Le Retour de Silberman* (1930), *Les Hauts Ponts* (4 vols., 1932–5), *Le Demi Dieu, ou le voyage en Grèce* (1944), *La Vie privée de Racine* (1949), *Le Pour et le contre* (1953) and *Deux cœurs simples* (1953).

**La Fayette, Marie Madeleine Pioche de la Vergne de** (1634–1693), French novelist. Born of noble family in Paris, she married the comte de La Fayette in 1655 and lived with him in Auvergne, but tired of marriage and the country she returned to Paris, living from 1665 until his death in 1680 with La Rochefoucauld (q.v.). She had published a long, slow-moving novel called *La Princesse de Montpensier* in 1662, but in subsequent works gradually freed herself from the old, dull, rambling style. *Zaïde* (1670) marks a new approach, realism taking the place of classical romanticism, and when we reach *La Princesse de Clèves* (1678; Eng. trans. by H. Ashton, 1925; and by N. Mitford, 1950) we find ourselves in a new world, a psychologically satisfying plot in a real court atmosphere. In this book we see the stage set for all the great fiction of France. Madame de La Fayette died in Paris.

**La Fontaine, Jean de** (1621–1695), French poet and fabulist. Born at Château-Thierry, in Champagne, the son of an official who had either inherited or bought the post of master of forests of the duchy of Château-Thierry, he was first educated for the Church but changed to law, which in turn he gave up in 1647, having succeeded to his father's mastership. He was ambitious, and by 1659 was in Paris, his wit and charm of manner gaining him access to every *salon*. Most important of all was the patronage of Fouquet, the chancellor, who before his fall in 1661 launched La Fontaine. His first successful piece of writing was his *Élégie aux nymphes de Vaux* (1661), and this was followed by the *Voyage en Limousin* (1663), but he produced nothing of permanent value until the first volume of *Contes* (1664). The *Contes*, the second volume of which appeared in 1668, the third in 1671 and the fourth in 1674, are taken from such writers as Boccaccio, Ariosto and Rabelais, and though often gross are exceedingly well related in brilliant if not great verse. But it was with the inimitable *Fables* (vol. i, 1668; ii, 1679; iii, 1693; crit. ed., 2 vols., 1926; Eng. trans. *La Fontaine's Fables*, by E. Marsh, 1934; rev. ed., 1952) that he made his name and secured immortality. In the *Fables* he came forward as a story-teller who breathed new life into Aesop's and other fables which had been exploited and worn out during the Middle Ages. With perfect ease and mastery in his verse, he is able to call to his aid his feeling for nature and his understanding of animals and men. His upbringing in the forest-lands of Champagne, and his experience of many a great house in Paris are blended to form a work of urbanity, wit and sagacity, to which an equal can scarcely be found in literature. Patrons were eager to claim him, and he lived for the rest of his life on their pensions. Of his host of friends none were more prized by him than Molière, Racine and Boileau (q.v.), with whom he formed one of the most celebrated of literary quartets. Unpractical, absent-minded and ingenuous in ordinary life, he does not seem to have been able to make use of his store of worldly wisdom in his own day-to-day existence. After some years of bad health he died in Paris. See his *Œuvres complètes* (11 vols., 1883–92) in the series *Les Grands Écrivains de la France*.

**Laforet, Carmen** (1921–    ), Spanish novelist. Born in Barcelona, she had a Europe-wide success with *Nada* (1945), with which new, harsh, unsentimental youth first broke upon the public eye of Spain. The dialogue is good and the description, the very 'feel' of Barcelona, remarkable. Her later works, such as *La isla y los demonios* (1952), *La muerta* (1952), *El piano* (1952), *Un noviazgo* (1953), *La niña* (1954), *El viaje divertido* (1954) and *La mujer nueva* (1955), are not up to this standard.

**Laforgue, Jules** (1860–1887), French poet and prose-writer, was born in Montevideo, Uruguay. He lived for five years of his short life at the court of Berlin, where he was reader and secretary to the Empress Augusta of Prussia. Becoming tubercular, he returned to Paris to marry and to die. His publications were crowded into the last two years of his life, and consist of *Les Complaintes* (1885), *L'Imitation de Notre-Dame la Lune* (1886), *La Concile féerique* (1886) and the prose work *Moralités légendaires* (1887). But it is the appearance of the free verse, *Les Derniers Vers de Jules Laforgue* (1890), that marks an important stage in poetry. The new possibilities for poetry which it disclosed were a revelation to a new generation, and the influence of the book is not yet over. See *Œuvres complètes* (6 vols., 1922–30).

**Lagerkvist, Pär Fabian** (1891–    ), Swedish novelist. Born at Växsjö, he settled down to a life of letters, working out his system of welding together humanitarian traditions, and, calling on neither thought nor devotion, appealed to natural right feeling in man as a means to outlaw the political horrors of the world, which in his time seemed to threaten the very foundations of civilization. He started with *Gäst hos verkligheten* (1925; Eng. trans. *Guest of Reality*, 1936), but by the time we reach *Dvärgen* (1944; Eng. trans. *The Dwarf*, 1945) we find ourselves locked in a death-struggle with all the powers of evil let loose. In *Barabbas* (1950; Eng. trans. 1952) man has still not found his right path. In *Sibyllan* (1956) he is still investigating. He gained the Nobel Prize for literature in 1951.

**Lagerlöf, Selma Ottilia Lovisa** (1858–1940), Swedish novelist and story-writer. Born at the manor of Mårbacka, near Ämtervik in Värmland, she was educated in Stockholm and was a schoolmistress at the Girls' High School, Landskrona, from 1885 to 1895, after which she gave herself up entirely to writing. She had already been noticed as a more than promising author when *Gösta Berlings saga* appeared in 1891 (Eng. trans. 1898). In it is to be found the key to her literary position; a love for the past, a dislike of the noisy materialism of her own day, and a sympathy with simple life and character. Other early works are *Osynliga länkar* (1894; Eng. trans. *Invisible Links*, 1899), *Antikrists mirakler* (1897; Eng. trans. *The Miracles of Antichrist*, 1899), *Drottningar i Kungahälla* (1899; Eng. trans. *The Queens of Kungahälla*, 1917) and *En herrgårdssägen* (1899; Eng. trans. *The Tale of a Manor*, 1922). Then came the great experience of her life, the discovery, while on a tour of Palestine in 1900, of a settlement of Swedish peasants who had emigrated to Jerusalem a few years previously to live in accordance with the ways of primitive Christianity. The novel which this inspired, *Jerusalem* (2 vols., 1901–2; Eng. trans. 1915), brought her universal recognition. After that she returned to a more familiar manner, but now with a still surer touch and conviction. Of her later work *Herr Arnes penningar* (1904; Eng. trans. *Herr Arne's Hoard*, 1923) and *Kristuslegender* (1904; Eng. trans. *Christ Legends*, 1908), a collection of short stories, may be particularly singled out as typical of the novel and the gathering of tales, many more of which she was to publish in the future. Different was her school textbook, *Nils Holgerssons underbara resa genom Sverige* (2 vols., 1906–7; Eng. trans. *The Wonderful Adventures of Nils*, 1907; and *Further Adventures of Nils*, 1911), a true piece of literature in its way. After this the quiet dignified domestic novel or the mythical or symbolical tales are continued in *Liljecronas hem* (1911; Eng. trans. *Liliecrona's Home*, 1913), *Körkarlen* (1912; Eng. trans. *Thy Soul Shall Bear Witness!*, 1921), *Kejsaren av Portugallien* (1914; Eng. trans. *The Emperor of Portugallia*, 1916), *Bannlyst* (1918; Eng. trans. *The Outcast*, 1920), the trilogy consisting of *Löwensköldska ringen* (1925), *Charlotte Löwensköld* (1925) and *Anna Svärd* (1928), the three translated into English as *The Ring of the Löwenskölds* (1931), and finally *Höst* (1933; Eng. trans. *Harvest*, 1935). Awarded the Nobel Prize for literature in 1909, she died in the manor house where she was born.

**La Harpe, Jean-François de** (1739–1803), French dramatist and critic. Born in Paris, he succeeded with his tragedy, *Le Comte de Warwick* (1763), and from time to time produced others in the same manner, such as *Les Barmécides* (1778), *Jeanne de Naples* (1781) and *Coriolan* (1784). It was, however, as a critic clearly reflecting the accepted tastes of his time that he made his mark. His tastes and views are to be seen in *Lycée, ou Cours de littérature* (1799) and *Correspondance littéraire* (1801). He died in Paris.

**Lamartine, Alphonse-Marie-Louis de Prat de** (1790–1869), French poet and prose-writer. Born at Mâcon, the son of a landowner, he was educated by the Jesuits, the influence of whom remained all his life. In 1811–13 he paid a visit to Switzerland and went on to Italy, and the impact of new beauties of nature and of art which this journey brought, coupled with his love for a dying young woman whom he met at Aix-les-Bains in 1816, stirred his latent gift for poetry. The result was *Méditations poétiques* (1820; crit. ed., 2 vols., 1915), a collection of lyrics, many of deep and moving beauty, which is usually accounted the beginning of the romantic movement in France. The same year he married an English girl, Marianne Birch, and shortly afterwards entered the diplomatic service, serving in Italy until 1829. He continued meanwhile to produce much poetry; quiet, thoughtful, religiously inclined, romantic and sonorous, such as *Nouvelles méditations poétiques* (1823), *La Mort de Socrate* (1823), *Le Dernier Chant du pèlerinage d'Harold* (1825), and his finest work, *Les Harmonies poétiques et religieuses* (1830), full of faith, optimism, harmony with nature, all expressed in romantic style. After 1830 he took an increasing interest in politics, was elected a deputy in 1832 and gained an increasing reputation as a Christian Liberal. In 1835 he published his first important prose work, *Souvenirs d'un voyage en orient*, revealing considerable descriptive power, while *Jocelyn* (1836) and *La Chute d'un ange* (1838) are fragments of a Christian epic never carried through to the end. *Les Recueillements poétiques* (1839) is his last important poetical publication. Side by side with his growing concern with politics went his interest in history, and with the *Histoire des Girondins* (1847; Eng. trans. *History of the Girondists*, 3 vols., Bohn's Library) he entered the field as historian. The revolution of February 1848 gave him his chance, and he was elected a member of the executive committee of the provisional government, but he was too honest and too peaceable to face successfully the rough and tumble of crude politics: it was one thing to be an orator in the chamber, another to out-trick the tricksters of Louis Napoleon. He stood for the presidency in 1849 and failed. Thereafter he was forced to write for a living, although he was later aided by a government pension. Of his remaining work, *L'Histoire de la Révolution de 1848* (1849; Eng. trans. Bohn's Library) and *Mémoires politiques* (1863) are of interest as first-hand accounts of outstanding events, but he is no historian, often preferring effect to truth. He died in Paris. It is as a poet that Lamartine must always be considered of importance as the link between the neo-classical and Victor Hugo. Without Lamartine the transition could have been far more difficult and the whole French romantic movement might well have been delayed or have taken another form. While his poetry has many qualities, as stated above, it is often too conventional, lacking in strength and limited in scope. His *Œuvres complètes* appeared in twenty-two volumes (1900–7).

**Lamennais, Hugues Félicité Robert de** (1782–1854), French prose-writer. Born at St Malo the son of a shipowner, he published *Réflexions sur l'état de l'Église* (1808), in which by demanding radical reorganization of the Church he exerted an enormous influence on ultramontanism (*see* J. M. de Maistre), although Napoleon's government tried to suppress it. Ordained priest in 1815, the following year he wrote the first volume of his greatest book, *Essai sur l'indifférence en matière de religion* (2 vols., 1818–24), in which he pleased Rome by arguing the dangers of allowing too much freedom of judgment and toleration, since society can only be held together if there is unity of belief. But his religious standpoint was much affected by his growing liberalism, as is to be seen in *Progrès de la révolution* (1829), and he was completely won over by the July revolution of 1830, founding in September *L'Avenir*, in which opinions, such as would later be called Christian socialism, were advocated by him and Montalembert (q.v.). In 1831 the paper was suspended by the ecclesiastical authorities, and Lamennais submitted. But his disillusionment gave rise to his beautifully written *Paroles d'un croyant* (1834), in which in rhythmical prose he gave voice to his belief in primitive Christianity. This marked the end of his priesthood, and thereafter he took a definite part in politics, being active in the revolution of 1848 and in the Constituent Assembly (1848–51). His *Esquisse d'une philosophie* (1840–6) contains his final summing-up of his ideas. He died in Paris unreconciled with the Church and was buried without religious rites in a pauper's grave at Père-la-Chaise. His influence on his generation was very great.

**La Mettrie, Julien Offroy de** (1709–1751), French prose-writer. Born at St Malo, he became so free a thinker that he found it advisable to settle in the Netherlands. In a trenchant style he set down his purely materialist philosophy, in which he expatiates on the death of the soul with the body, on life as a farce and on hedonism as the only answer. His work, of which *L'Homme machine* (1748; Eng. trans. 1750), *L'Art de jouir* (1751) and *Vénus métaphysique* (1752) are prime examples, marks the high-water mark of eighteenth-century materialism, and was fiercely contested. Invited in 1748 to Berlin by Frederick the Great, he died there.

**La Motte, Antoine Houdart de** (1672–1731), French dramatist, fabulist and literary critic. Born in Paris, he took part on the side of the moderns in the literary war caused by the controversy about the respective merits of ancient and modern literature and learning and the stultifying effect of academic rules. His finest prose work is *Réflexions sur la critique* (1716); his best play is *Inès de Castro* (1723). His *Fables* appeared in 1719. He died in Paris.

**Lampedusa,** *see* **Tomasi di Lampedusa, G.**

**Landesmann, Heinrich,** writing under the pseudonym of **Hieronymus Lorm** (1821–1902), German poet born at Nikolsburg, Moravia. Deaf from birth and ultimately blind, his darkly despairing *Gedichte* (1870) is at the core of the mood of pessimism, which, induced by the philosophy of E. von Hartmann's (q.v.) *Philosophie des Unbewussten* (1869), swept German literature in the 1870's. He died at Brünn.

**Langgässer, Elisabeth,** pseudonym of **Elisabeth Hoffmann** (1899–1950), German poet and novelist, born at Alzey. In all her works she explored the problem of the dichotomy of life, the forces of good and evil. Chief among them are the volumes of poetry, *Wendekreis des Lammes* (1924), *Die Tierkreisgedichte* (1935), *Kölnische Elegie* (1948) and *Metamorphosen* (1949), and the novels *Triptychon des Teufels* (1932), *Das unauslöschliche Siegel* (1946) and *Das Labyrinth* (1949). She died at Rheinzabern.

**Lannoy, Johanna Cornelia de** (1738–1782), Dutch poet and dramatist. Born in Breda, she wrote lyrics which she collected and published as *Dichtkundige Werken* in 1780. As a dramatist she is at her best in the tragedies *Leo de Groote* (1767) and *Cleopatra, Koningin van Syrië* (1776). She died in Geertruidenberg. An edition of her works was prepared by Bilderdijk (q.v.) in 1783.

**Lanson, Gustave** (1857–1934), the greatest French academic critic of his day, was born in Orléans. A professor at the Sorbonne, his books, above all his *Histoire de la littérature française* (1894), straightforward and excellently documented, have been source books for three generations of *lycée* students. His *Manuel bibliographique* (1909, 1912) is of the greatest value. He died in Paris.

**Laonicus Chalcocondylas,** *see* **Chalcocondylas.**

**Laprade, Victor de** (1812–1883), French poet. Born at Montbrison, he became a member of the faculty of letters at Lyon, where he died. His reflective poetry invested with quiet religious feeling and a love of nature is to be found in such collections as *La colère de Jésus* (1840), *Poèmes évangéliques* (1852), *Symphonies* (1855) and *Poèmes civiques* (1873). He edited his *Œuvres poétiques* (6 vols., 1878–81). His masterpiece is 'La Mort d'un chêne', the condemned tree becoming symbolic of nature and freedom destroyed by the inroads of 'civilization'. He stood apart from the literary schools of his time.

**Larbaud, Valéry** (1881–1957), French novelist. Born at Vichy, he was left a fortune which enabled him to indulge his taste for travelling and for literature. *Fermina Marquez* (1911) describes a youthful love-affair of his own, but it was with *A. O. Barnabooth* (1913), the tale of a millionaire who finds himself a slave of his own fortune, that he made his name. *Enfantines* (1918) and even more *Amants, heureux amants* (1923) reveal the great influence of James Joyce, whose *Ulysses* he translated. Later works are *Ce vice impuni, la lecture, domaine français* (1941) and *Le Vaisseau de Thésée* (1946). *Lettres à André Gide* appeared in 1948. He died at Vichy.

**Larguier, Léo** (1878–1950), French poet and prose-writer. Born at La Grand' Combe, he settled in Paris early, becoming known as a poet with *La Maison du poète* (1903) and *Les Isolements* (1906), an art critic with *En compagnie des vieux peintres* (1927), and an enthusiastic admirer of his adopted city with *Saint-Germain-des-Prés mon village* (1938), in which he died.

**Larivey, Pierre** (1545?–1612), French playwright. Born at Troyes, his family being of Italian origin, he adapted many prose comedies from the Italian, such as *Les Écoliers* (1579) and *Les Trompeurs* (1611). Several of his plays suggested plots to Molière. He died in Troyes. His work is printed in *Ancien Théâtre Français* (1855, vols. v, vi and vii).

**Laroche, Sophie von** (1730–1807), German novelist. Born at Kaufbeuren, *née* Gutermann, her love affair with Wieland (q.v.) was well known. She married G. von Laroche, a court official at Trier, and moved on the edge of literary circles. Her domestic novels following on from Gellert (q.v.) and Richardson are such as *Geschichte des Fräuleins von Sternheim* (1771), *Rosaliens Briefe* (1780), *Geschichte von Miss Lony* (1789) and *Fanny und Julia* (1802). She died at Offenbach and was the grandmother of Clemens Brentano (q.v.).

**La Rochefoucauld, François de** (1613–1680), French prose-writer. Born of noble family in Paris, his father being raised to the dukedom in 1622, he entered the army and took an active part in the wars of the Fronde, always an enemy of Mazarin, who banished him to his country estates, his health and fortune gone. After the death of Mazarin in 1661 he was able to return to Paris and became a king of the *salons*. In retirement he had been at work on his *Mémoires* (1662) and on his *Maximes*, on which his reputation rests. After a trial publication at The Hague in 1664, they issued forth in Paris in 1665 as *Réflexions ou Sentences et maximes morales*, and were revised and reprinted in 1666, 1671, 1672 and 1678, the last, his final revision, being the version used ever since in numerous republications. The best English translations are those by G. H. Powell (1903), F. G. Stevens (1939) and L. W. Tancock (1959). Few books contain so much urbane thought in such a clear and compressed style. Exquisitely expressed, here is the best of all mundane wisdom, knowledge of human nature. Partially crippled in his later years, his close friendship with Madame de la Fayette (q.v.), in whose house he lived for the last fifteen years of his life, was a source of consolation. He died in Paris. The best edition of his complete works, which means besides the *Maximes* only the *Mémoires* and letters, is that of 1935.

**Larousse, Pierre Athanase** (1817–1875), French lexicographer, born at Toucy (Yonne), he was responsible for the compilation of the indispensible *Nouveau Dictionnaire illustré* (1854), from which the famous *Petit Larousse illustré* is derived. His greatest undertaking was the *Grand Dictionnaire universel du XIXe siècle* (1866–76), which he had just completed at the time of his death in Paris.

**Larra, Luis Mariano de** (1830–1901), Spanish playwright. Born in Madrid the son of M. J. Larra (q.v.), he is remembered as the author of excellent operettas (*zarzuelas*), the most famous *El barberillo de Lavapiés* (1874). He died in Madrid.

**Larra y Sánchez de Castro, Mariano José** (1809–1837), Spanish prose-writer and poet. Born in Madrid where his father held a post under Joseph Bonaparte during the French occupation of Spain, his family fled with the French when they withdrew, and young Larra received an entirely French education, which was to make him the most international Spanish writer of the first half of the nineteenth century. Returning to Spain he took to journalism, and, as 'Figaro', became the finest and highest paid journalist of his time. An idealist, he had practical answers to the state of affairs in Spain that had produced a society which he lashed and ridiculed with all his very varied powers. All his articles were collected as *Artículos completos* (1944). Apart from his journalism he wrote the satire *El doncel de Don Enrique el doliente* (1834) and the verse-drama *Macías* (1834). His precocious marriage was a disaster, and after the breakdown of an unhappy liaison he committed suicide in Madrid.

**La Sal(l)e, Antoine de** (1388–1470?), French writer. Born probably in Burgundy, he was tutor at the courts of Anjou, Luxembourg and Burgundy in turn. His first works, such as *La Salade* (1442) and *La Sale* (1451), are educational treatises prepared for his pupils; but he is best known for *L'Hystoire et plaisante cronicque du petit Jehan de Saintré* (1456; Eng. trans. 1862), a tale of knightly training not in good conduct but misconduct. After references to him as a court official he vanishes from view.

**Las Casas, Bartolomé de** (1474–1566), Spanish prose-writer. Born in Seville, he went to Hispaniola in 1502 and was ordained priest there, the first ordination in the New World. He returned to Spain in 1515 to protest to the court against the revolting cruelty shown by his countrymen towards the Indians, which he afterwards discussed in *Brevísima relación de la destrucción de las Indias* (1552; Eng. trans. *A Briefe Narration of the Destruction of the Indies by the Spaniards* in Purchas's *Pilgrims*, 1625, Hakluyt Society), a noble and eloquent document, eagerly seized on by the enemies of Spain in Europe, which had the effect of the Spanish government's decision to forbid the further enslavement of the Indians. Returning to the New World, he founded a colony in Venezuela in 1520, which the Indians destroyed, and Las Casas thereupon retired to a Dominican monastery in Hispaniola, where he wrote his *Historia General de las Indias*, a fine piece of prose (mod. ed., 3 vols., 1927, which supersedes the ed., vols. lxii–lxvi in *Colección de documentos inéditos para la historia de España*, 1875–6). In 1544 Las Casas became Bishop of Chiapa in Mexico, but returned to Spain three years later. He died in Madrid.

**Lasker-Schüler, Else** (1876–1945), German poet and prose-writer, born at Elberfeld. A collection of her difficult poetry appeared in 1917 as *Gesammelte Gedichte*, while as a prose-writer she is to be judged by *Der Wunderrabbiner von Barcelona* (1921) and *Das Hebräerland* (1937). A keen Zionist, she died in Jerusalem.

**La Taille, Jean de** (1533?–1608?), French dramatist and critic, born at Bonderoy. His religious dramas, *Saül le furieux* (1572) and *La Famine, ou les Gabéonites* (1573), are generally held to be the best of their kind of the age in France. As a critic in *De l'art de la tragédie* (1572; mod. crit. ed., 1939) he insists on the Aristotelian dramatic unities. The whereabouts of his death and the exact date are unknown.

**La Tour du Pin, Patrice de** (1911–    ), French poet. Born of good family in Paris, his first book, *Quête de joie* (1933), brought him high consideration, which steadily increased with *La Lucernaire* (1936), *Le Don de la Passion* (1937), *Psaumes* (1938) and *La Vie recluse en poésie* (1938; Eng. trans. *The Dedicated Life in Poetry*, 1948). A difficult poet, intensely Christian, and using a complex symbolism to express his thought, in *Une Somme de poésie* (1945) he brought his craft near perfection, not advanced upon in *Les Contes de soi* (1946) and *La Contemplation errante* (1948).

**La Tour Landry, Geoffroi de** (*fl.* 1370), author of the fascinating treatise on the education of women designed for his daughters, incidentally giving much information about himself and contemporary social life, *Le Livre du chevalier de la Tour Landry pour l'enseignement de ses filles* (ed. A. de Montaiglon, 1854; Eng. trans. 1906).

**Laube, Heinrich** (1806–1884), German novelist and playwright. Born at Sprottau, Silesia, he knew as a journalist and theatrical producer what would sell well and act well, and though frowned on by the highbrows had much popular success. As a playwright he was strongest with his costume pieces, such as *Rococo oder die alten Herren* (1846), *Struensee* (1847), *Die Karlsschüler* (1848), a comedy about Schiller's youth, and *Graf Essex* (1856), a blank verse tragedy about Queen Elizabeth and Essex. He was on less sure ground as a novelist, but here again when he takes to the historical, as in the nine-volume novel on the Thirty Years War, *Der deutsche Krieg* (1863–6), he is far more competent than when trying to survey the contemporary scene in *Das junge Europa* (3 vols., 1833–7), which purports to be a saga of the age. His miscellaneous prose is unimportant, except for his works about the theatre and stagecraft, *Das Burgtheater* (1868), *Das norddeutsche Theater* (1872) and *Das Wiener Stadttheater* (1875). More important than all, from 1850 onwards Laube was the greatest and most influential German theatre-director of the age, first of the Hofburgtheater, Vienna, then of the Leipzig municipal theatres, returning at last to Vienna as director of the Stadttheater and dying in that city.

**Lautréamont,** *see* **Ducasse, I.-L.**

**Lavater, Johann Kaspar** (1741–1801), Swiss poet and prose-writer. Born in Zürich, he became a Protestant pastor there in 1769, and was the friend of Bodmer (q.v.), Klopstock (q.v.) and Goethe (q.v.). Early interest in aesthetics and his strong religious feelings led him to poetry, and between 1767 and 1780 he produced five volumes of verse, the most characteristic being *Schweizerlieder* (1767), the long *Jesus Messias* (1783–6) and *Das menschliche Herz* (1780). It was his conviction that the outward and actual was the result of what was behind and within that led him to the only work for which he is now remembered, that system of physiognomy, *Physiognomische Fragmente* (1775–8; Eng. trans. 1793) which swept Europe. Wounded while acting as a civilian stretcher-bearer at Masséna's capture of Zürich (September, 1799), he died of the wound well over a year later.

**Lavedan, Henri** (1859–1940), French dramatist, born in Orléans, he lashed the hidden evils of polite society in such strong, well set up plays as *Les Deux Noblesses* (1894), *Les Viveurs* (1895), *Le Vieux Marcheur* (1895), *Le Marquis de Priola* (1902), *Le Duel* (1905) and *Le Goût du vice* (1911). He died in Paris.

**Lavrenyov, Boris Andreyevich** (1891–1959), Russian Soviet short-story writer and dramatist, was born at Kherson, and became known for his well-written, romantically inclined short stories, with a dash of humour, such as those in the collection *Shalye povesti* (1926, 'Crazy Tales'). Some of his stories appeared in English translation as *Stout Heart and Other Stories* (1943). As a playwright he is known especially for his two well-constructed plays on the civil war in Russia of 1918–21, *Dym* (1925, 'Smoke') and *Razlom* (1928, 'The Rout'). He died in Moscow.

**Lavrov, Peter Lavrovich** (1823–1900), Russian prose-writer, born at Melekhovo, Pskov. Exiled in 1868, he became one of the leaders of revolutionary political thought operating as a journalist from Paris, where he died. His most lasting work is *Istoricheskie pis'ma* (1879, 'Historical Letters'), which brings Hegelian dialectics to bear on history, stressing the importance of the individual. His collected works were published (7 vols.) in 1919–20.

**Laxness, Halldór Guðjónsson Kiljan** (1902–    ), Icelandic novelist and essayist. Born at Reykjavík, his family was sufficiently well-to-do for him to travel at his leisure. He took advantage of his opportunity, saw the world, was converted to Catholicism, and then threw in his lot with Communism the next minute. In his promising novel, *Vefarinn mikli frá Kasmir* (1927), he describes his conversion to Catholicism, while in his essays, *Alþýðubókin* (1929), he considers his new found Communism. In 1930 he settled in Iceland, his travels over, and began to take stock of his own people, above all in *Sjálfstætt fólk* (2 vols., 1934–5; Eng. trans. *Independent People*, 1945). Later works are *Hús skáldsins* (1939), *Íslandsklukkan* (1943), *Eldur í Kaupinhafn* (1946) and *Atómstöðin* (1948), in all of which he is an incisive political and social critic. A later work is *Heiman ek fór* (1952).

**Lazhechnikov, Ivan Ivanovich** (1792–1869), Russian novelist, born at Kolomna. His feeling for the past stood him in good stead as a writer of historical fiction, his best works being *Ledyanoy dom* (1835; Eng. trans. *The Palace of Ice*, 2 vols., 1860–1), which the elder Dumas (q.v.) adapted as *La Maison de Glace*, and *Basurman* (1838). He died in Moscow.

**Léautaud, Paul** (1872–1956), French man of letters. Born in Paris, he became précis writer and indexer of the *Mercure de France*, a post he held from 1908 to 1940. Of his own few works the best known are the novel *Le Petit Ami* (1903) and *Le Théâtre de Maurice Boissard* (1927), a collection of his dramatic criticism which he wrote under that pseudonym for the *Mercure*, *La Nouvelle Revue française* and *Nouvelles littéraires*. His *Journal littéraire* (11 vols., 1954–61) revealed his widely ranging, tolerant views, and freedom from any kind of anxiety complex. His *Entretiens avec Robert Mallet* (1952) were brilliant dialogues written for the wireless. He died in Paris.

**Leblanc, Maurice** (1864–1941), French novelist, born in Rouen. He became one of the greatest writers of detective novels of his day, being the creator of the detective Arsène Lupin. He died in Perpignan.

**Le Braz, Anatole** (1859–1926), French poet and prose-writer. Born at Duault, Brittany, he pursued an academic career, joining the staff of Harvard University, U.S.A., in 1906. His most famous book is the prose work *La Légende de la mort chez les Bretons-armoricains* (1903; new ed., 1922). Of his poetry the best is perhaps to be found in *La Sang de la Sirène* (1901), *Contes du soleil* (1903) and *Poèmes votifs* (posthumous in 1927). He died in Paris.

**Lécavelé, R.,** *see* **Dorgelès, R.**

**Le Clerc, Jean** (1657–1736), Swiss lexicographer. Born in Geneva, he became in 1684 professor of philosophy in a Remonstrant seminary in Amsterdam. It was here that he published his *Bibliothèque universelle et historique* (25 vols., 1686–93) containing among many others articles on theology, biblical criticism and exegesis, which by applying cool scientific methods to the historical basis of the Pentateuch and subjecting the question of miracles to analysis paved the way for deism, which until then had as it were been working underground. Le Clerc brought down attacks on himself from all sides, and, forced to resign, spent the rest of his life working on less compromising compilations. He died in Amsterdam.

**Lecomte, Georges** (1867–1958), French novelist and miscellaneous writer, was born at Mâcon. As a novelist he is represented by *Les Valets* (1897), *Les Cartons verts* (1901), *Les Hannetons de Paris* (1905) and *Le Mort saisit le vif* (1925). He was also well known as a writer of biographies. He died in Paris.

**Leconte de Lisle, Charles-Marie-René** (1818–1894), French poet and translator. The son of a Breton sugar-planter, he was born on the Island of Réunion, spent much of his youth there, and was profoundly influenced all his life by his exotic environment, studied law at Rennes in France and in 1845 settled in Paris as a journalist and man of letters. With all his gifts, there was something lacking in his character which deprived him of the directive force needed for his success in life as the man of action he wished to be. Probably this was the result of his upbringing in the Far East and his distaste for the politics of France after the failure of the 1848 revolution. On the other hand, his wide reading and his highly trained appreciation of the form and colour of nature enabled him to excel as a descriptive poet and to express himself in a faultless style. But the static presentation is not enough and the acknowledged head of the Parnassians is fatally impersonal. It was in reaction against the subjectivity and extravagance of romanticism that Parnassianism arose with its classical restraint, plastic-like beauty, intellectualism, pessimism and love of nature. All this is to be found at its height of achievement in his three great books of poetry, *Poèmes antiques* (1852; rev., 1872), *Poèmes barbares* (1862; rev. 1874 and 1878) and *Poèmes tragiques* (1884), the last being inferior to the other two. His fine Greek scholarship was brought to bear on excellent translations into French, and he succeeded particularly well with Homer and Theocritus. His prose is of little account except for the posthumous *Contes en prose et impressions de jeunesse* (1911) which possesses much charm. He was appointed librarian to the Senate in 1872 and died, the most respected poet of the day, at Louveciennes. His *Poésies complètes* were published (4 vols.) in 1927–8.

**Ledeganck, Karel Lodewijk** (1805–1847), Flemish poet. Born of working-class parents at Eeklo, he was at first a weaver and by sheer ability and character raised himself to be a local magistrate and school-inspector. He lives now solely by reason of his powerful verse trilogy, *De drie zustersteden* (1846, 'The Three Sister-Cities'), in which he celebrates and compares Ghent, Bruges and Antwerp. He died, prematurely worn out, in Ghent.

**Leffler, A. C.,** *see* **Edgren, A. C.**

**Le Fort, Gertrud von** (1876–    ), German novelist, born at Minden. The two subjects on which her best work is founded have been her Roman Catholicism, which she embraced in 1926, leading to the novels *Das Schweisstuch der Veronika* (2 vols., 1927, 1946; Eng. trans. of the first, *The Veil of Veronica*, 1932), and *Der Papst aus dem Ghetto* (1929; Eng. trans. *The Pope from the Ghetto*, 1934), and her belief in the mission of women in life, leading to *Die Letzte am Schafott* (1931; Eng. trans. *The Song at the Scaffold*, 1933), *Die Opferflamme* (1938) and *Das Gericht des Meeres* (1944). *Die Magdeburgische Hochzeit* (1936) is an historical novel about the fall and destruction of Magdeburg during the Thirty Years War.

**Léger, Alexis,** *see* **Saint-John-Perse.**

**Legouvé, Gabriel Ernest** (1807–1903), French novelist, playwright and publicist, son of the poet and dramatist, J.-B. Legouvé, was born in Paris. He began his literary career with novels such as *Max* (1833) and *Édith de Falsen* (1840), but it was as the joint author with Scribe (q.v.) of the drama *Adrienne Lecouvreur* (1849), the heroine being the great tragic actress of the eighteenth century, that he gained his prestige in the literary world. His classical tragedy *Médée* (1855), though well composed, is not really in his true vein, but it was highly acclaimed at the time. Thereafter he devoted himself more and more to his work on behalf of the emancipation of women and universal primary education for children. *La Femme en France au XIX$^e$ siècle* (1864) is a forceful exposition of women and their place in society, while *Messieurs les enfants* (1868) deals seriously with the rights of children. He died in Paris.

**Leibniz, Gottfried Wilhelm von** (1646–1716), German prose-writer in Latin, German and French, was born the son of a university professor at Leipzig, and after a brilliant academic career became counsellor to the elector of Mainz in 1667, being engaged in politics and in scientific speculation until, longing for a quieter life, he accepted the post of librarian to the Duke of Brunswick in 1676. Here he reformed methods of mining, of coinage, of the library system at Wolfenbüttel, where Lessing (q.v.) was to be librarian later in the century, and was in touch with savants throughout Europe. His purely scientific activities and writings have no place here, and though one would be hard put to it to name anything by him of actual literary quality, except for *La Monadologie* (1714), his philosophical system, formulated in a tense, concentrated style, exactly sums up the political and social theory of the baroque world, and paved the way for the Enlightenment. His *Gedanken betreffend die Ausübung und Verbesserung der deutschen Sprache* (1717), in which, following in the steps of C. Thomasius (q.v.) he advocates the use of German as a literary language, should also be mentioned here. The greatest all-rounder of his age, who had perfected the calculus and had been responsible for getting the Prussian Academy founded, died in comparative neglect in Hanover, the subject of George I of England as much as was Newton, his rival. The best edition of his works is the French one of 1859–75 (7 vols.).

**Leip, Hans** (1893–    ), German poet and novelist, born in Hamburg.
The bulk of his verse is contained in the three volumes, *Die Nächte-
zettel der Sinsebal* (1927), *Die kleine Hafenorgel* (1937) and *Heimkunft*
(1947), but the work by which he became known all over the world
during the Second World War was the song 'Lili Marlene'. Of his
novels *Jan Himp und die kleine Brise* (1933), *Drachenkalb singe* (1949)
and *Der grosse Fluss im Meer* (1954) should be mentioned.

**Leisewitz, Johann Anton** (1752–1806), German dramatist. Born in
Hanover, he studied law at Göttingen, meeting there Hölty (q.v.)
and other members of the then flourishing *Göttinger Hain*. Becoming
a lawyer in Brunswick, he grew to be a friend and disciple of Lessing
(q.v.), then librarian at Wolfenbüttel close by. From him he learned
the art of the playwright and entered his play *Julius von Tarent* for
the Hamburg dramatic competition of 1776. The prize went to the
forceful though dramatically and technically inferior *Die Zwillinge*
of Klinger (q.v.), and Leisewitz, who seems to have lacked self-
confidence, gave up all literary ambition and destroyed his manuscripts. He died in the ducal service at Brunswick. In spite of contemporary judgment *Julius von Tarent* is by far the best play both
from the point of view of literature and theatre of the *Sturm und
Drang* movement.

**Lemaire de Belges, Jean** (1473–1524?), French man of letters from
Hainault, perhaps Bavai, was the first literary representative of the
full Renaissance in France. Employed at the court of Louis XII, he is
the author of the humorous *Épîtres de l'amant vert* (1510; mod. ed.,
1948) and *La Concorde des deux langages* (1511; mod. ed., 1947), in the
second of which he demands that France and Italy should be united
to form one kingdom of art presided over by Venus. The definitive
edition of his works is that by J. Stecher (4 vols., 1882–91).

**Lemaître, François Élie Jules** (1853–1914), French playwright, short-
story writer and critic. Born at Vénnecy (Loiret), he became a forceful
dramatic critic on the *Journal des Débats* and the *Revue des Deux
Mondes*, a playwright with *Le Député Leveau* (1891), *L'Âge difficile*
(1895) and *L'Aimée* (1898), and a short-story writer with *En marge
des vieux livres* (1905). A practising author and critic, the counterpart
of Brunetière (q.v.) and purely academic critics, Lemaître died at
Tavers (Loiret).

**Lemercier, Louis Jean Népomucène** (1771–1840), French poet and
dramatist. Born in Paris, he was much appreciated during the
revolution as a purveyor of melodramas with classical plots such as
*Le Lévite d'Éphraim* (1795) and *Pinto, ou la journée d'une conspiration*
(1800). His only really satisfactory play is, however, the historical
comedy *Agamemnon* (1797). He died in Paris having long outlived his
literary reputation.

**Lemierre, Antoine Marin** (1723–1793), French dramatist and poet,
born in Paris. He comes at the tail end of the old outworn school of
rhetorical, static drama. Such plays are *Hypermnestre* (1758),
*Guillaume Tell* (1766) and *La Veuve du Malabar* (1770), which last
had a vogue in England in translation. As a poet he is represented by

two descriptive poems of some length, *La Peinture* (1769) and *Les Fastes* (1779), the latter evidently inspired by Ovid's *Fasti*. He died at St-Germain-en-Laye. His *Œuvres* appeared in 1810.

**Lemonnier, Antoine Louis Camille** (1844–1913), Belgian novelist and dramatist, was born at Ixelles and came under the influence of the work of the Goncourts (q.v.) and Zola (q.v.) as can be seen in his earlier novels, *Les Charniers* (1881), *Le Mort* (1882), *L'Hystérique* (1885), *Happe-chair* (1886) and *Madame Lupar* (1888). This uncompromisingly naturalistic stage passed and was succeeded by a quieter, more sensitive, imaginative one exemplified in such works as *L'Arche* (1894), *Le Vent dans les moulins* (1901) and *Comme va le ruisseau* (1903). He also wrote a tragedy, *Édénic* (1912), performed with some success. He died in Brussels.

**Lenau, Nikolaus,** pseudonym of **Nikolaus Franz Niembsch von Strehlenau** (1802–1850), Austrian poet. Born at Csatad, Hungary, he grew up gifted, spoilt and wilful, and was for ten years a student, first of law and then of medicine, without result. At last breaking free from all restraint he went to Stuttgart where, showing round the poetry he had already written, he gained enough supporters for the publication of his first book, *Gedichte* (1832), in which was revealed an unusual power of interpreting nature and approximating its moods to human ones. A short visit to the U.S.A. (1832–3) was a failure, and he returned to plunge into two subjective Byronic poems, *Faust* (1836) and *Savonarola* (1837), which apart from the lyrics found dispersed in them are of little permanent value. On the other hand, in *Neuere Gedichte* (1838), *Gedichte* (1844) and the posthumous *Nachlass* (1851), there are a lyric depth of feeling and a musical quality unusual in German literature. Lenau became insane in 1844 and in that state remained until his death at Oberdöbling, near Vienna. His collected works appeared (6 vols.) in 1910–23.

**Lennep, Jacob van** (1802–1868), Dutch poet and novelist, born in Amsterdam. He studied law, and while practising it produced both novels and verse in the manner of Sir Walter Scott. As a poet his most considerable work is *Jacobaas Weeklacht op het Huis te Teylingen* (1839; Eng. trans. *Jacoba's Lament at the House of Teylingen*, n.d.). The most characteristic of his novels are *De Pleegzoon* (2 vols., 1833; Eng. trans. *The Adopted Son*, 1847), *De Roos van Dekama* (2 vols., 1836; Eng. trans. *The Rose of Dekama*, 1847), *De lotgevallen van Ferdinand Huyck* (2 vols., 1840; Eng. trans. *The Count of Talavera*, 1880), and the only one of his novels in a contemporary setting, *Klaasje Zevenster* (5 vols., 1865; Fr. trans. *Aventures de Nicolette Sept-étoiles*, 1878). He died at Oosterbeek.

**Lenormand, Henri-René** (1882–1951), French playwright. Born in Paris, he drew attention to himself with his play *Les Possédées* (1909) but did not gain a sure position in the theatre until the production under Georges Pitoëff, the actor-manager, of *Le Temps est un songe* (1919). *Les Ratés* and *Le Simoun* (both 1920) strengthened his claims to wide recognition, and after *Le Mangeur des rêves* (1922) he was regarded as a leading exponent of psychological drama in the wake of Freud. Later plays were *Sortilèges* (1932) and *Crépuscule du théâtre* (1934). His *Théâtre complet* came out in ten volumes at intervals between 1921 and 1942. He also wrote *Confessions d'un auteur dramatique* (3 vols., 1949–52). He died in Paris.

**Lenz, Jacob Michael Reinhold** (1751–1792), German dramatist and translator. Born the son of a well-to-do clergyman at Sesswegen, Livonia, he began to read theology, but broke off to go to Strassburg, where he met Goethe, and, impressionable as he was, began to try to ape Goethe's ways, even courting Friederike Brion, whom Goethe had loved and rejected. Caught up in the *Sturm und Drang* movement, he studied Shakespeare, and before long became one of the chief exponents of the new manner. His *Anmerkungen übers Theater* (1774), which was accompanied by a prose translation of Shakespeare's *Love's Labour's Lost* entitled *Amor vincit omnia*, shows him as a leading spokesman of the new drama, and he followed this up with several plays, the best of them *Der Hofmeister* (1774), *Der neue Menoza* (1774), and above all *Die Soldaten* (1776), all on contemporary social subjects, the last a confrontation between the supercilious Junker class and the insulted bourgeoisie. The rest of his work is of no importance. Without talent for constructing his plays as a whole entity, he was second only to Goethe himself as a creator of real living characters. In Weimar for a time in 1776, he became insane, but recovered and continued his wanderings, which had led him as far as Moscow, where one night he was found dead in the street. This strange eccentric character appealed greatly to the young romantics, of whom Tieck (q.v.) edited his works (3 vols., 1828) and Georg Büchner (q.v.) in the next generation wrote a long short-story about him. There is a good edition of his collected works by F. Bley (5 vols., 1909–13).

**León, Luis de** (1527?–1591), Spanish poet and prose-writer, was born at Belmonte, Cuenca, became an Augustinian and lectured at the University of Salamanca, fell foul of the Inquisition over his splendid translation of the Song of Solomon, *Cantar de cantares* (1572; mod. ed., 1936), but was released and became provincial of his Order. His lyrics, some of them of fine quality, were not collected until long after his death by Quevedo (q.v.) in 1631. He also wrote commentaries on the Bible, one of which on a passage in Proverbs, entitled *La perfecta casada* (mod. ed., 1917), is a model of Spanish prose. By many his greatest work is considered his devotional dialogue *De los nombres de Cristo* (mod. ed., 3 vols., 1914–21). He died at Madrigal. His poetical works are best consulted in Llobera's edition (2 vols., 1932–3). His lyrics, Horatian in form, served as the basis for Spanish eighteenth-century classicism.

**León, Ricardo** (1877–1943), Spanish novelist. Born in Malaga, he became a clerk in a bank. He was a favourite with that great majority of middle-class readers who were growing weary of the continual attacks by intellectualist novelists on long accepted values. Typical of his work is *Casta de hidalgos* (1908; Eng. trans. *A Son of the Hidalgos*, 1921), and others are *La escuela de los sofistas* (1910),

*Los centauros* (1912) and *Los caballeros de la cruz* (1916). He died in Madrid.

**Leone Ebreo,** *see* **Abarbanel, L. E.**

**Leonora Christina of Slesvig-Holstein** (1621–1698), Danish prose-writer. An illegitimate daughter of Christian IV of Denmark, she was born at Frederiksborg, marrying in 1636 Count Ulfeldt. Guiltless of treason, she was accused of it together with her husband and, simply to satisfy a grudge which the queen-dowager had against her, spent most of the period between 1659 and 1685 in prison. During those long years she wrote her autobiography, *Jammersminde* (first publ., 1869; Eng. trans. *Memoirs of Leonora Christina,* 1872, reprinted 1931), a splendid piece of writing, which entitles her to be considered the best woman writer of Denmark. She died a secular abbess at Maribo.

**Leonov, Leonid Maximovich** (1899–     ), Russian Soviet novelist, born at Polukhino. He has generally been considered the most traditional of Soviet writers, both in style and content having closer proximity to the nineteenth-century realists than any of his con-temporaries. Such works as *Barsuki* (1925; Eng. trans. *The Badgers,* 1947), *Vor* (1926; Eng. trans. *The Thief,* 1931), *Sot* (1929; Eng. trans. 1931) and *Skutarevsky* (1932; Eng. trans. 1936) certainly give this impression.

**Leopardi, Giacomo** (1798–1837), Italian poet and prose-writer, born at Recanati of noble family. His father had greatly neglected the family's affairs and spent his time in his fine library which Giacomo was encouraged to use. Before long the boy developed into a prodigy, tutors were dispensed with, and he toiled on alone day after day, until at sixteen he had read all the great classical texts in Latin and Greek, knew English, French, Spanish and Hebrew and was at work on a commentary on Plotinus. Meanwhile instead of checking him his parents looked on approvingly until his eyesight was permanently injured (he eventually lost the sight of one eye) and he developed curvature of the spine. About the age of twenty he at last seems to have looked up from his books and come to terms with himself. Life was tedious, purposeless, optimism for the future was nonsense; happiness lay in illusion; technical advance, far from helping on the millennium, was going to lead to human misery. It is the poet's mission to recreate the illusion of happiness which, glimpsed at in childhood, has afterwards been snatched away from us. Along these lines he wrote his poetry, at its best of remarkable individuality. An example of his earlier style is *Alla primavera* (1822), but it is with *La quieta dopo la tempestà* (1829) that he reaches maturity. *Canto notturno* (1830) is moving, *Canti* (1831) contains much of his finest work, and in *Amore e morte* (1832) he is at his best. In 1833 his good friend Ranieri, realizing that he must live in a warmer climate if he were to survive, took him off to Naples. There, increasingly suffering in mind and body, he wrote *Palinodie* (1834), *Ad Aspasia* (1834), *I nuovi credenti* (1835) and a satirical 'Continua-tion of the Battle of the Frogs and Mice' (referring to the pseudo-Homeric poem), *Paralipomeni della Batracomiomachia* (1837). He

died in Naples. It was as a prose-writer, the author of *Operette morali*
(1827; mod. ed., 1940; Eng. trans. *Essays and Dialogues*, 1882;
*Essays, Dialogues and Thoughts of Count Giacomo Leopardi*, 1905),
that he first gained European fame, and it was as a moralist that
Gladstone and Sainte-Beuve (q.v.) acclaimed him. His high reputation as a poet, both within his country and outside it, was reached
long afterwards. The best way to sample his work in the original is
to read *Canti* (ed. I. Sanesi, 1943), while *The Poems of Leopardi* (by
G. L. Bickersteth, 1923) has the Italian text and an English translation in verse. Other English translations are those by R. C. Trevelyan
(1941) and J. Heath-Stubbs (1946). See also *Selected Prose and Poetry*
in Oxford Library of Italian Classics.

**Leopold, Jan Hendrik** (1865–1925), Dutch poet. Born at 's-Hertogenbosch, he became a schoolmaster, a life thoroughly uncongenial, and
his days were embittered by increasing deafness which finally incapacitated him for ordinary social activities. In his first two books
of poetry, *Verzen* (1912 and 1913), we see him mastering poetic
diction, which he was to bring to perfection in his third collection,
brought out posthumously in 1926, but except for *Cheops* (1915;
Eng. trans. 1947), there is never the poetic urgency to match it. He
died in Rotterdam.

**Lermontov, Mikhail Yuryevich** (1814–1841), Russian poet. Born, of
Scottish extraction (Learmonth), in Moscow, the son of an army
officer, he entered a cadet school in 1832 and soon obtained a commission in the guards. He first attracted attention as a poet with
*Na smert' Pushkina* (1837, 'On the Death of Pushkin'), in which he
accused the government of cynically arranging the events leading to
the duel which caused the poet's death, and was promptly transferred
to the army of the Caucasus. A complex character, gloomily romantic
and obsessed by his feeling of being an outcast, he found in the
magnificence of Caucasian scenery an inspiration which led to the
writing of the splendid long narrative poem *Demon*, not published
till 1856 (best of several Eng. trans. *The Demon* by Ellen Richter,
1910; and R. Burness, 1918). In 1839 he was allowed to return to
Petersburg, bringing with him many lyrics and a half-finished novel.
This novel, *Geroy nashego vremeni* (1840; Eng. trans. *A Hero of
Nowadays* by S. Phillimore, 1920; *A Hero of our Time* by R. Merton,
1928; and *A Hero of our Own Times* by E. and C. Paul, 1940), is a
remarkable analysis of the *mal de siècle*, the hero, that is Lermontov
himself, being a typical product of Byronic romanticism with all its
attendant problems. For engaging in a duel with the son of the French
ambassador he was again exiled to the Caucasus in 1840, and the
following summer while staying at the Caucasian resort, Pyatigorsk,
he had a chance quarrel with another officer, and in the resultant duel
was killed. There was no question of this having been arranged by the
government as in Pushkin's case. In his short life he had come to be
regarded as second only to Pushkin as a poet, and to modern eyes he
is perhaps even more remarkable as a novelist. A collection of his
lyrics first appeared in 1840; for English translations of some see
*Poems by Pushkin, Lermontov, Tyutchev* (1947) and see also *A Song*

*about Tsar Ivan Vasilyevich* (1929), and various translations in Bowra's *Book of Russian Verse* (2 vols., 1943, 1947).

**Lersch, Heinrich** (1889–1936), German poet and novelist. Born of a working-class family at München-Gladbach, he himself became a factory hand. Never able to make up for defects in his education, there are deep technical faults in all his work, but some of his poetry is saved by his eagerness and idealism. This is particularly true of his war poems, *Kriegsgedichte*, which appeared in ten volumes between 1915 and 1918. *Stern und Amboss* (1926) is characteristic of his technically more satisfactory later poetry, but it has lost its fire. Of his novels possibly the best is *Hammerschläge* (1930). He died at Remagen. His poetical works were collected in 1937.

**Le Sage, Alain-René** (1668–1747), French novelist and playwright. Born at Sarzeau, Morbihan, Brittany, he went to Paris in 1692 to read law, but an early marriage compelled him to find money more rapidly and he took to writing. His friend, Abbé de Lionne, gave him the freedom of his excellent Spanish library, and made him an allowance so that he might study it in peace, and the result was that during the next eight years he gained a knowledge of Spanish literature almost unrivalled in the France of his day. His adaptations and translations of various plays, especially those by Lope de Vega (q.v.), Calderón (q.v.) and F. de Rojas Zorrilla (q.v.), met with some success, but he did not achieve full recognition until his novel *Le Diable boiteux* (1707; first Eng. trans. *The Devil upon Two Sticks*, 1708), founded on L. Vélez de Guevara's (q.v.) *El diablo cojuelo*, appeared. For a moment he turned away from Spanish literature, and in *Turcaret, ou Le Financier* (1709) followed in the tradition of Molière (q.v.) to produce an excellent satirical play on crooked speculators, yet he never returned to anything like this. But the crown of his achievement is *Gil Blas* (vols. i and ii, 1715; vol. iii, 1724; and vol. iv, 1735; crit. ed., 1935; first Eng. trans. T. Smollett, 1749), a picaresque novel, not founded on any particular original or originals, but the result of a general 'feel' for Spanish literature and for Spain, a country which he never visited. And if the setting is Spanish, the satire is definitely French. Voltaire (q.v.), whom Le Sage heartily disliked and let him know it, was the first to pretend that *Gil Blas* was merely a translation, and in Spain Isla (q.v.) perpetuated the injustice. Other novels, all with the exception of *Les Aventures de Monsieur Robert Chevalier de Beauchêne* (1732) having Spanish themes, are *Guzman d'Alfarache* (1732), *Estébanille Gonzalès* (1734) and *Le Bachelier de Salamanque* (1736). In his last years he lived at Boulogne, and died there. His *Œuvres complètes* appeared in twelve volumes (1821).

**Leskov, Nikolay Semyonovich** (1831–1895), Russian novelist and short-story writer, was born at Gorokhovo, and in his youth travelled much in Russia and made himself conversant with all manner of men, an experience which stood him in good stead when he wrote. Settling in Petersburg in 1861 he began to write in earnest, the result being two novels, *Nekuda* (1864, 'Nowhere') and *Na nozhakh* (1871, 'At Daggers Drawn'), powerful social studies, in which he turns on radicals and other hot-house theorizers, who from their armchairs seek to turn society upside down. He then withdrew from the contemporary scene, in *Soboryane* (1872, 'Cathedral Folk') turning to the historical novel. But perhaps he deserves the highest praise for his short stories, outstanding among them *Ledi Makbet Mtsenskogo uyezda* (1865; Eng. trans. *The Lady Macbeth of the Mtsensk District* in *Representative Russian Stories*, 1946). A selection of his short stories has been made in English as *The Tales of Leskov* (1944). He died in Petersburg. Underestimated in his own day, his novels, with their remarkable gallery of portraits, exerted much influence on young writers at the turn of the twentieth century, notably Gorky (q.v.).

**Lespinasse, Jeanne Julie Éléonore de** (1732–1776), French prose-writer. Born in Lyon, she joined that great *salon* queen Madame du Deffand in Paris in 1754. In 1764 they parted in anger, and Julie set up a rival *salon* which was soon frequented by the Encyclopédistes, one of whom, D'Alembert (q.v.), fell hopelessly in love with her. Charming but frigid, two other love affairs came to nothing. A copious correspondent, only her letters written between 1773 and 1776 have been preserved. They were published in 1809, and were later highly praised by Sainte-Beuve (q.v.) as outstanding examples of the epistolary art. She died in Paris.

**Lessing, Gotthold Ephraim** (1729–1781), German dramatist and general prose-writer, the true founder of modern German literature, was born, the son of a Lutheran pastor, at Kamenz, in Saxony, and went to school at Meissen. When he entered the University of Leipzig it was to read theology, but soon his literary and particularly his dramatic interests began to predominate, and in 1748, not yet twenty, his comedy, *Der junge Gelehrte*, was produced at the Leipzig theatre. *Die Judin* (1749, 'The Jewess') followed, and he felt he was on his way to his ambition of becoming 'the German Molière', but his pious father was horrified, and he left Leipzig in disgrace to plunge into the world of literature in Berlin, where he remained until 1755. After a difficult start he prospered from the time when he was appointed literary critic of the *Vossische Zeitung* in 1751, and as the editor of the *Theatralische Bibliothek* (1754–8) he followed in the footsteps of Elias Schlegel (q.v.) to become in time the leading German dramatic critic of the day. But Lessing was not just a critic, he was a performer, and with his play, *Miss Sara Sampson* (1755), produced the first modern domestic tragedy in Germany. Not only the title but the whole play is inspired by England, the breath of its being derived from George Lillo's *George Barnwell* (1731), a bourgeois tragedy, while the characters are taken from Richardson's novel *Clarissa Harlowe*. It was the beginning of his long and eventually successful struggle to oust artificial French drama from the stage and replace it by the 'natural' English drama. *Miss Sara Sampson* was a great success, but Lessing soon left the crude realism of it behind him, and after a spell in Leipzig returned once more to Berlin, where he tried out his hand on a fine one-act tragedy on the ancient Greek model, *Philotas* (1759). He then joined forces with Moses Mendelssohn (q.v.) and J. C. F. Nicolai (q.v.) in writing a literary magazine, *Briefe, die* *neueste Literatur betreffend* (1759–65), as a result of which he became the unchallenged literary critic of Germany. Having finally demolished Gottsched's (q.v.) pretensions in the *Briefe* he turned to the necessity of supplementing a still very modest income, and in 1760 became secretary to the military governor of Breslau. During the five years he spent there several plans were germinating in his mind, one to evolve a new system of aesthetics, which appeared to Lessing to have been unsatisfactorily treated by Winckelmann (q.v.) owing, for example, to faulty premises and confusion of terms; another plan was to create a national German stage. Thus it was that in 1765 he returned to Berlin where in *Laokoon* (1766) he, with a knowledge of classical culture surpassing Winckelmann's, brilliantly refuted the latter's insistence that the plastic arts were superior to literary description, proving that comparison between different media was idle. A by-product of this controversy was the essay *Wie die Alten den Tod gebildet* (1769, 'The Representation of Death by the Ancients'). With *Minna von Barnhelm* (1767) he succeeded in writing a comedy on a contemporary theme (it is set in the period of the Seven Years War), and he had the satisfaction of proving that the writer in him matched the critic. Then came a crisis in his life. Voltaire having reported against him to Frederick the Great, Lessing failed to obtain the directorship of the Royal Library, Berlin. He left Prussia for good, and went to Hamburg to take up the second-rate post of house critic to the theatre there; perhaps, at any rate, it might become the theatre of his dreams. Although he was to be disillusioned, all the same the appointment led to the writing of the *Hamburgische Dramaturgie* (1767–8), 'the ripest opinions which eighteenth-century classicism attained to on the subject of the drama'. Sophocles and Shakespeare as writers, Aristotle as critic are the three great figures before whom all dramatists should make obeisance; but even so he is broad-minded enough (and this tolerance was a feature of his later years) to admit the genius of other schools of drama with other critical standards, outstandingly the Spanish. But on the material side the sojourn in Hamburg was a disaster; his scheme for the national theatre, into which he had sunk the greater part of his savings, collapsed, as did a printing business which he had partly financed. An anxious time followed, which was only ended by the offer of the librarianship of Wolfenbüttel Ducal Library, a post which he gladly accepted (1770). In this quaint, quiet, decayed old town he spent eight years, and he wrote one more dramatic work, the dignified, classically inspired tragedy *Emilia Galotti* (1772), before plunging into the presses of the silent, dusty library to find forgotten or undiscovered treasures and publishing them from 1773 onwards in a series entitled *Zur Geschichte und Literatur*. Out of such seemingly peaceful pursuits a veritable tempest grew. In several of the numbers he had published writings by Reimarus (q.v.), as *Fragmente eines Ungenannten* ('Fragments of an Anonymous Author'), which denied the supernatural origin of Christianity. Lessing was now attacked by the orthodox led by the chief pastor of Hamburg, J. M. Goeze, with a virulence and bitterness reminiscent of the sixteenth century. Lessing had the last word in

*Anti-Goeze* (1778), but was forbidden by authority to engage in any more such disputes, and it was then that he conceived the plan of *Nathan der Weise*. This work, not intended as a drama for the stage, was so framed as to escape from the ban on his further controversial prose-writings. It is a plea for toleration disguised as a verse play. Lofty and idealistic, it is the finest flower of the Enlightenment in Germany, and demands the brotherhood of men. Political nationalism had always been hateful to Lessing, and so were religious divisions. *Nathan* appeared in 1779, and for all its shortcomings both as to plot (without the use of the episode of the three rings in Boccaccio's *Decameron* what movement would it have?) and even to verse, it soon came to be valued as the final judgment on life of a great European. He had already, in *Ernst und Falk: Gespräche für Frei-maurer* (1778), shown his faith in freemasonry as a force for good among men and nations, and in his last work, *Die Erziehung des Menschengeschlechts* (1780, 'The Education of the Human Race'), with its generous breadth, he forestalls the best of nineteenth-century liberalism. Florid in appearance and optimistic in disposition, behind this front had been many disappointments and frustrations, the strain of controversy, and domestic sorrow, all of which led to his premature death from apoplexy in Brunswick. See *Sämtliche Werke* (30 vols., 1791–4; 24 vols., 1886–1924; and 25 vols., 1925). For English translations see Bohn's Library for *Dramatic Works* (vol. i, *Tragedies*, vol. ii, *Comedies*) and *Prose Works* (containing *Laokoon, Dramatic Notes* and *The Representation of Death by the Ancients*). There is also a volume in Everyman's Library containing *Laocoön, Minna von Barnhelm* and *Nathan the Wise*.

**Levi, Carlo** (1902–     ), Italian prose-writer. Born in Turin, it was his exile as an anti-Fascist to Lucania in the south of Italy that led him to discover his talent, for it was while there, uprooted from accustomed pursuits, that he wrote his remarkable account of the daily round in this distant region, *Cristo s'è fermato a Eboli* (1946; Eng. trans. *Christ Stopped at Eboli*, 1947). A love of man and nature pervades it. Other books in the same strain are: *Paura della libertà* (1947; Eng. trans. *Of Fear and Freedom*, 1950), *L'orologio* (1950; Eng. trans. *The Watch*, 1951), *Il futuro ha un cuore antico* (1956) and *La doppia notte dei tigli* (1959).

**Lewald, Fanny** (1811–1889), German novelist. Born in Königsberg of Jewish family, she was converted to Christianity in 1829. A champion of women's rights, she was a great publicist in this cause. As a novelist her best works were *Von Geschlecht zu Geschlecht* (1864, 'From Race to Race') and *Stella* (1883; Eng. trans. 1884). She died in Dresden.

**L'Hermite, François,** *see* **Tristan L'Hermite.**

**Libedinsky, Yury Nikolayevich** (1898–1959), Russian Soviet novelist, born in the Urals region. A leading working-class writer and literary ideologist, he opened his career with *Nedelya* (1922; Eng. trans., *A Week,* 1923). Other novels include *Komissary* (1925, 'Commissars'), *Rozhdenie geroya* (1930, 'Birth of a Hero') and *Gory i lyudi* (1947, 'Mountains and People').

**Lichtenberg, Georg Christoph** (1742–1799), German satirist born at

Oberramstädt near Darmstadt, was educated at the University of Göttingen, where from 1769 till his death he was professor of physics. With his clear and trenchant prose he ridiculed the craze for physiognomy initiated by Lavater (q.v.) in *Über Physiognomik wieder die Physiognomen* (1773). He frequently visited England, and his *Briefe aus England* (1776–8) is a most attractive account of the impact of that country on him. An appreciation of Hogarth's engravings led him to some of his most outstanding writing, *Ausführliche Erklärung der Hogarthischen Kupferstiche* (1794–9; Eng. trans. *Lichtenberg's Commentaries on Hogarth's Engravings*, 1966). He died in Göttingen. His collected works were published (2 vols.) in 1949.

**Lidin, Vladimir Germanovich,** pseudonym of **Vladimir Gomberg** (1894–    ), Russian Soviet novelist born in Moscow, author of *Idut korabli* (1926, 'The Ships Sail'), *Otstupnik* (1927; Eng. trans. *The Apostate*, 1931), *Iskateli* (1929, 'The Seekers') and *Mogila neizvestnogo soldata* (1932, 'The Grave of the Unknown Soldier').

**Lie, Jonas Lauritz Idemil** (1833–1908), Norwegian novelist. Born at Eiker, he spent his youth in Tromsø, where the north Norwegian scenery made a lasting impression on him and which colours all his work. He took up law and prospered until 1868, when he went bankrupt as a result of unfortunate speculations. Taking to his pen for a living, he soon succeeded with his novel *Den Fremsynte* (1870; Eng. trans. *The Visionary*, 1894), and this success continued with another book about the far north, *Tremasteren ' Fremtiden' eller Liv Nordpaa* (1872; Eng. trans. *The Barque ' Future' or Life in the Far North*, 1879). He then turned to an even happier vein, that of middle-class and lower middle-class Norwegian family life, his best novels on this theme being *Lodsen og hans Husfru* (1874; Eng. trans. *The Pilot and his Wife*, 1877), *Livs-slaven* (1883; Eng. trans. *One of Life's Slaves*, 1895), *Familjen paa Gilje* (1883; Eng. trans. *The Family at Gilje*, 1920), *Kommandørens Døtre* (1886; Eng. trans. *The Commodore's Daughters*, 1892) and *Niobe* (1893; Eng. trans. 1897). *Trold* (2 vols., 1891–2) shows his predilection for the strange. It was translated into English as *Weird Tales from Northern Seas* (1893). He died at Fleskum.

**Ligne, Charles-Joseph de** (1735–1814), Belgian letter-writer and historian. Born in Brussels, Prince de Ligne found time during a busy life to write fascinating letters and pen portraits, which make forgotten incidents and figures live. The bulk of his work is to be found in *Lettres à la Marquise de Coigny* (1787) and *Mélanges littéraires, militaires et sentimentaires* (1795), both of which are incorporated in *The Letters and Memoirs of the Prince de Ligne* (Eng. trans. by L. Ashton, 1927). He died in Vienna.

**Liliencron, Friedrich Adolf Axel Detlev von** (1844–1909), German poet and short-story writer. Born in Kiel of noble though diminished family, he entered the army, but by his early thirties he had run so heavily into debt that he was forced to resign, married money and gave up the rest of his life to literary work. His book of verse, *Adjutantenritte und andere Gedichte* (1883), is powerful and original,

full of the raciness of the keen air of north Germany with army life
to the fore. In *Der Heidegänger und andere Gedichte* (1890) the
tramp of soldiers' feet melts into the distance and one is left in
the stillness of the flat plains with their wide skies. His collected
poems were published in three volumes (1897–1900). By this time
he had become the acknowledged father of the younger generation
of poets who were impatient of the still lingering romantic traditions
in poetry, and there is no doubt that he was responsible for leading
German verse into new fields and opening up new possibilities to it.
He was also a good long short-story writer, as *Unter flatternden
Fahnen* (1888) and *Kriegsnovellen* (1895) prove. He died at Alt-
Rahlstedt, near Hamburg. His collected works appeared (8 vols.)
in 1922.

**Limburg Brouwer, Petrus Abraham Samuel van** (1829–1873), Dutch
novelist. Born in Liège, he was a well-known philosopher, writing on
Fichte (q.v.), Spinoza (q.v.) and Schopenhauer (q.v.), but as far as
literature goes he is important for his novel *Akbar* (1872; Eng. trans.
1879). He died in The Hague.

**Linati, Carlo** (1878–1949), Italian novelist. Born at Como, he wrote
excellent prose whether he tackled literary criticism, the general essay
or fiction. His best novels belong to the later period and are: *Due*
(1928), *Concerto variato* (1933), *Sinfonia alpestre* (1937), *A vento e
sole* (1939), *Un giorno sulla dolce terra* (1941), *Nerone secondo* (1943)
and *Due tempi in provincia* (1944). He died at Rebbio.

**Lindau, Paul** (1839–1919), German dramatist. Born in Magdeburg,
he began early to write for the stage and gained success with *Marion*
(1868). In 1895 he became chief playwright to the Meiningen Court
Theatre, writing about the time of his appointment his masterpiece
*Der Abend* (1896). His novels had no permanent value. He died in
Berlin.

**Lindorm, Erik** (1889–1941), Swedish writer. Born in Stockholm, where
he died, he is best known outside his own country as the inventor of
the so-called 'book film', an arrangement of newspaper and magazine
cuttings to make up a narrative of historical events, the skill in
handling of the material being considered the 'authorship'. To some
this was little more than a gimmick, to others comparable to Picasso's
use of paper and metals in his pictures. Brilliant examples of this are
*Oscar II och hans tid* (2 vols., 1934) and *Gustav V och hans tid* (3 vols.,
1936–40).

**Lingg, Hermann von** (1820–1905), German poet. Born at Lindau, he
became an army physician, but later retiring and going to Munich he
discovered his talent for verse, and embarked on an ambitious epic,
*Die Völkerwanderung* (1866–8). But it was with short poems, powerful
if graceless in style, that he made his name. They have a vigour and
lack of sentimentality unusual for the time. See the collection of
them made by Paul von Heyse (q.v.) in 1905. Some of them were
translated into English in F. D'Anvers's *English Echoes of German
Song* (1877). Lingg died in Munich.

**Linnaeus, Carl,** from 1757 **Carl von Linné** (1707–1778), Swedish prose-writer. The great naturalist, whose scientific works have no place here, but whose general culture and travel-books give him a niche in literature, was born the son of the village clergyman at Råshult, near Stenbrohult, Småland, and became director of the botanic gardens at the University of Uppsala; he died there as professor of botany. Of his voluminous writings the three accounts of his visits to remote corners of Sweden and other parts of Europe have all the charm of true literature. They are: *Carl Linnaei Öländska och Göthlandska resa* (first publ., 1940), *Carl Linnaei Wästgöta resa* (first publ., 1928) and *Carl Linnaei Skånska resa* (first publ. 1940).

**Littré, Maximilien Paul Émile** (1801–1881), French author. Born in Paris, he studied languages, philology and philosophy. He became, after Comte (q.v.), the chief representative of the Positivists, but as he showed in his *Paroles de la philosophie positive* (1859) he absolutely disapproved of their mysticism. It is, however, as a philologist that he is remembered, and here his *Dictionnaire de la langue française* (4 vols., 1863–72) is his finest work and one of the supreme results of French scholarship. An uncompromising republican, he gained little official recognition until after the fall of Napoleon III. He died in Paris.

**Liutprand** (922?–972), Italian historian writing in Latin. Born probably in Pavia, he was chief envoy of the Emperor Otto I, and was consecrated Bishop of Cremona in 961. His principal work is his lively *Relatio de Legatione Constantinopolitana* (Eng. trans. 1896), describing his mission to the Byzantine court and his impressions and experiences there. His *Gesta Ottonis*, a life of the Emperor Otto, is an example of good tight Latin prose. His *Opera* appeared in a critical edition in 1915.

**Lobo, Francisco Rodrigues** (1580–1622), Portuguese novelist and poet. Born at Leiria, he gained an office at the court of the Duke of Bragança, having there plenty of opportunity to pursue his taste for writing. He produced three pastoral novels forming a trilogy, full of charming lyrics, *A primavera* (1601), *O pastor peregrino* (1608) and *O desenganado* (1614), and a collection of didactic eclogues, *Églogas* (1605; mod. ed., 1928), but his best work is *Corte na aldeia e noites de inverno* (1619; mod. ed., 1945), modelled on the *Cortegiano* of Castiglione (q.v.) though with little of the original's lofty idealism. Lobo was accidentally drowned in the Tagus, near Belem. See his *Obras políticas e pastorais* (4 vols., 1774). There is a modern edition of all his poetry (1940).

**Lohenstein, Daniel Casper von** (1635–1683), German dramatist, novelist and poet. Born at Nimptsch, he became a member of the Hofmannswaldau (q.v.) circle at a very early age, having written his first play, *Ibrahim Bassa* (1653), while still a schoolboy. He prospered as a lawyer in Breslau, at the same time working on his elaborate baroque plays, which include *Cleopatra* (1661), *Epicharis* (1665), *Ibrahim Sultan* (1673) and *Sophonisbe* (1680). His formal and intricate lyrics were collected as *Blumen* (1680). At the time of his death in

Breslau he left unfinished a bulky novel, *Grossmüthiger Feldherr Arminius* (2 vols., 1689), which promised well.

**Lomonosov, Mikhail Vasilievitch** (1711–1765), Russian poet. Born on the Island of Denisovka, near Archangel, the son of a fisherman, Lomonosov after great trials became professor of chemistry at Petersburg, and later rector. As a poet he spent all his energies on his epic, *Peter Velikiy* ('Peter the Great'), and on his twenty-four odes, all showing strength, rhetorical power, and the wide sweep of a far-ranging mind. He had as a philologist an extraordinary influence on the development of the Russian language, advocating the literary use of a middle language half way between colloquial Russian and ecclesiastical Slavonic. Also a scientist of no mean order, his essays in this field were models of conciseness. He died in Petersburg. His *Sochineniya* were collected in five volumes (1891–1902).

**Löns, Hermann** (1866–1914), German poet, novelist and short-story writer, was born at Kulm. His charming nature verse is to be found in *Mein goldenes Buch* (1901), *Mein blaues Buch* (1909) and especially in *Der kleine Rosengarten* (1911; Eng. trans. *The Little Garden of Roses*, 1929). His short stories, to be found in the collections *Mein grünes Buch* (1901), *Mein braunes Buch* (1906) and *Der Mümmelmann* (1909), deal with animals, nature and peasants. There is in some of them, as in the full-length novel *Der Wehrwolf* (1910; Eng. trans. *Harm Wolf*, 1931), more than a hint of the weird and the not always amusing grotesque. He is outstanding as a descriptive writer. He died in Reims, France, shortly after the outbreak of the First World War.

**Lope de Vega,** *see* **Vega Carpio, L. F. de.**

**Lopes, Fernão** (1380?–1460?), Portuguese chronicler. Little is known of his life beyond the facts that he came of a poor family and was historiographer to the kings of Portugal. The greatest historian of medieval Portugal and one of the finest of Europe, he produced three works, *Crónica de Dom Pedro* (mod. ed., 1932), *Crónica de Dom Fernando* (mod. ed., 2 vols., 1933, 1935) and *Crónica de Dom João I* (mod. ed., 2 vols., 1946–9). His manner of writing is excellent, he knows human nature just as he knows how to handle his materials, and substantiates the views he takes by deftly yet honestly making use of the evidence.

**López de Ayala, Adelardo** (1829–1879), Spanish dramatist. Born at Guadalcanal, near Seville, he read law, entered politics and at his death in Madrid was prime minister. As a dramatist he is known for several comedies of manners in which light satire plays a leading part, the best *El tanto por ciento* (1861) and *Consuelo* (1870).

**López de Ayala, Pero** (1332–1407), Spanish chronicler and poet. Born at Vitoria, after a varied and disturbed life with many changes of fortune he became chancellor of Castile in 1399. His great work is his chronicle of Spain from about 1350 to 1400 (first trustworthy ed. as *Crónicas de los reyes de Castilla*, 1779), written with much dramatic feeling and in general with accuracy. As a poet he wrote the long satire on abuses in the contemporary world, *Rimado de palacio* (mod. ed., N.Y., 1920).

**López Picó, Josep María** (1886–1959), Catalan poet and literary critic, born in Barcelona, where he died. As founder-editor of *La Revista* he became the enlightened dictator of Catalan literature, and published a number of well-regarded volumes of verse, including *Amor, Senyor* (1912), *Canto i allegoríes* (1917), *Elegia* (1925), *Antologia lírica* (1931), *Museu* (1934) and *A contraclaror del seny* (1936), a reflection on the violence and divided aims which heralded the outbreak of the civil war. *Intermezzo mallorquí* (1946) and *Lloa zodiac i triomf de Barcelona* (1947) are typical of his later work.

**López Silva, José** (1860–1925), Spanish poet and playwright, was born in Madrid. As a poet he is at his best in *Los barrios bajos* (1894), *Los Madriles* (1896), *La gente del pueblo* (1908) and *La musa del arroyo* (1911), which show an intimate understanding of and feeling for the humbler life of Madrid. His best-known work, however, is the play *La revoltosa* (1897). He died in Madrid.

**López Soler, Ramón** (1806–1836), Spanish novelist. Born in Barcelona, he took up literary journalism and was soon a well-known exponent of the romantic novel, following Scott in *Los bandos de Castilla* (1830) and Victor Hugo (q.v.) in *La catedral de Sevilla* (1832). He died in Madrid.

**Lorca,** *see* García Lorca, F.

**Lorenzo de' Medici,** *see* Medici.

**Lorm, H.,** *see* Landesmann, H.

**Lorris,** *see* Guillaume de Lorris.

**Loti, Pierre,** pseudonym of **Louis Marie Julien Viaud** (1850–1923), French novelist. Born at Rochefort, he joined the navy and saw the world, his experiences providing material for his exotic novels with himself nearly always in a leading part, surrounded by charming and ingenuous natives. His first piece of fiction was *Aziyadé* (1879), about Turkey, the second, *Rarahu* (1880; reprinted as *Le Mariage de Loti*, 1882), brought him fame with its Polynesian setting, its splendid description and its sad sentimentalism. In *Mon Frère Yves* (1883) and the celebrated *Le Pêcheur d'Islande* (1886) he turned for a moment to Breton fishermen for his inspiration, but returned to the East with *Madame Chrysanthème* (1887) and *Fantôme d'Orient* (1891). He soon outwrote himself, and had little more to say after this. His melancholy can depress, his precious style may irritate, but at his best he is one of the foremost descriptive writers in French literature of the nineteenth century. He died at Hendaye. His *Œuvres complètes* were published (11 vols.) between 1894 and 1911.

**Lotichius Secundus, Petrus** (1528–1560), German poet writing in Latin, born at Niederzell, near Schlüchtern. One of the greatest of modern Latin poets, he took Virgil, Horace, Tibullus and Ovid as his models and produced verse not only of formal beauty but of true feeling. He published *Elegiarum liber et carminum libellus* in 1551 (collected editions appearing in 1586, 1754 and 1773, and a modern selection in 1926). He died in Heidelberg.

**Louÿs, Pierre,** his surname originally **Louis** (1870–1925), French prose-writer and prose-poet. He was born in Ghent, son of a rich business family from Paris, to which city his parents soon returned. Brilliant and personable, he founded in 1891 the literary magazine *La Conque*, which soon had as contributors not only the young writers Valéry (q.v.) and Gide (q.v.), but Verlaine (q.v.), Maeterlinck (q.v.) and Mallarmé (q.v.). With a surprising gift for languages he buried himself in the classics and the most obscure Hellenistic and late Latin authors, reading also oriental works. In 1893 he published *Chrysis*, which afterwards became the first chapter of the extremely frank and uncompromising novel about an Alexandrian courtesan, in which he extolled the glories of the body to the confusion of Christian morality. *Les Chansons de Bilitis* (1894) was a cycle of prose poems of great beauty on lesbianism in ancient times. *Aphrodite* (1896), a continuation of *Chrysis*, was acclaimed first by Coppée (q.v.), and widely read. *La Femme et le pantin* (1898) is a colourfully realistic novel about Spain based on an episode in the adventures of Casanova (q.v.); *Les Aventures du Roi Pausole* (1901) satirizes conventional morality. A later work is *Le Crépuscule des nymphes* (1925). He died in complete seclusion in Paris. *Aphrodite, Les Chansons de Bilitis* and *Les Aventures du Roi Pausole* appear in English translation in *Collected Works of Pierre Louÿs* (N.Y., 1951).

**Loyola, Ignatius,** his real name **Íñigo López de Recalde** (1491–1556), Spanish devotional writer, was born of noble family in the castle of Loyola, in Guipúzcoa. Beginning life as a page at the court of Ferdinand and Isabel, he next became a soldier and, after recovering from a severe illness occasioned by a wound received at the defence of Pamplona against the French (1521), was converted; and at Manresa (1522) wrote his *Ejercicios espirituales* (first publ., 1548; Eng. trans. *Spiritual Exercises*, one version, 1915, another, 1919), one of the most influential religious works in modern times. Strong and unadorned, they constitute a fine example of pure Spanish prose. The rest of his life hardly concerns literary history. The founder of the Society of Jesus, he died in Rome.

**Ludwig, Emil** (1881–1948), German prose-writer. Born in Breslau of Jewish family, his real surname being Cohn, he read law at Heidelberg and entered on a commercial career, which he left for literature. Although books on Richard Dehmel (q.v.) and Wagner (q.v.), both published in 1913, showed considerable promise, it was not until after the First World War, during which he was employed in the German Ministry of Information, that he made his name as the outstanding exponent of 'dramatized biography', a form of biography, half true biography, half historical novel, which became popular throughout Europe during the twenties and thirties, particularly in France and Russia. His best books of this kind were *Goethe* (3 vols., 1920; Eng. trans., 2 vols., 1928), *Napoleon* (1925; Eng. trans. 1927) and *Bismarck* (1926; Eng. trans. 1927). He died at Ascona, in Switzerland.

**Ludwig, Otto** (1813–1865), German playwright and long short-story writer, was born at Eisfeld, in Saxe-Meiningen. He studied music under Mendelssohn in Leipzig, but by 1842 had decided on a literary career. A man without strong will, very sensitive and weak in health, he lived a quiet, unsuccessful life, isolated from the world. He was not stimulated by personal contact with other writers, and becoming increasingly and stubbornly immersed in his Shakespeare studies (*Shakespeare-Studien*, 1871) wore himself out to little purpose. Although not fitted for writing stageworthy plays, owing to lack of experience, he yet composed two pieces, *Der Erbförster* (1850; Eng. trans. *The Hereditary Forester* in *German Classics of the Nineteenth and Twentieth Centuries*, 1913) and *Die Makkabäer* (1854), which are among the best representatives of the realistic drama in Germany. They are interesting to compare with Hebbel's (q.v.) plays, and we find that, in the work of both, character heads the action, although Ludwig knows nothing of the psychology which Hebbel understood how to use. It is, however, as a story-writer that he has survived, and in *Die Heitherethei* (1854), *Zwischen Himmel und Erde* (1856; Eng. trans. *Between Heaven and Earth*, 1928), the best, and *Aus dem Regen in die Traufe* (1857) he is worthy to stand beside the best writers in the long tradition of the *Novelle*. Completely incapacitated from 1860 onwards by a nervous disease, he died in Dresden.

**Lull, Ramón** (1235?–1315), Catalan poet and prose-writer in Catalan and Latin. Born at Palma de Mallorca, he led an idle, licentious life until a sudden change of feeling in 1266 caused him to embrace the religious life. After some years of study and contemplation he set up a school of missionaries, where, having learnt Arabic and Hebrew, he was able to instruct his pupils in these languages, his purpose being to enable them to stand up to Jews and Mohammedans on equal terms which former missionaries in their ignorance had not been able to do. His entry into English literature as 'Raymond Lully', a magician, is derived from an eccentric side of his character, his claim to have discovered a method of thinking with the help of geometrical signs which he termed *Ars Magna*. Otherwise, there is much that was practical in him. He ran his missionary school, travelled as a missionary himself in Cyprus, north Africa and in Armenia, lectured and debated in France and Italy, and wrote enormously. He was a lexicographer, editor, poet and romance-writer. His principal works are *Blanquerna* (1283), in which he writes of the ideal state, the two beautiful poems, *El desconhort* (1295) and *Lo cant de Ramón* (1299), a religious encyclopaedia, *Libro de conexença de Deu* and a scientific encyclopaedia, *Felix*. His Latin *Principiorum Philosophorum Contra Averroistas* (about 1308) was a powerful doctrinal work. He continued his missionary work to the end, appealing to popes and kings, troubling their often easy consciences by demanding crusades and greater efforts to convert the infidels. He died of wounds received from stoning at the hands of a mob at Bugia, Algeria. The pioneer collection of his works is that by Salzinger (1721–42), and the standard one is by

Rossello (1886). His followers the Lullists soon degenerated into quasi-religious alchemists and intensified the impression of 'Lully', the wizard.

**Lunacharsky, Anatoly Vasilyevich** (1875–1933), Russian Soviet playwright and critic, born in Poltava. A social, political and literary theorist in the service of Bolshevism, he is chiefly known to Western readers for three of his plays which were translated in L. A. Magnus's *Three Soviet Plays* (1923) as *Vasilisa the Wise*, *Faust and the City* and *The Magi*. He died in Moscow.

**Lundegård, Axel** (1861–1930), Swedish novelist. Born at Sallerup, he wrote fiction of a variety of kinds, but it was as an historical novelist that he made his mark in such works as *Struensee* (3 vols., 1898–1900), *Drottning Filippa* (1907) and *Drottning Cilla* (1910). He died in Stockholm.

**Lundkvist, Artur** (1906–    ), Swedish prose-writer. Born at Oderljunga, all his best work, such as *Atlantvind* (1932), *Himmelsfärd* (1935), *Ikarus' flykt* (1939) and *Indiabrand* (1950), has been inspired by his wide-ranging travels.

**Luther, Martin** (1483–1546), German religious reformer and writer. Born at Eisleben, the son of a miner, he was sent by patrons to the University of Erfurt in 1501. He joined the Augustinian Order in 1505 and lectured at the University of Wittenberg from 1508 onwards. Then in 1517 the controversy about indulgences began, followed by his excommunication. In this year (1520) he wrote several sturdy tracts, including *An den christlichen Adel deutscher Nation* ('To the Christian Nobility of the German Nation') and *Von der Freiheit eines Christenmenschen* ('Of the Freedom of Christians'), which showed how powerful a weapon was his pen; a German of the Germans, he knew how to appeal to their inmost aspirations and in their own way, seeming inconsistences being hammered together into some kind of cohesion which compelled without persuading. Condemned at the Diet of Worms (1521), the following year, while lodged for his own safety in the Wartburg, he translated the New Testament from the Greek version of Erasmus (q.v.) into racy, homespun German, and between 1523 and 1534 he laboured at a translation of the Old Testament. By no means literal, both are interpretations of enormous ability. Luther also called his poetic gifts to his aid, knowing how much hymns could impress the ordinary people, and thus from 1524 onwards he produced a number of *Geistliche Lieder* (mod. ed., 1923; Eng. trans. 1883), of strength and verve, among them the celebrated 'Ein' feste Burg' (The Old Hundredth). The Augsburg Confession (1530) had assured the new Church of firm foundations, and for the rest of his life Luther continued to build on them. In doing so he still further made use of his literary talents, issuing moral fables based on Aesop, *Fabeln* (1530; mod. ed., second ed., 1911), and showed how religious plays could do much to spread the Reformation feeling (*Vorreden auf Buch Judith und das Buch Tobias*, 1534). His *Tischreden* (1566; mod. ed., 1903; Eng. trans. *Table Talk*, 1848; *Conversations*, 1915) do much to reveal the character of the man, whereas his *Briefe*

(18 vols., 1884–1914; Eng. trans. (selection), *Luther's Correspondence,* 1913) reveal his aims. He died at Eisleben. Of many editions of his works the most useful for the general reader are the selective one by G. Buchwald (10 vols., fourth ed., 1924) and the still more selective one in three volumes by A. E. Berger (1917). There is an English translation of the *Works* (ed. P. Holmann, 1915).

**Luzzato, Moses Hayyim** (1707–1747), Hebrew mystic. Born in Padua, he became a rabbi, was driven out of many congregations for alleged unorthodoxy, and most of his writings were destroyed. He is remembered for his *Mesilat Yesharim* (1740; Eng. trans. *Mesilat Yesharim, the Path of the Upright*, 1936), a work on the good and upright life. This was written in Amsterdam, but he later left for the Middle East, and died in Acre.

# M

**Maartens, Maarten,** pseudonym of J. M. W. van der Poorten Schwarz (1858–1915), Anglo-Dutch novelist, born in Amsterdam. He spent part of his boyhood in England, then went to Germany, and later read law at Utrecht. He wrote a number of novels on the burgher and farming life of the Netherlands, all appearing simultaneously in Dutch and English, such as *The Sin of Joost Aveling* (1889), *God's Fool* (1893) and *Harmen Pöls, Peasant* (1910). He died at Doorn.

**Mácha, Karel Hynek** (1810–1836), Czech poet. Born in Prague of poor family, he yet managed to study law at the university there, but followed no occupation. He read much romantic literature—he knew German well and English slightly—and wandered about Bohemia and even went as far as Italy, which made a great impression on him. At length, forced by absolute poverty to accept the post of clerk in a lawyer's office at Litoměřice, he died there a month later. Shortly before he had published his wild epic *Máj* (Eng. trans. 1932 and 1949), a vagabond romance set against backgrounds of wild natural beauty such as he had found in the course of his wanderings.

**Machado y Ruiz, Antonio** (1875–1939), Spanish poet, one of the most important of this century, was born the son of an intellectual family and the younger brother of Manuel Machado (q.v.) in Seville. He was a schoolmaster for many years and was of a retiring disposition. He wrote little, but what he did write— the *Soledades* (1903), the well-known *Campos de Castilla* (1912), the rest of his work appearing in *Poesías completas* (1917) and in the four-volume edition of his and his brother's works (1947)—shows his marked individuality of style. A mystic, and inspired by the open spaces and sharp air of Castile, his plain, misleadingly simple-looking manner is replete with overtones and undertones of profound thought and feeling. An ardent supporter of the republic, on its virtual destruction in 1938 he made for France on foot, never recovering from the hardships of body and sorrow of mind which the ordeal of war and flight occasioned. He died a few miles inside the French border. For an English translation, see W. Barnstone's *Eighty Poems of Antonio Machado* (1959).

**Machado y Ruiz, Manuel** (1874–1947), Spanish poet. Born in Seville, elder brother of Antonio (q.v.), he divided his active life between librarianship and literary journalism. A poet of the senses, the colours of Andalusian life were more to his taste than his brother's Castile; there are folk rhythms to be found in his verse, and he gives glowing accounts of pictures and architecture, while love-poetry is there in abundance. Outstanding among his publications are *Museo* (1910), *Cante hondo* (1912), *Sevilla y otros poemas* (1921) and the poetic drama *La Lola se va a los puertos* (1930), with the last of which Antonio assisted. He died in Madrid.

**Machar, Josef Svatopluk** (1864–1942), Czech poet. Born at Kolín, he went in for banking in Vienna, where he remained till 1917. While there he became prominent in Czech literary and political circles, and in his late twenties and early thirties was particularly active as a poet. Thus his *Confiteor* (3 vols., 1887–92) is a collection of his romantic, idealistic lyrics, while *Tristium Vindobona* (1893) is devoted to the problems and future hopes of Czech nationalism. His experiences in the First World War resulted in *Kriminál* (1918; Eng. trans. *The Jail*, 1921). A close friend of T. G. Masaryk (q.v.), he became the Republic of Czechoslovakia's first inspector-general of the army (1919–24). He died in Prague.

**Machaut, Guillaume de** (1300 ?–1377), French poet. Born at Machaut, in Champagne, he entered the royal service of Bohemia, later that of Normandy, and in 1350 that of the king of France. His works, which are technically interesting, are most impersonal and frigid, but they had a great influence on Froissart (q.v.) and Chaucer. They are the panegyric, *Le Jugement du roi de Navarre*, the epic, *La Prise d'Alexandrie*, and *Le Livre du voir-dit*, his last work, written about 1364 (crit. ed., 1875). He also wrote lyrics (*Poésies lyriques*, 2 vols., 1909).

**Machiavelli, Niccolò di Bernardo dei** (1469–1527), Italian political theorist, historian, scholar, dramatist and novelist, was born in Florence of a legal family. He seems to have received all his education at home, but little is known of him until 1494, when he entered the service of the Florentine Republic on the downfall of the Medici. In 1498 he became secretary to the Chancery of the Ten, and carried out his work with enthusiasm, seeing in the republic which he served a new Roman republic on the ancient pattern that as a humanist he so much admired. During the years 1499 to 1509 he travelled widely on diplomatic missions which enabled him to study the ways of foreign courts at close quarters. During the next three years he was the life and soul of Florence in resisting the return of the Medici, but his efforts proved unavailing in the end and the tyranny returned (1512). As one of their most outstanding enemies Machiavelli was kept under surveillance by the Medici, but was otherwise allowed to move freely so long as he did not leave Florence. Involved in the great anti-Medicean conspiracy of 1513, he was imprisoned and even tortured, but since nothing could be proved against him he was allowed to go into the country to San Casciano, outside Florence, where he turned to literary work. Here he wrote that very year (1513) his famous *Il Principe* (standard ed. L. Russo, seventh ed., 1940; Eng. trans. by N. H. Thomson, second ed., 1897; by L. Ricci, 1903; and in Everyman's Library). Having discussed in it principalities, he set about dealing with republics, and between 1513 and 1521 was engaged on his *Discorsi della prima deca di Tito Livio* (Eng. trans. *The Discourses of Niccolò Machiavelli*, 2 vols., 1950). Feeling that even though the Medicis were firmly re-established in power this need not be incompatible with some form of republican government, he made peace with the family, and in 1519 was allowed to attend the court and asked to write the history of Florence by Giulio de' Medici (afterwards Pope Clement VII). Thus Machiavelli's *Istorie fiorentine* (Eng. trans. *History of Florence* in Everyman's Library) came to be written, and was completed in 1525. The patronage had another result, for in *Dell'arte della guerra* (1521) he fulfilled Giulio's demand that he should instruct him in the art of war. His literary gifts lay in other directions also, as is shown by his excellent comedy, *La Mandragola*, written between 1513 and 1516, and by his fictional work *Belfagor*, first published in 1545. Ill fortune dogged Machiavelli, for, just when he had won full favour with the Medici, the family was once more expelled following the sack of Rome (1527). He now expected office under the new republic, but he was looked upon as one not to be trusted. His disappointment is said to have led to the illness of which he died in Florence. *The Prince* needs a word about it. The main theme of the work is the supremacy of the secular state, to preserve which a ruler is justified in using any means at his disposal. The world remains constantly the same, and the people in it fundamentally grow neither better nor worse from age to age. For this reason Machiavelli has come to be regarded as the opportunist *par excellence*, even an evil influence. But he never attacked private virtue, and was ready to impress upon his readers his belief that such morality lay at the root of a nation's life. His fatal mistake was to place public and private virtues in separate compartments, judging family life by ethics, but divorcing political science from any ethical consideration. The style of the treatise is beyond praise. See *Tutte le opere storiche e letterarie* (1929), the English translation of the principal prose works by C. E. Detmold (1891), and *The Literary Works* (Oxford Library of Italian Classics).

**Macías Picavea, Ricardo** (1847–1899), Spanish novelist and writer on sociology and education, was born at Santoña and taught classics in the Valladolid Institute, dying in that city. He is the author of three books, all valuable in their own way: *La instrucción pública en España y sus reformas* (1882), a work which should be reprinted, since many of the questions raised have not yet been rectified in the Spain of today, *Tierra de campos* (2 vols., 1897–8), a strong novel of country life in Castile, and a splendid analysis of Spain with the disasters of 1898 fresh in mind, with cogent proposals (not yet followed), *El problema nacional* (1899).

**Madách, Imre** (1823–1864), Hungarian poet. Born at Alsó-Sztregova, he took part in the 1848 Revolution, after which his life became increasingly gloomy and frustrated. His best work is the dramatic poem *Az ember tragédiája* (1861; Eng. trans. *The Tragedy of Man*, 1933), full of nebulous if sometimes splendid thought, but couched in language which will hardly bear the strain. He died at Alsó-Sztregova.

**Madariaga, Salvador de** (1886–    ), Anglo-Spanish prose-writer, writing in Spanish, English and French. Born at La Coruña, he was educated at the École Polytechnique, Paris, for an engineering career, but in 1921 joined the staff of the League of Nations and was secretary of the disarmament commission (1922–7). He was then appointed to the new chair of Spanish studies at Oxford, leaving that in 1931 to become ambassador of the Spanish Republic to the U.S.A., exchanging this a year later for a similar post in France. On the collapse of the republic he went into exile and later settled in Oxford. An excellent writer, with a penetrating yet graceful style in whichever of the three languages he writes, he is the most internationally minded of all Spanish authors. His chief books are: *The Genius of Spain* (1923), *Englishmen, Frenchmen, Spaniards* (1927), *Don Quixote, An Introductory Essay* (1935), *Colón* (1940, 'Columbus'), *Hernán Cortés* (1942), *The Fall of the Spanish American Empire* (2 vols., 1947), *On Hamlet* (1948), *Bolívar* (1952), *El ciclo hispánico* (2 vols., 1957), *Democracy versus Liberty* (1958) and *General, márchese Usted* (1960), in all of which he shows that scholarship can be not only vivid but also, which is much rarer, literature. Of his fiction, mention should be made of: *El enemigo de Dios* (1926), *Sir Bob* (1930), *El corazón de piedra verde* (1942; Eng. trans. *The Heart of Jade*, 1956), *Ramo de errores* (1952), *Guerra en la sangre* (1956) and *Una gota en el tiempo* (1959). He has also published poetry and plays, including *El toisón de oro* (1940) and *Don Juan y la donjuanía* (1950).

**Madelin, Louis** (1871–1956), French historian. Born at Neufchâteau in the Vosges, he was on the staff of the Sorbonne (1905–10). His *La Révolution française* (1911) showed how the findings of distinguished scholarship could be expressed in an excellent literary style, a combination unhappily so rarely found. *Danton* (1914) has similar qualities. In *Verdun* (1919) and *Le Maréchal Foch* (1926) he brought his gifts to bear on contemporary events. His masterpiece was *Histoire du Consulat et de l'Empire* (16 vols., 1937–54). He died in Paris.

**Maerlant, Jacob van** (1235?–1295?), Flemish poet. Born at Vrije van Brugge, he became a scribe and was first an ecclesiastical clerk and afterwards a law clerk at Damme, where he died. His great work is his *Spieghel Historiael* (begun 1283), a history of the world, evidently derived from the *Speculum Historiale* of Vincent of Beauvais. It remained unfinished. His *Rijmbijbel* (1271, 'The Rhymed Bible') had brought him into collision with the Church and no doubt led to his taking to civil employment. A man of great erudition, he was one of the deepest thinkers of his time.

**Maeterlinck, Maurice** (1862–1949), Belgian poet and dramatist. Born in Ghent, he was educated by the Jesuits and became an advocate, although he was more at home in literary circles. His first success was won as a poet with *Serres chaudes* (1889; Eng. trans. *Hot Houses*, 1915), completely symbolist, but it was his particular gift to transfer symbolism to the theatre, which no one before had attempted. This he did in the three plays (all 1890), *La Princesse Maleine* (Eng. trans. 1915), *L'Intruse* and *Les Aveugles*. *Pelléas et Mélisande* (1892; Eng. trans. 1894), one of his most attractive works, formed the libretto of Debussy's opera of that title (1902). *La Mort de Tintagîle* (1894) was an excursion into the marionette play, while his tendency to philosophize, though beginning well with his study of Novalis (q.v.) and the translation of his *Lehrlinge zu Saïs* (1895), resulted in shallow and pretentious work such as *Le Trésor des humbles* (1896; Eng. trans. *The Treasure of the Humble*, 1897) and *La Sagesse et la destinée* (1898). A preoccupation with natural history was also turned to literature and given new symbolic significance, in, for example, that great success, *La Vie des abeilles* (1901; Eng. trans. *The Life of the Bees*, 1901). He, however, left symbolism after *L'Oiseau bleu* (1908; Eng. trans. *The Blue Bird*, 1909), in which Novalis's blue flower of happiness in *Heinrich von Ofterdingen* becomes a spirit of the air. *La Mort* (1913) shows a reaction from mysticism, which came to the full in the realistic war plays, *Les Fiançailles* (1918; produced in London as *The Betrothal*, 1919) and *Le Bourgmestre de Stilemonde* (1918; produced in London as *The Burgomaster of Stilemonde*, 1920). In his later works he returned to natural history with a pantheistic interpretation, as in *La Vie des termites* (1927; Eng. trans. *The Life of the White Ant*, 1927), *La Vie de l'espace* (1928) and *L'Araignée de cristal* (1932). He was awarded the Nobel Prize in 1911, but his reputation has greatly declined since then and continues to do so. He died in Nice.

**Maffei, Francesco Scipione** (1675–1755), Italian dramatist and archaeologist, was born of noble family in Verona. His verse tragedy, *Merope* (1713), was a great success and marks the acclimatization of the French classical style to Italy. It in fact paved the way for Alfieri (q.v.) later in the century. His comedy, *Le ceremonie* (1728), was also successful. *Verona illustrata* (4 vols., 1731–2) represents him as an archaeologist of merit. These are only a fraction of his enormous output (*Opere*, 21 vols., 1790; sel. ed. *Opere drammatiche e poesie varie*, 1928). He died in Verona.

**Magny, Olivier de** (1529?–1561), French poet. Born at Cahors, he became secretary to various powerful patrons, one of whom he accompanied to Rome, on his way meeting Louise Labé (q.v.) in Lyon and inspiring in her the unrequited love which is the subject of many of her poems (1555–6). In Rome he became the friend of Du Bellay (q.v.), and under his influence and that of Ronsard (q.v.) published *Les Soupirs* (1557), a collection of sonnets and his best work, and *Les Odes* (1559). He died in Paris. His collected poetry (mod. ed., 6 vols., 1871–80) contains also the *Amours* (1553) and *Gaietés* (1554), charming if sometimes faulty work. There is a selective edition of his verse (1913).

**Mai, Angelo** (1782–1854), Italian classical scholar. Born at Schilpario, in Lombardy, he was educated by the Jesuits and became a secular priest. He was at first librarian of the Ambrosian Library at Milan, where his discoveries of long-lost manuscripts made a great impression on the literary world. Later, appointed to the Vatican and made a cardinal, he discovered more lost works and produced masterly editions containing them, such as *Scriptorum Veterum Nova Collectio* (1825–38), *Classicorum Auctorum Collectio* (1828–38) and *Patrum Nova Bibliotheca* (1845–53). He died in Rome. It is no exaggeration to say that his work is the most extensive and important of its kind in modern times, and that directly or indirectly his influence on the literary world was profound.

**Maimon, Salomon** (1754–1800), German prose-writer and philosopher. Born of Jewish family at Neschwitz, Lithuania, he became a prodigy of learning, publishing in 1770 a commentary on the *Moreh Nevu-Khim* of the great Maimonides (q.v.), whose name he assumed in token of respect. He next went to the University of Berlin and, after completing his studies in philosophy and languages there, settled in that city as a hack. He later took to a wandering, improvident life, made some friends but more enemies, and was often on the verge of starvation. Yet he contrived to write his *Versuch über die Transcendentalphilosophie* (1790), which elicited the praise of Kant (q.v.). He claimed to have been the author of the 'principle of sufficient reason' in his attractive *Autobiographie* (1792; Eng. trans. 1888), which tells much of contemporary Jewish communities. He died in utter destitution at Niedersiegersdorf, Silesia.

**Maimonides, Moses, or Moses ben Maimon** (1135–1204), Spanish Hebrew and Arabic writer. Born of Jewish parents in Cordoba, he left Spain with his family in 1160, spent some time in Morocco and then in Palestine, and settled in Cairo as physician to the sultan and rabbi to his people. The greatest Jewish scholar of the Middle Ages, he completed in 1180 his all-embracing commentary on Jewish law, the *Mishneh Torah* (Eng. trans. *The Code of Maimonides*, 15 vols., 1949 ff.). But it is as the author of the *Dalālat al-Hā'irīn* in Arabic (in Hebrew *Moreh Nevu-Khim*; Eng. trans. *The Guide of the Perplexed*, 3 vols., 1881–5; sel. trans., 1952), finished about 1190, that he is above all famous, for this complete elucidation of the Jewish religion set out in the schoolmen's Aristotelian manner has not only had a profound influence on Jewish thought from then onwards down to the present, but from the thirteenth century, when a Latin translation, *Doctor Perplexorum*, appeared and was quickly copied in monasteries throughout Europe, on Christian thought also. By rejecting much outworn rabbinical tradition he gave new life to Jewish faith and culture. Maimonides died in Cairo.

**Maistre, Joseph Marie de** (1754–1821), French prose-writer. A Savoyard, elder brother of Xavier de Maistre (q.v.), he was born at Chambéry of noble family, and when Savoy was occupied by the French (1792), he went first to Lausanne and later accompanied the Sardinian court to Sardinia. He was Sardinian envoy to Petersburg (1803–17). He viewed the new world created by the French Revolution with a feeling resembling hatred (*Considérations sur la France*, 1796), and it was not long before he came to realize that the papacy offered about the only hope of a return to traditional ways of life. It is as the reviver of ultramontanism, which has played such a part in European politics, that he is now remembered, his chief work being *Du Pape* (2 vols., 1819). He died in Turin. Among the books which were published after his death the most interesting are *De l'Église gallicane* (1822) and *Les Soirées de Saint Petersbourg* (2 vols., 1821–2).

**Maistre, Xavier de** (1763–1852), French novelist. Younger brother of the religious and political writer J. M. de Maistre (q.v.), he was born at Chambéry. He entered the army first with the Piedmontese and in 1799 with the Russians. It was while serving a term of imprisonment for taking part in a duel that he wrote (1794) that charming flight of fancy, *Voyage autour de ma chambre,* upon which his reputation mainly rests. A sequel, *Expédition nocturne autour de ma chambre,* was published in 1825, in which year his collected works, including among other novels *Le Lépreux de la cité d'Aoste* (1811) and *Les Prisonniers du Caucase* (1815), appeared. He died in Petersburg.

**Malaparte, Curzio,** pseudonym of **Curzio Suckert** (1898–1957), Italian novelist. Born at Prato, near Florence, he early became identified with Fascism, and such works of fiction as *Avventure di un capitano di Sventura* (1927), *Sodoma e Gomorra* (1931) and *Sangue* (1937) all have more than a slant in that direction. Of modest talent only, he attempted in two Second World War novels, *Kaputt* (1945; Eng. trans. 1948) and *La Pelle* (1949; Eng. trans. *The Skin,* 1952), to win a public which had remained generally unimpressed by his work, by a liberal amount of lurid sensationalism. In *Kaputt* his personal experiences in Russia are laid bare; in *La Pelle* all the sordid details of life at the time of and just after the liberation of Naples are put before us. With them he succeeded at last in winning vast popularity —not, however, for literary reasons. Later works are *Storia di domani* (1949), *Maledetti toscani* (1956) and *Racconti italiani* (1957).

**Malczewski, Antoni** (1793–1826), Polish poet, born at Kniahinin. He took some part in the later stages of the Napoleonic wars, travelled, settled in Warsaw and became involved in a love affair which inspired his main poetical work, *Marja* (1825; Eng. trans. 1935). He died in Warsaw. His collected works were published (2 vols.) in 1857.

**Malebranche, Nicolas** (1638–1715), French prose-writer, one of the finest in the whole range of the literature of France, was born in Paris and became an Oratorian. Originally a follower of Descartes (q.v.), he gradually became a quietist, that is, he subjected all free human will to the will of God. His most important books are *La Recherche de la vérité* (1674–5; mod. crit. ed., 1880), *Entretiens sur la métaphysique et la religion* (1688; mod. crit. ed., 1922) and *Traité de l'amour de Dieu* (1697; mod. crit. ed., 1923). He died in Paris. His one English disciple was John Norris of Bemerton (1657–1711).

**Malherbe, François de** (1555–1628), French poet and translator. Born in Caen, the son of a Huguenot lawyer, he refused to follow in his father's footsteps and eked out his mediocre earnings derived from work for booksellers, including good translations of the classics, such as Livy and Seneca the Younger, until in 1605 he at last found a patron, none other than King Henri IV. Thereafter he lived on a modest pension, continued by Louis XIII, deriving some satisfaction from being at last regarded as the supreme arbiter of poetic taste. Cold and correct, he can at times, as in his famous *Consolation à Dupérier* (1601), reach a majestic style to suit the solemnity of his thought. As an absolute opponent of Ronsard (q.v.) and his associates.

whom he roundly condemns in *L'Académie de l'art poétique* (1610) and elsewhere for their lack of correctness, he was to be held up to praise by Boileau (q.v.) in *L'Art poétique* (1674) as the pride of the classical ode. Besides the *Consolation* mentioned above his most important works are *Les Larmes de Saint-Pierre* (1587), *Ode au roi Henri le Grand* (1600), *Prière pour le roi Henri le Grand* (1605) and *Ode au roi Louis XIII allant châtier les Rochelois* (1628). A somewhat unsympathetic figure, Malherbe died in Paris. His *Œuvres poétiques* appeared in 1630. See *Œuvres complètes* (5 vols., 1862).

**Mallarmé, Stéphane** (1842–1898), French poet and prose-writer. Born in Paris, he visited England in 1862 to become proficient in English in order to teach it and in order to read its literature. He spent nearly a year there, returned to Paris, gained his certificate to teach and was a schoolmaster for over thirty years, for the greater part of that period in provincial *lycées*, but finally in Paris, where he was acknowledged as the leader of symbolism, that revolt against the actual, the concrete in poetry which the Parnassians had stood for. He first became known for his felicitous translation of Edgar Allan Poe's *The Raven* (1875), but in the following year came that masterpiece, *L'Après-midi d'un faune*, which was to inspire one of Debussy's loveliest compositions. Here is the ideal world with peace, warmth and light, a haven in the midst of this modern blaring one, which, however, everyone must pass through and suffer from before eventually reaching the promised land. He published *Poésies* (1887), *Album de vers et de prose* (1893), while a prose work, *Divagations*, appeared in 1897. He retired from schoolmastering in 1894 and immediately left Paris for Valvins, near Fontainebleau, where he died. Besides the titles mentioned above are the two prose works, *Les Dieux antiques* (1880) and *Les Poèmes d'Edgar Poe* (1888). The best edition of his collected works is that of 1945. See the English translation, *Selected Prose, Poems, Essays and Letters* (1956).

**Malmberg, Bertil** (1889–1958), Swedish prose-writer. Born at Härnösand, he can be said to have succeeded only with autobiography, the supreme example of which is the account of his boyhood, *Åke och hans värld* (1924; Eng. trans. *Åke and his World*, 1940). His play about Hitler's Germany, *Excellensen* (1943), has faded.

**Malot, Hector Henri** (1830–1907), French novelist. Born in Rouen, he spent several years as a correspondent for French newspapers in London. His many novels, such as *Victimes d'amour* (1858), are set in the sultry atmosphere of the Second Empire. He died at Fontenay-sous-Bois (Vincennes).

**Malraux, André** (1901–    ), French novelist and essayist. Born in Paris, he studied archaeology and went on an archaeological expedition to Indo-China, and it was then that contemporary events caught him up and he became a man of action. His experiences provided the raw material for his literary work. He was active in China during the revolution of 1926, which resulted in the novels *Les Conquérants* (1928; Eng. trans. *The Conquerors*, 1929) and *La Voie royale* (1930; Eng. trans. *The Royal Way*, 1935), and was involved in the Sino-

Japanese War, which he describes powerfully in *La Condition humaine* (1933; Eng. trans. *Storm over Shanghai*, 1934). A stay in the new Germany of Hitler led to the novel *Le Temps du mépris* (1935; Eng. trans. *Days of Contempt*, 1938), whose very title is enough to show how it struck him. Organizer of the Spanish Republican Government's air force during the civil war, he turned that experience into the novel *L'Espoir* (1937; Eng. trans. *Days of Hope*, 1938). During the German occupation of France he was a vigorous leader of the Resistance movement, and smuggled out another topical novel, *La Lutte avec l'ange* (1943), to be published in Switzerland. After the war he attached himself to De Gaulle, and has held office in his cabinet. As an essayist, his *Tentation de l'Orient* (1926) is a vivid and highly personal study of what the westerner expects from the East and what its impact was on him. His trilogy, *Essais de psychologie de l'art*, is a remarkable confession of faith in humanism, comprising *Le Musée imaginaire* (1947), *La Création artistique* (1948) and *La Monnaie de l'absolu* (1950), the first two in English translation as *The Psychology of Art* (1949). *Saturne, essai sur Goya* (1950), *Du musée* (1955) and *La Métamorphose des dieux* (1957) show his increasing absorption in various aspects of art.

**Malyshkin, Alexander Georgievich** (1892–1938), Russian Soviet novelist, best known for *Sevastopol* (1929), in which is described the effect of the Kerensky Revolution on the Black Sea Fleet.

**Mameli, Goffredo** (1827–1849), Italian poet, born in Genoa. He spent all his life in working for Italian freedom, attached himself to Mazzini (q.v.), joined Garibaldi and was killed in Rome in defence of the short-lived Roman Republic. He wrote the Italian national anthem, 'Fratelli d'Italia'. There is a critical edition of his poetry (1927).

**Manasseh ben Israel** (1604–1657), Jewish prose-writer in Latin, Spanish, Portuguese, Hebrew and English, was born at La Rochelle, France, but was with his family in Amsterdam by 1620. He became a rabbi and publisher and wrote much, and in different languages, on the Old Testament and on the Jewish people. Well known throughout Europe, and an honoured friend of Rembrandt, his principal works are: *El Conciliador* (4 vols., 1632–51; Eng. trans. *The Conciliator, a Reconcilement of the Apparent Contradictions in Holy Scripture*, 2 vols., 1842), *Esperança de Israel* (1650; Eng. trans. *The Hope of Israel*, 1650), *Humble Addresses to the Lord Protector* (1655), with which he began the negotiations which led to the admittance of Jews to England in 1657, and *Vindiciae Judaeorum* (1656). He died in Middelburg.

**Mann, Heinrich** (1871–1950), German novelist, brother of Thomas Mann (q.v.) was born in Lübeck, the son of a wealthy manufacturer. The trouble with his many very successful novels is that he was never able to become objective and mould his material to unentangled art as was his so much greater brother. Thus he is always inclined to preach and to rail against the upper middle classes, from among whom he came. His principal works are *Das Wunderbare* (1897), *Im Schlaraffenland* (1900; Eng. trans. *In the Land of Cockaigne*, 1929),

*Professor Unrat* (1905; Eng. trans. *The Blue Angel*, 1932), his most famous work, filmed with Marlene Dietrich as the star, *Die kleine Stadt* (1909; Eng. trans. *The Little Town*, 1930), *Die Armen* (1917), *Der Untertan* (1918), *Macht und Mensch* (1919), *Mutter Marie* (1927; Eng. trans. *Mother Mary*, 1928), *Eugénie* (1928; Eng. trans. *Royal Woman*, 1930), *Das Herz* (1931) and *Ein ernstes Leben* (1932; Eng. trans. *Hill of Lies*, 1934). Exiled from Germany in 1933, he went to the U.S.A., where he died at Santa Monica, California.

**Mann, Thomas** (1875–1955), German novelist and short-story writer. Born the son of a wealthy merchant at Lübeck, the younger brother of Heinrich (q.v.), it was his own family with its rise and fall in fortune—for at his father's early death the Manns were left in reduced circumstances—that inspired his first and great book, *Die Buddenbrooks* (1900; Eng. trans. *Buddenbrooks*, 1924). Long before this the family had left Lübeck for Munich, and Thomas had already completed his university course and had been for some time in business, though giving more and more of his time to journalism. *Buddenbrooks* showed very wide reading, a dispassionate judgment and an individuality of style extraordinary in one so young. The fortunes of a nineteenth-century German mercantile family are turned into an epic. For many years after this Mann found the long short story more suited to his literary expression, the artist confronted with the conventional being an especially favoured theme as in those masterpieces, the greatest of their kind of the century, *Tonio Kröger* (1903), *Tristan* (1903), *Der Tod in Venedig* (1913; the three trans. into Eng. together, 1925) and *Felix Krull* (1922). Then came his second full-length novel, *Der Zauberberg* (1924; Eng. trans. *The Magic Mountain*, 1927), which proved that he was able to maintain the reputation gained almost a quarter of a century before. While still preserving the elements of the traditional German novel, the plot is no longer built round a single group, but is spread out far and wide over a tremendous canvas, now shining on one part of it, now on another, the whole yet bound together into a satisfying unity. The bestowal of the Nobel Prize on him in 1929 fitly acknowledged his position as the greatest novelist in Europe. He next turned to his most ambitious undertaking, a novel in four parts under the collective title of *Joseph und seine Brüder*, consisting of *Die Geschichten Jaakobs* (1933; Eng. trans. *Tales of Jacob*, 1934), *Der Junge Joseph* (1934; Eng. trans. *The Young Joseph*, 1935), *Joseph in Ägypten* (1936; Eng. trans. *Joseph in Egypt*, 1938) and the long-delayed *Joseph der Ernährer* (1944; Eng. trans. *Joseph the Provider*, 1944). ' Joseph and his Brethren' is the story contained in the later part of Genesis but penetrated by modern thought, turned inside out and given the significance of a modern political tale symbolistically expressed—freedom of the individual against tyranny. On the arrival of the Nazis Mann had had to leave Germany and finally settled in the United States. As the war approached he turned back for the moment to the luxury of escapism in the world of Goethe, recreating an incident in the great man's life and treating it with delicacy and charm in *Lotte in Weimar* (1939; Eng. trans. 1940). The horrors of war, the near breakdown of a civilization stimulated Mann's last major work, and he gathered up all his strength to produce *Doktor Faustus* (1949; Eng. trans. *Doctor Faustus*, 1950). Here, using the old story, he analyses Germany: Germany is Faust, the mixture of genius and madness. In this titanic work he calls to his aid every kind of device, and out of a welter of interpretations derived from different art media creates a new and challenging world. An excellent collection of English translations of his shorter stories is *Stories of Three Decades* (1936).

**Manrique, Jorge** (1440?–1479), Spanish poet, born at Paredes de la Nava of noble family. He is remembered by reason of his exquisitely moving elegy on the death of his father, *Coplas por la muerte de su padre don Rodrigo* (1477; mod. ed. 1912), well translated by Longfellow (1833). He was killed in battle at Calatrava during the civil wars.

**Manzini, Gianna** (1899–     ), Italian novelist and short-story writer, born at Pistoia. She is the representative of the 'stream of consciousness' style in her country's literature. Examples of her writing are: *Tempo innamorato* (1928), *Un filo di Brezza* (1936), *Rive remote* (1940), *Lettera all'editore* (1945), *Forte come un leone* (1947), *Animali sacri e profani* (1953), *Foglietti* (1954) and *Arca di Noè* (1960).

**Manzoni, Alessandro** (1785–1873), Italian novelist and poet. Born in Milan of noble family, his mother the daughter of Beccaria (q.v.), the famous jurist, his parents separated in his youth and he went to Paris to join his mother in 1805. He there came into contact with new literary developments in Europe, and five years later was reconciled to Roman Catholicism, from which he had fallen away. His deep faith, from which he never afterwards swerved, is expressed in such religious poetry as *La Risurrezione* (1812), *Passione* (1814), *Pentecoste* (1817) and *Inni sacri* (1824), the last still retaining its popularity. With the verse tragedies, *Il conte di Carmagnola* (1820) and *Adelchi* (1822), he ushered in a new epoch in Italian drama by breaking with classical tradition and making Shakespeare his model. But it is his historical novel about Milan under Spanish rule in the seventeenth century, *I promessi sposi* (1827; mod. ed., 1940; Eng. trans. *The Betrothed*, 1951), that made him famous the length and breadth of Europe. Perhaps the greatest piece of Italian literature of modern times, the derivation of the work is from the Waverley Novels of Sir Walter Scott, but *I promessi sposi* goes far deeper than any Scott novel and sounds the very foundations of human life. In spite of his devout Catholicism he believed in a united Italy, which led him to choose Florentine as its official literary language, and with this in mind he rewrote *I promessi sposi* in Florentine dialect as *La storia della Colonna infame* (1840; Eng. trans. *The Column of Infamy*, 1964), but it is no improvement on the story and is of interest purely to the philologist. His *Tragedie e poesie* were collected in 1852, after which he wrote nothing more of importance. A man of singularly fine character, he died in Milan. Verdi's Requiem Mass is a memorial to him. See the editions of *Le Tragedie, Gl'Inni Sacri, Le Odi* (by M. Scherillo, 1922) and *Liriche e Tragedie* (by M. Apollonio, 1940).

**Mapu, Abraham** (1807–1867), Hebrew novelist. Born at Slobodka-Kovna, he is the author of that remarkable novel, *Ahabat Zion* (1853; Eng. trans. *Amnon, Prince and Peasant*, 1887; and *In the Days of Isaiah*, 1902), an historical romance influenced by contemporary European romanticism and the first work of fiction written in Hebrew. Mapu died in Königsberg.

**Márai, Sándor** (1900–    ), Hungarian novelist, born at Kassa (Košice). He discusses in his well-written works of fiction the problem of the bourgeoisie to accommodate itself to rapidly changing social conditions. Chief among his books, which have been far more popular in Germany and Austria than in English-speaking countries, are *A zendülük* (1930, 'The Rebels'), *A féltékenyek* (2 vols., 1937, 'The Jealous Ones'), *Vendégjáték Bolzanóban* (1940, 'Guest Production in Bolzano'), *Napló* (1944, 'Diary'), *A nővér* (1946, 'The Sister'), *Sértődöttek* (1947, 'The Offended Ones') and *Béke Ithakában* (1952, 'Peace in Ithaca'). His *San Gennaro vére* ('The Blood of San Gennaro') appeared in 1965.

**Marañón, Gregorio** (1887–1960), Spanish prose-writer, born in Madrid, became a medical practitioner. He brought his powers of scientific analysis to bear on biography, and was an attractive writer and clever theorist even when he did not convince. His most important works are *Enrique IV de Castilla* (1930), *Don Juan* (1940) and *Tiberio* (1939; Eng. trans. *Tiberius, A Study in Resentment*, 1956), in which his ideas about heredity and sex are aired with considerable vigour. He is likely to last by reason of his appreciation of the scientific gifts of Feijóo (q.v.) in *Las ideas biológicas del Padre Feijóo* (1934), a subject wholly fitted to his scientific training and his style of writing; but it was *Don Juan* which first gained him a reputation by its controversial nature. He died in Madrid.

**Marcel, Gabriel** (1889–    ), French prose-writer and playwright. Born in Paris, he became one of the leading Catholic existentialists. Notable specimens of his philosophical outlook, written in a not particularly distinguished manner, are: *Être et avoir* (1935), *Du Préfus à l'invocation* (1942), *Homo viator* (1944), *Le Mystère de l'être* (2 vols., 1951), *Les Hommes contre l'humain* (1951), *Le Déclin de la sagesse* (1954), *L'Homme problématique* (1955) and *Présence et immortalité* (1959). As a playwright he simply projected his ideas on to the stage, both in those pieces like *Le Seuil invisible* (1914), *Un Homme de Dieu* (1925) and *La Chapelle ardente* (1925), in which he was seeking faith, and in those such as *Le Chemin de crête* (1936), *Le Dard* (1936), *Le Fanal* (1938) and *Rome n'est plus dans Rome* (1951), by which time he had found it. Though having great prestige with intellectual audiences, he cannot be said to have broken through to a wider public, largely because he was content to allow his characters to be merely mouthpieces for his ideas. As a critic he is best represented by *L'Heure théâtrale: De Giraudoux à Jean-Paul Sartre* (1959).

**Marchena, José** (1768–1821), Spanish poet. Born at Utrera, he became a priest, but later as a follower of French encyclopaedism abandoned his Orders and went to France, where he took some part in the revolution and remained there for many years, dying, however, in poverty in Madrid. A representative of that very scanty band, the 'enlightened' Spanish ecclesiastic, most of his work is ephemeral, except for the moving 'Oda a Cristo crucificado'. See his *Obras* (2 vols., 1896).

**Marguerite de Navarre** (1492–1549), French poet, playwright and prose romance writer, was born at Angoulême, the sister of King Francis I of France. Married first to Charles, duc d'Alençon, and secondly to Henri, King of Navarre, she was a patroness of poets, a sympathizer with the Reformation, and one of the few outstanding women writers of Europe. As a poet she writes in a difficult symbolistic manner and her ideas incline greatly towards neo-Platonism. Outstanding among her poetry is *Le Miroir de l'âme pécheresse* (1531; Eng. trans. *A Godly Meditation of the Soul*, 1548; rev., 1897). *Les Marguerites de la Marguerite des princesses* also appeared in her lifetime (1547). Her poetical works are gathered together in *Les Poésies de Marguerite de Navarre* (4 vols., 1880). She also wrote several plays, including *La Nativité* (mod. ed., 1939), and other non-religious plays are to be found in *Théâtre profane de Marguerite de Navarre* (1946). It is, however, above all for her *Heptaméron*, a series of stories in imitation of the *Decameron*, that she is remembered. The collection was left unfinished at her sudden death at Odos, near Tarbes, and was published as *Histoires des amans fortunez* in 1558, and given its familiar title by C. Gruget, who edited the second edition of 1559. There is a modern edition of it (1943) and English translations (1886 and 1894).

**Margueritte, Paul** (1860–1918), French novelist. Born at Laghzouat, Algeria, the son of a general, he was in the army himself for a time, but left it in 1881. He then took up writing, produced *Mon père* (1884), a life of his father who had been killed in the Franco-Prussian War, and began his career as a novelist with *Tous Quatre* (1885), following this up with *Amants* (1889), *Jours dé'preuve* (1889), *La Force des choses* (1890), *Ma Grande* (1892) and *La Tourmente* (1893). His younger brother, **Victor Margueritte** (1866–1942), born at Blida, who had also entered the army, left it in 1896 and joined his brother for twelve years as a novelist in collaboration. Beginning with *Le Pariétaire* (1896) and *Le Carnaval de Nice* (1897), they wrote a number of highly successful novels, many of them historical, including *Une Époque* (4 vols., 1898–1904), striking stories of the war of 1870, *Femmes nouvelles* (1899), in which they supported the feminine emancipation movement, *Quelques idées* (1905), *Le Prisme* (1905) and *Sur le vif* (1906). They separated in 1908 and Paul wrote alone such novels as *La Flamme* (1909), *La Maison brûle* (1913) and *Jouir* (1918). Paul died at Hossegor. Victor, delighted at the eventual emancipation of women after the First World War, celebrated it in the single novel *Les Coupables* (1922) and in the trilogy, *La Femme en chemin*, which consisted of *La Garçonne* (1922), which gained particular notoriety, *Le Chant du berger* (1930) and *Debout les vivants* (1932). Victor died at Monestier.

**Marie de France** ( *fl.* 1181–1216), Anglo-French poet, born probably in Anjou, the natural daughter of Geoffrey IV of Anjou. She became abbess of Shaftesbury. Her *Lais* (1185–8; mod. ed., 1925 and 1944; paraphrased by A. O'Shaughnessy as *Lays of France*, 1872) are her main work and consist of fourteen poetical narratives which closely resemble folk tales and are probably derived from them.

**Marinetti, Filippo Tommaso** (1876–1944), Italian novelist, poet and playwright, writing also in French, founder of Futurism, was born in Alexandria, and after some unheeded volumes of verse (*Destruction*, 1904 and *La Vie charnelle*, 1908) burst upon the world with his novel *Mafarka il futurista* (1910), following this up with lectures and demonstrations demanding that the past should be forgotten and that in the arts and in politics alike beauty and inspiration should be sought after and found in the present. His next poetry, *Guerra sola igiene del mundo* (1915), welcomed war and Italy's participation in the European conflict as a break with the past and a source of strength for the future. His later work, still futurist, included two novels, *1 manifesti del futurismo* (1919) and *Elettricità sessuale* (1920), the political *Futurismo e fascismo* (1922) and the play *Tamburo di fuoco* (1932). He died at Bellagio on Lake Como.

**Marini** or **Marino, Giambattista** (1569–1625), Italian poet, born in Naples. He was first employed in Rome as an ecclesiastical clerk, then went to Turin, where he fell foul of the law and lived in Paris under the protection of Marie de' Medici (1615–23), and having made his reputation and fortune with *L'Adone* (1623; mod. ed., 1922), an epic romance on the loves of Venus and Adonis, returned to Naples, where he died. His rich, sensuous style, studded with glittering conceits of all kinds, brought about the rise of the school of poetry called Marinism, which dominated seventeenth-century Italy and spread to other parts of Europe. His other poetry is of slight importance, but the following may be mentioned: *La lira* (2 vols., 1608, 1614), *La galeria* (1620; mod. ed., 1926), and *La strage degli innocenti* (1632; Eng. trans. *The Slaughter of the Innocents by Herod*, 1675). See *Poesie varie* (1913).

**Maritain, Jacques** (1882–    ), French writer. Born in Paris of Huguenot parents, he was converted to Roman Catholicism in 1906, the natural turning point in his life. Opposed to Bergson (q.v.) he began as an uncompromising Thomist (*see* Thomas Aquinas), but modified this in time in accordance with modern trends. Typical of his style and thought are: *La philosophie bergsonienne* (1914), *Éléments de philosophie* (2 vols., 1920–3; Eng. trans. *An Introduction to Philosophy*, 1930), *Trois réformateurs* (1925; Eng. trans. *Three Reformers*, 1928), *Primauté du spirituel* (1927; Eng. trans. *The Things that are not Caesar's*, 1930), *Humanisme intégral* (1936; Eng. trans. *True Humanism*, 1938), *Christianisme et démocratie* (1943; Eng. trans. 1945), which shows him facing democracy and its implications squarely and finding the Left acceptable to his Christian standpoint, *Principes d'une politique humaniste* (1944) and *Pour la justice* (1945). He was French ambassador to the Vatican (1945–8). Later he became professor *emeritus* at Princeton University (1948–53) and has published in English *Man and the State* (1951) and *Creative Intuition in Art and Poetry* (1953).

**Marivaux, Pierre Carlet de Chamblain de** (1688–1763), French playwright and novelist. Born in Paris of an old Norman family, he was brought up in comfort with money to spare, and enjoyed himself to the full in the easy life of the Regency, dabbling in literature with his burlesque of the *Iliad*, *L'Homère travesti* (1716), until in Law's financial crash of 1722 he found himself practically ruined. Forced to earn a living, he turned to writing for the stage and soon discovered his gift as a writer of comedies. Between 1723 and 1740 a host of them appeared with remarkable success, including *La Double Inconstance* (1723), *La Seconde Surprise de l'amour* (1727), *Le Jeu de l'amour et du hasard* (1730), his best, *Le Triomphe de l'amour* (1732), *La Méprise* (1734), *Les Fausses Confidences* (1737), *Les Sincères* (1739) and *L'Épreuve* (1740). Excellent dialogue, emotional interest—fatally lacking in the French theatre before this—but a preciousness of style ('marivaudage') mark these plays. Marivaux is interested in revealing the character hidden beneath the mask of convention, and as such an analyst he succeeds admirably. Whether he is a good dramatist is another matter. As a picaresque novelist (a French Defoe) he is to be seen at his very best in *La Vie de Marianne* (11 parts, 1731–41) and at his second best in the unfinished *Le Paysan parvenu* (1735). He died in Paris. See his *Théâtre complet, Romans* (2 vols., 1949).

**Markevich, Boleslav Mikhaylovich** (1822–1884). Russian novelist, noted for his reactionary views, such as that the liberation of the serfs in 1861 and the other reforms of that decade were misguided. He is best known for his novel *Marina iz Alogo Roga* (1878, 'Marina from Aly Rog') and for his unfinished trilogy *Chetvert veka nazad* (1878, 'A Quarter of a Century Ago'), *Perelom* (1880, 'Turning Point') and *Bez dna* (1883, 'Abyss'). His *Zabyty vopros* (1872) was translated into English as *The Neglected Question* (1875). A second edition of his complete works (11 vols.) was published in Moscow in 1911.

**Markov, Evgeny Lvovich** (1835–1903), Russian novelist. Born in the Province of Kursk, he wrote two novels extolling the mission of the country squire as a power for good as opposed to town-dwellers and their soulless industrial way of life. These are *Barchuki* (1875, 'Young Nobles') and *Chernozyomnye polya* (1878, 'Black Earth Fields'). He died in Voronezh.

**Marmontel, Jean-François** (1723–1799), French novelist and dramatist. Born at Bort, in the Limousin, he came to Paris in 1745 encouraged by Voltaire, and made his reputation with tragedies after the manner of Crébillon *père* (q.v.) such as *Cléopâtre* (1750). Patronized by Madame de Pompadour, he gained a court appointment, and now editor of the *Mercure de France* began to print in it his tales of virtue and its rewards, published together as *Contes moraux* (1761; Eng. trans. *Moral Tales*, 1895). Fairly set as a public censor, he wrote the heavily sententious novel *Bélisaire* (1766; Eng. trans. 1767), replete with exhortations to tolerance, which aroused much opposition, and demanded the abolition of slavery in *Les Incas* *ou La Destruction de l'Empire du Pérou* (1777). His contributions to the *Encyclopédie* were published as *Éléments de Littérature* (1787). He died at Gaillon, Normandy. His *Œuvres complètes* appeared (19 vols.) in 1818.

**Marnix, Philips van** (1540–1598), Dutch poet and prose-writer. Born in Brussels of the noble family of St Aldegonde, he studied at Louvain, became a Protestant in 1560 and worked with Beza (q.v.) and Calvin (q.v.) in Geneva. Returning to the Netherlands in 1566 he came to be an intimate friend of William the Silent, took part in the first meeting of the Estates of the United Provinces at Dort (1572), and later defended Antwerp against the Spaniards, but capitulated finally and retired into private life. He is said to be the author of the patriotic *Wilhelmus* song, although there is much doubt about this; but he is to be remembered for his great prose satire against Catholicism, the *Biencorf der H. Roomsche Kercke* (1569, 'The Beehive of the Holy Roman Church,' mod. ed. 1862) and for his metrical translation of the Psalms (1580). He died in Leiden.

**Marot, Clément** (1469–1544), French poet. Born at Cahors, he became a retainer at the court of Margaret, Duchess of Angoulême, in 1519. In 1526 he was imprisoned for a short time as a suspected Protestant, but as likely as not it was a false charge made against him by the many enemies he had won by reason of his biting satires. In 1532 appeared his most attractive book, *L'Adolescence Clémentine*, a collection of his poetry up to that date, showing his mastery of every kind of metrical form, a book indeed which, for all the passing fashions which have eclipsed it from time to time, has never lost its place in French literature. Again accused of heresy in 1535, he fled to the court of that sympathizer with Protestantism, Marguerite de Navarre (q.v.), and later to the court of Ferrara. He returned to Paris when the storm had blown over in 1536 and took in hand his metrical version of the Psalms, completed in 1543. On its condemnation by the Sorbonne Marot left for Geneva, but disliking Calvin (q.v.) went on to Turin, where he died. As a graceful satirist Marot had few equals in the whole range of French literature, and he is the link between French medieval and modern poetry. See *Œuvres complètes* (5 vols., 1875–1931).

**Marotta, Giuseppe** (1902–1963), Italian short-story writer. Born in Naples, which city has provided the material for his slick sketches such as: *L'oro di Napoli* (1947; Eng. trans., *Neapolitan Gold*, 1950), *San Gennaro non dice mai no* (1948; Eng. trans. *Return to Naples*, 1951), *Gli alunni del sole* (1952; Eng. trans. *Enchanted in the Sun*, 1953), *Le madri* (1952), *Coraggio, guardiamo* (1953), *Mi voglio divertire* (1954), *Salute a noi* (1955), *Mal di galleria* (1958) and *Gli alunni del tempo* (1960; Eng. trans. *The Slaves of Time*, 1964).

**Marpicati, Arturo** (1891–    ), Italian novelist and general prose-writer, born at Ghedi, Brescia. A second-rate writer, his best novel is the straight descriptive *Quando fa sereno* (1937). An apologist for Fascism, he is most at home when extolling that ideology as in *Il partito fascista* (1935). Other books are *Questi nostri occhi* (1953) and *Sole sulle vecchie strade* (1956).

**Marquina, Eduardo** (1879–1946), Spanish poet. Born in Barcelona, he became one of the finest lyrical poets of his generation, deriving his inspiration from ancient Mediterranean culture, a kind of neo-paganism, as is to be seen in that fine volume, *Vendimión* (1909). But before long he grew concerned with social and political questions, and the result was *Canciones del momento* (1916), in a completely different manner. Siding with the republic, he went into exile on Franco's victory (1939) and died in New York.

**Marshak, Samuil Yakovlevich** (1887–1964), Russian Soviet author of books for children, some of them translated into English, e.g. *The Ball* (1943), *The Ice-Cream Man* (1943) and *The Circus* (1945). Born in Voronezh, he was also an outstanding translator of English poetry into Russian, in particular of Shakespeare's Sonnets and of Burns.

**Marsman, Hendrik** (1899–1940), Dutch poet and essayist. Born at Zeist, he was a strong, introspective, gloomy poet, influenced by Trakl (q.v.) as is to be seen in *Penthesileia* (1925), *Voorpost* (1931), *Porta Nigra* (1934) and *Tempel en Kruis* (1940). As an essayist he wrote *De Vliegende Hollander* (1927), *De Lamp van Diogenes* (1928), *De Vijf Vingers* (1929) and *Herman Gorter* (1937). He was drowned when the ship in which he was escaping from France to Britain was torpedoed.

**Martin du Gard, Roger** (1881–1958), French novelist. Born at Neuilly, he spent a retired life wholly devoted to literary work. *Devenir* (1908) and *Jean Barois* (1913; Eng. trans. 1949) give deeply considered pictures of the moral malaise of the younger generation soon to be swallowed up in the holocaust of 1914. His great work is *Les Thibault* (8 vols., 1922–1940; Eng. trans. *The World of the Thibaults*, 1939–41), a family chronicle, dealing with the average bourgeois family's experiences in the years before the First World War and during it. The constituent parts of it are *Le Cahier gris* (1922), *Le Pénitencier* (1922), *La Belle Saison* (1923), *La Consultation* (1928), *La Sorellina* (1928), *La Mort du père* (1929), *Été 1914* (1936) and *Épilogue* (1940). A writer of majestic prose, he was awarded the Nobel Prize in 1937. He died at Bellême (Orne).

**Martínez de la Rosa, Francisco** (1787–1862), Spanish poet, dramatist and novelist. Born in Granada, he entered political life in 1813 and became prime minister of the Liberal government in 1822. Banished in 1823 on the return of Ferdinand VII and autocracy, he went to Paris. He later returned to Spain under Isabel II and was Spanish ambassador in Paris, 1847–51. As a lyric poet he develops from a classical writer to a romantic, but if he is remembered today it is for his well-written romantic drama *La Conjuración de Venecia* (1834) and his historical novel *Doña Isabel de Solís* (1837). He died in Madrid. His collected works were published in three volumes (1866).

**Martínez Ruiz, José**, using the pseudonym **Azorín** (1874–1967), Spanish novelist, story-writer and essayist. Born at Monóvar near Alicante, he read law at Valencia, but settled in Madrid in 1896, spending most of his time as a literary journalist and taking some part in politics. His first novel *La voluntad* (1902) gave good promise, and with *Antonio Azorín* (1903; rewritten 1933) his particular gifts were revealed. His stories about the Castilian countryside, of which perhaps the best are *Los pueblos* (1905) and *Castilla* (1912), prove him to have been at his most happy when writing on a miniature scale. He was an elegant critic, e.g. *Al margen de los clásicos* (1915), *Rivas y Larra* (1916) and *Una hora de España, 1560–1590* (1924; Eng. trans. *An Hour of Spain, 1560–1590*, 1933). His *Obras selectas* appeared in 1943; his *Obras completas* (9 vols.) in 1947–53. He died in Madrid.

**Martínez Sierra, Gregorio** (1881–1947), Spanish playwright, born in Madrid, gained European fame with *Canción de cuna* (1911), which he maintained with *El reino de Dios* (1916), *Sueño de una noche de agosto* (1918) and *Triángulo* (1930). He was also the librettist for *Las golondrinas* (1913), an opera with music by Uzandizaga. He died in Madrid. His *Obras* were published (3 vols.) in 1948. See *The Plays of Gregorio Martínez Sierra*, the English translation in two volumes (1923).

**Martinson, Harry** (1904–   ), Swedish novelist. Born at Jämshög, he spent much of his early life as a wanderer by sea and land, projecting his experiences in fiction such as *Kap Farväl* (1933; Eng. trans. *Cape Farewell*, 1934), *Nässlorna blomma* (1935; Eng. trans. *Flowering Nettle*, 1936) and *Vägen till Klockerike* (1948).

**Martorell, Joanot** (*d.* 1488?), Catalan novelist. Born in Valencia, he seems to have been a diplomat and to have visited Portugal and England in his youth. He is the author of the romance *Tirant lo blanc*, which he began about 1460, and which was published in 1490 (Spanish trans. 1511). Full of knightly adventures with descriptions of England (first hand) and of the Levant (from Muntaner, q.v.), the work is too drawn out and becomes almost intolerable towards the end. Cervantes (q.v.) read it and noticed it in *Don Quijote*. There is a modern edition by A. M. Huntingdon (1904).

**Martyr, Peter,** the name by which **Pietro Martire d'Anghiera** (1459–1526) is known in English, Italian-Spanish prose-writer. Born at Arona on Lake Maggiore, he settled in Spain in 1487, was given high ecclesiastical preferment, finally the bishopric of Jamaica, also held diplomatic posts, and in 1511 published *Decades de Orbe Novo* (first *in extenso*, 1530; Eng. trans., 2 vols., 1912), the first account of the discovery of America. His *Opus Epistolarum*, published posthumously in 1530, is a history of the period 1488–1525 in the form of letters. He died in Granada.

**Marx, Heinrich Karl** (1818–1883), German political theorist, was born at Trier, of Jewish middle-class parents, was educated at Bonn and Berlin, and suddenly turning away from an intended academic career took up journalism as editor of the advanced *Rheinische Zeitung* (1842). On its suppression the following year he went to Paris, where he studied economics and, using the by now creaking regime of Louis-Philippe as an example, wrote the *Deutsche-Französische*

*Jahrbücher* (1843) and *Vorwärts* (1844). Exiled from France in 1845 he went to Brussels, where there followed the friendship with Engels and the reorganization of the Communist League, for which the *Manifesto* (1848) was written. Then followed his participation in the revolution of 1848 and his final settling down in London in 1849, where in the British Museum he worked on what was to develop into *Das Kapital* (vol. i, 1867; vols. ii and iii, ed. F. Engels, 1885, 1895; Eng. trans. *Capital*, 1938, best of several). It goes without saying that all literatures have been more or less affected by Marx's thought at some point, Soviet literature fundamentally so, but as literature his works are valueless, and *Das Kapital* with all its verbiage is a monument to the hideousness which German in particular can become in the hands of a literary philistine. Marx died in London.

**Masaryk, Tomáš Garrigue** (1850–1937), Czech author writing also in German. Born at Hodonín, Moravia, the son of a coachman, he was apprenticed to a blacksmith, but was enabled to go to the University of Vienna and was appointed to the chair of philosophy in Prague. Entering the Austrian Reichsrath in 1891 the next period of his life was devoted to forming an independent state for the Czechs and Slovaks, his efforts being successful in 1919. Even so he found time for much writing, and if he had done nothing else but write he would have been sure of recognition. His most noteworthy books are those on Czech history, especially *Česká otázka* (1895, 'The Czech Question') and *Jan Hus* (1896), then his ethical work *Ideály humanitní* (1901; Eng. trans. *The Ideals of Humanity*, 1938), and then his two widely read studies of contemporary politics, *Russland und Europa* (1913; Eng. trans. *The Spirit of Russia*, 1918) and *Světová revoluce* (1925; Eng. trans. shortened, *The Making of a State*, 1927). Masaryk died, President of Czechoslovakia, at Lány.

**Massillon, Jean-Baptiste** (1663–1742), French prose-writer and orator. Born at Hyères in Provence, he became court preacher to Louis XIV in 1699 and soon gained a reputation as an outstanding orator without a trace of dogmatism. His noble funeral discourse on the death of Louis XIV (1715) is a masterpiece. In 1717 he became Bishop of Clermont, and the following year preached before Louis XV a series of ten Lenten sermons, *Le Petit Carême*, on which his ultimate reputation as the greatest of all French religious orators, not excluding Bossuet (q.v.) and Bourdaloue, rests. He died of apoplexy at Clermont. His collected works were published in 1745–6.

**Mastriani, Francesco** (1819–1891), Italian novelist. A lifelong resident of Naples, he was a prolific novelist dealing with the lives of the poor of his native city. His best and most famous work is *La cieca di Sorrento* (1852).

**Matthisson, Friedrich von** (1761–1831), German poet. Born at Hohenbodeleben, near Magdeburg, he became a schoolmaster and travelling tutor, and after 1801 a court official in Baden and Württemberg. A man of taste and attractive manners, of a type which one associates in English literature with Richard Cumberland or Jerningham, his facile sentimental lyrics, collected as *Lieder* (1781) and

*Gedichte* (1787), were used for songs by Mozart, Beethoven and Schubert. His rambling memoirs (5 vols., 1810–15), though not well written, are of some historical interest. He died at Wörlitz.

**Maupassant, Henri René Albert Guy de** (1850–1893), French short-story writer and novelist. Born in Normandy at Tourville-sur-Arques, he was the son of a stockbroker who claimed to be of noble descent, and of the sister of Alfred Le Poittevin, the close friend of Flaubert (q.v.). In 1861 his parents parted and the boy was brought up by his mother, who repeatedly turned to Flaubert for advice, and so it came about that the famous novelist kept a watch on his education and encouraged his entry into the civil service. In 1872 Maupassant became a clerk in the Ministry of Marine in Paris, spending his spare hours in swimming and boating on the Seine (he was a giant of a man of splendid physique, 'the Normandy Bull') and also attending literary gatherings which from time to time Flaubert held on his infrequent visits to Paris. Here came Zola (q.v.), Daudet (q.v.), Turgenev (q.v.) and Mendès (q.v.). The young man listened and said little; before long he was trying out his hand as a short-story writer, visiting Flaubert privately and gaining from him the literary advice from which he was so greatly to profit. His first publication, however, was a book of salacious verse, *Des Vers* (1880), which when he was threatened with a prosecution he hurriedly suppressed; but this year was memorable for something far more worthy. Under the aegis of Zola and Huysmans (q.v.), a collection of realist short stories, *Les Soirées de Médan*, appeared, to which Maupassant contributed *Boule de Suif*, that masterpiece of an incident in the Franco-Prussian War, pathetic without being sentimental, and beautifully written. The hitherto unknown young man in a stroke had won a reputation which his next publication, *La Maison Tellier* (1881), only confirmed. *Mademoiselle Fifi* (1882) followed and in 1883 came the full-length novel *Une Vie*, a powerful, uncompromising study of a girl whose life is a series of disillusionments. He had already resigned from the civil service, and had become a professional writer, in fact a commercial writer, and, as he claimed, one who wrote because he wanted to earn plenty of money in order to live well. Unfortunately, living well for him meant less and less the athletic life of the past and more and more drink, drugs and women. For the moment he was at the height of his powers and there appeared in quick succession the books of short stories, *Contes de la bécasse* (1883), *Clair de lune, Miss Harriet* and *Les Sœurs Rondoli* (all 1884), the attractive essays, *Au Soleil* (1884), more books of short stories, *Yvette, Contes et nouvelles, Monsieur Parent* and *Contes du jour et de la nuit* (all 1885), and his second full-length novel *Bel-Ami* (1885), a study of a man who uses his physical assets to win success. The books of short stories, *Toine* and *La Petite Roque*, belong to 1886, *Mont-Oriol*, his third novel, and the terrifying *Le Horla* to 1887. In *Le Horla* are definite signs of mental derangement, although with the aid of drugs he was able for nearly three years longer to produce works, some of them touched with a new sympathy and understanding lacking in the earlier works, as if he had become mellowed with suffering. To this last period belong the book

of short stories, *Le Rosier de Madame Husson,* the most deeply felt of
his novels, *Pierre et Jean,* and a book of sketches about sailing, *Sur
l'Eau* (all of these 1888), while to 1889 belong the short stories *La
Main gauche,* proof of failing powers, and the stronger full-length
novel *Fort comme la mort.* Then came the last year of work (1890) with
a novel, *Notre cœur,* a volume of travel sketches, *La Vie errante,* and
a book of short stories, *L'Inutile Beauté.* The rest of his career was a
death in life, and the shattered brainless wreck, ravaged by syphilis,
died three years later in Paris. One of the most popular authors of the
age, his bright, sharp craftsmanship amounts to genius. He modernized his mode of expression and swept away literariness, and yet
generally not at the expense of good style. Good taste in fact never
deserted the man who frankly wrote for the many, and even sordid
subjects are elevated by his feeling and insight. Right until the end
there is a healthiness in his approach which makes a sad contrast
to his tragic personal life. Hereditary mental unbalance, and a
mother's doting, together with handsomeness and easy success with
women had made of Maupassant a Samson enslaved. See his *Œuvres
complètes* (15 vols., 1934–8) and the English translation, *The Works
of Guy de Maupassant,* by M. Laurie (10 vols., 1923–9).

**Mauriac, François** (1885–    ), French poet, novelist, essayist and
playwright. Born in Bordeaux, he turned from thoughts of an
academic career to one of literature, and became known for his
religious poems, *Les Mains jointes* (1910), in which, as in all the works
which followed, he dealt with the eternal struggle between the material
and the spiritual. The world for him is full of passions of every kind,
and it is unavoidable that men should indulge them, a particular
passion being preferred by everyone according to his or her nature;
but just as it is easy to indulge oneself so is it very difficult to obtain
forgiveness. Of his many novels these are the chief: *La Chair et le
sang* (1920), *Le Baiser au lépreux* (1922; Eng. trans. *A Kiss for the
Leper,* 1950), *Génitrix* (1923; Eng. trans. 1950), *Le Désert de l'amour*
(1925; Eng. trans. *The Desert of Love,* 1949), *Thérèse Desqueyroux*
(1927; Eng. trans. 1947), *Ce qui était perdu* (1930; Eng. trans. *That
which was Lost,* 1951), *Le Nœud de vipères* (1932; Eng. trans. *The
Knot of Vipers,* 1951), *Le Mystère Frontenac* (1933; Eng. trans. *The
Frontenac Mystery,* 1952), *Le Mal* (1935; Eng. trans. *The Enemy,*
1949), *Les Anges noirs* (1936; Eng. trans. *The Dark Angels,* 1951),
*Les Chemins de la mer* (1939; Eng. trans. *The Unknown Sea,* 1948),
*La Pharisienne* (1941; Eng. trans. *A Woman of the Phari-
sees,* 1946) and *Le Sagouin* (1951; Eng. trans. *The Little
Misery,* 1952). His religious honesty is to be seen in *La Rencontre
avec Pascal* (1926) and *Souffrances et bonheur du chrétien* (1929).
Insight into his approach to his work as a novelist is to be sought in
*Le Romancier et ses personnages* (1933), while his *Vie de Jésus* (1936;
Eng. trans. 1937) is an interpretation as beautiful as it is unusual.
His *Cahier noir* (1943) is an eloquent memorial of his part in the
Resistance movement against the Germans. As a playwright his most
significant contributions to the literature of the theatre are: *Asmodée*
(1938; Eng. trans. *Asmodée, or the Intruder,* 1939), *Les Mal Aimés*

(1945), *Le Feu sur la terre* (1951) and *Le Pain vivant* (1955). He was awarded the Nobel Prize in 1952. His narrative, *L'Agneau* (1954; Eng. trans. *The Lamb*, 1961), should also be mentioned.

**Maurois, André,** pseudonym of Émile Herzog (1885–1967), French novelist, essayist and biographer. Born at Elbeuf, Normandy, of well-to-do Alsatian parents, he studied philosophy at the Lycée Corneille, Rouen, under Émile Chartier (q.v., better known by his pseudonym Alain), who had a lasting influence on him. Entering the family cloth factory at Elbeuf he remained there until the outbreak of war in 1914. Appointed a liaison officer with the British Army he gained that insight into the British character which he turned to excellent account in his two studies of men and opinions, *Les Silences du colonel Bramble* (1918; Eng. trans. 1919) and *Les Discours du docteur O'Grady* (1922). His first biography, *Ariel, ou la vie de Shelley*, was published in 1923 (Eng. trans. 1924). Three years later he left Elbeuf and went to Paris determined to follow an exclusively literary career. Soon after his arrival appeared his partly autobiographical novel, *Bernard Quesnay* (1926; Eng. trans. 1927); and two further books dealing with moral problems in a domestic setting, *Climats* (1928; Eng. trans., *Atmosphere of Love*, 1965), and *Le Cercle de famille* (1932; Eng. trans. 1932), increased his growing popularity. Two more biographies of Englishmen belong to this period, *La Vie de Disraëli* (1927; Eng. trans. 1927) and *Don Juan, ou la Vie de Byron* (1930; Eng. trans. 1930). *Le Peseur d'âmes* (1931; Eng. trans. *The Weigher of Souls*, 1931) best represents his novels of fantasy, while his philosophical approach is to be found in *La Machine à lire les pensées* (1937; Eng. trans. *The Thought-Reading Machine*, 1938). His views on social problems are expressed in *Dialogues sur le commandement* (1924; Eng. trans. *Captains and Kings*, 1925) and *Sentiments et coutumes* (1934), his taste for English literature is displayed in *Magiciens et logiciens* (1935; Eng. trans. *Prophets and Poets*, 1935), and his *Histoire d'Angleterre* (1937; Eng. trans. 1937) exemplifies his very personal and appreciative approach to English history. In 1939 he enlisted in the army, but on the collapse of France went to the U.S.A., writing there among other topical books *L'Histoire des États-Unis* (1943). He returned to France after the liberation. A writer of wide culture, sanity and courage, the keynote of his work is charity and optimism. Among his later works may be mentioned his biographies, *Lélia, ou la Vie de George Sand* (1952; Eng. trans. 1953), *Olympio, ou la Vie de Victor Hugo* (1954), *Les Trois Dumas* (1957) and *Adrienne, ou la Vie de Madame de La Fayette* (1960), and his book of literary criticism, *De Proust à Camus* (1962). Later novels included *Terre promise* (1946) and *Les Roses de septembre* (1956; Eng. trans. 1958). Other prose works were: *Cinq Visages de l'amour* (1942; Eng. trans. *Seven Faces of Love*, 1943), *Retour en France* (1947), *Alain* (1949), *Les Nouveaux Discours du docteur O'Grady* (1950; Eng. trans. *The Return of Doctor O'Grady*, 1951), *Destins exemplaires* (1952; Eng. trans. *Profiles of Great Men*, 1954) and, with Aragon (q.v.) *Histoire parallèle des U.S.A. et de l'U.R.S.S.* (1962; Eng. trans. 1964). He died in Paris.

**Maurras, Charles** (1868–1952), French poet and prose-writer. Born at Martigues, he grew up ultramontane in religion and royalist in politics. His purely literary works are such as *Le Chemin de paradis* (1891) and *Anthinéa* (1901), but as soon as he joined the staff of *L'Action Française* he became almost entirely a political writer. In 1908, with the help of Léon Daudet (q.v.), he converted *L'Action* into a daily paper, and turned it towards a policy, which he had already advocated in *L'Avenir de l'intelligence* (1905), of the restoration of the monarchy and a state system which much resembled what afterwards became known as Fascism. *Les Conditions de la victoire* (1916) was violently anti-German, and after the war such speculative volumes as *L'Allée de philosophes* (1924), *Romantisme et révolution* (1925) and *Les Idées royalistes sur les partis* (1925) brought him into collision with Church and state. In 1940 he collaborated with Pétain in the Vichy government and was condemned to imprisonment for life. He died at Saint-Symphorien.

**May, Karl** (1842–1912), German novelist. Born at Hohenstein-Ernstthal of very poor family, he was completely self-taught, and wrote vivid adventure stories, set in every part of the world although he never left Germany. Among his best are *Durch die Wüste* (1892) about the Middle East, *Winnetou* (3 vols., 1893), about cowboys and pioneers in the Far West, *Der Schatz im Silbersee* (1894), in the tradition of *Treasure Island*, and *Im Lande des Mahdi* (1896), topical and Sudanese. His complete works fill sixty-five volumes (1892–1945), and for all their shallowness and weak plots they can still appeal by reason of the author's soaring imagination which carries the reader along. He died at Radebeul.

**Mayakovsky, Vladimir Vladimirovich** (1894–1930), Russian Soviet poet and playwright. Born at Bagdady, he went to Moscow and mixed in literary circles just at the moment when futurism was coming in from France, and his early poetry is purely experimental. But *Voyna i mir* (1916, 'War and Peace') proves how a definite inspiration had canalized his gifts into something worthwhile, for the coming revolution was already in the air and he revelled in the idea of its coming. There followed the distasteful play parodying various aspects of the Christian religion, *Misteriya-Buf* (1917, 'Mystery-Bouffe'), in which he hailed the revolution's arrival. But however much he might rejoice in public events, his private life was a failure, and love and satisfactory friendship seemed denied him. In *Lyublyu* (1922, 'Love') he hints at his failure to win personal happiness. In another poem, *Vladimir Ilyich Lenin* (1924), in which he mourns the death of Lenin, he again hints, but this time at his fear of an even more barren and frustrated personal life now that lesser men without vision will take control of Russia's affairs. Among his last works are two plays, *Klop* (1928, 'The Bed-bug') and *Banya* (1929, 'The Bath'), in which fellow-travellers of the regime are harshly criticized. He committed suicide in Moscow. A great deal of his work has been translated into English, in *Mayakovsky*, by Herbert Marshall (last and best edition, 1965).

**Maykov, Apollon Nikolayevich** (1821–1897), Russian lyric poet born in Moscow, whose first volume of verse appeared in 1842. He was also a noted translator from the western European and Slavonic languages. He died in Petersburg.

**Mažuranić, Ivan** (1814–1890), Croat poet. Born at Novi Vinodolski, he became a lawyer and literary journalist, and in 1846 published his chief work, the epic *Smrt Smail-age Čengića* (Eng. trans. *The Death of Smail-aga Čengić*, 1925), set in Montenegro. In 1873 he was appointed governor of Croatia and proved immensely popular and successful. He founded Zagreb University, and died in that city.

**Mazzini, Giuseppe** (1805–1872), Italian prose-writer. He was born in Genoa and educated for the law, but soon became involved in anti-Austrian activities, which culminated in his joining the Carbonari in 1827 and being exiled in 1830. Two years later he was exiled from France whither he had gone, and after an unsuccessful attack on Savoy, he settled in London in 1837 to work for the liberation of his country. In Britain he won many friends and sympathizers and continued his activities until the 1848 Revolution came. Elected one of the triumvirs of the Roman Republic (1849), his triumph was short-lived, and on the French suppression of the republic he returned to London, where his influence over the Risorgimento was supreme until in 1858 he fell out with Cavour's policy, which he considered a compromise and a betrayal of true republican democracy. He opposed Victor Emmanuel's regime for the rest of his life, and, settling at Lugano, just over the border, plotted against it. He refused Victor Emmanuel's amnesty, but sometimes visited Italy incognito. He was at Pisa on such a visit under the name of Brown when he died. As a writer, Mazzini subordinated art to patriotism, and so in *Dell'amor patrio di Dante* (1826) Italy's greatest poet is discussed from that angle. *La filosofia della musica* (1836) is a graceful treatise, while *Byron e Goethe* (1847) displays his views on literature in general. *I doveri dell'uomo* (1860; Eng. trans. *The Duties of Man*, 1862; *The Duties of Man and Other Essays*, Everyman's Library ed., 1907; reprinted, 1936), is a fine exposition of his ethical views, written when he had come to believe that the working classes represented what was best in Italy. He was an accomplished journalist, as is to be seen from his many writings scattered throughout his various political papers, such as *La Giovine Italia* (1832–6), *L'Italia del popolo* (1848–51), *Pensiere ed azione* (1859–60) and *La Roma del popolo* (1870–2). See *Life and Writings of Joseph Mazzini* (6 vols., 1864–70; new ed., 1890–1).

**Medici, Lorenzo de'** (1449–1492), Italian poet and dramatist, was born the grandson of the great Cosimo, who founded the fortunes of the family, in Florence. In 1469 he became joint ruler of Florence together with his brother, and after the latter's assassination in 1478 he governed alone. With Lorenzo, called 'The Magnificent', Florence reached the height of artistic glory. Licentious, crafty and cruel, as the panel by Vasari in the Uffizi Gallery amply shows, he loved all the arts and was a lavish patron of poets and painters, sculptors and antiquaries. As a poet his *Rime* are Petrarchan, his *Selve d'amore* reveal deep appreciation of nature, and there is great ability in his *Trionfi e canti carnascialeschi* and *Canzoni a ballo.* He parodies Dante and even his master Petrarch, from both of whom it seems impossible for an Italian writer to escape, he appears to feel, in *Il Simposio o I Beoni.* He wrote and acted in a religious play, *San Giovanni e San Paolo,* in 1489. He died at Careggi, having by his brilliant diplomacy secured for his state a much-needed period of rest from war. He was patron of Leonardo da Vinci, enormously enriched the Laurentian library, founded an academy of philosophy, while his collection of ancient classical sculpture was among the choicest in Europe. The best edition of his collected works is that by A. Simioni (2 vols., 1913–14, new. ed., 1939).

**Meilhac, Henri** (1831–1897), French playwright. Born in Paris, he worked in a bookshop before becoming a journalist, wrote vaudevilles, such as *L'Autographe* (1859) and *Le Petit-fils de Mascarille* (1861), and then joined with Halévy (q.v.) to help the Second French Empire to amuse itself. In this he prodigiously succeeded by providing Offenbach with libretti for his operettas, Halévy often collaborating, such as *La Belle Hélène* (1864), *Barbe-Bleue* (1866), *La Vie Parisienne* (1866), and *La Grande Duchesse de Gérolstein* (1867). *Froufrou* (1869), which enjoyed an immense success, is a straight comedy. He died in Paris. See *Le Théâtre de Meilhac et Halévy* (8 vols., 1900–2).

**Meinhold, Johann Wilhelm** (1797–1851), German novelist, was born on the Island of Usedom and became a clergyman. His two sensational novels, *Maria Schweidler, die Bersteinhexe* (1843; Eng. trans. *The Amber Witch,* 1844) and *Sidonia von Bork, die Klosterhexe* (1847; Eng. trans. *Sidonia the Sorceress,* 1894), are precursors of the melodramatic and exotic fiction exemplified in the English-speaking world by the novels of Sax Rohmer. Meinhold died at Rehwinkel.

**Meissner, Alfred von** (1822–1885), Austrian novelist, who also wrote poetry and plays long since forgotten, was born at Teplitz. His chief novels are *Der Pfarrer von Grafenried* (1855), a particularly attractive rendering of the domestic scene, *Schwarzgelb* (2 vols., 1862, 1865) and *Norbert Norson* (1883). His collected works, without the slightest reference to his collaborator F. Hedrich, appeared in eighteen volumes in 1872. A literary storm followed with subsequent disgrace and remorse as Meissner's portion. He died at Bregenz.

**Melanchthon, Philipp** (1497–1560), German theological writer. Born at Bretten in Baden, his real name, of which Melanchthon was a Greek translation, being **Schwarzerd,** he was educated at Heidelberg; he lectured at Tübingen, and in 1518 was appointed professor of Greek at Wittenberg, where he came under the influence of Luther (q.v.). His great work is that model of theological dogmatism, *Loci Communes Rerum Theologicarum* (1521; mod. ed., 1925; Eng. trans. 1944). The drawing up of the Augsburg Confession was largely his work. Tolerant and urbanely learned, he exercised a civilizing and restraining influence on the coarser and more violent elements of the Reformation, although after Luther's death he began to lose control. He died in Wittenberg. See his *Opera* (28 vols., 1834–60, suppl., 4 vols., 1910–26).

**Meléndez Valdés, Juan** (1754–1817), Spanish poet. Born at Ribera del Fresno, Badajoz, he went to the University of Salamanca, then enjoying a revival, meeting there Cadalso (q.v.) and Jovellanos (q.v.), the latter of whom became a lifelong friend. He began to write poetry, while reading much and becoming a proficient classical scholar, and he was appointed to the chair of classical literature at Salamanca, in 1780 carrying off the Spanish Academy's prize for poetry. Although Meléndez can be distressingly conventional, glancing back to outworn eighteenth-century diction and spirit, he can rise to sympathy not only for a fallen giant of the forest, but for a beggar, even a criminal. In his *Poesías* (1785) there is a wealth of lyric verse of all kinds, most significant of all being the symbolical apostrophes to justice, which show him to be a son of the ill-starred Spanish Enlightenment. Appointed a judge of the court of Zaragoza (1789) through the influence of Jovellanos, he was able to exercise his humanitarianism. He was a member of the Treasury Department in Madrid (1793–8) until he was exiled with Jovellanos. A man of the same introverted, uncertain spirit as the younger Moratín (q.v.), Meléndez was unsure what to do at the time of the French invasion of 1807, but accepted office under Joseph Bonaparte, and was forced to go into exile in France in 1813 when the French withdrew. He died in Montpellier. A full edition of the *Poesías* was published in 1820, and his complete work is to be found in *Biblioteca de Autores Españoles* (vol. lxiii). There are some English translations of his poems in Longfellow's *Poets and Poetry of Europe* (1888).

**Melnikov-Pechersky, Pavel Ivanovich** (1819–1883), Russian novelist. Born in Nizhny Novgorod, where he died, he wrote two unusual works about the sect of the 'Old Believers' living in complete isolation from the world and clinging to beliefs and a way of life which dated from the seventeenth century. The first, *V lesakh* (1871–5, 'In the Forests'), is set on the upper reaches of the Volga, while the other, *Na gorakh* (1875–81, 'On the Mountains'), takes place in the Urals. Melnikov had an immense capacity for depicting unusual characters, but had little idea of literary 'architecture', and his books are overweighed with detail which adds to their almost unbearable length.

**Melo, Francisco Manuel de** (1608–1666), Portuguese poet and prose-writer, writing almost entirely in Spanish. Born of noble family in Lisbon, he joined the army, which meant at that period (1580–1640) the Spanish army, since Portugal had been annexed. He took part in the Catalan rebellion on the side of the government, of course, and seemed to be on a fair way to a successful career when in 1644 he was suddenly imprisoned, no charge forthcoming, and afterwards sent to Brazil. He was before long allowed his freedom on parole, but was not officially pardoned until 1657. As a poet he is at his best in *Las tres musas del Melodino* (1649; Eng. trans. *Relics of Melodino*, 1815; second ed., 1820), and as a prose-writer he is at his most humorous in his satire on married life, *Carta de guía de casados* (1651; Eng. trans. *The Government of a Wife*, 1697), and at his most serious, the master of an excellent prose, in *Historia de los movimientos y separación de Cataluña* (1645; mod. ed., 1912). His letters, *Cartas familiares* (1664) are of much interest. He was employed as a diplomat in his later years, and died at Alcántara.

**Mendelssohn, Moses** (1729–1786), German prose-writer. Born at Dessau, in Anhalt, after early privations he went into business, but spent all his spare time in writing and in cultivating the friendship of literary men, one of whom, Lessing (q.v.), became a collaborator and wrote his *Nathan* with him in view. A man of elevated mind, he was an orthodox Jew but shared in the Enlightenment of his day. His main works are *Philosophische Gespräche* (1755), in which he joined with Lessing and discussed Alexander Pope, *Briefe über die Empfindungen* (1755, 'On the Sensations'), *Phädon oder über die Unsterblichkeit der Seele* (1767), a Platonic dialogue on the immortality of the soul, *Jerusalem* (1783), in which he defended Judaism and asked for the emancipation of the Jews, and *Morgenstunden oder über das Dasein Gottes* (1785), essays against Pantheism and the doctrines of Spinoza (q.v.). One of the finest examples of the best aspects of eighteenth-century toleration, he died in Berlin. He was the grandfather of the composer. His collected works appeared (7 vols.) in 1843–5.

**Mendès, Catulle Abraham** (1841–1909), French poet, novelist, play-wright and essayist, was born of Jewish family in Bordeaux, and as early as 1859 founded *La Revue Fantaisiste*, a rallying-point of the Parnassians. He began his literary career with volumes of verse such as *Philoméla* (1864) and *Odelette Guerrière* (1870), and then turned to the novel and short story, producing brilliantly written, well-con-structed and voluptuous works, such as *Zo'har* (1886), *La Dernière Maîtresse* (1887), *La Grande Maguet* (1888) and *La Femme enfant* (1891). He wrote such plays as *Médée* (1898) and *La Vierge d'Avila* (1906), while as a critic and essayist his *La Légende du Parnasse contemporain* (1884), *L'Art du théâtre* (3 vols., 1895–1900) and *Rapport sur le mouvement poétique français, 1867–1900* (1902) are all valuable contemporary comments on literary movements in which he had taken so great a part. He was killed in a street accident at St-Germain-en-Laye.

Mendes Pinto, F., *see* Pinto, F. M.

**Menéndez Pidal, Ramón** (1869–    ), Spanish scholar. Born at La Coruña, he was appointed to the chair of Romance philology at the University of Madrid in 1899, retaining the post for forty years, and became director of the Spanish Academy in 1925. He was first known as a philologist when his masterly account of the history of the Spanish language, *Manual de gramática histórica española* (1904), came out, and as a great authority on Spanish literature when he published his critical edition of the Cid, *Cantar de mio Cid* (3 vols., 1908–12), and that brilliant work about the Cid and his time, *La España del Cid* (1920; Eng. trans. *The Cid and his Spain*, 1934). A later work is *Los orígenes del español* (1926). *Reliquias de la poesía épica española* (1951), *Romancero hispánico* (2 vols., 1953), *Los godos y el origen de la epopeya española* (1955) and *La Chanson de Roland y el neotradicionalismo* (1959) showed him still working on with unclouded mind at an advanced age.

**Menéndez y Pelayo, Marcelino** (1856–1912), Spanish scholar. Born in Santander, he was appointed to the chair of Spanish literature at Madrid at twenty-two, a special act of the Cortes being necessary to accomplish this. He held this post till 1898 when he became director of the national library at Madrid, an office which he occupied at the time of his death in Santander. In an unimpeachable style he wrote on a wide variety of subjects, and was not afraid of generalizations which, though flaws have since been found in some, stimulated thought and still do. This is particularly true of *La ciencia española* (3 vols., 1876–88; rev. ed., 1933), and that mine of information, *Historia de los heterodoxos españoles* (2 vols., 1880–2; better edition, 3 vols., 1911–17), in which he seldom if ever allows his strong Catholicism to overpower his judgment. Valuable and maturer works are *Historia de las ideas estéticas en España* (9 vols., 1883–91; improved edition, 1890–1912) and the prologues (but not the often unreliable texts) of the *Antología de poetas líricos castellanos* (13 vols., 1890–1908). These prologues were extracted from the rest and published as *Historia de la poesía castellana* (3 vols., 1911–16). His works fill forty-nine volumes (1940–5).

**Mercanton, Jacques** (1910–      ), Swiss novelist, born at Lausanne. His conversion to Roman Catholicism has coloured his whole life. His serious works deal with mankind's fundamental problems in confrontation with the world. They are *Thomas l'incrédule* (1943), *Le Soleil ni la mort* (1948) and *La Joie d'amour* (1951).

**Merezhkovsky, Dmitri Sergeyevich** (1865–1941), Russian prose-writer. Born in Petersburg, he joined modernist literary circles intent on winning back literature for religion. In order to do this he looked into the question of the rise and fall of cultures and beliefs, the result being his highly individualistic trilogy, consisting of *Yulian Otstupnik* (1894; Eng. trans. *The Death of the Gods*, 1901), about Julian the Apostate and his feverish bid to preserve paganism from the inroads of Christianity, *Voskresshie bogi* (1896; Eng. trans. *The Resurrection of the Gods*, 1938), set in Florence with Leonardo da Vinci as hero, and *Pyotr i Alexey* (1905), the last 'the tragedy of the gentle Tsarevitch Alexis, servant of the Galilean, . . . victim . . . of human will incarnate in the genius of Peter [the Great], lifting itself above good and evil'. In his literary periodical, *Novy put'* (1903–4, 'New Path'), he continued his campaign for religion in literature. Another trilogy, a play, *Pavel I* (1908), and two novels, *Alexander I* (1911) and *14. dekabrya* (1918; Eng. trans. *December the 14th*, 1923), is the vehicle for a further assessment of religion, this time centred on the mysticism of Alexander I with violence on either side of him. As might be expected Tolstoy was an inspiration to Merezhkovsky, and it was his example which had led to the foundation of the Religious-Philosophic Society, a headquarters of the religiously minded intellectuals in Petersburg before the revolution. In 1920 Merezhkovsky settled in Paris, where he never ceased in pamphlet and in book to harry Communism and open the vials of his wrath on the Soviet government. Few of his publications during these later years have much literary value, with the exception of *Tayna Zapada* (1930; Eng. trans. *The Secret of the West*, 1933), a beautifully written piece of work about ancient civilizations, memorably the lost land of Atlantis and the religious beliefs of the Aztecs and Incas. He died in Paris.

**Mérimée, Prosper** (1803–1870), French novelist and short-story writer, was born in Paris, the son of an artist. He studied law, discovered an unusual gift for languages, became interested in archaeology, and dabbled in literature. His two literary hoaxes, *Le Théâtre de Clara Gazul* (1825), supposed to be a collection of plays by a Spanish actress which he had translated into French, and *La Guzla* (1827), which he let loose on his public as a translation by him of Illyrian folk-songs, brought him some success. He became a civil servant, and was appointed an inspector of historic monuments, a post which exactly suited him, in 1834. He had meanwhile failed in his attempt to write a full-scale historical novel, *La Chronique du règne de Charles IX* (1829), but found the long short story more to his taste. His first collection, *Mosaïques* (1830; Eng. trans. 1903, in ' French Novels of the Nineteenth Century '), contains such masterpieces as 'Tamango' and 'Le Vase étrusque'. *La Vénus d'Ille* (1837; Eng. trans. *The Venus of Ille and Other Stories*, 1964) is another excellent story. But it is with *Colomba* (1841) and *Carmen* (1845; the two in Eng. trans. 1923, in 'Masterpieces of French Romance') that he reached his height. Here with studied detachment in a precise restrained style he describes violence and passion, in *Colomba* in Corsica, in *Carmen* in Spain, the latter country one which had so much impressed him on his first visit there in 1830. After *Carmen* his inspiration seemed to flag and he had little more to say except at the end of his life when he wrote *Lokis* (1869; Eng. trans. 1903) and proved that he still retained his old cunning. He had been for long a friend of her family when Eugénie married Napoleon III. Mérimée, who was made a senator in 1853, was from then on *persona grata* at court, and there this singular man, who affected the dress and the reserve of an Englishman, would send a flutter through the court-ladies as in a monotonous voice he would read his tales of evil, violence and passion. The collapse of the empire (1870) broke him down, and suffering severely from asthma he went to Cannes, where he died, as Edmond de Goncourt (q.v.) maliciously recorded in his diary, ' sandwiched between two old governesses, one of the saddest ends in the world '. His collected works, which contain some formal history and a great many archaeological reports and diaries of travel, appeared in twelve volumes in 1927. In *Lettres à une inconnue* (1873) we find Mérimée at last almost in love.

**Metastasio, Pietro,** Metastasio being the Grecized form of his real surname, **Trapassi** (1698–1782), Italian poet and librettist. He was born of poor and humble family in Rome, but was adopted by the wealthy lawyer and man of letters, G. V. Gravina (q.v.), who educated him well and on his death (1718) left him his fortune. Metastasio, having joined the Arcadian Academy at Rome, the literary canons of which he adhered to and developed, left Rome in 1719 and went to Naples. There he wrote a series of operas, the most famous *Didone abbandonata* (1723), which were set to music by such composers as Porpora, Pergolese, Durante and Scarlatti, and had such a success that in 1730 he was invited to succeed Apostolo Zeno (q.v.) as imperial court poet in Vienna. He accepted and remained in Vienna holding that office for the rest of his life. Here he wrote well over twenty more operas, e.g. *Demetrio* (1730) and *Demofoönte* (1740), classical, calm and luminous, 'like a quiet sky over Palladian architecture'. The lines sang before the composer set them to music. It is a quiet Arcadian world, graceful and lightly sentimental but not static, although even when Metastasio attempts tragedy on the French model, as in *Attilio Regolo* (1740), it is softened and smoothed away to sad elegance. In his later years suffering from 'mental and moral ennui', the greatest of all writers of opera libretti died in Vienna. The best edition of his works is that by Brunelli (3 vols., 1943–52) to be supplemented by the edition of Nicolini (4 vols., 1912–14). The Paris edition (12 vols., 1780–2) is exhaustive and a bibliographical curiosity. There is the classic English translation, *Dramas and Other Poems*, by J. Hoole (3 vols., 1800). Metastasio's fall from favour during the last century was not only a question of change of taste but was political also. One who had taken office under the hated Austrian was hardly attractive to the literary men of the Risorgimento. It was Carducci (q.v.) who reinstated him by editing his letters (1883) and pointing out his unique qualities.

**Meung, Jean de,** otherwise known as **Jean Clopinel** (1250?–1305?), French poet, of whose life little is known beside the fact that he was in Orders and lived in Paris during the reign of Philippe le Bel. He may have been born at Meun-sur-Loire. He was much employed as a translator. He lives, however, as the author of a lengthy continuation of *Le Roman de la Rose* by Guillaume de Lorris (q.v.). The plot is adhered to, but the standpoint is given a complete twist, and cynical satire takes the place of romantic allegory. A contempt for the Church, for royalty and for women is uppermost in Jean de Meung's mind. He also wrote *Le Testament maistre Jehan de Meung*, a witty pseudo-autobiography. A good edition of his works is that by E. Méon (1814).

**Meurice, François Paul** (1818–1905), French playwright and novelist. Born in Paris, he took up political journalism, and as editor of Victor Hugo's *L'Évènement* was imprisoned in 1848. He adapted several of the novels of Hugo and George Sand (q.v.) for the stage, collaborating also with Gautier (*Falstaff*, 1842) (q.v.) and Dumas *père* (*Hamlet*, 1847). On his own account he wrote *Benvenuto Cellini* (1852) and *Fan-fan la Tulipe* (1858). He also brought out several novels, some under the name of Dumas, and others under his own name, which include *Les Tyrans de village* (1857), *Césara* (1869) and *Le Songe d'amour* (1889). He died in Paris.

**Mey, Lev Alexandrovich** (1822–1862), Russian dramatic poet. Born of a well-to-do family in Moscow, he is the author of *Tsarskaya nevesta* (1849; Eng. trans. *The Tsar's Bride*, 1914) and *Pskovityanka* (1860; Eng. trans. *The Pskov Maiden*, 1931), both of which provided libretti for Rimsky-Korsakov. Mey died of drink in Moscow.

**Meyer, Conrad Ferdinand** (1825–1898), Swiss poet, novelist and short-story writer. Born in Zürich of wealthy family, he grew up pampered and neurotic and was unable to find even an interest in anything, let alone do anything active. Another problem was that being bilingual in French and German he could not make up his mind which to use for literary expression, and it was not until the rise of Prussia in the mid 1860's that he finally decided in favour of German. When at length he broke into print with *Zwanzig Balladen von einem Schweizer* (1867) he showed great taste and a consummate mastery of language which is to be found in all his work. Of other books of poetry, *Huttens letzte Tage* (1871), about the death of Ulrich von Hutten (q.v.), the knight of the Reformation, is outstanding. The second part of his literary life is almost entirely confined to prose, the novel and long short story, above all exemplified in *Jürg Jenatsch* (1876), *Der Heilige* (1880; Eng. trans. *Thomas à Beckett*, 1885), *Die Hochzeit des Mönchs* (1884; Eng. trans. *The Monk's Marriage*, 1913), *Die Richterin* (1885) and *Die Versuchung des Pescara* (1887; Eng. trans. *The Tempting of Pescara*, 1890). All these works are historical with ecclesiastical themes predominating. Meyer died at Kilchberg. His collected works were published (14 vols.) in 1925.

**Michaëlis, Karin Marie Bech,** *née* **Brøndum** (1872–1950), Danish novelist. Born at Randers, she married the poet Sophus Michaëlis and gave up a musical career for letters. A fine psychologist, especially when dealing with children, her first considerable work was *Barnet* (1902; Eng. trans. *The Child: Andrea*, 1904), another excellent early book being *Trold* (1904; Eng. trans. *Little Troll*, 1946). But it was *Den farlige Alder* (1910; Eng. trans. *The Dangerous Age*, 1911), in which she describes a woman at the moment of her change of life, that gave her a European reputation, at the same time arousing a storm of protest from those who could not face its candour. She continued her literary career with such works as: *Elsie Lindtner* (1912; Eng. trans. 1912), *Grev Sylvains Hævn* (1913; Eng. trans. *The Governor*, 1913), *Don Juan—efter Døden* (1919), *Mette Trap og hendes Unger* (1922; Eng. trans. *Venture's End*, 1927), the excellent series about the little girl Bibi, *Bibi-Bøgerne* (1929; Eng. trans. *Bibi*, 1933; and *Bibi goes Travelling*, 1934), *Mor* (1935) and *Den grønne Ø* (1937; Eng. trans. *The Green Island*, 1938); and these are only the most outstanding of a very large output. She died at Thurø.

**Michaux, Henri** (1899–     ), Belgian poet and satirist, born at Namur, but educated and living in France. His work, which has been described as a kind of instantaneous dream photography full of rich flights of the imagination, includes: *Un Barbare en Asie* (1932; Eng. trans. 1949), *Voyage en Grande-Garabagne* (1936), *Plume* (1938), *Au pays de la magie* (1941), *Arbres des tropiques* (1942), *L'Espace du dedans* (1944; Eng. trans. *Selected Writings or The Space Within*, 1951), *Arriver à se réveiller* (1947), *Ailleurs* (1948), *Veille* (1951), *Tranches de savant* (1953), *L'Infini turbulent* (1957), *Paix dans les brisements* (1959) and *Connaissance par les gouffres* (1961). He is also an artist of talent.

Michelangelo, *see* Buonarotti.

Michelet, Jules (1798–1874), French prose-writer. Born in Paris, the son of a printer, his chance came when after the revolution of 1830 he was given a post in the Archives of France and made assistant to Guizot (q.v.), professor of history at the Sorbonne, and he gained the chair of history at the Collège de France in 1838. From then on until the seizure of power by Napoleon III in 1852 he worked as historian and as writer on social questions. His most ambitious work was the *Histoire de France*, begun in 1833 and completed in eighteen volumes in 1867. Other historical works are *Origines du droit français* (1837), *Mémoires de Luther* (1845) and *Le Procès des Templiers*, finished in 1851. As a social critic he showed himself to be an enthusiastic democrat, over-simplifying contemporary problems, and, as in *Le Prêtre, la femme et la famille* (1845), appealing to popular prejudice, in this case anti-clericalism. *Le Peuple* (1846) shows all the dangers of generous enthusiasms but little thinking. Then came the Empire, Michelet's refusal to take the oath of allegiance to Napoleon III and the loss of his appointments. He tried living in Brittany for a time, then settled on the Riviera and wrote several quasi-scientific books of much charm, for instance *L'Oiseau* (1856; Eng. trans. *The Bird*, 1874) and *La Mer* (1861; Eng. trans. *The Sea*, 1875), and another specimen of 'social philosophy', *La Bible de l'humanité* (1864). His *Histoire du dix-neuvième siècle* (3 vols., 1876) remained unfinished at his death at Hyères.

Mickiewicz, Adam Bernard (1798–1855), Polish poet, playwright and novelist. Born of a small landowning family at Zaosie, near Novogrodek, Lithuania, he became a schoolmaster at Kovno and published a book of verse, *Ballady i romanse* (1822), which may be accounted the beginning of the Polish romantic movement. Exiled to Russia for political reasons in 1824 he met Pushkin (q.v.) and visited the Crimea, which led to the beautiful sonnets inspired by nature, *Sonety krymskie* (1826). Under Pushkin's influence he now read Byron and Scott and wrote the poetic drama, *Dziady* ('Forefathers' Eve', completed 1827), and the two 'poetic' novels, *Grazyna* (1827) and *Konrad Wallenrod* (1828; Eng. trans. 1925). Allowed in 1829 to travel abroad he went to Rome where he wrote his masterpiece *Pan Tadeusz* (1834; Eng. trans. 1886, 1917 and 1932, Everyman's Library), a splendid account of Polish life about 1800. Appointed professor of Slavonic literature at the Collège de France in Paris in 1840, he was dismissed in 1844 for bringing political propaganda into his lectures. He died in Constantinople.

**Mikszáth, Kálmán** (1847–1910), Hungarian novelist, born at Szkla-bonya, held up his countrymen to kindly ridicule in *A jó palocok* (1882; Eng. trans. *The Good People of Palócz*, 1893) and *Szent Péter esernyője* (1895; Eng. trans. *St Peter's Umbrella*, 1900). He died in Budapest.

**Milosz, Oscar Wencelas de Lubicz** (1877–1939), French poet. Born at Czereïa, Lithuania, of an aristocratic family, he was Lithuanian consul-general in France from the proclamation of the republic until 1926. He then took out French naturalization and settled in Fontainebleau. He had been writing poetry from his early years, difficult in expression, exotic, very troubled. Examples of his work are to be found in *L'Amoureuse Initiation* (1910), *Miguel Nañara* (1912), *La Confession de Lémuel* (1926) and *Poèmes* (1938). He died at Fontainebleau.

**Mirandola, Giovanni Pico della** (1463–1494), Italian humanist writing in Latin. Born of noble family at Mirandola, near Modena, he was an infant prodigy, being accounted a scholar of standing at the age of ten. He studied at the universities of Paris, Bologna, Pavia and perhaps Padua, and set to work to try to reconcile Aristotelianism with Platonism, that bugbear of the schoolmen. By 1486 he had prepared his nine hundred theses, *De omni re scibili* ('Concerning all things knowable'), which were condemned as heretical by the Church, still the enemy of Platonism (1487). At the same time he composed his fine *Oratio de hominis dignitate* (1486). Exiled to France, he was back in Florence in 1488, and armed with his *Apologia* sought papal forgiveness, which was not acceded to till 1493, in which year Mirandola was persuaded by Savonarola (q.v.) to enter the Dominican Order. He died by poison in Florence. His *editio princeps* is that of 1495 (2 vols., best mod. ed., 1942).

**Mirbeau, Octave Henri Marie** (1850–1917), French novelist and playwright, was born at Trevières (Calvados). He soon moved to Paris, where he became known as a writer with strong left-wing ideas, employing a style at once crude and telling. His *Lettres de ma chaumière* (1886) gained him esteem which grew into notoriety when he followed it up with *Le Calvaire* (1887) and *Sébastien Roch* (1890), both bitterly anti-clerical, the latter a cruel attack on the Jesuits. He now turned to the stage and scored two outstanding successes, *Les Mauvais Bergers* (1897) and his withering attack on the immorality of big business, *Les Affaires sont les affaires* (1903; Eng. trans. *Business is Business*, 1905), undoubtedly his best work. Later novels are *Le Journal d'une femme de chambre* (1900; Eng. trans. *A Chambermaid's Diary*, 1934) and *Dingo* (1913). He died in Paris. His collected works appeared (9 vols.) in 1934–6.

**Miró, Gabriel** (1879–1930), Spanish novelist. Born in Alicante, he became a desultory lawyer and freelance journalist, slow, kindly and for ever burdened with domestic cares. His books, which are slow moving, deficient in dialogue and hardly well put together, contain on the other hand abundance of fine descriptive passages. Among these works the best are: *Las cerezas del cementerio* (1904), *El libro de Sigüenza* (1916), *Figuras de la Pasión de Nuestro Señor* (1916; Eng. trans. *Figures of the Passion of Our Lord*, 1924) and *Nuestro Padre San Daniel* (1921; Eng. trans. *Our Father Daniel*, 1930). He died in Madrid.

**Mistral, Joseph Étienne Frédéric** (1830–1914), French poet writing in Provençal. Born at Maillanne (Bouches du Rhône), he was educated at Avignon and then read law at the University of Aix-en-Provence. Deeply devoted to the restoration of Provençal literature, he in 1854 founded the Félibrige school for this end. His great rustic epic in verse, *Mirèio* (1859), on which Gounod based his opera *Mireille*, made him known throughout France, and he eventually became sharer of a Nobel Prize (1904). The best of his other works are *Calendau* (1867), *Lis Isclos d'or* (1875), *Nerto* (1884), *Lou Tresor doú Félibrige* (1885). a philological treasure-house of the *langue d'oc*, *Lou pouèmo doú Rose* (1897; Eng. trans. *The Song of the Rhône*, 1937) and *Moun Espelido, memòri e raconte* (1906; Eng. trans. *Memoirs of Mistral*, 1907), his autobiography. He died at Maillanne.

**Moberg, Carl Artur Vilhelm** (1898–      ), Swedish novelist. Born at Algutsboda, he has depicted town life as in *A. P. Rosell, bankdirektör* (1932), but his heart is with the peasants of Sweden, whether in the historical past, *Rid i Natt* (1941; Eng. trans. *Ride This Night!*, 1943) or at the present time, *Utvandrarna* (1949; Eng. trans. *The Emigrants*, 1956). Other notable works are: *Mans kvinna* (3 vols., 1933–9; Eng. trans. *Fulfilment*, 1953), *Soldat med brutet gevär* (1944; Eng. trans. *When I was a Child*, 1957), *Brudernas källa* (1946), *Den okända släkten* (1950), *Invandrarna* (1953; Eng. trans. *Unto a Good Land*, 1957), *Bönder på havet* (1954), *Nybyggarne* (1956) and *Sista brevet till Sverige* (1959), the last two in English translation as *The Last Letter Home* (1961).

**Moe, Jørgen Engebretsen** (1813–1882), Norwegian poet and writer of tales. Born at Hole, Ringerike, he became an ecclesiastic, later attaining the rank of Bishop of Kristiansand, where he died. He published two volumes of lyrics (1850 and 1855), but it is as the part collector with P. C. Asbjørnsen (q.v.) of *Norske folkeeventyr* (2 vols., 1842–4) that he is remembered. Many English translations have been made of this, sometimes including later collections, such as those of 1845–8, 1852 and 1871, which are by Asbjørnsen alone. Some of the translations are: *Popular Tales from the Norse* (1859), *Norwegian Fairy Tales* (1895), *Fairy Tales from the Far North* (1897) and *Norwegian Fairy Tales* (1924).

**Molière**, name used by **Jean-Baptiste Poquelin** (1622–1673), French dramatist. Born in Paris, the son of a well-to-do court upholsterer, who held the hereditary post of *valet-tapissier du roi*, he was educated at the Collège de Clermont, going on in 1641 to read law at the University of Orléans. He was expected to follow in his father's footsteps, but having inherited some money from his dead mother, decided to follow his true bent, the stage, and joined his friends, the

Béjart family, in founding a theatrical company, which they named the Illustre Théâtre in 1643, in Paris. Two years later, however, having met with scant success, they decided to tour the southern provinces, and after thirteen hard but growingly successful years were recalled to Paris to act under the patronage of Louis XIV's brother, the duc d'Orléans (1658), and were installed in the hall of the Petit-Bourbon, where Molière's *L'Étourdi*, written in 1653, was produced with success and made certain the troupe's permanency in the capital. This and other early works are thoroughly Italian in character, but with *Les Précieuses ridicules* (1659) Molière broke new ground, replacing the stock plots and characters of the *commedia dell'arte* with dramatized satire on French cultured life and society. Such is *Sganarelle, ou Le Cocu imaginaire* (1660) and *L'École des maris* (1661). His serious *comédie héroïque*, *Dom Garcie de Navarre, ou Le Prince jaloux* (1661), was not in his true vein and this style was not repeated. *Les Fâcheux* (1661) is the first of the court entertainments in which he employed ballet, but this is not typical of his great work. With *L'École des femmes* (1662), in verse, the first mature comedy in French literature, in which he deals with the part played by women in social life, he set out on his great and characteristic plays. It aroused much opposition, and from that time onwards Molière had to face the attacks of certain members of the court and of rival troupes such as those of the Théâtre du Marais and of the Hôtel de Bourgogne. His own actors, however, stood loyally at his side, and with his new headquarters at the Palais-Royal (where he remained till his death) and with the increasing interest of Louis XIV, who in 1665 replaced the duc d'Orléans as his patron, he had little to fear. His marriage, however, to Armande Béjart, a member of his company, and very young and flirtatious, in 1662, led to much unhappiness for him. He was now at the height of his genius, and in the following years produced a host of works, outstanding among which are: *Le Tartuffe, ou L'Imposteur*, in verse, an attack on religious hypocrisy, which answered not only the Jesuits but the Jansenists as well, first acted at Versailles in 1664, but not officially authorized until 1669, *Dom Juan ou Le Festin de pierre* (1665), in prose, a satire on free-thinking and loose living, soon withdrawn under pressure from the court but published in 1682 with his complete works in the changed climate of a court grown serious under the influence of Madame de Maintenon, *Le Misanthrope* (1666), in verse, a masterpiece of dramatic movement in spite of there being little or no action, *Georges Dandin* (1668), with its wonderful characterization of the man who marries above his station and suffers the consequences, *Amphitryon* (1668) and *L'Avare* (1668), in prose. A breakdown in Molière's health, probably tubercular, in 1665 brought him face to face with the medical profession, whom he mercilessly satirized for their pomposity and general ineffectiveness in *L'Amour Médecin* (1665) and *Le Médecin malgré lui* (1666). Not only was he managing, writing and acting during all this time, but he had to provide ballets and other entertainments for the court at Versailles, Chambord and Saint-Germain, typical of this work being *L'Impromptu de Versailles* (1663), *Les Plaisirs de l'Île Enchantée* (1664), a pageant, *Mélicerte* (1666), a pastoral, and *Pastorale comique* (1667), verses for a ballet. But even he had to rest (1668–9) while his lung trouble increased, and it was not until 1670 that in his *comédie-ballet, Le Bourgeois Gentilhomme*, he was able to show the world what he could still do so brilliantly. To 1671 belong *Psyché*, a *tragédie-ballet*, in which he collaborated with Quinault (q.v.) and Pierre Corneille (q.v.), and *Les Fourberies de Scapin*. His last great works were *Les Femmes savantes* (1672), in verse, a satire on affected learning, a subject on which he had touched with far less ability in the early *Les Précieuses ridicules*, on bluestockings, and *Le Malade imaginaire* (1673), a last jibe at the medical profession. Molière took the part of the invalid in the play, although suffering from slight pneumonia and, breaking a blood-vessel during an attack of coughing towards the end of the performance, died half an hour later in his house in the rue de Richelieu. The art of this supreme master of comedy rests above all on his amazing understanding of dramatic effect and his sharp perception of the basic ludicrousness of many human actions. Any faults of style—and there is little that is classical about it—are amply made up for by liveliness and naturalness. There is an early edition of his works by Lagrange and Vinot (1682), but the standard one is that by Despois and Mesnard (14 vols., 1873–1900). The best of English translations are those by A. R. Waller (8 vols., 1926), in which the French texts are also given. C. H. Wall's English translations (1901) are also worth looking at.

**Molina, Tirso de,** pseudonym of **Gabriel Téllez** (1584?–1648), Spanish dramatist and writer of fiction, was born in Madrid and took his vows as a friar in Guadalajara in 1601. He seems to have lived for some years in Santo Domingo in the West Indies and to have later resided in Barcelona, although he died at Soria. His first publication was an extraordinary miscellany, *Los cigarrales de Toledo* (1621), consisting of a treatise on the contemporary theatre, highly praising Lope de Vega (q.v.), whose style of drama Molina followed, plays and novels of varying quality. Then between 1624 and 1633 he published five volumes of plays, his best being *El burlador de Sevilla y convidado de piedra*, the first drama about Don Juan, *La prudencia en la mujer*, a chronicle play, and a religious play, *El condenado por desconfiado*. His second miscellany, *Deleitar aprovechando* (1635) is entirely religious in character. His work is to be found in the *Biblioteca de Autores Españoles* (vols. v and lviii) and *Nueva Biblioteca de Autores Españoles* (vols. iv and ix). There is a good critical edition of *La prudencia en la mujer* (ed. W. McFadden, 1933).

**Molinos, Miguel de** (1627–1696), Spanish devotional writer. Born of noble family at Muniesa, near Zaragoza, he was educated at Pamplona and Coimbra, took Orders and in 1669 went to Rome. There he published his excellently written *Guía espiritual* (1675; mod. crit. ed., 1906; Eng. trans. *The Spiritual Guide*, 1688; rev., 1907). It was not until 1687 that the Inquisition came to see in it the danger of quietism (i.e. denying man's free will, with God as the all-powerful Disposer), a doctrine running counter to the doctrine of Redemption as proposed by Augustine. Molinos was cited before the Holy Office and condemned to perpetual imprisonment in a monastery in Rome, where he died. 'Molinism' was, however, not so easily disposed of, and has remained a thorn in the flesh of orthodoxy until the present day.

**Möllhausen, Heinrich Balduin** (1825–1905), German novelist. Born at Jesuitenhof, near Bonn, he travelled widely, making use of his experiences as matter for his sensational, fast-moving novels of adventure, chief of them *Das Mormonenmädchen* (6 vols., 1864), *Der Hochlandpfeiffer* (6 vols., 1868), *Das Loggbuch des Kapitäns Eisenfänger* (3 vols., 1887) and *Kaptein Meerrose und ihre Kinder* (3 vols., 1893). Their mere length has killed them. Möllhausen died court librarian in Berlin.

**Molnár, Ferenc** (1878–1952), Hungarian novelist and playwright, was born in Budapest. The most widely known author produced by his country, he began his masterly fiction, set in cities, with *A Pál-utcai fiúk* (1907; Eng. trans. *The Paul Street Boys*, 1928) and *Rabok* (1907; Eng. trans. *Prisoners*, 1925) before turning to his well-constructed and well-written plays, of which the best are *A hattyú* (1926; Eng. trans. *The Swan*, 1929) and *Harmonia* (1932; Eng. trans. *Girl Unknown*, 1936). He had by this time settled in New York, where he died. The most outstanding of his later novels was *A zenélő angyal* (1933; Eng. trans. *Angel Making Music*, 1934). Superior as a playwright, all his dramatic works were translated into English in 1927.

**Mombert, Alfred** (1872–1942), German poet. Born in Karlsruhe, he wrote formless but exquisitely toned verse, such as 'Schlummerlied', derived from Max Dauthendey (q.v.), but whereas, writes Jethro Bithell, 'Dauthendey roams dream-rapt in his earthly paradise, Mombert, spellbound, floats through the vasty empyrean: he is lord of the cosmos he creates from chaos'. Among his many volumes the following may be listed: *Die Schöpfung* (1897), *Der Sonne-Geist* (1905), *Aeon von Syrakus* (1912), *Der Held der Erde* (1919) and *Aiglas Tempel* (1931). Persecuted as a Jew under Hitler, he managed to reach freedom from concentration camps, dying at Winterthur in Switzerland.

**Monnier, Henri Bonaventure** (1799–1877), French writer of sketches and light plays. Born in Paris, he began his career as an artist, publishing his work in magazines. Among his numerous publications in which he satirized the comfortable and pompous middle classes, inventing the prototype Monsieur Joseph Prudhomme, are: *Scènes populaires dessinées à la plume* (1830), *Nouvelles Scènes populaires* (1835), *Les Mémoires de M. Joseph Prudhomme* (2 vols., 1857), and the short witty plays, *Grandeur et décadence de M. Joseph Prudhomme* (1852) and *Le Roman chez la Portière* (1855). He died in Paris.

**Montaigne, Michel Eyquem de** (1533–1592), French essayist. Born at the Château de Montaigne, in the Dordogne, of a landed upper-middle-class family, he was carefully if eccentrically educated at home according to his father's particular precepts, and afterwards had his classical studies rounded off at the Collège de Guienne in the University of Bordeaux, where he had as a fellow student George Buchanan. He next studied law, and in 1555 succeeded his father as *advocat* of the Cour des Aides of Périgueux. Later he was a judge of the Parlement of Bordeaux. There he made the friendship of another judge called La Boëtie, who at his death not long afterwards bequeathed to Montaigne his valuable library. At first he made little use of it, and led a life of pleasure amounting at times to excess, as he records in his essays; but after his loveless marriage in 1565 he turned to study, and for his own use made a translation into French of a Latin treatise *Theologia Naturalis* by the Catalan Ramón Sebon, which he completed in 1568; and this led to an essay in scepticism, *L'Apologie de Raimond Sebon* (mod. ed., 1937), which shows him reaching a philosophical standpoint that he preserved for the rest of his life. In 1571, having succeeded to the family estates on the death of his father, he gave up his official posts, and retired to the Château de Montaigne to pursue a scholarly and contemplative life in his study in a tower which he had built. The result of this studious life was the famous *Essais* (he is the original essayist and he coined the word 'essay' in its literary sense), the first two volumes of which were published in 1580. But his sedentary life had brought on gout and kidney troubles, and in pursuit of health he visited Germany and Italy and their spas. His *Journal de Voyage*, an account of his journey, was for long lost and was not published till 1774 (mod. crit. ed., 1942; Eng. trans. 1929). Hearing while abroad of his election as mayor of Bordeaux, he returned in 1581 and held that office until 1585, his practical experience gained during those years going to broaden the scope of his third and final volume of *Essais* (1588). He died at the Château de Montaigne. The *Essais* (best mod. ed., 5 vols., 1906–33, other handy editions such as that by Thibaudet, 1934; Eng. trans. by J. Florio, 1603; C. Cotton, 1685; G. B. Ives, 1925; and Everyman's Library) are the earliest and finest of their kind in literature. Starting from the delightfully urbane lucubrations of a country gentleman they develop into the search for a philosophy. He takes the reader into his confidence without affectation or condescension, and his fairmindedness has made him the companion of men of all persuasions.

**Montale, Eugenio** (1896–      ), Italian poet. Born in Genoa, he attached himself to Ungaretti (q.v.) and the so-called 'hermetic'—one might rather call it 'philological'—school. Although they contain some distinguished pieces of poetry, his volumes, *Ossi di seppia* (1920–7), *Meriggi e ombre* (vol. i, 1922–4; vol. ii, 1926–7), *Da Mediterraneo* (1924), *La casa dei doganieri* (1932), *Le occasioni* (1928 and 1939) and *Finisterre* (1943) are spoilt by obscurity and a straining after the unusual. Much later, but as difficult as those before, is *La bufera e altro* (1956). A small man, silent, withdrawn and preoccupied, he lives a life of semi-seclusion. See the English translations *Poesie/Poems* (1964) and *Selected Poems* (1966).

**Montalembert, Charles Forbes René de** (1810–1870), French prose-writer, was born the son of a noble *émigré* and an English mother in London. He was educated in Fulham and lived for a time in Sweden and Ireland. In 1831 he went to Paris where in conjunction with Lamennais (q.v.) and Lacordaire he became known as a liberal but

yet ultramontane, educationalist. His modernistic approach to
Catholicism in the periodical *Avenir* led to his condemnation by
the Pope in 1831, after which he lived for a time in Germany. He
returned to France in 1835, wrote much which is hardly of literary
value, and lived a stormy political career, being in opposition to
Napoleon III from 1852 onwards. His most lasting work, written in
dignified prose, is his *Les Moines d'Occident* (5 vols., 1860–7, 5th ed.,
1893). His other most important publication was *L'Église libre dans
l'état libre* (1863), in which he discusses the problems of the Church
in an increasingly democratic world. He died in Paris.

**Montchrestien, Antoine de** (1575?–1621), French dramatist. Born of
noble Huguenot family at Falaise, he led a wild youth and had to
escape to England where he remained for some time, flourishing
there as a cutler. His best work by far is the tragedy, *L'Écossaise*
(1601; mod. ed., 1905), about Mary Queen of Scots. Among his other
plays is *Hector* (1604), after which date he wrote no more. He was
killed fighting against the Catholics at Tourailles, near Falaise.
There is an edition of his tragedies by L. Petit (1901).

**Montemayor, Jorge de** (1520?–1561), Spanish pastoral novelist. Born
the son of a Portuguese Jewish silversmith at Montemor-o-Velho, he
went early to Spain to seek his fortune and held a post at court.
He wrote some poetry, both secular and religious, but owes his
reputation solely to his pastoral novel (the first in Spanish), *La
Diana* (1559; mod. crit. ed., 1946; Eng. trans. T. Wilson, 1596,
repr., 1920; and B. Young, 1598), couched in a quiet, smooth prose. It
was one of the most popular works of its day, not only in Spain but
in France and England, and had undoubted influence on Sir Philip
Sidney's *Arcadia*. A small number of charming lyrics are to be found
in *El cancionero del poeta Jorge de Montemayor* (mod. ed., 1932). He
was killed in a duel in Italy.

**Montesquieu, Charles-Louis de Secondat de La Brède et de** (1689–
1755), French prose-writer. Born of noble family at the Château de
La Brède, near Bordeaux, he read law and became an advocate of
the Parlement of Bordeaux in 1714 and president two years later, in
his leisure time devoting himself to scientific pursuits, both physics
and physiology. Soon this man of inquiring mind turned his attention
to the state of his own country, and in his *Lettres Persanes* (1721;
mod. crit. ed., 1929), damagingly satirized the corrupt state of
French manners under the Orléans Regency. The brilliant success of
the *Lettres* led him to Paris, where he fell in for a time with the
sceptical ways of free-thinking society and produced two works, *Le
Temple de Gnide* (1725) and *Le Voyage à Paphos* (1727), in which he
shrewdly commented on the shallow opinions then floating on the
fashionable air and which he daily heard; for while seeming to be a
thorough-paced hedonist in *Le Temple*, he saw through such an
attitude, and chose the title of *Le Voyage* as a commentary on the
court's attitude of make-believe rather than face reality, as Watteau
had done in his *Cythère* picture. His travels in Europe and especially
his visit to Britain (1729–31) were the turning point of his life. The
British constitution seemed to provide the answer to France's

problems, while as a result of his varied experiences his awareness of comparisons between different nations was sharpened. Returning to France, he passed his time between his estates at La Brède and Paris. His *Considérations sur la cause de la grandeur des Romains et de leur décadence* (1734) was the first-fruit of his widened view of history; here was a prime example of a great nation and empire destroyed because the virtues of that nation had been lost. Those who felt so inclined might also interpret this as a reflection on France. Environmentalism as preached by Locke, the gathering together of data as exemplified by Bayle (q.v.), uninhibited criticism in which Le Clerc (q.v.) had shown the way, all these are facets of his brightly written *L'Esprit des lois* (1748; Eng. trans. 1793; rev. ed., 2 vols., 1896-7), a great marshalling of facts with masterly deductions, a herald of the *Encyclopédie* and of the Enlightenment, a veritable gold-mine for the intellectual middle classes, now growing to the height of their importance, to make use of for the improvement, not the destruction, of society. Montesquieu died blind in Paris. See his *Œuvres* (7 vols.), 1875-9. An English translation of his complete works came out in 1777.

**Montherlant, Henry de** (1896– ), French novelist and playwright. Born at Neuilly of good family, he found himself plunged into the First World War at eighteen. Afterwards, following the cult of self-expression and D'Annunzio's (q.v.) self-conscious religion of virility and violence, he went big-game hunting in Africa and bull-fighting in Spain, his enthusiasm for such 'manly' exercises being extinguished after an unsatisfactory encounter with a bull in the ring. He now turned his self-assertiveness from animals to books, and developed a philosophy of aloofness and sensualism as an end in itself, with women as instruments to that end and nothing more, but all the same a sense of duty to oneself and the *élite*, which latter is all that is worthy of preservation in society. Those who fail their class by faults of character, or lack of it, are mercilessly attacked. The influence of Nietzsche (q.v.) is also present in the rejection of pity. His work includes: *La Relève du matin* (1920; Eng. trans. 1951), *Les Olympiques* (1924), *Chant funèbre pour les morts de Verdun* (1924), *Les Bestiaires* (1926; Eng. trans. *The Bullfighters*, 1927), *Les Célibataires* (1934; Eng. trans. *Lament for the Death of an Upper Class*, 1935 and 1960), *Les Jeunes Filles* (2 vols., 1935-9; Eng. trans. of vol. i, *Pity for Women*, 1937; of vol. ii, *The Lepers*, 1940), and the plays, *La Reine morte* (1942), *Malatesta* (1946; Eng. trans. 1962) and *Le Maître de Santiago* (1947; Eng. trans. 1962). Other novels are: *Croire aux âmes* (1944), *La Vie amoureuse de M. de Guiscart* (1946), *Pages d'amour de la Rose de Sable* (1948), *Histoire d'amour de la Rose de Sable* (1951; Eng. trans. *Desert Love*, 1957), *Les Auligny* (1956), *La Muse libertine* (1957) and *Le Chaos et la nuit* (1963; Eng. trans. *Chaos and Night*, 1964). His *Carnets, 1935-1939* (1947) and *Carnets, 1942-1943* (1948) are of great autobiographical interest.

**Monti, Vincenzo** (1754-1828), Italian poet and prose-writer. Born at Alfonsine, in the Romagna, he became a member of the Arcadian Academy in Rome, in which city he held librarianships and secretaryships. He showed his anti-French Revolution feelings in his poem in defence of Louis XVI, *La Bassvilliana* (1793). By 1800 he was ready to praise Bonaparte in *La Mascheroniana*, and this served him well in helping him to obtain a chair at Pavia. His translation of the *Iliad* (1810) is regarded as an Italian classic. He died in Milan. His *Opere* appeared (6 vols.) in 1839–43, and there is a modern edition of his *Tragedie, poemetti e liriche* (1927).

**Móra, Ferenc** (1879–1934), Hungarian novelist, born at Kiskun-félegyháza, and known for his fictional work dealing with the countryside, *Ének a búzamezőkről* (1927; Eng. trans. *Song of the Wheatfields*, 1930). He died at Szeged.

**Morais, Francisco de** (1500?–1572), Portuguese novelist. Nothing is known of his early life, but he was appointed for a time treasurer of the household to King John III of Portugal, and in 1540 was a member of the ambassadorial staff in Paris, where he fell in love with a court lady, did not prosper in his suit, and later on in retirement wrote a romantic knightly novel, revealing in the course of it strong anti-feminist feelings. This is *Primeira e segunda parte do Palmeirim de Inglaterra* (1567; mod. ed. as *Crônica de Palmeirim de Inglaterra*, 1946; Eng. trans. *The History of Prince Palmerin of England*, by Anthony Munday, 1609 and emended by Robert Southey, 4 vols., 1807). Morais was murdered at Évora.

**Morales, Tomás** (1885–1921), Spanish poet. Born in the Canary Islands at Moya. His work is sturdy and full of the sea, and is contained in *Poemas de la gloria, del amor y del mar* (1908) and *Las rosas de Hércules* (second and full ed., 1922), in the latter the added attraction of undertones of the classical world. He died at Las Palmas.

**Morand, Paul** (1888–    ), French novelist and short-story writer, was born in Paris and became a diplomat (see *Journal d'un attaché d'ambassade*, 1948). He first gained recognition as a literary figure with his books about the hectic life of the twenties: *Ouvert la nuit* (1922; Eng. trans. *Open all Night*, 1923), *Fermé la nuit* (1923; Eng. trans. *Closed all Night*, 1924), *Lewis et Irène* (1924; Eng. trans., 1925), *L'Europe galante* (1925; Eng. trans. *Europe at Love*, 1926) and *L'Innocente à Paris* (1927). Later he developed into a writer who found inspiration, as did many authors of his generation, in his varied travels. Examples of this kind of fiction are: *Rien que la terre* (1926; Eng. trans. *Earth Girdled*, 1928), *Bouddha vivant* (1927; Eng. trans. 1927), *Magie noire* (1928; Eng. trans. 1929), *Nœuds coulants* (1928), *Hiver caraïbe* (1929), *Champions du monde* (1930; Eng. trans. *World Champions*, 1931), *Flèche d'Orient* (1932; Eng. trans. *Orient Air Express*, 1932), *Air indien* (1932; Eng. trans *Indian Air*, 1933) and *London* (1933; Eng. trans. *A Frenchman's London*, 1934), which was followed by the collection of long short stories *Je brûle Moscou* (1934), full-length narratives being continued with, among others, *Mes débuts* (1934), *Les Extravagants* (1936), *L'Homme pressé* (1941), *Propos de 52 semaines* (1942) and *Milady* (1944). Since the war he has published another collection of long short stories, *À la fleur* *d'orangier* (1946), and the novels, *Montociel, rajah aux grandes Indes* (1946; Eng. trans. 1962), *Le Flagellant de Séville* (1951; Eng. trans. 1953), *L'Eau sous les ponts* (1954), *La Folle Amoureuse* (1956), *Fin de siècle* (1957) and *Le Prisonnier de Cintra* (1958).

**Moratín, Leandro Fernández de** (1760–1828), Spanish playwright, poet and translator. Born in Madrid, the son of Nicolás (q.v.), he was apprenticed to a goldsmith, but on his father's death was helped by Jovellanos (q.v.) who procured for him a post in the Spanish embassy in Paris, where he imbibed 'enlightened' ideas and was taken up by the dictator Godoy, who employed him on various diplomatic missions. It is as the only Spanish writer who can be said to have succeeded in acclimatizing the French comedy to his country's stage that Moratín is noteworthy, and his two masterpieces, *La comedia nueva* (1792), in which he mocks at Spanish dramatic traditions perpetuated by writers who hardly understand the meaning of those traditions, and *El sí de las niñas* (1805), in which he confronts the older with the younger generation, judging in favour of the latter, are inimitable. Throughout his life he wrote a great deal of fugitive poetry, none of it of the first quality. As a translator of Molière (q.v.) into Spanish he was excellent. As a translator of Shakespeare he was less good. He welcomed the French invaders in 1807, seeing in them, as did other Spanish intellectuals, the means by which an end could be made of monarchical and clerical reaction. He became librarian to Joseph Bonaparte in Madrid, left when the French did in 1813, returned to Spain for a time, but fearing the reinstated Inquisition left his country for good in 1814 and died in Paris. A reserved, gloomily inclined, timorous person, he was a close friend of Goya, who painted a memorable character-study portrait of him. His works appear in *Biblioteca de Autores Españoles*, vol. ii. A good modern edition of his *Teatro* is that by R. Morcuende (1924).

**Moratín, Nicolás Fernández de** (1737–1780), Spanish poet and dramatist. Born in Madrid he intended to pursue a legal career, but took to writing instead, and in his *Desengaños al teatro español* (1763) led the way in modernizing the Spanish stage and ridding it of the remnants of clericalism which the *autos sacramentales* (or religious morality plays) had become, seeking at the same time to replace traditional Spanish dramatic style by a French one; but he was far too Spanish himself to be able to practise what he preached, and his trilogy, *Lucrecia* (1763), *Hermesinda* (1777) and *Guzmán el Bueno* (1777), is little more than unfelt posturing. Similarly his comedies had no life. It is only as the poet of 'Fiesta de toros en Madrid' and 'Oda a Pedro Romero' that he can be said to survive at all. He died in Madrid. His complete works are to be found in the *Biblioteca de Autores Españoles*, vol. ii.

**Moravia, Alberto,** pseudonym of **Alberto Pincherle** (1907–    ), Italian novelist. Born in Rome the son of an architect, he suffered much from ill-health in youth, but in his enforced leisure read widely and became master of several languages. He took up journalism in Turin and was at one time a foreign correspondent in London. A disillusioned, even cynical, writer, he gained recognition with *Gli indifferenti* (1929; Eng. trans. *The Indifferent Ones*, 1932), following this up with *La bella vita* (1935), but became more and more involved in politics until his books were banned by the Fascists and he was forced to go into hiding until the British victories (1944). *La mascherata* (1941; Eng. trans. *The Fancy Dress Party*, 1947) had in the meantime been published, and this was now followed up in quick succession by *Agostino* (1944; Eng. trans. 1947), *La Romana* (1947; Eng. trans. *The Woman of Rome*, 1949), his best known book, an uncompromisingly realistic work about a prostitute, *Disubbidienza* (1948; Eng. trans. *Disobedience*, 1950), *L'amore congiugale* (1949; Eng. trans. *Conjugal Love*, 1951), *Il conformista* (1951; Eng. trans. *The Conformist*, 1952), *Il disprezzo* (1954; Eng. trans. *A Ghost at Noon*, 1955) and *Racconti romani* (1954; Eng. trans. *Roman Stories*, 1956). His style is undistinguished, but his dialogue is good and he has a power of narrative.

**Morax, René** (1873–1963), Swiss playwright, born at Morges. He built the Théâtre du Jorat at Mézières, in the canton of Vaud, which became the centre of Swiss dramatic activity, and here he infused new life into the stage of his country with his own productions, such as *La Nuit des Quatre-Temps* (1901), *La Dîme* (1903) and *Guillaume Tell* (1914). Later plays, more and more spectacular and often with musical accompaniment, were *Le Roi David* (1921) and *Charles le Téméraire* (1944). He died at Morges.

**Moréas, Jean,** pseudonym of **Jannis Papadiamantopoulos** (1856–1910), French poet of Greek birth from Athens, who settled in Paris in 1880. He set out as a symbolist with *Les Syrtes* (1884), but withdrew and turned back to classical forms and clear and incisive thought, which he realized were fatally lacking in the work of the symbolists. His books of verse, such as *Énone au clair visage* (1893), *Sylves* (1894), *Sylves nouvelles* (1895) culminating in *Les Stances* (final version, 1905), reveal his gradual path towards self-discipline in thought and form. He died in Paris.

**Morgenstern, Christian** (1871–1914), German poet. Born into a family of artists in Munich, he was of delicate health for the whole of his short life. There are two characteristics to be seen in his work, the first a playing about with, a 'prodding' of words, which he juggles with as if to find out whether as symbols of life and thought they have any meaning, and whether in fact life itself has any definite meaning, and the second the love element which came to fruition at the end of his life in his association with Margarete Gosebruch. His most notable books are *Ich und die Welt* (1898), *Ein Sommer* (1899), *Einkehr* (1910), *Ich und Du* (1911) and *Wir fanden einen Pfad* (1914). He died at Meran.

**Mörike, Eduard Friedrich** (1804–1875), German poet and prose-writer, born at Ludwigsburg, the son of a physician, and educated at Tübingen. His love affair while a student with a strange, unbalanced girl, Maria Meyer, was a failure, but was the spring-board which was to plunge him into his poetry. He unwillingly entered the Lutheran Church and in 1834 was appointed vicar of Cleversulzbach, but from the start he disliked his work, spent as much time as was decently possible roaming the countryside, and dreaded preaching so much that he was continually malingering. In 1838 appeared *Gedichte*, probably the most uniformly excellent collection of lyrics in the German language, containing such gems as 'Jung-Volker', 'Das verlassene Mädchen', 'Agnes', 'Schön-Rohtraut' and 'Ein Stündlein wohl vor Tag'. Hallmarks of his verse are simplicity, absolute fidelity of diction and fitness of expression, nature being won into service as a mirror of the passions, as in Eichendorff (q.v.), but with even greater delicacy. In *Klassische Blumenlese* (1840) he is less successful, being hindered by adherence to classical metres. As a prose-writer he had already published *Maler Nolten* (2 vols., 1832), a rambling, formless novel, though studded with passages akin to the lyric beauties of his verse. He succeeded, however, in prose-works of smaller compass, especially in the fairy-tale, *Das Stuttgarter Hutzelmännlein* (1853), and above all in that classic of the long short story, the gem *Mozart auf der Reise nach Prag* (1856; Eng. trans. *Mozart on the Way to Prague*, 1934), to read which is an unforgettable experience. He had retired from his clerical life with a very small pension (1843), and having at last attempted marriage—he had been on the brink of it before—found himself (1851) forced to supplement his income as a schoolmaster, in Stuttgart, teaching girls literature. He wrote practically nothing after 1856 except letters to his many literary friends, including Theodor Storm (q.v.). His marriage, owing to the intrigues of his sister, was a disaster, and was terminated in 1872. Mörike died in Stuttgart. His collected works appeared in three volumes in 1909–14.

**Moritz, Karl Philipp** (1756–1793), German prose-writer. Born at Hamelin of simple family, he was in turn actor, schoolmaster and clergyman. He had already tried his hand at a novel, *Blunt, oder der Gast* (1781), when he paid his visit to England in 1782, which he immortalized in his *Reisen eines Deutschen in England* (1792; Eng. trans. *Travels . . . through Several Parts of England in 1782*, 1795; reprinted Cassell's National Library, 1886). In these keenly observant and charmingly ingenuous letters to his friend Gedike he has produced a short travel book of rare quality, at the same time revealing himself as an unusually attractive person. On his return to Germany he became a literary journalist and began the masterly novel *Anton Reiser, ein psychologischer Roman* (4 vols., 1785–90; Eng. trans. 1926), autobiographical and almost modern in its handling of character. Meanwhile he had gone to Italy in 1786, where he met Goethe, and was inspired to make an interesting contribution to aesthetics, *Über die bildende Nachahmung des Schönen* (1788), as a result of the impact which Italian art had made on him. This and Goethe's support procured for him a post at the Academy of Arts in Berlin (1789). He married on the strength of it, but a settled life was not for such a wanderer as he. After tiring himself out travelling in Italy again and producing *Reisen eines Deutschen in Italien* (1792–3) he returned to Berlin, only to die.

**Mosen, Julius** (1803–1867), German man of letters. Born at Marieney, he was trained as a lawyer and set up in practice in Dresden, but finished his career as a theatre-director in Oldenburg. Best known as a lyric poet inspired by oppressed nationalistic movements, his principal works are *Das Lied vom Ritter Wahn* (1831), the novel *Der Kongress zu Verona* (2 vols., 1842) and *Bilder im Moose* (2 vols., 1849). His *Sämtliche Werke* were published (6 vols.) in 1880.

**Möser, Justus** (1720–1794), German prose-writer. Born at Osnabrück, he was an important official in the town's administration. With Herder (q.v.) and Goethe he was the third collaborator in *Von deutscher Art und Kunst* (1773), which is generally considered the manifesto of the *Sturm und Drang* movement. Möser slanted his contribution to the historian's standpoint, regarding Germany's medieval past as a glorious one but a lost ideal, and it was in conformity with Herder's evolutionist theory that he wrote his excellent piece of local history *Osnabrückische Geschichte* (1768). In his other considerable book, *Patriotische Phantasien* (1774), he is stridently against eighteenth-century rationalism and already looks forward to something approaching romanticism. His *Über die deutsche Sprache und Literatur* (1787) is interesting as a survey of the German language and literature at so formative a period and as being written by one who had been in the thick of the movement which transformed them. He died at Osnabrück.

**Müller, Friedrich,** known as 'Maler' ('Artist') **Müller** (1749–1825), German poet and dramatist. Born at Kreuznach of simple parentage, he was enabled by patrons to train as an artist, and had already set up his studio in Mannheim when in 1775 he met Goethe, who discovered that he had also written poetry, and encouraged him to publish. The result was the appearance that same year of three idylls in the manner of Gessner (q.v.), *Der Faun, Der erschlagene Abel* and *Der Satyr Mopsus*. After another idyll, *Die Schafschur* (1776), his best work, Müller became a firm adherent of the *Sturm und Drang*, his drama, *Fausts Leben dramatisiert* (1778), depicting in Shakespearean terms the struggle of a man to gain the mastery of life. In 1778 he left Germany for good and settled in Rome, painting a little, acting as a guide to visitors and continuing a desultory literary career, completing the drama *Golo und Genoveva*, begun in 1775, in 1781. It was not, however, published until 1811, in which year another idyll, *Das Nusskernen*, written in 1774, also appeared, together with the rest of his works in three volumes. He died in Rome. A selective edition of his writings was made by M. Oeser (2 vols., 1916).

**Müller, Johannes von** (1752–1809), Swiss prose-writer. Born at Schaffhausen, he studied at Göttingen, and from 1774 to 1780 was a schoolmaster in Geneva. In 1786 he was appointed librarian to the elector of Mainz, at once beginning to publish his *Geschichte schweizerischer Eidgenossenschaft*, at which he had been at work for some time, and of which he completed the fifth and last volume in 1808 (new ed., 1826). In 1804 he was appointed Royal Historiographer of Prussia, and in 1807 Napoleon appointed him a secretary of state for Westphalia. He died at Cassel. Müller's history of Switzerland is the first historical work in German with claims to literary quality. It was eagerly read by Schiller (q.v.) and the graphic treatment of the subject by Müller suggested to him his drama of *Wilhelm Tell*. A striking feature of Müller's work are his powerful descriptions of nature, which he as it were sets up as a backcloth.

**Müller, Wilhelm** (1794–1827), German poet. Born at Dessau, he went to Berlin, before long making his name with his lyrics on Greece, *Lieder der Griechen* (5 vols., 1821–4). Piquancy was added to them by the fact that the Greek War of Independence was just taking place. They have not stood the test of time, ringing hollow now and unbearably monotonous. It is by his two collections of charmingly fresh lyrics and song cycles, *Siebenundsiebzig Gedichte aus den hinterlassenen Papieren eines reisenden Waldhornisten* (2 vols., 1821–4) and *Lyrische Reisen und epigrammatische Spaziergänge* (1827), that he is particularly remembered. His love of the Mediterranean lands was at last worthily celebrated in the cycle, *Lieder aus dem Meerbusen von Salerno* (1827). His immortality is assured as the author of the *Müllerlieder* and *Winterreise* set to music by Schubert. He died at Dessau. He was the father of the philologist Max Müller.

**Müllner, Gottfried Adolf** (1774–1829), German dramatist. Born at Langendorf, near Weissenfels, he became an advocate at Weissenfels and built his own private theatre there. He had a taste for the exaggeratedly macabre, and after winning recognition with *Der 29. Februar* (1812), a fate drama, in which he leaned heavily on Zacharias Werner (q.v.), he gained enormous success with *Die Schuld* (1815; Eng. trans. *Guilt*, 1819), a lurid melodrama in verse, first produced in Vienna. Further plays in the same style, such as *König Yngurd* (1818) and *Die Albaneserin* (1820), failed. His collected dramatic works were published (7 vols.) in 1828. He died at Weissenfels.

**Multatuli,** pseudonym of **E. D. Dekker** (1820–1887), Dutch novelist, born in Amsterdam. In 1838 he entered the service of the Dutch East India Company in Java, became an unsparing critic of the administration, and, siding with the natives against the Dutch government there, was suddenly dismissed. His best-known novel, *Max Havelaar* (2 vols., 1860; Eng. trans. 1927), while so extremely biased against the European as to be unjust, yet springs to life by reason of its burning hatred of exploitation of the Javanese. His only other work which calls for notice is his autobiographical novel *De Geschiedenis van Woutertje Pieterse* (written some time before 1877; ed., 1890; Eng. trans. *Walter Pieterse; a Story of Holland*, 1904). He died at Nieder-Ingelheim.

**Munk, Kaj Harald Leininger** (1898–1944), Danish playwright and essayist. Born at Maribo, he became a clergyman in Jutland and was a most successful and highly esteemed dramatist. Outstanding are *En Idealist* (1928), about Herod the Great, *Ordet* (1932), *Sejren* (1936), *Pilatus* (1937), *Niels Ebbesen* (1942), *Ewalds Død* (1943), about the great Danish poet (q.v.), and *Før Cannae* (1943), with its theme of humanism faced with brute force. *Ved Babylons Floder* (1941; Eng. trans. *By the Waters of Babylon*, 1945) is a good example of his straight prose. As an active member of the Resistance movement in Denmark against the Germans, he was murdered by them near his vicarage at Hørbylunde, near Silkeborg. Translations of his writings are to be found in R. P. Keigwin's *Kaj Munk, Playwright, Priest and Patriot* (1944).

**Muñoz Seca, Pedro** (1881–1936), Spanish playwright. Born at Santa María, near Cadiz, he wrote brilliant farces, such as *El contrabando* (1904), parodies of pretentious dramas, such as *La venganza de Don Mendo* (1918) and satires of empty plays, like *Los extremeños se tocan* (1926). He was murdered in Madrid at the beginning of the civil war.

**Muntaner, Ramón** (1265–1336), Catalan chronicler. He may have been born in Barcelona, but what is certain about his life is that he was a soldier, took part in various Catalan expeditions to the Levant, settled in Valencia about 1325 and wrote his *Chrónica, o descripció dels fets, e hazanyes del inclyt rey Don Iaume primer Rey Daragó* (first printed, 1558; Eng. trans. *The Chronicle of Muntaner*, 1920). It is written with such enthusiasm that, like an adventure story, it carries the reader away. It is a document of the greatest value.

**Munthe, Axel** (1857–1949), Swedish prose-writer. Born at Oskarshamm, he became a physician, wandered about the world and wrote in English *Memories and Vagaries* (1908; rev. ed., 1930), *Red Cross and Iron Cross* (1917) and that remarkable self-revelation of a proud, retired, pessimistic, nature-loving man, *The Story of San Michele* (1929), composed in the fastness of his beautiful Italian villa on Capri. He died in Stockholm.

**Muratori, Lodovico Antonio** (1672–1750), Italian scholar, born at Vignola, Modena, was appointed, after taking Orders, Ambrosian librarian at Milan (1695), and five years later ducal librarian and archivist at Modena. After writing two short works, *Della perfetta poesia italiana* (1706) and *Riflessioni sopra il buon gusto* (1708), which wielded an enormous influence on Italian letters, he spent the rest of his life on historical research of the most exacting kind, the flower of all this labour being *Rerum italicarum scriptores* (27 vols., 1723–38; supplementary vol., 1751), a collection of medieval documents of the highest value, edited with great ability, and *Antiquitates italicae medii aevi* (6 vols., 1738–43), containing learned treatises on the social history of medieval Italy. He then turned to the task of writing a general history of Italy from early Christian times to the present, *Annali d'Italia* (12 vols., 1744–9), which occupied him almost up to the time of his death in Modena.

**Murger, Henry** (1822–1861), French novelist. Born in Paris, he tried his hand at painting, learning very early what it was like to be down and out but buoyed up by youthful optimism in the Latin Quarter. After a spell as secretary to Alexander Tolstoy he became a freelance journalist and began in 1847 to publish his *Scènes de la vie de Bohème* as a serial which was completed in 1849 (Eng. trans. *The Latin Quarter*, in French Novels of the Nineteenth Century, vol. ii, 1901). The same year it was dramatized and in this form provided the libretto for Puccini's *La Bohème*. He had created a world founded on fact, but, as Haussmann's Paris encroached on the old quarters, his world of *grisettes* and students and a happy-go-lucky life of garrets and narrow streets of tottering old houses became a world of golden nostalgia. All France wanted more. Murger provided it fitfully and waywardly in such works as *Claude et Marianne* (1851), *Le Pays latin* (1851), *Adeline Protat* (1853), *Le Roman de toutes les femmes* (1854), *Les Buveurs d'eau* (1855), *Le Dernier Rendezvous* (1856), *Le Sabot rouge* (1860) and *Le Serment d'Horace* (1861). But he was falling more and more into a life of dissipation, and died destitute in a public hospital in Paris. Several more volumes by him were published posthumously, the best being the wistful and graceful book of poetry *Les Nuits d'hiver* (1864; some in Eng. trans. in *Ballads and Lyrics of Old France* by Andrew Lang, 1872).

**Musäus, Johann Karl August** (1735–1787), German novelist and story-writer. Born at Weimar, he read theology at Jena, but was refused a pastorship having been seen dancing in public. He was a tutor at the ducal court of Weimar (1763) and became a schoolmaster there in 1770. Already he had attracted attention in the literary world with his parody of Richardson's *Sir Charles Grandison*, the novel *Grandison der Zweite* (1760). A second novel, *Physiognomische Reisen* (1779), satirizes the works on physiognomy by Lavater (q.v.). But it is as a writer of fairy-tales and folk stories that he has the largest claim to be remembered. These are known collectively as *Die Volksmärchen der Deutschen* and appeared between 1782 and 1786 (see T. Carlyle's *German Romance*, 1826, for rather second-rate trans. of some of these tales). He returned to the satirical novel with *Freund Heins Erscheinungen in Holbeins Manier* (1785), and at his sudden death at Weimar left a further volume of tales, *Straussfedern*, unfinished.

**Musil, Robert** (1880–1942), Austrian novelist. Born at Klagenfurt, he owed his, for the most part, posthumous reputation to the enormous rambling novel *Der Mann ohne Eigenschaften* (3 vols., 1930–43, Eng. trans. *The Man without Qualities*, 3 vols., 1953–60), describing the thoughts and standpoint of 'the average man' in the last stages of the Habsburg regime. His other works, *Die Vermirrungen des Zöglings Törless* (1906; Eng. trans. *Young Törless*, 1955), *Vereinigungen* (1911), *Die Schwärmer* (1921) and *Drei Frauen* (1924), are of quite secondary importance. He died in Geneva.

**Musset, Louis-Charles-Alfred de** (1810–1857), French poet and dramatist. Born in Paris, the son of a War Office official, he grew up spoilt and idle yet brilliant. He tried studying first law and then medicine, gave up both and turned his attention to literature. Here his wit, charm and physical attractiveness were of the greatest value, for they made easy his entry into the literary *salons*. By 1828 he had gained the friendship of Victor Hugo (q.v.) and was the spoilt darling of literary society. His first book of poetry, *Contes d'Espagne et d'Italie* (1830), was well received and was in the high romantic manner, but he was too particular in his taste to care for the full blare of romanticism; what appealed to him was Byronic disdain and a well-bred eighteenth-century clarity, which he could, however, only command when not carried away by gusts of passion coming from his super-sensitive nature. His second volume of poetry, *Un Spectacle*

*dans un fauteuil* (1832), is thus a step away from the full romanticism
of Hugo. But he needed a deep emotional experience to bring out the
true poet in him, and this he found in his short and disastrous liaison
with George Sand (q.v.) ending in their angry parting in Venice early
in 1835. This breakdown of the great love affair of his life led to his
best poetry, some of the most memorable in French romantic literature, *Les Nuits* (1835–7), which includes 'Nuit de décembre', 'Nuit de
mai' and 'Nuit d'août'. It was at this time also that he began the series
of *Poésies nouvelles* with such outstanding pieces as *Lettre à Lamartine*
(1836) and *L'Espoir en Dieu* (1838). He had meanwhile written
several plays. His first, *La Nuit vénitienne* (1830) had been a failure,
but in *André del Sarto* (1833) and *Les Caprices de Marianne* (1833)
he produced exquisite tragi-comedies. *Fantasio* (1834) and *On ne badine
pas avec l'amour* (1834) are also excellent plays in their way, and he
gathered some more together as *Comédies et proverbes* in 1840. He
was already at thirty an old young man, excessive in sexual adventures and in drinking, broken in health and prone to something
resembling epilepsy. His appointment as librarian to the Home
Office in 1838 did something to arrest his downward course for a
time, but in the end he lost interest in the work. He had already by
fits and starts completed his very personal and attractive *Confession
d'un enfant du siècle* (1836). The one bright spot in his life in the
forties was the increasing interest of the public in his dramatic works.
Since the failure of *La Nuit vénitienne*, none had been staged but only
printed in magazines; now they were produced at the Comédie
Française with acclaim. Encouraged, he wrote a few more, such as
*Il faut qu'une porte soit ouverte ou fermée* (1842) and *Un Caprice*
(1847). By 1852 he had brought his collection of *Poésies nouvelles* to
an end; by 1855 his *Nouvelles Comédies et proverbes*. The last were
sorrowful years, to which period belongs the story of a meeting of the
Academy at which, when the poet's name was called and there was
no reply, one of his fellow academicians mockingly answered:
'Absynthe (absent)'. He died of heart disease in Paris. See his
*Œuvres complètes* (3 vols., 1933–8).

**Mussolini, Benito** (1883–1945), Italian politician and prose-writer.
Born at Predappio, he was an accomplished journalist who found
time from his almost overwhelming career to write such virile prose
works as: *Il mio diario di guerra* (1923), *Roma antica sul mare* (1926),
*Vita di Arnaldo* (1932) and *Storia di un anno* (1948; Eng. trans. *The
Mussolini Memoirs 1942–43*, 1949). He also produced a novel and a
play of no particular value. Deposed from the headship of the Italian
state in 1943, he was executed at Dongo, near Lake Como, by partisans.

**Nabokov, Vladimir Vladimirovich,** also writing under the pseudonym **Vladimir Sirin** (1899–    ), Russian-American novelist and short-story writer in Russian and English. Born in Petersburg of an aristocratic family, he left Russia for Britain at the revolution and was educated at Cambridge. In 1940 he settled in the United States. In his early works, all in Russian, he treats his characters coldly, but the influence of Dostoyevsky, while still further deepening his pessimism, humanized him. *Camera Obscura* (1932; Eng. trans. *Laughter in the Dark*, 1938) marks the transitional stage. From 1944 onwards he has written almost entirely in English, in which year his striking *Nikolai Gogol*, a brilliant study of the Russian novelist, appeared. *The Real Life of Sebastian Knight* (1945), a clever delineation of personality as revealed in the narrative of a second person, was his best work to date. *Pnin* (1957) shows deeper feeling, and is in fact a moving account of the sorrows of exile. The brashness, even cruelty, of the new civilization as revealed in the United States now haunted him, as he had already shown in that much misunderstood novel *Lolita* (Paris, 1955; N.Y., 1958; London, 1959), which is a terrible denunciation of the hideous modern world and its corrupt values.

**Nałkowska, Zofia** (1885–1954), Polish novelist and essayist, was born in Warsaw, where she died. Her style and approach to the quieter social problems were much admired. Examples of her novels are *Kobiety* (1906; Eng. trans. *Women*, 1920) and *Chaucas* (1927; Fr. trans. 1936). Of her essays *Medaliony* (1954, 'Medallions') is representative.

**Nansen, Peter** (1861–1918), Danish novelist. Born in Copenhagen, he became a publisher. His three novels, *Julies Dagbog* (1893), *Maria* (1894) and *Guds Fred* (1895), which were translated together as *Love's Trilogy* (1906), were considered very daring in their day. They show application of the principles of the French realist school to domestic problems to an uncompromising extent. Nansen died at Mariager.

**Narezhny, Vasily Trofimovich** (1780–1825), Russian novelist, born at Mirgorod. His satirical novel, *Rossiyskiy Zhil Blas* (1814), is as its name implies inspired as to manner at least by the *Gil Blas* of Lesage (q.v.). It contains good accounts of Russian life, and was republished as recently as 1938. He died in Petersburg.

**Naruszewicz, Adam** (1733–1796), Polish poet. Born at Pinsk, he became a Jesuit and a schoolmaster at the Order's college at Vilna. He is the best example of the poet of the pastoral idyll in Polish literature, as his *Liryka* (1778) show. Royal historian of Poland, his work in that line can hardly be accounted of literary value. He died at Janów.

**Nascimento, Francisco Manuel do** (1734–1819), Portuguese poet. Born in Lisbon, he became a priest and a member of the Arcadian Academy there, assuming the name of **Filinto Elysio**. By this time the academies were changing in character in every country and were taking on a less literary and more political shade. Playing about with what were considered dangerous ideas, Nascimento escaped to France to avoid the Inquisition in 1778 and spent the rest of his life in Paris. Classical in presentation and feeling, there is yet a richness of style in his poetry which seems to look towards the near-romantics of the next generation. The turbulent Bocage (q.v.), for all his waywardness, owes to him many of the better points of his poetic diction. There is a useful anthology of his work, *Filinto Elísio: Poesías*, by J. Pereira (1941).

**Nekrasov, Nikolay Alexeyevich** (1821–1877), Russian poet. Born at Greshnevo, the son of an army officer, he refused to follow in his father's footsteps and was disinherited. Fighting his way to a position of influence in Petersburg journalism, in 1847 he bought a newspaper which he made use of to attack the government. When in 1866 it was suppressed he bought another which even more clearly than the first became a rallying point of radicalism. A very unequal writer, he survives thanks to his long unfinished poem, *Komu na Rusi zhit' khorosho* (1876; Eng. trans. *Who can be Happy and Free in Russia?*, 1917), and to some of his lyrics, a selection of which have been translated into English by J. Soskice (1920). Nekrasov died in Petersburg.

**Nelli, Jacopo** (1673–1767), Italian dramatist. Born in Siena, he became a priest and tutor, and was a prominent member of the Arcadian Academy of Rome. A close student of the French stage, especially of Molière (q.v.), Nelli was responsible for introducing the comedy of manners into Italy and so paving the way for Goldoni (q.v.). He died at Castellina del Chianti. His best work is considered to be *La serva padrona* (1709). Some of his plays were collected as *Commedie* (3 vols., 1883–9), following the eighteenth-century edition; others still remain in manuscript.

**Nelli, Pietro** (1511?–after 1572), Italian poet, born in Siena, where he died. Bitter when dealing with the evils of Spanish rule in Italy (*Satire alla carlona*, 1547), he is otherwise playful and optimistic. He collected his *Sonetti ed epigrammi* in 1572.

**Němcová, Božena**, *née* **Panklová** (1820–1862), Czech novelist born in Vienna, her father being a coachman to a noble family in the north of Bohemia. On her marriage in 1837 she went to live in Prague, where she quickly found herself in literary circles. Her marriage proved a failure, her health broke down, until finally the only happiness in her life that remained was the memory of her early days in the country, and this she celebrated in her moving *Babička* (1855, 'The Grandmother'), a series of beautiful tableaux of youth and nature. She died in Prague.

**Nemirovich-Danchenko, Vasily Ivanovich** (1848–1936). Russian novelist. Born at Tiflis, he became a journalist and wrote countless novels with a straightforward, brisk narrative style, which became popular, three of them in their translations, *The Reminiscences of General Skobeleff* (1884), *The Princes of the Stock Exchange* (1914) and *Peasant Tales of Russia* (1917), being much read in Britain. Nemirovich died in self-imposed exile, in Prague.

**Néricault, P.,** *see* **Destouches.**

**Neruda, Jan** (1834–1891), Czech poet and prose-writer. Born in Prague the son of the keeper of the canteen of the military barracks, he received a good schooling and became a journalist in 1858, soon making a name for himself as a literary critic. The pearl of his books of lyric verse is *Balady a romance* (1883), while *Malostranské povídky* (Pt. I, 1878; Pt. II, 1885, 'Tales of Malá Strana'), admirable short stories set in Prague, is representative of his prose. He died in Prague a lonely egoist.

**Nerval, Gérard de,** pseudonym of **Gérard Labrunie** (1808–1855), French poet and prose-writer. Born in Paris the son of an army surgeon, after an unhappy childhood he was praised for his translation of Part I of Goethe's *Faust* (1828), and shortly afterwards set out on journeys all over Europe and in the East. The course of his life from then on consisted of restless travel, fits of dissipation, brilliant work at intervals, and an unhappy (perhaps not very deep, but certainly romantic) love affair. The exotic and the mentally unbalanced are both very clear in his work and undoubtedly add to its strange charm. The finest examples of his beautiful and haunting prose are: *Scènes de la vie orientale* (2 vols., 1850), *Voyage en orient* (1852), *Les Filles du feu* (1854), containing his poetic masterpiece *Les Chimères*, later issued as a separate book, and *Aurélia* (1855; Eng. trans. 1932). Nerval, very much a figure in the Latin Quarter, of whose eccentricity many stories are told, such as his exercising his tame lobster in the street, committed suicide one winter night by hanging himself from a lamp-post. The definitive edition of his *Œuvres complètes* was issued in ten volumes (1927–31).

**Neumann, Alfred** (1895–1952), German novelist and short-story writer, was born at Lautenburg, and became one of the most popular historical novelists in Europe in the mid twenties, his success continuing till towards the end of the thirties. Of novels may be mentioned: *Der Teufel* (1926; Eng. trans. *The Devil*, 1928), *Rebellen* (1927; Eng. trans. *The Rebels*, 1929), *Der Held* (1930; Eng. trans. *The Hero*, 1931), *Narrenspiegel* (1933; Eng. trans. *The Mirror of Fools*, 1933), *Neuer Cäsar* (1934; Eng. trans. *New Caesar*, 1934) and *Kaiserreich* (1936; Eng. trans. *Gaudy Empire*, 1937). After the Second World War he kept to the same vein, as in *Die Volksfreunde* (1951). His principal collection of short stories was *König Haber* (1926; Eng. trans. *King Haber and Other Stories*, 1930). He died in Lugano.

**Neumann, Robert** (1897–    ), Austrian novelist, born in Vienna. He made a name for himself as a powerful writer with *Sintflut* (1929; Eng. trans. *Flood*, 1930), and sustained it with *Die Macht* (1932; Eng. trans. *Mammon*, 1933) and *Zaharoff* (1934; Eng. trans. 1935).

In disfavour with the Nazis, he left his country for England in 1934, becoming a British subject. Since then he has written, in both German and English, such works as the following: *On the Waters of Babylon* (1939), *The Inquest* (1945), *Blind Men's Buff* (1949), *In the Steps of Morell* (1952) and *Festival* (1962). At present he lives in Locarno.

**Neverov, Alexander Sergeyevich**, his real surname being **Skobelev** (1886–1923), born at Novikovka, Russian Soviet author of *Tashkent gorod Khlebny* (1921; Eng. trans. *Tashkent*, 1930), which describes the impact of the revolution on remote communities.

**Neveux, Georges** (1900–    ), French dramatist, born in Poltava, Russia. A surrealist of the stage and later a lesser disciple of Giraudoux (q.v.), the best example of his first manner is *Juliette, ou la Clef des songes* (1930), of the second *Le Voyage de Thésée* (1943).

**Nexø, Martin Andersen** (1869–1954), Danish novelist. Born in near poverty in Copenhagen, he took up various menial jobs, and later threw in his lot with socialism, becoming a leader of Danish Communism after the Russian Revolution. His chief works are lengthy and powerful novels about the working classes: *Pelle Erobreren* (4 vols., 1906–10; Eng. trans. *Pelle the Conqueror*, 4 vols., 1913–16) and *Ditte Menneskebarn* (5 vols., 1917–21; Eng. trans. *Ditte: Girl Alive!*, 1920; *Ditte: Daughter of Man*, 1922; and *Ditte: Towards the Stars*, 1923). He was a skilled short-story writer, and his various volumes of memoirs, such as *Under aaben Himmel* (1935; Eng. trans. *Under the Open Sky*, 1938) are excellently written. He died in Dresden.

**Nezval, Vítězslav** (1900–1958), Czech poet, born at Biskoupky. A great enthusiast for Communism from his early days, he unashamedly lent his poetry to effusive praise of the Soviet regime. His books like *Stalin* (1949) and *Zpěv míru* (1950; Eng. trans. *Song of Peace*, 1951) are mere propaganda, but earlier volumes showed him to have been capable of better work. He died in Prague.

**Niccodemi, Dario** (1874–1934), Italian playwright, born in Leghorn. After living in South America he settled for a time in Paris where he gained some experience in production and stage-management. Back in Italy in 1915 he wrote plays depicting rather than analysing the transformation of society and its dangerous restlessness; among them may be mentioned *L'ombra* (1915) and *La Madonna* (1927). He died in Rome.

**Niccolini, Giambattista** (1782–1861), Italian dramatist, was born at Lucca. He is remembered as the author of the greatest play of the early Risorgimento, *Arnaldo da Brescia* (1838), in which he voices his dislike of the papacy in the person of the reactionary Gregory XVI and warns his countrymen against clerical wiles; but the work, unlike so much propaganda, is a great piece of art in itself. Niccolini died at Pistoia.

**Nicolai, Johann Christoph Friedrich** (1733–1811), German critic and novelist, was a Berliner and in that city he lived and died. For the greater part of his life he carried on business as a bookseller. In 1754 he became a member of that literary circle, including Lessing (q.v.) and Moses Mendelssohn (q.v.), which sought to bring new influences into German letters by breaking down the French and pseudo-classical bondage imposed by Gottsched (q.v.) and other academics, and putting in its place a style derived from true classical and English models. With this in mind he founded the journal *Bibliothek der schönen Wissenschaften* in 1757, and it ran until 1760. In 1759 with the same end in view he started another literary magazine in collaboration with Lessing, *Briefe, die neueste Literatur betreffend*, which lasted until 1765. This famous publication caused Nicolai to be regarded as one of the greatest literary critics of Germany, and having reached that pinnacle he sought to preserve his position with the third of his periodicals, *Allgemeine deutsche Bibliothek*, which he edited from 1765 to 1800, and in which he made strong attacks on the new literature of the *Sturm und Drang*, falling foul of Goethe and Schiller for denouncing what he termed their extravagance. In order to expose what he believed was the dangerous decadence of Goethe's *Werther* he produced the novel *Die Freuden* ('Joys') *des jungen Werthers* (1777–8), and for over twenty years after that he tirelessly berated the Weimar school, while enemies of the Goethe circle—and there were many—found a ready welcome in Berlin. Goethe's and Schiller's cruel diatribes against Nicolai (as in the *Xenien*, for example) have blinded people to the fact that he was a man of integrity whose writing was always on the side of sanity and toleration. His two semi-autobiographical novels, in their self-revelation reminding one of similar works of the next century such as Keller's (q.v.) *Grüne Heinrich*, are *Magister Sebaldus Nothanker* (1773–6) and *Sempronius Gundibert* (1798), in which there is an interest in the occult particularly striking.

**Nietzsche, Friedrich Wilhelm** (1844–1900), German prose-writer. Born at Röcken, Saxony, the son of a well-known Lutheran pastor who died young, he was brought up in a household of women—he tried all his life to escape from the domination of female relatives—before being sent to the famous Pforta gymnasium, after which he attended the universities of Bonn and Leipzig. He took his doctorate in 1868 at Leipzig, having by this time become so well known as a classical scholar of enormous promise that he was appointed to the chair of classics at Basel in 1869. Under the influence of Richard Wagner (q.v.) with whom he now formed a temporary friendship, and inspired by Schopenhauer's (q.v.) work, he set about a study of the Greek genius, the main argument of his resultant brilliant book, *Die Geburt der Tragödie* (1872, 'The Birth of Tragedy'), being that the Greeks naturally lent themselves to the instinctive, joyful creativeness which is the aim of man, 'the Dionysiac', but that later this marvellous dawn was clouded by succeeding cultures with their over-intellectualism and rigid moral codes, especially those brought about by religions. This thesis led him to explore the culture and social life of his own day in various essays which became still more sharply critical of contemporary values just before and just after his resignation from the professorship as a result of ill health in 1879. Characteristic of this middle period, as it is usually termed, are *Menschliches, allzumenschliches* (1878–80, 'Human, All Too Human') and

*Die fröhliche Wissenschaft* (1882, 'The Joyous Wisdom'). These works had in reality been destructive, and Nietzsche now sought to build up a new philosophy from the ruins. Living on his university pension of £120 a year and a few other slight resources, first in Italy and then in Switzerland, he wrote his greatest book *Also sprach Zarathustra* ('Thus Spake Zarathustra'), three parts of which appeared between 1883 and 1884 and a fourth in 1892. He had by this time given up his Wagner worship, above all disgusted by the 'Parsifal cult' in which he saw the composer's Greek ideals of the drama abandoned for what he considered cloudy, deluded mysticism. Nietzsche now turned to Schopenhauer's idea of the 'Will to Power'. It is, he teaches, the only effective life force; everything will yield to power, and men must not be afraid of a belief in impulse and in self-sufficiency, with the proviso that the strong must also exercise self-discipline. But here it is his work as literature which is the chief concern. Nietzsche at his best is, with Goethe and Schopenhauer, one of the finest prose-writers in German, and much of his writing, especially in *Zarathustra*, rises to prose-poetry of indefinable beauty. Interpreted and mis-interpreted to suit various political codes, he remains an idealist for whom the hypocrisies of modern Europe and its worship of Mammon are alike detestable. His health had been long precarious when apoplexy in 1888 hastened the insanity which had threatened him, and from 1889, all hope of recovery having vanished, until his death he lived in his sister's house at Weimar. It was Georg Brandes' (q.v.) essay of appreciation in 1890 which brought him the fame and influence denied him before, by a stroke of irony when he could know nothing of it. All his works were translated into English in O. Levy's edition (1900–13).

**Nievo, Ippolito** (1831–1861), Italian novelist. Born in Padua, he wrote a fine novel, *Le confessioni di un italiano*, in 1858, but it was not published until 1867, after his death, being then given the title of *Confessioni d'un ottuagenario*. It is an account in the first person of the Italian bid for freedom from the French invasion of Italy under Bonaparte to the days of Garibaldi. Nievo was in fact a volunteer under Garibaldi in the Sicilian campaign of 1860, a vivid account of which he gives in *Amori garibaldini* (1860). The next year he was drowned in the Tyrrhenian Sea.

**Nilsson-Piraten, Fritiof** (1895–    ), Swedish novelist, born at Vollsjö. Although he developed a disturbing manner and strange treatment of his plots, it is his straightforward ones founded on the experiences of his youth which are probably his best contribution to literature. They are *Bombi Bitt och jag* (1932; Eng. trans. *Bombi Bitt*, 1933), *Tre Terminer* (1943) with its description of student life in the old university city of Lund, and *Bombi Bitt och Nick Carter* (1946).

**Noailles, Anna de** (1876–1933), French poet and novelist. Born in Paris, the daughter of Prince Bibesco, a Rumanian, in 1897 she married a grandson of the duc de Noailles. Of her poetry, intense, musical and exotic, the best-known volumes are: *Le Cœur innombrable* (1901), *Les Éblouissements* (1907), *Les Vivants et les morts* (1913), *Le Poème de l'Amour* (1925) and *L'Honneur de souffrir* (1927). Of her novels the best known are *La Nouvelle Espérance* (1903) and *Le Livre de ma vie* (1932). She died in Paris.

**Nodier, Jean Charles Emmanuel** (1780–1844), French writer. Born in Besançon, he was a revolutionary idealist in his youth, and was imprisoned in 1803 for writing a skit on Napoleon. On his release he left France, not returning until 1815 when he became a journalist. In 1824 he was appointed librarian of the Bibliothèque de l'Arsenal, for recreation holding gatherings of young romantic literary men in his house in the evenings. By 1830 he had become the centre of the romantic movement, and this was his role rather than being a conspicuous creator, although *La Fée aux miettes* (1832), *Le Dernier Banquet des Girondins* (1833), *Inès de las sierras* (1837) and *La Neuvaine de la Chandeleur* (1839) deserve mentioning. Nodier died in Paris.

**Nordau, Max Simon** (1849–1923), German-Hungarian author, was born of Jewish parents in Budapest, his real name being **Südfeld**, and became for a time a medical practitioner in Paris. It is, however, as the author of works in which he weighs up the civilization of the late nineteenth century and finds it decadent and neurotic that he became well known. In *Conventional Lies of Civilization* (1883), written in excellent English, he throws down the gauntlet and attacks among other institutions the Christian churches as manifestations of society's essential hypocrisy. In his best-known book, *Entartung* (1892; Eng. trans. *Degeneration*, 1893), he routs out the contemporary arts, heaping scorn on them, and in his strongest play, *Das Recht zu Leben* (1894; Eng. trans. *The Right to Live*, 1894), he takes aggressively active measures against a hidebound moral code. He died in Paris.

**Novalis,** pseudonym of **Friedrich Leopold von Hardenberg** (1772–1801), German poet and prose-writer. Born at Oberwiederstedt, near Halle, the son of a landed nobleman, gloomy and deeply religious in a pietistic, Protestant manner, Hardenberg studied at the universities of Jena (where he came under the influence of Schiller, then professor of history there, 1789–91), of Leipzig (where he met F. Schlegel, q.v.) and of Wittenberg, graduating in 1794. He became an inspector at the Saxon Salt Works. Latent tuberculosis, of which he was to die, undoubtedly rendered him precocious, and he is the embodiment of the first generation of the romantics. His love for the child Sophie von Kühn, who died at the age of fifteen, was a highly rarefied affair set in the medieval surroundings of the Kühns' castle home; but it did bring about the inspiration needed to drive Novalis (he had taken this pseudonym, meaning 'untilled field', from the traditional name of certain acres on his father's estate) into the remarkable literary activity which filled the rest of his short life. *Blütenstaub* (1798, 'Flower-pollen') is a collection of axioms, the general drift of many of which is the necessity to face life with the help of hidden transcendental powers hovering near us. The full tide of Novalis's mysticism was now in. In his next work, *Die Christenheit oder Europa* (1799), we have a very interesting discussion on the possibility of the unification of European culture, and here the medievalism of the romantic movement clearly comes out with a wistful harking back to the unity of Europe before the shocks of the Reformation. This book marks the change in European thought from romantic, free-thinking idealism to a desire for some straighter, more disciplined path, leading to the work of Chateaubriand (q.v.) and J. M. de Maistre (q.v.), and to the eventual turning to Catholicism of such utter romantics as F. Schlegel and Z. Werner (q.v.). Not that Novalis ceased to be a pietistic Protestant, but his next publication, the beautiful *Hymnen an die Nacht* (1800, 'Hymns to the Night'), contains poetry of the deepest spirituality with Catholic symbolism clearly introduced. His other works appeared posthumously in the edition of his writings prepared by his friends F. Schlegel and L. Tieck (q.v.) in 1802. They consist of more poetry, *Geistliche Lieder*, and two unfinished novels, *Heinrich von Ofterdingen*, with a medieval setting and famous for the symbolism of the 'blue flower of happiness', and *Die Lehrlinge zu Saïs* (Eng. trans. *The Disciples at Saïs* by U. Birch, 1907, which volume also contains translations of the *Blütenstaub* and *Hymnen*), set in ancient Egypt. Novalis died at Weissenfels.

**Novikov-Priboy, Alexey Silych** (1877–1944), Russian novelist, born in Tambov province. He originally served in the Russian Imperial Navy, and later, under the Soviet regime which he supported, he wrote several novels based on first-hand knowledge dealing with the Czarist fleet. The two outstanding are *Tsushima* (2 vols., 1932–5; Eng. trans. 1936), the subject of which is the Russian Navy in the Russo-Japanese War of 1905, and *Kapitan I-go ranga* (1943; Eng. trans. *The Captain*, 1946).

**Nowakowski, Zygmunt,** pseudonym of **Zygmunt Tempka** (1891–     ), Polish novelist. Born in Cracow, he followed a military career, later settling down as a writer. His best-known work is the novel *Przylądek Dobrej Nadriei* (1931; Eng. trans. *The Cape of Good Hope*, 1940).

# O

**Obey, André** (1892–   ), French playwright. Born in Douai, he became director of the Comédie Française in 1945. He made his name with *Le Viol de Lucrèce* (1931), but he has not lived up to earlier expectations. His later work includes *Maria* (1946) and *Lazare* (1951).

**Obstfelder, Sigbjørn** (1866–1900), Norwegian poet and novelist. Born at Stavanger, he later moved to Copenhagen, where he died. His country's sole representative of the thorough-paced *fin-de-siècle* manner of thought and style, he is best studied in his book of verse *Digte* (1893). His collected works (*Samlede skrifter*, 3 vols., 1950) contain several novels. In both verse and prose there is a diffuse beauty tinged with a kind of unhappy, half-suppressed longing, and also an ever-present touch of anxiety sometimes developing into actual fear.

**Ochoa, Eugenio de** (1815–1872), Spanish archivist, novelist and translator. Born at Lezo, Guipúzcoa, in his youth he had influential friends, and making his home in Madrid eventually became a member of the council of state. Besides his valuable work in cataloguing Spanish manuscripts and his translations, some of which introduced Victor Hugo's writings to Spain, he wrote an historical novel, *El auto de fe* (1837), which caused something of a scandal and led to Ochoa's seven years exile, spent in France. His memoirs give a most interesting social, literary and political account of the time (*Miscelánea de literatura, viajes y novelas*, 1867). He died in Madrid.

**Oehlenschläger, Adam Gottlob** (1779–1850), Danish poet, dramatist, and short-story writer, was born and died in Copenhagen. His meeting in 1802 with Henrik Steffens (q.v.), who had just arrived hotfoot from Germany full of ideas of the Goethe and the Weimar circle, set him on his literary way, and that very year he published his first long poem in full romantic style, *Guldhornene* (Eng. trans. *The Golden Horns*, 1913). From then on until about 1820 he published a stream of poems and dramas, the like of which for variety of subject, style and versification have not been equalled in Danish literature. At this time he travelled in Germany, where he met Goethe, Tieck (q.v.) and the Schlegels (qq.v.), and in Italy. In 1810 he became professor of aesthetics at Copenhagen University. To these years belong volumes of poetry, such as *Vaulundurs Saga* (1812; Eng. trans. 1847) and *Nordens Guder* (1819; Eng. trans. *Gods of the North*, 1845)—he had written enough by 1805 to have a two-volume edition of *Poetiske Skrifter* published; while among his plays are *Palnatoke* (1809; Eng.

trans. 1855), *Axel og Valborg* (1810; Eng. trans. *Aksel and Valborg*, 1851), and especially *Aladdin eller den forunderlige Lampe* (1820; Eng. trans. *Aladdin or The Wonderful Lamp*, 1857). Among his stories may be mentioned *Den lille Hyrdedreng* (1818; Eng. trans. *The Little Shepherd-Boy* 1827). After about 1820 his work declined in quality. The most recent and useful collection of his work is *Poetiske Skrifter i Udvalg*, edited by H. Topsøe-Jensen (5 vols., 1926–30).

**Ognyov, N.,** *see* **Rozanov, M. G.**

**Ojeda, D. de,** *see* **Hojeda, D. de.**

**Olesha, Yury Karlovich** (1899–1960), Russian Soviet novelist and playwright, was born in Elisavetgrad. An opponent of the materialism and damage done to family life by Bolshevism, he denounced these aspects of the new Russia in a novel, *Zavist'* (1927; Eng. trans. *Envy*, 1936), which caused much discussion. He was arrested shortly afterwards, and ignored by the Soviet press until 1956. In 1957 the republication of his selected works marked his official rehabilitation. He died in Moscow.

**Oliveira, Francisco Xavier de** (1702–1783), Portuguese prose-writer. Born of good family in Lisbon, he was destined for a diplomatic career but his religious opinions forced him to leave Portugal, and after a period in the United Provinces he settled in London. For a long time verging on it, he finally became a Protestant. He had already roundly attacked the Inquisition and Church in Portugal, while in Amsterdam he published the famous *Cartas familiares, históricas, políticas e críticas* (3 vols., 1741–2; appearing for the first time in Portugal in 1855). In this work he lays bare the backwardness of his native country, placing the reason for most of its shortcomings at the door of the clergy. Besides this, his work is most interesting for its account of pre-Pombal Portugal. Burnt in effigy at Lisbon in 1761, Oliveira died at Hackney. A selection from the *Cartas* was made by A. Ribeiro in 1942.

**Olivier, Juste** (1807–1876), Swiss poet. Born in the Canton of Vaud, he taught literature and history in various institutions before settling in Paris in 1845, where he remained until the fall of Napoleon III in 1870. A poet of strong Swiss national feeling, his best work, such as that found in *Poèmes suisses* (1830) and *Les Chansons lointaines* (1847), is steeped in traditional lore. His *Œuvres choisies* were published in 1879. He died in Geneva.

**Oller i Moragues, Narcís** (1846–1930), Catalan novelist, was born in Barcelona, where he died. Greatly influenced by the Russian novels of Tolstoy and Turgenev (q.v.), he was a personal friend of Zola (q.v.). His outstanding work is *Pilar Prim* (1906), which deals with comfortable middle-class society, and is undoubtedly one of the very best Catalan novels. His collected works were published between 1928 and 1930.

**Olofson, Georg** (1598–1672), Swedish poet, took the name of **Lilia** (1614) and was ennobled as **Stjernhjelm** in 1631. Poetry was only one among his many attainments: born at Wika, he was well known as a scientist and lawyer, becoming also court poet, in which capacity he produced words for songs and ballets, a good example of the latter being *Parnassus triumphans* (1651). His epic poem, *Hercules* (1658), was long admired. The very fact that such a man should pursue letters improved the status of literary men in Sweden. Stjernhjelm died in Stockholm.

**Ongaro, F. dall',** *see* **Dall' Ongaro, F.**

**Opitz von Boberfeld, Martin** (1597–1639), German man of letters, whose influence as a stylist did much to pave the way for the rise of his country's literature during the latter half of the seventeenth century, was born at Bunzlau, Silesia. Educated at Heidelberg and in the United Provinces where he went in 1620 to escape the plague and the Thirty Years War, he afterwards served several German princes, and finally became historiographer to King Ladislaus IV of Poland, dying at Danzig of the plague he had sought to avoid nearly twenty years before. As a poetic theorist his ideas are most clearly seen in *Aristarchus* (1617) and in the *Buch von der teutschen Poeterey* (1624), which revealed to German literary men the new poetry of other nations, such as the work of the French Pléiade (*see* Ronsard). His *Teutsche Poemata* (1624) exemplifies his cold, unimaginative, pedantic original work, although in it he produced a kind of baroque copy-book for others to follow. He adapted Sidney's *Arcadia* as *Arcadia der Gräfin von Pembrock* (1629), and made translations from Sophocles, Seneca, Heinsius, Grotius (q.v.) and the Bible.

**Opzoomer, A. S. C.,** *see* **Wallis, A. S. C.**

**Oresme, Nicole** (1320?–1378?), French scholar, became Bishop of Lisieux. He is remembered as the translator of Aristotle's *Ethics*, thereby greatly influencing French thought and letters. His *Livre de l'Éthique d'Aristote* has been edited by A. D. Menut (1940).

**Oriani, Alfredo** (1852–1909), Italian novelist and political theorist, was born at Faenza. His novels may be divided into two kinds. During the first period from *Memorie inutili* (1876) to *Quartetto* (1883) he gives expression to violent opposition to established moral codes, a point of view to which he returns in the autobiographical *Olocausto* (1902). In the 1890's, however, as in *Vortice* (1899) he writes in a romantic, even sentimental manner. As a theorist he was a Neo-Hegelian, harping on the importance of the family as the nucleus of the power of the state and discoursing on the greatness of Italy's past and her future destiny (*La rivolta ideale*, 1908). Little wonder that Oriani was much approved of by the Fascists. His *Opera omnia* were edited by B. Mussolini (30 vols., 1923–33). He died at Il Cardello.

**Orléans, Charles duc d'** (1391–1465), French poet, was the fourth son of Louis, duc d'Orléans, brother of King Charles VI. In 1406 he married Isabella, widow of Richard II of England. In command at Agincourt (1415), he was taken prisoner and brought to England, where he spent a pleasant quarter of a century in honourable and easy captivity. In 1440 he was allowed to return to France, and during the last part of his life kept a kind of literary court at Blois, dying, however, at Amboise. His son became Louis XII of France. His

ballades, rondels and other lyrics are simply expressed, fresh and
sincere. He also wrote some poems in English. His *Poésies* have been
edited by P. Champion (2 vols., 1923–7). For the English poems see
R. Steele's *The English Poems of Charles of Orléans* (1941). An account
of him appears in R. L. Stevenson's *Familiar Studies* (sixth ed.
1892).

**Ortega y Gasset, José** (1883–1955), Spanish prose-writer and theorist,
was born in Madrid into an intellectual family. Educated by the
Jesuits and at Madrid University, he did not have the chance of
ranging widely over intellectual and philosophical problems until he
went to Germany. He returned to become professor of metaphysics at
Madrid, from which position he was always ready as speaker and as
writer to put his views, often controversial, before the public; and he
soon became an influential member of that renowned literary club,
the Ateneo. This tendency increased with the years and there is little
doubt that with his restless intervention in the political affairs of the
moment he dissipated his energies. The philosopher had become a
theorist, a prime example of the Spaniard spoilt by Germany. The
decadent theories of Nordau (q.v.) and Spengler (q.v.), for example,
took root in him, and in *España invertebrada* (1921; Eng. trans.
*Invertebrate Spain*, 1937) he advances plausibly, sometimes brilliantly,
theories for the causes of Spanish decadence. In *El tema de nuestro
tiempo* (1923; Eng. trans. *The Modern Theme*, 1933) he attacks
rationalism, but does not find a viable substitute. He attacks modern
trends in the fine arts in *La deshumanización del arte e ideas sobre la
novela* (1925; Eng. trans. *The Dehumanization of Art and Notes on
the Novel*, 1948), and here, cogent though many of the ideas he
advances are, it must be admitted that his premises are often
insecurely laid. But it was his *La rebelión de las masas* (1930; Eng. trans.
*The Revolt of the Masses*, 1932) that brought him world-wide acclaim.
Here in impressive, though somewhat over-elaborate style, he marshals the ideas that go to form his pessimism about the present state
of and future outlook for Western civilization. The crux of the
matter for Ortega is the mass revolt against the *élite* which has up to
now from its dawn guided our civilization. Although it is tempting
to see a refined Nietzsche (q.v.) behind this standpoint, this would be
to misunderstand the basis of the view here presented. Ortega y Gasset
sets down with uncompromising clarity the dilemma of the refined
intellectual faced with social revolution. What he, however, fails to
see is that apparent decadence may perhaps be the starting-point of
a new chapter in civilization, and that the intellectual must cross
'the howling wilderness' in Carlylean style if he is to reach the
promised land. The result of the Spanish Civil War sent him into
exile, but he returned for a time in 1945. The regime was not to his
liking and he left once more, only to go back at the very end of his
life to die and be given a public funeral in Madrid by a government
he could hardly approve of. Too much a man of his time to create a
lasting impression, Ortega y Gasset brought his very extensive gifts
to bear on what then seemed the insurmountable problems of the
intellectual.

**Orzeszkowa, Eliza** (1841–1910), Polish novelist. Born at Miłkowszczyzną and educated at Warsaw, she married Peter Orzeszko, who was exiled to Siberia after the Polish revolt against Russia in 1863. In 1866 she moved to Grodno and turned novelist, in her work, which is well-written and depicts sympathetically the life of the Jews, peasants and impoverished gentry, proving herself to be a supporter of women's emancipation. Outstanding among her books are: *Eli Makower* (1875; Fr. trans. *Histoire d'un Juif*, 1888), *Meir Ezofowicz* (1878; Eng. trans. *An Obscure Apostle*, 1898) and *Argonauci* (1899; Eng. trans. *Modern Argonauts*, 1901). She died at Grodno.

**Osorgin, Mikhail Andreyevich**, pseudonym of **M. A. Ilyin** (1878–1942), Russian novelist, who went into exile at the revolution of 1905, settling in Paris. His best-known work is the novel *Sivtsev Vrazhek* (1928, Eng. trans. *A Quiet Street*, 1930). Other novels include *Svidetel' istorii* (1932, 'An Eye-Witness to History').

**Osório, Jerónimo** (1506–1580), Portuguese historian writing in Latin, was born in Lisbon. A typical product of Portuguese humanism, he was educated in Spain, Italy and France, and became a professor at Coimbra and finally Bishop of Silves. His great Latin history which did so much to make known his country's eastern discoveries is *De rebus Emmanuelis regis Lusitaniae invictissimi virtute et auspicio gestis libri duodecim* (1571). It was translated into English by J. Gibbs in 1762 as *The History of the Portuguese during the reign of Emmanuel [i.e. Manuel] containing all their discoveries.* . . . Osório died at Tavira.

**Ossendowski, Antoni Ferdynand** (1876–1945), Polish writer. Born at Vitebsk, he fell foul of the Czarist regime and spent some time in imprisonment in Siberia, as a result of his treatment publishing several books which brought about a partial reform of the prison system. Opposed to the Bolshevik Revolution, he joined Admiral Kolchak at his anti-Bolshevik government headquarters at Omsk in 1918. On the fall of Kolchak in 1920 he managed to escape into Mongolia, and finally after extraordinary experiences he reached Warsaw. All this he vividly if sometimes inaccurately describes in such books as *Przez kraj zwierząt ludzi i bogów* (1923; Eng. trans. *Beasts, Men and Gods*, 1923), *Od szczytu do otchłani* (1924; Eng. trans. *From President to Prison*, 1925), *Pod smaganiem Samumu* (1926; Eng. trans. *The Breath of the Desert*, 1927) and *Niewolnicy słońca* (1928; Eng. trans. *Slaves of the Sun*, 1928), these last two inspired by African and Middle Eastern travel. He also wrote a biographical novel, *Lenin* (1929; Eng. trans. *Lenin, God of the Godless*, 1931). Ossendowski died at Żółwin.

**Ostrovsky, Alexander Nikolayevich** (1823–1886), Russian playwright. Born in Moscow, he began to write under the influence of Gogol in 1847, the lives of Moscow merchants being his particular theme. His first plays were comedies, but in the 1860's the trend to tragedy is apparent and he had come to include in his field gentry and actors as well. In 1884 he became director of the Moscow Theatre and was the founder of the Russian Academy of Dramatic Art. He was the greatest playwright of the Russian 'realistic period'. He is best known in Britain for *Groza* (1860; Eng. trans. *The Storm*, 1898 and 1930). Four more plays were translated by G. R. Noyes in 1917, and three more by D. Magarshack in 1944. He was fearless in his denunciation of government abuses, but so carefully are his strictures embedded in his plots that he escaped the censorship. He died in the country near Moscow.

**Ostrovsky, Nikolay Alexeyevich** (1904–1936), Russian Soviet novelist, born at Vilizha, Volhynia. Wounded during the Red and White civil war in 1921, in which he eagerly took the Bolshevik side, he gradually became blind and paralysed. He nonetheless thereupon wrote a bright and happy autobiographical novel, *Kak zakalyalas' stal'* (1932–4; Eng. trans. *The Making of a Hero*, 1937), which became the most widely read book published in Soviet Russia, over six million copies being sold in sixteen years. A man of the working-class, Ostrovsky was largely self-educated. He died in Moscow.

**Oswald von Wolkenstein** (1377–1445) was a Tirolean poet whose work in every kind of style is the most attractive in later Middle-Age Germany. The principal edition of his 125 poems is that by J. Schatz (second ed. 1904).

**Otero, Blas de** (1916–     ), Spanish poet, born in Bilbao. His strange tortured poetry, rough in style, is exemplified in *Ángel fieramente humano* (1950) and *Redoble de conciencia* (1951). These works reveal the poet as preoccupied with religion and spiritual conflicts. Later, losing faith in religion, Otero turned to politics as the last hope, and his *Pido la paz y la palabra* ('I beg for Peace and the Freedom to Speak') was published in Spain in 1955, having escaped censorship. This book and others, hostile to the regime, which followed have since been banned. Six of Otero's poems appear in the revised edition of *The Penguin Book of Spanish Verse*.

**Oudaen, Joachim** (1628–1692), Dutch poet. Born in Rijnsburg, he took up tilemaking in Rotterdam, there becoming head of a Protestant literary coterie opposed to Vondel (q.v.). His play *Johanna Gray* (1648) is a counterblast to Vondel's *Maria Stuart*. His poem, *De neergeplofte Lucifer* (1659), deals with the death of Cromwell. He took an interest in all the arts, so typical of his time, being an amateur musician, painter and glass-engraver. He died in Rotterdam.

# P

**Pagnol, Marcel** (1895–   ), French playwright and script-writer, was born at Aubagne (Bouches-du-Rhône). He became a trenchant critic of official society with *Les Marchands de gloire* (1924, in collaboration with P. Nivoix), attacked contemporary social values in *Jazz* (1926), and scored a hit with his damaging farce, *Topaze* (1928), directed against self-important and none too scrupulous functionaries. His most significant work is the trilogy *Marius* (1929), *Fanny* (1931) and *César* (1936), the last written first as a film script and immediately converted into a stage play. Later, as the film *César et Marius*, this vivacious study of Marseille life lost its fire and appeared long-winded to an almost unbearable degree. After a long period of writing film scripts, such as *La Fille du puisatier* (1940), *La Belle Meunière* (1948), *Manon des sources* (1953) and *Lettres de mon moulin* (1954), he returned to writing for the stage and produced *Judas* (1955) and *Fabien* (1956). He then published three delightful books on his childhood, *La Gloire de mon père* (1957), *Le Château de ma mère* (1958) and *Le Temps des secrets* (1960).

**Pailleron, Édouard** (1834–1899), French playwright. Born in Paris, he set out to be a lawyer, but his marriage to the daughter of the owner of *La Revue des Deux Mondes* ushered him into the literary world. After trying his hand at verse plays he settled down to producing brilliant prose plays in which he pilloried contemporary society. Among the best are: *Les Faux Ménages* (1869), *Hélène* (1872), *L'Étincelle* (1879) and his satire on university life from the professorial point of view, *Le Monde où l'on s'ennuie* (1881). He died in Paris.

**Palacio, Manuel del** (1832–1906), Spanish poet and prose-writer. Born at Lérida, he became a journalist and was soon involved in politics. A collection of his political articles, *De Tetuán a Valencia haciendo noche en Miraflores* (1865), proved the excellent quality of his prose but angered the government of Isabel II, and he found himself in exile in Puerto Rico. On his return he turned more and more to pure literature, producing his finest and more enduring publication, *Veladas de otoño*, in 1884. A master of the sonnet, Palacio died in Madrid. His *Poesías escogidas* appeared in 1916. Some translations into English of his poetry are to be found in T. Walsh's *Hispanic Anthology* (1920).

**Palacio Valdés, Armando** (1853–1938), Spanish novelist. Born at Entralgo, Asturias, he turned to law for a career, but gained enough literary success to abandon the profession. His realistic manner interfused with a good deal of sentimentality, though not unpleasant, is to be seen at its best in *La hermana San Sulpicio* (1889; Eng. trans. *Sister Saint Sulpice*, 1890; new ed., 1925). The plot is laid in Seville and the local characters and colour are presented with great vivacity. Other novels include *Fé* (1892; Eng. trans. *Faith*, 1892), *Tristán o el pesimismo* (1906; Eng. trans. 1925), *La novela de un novelista* (1921) and *Testamento literario* (1929). He died in Madrid.

**Palamas, Kostes** (1859–1943), Greek poet, playwright and short-story writer, born at Patras. He soon turned to politics and poetry, in both of which he showed himself to be an ardent patriot. His first accomplished work is the volume of poetry, *Tragoudia tes patridos mou* (1886, 'Tragedy of my Country'). Works such as *Hymnos eis ten Athenan* (1889, 'Hymn to Athens'), *Iamboi kai anapaistoi* (1897, 'Iambics and Anapaests') and *O taphos* (1898, 'The Grave') followed. This last had been inspired by the ruinous war with Turkey of 1897, which led him to seek rejuvenating influences for a future Greece in folk-themes, regarded by him as leading the way back to healthy and uncomplicated origins. He next turned to the short story, and *Thanatos Pallikariou* (1901; Eng. trans. *A Man's Death*, 1934) contains some excellent specimens in this *genre*. With the play *Triseueni* (1903; Eng. trans. *Royal Blossom*, 1923) he made a successful attempt in another field, before returning to poetry with *Asalephte zoe* (1904; Eng. trans. *Life Immovable*, 1919, being the first part and *A Hundred Voices*, 1921, being the second). In his later work, such as *Pentasyllaboi* (1925), the thinker obscures the poet. Palamas died in Athens.

**Palazzeschi, Aldo Giurlani** (1885–    ), Italian poet and novelist, born in Florence. He became a follower of the futurist Marinetti, and inspired by an unorthodoxy that seemed like freedom, produced a host of poems which form the most interesting part of his collected poetry (1930). His posturings and self-advertising mannerisms are to be found in such novels (often hardly convincing) as *Stampe dell' ottocento* (1932), *Le sorelle Materassi* (1934) and *I fratelli Cuccoli* (1948). Some, however, find in him a writer of delicate irony.

**Paleario, Aonio** (1503?–1570), Italian poet writing in Latin, was born at Veroli. His great work is *De Immortalitate Animorum* (1536), which had violent repercussions in the Church. Long suspected of Pro-testantism he was burnt in Rome. The *Trattato utilissimo del beneficio di Giesù Cristo crocifisso* is not by him but by Benedictus Mantuensis. Paleario's *Opera* (1696) contains some damaging attacks on the papacy.

**Palladius, Peder** (1503–1560), Danish prose-writer. Born at Ribe, he took Orders, became a schoolmaster and later the first Lutheran Bishop of Zealand. Apart from his many religious works, some of which were much read in translation in England in Elizabethan and Jacobean times, he is highly regarded as the author of his delightfully individualistic *Visitatsbog*, not discovered until 1866. He died in Copenhagen. His collected works were published (5 vols.) in 1911–26.

**Palmblad, Vilhelm Fredrik** (1788–1852), Swedish man of letters, was born at Skönberga. Lamed as the result of an accident in 1802, he turned to books as his sole resource and became a voracious reader. He established himself as a critic of discernment with *Dialog över romanen* (1812), an interesting sidelight on the romantic movement as seen from Scandinavia. Two years before this he had set up a printing press which until he gave it up after being appointed professor of Greek at Uppsala in 1835, exerted much influence on the literary life of Sweden. His extended novels dealing with contemporary life, *Familjen Falkenswärd* (1844) and *Aurora Königsmarck* (1846), though long-winded, contain passages of considerable charm. Well known also for his academic work, Palmblad died at Uppsala.

**Palmieri, Matteo** (1406–1475), Italian prose-writer, born in Florence where he died. He is remembered as the author of a well-written and interesting dialogue on ideal citizenship, *Della vita civile*, first published in 1529 (mod. crit. ed., 1944).

**Pálsson, Gestur** (1852–1891), Icelandic short-story writer, was born the son of a farmer at Miðhús, Reykhólasveit, and spent some years in Copenhagen, a formative experience. In 1882 he was back in Iceland as a journalist in Reykjavík, publishing his best work, *Sagan af Sigurði formanni*, in 1887 (Eng. trans. *The Tale of Sigurdur the Fisherman* in *Icelandic Poems and Stories*, trans. M. Perkins, 1943). Opposed to the narrow life of his native capital he left in 1890 for Canada, but died in Winnipeg not long afterwards. His influence on Icelandic letters has been considerable.

**Paludan, Stig Henning Jacob Puggaard** (1896–      ), Danish novelist. Born in Copenhagen, he became a pharmaceutical chemist before going to Ecuador. Later, New York life proved distasteful, and he returned to Denmark full of fear that American materialism would swamp Europe. This impression remained long in his mind, and in fact deepened with the years, and he gave expression to his fears in such novels as *En Vinter lang* (1924) and *Fugle omkring Fyret* (1925; Eng. trans. *Birds around the Light*, 1928). His most ambitious work is *Jørgen Stein* (2 vols., 1932–3), set in the Denmark of the very end of the pre-1914 era. Here he attacks his countrymen, as did H. Pontoppidan (q.v.), for lack of moral fibre and for worship of Mammon.

**Paludan-Müller, Frederik** (1809–1876), Danish poet. Born at Kjerteminde, he read law at Copenhagen University, and by 1836 had written enough romantic poetry to fill two volumes. Then a change in his whole approach to life took place. The follower of Byron became a stern moralist, deriving inspiration from the Bible and style from the Greek classics. The withdrawn misanthropist pointed out that the life of the flesh was a snare and a delusion; only God was great and to be obeyed. Such a solemn message is the burden of his greatest work, *Adam Homo* (3 vols., 1841–8), an epic containing the sonnet sequence *Alma*. Other works of importance are *Paradiset* (1862) and *Adonis* (1874). He died at Fredensborg.

**Panfyorov, Fyodor Ivanovich** (1896–1960), Russian Soviet novelist, whose propagandist *Bruski* (4 vols., 1928–37; Eng. trans. (part only) 1930; and vol. iv as *And then the Harvest*, 1939) has not stood the test of time. *Svoimi glazami* (1942; Eng. trans. *With their Own Eyes*, 1942) is a test piece for his shorter work. His other novels are of frankly bad quality. He was for a long time editor of the influential *Oktyabr* ('October'). He died in Moscow.

**Panova, Vera Fyedorovna** (1905–    ), Russian Soviet novelist. Her novels were just what Stalin wanted. Such are *Sputniki* (1947; Eng. trans. *The Train*, 1948) and *Kruzhilikha* (1948; Eng. trans. *The Factory*, 1949). The literary value of these dreary works is slight.

**Panzini, Alfredo** (1863–1939), Italian novelist, born at Senigallia. He led a quiet life in Rome, where he died, producing many prose works ranging from scholarly monographs to novels and short stories. Of his fiction may be named *La lanterna di Diogene* (1907), *Il mondo è rotondo* (1921) and *Il bacio di Lesbia* (1937).

**Paoli, Betty,** pseudonym of **Barbara Elisabeth Glück** (1814–1894), Austrian poet and prose-writer, born in Vienna. Following in the footsteps of Annette Droste-Hülshoff (q.v.) she produced several volumes of sad and dignified verse, such as *Nach dem Gewitter* (1843), *Romanzero* (1845) and *Neue Gedichte* (1850). Greatly regarded in her day, she was for many years companion to Princess Schwarzenberg. As a prose-writer she is represented by *Die Welt und mein Auge* (3 vols., 1844). Her collected poems appeared in 1895. She died at Baden, near Vienna.

**Papini, Giovanni** (1881–1956), Italian prose-writer. Born in Florence, he wrote a famous autobiographical novel, *Un uomo finito* (1912; Eng. trans. *A Man—Finished*, 1924). Soon after he had reconciled himself with a Church which he had bitterly attacked earlier, he produced *La storia di Cristo* (1921; Eng. trans. *The Story of Christ*, 1923) and *Sant' Agostino* (1929; Eng. trans. *St Augustine*, 1930). In *Gog* (1931) he attacked contemporary culture. His *Il Diavolo* (1953; Eng. trans. *The Devil*, 1955) caused a stir in the Vatican. He died in Florence.

**Paracelsus, Philippus Aureolus Theophrastus,** the Latin names of **Theophrast Bombast von Hohenheim** (1493–1541), Swiss Latin and German prose-writer. Born the son of a physician just outside Einsiedeln, canton of Schwytz, he took his medical degree at Ferrara in 1515. An eccentric with an undisciplined mind, but with flashes of genius, he helped to revolutionize the approach to medicine by rebelling against old methods. Every patient, he protested, must be treated differently, and he attacked complicated prescriptions and urinoscopy. He was city physician at Basel (1526) and was soon lecturing in the medical faculty of the University, where his loudness of manner and strong comments against the academic medicine-men led in 1528 to his being almost forced out of his post. After that he had no fixed abode, but wandered about Germany teaching and practising, writing the *Opus Paramirum* (1531; mod. ed. by J. Achelis, 1928), on the causes and nature of diseases, and *Das Buch Paragranum* (ed. F. Strunz, 1903), on the principles of medicine. Whether he writes in Latin or in German, on medicine or psychiatry, and indulges in mysticism or even abuse of his purblind colleagues, there is nearly always behind the utterance of this 'more than Celsus' something great. A quaint old English translation (by J. Hester, 1633) of some of his work seems to convey more of the essential flavour of Paracelsus than the far more accurate and scholarly *Selected Writings* translated by N. Gutermann (1951). Paracelsus died in Salzburg, worn out by his wanderings and feverish labours. The great edition of his collected works is that by K. Sudhoff and W. Matthiessen (14 vols.), 1922–33.

**Parandowski, Jan** (1895–     ), Polish novelist and short-story writer, born at Lwów. With an excellent style in which to express his knowledge of and feeling for the ancient world, he is well represented by his book of stories, *Eros na Olimpie* (1924) and by his full-length novel *Dysk olimpijski* (1933; Eng. trans. *The Olympic Discus*, 1939 and 1964). More recently he has published a volume of reminiscences, *Wspomnienia i sylwety* (1960).

**Pardo Bazán, Emilia** (1852–1921), Spanish novelist, short-story writer and essayist. Only child of the Conde de Pardo Bazán, she was born at La Coruña. Let loose in her father's extensive library she profited so much from the opportunity that she became the leading intellectual woman in the Spain of her day, even holding government posts in the Ministry of Education. A French scholar she introduced contemporary French literature into her own country, heralding the Spanish naturalistic school with *La cuestión palpitante* (1883). She was at her best, however, when she simply wrote realistic regional fiction, such as *Los Pazos de Ulloa* (1886; Eng. trans. *The Son of a Bondwoman*, 1908) and *La madre naturaleza* (1887), both rich in the lore of Galicia. Her short stories, *Cuentos de Marineda* (1892), are of excellent quality. As a literary critic she brought before her countrymen the significance of Russian literature in *La revolución y la novela en Rusia* (1887; Eng. trans. *Russia, its People and its Literature*, 1890). She died in Madrid.

**Parini, Giuseppe** (1729–1799), Italian poet and prose-writer. Born at Bosisio, Brianza, near Milan of modest family, he was educated for the priesthood and became tutor to the aristocratic Serbellonis (1754–62), in whose household he was treated almost as a servant, storing up information, of which he was to make such brilliant use in the future. In 1757 he began his series of *Odi* of Horatian purity of style, and he continued to write in this manner almost until the end of his life. But it is for his *Il giorno*, a long poem in four parts, consisting of *Mattino* (1763), *Mezzogiorno* (1765), *Vespro* and *Notte* not being published until 1801, that he is remembered. In this work, a social satire, urbane but sharp in its delineation of the idleness of the powerful and wealthy Italian of the day, we see a new climate beginning to settle over Europe, the first-fruits of Rousseau's (q.v.) teaching, the belief in the natural equality of all men. *Il giorno* (among the many editions of it is that by A. Momigliano, 1925; and there is an Eng. trans. *The Day*, 1927) shows Parini's complete control of a compendious irony. His prose, *Dialogo sopra la nobiltà* (1757), is another damaging exposure of mere aristocracy, since it is compared to true idealistic nobility. He was also a keen academician and joined in such literary battles as that discussed in the very persuasive prose of *Contra il Padre Branda* (1760). While under the patronage of Count Firmian, Austrian minister at Milan, he met the young Mozart, who put his *Ascanio in Alba* (1771) to music. As might have been expected he welcomed the arrival of the French in 1796, and held high appointments in the new Cisalpine Republic, but not being amenable enough for the liking of the French Directory he was forced to resign. He died in Milan. The best edition of his works is that by G. Mazzoni (1925).

**Parny, Évariste-Désiré de Forges de** (1753–1814), French poet. Born of noble family in Île de Réunion, he is the outstanding representative of French classical-sentimental poetry. Steeped in the classics and influenced by the idylls of Gessner (q.v.) he produced *Poésies érotiques* (1784), *Chansons madécasses* (1787) and *Le Portefeuille volé* (1805). The best edition of his *Œuvres* is that by A. J. Pons (1862). He died in Paris.

**Paruta, Paolo** (1540–1598), Italian prose-writer, a Venetian by birth, he held high appointments such as the ambassadorship to Rome and the procuratorship of St Mark. His principal work is his *Historia Vinetiana* (1605), which has been selected and edited by G. Paladino (1913). He left many works on politics of more than literary competence, and often set in dialogue form (*Opere politiche*, ed. C. Monzani, 2 vols., 1852). As an historian Guicciardini (q.v.) and Bembo (q.v.) are his masters, as a politician Machiavelli (q.v.). He died in Venice.

**Pascal, Blaise** (1623–1662), French prose-writer, was born in Clermont-Ferrand, his mother dying in his infancy, his father a legal official who took a keen interest in his son's education. The family (Blaise had two sisters) moved to Paris in 1631, and by the time it again moved ten years later to Rouen the boy had shown that he was a mathematician of genius. In his *Essai sur les coniques* (1640), a model of scientific writing which is also dignified prose, he propounded the theorem of collinearity. Always delicate he ruined his health by overwork at Rouen, but his life became increasingly fruitful and interesting. He got to know Descartes (q.v.) and P. Corneille (q.v.), and (of great significance for the future) began to move in Jansenist circles. On the death of their father, Pascal's younger sister immediately became a nun at Port Royal (1651). Three years later Pascal himself entered this Jansenist convent to lead the life of a recluse. It was the attacks made by the Jesuits on the Jansenists and in particular on the superior of Port Royal, Antoine Arnauld, which led Pascal to write his *Lettres Provinciales*, the eighteen letters coming out in 1656–7, in which appear quiet irony and perfect wit couched in noble prose. The Jesuits, rounded on for their easy conception of morality, were so discomfited that they did not rest until they had had the *Provinciales* publicly burnt in 1660, but already the popularity of the book was assured. In 1658 Pascal began his second great task, *Pensées sur la religion et sur quelques autres sujets*, which still remained in note form at his death, but this does not detract from its enormous power and the evidence of an unusually mighty intellect at work. Pascal reveals his standpoint here. He is sceptical of reason because reason attacks faith, and man with his terrible destiny cannot afford to lose faith. He himself is a convinced believer; it is his purpose to win men over to a belief in the truth of revealed religion. Left in an unfinished state the *Pensées* were not reliably edited until 1844 (by A. P. Faugère), but they soon after Pascal's death began to exert the enormous influence they have maintained ever since. Becoming desperately ill Pascal left Port Royal and died in Paris in the house of his elder sister, Madame Périer, with whose husband Pascal had in 1647 carried out the experiment on the Puy de Dôme, leading to the establishment of the nature of atmospheric pressure. Périer edited the brilliant *Traité du triangle arithmétique* (1665) in which Pascal laid down a scheme for determining the coefficients of expansion. This remarkable scientist, who was no less a Christian believer, may be called the founder of hydrodynamics. The best collected edition of his works is that by L. Brunschvicg, P. Boutroux and F. Gazier (14 vols., 1904–14). A separate edition of the *Lettres Provinciales* is that by Z. Tourneur (2 vols., 1944). For the *Pensées* see H. F. Stewart's edition, with English translation (1950).

**Pascoli, Giovanni** (1855–1912), Italian poet. Born at San Mauro di Romagna, he spent an unhappy childhood and youth, then went to the University of Bologna and became a student under Carducci (q.v.). After imprisonment for political offences he had settled down into calmer waters by 1882, and he entered academic life, finally becoming professor of Latin at his old university and living at Castel-vecchio, outside Bologna, where he died. His first book of poetry, *Myricae* (1891), is sombre and full of unsolved problems concerning life and death, but the *Canti di Castelvecchio* (1903; rev. ed., 1907) show a new love of nature and an approach to a happy standpoint. His classically inspired *Poemi conviviali* (1904) are somewhat stiff, though exceedingly well-bred. *Primi poemetti* (1904) and *Nuovi poemetti* (1909) are full of the breath of the *Georgics* with Carducci near at hand. Such later works as his nationalistic *Poemi del Risorgimento* (1913) somehow strike a blatant and disagreeable note. Pascoli also wrote Latin poetry with much grace and fluency, as his *Carmi latini* (1914) show. A useful edition of his Italian poetry is that of 1939, *Tutte le poesie italiane di Giovanni Pascoli*.

**Passeroni, Gian Carlo** (1713–1803), Italian poet. Born at Condamine, near Nice, he became a priest and was an active member of various literary academies. A close friend of Parini (q.v.) he was like him a moralist as his most considerable work the didactic poem, *Il Cicerone* (6 vols., 1755–74), shows. Into this rhymed life of Cicero he works many an attack on the futility of contemporary Italian life. The work is hardly readable today, although it throws much light on social affairs of the time. As a fabulist and epigrammatist he is, however, still attractive with his *Favole esopiane* (7 vols., 1779–88) and especially *Epigrammi greci* (1786). A typical literary *abate* of the day with a tolerant, urbane outlook, he died in Milan.

**Passeur, Stève**, pseudonym of **Étienne Morin** (1899–      ), French dramatist, born at Sedan. A noisy, undisciplined writer, who owed much to his producers, his iconoclasm is revealed in all he wrote. His chief works are: *La Maison ouverte* (1925), *Suzanne* (1929), *L'Acheteuse* (1930), *Le Témoin* (1936), *Le Château de cartes* (1937), *Le Pavillon brûle* (1941), *La Traîtresse* (1946), *Le Vin du souvenir* (1947), *107 Minutes* (1948) and *N'importe quoi pour elle* (1954). He has written many film scripts.

**Pasternak, Boris Leonidovich** (1890–1960), Russian Soviet poet, short-story writer and novelist. Born in Moscow the son of an artist of some note, he took up music and read philosophy at Moscow and Marburg. Joining various literary circles, he passed through a futurist stage, and writing some tentative verse gained some notice; but it was not until 1922 when he published *Sestra moya zhizn'* (written in 1917, 'My Sister, Life') that he won fame, which was increased by *Temy i variatsii* (1923, 'Themes and Variations'). He then turned for a moment to the short story which he had cultivated for a time in 1918; the result was a collection of tales including *Detstvo Luversa*, which gave the book its title (1925; Eng. trans. *Childhood*, 1941). Returning to poetry he less successfully attempted the narrative with *Spektorski* (1926), autobiographical in content, *1905* (1926) and *Lieutenant Schmidt* (1927), the two last both being accounts of the course of revolution. In 1932, however, Pasternak triumphantly returned to the lyric with his *Vtoroye rozhdenie* (1932, 'The Second Birth'), full of graphic descriptions of the Caucasus and influenced by Lermontov (q.v.). In spite of the difficulty of his work and its lapses in taste he had by this time become the leader of the younger poets of Soviet Russia, but he was not able readily to accept the Bolshevik regime and was looked upon with suspicion by the authorities. His autobiography in prose, *Okhrannaya gramota* (1931; Eng. trans. *Safe Conduct* in *Selected Writings of Boris Pasternak*, 1949), clearly shows his position. In an increasingly hostile atmosphere he turned to translation, succeeding particularly well with Shakespeare, until during the Second World War the Soviet government in desperate straits relaxed its party hold in the face of a wider patriotism. This enabled him to publish two more collections of verse, *Na rannikh poyezdakh* (1941, 'On Early Trains') and *Zemnoy prostor* (1945, 'The Wide World'). See *The Collected Prose Works of Boris Pasternak*, translated by R. Payne and B. Scott (1945), *Selected Poems*, translated by J. M. Cohen (1947), and *In the Interlude. Poems, 1945–60* (1962). In 1957 he allowed his *Doktor Zhivago* (Eng. trans. 1958) to appear and its success was worldwide. An offer of the Nobel Prize was made in 1958, but this his own country refused to allow him to take up. He died in seclusion and under a cloud at Peredelkino, near Moscow.

**Pavese, Cesare** (1908–1950), Italian poet and novelist. Born at Cuneo, he brilliantly depicted the spirit of disillusionment of men faced with the destruction of culture and the consequent purposelessness of life by political totalitarianism either from above (Fascist government) or from below (the alternative power of the masses) with total war as the final destroyer. Such novels as *La spiaggia* (1942), *Feria d'agosto* (1946), *Il compagno* (1947; Eng. trans. *The Comrade*, 1959), *La bella estate* (1949) and above all his masterpiece *La luna e i falò* (1950;

Eng. trans. *The Moon and the Bonfire*, 1952) give powerful utterance
to his state of mind. He committed suicide in Turin. His most considerable volume of verse, *Verrà la morte*, appeared the year after his
death.

**Pavlenko, Peter Andreyevich** (1899–1951), Russian Soviet novelist
born in Petersburg. He gained his reputation with *Barrikady*
(1932) about the Paris Commune of 1871. *Na vostoke* (1936; Eng.
trans. *Red Planes Fly East*, 1938) is concerned with Siberia and the
approaching inevitable war with Japan. *Schastie* (1947, 'Happiness')
is a disgraceful travesty of the Yalta Conference.

**Péguy, Charles Pierre** (1873–1914), French poet and prose-writer.
Born in Orléans, the son of peasants and largely self-educated, he
went to Paris and studied under Bergson (q.v.). He first attracted
attention with a book on labour problems from a socialistic point of
view, *De la cité socialiste* (1897), and the same year he produced
*Jeanne d'Arc*, a poetic drama, deeply catholic in tone, in collaboration
with Marcel Baudouin, whose sister, Charlotte, he married soon
afterwards. In 1900 he started the famous literary paper, *Cahiers
de la Quinzaine*, which ran till 1914 and had such an influence on its
generation. He took a leading part in the defence of Dreyfus, returning to the affair in memorable terms in *Notre jeunesse* (1910). By 1905
he had come to realize that Germany intended France's ultimate ruin,
and from then on all his efforts were bent on extolling his love for
France and invoking her guardians, Jeanne d'Arc and Saint Geneviève.
*Le Mystère de la Charité de Jeanne d'Arc* (1910; Eng. trans. 1950) is a
truly vivid work on Christ's Passion, and this was followed up by
*L'Argent* (1912) and *La Tapisserie de Sainte Geneviève et de Jeanne
d'Arc* (1913). This mystical work has had an enormous influence on
modern French literature. He was killed in action at Plessis-l'Évêque,
during the Battle of the Marne. His *Œuvres complètes* appeared (15
vols.) between 1917 and 1934. See also *Œuvres poétiques complètes*
(1941).

**Peire Cardenal** (1225?–1272), Provençal troubadour. Born at Puy-en-
Velai or thereabouts, he took a serious view of his poetic mission,
attacking in his sixty-five poems the vices of courts and above all
the immorality of the clergy and the crying scandal of the Albigensian
crusade. Dante honoured him (*Paradiso*, xxvi). See A. Kolsen,
*Dichtungen der Trobadors* (1916).

**Peire Rogier** ( *fl.* 1160–1180), Provençal troubadour, probably from
Auvergne. He was famous in the Middle Ages for his courtly poetry,
much of it addressed to the Lady Ermengarde of Narbonne. See
C. Appel, *Leben und Lieder des Trobadors Peire Rogier* (1882).

**Peire Vidal** (1180?–1206), Provençal troubadour, born in Toulouse,
the son of a farrier. A wanderer all over southern Europe, reaching the
Balkans and even the Byzantine Empire, he sang his way from court
to court during his short and vivid life, celebrating love and the
happiness of the open road. The best edition of his work is *Les
Poésies de Peire Vidal* by J. Anglade (second ed., 1933).

**Peletier du Mans, Jacques** (1517–1582), French poet, born at Le Mans, became closely associated with the Pléiade. His two most considerable volumes are *Œuvres poétiques* (1547; ed. L. Séché, 1904) and *L'Amour des Amours* (1555; ed. A. van Bever, 1926), the quality of the latter being at times excellent, especially in the lyrics. *La Savoie* (1572; ed. C. Pagès, 1897) reveals descriptive qualities. He died in Paris.

**Pellico, Silvio** (1788–1854), Italian dramatist and autobiographer, was born at Saluzzo, Piedmont, became a journalist and gained a reputation with his plays, above all *Francesca da Rimini* (1818; Eng. trans. 1856). Becoming a member of the Carbonari in 1819, he was accused of treason by the Austrians the following year, and from 1822 to 1830 was imprisoned in the Spielberg in Moravia. After his release he published *Le mie prigioni* (1832; Eng. trans. *My Prisons*, 1833) giving a moving account of his sufferings in gaol, in a manner all the more damaging to his Austrian persecutors because of its spirit of patience and quiet endurance. He always refused to preach defiance, and this turned many militant Italians against him, yet in the end the book proved more telling than manifestos. His later works do not call for mention. He died in Turin.

**Pellisson-Fontanier, Paul** (1624–1693), French prose-writer and poet. Born at Béziers, he rose in the literary and social world thanks to his friendship with Madeleine de Scudéry (q.v.), but fell foul of Louis XIV in 1661 and was imprisoned for five years. Having gained his release by renouncing Protestantism, he was appointed historiographer royal in 1666, but owing to court and literary intrigues he lost the post in 1677. As a prose-writer he gained celebrity with his dignified *Histoire de l'Académie françoise* (1652), on which all future histories of the subject are based, and his verse contributions to the *Recueil de pièces gallantes en prose et vers* (1664) show his poetic qualities. He died in Paris. Sainte-Beuve (q.v.) regarded him highly.

**Pemán, José María** (1898–    ), Spanish poet and playwright. Born in Cadiz, he became as strong an apologist for Catholicism as for right wing politics and even totalitarianism. *El barrio de Santa Cruz* (1931) is his first important book of verse and showed him anchored squarely in the past, drawing inspiration from folk-song. The setting up of the Spanish Republic drew from him *Elegía a la tradición española* (1931), but it was as a playwright that he had the most impact, above all in *El divino impaciente* (1935; Eng. trans. *A Saint in a Hurry*, 1935). Other plays are *La santa virreina* (1939) and *Metternich* (1943), the latter a highly significant theme for an upholder of Franco's Fascist government. His later works include *La destrucción de Sagunto* (1954), *Édipo* (1954), *La noche de San Martín* (1955), *Tyestes* (1958) and *Los tres etcéteras de Don Simón* (1959).

**Perdigon** (*fl.* 1190–1212), Provençal troubadour, the son of a fisherman he was patronized by the Dauphin d'Auvergne. Later he became a Cistercian monk. His tender lyrics are very personal and he is a master of style. See *Les chansons de Perdigon* (ed. H. J. Chaytor, 1909; rev. and extended 1926).

**Pereda y Sánchez de Porrúa, José María de** (1833–1906), Spanish novelist. Born at Polanco, near Santander, of a wealthy landed family, he entered the army, but left it to devote himself to looking after the estate. A man of strong reactionary views, some of his novels, such as *Don Gonzalo González de la Gonzalera* (1878; part Eng. trans. *Don Gonzalo* by W. H. Bishop in *Library of the World's Best Literature*, 1942) were mere vehicles for prejudice. His best work is, however, to be found in his accounts of peasant and seafaring life in the neighbourhood of Santander, and such novels as *Escenas montañesas* (1864) set in the countryside, *Sotileza* (1884; part Eng. trans. in *Library of the World's Best Literature*, 1942) by the sea, and *Peñas arriba* (1894) in the mountains, are, in spite of shallow plots, vivid sketches. He died in Santander.

**Pérez de Ayala, Ramón** (1880–1962), Spanish novelist. Born in Oviedo, he was educated by the Jesuits and at Oviedo University under Clarín (q.v.). He then travelled widely, but the failure of the family business and his father's sudden death brought him home faced with the necessity of earning his living. He turned to writing, and with his gifts of style (he was one of the finest prose-writers of his generation), his sharp intellect, his grasp of situation and his power of analysis of character he succeeded from the start. *Tinieblas en las cumbres* (1907) is autobiographical, *A.M.P.G.* (1910) is a somewhat cruel satire on the Jesuits, *Prometeo* (1916; Eng. trans. *Prometheus* in *Stories by Pérez de Ayala*, 1920) and *La máscara* (1918) show a more objective approach, which is fully reached in *Belarmino y Apolonio* (1921) and *Bajo el signo de Artemisia* (1924). His last important novels were *Tigre Juan* (1926; Eng. trans. *Tiger Juan*, 1933) and *El curandero de su honra* (1926). In 1931 he became the first ambassador of the Spanish Republic to Britain, but later made his peace with Franco and was cultural attaché in Argentina (1942). He returned to Spain in 1949 and settled as a free-lance journalist in Madrid where he died.

**Pérez de Hita, Ginés** (1542?–1619?), Spanish novelist, born somewhere in Murcia. Early he entered the army, but left it in 1571 to lead a life of letters, the chief result of which was his *Guerras civiles de Granada* which appeared in two parts, the first in 1595, the second in 1619. Both deal with Moorish life, which had fascinated Pérez since he had taken part in the expedition to quell the Moorish revolt in the Alpujarras mountains of the Sierra Nevada in 1568. But the two parts are absolutely different. The first, which purports to be a history of the Moors in Granada down to 1492, is highly coloured and full of literary life but is little more than a novel, whereas the second, which continues the history of the Granadine Moors down to 1568, is a genuine piece of history. The master edition is that by P. Blanchard-Demouge (2 vols., 1913–15). The first part has had among its devotees Chateaubriand (q.v.) and Washington Irving; the second Calderón (q.v.). The whereabouts of Pérez de Hita's death, as in fact its very date, are unknown.

**Pérez Galdós, Benito** (1843–1920), Spanish novelist. Born in Las Palmas, Canary Islands, he read law at Madrid, but in 1870 gave up a legal career to devote himself to writing. His forty-six volumes of novels depicting Spanish life from the Battle of Trafalgar (1805) to the restoration of the monarchy in 1874 are comprised in *Episodios nacionales* (1873–1912). This series has often been compared to Balzac's (q.v.) *Comédie humaine*, though the narratives are more lively and attractive if not so true to life as the Frenchman's. Galdós was at the same time writing separate novels on contemporary life, and it is on these, rather than on the *Episodios*, that his fame now rests. In these non-historical books, delightfully humorous though at the same time penetrating studies of domesticity, Dickens, whose work he had learnt to love while in the English school which he attended in Las Palmas, is his master. *Doña Perfecta* (1876; Eng. trans. *Lady Perfecta*, 1894) is typical of his best work as with mastery he unfolds the battle between the old and new ways of life in Spain. Other outstanding books not in the *Episodios* series are *Gloria* (1877; Eng. trans. 1897), *La familia de León Roch* (1878; Eng. trans. 1888), *La de Bringas* (1884; Eng. trans. *The Spendthrifts*, 1952), *Tormento* (1884; Eng. trans. 1952) and *Marianela* (1878; Eng. trans. 1893). But his masterpieces are undoubtedly *Fortunata y Jacinta* (2 vols., 1886–7) and *Ángel Guerra* (2 vols., 1891–2), also detached novels. *Fortunata* is a magnificently successful account of the city scene. A later work is *Electra* (1901; Eng. trans. 1901). A lifelong bachelor, no one has described better than he all the little daily problems of domestic life, and with such humour and tolerance. He became blind in 1912 and died in Madrid. His *Obras completas* appeared (6 vols.) between 1942 and 1945.

**Pérez Lugín, Alejandro** (1870–1926), Spanish journalist and novelist, born in Madrid. After reading law at the University of Santiago de Compostela, he became a journalist first in Santiago and afterwards in Madrid. His fame as a novelist began with *La casa de la troya* (1915), depicting student life in Santiago. It received the prize of the Academia Española and was subsequently dramatized. He died at El Burgo (Coruña) before the publication of his more mature works, *Arminda Moscoso* (1928) and *¡La Virgen del Rocío ya entró en Triana!* (1929). His *Obras completas* were published in 1946.

**Pergaud, Louis** (1882–1915), French short-story writer. Born at Belmont, he became a schoolmaster until, realizing his powers, he moved to Paris and gave himself up to a literary career. He succeeded with his excellent books of animal stories, *De Goupil à Margot* (1910; Eng. trans. *Tales of the Untamed*, 1911) and *La Revanche du corbeau* (1911; Eng. trans. *The Vengeance of the Crow*, 1930). Before he died at Marcheville, a victim of the First World War, he had produced several other works of a similar kind, including *Le Roman de Miraut* (1913) and *La Vie des bêtes*, published posthumously in 1923.

**Perk, Jacques Fabrice Herman** (1859–1881), Dutch poet, was born at Dordrecht. Paralyzing inhibitions upset his emotional life, but he was enabled to sublimate his love for Mathilde Thomas into his fine sonnet sequence *Mathilde-Krans* (left in MS. and not ed. till 1941, 3 vols.). Here we have the adoration of love dignified by distance into cool and transcendent beauty such as is to be found in Dante (q.v.)

and Novalis (q.v.), both of whom had deeply influenced Perk. His cerebral *Gedichten* first appeared in 1882, but it was not until H. A. Mulder's edition (1942) that all his poetry became available in a reliable text. He died in Amsterdam.

**Perrault, Charles** (1628–1703), French fabulist and general prose-writer. Born in Paris of a legal family, he served under Colbert, becoming an official in charge of the royal buildings. In the literary field he was involved in the controversy over the respective merits of the ancients and moderns, in which Boileau (q.v.), his chief opponent, may be accounted victor. Perrault's *Parallèle des anciens et des modernes*, spun out from 1688 to 1697, is a dignified exposition of the superiority of the moderns, while his *Hommes illustres qui ont paru en France pendant le dix-septième siècle* (1687–1701) is a modern portrait gallery of some interest. But it is as a fabulist that he is in reality remembered. In his charming *Histoires ou Contes du temps passé* (1699) such stories as 'Little Red Riding Hood', 'The Sleeping Beauty', 'Bluebeard' and 'Puss in Boots', half-forgotten folk tales before, were first brought out into the modern light. He died in Paris.

**Perse, Saint-John,** *see* **Saint-John-Perse.**

**Perventsev, Arkady Alexeyevich** (1905–     ), Russian Soviet novelist, who leapt to fame with yet another book on the well-worn theme of the Russian civil war of 1918–21, *Kochubey* (1937; Eng. trans. *Cossack Commander*, 1939).

**Pessoa, Fernando** (1888–1935), Portuguese poet born in Lisbon, spent his childhood in South Africa. Returning to Portugal in 1905, he soon became prominent in the Modernist movement, collaborating in the literary review, *Orpheu*, from 1915 onwards. Pessoa wrote— apart from his own name—under three pseudonyms, each of which he claimed represented distinct personalities: 'Alberto Caeiro', 'Ricardo Reis' and 'Álvaro de Campos'. During his lifetime he pub-lished only two works, *English Poems* (3 vols., 1918–21) and the epic, *Mensagem* (1934), the former being a result of his South African education, and the bulk of his poetry was not collected until after his death, as *Obras completas* (5 vols., 1945–51). He died in Lisbon. His influence on twentieth-century Portuguese poetry cannot be overestimated.

**Pestalozzi, Johann Heinrich** (1746–1827), Swiss prose-writer. Born at Zürich, he began at an early age to devote himself to charitable work. Influenced by Rousseau into believing that only rural life would lead to regeneration, he bought a farm in the canton of Aargau and started an agricultural school for the children of the very poor, which, owing to his complete lack of understanding of finance, failed. He withdrew for the time being to reconsider his theories of education, the importance of which he had come to see more and more clearly, and the result of his speculations appeared as *Die Abendstunde eines Einsiedlers* (1780, 'Evening Hours of a Hermit'). A long, but interest-ing novel of a didactic, philanthropic kind, *Lienhard und Gertrud* (4 vols., 1781–7; Eng. trans. *Leonard and Gertrude*, 1824) describes the reform of a miserable village, thanks to the efforts of the school-master and the heroine. *Christoph und Else* (1782) was a flight in the same direction. In 1798 he opened an orphanage at Stanz on Lake Lucerne, which was broken up by the French the following year. He retired once more and wrote the textbook of the Pestalozzi method of teaching, *Wie Gertrud ihre Kinder lehrt* (1801; Eng. trans. *How Gertrude Educates her Children*, 1894). Here can be seen his knowledge of child psychology, and his conviction that the individual child is more important than the subject he is taught. In 1805 Pestalozzi was able to open a new school at Berthoud, later moved to Yverdun, which attracted pupils from all over Europe; but once more his fortune was dogged by lack of practical ability and by the enmity of orthodox schoolmasters until its numbers began to fall rapidly, and it was closed in 1825. His optimism at length gone, Pestalozzi went to live at Neuhof, near Brugg in the canton of Aargau, where he died. His last year was spent in writing his reminiscences, *Meine Lebens-schicksale* (1826).

**Peter of Eboli** (1160?–1219), Italian poet writing in Latin. Born at Eboli, he was probably a member of the faculty of medicine at Salerno University. He was patronized by the Emperor Henry VI, to whom he dedicated an elaborate poem. His poem on the Roman baths of Puteoli is of considerable literary merit besides being of much antiquarian interest. **Petrus Ansolinus,** as he is sometimes called, seems to have died in Sicily. See E. Rota's *Petri Ansolini de Ebulo de rebus Siculis carmen*, 1904.

**Peter the Venerable** (1093–1155), French prose-writer and poet in Latin, was Benedictine abbot of Cluny from 1122 until his death, and gave the persecuted Abélard (q.v.) refuge in his monastery in his last years. Keenly interested in Islamic studies, he patronized a Latin translation of the Koran, and was the author of devotional prose works and hymns. See J.-P. Migne's *Patrologia Latina* (vol. clxxxix).

**Peters, Gerlach** (1378–1411), Dutch mystic writing in Latin, was born at Deventer and became a monk at Windesheim where he died. His great work is his devotional *Soliloquium*, composed between 1403 and 1411 (ed. J. Strange, 1849; Eng. trans. *The Divine Soliloquies*, 1920, which includes an earlier work, the *Breviloquium*).

**Petersen, Nils** (1897–1943), Danish novelist and poet, who was born at Vamdrup, took up journalism before making for the open road. A neurotic who could not face an ordinary straightforward life, he wandered from place to place earning a precarious living in all manner of ways, but found time to publish a large number of books, none of which enjoyed success until he turned to the historical novel. The first of these, set in ancient Rome, is *Sandalmagernes Gade* (1931; Eng. trans. *The Street of the Sandalmakers*, 1933), and it achieved much European popularity. His only other novel, *Spildt Mælk* (1934; Eng. trans. *Spilt Milk. A Story of Ireland*, 1935), deals with Ireland in the time of the civil war. The best of his poetry, the self-revelations of a tortured man, is to be seen side by side with much inferior work in *Samlede Digte* (1949). He died at Laven.

**Petőfi, Sándor** (1823–1849), Hungarian poet. Born at Kiskőrös, he was brought up as a Calvinist, but ran away from his strict and loveless home to become an actor. Failing in this he joined the army, but thanks to friends he had made in the meantime he was able to settle down in Pest as a literary man. *Versek 1842–44* (1844) carried him into a prominence brought out into further relief by *Versek 1844–45* (1845) with its plenitude, like the former, of remarkable short lyrics. For a translation of some of his poems see *Sixty Poems by Andor* (*sic*) *Petőfi* by E. B. Pierce and E. Delmár (1948). Petőfi, a keen Hungarian nationalist, was killed in action at the Battle of Segesvár, Transylvania. He is unquestionably the greatest Hungarian lyric poet.

**Petrarch (Petrarca), Francesco** (1304–1374), Italian poet and prose-writer in Italian and Latin. Francesco Petracco (as his name originally was) was born at Arezzo, Tuscany, into a legal family, exiled from Florence on account of its support of the White Party. In 1313 the boy was taken by his parents to Avignon, papal territory, and in 1319 entered the University of Montpellier to read law. He was there for four years, going on to Bologna to complete the course. On the death of his father in 1326, however, he renounced a legal career for good and took minor Orders. Almost at once there followed the incident which coloured his whole life, his falling in love with Laura de Noves, wife of Hugues de Sade, at Avignon (1327). This meeting led to the composition of *Le Rime*, that incomparable series of love-poems. Already courted by the great, Petrarch availed himself of their patronage to travel widely in Europe, and from 1333 for the next twenty years was often on the move in the Low Countries, France, Spain and even Hungary. A temporary breakdown of health led to heart and mind searchings in retirement at Vaucluse (1336); but he recovered to receive the laureate's crown in an impressive ceremony on the Capitol in Rome (1341). He had by this time written many poems of the Laura cycle as also the splendid ode *All' Italia*, and had composed the greater part of his Latin verse epic *Africa* (left incomplete, 1339) on the life of Scipio Africanus. Petrarch settled in Parma in 1347, but the Black Death of 1348–9 brought him many sorrows, above all the death of Laura in the first year of it. His conscience again pricked him as it had done twelve years before, reminding him of the vanity of the world. He made a pilgrimage to Rome (1350) and visited Florence where he met Boccaccio (q.v.), a friendship which lasted till his death. On his return to Avignon he was offered a papal secretaryship, but refused it, leaving the city finally (1353). He now joined the Viscontis' court at Milan, and was employed by Giovanni Visconti as ambassador to foreign courts, where his dignity of manner and his fame resulted in successful missions. The greatest poetry in the vernacular which he wrote during these years is *I Trionfi* (begun 1352), highly allegorized poems in praise of Laura, the whole conception influenced by Dante. As a latinist he produced about this time magnificent imitations of Virgil and the Horace of the *Epistles*. His last important diplomatic mission was to the French court in 1360, and not long afterwards he retired to Arquà, near Padua, devoting himself to unceasing study until his death. His life and work shows the Renaissance bursting out of its bonds: spiritual austerity and literary sensualism exist in the man simultaneously, the reverence for the age-old Latin language is balanced by the love of the newly flowered Italian language; the traveller and the recluse, the laureate and the ascetic live side by side. Petrarch's influence as a humanist and as a lyric poet were, and have been since, overwhelming. His *Rime* with their depth of feeling discredited for ever the far too often soulless Provençal courtly poetry. Here was a new poet of the living language who had every literary grace at his command, and a craftsman who brought many a verse scheme to perfection, above all the sonnet, virtually introduced by him to Europe. Of editions of his works the best is *Rime, Trionfi e Poesie latine* (ed. Neri and others, 1951). The earliest complete edition of all his works including prose—and his Ciceronian letters, *Rerum familiarum* and *Rerum senilium* are fascinating accounts of the life and thought of his time—is the Basel edition of 1554. The *Rerum familiarum* appeared in four volumes (1933–42) and there is an edition of the *Rerum senilium* (1869). Many have attempted to translate Petrarch's *Rime* into English. Perhaps the best effort is *Some Love Songs of Petrarch*, translated and annotated by W. D. Foulke (1915).

**Petrov, E. P.,** *see* **Ilf, I. A.**

**Petrović, Petar Njegoš** (1813–1851), Montenegrin poet. Born at Njeguši, he studied for the Church, and became Prince-Bishop of Montenegro before he was twenty. A great patriot, always alive to the dangers to his country from the Turks, he is the author of three poetical works which entitle him to pride of place in Yugoslav literature. The first is a speculative poem, *Luča Mikrokozma* (1845, 'Microcosmic Ray'), full of high flights of thought accompanied by magnificent descriptive passages. Then there is the narrative poem *Laž'ni Car Šćepan Mali* (1851, 'The False Czar Šćepan Mali'), inferior in general to the former, but revealing new lyrical powers. His masterpiece is *Gorski Vijenac* (1847; Eng. trans. *The Mountain Wreath*, 1930), in which every kind of quality appears and a gigantic panorama of Montenegrin life is spread out before us, with the struggle between Turk and Montenegrin magnified to a tremendous battle between the powers of good and evil. Petrović died at Cetinje.

**Petrus de Dacia** (1230?–1289), Swedish Latin prose-writer. Born in Gotland, he studied at Cologne and Paris, and later became a Dominican monk, and died prior of Visby monastery. His meeting while in Cologne with a nun called Kristina von Stommeln (1266) led to a lifelong correspondence and an appreciation of her, *Vita Christinae Stumbelensis* (ed. J. Paulson, 1896), which borders on love.

**Pétursson, Hallgrímur** (1614?–1674), Icelandic religious poet. The place and date of his birth are unknown, and he grew up in very poor surroundings until patronage allowed him to gain some grammar-school education followed by a lengthy stay in Denmark. On his return to Iceland he became a clergyman. He died at Ferstikla. His most famous work and the greatest example of Icelandic devotional poetry is *Fimmtíu Passiusálmar* (1666). A modern edition of his collected works is *Sálmar og Kvæði* (ed. G. Thomsen, 2 vols., 1887–1890). For translations see *The Passion Hymns of Iceland* (1913) and *Icelandic Christian Classics* (1950), both by C. Venn Pilcher.

**Peyrefitte, Roger** (1907– ), French novelist, born at Castres. He entered the diplomatic service in 1931, remaining in it until 1945. He has been an unsparing critic of the circles in which he has moved, in such books as: *Les Amitiés particulières* (1945), *Les Ambassades* (1951; Eng. trans. *Diplomatic Diversions*, 1953), *La Fin des ambassades* (1953; Eng. trans. *Diplomatic Conclusions*, 1954), *Les Clés de Saint Pierre* (1955), *Les Chevaliers de Malte* (1957; Eng. trans. *Knights of Malta*, 1959), *Les Fils de la lumière* (1961) and *Notre amour* (1967).

**Pfeffel, Gottlieb Konrad** (1736–1809), German poet and playwright. Born in Colmar, Alsace, his law studies were ended by blindness in 1757. He then turned his attention to the education of children, forestalling Pestalozzi (q.v.) as an enlightened pedagogue and directing a most successful school in his native town. An accomplished metrist he published two attractive volumes of poetry, *Poetische Versuche* (1761) and *Fabeln* (1783). His collection of plays for children, *Dramatische Kinderspiele* (1769) show an understanding of the child mind most unusual in that age. He died in Colmar.

**Philippe, Charles-Louis** (1874–1909), French novelist born at Cérilly of poor parents, he worked for some time as a clerk in Paris before making a reputation with *La Mère et l'enfant* (1900), founded on his own experiences. This was set in the country, but he soon found inspiration in the life of the Paris poor which is treated in a direct manner, with an underlying current of romanticism in *Bubu de Montparnasse* (1901), *Le Père Perdrix* (1903), *Marie Donadieu* (1904; Eng. trans. 1949) and *Croquignole* (1906). Always weak in health he had barely completed *Charles Blanchard* (posthumously, 1913) when he died in Paris. He exercised an undoubted influence on Giraudoux (q.v.).

**Philippe de Remy de Beaumanoir** (1248?–1296), French poet and prose-writer who eventually held official appointments in Poitou, wrote *La Manekine* (1276) and *Jehan et Blonde* (1278), both romances but differing greatly in treatment, the first being credulous and replete with fantastic stories, the second thoroughly natural and down-to-earth. In addition he composed short love-poems and a variety of other lyrics and the famed legal work, *Les Coutumes de Beauvoisis* (1283; ed. A. Salmon, 2 vols., 1899, 1910). His *Œuvres poétiques* (ed. H. Suchier) appeared in two volumes, 1884–5.

**Philippe Mousqués** (1215?–1268?), French poet, born at Tournai. Little is known of his life, towards the end of which he composed his *Chronique rimée*, an enormous work dealing with the history of the French kings down to his own time, much of the earlier part merely fabulous. It is interesting as a general repository for chronicles and stories of many kinds and from many sources, but it owes its framework to the Latin history of France, the *Abbreviatio* composed by the monks of St Denis. The time and place of his death are both unknown. The *Chronique rimée* was edited by F. J. de Reiffenberg (1836).

**Piachaud, René-Louis** (1896–1941), Swiss poet, born in Geneva. His strong and lucid verse, set in a variety of metrical schemes, is to be found in such volumes as *L'Indifférent* (1923), *Le Poème paternel* (1932) and *Le Chant de la mort et du jour* (1937), their inspiration derived from love of family and of his native land. He died in Geneva.

**Pibrac, Guy du Faur de** (1529–1584), French poet. Born of noble family at Pibrac, near Toulouse, he became a famous man of law and served on various foreign missions. He is known for his bucolic poem, *Plaisirs de la vie rustique* (1574), and for his two collections of axiomatic verse, *Quatrains moraux* (1574–6). He died in Paris.

**Piccolomini, Enea Silvio, Pope Pius II** (1405–1464), Italian Latin prose-writer. Born at Corsignano-Pienza, he entered the imperial service and lived a wild and irregular life even after becoming secretary to the Bishop of Fermo at the Council of Basel. Later he was employed in various embassies until his ordination. His rise in the Church was rapid; he was soon Bishop of Trieste, was made a cardinal in 1456, and on the death of Callixtus III (1458) he was elected Pope as Pius II. By now famed throughout Europe as a humanist with such a diversified literary performance as his poetry, his *De curialium miseriis epistola* (ed. W. P. Mustard, 1928), a flight into stylish moralizing, a Terentian comedy, *Chrysis* (ed. I. Sanesi, 1941), a history of his own times, *Commentarii rerum memorabilium quae temporis suis contigerunt* (first publ. 1584), and the popular love-tale, *De duobus amantibus historia* (ed. J.-J. Dévay, 1904; Eng. trans. *Euryalus and Lucrezia*, 1929), he showed strength of character in his efforts to raise a European army to face the Turks which took up most of his pontificate. He died at Ancona. His *Opera* first appeared in 1551.

**Pichler, Karoline** (1769–1843), Austrian novelist, born in Vienna, of which she was a lifelong resident. She produced a vast number of novels of varying style, quality and plot, most characteristic being the 'heroic' *Frauenwürde* (1808) and *Die Belagerung Wiens* (1824).

**Pico della Mirandola,** *see* **Mirandola.**

**Picón y Bouchet, Jacinto Octavio** (1852–1923), Spanish novelist. Born in Madrid, he was educated partly in France, which introduced him to anti-clericalism and natural (one might just as soon call it free) love. The first is to be seen in the well-written, perhaps too well-written, *Lázaro* (1882) and *El enemigo* (1887). His novels of the other kind include *La hijastra del amor* (1884), *La honrada* (1890), *Dulce y sabrosa* (1891), *Juanita Tenorio* (1910) and *Sacramento* (1914). There are English translations of several novels by C. B. MacMichael (Kansas, 1926–7). Picón died in Madrid.

**Piferrer y Fábregas, Pablo** (1818–1848), Spanish poet. Born in Barcelona of working-class family, he became professor of rhetoric and belles-lettres at the university there. His knowledge of and feeling for folk tales are revealed in his charming lyrics and longer narratives enshrining legends. They appear in the collection of three poets, *Composiciones poéticas de Pablo Piferrer, Juan Francisco Carbó, y José Senis y Meusa* (1851). Piferrer died in Barcelona.

**Pignotti, Lorenzo** (1739–1812), Italian poet, born at Figline in the Val d'Arno, became professor of physics at the University of Pisa in 1774. Resident in Florence, he was a leading light in the Accademia della Crusca there and took part in *The Florence Miscellany* (1785), a work by several members of the English colony in the city, including Mrs Piozzi and Robert Merry. His best-known work is his *Favole e novelle* (1782), and his enthusiasm for English literature, which until that time had been imperfectly known in Italy, is to be seen in such works as *La tomba di Shakespeare* (1779) and *L'ombra di Pope* (1781). His 'Homeric' epic, *Roberto Manners* (1783; Eng. trans. *Robert Manners* by R. Merry, 1785), is an enthusiastic pro-British and anti-French account of the Battle of the Saints (1782). He became Royal Historiographer of Tuscany in 1801, and in this capacity wrote his *Storia della Toscana*, posthumously published in 1813. He died in Pisa. His collected *Poesie* appeared in 1820.

**Pijpers, Pieter** (1749–1805), Dutch poet and dramatist. Born at Amersfoort, he became well known in politics. His patriotic *Vaderlandsche Gedichten* (1784–7) comprise his most considerable poetic efforts. A Dutch Alfieri (q.v.), inspired by the classics, his most characteristic play is *Spartacus* (1805) breathing a love of freedom and confusion to tyrants. He died at Amersfoort.

**Pilnyak, Boris**, pseudonymn of **Boris Andreyevich Vogau** (1894–1940?), Russian Soviet novelist, born at Mozhaysk. After entering into the 1917 Revolution with gusto and bringing his experiences to bear on several works, he became critical of the new regime and had to redeem himself. The result was his pro-Stalinist *Volga vpadayet v Kaspiyskoye more* (1930; Eng. trans. *The Volga Falls to the Caspian Sea*, 1931). After this he was allowed to travel freely abroad, and his experiences only brought about a renewed distaste for the materialistic ideals of the new Russia. He fell foul of the party once more, and after a few more novels, such as *Kamni i korni* (1935, 'Stones and Roots'), he disappeared from view and has not been heard of since 1938. He is said to have been shot in the Urals about 1940. See the collection of Pilnyak's stories in English translation, *Tales of the Wilderness* (1924).

**Pindemonte, Ippolito** (1753–1828), Italian poet, prose-writer and translator, was born in Verona. Brought up in cultured surroundings, he travelled in many parts of Europe and added cosmopolitanism to his classical culture. Associated (1785) with the Accademia della Crusca at Florence, where he was on friendly terms with several of the English residents, he and Lorenzo Pignotti (q.v.) were among the first to foster that atmosphere of mutual goodwill between Italian and English men of letters which led to Dante studies and enthusiasm for the Risorgimento in nineteenth-century England. His *Gibilterra salvata* (1783) was an elaborate panegyric on the British defence of Gibraltar by General Eliott, and his *I sepolcri* (1785), inspired by the

Grand Duke Leopold of Tuscany's Burial Decrees, influenced his young friend Foscolo's (q.v.) *De' sepolcri* (1807). But the political idealist Pindemonte, who trod over the ruins of the Bastille with Alfieri (q.v.) in 1789, was happiest in his beautiful collection of lyrics *Poesie campestri* (1785). He made a notable translation of the Odyssey, *L'Odissea* (1805–19; ed. Reichenbach, 1928). See his collected poetry, *Poesie originali di Ippolito Pindemonte* (ed. Torri, 1858). He died in Verona.

**Pinto, Fernão Mendes** (1510?–1583), Portuguese prose-writer, born at Montemoro-Velho. His extraordinary career began when in 1537 he set out for the East, and embarked on an adventurous life which took him to Arabia, India, Burma and Japan. After more than twenty colourful years, during which he suffered imprisonment, being even sold into slavery, and turned his hand to every kind of occupation and trade, he came back to Portugal to write his astonishing account of his experiences, *Peregrinaçam de Fernam Mendez Pinto*, begun in 1558 (first publ. 1614; mod. eds., 4 vols., 1908–10; 7 vols., 1930–1; 7 vols., 1944–5; Eng. trans. *The Voyages and Adventures of Ferdinand Mendez Pinto, a Portugal*, 1663; abridged ed., 1891). Under the influence of Saint Francis Xavier he entered the Jesuit Order, but later left it. He died at Almada.

**Pinto Delgado, João** (*d.* 1639?), Spanish poet. A Portuguese Jew, he was born in Tavira, Portugal, but in order to avoid persecution left the country for France at an early age and settled in Rouen, where he published the beautiful *Poema de la Reyna Ester* (1627) inspired by the Old Testament. Finally threatened with imprisonment for his faith he went to Amsterdam, where he died.

**Pirandello, Luigi** (1867–1936), Italian playwright, novelist and short-story writer, was born at Girgenti, Sicily. He was educated at the universities of Palermo, Rome and Bonn, returning to Rome as a schoolmaster in a high school for girls. It was as the author of the realistic, slightly cynical novel, *Il fu Mattia Pascal* (1904; Eng. trans. *The Late Mattia Pascal*, 1923), that he gained a reputation. Not until 1912 did he venture to the stage, but in doing so he discovered the medium best suited to his gifts. He experimented at first in such plays as the one-act *La morsa* and the full-length *Pensaci, Giacomino!* (1916). With *Così è—se vi pare* (1918; Eng. trans. *Right You Are—If You Think So* in *Three Plays* by A. Livingston, 1923) he is in his full element; in *Sei personaggi in cerca d'un autore* (1921; Eng. trans. *Six Characters in Search of an Author* in *Three Plays*, 1923) he is triumphant. With *Enrico IV* (1922; Eng. trans. *Henry IV* in *ibid.*) he became world famous. Many of his plays were produced on the British stage, and were enjoyed, praised, reviled and constantly misunderstood. But out of the welter of themes and systems of philosophy comes this Pirandellian message, that each man must learn to face himself and know himself, for he stands alone in the universe with no one who can help him, since there is no one else sufficiently like him in the whole of creation to understand him. Pirandello's characters are definitely the ordinary men of the world, but he leads the

modern stage in investing such characters with universal significance.
He died in Rome. See the English translation, *Short Stories* (1959).

**Pirckheimer, Willibald** (1470–1530), German man of letters. This all-round personality was born at Eichstätt. He eventually moved to Nuremberg, of which city he became a councillor, gathering about him many literary and artist friends, including Albrecht Dürer. His *Schweizerkrieg* (ed. K. Rück, 1895) is a vivid account of the Swiss war in which he took part, and it seems now likely that he is the author of the Latin satire concerning the Reformation, *Eccius Dedolatus* (ed. A. E. Berger, 1931). His collected works, for the most part in Latin, first appeared in 1610. He died in Nuremberg.

**Pisan, Christine de,** *see* **Christine.**

**Pisarev, Dmitry Ivanovich** (1840–1868), Russian political writer and literary critic, was born in the province of Orel. He is the prototype of the younger generation in uncompromising revolt against tradition. Unpleasant in character, probably unbalanced mentally, his outrageous attacks on Pushkin (q.v.), who had by now come to be regarded as a classic, brought him many enemies, but no one could deny the brilliance of his style. He was drowned near Riga. His collected works were published (6 vols.) in 1894. In recent times his work has been taken out of the lumber room and dusted by the Soviet Union.

**Pisemsky, Alexey Feofilaktovich** (1820–1881), Russian novelist and short-story writer, born in the province of Kostroma. Of a gloomy, critical nature, he set out to undermine the upper middle classes in his first novel, *Tyufyak* (1850, 'The Mattress'). His masterpiece, *Tysyacha dush* (1858, 'A Thousand Souls'; Fr. trans. *Mille âmes*, 1886), is almost great. Good is his novel about the peasants, *Gor'kaya dolya* (1859; Eng. trans. *A Bitter Fate*, 1933). He died in Moscow, having become a reactionary outcast from radical circles.

**Pixérécourt, René Charles Guilbert de** (1773–1844), French melo-dramatist. Born in Nancy, he became a prolific purveyor of popular plays, often with exciting, fast-moving plots, spiced with horror, suggested by the 'gothick' literature of Horace Walpole, Mrs Rad-cliffe and 'Monk' Lewis. Such are *Le Château des Appenins, ou les Mystères d'Udolphe* (1797), *Victor, ou l'Enfant de la forêt* (1798) and *Le Chien de Montargis, ou la Forêt de Bondy* (1816). His work led the way to the popular sensational 'Murder at the Red Barn' theatre of the first half of the nineteenth century. Pixérécourt died in Nancy.

**Platen-Hallermünde, August von** (1796–1835), German poet. Born of noble family at Ansbach, he entered the army and took part in the war of 1813. In 1818 he gave up his military career completely, and studied at the universities of Erlangen and Würzburg, where he showed a great gift for languages. Oriental studies were in the air, thanks to the Viennese Orientalist J. von Hammer-Purgstall, and these led Platen to his first notable publications, *Ghaselen* (1821) and *Neue Ghaselen* (1824). His *Sonette aus Venedig* (1825; Eng. trans. *Sonnets*, 1923) is his most satisfying work, and showed that though a romantic he did not allow himself to become undisciplined. In 1826 he settled in Italy and had little further communication with his German contemporaries. In fact, as can be seen from his sharp *Der romantische Oedipus* (1829), in which he attacked K. L. Immermann (q.v.), he regarded himself as the last upholder of true romanticism in an age of literary decadence, and despised his compatriots. Later works are the *Polenlieder* (1831), in which he sympathized with Poland in her struggle against Russia, *Die Liga von Cambrai* (1833) and *Die Abassiden* (1834), for which last he again sought inspiration in the East. He died in Syracuse. His collected works were published in 1839. As a master of form and expression Goethe is his only equal in the whole range of German literature.

**Platina,** *i.e.* **Bartolomeo Sacchi** (1421–1481), Italian prose-writer. Born at Piadena, he sought his fortune in Rome, where after varying fortune he was made librarian to Pope Sixtus IV. His main work is his *Liber de vita Christi ac omnium pontificum* (completed 1474; Eng. trans. *Lives of the Popes* (1685; mod. ed. 1888), the earlier parts untrustworthy, the last full of interest and a valuable source. He died in Rome.

**Platter, Thomas** (1499–1582), Swiss autobiographer. Born in Grächen in the Valais, he tried many trades, finally becoming a printer in Basel, where he died. His *Selbstbiographie* (1547) is an autobiography of extraordinary attraction, both as a picture of the time and a piece of literature. An English translation of it appeared in 1839.

**Plievier, Theodor** (1892–1955), German novelist. Born in Berlin of working-class parents, when he turned to writing at the end of the First World War it was as a keen critic of autocracy in any form. Such were *Des Kaisers Kulis* (1930; Eng. trans. *The Kaiser's Coolies*, 1932) and *Der Kaiser ging, die Generäle blieben* (1932; Eng. trans. *The Kaiser Goes, the Generals Remain*, 1933). As a critic of militarism he had to lie low during the rule of Hitler, but the Second World War inspired him to write his greatest work, the trilogy *Stalingrad* (1945; Eng. trans. *The Death of an Army*, 1948), *Moskau* (1952) and *Berlin* (1954). Here the grief, suffering and destruction of war are brought starkly before us as we see the German disaster in Russia and the subsequent agony of Berlin. He died at Avegno, Switzerland.

**Plisnier, Charles** (1896–1952), Belgian novelist, born at Ghlin-les-Mons. He became a lawyer and an enthusiastic Communist, but later, seeing the other side of the picture, retracted. *Mariages* (1936; Eng. trans. *Nothing to Chance*, 1938), *Faux Passeports* (1937; Eng. trans. *Memoirs of a Secret Revolutionary*, 1938), *Meurtres* (comprising *Prologue et mort d'Isabelle*, 1939; *Retour du fils*, 1939; *Martine*, 1940; *Feu dormant*, 1940; and *La Dernière Journée*, 1941) and *Mères* (comprising *Mes bien-aimés*, 1946; *Nicole Arnaud*, 1948; and *Vertu du désordre*, 1950), were excellent studies of middle-class life. He died in Brussels.

**Poerio, Alessandro** (1802–1848), Italian poet. Born in Naples, he soon became a member of various anti-Austrian movements, being exiled (1815–18 and 1820–35). During his second exile he went to

Germany and became a disciple and friend of Goethe at Weimar. Returning to Italy after fifteen years with his ardour for Italian nationalism unabated, he began to write those stirring and moving poems, chief of them all 'Il Risorgimento', which were collected as *Liriche* (1843). The influence of Leopardi (q.v.) is evident in them. He was mortally wounded in battle against the Austrians near Mestre, and died in Venice. The savage treatment meted out to his brother Carlo after the unsuccessful war of 1848–9 against Austria led to the exposure of Ferdinand of Naples and his government by Gladstone.

**Poggio Bracciolini, Gian Francesco** (1380–1459), Italian prose-writer and scholar. Born at Terranuova d'Arezzo, he became secretary to the Roman curia, and in the following years made a reputation by his recovery of important classical Latin manuscripts, including some of Lucretius, Quintilian and Vitruvius. His elegantly written satire on the contemporary Church and society, *Liber Facetiarum* (1438–52; Fr. trans. and ed. by Lisieux, 1878), is an excellent example of Renaissance literature. He died in Florence. His *Opere* appeared at Strassburg in 1510.

**Polenz, Wilhelm von** (1861–1903), German novelist, born at Ober-kunewalde, Lusatia. In such fiction as *Der Pfarrer von Breitendorf* (1893), *Der Büttnerbauer* (1895; Eng. trans. *Farmer Büttner*, 1913) and *Das Land der Zukunft* (1903; Eng. trans. *The Land of the Future*, 1904) he gives a realistic account of country life, never glossing over its less pleasing aspects, but at the same time remaining uncompromisingly hostile to the new-fangled inventions and attitudes of modern urbanism. He died in Breslau. His works were collected in ten volumes in 1909–11.

**Poliziano, Angelo,** latinized **Politianus** (1454–1494), Italian poet. Born at Montepulciano (*Mons Politianus*), he was called after his birthplace, his real name being **Angiolo Ambrogini**. He studied Greek and Latin in Florence, and in 1475 was appointed tutor to Piero de' Medici, son of Lorenzo; but he quarrelled with the Medici family, and in 1479 left Florence for Mantua, where he was patronized by the Gonzagas, leaving unfinished an epic in honour of the Medicis, *Stanze per la Giostra*, a beautiful poem, which he never resumed. It was in Mantua that he wrote his finest work *Orfeo* (1480), accounted the first pastoral drama in Italian literature and heralding the opera. The greatest classical scholar of his time and the most distinguished literary practitioner in the ancient languages of his age, he wrote a Latin *Iliad*, an outstanding essay in Virgilian verse, and Latin lyrics and Greek epigrams which all have the authentic ring. Soon after completing the *Orfeo* he made his peace with the Medici and returned to Florence, where he was ordained, becoming canon of the cathedral, and was given the chair of classics at the university. He died in Florence. There is an excellent edition of *Le Stanze, l'Orfeo, rime e versi latini* (ed. A. Donati, 1942). A handy edition of the *Poesie italiane e latine* is that by A. Polvara (1948). There is an incomplete *Opere* (1553).

**Polo, Marco** (1254–1324), Italian traveller, born of noble family in Venice. In 1271 he set out with his father and brother on a cultural and mercantile expedition to the court of Kublai, prince of Cathay (China), and after four years' travel across the Middle East, over the Pamir and even across the Gobi Desert, arrived at the palace of Kublai Khan. Marco soon became the great favourite of the Khan, who, having sent him on special missions to Burma, Cochin China and India, appointed him governor of Yang Chow. Marco returned to Venice, after further remarkable journeys, in 1295 the possessor of enormous riches. On the outbreak of war between Genoa and Venice he commanded a galley at his own expense (1298), being taken prisoner and imprisoned for a year in Genoa. It was while in prison that he dictated an account of his journeys to a fellow captive, Rusticiano of Pisa, who copied them down in French. *Il Milione*, as the book was called after a Polo family nickname, was translated into Latin and Italian, and later into many other languages. The original French text was published in 1824, having been neglected for countless years, earlier editions following either the Latin or Italian texts. The best Italian edition is that by L. F. Benedetto (1942); the best English translation by H. Yule (1871; new ed. 1899), taken from an eclectic text. Polo was released in 1299 and died in Venice. Only the Prologue contains personal narrative; the rest of the work is concerned with the state of affairs in the various countries of Asia, interspersed with stories of the marvellous. A passage in the work inspired S. T. Coleridge's *Kubla Khan*.

**Ponsard, François** (1814–1867), French dramatist. Born at Vienne (Isère), he became an opponent of the out-and-out romantic school of Victor Hugo (q.v.) with his *Lucrèce* (1843), following this up with *Agnès de Mérane* (1846), *Charlotte Corday* (1850) and *L'Honneur et l'argent* (1853). His work thereafter is unimportant. He died in Paris. His *Œuvres complètes* were published (3 vols.) between 1865 and 1876.

**Ponson du Terrail, Pierre-Alexis** (1829–1871), French novelist. Born at Montmaur, he made his name as a sensational fiction writer with *Les Exploits de Rocambole* (1859), sequels to which, such as *Les Drames de Paris* (1865), *Le Dernier Mot de Rocambole* (1866) and *La Vérité sur Rocambole* (1867), resulted in the term 'Rocambolesque' being applied to plots exemplified in these works, which foreshadow the detective novel and science fiction. He died in Bordeaux.

**Pontano, Giovanni** (1422–1503), Italian Latin poet, was born at Cerreto. From 1447 he served the Aragonese kingdom of Naples, becoming chancellor of it in 1486, and being dismissed in 1495 for agreeing to capitulate to the French. He died in Naples. A foremost Latin poet of the Italian Renaissance, his *Carmina* (ed. B. Soldati, 2 vols., 1902) contain a wide variety of lyrics, all inspired by Naples and its people.

**Pontoppidan, Erik** (1698–1764), Danish prose-writer. Born at Aarhus, he became professor of theology at Copenhagen University (1738) and nine years later Bishop of Bergen. His chief work, written in an engaging style, is his *Norges naturlige historie* (1752–4; Eng. trans.

*The Natural History of Norway*, 1755), full of accounts of the marvellous. His description of the fabulous sea-serpent, the Kraken, caused reverberations in contemporary and romantic literature. He died in Copenhagen.

**Pontoppidan, Henrik** (1857–1943), Danish novelist. Born at Fredericia a clergyman's son, he studied engineering at Copenhagen, but soon took to writing. Dissatisfied with his countrymen's superficiality and easy confidence, he lashed them in *Det forjættede Land* (3 vols., 1891–5; Eng. trans. of two of the vols., *Emanuel, or Children of the Soil*, 1892; and *The Promised Land*, 1896). In this work attention was drawn to the plight of the Danish countryside and its people in the face of the new prosperity of the towns. Two other extended novels, *Lykke-Per* (8 vols., 1898–1904) and *De Dødes Rige* (5 vols., 1912–16), are further explorations into the Danish character and way of life. Nobel Prize winner in 1917, Pontoppidan died at Ordrup.

**Ponz, Antonio** (1725–1792), Spanish prose-writer. Born at Beché, Province of Valencia, he travelled much in southern Europe, studying remains of classical art in Italy and Greece especially. He is, however, chiefly remarkable as the author of that astonishing account of Spanish art, to collect materials for which he journeyed throughout the country, *Viaje de España* (18 vols., 1772–84). He was predisposed against post-Renaissance architecture, which in more recent times when the baroque has come into its own, has lost for him a good deal of his authority; but on the romanesque and gothic he still holds his own, and his inventories of works of art in churches and conventual buildings are invaluable. The standard of his prose is, considering the length of the work, excellently maintained. He died in Madrid. He was an artist of some account.

**Poot, Hubert Korneliszoon** (1689–1733), Dutch poet. Born into a family in very straitened circumstances living at Abtswoude, he was largely self-taught. His longer works written in an overelaborate style are little more than period pieces now, but his lyrics have a certain charm. See his *Gedichten* (3 vols., 1722–35). Poot died in Delft.

**Poot, L.** *see* **Döblin, A.**

**Popov, A. S.,** *see* **Serafimovich, A.**

**Porché, François** (1877–1944), French dramatist. Born at Cognac, he was led by his admiration for Rostand (q.v.) to write all his earlier plays, such as *Les Butors et Finette* (1917), *La Jeune Fille aux joues roses* (1919) and *Dauphine* (1921), in verse at the period between 1914 and 1930 when poetical plays were out of fashion. These plays have scarcely survived, but his prose plays, *Le Tsar Lénine* (1931), *Un Roi, deux dames et un valet* (1939) and *Le Lever du soleil* (1947) were all successful, and are of excellent quality. He died at Vichy.

**Porto-Riche, Georges de** (1849–1930), French poet and dramatist, born in Bordeaux, made the public take notice of him when his *La Chance de Françoise* appeared in 1890. In this work, as in *Amoureuse* (1891), *Le Passé* (1897) and *Le Marchand d'estampes* (1917), he uncompromisingly enthrones physical love as the only guiding force in human relations. Psychologically faulty, all his books are redeemed by brilliant dialogue. He died in Paris.

**Poruks, Janis** (1871–1911), Latvian short-story writer and poet, was born at Druviena. He went to Germany with a view to a musical career and studied for some years in Dresden, the while imbibing cloudy and diluted Nietzschean thought. The result was wasted time and a return home with consequent failure to find a suitable post in Riga. Of his collections of stories the best undoubtedly is *Romas atjaunotāji* (1900; Eng. trans. *Builders of New Rome*, 1924). His output of verse is enormous; a few have been translated in W. K. Matthews's *Tricolour Sun* (1936). Poruks, who had a great influence on the development of modern Latvian literature, died insane at Tartu.

**Postl, K. A.,** *see* Sealsfield, C.

**Potgieter, Everhardus Johannes** (1808–1875), Dutch poet, born at Zwolle, from 1826 to 1830 held a commercial post in Antwerp, and then in 1831 settled in Amsterdam, living as a literary editor first of *De Muzen* and later of *De Gids*. His three notable volumes of poetry are *Liedekens van Bontekoe* (1840), *Florence* (1868) and *De nalatenschap van de landjonker* (1875), the last remarkable for its vivid psychological symbolism. His *Poëzy* were collected (2 vols.) in 1868 and 1875. He died in Amsterdam.

**Potocki, Wacław** (1625–1696), Polish poet and prose-writer. Born at Wola Łużańska of a landed family, he lived on his estate devoting his ample leisure to literary work. Although he is very much a derivative writer, his long poem, *Argenida* (1697), being founded on Barclay's *Argenis*, his *Syloret* (1764) on Heliodorus and his *Moralia* (1688; mod. ed., 3 vols., 1915–18) on the *Adagia* of Erasmus (q.v.), he yet has a distinctive style. His epic poem *Wojna chocimska* (1850, 'The War of Chocim'; crit. ed. by A. Brückner, 1924) is second only to Mickiewicz's (q.v.) *Pan Tadeusz* in Polish literature. His interesting epigrams (*Fraszki*) were published as *Ogród fraszek* (2 vols.) in 1907.

**Potvin, Charles** (1818–1902), Belgian poet and prose-writer. Born at Mons, he devoted himself to a literary life. His name was made with his ringing celebration of Belgian nationalism, *1830: Chansons et poésies* (1847). The European revolutions of 1848 led him to write *Poèmes politiques* (1849), which was followed by *Le Drame du peuple* (1850), *Satires et poésies* (1852) and in different vein, *Le poème du soleil* (1855) and *Marbres antiques* (1857). A close friend of that painter of the macabre A. J. Wiertz, on that artist's death in 1865 Potvin was responsible for converting his studio into a memorial picture gallery to him in Brussels, the Musée Wiertz, of which he became the first curator. *L'art flamand* was an incursion into art criticism, and he reveals his powers as a literary critic in *Un cours d'histoire des lettres en Belgique* (1870) and as a dramatic critic in *Essais de littérature dramatique* (1880). He died in Brussels.

**Pourrat, Henri** (1887–1959), French novelist. Born at Ambert (Puys-de-Dôme), he lived all his life in Auvergne, and his novels are full of the peasant types and natural descriptions of that region. Of his many books, all evincing strong belief, the most important are: *Sur la Colline ronde* (1912), *Les Montagnards* (1919), *Vaillances, farces et gentillesses de Gaspard des Montagnes* (1922), his masterpiece, and its sequels, such as *Le Mauvais Garçon* (1925) and *La Veillée de novembre: vie de Cécile Sauvage* (1931). There followed separate books, such as *Les Sorciers du canton* (1933), *Le Secret des compagnons* (1937) and *Le Chemin des chèvres* (1947). His final work was the long series *Le Trésor des contes* (12 vols., 1948–62). He died at Ambert.

**Pourtalès, Guy de** (1881–1941), Franco-Swiss novelist, born in Geneva, produced two first-rate novels, *Marins d'eau douce* (1919) and *La Pêche miraculeuse* (1937), besides a quantity of ephemeral musical criticism. He died a naturalized Frenchman at Lausanne.

**Pratolini, Vasco** (1913– ), Italian novelist. Born in Florence of very poor parents, his realistic novels depict the life of city workers. Such are *Il quartiere* (1944; Eng. trans. *A Tale of Santa Croce*, 1952), *Cronache di poveri amanti* (1947; Eng. trans. *A Tale of Poor Lovers*, 1949) and *Eroe del nostro tempo* (1949; Eng. trans. *A Hero of To-day*, 1951). The second of these is considered his best, but even here the style is pedestrian and overloaded with detail. It is when he indulges in pure description that Pratolini comes into his own. *Metello* (1955) was the first volume of a trilogy dealing with a Tuscan family *Una storia italiana*. The others were *Lo scialo* (1960) and *Allegoria e derisione* (1966).

**Prešeren, France** (1800–1849), Slovene poet, born at Vrba, near Bled, he received a good and broad education and by his influence made Slovene literature something to be reckoned with in the Balkans. His unhappy love affairs and disordered life are mirrored in his *Poezije* (1847; Ger. trans. *Gedichte*, 1936; Eng. trans. of some of the poems in P. Selver, *Anthology of Modern Slavonic Literature*, 1919, and see also W. K. Matthews, *A Selection of the Poetry of France Prešeren*, 1953). He died at Kranj.

**Prévert, Jacques** (1900– ), French film-script writer and poet. Born at Neuilly-sur-Seine, he is the author of *Drôle de drame* (1937), *Le Quai des brumes* (1938) and *Les Enfants du Paradis* (1943), three of the finest scripts ever written. A surrealist, his ideas have proved self-destructive both in his novels and his poetry. The latter is to be found in the three collections, *Paroles* (1948), *Spectacle* (1951) and *La Pluie et le beau temps* (1955).

**Prévost, Eugène Marcel** (1862–1941), French novelist. Born in Paris, he came to be employed in the tobacco industry and later qualified as a government engineer-inspector in Lille factories. In 1891 he abandoned this career for literature. He had already such novels of domestic life to his credit as *Le Scorpion* (1887) and *Mademoiselle Jauffre* (1889), and he now with deeper psychological discrimination considered the question of disasters caused by a failure of the natural impulse either in men, as in *Les Demi-Vierges* (1894), his most powerful work, or in women, *Le Mariage de Juliette* (1896). Other books are:

*L'Heureux Ménage* (1901), *Lettres à Françoise mariée* (1908), an example of a growing tendency to pontify along feminist lines which soon damaged his work, *Les Anges gardiens* (1913), *La Retraite ardente: l'homme vierge* (1927) and *Mort des ormeaux* (1938). Several of his novels were dramatized, the most successful adaptation being *Le Plus Faible* (1904). He died at Vianne (Lot-et-Garonne).

**Prévost, Jean** (1901–1944), French prose-writer. Born in Paris, he became a journalist, beginning as a sports critic. A volume of studies of his boyhood, *Dix-huitième année* (1929), made a very good impression, and was followed up by *Les Frères Bouquinquant* (1930), a novel of working-class life. Whether he wrote on politics or letters or penned novels, he displayed the same vivacity of style and clarity of thought as is to be seen in his later books, such as *La Chasse du matin* (1937), *Usonie* (1939) and *Apprendre seul* (1940). During the German occupation he was in the Resistance movement, but was caught and shot at Sassenage, near Grenoble.

**Prévost d'Exiles, Antoine François** (1697–1763), French novelist and man of letters. Born at Hesdin, Artois, he was educated by the Jesuits, served in the army (1716–19) and joined the Benedictines in 1721, but left them about the time of the publication of his long fictional work *Mémoires et aventures d'un homme de qualité* (vols. i-iv, 1728; vols. v-vii, 1731; Eng. trans. *Memoirs of a Man of Quality*, 2 vols., 1742), volume seven of it being formed by the story of *Manon Lescaut*, which since 1753 has been published alone (a mod. Eng. trans. by L. W. Tancock, 1949). A beautifully fresh tale, it has inspired the operas of Massenet and Puccini. Greatly influenced by the novels of feeling of Samuel Richardson, some of which he translated into French, he wrote *Le Philosophe anglais ou Histoire de M. Cleveland* (1732; Eng. trans. *Life of Mr Cleveland*, 1734) and *Le Doyen de Killerine* (1735; Eng. trans. *The Dean of Coleraine*, 1742). He catered for the growing taste for fictionalized travel-books and memoirs with *L'Histoire d'une grecque moderne* (1740; Eng. trans. *History of a Fair Greek*, 2 vols., 1741) and *Mémoires d'un honnête homme* (1745) respectively. He remained in the Church as a nominal secular priest and obtained the sinecure of Prior of St Georges de Gesnes in 1754. He died suddenly of an aneurysm at Chantilly. His *Œuvres choisies* appeared (39 vols.), 1783–5.

**Prishvin, Mikhail Mikhailovich** (1873–1954), Russian Soviet writer of animal stories of excellent quality, collected in *Sobranie sochineniy* (6 vols., 1927–31). Some of them have been translated into English, such as *The Blue Hare* (1945) and *The Black Arab, and other Stories* (1947). He was born at Khrushchevo in central Russia and died in Leningrad.

**Proust, Marcel** (1871–1922), French novelist and short-story writer. Born in Auteuil on the outskirts of Paris, the son of a distinguished physician, later a professor of medicine at the University of Paris, and a wealthy Jewish heiress, he was delicate from boyhood. Precocious, physically attractive and a brilliant conversationalist, he was freely admitted to the most select society, which enabled him to

write later with such authority of a world which was closed to so
many. He published nothing until 1896, when his finely wrought short
stories *Les Plaisirs et les jours* appeared, but by the turn of the
century his increasing asthma drove him further and further towards
a retired life, to which after the death of his parents (both were dead
by 1905) he entirely withdrew. In 1907 he was entrenched in a flat
in the heart of Paris working on notes and sketches on which he had
been engaged since 1896 when he had written a draft of a prologue
to what became *À la recherche du temps perdu*, that supreme novel
cycle of modern times. (The draft, *Jean Santeuil*, was first published in
1952.) By 1909 he was fully engaged on this work which he continued
to compose right up to the time of his death. In *À la recherche*, founded
on his experiences during the first thirty years of his life, he not only
describes that life with its social successes and failures, its loves and
its sorrows, with a leisurely amplitude of description and a savouring
of moods and atmospheres such as had never been attempted before,
but he binds the whole of the series together by giving this progress
through youth to early manhood the character of a spiritual search
for the undying values which underlie the actions of this ephemeral
existence. There are three stages of life: the purity and untrammelled
awareness of childhood, the ardours, sins and sorrows of youth, and then
out of the consequent disillusionment grows wisdom when the soul is
purified. The first part of *À la recherche*, *Du Côté de chez Swann* (1913)
made little stir, but the second *À l'Ombre des jeunes filles en fleurs*
(1918) was received with acclamation and soon made him famous
throughout Europe. There followed the first half of *Le Côté de
Guermantes* (1920), the second part of *Le Côté* and the first part of
*Sodome et Gomorrhe* (1921), and the second part of the same in 1922,
the year of Proust's death in Paris, hastened by overstrain and his
unhealthy enclosed life. But he had already completed *À la recherche*,
and its final volumes appeared as *La Prisonnière* (1923), *Albertine
disparue* (1925) and *Le Temps retrouvé* (1927). The whole work has
been splendidly translated into English by C. K. Scott-Moncrieff (12
vols., 1941). His fascinating *Correspondance générale* was published
(6 vols.) in 1930–6 (Eng. trans. *Letters of Marcel Proust*, 1950).

**Provence, M.,** *see* **Jouhandeau, M.**

**Prudhomme, R. F. A.,** *see* **Sully Prudhomme.**

**Prus, Bolesław,** pseudonym of **Aleksander Głowacki** (1847–1912),
Polish novelist and short-story writer. Born at Hrubieszów, he
started life as a factory hand before becoming a journalist, in which
capacity he gained a reputation as a humorist. He was by this time in
Warsaw, the life of which he came to know intimately from many
angles, and this and his sympathy with the peasant life he had grown
up to know provided him with abundant material for his books.
Chief of his collections of short stories is *Kamizelka* (1882; Eng. trans.
*The Waistcoat* in 'Slavic and East European Review', IX, 1930). Of
his novels the best and best known are *Pałac i rudera* (1874, 'Palace
and Hut'), *Placówka* (1885; Eng. trans. *The Outpost* in *Polish Tales*
by S. C. M. Benecke and M. Busch, 1921), about a Polish peasant

family, *Lalka* (2 vols., 1887, 1889), about contemporary mercantile society, *Emancypantki* (4 vols., 1891–3), a satire on feminists, and *Faraon* (1895; Eng. trans. *The Pharaoh and the Priest*, 1902), set in ancient Egypt. A man of broad humanity, he died in Warsaw.

**Pucci, Antonio** (1309?–1388), Italian poet, born in Florence. He is chiefly remembered for his didactic poem *Le Noie*, written probably in the earlier part of his life. He was a lyric poet of no mean order, as is to be seen from his *Fiore di leggende, cantari antichi* (1914), in which much of his most interesting work is to be found. The Arthurian legend is a much favoured theme in these poems. He died in Florence.

**Pückler-Muskau, Hermann Ludwig Heinrich von** (1785–1871), German travel-writer and poetaster. A hereditary prince who had a passion for landscape gardening and travel, he is the archetype of the inverted romantic dilettante, for ever trying to escape from himself, but in vain. His chief works are *Briefe eines Verstorbenen* (4 vols., 1831; Eng. trans. *A Tour in Germany, Holland and England 1826–1828*, 1832) and *Tutti Frutti* (5 vols., 1834; Eng. trans. 1839). More of a literary curiosity than anything else, Fürst von Pückler-Muskau died at Cottbus.

**Puffendorf, Samuel von** (1632–1694), German prose-writer, writing for the most part in Latin. Born at Chemnitz, he was educated at the universities of Leipzig and Jena and went into the diplomatic service. He became professor of international law at Heidelberg in 1661, moving to Lund in 1670, and it was there that he composed *De Jure Naturae et Gentium* (1672) in dignified and sonorous prose, which had untold influence on European political thought for three generations. Both this and *De Officio Hominis et Civis* (1673), another noble plea for internationalism, were extensively translated into English. A sample of his German prose is to be found in his *Einleitung zur Historie der vornehmsten Reiche* (1685). The influence of Grotius (q.v.) is apparent in all he wrote. In 1688 on the death of the 'Great' Elector, his son, Frederick III, invited him to come to Berlin to write a life of his father. He therefore left his Swedish court appointments, which he had held since 1677, and settled in Berlin, where he died.

**Pulci, Luigi** (1432–1484), Italian poet. Born in Florence, he was a great favourite with the Medicis and became a close friend of Lorenzo, who employed him as ambassador to Pisa and Naples. His chief work is *Il Morgante maggiore* (1482), a chivalrous romance, but withal a burlesque, and full of wild comedy. The chief modern editions of the work are those of G. B. Weston (2 vols., 1930) and G. Fatini (2 vols., 1948). Byron translated the first of the twenty-eight cantos in 1823. He was also a sonneteer (*Sonetti di Matteo Franco e di Luigi Pulci*, 1759). See his extremely interesting *Lettere a Lorenzo il Magnifico e ad altri* (ed. S. Bongi, second ed., 1886). He died in Padua.

**Pushkin, Alexander Sergeyevich** (1799–1837), Russian poet and dramatist, born in Moscow of a noble family holding estates at Pskov. There was Abyssinian blood on his mother's side, which accounts for his swarthy appearance. At the academy at Tsarskoe Selo he received an eclectic education, being greatly addicted to

French and English literature, while before that a much-loved children's nurse, a truly peasant woman, had kept him in touch with the ideas of the common people. Thus, while on the one hand he was very much of the European, on the other he never lost his understanding of the people of the soil of his own country. He entered the civil service in 1817 and lived as a young man about town in Petersburg, gaining recognition as a poet with his light-hearted epic *Ruslan i Ludmila* (1820), later to inspire Glinka's opera. Shortly afterwards, for some political epigrams offensive to the government, he was exiled to the Caucasus, read Byron, and produced *Kavkazskiy plennik* (1822, 'The Prisoner of the Caucasus'), a thoroughly romantic, subjective work depicting in Byronic manner the outcast of society. Pardoned by the Czar Nicholas I in 1826 he was allowed to return to Petersburg, and the same year published his blank-verse historical drama (influenced by Shakespeare) *Boris Godunov*, from which Moussorgsky's opera is derived. He had already begun his poem on the flood at Petersburg of 1824, *Evgeny Onegin* (completed 1831; Eng. trans. *Eugene Onegin* by D. P. Radin and G. Patrick, 1937; and by O. Elton, second ed., 1943), later to inspire Tchaikovsky. It depicted the life of the simple clerk Evgeny, ruined by the spirit of Peter the Great, who one hundred years after his death still haunts Russia. It is the story of individual happiness sacrificed to national demands. The year of the completion of *Evgeny* he married the exquisitely beautiful Natalia Goncharova; but unfortunately she was light and empty, and soon her flirtations in Petersburg became a continual trial to him, involving him in scandalous gossip. Moreover, a new generation was growing up, the rising *nouveaux riches* who were tired of poetry and wanted prose. Pushkin took the hint and turned almost entirely to story-writing after his brilliant narrative on Peter the Great, *Medny vsadnik* (written 1833; publ. 1841, 'The Bronze Horseman'). As a writer of prose fiction Sir Walter Scott's influence was strong, but he avoided Scott's prolixity. The period of his prose works begins with *Povesti Belkina* (1830, 'The Tales of Belkin'), and continues with *Dubrovsky* (1832), the weird *Pikovaya dama* (1834, 'The Queen of Spades'), followed by the excellent short novel, *Kapitanskaya dochka* (1836; Eng. trans. *The Captain's Daughter and other Tales*, 1933; cf. Scott's *The Surgeon's Daughter*). Meanwhile the attentions shown by Baron d'Anthès, a French exile in Russian military service, to his wife Natalia had become intolerable. Pushkin challenged him to a duel, but was mortally wounded in Petersburg, an incident which, it was said, was purposely provoked by the government, d'Anthès being employed as an *agent provocateur*. The young Lermontov (q.v.) voiced this feeling. The essential greatness of Pushkin lies, as Dostoyevsky (q.v.) realized, in his ability to blend Western and Russian culture. His influence on Russian literature has been incalculable. Modern Soviet critics have tried, as did the Nazis with Goethe and Schiller, to turn him into an incipient Communist and have denied the great influence of Western literature on him. Such attempts are ridiculous. Pushkin, like all great writers, has no party ticket, is for all time and freely participates in universal art. Collected editions of his works are that of 1890 (10 vols.) and the 1935–8 edition (9 vols.). Turgenev (q.v.) translated some of his works into French as *Poèmes dramatiques* (1862). Of English translations, apart from those mentioned above, the following are to be recommended: *The Works of Alexander Pushkin* (ed. A. Yarmolinsky, 1936), uneven, but some translations good, *Poems* by Maurice Baring (1931), *Pushkin's Poems* by W. Morison (1945) and *The Fairy Tales of Pushkin* by T. Panchev (1947). *The Complete Prose Tales of Pushkin* by G. R. Aitken appeared in 1967.

# Q

**Quasimodo, Salvatore** (1901–    ), Italian poet, was born in Syracuse, Sicily, and settled in Milan. His first volume, *Acque e terre* (1930), is remote with its reflections of distant, static nature and a recurrent personal note of anxiety about life and fear of being alone. In *Oboe sommerso* (1932) the imagery is particularly fine while the same remoteness remains; but by 1936 when *Erato e Apollion* appeared, ordinary earthly problems begin to intrude. The impact of the war on Quasimodo was profound, and in his *Nuove poesie* (1942) he voices his profound disillusionment, which deepens in *Giorno dopo giorno* (1947), when with a kind of horror he surveys Italy's war guilt. From then on he has sought to find a solution to world problems as in *La vita non è sogno* (1949) and *Il falso e vero verde* (1956), the latter pro-Communist and anti-Christian, but he cannot be said to have succeeded. In fact one can be sure that his preoccupations have damaged his poetry. None the less he was awarded the Nobel Prize for Literature in 1959. Some of his poems are translated into English in S. Pacifici's *The Promised Land* (1957) and in G. Kay's *Penguin Book of Italian Verse* (1958).

**Queirós, J. M. de Eça de,** *see* Eça de Queirós.

**Queneau, Raymond** (1903–    ), French novelist and poet. Born at Le Havre, son of a shopkeeper, he began to write poetry in the Surrealist manner, and although he outwardly broke with the movement in 1930 his style has ever since preserved many surrealistic characteristics. His poetry, which strikes one rather as a series of clever linguistic exercises than true inspiration, is most accessible in the collection *Si tu t'imagines* (1952). It is as a novelist, however, that he has really made his mark, and in *Un Rude Hiver* (1939; Eng. trans. *Hard Winter*, 1948), *Pierrot mon ami* (1943; Eng. trans. *Pierrot*, 1950), *Le Dimanche de la vie* (1951) and *Zazie dans le Métro* (1959; Eng. trans. *Zazie*, 1960) he sketches with kindly humour and with an eye for the grotesque the everyday life of the French lower middle classes. His dialogue is excellent and is free from any literariness, although his phonetic spelling and other peculiarities often seem to defeat their own ends. His complete mastery of every kind of linguistic manner is to be seen in his *tour de force*, *Exercices* (1947; Eng. trans. *Exercises in Style*, 1958). A further collection of poetry, *Courir les rues*, appeared in 1967.

**Quental, Antero Tarquínio de** (1842–1891), Portuguese poet. Born at

Ponta Delgada in the Azores, Quental was educated at Coimbra. Later he studied German philosophy, became a Socialist, and started various literary magazines in which he sought to discredit romanticism in poetry. After some volumes of verse inclining to that very romanticism which he condemned, he broke new ground with *Odas modernas* (1865), but it is in his sonnets, collected by J. P. Oliveira Martins in 1886 as *Os sonetos completos de Antero de Quental*, that his best work is to be found. In these poems can be traced his spiritual odyssey with abundant evidence of the pain suffered by an idealist who finds mundane existence always falling short of his aspirations. For some years involved in the political life of Lisbon, ill-health compelled him to retire, and he returned to the Azores where he died by suicide the same year.

**Querol, Vicente Wenceslao** (1836–1889), Spanish poet from Valencia, in which province he died. He was equally at home in both Castilian and Catalan, and his favourite themes were domestic and religious. A quiet romantic, he was able successfully and with much taste to blend classical and biblical styles of expression together in his work, while he was also ready to learn from contemporary literary developments. The greatest single influence on him was undoubtedly Byron, several of whose works, notably *Childe Harold*, he translated in collaboration with L. Llorente. The main collection of his verse published in his lifetime appeared in 1877 as *Rimas*. This with further additions was gathered after his death by Llorente under the same title in 1891. A complete edition of his work was published as *Poesías* in 1924.

**Quevedo y Villegas, Francisco Gómez de** (1580–1645), Spanish prosewriter, dramatist and poet. Born in Madrid, where both his parents, who were of excellent family, held court appointments, he grew up in that atmosphere of intrigue and place-hunting which he was later to satirize so successfully and so unmercifully. After a brilliant career at the University of Alcalá, he joined the retinue of the Duke of Osuna, Viceroy of Sicily, whose trusted envoy he soon became, being constantly employed as his go-between with the court at Madrid. When Osuna was promoted Viceroy of Naples he took Quevedo with him as minister of finance. But with his patron's sudden fall in 1619 the still young diplomat and politician found himself not only without employment, but imprisoned and then banished to his estates in the Sierra Morena. He was allowed to return to Madrid in 1623, having in the meantime published his first book, a devotional one, *Vida de San Tomás de Villanueva* (1620). He was soon in high favour with the new king Philip IV, whom he did his best to try to influence against the attractions of a lax court led by the minister Olivares. It was for Philip that Quevedo now wrote his noble *Política de Dios* (1626), in which he appealed to him to be more than a king merely in name, but the steward of God who has a duty to his people and the realm. Yet the moralist could turn to other styles and subjects, and that same year (1626) produced one of his most popular works, a book of far-reaching influence, *Vida del Buscón, llamado Don Pablos*, an extraordinary picaresque novel written as the autobiography of an

unrepentant reprobate. *El Buscón,* one of the satirical masterpieces
of European literature, reveals Quevedo's cynical view of the world
and all its ways, but it is relieved by striking humour. It was first
translated into English (from French) as *Buscon, the Witty Spaniard,*
by J. Davies (1657). The following year (1627) he struck another mine
of his varied talent with his *Sueños,* usually known in English as
*Visions,* in which in the form of burlesques he witheringly describes
the follies of the world and consequent hell and judgment. This
extraordinary work's lurid side is counterbalanced by wild humour
and penetrating satire, but it had to be shockingly mutilated to
escape censorship, and it is only in comparatively modern times that
it has been printed as Quevedo intended. It was the first of Quevedo's
works to be translated into English (from French), and it remained
very popular and influential in England from the time of Richard
Crashawe's translation of it as *Visions or hels kingdome strangely
displaied* (1640) until the middle of the eighteenth century. Another
well-known translation of it was by Sir Roger L'Estrange (*The
Visions of Quevedo*), published in 1667. In spite of his continued
literary attacks on the vanity of the court and the follies of men
greedy for power, he remained on reasonable terms with Olivares,
who offered him several posts to try to bribe him to keep silent. He
would accept nothing, however, except the honorary title of Royal
Secretary (1632). At last in 1639 Quevedo, denounced to Olivares as
the author of a petition to the king on the wretched state of the
country, was imprisoned in a monastery at León, where the treatment
meted out to him broke his health for good. The fall of Olivares in
1643 allowed him to return to Madrid, and there he finished two
works on which he had been engaged during his confinement, a great
political commentary on Plutarch's *Brutus,* *La vida de Marco
Bruto,* and a life of St Paul, both published in 1644. His disastrous
marriage to Esperanza de Aragón (1634) had broken down years
before. He died in complete retirement at Villanueva de los Infantes.
Quevedo was also a poet of distinction, though very little of his work
in this field was known during his lifetime or for long afterwards,
apart from his contributions to P. Espinosa's (q.v.) *Flores* (1605).
He also wrote *entremeses* ('interludes') and comedies. The greatest
edition of Quevedo is the *Obras completas* edited by A. Fernández-
Guerra and M. Menéndez y Pelayo (3 vols., 1897–1907), and there is
another edition in two volumes edited by L. Astrana Marín (revised,
1943). Mention should also be made of A. Castro's edition of the *Vida
del Buscón* (revised, 1927) and that of *Los sueños* by J. Cejador (2
vols., 1916–17, 1922). Of English translations, besides those mentioned
above, several of the works, including *Buscón,* were well translated
straight from Spanish by John Stevens between 1697 and 1707.
These and other renderings by various English translators were
collected in *Quevedo's Works* (1798). See also *The Choice Humorous
and Satirical Works of Quevedo,* edited by C. Duff (1926).

**Quinault, Philippe** (1635–1688), French dramatist and opera-writer,
who was born and died in Paris. He was active as a writer of second-
rate comedies between 1653 and 1665, and of smooth, sentimental

tragedies and tragi-comedies between 1658 and 1671. Examples of the first are *L'Amant indiscret* (1654) and *La Mère coquette* (1665), of the second (all of these being either historical or mythological), *Stratonice* (1660), *Pausanias* (1668) and *Bellérophon* (1671). In spite of a certain grace which at their best the latter have, they were so mercilessly mocked for their preciosity and false gallantry by Boileau that Quinault turned to opera, in which, having a good musical ear, he was more successful. As the famous composer Lulli's librettist he produced many operatic works, such as *Cadmus et Hermione* (1673), *Thésée* (1675), *Isis* (1677), *Persée et Andromède* (1682), and *Armide* (1686), all of which contain charming lyrics. His collected works were published in 1778.

**Quinet, Edgar** (1803–1875), French historical, philosophical and religious writer, was born at Bourg. Having spent his student days in France, Switzerland and Germany, completing his studies at Heidelberg, he caught the eye of Victor Cousin (q.v.), then in the van of the new academic thought emanating from the University of Paris, with his translation, accompanied by a brilliant introduction, of Herder's (q.v.) *Auch eine Philosophie der Geschichte* ('Philosophy of History'). This appeared in 1825 and at once opened literary Paris to him, and in 1829 he was chosen to accompany a government mission to newly free Greece, the result of which was his interesting study of the country, *La Grèce moderne* (1830). In his poem *Ahasvérus* (1833), the history of the Wandering Jew, he revealed himself in a new light in what has been termed 'a spiritual imitation of the ancient mysteries'. By 1838 he successfully parried the growing rationalistic interpretations of Christianity led by D. F. Strauss with his *Examen de la vie de Jésus*, in which he shows how erroneous it is to try to subject matters of faith to intellectual analysis. The following year he was appointed professor of foreign literature at Lyon, in 1841 exchanging this for a similar appointment at the Collège de France. Lectures delivered during these years went to form the basis of his brilliant *Du génie des religions*, published in 1842. His closest friend was now Michelet (q.v.), whose influence turned his attention to politics, and he became one of the leaders of the growing dissatisfaction with the rule of Louis-Philippe. He attacked the interference of the religious orders in politics in *Les Jésuites* (1843), and by 1846 his freely expressed opinions had become so obnoxious to the authorities that he was forced to resign his professorship. He took part in the street fighting in Paris in 1848, and was on the extreme left of the National Assembly. Exiled at the *coup d'état* of 1851, he lived in Brussels until 1857, in which year his *La Révolution religieuse au XIX<sup>e</sup> siècle* appeared. He then went to Switzerland where he remained until the fall of Napoleon III in 1870, when he returned to France. While in Switzerland he produced his most considerable later book of verse, *Merlin l'Enchanteur* (1860), and historical, political, and religious works, such as *L'Histoire de la campagne de 1815* (1862), *Pologne et Rome* (1863) and *La Révolution française* (1865). A leading patriotic figure during the siege of Paris and in the early years of the National Assembly of the Republic of 1871, his recapitulation of his glowing faith in democracy, *L'Esprit nouveau,* appeared in 1874, and *Le Livre de l'exilé* (1875) came out a short time before his death at Versailles.

**Quintana, Manuel José** (1772–1857), Spanish poet and prose-writer, who was born and died in Madrid. His education at Salamanca University, then the centre of the new literary and philosophical outlook growing up under the influence of Meléndez Valdés (q.v.) and Jovellanos (q.v.), had a lasting effect on him. A patriot and liberal politician, as a poet his majestic odes on national events are the most noteworthy, his style being neo-classical without a trace of the romantic. His excellent prose is chiefly known from his series of critical biographies, *Vidas de españoles célebres* (1807–33). Quintana corresponded with the famous Lord Holland, especially on Spanish politics, and these letters were collected and published in 1852. His plays are of no literary value. Director of Education in the Liberal government of 1820–23, he afterwards made peace with the royal family, and was tutor to Isabel II. Longfellow's interesting translations of some of his poetry appeared in *Outre-Mer* (Boston, 1833).

**Quintero, S. and J. Álvarez,** *see* **Álvarez Quintero.**

# R

**Raabe, Wilhelm** (1831–1910), German novelist who wrote under the pseudonym of **Jakob Corvinus**, was born at Eschershausen. After working as a bookseller he took to a literary life, settling in the quiet, old-fashioned town of Wolfenbüttel. It was here that he wrote his striking study of provincial life and character, *Die Chronik der Sperlingsgasse* (1857) with its Dickens-like characterization and description, often humorous; but with his move to Stuttgart in 1864 a new period begins. He leaves his quiet optimism behind and starts to look on life as a useless struggle against great odds. This pessimistic approach invests the whole of his long novel *Abu Telfan, oder Die Heimkehr vom Mondgebirge* (1867; Eng. trans. *Abu Telfan, Return from the Mountains of the Moon*, 1881). In 1871 Raabe left Stuttgart for Brunswick where he died. During this last period he wrote with a new serenity such novels as *Stopfkuchen* (1891) and *Hastenbeck* (1899). The best known of his works, though not the best, is *Der Hungerpastor* (1864; Eng. trans. *The Hunger-Pastor*, 1885). It is written in his early Wolfenbüttel style.

**Rabelais, François** (1490?–1553), French writer, was born the son of a prosperous lawyer on his father's estate La Devinière, near Chinon in Touraine. Nothing of his early days is known, and we do not hear of him again until 1521 when he was a Franciscan monk in Poitou. He had already made the acquaintance of Budé (q.v.) and other humanists, and it was in order to facilitate greater opportunities for moving in intellectual circles that in 1524 he asked and obtained permission to change his Order to that of the less austere Benedictines. But he was verging on secular life, and after a period of service to Geoffroy d'Estissac, abbot of the monastery of Saint Pierre, Maillezais, in 1527 he changed from being a regular to a secular priest and read medicine at Montpellier, becoming bachelor in 1530 and doctor in 1537. Five years before the doctorate he had settled in Lyon with a mistress and two illegitimate children as physician and lecturer in anatomy at the Hôtel-Dieu. At this time he proved his scholarship by editing the Greek text of the *Aphorisms* of Hippocrates (1532). That very year was published the first book of *Pantagruel* by 'Alcofribas Nasier', the anagram of François Rabelais. *Gargantua* followed in 1534, the *Tiers Livre* in 1546, the *Quart Livre* in 1552, the fifth part not coming out until 1562 (authenticity uncertain). The hue and cry against the man who dared to attack the abuses of the Church had begun as soon as *Pantagruel* was published, and it was to prove fortunate for Rabelais that he had gained the patronage of a prominent cleric Cardinal Jean Du Bellay, uncle of the poet (q.v.). Thus when he was condemned by the Sorbonne and threatened with prosecution for heresy he was protected by the family; but by 1546 the danger seemed so great that Rabelais suddenly fled to Metz, becoming town physician there. In 1548 his faithful patron took him with him to Rome, and the following year hearing that the attacks had died down Rabelais returned to France. He settled near Paris, perhaps at Saint-Maur, of which abbey he had been canon *commendataire* for many years, and died there. Rabelais, one of the most prominent figures of the later Renaissance, bravely faced the orthodoxy that opposed the new ideas and tried to distort truth out of fear of change. A satirist, there is nothing bitter about his satire, and his much advertised coarseness is the result of a purely natural pagan temperament which despised hypocrisy, and salacity is absolutely foreign to it. Out of his enormous burlesque, which at times seems aimless, grows a sincere purpose, the bid for progressive thought and action, the desire to break down every barrier that hinders the good of humanity. The authoritative edition of the *Œuvres complètes* is that carried out under the editorship of A. Lefranc (5 vols., 1913–31). The classical English translation is by Urquhart (Bks I–III, 1653) and Motteux (Bks IV–V, 1694). There have been numerous reprints of this. There are modern translations of merit by W. F. Smith (1893) and J. M. Cohen (1955).

**Rabener, Gottlieb Wilhelm** (1714–1771), German poet. Born at Wachau, near Leipzig, he became a civil servant. He was a quiet and kindly satirist of the social extravagances of his day, and sometimes allowed himself a passing jibe at Gottsched (q.v.) and his literary pedantry. Rabener died in Dresden. His works were collected in *Sämtliche Schriften* (1777), and a revised edition appeared in 1839.

**Racan, Honorat de Bueil de** (1589–1670), French poet. Born at Champmarin, Touraine, the family estate, he followed a military career, cultivating the muse in his spare time. A Latin and Italian scholar and a follower of Malherbe (q.v.) he wrote charmingly in the pseudo-classical arcadian style of the day. He also wrote devotional poetry. Of the first manner *Les Bergeries* (1625), a long pastoral dialogue in the style of Guarini (q.v.), is the most characteristic, of the second *Psaumes et poésies chrétiennes* (1660). Racan died in Paris.

**Racine, Jean** (1639–1699), French dramatist, was born at La Ferté-Milon (Aisne) and, early left an orphan, was brought up by his grandmother, a severe Jansenist. His education by the Jansenists at Port Royal had a profound effect on him for life, not only because it brought him face to face with a concept of religion which made the devotee so aware of moral problems, a theme that Racine was later to treat so grandly and explore to its very fundamentals, but because it grounded him firmly in the classics. That serenity of presentation and that purity of expression, which make Racine perhaps the greatest classical writer of modern times, were the fruits of his schooling. Little, however, did his masters realize that while he was poring over Sophocles and Virgil, he was already dreaming of writing for the stage. He was to follow in his dead father's footsteps and become a lawyer. Rebelling against this he was sent to read philosophy at the Collège d'Harcourt, a constituent part of the University of Paris; but city pleasures and the fraternity of men of letters proved too enticing, and breaking his connections with academic life and Port Royal, he soon found himself in the congenial company of Molière, La Fontaine and Boileau. He now began to write poetry, stilted work which gives no indication of the greatness to come, but one of his pieces, *La Nymphe de la Seine*, on Louis XIV's marriage to Maria Teresa of Spain, had a practical result in bringing him to the king's notice. This even so was not pleasing to his family, who urged him to go to his uncle who was vicar-general of the diocese of Uzès, Languedoc, and Racine obeyed. He remained there from 1661 to 1663, his delightful letters while there revealing a shrewd eye for what went on round him and a keen sense of humour. The study of theology was suggested, but after toying with it he was back in Paris. By 1664 he had again pleased the king with an ode, and with another, *La Renommée aux muses*, his acquaintance with Boileau ripened into lifelong friendship. In the same year his first play, *La Thébaïde ou Les Frères ennemis*, was performed by Molière's troupe at the Palais Royal, which also acted his *Alexandre le Grand* (1665). Both were tentative and no better and no worse than similar contemporary works, but they caused a complete break with his family and with Port Royal. An unfortunate quarrel with Molière also took place half way through the production of *Alexandre*, and led to the withdrawal of the play from Molière and Racine's placing it in the hands of the rival Bourgogne company. This unedifying episode was intensified by Racine's disrespectful behaviour towards the venerable Corneille. It was after that, however, that the true greatness of Racine emerged, and between 1667 and 1677 he wrote his magnificent tragedies with one comedy, *Les Plaideurs*, a satire on lawyers, in 1668. The tragedies began with *Andromaque* (1667), a study of the terrible moral degeneration of a woman scorned, and to it succeeded *Britannicus* (1669), *Bérénice* (1670), with its theme of the renunciation of love for duty, *Bajazet* (1672), in which revenge is depicted, *Mithridate* (1673), the tragedy of the rivalry between the old and the young, *Iphigénie* (1675), a masterpiece of pathos, and *Phèdre* (1677), one of the world's greatest studies of human agony of mind. The works of this decade, the result of his moral and literary training allied in a marvellous way, reveal Racine as the equal if not the superior of Corneille as a playwright while he is undeniably the greater poet. As a dramatist he replaced Corneille's tragedy of character by the tragedy of passion as with unrivalled psychological depth he depicted his *personae* not as pitting themselves against their fate but as already the victims of it. The themes are elementally simple, the plots are stark, the stage is bare and the clutter of antiquarian property is dispensed with. We are confronted with strong, clear human conflicts. Adhering to the unities Racine builds up his work into the symmetry of classical architecture, and he is absolutely Virgilian in that phrases, even stray words, seem to reach out to convey meanings and to create images beyond the power of ordinary language. He certainly brought to the French language a flexibility without parallel in the history of its literature, and a grace of rhythm beside which Corneille seems stiff. After 1677 he wrote no more for twelve years. He had to pay in the first instance the price for his success, and the hornets of the literary world were out against him; but apart from that the old Port-Royal conscience was stirring in him and he felt that as a writer for the theatre he had sinned. Full of remorse he decided to give up the stage and for a time thought of becoming a monk, but instead, before the end of 1677, married and settled down to quiet family life, being immediately reconciled with Port Royal. At the same time he was appointed the king's historiographer jointly with Boileau, and from then on until his fall from grace with Louis XIV for his continued Jansenism in 1695, he divided his time between his growing family and his official duties. In 1689, however, he took pen in hand once more when Madame de Maintenon asked him to write a sacred drama for the girls' school at St Cyr which she patronized. The result was *Esther*, its scope limited by the fact that in the circumstances it could hardly be dramatic and was rather a transposition of the biblical story into dramatized verse; but it had aroused the old feelings for the stage put by for so long and led to Racine's last play, *Athalie* (1691). This, his swan song, is in perfection of style, nobility of feeling and characterization, if not in dramatic intensity, as fine in its own way as anything that went before. Some devotional poetry and a history of Port Royal were the productions of his last years, and he died in Paris at the age of fifty-nine, being buried at Port Royal. See his *Œuvres complètes* (ed. P. Mesnard, 8 vols., 1865–73) and the more handy *Œuvres* (ed. E. Pilon, R. Groos and R. Picard, 2 vols., 1951–2). There is a readily available translation into English of *The Best Plays of Racine* by L. Lockert comprising *Andromaque*, *Britannicus*, *Phèdre* and *Athalie* (1957).

**Radičević, Branko** (1824–1853), Croat poet, the greatest in Yugoslav literature, was born at Brod, but went to Vienna to read law, remaining there for the rest of his life. Although he wrote several epics and other lengthy poetry, he was at his greatest in his short lyrics. The collection of his work, *Pesme*, was begun in 1847, but not completed until 1911, and comprises four volumes.

**Radiguet, Raymond** (1903–1923), French novelist of a precocity seldom equalled, was born at St Maur. A protégé of Jean Cocteau (q.v.) he wrote two amazingly mature novels in a style of the purest classical precision before he was twenty. They are *Le Diable au corps* (1923; Eng. trans. *The Devil in the Flesh*, 1949), a study of the impact of the First World War on a youth, and *Le Bal du Comte d'Orgel* (1924; Eng. trans. *Count d'Orgel Opens the Ball*, 1952). Radiguet died in Paris aged twenty and a half years old.

**Radishchev, Alexander Nikolayevich** (1749–1802), Russian prose-writer and poet. Born in the region of Saratov, he spent his youth in Petersburg, taking a keen interest in political and social conditions. His lyric poetry contained evocations of liberty and veiled criticism of the regime and was to have an influence on the great movement of the early nineteenth century headed by Pushkin (q.v.). But there was nothing veiled about the brave attacks against Catherine II's tyranny and the scandals of serfdom contained in his prose work *Puteshestvie iz Peterburga v Moskvu* (1790; Eng. trans. *A Journey from St Petersburg to Moscow*, 1958). For this he was condemned to death, but at the last moment was reprieved and sent to Siberia. He was set at liberty by the Emperor Paul in 1797 and returned to Petersburg, but committed suicide there five years later. His attitude to czarism was very pleasing to the Bolsheviks, and several Soviet scholars have been at work on Radishchev since 1917. A new edition of his poetry appeared in 1938 and of the *Puteshestvie* in 1950.

**Raimann, Ferdinand,** who called himself **F. Raimund** (1790–1836), Austrian playwright. Born in Vienna of humble family he became an actor and was director of the Leopoldstadt Theatre from 1828. His strange nature, a mixture of wild happiness and depression, the latter being increased by his unsatisfactory marriage contracted in 1820, comes out very clearly in his work. His fantastic *Der Barometermacher auf der Zauberinsel* (1823) and *Der Alpenkönig und der Menschenfeind* (1828; Eng. trans. *The King of the Alps*, 1850) are typical of his very personal work. Afraid that he had caught rabies he committed suicide in Vienna.

**Raimbaut de Vaqieras** (1155?–1207), Provençal troubadour. Born at or near Orange, he entered the service of Boniface I of Montferrat and went with him to Greece on the crusade where he is said to have been killed in battle. His troubadour lyrics are in most varied forms and among them is the well-known *Calenda Maya*. His work appears in G. Carducci's *Nuova Antologia*, lxxiv (1885).

**Ramler, Karl Wilhelm** (1725–1798), German poet and critic. Born at Kolberg, he became a member of Lessing's university circle at Leipzig and collaborated with him in editorial work. He settled in Berlin as a schoolmaster in 1748. Although he published two volumes of well-written if somewhat frigid poetry, *Lyrische Gedichte* (1762) and *Oden* (1767), it was as a literary critic that he was chiefly regarded. His anthologies, in which he included his translations of French and English poetry, particularly of Dryden, had much influence. Representative of these is *Lyrische Blumenlese* (2 vols., 1774–8).

**Ramos, João de Deus Nogueira** (1830–1896), Portuguese poet, born at San Bartolomeu de Messines. After a protracted education at Coimbra, where he met many future men of letters with progressive ideas for rejuvenating Portuguese literature, he became a journalist in Lisbon where he died. In spite of the literary views of the majority of his contemporaries he remained within the bounds of traditionalism in his lyrics, but his marked feeling for nature, which he associated with human passion, causes him to be regarded as Portugal's link between neo-romanticism and realism. His poetry was collected as *O campo de flores* (1893).

**Ramuz, Charles Ferdinand** (1878–1947), Swiss novelist. Born in Lausanne, he went later to Paris, spending twelve years there engaged in literary work, which had a great influence on his style and method. Returning to Switzerland he settled in the Vaud canton, his native one, and made a name within his own country with *Le Petit Village* (1903). It was not, however, until *La Présence de la mort* (1922; Eng. trans. 1946) that he gained a European reputation. Thereafter his powers of description, his characterization, and even more his ability to see deep into peasant thought and to portray aspects of natural forces rarely successfully attempted before, lent to his works, such as *Beauté sur la terre* (1927; Eng. trans. *Beauty on Earth*, 1929) and *Derborence* (1934; Eng. trans. *When the Mountain Fell*, 1949), increasing authority, although there were some who considered that his sometimes unconventional methods, such as great freedoms with syntax, detracted from the whole effect. His *Journal*, covering forty-five years of his life, was published in 1943, and he died at Pully four years later.

**Raoul de Houdenc** (1180?–1235?), French poet from the Low Countries, but the whereabouts of his birth and death are unknown. He was the author of one of the best of the Arthurian romances, *Méraugis de Portlesguez*, which though its style is disagreeably laboured yet shows great narrative ability. He also wrote a satire on pilgrimages, *Songe d'Enfer*, and a dignified account of the aims of a knight, *Le Roman des ailes*. The definitive edition of *Méraugis* was published in 1897, while Raoul's two other works appear in A. Scheler's *Trouvères belges*, vol. ii (1879).

**Rashi**, i.e. **Solomon ben Isaac** (1040–1105), French Hebrew poet and scholar. A native of Troyes where he founded an academy for Hebrew studies, he wrote much fine religious poetry (S. Bernstein, *Rashi betor paytan*, 1940). He is, however, better known as the author of a famous commentary on the Pentateuch, so much esteemed in the Middle Ages that it was the first Hebrew book ever to be printed (at Reggio, Calabria, 1475). It has indeed stood the test of time as the greatest work on the subject. He also wrote a commentary on the Talmud and finally completed one on the whole of the Old Testament. He greatly influenced not only Jewish but Christian writers, as is apparent in Luther's translation of the Bible.

**Raspe, Rudolf Erich** (1737–1794), German man of letters and adventurer, was born in Hanover and educated at Göttingen and Leipzig. Appointed keeper of medals and gems at Cassel, on being found to be stealing and selling from the collection he escaped to Britain and took a post in a Cornish tin-mine. He died of 'fever' at Muckross, Donegal. He is well known as the author of the fantastic *Baron Munchausen's Narrative of his marvellous Travels and Campaigns in Russia*, first published in English in London in 1785. The German translation, undertaken by G. A. Bürger (q.v.) appeared the following year. *Munchausen* is based to a great extent on sixteenth-century German jest-books, while the work also contains Raspe's own satire on the numerous travel-books which were at that time the public rage. In so doing he mocked the true as well as the false, including Bruce's *Abyssinia* among the former. The real Baron von Münchhausen (1720–1797), a professional soldier whom Raspe had met in Hanover, was a great spinner of exaggerated yarns. He did not write a word of the book, however; the tales were merely grafted on to his name. Of the numerous editions, the best is that of 1895.

**Raupach, Ernst Benjamin Salomon** (1784–1852), German playwright. Born at Straupitz, after much wandering he settled at Berlin in 1823 where he remained for the rest of his life. His output was enormous and so was his success, equalling Kotzebue's (q.v.) and arousing the hostility of the superior literary world. Facile and of second-rate quality, at any rate his plays could be acted. The two best known are *Die Leibeigenen, oder Isidor und Olga* (1826; Eng. trans. *The Serfs*, 1828) and *Der Nibelungenhort* (1834; Eng. trans. *The Nibelung Treasure*, 1847).

**Raynal, Paul** (1885–      ), French playwright, was born in Narbonne. A fine dramatist in the heroic French tradition, although cried down by the surrealists and other coteries, his best-known work is *Le Tombeau sous l'Arc de Triomphe* (1924; Eng. trans. *The Unknown Warrior*, 1928). Others include *La Francerie* (1933) and *A souffert sous Ponce-Pilate* (1939).

**Rebhuhn, Paul** (1498–1546), German dramatist. Born at Waidhofen, he was a student under Luther and Melanchthon at Wittenberg, and became a Protestant clergyman. His one surviving work is his remarkable religious play *Susanna* (1536), a landmark in German poetical development. *Susanna* was critically edited in 1868. Rebhuhn died at Ölsnitz.

**Rebora, Clemente** (1885–1957), Italian poet. Born in Milan, he published poems in traditional manner, but shot through with that very modern malady which comes from an inability to get to grips with loneliness (*Canti anonimi*, 1922). He became a regular priest in 1930, and his *Poesie religiose* (1936) shows a change to mysticism and a sense of securely won peace.

**Redi, Francesco** (1626–1698), Italian poet. Born at Arezzo, he became physician to the Medici grand dukes at Florence. An expert linguist, he was particularly interested in Italian dialects and gained renown as a philologist, but he is now chiefly remembered for his thousand-line dithyrambic poem, *Bacco in Toscana* (1685), in which in gay, freely rhymed verse he exploits to full advantage his connoisseurship of poetry and wine. Such an irresistible piece has found many admirers, translators and imitators, among the English ones Leigh Hunt, whose translation, *Bacchus in Tuscany*, was published in 1825. Redi, who as a scientist may be said to have laid the foundations of modern biology, died in Pisa.

**Regnard, Jean François** (1655–1709), French dramatist and novelist. Born in Paris, the son of a rich shopkeeper, he was left at twenty with a large fortune and decided to travel. He went to Provence and with a newly acquired mistress set sail for the East. In his autobiographical romance, *La Provençale* (1682), he describes how they were captured by Algerian pirates, sold as slaves in Constantinople, and finally ransomed (1678–80). In 1683 he settled in Paris and began to produce a series of successful comedies, which, though they cannot stand comparison with Molière's, are full of life. Among them may be mentioned *Le Joueur* (1696), *Le Retour imprévu* (1700), and his masterpiece, *Le Légataire universel* (1708). He died at the Château de Grillon, Normandy which he had bought. His works were first collected in the Didot edition (1820–2), and of later editions that by Moland (1893) is good.

**Régnier, Henri François Joseph de** (1864–1936), French poet and novelist. Born at Honfleur, he went to Paris where he identified himself with the symbolists, became a disciple of Verlaine (q.v.) and Mallarmé (q.v.), and married into the family of the poet of the sonnet, J. M. de Hérédia (q.v.). His first works were all verse, such as *Poèmes anciens et romanesques* (1890), *Les Médailles d'argile* (1900) and *La Cité des eaux* (1902). He turned to the novel with *Le Trèfle noir* (1895), and became acknowledged head of the younger generation of symbolists in prose with *Les Vacances d'un jeune homme sage* (1903). Thereafter he moved away from the school in novels such as *La peur de l'amour* (1907), but even in so late a work as *L'Escapade* (1926) many features of his early affiliations remain. He became a member of the French Academy in 1911 and died in Paris.

**Régnier, Jean** (1390?–1468), French poet, born probably at Auxerre. He took service under the House of Burgundy, but was captured by French royalists in 1432 and imprisoned at Rouen. It was there that he wrote the greater part, if not the whole, of his *Livre des Fortunes et Adversitez*, a long, very personal, philosophizing poem with lyrics here and there. Not great in itself, it has a quiet attractiveness and its style influenced Villon (q.v.) among others. The *Livre* was well edited by E. Droz (1923).

**Régnier, Mathurin** (1573–1613), French poet, was born in Chartres. He was intended for a clerical life and was tonsured at nine years old. Henry IV gave him a canonry, but that is as far as he went since he preferred an improvident, dissipated life. He did not write much poetry, but what he did produce, for the most part satires, was praised by Boileau (q.v.) who acknowledged his debt to him. He did much to break the influence of the contemporary literary dictator Malherbe (q.v.), preferring Ronsard and the Pléiade. His nineteen *Satires* are the first masterpieces of their kind in French literature, and the best of these is *Macette ou l'Hypocrisie déconcertée*, an attack on pious hypocrites. Régnier died in Rouen. See *Œuvres complètes*, edited by J. Plattard (1930).

**Reimarus, Hermann Samuel** (1694–1768), German critic and thinker, was born in Hamburg. He was first rector of a gymnasium at Wismar and then in 1728 returned to Hamburg as professor of oriental literature and language. It is as the author of *Fragmente eines Ungenannten Wolfenbüttelsche*, essays published after his death by Lessing in 1774–8, that he is best known. In this work Reimarus denied the supernatural origin of Christianity, and in Lessing's hands this became yet another means of forcing the intellectual world of his time, entrenched behind conventional official thought, to reconsider its position. In modern times the standpoint of Reimarus has had a profound influence on Albert Schweitzer. David Strauss's life appeared in 1860 and was translated into English in 1879 by Charles Voysey, head of the English Theistic Church.

**Reina, Manuel** (1856–1905), Spanish poet. Born at Puente Genil, Cordoba, where he died, he lived a retired life on his estates as a wealthy dilettante. In his strange, sensual poetry, such as *Andantes y alegros* (1877), *La vida inquieta* (1894) and *Poemas paganos* (1896), he unwittingly led the way towards the new approach to poetic values which began in Spain about the turn of the century.

**Rejment,** *see* **Reymont.**

**Rellstab, Ludwig** (1799–1860), German novelist, was born in Berlin where he died. A popular, facile historical novelist, his best-known novel is the long Napoleonic saga, *1812* (1834; Eng. trans. 1849). In his earlier years he was an influential music critic.

**Remarque, Erich Maria,** pseudonym of **Erich Paul Remark** (1898– ), German novelist, born at Osnabrück, went into the army straight from school and fought all through the 1914–18 War. As a result of his war experiences he published in 1929 the autobiographical *Im Westen nichts Neues* (Eng. trans. *All Quiet on the Western Front*, 1930), which, translated into many languages, had a world-wide success. This memorable book, with its naked realism but full of deep sympathy for human suffering, was succeeded by an equally powerful study of post-war disillusion, *Der Weg zurück* (1931; Eng. trans. *The Road Back*, 1931). Of his later work in the same vein may be mentioned *Drei Kameraden* (1938) and *Der Funke Lebens* (1952; Eng. trans. *The Spark of Life*, 1952).

**Remizov, Alexey Mikhailovich** (1877–1957), Russian *émigré* writer, considered by some the most original Russian novelist, after A. Bely (q.v.), of the last fifty years. Born in Moscow, he published many novels before the Revolution, including *Prud* (1907, 'The Pond') and *Krestovye sestry* (1910, 'Sisters in the Cross'), and a volume of short stories, *Pyataya yazva* (1912; Eng. trans. *The Fifth Pestilence*, 1927). After 1921 he lived abroad, producing further novels, such as *V pole blakitnom* (1922; Eng. trans. *On a Field Azure*, 1946) and *Olia* (1927). His style is tortured, a weird mixture of the comic and the pathetic, and he delights in words for their own sake, creating a world of surrealistic visions and grotesque fantasy. His work undoubtedly influenced the younger neo-realist writers such as Bulgakov (q.v.) and Pilnyak (q.v.). He died in Paris.

**Renan, Joseph Ernest** (1823–1892), French historian and philosopher. Born at Tréguier, Brittany, he was early on intended for the priesthood, but by 1845 he found himself unable to accept orthodox theology, and with the help of his devoted sister, Henriette (*d.* 1861), he settled down to private study, especially in oriental philosophy and philology. The result of this appeared in 1852 with his book on Arabic philosophy, *Averroès et l'averroïsme,* which he followed up with *L'Histoire générale des langues sémitiques* (1852). In his *Essais de morale et de critique* (1859) he elaborates his philosophical standpoint that the modern world will only be regenerated by a return to feudalism. His growing fame resulted in his appointment as professor of Hebrew at the Collège de France in 1861, but owing to clerical opposition it did not become effective till 1870. In 1863 appeared his best-known work, *La Vie de Jésus* (Eng. trans. *The Life of Jesus*, 1864), which was widely condemned and widely read. It was the first volume of a great undertaking, *L'Histoire des origines du Christianisme*, completed in 1883, and he was engaged on another titanic task, *L'Histoire du Peuple d'Israël*, from 1887 until shortly before his death. Renan lives today as a vivid manifestation of the thought of the period and of the first serious inroads of science into orthodox belief which intensified the pride and optimism of knowledge, rather than for his general works. The two exceptions are *Averroès*, which still remains an impressive piece of scholarship, and his most abiding literary work, *Souvenirs d'enfance et de jeunesse* (1883; Eng. trans. *Recollections of My Youth*, 1883). Although he married in 1856 his wife never took the place of his sister, and his tribute to her, *Ma Sœur Henriette*, appeared in 1895. He died in Paris.

**Renard, Jules** (1864–1910), French novelist and playwright, was born at Chalon-sur-Mayenne. Although a contributor to Paris journalism he continued to live in the country, and became an accurate observer of country life. The deep love and understanding of nature and peasant life, which he gained from thus continually communing with them, are well illustrated in his two series of *Histoires naturelles* (1896 and 1904; Eng. trans. 1948). As a playwright he is best represented by *Poil de carotte* (1900; Eng. trans. *Carrots*, 1946), a study of a boy and a work of genuine pathos. It has been made into a successful film in recent years. The complete edition of his works appeared in 1925, and ten years later his *Journal intime* revealed a rarely beautiful mind facing day to day life.

**Renaut** (thirteenth century), French poet (not Renart) known for his *Galeran de Bretagne*, a love-story with a dull style but a most striking human interest far in advance of its time. The most modern edition of it is that by L. Foulet (1925).

**Renaut de Beaujeu** (thirteenth century), French poet, author of an Arthurian romance, *Le Bel Inconnu* (1220?). It has been edited by G. P. Williams (1929).

**Resende, Garcia de** (1472?–1536), Portuguese poet and anthologist. Born at Évora, he served at the royal court. His *Cancioneiro Geral* (1516) is a large collection of courtly verse, some of it his own, from which one learns much of the social life of the time. This and his later work was collected as *Livro das obras de Garcia de Resende* (1545, with additions in the second ed. of 1554).

**Restif, Nicolas Edmé** (1734–1806), generally known as **Restif de la Bretonne**, French novelist. Born at Sacy, he worked for a time as a journeyman printer, and composed some of his vast output of well over two hundred volumes straight into print. A moralist who has caught something of the Rousseauesque state of mind, he tries to set before the reader broad descriptions of the world he knows (lower middle-class and working-class life). *Lucile, ou les Progrès de la vertu* (1768) and *Le Paysan perverti* (1776) are prime examples of his work. If he approaches very near to the salacious on some occasions it is only in the interest of the reformation of society which he takes so seriously. *Monsieur Nicolas, ou le Cœur humain dévoilé* (16 vols., 1796–7; Eng. trans. 6 vols., 1930–31) is autobiographical. Restif died in Paris. The definitive edition of the works worth retrieving appeared in 1930–2.

**Reuchlin, Johann** (1455–1522), German scholar and man of letters. Born at Pforzheim, Baden, he was educated at Basel where he wrote his Latin dictionary (1476), and after travelling in France set up as a lecturer at Tübingen in 1481. Before long he was off again partly on state affairs and partly in a private manner, paying especially profitable visits to Italy. In 1496 he went to Heidelberg, becoming the leading Hebrew scholar of the day, and with Erasmus introducing the study of Greek into Germany. His *Rudimenta Linguae Hebraicae* (1506) gave a remarkable impetus to the study of the Hebrew text of the Bible, and his editions of Greek texts were highly regarded also. A learned cabbalist, his two great works on that subject are *De Verbo Mirifico* (1494) and *De Arte Cabbalistica* (1517). Reuchlin, who in 1500 had become a judge of the Swabian League, in 1510 came to verbal blows with less broadminded scholars over his tolerant attitude to Jews and Hebrew sacred books, and the quarrel which followed is enshrined in the famous and very readable *Epistolae Obscurorum Virorum* (1516), written by Reuchlin's supporters Crotus Rubeanus and Hutten (q.v.) against the Dominicans and other devotees of scholasticism. Reuchlin's two Latin comedies, *Sergius* (1496) and *Henno* (1497), are the first genuine comedies written in Germany. Reuchlin died at Bad Liebenzell.

**Reuter, Heinrich Ludwig Christian Friedrich (Fritz Reuter**, 1810–1874), German novelist, writing in Low German. Born at Stavenhagen, Mecklenburg-Schwerin, he became a law student first at Rostock and then at Jena, where in 1833, as a member of a political group within the students' union, he was condemned to death by a Prussian court. This was commuted to thirty years' imprisonment, but he was released in 1840 after serving seven, broken in health and with his career ruined. He took to farming, gradually recovered, and married in 1851. After some volumes of verse in Low German, the first in 1853, which proved popular, and included *Kein Hüsung* (1858), a tragic poem on the wretchedness of the almost serfs of Mecklenburg, he turned to novels also written in Low German. Of these the best are *Ut mine Festungstid* (1862), in which he tells of his ruined youth in prison, and his finest work, *Ut mine Stromtid* (1863–1864; Eng. trans. *An Old Story of My Farming Days*, 1878). *Ut de Franzosentid* (1860; Eng. trans. *The Year '13*, 1873), is a reconstruction of information gained from the peasants themselves of the War of Liberation of 1813 in Mecklenburg. Fritz Reuter raised *Plattdeutsch* to the status of a literary language. His particular gifts were fluency, whether in prose or verse, and delicate mingling of humour and pathos. He died at Eisenach.

**Reymont** (or **Rejment**), Władysław Stanisław (1867–1925), Polish novelist. Born in Kobiele Wielkie the son of the village organist, he led an unsettled life doing many varied jobs until 1891, when he settled in Warsaw determined to pursue a literary life. Success came to him in 1896 with his novel on the life of the theatre, *Komediantka* (Eng. trans. *The Comedienne*, 1921), and this he followed up with *Ziemia obiecana* (1899; Eng. trans. *The Promised Land*, 1927), with factory life as its theme, and *Sprawiedliwie* (1899; Eng. trans. *Justice*, 1925). His greatest book is generally considered to be *Chłopi* (4 vols., 1904–9; Eng. trans. *The Peasants*, 1925–6), featuring the peasant life of Poland on a gigantic scale. Reymont, who received the Nobel Prize for literature in 1924, died in Warsaw.

**Riba Bracons, Carles** (1893–1959), Catalan poet and translator. Born in Barcelona, where he died, he became professor of Greek at the university there, but was deprived of his post as a Catalanist in 1939. His best original work is to be found in his volume of poetry, *Estances* (1933). The variety of his translations into Catalan, ranging from Sophocles to Hölderlin (q.v.) and E. A. Poe, is truly amazing. See *Obra poética: antología*, with Catalan and Spanish versions (1956).

**Ribeiro, Bernardim** (1484?–1552), Portuguese pastoral prose-writer, born at Torrão. Practically nothing is known of his life except that since a few of his verses appear in G. de Resende's (q.v.) *Cancioneiro Geral* (1516), he must have been a member of the royal court, and there is a tradition that he died insane. He is remembered solely as the author of a pastoral novel comprising several eclogues, *Menina e Moça* (1554). This can be found in his *Obras completas* (2 vols., 1949–50).

**Richard I** (1157–1199), King of England and French troubadour. Born in Oxford, he was yet a foreigner in England and almost entirely French speaking. The influence of his mother, Eleanor of Aquitaine, a patroness of poets, was very strong, and his love for her was about the only personal attachment he seems to have had in his life; it was at his express desire that he was buried beside her in the abbey of Fontevrault after his death at the siege of Chaluz. His most striking poetical work is his *Rotrouenge*, written while a prisoner of the Emperor Henry VI in the castle of Dürenstein, near Vienna (1192–3). His verse has been collected in J. Brakelmann, *Les plus anciens chansonniers français* (1896).

**Richepin, Jean** (1849–1926), French poet, playwright and novelist, was born at Médéa, Algeria, and went to Paris where he became known as a literary iconoclast, being imprisoned for his book of verse, *Chanson des gueux* (1876), which was officially regarded as detrimental to popular morality. *Les Blasphèmes* (1884), as its title indicates, was still rebellious but less so, and he gradually renounced his earlier violent style, becoming acceptable in official circles. The rebel ended his days as chancellor of the French Academy and director of the Comédie Française. His novels include the violent *Les Morts bizarres* (1876) and the considerably softer *Flamboche* (1895) at the end of the series. It was, however, as a playwright that he wrote lasting work. In verse and in the grand tradition his plays, which were collected in four volumes in 1919, attracted Sarah Bernhardt, who acted in several of them opposite Richepin himself. He died in Paris. See A. G. Cameron's *Selections from Richepin* (1905).

**Richter, Johann Paul Friedrich,** known as **Jean Paul** (1763–1825), German novelist. Born at Wunsiedel, in northern Bavaria, he was sent in 1781 to Leipzig to study theology, but left the university without a degree and had to retire to his mother's poverty-stricken cottage. Here he wrote *Grönländische Prozesse oder satirische Skizzen* (1783, 'The Greenland Lawsuits') which was bought by a Berlin publisher, but it was a failure on publication, and in 1787 he was forced to take to teaching, continuing with it until 1796. He continued writing and in 1793 scored a success with *Die unsichtbare Loge* (Eng. trans. *The Invisible Lodge*, 1883), a foretaste of his individual style and whimsical humour. With *Hesperus, oder 45 Hundspostlage* (1795; Eng. trans. 1865) he reached fame, and followed this up with *Das Leben des Quintus Fixlein* (1796; Eng. trans. by Thomas Carlyle, 1827) and *Blumen-, Frucht-, und Dornstücke, oder Ehestand, Tod und Hochzeit des Armenadvokaten Fr. S. Siebenkäs* (1796; Eng. trans. *Flower, Fruit and Thorn Pieces*, 1845). Invited by one of his many female admirers, Charlotte von Kalb, to Weimar in 1796 he was cold-shouldered by Goethe and Schiller but received enthusiastically by Herder (q.v.). He ventured into philosophical realms with *Das Kampaner Thal* (1797) on the immortality of the soul, but happily returned to the idyll, in which he had proved how he could excel in *Dominie Wuz* (1793), with *Palingenesien* (1798, 'Prospective Autobiography'). After visiting Weimar again in 1799 he went the following year to Berlin, and married in 1801. A gigantic romance, *Titan*, which he had begun to publish in 1800, was completed in 1803 (Eng. trans. 1862), and after venturing into near-philosophy once more with *Vorschule der Ästhetik* (1804), he projected his personal idiosyncracies in *Flegeljahre* (1804–5, 'Wild Oats'). In *Levana, oder Erziehungslehre* (1807; Eng. trans. 1848) he set up as an oracle on education, before resuming his accustomed manner in *Des Feldpredigers Schmelzles Reise nach Flätz* (1809; Eng. trans. by Thomas Carlyle, *Army Chaplain Schmelzle's Journey*, 1827). His last great effort was *Nicholas Markgraf oder Der Komet* (1820–2), in which the Jean Paul diffusiveness has reached such a height as to make the book almost unreadable. His autobiography, a charming work, was not completed owing to failing eyesight. He died blind at Bayreuth where he had lived since 1804. Richter's quaintness, his sentimental feelings and his romantic descriptive powers fascinated his contemporaries, who delighted in his emotional formlessness and ungoverned bizarrerie; but the belated south German romantic baroque, to which Carlyle fell a willing victim, has not stood the test of time except in the idylls, the autobiographies, and some passages of the *Thorn Pieces*, which have undeniable and lasting charm.

**Rilke, Rainer Maria** (1875–1926), German poet and prose-writer, was born in Prague. A psychopathological case, Rilke was always afraid of the world, and fear of ties and obligations made him a wanderer on earth and a hovering visitor on the edge of society. His first period, the time of the influence on him of the folk-song and nature, was succeeded by one of an increasing complexity of thought and style, mysticism taking the place of the earlier definite religious creed. To this time belongs *Geschichten vom lieben Gott* (1900–4; Eng. trans. *Stories of God*, 1931). From about 1904 to 1913 Rilke is under French influence, the finest flower of this period being *Neue Gedichte* (1907–8), while his best prose belongs to this time: *Die Weise von Liebe und Tod des Cornets Christoph Rilke* (1906; Eng. trans. *The Tale of Love and Death of Cornet Christopher Rilke*, 1932) and *Aufzeichnungen des Malte Laurids Brigge* (1910; Eng. trans. *Notebook of Malte Laurids Brigge*, 1930). Then comes the final period of the deepened wisdom of experience, sometimes sad, at others passionate or near despair with *Duineser Elegien* (begun 1911, not completed until 1922; Eng. trans. *Duino Elegies*, 1939) and *Sonette an Orpheus* (1922; Eng. trans. *Sonnets to Orpheus*, 1936). See also *Translations* (N.Y., 1938). Rilke died at Val-Mont, near Montreux.

**Rimbaud, Jean Nicolas Arthur** (1854–1891), French poet and prose-writer. Born in Charleville, he went to Paris in 1871 where he immediately won the friendship of Verlaine (q.v.), with whom he spent some time in London. Between then and 1873 he wrote practically all his work, publishing for the first and last time on his own initiative a remarkable prose volume, *Une Saison en enfer*, that year. In this he describes with immense power and faultless technique a battle with disillusionment in all things mental which ends in the repudiation of art. Acting on this loss of faith he gave up a literary life for good and set out on his wanderings, earning his living in many ways, which led him to Harrar in Abyssinia where he was a merchant, gun-runner and slave dealer. Contracting syphilis he returned to France, where he died after the amputation of his leg at Marseille. In 1886 Verlaine, believing him to be dead, published an early work of his belonging to the *Saison* period called *Les Illuminations*, containing poems in verse and prose. This astonishing book, full of visions of a kind of wild, untamed universe, in which colours and sounds play a significant symbolistic part, can be matched only by another of his creations, *Le Bâteau ivre*, written when he was sixteen. This latter (Eng. trans. *The Drunken Boat*, 1952) did not appear until his works were collected in 1895. The latest edition of the *Œuvres complètes* is that of 1946.

**Rinaldo d'Aquino** (1208?–1280?), Italian poet, believed to be of the same family as St Thomas Aquinas (q.v.), wrote some moving lyrics including one, the subject of which is a girl mourning for her lover who is about to set out on a crusade. These are included in G. Lazzeri's *Antologia dei primi secoli della letteratura italiana*, vol. ii (1942).

**Rinuccini, Ottavio** (1562–1621), Italian poet and melodramatist, who was born and who died in Florence. His great feeling for music is reflected in his pastoral melodramas *Dafne* (1594), *Euridice* (1600) and *Arianna* (1607). Never before had a poet written with an eye to the musician's point of view, and in this way Rinuccini may be said to have been one of Europe's earliest and first satisfactory librettists, as he is the first true melodramatist. He also published a volume of verse in 1622. His *Drammi per musica* appeared in a definitive edition in 1926.

**Rivarol, Antoine** (1753–1801), French satirist, was born at Bagnols, Languedoc, arrived in Paris in 1780 and made a hit with his *Petit Almanach de nos grands hommes* (1788) in which he mocked the old regime. When he did the same for the revolution in the *Petit Dictionnaire de nos grands hommes de la Révolution* (1790) it was less well appreciated, and he went into exile in 1792. Now turned royalist and pensioned by the *émigrés* he was busy writing propagandist pamphlets in the royalist interest in Brussels, London, Hamburg and Berlin, where he died. The best edition of his *Œuvres* is the second (1880).

**Rivas, Ángel de Saavedra y Ramírez de Baquedano de** (1791–1865), Spanish poet and playwright, was born of noble family at Cordoba. He became conspicuous as a liberal politician, escaping the revenge of Ferdinand VII in 1823 by leaving Spain. During his eleven years of exile, including a long period in London, he fell under the influence of the work of Scott and Byron. Rivas is important as the author who more than anyone else broke up the neo-classicism which still lingered in Spain and replaced it by romanticism. This change was particularly due to the publication of his narrative poem with a highly colourful Moorish background in the manner of Moore and Byron, *El moro expósito*, in 1834, and the year after he followed this up with an even more successful play, *Don Álvaro o la fuerza del sino*, a work absolutely steeped in romanticism, from which later the libretto for Verdi's *La forza del destino* was made. The most lasting of Rivas's works is his collection of ballads on historical subjects, *Romances históricos* (1841). After his work and that of Espronceda (q.v.) romanticism was bound to triumph. On his return to Spain in 1834 he had inherited the dukedom, but by this time his liberalism was cooling and he lived to become Isabel II's prime minister and ambassador in Paris. He died in Madrid. His complete works in seven volumes appeared between 1894 and 1904. There have been English translations of some of his poetry, but they are not worth reading.

**Robbe-Grillet, Alain** (1922–   ), French novelist, born in Brest. Trained as an agricultural engineer, he became a research biologist and then turned to writing as a profession. One of the leaders of the *avant-garde*, he became known in 1957 for two novels published that year, *Le Voyeur* (Eng. trans. *The Voyeur*, 1959) and *La Jalousie* (Eng. trans. *Jealousy*, 1960), two slow-moving works with everything concentrated on the hero obsessionally analysing his own and the actions of others which have brought him to the uncomfortable position he finds himself in. In his article 'Nature, humanisme et tragédie' (Eng. trans. *London Magazine*, Feb., 1959—'Old "Values" and the New Novel') he declares his coldly scientific approach to literature, the purpose of which is to describe human motives without relation to moral values. The mental and physical, he believes, run on different planes and can never be brought together. His script for the prize-winning film, *L'Année dernière à Marienbad* (1961), was translated in 1962 as *Last Year at Marienbad*.

**Robert de Blois** (thirteenth century), French poet, employed by Hugo de Poix, he wrote some dull rhymed etiquette books, including the *Chastoiement des Dames*, a moderate Arthurian romance, *Beaudous*, and a pleasing short-verse tale, *Floris et Liriopé*, very much in the late Greek romantic style, which found its way westwards in Latin versions, but all his work is spoilt by his besetting sin of lecturing his readers.

**Robert de Borron** ( *fl.* 1186–1214), French poet, author of the first Grail romance, *Joseph d'Arimathie*, came from the Belfort area. *Joseph* was edited by W. A. Nitze in 1927.

**Roblès, Emmanuel** (1914–    ), French novelist. Born in Oran, Algeria, he became a journalist and travelled widely. His study of working-class life, *Travail d'homme* (1942), established him and he continued the social novel in such books as *Les Hauteurs de la ville* (1948), and *Les Couteaux* (1956; Eng. Trans. *Knives*, 1958).

**Rod, Édouard** (1857–1910), Franco-Swiss novelist, was born at Nyon in the canton of Vaud. After education at Lausanne, Bonn and Berlin, he settled in Paris where he remained for many years and was editor of *La Revue Contemporaine*. On the whole pessimistic with a severe style, he first adhered to Zola and the naturalistic school as in *La Chute de Miss Topsy* (1882), but later turned to mental processes and moral problems, in *La Vie privée de Michel Teissier* (1893) and *La Seconde Vie de Michel Teissier* (1894) producing impressive studies of conscience and desire and duty. He died at Grasse, France.

**Rodenbach, Georges-Raymond-Constantin** (1855–1898), Belgian poet and novelist. Born at Tournai, he published his first book of poetry, *Le Foyer et les champs*, in 1877, and this was succeeded by *Les Tristesses* (1879). Of his later poetry *Le Règne du silence* (1891) and *Les Vies encloses* (1896) are fine. His novel about Bruges, *Bruges-la-Morte* (1892), like his poetry is full of the quiet, long-vista'd, slightly sad greyness of Flanders, the atmosphere sometimes thickening into misty melancholy. His short stories in *Le Rouet des brumes* (post-humously, 1901) have the same haunting quality. Rodenbach died in Paris where he had become something of a celebrity in literary circles.

**Rodríguez de la Cámara, Juan** (1405?–1445?), Spanish novelist. Born at Padrón (hence sometimes called **Rodríguez del Padrón**), he served as a page at the court of Castile. His autobiographical novel, *El siervo libre de amor* (1430?), is well written and reveals a strong and interesting character. A modern edition of it was published at Buenos Aires in 1943.

**Roger de Beauvoir,** *see* **Beauvoir.**

**Rojas Zorrilla, Francisco de** (1607–1648), Spanish dramatist, was born in Toledo. He settled in Madrid and was in high favour with Philip IV. He was murdered there by an unsuccessful candidate for a prize while acting as the judge of a poetical contest. Influenced in tragedy by Calderón, his best play in that direction is *García del Castañar*, but when he relies on his native humour as in *Entre bobos* *anda el juego* he is more at his ease and more convincing. He was plundered for plots by French playwrights, Scarron (q.v.) especially. *García* and *Entre bobos* appear in *Teatro de F. de Rojas Zorrilla* (1917).

**Rolland, Romain** (1866–1944), French novelist, playwright and biographer, was born at Clamecy, Nièvre, of a well-to-do family. In 1896 he was appointed professor of the history of music at the École Normale, Paris, and later became professor of the same subject at the Sorbonne. He first appeared in print with *Les Origines du théâtre lyrique moderne* (1895), a landmark in historical criticism. He next began to take an increasing interest in original writing, displaying his great gift of psychological insight into character, which was his strongest vein, in a series of plays on the French Revolution of 1789. Poorly constructed and really unfit for dramatic presentation, some of them, such as *Danton* (1900; Eng. trans. 1918) and *Le Quatorze Juillet* (1902; Eng. trans. *The Fourteenth of July*, 1928), are incisive studies of men, ideas and motives. In 1904 he began to contribute to *Les Cahiers de la Quinzaine*, the early parts of his long romance, 'the tragedy of a generation that had disappeared', *Jean-Christophe* (published in book form, 1904–12, and in a rev. ed. 1931–4; Eng. trans. *John Christopher*, 4 vols., shortened, 1910–13). Speaking through his musician hero, an amalgam of all that is best in French and German culture, Rolland in this lengthy, almost rambling work, presents his views on every kind of aspect of life. While engaged on this he had embarked on his dramatized biographies of great artists and idealists, such as *Vie de Beethoven* (1902; Eng. trans. 1907), *Vie de Michel-Ange* (1906; Eng. trans. 1912) and *Vie de Tolstoï* (1911; Eng. trans. 1911). On the outbreak of war in 1914 he left France for Switzerland, and there wrote a number of pacifist pamphlets, collected as *Au-dessus de la mêlée* (1915), being awarded the Nobel Prize the same year. After the war, as optimistic as ever about the final perfectibility of man, he returned to the studies of his heroes with *Mahatma Gandhi* (1924; Eng. trans. 1924), a memorable study of spirituality, and the still more remarkable *Beethoven, les grandes époques créatrices* (1930; recast and publ. posthumously in 1945), perhaps his greatest work. Another huge *roman-fleuve* in the manner of *Jean-Christophe* belongs to the later years, being published as *L'Âme enchantée* (7 vols., 1927–1933; Eng. trans. *The Soul Enchanted*, 6 vols., 1927–35). He died at Vézelay. His *Journal des années de guerre, 1914–19*, edited by his widow Marie Rolland, appeared in 1953.

**Rolli, Paolo** (1687–1765), Italian poet, born in Rome. He came to London in 1715 and stayed there for nearly thirty years, being at the forefront of the movement to popularize still more the Italian opera, a rage which had begun in the last years of Queen Anne's reign. As such Rolli produced many libretti for Handel, Buononcini and other composers, his style being copied by such English librettists as Aaron Hill and the younger Stillingfleet, and his influence continued until late in the eighteenth century. His lyric poetry is smooth and sweet, its precision of language gained from a true understanding of such classical Latin poets as Horace and Tibullus. An excellent example of his verse is to be found in the volume, *Le rime* (1717). His *Poetici* *componimenti* appeared in 1753, and there is a very informative edition of the *Liriche* (1926). Rolli, who returned to Italy in 1744, died at Todi.

**Rollinat, Jean Auguste Maurice** (1846–1903), French poet, born in Châteauroux. A late derivative of Baudelaire's (q.v.) earlier macabre manner, he first drew attention to himself with his decadent volume of verse, *Les Névroses* (1883), which remains his best and most characteristic work. Of his later publications in the same vein, *L'Abîme* (1886) and *Les Apparitions* (1896) may be mentioned. He went mad and died at Ivry-sur-Seine, near Paris.

**Romains, Jules,** pseudonym of **Louis Farigoule** (1885–    ), French novelist, dramatist and poet, born at Saint-Julien-Chapteuil. As soon as he started to write he proclaimed himself the head of a new school which eventually brought collective psychology into literature, thus foreshadowing what was to come about later in the days of the dictators. His doctrine of the spirit of collective society being superior to that of the individual was displayed in his book of poems, *La Vie unanime* (1908), while in *Le Manuel de déification* (1910) he went further and considered a new religion which should, better than Christianity with its accent on the individual, more nearly represent the new collective social forces of the world. A straight social novel founded on his early life, *Les Copains*, his most popular work, appeared in 1913, and was followed by a volume of short stories, *Sur les quais de la Villette* (1914). In the 1920's he turned for a time to plays, and produced two outstanding ones, each satirizing an abuse in modern society. These are *Knock* (1924; Eng. trans. *Dr Knock*, 1925), in which he pillories an unscrupulous member of the medical profession and at the same time touches on mass-feeling, and *Donogoo* (1931), an attack on speculators mad for money. After this he set about his ambitious series of novels dealing with French society between 1908 and 1933, *Les Hommes de bonne volonté* (1932–46; Eng. trans. *Men of Good Will*, 1933–48). The result, as was almost inevitable, falls far short of Balzac and Proust (q.v.), although several volumes are immensely readable, and a firm style and good dialogue seldom fail.

**Romanov, Panteleymon Sergeyevich** (1884–1936), Russian Soviet novelist. In his lengthy novel, *Rus'* (4 vols., 1924–36, 'Russia'), he made a bold attempt to deal with the problems which faced his own generation astride two completely different ways of life. He is well known for his short story, *Bez cheryomukhi* (1926; Eng. trans. *Without Cherry Blossom*, 1930).

**Ronsard, Pierre de** (1524–1585), French poet. Born at the Manoir de la Possonnière, Couture, near Vendôme, he was intended for a military and diplomatic career, and as a preliminary was sent to court as a page, visiting Scotland in the retinue of Mary of Guise in 1538. He remained at court on his return, had a severe illness in 1542 which left him permanently partially deaf, and soon afterwards he became a student at the Collège de Coqueret, where he met Baïf (q.v.) and Du Bellay (q.v.), who were later to be associated with him as poets of the Pléiade. While at the Collège he gained a great knowledge of classical literature, the inspiration of his *Odes*, which came out in two series (1550 and 1552). It could be seen at once how Horatian and Pindaric styles had enriched French poetry, and to increase this element became the Pléiade's avowed object. Next he published his first book of *Amours* (1553), inspired by his hopeless, or perhaps idealized love for Cassandre de Salviati whom he met at a ball at Blois; but with his second and third book of *Amours* (1555-6) we find ourselves in a different world of feeling: sensual love for a peasant girl. At the very same time that he was publishing these, Ronsard was preparing for publication *Hymnes* on the Homeric model, majestic addresses to friends and patrons (1556). By 1560 he and the other members of the Pléiade had definitely displaced medieval style by the new humanism. Ronsard, who first collected his poems that year, had reached the height of fame and prosperity. Next begins his later literary period of the alexandrine with *Les Discours* (1560-70), dealing with the religious wars from a nationalist and Catholic standpoint, the *Élégies, Mascarades et Bergerie* (1565), the stiff, unfinished epic, *La Franciade* (1572)—Ronsard was essentially a lyric poet—and what is nowadays considered his masterpiece, *Sonnets pour Hélène* (1578), addressed to a maid-of-honour, Hélène de Surgères. In his last years Desportes (q.v.) took the place of Ronsard as favourite poet, and after his death the condemnation of him by that dictator of letters, Malherbe (q.v.), put Ronsard out of view for a considerable time. Ronsard died at the abbey of Saint-Cosme, Touraine, crippled with arthritis. The *Œuvres complètes* have been edited by P. Laumonier (8 vols., 1914-19), and this is considered the definitive edition. See also *Sonnets pour Hélène*, edited by J. Lavaud (1947). There is an English translation, *Songs and Sonnets of Pierre de Ronsard* by C. H. Page (1903).

**Ropshin, V.,** *see* **Savinkov, B.**

**Rørdam, Valdemar** (1872-1946), Danish poet, born at Dalby, the son of a clergyman. A prolific writer, he was particularly successful in his patriotic poetry (*Danske Tunge*, 1901; *Den gamle Kaptajn*, 1906-7; and *Sangen om Danmark*, 1923) and as a translator (*Drömmerier*, 1924, translations from Yeats). Prominent among his later work was *Danmark i tusind Aar* (1940). When Germany occupied Denmark he became notorious as a collaborationist and died completely discredited.

**Rosegger, Peter,** who changed his name from **Petri Kettenfeier** (1843-1918), Austrian short-story writer, was born of a peasant family at Alpl, Styria. Self-educated, he became a travel-agent for Alpinists, in his spare time writing his many popular volumes of short stories on country life. *Die Schriften des Waldschulmeisters* (1875; Eng. trans. *The Forest Schoolmaster*, 1901) and *Waldheimat* (1877; Eng. trans. *The Forest Farm*, 1912) are good examples of his facile though pleasing work. For the greater part of his life he lived in Graz, but died at Krieglach.

**Rosny, J. H.,** pseudonym until 1908 of the brothers **Joseph-Henri**

Boëx (1856–1940) and Justin Boëx (1859–1948), both of whom were born in Brussels and died in Paris. After 1908 they wrote their books separately as Rosny *aîné* and Rosny *jeune* respectively. Their large number of novels, generally historical, range over a very wide period and are written in an urgent, compelling style, which even after they ceased to collaborate remained very similar. They were naturalists, but are of the school of Flaubert's (q.v.) *Salammbô* rather than of Zola (q.v.). The following of their novels may be mentioned: as J. H. Rosny, *L'Immolation* (1887) and *L'Impérieuse Bonté* (1905); as Rosny *aîné*, *La Vague rouge* (1910), *L'Appel au bonheur* (1919) and *Les Pécheresses* (1928); and as Rosny *jeune*, *Sépulcres blanchis* (1913) and *La Pantine* (1929).

**Rossetti, Gabriele** (1783–1854), Italian poet and literary critic. Born at Vasto, Abruzzi Citeriore, he became keeper of ancient bronzes in the Naples museum, and was a member of Murat's provisional government there (1813). After the restoration of the Neapolitan Bourbons in 1815 he joined the Carbonari and made a reputation as a patriotic poet. Forced to leave Italy for his political opinions in 1821, he reached London in 1824 and in 1831 became professor of Italian at King's College, London, in which city he died. He was the father of Christina and D. G. Rossetti. Besides his work as a Dante scholar, still much appreciated today, he wrote some good poetry inspired either by hopes for Italian unity, as *Iddio e l'uomo salterio* (1833), or by religious feeling, such as *L'Arpa evangelica* (1852). Carducci (q.v.) edited his poetical works in 1879.

**Rostand, Edmond Eugène Alexis** (1868–1918), French dramatist. Born in Marseille, he had his first success with *Les Romanesques* (1894; produced in England in translation as *The Fantasticks* the same year), and he gained further high praise with *La Princesse lointaine* (1895), in which Sarah Bernhardt took the leading part, and *La Samaritaine* (1897), all of these showing great poetic gifts, dramatic intensity, and clearly in the tradition of Victor Hugo (q.v.). Then in the same year as *La Samaritaine* appeared that fine heroic verse drama, *Cyrano de Bergerac* (Eng. trans. 1937), which made him world-famous. The seventeenth-century French poet of that name (q.v.) is the hero. There followed *L'Aiglon* (1900; Eng. trans. *The Young Eagle*, 1927), a tragedy of the life of Napoleon's unfortunate son, the duc de Reichstadt. His symbolical animal play, *Chantecler* (1910), was in no way equal to his previous work. The final representative of the French romantic playwrights, Rostand, who had been elected to the French Academy in 1901, died in Paris. He left behind another play which is fine literature rather than drama, *La Dernière Nuit de Don Juan*. It was published in 1921.

**Rostand, Maurice** (1891–      ), French playwright. Son of Edmond (q.v.), he was born at Cambo, and made a name with his historical play in verse, *La Gloire* (1921). Among his later plays may be named *Le Dernier Tzar* (1929) and *Le Procès d'Oscar Wilde* (1935). In 1948 he produced a volume of memoirs, *Confession d'un demisiècle*.

**Rostworowski, Karol Hubert** (1877–1938), Polish playwright. Born at

Rybna of an old aristocratic family, he had a musical training and then in his late thirties settled in Cracow where he spent the rest of his life. A man of deeply religious feeling, he set himself to investigate in his plays the motives behind the actions of men judged harshly by history. Thus in *Judasz z Kariothu* (1913) and *Kajus Cezar Kaligula* (1917) he takes two obviously shady characters and tries with sympathy to understand why they committed the crimes for which they stand condemned. This approach is broadened and deepened in *Antychryst* (1925). In his later years Count Rostworowski turned to straight dramatic studies of peasant life, as in the trilogy *Niespodzianka* (1929, 'The Surprise'), *Przeprowadzka* (1930, 'The Removal') and *U mety* (1932, 'At the Finish').

**Roth, Eugen** (1895–        ), German humourist in verse and prose, was born in Munich. He successfully held up his glass to the follies of social life in such books as *Ein Mensch* (1935). *Mensch und Unmensch* (1948) is representative of his post-war publications.

**Rotrou, Jean de** (1609–1650), French dramatist, born at Dreux. Making his way to Paris to try his fortune, he was employed by Richelieu to produce propagandist plays in support of his dictatorship. These were written in the 'cloak and sword' style of Lope de Vega (q.v.). Later, freed from official interference, especially after Richelieu's death (1642), he wrote in a more concentrated classical style, producing three excellent pieces, *Saint-Genest* (1646), a tragedy of Christian martyrdom, *Venceslas* (1647), a drama with a strong love interest set in Poland, and a very competent comedy, *Don Bertrand* (1648). His output was enormous, and, after his death from plague at Dreux, other playwrights were not slow to profit from his numerous and attractive plots. Racine (q.v.) learnt much from him, and *Saint-Genest* was a model for his own religious dramas *Esther* and *Athalie*. His *Œuvres* were collected in 1820.

**Roucher, Jean-Antoine** (1745–1794), French poet. Born in Montpellier, he was guillotined as a royalist in Paris during the reign of terror. He is known for his pseudo-classical *Les Mois* (1779), a cycle in twelve parts on the countryman's year, which has a distinct Virgilian charm.

**Rouget de Lisle, Claude-Joseph** (1760–1836), French poet born at Lons-le-Saulnier, Jura. It was when stationed in 1792, as a captain of engineers at Strassburg that he wrote the first six verses of 'Le Chant de guerre de l'armée du Rhin, renamed shortly afterwards 'La Marseillaise'. The last verse is not his, and whether the music is his remains enigmatical. He was wounded at the Battle of Quiberon in 1795 and, leaving the army, published *Essais en vers et en prose* (1797). He lived in rather poor circumstances in Paris, publishing *Chants français* in 1825, until granted a small pension by Louis-Philippe in 1830. He died at Choisy-le-Roi.

**Rousseau, Jean-Baptiste** (1671–1741), French poet. Born in Paris, the son of a shoemaker, he took to writing poor plays in 1694, and frequented the well-known Café Laurent, gaining notoriety from his lampoons. A man of the most unpleasant character, he made enemies wherever he went, and he finally received official sentence of perpetual banishment from France in 1712, after which he wandered about Europe always on the edge of poverty, dying in Brussels. His *Odes et cantates*, published in London in 1723, were once much admired, but today seem insipid. His entire collected works appeared in 1868.

**Rousseau, Jean-Jacques** (1712–1778), French writer and philosopher, was born at Geneva, the son of a watchmaker of French Calvinist ancestry. His mother died at his birth and his ne'er-do-well father made his son over to various relatives. Thus his childhood was unstable and, left much to himself, he became a precocious half-thinker and, in the solitude he preferred, a dreamer. After being apprenticed to an engraver, he ran away from Geneva at the age of sixteen, and from then on for the next dozen years led a wandering life first in Savoy, and later in Piedmont and France. During these years what most nearly approximated to his home was the house of a sentimental, slightly hysterical widow, Madame de Warens, who arranged for his (temporary) conversion to Roman Catholicism, and who probably became his mistress. They lived together first in comparative comfort in Annecy, and, after the loss of part of her capital in foolish speculation, in worse circumstances at Chambéry. Most of this period of his life is known only from his untrustworthy *Confessions*, but his history is clear from the time that he settled in Paris in 1741. Here his first act was to form a liaison with an uneducated, vulgar girl, Thérèse Levasseur, and during the following years five children were born to them, and—thus do the theories of some idealists go for naught in real life—the couple abandoned them in a foundling hospital. That he married Thérèse, as he claims in the *Confessions*, is without foundation. In Paris Rousseau passed some hard years eking out a living by literary hack-work and music-copying, but gradually, aided by his natural charm, he insinuated his way into the good graces of leading men of letters, his first meeting of importance being with Condillac (q.v.), the philosopher, who lodged in the same building as he for a time. Through Condillac he got to know Diderot (q.v.), Fontenelle (q.v.) and others, and for a few faintly disreputable months was in Venice as a secretary of legation. It was the friendship with Diderot which was the most beneficial connection that he had, and it was thanks to this generous man that Rousseau became a contributor to the famous *Encyclopédie* which began to appear in 1751. The year before he had made a name with his essay on the subject, set for a prize by the Académie de Dijon, *Si le progrès des sciences et des arts a contribué à corrompre ou à épurer les mœurs*. His perverse answer, in which he condemned such progress, was entirely in tune with the disillusionment of the time and he won the prize. The trend of his future thought is ascertainable from this point, and this is still more clearly seen in his *Discours sur l'origine et les fondements de l'inégalité parmi les hommes* (1755), a condemnation of private property. In 1760 appeared the first of his great works, *La Nouvelle Héloïse*, in which, influenced by the work of Samuel Richardson, he propounds in novel form his doctrine of the superiority of the

natural unit, the family, to artificial society. It brought Rousseau
immediate fame and in the long run was to exercise untold influence
on the course of European fiction. Then in 1762 came *Du Contrat
social ou Principes du droit politique*, one of the books that literally
shook the world by providing the French Revolution with a philosophical basis for interpreters (among them Robespierre), to whom,
quite mistakenly, it seemed to be a justification for the destruction
of existing despotism to be replaced by something very like new
despotism on what was supposed to be a rational foundation. But
the work is by no means revolutionary; it is a plea in the context of
enlightened absolutism for a nobler relationship between the elements
which compose society. In *Émile ou De l'éducation*, published the
same year, we find him advocating natural religion as against set
forms. In the fourth part of this work appears the memorable *La
Profession de foi du Vicaire Savoyard*, a magnificently written confession of personal faith, which more than anything brought in a
spirit of theism in place of cynical scepticism; hence Robespierre's
insistence that a belief in God was necessary to state and society.
Threatened with persecution in France he fled to Switzerland, but in
1764, such was his local unpopularity, he was forced to abandon that
retreat, and in 1765 arrived in England at the invitation of David
Hume. He remained at Wootton in Staffordshire for eighteen months,
where he composed a large part of his *Confessions*, begun in Switzerland. By now, however, he was showing signs of mental derangement
which took the form of persecution mania, and before long he quarrelled with all his friends. He returned to France in 1767 and, after
further wanderings, settled in Paris in 1770. He had already interested
himself in Corsican politics; now he took up the Polish question, and
on the eve of the First Partition published *Considérations sur le
gouvernement de la Pologne* (1772). His last work of importance was
*Rêveries d'un promeneur solitaire* (1776–8), a beautifully written, calm
idyll in marked contrast to his later letters and various essays which
are strange and unbalanced. He died suddenly at Ermenonville,
outside Paris. See J. Sénelier's *Bibliographie générale des œuvres de
Jean-Jacques Rousseau* (1950). The main works are available in
numerous English translations. Publication of Rousseau's correspondence was begun in 1924.

**Roussin, André** (1911– ), French dramatist. Born in Marseille,
he became an actor and later a well-known experimental producer in
Paris where he made a name for himself with his staging of English
Elizabethan and Jacobean plays, notably Webster's *Duchess of
Malfi* (1937). As a playwright, after an aggressive start as the author
of uncompromisingly revolutionary pieces, he settled down into satire
in 1948 with *La Petite Hutte* (Eng. trans. 1950), *Nina* (1950) and
*Lorsque l'enfant paraît* (1951).

**Roux, Paul,** *see* **Saint-Pol-Roux.**

**Rovetta, Girolamo** (1851–1910), Italian playwright and novelist,
born in Brescia. His facile novels, of which *Le lacrime del prossimo*
(1888) is the best, were very popular. Of his plays, for the most part
historical, the best known is *Romanticismo* (1901). He died in Milan.

**Rozanov, Mikhail Grigorievich** (1888–1938), Russian Soviet novelist. The son of a provincial lawyer, Rozanov (who wrote under the pseudonym of **Nikolai Ognyov**) produced morbid and unlikely short stories while engaged in underground revolutionary activities previous to 1917. After the revolution he published novels in which he contrasted the chaos and superstition of peasant life with the rational and ordered coherence which he found resulting from Soviet rule. Always ready to regard affairs from an intellectualist point of view, he found himself and won popularity with his two vivid, humorous and at the same time pathetic studies, *Dnevnik Kosti Ryabtseva* (1927; Eng. trans. *The Diary of a Communist Schoolboy*, 1928) and *Iskhod Nikpetozha* (1928; Eng. trans. *The Diary of a Communist Undergraduate*, 1929). They ably portray the difficulties of the first generation of those educated under Soviet government.

**Rozanov, Vasily Vasilyevich** (1856–1919), Russian prose writer, born at Vetluga. His work, mostly in the form of essays and sketches, is particularly notable for a penetrating analysis of mental processes and of the emotions. Human relationships, especially sexual ones, are dealt with uncompromisingly. It was natural that Dostoyevsky should be the fountainhead of his inspiration, and it was Rozanov's book *Legenda o velikom inkvizitore* (1890, 'The Legend of the Grand Inquisitor') which caused a return to an interest in his master. Literary criticism in Rozanov's best manner is to be found in *Uyedinyonnoye* (1912; Eng. trans. *Solitaria*, 1927) and *Literaturnye izganniki* (1913, 'Literary Exiles'). There is an arresting quality about *Opavshie list'ya* (1913–15; Eng. trans. *Fallen Leaves*, 1929). At the outbreak of revolution in 1917 he left Moscow and went to live in a monastery outside the city. There he wrote a strange work, *Apokalipsis nashego vremeni* ('The Apocalypse of our Day'), revealing the half mystical, half mistrustful mood in which he faced the cataclysm. He died in the monastery.

**Rubió i Ors, Joaquim** (1818–1899), Catalan critic and man of letters, a native of Barcelona, where he died professor of literature at the university, was one of the most conspicuous among the revivers of Catalan as a literary language. Rather than as an original writer, he is to be remembered above all for his restoration of the *Jocs Florals*, a rallying point of the Catalan literary revival, in 1859.

**Rückert, Friedrich** (1788–1866), German poet and orientalist, was born at Schweinfurt, and became professor of oriental languages first at Erlangen (1826–41) and then at Berlin (1841–8), having been under the influence of the famous scholar of eastern literature, J. von Hammer-Purgstall, when staying at Vienna. Besides many translations, adaptations and straight critical works, which did much to make his generation familiar with Persian, Indian and Chinese literature, he wrote many attractive lyrics, the most famous being those in the volume *Liebesfrühling* (1844), especially 'Aus der Jugendzeit!' His metrical skill is one of the most remarkable in European literature. He died at Neusess, near Coburg.

**Rudel,** *see* **Jaufré.**

**Rueda, Lope de** (*d.* 1565), Spanish dramatist, born in Seville. As actor-manager of a strolling company, later patronized by Philip II, he introduced plays founded on Italian models to Spain. His own racy one-act pieces show his mastery of excellent dialogue. His influence on Lope de Vega (q.v.) was enormous. He died in Cordoba. A critical edition of his complete *Obras* appeared in 1908.

**Ruffini, Giovanni Domenico** (1807–1881), Anglo-Italian novelist. Born at Genoa, he was a political exile in Britain from 1836 to 1875. His two best works are *Lorenzo Benoni: Passages in the Life of an Italian* (1853), which is founded on his experiences as a member of the 'Young Italy' movement, and *Doctor Antonio* (1855; new ed. 1945). Both were written in English. The libretto of Donizetti's comic opera *Don Pasquale* (1843) is by Ruffini. He died at Taggia on the Italian Riviera.

**Ruiz, Juan** (1283?–1350?), Spanish poet known from his office as the **Arcipreste de Hita.** Thought to have been a native of Alcalá, he is famous for his poetical miscellany, *El libro de buen amor* (1330), a kind of gold-mine of influences of all kinds derived from Latin and Arabic literature, an extraordinary mixture of devotional and erotic inspiration. There is a good modern critical edition by J. Corominas (1967) and an English translation, *The Book of Good Love of the Archpriest of Hita,* by E. K. Kane (1933). Juan Ruiz's place of death is unknown.

**Ruiz Aguilera, Ventura** (1820–1881), Spanish poet, born in Salamanca. His *Elegías* (1862), on the death of his daughter, is a quietly moving volume. Another such is *Las estaciones del año* (1879). Ruiz died director of the Archaeological Museum at Madrid.

**Ruiz de Alarcón,** *see* **Alarcón.**

**Runeberg, Johan Ludvig** (1804–1877), Swedish-Finnish poet writing in Swedish, was born at Jakobstad, Finland, and settled in Helsingfors in 1828. He lived as a schoolmaster and journalist until he retired in 1857, and died at Borgå. His first popular volume of poetry was *Elgskyttarne,* which was published in 1832. His masterpiece is *Kung Fjalar* (1844; Eng. trans. *King Fjalar,* 1904), a romantic national saga in strictly classical form, while his most popular was *Fänrik Ståls sägner* (first series 1848, second series 1860; Eng. trans. *The Songs of Ensign Stål,* 1925), a lyric in which has become the national anthem of Finland.

**Rydberg, Abraham Viktor** (1828–1895), Swedish poet and novelist. Born at Jönköping, he had an unsatisfactory, restless childhood and something of a wandering youth and early manhood before settling down as lecturer and freelance journalist. His critical works on history, the fine arts and culture can hardly be classed as literature, and his political and philosophical novels have scarcely stood the test of time; but his poetry, written late in life (*Dikte,* 1882 and a second vol. in 1891), is particularly pertinent and telling today since in it he tries to face from a spiritual standpoint the seemingly insurmountable problems caused by the spread of science. He died in retirement at Djursholm.

**Ryleyev, Kondraty Fedorovich** (1795–1826), Russian poet born on his father's estate at Batovo, Petersburg. Executed at Petersburg for his part in the Decembrist revolt of 1825, he wrote some narrative poetry in the Byronic vein and some of the best revolutionary poetry in Russian literature. He was a close friend of Pushkin (q.v.). His *Sochineniya* were published at Berlin in 1860, and see *The Poems of K. F. Ryleieff*, an English translation of a selection by R. Hart-Davies (1887). As a victim of czarist tyranny he has become a favourite with Soviet critics.

**Rzewuski, Henryk** (1791–1866), Polish novelist, writing under the pseudonym J. Bejła. An aristocrat who took a prominent part in politics by no means patriotic, at any rate in later life, he is noteworthy as the author of *Listopad* (3 vols., 1845–6; Eng. trans. *November*, 1857), which deals with the life of the Polish upper classes in the eighteenth century. Count Rzewuski died at Cudnów. His work was particularly popular in Germany.

# S

**Saar, Ferdinand von** (1833–1906), Austrian short-story writer, a native of Vienna, the life of which at all levels was his inspiration, as is to be seen in his collections, *Novellen aus Österreich* (vol. i, 1876; vol. ii, 1897). Dogged all his days by economic difficulties, he finally developed an incurable disease, and died in Vienna by suicide. Some of his work appears in translation in Francke and Howard's *German Classics of the Nineteenth and Twentieth Centuries*, vol. xviii (1913–15).

**Saavedra y Ramírez de Baquedano,** *see* **Rivas.**

**Saba, Umberto** (1883–1957), Italian poet, born in Trieste. A pessimist, all his work, written in a traditionalist manner, voices his unhappiness. The influence of Petrarch is apparent, and it is significant that his collected poems are entitled, *Il Canzoniere* (second ed., 1946). *Mediterranee* (1947; revised, 1950) contains further poetry in the same style. He died at Gorizia.

**Sacchetti, Franco** (1330?–1400). Italian prose-writer, whose date and place of birth are unknown. He settled in Florence where he held important offices. In literature he is remembered as the author of the *Trecentonovelle*, a collection of vigorous stories first published in 1724 (a handful trans. by T. Roscoe in his *Italian Novelists*, 1825). He died in Florence.

**Sacher-Masoch, Leopold von** (1835–1895), Austrian novelist. Born in Lemberg, he became a lawyer, and writing in his spare time gained a reputation for his studies of small-town life in Poland and the relationship between Jew and Gentile in such works as *Don Juan von Kolomea* (1866). Later, having become a sexual pervert of the kind now known after him as masochist, he produced erotic fiction, such as *Das Vermächtniss Kains* (1869) and *Die Messalinen Wiens* (1873). He died at Lindheim in Hesse.

**Sachs, Hans** (1494–1576), German poet and dramatist, was born in Nuremberg, and, after serving his apprenticeship and travelling through Germany, returned to his native town, remaining there as a master cobbler until his death. Early in his life he had been initiated into the art of the *Meistersinger* (and so Wagner, q.v., celebrated him in *Die Meistersinger von Nürnberg*). He became a keen supporter of Luther (q.v.) in 1523 and in that year published *Die Wittenbergische Nachtigall*, in which he praised the Reformation movement. His output from then on was extraordinary with over four thousand *Meisterlieder*, rough, homely verse dealing with every-day life, full of humour, well-informed, highly amusing dialogues, *(Schwänke)*, serious tales and religious poems and dramas, besides translations of Middle High German. Sachs with his broad humanity, free from every kind of meanness, is one of the most memorable men of his day. His *Sämtliche Werke*, edited by Keller and Goetze, appeared in twenty-six volumes (1870–1908). Selections have been made by Goedeke and Tittmann, the latest edition of which was edited by Merker and Buchwald (2 vols., 1923).

**Sá de Miranda, Francisco de** (1481–1558), Portuguese poet and play-wright, was born in Coimbra, studied law and attended the royal court at Lisbon. It was his visit to Italy (1521–5) which proved the turning point of his life, for it was there that he imbibed all those Renaissance influences which enabled him to revivify Portuguese literature and open the path for Camões (q.v.). His poems *(Poesias,* ed. C. M. de Vasconcelos, 1885) are particularly strong in eclogues and moralizing epistles. His most important single works are his comedies in classical Italian style, *Comédia dos Estrangeiros* (1559) and *Comédia dos Vilhapandos* (1560). He died at or near Ponte do Lima, possibly at Tapada.

**Sade, Donatien Alphonse François de** (1740–1814), French writer. Born into an old noble family with a marquisate to which he suc-ceeded, he entered the army and saw service in the Seven Years War, but resigned his commission in 1768. In 1772 he was condemned to death for sexual offences, but reprieved, soon to be convicted again at Vincennes, being imprisoned there and afterwards in Paris until 1804. During the last dozen years or so of his imprisonment he was allowed a certain amount of freedom, using his opportunity to publish some of the highly erotic romances written in his cell. There are many still in manuscript, but those that appeared in his lifetime are: *Justine ou les Malheurs de la vertu* (1791; Eng. trans. 1953), *Aline et Valcourt* (1793), *La Philosophie dans le boudoir* (1795; Eng. trans. *The Bedroom Philosophers,* 1953), *Juliette ou les Prospérités du vice* (1797; Eng. trans. 1958) and *Les Crimes de l'amour* (1800). In recent times *Les 120 Journées de Sodome* was published in 1904 (rev. ed. 1935; Eng. trans. 1954). Sade, with his fierce insistence on the right of the individual to satisfy himself as he wishes, represents the culmination of Rousseauism in hysteria, but such a wild bid for licence, heightened as it was by madness, stirred echoes in romanti-cism and liberal thought in the years to come. A renewed interest in Sade has set in in our own day. He died insane at Charenton. See his *Œuvres complètes* (12 vols., 1966–7).

**Sagan, Françoise,** pseudonym of **Françoise Quoirez** (1935–      ), French novelist, born at Cajarc (Lot) of a middle-class family. She read philosophy and letters at the Sorbonne, after which she turned to literature. Her first novel, *Bonjour, tristesse* (1954; Eng. trans. 1955), was widely acclaimed and discussed, and certainly showed that she could handle narrative with great ability, while the theme forcibly summed up certain aspects of the time. Her next novel, *Un*

*Certain Sourire* (1956; Eng. trans. *A Certain Smile*, 1956), able as it also was, suffered somewhat by comparison with her previous book, while *Dans un mois, dans un an* (1957; Eng. trans. *Those without Shadows*, 1957) was an experimental failure. *Aimez-vous Brahms?* (1959; Eng. trans. 1960) revealed an intensification of that cynicism which, however brilliant, was repulsive to many. Until then she had been an interpreter of her generation, but there are signs now, as in her fifth novel, *Les Merveilleux Nuages* (1961; Eng. trans. *Wonderful Clouds*, 1961), that she is falling behind it. In her small range Françoise Sagan shows undoubted gifts of interpretation; but her one theme is in danger of becoming monotonous and her creative gifts do not seem to be advancing. Her play, *Château en Suède* (1960), had at most a *succès d'estime*. More recently have appeared: *Les Violons parfois* (1962), *La Robe mauve de Valentine* (1963), *Toxique* (1964; Eng. trans. 1965), *La Chamade* (1965; Eng. trans. 1966).

**Sagarra i Castellarnau, Josep Maria** (1894–1961), Catalan poet and playwright born in Barcelona, representative of naturalism. He has a strength and fluidity, seen to advantage in such books of verse a *Cançons de taverna i d'oblit* (1922) and *El Comte Arnau* (1928), which deals with Catalan legends. His plays include *Marçal Prior* (1926) and *L'hostal de la Glòria* (1931). A great Catalan nationalist, he naturally fell foul of Franco's regime, and his epic, *Montserrat* (written 1942–8), was banned by the censorship and its publication withheld. This political interference seriously impeded his later output. His poetry was collected as *Obra poètica* in 1947 and his *Memories* were published in 1954. He died in Barcelona.

**Saint-Amant, Marc-Antoine de Gérard de** (1594–1661), French poet. Born in Rouen, he led an active life with varied experiences, all of which he seems to have enjoyed with gusto. His strange work is wildly undisciplined but infectiously happy. *Les Visions* (1628), *Moïse sauvé* (1653) and *La Solitude* (1654) are characteristic of his style. He died in Rouen.

**Saint Bridget,** *see* **Bridget.**

**Saint Catherine of Sienna,** *see* **Caterina da Siena.**

**Sainte-Beuve, Charles Augustin** (1804–1869), French critic, poet and novelist. Born at Boulogne, the posthumous son of a commissioner of taxes, after schooling locally and in Paris he enrolled as a medical student, but abandoned medicine in 1827 for journalism, becoming a contributor to a new liberal paper, *Le Globe*. His articles which appeared in it were collected as *Le Tableau de la poésie française au XVIᵉ siècle* (1828) and show his enthusiasm for the romantic movement. The year before an appreciative review of V. Hugo's (q.v.) *Odes et ballades* had led to a close friendship between the two men which was destroyed in 1834 when Hugo discovered that Sainte-Beuve was his wife's lover. From that time onwards Sainte-Beuve drifted away from the thorough-paced romantics. His romantic phase can be studied in his three books of poetry, *La Vie, les poésies et les pensées de Joseph Delorme* (1829), *Les Consolations* (1830) and *Pensées d'août* (1837), which show the influence of the English Lake

Poets, and his powerful novel with a modern ring, *Volupté* (1834), largely autobiographical. Invited to lecture at Lausanne in 1837 he chose Port Royal (*see* Racine) as his subject, and out of this grew his first great work, *L'Histoire de Port-Royal* (3 vols., 1840–8; third ed. 7 vols., 1867). From 1840 to 1848 he was librarian of the Mazarin Library, Paris, leaving this post to become a temporary professor at Liège (1848–9), his lectures given in that capacity being published in 1860 as *Chateaubriand et son groupe littéraire*. In 1851 he started out on his great period of journalistic activity and soon became famous for his Monday critical articles in the *Constitutionnel* (1851–61 and 1867–9), and afterwards in the *Moniteur* (1861–7) and *Le Temps* (1869). These *Lundis* were published in three groups as *Causeries du lundi* (11 vols., 1851–62), *Nouveaux lundis* (13 vols., 1863–70) and *Premiers lundis* (3 vols., 1874–5), and they stand among the greatest examples of European literary criticism of modern times. Throwing in his lot with the Empire, much to the disgust of many friends, he enjoyed all the benefits of adherents to the regime, becoming professor at the Collège de France (1854–7) and at the École Normale (1857–61). He was made a senator in 1865 and died in Paris. As a man he was smaller physically and morally than his work, even a pathetic figure, alone in later years in his bachelor rooms and picking up street-girls after dark, something of a toady and lacking in the moral courage needed in ordinary life. There criticism must end and give place to admiration for his great honesty as a critic and the loftiness of spirit which prevented him from allowing personal prejudice ever to intervene, all the more so since he had strong likes and dislikes, the latter revealed in *Mes poisons* (1926). The *Lundis* have appeared in several later shortened editions, and among other works not mentioned above should be named: *Critiques et portraits littéraires* (5 vols., 1836–9), *Portraits contemporains* (1846; rev. ed., 3 vols., 1869–71), *Étude sur Virgile* (1857) and *Souvenirs et indiscrétions* (1872). See also *Correspondance générale*, edited by J. Bonnerot (6 vols., 1935–49).

**Saint-Évremond, Charles de Marguetel de Saint-Denis de** (1616–1703), French critic and satirist, was born of an old landed family at Saint-Denys-le-Guast, Cotentin, Normandy. He turned soldier and took part in the Thirty Years War, being present at the battles of Nördlingen and Rocroi, remained loyal during the Fronde, but having attacked Mazarin on the Peace of the Pyrenees (1659), he escaped to the Low Countries and in 1661 made his home in England. He soon found an honoured place at Charles II's court, writing such works as *Réflexions sur les divers génies du peuple* (1663), *De la tragédie ancienne et moderne* (1672) and *Sur les poèmes des anciens* (1685). For many, however, he is the author of his excellent satire *La Comédie des Académistes*, a veiled attack on Richelieu and his Academy, written in 1643 but not published until 1650. Saint-Évremond died in London and was buried in Westminster Abbey.

**Saint-Exupéry, Antoine de** (1900–1944), French writer, the philosopher prose-poet of the air, was born in Lyon into an aristocratic family with little wealth remaining. Intended for the navy he failed to pass his examination and entered the French Air Force. Later he was engaged in commercial aviation and did great work in opening up an air-mail service across the Sahara to Dakar and across the Andes in South America. His first book, *Courrier-Sud* (1928; Eng. trans. *Southern Mail*, 1933), described his adventures. *Vol de nuit* (1931; Eng. trans. *Night Flight*, 1932) went further and showed that at last aviation was to be served as the navy had so long been, to be given its due as a new dimension to life. It was a new means to nobility and freedom. *Terre des hommes* (1939; Eng. trans. *Wind, Sand and Stars*, 1939) reached a still wider public, but many failed to realize that he had ceased to care very much for nature or even for men, and his book dealing with his war experiences, *Pilote de guerre* (1942; Eng. trans. *Flight to Arras*, 1942), shows great detachment. *Le Petit Prince* (1943, but written earlier; Eng. trans. *The Little Prince*, 1944) on the other hand proves his love and understanding of children. After France fell he seemed to have nothing left to live for, since Pétainists and Gaullists were equally hateful to this romantic idealist. He died mysteriously on a flight over the Mediterranean.

**Saintine, Xavier Boniface**, pseudonym of **J. X. Boniface** (1798–1865), French man of letters, born in Paris. He became known for the famous sentimental story, *Picciola* (1836; first of many Eng. trans. 1837), translated into many languages. He was a facile dramatist and often found a congenial collaborator in Scribe (q.v.). Saintine died in Paris.

**Saint John of the Cross,** *see* **Juan de la Cruz.**

**Saint-John-Perse,** pseudonym of **Alexis Léger** (1889–    ), French poet. Born at Pointe-à-Pitre, Guadeloupe, West Indies, he became a diplomat; Secretary-General for Foreign Affairs, 1933–40. With the fall of France in 1940 he went into exile and settled in the United States in 1945. Although he had been writing and publishing poetry since 1904, it was not until 1926 that he gained any following with the surrealistic *Anabase*. Translations of his work into English in 1930 by T. S. Eliot brought him into wider notice on both sides of the Atlantic; but it was *Exil* (1942) with its bid for a new faith and optimism after the sorrows and ruins of war that made him really well known as a foremost poet of his time. A growing amplitude of inspiration is discernible in his latest works, *Vents* (1946), *Amers* (1957) and *Chronique* (1960). In 1960 he was awarded the Nobel Prize for literature.

**Saint-Lambert, Jean-François de** (1716–1803), French poet. Born at Nancy, he became an army officer and later a chamberlain at the court of Louis XV's father-in-law, Stanislaus Leszczinski, Duke of Lorraine. In literary history he holds the extraordinary position of having been the lover of Voltaire's mistress, Madame du Châtelet and of Rousseau's idealistically adored Sophie, Madame d'Houdetot. In this he was more original than in any literary work he produced, the chief of which, *Les Saisons* (1769), a poor imitation of James Thomson's *The Seasons*, cannot bear comparison with contemporary French pastoral poetry such as J.-A. Roucher's (q.v.) *Les Mois*. Saint-Lambert also produced stories, *Contes* (1770), of even less interest. He died in Paris.

Saint-Pierre, *see* Bernardin de Saint-Pierre.

**Saint-Pol-Roux,** pseudonym of **Paul Roux** (1861–1940), French poet and librettist. Born at St Henry, he evolved a world of his own inspired by regional cultures, such as those of the Ardennes and Brittany, in publications like *Les Reposoirs de la procession* (incomplete, 1893; third ed., complete, 3 vols., 1907), *La Dame à la faux* (1899) and *Ancienneté s* (1903; rev. ed., 1946). He was also the author of the libretto, *Louise* (1900), the very successful light opera set to music by Georges Charpentier. When in his eightieth year he was murdered by German soldiers at Brest for speaking boldly in public against the enormities of the regime they represented.

**Saint-Simon, Claude-Henri de Rouvroy de** (1760–1825), French writer. Born in Paris a member of the great ducal family to which Louis, duc de Saint-Simon (q.v.) belonged, he took part against Britain in the American War of Independence. During the French Revolution he was imprisoned as an aristocrat, lost much money in consequence, but made a small fortune by speculation. His marriage in 1801 ended in divorce and his eccentricity resulted in his losing what money he had saved. He thereupon turned author and produced *Lettres d'un habitant de Genève à ses contemporains* (1803). He began to evolve what became known as Saint-Simonism, a kind of socialism, harking back to some tenets of the physiocrats, which was to take the place of traditional government and religion. Society was to be reorganized, for the revolution and Napoleon had been negative, relying as both had done on arms and the Church, each hopelessly reactionary. Production, both industrial and intellectual was to be accorded precedence over capital, while science in its broadest sense was to be the new religion with scientists and intellectuals as its priests. Although a muddled thinker, such of his works as *L'Industrie, ou Discussions politiques, morales et philosophiques* (1817), *L'Organisateur* (1819), *Du système industriel* (1821), *Le Catéchisme des industriels* (1824) and *Le Nouveau Christianisme* (1825) had a profound effect on various aspects of romantic thought, on liberalism, socialism and positivism. Living on the charity of friends for many years, Saint-Simon tried to shoot himself in a fit of despair, blinding himself in one eye in the attempt. He died in Paris less than two years later.

**Saint-Simon, Louis de Rouvroy de** (1675–1755), French prose-writer, was born in Paris, the son of a former favourite of Louis XIII who had become duke in 1636. Entering the army in 1691, he fought at Namur (1692) and Neerwinden (1693), having succeeded to the dukedom on his father's death in 1693. In 1702, dissatisfied with his chances of promotion, he left the army and went to Versailles, spending his time in quarrels about precedence and in intrigue for power. He secured the friendship of the Duke of Orleans, and on the death of Louis XIV became a right-hand supporter of the new regent, on whose death in 1723 he retired to his estate at La Ferté Vidame, near Chartres. A man who by his disagreeable character had thrown away every advantage, he now turned his bitterness at his ruined career to good account by writing up his diary which he seems to have kept from about 1698, if not earlier, until 1723 and joining to it an expanded version of Philippe de Dangeau's *Mémoires* (1684–1720). The result is a marvellous account of court life and personalities in the latter part of Louis XIV's reign and during the regency. What is remarkable about the *Mémoires* of Saint-Simon, which he had written completely by 1752, although the first authentic edition did not for political reasons appear until 1830 (Eng. trans. *Historical Memoirs of the Duc de Saint-Simon*, vol. i, 1967), is that he is a creative writer who builds up scenes and presents persons to us, the result being if not historically accurate at any rate a stupendous evocation of the past hardly matched elsewhere. Whether Louis XIV and Madame de Maintenon were actually sitting talking that particular evening when Racine made the unfortunate remark about Scarron (q.v.) is a matter for the historian. Saint-Simon the artist paints the picture and leaves us to admire his art. His last years were unhappy with death busy in the family, and he died bankrupt in Paris.

**Saint Teresa of Avila,** *see* **Teresa de Jesús.**

**Salacrou, Armand** (1899–      ), French playwright, was born in Rouen. He began as a surrealist with a one-act play, *Le Casseur d'assiettes* (1924). *Tour à terre* (1925) and *Le Pont de l'Europe* (1927) are full length and in the same manner. In the thirties he took an increasing interest in social affairs, as can be seen in *Une Femme libre* (1934), *Les Frénétiques* (1934), a powerful satire directed against Hollywood, *L'Inconnue d'Arras* (1935), with a new tenderness which showed that he had put his earlier noisy sensationalism behind him, *Un Homme comme les autres* (1936) and *La Terre est ronde* (1938). The pessimism and disillusionment which the war provoked in him are reflected in: *Les Fiancés du Havre* (1944), *Les Nuits de la colère* (1946) and *L'Archipel Lenoir* (1948). Latest plays include: *Les Invités du Bon Dieu* (1953), *Une Femme trop honnête* (1956) and *Boulevard Durand* (1960).

**Salias de Tournemir, Evgeny Andreyevich** (1840–1908), a popular Russian historical novelist, at his best between 1869 and 1894, in which year a collected edition of his works, *Sobranie sochineniy*, began to appear and filled twenty-seven volumes on its completion in 1901. He died in Moscow.

**Salinas, Pedro** (1891–1951), Spanish poet and translator, was born in Madrid, travelled and held academic posts at the Sorbonne and Cambridge before becoming professor of literature at Seville. His *Poema del Cid* (1925) was a successful translation of that classic into modern Spanish, and his critical editions of various standard works raised his reputation. The civil war of 1936 broke his career and he emigrated to the United States, holding university posts there and publishing an important piece of criticism in English, *Reality and the Poet in Spanish Poetry* (1940). Meanwhile there had been a steady output of poetry, the impressiveness of which was revealed in 1942 when *Poesía junta*, containing all that he had written up to date, appeared. Two volumes of new poetry, *El contemplado* (1947) and *Todo más claro* (1949) were published before his death in Baltimore.

A selection of his poetry, *Poemas escogidos* (1953), was followed by his complete poetical works, *Poesías completas* (1955), a triumphant reaffirmation of his claim to be one of the great Spanish poets of his generation. For English translations see *Lost Angel and Other Poems* (1938) and *Truth of Two and Other Poems* (1940).

**Salis-Seewis, Johann Gaudenz von** (1762–1834), Swiss poet. Of noble family he was an officer in the famous Swiss Royal Guard at Versailles. but resigned in 1789 and returned to Switzerland, the impact of which on him after years away inspired his charming *Gedichte* (1793). After a lengthy period in the civil service and a long retirement, he died at Bothmar, the place of his birth.

**Salmon, André** (1881–     ), French poet. Born in Paris, he became a journalist travelling much in that capacity. It was in 1921 when his long surrealist poem on the Russian Revolution, incidents of which he saw with his own eyes, was published as *Prikaz*, that he became well known. His strange style, at once a mixture of journalism, surrealism and classical precision, is well exemplified in such books as: *Le Manuscrit trouvé dans un chapeau* (1924), *Vénus dans la balance* (1926), the connected poems, *Tendres Canailles* (1931) and *Monstres choisis* (1938), and *L'Air de la butte* (1945). His autobiography, *Souvenirs sans fin*, appeared between 1955 and 1961.

**Saltykov-Shchedrin, Mikhail Evgrafovich** (1826–1889), Russian novelist and journalist. Born in the province of Tbep, he became known as a radical journalist, bringing all his powers of satire to bear on the well-to-do middle classes. His great work is *Gospoda Golovlyevy* (1876; Eng. trans. *The Golovlev Family* by A. Ridgway, 1916; *The Golovlyov Family* by N. Duddington, 1931). It is a memorable novel describing the decline of a landed household. His political *Basni* (1880–5; Eng. trans. *Fables*, 1931) are still of some interest. He died in Petersburg.

**Saluzzo, Diodata** (1775–1840), Italian poet, who spent all her life in Turin. Her epic poem, *Amazzoni* (1795), was a *tour de force* as much as anything. Her short poems, collected as *Versi* (1817), are, on the other hand, of undoubted quality, and are interesting as one example of the bridging of the gap between the Italian classical and romantic schools.

**Salvaneschi, Nino** (1886–     ), Italian novelist. Born in Pavia, he was a journalist, founding in Brussels *L'Époque Nouvelle*, but had to retire owing to blindness in 1924. A return to religious faith resulted, and the novels which he began to write are remarkable for profound mysticism and perfect style. Among them are: *Il fiore della notte* (1928), *La cattedrale senza Dio* (1930), *Il sole nell'anima* (1937) and *Il bel viaggio insieme* (1942). A moving and deep invitation to consider the way to belief, not a novel, is *Saper credere* (1946). *Le stelle, la sfinge, la croce* (1951) is in the same vein and was followed up with *L'ultima rivolta* (1953) and *Saper vivere in due* (1957). His latest novels have been religious in inspiration, *Frate Francesco* (1954) and *Il santo di Padova* (1955).

**Samain, Albert** (1858–1900), French poet. Born in Lille, he led a sad life of ill-health, loneliness and family troubles. Partly through disinclination, partly through physical weakness, he resigned from his third-rate civil service post and became a literary journalist in Paris, helping to found the *Mercure de France* in 1890. Identified with the symbolists, he has a distinct quality, a compound of nostalgia and an unusually sensitive balance between words and shades of meaning. In his first book of poetry, *Au Jardin de l'Infante* (1893), there is an all-pervading sadness and an exquisite musical beauty. In his later work, as exemplified by *Aux Flancs du vase* (1898) and *Le Chariot d'or*, posthumously published in 1901, he left these atmospheric nuances for the definite inspiration of ancient Greece, which became an idealized world of his own creation. Tuberculosis overcame him in the end and he died in the country at Magny-les-Hameaux. His Greek drama *Polyphème* was played in 1904. His *Œuvres complètes* were published (3 vols.) in 1911–12.

**Samaniego, Félix María** (1745–1801), Spanish poet, of landed family, was born at Laguardia where he died. A typical example of the French-inspired Enlightenment in Spain, he wrote many ephemeral works in the spirit of the *Encyclopédie*. The only work of his that may be said to survive is his *Fábulas morales* (1781), containing translations and adaptations of earlier fabulists of various literatures, classical and modern. He will not bear comparison with Iriarte (q.v.) with his far greater originality and superior technique.

**Sanctis, Francesco de,** *see* **De Sanctis.**

**Sand, George,** pseudonym of **Amandine-Aurore-Lucie Dupin** (1804–1876), French novelist. Born in Paris, her father, Maurice Dupin, an army officer, was the son of a natural daughter of the famous Marshal Saxe, but her mother Sophie Delaborde was a simple dressmaker. Aurore's father was killed when she was still a child and she was brought up at Nohant by her paternal grandmother, Aurore de Saxe, who looked down on her plebeian grandchild. At the age of thirteen she was sent to the English convent in Paris, where she remained until 1820, and two years later she married Casimir Dudevant, natural son of a Gascon landowner. The marriage broke up quite amicably in 1831 after the birth of a son and daughter, and Aurore Dudevant went to Paris, and by sheer force of personality won a position on the staff of the *Figaro*. She soon became well known in literary circles of the Bohemian kind, adopting men's dress and smoking pipes and cigars, and being decently promiscuous. With one of her lovers, Julien Sandeau (q.v.), she collaborated in the writing of *Rose et Blanche* (1831), a novel by ' Jules Sand'. *Indiana* (1832) was written alone under her pseudonym from henceforth of George Sand, *Valentine* (1832) following shortly afterwards. Then in the summer of 1833 she met Alfred de Musset (q.v.), with whom she lived in Venice for a short and stormy time. *Lélia* (1833) clearly shows her in the full tide of romantic revolt against the constraints of society. After the quarrel and parting of the lovers, George stayed on in Venice writing *Jacques* (1834), a violent attack on marriage, and described the whole unhappy episode years later in *Elle et lui* (1859). But more famous and long lasting was her liaison with Chopin the composer, which ran from 1838 for ten years. Here she proved herself to be an unselfish lover and friend, and in fact it is one of her undoubted charms that, for all her failings, she was great-hearted. Calling herself an artist of the people writing for the wide public, she set no particular store by the criticism of her work, simply trying in her hundred books to express her large humanity. *Mauprat* (1837), one of her best novels to date, and *Spiridion* (1839) close the first period, after which while continuing to write novels, such as *Consuelo* (1842), *La Mare au Diable* (1846; Eng. trans. *The Devil's Pool*, 1895) and *François le champi* (1846; Eng. trans. *François the Waif*, 1889), she turned increasingly to politics. After the revolution of 1848 she left Paris and settled at Nohant, owner now, thanks to a legal decree of 1836, of the manor-house and land there. Other novels include: *La Petite Fadette* (1849), *Les Beaux Messieurs de bois doré* (1858), *Le Marquis de Villemer* (1861; as a play, 1864), *Monsieur Sylvestre* (1866) and *Mlle de Merquem* (1868). She had now subsided into a quiet elderly age, the good friend and correspondent of Flaubert (q.v.) and Sainte-Beuve (q.v.). She died at Nohant. Her *Journal intime*, very much a period piece, was published in 1926. Michel Lévy's edition of her works (1868) consists of 105 volumes.

**Sandeau, Léonard Sylvain Julien,** called **Jules** (1811–1883), French novelist and dramatist. Born at Aubusson, he came to Paris to study law, became the lover of Aurore Dudevant, who took her pen-name of George Sand (q.v.) from his surname, and turned to letters, the two collaborating as 'Jules Sand' in the novel *Rose et Blanche* (1831). Having broken with George Sand in 1833, Sandeau began to write on his own and produced such novels as *Madame de Sommerville* (1834), *Marianna* (1840), an enormous success, and *Mademoiselle de la Seiglière* (1848), his best. Besides many other novels, which gradually became less romantic and more realistic, he joined with Augier (q.v.) in writing plays, the best result of this association being *Le Gendre de Monsieur Poirier* (1854). He became keeper of the Mazarin Library, Paris in 1853 and librarian of the Royal Library, St Cloud, six years later, and there he died.

**Sandemose, Aksel** (1899–1965), Norwegian novelist of Danish family, was born at Nykøbing. He claimed and received much attention with his extraordinary work of fiction, *En flyktning krysser sitt spor* (1933; Eng. trans. *A Fugitive Crosses his Tracks*, 1936), containing a keen analysis of contemporary society, and he followed this up with *Vi pynter oss med horn* (1936; Eng. trans. *Horns for Our Adornment*, 1939). His novels after the war included *Alice Atkinson* (1949) and *Rejsen til Kjørkelvik* (1954). He died in Copenhagen.

**Sannazaro, Jacopo** (1458–1530), Italian poet. Born in Naples, probably of Spanish descent, he became a member of the Neapolitan Academy. He is famed for his pastoral romance in verse and prose, *L'Arcadia* (first complete edition, 1504), which led the way to the pastoral drama and novel, later to be cultivated by Tasso (q.v.), Guarini (q.v.), Spenser and Sir Philip Sidney, who particularly spring to mind in this connection. Among his Latin works may be mentioned the *Piscatoriae* (1526; Eng. trans. 1726), eclogues with fishermen replacing the shepherds of L'Arcadia. He died at Mergellina, near Naples.

**San Pedro, Diego de** (late fifteenth century), Spanish novelist. Little if anything is known of his life, but it has been suggested that he was of Jewish descent and was in some kind of service in a noble household, to amuse the members of which he wrote prose romances. The two which have survived are *Arnalte y Lucenda* (1491; Eng. trans. *The pretie and wittie historie of Arnalte and Lucenda*, by C. Holyband, 1575) and *La cárcel de amor* (1492; Eng. trans. *The Castel of Love* by Lord Berners, 1541).

**Santeuil, Jean-Baptiste de** (1630–1697), French hymn-writer. Born in Paris, he became one of the greatest Latin scholars of the day, yet is now remembered not as the unnecessary translator of Corneille into Latin or as the unblushing sycophant of Louis XIV, but as the writer of some fine and sonorous hymns, with vivid imagery, chief among them perhaps the one used in the Church of England as 'Disposer Supreme and Judge of the Earth'. He died in Dijon. His collected works appeared in 1729.

**Santillana, Íñigo López de Mendoza** (1398–1458), Spanish poet, who succeeded to the marquisate and estates at Carrión de los Condes, where he was born. Combining close interest in state affairs and humanism, he tried his hand at translating Horace, wrote *La comedieta de Ponza*, a poem in praise of King Alfonso V of Aragon, and the didactic poem, *Los proverbios* (Eng. trans. *The prouerbes of Sir J. Lopez de Mendoza* by B. Googe, 1579).

**Santos, Francisco** (1617?–1697?), Spanish prose-writer, a native of Madrid. A soldier by profession, he is best known as the author of a series of sketches of the underworld of his city, *Día y noche de Madrid* (1663; republ. in *Biblioteca de Autores Españoles*, vol. xxxiii), used by Le Sage (q.v.) in his *Diable boiteux*.

**Sanz del Río, Julián** (1814–1869), Spanish philosopher, whose influence has been felt in every branch of thought and letters, especially during the years of intellectual liberty prior to 1936, was born near Soria and became professor of philosophy at Madrid where he died. His ideas, derived broadly from the work of the German philosopher K. C. F. Krause (1781–1832), are liberal and ethical and anti-dogmatic, hence anathema to orthodox catholicism which in Spain has done its best to crush *krausismo*. The most characteristic of Sanz del Río's works are *Ideal de la humanidad por la vida* (1860) and *Filosofía de la muerte* (1877).

**Sanz y Sánchez, Eulogio Florentino** (1822–1881), Spanish playwright and translator from Avila. Besides his brilliant translations, which did much to introduce German romantic poetry into Spain, he is the author of an excellent romantic historical play, *Don Francisco de Quevedo* (1848), the subject being the famous author (q.v.) set against a splendidly evoked background of the court of Philip IV. Sanz died in Madrid.

**Saponaro, Michele** (1885–1959), Italian novelist and short-story writer, was born at San Cesario di Lecce. With considerable narrative power and gifts of description he turned his own experiences of life to good account in *L'adolescenza* (1925) and *La giovinezza* (1927). Provincial life is pin-pointed in the collection of short stories, *Avventure provinciali* (1931), and there is much that is of high quality in the full-length novel, *Il cerchio magico* (1939). With the war he turned more and more to literary and historical criticism, but he maintained his hold on the novel with *L'ultima ninfa non è morta* (1948) and *Il romanzo di Bettina* (1959). He died in Milan.

**Sardou, Victorien** (1831–1908), French playwright, born in Paris. After several failures, he met and married the well-known actress Brécourt who introduced him to a prosperous theatre-manager called Déjazet. His two plays, commissioned by him, *Monsieur Garat* and *Les Prés Saint-Gervais*, were both produced in 1860 and brought Sardou money and popularity. From this point he followed in the footsteps of Scribe (q.v.), in a few years amassing a fortune. He became the most uniformly successful dramatist of his day and was extensively translated. The two plays of his most popular with English-speaking audiences were *A Scrap of Paper* (the translation of *Les Pattes de mouche*, 1860) and *Diplomacy* (that of *Dora*, 1877). Psychologically superficial he was yet one of the greatest of all masters of stagecraft. *La Tosca* (1887), celebrated as the source of the libretto for Puccini's opera, was written for Sarah Bernhardt, as *Robespierre* (1899) was for Henry Irving. Sardou, who was an excellent producer, died in Paris. His *Théâtre complet* in eleven volumes was published in 1950.

**Sarpi, Pietro,** religiously **Fra Paolo** (1552–1623), Italian prose-writer, was a Venetian, and in 1575 was made professor of philosophy at the Servite monastery there. A man of extraordinary erudition in both arts and sciences, he became the spokesman of the republic in its quarrel with the Papacy over clerical immunity and freedom of thought. He answered papal threats with his incisive *Trattato dell' Interdetto di Paolo V* (1606). On his being summoned to Rome to account for his conduct he refused to go, was excommunicated, and was wounded by hired assassins. The rest of his life was spent at Venice writing his fine account of the Council of Trent, *Istoria del Concilio Tridentino*, published in London in 1619, one of the greatest works both from the literary and academic points of view of Italian history. An excellent translation by Sir Nathaniel Brent appeared in 1620.

**Sarraute, Nathalie** (1902–      ), French novelist. She was born in Russia but left it when under two years old. She became an advocate and practised for a time, but turned to letters and family commitments after 1939. Her principal works are: *Tropismes* (1939; Eng. trans. 1963), *Portrait d'un inconnu* (1947), *Martereau* (1953; Eng. trans. 1967), *L'Ère du soupçon* (1956) and *Le Planétarium* (1959).

**Sartre, Jean-Paul** (1905–      ), French prose-writer, novelist and dramatist, was born in Paris, the son of a sailor, and spent much of his youth in La Rochelle. On the death of his father he went back to Paris and was educated at the École Normale Supérieure, winning a brilliant *agrégation de philosophie*. He taught for a time at Le Havre before becoming a member of the staff of the French Institute at Berlin, where he gained a sound knowledge of modern German philosophy, which was to influence him greatly. By the time the 1939–45 war came he was back in Paris and soon took a leading part in the Resistance. When the war ended he travelled widely, visiting the U.S.A. among other countries, and finally settled down with Simone de Beauvoir (q.v.) to face every kind of contemporary problem in his brilliant review, *Les Temps Modernes*. His philosophy, existentialism, has had an enormous formative effect on the intellectuals of the war and post-war period. His ideas have their origin particularly in the work of Kierkegaard (q.v.), who believed that existence had purpose and direction, the source of such purposefulness of existence and the prime mover being God. Sartre, a Marxian Communist, removed God as the fountainhead of existence and replaced Him by political idealism, whose doctrine was that freedom is acceptance of responsibility. Lack of freedom results in disgust, and this was the subject of his first novel, *La Nausée* (1938; Eng. trans. *The Diary of Antoine Roquentin*, 1949), a powerful evocation of the mental state and physical feeling of individual uselessness in society. His existentialism is explained in *L'Existentialisme est un humanisme* (1946; Eng. trans. *Existentialism and Humanism*, 1948). But it is as a novelist, playwright and short-story writer that he has, by reason of his extraordinarily vivid and penetrating style, appealed to a wide circle of readers as one of the most deep thinking representatives of an intellectual approach in literary form to the problems of life of his generation, although Communism is a constant source of bias. Of his novels none can be more significant than *Les Chemins de la liberté*, which consists of three parts, *L'Âge de raison* (1945; Eng. trans. *The Age of Reason*, 1947), *Le Sursis* (1945; Eng. trans. *The Reprieve*, 1947) and *La Mort dans l'âme* (1949; Eng. trans. *Iron in the Soul*, 1951). An account of France during the troubled thirties down to the collapse of 1940, it is, however, a highly subjective piece of work, the purpose of it being to proclaim freedom as the definition of the ego. It is secondarily an apology for Communism as the only alternative to outworn democracy in facing Fascism. Of his plays, *Les Mouches* (1943; Eng. trans. *The Flies*, 1947) is a powerful proclamation of liberty, veiled in a classical myth which deluded the German censorship; *Huis-Clos* (1944; Eng. trans. *In Camera*, 1946) is a piece of symbolism depicting hell on earth; in *Crime passionnel* (1948; Eng. trans. *Dirty Hands*, 1949) he criticizes Communism in spite of himself, a source of embarrassment to him afterwards, although the Hungarian Revolt of 1956 has greatly modified his views; *Le Diable et le bon Dieu* (1951; Eng. trans. *Lucifer and the Lord*, 1953), set in the epoch of the Thirty Years War, is on the theme of public and private integrity; *Nekrassov* (1956; Eng. trans. 1956) is an attack on journalism; and *Les Sequestrés d'Altone* (1959; Eng. trans. *Altona*, 1961) is a study of Nazism and the guilty conscience growing up in the long

after-years of reflection. *Sartre* by I. Murdoch gives a general introduction to his philosophy. S. de Beauvoir's *Les Mandarins* (q.v.) is
a fictional account of Sartre and Camus (q.v.) in Paris in 1945. Much
comment was aroused in 1965 by his refusal of the Nobel Prize.

**Savinio, Alberto,** pseudonym of **Andrea de Chirico** (1891–1952),
Italian novelist, playwright, essayist, painter and musician, one of the
most variously gifted of modern men of letters, was born in Athens.
In Paris he became a close friend of Apollinaire (q.v.) and later of
Cocteau (q.v.). His tendency to surrealism is excellently balanced by
his classicism and lends form to his extraordinary work. There is
originality in everything he wrote whether novels, such as *Angela o
la notte di maggio* (1927) and *Tutta la vita* (1945), plays, such as *Il
Capitano Ulisse* (1934) and *Alcesti di Samuele* (1949), prose studies,
such as *Achille innamorato* (1938), and the ballets, *Perseo* (1924), *La
morte de Niobe* (1927) and *La vita dell' uomo* (1946), the last performed
with great success at the Scala, Milan, all the scenery and costumes
being designed by him. He died in Rome. His wireless play, *Cristoforo
Colombo*, appeared posthumously in 1952.

**Savinkov, Boris,** pseudonym **V. Ropshin** (1877–1925), Russian Soviet
novelist born in Vilna, who acted as a Bolshevik spy, informer and
even political terrorist when the occasion demanded. But it was in
pre-revolutionary days that he wrote that powerful psychological
study of a terrorist, *Kon'bledny* (1913; Eng. trans. *The Pale Horse*,
1917), thus in a remarkable way forestalling the future development
of his own character without realizing it. After Lenin's death he
became hopelessly entangled in cut-throat politics, from which he
freed himself by suicide in Moscow.

**Savoir, Alfred** (1883–1934), French dramatist. A Pole by birth from
Łódz, his real name being **Posznański,** he wrote comedies in which he
ridiculed many accepted values in a highly intellectualized style.
Among them are *La Huitième Femme de Barbe-Bleue* (1921; Eng.
trans. *Bluebeard's Eighth Wife*, 1921) and *La Petite Catherine* (1930;
Eng. trans. *Little Catherine*, 1930), both acted in London. His most
ambitious work was the trilogy, *Trois Comédies d'avant-garde*
(1923; 1925; 1926). He died in Paris.

**Savonarola, Girolamo** (1452–1498), the great Italian preacher and
reformer, lives in literature as the author of *Trattato circa il reggi-
mento della città di Firenze*, his treatise on his ideal Florentine Republic (standard ed. by A. de Rians, 1847), his poetry, *Rime* (ed.
Guasti and Lungo, 1914), and his sermons, *Prediche italiane ai
fiorentini* (3 vols., 1930–5). All show his extraordinary powers, and
his fervid style is everywhere evident. Born in Ferrara, he was
executed in Florence.

**Saxo Grammaticus** (1140?–1222?), Danish chronicler, of whom little
is known except that he was born in Zealand and was secretary to the
Archbishop of Rœskilde. His Latin *Gesta Danorum*, written between
about 1185 and 1222, is inaccurate as history, but is splendid literature. Making use of ancient legends and poems, some going back to
the fourth century A.D., it was his purpose to show Europe that the

Danish nation was of great antiquity. One of the stories, that of Amleth, suggested the plot of *Hamlet* to Shakespeare. The *Gesta Danorum* was first published in Paris in 1514; a modern edition in two volumes appeared between 1931 and 1948. Part of the work was translated into English as *The First Nine Books of the Danish History of Saxo Grammaticus* by O. Elton (1894).

**Scaliger, Joseph Justus** (1540–1609), French scholar. Born at Agen, third son of J. C. Scaliger (q.v.), by whom he was educated, he became the most remarkable scholar in classics and oriental languages of his day and one of the foremost critics and scholars of all time. Turning Protestant he left France after the massacre of St Bartholomew (1572) and became a professor in Geneva, then returned to France and lived in retirement before in 1593 settling as professor in Leiden, where he consolidated his position as scholar, critic, chronologist and historian. His influence on both scholarship and literature was incalculable especially in the Netherlands. He died in Leiden.

**Scaliger, Julius Caesar** (1484–1558), Franco-Italian poet writing only in Latin. According to his son J. J. Scaliger (q.v.) he was born at Riva Castle on Lake Garda, a son of the nobleman Benedetto della Scala, and was even a cousin of the Emperor Maximilian! Others have said that he was of a burgher family of Padua, and others yet again that he was the son of a Verona sign-painter. Whatever his origin was he was a notable humanist of his day, fought in the Franco-Italian wars, quarrelled with Erasmus (q.v.) and attacked him in some scurrilous orations, became a Franciscan monk, renounced his vows and became a physician at Agen in France, where he died. His *Poetices libri septem*, entirely influenced by Aristotle, greatly affected French literature right down to the time of Boileau (q.v.) and beyond.

**Scarron, Paul** (1610–1660), French poet, novelist and playwright, was born in Paris where he spent a dissipated youth, became an *abbé commendataire* though not in Orders, went to Italy, but in 1638 was attacked by tuberculosis of the spine which in five years left him an absolute cripple. Often in pain, his life ruined, he showed a noble fortitude, never complaining, always gay and writing for a living. His house became a literary centre, refined after his marriage in 1652 to the young and charming, though poor, Françoise d'Aubigné (*see* Aubigné), later to be so well known as Madame de Maintenon, who proved a devoted wife. As a poet he excelled in burlesque in such works as *Typhon ou la Gigantomachie* (1644), while *Virgile travesti*, which appeared in two parts (Part I, 1648; Part II, 1659) was much esteemed. *Poésies diverses* (ed. M. Cauchie, 1948) is a useful modern selection. Of all his works his novel, *Le Roman comique*, published between 1651 and 1657, proved the most long lasting, and not only helped to break down the influence of the affected Scudéry (q.v.) school, but prepared the way for Le Sage (q.v.), Defoe and the picaresque novelists of the following century. In all his work Spanish literature was his inspiration; in his plays, the best of which are *Jodelet, ou le Maître valet* (1643), *Les Boutades du Capitan Matamore* (1645), *Le Marquis* *ridicule* (1655) and *La Fausse Apparence* (1657), he plundered it. When, however, one considers that his *L'Écolier de Salamanque* (1654) led to Le Sage's *Le Bachelier de Salamanque* (1736) one can gauge his genius for converting things Spanish into French, making them all his own, and tapping new mines for others to make use of. He died in Paris.

**Scève, Maurice** (1501–1560), French poet, was born and died in Lyon. He seems to have been responsible for introducing Italian influences into French poetry. His main work is *Délie, object de la plus haulte vertu* (1544), a rarefied love-poem, and besides he wrote *La Saulsaye, églogue de la vie solitaire* (1547) and a religious poem, *Microcosme* (1562). Scève with his stiffness of manner compares very unfavourably with Ronsard (q.v.) and other poets of the Pléiade, only a generation after him. He now makes little more than specialist reading.

**Schack, Adolf Friedrich von** (1815–1894), German poet and critic, was born at Brüsewitz, near Schwerin. A patron of the arts (his collection of nineteenth-century painting is exhibited in Munich), he was a keen devotee of Spanish literature, his work on Spanish drama, *Geschichte der dramatischen Literatur und Kunst Spaniens* (3 vols., 1845–6), having wide influence. Among his volumes of poetry may be named *Lothar* (1872), *Nächte des Orients* (1874) and *Timandra* (1879). Graf von Schack died in Rome.

**Schack, Hans Egede** (1820–1859), Danish novelist, born at Sengeløse, and who died in Copenhagen, was the author of that remarkable investigation of daydreaming, *Phantasterne* (1857).

**Scheffel, Josef Viktor von** (1826–1886), German poet and novelist, was born in Karlsruhe. A man of difficult character, always restless and discontented, trying first law and then turning to painting, he made his name with his poem, *Der Trompeter von Säkkingen* (1854; Eng. trans. 1893), which has been through well over three hundred editions, and is a narrative of the Thirty Years' War. *Ekkehard* (1857; Eng. trans. 1867) is a tale of the tenth century, the plot largely autobiographical. This has been through more than two hundred editions. His other success was *Gaudeamus, Lieder aus dem Engern und Weitern* (1869; Eng. trans. 1872), a collection of songs. Less successful was *Bergpsalmen* (1870; Eng. trans. *Mountain Psalms*, 1882). He also wrote two romances, *Juniperus* (1867) and *Hugideo* (1884). His marriage broke down after three years and he died in a state almost of melancholia in Karlsruhe.

**Schelling, Friedrich Wilhelm Joseph von** (1775–1854), German prose-writer and philosopher, was born at Leonberg, Württemberg, and became a fellow student of Hegel (q.v.) and Hölderlin (q.v.) at Tübingen. In 1798 on the recommendation of Goethe he came to Jena and lectured there, soon joining the group which included the Schlegels (q.v.) and becoming the acknowledged philosopher of the early romantic movement. Extraordinarily precocious, during his five years (ending in 1803) at Jena he gained a great reputation, and his main works, on which during the rest of his long life he made no perceptible advance, date with one exception from this period. They are *Ideen zu einer Philosophie der Natur* (1797), *Von der Weltseele* (1798) and *System der tranzendentalen Idealismus* (1800; Eng. trans. *Introduction to Idealism*, 1871). In these works Schelling reveals himself as above all concerned with nature, with the world spirit which invests it (Pantheism), and with the plastic arts, which, as he declares in *Das Verhältnis der bildenden Künste zur Natur* (1807; Eng. trans. *On the Relation of the Plastic Arts to Nature*, 1913–15), he regards as the action of this spirit on the mind of man confronted with the phenomena of nature. He was thus in no way a scientific philosopher and his philosophy is poetically imaginative rather than intellectual. An affair with Caroline, the wife of A. W. Schlegel (q.v.), whom the latter divorced in 1803 and whom Schelling married the same year, led to his departure from Jena to a professorship at Würzburg. He next went to Munich, where he remained until 1841, when he was invited to the chair of philosophy at Berlin by the King of Prussia, who hoped that he would be able to stem the tide of Hegelianism which they both hated, but the tide was too strong. When he died at Bad Ragaz, Schelling had long outlived himself. He like Schopenhauer (q.v.) reveals the current influence of oriental thought. A poet in a world of philosophers, he could hardly stand the pace, but as an ally of the German romantics his best work is a challenging and sometimes (for he often lacks clarity) attractive proposition.

**Schendel, Arthur Franciskus Emil van** (1874–1946), Dutch novelist, born in Batavia, Java. He lived much in England and was at one time a schoolmaster there. He was also for a period in Italy. The two influences on his work were medieval Italy and the Netherlands. Of the first may be noted: *Angiolino en de Lente* (1923), *Oude italiaansche steden* (1924), *Merona, een Edelman* (1927) and *Florentijnsche Verhalen* (1929). To the later and much more important period belong: *Het Fregatschip Johanna Maria* (1930; Eng. trans. *The 'Johanna Maria'*, 1935), *De Waterman* (1933), *Een hollandsch Drama* (1935; Eng. trans. *The House in Haarlem*, 1940), *Avonturiers* (1936), *De Grauwe Vogels* (1937; Eng. trans. *Grey Birds*, 1939), *Een Spel der Natuur* (1942), *Sparsa* (1944), *Het oude Huis* (1946), generally considered his best work, and posthumously *De Pleizier-vaart* (1951). He was the greatest Dutch prose-writer of his day. He died in Amsterdam.

**Schenkendorf, Gottlob Ferdinand Max Gottfried von** (1783–1817), German poet, was born at Tilsit, son of a Prussian army officer. At Königsberg University he gained the friendship of Arnim (q.v.) and like him endeavoured to stir up patriotic resistance to Napoleon and tried to liberalize Prussianism. His poetry of this character is to be found in *Studien* (1808) and *Gedichte* (1815). A convert to Roman Catholicism, his religious poetry is seen in *Christliche Gedichte* (1814). He died in Coblenz. Some of his work was translated into English by C. W. Dulcken in *The Book of German Songs* (1856).

**Scherenberg, Christian Friedrich** (1798–1881), German poet, born in Stettin. After shaky beginnings he gained renown in the little exploited field of war poetry. *Ligny* appeared in 1846, *Waterloo* in 1849, *Abukir, die Schlacht am Nil,* an account of the Battle of the Nile, in 1856. Of his later books, *Hohenfriedberg* (1868) was the most widely appreciated. They lent themselves to the favourite drawing-room declamations of the time. Scherenberg died at Zehlendorf, Berlin.

**Scherfig, Hans** (1905–    ), Danish novelist, born in Copenhagen. Beginning as an artist, he turned to writing detective stories which were often attacks on the various follies of society, such as, for example, his best-known book, *Idealister* (1945; Eng. trans. *The Idealists,* 1949), in which he mocks contemporary idealisms and their advocates. But he himself is, as many must acknowledge, a self-deceiving Communist idealist, as is to be seen in his account of Russia, *Rejse i Sovjetunionen* (1951).

**Schermer, Lucas** (1688–1711), Dutch poet and playwright, was born and died in Haarlem. His health broke down while he was a student and he became a permanent invalid. His work has great charm and is inspired by a classical mythological world, described in his three posthumously published books, the volume of verse, *Gedichten* (1712), and the two plays, *Atalante in den hof van Kalidon* (1711) and *Meleager en Atalante* (1712).

**Schickele, René** (1883–1940), German novelist, born at Oberehnheim, Alsace, where he was brought up to become acutely conscious of the evils of armed power and national antagonisms. His main work is the three-volume novel, *Das Erbe am Rhein* (1925–31), the second volume of the trilogy being translated into English as *The Heart of Alsace* in 1929. He died, broken-hearted at the failure of all his hopes for peace, at Sanary, France.

**Schiller, Johann Christoph Friedrich von** (1759–1805), German poet, dramatist and philosopher, was born the second child of an army surgeon at Marbach, Württemberg. After several moves (for the Seven Years War was not yet over, and because of his duties the surgeon could not provide a settled home), the Schiller family at last came to rest at Ludwigsburg. Here young Schiller grew up in an atmosphere of discomfort and uncertainty, for his father's pay was often in arrears and they always feared other enforced moves. The boy's vague desire to enter the Church was crushed when in 1773 Duke Karl Eugen of Württemberg, in whose service the elder Schiller was, conscripted Friedrich for his newly founded military academy, called The Solitude, near Ludwigsburg. Under military discipline Schiller was forced to study law, which he hated, but life was made bearable by his friends and fellow-sufferers. In 1775 a slight change for the better occurred when the academy was moved to Stuttgart, and a medical faculty was started. Schiller at once transferred to medicine, passing out as regimental surgeon in 1780. Reading medicine had not, however, been his sole occupation during these years. He had found opportunities to read such plays of the 'Storm and Stress' school as Goethe's *Götz von Berlichingen* and Klinger's (q.v.) *Die Zwillinge,* with their message of freedom from

restraint and their hostility to the present state of society. Out of
his reading, thought and friendships, out of all the suffering that a
petty tyrant had caused him, grew his own play, *Die Räuber*, the
great revolutionary drama of German literature, which was published
privately and anonymously in 1781. It was received by a wide public
with such enthusiasm that a second edition was immediately called
for, but it soon came to Duke Karl's ears that his own regimental
surgeon was its author, and he gave a peremptory command that
Schiller was not to write again. Schiller realized that he must take a
bold decision. First he disobeyed orders by going to Mannheim to see
his play performed, and then fled beyond Württemberg territory. In
the quiet village of Bauerbach he completed his second tragedy,
*Fiesko*, whose plot, unlike that of *Die Räuber*, which is set in
modern times, is laid in sixteenth-century Genoa. It is in no sense
a worthy successor, and was tepidly received when acted at Mannheim in 1783. In the following year Schiller produced, however, a
tragedy very much more attuned to his abilities. This was *Kabale
und Liebe* ('Intrigue and Love'), an indictment of political intrigue
in high places which results in the blighting of youth and love,
sacrificed to the caste system. With this his one-year contract with the
Mannheim theatre came to an end and was not renewed. Schiller had
won esteem but little money, and he now turned to journalism for a
living. In 1785 his paper, *Rheinische Thalia*, began to come out and
lasted until 1793. Meanwhile an unhappy love affair was making life
in Mannheim unbearable, and he gladly accepted an offer of hospita-
lity from several admirers of his in Leipzig, chief among them
C. G. Körner. His delight in this circle, none of whom he had
known before, is celebrated in his poem 'An die Freude' ('To Joy'),
which inspired Beethoven's Ninth Symphony many years later.
When Körner moved to Dresden, Schiller followed, and it was near
there that he completed his next drama, *Don Carlos*, his first in
verse, a tragedy of the court of Philip II of Spain. The blank verse is
majestic and sonorous, the idealization of liberty notable, and the
characterization impressive. That same year (1787) he paid his first
visit to Weimar, but was disappointed. Goethe was in Italy, and when
Schiller read his *Don Carlos* at court it was coldly received. This
made him turn to another sphere of writing, and during the next two
years he produced his best historical work, *Geschichte des Abfalls
der vereinigten Niederlande von der spanischen Regierung*, and an
indifferent novel, *Der Geisterseher* (1789, 'The Ghostseer'), its improbable plot eked out by unconvincing magic. His historical work
had meanwhile attracted the attention of Goethe, who had returned
to Weimar, where Schiller was now living, and through his influence
the dramatist-turned-historian was offered and accepted a professorship at nearby Jena. Small though the salary was, he was now
sure of a livelihood, and was enabled to marry Charlotte von Lenge-
feld, a lady-in-waiting at the Weimar court, in 1790. The following
year, however, he fell seriously ill and had to resign his post, but
thanks to a pension from some Danish admirers he was free to
continue his historical studies. His *Geschichte des dreissigjährigen
Krieges* ('History of the Thirty Years War') was completed in 1793,

whereupon he turned to philosophy, becoming a keen adherent of Kant (q.v.). He still wrote some poetry at this time, 'Die Götter Griechenlands' ('The Gods of Greece') and 'Die Künstler' ('The Artists') being noteworthy; but he might have become a purely academic thinker had it not been for his friendship with Goethe, which after years of distant mutual esteem at best began in earnest in 1794. With Goethe's encouragement he produced his finest philosophical lyrics in 1795–6 and his ballads in 1797, rounding off his inquiries into aesthetics with his treatise, *Über naïve und sentimentalische Dichtung* (1795–6). Schiller and Goethe now joined forces in literary journalism (*Die Horen*, 1795–7), laying somewhat cruelly about their many opponents in the satirical *Xenien* (1796–7); but Schiller was just about to embark on the last and most memorable period of his literary life. Goethe, manager of the Weimar theatre, pressed him to take once more to writing for the stage, and Schiller responded. The result was his magnificent tragedy, the trilogy *Wallenstein*, inspired by his past study of the Thirty Years War, which was performed at Weimar with great success, the first two parts being completed in 1798 and the third in 1799. The second part, *Die Piccolomini*, and the third, *Wallensteins Tod*, were splendidly translated by S. T. Coleridge (1799–1800). In 1800 *Maria Stuart*, a sympathetic study of Mary, Queen of Scots, was performed, and in 1801 another play, *Die Jungfrau von Orleans*, an idealized history of Joan of Arc, showed Schiller's stagecraft at its best. *Die Braut von Messina*, an experiment in classical drama with choruses as in Greek tragedy, but not wholly satisfactory, appeared in 1803; but *Wilhelm Tell* (1804) with its dramatic portrayal of a nation in its struggle for independence, was a triumph. Schiller, who had constantly battled with ill health since 1791, died a year later, prematurely worn out by overwork and tubercular disease. Germany's greatest dramatist, he is a champion of high ideals expressed in noble rhetoric. His prose is that of a poet, luminous and impassioned, while as a poet he has written lyrics in which grace is seldom sacrificed to the deep thought which they usually contain. All his life he struggled manfully with every kind of difficulty and overcame them all except health. There is a uniform edition in Bohn's Library of English translations of the greater part of his works. It is useful if uninspired.

**Schimmel, Hendrik Jan** (1823–1906), Dutch novelist and playwright. Born at The Hague, he went into business, at the same time taking a great interest in literature. He cultivated the historical style both in his prose fiction and his dramas. Chief among the former are: *Mary Hollis* (1860; Eng. trans. 1872), *Mylady Carlisle* (1864), *Sinjeur Semeyns* (1875) and *De Kaptein van de lijfgarde* (1888; Eng. trans. *The Lifeguardsman*, 1896). Of his plays may be mentioned the romantic *Joan Woutersz* (1847) and *Giovanni di Procida* (1848), and the realistic *Struensee* (1868), the dialogue of which is excellent. He died at Bussum.

**Schlegel, August Wilhelm von** (1767–1845), German man of letters, was born in Hanover, the nephew of J. E. Schlegel (q.v.). After a long and careful academic training at Göttingen, followed by a spell of tutoring in the Netherlands, he went to Jena, there joining forces with his brother (q.v.), Novalis (q.v.) and Tieck (q.v.) in 1796, being welcomed at first by Schiller, although Goethe regarded the whole group with suspicion. Self-opinionated and exceedingly vain, Schlegel was yet a forceful critic who gave direction to the romantic school, as in *Charakteristiken und Kritiken* (1801), in collaboration with his brother, F. Schlegel being the initiator of ideas and theories, A. W. ordering and directing them. They were in fact the most robust element in the early romantic movement. A. W. Schlegel, having quarrelled with Schiller, Goethe and at last with his own brother, went to Berlin, where he wrote and lectured and produced his cold pseudo-Greek tragedy, *Ion* (1803); his equally chilly *Gedichte* had appeared in 1800. It was, however, not as an original writer that he was to serve literature but as a translator and critic. As a translator, with the later help of L. Tieck (q.v.), he turned the works of Shakespeare into German with incomparable mastery (1797–1810). It is indeed one of the finest examples of translation in any language. He did the same with the Spanish stage in *Spanisches Theater* (2 vols., 1803–9), and in 1804 made an anthology in translation of Italian, Spanish and Portuguese verse, *Blumensträusse italienischer, spanischer und portugiesischer Poesie*. His study *Über dramatische Kunst und Literatur* (3 vols., 1809–11; first Eng. trans. *A course of Lectures on Dramatic Art and Literature*, 1815; and in Bohn's Library) is probably the most attractive today of all his works apart from his translations. From 1801 to 1804 he was tutor to the sons of Madame de Staël (q.v.), and afterwards as her literary adviser moved much in her circle until her death in 1817. The following year he became professor of literature at the newly founded University of Bonn, where he remained, engaged particularly in Sanskrit studies and paying several visits to England, until his death. Small and dapper, he was long remembered declaiming his evening lectures, a liveried servant standing near him holding aloft a silver candelabra to light his manuscript.

**Schlegel, Carl Wilhelm Friedrich von** (1772–1829), German man of letters. Born in Hanover, the younger brother of A. W. Schlegel (q.v.), he went to Leipzig University, and after studying classical archaeology for some years made for Jena like his brother, lectured there and became the chief contributor to *Das Athenäum* in 1798. He fired the romantic movement, and by the warmth of his personality drew off some of the esteem from the Olympian Goethe and Schiller to his own circle. His complete break not only with accepted literary values but also with conventional moral standards was soon shown by his abduction of Dorothea Veit, daughter of the famous Moses Mendelssohn (q.v.), from her wealthy husband (a blow against the bourgeoisie), and the publication (1799) of the erotic novel *Lucinde* (Eng. trans. 1913–15), inspired by the affair. By this time he had made enemies on every hand and quarrelled even with his brother. *Das Athenäum* ceased in 1800, and after editing with Tieck (q.v.) the works of the deceased Novalis (q.v.) and publishing an interesting but hardly stageworthy tragedy, *Alarcos* (both 1802), he went to Paris, where he studied Greek and Sanskrit, the result of the first being an edition of Euripides, of the second *Über die Sprache und Weisheit der Indier* (1808), containing some most important contributions to philosophy, which marks a stage in the swift advance of oriental studies. His last effort at original work appears in the *Gedichte* (1809), but many of the poems had been written years before. His increasing concern to formulate his approach to literature and history led to the writing of *Vorlesungen über die neuere Geschichte* (1811), the biased opinions expressed in which are the results of his rampant Roman Catholicism, for having been converted in 1808 he had grown into a thorough reactionary, had entered the Austrian public service, and was responsible for the manifesto against Napoleon published by the government to whip up national feeling. His *Geschichte der alten und neuer Literatur* (1815; Eng. trans. *On the History of Literature*, by J. G. Lockhart, 1818) was worked up from earlier lectures. His attempt at metaphysics, *Philosophie des Lebens* (1828), gives promise of something unfulfilled, but his last work, *Philosophie der Geschichte* (1829; Eng. trans. *The Philosophy of History*, 1835; and in Bohn's Library), contains all his best qualities. It was published a few months after his death in Dresden. There is little doubt that F. Schlegel was the master mind behind the German romantic movement in its early stages.

**Schlegel, Johann Elias** (1719–1749), German dramatist and critic, born at Meissen, was educated at the University of Leipzig, where he was greatly influenced by Gottsched (q.v.), then at the height of his literary power, and according to whose specifications he wrote stiff tragedies (*Hermann*, 1741) and anaemic comedies (*Der Triumph der guten Frauen*, 1748). Even so he showed an appreciation of Shakespeare, a pointer to the future, in *Vergleichung Shakespeares und Andreas Gryphs* (1742), in which he contrasts the English dramatist with A. Gryphius (1616–64, q.v.). Schlegel went to Denmark to take up the post of schoolmaster and died there at Sorø. He was the uncle of A. W. and F. Schlegel (qq.v.).

**Schleiermacher, Friedrich Daniel Ernst** (1768–1834), German writer. Born at Breslau, he was brought up strictly as a Moravian, but became a Lutheran pastor, having studied at Halle. His interest from the literary point of view begins about 1797, when he made the acquaintance of several leaders of the romantic movement, including Friedrich Schlegel (q.v.), whose greatly traduced *Lucinde* he defended in *Vertraute Briefe über F. Schlegels Lucinde* (1800). Already in *Über die Religion* (1799; Eng. trans. 1893) he had questioned the validity of Kant's religious ideas, and in his sermons—he was one of the finest preachers of the day—and in such persuasive works as *Monologen* (1800; Eng. trans. *Soliloquies*, 1926) attacked the still lingering influence of the Enlightenment which he thought conditioned by feudalism. In these and other works, especially *Grundlinien einer Kritik der bisherigen Sittenlehre* (1803), he postulated the romantic theory of religion. It was, he insisted, a purely personal matter. Dogmas concerning supernatural occurrences such as miracles were of secondary importance; religion was a manifestation of the Spirit of God at work in the world, but so were the arts of music, poetry and painting.

As can be imagined, he was looked upon askance by many churchmen, but after he had become professor of theology at the new University of Berlin in 1810 his influence was little challenged, and he was able to bring about the union of the Lutheran and Reformed Churches of Prussia in 1817, a feat undreamt of a little while before. The most attractive of his purely devotional works and his best contribution to pure literature in his *Die Weihnachtsfeier* (1806; Eng. trans. *Christmas Eve, a dialogue*, 1890). Another work worth reading as revealing his theological ideas in the light of his philosophy is *Der christliche Glaube nach der Grundsätzen der evangelischen Kirche* (2 vols., 1821–2). Schleiermacher died in Berlin.

**Schlumberger, Jean** (1877– ), French novelist and essayist, was born of a Protestant family at Guebwiller, Alsace. Becoming a friend of Gide (q.v.) he was greatly influenced by him, but Schlumberger's literary self-discipline and strong moral sense separate the two. Outstanding among his novels is *Saint-Saturnin* (1931), a heart-rending family history. Of the others prominent are: *Un Homme heureux* (1921), *L'Enfant qui s'accuse* (1927), *L'Histoire de quatre potiers* (1935) and *Stéphane le Glorieux* (1940), in all of which pessimism is marshalled into something positive and fruitful. He has celebrated his debt to Corneille (q.v.), whose heroic approach to life he so much admired, in the essays, *Plaisir à Corneille* (1936). His memoirs, *Éveils*, came out in 1949, and a novel, *Passion*, in 1956.

**Schnabel, Ernst** (1913– ), German novelist and essayist born at Zittau. From the first of his publications, *Die Reise nach Savannah* (1939), he seemed bent on new experiments in technique. In *Nachtwind* (1941) and *Schiffe und Sterne* (1943) he was finding his way with success; but ultimately he was to discover his true field in wireless plays, such as *Der 29. Januar* (1947) and *Interview mit einem Stern* (1951).

**Schnabel, Johann Gottfried,** pseudonym **Gisander** (1692–1752?), German novelist. Born near Bitterfeld, he became an army surgeon, retired and went to live at Stolberg, where he died. As an imitator of Daniel Defoe he wrote, among other works in his style, *Die Insel Felsenburg* (4 vols., 1731–43), a heavier, Teutonic, moralizing *Robinson Crusoe*. It became a favourite family book.

**Schnitzler, Arthur** (1862–1931), Austrian playwright and novelist. Born in Vienna, where he died, Schnitzler took up medicine, giving more and more time to the exercise of his literary gifts which particularly fitted him to be a witty (if saddened) commentator on fast declining Viennese society. Of his plays may be mentioned: *Anatol* (1893; Eng. trans. 1911), *Liebelei* (1896; Eng. trans. *The Reckoning*, 1907), *Reigen* (1900; Eng. trans. *Hands Round*, 1920), which was made into a highly publicized film *La Ronde* (1950), *Der grüne Kakadu* (1899; Eng. trans. *The Duke and the Actress*, 1910), *Der einsame Weg* (1903; Eng. trans. *The Lonely Way*, 1915) and *Professor Bernhardi* (1912; Eng. trans. 1927). The most outstanding of his novels are: *Der Weg ins Freie* (1908; Eng. trans. *The Road to the Open*, 1923), *Dr Graesler* (1917; Eng. trans. 1923), *Casanovas Heim-*

*fahrt* (1918; Eng. trans. *Casanova's Homecoming*, 1921), *Fräulein Else* (1924; Eng. trans. 1925) and *Flucht in die Finsternis* (1931; Eng. trans. *Flight into Darkness*, 1931).

**Schopenhauer, Arthur** (1788–1860), German prose-writer. Born in Danzig, the son of a well-to-do merchant banker of Dutch origin, who later committed suicide, and an excitable mother, Johanna, later to become an emancipated literary woman, his antecedents were not conducive to mental balance for himself. His whole life, in fact, shows that for all the brilliance and clarity of his mind he was not normal. After a brilliant university career at Göttingen, Berlin and Jena, where he graduated master and doctor in 1813, he visited Goethe at Weimar and began the study of oriental philosophy which was to exercise untold influence on him. He then went to Dresden, where he carried out research in optics, publishing *Über das Sehen und die Farben* (1816) which largely anticipated Goethe's book on the same subject, and working out his famous philosophy. His great *Die Welt als Wille und Vorstellung* (Eng. trans. *The World as Will and Idea*, by Haldane and Kemp, 3 vols., 1883–6) came out at the end of 1818, although the date 1819 appears on the title-page. Together with *Über den Willen in der Natur* (1836; Eng. trans. *Will in Nature*, 1900), in which he sought to illustrate his philosophy with concrete examples of the operation of the 'will' in the world of nature, and *Parerga und Paralipomena* (1851; Eng. trans. 1891), it forms almost the sum total of his philosophic work. Without here taking into account his philosophy, the influence of which has been incalculable, from a literary point of view his prose, together with that of Nietzsche (q.v.) and to a lesser extent of Goethe, is the finest in modern German. Schopenhauer, who had lived in retirement at Frankfurt-am-Main since 1831, died there having seen his philosophy at last gain acceptance.

**Schubart, Christian Friedrich Daniel** (1739–1791), German poet. Born at Obersontheim in Swabia, he became a schoolmaster and organist, but his lack of self-discipline led to his dismissal from his posts. His next venture was into journalism at Augsburg, where he became editor of *Die deutsche Chronik* (1774–7), a newspaper in which he freely discussed the tyrannical behaviour of some of the German princes. Because of this, and especially because of a much-read poem on despots, *Die Fürstengruft* (1777, 'The Grave of Princes'), Schubart became particularly obnoxious to Duke Karl Eugen of Württemberg, who had him enticed into his territory and then imprisoned without trial in the castle of Hohenasperg. There he remained for ten years, a martyr in the eyes of Schiller and the other young writers of the aftermath of the *Sturm und Drang* movement. While in prison he published the bulk of his poetry (*Gedichte*, 1785), notable for its appreciation of nature. On his release in 1787 he went to Stuttgart, where he became manager of the theatre, and there he died, having prepared for publication his autobiography (publ. posthumously, 1791–3). He seems to have borne no bad will towards the duke and even curried favour with him. All in all he was hardly worthy of the championship of Schiller and his friends, but was a rallying-point for the rising German middle classes imbued with Rousseauism and other new theories.

**Scribe, Augustin Eugène** (1791–1861), French dramatist and librettist, was the son of a wealthy silk mercer and was born in Paris. He began to write for the stage in 1811, and five years later had achieved such success that he set up a kind of 'factory' for the production of plays and libretti, many of which he did little more than supervise. Indifferent as literature, the plays of Scribe have good, strong-moving plots and easy dialogue, and they include such favourites in their day as *Une Chaîne* (1842), a comedy, *Un Verre d'eau* (1842), an historical drama, and *Adrienne Lecouvreur* (1849, with E. Legouvé, q.v.), an emotional *tour de force*. He also wrote the libretti for over sixty operas, including *La Muette de Portici* (1828), *Masaniello* (1828) and *Fra Diavolo* (1830), all of these for Auber, the composer; and *Robert le Diable* (1831), *Les Huguenots* (1836) and *Le Prophète* (1849), all for Meyerbeer. His influence in his field in Europe was immense. He died in Paris.

**Scudéry, Georges de** (1601–1667), French playwright, poet and critic. Born at Le Havre of a substantial upper middle-class family, he became a well-known (and ridiculous) figure in Parisian literary circles in conjunction with his sister Madeleine (q.v.). Besides helping her with her novels he wrote heroic plays on classical themes such as *Le Grand Annibal* (1631) and *L'Amour tyrannique* (1639), verse epics such as *Alaric, ou Rome vaincue* (1654), and very conservative literary criticism such as *Observations sur le Cid* (1637), an attack on Corneille. He died in Paris.

**Scudéry, Madeleine de** (1607–1701), French romance writer. Born at Le Havre, she became a leading light in the literary *salon* of the Hôtel Rambouillet in Paris. The sentimental near-historical novels, though published under her brother's name, seem to have been almost entirely written by her. Unreadable as such works as *Artamène ou le Grand Cyrus* (10 vols., 1649–53) or *Clélie, histoire romaine* (10 vols., 1654–60), that 'encyclopedia of love', now seem to be, with their chivalrous adventures, tenderness, rhetoric and allusions to well-known people of the time, they proved irresistible to her contemporaries. She died in Paris at the age of ninety-four.

**Sealsfield, Charles,** pseudonym of **Karl Anton Postl** (1793–1864), German novelist, born at Poppitz in Moravia. Leaving Germany for America in 1823, he wrote several interesting novels under the name of Sealsfield which give a good idea of American life during the first half of the nineteenth century. Among these may be named: *Der Virey und die Aristokraten* (1834; Eng. trans. *The Viceroy and the Aristocracy*, in *Blackwood's Magazine*, vol. lvii, 1845), *Die deutsch-amerikanischen Wahlverwandtschaften* (1839; Eng. trans. *Rambleton*, 1844) and *Das Kajütenbuch* (1841; Eng. trans. *The Cabin Book*, 1844). He died at Solothurn, Switzerland.

**Sedaine, Michel** (1719–1797), French dramatist and poet, was born in Paris, where he died. A master mason by trade, he was a successful librettist for light opera, producing for Grétry, the composer, and others such graceful verse as *Les Sabots* (1768) and *Richard Cœur de Lion* (1784), while with his straight play, *La Gageure imprévue* (1768), he is about the only representative of the drama of bourgeois life in France.

**Seferis, Jorgos** (1900–     ), Greek poet, born in Smyrna. Influenced by the ancient literature of his country, he yet gave it a modern character. The *Odyssey* was the book round which he built his work; a study of T. S. Eliot presented him with the technique within which to express himself. An Ionian Greek, he lost his home for good when the Turks invaded the west coast of Asia Minor in 1922 and deprived him of the world of the *Odyssey*, the source of his inspiration, which later the German invasion of 1940–1 was to heighten. His *Poiemata*, the collected edition of his poetry, appeared in 1951. Of translations into English there are *The Kings of Asine and Other Poems* (1948) and *Poems* (trans. R. Warner, 1960).

**Seghers, Anna,** pseudonym of **Netty Radvanyi** (1900–     ), German novelist. Born in Mainz, she made her name with *Der Aufstand der Fischer von Sankt Barbara* (1928). A strong opponent of the Nazi regime, she left Germany for France in 1933 and in 1939 went to Mexico. In exile she asserted her faith in the future of democracy in Germany, and in *Das siebte Kreuz* (1941) she gave a moving account of German resisters of the Hitler regime and of their suffering in concentration camps. *Transit* (1947) deals with emigration, while *Die Toten bleiben jung* (1949) is a long saga of German political life from 1918 to 1945. In 1947 she settled in East Germany.

**Seidel, Ina** (1885–     ), German poet and novelist. Born in Halle, the grand-daughter of Georg Ebers (q.v.), antiquary and novelist, she married a writer, H. W. Seidel. Ill health gave her much time for thought, and religion and nature are considered deeply and beautifully in her collection of verse, *Gedichte* (1914). It was with her novels that she made an impact on European literature, finding an inspiration in the life of J. G. A. Forster (q.v.), the eighteenth-century traveller and naturalist, for his life forms the plot of *Das Labyrinth* (1922; Eng. trans. 1932). *Das Wunschkind* (1930; Eng. trans. *The Wish Child*, 1935) is far more personal, and is indeed a fine study of motherhood, set in the time of the Prussian war of liberation. She has written an autobiography, *Meine Kindheit und Jugend* (1935). Of recent novels the best known is *Das unverwesliche Erbe* (1954). As a literary critic she has concentrated on the romantics Brentano (q.v.) and the Arnims (q.v.), as in *Drei Dichter der Romantik* (1956).

**Seifert, Jaroslav** (1901–     ), Czech poet, born in Prague. His earliest work was pure socialism, but with a deep human sympathy which prevented it from becoming mere propaganda, *Město v slzách* (1920, 'A City in Tears'). His next period, exemplified by *Na vlnách T.S.F.* (1925, 'On Wireless Waves'), shows him at his most experimental, while *Ruce Venušiny* (1936, 'The Hands of Venus') is more true and integrated and its style is excellent. The shock of the German invasion of 1938 is to be clearly seen in *Světlem oděná* (1940, 'Clothed in Light').

**Selgas y Carrasco, José** (1822–1882), Spanish poet and novelist, born at Lorca, Murcia. He wrote poetry in a restrained romantic style such as in the volume *Primavera* (1850). His lengthy novel *La manzana de oro* was published in 1872. He died in Madrid.

**Semyonov, Sergey Alexandrovich** (1893–1943), Russian Soviet novelist, who was one of the main voices of the Soviet Union in its first years. Typical of his 'proletarian' work is *Golod* (1922, 'Hunger'), crammed with documentary evidence.

**Sénancour, Étienne Pivert de** (1770–1846), French prose-writer, was born in Paris. Intended for the priesthood, he escaped from his home and went to Switzerland in 1789, marrying a year later. Left a widower with small children, he returned to France in 1798 and lived by his pen during the rest of his financially restricted life, for his family property had been lost for good and journalism hardly filled the gap. A follower of Rousseau but tormented by scepticism, he expresses his sincere feelings with sad eloquence in his famous epistolary novel, *Obermann* (1804; Eng. trans by A. E. Waite, 1898), which, although neglected at the time, was later to become the delight of George Sand (q.v.) and Matthew Arnold, the latter dedicating two elegies on 'Obermann' to his memory. His other important work is *Rêveries sur la nature primitive de l'homme* (1799), in which the idealist struggles with necessitarianism. Sénancour died at Saint-Cloud.

**Sender, Ramón José** (1901–    ), Spanish novelist and general prose-writer, born at Alcolea de Cinca, near Huesca, Aragon. After serving in the Moroccan campaign he turned his experiences to account in *Imán* (1930; Eng. trans. *Earmarked for Hell*, 1934). During the last years of the dictatorship of Primo de Rivera he had begun to take part in politics, suffering arrest in 1926, and he did much as a journalist to foster the republican movement after his release, while in the following years, especially after the establishment of the republic in 1931, he travelled widely. *Siete domingos rojos* (1932; Eng. trans. *Seven Red Sundays*, 1936) increased his reputation with its account of labour troubles and politics in Spain. The Cartagena revolution of 1873 is the subject of *Míster Witt en el Cantón* (1935; Eng. trans. *Mr Witt among the Rebels*, 1937), and this was awarded the Spanish National Prize for Literature. *Contraataque* (1938; Eng. trans. *Counter Attack in Spain*, 1938) is a vivid account of the civil war in which he fought as major in the republican army. On the insurgent victory in 1939 he went to France, and settled in 1942 in the United States, where he has been professor of Spanish literature at the University of Albuquerque (New Mexico) since 1947. *Epitalamio del prieto Trinidad* (1942; Eng. trans. *Dark Wedding*, 1943) describes the influence on him of war and exile. *Ariadna* (1955) is a long and ambitious novel on the civil war.

**Sepheriades, G.** *see* **Seferis, J.**

**Serafimovich, Alexander,** pseudonym of **A. S. Popov** (1863–1949), Russian Soviet novelist born at Nizhne-Kurmayaskaya, author of *Zhelezny potok* (1924; Eng. trans. *The Iron Flood*, 1935), which has

has for its theme the civil war in the Caucasus during the Bolshevik Revolution. He died in Moscow.

**Serao, Matilde** (1856–1927), Italian novelist. Born at Patrasso in Greece, she returned with her family to Naples where she became a well-known journalist. She wrote a great number of novels about lower middle-class Neapolitan life, frankly popular and without any literary graces. Chief among them are *Il romanzo della fanciulla* (1886), *La ballerina* (1899) and *Suor Giovanna della Croce* (1901). She died in Naples.

**Sercambi, Giovanni** (1347–1424), Italian prose-writer, a native of Lucca, where he lived and died. Apart from political works and a history of Lucca which can hardly be classed as literature, he wrote a number of vivacious if erotic *Novelle* (ed. by G. Renier, 1889) of real quality.

**Sergeyev-Tsensky, Sergey Nikolayevich** (1876–1945), Russian Soviet novelist. He developed late, but finally settled down into the type of historical fiction writer so much relished in Russia between the two world wars. His *Mikhail Lermontov* (1933) is a dramatized biography, *Sevastopol'skaya strada* (3 vols., 1939–40, 'The Trials of Sebastopol') is an epic of the Crimean War. In another style is *Brusilovskiy proryv* (1944; Eng. trans. *Brusilov's Breakthrough*, 1945). He died in the Crimea.

**Sestini, Bartolomeo** (1792–1822), Italian poet, born in Pistoia, whose verse (*Poesie del Sestini*, 1855) recommended itself to Rossini, Bellini and Donizetti as suitable for putting to music. He died a political exile in Paris.

**Seume, Johann Gottfried** (1763–1810), German poet and topographical writer. Born of poor parents near Weissenfels in Saxony, he was pressed into service with Hessian mercenaries while a student and so fought against the Americans in the War of Independence. On his return to Germany at the end of the war he deserted, went back to his studies (1783), and thereafter led a restless life, serving in the Russian army for a time, and later touring about Europe. His poetry, *Gedichte* (1801), has some interest, but much more characteristic, and of particular value as expressing the impact of the classical world on the romantics, is *Spaziergang nach Syrakus* (1802; Eng. trans. *A Stroll to Syracuse*, 1964). Attractive also is *Mein Sommer im Jahre 1805* (1807). Seume died at Teplitz.

**Seuse, Heinrich** (1295?–1366), German mystical writer and one whose prose is particularly good from the literary point of view. Born at Überlingen, he became a Dominican, and is known as the author of *Büchlein der ewigen Weisheit* (1328; Eng. trans. *Little Book of Eternal Wisdom*, 1952). It was well known in the Middle Ages in its Latin translation *Horologium Sapientiae*. Seuse died in Ulm.

**Séverin, Fernand** (1876–1931), Belgian poet. Born at Grand-Manil, he became professor of literature at Ghent University, dying in that city. Writing in classical style, he celebrated nature. There is a softness, a sadness about his slightly misty works, among which should be named

*La Solitude heureuse* (1904), *La Source au fond des bois* (1924) and *Poèmes* (1930).

**Severyanin, Igor,** pseudonym of I. G. **Lotaryev** (1887–1942), Russian poet born in Petersburg, who gained a great reputation as the author of a futurist work, *Kubok gromokipyashchiy* (1913, 'The Thunder-seething Goblet') which was a best-seller and revealed a remarkable command of language and metrical virtuosity. Going into exile in 1917, Severyanin died in France, having long survived his reputation.

**Sévigné, Marie de Rabutin-Chantal de** (1626–1696), French writer. Born in Paris, she was left an orphan at an early age, but received a good education, and at eighteen was married to Henri, marquis de Sévigné, who was killed in a duel in 1651. After being widowed she lived a quiet life devoting herself to her two children, to one of whom, her spoilt daughter (afterwards Madame de Grignan), she wrote many of her unsurpassed letters. Some were first published in the *Mémoires et Correspondance* of her cousin Roger de Bussy-Rabutin (q.v.). Madame de Sévigné died at Grignan, the estate of her son-in-law, who called her letters 'delicious companions', a succinct commentary on their particular quality, that liveliness, that confidence in her reader which brings back so clearly the age in which she lived. There is a monumental edition of the *Lettres* (14 vols., 1862–7). The most convenient is the *Lettres choisies*, edited by A. Vigneron (1937).

**Shishkov, Vyacheslav Yakovlevich** (1873–1945), Russian Soviet novelist born at Biezhetsk, near Kalinin, whose novel *Ugryum reka* (1933; Eng. trans. *Children of Darkness*, 1936) made him well known abroad, while *Emelyan Pugachov* (1943), set in the Urals at the time of the rebellion of the Cossacks against Catherine the Great, brought him a last-minute celebrity in his own country. He died in Moscow.

**Shmelyev, Ivan Sergeyevich** (1875–1950), Russian novelist born in Moscow, the author of two excellent novels. The first, pre-revolution, was in realist style, the subject being the life of a poor old waiter and his family, *Chelovek iz restorana* (1910, 'The Man from the Restaurant'). The second was a kind of surrealistic account of the civil war in the Crimea, *Solntse myertvykh* (1923; Eng. trans. *The Sun of the Dead*, 1927). He died in Paris.

**Sholokhov, Mikhail Alexandrovich** (1905–    ), Russian Soviet novelist, born at Kruzhilin in Kuban, left school in the middle of the revolution and spent the following years wandering and taking on all kinds of jobs. After a trial of his now developing talent in the series of short stories, set in his own Cossack country, *Donskie rasskazy* (1926, 'Tales of the Don'), he turned to his masterpiece, the long novel *Tikhiy Don*, which appeared in four volumes between 1928 and 1940 (Eng. trans. vols. i and ii, *And Quiet Flows the Don*, 1934; vols. iii and iv, *The Don Flows Home to the Sea*, 1940). The theme is the life of the Don Cossacks, confronted first by the revolution and then by the ensuing civil war. This work, which at once made him the leading Soviet novelist, is a powerful and sombre one, and proved that the realistic novel in the great tradition of Russia was still the finest vehicle for describing national life, however much changed. In a separate piece of fiction, *Podnyataya tselina* (1932; Eng. trans. *The Virgin Soil Upturned*, 1935), the collectivization of the land is considered. The most outstanding of his subsequent novels, still dealing with the Don Cossacks, is *Oni srazhalis' za rodinu* (1944, 'They Fought for their Country'), which describes the Cossacks facing the German invasion. *Tikhiy Don* and *Podnyataya tselina* have been successfully filmed, the latter having been also adapted for the stage. Active in the Communist Party in peace and during the war at the front as interpreter, journalist and organizer of cultural activities of a naturally propagandist nature, he was awarded the Order of Lenin. He gained the Nobel Prize in 1966.

**Sienkiewicz, Henryk Adam Alexander Pius,** pseudonym **Litwos** (1846–1916), Polish novelist. Born at Wola Okrzejska of a family of small landowners, he graduated in 1870 at Warsaw University, and henceforth divided his time between writing and travel. He began his literary career cautiously with the novel *Na marne* (1872; Eng. trans. *In Vain*, 1889) and followed this up with an excellent collection of short stories, *Stary sługa* (1875, 'The Old Servants'; Eng. trans. in *Tales*, Everyman's Library). Other volumes of short stories followed, including *Hania* (1876; Eng. trans. in *Tales*, Everyman's Library) and *Bartek Zwycięzca* (1882, 'Bartek the Conqueror'; Eng. trans. in *Tales*, Everyman's Library); but it was with his trilogy of seventeenth-century Poland, the first part of which was *Ogniem i mieczem* (4 vols., 1884; Eng. trans. *With Fire and Sword*, 1895), the second, *Potop* (6 vols., 1886; Eng. trans. *The Deluge*, 2 vols., 1895) and the third, *Pan Wołodyjowski* (3 vols., 1887–8; Eng. trans. *Pan Michael*, 1895), that he conquered his public. Written in an impeccable style, full of interest and colour and excellently planned, the works of Sienkiewicz gained further devotees with *Bez dogmatu* (1891; Eng. trans. *Without Dogma*, 1893) and *Rodzina Połanieckich* (3 vols., 1895; Eng. trans. *Children of the Soil*, 1895), until with his novel of Roman times, *Quo Vadis?* (3 vols., 1896; Eng. trans. 1898, etc.) he reached world renown. After this he produced further novels, *Krzyżacy* (4 vols., 1900; Eng. trans. *The Teutonic Knights*, 1943), *Na polu chwały* (1906; Eng. trans. *On the Field of Glory*, 1906), *Wiry* (2 vols., 1910; Eng. trans. *Whirlpools*, 1910) and *W pustyni i w puszczy* (2 vols., 1911; Eng. trans. *In the Desert and Wilderness*, 1912). He had been awarded the Nobel Prize in 1905. The outbreak of the First World War found him in Switzerland engaged on an historical novel about Poland at the end of the eighteenth century, *Legiony*. He left it and it was never completed, for he gave all his remaining strength to international war work; but his new and unfamiliar tasks were too much for him, and after two years he died at Vevey.

**Sieroszewski, Wacław,** pseudonym **Sirko Bagrynowski** (1858–1945), Polish novelist and short-story writer. Born at Wólka Kozłowska, he became a technological student, but for participation in anti-Russian activities was exiled to Siberia, not being freed until 1900, having in the meantime published a few novels, notably *Na kresach lasów*

(1894; Fr. trans. *Sur la lisière des forêts*, 1929). Travels in the East and in Europe from 1902 onwards led to an inevitable broadening of horizons, which he exploited with great effect in his often moving and always sympathetic works. *Ucieczka* (1904; Eng. trans. *A Flight from Siberia*, 1909) is founded on vivid personal experience, Korea is the setting for *Ol-Soni-Kisan* (1906; Fr. trans. *La Danseuse coréenne*, 1938), China for *Zamorski diabeł* (1909; Fr. trans. *Yang-Hun-Tsy, le diable étranger*, 1909), Japan for *Miłość samuraja* (1926; Fr. trans. *L'Amour du Samourai*, 1932) and Tibet for *Dalaj Lama* (1927; Ger. trans. 1928). The best collection of his short stories is *Małżeństwo* (1909; Fr. trans. *Amours d'exilés*, 1923). Sieroszewski fought against the Bolsheviks in 1920, and, surviving German rule in Poland during the Second World War, died in Warsaw about the time that the Soviet armies entered it. His memoirs (*Pamiętniki i wspomnienia*) were published after his death, in 1959.

**Sigurjónsson, Jóhann** (1880–1919), Icelandic-Danish dramatist. Born at Laxamýri, he went to the University of Copenhagen and remained in that city for the rest of his life. He wrote in Danish romantic plays historically inspired, including *Bóndinn á Hrauni* (1908) and *Bjærg-Ejvind og hans Hustru* (1911), which were translated as *The Hraun Farm* and *Eyvind of the Hills* respectively in H. K. Schanche's *Modern Icelandic Plays* (1916).

**Sillanpää, Francs Eemil** (1888–1964), Finnish novelist and short-story writer, born at Hämeenkyrö. He leapt to European fame with a novel of power, grace, and with realism and idealism nicely balanced, *Hurskas kurjuus* (1919; Eng. trans. *Meek Heritage*, 1938), and with *Nuorena nukkunut* (1931; Eng. trans. *Fallen Asleep While Young*, 1933) he made good his claims to be regarded as a leading novelist of his time. He received the Nobel Prize in 1939. He died in Helsinki.

**Silone, Ignazio,** pseudonym of **Secondo Tranquilli** (1900–     ), Italian novelist. Born at Pescina dei Marsi, Abruzzi, he lost his whole family in an earthquake when a child and spent a poverty-stricken youth. Drifting to the town, he became a journalist and took part in founding the Italian Communist Party before being driven into exile as an opponent of Mussolini's regime. From Zürich he now issued novels, strongly anti-Fascist, which brought him world-wide fame. Chief of them are: *Fontamara* (1933; Eng. trans. 1934), *Pane e vino* (1936; Eng. trans. *Bread and Wine*, 1936) and *Il seme sotto la neve* (1940; Eng. trans. *The Seed beneath the Snow*, 1943). His political work *La scuola dei dittatori* (1938; Eng. trans. *The School for Dictators*, 1939) made a great impression. The output of Silone since his return to Italy after the war has been much smaller, and his novels flow in quieter channels, although probably with a gain in literary quality. Of these works the best are: *Una manciata di more* (1952; Eng. trans. *A Handful of Blackberries*, 1954), *Il segreto di Luca* (1958; Eng. trans. *Luca's Secret*, 1959) and *La volpe e le camelie* (1960).

**Silva, António José da** (1705–1739), Portuguese dramatist. Born in Rio de Janeiro, he went to Lisbon with his family in 1713, and was tortured by the Inquisition for his religion as a Jew. He abjured, became a lawyer, and made a name for himself as a playwright, especially for marionette shows. His three best are the comedies *Vida do grande D. Quixote e do gordo Sancho Pança* (1733; mod. ed. 1905), *Encantos de Medeia* (1736) and *Guerras do Alecrim e Mangerona* (1737; mod. ed. 1905). Unhappily he was reported to the Inquisition in 1737 for the supposed anti-Christian tendencies of these plays, imprisoned, strangled and his body burnt as a lapsed Catholic in Lisbon. He was without doubt the most gifted Portuguese dramatist of his time.

**Silva, Luís Augusto Rebelo da** (1822–1871), Portuguese novelist, the author of an eighteenth-century historical novel, *Lágrimas e tesouros* (1863) in which the English eccentric millionaire, William Beckford, appears. His *A Última corrida de touros em Salvaterra*, was published in 1848 (Eng. trans. *The Last Royal Bull-fight at Salvaterra*, 1909). He spent all his life in Lisbon.

**Simenon, Georges,** pseudonym of **Georges Sim** (1903–    ), Belgian novelist, born in Liége, of Franco-Dutch parentage, he became a reporter on the *Gazette* of his native city, and wrote many ephemeral 'pot-boilers'. With *L'Affaire Saint-Fiacre* (1932), he turned, however, to more serious work, and has produced a bewildering number of detective and straight novels, about a third of which have been translated into English with very varying success. His famous creation is the detective Maigret, first introduced in *Maigret* (1934). At first reading they may seem to be sordid stories in a sordid setting, but at bottom they are intense studies of human life and character (or the failure of it). Many deal with crime, but not as an end, rather as a shocking incident luridly lighting up the general drabness and aimlessness of life in a world of rain and fog.

**Simonov, Konstantin Mikhailovich** (1915–    ), Russian Soviet novelist and dramatist, born in Petrograd. It was his novel about the battle of Stalingrad, *Dni i nochi* (1943; Eng. trans. *Days and Nights*, 1945) that made his name. In this he brought to fiction the same power that he had already displayed in his drama *Russkie lyudi* (1942; Eng. trans. *The Russians*, 1944). His *Voyennye dnevniki* (1945, 'War Diaries') reveal the same kind of urgency of feeling and of style to match it. A new war novel, *Tovarishchi po oruzhiyu* (1952, 'Comrades in Arms'), describes the undeclared war with Japan in Mongolia in 1939. Another well-known novel is *Zhivye i myortvye* (1959; Eng. trans. *The Living and the Dead*, 1962).

**Simrock, Karl Josef** (1802–1876), German poet, born in Bonn. After a revolutionary phase, he settled down as professor of Old German at Bonn, where he died. He did much by his editing of the old writers, such as Hartmann von der Aue (q.v.) and Walter von der Vogelweide (q.v.), to revive interest in the early days of German literature. He also made two important collections of folk-poetry, *Das deutsches Heldenbuch* (6 vols., 1843–9) and *Die deutsche Volksbücher* (13 vols., 1845–67). Two volumes of his original verse appeared in 1844 and 1863.

**Siwertz, Sigfrid** (1882–    ), Swedish poet and novelist, born in Stockholm. In his collected verse, *Samlade dikter* (1944), can be traced his change from early pessimism to a more sturdy acceptance of life and a deeper philosophic content derived from Bergson (q.v.). As a novelist he developed from *Margot* (1906) to the searching analysis of war racketeers in Stockholm in *Selambs* (1920; Eng. trans. *Downstream*, 1922). Another book on social matters, *Det stora varuhuset* (1926; Eng. trans. *Goldman's*, 1929), proved equally popular.

**Six, Jan** (1618–1700), Dutch dramatist and patron of the arts, whose *Medea* (1648) was furnished with an illustration by Rembrandt, a beneficiary of his.

**Skekely-Lulofs, Madelon Hermine** (1899–    ), Dutch novelist, born at Surabaya. Her novels, full of life and colour, but not deep enough to suit the canons of the literary-minded, are set in the Dutch East Indies. Among them are: *Rubber* (1931; Eng. trans. 1933), *Koelie* (1932; Eng. trans. *Coolie*, 1936), *De andere Wereld* (1934; Eng. trans. *The Wealthy Beggar*, 1935), *Van Oerwoud tot Plantage* (1935; Eng. trans. *Tropic Fever*, 1939), *Onze Bedienden in Indië* (1945) and *Tjoet Nja Din* (1948).

**Skram, Bertha Amalie** (1847–1905), Norwegian novelist, was born at Bergen, and was twice married. Her novels of domestic life include *Constance Ring* (1885) and *Professor Hieronimus* (1895; Eng. trans. 1899). She died in Copenhagen.

**Sládkovič, Andrej**, pseudonym of **Ondrej Braxatoris** (1820–1872), Slovak poet, born at Krupina, is best known as the author of *Marína* (1846), its love-theme suggested by Pushkin's (q.v.) *Onegin*. He also wrote an historical epic poem, *Detvan* (1853). He died at Radvaň.

**Slaveykov, Pencho** (1866–1912), Bulgarian poet, son of the folklorist Petko Slaveykov, was born at Trevna. An accident which he sustained as a young man left him permanently crippled, and this and a very unhappy social life made such an impression on his work that he is known as the 'poet of darkness'. His longer poems have not stood the test of time, but his lyrics, collected as *Sån za shtastie* (1906, 'Dreams of Happiness') are of high quality. He died at Commo Brumatte in Italy.

**Słowacki, Juliusz** (1809–1849), Polish poet and dramatist, was born at Krzemieniec. Brought up in comfortable circumstances, he suddenly left his sheltered home to take part in the abortive Polish revolution against Russia in 1831, had to leave his country and never returned. The year before his exile he wrote and published a long poem in Byronic style, *Hugo*, and followed this up with several others such as *Jan Bielecki* and *Arab*. From 1832 to 1839 he wandered in Italy, Greece and the Middle East, and settled in Paris in the latter year. Love affairs resulted in *W Szwajcarii* (1836, 'In Switzerland'), while his meeting in 1842 with the mystic Towiański inspired his greatest poem, *Król Duch* (1847, 'King-Spirit'). Many beautiful lyrics belong to these years, as do the poetic dramas such as *Balladyna* (1839), *Mazepa* (1840; Eng. trans. 1930), *Lilla Weneda*, his best (1840) and *Ksiądz Marek* (1843). He died in Paris. There is a complete French translation of his works, *Œuvres complètes*, all in prose (3 vols., 1870–1911). He and Mickiewicz (q.v.) are without doubt the greatest poets Poland has produced.

**Smidovich, V. V.,** *see* **Veresayev, V.**

**Smolenskin, Perez** (1842–1885), Russian Hebrew novelist, born at Monastyrshchina, who, after a period as a journalist at Odessa, became a highly successful printer in Vienna. Of his novels *Kheburath Khmor* (1884, 'The Burial of an Ass') is looked on as his best. He died at Meran.

**Snoilsky, Carl Johan Gustaf** (1841–1903), Swedish poet, was born and died in Stockholm. Latin countries fascinated him and they inspired such volumes of verse as *Dikter* (1869) and *Sonetter* (1871). Until 1879 he was in the diplomatic service, but a scandal in his private life put an end to this career, and he lived abroad for ten years, being appointed librarian-in-chief of the Royal Library, Stockholm, on his return in 1889. His later poetry is often nationalistic. His *Samlade dikter* were collected in five volumes (1903–4).

**Snorri Sturluson,** *see* **Sturluson.**

**Sobolev, Leonid Sergeyevich** (1894–      ), Soviet novelist. His sea stories include *Kapital'nyi remont* (1932; Eng. trans. *Storm Warning*, 1935) and *Morskaya dusha* (1943; Eng. trans. *The Soul of the Sea*, 1946). More recent is *Zelenyi Luch* (1956; Eng. trans. *The Green Light*, 1956).

**Söderberg, Hjalmar** (1869–1941), Swedish novelist and short-story writer, was born in Stockholm and became a civil servant before deciding to live by his pen. His first success was *Historietterna* (1898), a collection of short stories, and he followed this up with the striking novels, *Martin Bircks ungdom* (1901; Eng. trans. *Martin Birck's Youth*, 1930) and *Doktor Glas* (1905; Eng. trans., 1963). A selection of his many short stories was translated into English by C. W. Stork in 1935. Söderberg died in Copenhagen.

**Søiberg, Harry** (1880–1954), Danish novelist and short-story writer. Born at Ringkøbing, Jutland, he became a bookbinder and a left-wing politician, and turned author. His work deals with fisher-folk and peasants, for whom he had a deep sympathy and understanding. *Hjemlig Jord* (1914), *De Levendes Land* (1920) and *Søkongen* (3 vols., 1926–30; Eng. trans. *The Sea King*, 1928) are excellent examples of the novels; *Fra Hjertets Krinkelkroge* (1932) and *Af Jordens Slægt* (1945) of the short stories. He died in Copenhagen.

**Sologub, Fyodor,** pseudonym of **Fyodor Kuzmich Teternikov** (1863–1927), Russian novelist and short-story writer, was born in Petersburg of humble family. He became a schoolmaster in the provinces, and he depicted the life there in excellent style in *Melkiy bes* (1907; Eng. trans. *The Little Demon*, 1916), which first brought him recognition. Later he developed into a morbid fantasist showing signs of a split personality, as in *Tvorimaya legenda* (1916; Eng. trans. *The Created Legend*, 1916). In this trilogy a romantic dream-world is inset in a workaday one with a hero as opposed in the two sides of his character as Dr Jekyll and Mr Hyde. Sologub died in complete retirement in Petersburg, hating the new regime but unable to bring himself to leave Russia.

**Solomos, Dionysios** (1798–1857), Greco-Italian poet from the Ionian Islands. Born in Zante, he died in Corfu. The illegitimate son of an Italian count, he was educated in Italy and lived there until 1818, when he returned to Zante. Writing in the everyday Greek which writers (such as there had been) were unwilling to do, preferring the classical style, he made a name for himself with *Hymnos eis ten Eleutherian* (1823, 'Hymn to Liberty'). His lengthy ode on Byron's death (1825) is his most satisfying composition. After his removal to Corfu in 1828 his inspiration was overpowered by self-criticism and, increased by his habitual laziness, died away. Much of his later work is fragmentary. The first volume of the 1948 edition of his collected works by Polites contains all the Greek poems. The Italian poems were collected as *Ta Italika Poiemata* with a Greek translation in 1921.

**Sønderby, Knud** (1909–    ), Danish novelist and playwright, born at Esbjerg, who as a follower of Ernest Hemingway wrote of smart young people, amoral on the surface, but troubled and insecure at heart, typical of the Jazz Age. Such a novel is *Midt i en Jazztid* (1931); but by 1940, when *De kolde Flammer* was published, his disillusionment was coming undisguisedly to the fore. A most accomplished prose-writer, as his essays (e.g. *Grønlandsk Sommer*, 1941) show, he wrote some good plays, such as *Krista* (1947).

**Sorel, Charles,** *see* Souvigny, C. S. de.

**Soulary, Joseph-Marie** (1815–1891), French poet, was born and died in Lyon. After trying several careers he ended as a librarian at the Palais des Arts in his native city. His volumes of romantic poetry, showing a mastery of verse forms, include *Les Éphémères* (1846, second ed., 1857), *Sonnets, poèmes et poésies* (1864), and *La Chasse aux mouches d'or* (1876).

**Souvigny, Charles Sorel de** (1600–1674), French novelist of a humoristic turn, was born in Paris, where he died. He is known for two works, *La Vraie Histoire comique de Francion* (1623), a vivacious novel of low life, and *Le Berger extravagant* (1627), a parody of the pastoral novel.

**Spangenberg, Cyriacus** (1528–1604), German religious poet and dramatist. Born at Nordhausen, he became a pastor and was a friend of Luther (q.v.). He wrote many fine hymns such as those to be found in *Christliches Gesangsbüchlein* (1568). His religious drama, *Von dem Cananeischen Weiblein* (1589), is notable. He died in Strassburg.

**Spengler, Oswald** (1880–1936), German philosophical writer. Born at Blankenburg, after a spell of teaching in Hamburg he settled in Munich in 1911 to write. The first volume of his *Der Untergang des Abendlandes* appeared in 1918 and was an immense success, reflecting as it did the determinism and fatalism alive in post-war Germany. The second volume was published in 1923, both being translated as *The Decline of the West* (2 vols., 1926–9), creating a great impression in Britain and America. Spengler argued that Western culture was on the downward trend and that democratic government was soon to be swallowed up by Caesarism or dictatorship, the necessity for which he seemed to imply. No wonder that Fascists and Nazis welcomed him, but when all is said Spengler did honestly bring his great learning to bear on what seemed to be a disintegrating society. His prose is forceful and pliant enough to serve the sometimes very difficult purposes to which he turned it. The best known of his other books was *Der Mensch und die Technik* (1931; Eng. trans. *Man and Technics*, 1932). He died in Munich.

**Spielhagen, Friedrich** (1829–1911) German novelist. Born in Magdeburg, he took an active part in left-wing politics while still at the universities of Berlin and Greifswald, and afterwards became an actor and journalist before settling down as a writer in Berlin in 1862. His first novels, such as *Problematische Naturen* (1861; Eng. trans. *Problematic Characters*, 1869), *Durch Nacht zum Licht* (1862; Eng. trans. *Through Night to Light*, 1870) and above all *Hammer und Amboss* (1869; Eng. trans. *Hammer and Anvil*, 1870), which established his reputation, deal with working-class problems. After this he turned to more generalized social questions, treating of them in a highly sensational manner, the most powerful of his novels in this style, and in fact his generally considered masterpiece, being *Sturmflut* (1876; Eng. trans. *The Breaking of the Storm*, 1877). Later works include *Susi* (1895) and *Faustulus* (1897). His autobiography, *Finder und Erfinder* (1890), is of some interest, but the prolixity of all his work has damaged his reputation. He died in Berlin.

**Spiess, Henry** (1876–1940), Swiss poet, born in Geneva, where he died. Greatly influenced by French Parnassian and symbolist literature, the two most substantial collections of his lyrics are *Rimes d'audience* (1903, with additions, 1917) and *Le Silence des heures* (1904). His last publication was the religiously inspired volume *Chambre haute* (1928).

**Spinoza, Baruch** (1632–1677), Dutch philosopher, was born in Amsterdam, the son of Portuguese Jews who had fled from persecution. Carefully brought up and given a rabbinical education, he clandestinely studied modern philosophy, especially Descartes (q.v.), and science, and in 1656 was accused of heresy, banished from the synagogue, an attempt being made on his life, and with the concurrence of the more conservative elements among the Protestants he was driven from Amsterdam. For some years he lived in near poverty, eking out a living by lens-polishing, the while writing a striking work, the germ of the famous *Ethica*, entitled *Korte verhandeling van God, de Mensch en deszelfs Welstand* (discovered and publ. 1852; Eng. trans. *Short Treatise on God, Man and his Well-Being*, 1910). In 1661 he moved to Rijnsburg, near Leiden, two years later making for Voorburg, and finally settling in The Hague (1671), where his gentleness, high character and intellectual brilliance gained him a circle of admirers. He had changed his first name to Benedictus in 1656 on his break with Jewry, at which period he became closely acquainted with Rembrandt, who twice painted his portrait under anonymous titles. Besides the treatise already mentioned, two more works were published in his lifetime, *Renati des Cartes principiorum philosophiae, mori geometrico demonstratae* (1663), which shows his breakaway from Cartesian dualism to monism, and the *Tractatus Theologico-Politicus*

(1670), written in support of the liberal minded brothers de Witt, with its plea for religious and political toleration and a new critical and rationalistic approach to the Bible. The rest, though freely handed about in manuscript among his friends and expounded to his disciples, were not published until 1677, some months after his death at The Hague, as *Opera Posthuma*, edited by his close friend Lodewijk Meyer, who received last instructions from Spinoza, dying of tuberculosis brought on by overwork and ascetic ways. This being so, there has been little difficulty in establishing the texts, which all had the philosopher's approval. Chief of these, and indeed the two masterworks, are the *Ethica* and *De Intellectus Emendatione*. In these two great pieces many men of different shades of thought have found inspiration. At first sight, set as they are in apparently uncompromising geometric form (*ordine geometrico demonstrata*), one is surprised that Herder (q.v.) and Goethe should have found him a kindred soul and that Novalis (q.v.) should have termed him *ein Gottbetrunkener Mensch* ('a man drunk with God'); but one soon discovers that there is inspiration to be found in his pantheism; God is Nature, Nature is God, any man may by self-knowledge become part of this universal oneness. This teaching of salvation reveals a warm humanity, unrealized when looking at the exterior of the system. Few philosophers have ever shown so human an approach in what so often comes to be a forbidding science, or opened up so wide a path free from scholastic conventions. The best edition of Spinoza is by Gebhardt (4 vols., 1926). There is a useful English edition of the *Ethics* and *De Intellectus Emendatione* in Everyman's Library. The *Tractatus Theologico-Politicus* was first translated into English as *A Treatise, partly Theological, partly Political* in 1689. A complete translation into English of all the works has been made by Abraham Wolf (1928).

**Spitteler, Carl Friedrich Georg** (1845–1924), Swiss poet and prose-writer. Born at Liestal, he studied at the universities of Basel and Heidelberg and then visited Russia. After trying journalism he lived at Lucerne, where he remained for the rest of his life. Nietzsche (q.v.) first attracted him and this influence was responsible for the highly individualistic prose-poetry contained in the two volumes, *Prometheus und Epimetheus* (1881; Eng. trans. 1931) and *Extramundana* (1883), both published under the *nom de plume* 'Carl Felix Tandem' which he did not employ again. His satire *Lachende Wahrheiten* (1898; Eng. trans. *Laughing Truths*, 1927) displayed an unsuspected penetrating wit brought to bear on the follies of contemporary life, while *Conrad der Leutnant* (1898) is a powerful, straightforward novel. Most distinctive of all his works, however, is his strange Homeric extravaganza *Olympischer Frühling*, published in five parts between 1900 and 1910. On the outbreak of war he published an eloquent statement of Switzerland's position in European affairs, *Unser schweizer Standpunkt* (1914). He wrote on to the end, publishing *Prometheus der Dulder* shortly before his death. He won the Nobel Prize in 1919.

**Staël, Anne-Louise-Germaine de,** *née* **Necker** (1766–1817), French prose-writer. Born in Paris, the only child of the financier Necker, later to be so famous in the events leading to the French Revolution, her mother having once been the object of the historian Edward Gibbon's love, she was given an unusually full education for girls of her day and was busy with her pen before she was twenty. In 1786 she married the impecunious Swedish ambassador in Paris, Baron de Staël-Holstein, formally separating from him in 1797 after she had borne him three children. A woman of a rich and varied character, full of enthusiasm and without prejudice, she was soon one of the social and intellectual celebrities of Paris, but the revolution took her by surprise and forced her to take refuge in Switzerland in 1792, and later at Mickleham, Surrey. Returning to Switzerland in the early summer of 1793 she published *Réflexions sur le procès de la Reine* in which she made a vain attempt to save Marie Antoinette. Formally allowed back to Paris in 1797, she gathered round her men of letters in opposition like Benjamin Constant (q.v.) and disaffected generals like Moreau, and in 1800 published her clever *Littérature et ses rapports avec les institutions sociales*, in which she gauges the influence of climate and social conditions on literature. Side by side with this serious work stands her passionate feminist novel *Delphine* (1802). By now on the worst of terms with Bonaparte the Consul, she was ordered by him to leave Paris (1803), and at the end of the year she made for Germany, descending like a shower of sparks on Weimar and startling the by now sober Goethe and Schiller and the earnest little court. She next set out for Berlin, attaching A. W. Schlegel (q.v.) and later W. von Humboldt (q.v.) and Bonstetten (q.v.) to her train, and with them toured Italy, returning to Switzerland to publish *Corinne* (1805, rev. 1817), a stronger *Delphine*, which consolidated her reputation. Meanwhile she had been at work on *De l'Allemagne*, which reflected her experiences of Germany, and showed how much impressed she had been by German literature and thought. To oversee its publication she journeyed back to Paris, but just when the book was about to appear the whole impression was destroyed by order of Napoleon and she herself ordered to leave. She managed, however, to smuggle her manuscript out of the country and it was published in London in 1813. Her husband had died in 1802, and in 1811 she married a young Italian officer, Albert de Rocca. The fall of Napoleon allowed her to return to Paris, where she died, leaving unfinished her *Considérations sur la révolution française* (1818), praised by Sainte-Beuve (q.v.) for its literary qualities. Her *Œuvres complètes* are most easily accessible in the Didot edition of 1836. Her autobiographical *Dix ans d'exil* (1821) was republished in a critical edition in 1904. A phenomenon of the age, Madame de Staël is a forerunner of the emancipated woman whom the nineteenth century was to see before its end.

**Stagnelius, Erik Johan** (1793–1823), Swedish dramatist and poet. Born at Gärdelösa, the son of a bishop, he illustrates his country's literary transition from classical to romantic. Stagnelius, by temperament an idealist, suffered almost from a split personality, tormented by sensualism while he sought to rise above it, and the result of this, coupled with drug-taking to which he resorted to avoid the pain caused by heart disease, led him to an originality of style and feeling unmatched in Scandinavian literature. *Bacchanterna* (1822) is a prime example of his work. A modern edition of his *Samlade skrifte* appeared in five volumes in 1911–19. Stagnelius died in Stockholm.

**Steffens, Henrik** (1773–1845), Danish-Norwegian philosopher and literary critic writing also in German, was born at Stavanger. His main importance from the literary point of view is that he introduced the new German romanticism as propounded by Tieck (q.v.) and the Schlegels (qq.v.) to Copenhagen and so to Scandinavia on his return after a stay in Jena in 1802. Oehlenschläger (q.v.) was his first and most important convert. *Über die Idee der Universitäten* (1809) is an interesting commentary by a university professor (Steffens had settled in Germany as one in 1804) on the role of academic life in a changing society and in face of new political ideas. His hefty memoirs, *Was ich erlebte* (10 vols., 1840–5), appeared in English in more reasonable proportions as *The Story of my Career* in 1863. Steffens died in Berlin, where he had been professor since 1832.

**Stendhal,** pseudonym of **Marie-Henri Beyle** (1783–1842), French novelist, short-story writer and critic. Born in Grenoble of well-to-do middle-class parents of remote Italian ancestry, he became a student at the École Polytechnique, Paris, in 1799, but never finished his studies, and entered the army, taking a small part in the second Italian campaign. Resigning his commission, he obtained minor civil office under the Napoleonic regime and in 1812 went to Russia as a secretary to the imperial staff. In 1814 on Napoleon's fall he left for Italy as French consul at Trieste, where he began to write on music and painting (*Les Vies de Haydn, de Mozart et de Métastase*, 1814; Eng. trans. *The Lives of Haydn and Mozart*, 1818; and *L'Histoire de la peinture en Italie*, 1817) and topography (*Rome, Naples et Florence*, 1817; Eng. trans. 1818). Supporting the bid for Italian freedom from Austria, he was forced to leave Trieste in 1821, but remained in Italy in non-Austrian territory and lived by his pen. In *De l'amour* (1822; Eng. trans. *On Love*, 1928) he promises much but accomplishes little, in *Racine et Shakespeare* (1823) he shows that he is well aware of contemporary dramatic criticism, while in *La Vie de Rossini* (1823; Eng. trans. *The Memoirs of Rossini*, 1824) he reveals his affinities with romanticism. But in 1827 he turned to the novel with *Armance* (Eng. trans. 1928), exploiting his egoism and experience to some, if not enough, advantage, showing however that he might well be fit to lead the way in giving a completely new turn to fiction. This expectation was fulfilled in *Le Rouge et le noir* (1830; Eng. trans. *Scarlet and Black*, 1926) in which he intensifies his theme of the rebel hero pitted against the conventions of society. Here excellent characterization, dissection of motive, and splendidly clear and concise prose reveal the absolute master, but the accompanying egoism and cynicism are distasteful. That same year (1830), with the fall of the French Bourbons, Stendhal found his feet in the diplomatic service once more, being appointed consul at Civitavecchia near Rome, at which post he remained until his health failed in 1841 and he returned to Paris to die. During this period besides various topographical works he wrote his masterpiece, *La Chartreuse de Parme* (1839; Eng. trans. *The Charterhouse of Parma*, 1926), a marvellous account of a small reactionary Italian state and the impact on it of Napoleonism. More objective than *Le Rouge et le noir*, characters, descriptions, actions set within an intricate plot, with all the intrigues of a complex and moribund society sharply revealed, Stendhal shows an exquisite sensibility, his style perfectly fitting the context. His other novels, not published till long afterwards, such as *Lamiel* (1889; Eng. trans. 1951), *Lucien Leuwen* (1894; Eng. trans., 2 vols., 1951, i. *The Green Huntsman*, ii. *The Telegraph*) and *La Vie de Henri Brulard* (1894; Eng. trans. 1925) while in no way matching up to this, have interesting qualities. Of short stories Stendhal wrote his fair share, especially worth reading being *L'Abesse de Castro* (1839; enlarged as *Nouvelles inédites*, 1855; Eng. trans. *The Abbess of Castro and other Stories*, 1926). Of literary as well as biographical value is *Souvenirs d'égotisme* (1892; Eng. trans. *Memoirs of an Egoist*, 1949). His *Journal* (5 vols., 1923–34) is a mine of information for the period, and from it various selective translations into English have been made.

**Stepnyak, Sergey,** pseudonym of **S. M. Kravchinsky** (1852–1895), Russian writer. Born in southern Russia, as a young man he became identified with a group of nihilists and in 1874 he was kept under surveillance, which did not, however, prevent him from being suspected as the assassin of Mesentzev, head of the Petersburg police (1878). He later escaped to Geneva and finally settled in London in 1885. His first work, *La Russia sotteranea*, was published in Milan in 1881 (Eng. trans. *Underground Russia*, 1883) and describes the nihilist movement. He thereafter wrote in English a novel, *The Career of a Nihilist* (1889; Russian trans. *Andrey Kozhukhov*, 1898), *Nihilism as it is* (1894), *King Stork and King Log* (1895), a general account of contemporary Russia, and *Russian Wit and Humour* (1895). He was killed by a train in a London suburban station.

**Stern, Daniel,** *see* **Agoult, Marie d'.**

**Stieler, Kaspar** (1632–1707), German poet. A native of Erfurt, where he was born and where he died, he became a soldier, wandered much and finally practised as a lawyer. He is remembered for two very different works, a delightful collection of lyrics, *Die Geharnischte Venus* (1660), taking the pseudonym of 'Filidor der Dorfferer', thus confusing the authorship which has until recently been assigned to others, and the drama *Bellemperie* (1680), founded on the Elizabethan dramatist Thomas Kyd's *Spanish Tragedy*, Bellimperia being the name of the heroine of that work.

**Stifter, Adalbert** (1805–1868), Austrian prose-writer, born at Oberplan in Bohemia, the son of a linen-weaver, he became a law student in Vienna and later an artist of some accomplishment. Later a private tutor in Metternich's household in Vienna, he gained the friendship of Lenau (q.v.) and others in literary circles. Beginning to try his hand as an author, he published *Der Kondor* in 1840, following this up with *Feldblumen* (1841), *Die Mappe meines Urgrossvaters* (1841; Eng.

trans. *Rural Life in Austria and Hungary*, 1850) and *Die Narrenburg* (1843; Eng. trans. in the collection *Pictures of Life* by Mary Howitt, 1847). All these contain quiet and beautifully felicitous descriptions of nature. With *Brigitta* (1844) he began to treat of human character against the background of nature, always choosing humble people, in whom he found the true nobility of life. His *Studien* (6 vols., 1844–1850) especially contain a rich store of all his qualities. Chafing in the end against his somewhat servile position, Stifter accepted an inspectorship of schools at Linz and left Vienna. Soon, however, he regretted his decision, missing his literary life in the provincial town. In this isolation he doggedly continued his work, publishing among other books two of strong emotional feeling, *Der Nachsommer* (3 vols., 1857) and *Witiko* (3 vols., 1865–9). He had been in failing health and deep depression of mind for a long time when he committed suicide at Linz, having realized that he was suffering from cancer.

**Stilling, H.,** *see* **Jung-Stilling, J. H.**

**Stinde, Julius** (1841–1905), German novelist, born at Kirchnüchel in Holstein, made his reputation with his lively and humorous accounts of Berlin family life, inventing for his purpose the Buchholz family. *Buchholzens in Italien* (1883), *Die Familie Buchholz* (3 parts, 1884–6) and *Frau Wilhelmine Buchholz' Memoiren* (1895) have on the whole lasted well. Stinde died at Olsberg, Westphalia.

**Stjernhjelm, Georg,** *see* **Olofson.**

**Stolberg, Christian zu** (1748–1821), German poet. Born in Hamburg, he was educated with his brother Friedrich (q.v.) at the universities of Halle and Göttingen and by 1775 had become a friend of Goethe. From 1777 to 1800 he served in the Holstein public administration. A follower of the *Sturm und Drang* movement, as can be seen from the volume of *Gedichte* which he published with his brother in 1779, he later became a keen advocate of Greek classicism, translating Sophocles (1787). He died at Eckernförde.

**Stolberg, Friedrich Leopold zu** (1750–1819), German poet and prosist, closely associated with his brother (q.v.). Born at Bramstedt, Holstein, he (like his brother) adhered to the *Sturm und Drang* movement, and was in the Holstein public service from 1777 to 1789 and in the diplomatic service from the latter year until 1800, when he retired with his brother. A lover of freedom in early life, his poetry being full of attacks on tyrants, he later became a Roman Catholic and a thorough-paced reactionary. Among his works may be mentioned his novel *Die Insel* (1788) and a travel book, *Reise in Deutschland, der Schweiz, Italien und Sizilien* (1794). He died at Osnabrück.

**Storm, Theodor Woldsen** (1817–1888), German poet and story-writer, was born at Husum, Schleswig, of an old landed family. He went to Kiel University, where he read law and was a fellow student of Theodor Mommsen, later to be the great historian, and his brother, together with them publishing a book of poems, *Ein Liederbuch dreier Freunde*, in 1843. That year he left Kiel and returned to Husum as a lawyer, but almost immediately was exiled since it was in Danish territory and he was associated with the German resistance to Danish rule. At the beginning of his enforced exile, which deeply affected him, he wrote little of importance, and it was not until 1852 that he was revealed as a new figure in the literary world with the publication of both *Immensee* (Eng. trans. 1863), a lovely prose idyll born of longing for the past and his family home, and his emotional lyrics, *Gedichte*. In 1854 appeared *Im Sonnenschein*, a deeply moving prose tale of similar inspiration. The year before he had accepted a good legal post at Potsdam, being later transferred to Heiligenstadt, which he left in 1864—when Prussia went to war with Denmark, as a result of which the greater part of Schleswig, Husum included, became Prussian—to fill the post of judge in his native town, retiring from office in 1880. By this time the sweet resigned sadness of the earlier work had given place to a more realistic approach. Such stories as *Viola Tricolor* (1873) and *Pole Poppenspäler* (1874) mark the transition, and by the time we reach *Psyche* (1877) the change is complete. Sadness has become tragedy and there is a delving into psychology which shows that Storm was aware of modern trends. With *Aquis submersus* (1877; Eng. trans. 1910) he enters on the final stage of his development with its admixture of history. *Renate* (1878), *Carsten Curator* (1878), *Die Söhne des Senators* (1880) and *Eekenhof* (1880; Eng. trans. 1908) show a steady increase in mastery of technique, which continued to the end. *John Riew'* (1886) is impressive and *Der Schimmelreiter* (1888; Eng. trans. *The Rider on the White Horse*, 1915) fittingly crowns his work. He died that year at Hademarschen. His large correspondence, that with Keller (q.v.) and Mörike (q.v.), both kindred spirits, being especially interesting, has been published at various times. The modern selected edition by B. Loets, *Storms Leben in Briefen* (1945) is very useful.

**Strachwitz, Moritz von** (1822–1847), German poet. Born at Peterwitz, Silesia, owing to weak health he spent much time in travel, and while on a journey he died in Vienna. His ballads were particularly admired. A collected edition of his works (*Sämtliche Lieder und Balladen*) appeared in 1912.

**Strauss, Emil** (1866–1960), German playwright and novelist, born at Pforzheim. His most successful plays are *Don Pedro* (1899), *Hochzeit* (1908) and *Vaterland* (1925). Prominent among his novels is *Der nackte Mann* (1912). He died at the advanced age of ninety-four at Freiburg-im-Breisgau.

**Strindberg, Johan August** (1849–1912), Swedish dramatist, novelist and short-story writer. Born in Stockholm, the son of a shipping agent and an ex-waitress, he passed a miserable childhood, and his career at Uppsala University soon ended owing to lack of money. In 1872, having become a master at an elementary school, he wrote a play, *Mäster Olof* (Eng. trans. 1915), influenced by Ibsen (q.v.), which, while a failure, proved his talent and had a great effect on subsequent Swedish drama. A black period followed, during which he felt himself an outcast from society, a state of mind reflected in another play written at this time, *Den Fredlöse* (written 1871; publ. 1880; Eng. trans. *The Outlaw*, 1913). In 1874, however, he fortunately obtained

an assistantship in the royal library, Stockholm, which gave him
time for study and authorship. In 1875 his love affair with Siri, the
wife of Captain Wrangel, began, ending in their marriage, with its
disastrous consequences, in 1877. Meanwhile he had rewritten *Mäster
Olof* in verse (publ. 1878), and in 1879 appeared his first novel, *Röda
Rummet* (Eng. trans. *The Red Room*, 1913), an attack on the seamy
side of Stockholm life. He returned to the drama with *Lycko-Pers
Resa* (1881; publ. 1882; Eng. trans. *Lucky-Peter's Travels*, 1930) and
in 1883 left Sweden for six years. A cynical volume of short stories
on married life, *Giftas* (1884, Eng. trans. *Married*, 1915), led to Strindberg's having to stand trial for an attack on Christianity. His acquittal
was regarded as a triumph for freedom of thought. Strindberg now
displayed signs of mental instability, it taking the form of hatred of
feminism and of Ibsen, whom he considered the leader of the feminist
movement. The novel *Hemsöborna* (1887), a masterly account of
Swedish island life, shows no signs of this, but in the plays *Fadren*
(1887, Eng. trans. *The Father*, 1899) and *Fröken Julie* (1888, Eng.
trans. *Miss Julie*, 1950) he gives full rein to his feelings. His marriage
ended in divorce in 1891, Strindberg accusing his wife of, among
other crimes, lesbianism. Other plays of this period were *Kamraterna*
(1888; Eng. trans. *Comrades*, 1914) and *Paria* (1890; Eng. trans.
*Pariah*, 1913). The autobiographical *Le Plaidoyer d'un fou* (1888, first
publ. in French, with additions, 1893; Eng. trans. *The Confession of
a Fool*, 1912) gives a particularly interesting account of his life down
to the break-up of the marriage. He is unwontedly objective on the
other hand in his novel *I Havsbandet* (1890; Eng. trans. *By the Open
Sea*, 1913). After this highly productive but miserable period, Strindberg in 1892 went to Berlin and there the following year married for
the second time. After a move to Paris this marriage also collapsed,
and out of the state of near-insanity which followed, when he dabbled
in alchemy and began to interest himself in something approaching
Swedenborgianism, grew his *Inferno* (1897; Eng. trans. 1912), a study
of mental abnormality. He returned to Sweden in 1898, began his
religious dramatic trilogy *Till Damaskus* (completed in 1904; Eng.
trans. *To Damascus*, 1913), and turned to historical plays such as
*Folkungasagan* (1899; Eng. trans. *The Saga of the Folkungs*, 1931).
Extraordinary power is revealed in the symbolistic play *Påsk* (1900;
publ. 1901; Eng. trans. *Easter*, 1929). In 1901 he married for the
third time, writing the same year a powerful drama of marriage,
*Dödsdansen* (Eng. trans. *The Dance of Death*, 1949), and following
this up with two volumes of short stories, *Fagervik och Skamsund*
(1902; Eng. trans. *Fair Haven and Foul Strand*, 1913) and *Sagor*
(1903; Eng. trans. *Tales*, 1930), and the delightful autobiography
*Ensam* (1903) with its pleasant tone so often missing in his work.
But his happiness was short-lived, for in 1904 the marriage broke
down, as had the other two. None the less the inspiration aroused by
his late actress-wife continued for a time. He became interested in
new theatrical experiments and wrote several plays in various styles,
including *Brända Tomten* (1907; Eng. trans. *After the Fire*, 1912).
His last years were spent in almost complete seclusion in Stockholm,
where, in a flat which he called 'Blå Tornet' ('The Blue Tower'), he

died of cancer. The greatest man of letters that Sweden has produced, Strindberg's influence on the whole of European drama was immense.

**Strubberg, Friedrich Armand** (1806–1889), German novelist, was born in Cassel. His experiences in the United States (1837–54) provided him with material for his novels which are important as preserving first-hand accounts of earlier days in America. Among them may be mentioned *Scenen aus den Kämpfen der Mexikaner und Nordamerikaner* (1859), *Sklaverei in Amerika oder Schwarzes Blut* (1862) and *Der Krösus von Philadelphia* (1870). He died at Gelnhausen.

**Stuckenberg, Viggo Henrik Fog** (1863–1905), Danish poet and story-writer. Born at Vridsløselille, he became a leading symbolist, the subjects of his quiet, sad poetry being domestic love and nature. Among his volumes of verse are *Digte* (1886), *Den vilde Jæger* (1894) and *Flyvende Sommer* (1898). His best-known book of stories is *Vejbred* (1899; Eng. trans. *By the Wayside*, 1917). He died at Frederiksborg.

**Sturluson, Snorri** (1178–1241), Icelandic poet and saga writer. The son of a chieftain, he was adopted by Jón Loptsson, one of the most important and most cultured men on the island. Sturluson's early marriage to a rich heiress stirred his ambition, and by 1218 when he visited Norway it was almost in the character of uncrowned king of Iceland that he went. Discovering that it was the King of Norway's intention to invade his country, Sturluson became his vassal to win him over, but found it difficult on his return to persuade his fellow chiefs of the wisdom of his move. For nearly twenty years, however, he bore with the difficult situation, until in 1237 he decided on a second mission to Norway. He remained there for two years intriguing with Earl Skúli against King Haakon. Almost immediately after his departure from Norway to Iceland in 1239, Skúli rebelled against the king, and Sturluson's position in Iceland having become desperate, Haakon had no difficulty in having him murdered by his agents. Snorri Sturluson lives as the greatest of all the old Scandinavian writers. He is the author of the prose *Edda*, an account of Icelandic and Norse mythology with rules for Bardic poetry, and also of the *Heimskringla*, a series of sagas on the Norse kings down to 1177, with a life of St Olaf. The *Edda* had been edited by F. Jónsson (1900), the *Heimskringla* by the same editor (4 vols., 1893–1901). Dasent's translation into English of the *Edda* (1842) is good. Among English translations of the *Heimskringla* are those by S. Laing (3 vols., 1844) and by William Morris (2 vols., 1893, third vol. by E. Magnússon, 1905).

**Sudermann, Hermann** (1857–1928), German novelist and dramatist, was born at Matziken, East Prussia, and, after earning his living in a chemist's shop, succeeded in reaching Königsberg University. He obtained a degree and became first a tutor and then a journalist. He won recognition with his novel *Frau Sorge* (1886; Eng. trans. *Dame Care*, 1891, which reached the 125th ed. in 1912), and in 1889 proved himself to be just as at home on the stage with his first play, *Die Ehre* (Eng. trans. *Honour*, 1915). From that time on he was prominent in both fields and exercised an enormous literary influence for a generation or more. Among his many other novels perhaps the most noteworthy are: *Der Katzensteg* (1889; Eng. trans. *Regina*, 1894), two far later works, *Der tolle Professor* (1926; Eng. trans. *The Mad Professor*, 1928) and *Die Frau des Steffen Tromholt* (1927; Eng. trans. *The Wife of Steffen Tromholt*, 1929), which show how well he retained his powers. Prominent among his plays are: *Heimat* (1893; Eng. trans. *Magda*, 1895, 1907, and filmed), *Schmetterlingsschlacht* (1894; Eng. trans. *The Battle of the Butterflies*, 1914), *Die drei Reiherfedern* (1899; Eng. trans. *The Three Heron's Feathers*, 1900) and *Der Bettler von Syrakus* (1911). Sudermann's autobiography appeared in English under the title *The Book of My Youth* in 1924. He died in Berlin.

**Sue, Marie-Joseph-Eugène** (1804–1857), French novelist, born in Paris. He became a surgeon, first in the French army in Spain (1823) and then in the navy, being present at the Battle of Navarino (1828). On leaving the services he took to journalism and wrote for *La Presse*, producing also absurd and sensational novels, such as *La Salamandre* (1832), as well as valueless books on naval history. His experiences as a journalist had meanwhile turned him into a Socialist and he exploited his knowledge of Parisian low life in the notorious *Les Mystères de Paris*, which was first published in the *Journal des Débats* (1842–3). It was widely read, as often as not—as is the case with such books treating of vice and crime—for the wrong reason; but the work had a serious side, for in depicting the underworld of Paris Sue was indicting modern civilization—the first serious impact of the industrial revolution in France began to be felt at this time— as responsible for driving its victims to crime. Sensationalism apart, the work evoked the atmosphere of the reverse side of the romantic age; the dark, ugly, cruel and twisted appear in a starkly modern guise, and a general malaise is laid bare in a manner unattempted by writers of even ten years before. His *Le Juif errant* (1844–5), another serial, was an equally sensational anticlerical piece of fiction and was also immensely successful. Other works were *Martin, l'enfant trouvé* (1846), *Les Sept Péchés capitaux* (1847–9) and *Les Mystères du peuple* (1849), which last was condemned by the courts as seditious. Sue entered politics at the revolution of 1848, and in 1850 was elected a republican deputy for the Seine department, but was unseated and driven into exile on Louis Napoleon's *coup d'état* in 1851. He died at Annecy, Savoy, then independent of France.

**Sukhovo-Kobylin, Alexander Vasilyevich** (1817–1903), Russian playwright, born in Moscow. He is the author of a gay trilogy, the first part appearing in 1855 and the second and third in 1869 (mod. coll. ed., *Trilogiya*, 1927), which, thanks to mastery of stagecraft and clarity of plot, still keeps the Russian stage today. He died in Moscow.

**Sully Prudhomme**, pseudonym of René François Armand Prudhomme (1839–1907), French poet, essayist and translator, was born in Paris and gave up science for a literary career. His first considerable volume of verse, *Stances et poèmes* (1865) was clearly influenced by Leconte de Lisle (q.v.) and the Parnassians, but by 1869 when *Les*

*Solitudes* was published he had dissociated himself from that school both in style (short, concise lyrics), in manner (symbolism) and in thought (philosophic and didactic). Introspection and nobility of ideas, grace and tenderness are the hallmarks of such poetry as *Les Destins* (1872), *La Justice* (1878) and *Le Bonheur* (1888). His excellent metrical translation of the first book of *De Natura Rerum* of Lucretius, *De la nature des choses*, appeared in 1869, and his collections of essays include *Testament poétique* (1901) and *La Vraie Religion selon Pascal* (1905). He received the Nobel Prize for literature in 1901. Almost incapacitated by paralysis in his last years, he died at Châtenay.

**Supervielle, Jules** (1884–1960), French poet, novelist and playwright, was born in Montevideo but educated in Paris. His symbolistic poetry is to be found in the earlier volumes such as *Les Poèmes de l'amour triste* (1919). With *Gravitations* (1925) he showed a complete change of manner, wistful, tender and very personal, which he continued to display in such books of verse as *Les Amis inconnus* (1934) and *La Fable du monde* (1938). During the war he was in self-imposed exile in Uruguay where he wrote the very moving *Poèmes de la France malheureuse* (1939–40). In his novels and collections of short stories he shows how, like W. de la Mare, though without his hidden terrors, he can so easily enter a child's world. Such are *L'Enfant de la haute mer* (1931), *L'Arche de Noé* (1938), and *Premier pas de l'univers* (1950). Of his plays those with the same streak of fantasy are the most successful, such as *Schéhérazade* (1939) and *Le Voleur d'enfants* (1949). He died in Paris.

**Suttner, Bertha von** (1843–1914), Austrian novelist, born in Prague, made a sensation with her strong pacifist work of fiction *Die Waffen nieder* (1889; Eng. trans. *Lay Down your Arms*, 1892). Alfred Nobel, the armaments king, was so struck with it that he decided to set up his Peace Prize. Bertha von Suttner was the first recipient. She died in Vienna.

**Svensson, Jón Stefán** (1857–1944), Icelandic writer of children's books. Born at Hörgárðalur, he was given a splendid education in France at the expense of Roman Catholic missionaries, finally taking up a teaching career in Denmark. From 1912 onwards he wrote in German a long series of adventure stories centred upon a boy called Nonni, inspired by memories of his youth in Iceland. They were extensively translated and read. Examples are: *Nonni und Manni* (1914; Eng. trans. *Lost in the Arctic*, 1927), *Die Feuerinsel im Nordmeer* (1933) and *Nonni erzählt* (1936). Svensson died in Cologne.

**Svevo, Italo,** pseudonym of **Ettore Schmitz** (1861–1928), Italian novelist. Born in Trieste, he became a friend of young James Joyce when the latter set up as a private tutor at Trieste and had him for a pupil for English lessons. It was Joyce who introduced him to French critics and in this way his much-neglected work came to the light. His best-known books, in which he is chiefly concerned with the mental process of facing a situation, are *Senilità* (1898; Eng. trans. *As a Man Grows Older*, 1932), *La coscienza di Zeno* (1923; Eng. trans. *Confessions of*

*Zeno*, 1930) and *La novella del buon vecchio e la bella fanciulla* (1930; Eng. trans. *The Nice Old Man and the Pretty Girl*, 1930). Svevo died at Motta di Livenza two years before the publication of this last work.

**Swedenborg, Emanuel** (1688–1772), Swedish Latin prose-writer, scientist and mystic. The son of Jesper Swedberg, Bishop of Skara and professor of theology at Uppsala, he was born near Falun. Young Swedberg—he did not change his name to Swedenborg, the province in which his father's diocese lay, until he was granted a pension and an estate in 1719—went to the University of Uppsala and after the completion of his studies there travelled in Britain, France and the United Provinces. His scientific training now complete, he accepted an excellent post in the Swedish department of mines in 1716, and for many years devoted himself to his official work in engineering and mineralogy. His drift away from the scientific to religious matters is first to be seen in his *Opera philosophica et mineralia* (1734), in which he discusses his theory of the constitution of matter, far in advance of the time. Soon afterwards he began anatomical researches in an endeavour satisfactorily to explain the relationship between soul and body, and his failure to do so led to a fundamental change of views. In 1743 he had some striking religious experience which ended in his declaring that he had received insight into the spiritual world, and he gave up his official post in 1747. His main works in which he propounds his ideas are *Arcana Cœlestia* (1756) and *Doctrina Vitae pro Nova Hierosolyma* (1763). All his religious works were collected under the title of *Urval av Swedenborgs religiösa skrifter* in 1925 with Latin texts and Swedish translations. All his main books were translated into English at various times by the Swedenborg Society, founded in 1810. He died in London. He himself had nothing to do with the foundation of the Church named after him.

**Sylva, Carmen,** *see* **Carmen Sylva.**

# T

**Taine, Hippolyte Adolphe** (1828–1893), French prose-writer, was born at Vouziers in the Ardennes and was educated at Paris. With his study of La Fontaine (q.v.), later expanded into a book, *La Fontaine et ses fables* (1860), he gained his *doctorat-ès-lettres*, and with his *Essai sur Tite Live*, a treatise on Livy not published until 1856, he won an Academy prize. In the following years he made a name for himself with *Les Philosophes classiques du XIXᵉ siècle en France* (1857), *L'Histoire de la littérature anglaise* (5 vols., 1864–9; Eng. trans. 1872–4) and *La Philosophie de l'art* (1865). In all these works and in his *Théorie de l'intelligence* (2 vols., 1870) he argues for the determinist point of view in opposition to the romantic school. His doctrine of racial and environmental influence on history, literature and the arts greatly appealed to the realist school of his day. His crowning achievement, to complete which he resigned in 1884 the chair at the École des Beaux Arts which he had occupied for twenty years, and which was still unfinished at his death, was *Les Origines de la France contemporaine*. It appeared between 1875 and 1894 (Part I, *L'Ancien Régime*, 1875; II, *La Révolution*, 1878–85; and III, the unfinished *Le Régime moderne*, 1890–4). Inspired to a large extent by the disaster of the Franco-Prussian war, it is pessimistic throughout, and in an age of brash optimism showed that though scientific discovery must be pursued it would come to little good seeing that man is the beast he is. Taine died in Paris.

**Tamayo y Baus, Manuel** (1829–1898), Spanish playwright, born in Madrid. One of the most cosmopolitan Spanish literary men of his generation, his profound knowledge of the French, Italian and German stages led him to success in his earlier historical plays, but it was Shakespeare and the Elizabethans who inspired his masterpiece, *Un drama nuevo* (1867; Eng. trans. *A New Drama*, 1915). He died in Madrid, permanent secretary of the Royal Academy.

**Tarasov-Rodionov, Alexander Ignatyevich** (1888–1930?), Russian Soviet novelist. He made a name for himself, though a Communist, with his outspoken attack on the regime in *Shokolad* (1922; Eng. trans. *Chocolate*, 1933). With *Fevral' 1917* (1928; Eng. trans. *February 1917*, 1931) he started out on what was to have been a panoramic novel of the revolution, but he seems to have fallen foul of authority and he vanished completely.

**Tardiveau, R.,** *see* **Boylesve, R.**

**Tasso, Torquato** (1544–1595), Italian poet. Born at Sorrento, the son of Bernardo Tasso, a poet himself and holding high office at various courts, he was educated in Naples by the Jesuits. In 1557 father and son went to Urbino, where Torquato grew up in the congenial atmosphere of the court until he went to Padua to study law. His time there, however, was spent in writing the epic poem *Rinaldo*, which when published in 1562 made his reputation. The turning point in his life came in 1565, when he was given a post in the household of Cardinal Luigi d'Este at Ferrara, and this led to his being nominated court poet to the cardinal's brother, Alfonso II, Duke of Ferrara in 1571. Two years later he had completed his most charming work, the pastoral idyll *Aminta* (publ. 1580), in its way the most perfect work since classical times, and in 1575 he finished his best known composition the *Gerusalemme Liberata*, an epic on the first crusade and the capture of Jerusalem by Godefroi de Bouillon (first authorized ed. 1581). Troubled by the pedantic criticisms of his work, religious scruples and (it is said) a hopeless love for the cardinal's sister Leonora d'Este, Tasso was overtaken by an attack of madness and was placed in confinement (1577), from which he escaped to his family at Sorrento. But in 1579 he was back in Ferrara, where he was almost immediately placed in a mental hospital, remaining there until 1586 although very well treated. On being freed he wandered about Italy, welcomed everywhere but happy nowhere, finally settling in Rome under papal protection. Here he set to work to remodel his *Gerusalemme* to conform to the criticism of the academies, and the unhappy result, *Gerusalemme Conquistata*, was published in 1593. Second-rate poetry and the failure of a tragedy, *Re Torrismondo* (1587), belong also to this later period. Made Poet Laureate, given other honours and an excellent pension (1594) it was too late for him to enjoy anything, and Tasso died insane at the monastery of St Onofrio, Rome. Tasso's influence on European opera and the epic was enormous, and *Aminta* and *Gerusalemme Liberata* are among the greatest poetical works of sixteenth-century Europe. There is a delightful English translation of *Aminta* by A. Fraunce (1591). As for *Gerusalemme Liberata*, apart from the classic but hardly accurate one by Fairfax (1600), the best is by J. H. Wiffen (1830). There is a mannered translation of *Rinaldo*, from which work a libretto was earlier produced for Handel, by J. Hoole, a member of Samuel Johnson's circle, in 1792.

**Tassoni, Alessandro** (1565–1635), Italian poet, a native of Modena, where he died. He spent his life in political service at various courts and was a ready critic of everyone and everything he came into contact with. He wrote much, but his only lasting work is his famous comic poem in heroic style, *La Secchia Rapita* (1622; Eng. trans. *La Secchia Rapita, or The Rape of the Bucket*, 1825), in reality a veiled satire on the follies of men.

**Tecchi, Bonaventura** (1896–    ), Italian novelist, was born at Bagnoregio, and wrote realistic novels with a firm grasp of characters and motives such as *Giovanni amici* (1940) and *L'isola appassionata* (1945).

**Tedaldi, Pieraccio** (1290?–1350?), Italian poet. A Florentine merchant, never happy and always wandering, he has left a clear portrait of himself in just over forty sonnets, some of them surprisingly gay. He died in Florence. See *Le Rime de P. Tedaldi* (1885).

**Tegnér, Esaias** (1782–1846), Swedish poet and novelist, was born the son of the pastor there at Kyrkerud, Vermland. His father's early death forced him at the age of eleven to decide on a livelihood, but friends appeared and helped him on his way, and he matriculated at Lund University in 1799. A brilliant academic career now opened, and in 1812 he became professor of Greek at Lund, having been ordained two years before. He was already regarded as an outstanding poet thanks to his stirring nationalistic poem *Krigssång för skånska lantvärnet* (1808). The quality of his verse increased still more in *Sång till solen* (1813), while religious experience is the keynote of the often lovely *Nattvardsbarnen* (1820; Eng. trans. by Longfellow, entitled *The Children of the Lord's Supper*, 1842). His love for the academic life of Lund is to be seen in *Epilog vid magisterpromotionen* (1820). Tegnér remained in Lund until 1826, two years after his appointment as Bishop of Växjö, where he now took up residence. He had brought the main part of his poetic career to a brilliant end with *Frithiofs Saga* (1825; Eng. trans. 1833). He died still Bishop of Växjö, though his mental powers had been greatly impaired since 1840, at Östrabo.

**Telesio, Antonio** (1482–1534), Italian poet and prose-writer in Latin, was a native of Cosenza. None of his works were written in the vernacular, and he used the latinized form of his name **Thylesius**. Professor of Latin at the University of Rome, he fled to Venice after the siege of 1527 and it was there that he wrote one of the finest Latin tragedies of the Renaissance, *Imber Aureus* (1529). His graceful lyrics in Horatian style were also celebrated, being published as *Antonii Thylesii Consentini Poemata* (1524). The first complete edition of his works dates from 1762. Telesio held official posts in Venice, but resigned them to return to Cosenza, where he died.

**Tencin, Claudine Alexandrine Guérin de** (1681–1749), French novelist. Born at Grenoble, she became a nun, but was allowed to renounce her vows and arrived in Paris in 1714 just in time for the Regency in which she was to play so great a social part. By 1716 her *salon* had become the most famous in Paris. Brilliant but unprincipled, she had among many lovers the Regent Orléans himself, Cardinal Dubois and Fontenelle (q.v.). D'Alembert (q.v.) was one of her natural children. Among her historical romances, which have an unusual power, especially in conveying a sense of fear of danger and an essential gloom, are *Mémoires du Comte de Comminges* (1735) and *Le Siège de Calais* (1739). *Les Malheurs de l'amour* (1747) is more personal. She died in Paris.

**Teodorescu, Dimitrie** (1892–      ), Rumanian novelist, who wrote social satires, among them *Robul* (1936; Eng. trans. *One House Contains Us*, 1939).

**Teresa de Jesús**, real name **Teresa Sánchez de Cepeda** (1515–1582), Spanish mystical writer, was born of mixed Jewish and Christian parentage at Ávila and entered a Carmelite convent in 1534, experienced a spiritual conversion in 1555, and in 1562 founded a reformed Carmelite convent at Ávila dedicated to St Joseph. Strongly opposed by ecclesiastical dignitaries, she none the less persisted in her reforms, aided by Philip II and leading laymen, as also by Juan de la Cruz (q.v.). A woman of extraordinary spiritual gifts and at the same time having a keen practical sense, her devotional works without being in any way remarkable for style are great by reason of their power to carry to the general reader the idea of the mystic life, rarely experienced and, even if experienced, seldom conveyed so clearly to others. Of her works, none of which were published in her lifetime, the most celebrated are her 'spiritual autobiography', *El libro de su vida*, *El camino de perfección*, a guide to her nuns, *Las moradas*, a mystical handbook, and *El libro de las fundaciones*, dealing energetically with the opposition she had to overcome in founding her reformed convents. A complete English translation appeared in 1946 made by E. A. Peers, who also translated her *Letters* (1951). Teresa died at Alba de Tormes, and was canonized in 1622.

**Testi, Fulvio** (1593–1646), Italian poet. Born in Ferrara, he took service under the Este family, plotted with agents of Savoy against it and died in prison at Modena. His love of the classics saved him from many of the extravagances of his contemporaries, and he was capable of achieving a majestic style, especially when inspired by patriotism. He published five volumes of poetry in his lifetime, and his poetic works were collected in 1653.

**Teternikov, F. K.,** *see* **Sologub, F.**

**Tetmajer, Kazimierz Przerwa** (1865–1940), Polish novelist and short-story writer. Born at Ludzimierz, he led a sheltered, even pampered life and died in Warsaw as a result of privations caused by the German invasion. As a short-story writer he is best represented by *Ksiądz Piotr* (1894; Eng. trans. *Father Peter* in 'Slavonic and East European Review', xvi, 1938) and *Na Skalnym Podhalu* (7 parts, 1903–12; Eng. trans. *Tales of the Tatras*, 1941). Of his novels *Anioł śmierci* (2 vols., 1898; It. trans. *L'angelo della morte*, 1930) is perhaps the best known.

**Tharaud, Jérôme** (1874–1953) and **Tharaud, Jean** (1877–1952), French novelists and short-story writers who collaborated as J.-J. Tharaud in many books with fast-moving plots and atmosphere and colour. Among them may be mentioned *Rabat* (1918) and *Marrakech* (1920), set in Morocco, *La Rose de Saron* (1927) and *Les Bien-aimées* (1932). Both brothers were born at Saint-Junien, but Jérôme, whose real Christian name was Ernest, died at Varengeville, while Jean, in reality Charles, died in Paris.

**Thoma, Ludwig** (1867–1921), German short-story writer and playwright. Born at Oberammergau, he became editor of that famous vehicle for social and political satire, the journal *Simplizissimus*. His collections of short stories included *Assessor Karlchen* (1900) and

*Tante Frieda* (1907), and among his comedies was *Moral* (1909; Eng. trans. *Morality*, 1909). His collected works appeared in 1922, the year after his death at Rottach.

**Thomasius, Christian** (1655–1728), German prose-writer, was born in Leipzig and on the foundation of the University of Halle in 1694 became its first professor of jurisprudence. One of the leaders of the new ideas which eventually ushered in the Enlightenment, he broke with tradition in lecturing in the vernacular instead of Latin, while he brought a commanding personality to oppose witchcraft trials and torture. His wide-ranging ideas are to be found in his sturdy *Gedanken und Erinnerungen* (1723–6). He died in Halle.

**Thoroddsen, Jón Thórðarson** (1819–1868), Icelandic novelist, the father of the novel of his country, is best known for *Piltur og stúlka* (1850; Eng. trans. *Lad and Lass*, 1890) which follows very much in the Walter Scott manner. Born at Barðaströnd, he died at Leirá.

**Thorsteinsson, Steingrímur** (1831–1913), Icelandic poet and translator. Born at Arnarstapi, the son of a provincial governor, he went to the University of Copenhagen, and remained in Denmark until 1872. He wrote much poetry, of which *Gilsbakka-ljóð* (1877; Eng. trans. *A Glenside Lay*, 1920) is a fair example; but it is as the introducer by translation of many European classics into Iceland, thereby deeply affecting its literature, that he is likely to be best remembered. He died in Reykjavík.

**Thümmel, Moritz August von** (1738–1817), German poet and novelist, was born at Schönefeld, near Leipzig, and became a Coburg government official, retiring in 1783, after which he travelled widely. Often described as the German Sterne, the blending of the wayward and the near-sensual as in the latter's work is to be found both in his novel *Wilhelmine* (1764) and in his book of poetry *Die Inokulation der Liebe* (1771). He died at Coburg.

**Tieck, Ludwig** (1773–1853), German man of letters, born in Berlin. An author in many fields, after becoming a literary journalist and writing for J. C. F. Nicolai's (q.v.) periodical *Straussfedern* in 1794, he completed a novel in English style, *Geschichte des Herrn William Lovell* (1796), which has some power, and then joined forces with W. H. Wackenroder (q.v.), helping him to write, and after his death completing *Herzensergiessungen eines kunstliebenden Klosterbruders* (1797). His interest in the medievalism of romanticism is shown in *Der blonde Eckbert* (1796), while folk tales as another vehicle for romanticism engaged him in *Peter Lebrechts Volksmärchen* (1797; enlarged and revised as *Phantasus*, 3 vols., 1812–17; Eng. trans. 1845, some of these having been trans. by T. Carlyle in 1827). *Franz Sternbalds Wanderungen* (2 vols., 1798) is a romantic projection of himself. Tieck next gained the friendship of the brothers Schlegel (qq.v.) and Novalis (q.v.) and was established in Jena by 1799. He tried his hand at poetic drama in *Genoveva* (1799), later an inspiration to the composer Robert Schumann, a style which was continued in *Kaiser Oktavianus* (1804), one of his most satisfying works artistically. One of the editors of Novalis's works (1802) he began to move away from original writing to literary criticism, making a valuable collection of ancient poetry in *Minnelieder aus dem Schwäbischen Zeitalter* (1803) and translating old English plays (*Altenglisches Theater*, 1811). A Shakespearian scholar, Tieck aided A. W. Schlegel in his magnificent translation of Shakespeare's works, brought out a series of essays, *Shakespeares Vorschule* (1823–9), and wrote a novel on Shakespeare's life, *Dichterleben* (1826). He had moved to Dresden in 1819, and remained there until 1842, when he returned to Berlin, where he died. The Dresden period is interesting as marking Tieck's return to original work, and he may be said to have considerably developed the art of the historical novel as, for example, in *Der Aufruhr in den Cevennen* (1826; Eng. trans. *The Rebellion in the Cevennes*, 1845).

**Timmermans, Felix** (1886–1947), Flemish novelist, born at Lier. An accomplished painter as well as writer, his literary career becomes important with the publication of his novel *Palleter* (1916; Eng. trans. 1924), in which the hero Palletier is studied in his relationship with God and nature. In his later work, such as in the novels *De harp van Sint-Franciscus* (1932; Eng. trans. *The Harp of Saint Francis*, 1949) and *Boerenpsalm* (1935; Fr. trans. *Psaume paysan*, 1942) a deeply religious concept of life is apparent. The fine arts as an ally of religion, or as a manifestation of it, is the keynote of such a novel as *Pieter Bruegel* (1928; Eng. trans. *Droll Peter*, 1930) and of the collection of short stories *Driekoningen-tryptiek* (1923; Eng. trans. *The Triptych of the Three Kings*, 1936). Timmermans died at Lier.

**Tinayre, Marguerite Suzanne Marcelle** (1872–1948), French novelist. Born at Tulle, Corrèze, she married the engraver Jules Tinayre. An apostle of women's emancipation, her witty novels are often vehicles for such beliefs. Among them are: *Avant l'amour* (1897), *Hellé* (1899), which was crowned by the French Academy, *La Rebelle* (1906), *L'Ombre de l'amour* (1910; Eng. trans. *Shadow of Love*, 1911), *Madeleine au miroir* (1912; Eng. trans. *Madeleine*, 1913) and *Sacrifice* (1916). She also wrote biographies such as *Madame de Pompadour* (1925) and travel books like *Terres étrangères* (1928). Mme Tinayre died at Grosrouvre (Seine-et-Oise).

**Tirso de Molina,** *see* **Molina.**

**Toller, Ernst** (1893–1939), German dramatist and poet, was born at Samotschin. His experiences during the First World War drove him far to the left in politics and led him to join the attempted Communist rebellion in Munich in 1919. Imprisoned for a time, on his release he became known as a powerful dramatist, revolutionary in ideas and technique, with *Masse Mensch* (1921; Eng. trans. *Man and the Masses*, 1924). Another side of him was revealed in his poetry such as *Das Schwalbenbuch* (1923; Eng. trans. *The Swallow-Book*, 1924). Other plays which had a profound effect on public opinion not only in Germany but in other parts of Europe also, especially Russia, were: *Die Maschinenstürmer* (1922; Eng. trans. *The Machine-Wreckers*, 1923), *Hinkemann* (1924; Eng. trans. *Brokenbrow*, 1926), and *Hoppla, wir leben!* (1927; Eng. trans. *Hoppla!*, 1928), which was performed in London. He attacked the Nazis and issued a warning on what would happen if they came to power in *Nationalsozialismus* (1930). When his worst fears were realized in 1933 he came to Britain, where he wrote *Eine Jugend in Deutschland* (1934; Eng. trans. *I Was a German*, 1934). He committed suicide in New York three and a half months before the outbreak of war.

**Tolstoy, Alexey Konstantinovich** (1817–1875), Russian writer, born in Petersburg. A distant relative of the great Tolstoy (q.v.), he is remembered as the author of the dramatic historical trilogy (*Dramaticheskaya trilogiya*) consisting of *Smert' Ivana Groznogo* (1866; Eng. trans. *The Death of Ivan the Terrible*, 1869, 1926 and 1933), *Tsar Fedor* (1868; Eng. trans. *Czar Fyodor Ivanovich*, 1923 and 1924) and *Tsar Boris* (1870). All these are in blank verse. He also wrote an historical novel, *Knyaz Serebryany* (1873; Eng. trans. *Prince Serebrenni*, 1874, *Prince Serebryani*, 1892, *A Prince of Outlaws*, 1927). Count Tolstoy died in Petersburg.

**Tolstoy, Alexey Nikolayevich** (1883–1945), Russian Soviet novelist. A member of the famous noble family, he left Russia at the revolution, but came to terms with the new order in 1923 and settled in Moscow, where he remained for the rest of his life. Two years before his return he had published a series of delicate sketches dealing with his childhood, *Detstvo Nikity* (Eng. trans. *Nikita's Childhood*, 1945), and had begun his trilogy of the last days of czardom, revolution, and the new age of Lenin, *Khozhdenie po mukam*, completed in 1941 (part trans. into Eng. as *Imperial Majesty*, 1932). Noteworthy also is the historical novel *Pyotr I* (i, 1929; ii, 1933; iii, 1945; Eng. trans. i and ii as *Peter the Great*, 1936).

**Tolstoy, Lev Nikolayevich** (1828–1910), Russian writer, was born on the family estate of Yasnaya Polyana, province of Tula. The family was prosperous and had been ennobled by Peter the Great. Young Tolstoy was at first educated at home and then sent to the universities of Moscow and Kazan, but in 1847 returned to Yasnaya. His father had been dead for some years, and, although the fourth son, the burden of the administration of the property fell on him. As yet he felt no interest in the life of a country landowner and went to Moscow, where he ran through all the pleasures of the city. In 1851, however, he suddenly renounced his aimlessness and enlisted in the army of the Caucasus, where he came face to face with the primitive Cossacks. Already his conscience was stirring, and in a longing to learn to know himself in order to make himself ready to get to grips with the fundamental problems of life and death he began in 1852 his autobiographical trilogy with *Detstvo* ('Childhood'). Drafted to the Crimea, he was present at the fall of Sebastopol (1855), but retired from the army shortly afterwards. A novel, *Kazaki* ('The Cossacks'), not published until 1862, notably sums up that period of his career. He now spent some years in Petersburg society, being to a fair extent lionized; but tiring of it all he retired to Yasnaya Polyana and married. His marriage was a great success, he became a model landlord, and in peace and prosperity he began his great novel, *Voyna i*

*mir* (1862–9, 'War and Peace'), one of the most magnificently conceived and executed works of fiction of all time. This story of Russia
and the Napoleonic war is panoramic, and the power of analysis when
dealing with character which Tolstoy shows is astonishing. The
subjectivity of his earlier work has given place to a clear narrative
from which the author has all but excluded himself, although on
closer inspection one realizes that the restless longing for the unobtainable which governs the actions of his main character is his
own. In 1875 he began the second of his greatest works, *Anna
Karenina*, completed two years later. He is still objective enough in
his approach to produce a perfect work of art, but Levin, the squire
with his longing to explain to himself the riddle of life, which unsolved
makes meaningless all the material comfort surrounding him, is more
stridently himself. After *Anna* Tolstoy's yearning was too strong to
allow him to continue in this style. In order to save himself from his
doubts he divested himself of all his former beliefs and manner
of living. Dressed as a peasant, a vegetarian, rejecting orthodox
Christianity, honouring the simplicity of peasant life as a means of
grace, Tolstoy was reborn. In fine prose he describes the change in
*Ispoved'* ('Confession'), written in 1878, but not published until 1882.
Although all his energies were now directed to new ethical ends and
much of his work from the literary point of view suffered accordingly,
he yet produced some books of an almost classical restraint. Among
them are *Smert' Ivana Ilyicha* (1884, 'The Death of Ivan Ilyich'),
*Khozyain i rabotnik* (1895, 'Master and Man') and *Hadji Murad*
(1901), which harks back to the ineffaceable memory of the Caucasus
experience of his youth. *Voskresenie* (1899–1900, 'Resurrection'),
with its rather disconcertingly opposed elements of artist and teacher
showing through, reverts to the older style, but not, one feels,
enough. For an end, that of spiritual certainty, which Tolstoy judged
to be of far more value than the artistry of this world, he deprived us
of many works which he could otherwise have written; but he has left
enough to be considered one of the great writers of modern times,
while his courage in creating a new faith out of despair is an inspiration to others. Tolstoy's family life had become unbearable by reason
of his beliefs, which his wife could not understand, and taking his
youngest daughter Alexandra, his only confidante, with him, he
escaped from home in October 1910. Taken ill at the little railway
station of Astapovo in central Russia, he died in the stationmaster's
room early in November. There is a complete English translation of
his works by A. and L. Maude (21 vols., 1928–37), and known as the
'Centenary Edition'. The most accessible Russian edition is that of
1948.

**Tomasi di Lampedusa, Giuseppe** (1896–1957), Italian prose-writer.
Born in Palermo of noble Sicilian family (he was Prince of Lampedusa), he took part in the First World War, but later became an
opponent of Fascism and travelled widely. He served in the artillery
during the Second World War. His palace in Palermo was destroyed
during the bombardment preceding the allied landing. He had for a
considerable time taken an interest in literature and after the war

frequented many literary gatherings. According to his wife he had had a book in mind for over twenty years before committing to paper in 1955–6 what was published after his death as *Il gattopardo* (1958; Eng. trans. *The Leopard*, 1960). This is a great saga of Sicily and especially the Sicilian aristocracy from 1860 to the end of the century, confronted by the new kingdom. Tomasi's minor writings were published as *Racconti* (1961). He died in Palermo.

**Tommaseo, Niccolò** (1802–1874), Italian poet and novelist, born in Dalmatia. Starting off as a pedant who attacked Leopardi (q.v.) for not writing pure Tuscan, thus harking back to the quarrels of the eighteenth-century academies, he proved with his verse tale *Una serva* (1837) that he was himself capable of good performance. In *Fede e bellezza* (1840) he produced a novel of excellent style, startlingly sensual and of great power. In 1848 he entered politics for a short time and settled in Florence. Totally blind by 1850, he was nothing daunted and set about his *Dizionario della lingua italiana*, which he had completed at his death, although the seventh and final volume did not appear until 1879. His influence on his friend Manzoni (q.v.) was great. He died in Florence.

**Topelius, Zachris** (1818–1898), Swedish-Finnish novelist and miscellaneous writer, was born at Kuddnäsi. He followed an academic career and was professor of history at the University of Helsingfors (Helsinki), 1853–78. Probably his best-known work is the long series of stories which appeared under the general title of *Fältskärns berättelser* (1853–67; Eng. trans. *The Surgeon's Stories*, 1872–84). He excelled also as a writer of children's books, as in *Läsning för barn*, another long series completed in 1896 (Eng. trans. *Fairy Tales from Finland*, 1896). He died in Helsinki.

**Töpffer, Rodolphe** (1799–1846), Swiss novelist and short-story writer. Born in Geneva, he started on an art career but had to abandon it because of bad sight, and founded an international boys' school, a pioneer in this field. His accounts of school excursions in the Alps are hardly literature, but his novel *Le Presbytère* (2 vols., 1839) and the collections of short stories, *La Bibliothèque de mon oncle* (1832) and *Nouvelles génevoises* (1841), have a flavour all their own. Töpffer died in Geneva.

**Torga, Miguel**, pseudonym of **Adolfo Correia da Rocha** (1907–    ), Portuguese short-story writer. Born at San Martinho de Anta, he is best known for his stories of regional life in the north-east of Portugal, such as *Montanha* (1941) and *Vindima* (1945), the first dealing with the highland country, the second with the Douro valley.

**Tormay, Cécile** (1876–1937), Hungarian novelist, born in Budapest. She had great success with her historical novels, such as *Emberek a kövek között* (1911; Eng. trans. *Stonecrop*, 1922) and *A régi ház* (1915; Eng. trans. *The Old House*, 1921). In a different style is *Bújdosó könyv* (2 vols., 1921–2; Eng. trans. *An Outlaw's Diary*, 1923). She died at Mátraháza.

**Torres Villarroel, Diego de** (1693–1770), Spanish prose-writer. Born in Salamanca, where later he became professor of mathematics, he led an unbalanced life of violence and superstition with half-crazy dabblings in the occult and alchemy, dying in the odour of sanctity as a member of a religious order, a character in fact just suited to the part of a hero fit for the general run of Spaniards. Two only of his works are worthy of comment, but these, *Sueños* (1743), a brilliant account of contemporary life in Madrid, and *Vida del doctor don Diego de Torres Villarroel, escrita por él mismo* (1743–58), one of the most remarkable autobiographies in literature, entitle him to a place in any literary history. Torres died in Salamanca, where his magnificent palace is still to be seen almost unchanged since his day.

**Toulet, Paul Jean** (1867–1920), French poet and novelist, born in Pau. His technically arresting poems, *Les Contrerimes*, appeared the year after his death, long after he had made a reputation with his cleverly constructed and telling society novels, such as *Le Mariage de Don Quichotte* (1901) and *Les Tendres Ménages* (1904). *La Jeune Fille verte* (1920) exemplifies the style of his later fiction. He died at Guéthary.

**Trakl, Georg** (1887–1914), Austrian poet. Born in Salzburg, he was a pronounced neurotic unable to face life without drugging himself. Ironically qualifying as a pharmaceutical chemist, he spent his spare time in a weird half-bemused world of terrible phantoms which was the inspiration for his macabre verse of death and decomposition. If there is any beauty in decay, like the hectic colours of some fungi, then Trakl has discovered it. Otherwise his work must surely be considered decadent and negative. Conscripted in 1914 and sent to the Galician front, he took his drugs with him and died of an overdose in hospital at Cracow. The definitive edition of his works was published in 1949. Some of his poems appeared in English translation as *Decline: Twelve Poems by Georg Trakl* (1952).

**Tranquilli, Secondo,** *see* **Silone, Ignazio.**

**Trenyev, Konstantin Andreyevich** (1878–1945), Russian Soviet short-story writer born in Kharkov, whose tales from various sources were collected in an edition translated into English as *In a Cossack Village* (1946). He died in Moscow.

**Trigo, Felipe** (1865–1915), Spanish novelist, born at Villanueva, near Badajoz. The leading example in Spain of French naturalism, his erotic novels, such as *La ingenua* (1901), *La bruta* (1904), *Sor demonio* (1908) and *La clave* (1910), sometimes stand on the borderline of pornography, though a probable moral purpose has been urged in extenuation of it. He died in Madrid.

**Triolet, Elsa** (1896–     ), French novelist of Russian origin, was born in Moscow. The sister-in-law of Mayakovsky (q.v.) and the wife of Louis Aragon (q.v.), she has written many works of fiction of good quality: *Bonsoir Thérèse* (1938), *Mille Regrets* (1941), *Le Cheval blanc* (1942), *Le Premier Accroc coûte deux cents francs* (1944), her best work, *Le Cheval roux* (1953), *Le Monument* (1957), and the trilogy, *L'Âge de nylon,* consisting of *Roses à crédit* (1959), *Les Manigances* (1962) and *L'Âme* (1963).

**Tristan L'Hermite,** pseudonym of **François L'Hermite** (1601–1655),

French poet, dramatist and novelist. Born at Solier, the ancestral estate, he led a roving life and was chronically short of money. His love-poetry in the Italian manner includes such volumes as *La Lyre* (1641), and another style is to be found in *Vers héroïques* (1648). He drifted to Paris about 1636 and earned his living by writing for the stage, classical tragedy being his forte. *La Morte de Sénèque* (1643) and *Osman* (1646) are fair specimens of this kind. *Le Parasite* (1653) is a comedy. *Le Page disgracié* (1643) is an autobiographical novel. He died in Paris.

**Trueba y Cossío, Joaquín Telesforo de** (1798–1835), Anglo-Spanish novelist and dramatist. Born in Santander, but educated in England, he became a member of the diplomatic corps in London and Paris before returning in 1822 to Spain, where he made a name for himself with his comedy *El veleta*. The return of Ferdinand VII and the absolutist party sent him once more into exile and he settled in London (1823) where he wrote, entirely in English from then on, *The Romance of the History of Spain* (1827), a retelling of old Spanish stories; the historical novels, *Gomez Arias* and *The Castilian* (both 1828), the latter in a contemporary setting; *The Exquisites* (1831), a comedy; *Call Again Tomorrow* (1832), a tragedy; *The Royal Fugitives* (1834), and some history and travel books. The death of Ferdinand (1833) allowed him to return to Spain, which he did in 1834, becoming secretary of the Cortes at Madrid. He died in Paris the following year.

**Tsvetayeva, Marina Ivanovna** (1892–1941), Russian Soviet poet of the modernist Pasternak (q.v.) school born in Moscow, who showed her qualities in *Stikhi* (1910, 'Verses'). After an unhappy life, caused by a final inability to accept the changed conditions caused by the revolution, she died by suicide.

**Tucholsky, Kurt** (1890–1935), German prose writer. Born in Berlin, he became a well-known Socialist journalist, one of the few to make political journalism into literature in the period between the wars. Such are his many contributions to *Die Weltbühne*. Among his books is *Schloss Gripsholm* (1931). He died in self-imposed and very necessary exile in Sweden two years after Hitler's rise.

**Tullin, Christian Braunmann** (1728–1765), Danish-Norwegian poet. Born in Kristiania, he became a student at Copenhagen, later a clergyman, and ended his strange short career in his native town as an industrialist. He is the most conspicuous example of the influence of English descriptive and didactic poetry in Danish literature. His works were collected (3 vols.) in 1770–3.

**Turgenev, Ivan Sergeyevich** (1818–1883), Russian novelist, short-story writer and dramatist, was born of landed gentry at Orel in central Russia. He studied in Moscow and afterwards in Berlin, already showing his interest in western Europe. On his return he tried his hand at poetry, but failing settled on prose. His sketches of rustic life, *Zapiski okhotnika* ('A Sportsman's Sketches'), appeared in 1852. Having been imprisoned for a month for writing an article on the death of Gogol (q.v.) the same year, on his release he found himself condemned to be banished to his estate. In 1861 he left Russia and, except for occasional visits home, spent the rest of his life in self-imposed exile for the most part in Paris and Baden. But it was of Russia that he continued to write, and of his own class doomed to frustration in knowing that the period in human history would soon be reached when it would no longer be needed. His work has been well described as having an autumnal character, for if sad it is also mellow. Of his novels perhaps especially noteworthy are: *Rudin* (1855), *Dvoryanskoe gnezdo* (1858, 'A House of Nobles'), *Nakanune* (1860, 'On the Eve'), *Ottsy i deti* (1861, 'Fathers and Sons'), a particularly important work in which the term 'nihilist' was used for the first time, and *Dym* (1867, 'Smoke'). Of his plays *Mesyats v derevne* ('A Month in the Country') is the best known. A giant of a man but completely lacking in self-assertiveness, he became the plaything of the singer Madame Viardot-Garcia, who refused to love him, and the intimate friend of another bachelor, Flaubert (q.v.), in whose company he was often to be found. The theme of the strong woman and the weak and ineffectual man is often present in his works. Turgenev died at Bougival, near Paris. There have been many separate translations of the novels, and there is a complete edition, *The Novels of Ivan Turgenev*, translated by C. Garnett (17 vols., 1919–23), and of the plays, *The Plays of Ivan Turgenev*, translated by M. S. Mandell (1924).

**Tynyanov, Yury Nikolayevich** (1894–1943), Russian Soviet novelist, born at Rezekne, Latvia. An exponent of historical novel writing in the form of romantic biography, so popular in Europe during the twenties and thirties, he can best be studied in *Smert' Vazir Mukhtara* (1929; Eng. trans. *Death and Diplomacy in Persia*, 1938) and in *Pushkin* (1937). He died in Moscow.

**Tyutchev, Fyodor Ivanovich** (1803–1873), Russian poet, born in the province of Orel. He became one of the Pushkin circle and began to write before going into the diplomatic service and spending a number of years in Germany and Italy. Apart from love-lyrics his outstanding work was the verse which conveyed his fear of the breakdown of ordered society, deepening at times to a terror almost of cosmic disintegration. In these powerful and concentrated lyrics Tyutchev employs a prosody which foreshadows Symbolism. He died in Petersburg. V. Nabokov (q.v.) translated a selection of his poems into English in *Pushkin, Lermontov, Tyutchev* (1947).

**Tzara, Tristan** (1896–1963), Franco-Rumanian poet. Born at Moineste, Rumania, he became a leading *dadaïste* in Switzerland in 1916. Three years later he arrived with his new ideas in Paris, and published his nonsensical, disintegrated language in *Sept Manifestes dada* (1920). He gradually disentangled himself from this through such intermediate works as *Mouchoir de nuages* (1925) and *L'Homme approximatif* (1930), after which he wrote good lyric poetry in a more natural manner as in *Grains et issues* (1935), *Le Cœur à gaz* (1938) and *Morceaux choisis* (1947). *Le Surréalisme et l'après-guerre* (1948) is an interesting assessment of the surrealist movement to which he had never really subscribed, but which he had come to regard as the one dynamic force in French poetry, in changed conditions. Tzara died in Paris.

# U

**Uberti, Fazio degli** (1305?–1368?), Italian poet, probably born in Pisa of a noble family exiled as Ghibellines from their native Florence. He spent his life as a courtier in various Italian cities, the last of them being Verona where he died. He is remembered for his strong lyric verse, some of it love-poetry and some dealing with political themes. In 1348 he seems to have experienced a spiritual conversion, celebrated in a lengthy allegorical poem called *Il Dittamondo*, which occupied him to within a year of his death, and even then remained unfinished. This description of a fabulous journey across the then known world is full of extraordinary colour. The *Liriche* can best be read in Renier's edition of 1883, *Il Dittamondo* in Corsi's (2 vols., 1852). Dante's influence on Uberti in *Il Dittamondo* is very marked.

**Uhland, Ludwig** (1787–1862), German poet, a native of Tübingen, where he spent all his life, being for a time (1824–33) a professor at the university there. It was the publication in 1807 of his first book of poetry that made him the heart and soul of the so-called 'Swabian movement' in German verse with its strong sense of the historic past. A short stay in Paris in 1810–11, where he spent much time studying medieval poetical manuscripts, quickly brought him to maturity, and from then on until 1817 he perfected German ballad poetry, catching the authentic Volkslied characteristics of the past. He is best known in English as the author of the ballad which Longfellow translated as 'The Luck of Edenhall'. After 1817 academic and political interests absorbed more and more of his time. A prominent member of the Liberal Party, at the 1848 Revolution he became a delegate in the German National Assembly. He collected his poetry in *Vaterländische Gedichte* (1817; Eng. trans. by W. W. Skeat, *Songs and Ballads of Uhland*, 1864). The modern critical edition is that by J. Hartmann and E. Schmidt (2 vols., 1898). Among his non-poetical works—his historical plays are of no account—the most noteworthy are *Minnesang* (1824) and *Schriften zur Geschichte der Dichtung und Sage* (8 vols., 1865–73). See also the uncritical edition of his works, *Sämtliche Werke*, by H. Fischer (6 vols., 1892).

**Ulloa y Pereira, Luis** (1584–1674), Spanish poet who was born and died at Toro (Zamora). A favourite of Olivares, he was employed as a civil servant at León. Amidst a wilderness of works he produced one outstanding poem on the love of King Alfonso VIII for the Jewess Raquel (1659). His collected works, *Obras, prosas y versos* first appeared in 1674, and the standard edition is in the *Biblioteca de Autores Españoles*, vol. xxix.

Ulrich von Lichtenstein (1200?–1275), Styrian poet of noble family,
was the author of a remarkable poetic autobiography, *Frauendienst*,
finished in 1255. This includes striking lyrics, some of them of the
*Tanzlieder* type, and the whole work was adapted under the same title
by L. Tieck (q.v.) in 1812. Ulrich's *Frauenbuch*, completed in 1257,
is a dialogue on the decay of chivalry. His lyrics all appear in *Deutsche
Liederdichter*, edited by K. Bartsch and W. Golther (1929). The best
edition of *Frauendienst* is that by R. Bechstein (1888).

Unamuno y Jugo, Miguel de (1864–1936), Spanish man of letters.
The most influential thinker that his country has produced this century, he was born in Bilbao and followed an academic career, being
rector of the University of Salamanca at his death. Great and clear
though his intellect was (perhaps because he was so uncompromisingly
honest), his ability to see both sides of everything produces a negative
result with one point of view militating against another, which can be
seen in his actions of daily life with its tragic end, first accepting
Franco and then bitterly denouncing him. Unamuno, a man of wide
European culture, first made his mark as an advocate of Spain's
taking her place in the general heritage. He hated her isolation, the
more so since he saw that after the disasters of 1898 the last vision of
empire and the Golden Age had been destroyed. Spain must therefore
be open to foreign trends, which does not mean to say that she must
forfeit her spiritual integrity. He was a man of the north, outwardly
as severe as the Castilian landscape he loved, but within him was a
fervent religious spirit wrestling with death for a clear belief in
immortality. His mature view of life is to be seen in his two masterpieces of religious philosophy, *Del sentimiento trágico de la vida* (1912;
Eng. trans. *The Tragic Sense of Life in Men and Peoples*, 1921) and
*La agonía del cristianismo* (1924; Eng. trans. *The Agony of Christianity*,
1928). In both these works Unamuno finds that man's earthly life is
from birth to death a tragedy, which formal Christianity can merely
palliate but cannot solve. Death is always round the corner and there
is no proof of the immortality of the soul which would make life
bearable. Some have rejected religion for this reason, but this was
impossible for Unamuno; in fact if there was any nobility in man,
especially in the intellectual, he was to be ready to accept a personal
deity against all the urgings of reason. In this line of approach he may
be said to have foreshadowed existentialism. In his novels, the best
being *Niebla* (1914; Eng. trans. *Mist, a Tragi-Comic Novel*, 1929),
*Abel Sánchez* (1917) and *Tres novelas ejemplares* (1921; Eng. trans.
*Three Exemplary Novels*, 1930, new ed., 1956), man is turned inside
out and all his wretched mortal doubts, fears and passions are
movingly examined. In *Vida de Don Quijote y Sancho* (1905;
Eng. trans. *The Life of Don Quixote and Sancho*, 1927) Unamuno
analyses the two opposing sides of Spanish life, love of tradition and
the half unwilling desire to accept innovation. His poetry, nobly
sombre, with again the ever-present awareness of death, its background the wide Castilian sierras, is most notably exemplified in 'El
Cristo de Velázquez' (1920), which appears in his *Antología poética*
(1942).

**Undset, Sigrid** (1882–1949), Norwegian novelist. Born of Norwegian parents at Kallundborg, Denmark, she was forced on the sudden collapse of the family's fortunes to work for a living in an office at the age of sixteen. This experience she turned to good account in her realistic novels, *Viga-Ljot og Vigdis* (1910; Eng. trans. *Gunnar's Daughter*, 1936) and especially *Jenny* (1911; Eng. trans. 1930), which deal with the place of women in modern society. In 1920–2 she broke new ground with her masterly historical trilogy, *Kristin Lavransdatter* (Eng. trans. 1930), which she followed up with a less successful four-volume saga, *Olav Audunssön i Hestviken* (1925–7; Eng. trans. *The Master of Hestviken*, 1934). She had become a Roman Catholic in 1924 and her marriage (to Anders Svarstad, 1912) broke down the following year. She now gave up her exploration of the Middle Ages and wrote in a modern setting, her plots greatly influenced by her new attitude to life caused by her conversion. Among her many novels published from this time on may be mentioned: *Etapper* (1929; Eng. trans. *Stages on the Road*, 1934), *Gymnadenia* (1929; Eng. trans. *The Wild Orchid*, 1931), *Den brœndende busk* (1930; Eng. trans. *The Burning Bush*, 1932), *Ida Elisabeth* (1932; Eng. trans. 1933), *Elleve aar* (1934; Eng. trans. *The Longest Years*, 1935), *Den trofaste hustru* (1936; Eng. trans. *The Faithful Wife*, 1937), *Norske helgener* (1937; the Eng. trans. from MS. having been published as *Saga of Saints* in 1934), *Madame Dorothea* (1939; Eng. trans. 1941), and *Catherina av Siena* (1951; Eng. trans. 1954). The greatest Norwegian writer of this century, she received the Nobel Prize in 1928. She died in Oslo.

**Ungaretti, Giuseppe** (1888–    ), Italian poet, was born in Alexandria, lived for a time in Paris, and for six years was engaged in university work in Brazil, returning to Italy in 1942. His great book was *Allegria di naufragi* (1919), inspired by his experiences in the First World War. Severe and simple, his lyrics achieve a clear spiritualized sensuousness allied with a compassion for all nature which he never reached again. One has only to compare the *Allegria* with *Un grido e paesaggi* (1952) to notice how the inspiration has flagged. A large selection of the *Allegria* has been edited but not very successfully translated by A. Mandelbaum, and appears in *Life of a Man* (1958).

**Unruh, Fritz von** (1885–    ), German playwright and novelist. Born in Coblenz, he took up a military career and became an officer in the Prussian Guard, but it was not long before he began reappraising the whole position of the soldier and society, bringing out a highly sensational play, *Offiziere* (1912), which caused a great deal of publicity. Others of the same kind followed, and when at the height of the war he published a pacifist novel, *Opfergang* (1916), he was sent to a lunatic asylum, which at least, things being as they were, saved him from a worse fate. Set at liberty at the end of the war, he continued to write pacifist plays, the last being *Bonaparte* (1926; Eng. trans. 1928). In 1928 *Opfergang* was translated into English as *The Way of Sacrifice* and produced a deep effect in Britain and America. Of his later novels none is more striking than *The End is not yet* (1947, in English; Ger. trans. *Der nie verlor*, 1949).

**Urfé, Honoré d'** (1567–1625), French novelist. Born in Marseille, he spent most of his life in the retinue of the Duke of Savoy, to whom he was related through his mother. Although turning sometimes to poetry, both secular and religious, it is on his novel *L'Astrée*, which appeared in five parts between 1607 and 1627, the last being completed by his secretary, that his fame rests. With its theme of idealized gallantry, redolent of a slow-moving, somewhat precious society, it became a kind of handbook of the art of good manners. The influence of such Italian pastorals as Guarini's (q.v.) *Pastor Fido* on this quietly sentimental romance is clear. Popular throughout the seventeenth century and beyond, it was plundered by a host of writers for plots. There is a modern edition of *L'Astrée* by H. Vaganay (1925–8).

**Uspensky, Gleb Ivanovich** (1840–1902), Russian novelist, was born at Tula of lower middle-class parentage. A close observer of peasant and suburban life from an early age, when he began to write it was to describe the impact of capitalism on the old ways of the land, and the treadmill which was so often the daily life of small town families, the victims of the new industrialism. A plain, straightforward writer who was too honest to romanticize the peasants' fate, in his best novel, *Vlast' zemli* ('The Power of the Soil', 1882), he describes village life in a masterly way. But if Uspensky was too honest to close his eyes he was too sensitive to be able to bear what he saw for ever. Moving to Petersburg he found the ethical bankruptcy of Russia even more staring there, and finally committed suicide in that city. His collected works, which by that time had reached a sixth edition, were published uniformly in 1908, and another was undertaken by the Soviet Academy in 1941.

**Usque, Samuel** (sixteenth century), Portuguese poet, of whom little is known beyond that he was born in Portugal of Spanish Jewish parents and died in Italy, perhaps in Ferrara, in the house of the most distinguished branch of his family. The work by which he is known is *Consolação às Tribulações de Israel* (1553), three pastoral pieces in which the sufferings of the Jews throughout the ages are recounted, the work ending on a triumphant note, that the persecuted race will finally be victorious. The *Consolação* has been edited by J. Mendes dos Remédios (3 vols., 1906–8).

**Uz, Johann Peter** (1720–1796), German poet, a native of Ansbach where he died. One of the circle of literary students at Halle, he was associated then and afterwards with Gleim (q.v.) and Götz (q.v.) as a writer of neat and sprightly verse, much of it anacreontic. Some of the best of it was published as *Lyrische Gedichte* (1749). His *Poetische Werke* were collected in 1768, long after he had ceased to be an influence in the German world of letters.

# V

**Våcårescu, Elena** (1866–1947), Rumanian poet and novelist born in Bucharest, writing in French and English. Maid of honour to Queen Elizabeth of Rumania (herself a woman of letters as 'Carmen Sylva', q.v.), she was supported in her love affair with the crown prince by the queen, but when this came to nothing on constitutional grounds she was exiled and went to Paris, where she died. Among her books of poetry may be mentioned *Le Rhapsode de la Dambovitza* (1885; Eng. trans. by Carmen Sylva, 1891), *Lueurs et flammes* (1903) and *Dans l'or du soir* (1928). Of her novels *Rada* (1896) particularly enjoyed a reputation, as did her semi-autobiographical works in English, such as *The Queen's Friend* (1908) and *Royal Lovers* (1909).

**Vailland, Roger** (1907–      ), French novelist. Born in Paris, he took a leading part in the Resistance movement, the experiences of which provided him with the material for his first book, *Drôle de jeu* (1945). In his later works, such as *Un Jeune Homme seul* (1952), *Beau Masque* (1954), *La Loi* (1957) and *La Fête* (1960), he showed signs of an increasing interest in Communism. His style has been compared to that of Stendhal (q.v.)

**Vair, Guillaume du** (1556–1621), French prose writer, critic and philosopher. Born in Paris, he became a priest and was made Bishop of Lisieux in 1617. His place in literature rests almost entirely on *De l'éloquence française* (1595), the notable style of it influencing, indeed inspiring, the language reforms of Malherbe (q.v.), which had so profound an effect on French poetry during the seventeenth century. His philosophical works were much read in England, two of the English translations appearing as *A Buckler against Adversity* (1622) and *The Moral Philosophy of the Stoics* (1664). He died at Tonneins.

**Valdés, A. Palacio,** *see* **Palacio Valdés.**

**Valdés, Juan de,** in Latin **Valdesius** (1495?–1545), Spanish prosist, was born at Cuenca. From 1528 involved in the movement for radical reform within the Church of Rome, he fell under the suspicion of the Inquisition and in 1531 went to Naples where he died. Although of great significance from the theological point of view, it is as a stylist that he is of importance here. His *Diálogo de la lengua* (not published until 1737; mod. crit. ed. by Montesinos, 1928) had great influence on Spanish prose in the sixteenth and early seventeenth centuries. In this work he insisted on a natural style and a carefully chosen vocabulary.

**Valera y Alcalá-Galiano, Juan** (1824–1905), Spanish novelist, critic and translator. Born at Cabra, Cordoba, he entered the diplomatic service in 1847 and in 1868 became Minister of Education. A man of wide culture, his prose is regarded as the finest in nineteenth-century Spanish literature. His letters are of enormous interest, his translation of Longus's *Daphnis and Chloe* is perfect of its kind, and there is superb mastery of style and urbanity if not of depth in his representative work of literary criticism, *Estudios críticos sobre la literatura* (1864). He did not publish his first novel, *Pepita Jiménez*, until 1874 (Eng. trans. 1927) and it was at once acclaimed a classic. This study of a theological student's first taste of love is splendidly told and he employs the epistolary form to great advantage. Of his other novels, *Comendador Mendoza* (1877; Eng. trans. *Knight Commander Mendoza*, 1893) and *Doña Luz* (1879; Eng. trans. 1891) are noteworthy. Appointed in turn Spanish ambassador in Lisbon, Washington, Brussels and Vienna, Valera died in Madrid.

**Valéry, Paul** (1871–1945), French poet and essayist, born at Cette. Going to Paris he was befriended by Mallarmé (q.v.), whose influence on him was great, but his first work was in prose, *Introduction à la méthode de Léonard de Vinci* (1895). Much more than mere art criticism, in this work he studies with great subtlety the mental processes and aims of a genius, thereby adumbrating his future standpoint with regard to the arts in general. Another prose work in the same manner was *La Soirée avec Monsieur Teste* (1906; Eng. trans. *Monsieur Teste*, 1951). It was not until 1920, however, that with *Album de vers anciens* his poetic fame was established, although his most perfect poem, *La Jeune Parque*, had already excited the greatest interest in him in 1917. *Les Charmes* (1922) contains his profoundest thought presented in poetry rich in marvellous imagery. After the middle twenties he wrote for the greater part in prose once more, his most considerable work being *Variété*, which filled five volumes between 1924 and 1944 and which contains his criticism in many fields. Of other works *L'Idée fixe* (1932) and *Mauvaises pensées* (1942) are particularly important. Valéry died in Paris. See J. Matthews, *The Collected Works of Paul Valéry in Translation* (12 vols.), 1951–62.

**Valle-Inclán, Ramón María del** (1869–1936), Spanish novelist and dramatist, was born in Galicia, spent part of his youth in Mexico and settled in Madrid, where he became the most picturesque and flamboyant character in 'Bohemia'. Self-assertive to a fault, he lost an arm as the result of a fight. His early work, representative of which is *Sonatas* (1902–5; Eng. trans. *The Pleasant Memoirs of the Marquis of Bradomín*, 1924), marks him as a decadent with the same pronounced sensualism which is to be found in the contemporary aesthetic school in France. The hero is not convincing and the ending is heavily contrived, but what is attractive is the description of the Galician countryside and peasantry. The World War of 1914 profoundly shocked him and he emerged as a pessimist whereas before his cynicism had been just as definite. In his tragedy, *Los cuernos de Don Friolera* (1921), he treats his characters literally as marionettes who are controlled by an evil hand. A novel, *Tirano Banderas* (1926; Eng.

trans. *The Tyrant*, 1929), describes with a good deal of power in episodic, near-dramatic form the ruin of a South American dictator. His despair at the prospect of man's future led him to turn his attention to his own country. The result was the series of novels forming the collection *Ruedo ibérico* in which he held up the latter part of the reign of Isabel II (1833–68) to harsh ridicule as the eternal pattern of the rottenness of Spanish public life. It began to appear in 1927, and the last volume came out in 1938 (an extract from it is translated as *The Golden Rose* in W. B. Wells's *Spanish Omnibus*, 1932). He died at Santiago de Compostela.

**Vallès, Jules** (1832–1885), French novelist. Born at Le Puy-en-Velay, he became a journalist. His many novels, written in a violent and bitter style, mirror his varied experiences. The most powerful of his works is the trilogy *Jacques Vingtras*, the three volumes of which are *L'Enfant* (1879), *Le Bachelier* (1881) and *L'Insurgé* (1886), the last containing a first-hand account of the Paris Commune of 1871, in which he took part as a communard. Several of his books were left unpublished at his death, one of them, *Le Proscrit*, appearing for the first time in 1950. A marked man after the failure of the Commune, he was allowed back after a while to France under an amnesty and died in Paris.

**Vallotton, Benjamin** (1877–1952), Swiss novelist, born at Gryon in the Vaud. Keeping his attention fixed on the Vaudois life round him, he reviewed it intimately and in kindly wise in such works as *Ce qu'en pense Potterat* (1915), Commissaire Potterat being his mouthpiece. Later he showed that the 1914–18 war had made an impact on him in such books as *Achille et Cie* (1921). He died at Sanary-sur-Mer.

**Van Lerberghe, Charles** (1861–1907), Belgian poet. Born in Ghent, he was left an orphan early and was taken into the family of a relation of Maeterlinck (q.v.). In such an atmosphere his latent poetic powers developed, and on the publication of *Les Flaireurs* (1889) he came to be looked on as a leader of the 'Young Belgian' movement in literature. *Entrevisions* (1898) deepened the impressions made by *Les Flaireurs*, while with *La Chanson d'Ève* (1904), a highly personal account of his spiritual happiness and sorrow, he produced his masterpiece. His last work, *Pan* (1906), appeared shortly before his mental collapse, and the following year he died insane in Brussels.

**Vančura, Vladislav** (1891–1942), Czech fictional writer. Born at Háje, he became a medical practitioner in Prague. A great stylist, he enormously increased the possibilities of the language, and his plots are strong. A love story breaking out across racial antagonisms is revealed in *Útěk do Budína* (1932, 'Flight to Buda'), while human relationships in the context of the First World War are forcibly dealt with in *Tři řeky* (1936, 'Three Rivers'), even though the style by its eccentricities does sometimes become unnecessarily distracting. He was shot by the Germans in Prague.

**Vauvenargues, Luc de Clapiers de** (1715–1747), French moralist. Born in Aix-en-Provence of an old and noble family (he succeeded to the marquisate), he entered the army and fought in the Italian campaign of 1733 and afterwards in the War of the Austrian Succession. At the Battle of Dettingen (1743) he was seriously wounded and permanently crippled, and shortly afterwards was terribly disfigured by smallpox. Failure to obtain a diplomatic post left him in Paris without a definite future, but a fortunate meeting with Voltaire (q.v.) led him to take to writing, and his famous *Introduction à la connaissance de l'esprit humain, suivie de réflexions et maximes*, inspired by his long and enthusiastic study of Seneca and Plutarch, was published in 1746 and 1747. His splendid optimism in spite of a life of disaster has been an inspiration to many, and contrasts very favourably with the cynicism of La Rochefoucauld (q.v.). Vauvenargues died in Paris. The latest edition of his works is that of P. Varillon (3 vols., 1929).

**Vazov, Ivan** (1850–1921), Bulgarian man of letters, the greatest his country has produced. Born at Sopot, he took part in politics in his earlier days, and it was not until the end of the century that he settled down entirely to literary work in Sofia where he died. His novel, *Pod Igoto* (1894), which describes Bulgarian life about 1875, is looked upon as the best in Bulgarian. Of his plays perhaps *Borislav* (1910) is the best known. His collected works fill over a hundred volumes. A selective edition in twelve volumes was brought out in 1938.

**Vega, Garcilaso de la,** *see* **Garcilaso.**

**Vega Carpio, Lope Félix de** (1562–1635), Spanish dramatist and poet, was born in Madrid and was educated at the University of Alcalá. He took part in the Azores expedition of 1582, and in connection with one of his numerous love affairs was banished from Madrid in 1588, in which year he married and took some part in the Armada against England. After this he lived for a time in Valencia and later was a member of the household of the Albas and the Sessas. His first wife died in 1595, and on the death of his second he became a priest in 1614, which, however, did not prevent him from indulging in a further amatory escapade. His last years in Madrid, where he died, were darkened by the death of his son and other domestic disasters. Self-imposed austerities hastened his own end. His literary activity was prodigious, and it seems that his five hundred extant plays represent only a part of what he actually wrote. Most of his plots were taken from Spanish history and were used as the base on which he built his intricate plots of intrigue, but what was different about them from what had been written before was that here was action and colour free from moralizing. This came to be known as the 'cloak and dagger' drama. He was equally at home in tragedy and comedy, and his dialogue was at all times excellent. It is difficult from this vast array to choose out some outstanding works, but *El alcalde de Zalamea, Fuenteovejuna, Peribáñez, La dama boba, El caballero de Olmedo, El perro del hortelano* and *El castigo sin venganza* are among the finest and best known. Of his other works, he attacked Drake and Queen Elizabeth in the epic *La dragontea* (1598), added a long continuation to Ariosto's (q.v.) *Orlando Furioso*, called *La hermosura de Angélica* (1602), while in *La corona trágica* (1627), another long poem, more than justice is done to Mary, Queen of Scots. Although attacked by the classicists like Góngora (q.v.), Lope de Vega submitted to Aristotle's 'unities', and thanks to his vitality he breathed new life into the stage. When he appeared Spanish drama was lifeless and stiff, and the plots and poetry poor. He produced new and vivid plots, new characterization and new dramatic language. Without him there could scarcely have been a Calderón (q.v.). There are three modern editions of his dramatic works, the best being by M. Menéndez y Pelayo (15 vols., 1890–1913) and by A. Cotarelo and others (13 vols., 1916–30). A selection of his non-dramatic poetry, *Poesías líricas*, by J. Montesinos appeared in two volumes (vol. i, 1927; vol. ii, 1941). *El alcalde de Zalamea, Fuenteovejuna* and *El perro del hortelano* were translated by J. G. Underhill, together with *Lo cierto por lo dudoso*, as *Four Plays* (1936).

**Vélez de Guevara, Luis** (1579–1644), Spanish novelist and playwright, born at Écija, Seville. While pursuing a brilliant career at the bar he is said to have written over four hundred plays. These are of little concern now, but his novel *El diablo cojuelo* (1641) is worthy of remembrance if only because on it Le Sage (q.v.) based his *Le Diable boiteux*. He died in Madrid.

**Veneziano, Antonio** (1543–1593), Italian poet. Born at Monreale, he led a wandering life, met Cervantes in the course of it and was for a short time a slave in Algerian galleys (1578). His most famous work is a long love-poem, *Celia*, in Sicilian dialect, but he also wrote many shorter works and sharp epigrams. He was killed by an explosion at Palermo. His works were not collected until 1861.

**Vercors**, pseudonym of **Jean Bruller** (1902–     ), French writer. Born in Paris, he became a journalist, a book-illustrator and typographer, but it was not until the war and the occupation of France that he made a name for himself. Putting his craftsmanship and journalism at the service of the Resistance he founded and ran the newspaper *Éditions de minuit*, which, stealthily circulated, did much to stimulate public opposition to Vichy. It was more than anything else Vercors's half-length novel serialized in that paper, called *Le Silence de la mer* (publ. secretly and separately, 1942; Eng. trans. *Put out the Light*, 1944) that helped to lay bare the treachery of the Pétain government. Another secret publication of war-time was *La Marche à l'étoile* (1943; Eng. trans. *Guiding Star*, 1946). With the return of peace he strove in his novels to put before a changed world the changelessness of humanistic values, as in *Les Yeux et la lumière* (1948) and *Les Animaux dénaturés* (1952).

**Veresayev, Vikenty**, pseudonym of **V. V. Smidovich** (1867–1946), Russian Soviet novelist. Born at Tula, he took up medicine, writing in his spare time. Becoming a Socialist he began to study the problems of the intellectual in an increasingly complex society, and this approach informs nearly all his earlier work, the best known of which is *Zapiski vracha* (1901, 'Sketches of a Physician'). Having wholeheartedly embraced the revolution he next appears as a Marxist novelist, his most outstanding books in this line being *V tupike* (1922; Eng. trans. *The Deadlock*, 1927) and *Sestry* (1933; Eng. trans. *The Sisters*, 1934). Veresayev died in Moscow.

**Verga, Giovanni** (1840–1922), Italian novelist and short-story writer, was born in Catania, Sicily. At first he cultivated the ordinary fashionable sentimental novel of the day as *I carbonari della montagna* (1861–2), *Eva* (1873) and *Eros* (1875), but in a collection of short stories, *Vita dei campi* (1880; Eng. trans. *Little Novels of Sicily*, 1925), he draws on the peasant life of Sicily for characters and background. Thereafter Sicily was the source of his inspiration, and he not infrequently wrote in Sicilian dialect. One of the stories in *Vita dei campi* is 'Cavalleria Rusticana', which provided the libretto for Mascagni's opera (1893), and itself was rewritten by Verga as a play (1896). Of his later work mention should be made of the full-length novel *Mastro Don Gesualdo* (1889; Eng. trans. *Master Don Gesualdo*, 1892) and *Don Candeloro* (1894). He died in Rome.

**Verhaeren, Émile Adolphe Gustave** (1855–1916), Belgian poet and playwright, was born at St-Amand, near Antwerp. Called to the bar, he soon tired of law and founded a literary review, *La Semaine*. From then on he became a leader of the new ideas in Belgian literature. In 1883 he published his first book of verse, *Les Flamandes*, naturalistic in character, but soon showed that he could be a Parnassian, cold and classical, as in *Les Moines* (1886). By 1895, when *Les Villages illusoires* came out, he had joined the symbolists and was writing in free verse. On the other hand *Les Heures claires* (1896; Eng. trans. *Bright Hours*, 1916) was a collection of love-lyrics. Soon after this he tried his hand at playwriting, but from *Les Aubes* (1898; Eng. trans. *The Dawn*, 1898) to *Hélène de Sparte* (1909; Eng. trans. 1916) none of them can be said to have been really successful. In his verse he reached a transitional stage with *Les Heures d'après-midi* (1905; Eng. trans. *The Sunlit Hours*, 1917) before producing his optimistic epic *Les Rythmes souverains* (1910), exuberant, Whitmanesque, revolutionary in literary style, at times verging dangerously on eccentricity, but on the whole a remarkable work, which made him the outstanding Belgian poet of his time. The war moved him deeply, as he showed in *Les Ailes rouges de la guerre* (1916). The German occupation of Belgium drove him to France. He was accidentally killed in Rouen railway station.

**Verlaine, Paul** (1844–1896), French poet. Born in Metz the son of a military engineer, he went to Paris in his teens and obtained a post as municipal insurance clerk. When office hours were over he would make for the Latin Quarter, and within a few years was on close terms with the younger members of the Parnassian circle, such as Coppée (q.v.) and Sully Prudhomme (q.v.). By 1866 he was able to publish his first poetry, *Poèmes saturniens*, which show the influence not only of a Parnassian like Leconte de Lisle (q.v.) but of Baudelaire (q.v.) also. That he stood midway between both extremes and was perfecting his own particular manner was to be seen in his charming Watteauesque *Fêtes galantes* (1869; Eng. trans. 1908) and his cheerful and somewhat sentimental *La Bonne Chanson* (1870). In the latter year he married, but the marriage was a failure and finally broke down in 1874. His meeting with Rimbaud (q.v.) in 1871 was a most important one, and during their short and intense friendship, in the course of which they visited England and Verlaine slightly injured his companion by shooting at him during a quarrel in a hotel, his powers rapidly developed. For the shooting incident Verlaine suffered two years' imprisonment, and on his release taught in schools or acted as a private tutor to earn a living. While in Mons jail he published *Romances sans paroles* (1874; Eng. trans. 1921), which marks a new approach to poetry and contains several features, including that subtle fascination of Verlaine, impressionism and a felicitous musical quality. The rest of his life was a battle between the two sides of his nature, devout Catholic belief and debauchery. The first of these is celebrated in the sincere and tender volume, *Sagesse* (1881), which contains his best religious poetry, while *Jadis et naguère* (1884) and especially *Parallèlement* (1889), with near obscenity disconcertingly mixed with pure religious poetry, illustrate his painful struggle between the spiritual and carnal. To the latter he unfortunately fell a complete victim, dying destitute in hospital. Among his later and much inferior work are *Bonheur* (1891), *Odes en son honneur* (1893) and *Invectives* (1896). Of his prose, which is of little literary importance, *Mes hôpitaux* (1891), *Mes prisons* (1895) and *Confessions* (1896; Eng. trans. 1950) are worth mentioning. His *Œuvres complètes* (5 vols.) appeared between 1898 and 1903.

**Verne, Jules** (1828–1905), French novelist. Born in Nantes, he went to Paris to read law but gave it up, and took to writing opera libretti, on several occasions collaborating with Dumas *fils* (q.v.). As a novelist he first scored a success with *Cinq semaines en ballon* (1862), the beginning of a lengthy series of adventure stories in which cunning and exciting use is made of science, then for the first time exerting a definite influence on a wide uncritical public. In anticipating inventions he never exaggerates, so that for his contemporaries his plots were always in the realm of possibility and the better for being so, while for us with our scientific sophistication his success in suggesting the practicality of his ideas and his literary gifts assure his work of continued popularity. Among his numerous books may be noted: *Voyage au centre de la Terre* (1864), *Une Ville flottante* (1867), which describes his voyage to America in the *Great Eastern* steamship, *Vingt mille lieues sous les mers* (1869), *Le Tour du monde en quatre-vingt jours* (1873), *L'Île mystérieuse* (three parts, 1874–5), *Le Rayon vert* (1882), *César Cascabel* (1890), *L'Île à hélice* (1895) and *La Phare au bout du monde* (1905). All these have been translated into English. Verne died in Amiens.

**Verwey, Albert** (1865–1937), Dutch poet and prose-writer. Born in Amsterdam of a clerical family, he became a journalist in that city before suddenly retiring to Noordwijk for private study, and this remained his home for the rest of his life. He was for a time professor of Dutch literature at Leiden. In spite of the many dogmatic claims made for him he was first and foremost a scholar and thinker, and his uncompromisingly harsh and difficult poetry is scarcely spontaneous. His first publications, such as *Persephone* (1883), are the more readable and smooth. His prose, much influenced by Goethe's ideas, was collected up to 1923 in *Proza* (10 vols.). He brought out a fine critical edition of Vondel (q.v.), *Vondel. Volledige dichtwerken*, in 1937.

**Viau, Théophile de** (1590–1626), French poet. He was born at Clairac, near Agen, and after wanderings with a troupe of travelling actors, for whom he wrote plays, took office in noble households, dying in the service of the Montmorencys at Chantilly, near Paris. Viau is chiefly remarkable for the free thought expressed in his often excellent lyrics. This brought him near to ruin on more than one occasion. His verse, far more natural than the general run of poetry of the time, was collected the year after his death, and there have been various other editions since, including a judicious selection by L. R. Lefèvre (1926).

**Viaud, L. M. J.,** *see* **Loti, P.**

**Vicente, Gil** (1470?–1540), Portuguese dramatist writing also in Spanish. Born at Guimarães, he was educated at Coimbra where he read law, but abandoned it and became attached to the courts of Manuel I and John III as dramatic entertainer. He died at Évora. Vicente left forty-four plays, seventeen of which are in Portuguese, fifteen in both Portuguse and Spanish, eleven in Spanish, and one in which he employs French and Italian also. His work consists of religious *autos*, tragi-comedies especially for the court, and comedies and farces for the popular stage. Representative of the first may be said to be the famous *Auto da Alma* (1518), of the second, *Don Duardos* (1525), written in Spanish, and *Romagem de Agravados* (1533), in Portuguese, while for the last one would perhaps single out the *Farsa de Inês Pereira* (1523). A great believer and yet an anti-clerical, he was not slow to attack the corruption of the Church, as in the *Auto da Feira* (1528). The standard edition of his works is that by Braga (6 vols., 1942–4). That great English scholar A. F. G. Bell made some good translations of Vicente's work: *Four Plays of Gil Vicente* (1920) and *Lyrics of Gil Vicente* (second ed., 1921).

**Viélé-Griffin, Francis** (1864–1937), French poet. Born at Norfolk in the United States, he was taken to France as a child, where he proved himself to be a symbolist of distinction in such volumes as *La Clarté de la vie* (1897), *Phocas le jardinier* (1898), *La Partenza* (1899) and *La Légende ailée de Wieland le forgeron* (1900), continuing in the same manner down to *La Sagesse d'Ulysse* (1925), but though the manner of approach did not change the form did, and we find him going over from academic metres to absolute free verse in his later work. He died at Bergerac.

**Vigny, Alfred Victor de** (1797–1863), French poet, prosist and playwright, was born of noble family at Loches (Indre-et-Loire), and served in the royal guards from 1814 to 1827. One of the 'frustrated generation that overheard the sounds of an age of grandeur which they arrived too late to take part in', it is this state of mind which is the keynote of his life and work, and the resulting frustration was increased by a disastrous marriage to an Englishwoman who was a brainless hypochondriac. His first work of note was *Éloa* (1824), a delightful poetic fantasy, and the high tide of the earliest period of his poetry is *Poèmes antiques et modernes* (1826), which contains ' Moïse' and 'Le Cor '. For a time the stage attracted him, but it was not until *Chatterton* (1835) that he gained his one and only success in this *genre*. Meanwhile he had turned to prose romance with *Cinq-Mars* (1826), the very attractive *Stello* (1832), in which he traces the harsh destiny of three young poets, Gilbert (q.v.), Chatterton and A. Chénier (q.v.), while in his masterpiece, *Servitude et grandeur militaires* (1835; Eng. trans. *The Military Necessity*, 1953), he gives a very personal interpretation of the soldier's life. This period of successful work coincides with the years of his liaison with the actress Marie Dorval, and on its breakdown he withdrew from social life, living very quietly, dividing his time between Paris and his country estate. From 1839 to 1844 he wrote his greatest poetry, in its dignity of style and nobility of thought unique in French literature. A pessimist with the will to endure he memorably sets out his philosophy in such major poems as ' La Mort du loup ', ' La Maison du berger ' and ' Le Mont des Oliviers '. His latest poetry, *Les Destinées*, appeared the year after his death from cancer in Paris. His interesting *Correspondance, 1816–63*, was edited in 1905. See his *Œuvres complètes*, edited by F. Baldensperger (2 vols., 1948–9).

**Vildrac, Charles,** pseudonym of **Charles Messager** (1882–     ), French dramatist. Born in Paris, he made a name for himself with *Paquebot 'Tenacité'* (1920) and sustained his reputation with *Michel Auclair* (1922) and *La Brouille* (1931). His later work included *L'Air du temps* (1938), *D'Après l'écho* (1949) and *Dommages de Guerre* (1961).

**Villaespesa, Francisco** (1877–1936), Spanish poet and playwright, was born at Laujar, Almería. Going as a young man to Madrid he soon found himself in his element in literary circles with advanced views, but it was not until 1911 that he was wholeheartedly accepted as a playwright with *El alcázar de las perlas*. His *Obras completas* (12 vols., 1927) comprise an astonishing variety of themes both in plays and poetry all set in a new style, dated now, but which then seemed excitingly modern. With the change in taste coming in during the 1920's his books rapidly lost popularity. Some of his work may be read in English translation in T. Walsh's *Hispanic Anthology* (1920) and in H. E. Fish's *Translations from Hispanic Poets* (1938). Villaespesa died in Madrid.

**Villehardouin, Geffroy de** (*d.* 1213?), French prose-writer. Born near Troyes, Champagne, he took part in the Fourth Crusade (1199), leading an embassy to Venice to come to an agreement with the Doge Dandolo about provisions and transport. Having accomplished that mission he led an army east and took part in the capture of Constantinople (1204). Thereafter he established the Latin empire of Romania and became marshal of it. He left an important historical work, the *Conquête de Constantinople*, worthy of notice not only by reason of its first-hand account of chivalry in action in a crusade, but as the first historical work concerned with medieval Europe which is of literary value. The first complete edition of it was published in Paris in 1585. A modern critical edition appeared in 1938–9 and there is an English translation in Everyman's Library.

**Villiers de l'Isle-Adam, Philippe-August-Mathias** (1838–1889), French poet and prose-writer. Born at St-Brieuc, Brittany, of an old and noble family claiming descent from a grand master of the Knights of Malta, he spent his life in proud poverty in Paris. Living in his own strange world of the imagination influenced by the satanism of Baudelaire (q.v.) and the bizarrerie of Hoffmann (q.v.) with its speculation in the realms of the occult, streaked with a sense of cruelty derived from Poe, he may be called the original Symbolist. His earliest work of importance was *Premières poésies* (1858), but *Isis* (1862) was the first of his publications to reveal his true style; it is a romance of the supernatural. Best known are the short stories in the two series of his *Contes cruels* (1883 and 1889), powerful fantasies, while his high-flying poetic drama, *Axel* (1890), contains his finest lyrical work. He died of cancer in Paris. His *Œuvres complètes* appeared in ten volumes between 1914 and 1929.

**Villon, François** (1431 ?–1466 ?), French poet, whose real name seems to have been **François de Montcorbier**, was born in Paris and graduated at the university there in 1452. Breaking away from the family of his relation, Guillaume de Villon, who had brought him up, he played fast and loose, was implicated in a murder and robbery with violence, and only escaped death by flight. After a time of lying low at Angers, he went to Blois in 1457 and gained some place at the court of Charles d'Orléans. Wandering on again he next confronts us in prison once more, and the last that is heard of him is sentence of perpetual banishment from Paris being passed against him. Apart from odd short pieces, Villon's work consists of two collections of poetry, *Les Lais* (1456) and *Le Testament* (1461), the latter containing the famous *ballades*. In his mingling of the happiness of earthly pleasures with thoughts of death lurking round the corner, and expressions of faith with obscenity, he reveals himself as the somehow likeable reprobate, very alive and very human. Above all it is his message of the vanity of human wishes, expressed half sadly, half whimsically, which has won the hearts of a wide variety of readers who could never be induced to contemplate a line of his remote contemporaries. Much busy scholarship has lately been at work to 'explain' Villon's literary ancestry, but it is better to read his poetry. There are editions of the *Œuvres* by L. Thuasne (1923) and A. Longnon and L. Foulet (1930). See the English translation, *Complete Poems of François Villon*, by B. Saklatvala (1968).

**Vinje, Aasmund Olafsen** (1818–1870), Norwegian man of letters, was born at Vinje in miserably poor circumstances. He took up journalism, became involved in the movement for New Norwegian and started a review in that language, *Dølen* ('The Dalesman'). After that he wrote only in New Norwegian, except for a book in English, *A Norseman's Views of Britain and the British* (1863). He died at Gran in Hadeland.

**Vinogradov, Anatoly Kornelyevich** (1888– ), Russian Soviet historical novelist. His easily written biographical novels include *Tri tsveta vremeni* (1930; Eng. trans. *Three Colours of Time*, 1946), about Stendhal (q.v.), and *Chyorny konsul* (1931; Eng. trans. *Black Consul*, 1934) about Toussaint of Haiti.

**Vishnevsky, Vsevolod** (1900–1956), Russian Soviet playwright, became known for his *Dramaticheskie proizvedeniya* (1932; Eng. trans. *An Optimistic Tragedy* in H. G. Scott and R. Carr's *Four Soviet Plays*, 1937). Since the war his *Nezabyvayemy 1919* (publ. 1950, 'The Unforgettable 1919') has been acclaimed and awarded a Stalin prize (1949), rather, it seems, for content than for literary value.

**Visnapuu, Henrik** (1890–1951), Estonian poet, the most considerable produced during his country's short independence, was born at Leebiku. He had tried many careers before war overtook him. After that he spent some miserable years in refugee camps and finally died in the United States. Although he wrote much narrative verse he is more noteworthy as a lyric poet, of love themes in the early period (*Amores*, 1917) and later of patriotic ones ranging in date from *Ränikivi* (1925) to *Mare Balticum* (1948). Some of his poetry appears in English translation in W. K. Matthews's *Anthology of Modern Estonian Poetry* (1953).

**Vittorini, Elio** (1908–1966), Italian novelist, born in Syracuse. A Communist who appeared after the war as an incompromising advocate of realism in literature, and wrote such a harsh, even crude book as *Le donne di Messina* (1949; Eng. trans. *Women on the Road*, 1961), he yet had earlier published in *Conversazione in Sicilia* (1941; Eng. trans. 1948) something poetical and delicate. It is, however, a style to which he never returned. He died in Milan.

**Vogt, Nils Collet** (1864–1937), Norwegian poet. Born in Kristiania of wealthy conservative parents, he rebelled against his class and took a part in the left wing politics of the latter half of the last century. One of the greatest of Norway's lyricists, his strong and independent character comes out in his work, powerful and sure in his earlier books, such as *Digte* (1887) and *September brand* (1907), sad and pondering in his later, such as *Hjemkomst* (1917) and *Vind og bølge* (1927). He died at Lillehammer.

**Voiture, Vincent** (1598–1648), French poet. A native of Amiens, where his father was a grocer, he became the petted, precious member of the Rambouillet *salon*, so important an institution in the literary and social life of Paris in the time of Louis XIII (*see* Scudéry). A stylist of taste and an accomplished metrist with real feeling for medieval poetry, his *Œuvres* were first collected in 1649, the year after his death from wounds received in a duel in Paris. An edition of selected work was produced by A. Arnoux (1907).

**Voltaire,** name assumed in 1718 by **François-Marie Arouet** (1694–1778), French dramatist, poet and prose-writer. He was born in Paris the fifth child of a well-to-do notary, received a sound classical education under the Jesuits at the Collège Louis-le-Grand, and then joined his father to serve his articles. Finding this life irksome in the extreme he made use of the generous allowance made to him by his father to win his way into influential circles, and he became the prized wit of several *salons*. It was now the time of the Regency when politicians and place-seekers were killing off their enemies with lampoons, and Voltaire's devastating abilities in this direction brought him social success, but also a spell in the Bastille (1717). He, however, turned this enforced leisure to good account by using it to write *Œdipe*, his first tragedy, acted with success in the winter of 1718. On his release earlier that year he had plunged into the financial speculations of Paris, and with his clear head so successful was he that before long he was master of a handsome fortune which was to stand him in good stead. Having gained a large and influential audience he next produced his *Henriade*, an epic poem in praise of Henri IV, religious toleration and Protestantism, which was published at Rouen in 1723 and, disguised under the title of *La Ligue ou Henri le Grand*, was smuggled into Paris. His reputation was increasing and he was successfully pushing his way at court when as the result of a quarrel he found himself once more in the Bastille, and was only released on condition that he left the country. He landed in England in the early summer of 1726, was made free of London literary circles, won the friendship of Chesterfield and Peterborough, and having gained a good knowledge of English was able to study British institutions, literature, philosophy and science. Locke's philosophy and Newton's astronomical physics particularly attracted him, and the English deists provided him with many of his future weapons. He remained in England until 1729, when he was allowed to return to France, taking with him his partly completed *Histoire de Charles XII* and material for *Lettres sur les anglais*, the first of which, the best and most lasting of his historical works, appeared in 1731, and the second in 1734, an English translation having been published the year before. In the meantime he was writing plays, having been fired by a study of Shakespeare to emulate him in the classical manner. *Brutus* was performed in 1730, *Zaïre*, his best and one of the best of its kind in French literature, in 1732, while *Mahomet* (1742) and *Mérope* (1743) were worthy successors. Meanwhile the happiest period of Voltaire's life had now opened with its domesticity in a fine country house; for in 1733 began his liaison with the beautiful and talented Marquise du Châtelet, whose husband's mansion they settled down in together until the 'divine Émilie's' death in 1749. Here at Cirey in Champagne he wrote a variety of works, such as the philosophical poem *Discours en vers sur l'Homme* (1738), the tale *Zadig* (1747), and the greater part of *Le Siècle de Louis XIV*, not published until 1751. In the latter year Voltaire accepted the invitation of Frederick II of Prussia to come to Berlin, where he was shown every mark of favour and made king's chamberlain. Jealousies with members of the Berlin Academy and disagreements with Frederick finally led to his return to France in 1753. His wealth having by now still further increased since the greater part of his investments were in army supplies and wars had not been lacking, he settled down to a country life of great comfort in the neighbourhood of Geneva, first at Les Délices and from 1758 at

Ferney just inside the French border. At Les Délices he showed his pessimism in the face of hostile natural forces in his didactic poem on the Lisbon earthquake, *Sur le désastre de Lisbonne et sur la Loi naturelle* (1756), while in *La Pucelle*, published the year before, he showed that he was as much as ever the enemy of superstition and the champion of toleration. After he had settled at Ferney this became even more strongly marked and the last twenty years of his life can be looked upon as not only a literary but a practical crusade against 'l'Infâme', that is, autocracy, tyrannical privilege and vested interests that crush the individual. He began with a devastating attack on the complacency of the time in *Candide* (1759), one of the most brilliant satires of the Age of Reason, while his *Pièces originales concernant la mort des Sieurs Calas* (1762) gives literary expression to the part he took in fighting against a terrible miscarriage of justice. His noble *Traité sur la tolérance* followed next year, and other books meant to bring home to a wide public the outrages against humanity carried out under the names of religion and patriotism were *Relation de la mort du Chevalier de la Barre* (1766) and *Fragments sur l'Inde et sur le Général Lalli* (1773). The Church of Rome then and since has thought fit to interpret Voltaire's 'Écrasez l'Infâme' as directed against Christianity, which is untrue; indeed when Holbach's (q.v.) *Système de la nature* (1770) declared for atheism Voltaire whole-heartedly opposed it. So his busy life continued until he was induced to come to Paris in 1778 to be present at the production of his play *Irène*. Fêted as a national hero the strain was too much for the veteran, who died at the end of May. The influence of the man has been even greater than the writer; his perfect style can be enjoyed in *Charles XII*, *Candide*, *Zadig*, *Zaïre*, and other works as pure literature; but it is as the keenly incisive moralist, the greatest of that clear-headed age, the Age of Reason, that he shook the world, applying the necessary alternative approach to Rousseau when the time came to overturn privilege and make the rights of man a reality. There is the great original edition of his works edited by Condorcet (q.v.), Beaumarchais (q.v.) and others between 1785 and 1789. The two standard critical editions are those by Beuchot (72 vols., Paris, 1829–40) and Moland (50 vols., Paris, 1877–83), but the correspondence must be studied in the Swiss Bestermann edition which began in 1953. The greater part of Voltaire's works—all the most important and many others—have been translated into English.

**Vondel, Joost van den** (1587–1679), Dutch dramatist and poet, was born in Cologne to Mennonite refugees from Antwerp. He became a hosier in Amsterdam where his business flourished, at the same time taking his place as a leading light in the literary circle which met in the house of the patron Roemer Visscher. Here his literary knowledge widened, and if one compares his first two dramas, *Het Pascha* (1612) and *Hierusalem verwoest* (1620), with his third, *Palamedes* (1625), one can see the narrow Mennonite with his Bible as his sole inspiration becoming a lover of the ancient classics through contact with such scholars as Vossius and Heinsius. *Palamedes*, written as a protest against the execution of Oldenbarneveldt, brought Vondel fame and he was commissioned to write for the national theatre. Unhappily, just when his affairs seemed brightest, domestic troubles fell on him; his wife and two of his children died, and he was left with a worthless son who so ruined him that he had to sell his business and take a job in a pawnshop. Adversity brought about a change of belief and he became a Roman Catholic in 1640, and now, alienated from his old friends, he withdrew more and more into himself, sustained by his new faith. Of his later dramas *Lucifer* (1654; Eng. trans. 1898; second ed., 1917) is the finest and is in fact his masterpiece. His own favourite was *Jephta* (1659), while *Noah* (1667) contains beautiful lyrics. His short poems, of which collections were published in 1647 and 1682, have, according to many critics, stood the test of time better than any of his other work. Vondel died in Amsterdam at the age of ninety-one. The monstrous charge made against Milton that passages in *Paradise Lost* and *Samson Agonistes* are plagiarisms from Vondel (E. Gosse, *Studies in Northern Literature*, 1879; and G. Edmundson, *Milton and Vondel*, 1885) is absolutely untrue, as was shown by a Dutch scholar J. J. Moolhuizen in his *Vondel's Lucifer en Milton's Verloren Paradijs* (1895). A complete edition of the works of Vondel appeared in ten volumes, 1927–40.

**Voronsky, Alexander Konstantinovich** (1884–1930?), Russian Soviet prose-writer. As a critic he exemplifies the more conservative Marxist approach, and as a literary editor of a well-known periodical brought trouble on himself for accepting the contributions of very tepid party members, as a result of which he was expelled from the party in 1927. That year his best-known book, *Za zhivoy i myertvoy vodoy* (Eng. trans. *Waters of Life and Death*, 1936), was published. He was readmitted to the party a year or so later and then disappeared for good. He was a native of Tambov province.

**Vörösmarty, Mihály** (1800–1855), Hungarian poet. Born at Kápolnásnyék, he achieved fame with *Zalán futása* (1825, 'The Rout of Zalán'), an epic poem celebrating the victory of Árpád, one of the masterpieces of Magyar literature. His lyrics, to be found in *Vörösmarty összes munkái* (his collected works, 8 vols., 1884–5), are considered excellent. He died in Pest.

**Vosmaer, Carel** (1826–1888), Dutch novelist and translator. Born in The Hague, he became a literary journalist and was regarded as a highly perceptive art critic, as is proved by his *Rembrandt* (1863). His original poetry is of little value, but his translations in hexameters of Homer (*Ilias*, 1879–80; *Odussee*, 1888) are brilliant and the best examples of their kind in Dutch literature. Of his novels the most celebrated is *Amazone* (1880; Eng. trans. *The Amazon*, 1884). He died at Montreux.

**Voss, Johann Heinrich** (1751–1826), German poet and translator. Born at Sommersdorf, he was educated at Göttingen and after graduating became rector of Otterndorf gymnasium. His literary career may be divided into three parts, the first being the period of his poetry influenced by Klopstock (q.v.) and romantic idealism, often with a mixture of sentimentality (*Die Leibeigenschaft*, 1776, *Selmas*

*Geburtstag*, 1776, and *Der Hagestolz*, 1779). But with his intense study of the classics, the first-fruit of which was his translation of the *Odyssey* (1781), his style changed and he produced several idylls of country life in hexameters, the finest of them, *Luise* (1783-4; recast 1795), exerting considerable influence on Goethe. In fact, Voss may well be considered the Greek guide of Goethe and Schiller especially after he settled in Jena in 1802. His third period begins with his highly successful translation of the *Iliad* (1793). Becoming professor of classics at Heidelberg in 1805 he brought out a translation of Horace the following year, and many others, including an unsuccessful one of Shakespeare's works which cannot stand comparison with that by A. W. Schlegel (q.v.). Voss died at Heidelberg.

**Voss, Richard** (1851–1918), German dramatist and novelist, born at Neugrape, Pomerania, became known for his sombre psychological plays, such as *Savonarola* (1878) and *Schuldig* (1892). A striking war book, *Brutus, auch Du*, appeared in 1917. He died at Berchtesgaden.

**Vrchlický, Jaroslav,** pseudonym of **Emil Frída** (1853–1912), Czech man of letters. Born at Louny the son of a business man, he became a professor of literary history at Prague. His literary output was enormous, and by its sheer bulk if nothing else might have been regarded as sure to dominate his country's literature. Certainly his poetry has merit, but is too diffuse in style and too derivative in manner to be considered great. What he did without doubt was to increase the possibilities of the Czech language and by nearly a hundred translations to introduce English and French literature into Czech letters, displacing the pre-eminent influence of German. His most permanent work is his epic, *Mythy* (two parts, 1879–80). Insane from 1908, he died at Domažlice.

# W

**Wachenhusen, Hans** (1822–1898), German journalist and writer of travel books. Born in Trier, he was one of the greatest war reporters of his day, and was noted for his accuracy and for his glowing style. Besides his reports on war in Italy (1859), Austria (1866) and France (1870) he wrote, among many others, an excellent book of travel in the Middle East, *Von Widdin nach Stambul* (1855) and sketches of Paris life, *Paris und die Pariser* (1855) and *Rouge et Noir* (1864). He died in Marburg.

**Wackenroder, Wilhelm Heinrich** (1773–1798), German essayist. Born in Berlin, the son of an overbearing Prussian civil servant, who forced him to follow his profession, he was a physically weak and timid dreamer, a kind of frail Novalis (q.v.). He exemplifies very clearly the hold which a shadowy medievalism as an escape from reality exercised over the young romantics at the turn of the century. A lover of Gothic architecture, he wrote a number of quietly brooding essays which seem to be lit by the colours of stained glass windows, and which were collected by his robust friend and protector Tieck (q.v.) with additions of his own as *Herzensergiessungen eines kunstliebenden Klosterbruders* (1797). In this and in *Phantasien über die Kunst*, another collection of essays on art, edited and published by Tieck in 1814, the religious implications of art are expounded, and the Roman Catholic revival, in which several of the German romantics, including F. Schlegel (q.v.) were involved, can be seen in embryo. Wackenroder seems to have sketched out the romantic novel which Tieck afterwards made his own as *Franz Sternbalds Wanderungen*. He died in Berlin.

**Wagner, Heinrich Leopold** (1747–1779), German dramatist. Born in Strassburg, he was a fellow student of Goethe at the university there in 1771 and fell under his influence. At the core of the so-called *Sturm und Drang* movement, his realistic plays clearly show the revolt of the young middle-class intellectuals against the outworn German social caste system and against a reactionary moral code dictated by the law and the Church. In his most notable play, the tragedy *Die Kindesmörderin* (1776), he passionately denounces a society which condemns to death a girl who in desperation at the result of her seduction has murdered her baby. Wagner died in Frankfurt-am-Main. The first volume of his *Gesammelte Werke* came out in 1923, but the edition has never been completed.

**Wagner, Richard** (1813–1883), German composer and dramatist. Born in Leipzig, he inherited from his father a love of drama and poetry scarcely less strong than his love of music, and in fact he was to make one the handmaid of the other, writing his own libretti for his musical works. An absolute romantic in his literary as in his musical creations, he approached everything in an idealistic, emotional, sensual light that certainly did not belong to the Middle Ages which he sought to evoke. Perhaps rather it is truer to say that he did not seek to recall the true epic days of Germany but to form his own idea of them. Without discussing his musical career it is enough to say that his work as a man of letters consists of the dramas for the stage as it then was and those for the new stage he wished to create. Of the first may be mentioned *Rienzi* (1842), *Der fliegende Holländer* (1843), *Tannhäuser* (1845) and *Die Meistersinger von Nürnberg* (1862), and in the new style for the music-drama, the almost religious rite of the *Festspiel*, are *Lohengrin* (1850), *Tristan und Isolde* (1859), *Der Ring des Nibelungen* (1863)—Hebbel's (q.v.) work on the same subject had appeared the year before—*Götterdämmerung* (1870) and *Parzifal* (1877). In all these he takes medieval German literary themes and creates from them his own works making them to accord with his ideal of the unity of the arts and elevating them together into a new plane of experience. The Bayreuth Theatre is the visible monument of his ambition to that end, a kind of temple of all the muses. Wagner died in Venice.

**Waiblinger, Wilhelm** (1804–1830), German poet. Born at Heilbronn, he wrote a strange, unbalanced novel, *Phaeton*, in 1823, a work streaked through with a near-genius that always eluded him. He visited the poet Hölderlin (q.v.), living by this time mad and in seclusion, and has left a vivid account of the meeting. Urged by Waiblinger's friends Uhland (q.v.) and Mörike (q.v.), Cotta the publisher provided him with funds to go to Italy and he made at once for Rome. This was fatal for him. He idled away much of his time, and died in very straitened circumstances, Cotta having refused to send him more money, in Rome. A large edition of his collected works was brought out by Canitz in 1839–40, but he is best read in the judicious selection of his poetry made by his faithful friend Mörike in 1844.

**Waller, Max,** *see* **Warlomont, M.**

**Wallin, Johan Olof** (1779–1839), Swedish religious poet, the greatest that his country has produced, was born at St Tuna and died an archbishop at Uppsala. He wrote many hymns for the official hymnary which he edited and completed in 1819. His best work is his poem inspired by the Swedish cholera epidemic, *Dödens ängel* (1834; Eng. trans. *The Angel of Death*, 1910).

**Wallis, A. S. C.,** pseudonym of **Adèle Sophia Cornelia van Antal,** *née* **Opzoomer** (1857–1925), Dutch novelist, was born in Utrecht and died in Rotterdam. She specialized in historical novels, her earliest being her best. Long, somewhat gloomy, they have a certain power, such as is to be found in *In dagen van strijd* (1878; Eng. trans. *In Troubled Times*, 1888) and *Vorstengunst* (1883; Eng. trans. *Royal Favour*, 1885).

**Walschap, Gerard** (1898–    ), Flemish novelist, the best of his generation, was born at Londerzeel. He made his name with *Adelaïde* (1929), an attack on Roman Catholicism and its culture in Flanders, which he regarded as merely superficial. He left the Catholic Church after this and turned to a humanistic concept of life, which developed into an ideal revealed in his finest book, *Houtekiet* (1940; Fr. trans. 1942). Of his later novels *Zuster Virgilia* (1951) may be mentioned.

**Walser, Martin** (1927–    ), German dramatist and novelist, born at Wasserburg, Bodensee, was conscripted in 1944 and two years later was able to pursue a university education. He was in business from 1951 to 1957. In his two most promising novels, *Ehen in Philippsburg* (1957) and *Halbzeit* (1960), he explores the various approaches to social life in the light of the different ideologies which have arisen since 1945, not least among them neo-Fascism. In *Eich und Angora* (1962) the problem is still pursued.

**Walther von der Vogelweide** (1168?–1230), German poet. Born near Sterzing in the Tirol, he studied poetry under Reinmar, the ducal court poet at Vienna, and was soon such an adept that he became a rival of his master and was forced to take to the road in 1198. He now wandered from court to court to earn his living as a Minnesinger, but his caustic satires pleased few and he sometimes lived on the edge of starvation. His patriotic poems, however, won him the patronage of the Emperor Frederick II ('Stupor mundi') in 1211 and he was granted land in the neighbourhood of Würzburg, where he died. His love-poetry is perhaps the best in medieval northern Europe, and he widened the scope of poets by introducing all manner of new subjects ranging from devotional themes to pleasant fooling. His finest body of verse is that inspired by his support of the empire against the Papacy. The Lachmann-Kraus edition (tenth ed., 1936) is the key one. For English translations of his work see *The Selected Poems of Walther von der Vogelweide* by W. Alison Phillips (1896), *Songs and Sayings of W. v. d. V.* by F. Betts (1938) and *I Saw the World* by I. G. Colvin (1938).

**Warlomont, Maurice** (1860–1889), Belgian novelist and editor, who wrote under the name of **Max Waller**, was born and died in Brussels, where as founder-editor of *La Jeune Belgique* he did more than any-one to free Belgium from almost entire literary dependence on France. Delicate in health, he wore himself out in this mission, which in fact was soon to have such noticeable results. His own work, e.g. the novel *Greta Friedmann* (1885), has hardly stood the test of time.

**Wassermann, Jakob** (1873–1934), German novelist. Born at Fürth, Bavaria, of Jewish parents, he became a journalist in 1895, and published his first novel, *Die Juden von Zirndorf*, in 1897 (Eng. trans. *The Jews of Zirndorf* 1933). This and later novels made him well known, especially for his treatment of social problems, his powers of characterization and his psychological insight. Strange twists of introspection as strange as some of his pen portraits, good dialogue, and plots, intricate but with movement, added to his popularity which was widened by a number of successful translations. The best known are *Christian Wahnschaffe* (1919; Eng. trans. *The World's Illusion*, 1920) and *Der Fall Maurizius* (1928; Eng. trans. *The Maurizius Case*, 1929). His best short stories are those contained in *Das Gänsemännchen* (1915; Eng. trans. *The Goose Man*, 1922), and he wrote an autobiography, *Mein Weg als Deutscher und Jude* (1921; Eng. trans. *My Life as German and Jew*, 1933). Elected a member of the Prussian Academy, he was deprived of his membership by the Nazis on their coming to power in 1933 and his books were banned. He never recovered from this persecution, dying soon afterwards at Alt-Aussee where he had lived since 1919.

**Wauchier de Denain** (early thirteenth century), French poet and translator, was in the service of Philip of Namur and for him translated pious works, but it is as the author of the latter part of the *Conte del Graal*, the rest being by Chrétien de Troyes (q.v.), that he is remembered. The *Conte* was edited by C. Potvin (1866).

**Wazyk, Adam** (1905–   ), Polish poet. Born in Warsaw, he became known as a translator, especially of Apollinaire (q.v.), and a playwright. But it is only in recent years that he has gained world-wide fame as the author of a savage attack on the evils of Communist bureaucracy in Poland, his poem known as *Poemat dla dorostych* ('Poem for Adults'), which was published in *Nowa Kultura*, journal of the Polish Writers' Association, in 1955. No action was taken against him owing to the fall of the Stalinists from power in Poland soon afterwards, and he and a growing number of Polish men of letters have continued to take their stand against official Communism. *Poemat dla dorostych* and some of Ważyk's other verse have been translated in R. Conquest's *Back to Life* (1958).

**Weckherlin, Georg Rudolf** (1584–1653), German poet. Born in Stuttgart, he joined the diplomatic service, came to England in 1610 on a visit, and in 1616 settled there definitely, married an Englishwoman and was employed in the Secretary of State's office in London. He published a collection of verse, *Oden und Gesänge*, in 1619, and his later poetry, showing the influence of Opitz (q.v.), appeared as *Gaistliche und Weltliche Gedichte* (Amsterdam, 1641). He was employed later as Latin secretary, being superseded by Milton, with whom, however, he remained on good terms. He introduced the sonnet form into German poetry, and came to be regarded as the most important link in the so-called transitional stage which joins Opitz to the German poets of the later seventeenth and early eighteenth centuries. Weckherlin died in Westminster.

**Wecksell, Josef Julius** (1838–1907), Finnish dramatist writing in Swedish, was born in Åbo. Very precocious, he had produced an impressive amount of highly gifted verse by 1860, and two years later brought out the greatest historical drama in Swedish during the nineteenth century, *Daniel Hjort*. Shortly afterwards he became insane and so remained until his death over forty years later in Helsinki. His works had been collected in 1868.

**Wedekind, Frank** (1864–1918), German dramatist. Born in Hanover, he became a journalist and later secretary of a circus before turning actor and producing his own plays. These, influenced by Strindberg (q.v.)

and the free moral thought coming out of Scandinavia, are erotic and harsh in tone with an admixture of symbolism. It is not surprising that they aroused controversy, and Wedekind was imprisoned for a time for his uncompromising opinions. His best-known play is *Frühlings Erwachen* (1891; Eng. trans. *Spring's Awakening*, 1923), and among the rest may be mentioned *Der Erdgeist* (1895; Eng. trans. *The Earth Spirit*, 1923) and *Die Büchse der Pandora* (1902; Eng. trans. *Pandora's Box*, 1923). Five of his plays were translated together as *Five Tragedies of Sex* in 1952. Wedekind died in Munich.

**Weil, R.,** *see* **Coolus, R.**

**Weil, Simone** (1909–1943), French prose-writer, born in Paris. She became a schoolmistress and in 1936 went to Spain to fight for the republic in the civil war. Back in France she joined the Resistance movement in 1942, but died in London. She gained posthumous fame as a writer with the publication of her manuscripts as *La Pesanteur et la Grâce* (1947; Eng. trans. *Gravity and Grace*, 1952), *La Connaissance surnaturelle* (1949), *L'Enracinement* (1949; Eng. trans. *The Need for Roots*, 1952), *Lettre à un religieux* (1951), *La Source grecque* (1953) and *Pensées sans ordre concernant l'amour de Dieu* (1962), nobly expressing her deep Christian faith and belief in social justice and human salvation.

**Weise, Christian** (1642–1708), German novelist and playwright, was born at Zittau, Saxony, where he died. As headmaster of the Hochschule there he wrote plays for his school all of a rationalistic strain as though to instil into his pupils the practical approach to life which would enable them to do well in the world. In his novels he takes the same standpoint. His plays were collected as *Zittauisches Theatrum* (1683). A good representative novel is *Die drey ergsten Ertznarren* (1672; ed. W. Braune, 1878). Weise in many ways a spokesman of the rising German middle classes, and in helping to condition them for their new role may be said to have had a considerable influence on the origins of the great bourgeois literature of the eighteenth century.

**Weisze, Christian Felix** (1726–1804), German playwright and translator. Born at Annaberg, he became a student friend of Lessing (q.v.) at Leipzig and from him imbibed ideas about the new currents of literature and especially of the theatre. He soon came into collision with Gottsched (q.v.), at that time the acknowledged dictator of letters. When Weisze's opera *Der Teufel ist los* was produced Gottsched loudly attacked it for not conforming to his dramatic rules, but Weisze won the day and may be said to have rounded off his victory with his essays on dramatic art, *Beitrag zum deutschen Theater* (5 vols., 1759–68), in which he included several translations of Shakespeare's tragedies, thereby at any rate giving German writers a taste of something new. His interesting *Selbstbiographie* was published in 1806, two years after his death in Leipzig.

**Welhaven, Johan Sebastian Cammermejer** (1807–1873), Norwegian poet and critic. Born in Kristiania, he was professor of philosophy at the university there from 1846–1868, and later became director of the Society of Arts. As one who believed it wrong to turn away from

Danish literature for purely political motives and concentrate on a self-conscious national literature, he became the spokesman of the conservative men of letters in Norway who ranged themselves against the nationalists led by Wergeland (q.v.). So acrimonious did the ensuing controversy become that Welhaven's engagement to Wergeland's sister was broken off, and the two enemy poets wasted years in a bitter paper war. His first work, the sonnet sequence, *Norges Dæmring* (1834, 'The Twilight of Norway') was an epoch-making publication, but was unfairly denounced as unpatriotic by his opponents as if patriotism had anything to do with the quality of literature. In spite of Wergeland's far greater power, his poetry often appears ragged and unfinished beside the smooth craftsmanship of Welhaven. His later collections, such as *Nyere Digte* (1845) and *Halvhundrede Digte* (1848), contain some of the most beautiful lyrics in the language. Welhaven died in Kristiania. His complete works were collected in the definitive edition of 1943.

**Wellekens, Jan Baptiste** (1658–1726), Dutch poet, an interesting link between the United Provinces and Italy, was born at Aalst. In 1676 he went to Italy to join the international artists' colony at Rome, and during his stay of ten years became a member of ex-Queen Christina of Sweden's Arcadian Academy. Bad eyesight forced him to abandon painting and he returned to the United Provinces where he devoted himself to literature at Amsterdam. His lyrics, some of them inspired by folk-song, others arcadian, others religious were collected in 1711. Of his plays, *Amintas*, a free adaptation of Tasso's (q.v.) work, appeared in 1715.

**Werfel, Franz** (1890–1945), Austrian poet and novelist, born in Prague. He early became identified with the literary circle which included Kafka (q.v.) and Max Brod (q.v.). Throughout his work there persists a mixture of Jewish-Oriental and Austrian-Catholic influence, and the ensuing emotionalism is to be seen in early poetry, such as *Der Weltfreund* (1911). His poetry was collected as *Gedichte aus den Jahren 1908–1945* (1948; Eng. trans. from MS., *Poems*, 1945). But his first popular success was the novel *Verdi* (1924; Eng. trans. 1925), which was followed by such other fiction as *Barbara oder Die Frömmigkeit* (1929; Eng. trans. *The Pure in Heart*, 1931) and *Die Geschwister von Neapel* (1931; Eng. trans. *The Pascarella Family*, 1932). By 1939 he had almost despaired of life when he published *Der veruntreute Himmel* (Eng. trans. *Embezzled Heaven*, 1940), but turning as a last hope to spiritual things became world famous with his novel on the theme of the miracle at Lourdes, *Das Lied von Bernadette* (1941; Eng. trans. *The Song of Bernadette*, 1942). Werfel had left Austria at the time of the German occupation (1938), but when the Germans caught up with him at Paris (1940) he managed to escape to California, where he died by suicide at Beverley Hills.

**Wergeland, Henrik Arnold** (1808–1845), Norwegian poet. Born at Kristiansand, he was the son of a clergyman much involved in political life, which had gained a new significance as a result of the granting of the Norwegian constitution in 1814. On becoming a student at Kristiania University where he read theology he began to write in verse and prose, evincing in all a love of freedom and of nature. Breaking with the conservative romantics, such as Welhaven (q.v.), he announced the necessity of a reassessment of Norwegian literature in the light of the new political nationalism and a re-appraisal of religion. His *Skabelsen, Mennesket og Messias* (1830) aroused considerable religious controversy and put an end to any hope of his entering the Church. Thereafter, until in 1840 he was appointed keeper of State Archives, he led the life of a Bohemian literary journalist, well known as a radical and gathering round him all the younger, noisier elements in Norwegian intellectual life. Although often marred by slackness of diction and hastiness of com-position his best poetry can reach such heights as no other Norwegian poet has attained. A complete edition of his works was published in 1918, and an English translation of many of his best poems appeared in 1929. He died in Kristiania of rheumatic fever as a result of catch-ing cold in damp muniment vaults.

**Werner, Friedrich Ludwig Zacharias** (1768–1823), German dramatist. Born in Königsberg to an eccentric professor of rhetoric and belles-lettres and a doting, slightly mentally deranged mother, his chances of growing up to be quite sound in mind were slight. It is not there-fore surprising that he did become one of the most notoriously unbalanced characters thrown up by romanticism. Wayward and undisciplined he yet attracted people, even those who secretly dis-approved of his scandalous domestic life (married and divorced three times). He first served in the Prussian civil service in the department of justice in Poland, as strange a recruit as E. T. A. Hoffmann (q.v.) was later to be, and came to rest at Warsaw for a time. Following in his mother's footsteps as a religious maniac, he soon began to indulge in mysticism and became a freemason of the esoteric variety. He now saw himself as a second Schiller, and in 1803 began to try his hand at drama with his inflated *Die Söhne des Tales* (Eng. trans. *The Brethren of the Cross*, 1892) and followed this up with *Das Kreuz an der Ostsee* (1806). Schiller having died in 1805, Werner made his way to Weimar and claimed his place as Schiller's successor with *Martin Luther* in his pocket (1807). Not for the first or last time Goethe's judgment failed him and he supported him to the exclusion of Kleist (q.v.). Certainly his later plays were actable, but all his dramas are of poor workmanship. As the author of *Der 24. Februar* (1810; Eng. trans. *The 24th of February*, 1903) he can at any rate claim to be the father of the 'fate drama', so worthily taken up seven years later by Grillparzer (q.v.). In 1811 the inevitable hap-pened, and the weary seeker after divine truth was not only received into the Roman Catholic Church but ordained priest at Rome. He later became a popular histrionic preacher at Vienna, where he died. Carlyle has a brilliant study of him in his *Critical Essays*. See also the interesting biography by L. Guinet (1964).

**Wessel, Johan Herman** (1742–1785), Danish writer. Although born at Jonsrud in Norway and of Norwegian ancestry, he settled early in Copenhagen and may be looked on as a purely Danish author. He lived a naturally Bohemian life which, while it hastened his death at forty-three, was very merry while it lasted, as merry as his clever light verses with their comic narratives which are still much esteemed in Scandinavia. According to E. L. Bredsdorff, a modern Danish critic, his chief play, *Kærlighed uden Strømper* (1772), is 'one of the most comic tragedies of world literature'. It is in heroic verse, and so effective was its irony that it made an end of pseudo-French and pseudo-Italian classicism in Danish letters. His collected works appeared in 1787, and in recent times there has been an edition of his poetry (1936).

**Wette, Hermann** (1857–1919), German author, a physician by profession, turned Chamisso's (q.v.) *Peter Schlemihl* into a play, but is chiefly known as the author of a powerful novel, *Wunderliche Heilige* (1913). His wife **Adelheid** (1858–1916) was the sister of the composer Humperdinck and composed libretti for his operas, including the famous *Hänsel und Gretel* (1893).

**Wickram, Jörg** (1518?–1560?), German dramatist and novelist. He was probably born in Colmar, Alsace, where he became town clerk and directed a school of Meistersingers from 1549. In 1555 he became town clerk of Burgheim, also in Alsace, and there he died. He is best represented as a playwright by *Tobias* (1551), but it is as the first German writer of fiction in prose after the Reformation that he is remembered now. Of his novels, which are full of graphic descriptions of contemporary life, the best are *Der Jungen Knaben Spiegel* (1554) and *Der Goldfaden*, published the same year, and considered his masterpiece. This latter was adapted by Brentano (q.v.) in 1809.

**Wieland, Christoph Martin** (1733–1813), German poet and novelist. Born of a wealthy family at Oberholzheim, near Biberach, Württemberg, he began to copy the style of Klopstock (q.v.) and spent some time in Switzerland as a guest of the influential critic Bodmer (q.v.). Leaving Zürich in 1760 he became a civil servant at Biberach, and having in his spare time translated over twenty of Shakespeare's plays (1762–6) was made professor of philosophy at Erfurt. He had by this time left behind him the religious manner of his poems of the Swiss period and allowed his love of the classics a free range, and it is in his clear, luminous, though sparing style that he stands out from his deeper, though often diffuse and turgid contemporaries, coming to be especially esteemed by Goethe and others when they had left the *Sturm und Drang* manner behind them. His sensuous humanism is apparent in his first really individualistic work, the philosophical romance *Agathon* (1766–7) and in such poetry as *Musarion* (1768), *Die Grazien* (1770) and *Der verklagte Amor* (1774). As a result of his educational novel, *Der goldene Spiegel* (1772), he was appointed tutor to the sons of the Grand Duchess of Saxe-Weimar, and he remained in Weimar for the rest of his life. In his quasi-philosophical, satirical novel, *Die Abderiten* (1774), he broke new ground, but it is as the author of his epic poem, *Oberon* (1780), that he is best known. This glowing work, based on the old French romance of Huon of Bordeaux, was translated into English in 1798, and the translation of it by John Quincy Adams, later President of the U.S.A., was edited in 1940. Wieland is also important as being one of the earliest to introduce the middle-eastern element into modern European literature. His works were first collected in forty-five volumes between 1794 and 1802.

**Wildenbruch, Ernst von** (1845–1909), German playwright and short-story writer, was born in Beirut, Syria, a member of a junior branch of the Hohenzollern family. At first in the army and later in the diplomatic service, he made his name as a writer of historical dramas. Realistic with a touch of pathos running through them, they stretch from *Harold* (1882; Eng. trans. 1891) to *Die Rabensteinerin* (1907; Eng. trans. *Barseba of Rabenstein*, 1909). Of his volumes of short stories the best known are *Der Meister von Tanagra* (1880; Eng. trans. *The Master of Tanagra*, 1886) and *Neid* (1900; Eng. trans. *Envy*, 1921). In his later years a very strong Prussian nationalist, Wildenbruch died in Berlin. His facile poetry hardly calls for notice.

**Wildermuth, Ottilie,** *née* **Rooschütz** (1817–1877), German novelist. Born at Rothenburg-am-Neckar, after her marriage in 1843 she moved to Tübingen where she died. She was well known in Swabian literary circles and numbered Uhland (q.v.) among her friends. Particularly a woman's novelist, in her quiet domestic stories she tells us much of the family life of her day. Typical of her work is *Im Tageslicht* (1861; Eng. trans. *By Daylight*, 1865) and *Beim Lampenlicht* (1878).

**Willy,** *see* **Gauthiers-Villars, H.**

**Winckelmann, Johann Joachim** (1717–1768), German art critic, whose influence in bringing classical taste to Germany and so to Goethe was very great, was born at Stendal, Saxony. He first became a private tutor, then rector of a gymnasium and next a librarian at Dresden, all the time devoting himself to the classics and to archaeological study. Next he turned Roman Catholic and having published his *Gedanken über die Nachahmung der griechischen Werke* (1755; Eng. trans. by H. Fuseli, 1765), the most influential of all his works, he went to Rome as Cardinal Albani's librarian, where he enjoyed every opportunity of following his archaeological pursuits. In 1758 he visited Pompeii, Herculaneum and Paestum, and offset these classical studies with renaissance ones at Florence. His masterly descriptions of the objects of art at Pompeii and Herculaneum break new ground in their scientific approach. He now turned to his monumental work on ancient art, *Geschichte der Kunst des Alterthums*, which was published in 1764, while his epigraphic studies resulted in *Monumenti Antichi Inediti* (1766). He had meanwhile been appointed superintendent of antiquities at Rome. While touring he was robbed and murdered by a fellow traveller at Trieste. Goethe paid tribute to him in his *Winckelmann und sein Jahrhundert* (1805). Winckelmann taught his age to see classical art as it really was, not through renaissance coloured glass. His *Werke* were published (13 vols.) in 1825–9.

**Winther, Rasmus Villads Christian Ferdinand** (1796–1876), Danish poet, was born at Fensmark, Zealand, and died in Paris. An undoubted derivative of Heine (q.v.) he had two subjects which he never tired of celebrating, women and nature, the first exemplified by a poem like

'Træsnit' and the second by the beautiful 'En Sommernat', in which nature and love are blended to form abstract love in the manner of Mörike (q.v.) and Eichendorff (q.v.). His longest and most ambitious work was *Hjortens Flugt*. It appeared in 1855 and deals in epic form with Zealand in the Middle Ages. A recent edition of his work is that by O. Friis (3 vols., 1927-9).

**Wolff, Christian von** (1679-1754), Germa 1 philosopher whose thought permeated German, Austrian and north European letters during the greater part of the eighteenth century, was born in Breslau and became a professor at Halle in 1707. Much appreciated by the free-thinking King Frederick I of Prussia, his rationalism offended his successor the Calvinist Frederick William I and Wolff was banished from Prussia in 1723. He then became professor at Marburg until Frederick the Great on his accession in 1740 recalled him to Halle as professor of international law, and in 1743 he became rector of the university. Wolff's most influential work was his *Vernünftige Gedanken von Gott, der Welt und der Seele des Menschen* (1719), which as the *Theologia Naturalis* became known throughout Europe. By and large it was a popularization of the work of Leibniz (q.v.). Optimistic, rationalistic, analytical, and fatally lacking any spiritual qualities, Wolff's thought was finally ousted by the various movements which from the 1760's sought to regain spiritual and natural values. He died in Halle.

**Wolff, Hans** (1888– ), German poet. Born at Guben, Lusatia, since 1940 he has lived in the U.S.A. The best example of his work, notable for its cool beauty, is *In den silbernen Nächten* (1950).

**Wolff, Julius** (1834-1910), German novelist. Born at Quedlinburg, he became a popular historical novelist of the straight costume type. Among his books may be named *Der Sülfmeister* (1883; Eng. trans. *The Salt Master of Lüneburg*, 1890) and *Der Raubgraf* (1884; Eng. trans. *The Robber Count*, 1890). Wolff died at Charlottenburg.

**Wolff-Bekker, Elisabeth** (1738-1804), Dutch novelist. Born at Flushing, she was something of a rebel in her youth and mixed in Dutch literary society on equal terms with men. Left a widow in 1777, she joined forces with her friend **Agatha Deken** (1741-1804) at The Hague where they began to collaborate as novelists. The two works by which they are chiefly known are *Historie van Sara Burgerhart* (1782) and the lengthy *Historie van den Herr Willem Leevend* (1784-6), a very fine psychological study of contemporary burgher life. Becoming increasingly advanced in their ideas they lived in revolutionary France until 1798, when returning to The Hague they found their fortunes lost under the new regime of the Batavian Republic. They died at The Hague within two months of each other.

**Wolfram von Eschenbach** (1170?-1220?), German poet. First in the service of the counts of Wertheim, it was at the court of Landgrave Hermann of Thuringia that he spent his best years, perhaps dying in his service. His great, and in fact only complete work is the celebrated *Parzival*, an epic, finest of all the Grail romances. It was finished about 1212, a deep and thoughtful work with a splendid unity built round the Grail, the stone of life. With its pilgrimage through loss of faith to the gaining of it again through humbleness of heart, and through desire remorse, and the learning of true devotion, it has little in common in feeling with the libretto, full of modern romantic violence, which Richard Wagner (q.v.) carved out of it. In the last book of Wolfram's *Parzival*, Lohengrin is introduced. The story is undoubtedly Provençal in origin as are the fragments, *Willehalm* and *Titurel*, which he left. A learned writer, he is sometimes obscure, but is rarely dull. *Parzival* has been translated into English verse by J. Weston (1894) and into English prose by M. F. Richey (1935).

**Wolzogen, Ernst Ludwig von** (1855–1934), German playwright and novelist. Born in Breslau into a family which in the past had befriended Schiller in his early days, Wolzogen first drew public attention to himself as the author of a successful play, *Lumpengesindel* (1892). He is best known, however, for his novel about Wagner and Liszt, *Der Kraft-Mayr* (1897; Eng. trans. 1914). He died in Munich.

**Würzburg, K. von,** *see* **Konrad von Würzburg.**

**Wyspiański, Stanisław Mateusz Ignacy** (1869–1907), Polish dramatist, was born in Cracow where he died. He first became known as a painter, but after the loss of a hand turned playwright. Among his allegorical plays with a bright dialogue, all permeated by strong Polish national feeling, may be mentioned *Meleager* (1898; Eng. trans. 1933), *Protesilas i Laodamia* (1899; Eng. trans. 1933), and his masterpiece *Wesele* (1900; Fr. trans. *Les Noces*, 1917).

**Wyss, Johann Rudolf** (1781–1830), Swiss author. Born in Bern, the son of a pastor, he became professor of philosophy at the university there in 1806. His famous *Der Schweizerische Robinson* appeared in four parts between 1812 and 1827, the first two parts being translated into English in 1820 as *The Swiss Family Robinson*. The story, which Wyss's father had told to his family, was written down from memory. It was eventually translated into every major European language, and has become a children's classic. Wyss died in Bern.

# Y

**Yevtushenko, Yevgeny Alexandrovich** (1933–    ), Russian Soviet poet born at Zima (Irkutsk), became well known both inside and outside Russia as a leading representative of the post-Stalin generation with such poems as the autobiographical *Stantsiya Zima* ('Zima Junction'), and *Babiy Yar* (1961), in which he courageously raised the issue of anti-semitism in the Soviet Union, 'Babiy Yar' being the name of a ravine near Kiev where many thousands of Jews were massacred during the Second World War. Since 1960 he has travelled widely, and has published three volumes of poetry: *Yabloko* (1960, 'Apple'), *Vzmakh ruki* (1962, 'A Wave of the Hand') and *Nezhnost* (1962, 'Tenderness'). See the English translation, *Selected Poetry of Yevtushenko* (1962).

# Z

**Zabaleta, Juan de** (1610?–1670?), Spanish prose-writer, was born and died in Madrid. Influenced by Gracián (q.v.) and writing in a good style he composed descriptions of a morning (*Día de fiesta por la mañana*, 1654) and an evening (*Día de fiesta por la tarde*, 1659) festival in Madrid, which together with other less attractive works were collected in his *Obras en prosa* (1667 and 1672).

**Zabłocki, Franciszek** (1750–1821), Polish playwright and poet, born at Volhynia. For many years a private tutor he became a priest late in life, dying at Końskowola. Before this he had written many comedies either adapted from or inspired by French plays, and his influence was great enough entirely to reform the Polish stage and give it new life and vitality. He also wrote odes and pastorals. His principal works are *Zabobonnik* (1781, 'The Superstitious Fool') and *Fircyk w zalotach* (1783, 'The Fop Goes A-Courting'), and his collected works, *Dzieła*, appeared in six volumes in 1829–30.

**Zachariä, Just Friedrich Wilhelm** (1726–1777), German poet. Born at Frankenhausen, he became in 1761 professor of the Carolinum, Brunswick, where he died. He is remembered today only for his satire on student life, *Der Renommist* (1744), a most colourful and amusing picture of the time. Among his other works may be mentioned *Die Tageszeiten* (1755).

**Zacuto (Zakkuth), Moses** (1625?–1697), Italian Hebrew dramatist, was born in Amsterdam and became a friend of Spinoza (q.v.). As a rabbi, he was appointed to Venice and later to Mantua where he died. He is important as the first Hebrew dramatist in Europe, his work such as *Yesod 'Olam* (1673, 'On Abraham') being modelled on the contemporary Italian style.

**Zamyatin, Yevgeny Ivanovich** (1884–1937), Russian novelist and short-story writer, born at Lebedyan, made a name for himself as a merciless satirist of bourgeois life at Petersburg in the last years before the revolution. The best example of this period of his writing is the long short story, *Na kulichkakh* ('At the World's End', 1914). This hatred of the middle-class business fraternity he took with him to Britain, where he stayed in 1916–17 supervising the building of ice-breakers for the Russian Navy. British war-profiteers are savagely attacked in *Ostrovityane* ('The Islanders', 1922). By 1920, however, Zamyatin had lost faith in the Bolshevik regime, which he now realized was as much if not more bent on destroying the individual than the czarist one had been. He began surreptitiously to write his best-known work, a sensational attack on the Soviet government, his novel *My*, the manuscript of which was smuggled abroad and published in Czechoslovakia in 1924 (Eng. trans. *We*, 1925; new ed., 1934). Zamyatin thereupon left the Soviet Union and settled in France where he died. *My* has naturally never been published in the Soviet Union, but it was as a short-story writer during the earlier period that Zamyatin had a profound influence on young Russian authors. Two of the best of his short stories have been translated into English: *Poshchera* (1922; trans. as *The Cave* in S. Konovalov's *Bonfire: Stories out of Soviet Russia*, 1932) and *Mamay* (1922; trans. in M. Slonim and G. Reavey's *Soviet Literature; an Anthology*, 1933).

**Zavattini, Cesare** (1902–    ), Italian short-story writer and film director, was born near Reggio Emilia, made films with De Sica, and became well known for his collections of stories, many of them humorous, in such volumes as *Parliamo tanto di me* (1931) and *Totò il buono* (1945).

**Zedlitz, Joseph Christian von** (1790–1862), Austrian poet and dramatist, was born at the Schloss Johannesberg, Austrian Silesia, and entered the Austrian civil service in Saxony. A romantic inspired by Byron, whose *Childe Harold* he translated (1836), Zedlitz became well known as a lyricist and ballad writer ('Die nächtliche Heerschau', 1832), and for his poetic narratives, such as *Das Waldfräulein* (1843). His dramas, such as *Turturell* (1821), popular in their day, have been long forgotten. After his retirement he lived in Vienna, where he died.

**Zeeus, Jacob** (1668–1718), Dutch poet. Born at Zevenbergen, where he died, he was first apprenticed to Houbraken the engraver, and later became surveyor-notary of his home town. A man of acute mind he was equally at home as a satirist, e.g. *De wolf int schaepsvel* (1711, 'The Wolf in Sheep's Clothing'), and as a lyricist in the Italian classical-idealist, or Arcadian, manner. His works in this latter style were collected posthumously in 1720 and 1726.

**Żeleński, Tadeusz** (1874–1941), Polish poet and critic writing under the name of **Boy**, was born in Warsaw, studied medicine at Paris, and settled in Warsaw in 1922, having already made his name as a writer of satirical occasional verse, collected as *Słówka* (1913). An ardent student of French literature he wrote an influential book on it, *Studia i szkice z literatury francuskiej* (1920), and *Molière* (1924). His advanced views and outspokenness held up his public career for a long time, but at last, in 1939, he was made professor of French literature at Lwów, where he was shot by the Germans two years later.

**Zeno, Apostolo** (1668–1750), Italian poet, was born in Venice. In 1710 he founded the influential literary journal, *Giornale dei letterati d'Italia*, in which he advocated a more dignified approach to dramatic writing. Called to Vienna in 1718 as Poet Laureate to the imperial court, he remained in that office until 1728 when he resigned and was succeeded on his own recommendation by young Metastasio (q.v.), who was to bring to perfection the dramatic style which Zeno himself had so long striven after. Between 1695 and 1737 Zeno wrote numerous libretti on classical heroic subjects, markedly influenced by Corneille and Racine, also oratorios on biblical subjects, and some comic operas. Many composers set his works to music, Handel and Pergolesi among them. His dramatic works were collected as *Poesie drammatiche* (10 vols., 1744). In later years he turned to literary scholarship, aiding Fontanini in his *Biblioteca dell' eloquenza italiana* (1753). He had already in earlier years shown his worth as a lexicographer and philologist in directing the 1705 edition of the famous dictionary of the Tuscan language, the *Vocabolario degli Accademici della Crusca*. The importance of Zeno's influence on the literature, scholarship and even music not only of his own country but of Europe cannot be overestimated. He died in Venice.

**Zermatten, Maurice** (1910–    ), Swiss novelist, born at Saint-Martin in the Valais, wrote convincingly of the peasant life of his wild canton in such novels as *La Colère de Dieu* (1940) and *Christine* (1944). More recently he has produced *Le Pain noir* (1947), *La Montagne sans étoiles* (1956) and *Le Bouclier d'or* (1961).

**Żeromski, Stefan,** who wrote under the pseudonyms of **Maurycy Zych** and **Józef Katerla** (1864–1925), Polish novelist, was born at Strawczyn of good family. Taking up veterinary surgery at Warsaw, while still a student he was arrested on insufficient grounds by the Russian police and imprisoned. The shock of this experience and his impaired health made an end of his hopes of an active professional career and he turned to writing. A man of warm heart and an idealistic approach to life while well aware of the enemies of justice, Żeromski always puts his ever-threatening pessimism to flight by turning to the nobility of individuals and the beauty of nature. Among his novels may be mentioned: *Popioły* (1904; Eng. trans. *The Ashes*, 1928), *Powieść o Udałym Walgierzu* (1906; Fr. trans. *Le roman de Walgour*, 1923), *Uroda życia* (1912; It. trans. as *La bellezza della vita*, 1920), and *Wierna rzeka* (1912; Eng. trans. *The Faithful River*, 1943). Żeromski died in Warsaw.

**Zesen, Philip von** (1619–1689), German novelist, was born at Prirau, spent much of his working life in Holland, where he lived by his pen, and died in Hamburg. He is to be remembered for his two novels, *Die Adriatische Rosemund* (1645), which is autobiographical, and *Assenat* (1670), on the Joseph and Potiphar's wife theme, both of them attempts to realize a German counterpart of the French school of novelists, such as Madeleine de Scudéry (q.v.) and Calprenède (q.v.), whose work he knew at first hand.

**Zhukovsky, Vasily Andreyevich** (1783–1852), Russian poet and translator, born the illegitimate son of a rich landowner at Tula, he turned to the study of German and English literature. By his masterly verse translations, the first of which was that of Gray's *Elegy* (1802), he paved the way for Pushkin and the great age of Russian poetry. His original work does not call for comment. Very much the westernizing, cosmopolitan Russian, he died at Baden Baden.

**Zieliński, Gustaw** (1809–1881), Polish descriptive poet, born at

Markowice. For his part in the revolution of 1830 he was exiled to Siberia where he remained from 1834 to 1842. His chief work is *Kirgiz* (1842) with its strong romanticism and vivid descriptions of the steppes.

**Zimmermann, Johann Georg von** (1728–1795), Swiss prose-writer, was born at Brugg, Switzerland. He became physician to George III of England at Hanover in 1768 and attended Frederick the Great of Prussia as physician during his last illness. His fame rests on his sentimental philosophical work, *An die Einsamkeit* (Eng. trans. *Solitude: on the Mind and the Heart*; various eds., best 1825), which first appearing in 1755 was translated into nearly every European language. It is representative of the style of thinking of that generation which had steeped itself in Young's *Night Thoughts* and was heading for Rousseau. He died in Paris.

**Zola, Émile Édouard Charles Antoine** (1840–1902), French novelist. The son of an engineer of mixed Italian and Greek ancestry, Zola was born in Paris. His university career ended disastrously, and he was thrown upon his own resources, striving for two years to live by his pen. In this he failed and was glad to accept the post of clerk with the publishers Hachette. While there he wrote some delightful short stories which appeared as *Contes à Ninon* in 1864, the favourable comments which the book received in certain places determining him to continue as an author. In 1866 he therefore left Hachette's and finished the full-length novel which he had in hand, *Thérèse Raquin*. It appeared the following year and was a pointer to the characteristics of his later work. Gloomy, even horrible in places, it yet smacks of true life, while the whole is invested with Zola's powerful and original imagination. *Thérèse* had considerable success, and thanks to the profits he gained from it and from his journalistic work, he was able to take in hand his plan for a history of a family, *Les Rougon-Macquart*, which came to consist of twenty volumes. The series was termed by its author 'a physiological history of the Second Empire', which gives a clue to Zola's reverence for scientific methods as became a leading expositor of a materialistic age. The first novel of the twenty, *La Fortune des Rougon*, was published in 1871, and the last, *Le Docteur Pascal*, in 1893. Comparable only to Balzac's *Comédie humaine* in its vast sweep of human nature, activity and thought, Zola's volumes were not as uniformly successful as his predecessor's, but some were enormously popular if not always for the right reason, such as *L'Assommoir* (1877; Eng. trans. 1962), concerning drink, and *Nana* (1880; Eng. trans. 1957), concerning sex. *La Faute de l'Abbé Mouret* (1875) is an example of those attacks on clerical celibacy which appeared in most European literatures about this time. *La Débâcle* (1892) is a powerful account of the Franco-Prussian War. Of others in the series may be mentioned *Pot-Bouille* (1882), an offensive account of middle-class life, *Germinal* (1885; Eng. trans. 1958), a description of life in the mines, and *La Terre* (1886; Eng. trans. *Earth*, 1958), which almost amounts to an attack on the crudities of peasant life. Many of the younger generation of literary men, prominent among them Maupassant (q.v.) and Huysmans (q.v.), became his acknowledged disciples. The last volume of his family chronicle having appeared in 1893, Zola immediately began a short series dealing with religious matters and called collectively *Les Trois Villes*, consisting of *Lourdes* (1894), *Rome* (1896) and *Paris* (1898; Eng. trans. *Trilogy of the Three Cities*, 3 vols., 1898), the mental journey of a priest from orthodoxy to free thought. In the last of these volumes the artistry appears to be wearing somewhat thin, and in the next and final series which he was to undertake there are signs of a tiring author. This was *Les Quatre Évangiles* (1899–1902). In these 'Four Gospels', *Fécondité* (1899), *Travail* (1900), *Verité* (1902) and *Justice*, left unfinished at his death, he deals with contemporary problems from a socialist standpoint. Until 1898 he had been content to influence his public through his literary productions, but the scandal of the Dreyfus affair and all that it implied seemed to him to call for a direct approach. Accordingly he wrote his open letter, ' J'accuse', to *L'Aurore* and electrified Paris by his belief in the innocence of Dreyfus and his condemnation of French justice, militarism and anti-semitism. This characteristically courageous action overturned French politics and finally led to the reinstatement of Dreyfus, but Zola did not live to see this, dying from asphyxia due to gas fumes caused by a defective flue in his bedroom in Paris. Among his non-literary and journalistic activities perhaps his interest in painting is the most significant, and his *Édouard Manet* (1880) celebrates his friendship with that artist. Zola's gigantic industry and will-power have been equalled by few, and if some of his work has died there remains enough alive to outweigh the achievements of most men of letters.

**Zorrilla y Moral, José** (1817–1893), Spanish poet and dramatist, born in Valladolid, left home in 1836 and the following year became known as the author of an elegy on the death of Larra (q.v.), the most outstanding Spanish literary figure of the time. In 1840 appeared his first play, *Cada cual con su razón*, an immediate success, while his treatment of legends, either as poetry, e.g. *Cantos del trovador* (1841), or drama, e.g. *El zapatero y el rey* (1841), was equally well received. But it is *Don Juan Tenorio* (1844) which has kept his name alive, and it is still performed. Here Zorrilla has created a popular hero saved from damnation by the love of a woman, and has given the whole story new life and vigour by adding new characters and new legends and by the strength of his melodious verse. Parting from his wife he went to France in 1850 and to Mexico in 1855 where he stayed for eleven years; but he found on his return to Spain in 1866 that his popularity had declined, and he lived for some years in poverty before receiving a pension. He married a second time in 1869, and his later years were cheered by a revival of his popularity, culminating with his public coronation as national Poet Laureate in 1889. He died less than four years later in Madrid.

**Zoshchenko, Mikhail Mikhailovich** (1895–1958), Russian short-story writer, the only real humorist the Soviet Union has so far produced, was born in Poltava. Coming early under the influence of Zamyatin (q.v.) he learned his craft from him, but later acknowledged Pushkin as his model. The 1920's was the period for Zoshchenko, in the days before the Party refused to allow any criticism of itself. His undoubted successes, *Rasskazy* (1923, 'Short Stories'), *Uvazhayemye grazhdanye* (1926, 'Respected Citizens') and *Nyervnyie lyudi* (1927, 'Nervous People'), all deal with the little bourgeois man-in-the-street, mocking him for his smallness in not being able to come to grips with the new world. Yet—and this was to be his ruin—Zoshchenko also had pity for this same little man bewildered by the march of events and said so in such a story as 'O chom pyel solovyei' ('What the Nightingale Sang Of'; Eng. trans, in E. Fen's *Modern Russian Stories*, 1943). After that he was continually in trouble with the Writers' Union, from which he was finally expelled. Of great sensibility and too honest to toe the Party line (although in later life he dismally tried to conform), the regime destroyed him as a writer. Besides the translation mentioned above, his work appears in English in *Russia Laughs* (1935) and in *The Woman who could not Read, and Other Tales* (1940). He died in Leningrad.

**Zschokke, Johann Heinrich Daniel** (1771–1848), German (afterwards naturalized Swiss) writer. Born in Magdeburg, he became first an actor and then a pastor at Magdeburg, before attracting attention with his sensational novel, *Abällino* (1793), dramatized as *Abällino der grosse Bandit* in 1795 and translated into English by M. G. Lewis in 1804 as *The Bravo of Venice*. In 1796 he settled in Switzerland becoming president of the educational department of the town of Aarau, and after 1801 served in the cantonal government of Aargau. As a publicist he was editor of a monthly paper, *Erheiterungen*, begun in 1811; as a novelist his *Des Schweizerlandes Geschichte* (1822) was popular, but if he is remembered today it is through his stories, such as *Das Goldmacherdorf* (1817; Eng. trans. *The Goldmaker's Village*, 1833), which influenced Gotthelf (q.v.), *Der Freihof von Aarau* (1826) and *Die Branntweinpest* (1837; Eng. trans. *The Rum Plague*, 1853). Zschokke died at Aarau. His autobiographical *Eine Selbstschau* (1842; Eng. trans. 1847) is of much interest.

**Zuckmayer, Carl** (1896–   ), German playwright and novelist, born in Nackenheim. His unorthodox opinions were given utterance in several well-written plays, which seem to contain every element necessary to the highest drama, such as *Der Hauptmann von Köpenick* (1931; Eng. trans. *The Captain of Köpenick*, 1932) and *Des Teufels General* (1946). A novel, *Salware oder Die Magdalena von Bozen* (1936), was translated into English as *The Moon in the South* (1937). More recent works are: *Barbara Blomberg* (1948), *Der Gesang in Feuerofen* (1950), *Das kalte Licht* (1955) and *Die Uhr schlägt eins* (1961).

**Zweig, Arnold** (1887–   ), German novelist and essayist, was born at Gross-Glogau, and after his experiences in the 1914–18 war set himself to explore the problem of total war and society, his findings on which problem he gives expression to in his striking novel *Der Streit um den Sergeanten Grischa* (1927; Eng. trans. *The Case of Sergeant Grischa*, 1927). A militant Zionist, he deals with this question in *De Vrient kehrt heim* (1932; Eng. trans. *De Vrient Goes Home*, 1933). The persecution of the German Jews called forth his essays,

*Bilanz der deutschen Judenheit* (1934; Eng. trans. *Insulted and Exiled*, 1937). Of his later novels the best known is *Das Beil von Wandsbek* (1947; Eng. trans. *The Axe of Wandsbek*, 1948), which was made into a film in 1951.

**Zweig, Stefan** (1881–1942), Austrian man of letters, born in Vienna, died by suicide in exile at Petropolis, Brazil. A lyric poet of ease and charm (*Die gesammelten Gedichte*, 1924) but with originality always just out of his grasp, as a biographer his gifts of vivacious description and presentation were exactly suited to his purpose. Among his works in that *genre* may be mentioned: *Drei Meister— Balzac, Dickens, Dostojewski* (1920; Eng. trans. 1930), *Die Heilung durch den Geist—Mesmer, Mary Baker Eddy, Freud* (1932; Eng. trans. *Mental Healers*, 1932), *Marie Antoinette* (1932; Eng. trans. 1933) and *Balzac. Der Roman seines Lebens*, which appeared after his death in 1946. His ambitious poetic drama, *Jeremias*, was published in 1917 (Eng. trans. *Jeremiah*, 1922 and 1929). As a short-story writer he is represented by the collections, *Amok* (1922; Eng. trans. 1931), *Verwirrung der Gefühle* (1925; Eng. trans. *Conflicts*, 1927) and *Schachnovelle* (1943; Eng. trans. *The Royal Game*, 1944).

**Zych, Maurycy,** *see* Żeromski, S.